The Top UK Perfume and Cosmetics Wholesalers

Profiles of the leading 3600 companies

John D Blackburn

Editor

First Edition

Summer 2019

ISBN-13: 978-1-912736-29-4

ISBN-10: 1-912736-29-2

All rights reserved. No part of this publication may be reproduced, distributed, or transmitted in any form or by any means, including photocopying, recording, or other electronic or mechanical methods, without our prior written permission, except in the case of brief quotations embodied in critical reviews and certain other non-commercial uses permitted by copyright law. For permission requests, please write to us.

Copyright © 2019 Dellam Publishing Limited

Printed in 8pt Nimbus Sans L

Designed by URW++ Design and Development GmbH

Dellam Publishing Limited

2 Heath Drive, Sutton, Surrey, SM2 5RP

Fax: 020 8770 7478   email: enquiries@dellam.com

SAN: 0177881   EAN/GLN: 5030670177882

Table of Contents

1 Acknowledgements iv

2 Introduction v

3 Total Assets League Table 1

- As a measure of size, total assets is preferable to turnover which is influenced by profit margins and whether companies are capital or labour intensive.

4 Age of Companies 17

- Each company is ranked by its date of incorporation. Newcomers are defined as those registered since 2017.

5 Geographic Distribution 37

- Each company is classed by county.

6 Company Profiles 57

- Full company name, date incorporated, net worth, total assets, registered office, activities, shareholders and parent company, directors (with date of birth, nationality and occupation) and number of employees (if available).

7 Index of Directorships 265

- Alphabetical list of directors showing their directorships. If several directors have identical names then their date of birth is shown.

8 Standard Industrial Classification 333

- These codes are used to classify businesses by the type of economic activity in which they are engaged.

9 *finis* 352

Acknowledgements

This is a long and detailed publication containing thousands of facts and figures. It is only to be expected, despite continuous and repeated editing and checking, that errors may occur. In such cases, once we are aware of any, we publish a correction on our website.

Readers are encouraged to check regularly at www.dellam.com/books for any corrections and updates.

Although we take extreme care to ensure accuracy and being up-to-date, we cannot accept responsibility for any errors or omissions.

Contains public sector information licensed under Open Government Licence v3.0. from The Charity Commission (England and Wales) and The Charity Commission for Northern Ireland. © Crown Copyright and database right (2018).

Contains information from the Scottish Charity Register supplied by the Office of the Scottish Charity Regulator and licensed under the Open Government Licence v.2.0. © Crown Copyright and database right (2018).

Contains OS data © Crown copyright and database right (2018)

Contains Royal Mail data © Royal Mail copyright and database right (2018)

Contains National Statistics data © Crown copyright and database right (2018)

Contains Office for National Statistics © Crown copyright and database right (2018)

Maps based on those produced by the Office for National Statistics Geography GIS & Mapping Unit (2012 and 2018).

Contains HM Land Registry data © Crown copyright and database right (2018).

Contains Parliamentary information licensed under the Open Parliament Licence v3.0.

House of Commons Library Briefing Papers licensed under the Open Parliament Licence v3.0.

Contains Food Standards Agency data © Crown copyright and database right (2018).

Contains Eurostat data, 1995-2018, copyright European Commission by the Decision of 12 December 2011.

Maps based on produced by ONS Geography GIS & Mapping Unit.

Contains Companies House data supplied under section 47 and 50 of the Copyright, Designs and Patents Act 1988 and Schedule 1 of the Database Regulations (SI 1997/3032).

We appreciate your interest in our publications, and your comments and suggestions are always welcome. Please contact us at enquiries@dellam.com.

Introduction

This study looks at all companies registered in the United Kingdom where they identify themselves as wholesalers of perfume and cosmetics.

This study includes companies that are dormant or non-trading some of which might be latent while others may operate under their owners' names but incorporate to protect the business name. In addition, all newly incorporated companies are included. The study will exclude those companies that do not specifically identify themselves as wholesalers of perfume and cosmetics.

The aim of this study is to provide an overview of the key movers and shakers in the UK perfume and cosmetics wholesale sector. Only key data has been isolated, particularly the company's net worth and total assets, but also its full name, date incorporated, registered office, other activities, shareholders, directors (with date of birth, occupation and nationality) and number of employees.

Two indicators of size are used: net worth and total assets. These are preferable to turnover which is influenced by profit margins and whether the companies are capital or labour intensive.

In the years 2016, 2017 and 2018, new company incorporations in the perfume and cosmetics wholesale sector were 291, 568 and 1179 respectively.

Product price inflation for years 2010-2018 was 100.0, 101.1, 100.4, 100.7, 101.6, 102.6, 102.1, 100.9 and 112.7.

The Cosmetic, Toiletry & Perfumery Association (CTPA) represents all companies involved in making, supplying and selling cosmetic and personal care products. It represents 80% of the market.

The market size is £ 9.769 billion (retail sales) and employs 200,000 people.

The breakdown is as follows: skin care £2.3 billion; toiletries £2.3 billion; perfumes and fragrances £1.8 billion; hair care £1.7 billion and make-up £1.6 billion.

Exports are £3.94 billion (2016) while imports were £4.28 billion. Exports to EU was 65%.

Cosmetics Europe is the European trade association for the cosmetics and personal care industry.

Valued at €77.6 billion at retail sales price in 2017, the European cosmetics and personal care market is the largest in the world. The largest national markets are Germany (€13.6 billion), France (€11.3 billion), the UK (€11.1 billion), Italy (€10.1 billion) and Spain (€6.8 billion).

The sector brings at least €29 billion in added value to the EU economy annually. €11 billion is contributed directly by the manufacture of cosmetic products and €18 billion indirectly through the supply chain.

Standard cataloguing guidelines for company names in the profile section have been used, but there will be occurrences when the name may not be strictly alphabetical. A certain licence was adopted where it was felt that strictly alphabetical could lead to improper cataloguing. Some company names have been shortened in the league tables for aesthetic reasons.

John D Blackburn
Editor

This page is intentionally left blank

The Top UK Perfume and Cosmetics Wholesalers　　　　　　　　　　　　　　　　dellam

Total Assets League Table

The Top UK Perfume and Cosmetics Wholesalers

Company	Revenue	Company	Revenue
Chanel Limited	£6,879,171,584	Sweet Squared Limited	£13,230,000
Estee Lauder Cosmetics Limited	£789,843,008	H & B Supplies Limited	£13,055,914
L'Oreal (U.K.) Limited	£561,248,000	KMI Brands Limited	£12,905,000
The Body Shop International Limited	£502,000,000	Innovaderma PLC	£12,810,000
DKH Retail Limited	£473,450,000	CBee (Europe) Limited	£12,713,475
Johnson & Johnson Limited	£204,111,008	Cowshed Products Limited	£12,586,555
Lush Ltd.	£133,899,000	Cosmetic Doctor at Work Limited	£12,198,167
HFC Prestige Products Limited	£106,194,000	Meller Design Solutions Limited	£11,733,302
Beiersdorf UK Ltd.	£103,750,000	United Retail & Sourcing Limited	£11,414,928
Colgate-Palmolive (U.K.) Limited	£92,973,000	Amelia Knight Limited	£11,315,489
Shaneel Enterprises Limited	£92,480,000	Bulldog Skincare Limited	£9,546,162
Boots International Limited	£74,912,000	Beauty Wholesale Limited	£9,373,346
Benefit Cosmetics Limited	£73,419,360	Guinot-Mary Cohr UK Limited	£9,200,507
Clarins (U.K.) Limited	£69,669,808	Beautynet Limited	£8,885,306
Per-Scent Limited	£68,810,000	Per-Scent Group Limited	£8,250,000
Fragrance Acquisitions Limited	£62,100,000	Vita Liberata Limited	£8,235,086
Gojo Industries - Europe Limited	£60,227,816	FB Beauty Ltd	£8,184,772
Hot (UK) Limited	£57,816,000	Perricone MD Cosmeceuticals UK Limited	£8,062,350
Revolution Beauty Limited	£49,814,564	Guerlain Limited	£7,892,760
Puig UK Limited	£48,891,000	Glendale S/S Limited	£7,720,000
Warpaint London PLC	£48,258,000	Iam Finance Limited	£7,646,464
Crabtree & Evelyn (Overseas) Limited	£47,446,560	Clive Christian Perfume Limited	£7,538,419
Parfums Christian Dior (U.K.) Limited	£45,344,508	This Works Products Limited	£7,457,314
Imperial Pharmaceuticals Limited	£43,300,000	Direct Supplies (2014) Limited	£7,294,925
Kenneth Green Associates Limited	£42,828,352	The Orange Square Company Ltd.	£7,251,013
Markwins Beauty Brands International Limited	£40,203,952	F A Commodities Ltd	£7,020,000
S A Designer Parfums Limited	£38,090,000	Mashco Limited	£6,896,520
CRM Trading Limited	£33,690,000	Ren Ltd	£6,821,000
Capital (Hair and Beauty) Limited	£29,652,584	Macks Ltd.	£6,780,867
Karium Ltd	£29,025,880	Comedic Limited	£6,675,613
Original Additions (Beauty Products) Limited	£27,130,652	Healthpoint Limited	£6,661,664
Dr. Organic Limited	£26,357,000	Brand Agency (London) Limited	£6,557,248
Scent Global Ltd	£26,120,000	Joy Limited	£6,390,251
Dermalogica (UK) Limited	£24,956,168	Dennis Williams Limited	£6,319,750
HCT Europe Limited	£24,520,000	Beauty Star Limited	£6,241,957
Neal's Yard (Natural Remedies) Limited	£24,280,000	Sanmex International Limited	£6,230,000
Arbonne UK Limited	£23,843,860	Trading Scents Group Limited	£6,196,438
Pricecheck Toiletries Limited	£23,155,352	Deciem UK Ltd.	£6,176,499
Doterra (Europe) Ltd	£22,412,516	Glorious Brands Ltd.	£6,115,543
Editions de Parfums Limited	£19,562,614	Affinity Fragrances Limited	£6,106,000
Warpaint Cosmetics Group Limited	£18,742,896	Pharmacare (Europe) Limited	£6,085,796
Space Brands Limited	£18,000,000	LVMH Fragrance Brands UK Limited	£5,940,969
Rainbow Cosmetics (Manchester) Limited	£17,311,892	Aspects Beauty Company Limited	£5,913,270
Salon Success Limited	£16,843,722	K.B. Salon Supplies Limited	£5,880,000
Optima Consumer Health Limited	£16,419,000	Trading Scents (2014) Limited	£5,596,729
Synlatex Limited	£16,274,429	Neal's Yard Remedies (Home) Limited	£5,570,000
Amelia Knight Holdings Limited	£16,228,597	M & N Traders Limited	£5,473,454
Warpaint Cosmetics (2014) Limited	£15,663,241	Fragrance Factory Limited	£5,415,582
Bluestar Enterprise Limited	£14,963,473	Kendo Brands Limited	£5,347,231
ESPA International (UK) Limited	£14,837,000	The Icon Consultancy Ltd	£5,290,676
F.D.D. International Limited	£14,650,000	The Lovely Distribution Company Limited	£5,183,221
Gazelli International Limited	£14,576,240	Warpaint Cosmetics Limited	£5,170,000
Almirall Limited	£14,548,521	N.S.I. (U.K.) Limited	£5,145,631
Elizabeth Arden (UK) Ltd	£14,282,117	I.S.O.D Limited	£5,140,190

The Top UK Perfume and Cosmetics Wholesalers

Company	Amount	Company	Amount
International Hair Cosmetics Limited	£5,100,000	Direct Cosmetics Limited	£2,367,745
Le Labo UK Limited	£5,038,555	Jerome Russell Limited	£2,265,709
Global Essence UK Ltd	£4,834,465	Varana UK Limited	£2,260,000
International Trade Corporation Limited	£4,610,000	Knight & Wilson Trading Limited	£2,254,243
Zainab Limited	£4,600,000	Sci Check Limited	£2,210,000
Acqua di Parma Limited	£4,486,617	The King of Shaves Company Limited	£2,190,000
P.S. Sahney & Co Limited	£4,480,000	Beauty Leisure Industry Supplies and Services Limited	£2,186,087
Holy Group Limited	£4,405,821	United Perfumes Limited	£2,147,091
La Prairie (UK) Limited	£4,370,000	Vivalis Beauty Limited	£2,140,637
Janson Limited	£4,234,088	Mainline Marketing U K. Limited	£2,132,736
Lottie London Limited	£4,227,193	Darklake Limited	£2,107,982
Fragrance and Beauty Limited	£4,210,000	I Love Cosmetics Limited	£2,083,616
Arnest International Limited	£4,206,000	Red Hot Products Limited	£2,045,250
Cyrano Limited	£4,070,000	Ray & Company (Hairdressers Sundries Men) Limited	£2,020,000
Re:New Beauty Ltd	£4,029,690	Adelphi Corporation Limited	£1,977,184
Asurex Limited	£4,027,577	Elegance By London Limited	£1,941,905
Per-Scent Fine Limited	£3,830,000	Universal Toiletries Corporation Limited	£1,933,357
Beauty Magasin Ltd	£3,814,213	Additional Lengths Ltd	£1,926,480
Teoxane UK Limited	£3,792,919	Star Qualities Ltd	£1,879,699
Fresh Cosmetics Limited	£3,775,909	Glow Consumer Products UK Limited	£1,854,338
Fragrance Group London Ltd	£3,702,898	Alvor Limited	£1,853,052
Strip Distribution Limited	£3,660,000	Sharp's Global Trading Limited	£1,852,485
Talza Limited	£3,582,667	Create Images Ion Limited	£1,850,000
Intertrade Group Ltd	£3,482,766	Nature's Dream Limited	£1,845,800
Pharmadose Limited	£3,458,054	Fox Group International Ltd	£1,831,570
Eden Parfums Limited	£3,450,000	Blissworld Limited	£1,818,324
Sisley UK Limited	£3,333,470	Bellapierre Cosmetics Limited	£1,797,884
Company NBN Limited	£3,300,000	Sterling Fragrances International Limited	£1,780,000
Headlines (Hair & Beauty Supplies) Limited	£3,299,255	Pern Consumer Products Limited	£1,770,000
Intercos UK Ltd	£3,172,919	Drammock International Limited	£1,765,066
Laurelle London Ltd	£3,104,143	Polex Limited	£1,760,319
Hive of Beauty Limited	£3,096,592	Geo. F. Trumper (Perfumer and Products) Limited	£1,759,021
Trading Scents Limited	£3,090,783	Beautypro Ltd	£1,750,000
Cosmeceuticals Limited	£3,084,327	M Beauty Ltd	£1,741,423
Roja Dove Limited	£3,070,000	Salon Connection (Wales) Limited	£1,731,733
Classic Beaute Limited	£3,061,265	Ambassadors Choice Limited	£1,729,580
Albert Roger Limited	£3,059,196	Australian Bodycare U.K. Limited	£1,727,205
Sarah Chapman Ltd.	£3,027,642	FM Cosmetics UK Ltd	£1,720,000
DMG Wholesale Limited	£3,020,000	EOS Products Limited	£1,667,435
Hairways (Hair & Beauty) Limited	£2,952,589	Kent Cosmetics Limited	£1,620,000
Herb U.K. Limited	£2,917,670	Mary Kay Cosmetics (U.K.) Limited	£1,615,294
The Skincare Sanctuary Limited	£2,899,590	Amber House Limited	£1,598,140
MGC Pharma (UK) Ltd	£2,896,542	Fragranceexpert Limited	£1,570,000
Protec Ingredia Limited	£2,895,331	So Susan Limited	£1,561,556
Anglia Enterprise (UK) Limited	£2,887,935	Forever Living Products Ireland Limited	£1,546,694
Beta Novis Limited	£2,790,000	Trade Smart Marketing Limited	£1,537,017
Acti Laboratories UK Ltd	£2,781,150	County Sales Limited	£1,530,087
Valorem Capital One Ltd	£2,749,421	Comfort Click Limited	£1,507,888
Adel Professional Limited	£2,708,869	Edenwest Limited	£1,480,743
Phils (Wholesale) Limited	£2,670,200	Tansi Packaging Solutions Limited	£1,452,988
Shure Enterprises (UK) Limited	£2,540,000	Vereer Limited	£1,452,182
General Healthcare Limited	£2,525,929	A B International Limited	£1,420,556
KPACA Limited	£2,496,459	Finders International Limited	£1,401,710
Ken Lamacraft Marketing Limited	£2,409,120	The Eyelash Design Company Limited	£1,350,000

Pixie Dust Products Limited	£1,322,901	Atkinson London 1799 Ltd	£856,114
B.Fairall (UK) Limited	£1,290,000	Harvey Pharma Ltd	£855,370
Oh My Scent Limited	£1,276,984	TWC Products Limited	£854,136
Perfume Holding UK Limited	£1,271,499	The Edge Nail & Beauty Limited	£836,626
Pharma Medico Limited	£1,265,051	Oud Milano UK Limited	£836,276
Carolina Herrera UK Ltd	£1,260,000	Dreamweave Products Ltd	£832,350
Fragrance & Beauty Creations Limited	£1,250,000	Shilcroft Limited	£810,280
Wrimes Cosmetics Ltd	£1,250,000	Belsay Ltd	£809,873
Designer Fragrances Limited	£1,230,000	Mancave Limited	£806,737
Simlar 2 Limited	£1,208,327	He-Shi Enterprises Ltd	£804,458
Fragrance Sales Limited	£1,205,000	Hair Ornaments UK Limited	£788,598
Transeur Export Finance Co. Limited	£1,200,660	Q River Limited	£787,788
Rouge Bunny Rouge UK Limited	£1,196,487	NBS Distribution Ltd	£787,000
Caudalie UK Limited	£1,188,945	Northdown Cosmetics Limited	£781,720
Perfume London Ltd	£1,182,925	Lovorika London Limited	£766,000
Kidlex Limited	£1,155,463	Uppercut Deluxe Co Limited	£763,275
Shay & Blue Ltd	£1,151,545	SES Wholesale Limited	£758,422
Phyto Therapeutics Limited	£1,150,000	Pole Position (Licensing) Limited	£752,000
Foundation Brands Ltd	£1,150,000	Soulful Beauty Ltd	£751,122
Angel Remy Ltd	£1,134,498	Mad Beauty Limited	£749,824
The Diverse Investment (London) Group Limited	£1,133,366	Profile Hair & Skin Care Limited	£744,844
M & M Cosmetics Limited	£1,120,525	Mellor & Russell Direct Distribution Ltd	£740,158
The Spirit of Dubai Limited	£1,109,323	Albert Roger & Partner France Limited	£707,857
Hampton Brands Limited	£1,090,000	Home & Bodycare Limited	£707,810
Cosimpex Ltd	£1,087,888	Allied Aerosols Limited	£705,444
Perfume Supplies Limited	£1,080,000	Ha-Derma Limited	£700,619
Aurelia Skincare Limited	£1,060,000	No.1 Nail Supply Limited	£694,950
Eve Taylor (London) Limited	£1,049,308	Fish London Limited	£687,770
Unique Cosmetics Limited	£1,040,000	Stantondown Limited	£686,153
Amalgamated Euro Products UK Ltd	£1,040,000	Regima UK Ltd	£685,726
Aglory Merchant Enterprises Limited	£1,028,863	Cool Blades Limited	£683,778
Orveda Limited	£1,012,170	Bioeffect Limited	£670,724
Thalgo UK Limited	£988,818	Enfield Distribution Ltd	£667,438
Ayursavvyveda Limited	£987,000	Annexa Solutions Limited	£652,176
Pure Natural Therapy Ltd	£984,000	Rosdon Group Limited	£641,530
Beauty Premier Limited	£977,466	Perfume Addict (UK) Ltd	£639,829
Winning Lines Limited	£971,312	Profusion Cosmetics UK Ltd	£638,398
Agenda Salon Concepts Limited	£970,994	Chris Adams Perfumes Ltd	£632,440
Fashion Fragrances & Cosmetics UK Ltd	£959,217	C Distribution UK Limited	£628,745
Graham Hair and Beauty Limited	£956,989	Simple Hair Limited	£627,080
Clinova Limited	£955,018	Erno Laszlo Group Ltd	£626,104
Universal Design Promotion Ltd	£945,380	BS Supply Ltd	£624,305
Hisamitsu UK Limited	£941,929	Pink Cosmetics London Limited	£621,593
Parkside Nails Supplies Ltd	£936,757	4 Corners Distribution Ltd	£617,647
L'Anza Europe Limited	£917,748	Worth Worldwide Property Limited	£613,412
Daniel Sandler Ltd	£917,310	Pellitier & Perkins Limited	£612,536
Allied Fragrances Limited	£898,170	Gold Class Hair Limited	£610,730
East End Cosmetics Limited	£897,837	Excel (GS) Limited	£607,348
Skinsense Ltd	£883,611	Anglo Indian Trading Limited	£605,866
PH Group UK Limited	£875,982	Inbeauting Ltd	£601,347
JS Marketing (N.I.) Limited	£875,495	Beaute Prestige International Ltd	£600,000
T.L.C. (Total Luxury Cosmetics) Ltd	£868,089	Legacy Wholesalers Limited	£595,000
Top Beauty Limited	£857,337	Mane (UK) Limited	£574,895
Innes McBeath Sourcing Ltd.	£856,872	Ozprodz Limited	£571,420

Company	Amount	Company	Amount
Fade Out Limited	£568,135	Takasago (U.K.) Limited	£403,593
Transformulas International Limited	£565,540	Anatomicals London (England, The World) Ltd	£400,702
P.H.A.B Wholesale Limited	£563,563	Brandaroma Limited	£395,594
Beautiful Body Limited	£547,213	Prism Parfums Limited	£395,430
Acering Limited	£547,190	Elko Electrical Ltd.	£393,944
Functional Fragrances Ltd	£545,940	Eurocosmetics Limited	£392,636
Vivatinell Limited	£545,860	The Berkeley Square Cosmetics Company Limited	£390,669
Pravera Ltd	£544,179	H2K Limited	£389,800
Crystal Spring Consumer Division Limited	£540,940	Kiss Products UK Limited	£388,868
Impulse Global Solutions Limited	£535,033	Skinmed Ltd	£388,090
Brandcare Group Limited	£528,874	Good Ventures Limited	£385,620
The Lemon Tree Beauty Limited	£528,236	Cosmetics R Us 1 Limited	£385,572
Jica Beauty Products Limited	£528,220	4T Medical Ltd	£385,008
Harpar Grace International Ltd	£519,252	Asabeauty Ltd	£383,133
Wonderful Life PHBS Ltd	£517,031	Linda Meredith Skin Care Limited	£380,824
Lukony Ltd	£514,939	Aesthetic Brands (Distribution and Management) Limited	£376,918
Waterman Corporate Enterprises Limited	£514,087	Mahrosh Beauty Ltd	£376,800
Fushi Wellbeing Limited	£509,340	Lock Stock & Barrel Grooming Company Ltd	£376,770
Sublyme Cosmetics Limited	£507,341	Galactix Ltd	£375,000
Makki Cosmetics Limited	£507,280	The Wildsmith Collection Limited	£373,484
SB Selected Beauty Ltd	£504,916	Dr.Lipp Ltd	£370,097
Mama Mio Limited	£503,000	Maximaliste Limited	£368,988
David Hart (Santo) Limited	£498,006	Hair Cosmetics Limited	£368,340
McCoey & Co. Limited	£495,320	Bays International Limited	£367,917
Fair Pharm Limited	£492,289	Beauty Innovator 2012 Ltd.	£367,704
Balmain Hair UK Ltd	£489,471	TLC - Tender Loving Care UK Limited	£366,340
Elemental Herbology Limited	£488,013	The Beauty School Limited	£363,492
Sawa Trading & Shipping Limited	£487,344	Menco International Limited	£362,197
Califa Ltd	£477,000	Unineed Limited	£362,090
New Era Hair Ltd	£476,007	Echo Hair Limited	£361,599
Phoenix Hair & Beauty (Ely) Limited	£475,143	BKSL Limited	£360,921
Organic Colour Systems Limited	£474,815	Brambles Farm Ltd	£360,142
Mark McDonald Consultancy Limited	£472,960	Salon Focus Ltd	£359,980
Rederm Limited	£466,808	Gentle Beauty Co Ltd	£358,498
Ellipsis Brands Limited	£456,789	Bracey Overseas Ltd	£358,034
Sai Enterprise Limited	£456,430	Butterwhips Ltd	£358,000
Sandaig Ltd	£455,633	Railworth Limited	£356,827
Freestyle (Trade) Ltd.	£454,271	Wiv Global Limited	£356,481
BSB Global Limited	£453,180	Arrow Hair & Beauty Supplies Limited	£355,627
Hair Dressing Supplies Lincoln Ltd	£452,800	Ultra Glow Cosmetics Limited	£354,418
Jigu Corporation Limited	£445,000	Hugworld Cristalinas UK Limited	£354,414
Prestige Perfumes Limited	£437,347	JMAR Op No 2 Ltd	£353,818
Incorporated Perfumery Distribution Limited	£429,567	Metropolitan Beauty Ltd.	£351,262
Ayesha Carolina Limited	£428,000	Lambsmead Limited	£350,601
Lab Brands Limited	£427,203	Interparcos U.K. Limited	£349,125
E.J. Contracts Limited	£419,125	Akoma International (UK) Limited	£348,160
Hommage International Ltd	£415,737	Cosmetic Traders Limited	£343,109
New Horizons (UK) Ltd	£413,513	G.P.B. Supplies Limited	£342,850
Healthcare Procurement Services Ltd	£411,847	Gentille Limited	£341,933
M & M Import Ltd	£411,410	Penny Price Aromatherapy Ltd	£340,260
Primoil Limited	£407,787	Isha Cosmetics Limited	£330,000
Kiara Sky Professional Nail Distribution Limited	£406,750	P.R. Professional Salon Supplies Limited	£329,774
Euro Aromas Limited	£406,260	Com4hospitality Ltd.	£328,589
Global Luxury Beauty Ltd	£404,122	Aroma Actives Limited	£328,000

Company	Amount	Company	Amount
Euro Perfumes (UK) Ltd	£323,725	Beached Limited	£241,170
North West Cosmetics Limited	£320,155	Global Couture (UK) Ltd	£241,117
The Scent Factory Limited	£320,085	Eutek Group Limited	£237,510
Elite Capital Limited	£318,958	Exquisite Cosmetics Limited	£237,027
Honeypot Cosmetics (Wholesale) Limited	£316,093	Lipoid Kosmetik Ltd	£236,532
Pearson Cosmetics Limited	£314,940	Kounga Ltd	£236,100
Meder Beauty International Ltd	£313,850	Salon Select (NI) Limited	£234,891
JGR UK Distributions Limited	£308,944	Optic Eye Wear Ltd	£234,020
Passion 4 Health International Limited	£304,832	Ila Asia Limited	£232,060
Nectar International Limited	£304,139	Opatra Limited	£225,560
Beauty Forever Cosmetics Limited	£302,530	Cosmetica Natural Oils Ltd	£223,780
Export Solutions (International) Limited	£299,669	The London Cosmetics Company Limited	£220,311
Swift Retail Limited	£299,541	Direct Salon Supplies Limited	£215,564
Inside Trading (Beauty) Limited	£298,546	JF Malcolm Ltd	£214,013
National Supplement Beauty Solutions Limited	£297,906	The Nail & Beauty Link Limited	£213,870
Protec Botanica Ltd	£295,602	The Rosebud Perfume Company Limited	£212,681
The Highland Soap Co. Limited	£294,882	Iam By Nature Ltd.	£210,488
Steam Cream Limited	£294,140	Maskhouse Wholesale Limited	£210,033
Gilmor Hair and Beauty (Newport) Limited	£291,872	CP Parfums Ltd	£209,429
TRS & Co (Europe) Limited	£291,791	Crystalnails4u Ltd	£208,360
Denbond Pharmaceuticals Limited	£290,359	EnhanceColor Limited	£207,826
Jean Christian Perfumes Limited	£289,970	Pispo Ltd	£207,170
ZS Beauty Ltd	£287,080	Season of Beauty Limited	£206,683
Rosmetics Aesthetics Limited	£287,071	Simply Nature Ltd.	£206,373
Adams General Ltd	£286,150	Alton Trading Ltd	£206,210
Azhar Academy Limited	£283,220	Creative Colours International Ltd	£205,480
Merumaya Limited	£281,102	Shared Beauty Secrets Limited	£204,414
Bramley Products Ltd	£280,976	Cosmetronic Global Limited	£203,124
Neroli Limited	£279,957	Lanolips Limited	£203,042
Basic Needs Ltd	£279,540	Green & Dionisi Ltd	£202,800
LW International Ltd	£275,056	JML Cosmetics Limited	£202,716
Apex Trading Limited	£273,796	Hairways 77 Limited	£200,438
RX Cosmetics Limited	£273,527	Georgie Salon Supplies Limited	£199,880
Cult 51 Ltd	£272,270	The Brighton Group Ltd	£198,261
Brands de Luxe Company Ltd	£271,623	Unigrand Group Limited	£197,451
San & Amad General Trade Company Ltd	£270,471	BBA Products Limited	£196,759
Flowscent Limited	£268,856	Hair North East Limited	£195,220
Bond Street Cosmetics Limited	£268,401	RDC (UK) Limited	£191,950
NB Beauty Limited	£265,980	Global Beauty Wholesale Ltd	£190,710
Beauty Fort Limited	£264,740	Watsoap.Com Limited	£189,709
Essential Beauty Supplies Limited	£264,446	Jacob's Well Limited	£189,362
Flirties Products and Training Ltd	£261,110	TLY Supplies Ltd	£188,002
Pharmaclinix Limited	£260,287	SMCK Hair Care Products Limited	£187,100
Seascape Island Management Limited	£256,211	The Skinsmith Limited	£186,819
House of Worth Limited	£255,450	Leslie International Ltd	£186,288
Gold 22 (UK) Limited	£254,300	Instant Effects Ltd	£185,100
Tarsago Ltd	£251,820	Code Beautiful Limited	£182,853
Evans Close Limited	£251,020	Scent N Essence UK Ltd	£182,741
Winter Hill No.2 Limited	£250,000	SMCK Limited	£181,800
Excelcia Limited	£248,890	Fleuroma Limited	£180,449
Predator Trading Limited	£248,210	Regima@Dr H Ltd	£179,661
Beauty Select Limited	£245,976	Perfume Essence Ltd	£179,342
Kazi Brothers Group Limited	£245,675	Firecrest Communications Limited	£178,957
London Links Trading Limited	£243,386	Eden Perfumes Limited	£178,380

ID Skincare Limited	£177,990	Savvy & Shine Ltd	£129,745
True Affinity Limited	£177,000	Grossmith Limited	£129,720
Plan Target Limited	£176,186	Pebbles Creative Ltd	£129,130
White Rose Aromatics Limited	£175,420	Mamado International Limited	£128,274
Active Skincare Limited	£172,716	Colbico Limited	£126,836
Jan Nails & Beauty Suppliers Ltd	£171,474	Jaydaw Limited	£126,224
GroundedBodyScrub Limited	£171,097	Saffron Beauty Ltd	£125,610
Bonfit UK Limited	£170,524	A.H. Francis Professional Beauty Limited	£125,440
Skindoc Formula Limited	£169,000	Logical Content Ltd	£124,980
Bits4hair Limited	£168,920	Dynamic Skincare Ltd	£124,536
SMC Cosmetics (UK) Ltd	£168,522	KDM Supplies Limited	£123,800
Yes To Carrots UK Limited	£167,483	Z & J Enterprises Limited	£123,104
Wish List Limited	£164,220	Zieseniss Limited	£122,910
Gracefruit Limited	£164,023	Vikenias UK Ltd	£122,013
72 Hair Limited	£163,840	Highfields Health Limited	£121,850
Fizzy Peach Ltd	£162,214	Lixir Skin Limited	£121,550
Total Beauty Network (UK) Limited	£159,913	Existo Limited	£120,933
Ijapan Ltd	£158,100	Medipro Pharma Limited	£120,062
Marque of Brands Limited	£158,067	Nov'max Keratin Limited	£119,915
Euro Healthcare Services Limited	£155,279	Bion Corporation Limited	£119,860
Fit Brands (UK) Ltd	£153,990	Lipolift Ltd	£119,390
Crane and Peach Limited	£152,363	Shahadah Ltd	£118,201
Universal Attraction (London) Ltd	£152,240	AJ Metals Ltd.	£117,527
Wild Brands Limited	£152,000	Essential Oils Direct Ltd	£117,050
Doris Michaels Cosmetics Ltd	£148,860	Oils4life Limited	£116,610
Natural Serenity Ltd	£148,315	HABM Ltd	£116,597
Neo Elegance Ltd	£146,986	Satya Life Ltd	£116,272
T L Brooks Limited	£146,975	SI & D (UK) Limited	£114,559
Neolife International Ltd	£146,835	The Harley Street Fulfilment Company Limited	£113,792
Lilyz Cosmetics UK Ltd	£146,204	Glitterati Distributions Limited	£112,684
Patagonia Consult Limited	£146,187	J K International Trading Ltd	£112,389
Beautivate Ltd	£145,995	Zurego Limited	£112,314
HCT Beauty Ltd	£145,520	Salon Depot Ltd	£111,940
Beauty Senses Limited	£145,472	White Lotus Anti Aging Ltd	£111,573
Lord & Berry Ltd	£144,600	Elequra Limited	£111,570
Sun-Glo Limited	£143,411	Glendale Group Limited	£110,100
Sasha Hair & Beauty Ltd	£143,140	Nu Essence Limited	£109,720
Aurelia Skincare (International) Limited	£142,750	Liqwd Limited	£108,810
Instant Beauty UK Limited	£142,476	Glasgow Nails & Beauty Supplies Limited	£108,579
Tom Daxon Limited	£141,944	Gaya Cosmetics Limited	£108,414
Republik Inc Limited	£141,730	Lescaro Health Limited	£108,300
Maverick Hair & Beauty Ltd	£141,711	Perfume World Limited	£108,056
CC Dist UK Ltd	£140,521	Skin Matrix Limited	£108,001
Lubatti Limited	£140,000	Mayfair Gate Limited	£107,270
Younghair AB Ltd	£139,790	CNI Services Limited	£106,950
Niko Pro Limited	£138,066	Pippa Beauty Limited	£106,730
CM Hair & Beauty Supplies Limited	£136,561	Beegood Enterprises Limited	£105,829
Viib Limited	£135,990	Haircosmetics (Sunderland) Limited	£105,421
Elysian Design Limited	£134,524	Dermatx Ltd	£105,315
Razaq & Iqbal Limited	£134,033	Fabdoo Limited	£105,180
Photonic Limited	£133,659	Brodie and Stone PLC	£104,987
Body Care Brand Development Ltd	£133,550	Orveda UK Limited	£104,514
Bleach Makeup Limited	£133,338	Jasper Conran Perfumes Limited	£104,270
Pound Ring Ltd	£131,003	Pareto Cosmedics Ltd	£103,849

Repechage Europe Limited	£103,051	Vida Aesthetics Ltd	£75,999
True Brit London Limited	£102,716	DHB (UK) Ltd.	£75,690
Blossom Colour Limited	£102,550	Louise Galvin Limited	£75,554
Revive Express Beauty Ltd	£102,130	Regima Zone Ltd	£75,336
The Daimon Barber Limited	£100,510	Leighton Denny Limited	£74,994
CHK (UK) Ltd	£100,294	XL Marketing Ltd.	£73,668
Cloud 19 Limited	£100,000	Melya & Co. Trading Ltd.	£73,173
Haircare of Sweden Ltd	£99,880	Previa UK Ltd	£72,853
Ved Healthcare Limited	£99,010	Biodeb Beauty Ltd	£72,032
Southend Hair and Beauty Limited	£98,709	D & L Hair Products Limited	£71,969
Omega Flax Limited	£97,558	ABC Beauty Limited	£71,140
Herc Ltd.	£97,450	RMG Hair Limited	£70,651
Outdoor Girl Limited	£96,931	Les Petits Parfums Limited	£70,480
AAA Edinburgh Ltd	£96,882	Grimas.co.uk Limited	£70,477
Skin Health Solutions Ltd	£94,711	Plantain Essential Oils Ltd	£69,976
Cutagen Ltd	£94,297	Eurasia Property Limited	£69,880
Splashes & Spills Ltd.	£94,290	Naturela Limited	£69,585
Natur Life Ltd	£94,174	La Personal Products Ltd	£69,150
Rapsodi London Ltd	£92,330	Eternal Beauty (UK) Ltd	£68,854
Zest Cosmetics Limited	£90,910	Latam HQ Health Ltd	£68,770
Palmsextra Limited	£90,603	Tabitha JK Limited	£68,375
Fine Fragrances and Cosmetics Limited	£90,392	Nail Perfection Limited	£68,280
Beever Haircare Ltd	£89,948	Egyptian Magic Ltd	£67,673
Imijo Ltd	£89,790	Arosci Trading Limited	£66,661
Beauty Link Wholesale Ltd	£89,494	Whitening World Ltd	£65,376
Albert Roger Portugal Limited	£87,977	Eurocare Impex Services Limited	£65,350
Serene House UK Limited	£87,844	Filberts Bees Limited	£65,260
Sama Perfumes Ltd	£87,790	Beautytrade Limited	£64,941
West Three Trading Limited	£87,562	Danlab Ltd.	£64,371
The Greenfrog Soap Company Limited	£86,916	Bluesky Products Limited	£64,123
The Perfume Lab Limited	£86,498	Nails and Co (Midlands) Limited	£64,107
The Nyasa Organics Limited	£85,481	Golden Rose Limited	£63,280
L.A.Tanning Company Ltd	£85,286	BM Beauty Ltd.	£63,268
Bottlemate UK Limited	£85,125	Holy Lama Naturals Ltd	£62,100
Gracetree Ltd	£84,566	Dovedale Limited	£61,365
Tiyati Ltd	£84,470	NYDG UK Limited	£61,058
Make-Up International Limited	£84,227	Connessioni UK Limited	£60,790
Myridium Active.Com Limited	£83,357	Sundome Leisure Products Limited	£60,769
Carbon Theory Limited	£81,620	Ecobeauty Ltd	£60,711
Spa Therapies Ltd	£79,606	Beauty Ideas Group Limited	£60,620
Daughter of The Soil Limited	£79,490	Werson International Ltd	£60,382
Jojoba Cosmetics Limited	£79,294	Discounted Cosmetics Limited	£60,291
MB Promotion Ltd.	£79,002	FreshBreathOnline Limited	£60,150
City Beauty Supplies (UK) Ltd	£78,872	Face Lace Limited	£60,130
Silk Oil of Morocco UK Limited	£78,850	Into Exports Limited	£60,082
Deism IT Solutions Ltd	£78,408	Natural Birthing Company Ltd	£59,947
Beyond Hair Ltd	£78,230	Fragrance Samples UK Limited	£59,930
Simple Beauty (UK) Limited	£77,410	One Beauty Ltd	£59,450
Votary Limited	£77,187	Direct Salon Limited	£59,198
Belensa Limited	£76,831	Loopy Hair & Beauty Ltd	£58,981
Iiuvo Limited	£76,759	Spa Voyage Limited	£58,922
Pure Thoughts Ltd	£76,362	ABX Beauty Limited	£58,500
Per Capelli Ltd	£76,324	Barefaced Beauty Ltd	£58,020
SB Beauty Marketing Limited	£76,240	Cath Collins Devon Ltd	£57,970

Veramic Limited	£57,765	Bouffe Limited	£43,778
Mayfair Export London Limited	£57,690	Brand Holdings Limited	£43,678
Purple Tree Skincare Limited	£57,545	Cancun Collection Limited	£43,659
Koreesa Limited	£57,233	Haresgraces Limited	£43,361
Fragrance London Limited	£57,222	Skinsider Cosmetics Ltd	£43,170
Clean & Care Facilities Management Limited	£56,410	SKN-RG Ltd	£42,945
Hera Beauty Ltd	£56,358	Elegance Gel UK Ltd	£42,890
McCarthy Inter Africa Ltd	£56,004	Bioactivebeauty Ltd	£42,822
USA Hair Extensions Ltd	£55,995	Westfield House Distributors Limited	£42,696
Twelve Beauty Ltd	£55,560	Hanfan (UK) Limited	£42,412
Salon Supplies 365 Limited	£55,194	Silk Route Impex Limited	£41,983
The London Skincare Company Ltd.	£54,400	Our Choice Gift Limited	£41,980
Initiative (UK) Limited	£54,329	In Situ Cosmetics Ltd	£41,432
EOB Distribution Ltd	£53,717	Hairshine UK Ltd	£41,111
Ecooner Cosmetics London Ltd	£53,593	Here We Flo Ltd	£41,030
Scrubd Ltd	£53,046	Alsons Beauty Ltd.	£40,839
Cosmetic Alchemy Ltd	£52,768	Corley Capital Limited	£40,666
Green World Spa Products Limited	£51,910	Shortt Investments2 Limited	£40,474
Arlenne Ltd	£51,536	Bullet and Bone Limited	£40,310
Calla Distribution Ltd	£51,380	Ximtrade (UK) Ltd	£40,258
Ashmira Botanica Ltd	£51,302	AJS Marketing Limited	£40,178
Perfect Look & Health Ltd	£51,190	Ukab Limited	£40,115
UK Direct Imports Ltd	£50,516	Lauren Stone Limited	£39,728
Salon Distribution Concepts Limited	£50,475	Thomas Kosmala Parfums Ltd	£39,284
Black Pearl Beauty Limited	£50,453	For All Dogkind Limited	£39,108
Le Keux Vintage Enterprises Limited	£50,392	Acorn Brokerage Limited	£39,089
4R Guest Supplies Limited	£50,312	Lyal Intertrading Ltd	£39,044
Five Dot Botanics Limited	£50,000	SKN Rehab Limited	£38,948
Essence Cosmetics Limited	£49,994	UK Mineral Make-Up Limited	£38,891
Andre Boyard Perfumes Limited	£49,878	Dazzlers & Toppers PTL Ltd	£38,723
Maryam Imports & Exports Ltd	£49,521	Tibetan Cosmetics Ltd	£38,592
Little Enterprises (NI) Ltd	£49,472	Polar Export Services Limited	£38,540
1st Choice Nails Limited	£49,440	Hair Fantastic Retail Limited	£38,530
Serendipity Herbals Ltd	£49,369	Joseph Lanzante Products Limited	£38,010
One Green Lab Ltd	£48,653	CFN 1 Limited	£37,806
Organii Limited	£48,517	W-Healthy Aging Limited	£37,497
Barber & Salon Supplies Ltd	£48,140	Jo Loves (Wholesale) Limited	£37,463
Paragon Enterprise Limited	£47,812	Sloane Home Ltd	£37,320
Choice of Nature Limited	£47,776	Alwais Ltd	£36,961
Glow Beauty Shop Ltd	£47,460	Kathleen Natural Limited	£36,890
Pouty Lipzz Limited	£47,010	First Choice Hair & Beauty Limited	£36,795
HSK Enterprises Ltd	£47,000	Gracy Hair and Makeup Ltd	£36,605
Knight & Wilson Limited	£46,892	Pink Beauty Supplies (UK) Ltd.	£36,520
Elite Salon Solutions Limited	£46,523	Purity Skincare Limited	£36,520
Real Looks Limited	£46,399	Green Sprouts Limited	£36,480
Nukua Limited	£46,201	Shivax International Ltd	£36,060
Sherhind Accessorize Limited	£46,144	Botanical Brands Ltd	£35,851
Batalveez Ltd	£45,887	Beauty Buddy Limited	£35,472
A & R Salon Enterprises Limited	£45,583	Cosmedi Limited	£35,337
Haych Cosmetics Limited	£45,429	Wild Celia Ltd	£35,326
Inovair Limited	£45,422	Thalia Erodotou Limited	£35,201
Beltech Limited	£45,170	Aqua Qualia Limited	£35,150
MacKenzie Cosmetics Limited	£44,870	Holistic Plant Technologies Ltd	£35,000
EJS Brand Management Limited	£43,990	Myego Ltd	£34,875

Company	Amount	Company	Amount
SZ Beauty Limited	£34,720	Ecocare Organic Limited	£24,715
Art Creative Limited	£34,645	Vanilla Blanc Limited	£24,570
Coll Gen Limited	£34,488	Hy-Brd Ltd	£24,410
Hair There & Everywhere Hair & Beauty Ltd	£33,779	Beautifully Bliss Ltd	£24,380
Aenea Cosmetics Ltd	£33,753	UK Vietnam Trade Ltd	£24,377
Seadrift Trading Limited	£33,670	BM Supplier UK & Europe Ltd	£24,270
Hairco Hair & Beauty Ltd	£33,601	Polish Cosmetics Distribution Centre UK Limited	£24,073
Slixir Ltd	£33,560	Humanity Cosmetics Limited	£24,045
Charlie Locks Ltd	£33,468	Better Nature International Ltd	£24,030
Nat & Co Limited	£33,468	Korebeauty Limited	£23,955
Pure Swiss Aesthetics Ltd	£33,162	Jazzy Hair Limited	£23,810
Varama Limited	£32,930	Natural British Limited	£23,236
Pampering Pattie International Limited	£32,643	Inspired Hair Supplies Limited	£23,174
40075 Limited	£32,600	Silvercleanse Health & Beauty Limited	£22,962
Sportclinix Labs Ltd.	£32,410	Hundred Acres Apothecary Limited	£22,895
Mindful Soulful Limited	£32,023	Pococks Absolute Rose Ltd	£22,869
NC Import Limited	£31,228	Sun Lounge Supplies Limited	£22,699
Hair Operating Products Limited	£31,211	The Serious Skin Care Company Ltd.	£22,465
Orange Balloon Ltd	£31,189	Pure Products Limited	£22,410
Guess Her Secret Limited	£30,916	MYNC Brands Limited	£22,365
Millennium Nails North West Limited	£30,539	Suzanne Neville Fragrance Limited	£22,246
Collection 1212 Limited	£30,130	JO Nielsen Limited	£22,028
The Skin Care Company Limited	£30,109	Amahla Limited	£21,989
Amly Limited	£29,807	Jealous Cow Limited	£21,784
Skin Matrix HD+ Cosmetology Limited	£29,668	Markwins Beauty Products Limited	£21,771
Bodygold Limited	£29,598	Fragrance Plus Limited	£21,720
ID Aromatics Limited	£29,595	Globe Intraworks Limited	£21,559
Deo Beauty Products Limited	£29,449	Vision Trading Limited	£21,556
MV Roberts & Co (UK) Ltd	£29,318	Salon Ambition Limited	£21,482
Greenwise Distribution Ltd	£29,200	Yasmin Karimi Ltd	£21,416
Best Choice FMCG Ltd	£29,130	Earth Mother Limited	£21,264
Smooth Image Beauty Limited	£28,961	Wellbeing Skincare Limited	£21,194
Ahwaz Ltd	£28,515	P & T PL Ltd	£21,100
Uni Supply Ltd	£28,408	Gruhme UK Limited	£21,070
Control Cosmetics Ltd	£28,283	Garda Service Ltd	£20,920
Beautyge Fragrances Holdings Ltd	£28,000	Europebro Wholesalers Ltd	£20,414
Angela Pickering Limited	£27,848	My Beauty World Ltd	£20,190
B & O Natural Cosmetics Ltd	£27,691	1962 Ltd	£20,125
My Pink Ltd	£27,435	Body Reform Limited	£20,001
Elite Beauty (London) Limited	£27,370	Aqua Bleu Limited	£19,860
Casa Cosmetics Ltd	£27,319	BLK Cosmetics Limited	£19,800
AMF Distribution Limited	£27,130	Luscious Lashes International Ltd	£19,800
Heavenly Riches Limited	£27,120	Pinoline Trading Company Ltd	£19,787
Incorporated Beauty Limited	£27,066	Bullingberg Limited	£19,508
Very British Baby International Limited	£27,001	The Natural Skincare Company Ltd.	£19,448
Doyin Tradings UK Limited	£26,917	Tassels UK Ltd	£19,342
Janiro Ltd	£26,710	Beuti Limited	£19,243
Ameera London Limited	£26,541	SGJ Perfumes Limited	£19,084
Gelmoment Limited	£26,389	Scent Retail Ltd	£18,970
Lola's Apothecary Ltd	£26,210	Imperial Bioscience Ltd	£18,581
Base Pro Artists Ltd	£26,184	Hair from India Limited	£18,551
Ebong and Brothers Ltd	£26,000	Dermashack Limited	£18,513
Lash House Eyelash Extensions Supplies Ltd	£25,156	Smart Skin Limited	£18,481
Diverse Solution Ltd	£25,140	Strategy M Ltd	£18,426

The Top UK Perfume and Cosmetics Wholesalers

Allure Beauty Supplies Ltd	£18,370	Denise Brown Limited	£13,807
Ella Nur Ltd	£18,370	Atlantic Beauty Store Limited	£13,779
ORA Naturals Limited	£18,214	Dee Doo Limited	£13,766
Aneen Ventures Limited	£18,109	Mega Mane Limited	£13,714
EBF Europe Ltd	£17,850	Essential Cosmetics Ltd	£13,680
Man & Diva's Ltd	£17,708	Maxibay Limited	£13,670
Ovis Liv Limited	£17,580	GBBC Ltd	£13,633
Ere Perez UK Limited	£17,550	Alico Exports Limited	£13,244
Rhona Gillmore Limited	£17,525	Goodscents Limited	£13,151
The Legends London Limited	£17,340	Noyras Ltd	£13,140
Romade Limited	£17,333	Beauty Solutions Limited	£13,070
Kingdom Scotland Limited	£17,190	Sue Moxley Beauty Limited	£13,049
Actuate Services (GB) Ltd	£17,152	Aqolade Ltd	£13,038
Super Yacht Spa Ltd	£17,139	Maddi Alexander Limited	£12,930
Calmer Solutions Limited	£16,916	Total Beauty Ltd	£12,912
Moyra UK Ltd	£16,751	Sara Post Ltd	£12,790
Alpha La Roche Limited	£16,727	Contour and More London Limited	£12,749
Pandhy's UK Sweet Cosmetics Ltd.	£16,670	Indigo Direct Ltd	£12,688
Snob Distribution Limited	£16,470	Luxe Associates Ltd	£12,670
NMB Property Limited	£16,441	Natrelle Limited	£12,450
Mitonia Company Limited	£16,350	Piggy Paint UK Ltd	£12,375
Fairy Dust Limited	£16,250	Fuzzique Limited	£12,330
Kamarino Limited	£16,146	Amberhue Limited	£12,220
Paiman Limited	£15,999	The Halal Cosmetics Company Limited	£12,190
Skin & Tonic London Ltd	£15,963	Beautysugaring Limited	£12,181
Image Hub Limited	£15,937	Alexandra de Markoff Limited	£12,180
Grautrans Limited	£15,870	Rose Tree Enterprises Ltd.	£12,099
Diamonds on Demand Ltd	£15,840	Venus Beauty Limited	£12,078
Kirimi Limited	£15,690	Jakor Limited	£12,054
Cosmetia UK Limited	£15,689	Santini Trade Ltd.	£11,923
Cor Europe Limited	£15,602	Neal's Yard Remedies (International) Ltd	£11,700
2M PH. Intl. Limited	£15,601	Perezoso Limited	£11,695
Modernist Fragrance Ltd.	£15,598	Chief Cosmetics Ltd	£11,591
Droplet Cosmetics Limited	£15,132	Laldhinio Limited	£11,571
Barnsley Card Ltd	£15,070	London Export Ltd	£11,417
By Sarah Limited	£15,020	L'Revolution Beauty Ltd	£11,393
Beard Zone Ltd	£15,000	Beauty Expression (UK) Limited	£11,389
HDDirect Limited	£15,000	Attar Mist Ltd	£11,220
Skincare Cornwall Ltd	£14,800	Regima Medic Ltd	£11,033
Cassolette & Co (Sales & Marketing) Limited	£14,774	Kenbar Beauty Products Limited	£11,000
Sahney Siblings Limited	£14,743	CHT Supplies Limited	£10,999
Warehouse.5 Limited	£14,634	Alliance SG Limited	£10,947
Eyeslices UK Limited	£14,568	AI Cosmetics Ltd	£10,930
PHB Franchise Limited	£14,439	Albert Roger Benelux Limited	£10,904
Abbliss Limited	£14,280	Paradise Organics London Ltd	£10,806
Solution Cosmetic Ltd	£14,228	Realine Beauty Limited	£10,710
Aurora Spa Health and Beauty Limited	£14,120	Aurum Argan Ltd	£10,679
Myroo Ltd	£14,070	Shalohm Ltd	£10,587
Rejuvapen UK Ltd	£14,042	Bath Spa Skincare Limited	£10,523
Temple Spirit Ltd	£14,020	Moyou Ltd	£10,430
Smiles Glasgow Limited	£13,980	Everyday Cosmetics Ltd	£10,330
Chirp Body Ltd	£13,970	QOD UK Ltd	£10,322
The Heath Consumables Ltd	£13,905	Vittoria Ventures Limited	£10,320
Argan Liquid Gold Limited	£13,810	Lumos Products Limited	£10,264

Company	Amount	Company	Amount
Santiago Distribution Limited	£10,223	Complexi-Light Ltd	£7,200
Belfast Beard Company Ltd	£10,180	Branded Hair Limited	£7,190
Ink Oil Limited	£10,001	Hamon Concepts Limited	£7,022
Bizi Bazzar Limited	£9,940	Buff Natural Body Care Ltd	£7,017
Green Harmony Limited	£9,939	Alianaz Ltd.	£7,010
Tir Chonaill London Ltd	£9,908	Daniele de Winter Monaco-UK Ltd	£7,000
Wrap N Pack Ltd	£9,880	Essentials4men Ltd	£6,990
Inga Permanent Make Up Limited	£9,816	Glute Plus Limited	£6,910
The Beauty Center Ltd	£9,810	Yorkshire Beauty Supplies Limited	£6,827
La Beauty Labs Ltd.	£9,807	Portland House International Trading Limited	£6,800
Anthony Braden Limited	£9,641	Spa and Salon Solutions Ltd	£6,790
Slim Line Club UK Ltd	£9,610	Sanchi Corp Limited	£6,697
A Pony Called Steve Ltd	£9,550	J & W Distribution Limited	£6,643
Razias London Ltd	£9,450	Pur3 Health Limited	£6,630
TM Brands Limited	£9,434	Online Motions Limited	£6,510
Iryna Stewart Ltd	£9,358	Diva Deva UK Limited	£6,500
Jedidiah Group Ltd	£9,254	Amassuna Limited	£6,500
Shyline Ltd	£9,236	Woldscot Limited	£6,410
United Solutions (UK) Limited	£9,180	Up Roar Ltd.	£6,404
Bellevue of London Ltd.	£9,174	Mann & Noble Europe Limited	£6,398
The Parfum Club Ltd	£9,163	Prispens Limited	£6,390
Beau Belle Brushes Ltd	£9,144	Need4health Limited	£6,380
Plectra Polish Limited	£9,084	LIV Organic Company Limited	£6,373
Mayjoy The Perfumer Ltd	£9,045	Miluv Ltd	£6,359
VIS International Corporation Limited	£9,000	Mupe Ltd	£6,244
Nomad Care Ltd	£8,992	Exentrique Limited	£6,206
Bedfordshire Beard Co. Limited	£8,947	BBT Products Limited	£6,203
Jennifer Myers Limited	£8,921	Dermaenhance Ltd.	£6,130
Miya Hair Limited	£8,721	La Tips Limited	£6,003
Janssen Cosmetics UK Ltd	£8,695	MJL Products Ltd	£5,934
Nut Dust Ltd	£8,620	Beauty Masks Limited	£5,924
Walking Pet Balloons (UK) Limited	£8,590	Shebelle Limited	£5,840
Nixsi Limited	£8,562	Sunspa UK Limited	£5,824
Disley Limited	£8,487	Brand Evangelists for Beauty Limited	£5,802
Bolm4 Limited	£8,480	Home Design 24 Ltd	£5,750
Rekze Laboratories Ltd	£8,433	Three Pears Online Limited	£5,585
J's Luxury Perfumery Ltd	£8,400	Allied Warden Marketing Limited	£5,579
Ruby Concepts Ltd	£8,218	Daly Beauty Limited	£5,540
Hexbomb Ltd	£8,053	DKB Essentials Ltd	£5,509
Naturally By Nature Ltd	£8,030	Elizabeth Cornelius Limited	£5,480
Indigo Nails Online Shop Ltd.	£8,029	Our-Scent Ltd	£5,469
Zipco Limited	£8,017	S & E Ventures Ltd	£5,430
Mil Iocshlainte, All Natural Balms Ltd	£7,978	Hazellbrook Limited	£5,410
Cool Essentials Limited	£7,910	Emel Trade Ltd	£5,400
Scented Home Limited	£7,649	Laurens Cosmetics UK Limited	£5,261
Ansor Supplies Ltd	£7,582	Shama Pharma Ltd	£5,253
Rokka Imagine Ltd	£7,580	Flores Distribution Limited	£5,240
Maringo Ltd	£7,520	Cosmetics 4U Limited	£5,237
Clarendon of London Limited	£7,440	Korban Beauty Limited	£5,193
Active Tan Limited	£7,410	Honeypie Minerals Limited	£5,152
Funky Skincare Limited	£7,337	Malvina Skin Care Limited	£5,144
Scope Cosmetics Ltd	£7,241	AJ Active Enterprises Ltd	£5,078
Lifestyle International Limited	£7,230	Anar Naturals Limited	£5,050
Natural Skincare London Limited	£7,210	Ileri Trading Limited	£5,032

Boutique Perfumes Limited	£4,912	Le Pure Limited	£3,089		
2B Enterprises Limited	£4,905	From Mini Acorns Ltd	£3,071		
Linrose Care Ltd	£4,865	Rabimed International Limited	£3,001		
Dunstan and Burr Ltd	£4,828	Jess Nails Limited	£3,000		
Anne Marie Beauty Products (U.K.) Limited	£4,670	Kiddeo Limited	£3,000		
Mono Naturoils Ltd	£4,660	Naturyl Glow Ltd	£2,977		
Olivia Kate Cosmetics Ltd	£4,607	Bes Hair Products Limited	£2,974		
Anglia-Perfumery Ltd.	£4,512	Lady T Limited	£2,966		
Heir & Grace Ltd	£4,500	Spartzy Lifestyle Brands Ltd	£2,940		
Yellbird Limited	£4,500	Impressions Beauty Limited	£2,910		
Aster & Bay Ltd.	£4,500	Karina Enterprise Ltd	£2,890		
Seba Trade Limited	£4,480	Crescent Soaps Ltd	£2,865		
Given By Nature Limited	£4,473	Swiss Arabian Perfumes (UK) Ltd	£2,807		
Beauty Bash Limited	£4,377	Miss Vivien Ltd	£2,731		
Julien Miguel Ltd	£4,345	Charms Europe Ltd	£2,713		
Lacomo Beauty Ltd	£4,310	Herba Skincare Limited	£2,679		
UK Fillers Ltd	£4,295	Diet Plan Unique Ltd	£2,645		
BeautyEmpireUK Ltd	£4,250	Hughes Evans Essentials Ltd	£2,642		
J. Rudzitis Ltd	£4,224	Cadden & Lee Limited	£2,632		
Medora of London Limited	£4,200	Winchpharma (Consumer Healthcare) Ltd	£2,538		
Glam Wholesale Limited	£4,182	Mirimiri Limited	£2,537		
Refan UK Ltd	£4,148	Juliajosh Limited	£2,393		
Wafson Ltd	£4,148	Beauty at The Avenue Online Limited	£2,364		
Charlotte Rhys UK Limited	£4,136	Kiki Body Limited	£2,314		
Philip Hansard Limited	£4,133	Jeunvie Ltd	£2,309		
Surreal Health & Beauty Limited	£4,100	Glamn Holding Ltd	£2,306		
Divine Natural Limited	£4,047	Nizz Cosmetics Ltd	£2,228		
Face Fodder Limited	£4,018	Moderna Aesthetics Ltd	£2,172		
Ferrara-Bardile Ltd	£4,000	Excellent Edges Ltd	£2,090		
PLTradeGroup Limited	£4,000	Angel Lash Limited	£2,090		
Sheabynature Ltd	£4,000	Amazon Healthcare Ltd	£2,088		
Luscious Skincare Ltd	£3,960	Crystal Nails No1 Ltd	£2,072		
BSB Fashion Limited	£3,899	Jigsaw International Holdings Limited	£2,050		
Alimacskincare Limited	£3,868	Madre Skincare Limited	£2,030		
Martha & Daughter Limited	£3,811	IR International Ltd	£2,026		
Myriad Skincare Limited	£3,770	Hi Life Health and Beauty (UK) Limited	£1,968		
Argan Vanity Ltd	£3,684	Meddiamonds Ltd	£1,964		
M.S.S (Micro Scientific Services) Limited	£3,610	Amazingface Limited	£1,947		
Innon Vision Limited	£3,559	STT Industries Ltd.	£1,920		
Sandine Zartaux Holding Ltd	£3,544	Okmarket24 Ltd	£1,862		
Irum Cosmetics Ltd	£3,501	Smart Nails (UK) Ltd	£1,841		
Aesthetic Cosmetic Ltd	£3,500	Skinnydip Skincare Limited	£1,830		
Lanko Naturals-UK (PVT) Ltd	£3,491	Xpoze International Limited	£1,812		
Rich 101 Ltd	£3,452	Rosense (UK) Ltd	£1,785		
Sopureoils Ltd	£3,421	Chando-UK Ltd	£1,783		
The Hair & Cosmetic Company Limited	£3,323	MSD Trading Services Limited	£1,700		
Fragrance and Gifts Limited	£3,289	Sai Darshan Limited	£1,670		
Paradoxx Ltd	£3,280	Monshea Limited	£1,659		
Pam Trading Limited	£3,260	Business Angels Syndicate Ltd	£1,618		
Azzy London Ltd	£3,230	Raynolds Ltd	£1,600		
Sanay Ltd	£3,212	Sculptola Ltd	£1,578		
Hotel Essentials Ltd	£3,180	Procare Women Health Limited	£1,548		
Rita Roberts Cosmetics Limited	£3,140	GS Fragrances Limited	£1,530		
Argan Secrets Limited	£3,125	Ars Nova (UK) Limited	£1,528		

Foad Wax Limited	£1,516	Adible Limited	£601
East Garden Ltd	£1,515	Akwaaba Social Enterprises Limited	£584
Mimi's Organics Ltd	£1,510	Gallya Deelya Ltd.	£560
Bigteal Industries Limited	£1,508	Celeb Products Ltd	£550
Nature et Bien-Etre Limited	£1,488	Dr Shea Ltd	£492
Sikania Ltd	£1,447	Leading National Training Ltd	£451
Bessacarr Ltd	£1,431	Sunspa Europe Limited	£445
Honor London Limited	£1,430	UK Make Up Limited	£426
Pherolec Global Ltd	£1,380	Smartway Pharma Limited	£426
Lino Rose Ltd	£1,288	Bush Oil Limited	£425
Occo London Limited	£1,242	Can Celebrity Brands Limited	£411
Sash Products Limited	£1,198	Butterflyy Productions Ltd	£400
Katherine Longhi Ltd	£1,187	Liaver Limited	£389
Vilhelm Parfumerie Limited	£1,170	Olfacstory Parfums Limited	£380
Cosmolab Limited	£1,140	Mounir's Ltd	£378
Neo Cosmetics Limited	£1,125	Aromeco Limited	£371
Julio & Ejder Ltd	£1,073	Unique Fragrances Limited	£368
Herra Hair Care Limited	£1,070	Ulric de Varens UK Limited	£354
S & P Cosmetics Limited	£1,066	True Scents Ltd	£344
20seven Limited	£1,062	Salt and Pamper Limited	£340
JZM International Limited	£1,055	Disciple Skincare Limited	£328
Hermossa Limited	£1,030	Sweden Eco Limited	£326
Deltagamma Limited	£1,027	Herbal Hakeem Ltd	£316
Nalla Skincare Ltd	£1,023	Etonigbo Limited	£259
Buy Perfumes London Limited	£1,021	Beauty Code Limited	£222
Beaming White Ltd	£1,015	AIGC Limited	£216
Sipro (UK) Ltd	£1,002	Arizona Botaniq Limited	£200
Evorin Pharma Limited	£1,000	Ozone Perfumes and Cosmetics Limited	£199
James & Jake Ltd	£1,000	Dermafood Limited	£191
Vancooler Ltd	£1,000	V@M Limited	£189
Florals of London Limited	£1,000	Quality Check Ltd	£140
Cedron Ltd.	£1,000	Vedaway Ltd	£139
Organica Skincare Ltd	£1,000	Samla Tribe Limited	£127
Posh Gift Ltd	£1,000	NA Medical Care Ltd	£124
Wild Organics Limited	£1,000	Ossulstone Hundred Limited	£124
Siam Skin Ltd	£1,000	Protective World Ltd	£120
London Ethnic Ltd	£992	Chronicles Medical Consulting Ltd	£120
GP Mediplus Ltd	£896	Luxury Consulting by Bethan Williams Limited	£112
Azur Interiors Limited	£868	Wellness Style Limited	£108
Beautifull Planet Ltd	£849	Pazery Bouffard and Company Limited	£100
Respect Male Grooming Ltd.	£833	Diva Cosmetics Limited	£100
Mary Jean Limited	£832	Hairways Direct Limited	£100
Mayfair Export UK Ltd	£771	Selfcare Corporation Ltd	£100
Nicfead Cosmetics & Fragrance Ltd	£747	Spa Skincare Limited	£100
UK Elements of Beauty Ltd	£735	Selective Fragrances Ltd	£100
U 2 Shine Limited	£722	Allies Network Ltd	£100
T A Trading Ltd	£712	Petersham Ventures Ltd	£100
Arahant Ltd	£697	Wild Beauty Ltd	£100
Simona Beauty Store Ltd	£686	Beauty Cosmetics (Bristol) Limited	£100
Motion Junkies Limited	£678	Beauty Cosmetics (Nottingham) Limited	£100
Goldshore (UK) Limited	£668	Interall Ltd	£100
Kailijumei Ltd	£662	Valiscious Limited	£100
Anthony Braden Online Ltd.	£629	Ibeautheart Limited	£100
JLE Trading Limited	£617	Pilaten EU Ltd	£100

The Top UK Perfume and Cosmetics Wholesalers   dellam

Ashley & Co UK Ltd	£100	Balm Balm Limited	£6
Acquaderm Ltd	£100	Victoria Pharma London Ltd	£2
Yehmea Limited	£100	Dermanor Ltd.	£2
Asante Distributors Limited	£100	Salonpas UK Limited	£1
Earth Aid Group Limited	£100	Hisamitsu Pharmaceutical UK Limited	£1
Urban Retreat Products Limited	£98	Bespoke Mr Ltd	£1
Gaya Minerals Limited	£51	Makeup54 Ltd	£1
Askett & English Ltd	£50	Orrwa Pharma Health & Beauty Limited	£1
Labrayon Cosmetiques France UK Ltd	£50	Kaxton Limited	£1
VR Consult Limited	£45	L & L Sunlight Importers and Exporters Limited	£1
The Essence of Esther Ltd	£42	Pharmafrance Ltd.	£1
Oilyspirit Ltd	£10	King's Vegan Grooming Ltd	£1
Ruxley Medical Aids Limited	£10		

This page is intentionally left blank

Age of Companies

1920-1929
Pazery Bouffard and Co Ltd
Chanel Limited
Colgate-Palmolive (U.K.) Ltd
Geo. F. Trumper (Perfumer and Products)

1930-1939
Guerlain Limited
L'Oreal (U.K.) Limited

1940-1949
Beiersdorf UK Ltd.
Brodie and Stone PLC
Pompadour Laboratories Limited
Ray & Company (Hairdressers Sundries Men)

1950-1959
Capital (Hair and Beauty) Ltd
McCoey & Co. Limited
Polex Limited
Dennis Williams Limited

1960-1969 [5]
HFC Prestige Products Limited
LVMH Fragrance Brands UK Ltd
Estee Lauder Cosmetics Ltd
Phils (Wholesale) Limited
Eve Taylor (London) Limited

1970-1979 [21]
Body Shop International Ltd
Crabtree & Evelyn (Overseas) Ltd
Denbond Pharmaceuticals Ltd
Direct Cosmetics Limited
Exquisite Cosmetics Limited
Glendale S/S Limited
Guinot-Mary Cohr UK Limited
Hair Cosmetics Limited
Headissimo Limited
Jica Beauty Products Limited
Kent Cosmetics Limited
Lambsmead Limited
Northdown Cosmetics Limited
Parfums Christian Dior (U.K.) Ltd
Pricecheck Toiletries Limited
Puig UK Limited
Railworth Limited
Shilcroft Limited
Transeur Export Finance Co. Ltd
Vivalis Limited
Winter Hill No.2 Limited

1980-1989 [42]
Acering Limited
Alico Exports Limited
Alvor Limited
Ambassadors Choice Limited
Anne Marie Beauty Products (U.K.)
Australian Bodycare U.K. Ltd
CRM Trading Limited
Clarins (U.K.) Limited
Comedic Limited
Dermalogica (UK) Limited
Dovedale Limited
Edenwest Limited
Fine Fragrances and Cosmetics Ltd
General Healthcare Limited
Glendale Group Limited

Graham Hair and Beauty Limited
HCT Europe Limited
Hairways (Hair & Beauty) Ltd
Camilla Hepper Sales Limited
ID Aromatics Limited
Intercos UK Ltd
Johnson & Johnson Limited
Kidlex Limited
Lipoid Kosmetik Ltd
Lynch-Staunton Cosmetics Ltd
Mainline Marketing U K. Ltd
Make-Up International Limited
Mane (UK) Limited
Neal's Yard (Natural Remedies) Ltd
Polar Export Services Limited
RDC (UK) Limited
P.S. Sahney & Co Limited
Salon Success Limited
Sandaig Ltd
Sanmex International Limited
Shaneel Enterprises Limited
Stantondown Limited
Synlatex Limited
Talza Limited
Thalgo UK Limited
Trade Smart Marketing Limited
Vivalis Beauty Limited

1990-1994 [43]
A B International Limited
Adelphi Corporation Limited
Aspects Beauty Co Ltd
Beautywise Limited
Crystal Spring Consumer Division Ltd
Drammock International Limited
ESPA International (UK) Ltd
Euro Healthcare Services Ltd
Eurocare Impex Services Ltd
Eurocosmetics Limited
F.D.D. International Limited
Finders International Limited
Fleuroma Limited
Rhona Gillmore Limited
Gojo Industries - Europe Ltd
Kenneth Green Associates Ltd
Haresgraces Limited
Headlines (Hair & Beauty Supplies)
Herb U.K. Limited
Hot (UK) Limited
Incorporated Perfumery Distribution
International Trade Corporation Ltd
Karium Ltd
Kenbar Beauty Products Limited
L'Anza Europe Limited
Lady T Limited
Charlie Locks Ltd
London Cosmetics Co Ltd
Lush Ltd.
M & M Cosmetics Limited
Mary Kay Cosmetics (U.K.) Ltd
N.S.I. (U.K.) Limited
Neolife International Ltd
Orange Square Co Ltd.
Organic Colour Systems Limited
Per-Scent Group Limited
Sharp's Global Trading Limited
Skin Care Co Ltd
Takasago (U.K.) Limited
Trading Scents Limited
Ultra Glow Cosmetics Limited
White Rose Aromatics Limited
Winning Lines Limited

1995 [10]
Beauty Star Limited
Berkeley Square Cosmetics Co Ltd
Bodygold Limited
E.J. Contracts Limited
Fragrance Factory Limited
Amelia Knight Limited
Ken Lamacraft Marketing Ltd
M & N Traders Limited
Phyto Therapeutics Limited
Sub Tropic Limited

1996 [11]
Aromaderme UK Limited
Beauty Leisure Industry Supplies and Services
Choice of Nature Limited
Classic Beaute Limited
Create Images Ion Limited
Healthpoint Limited
Imperial Pharmaceuticals Ltd
International Hair Cosmetics Ltd
North West Cosmetics Limited
Razaq & Iqbal Limited
Repechage Europe Limited

1997 [15]
Ajmal Perfume (UK) Limited
Arrow Hair & Beauty Supplies Ltd
Delights Beauty Co Ltd
Essential Beauty Supplies Ltd
Fragrance and Gifts Limited
Icon Consultancy Ltd
Jean Christian Perfumes Ltd
Kiss Products UK Limited
Mashco Limited
Passion 4 Health International Ltd
Ren Ltd
Serious Skin Care Co Ltd.
Skincare Sanctuary Limited
Three Pears Online Limited
Unique Cosmetics Limited

1998 [15]
Allied Fragrances Limited
Allied Warden Marketing Ltd
Beltech Limited
Cassolette & Co (Sales & Marketing)
Clive Christian Perfume Ltd
Cyrano Limited
Emvi Limited
A.H. Francis Professional Beauty
Galactix Ltd
H & B Supplies Limited
Mad Beauty Limited
Re:New Beauty Ltd
Sisley UK Limited
TLC - Tender Loving Care UK Ltd
Warpaint Cosmetics Limited

1999 [14]
AJS Marketing Limited
Apex Trading Limited
Aveda Limited
Awobajo Brother's Limited
Beauty Wholesale Limited
Bond Street Cosmetics Limited
Cowshed Products Limited
Deo Beauty Products Limited
Excel (GS) Limited

House of Worth Limited
Nature's Dream Limited
Primoil Limited
Universal Toiletries Corporation Ltd
Zipco Limited

2000 [38]

Elizabeth Arden (UK) Ltd
Azhar Academy Limited
Beaute Prestige International Ltd
Beautytrade Limited
Belsay Ltd
Benefit Cosmetics Limited
Blissworld Limited
Boots International Limited
Anthony Braden Online Ltd.
Jasper Conran Perfumes Ltd
Cool Essentials Limited
Cosmetics Direct Limited
County Sales Limited
DHB (UK) Ltd.
Diva Cosmetics Limited
Earth Mother Limited
Export Solutions (International) Ltd
H2K Limited
Hairways Direct Limited
Intermercantile Limited
JS Marketing (N.I.) Limited
Jazzy Hair Limited
Macks Ltd.
Markwins Beauty Brands International
Medora of London Limited
Myridium Active.Com Limited
PH Group UK Limited
Perfume World Limited
SB Beauty Marketing Limited
Scent Factory Limited
Serendipity Herbals Ltd
Simlar 2 Limited
Simply Nature Ltd.
Square Spots Limited
Starcount Limited
Three Beauties of London Ltd
Yummy Home Ltd
Zainab Limited

2001 [22]

Ars Nova (UK) Limited
Beauty Solutions Limited
Beauty Systems Group Ltd.
Denise Brown Limited
Designer Fragrances Limited
Essential Oils Direct Ltd
Evany Personal Care Limited
Freestyle (Trade) Ltd.
FreshBreathOnline Limited
Gentle Beauty Co Ltd
Global Essence UK Ltd
Intertrade Group Ltd
Jigsaw International Holdings Ltd
KMI Brands Limited
Nature et Bien-Etre Limited
Nectar International Limited
Pravera Ltd
S A Designer Parfums Limited
Skinmed Ltd
Specialist Hair Products Ltd
Value for Money (Cleethorpes) Ltd
Zieseniss Limited

2002 [36]

Akoma International (UK) Ltd
Aqua Bleu Limited
Asurex Limited
Andre Boyard Perfumes Limited
Caudalie UK Limited
Elemental Herbology Limited
Essential Bodycare Limited
Euro Aromas Limited
Fair Pharm Limited
Filberts Bees Limited
Firecrest Communications Ltd
Forever Living Products Ireland Ltd
G.P.B. Supplies Limited
Louise Galvin Limited
Hisamitsu Pharmaceutical UK Ltd
Hisamitsu UK Limited
Iam By Nature Ltd.
Inovair Limited
Janson Limited
KDM Supplies Limited
Lumos Products Limited
Minmar (1008) Limited
Natrelle Limited
P.H.A.B Wholesale Limited
Pro Impressions (UK) Limited
Rabimed International Limited
Rainbow Cosmetics (Manchester) Ltd
Real Looks Limited
Rita Roberts Cosmetics Ltd
Sai Enterprise Limited
Salonpas UK Limited
Sun-Glo Limited
Sundome Leisure Products Ltd
Transformulas International Ltd
Vett Limited
West Three Trading Limited

2003 [33]

Balmain Hair UK Ltd
Beauty Without Cruelty Limited
Calmer Solutions Limited
Collection 1212 Limited
Leighton Denny Limited
Direct Salon Limited
East End Cosmetics Limited
Elko Electrical Ltd.
F A Commodities Ltd
Fresh Cosmetics Limited
Hairways 77 Limited
David Hart (Santo) Limited
I Love Cosmetics Limited
J S Trading (UK) Limited
JGR UK Distributions Limited
Lemon Tree Beauty Limited
MacKenzie Cosmetics Limited
Linda Meredith Skin Care Ltd
Doris Michaels Cosmetics Ltd
Natural Skincare Co Ltd.
JO Nielsen Limited
Oils4life Limited
Palmsextra Limited
Parkside Nails Supplies Ltd
Penny Price Aromatherapy Ltd
Per-Scent Fine Limited
Salon Focus Ltd
Satya Life Ltd
Spa Voyage Limited
Ukab Limited
Ulric de Varens UK Limited
Vita Liberata Limited
Wisdom of Nature Limited

2004 [29]

2B Enterprises Limited
Agenda Salon Concepts Limited
Aglory Merchant Enterprises Ltd
Amber House Limited
Anglia-Perfumery Ltd.
Boutique Perfumes Limited
Anthony Braden Limited
Cosmetia UK Limited
Cosmetic Doctor at Work Ltd
Dee Doo Limited
Dr.Lipp Ltd
Face Boutique Limited
First Choice Hair & Beauty Ltd
Golden Rose Limited
Hair & Cosmetic Co Ltd
Healthcare Procurement Services Ltd
K.B. Salon Supplies Limited
Little Enterprises (NI) Ltd
Mama Mio Limited
Markwins Beauty Products Ltd
Mypure Limited
Original Additions (Beauty Products)
Per-Scent Limited
Perfume Supplies Limited
Pure Products Limited
Roja Dove Limited
Salon Ambition Limited
Salon Supplies Limited
Universal Attraction (London) Ltd

2005 [40]

Abbliss Limited
Barefaced Beauty Ltd
Beauty Buddy Limited
Sarah Chapman Ltd.
Comfort Click Limited
Direct Salon Supplies Limited
Edge Nail & Beauty Limited
Essence Pur Ltd.
B.Fairall (UK) Limited
Florascent Duftmanufaktur Ltd
Flores Distribution Limited
Fragrance Acquisitions Limited
Fragrance and Beauty Limited
Goldshore (UK) Limited
Grand By Designs Limited
Home & Bodycare Limited
Joy Limited
Lock Stock & Barrel Grooming Co Ltd
MB Promotion Ltd.
Martha & Daughter Limited
Millennium Nails North West Ltd
Jennifer Myers Limited
Pharmaclinix Limited
Pink Beauty Supplies (UK) Ltd.
Pippa Beauty Limited
Plan Target Limited
Pole Position (Licensing) Ltd
Rouge Bunny Rouge UK Limited
Sai Darshan Limited
Daniel Sandler Ltd
Santiago Distribution Limited
Season of Beauty Limited
Shure Enterprises (UK) Limited
Sun Lounge Supplies Limited
Teoxane UK Limited
Transformulas Limited
True Affinity Limited
UK Mineral Make-Up Limited
Victoria Pharma London Ltd
Xpoze International Limited

2006 [43]

ABC Beauty Limited
Acti Laboratories UK Ltd
Anatomicals London (England, The World, The Universe-Known and Unknown)
Arbonne UK Limited
BKSL Limited
Bains and Daughters Limited
Beauty Forever Cosmetics Ltd
Beauty Masks Limited
Beauty Premier Limited
Beauty Select Limited
Bellapierre Cosmetics Limited
Bits4hair Limited
Body Reform Limited
Brandaroma Limited
Bulldog Skincare Limited
Calbrook Cosmetics UK Ltd
Clinova Limited
Ecobeauty Ltd
Eyelash Design Co Ltd
Fabdoo Limited
Fish London Limited
Fragrance & Beauty Creations Ltd
Fragranceexpert Limited
Freestyle Trade (UK) Limited
Glitterati Distributions Ltd
Hanfan (UK) Limited
He-Shi Enterprises Ltd
Herc Ltd.
Highland Soap Co. Limited
M Beauty Ltd
Maison Danu (UK) Ltd
Meller Design Solutions Ltd
Myego Ltd
One Beauty Ltd
Purity Skincare Limited
RMG Hair Limited
Regima@Dr H Ltd
SI & D (UK) Limited
Salon Connection (Wales) Ltd
Simple Beauty (UK) Limited
Skinsmith Limited
Sunspa UK Limited
Sweet Squared Limited

2007 [42]

Additional Lengths Ltd
Adel Professional Limited
Almirall Limited
Amazingface Limited
Anglia Enterprise (UK) Limited
Argan Secrets Limited
Beauty School Limited
Beautynet Limited
Brambles Farm Ltd
Branded Hair Limited
CBee (Europe) Limited
Cosmeceuticals Limited
Danlab Ltd.
Dr. Organic Limited
Dynamic Skincare Ltd
FM Cosmetics UK Ltd
Fragrance Sales Limited
Gazelli International Limited
Good Ventures Limited
Hair Operating Products Ltd
Honeypot Cosmetics (Wholesale) Ltd
Horatio London Holdings Ltd
Impressions Beauty Limited
Initiative (UK) Limited

Jakor Limited
Koreesa Limited
Laurelle London Ltd
Leading National Training Ltd
Logical Content Ltd
Mamado International Limited
P.R. Professional Salon Supplies Ltd
Pampering Pattie International Ltd
Pern Consumer Products Limited
Pharmacare (Europe) Limited
Saffron Beauty Ltd
Smart Nails (UK) Ltd
Strip Distribution Limited
United Perfumes Limited
United Solutions (UK) Limited
Urban Retreat Products Limited
Watsoap.Com Limited
XSS Scotland Limited

2008 [48]

1962 Ltd
AAA Edinburgh Ltd
Annexa Solutions Limited
Bbeauty Lounge Cosmetics Ltd
Beauty Fort Limited
Beauty Senses Limited
Bioactivebeauty Ltd
Bolm4 Limited
Brandcare Group Limited
Brands de Luxe Co Ltd
Cilko Ltd
Clarendon of London Limited
Creative Colours International Ltd
Dazzlers & Toppers PTL Ltd
Dear Body Limited
Diva Deva UK Limited
Fushi Wellbeing Limited
Hair Ornaments UK Limited
Hairshine UK Ltd
Hampton Brands Limited
Herbline U.K. Limited
Iam Finance Limited
Innes McBeath Sourcing Ltd.
King of Shaves Co Ltd
Kirimi Limited
Kounga Ltd
Lubatti Limited
Mary Jean Limited
Menco International Limited
Miracle Herbs & Fruits Cosmetics Ltd
Nails and Co (Midlands) Ltd
Neal's Yard Remedies (International) Ltd
Occo London Limited
Perfect Look & Health Ltd
Perricone MD Cosmeceuticals UK Ltd
Plantain Essential Oils Ltd
Predator Trading Limited
Skincare Cornwall Ltd
Smooth Image Beauty Limited
Steam Cream Limited
Swift Retail Limited
United Retail & Sourcing Ltd
Universal Design Promotion Ltd
Vivatinell Limited
Walking Pet Balloons (UK) Ltd
Wild Brands Limited
Wild Organics Limited
Zarvis London Limited

2009 [72]

A & R Salon Enterprises Ltd

ABX Beauty Limited
Chris Adams Perfumes Ltd
Alton Trading Ltd
Beautifully Bliss Ltd
Beauty Forever Limited
Better Nature International Ltd
Brand Agency (London) Limited
T L Brooks Limited
Com4hospitality Ltd.
Cor Europe Limited
Elizabeth Cornelius Limited
Cosmolab Limited
DKH Retail Limited
Daly Beauty Limited
Doterra (Europe) Ltd
EnhanceColor Limited
FB Beauty Ltd
Fairy Dust Limited
Georgie Salon Supplies Limited
Gold 22 (UK) Limited
Green & Dionisi Ltd
Grossmith Limited
HSK Enterprises Ltd
Hair North East Limited
Haircare of Sweden Ltd
Hairganic Limited
Hi Life Health and Beauty (UK) Ltd
Highfields Health Limited
Himalaya Enterprise Limited
Hydrea London Limited
Ideal Beauty Products Limited
Imijo Ltd
Interparcos U.K. Limited
Ivaxane UK Ltd
Jojoba Cosmetics Limited
Le Labo UK Limited
Les Petits Parfums Limited
M & M Import Ltd
Mancave Limited
Maximaliste Limited
Neal's Yard Remedies (Home) Ltd
Suzanne Neville Fragrance Ltd
Novmedic Limited
Oyemam Ltd
Ozprodz Limited
Paragon Enterprise Limited
Patagonia Consult Limited
Pellitier & Perkins Limited
Pink Cosmetics London Limited
Red Hot Products Limited
Rich 101 Ltd
Rosebud Perfume Co Ltd
SMCK Limited
Scent Global Ltd
Scent Retail Ltd
Sci Check Limited
Shared Beauty Secrets Limited
Snob Distribution Limited
This Works Products Limited
USA Hair Extensions Ltd
Unique Fragrances Limited
Use Natural Ltd
VIS International Corporation Ltd
Varama Limited
Wellbeing Skincare Limited
Wish List Limited
Wiv Global Limited
Woldscot Limited
XL Marketing Ltd.
Yorkshire Beauty Supplies Ltd
Zaigul Wholesale Ltd

The Top UK Perfume and Cosmetics Wholesalers

January-June 2010 [37]
Bath Spa Skincare Limited
Bessacarr Ltd
Cloud 19 Limited
Colbico Limited
Cath Collins Devon Ltd
Crystalnails4u Ltd
D & L Hair Products Limited
Tom Daxon Limited
Divine Natural Limited
Glorious Brands Ltd.
Gracefruit Limited
Gracetree Ltd
Heath Consumables Ltd
Herra Hair Care Limited
Incorporated Beauty Limited
Julien Miguel Ltd
Lescaro Health Limited
Loopy Hair & Beauty Ltd
Mahrosh Beauty Ltd
Merumaya Limited
Natural Touch Enterprises Ltd
Naturally By Nature Ltd
Nixsi Limited
Opatra Limited
Perfume Addict (UK) Ltd
Perfume Holding UK Limited
Regima UK Ltd
SES Wholesale Limited
Serene House UK Limited
Shivax International Ltd
Skin Matrix Limited
Skinnydip Skincare Limited
Soulful Beauty Ltd
Sunspa Europe Limited
Tansi Packaging Solutions Ltd
Valorem Capital One Ltd
Vedaway Ltd

July-December 2010 [27]
Beauty Code Limited
Beautypro Ltd
Bioeffect Limited
Bluestar Enterprise Limited
Bonitec Ltd
Cosmetronic Global Limited
Diverse Investment (London) Group
Elegance By London Limited
Thalia Erodotou Limited
Heavenly Fragrance (UK) Ltd
Holy Lama Naturals Ltd
Istylists Limited
Kazi Brothers Group Limited
Mil locshlainte, All Natural Balms Ltd
Motion Junkies Limited
Pharmadose Limited
Portland House International Trading
Regima Medic Ltd
Ringley Trading Limited
Rosense (UK) Ltd
Savvy & Shine Ltd
Seventa Image Ltd
She Who Dares UK Ltd
TM Brands Limited
Temple Spirit Ltd
Westfield House Distributors Ltd
White Lotus Anti Aging Ltd

January-June 2011 [54]
Acorn Brokerage Limited
Maddi Alexander Limited
Anar Naturals Limited
Arnest International Limited
Askett & English Ltd
BM Beauty Ltd.
Balm Balm Limited
Beaming White Ltd
Beautysugaring Limited
Beta Novis Limited
Ayesha Carolina Limited
Cool Blades Limited
Deity World Ltd
Ebong and Brothers Ltd
Elite Beauty (London) Limited
Everyday Cosmetics Ltd
Fizzy Peach Ltd
Foad Wax Limited
Functional Fragrances Ltd
Garda Service Ltd
Hera Beauty Ltd
Hy-Brd Ltd
I.S.O.D Limited
ID Skincare Limited
In Situ Cosmetics Ltd
Jealous Cow Limited
L.A.Tanning Co Ltd
La Generale Limited
Erno Laszlo Group Ltd
Life's Big Stuff Ltd
Liplast Ltd
Madre Skincare Limited
Makki Cosmetics Limited
Maringo Ltd
Metropolitan Beauty Ltd.
Moderna Aesthetics Ltd
Nail & Beauty Link Limited
Natural Skincare London Ltd
Nov'max Keratin Limited
Optima Consumer Health Limited
Our Choice Gift Limited
Outdoor Girl Limited
PHB Franchise Limited
Plane Luxuries Limited
Protec Botanica Ltd
Protec Ingredia Limited
Rapsodi London Ltd
Sasha Hair & Beauty Ltd
Sebaroyale Ltd
Star Qualities Ltd
Unineed Limited
Whitening World Ltd
Worth Worldwide Property Ltd
Zurego Limited

July-December 2011 [39]
AMF Distribution Limited
Active Skincare Limited
Alliance SG Limited
Anglo Indian Trading Limited
Beautiful Body Limited
Beyond Hair Ltd
G & J Britton Consulting Ltd
Dermafood Limited
Design Essentials Limited
Elequra Limited
Excelcia Limited
Face Lace Limited
Fade Out Limited
Gallya Deelya Ltd.
Gaya Minerals Limited
Gracy Hair and Makeup Ltd
Into Exports Limited
Janiro Ltd
Just The Product Ltd
Karina Enterprise Ltd
La Prairie (UK) Limited
Linrose Care Ltd
Lola's Apothecary Ltd
London Ethnic Ltd
Monshea Limited
Nail Perfection Limited
Natural Birthing Co Ltd
Niki & Co Ltd
ORA Naturals Limited
Ozone Perfumes and Cosmetics Ltd
Pixie Dust Products Limited
Profile Hair & Skin Care Ltd
Charlotte Rhys UK Limited
Jerome Russell Limited
SKN-RG Ltd
Salon Select (NI) Limited
Sawa Trading & Shipping Ltd
Tabitha JK Limited
UK Make Up Limited

January-March 2012 [30]
4T Medical Ltd
Amalgamated Euro Products UK Ltd
Aurelia Skincare Limited
BSB Global Limited
Bion Corporation Limited
Bracey Overseas Ltd
British American Solutions Ltd
Crescent Soaps Ltd
Deltagamma Limited
Dreamweave Products Ltd
Euro Perfumes (UK) Ltd
Green Sprouts Limited
HCT Beauty Ltd
Hair Fantastic Retail Limited
Haircosmetics (Sunderland) Ltd
JCB Skincare Limited
Lacomo Beauty Ltd
Lactura Ltd
MYNC Brands Limited
NB Beauty Limited
Pispo Ltd
Prestige Perfumes Limited
Pure Thoughts Ltd
QOD UK Ltd
Reliant Overseas UK Limited
Rosdon Group Limited
Salon Depot Ltd
Shahadah Ltd
Space Brands Limited
Swiss Arabian Perfumes (UK) Ltd

April-June 2012 [22]
Aesthetic Brands (Distribution and Management)
Alimacskincare Limited
Art Creative Limited
Bays International Limited
Bonfit UK Limited
CHK (UK) Ltd
Calla Distribution Ltd
Dermaenhance Ltd.
Enfield Distribution Ltd
Flirties Products and Training Ltd
Green World Spa Products Ltd
Guess Her Secret Limited
Impulse Global Solutions Ltd
Lab Brands Limited
Le Keux Vintage Enterprises Ltd

Malvina Skin Care Limited
Nat & Co Limited
Pinoline Trading Co Ltd
Pound Ring Ltd
Shay & Blue Ltd
UK MUA Limited
Veramic Limited

July-September 2012 [21]
Actuate Services (GB) Ltd
Aesthetic Cosmetic Ltd
Asabeauty Ltd
Beauty Innovator 2012 Ltd.
Can Celebrity Brands Limited
Celeb Products Ltd
Code Beautiful Limited
Coll Gen Limited
Foundation Brands Ltd
Harley Street Fulfilment Co Ltd
Holy Group Limited
MJL Products Ltd
Miluv Ltd
New Horizons (UK) Ltd
Rashimex Trading Limited
Seadrift Trading Limited
Seascape Island Management Ltd
Selfcare Corporation Ltd
So Susan Limited
Waterman Corporate Enterprises Ltd
Winchpharma (Consumer Healthcare) Ltd

October-December 2012 [23]
Amazon Healthcare Ltd
Aroma Actives Limited
Bluesky Products Limited
Botanical Brands Ltd
Bramley Products Ltd
Cosmetics 4U Limited
Cutagen Ltd
Dermamaitre Ltd.
Home Design 24 Ltd
Honeypie Minerals Limited
Inspired Hair Supplies Limited
LCB Trading (UK) Limited
Joseph Lanzante Products Ltd
Lipstick and Black Coffee Ltd
Sue Moxley Beauty Limited
Organii Limited
Plectra Polish Limited
Santini Trade Ltd.
Silk Oil of Morocco UK Limited
Smartway Pharma Limited
Spa Skincare Limited
Super Yacht Spa Ltd
Wholesale Hair Extensions Ltd

January-March 2013 [47]
A & B Supply Co. Limited
Al Cosmetics Ltd
Alpha La Roche Limited
Aqolade Ltd
Attar Mist Ltd
Aurelia Skincare (International) Ltd
Beauty Expression (UK) Limited
Beegood Enterprises Limited
Body Care Brand Development Ltd
CM Hair & Beauty Supplies Ltd
DMG Wholesale Limited
Deciem UK Ltd.
Dilecta Cosmetics Limited
EJS Brand Management Limited

Eden Brands Limited
Galenti Limited
Gruhme UK Limited
Gymbar Limited
Halal Cosmetics Co Ltd
Hundred Acres Apothecary Ltd
Inside Trading (Beauty) Ltd
Jeunvie Ltd
Jolly Rogers Crew Limited
Just Beautiful Skin Ltd
Lipolift Ltd
Liqwd Limited
McCarthy Inter Africa Ltd
Moroccan Golden Sands Ltd
Naturela Limited
Noyras Ltd
Nu Essence Limited
Perfume Essence Ltd
Pharma Medico Limited
REN Skincare Limited
Realine Beauty Limited
Rederm Limited
Rogia Romini Limited
Sanay Ltd
Smiles Glasgow Limited
Southend Hair and Beauty Ltd
Sur Trading Limited
T.L.C. (Total Luxury Cosmetics) Ltd
Total Beauty Ltd
Vida Aesthetics Ltd
Vittoria Ventures Limited
Wellness Style Limited
Werson International Ltd

April-June 2013 [31]
40075 Limited
W. S Argan Limited
Basic Needs Ltd
Boz Ego Ltd
Cult 51 Ltd
Echo Hair Limited
Ellipsis Brands Limited
Eternal Beauty (UK) Ltd
GBBC Ltd
Glam Wholesale Limited
Hahydra Technologies Ltd
Harpar Grace International Ltd
Inbeauting Ltd
J's Luxury Perfumery Ltd
JMAR Op No 2 Ltd
Jaydaw Limited
La Tips Limited
London Skincare Co Ltd.
Mehron Limited
Mimi's Organics Ltd
Nalla Skincare Ltd
Neroli Limited
Oatany Ltd
Onya Limited
Pareto Cosmedics Ltd
Selective Fragrances Ltd
Sportclinix Labs Ltd.
Sublyme Cosmetics Limited
Surreal Health & Beauty Ltd
Thrifty Limited
Yes To Carrots UK Limited

July-September 2013 [34]
4M Cosmetics Limited
B & O Natural Cosmetics Ltd
Batalveez Ltd

Bella Rootz Limited
Biodeb Beauty Ltd
Black Pearl Beauty Limited
Bottlemate UK Limited
Bouffe Limited
Britexim Ltd
City Beauty Supplies (UK) Ltd
Cosmetic Alchemy Ltd
Dermashack Limited
Eden Parfums Limited
Funky Skincare Limited
Gilmor Hair and Beauty (Newport) Ltd
Goodscents Limited
KPACA Limited
LIV Organic Co Ltd
La Beauty Labs Ltd.
Labrayon Cosmetiques France UK Ltd
London International Inflammation Foundation
London Links Trading Limited
Neville Cut and Shave Limited
Pangaea Laser Ltd
Scope Cosmetics Ltd
Sculptola Ltd
Simple Hair Limited
Sipro (UK) Ltd
Skin & Tonic London Ltd
Spa Therapies Ltd
Daniele de Winter Monaco-UK Ltd
Wonderful Life PHBS Ltd
Ximtrade (UK) Ltd
Z & J Enterprises Limited

October-December 2013 [15]
Acqua di Parma Limited
Beauty Magasin Ltd
Deism IT Solutions Ltd
Demert Brands EU Ltd
Essential Cosmetics Ltd
Jan Nails & Beauty Suppliers Ltd
Just Cosmetics Ltd
Amelia Knight Holdings Ltd
Lanolips Limited
Nicfead Cosmetics & Fragrance Ltd
Albert Roger Limited
Rose Tree Enterprises Ltd.
Simply Untouched Ltd
Sloane Home Ltd
W-Healthy Aging Limited

January-March 2014 [31]
1st Choice Nails Limited
Akwaaba Social Enterprises Ltd
Allies Network Ltd
Angel Remy Ltd
BM Supplier UK & Europe Ltd
Brain Burgeon Ltd
Daimon Barber Limited
Daisy Anai Limited
Direct Supplies (2014) Limited
Dunstan and Burr Ltd
Evorin Pharma Limited
Gaya Cosmetics Limited
Gold Class Hair Limited
Good Skin Care Co Ltd
Grimas.co.uk Limited
London Beauty Limited
Lord & Berry Ltd
Mark McDonald Consultancy Ltd
Meder Beauty International Ltd
Niroshini Skincare Limited

P & T PL Ltd
Per Capelli Ltd
Pixie Porter Ltd
Previa UK Ltd
Refan UK Ltd
Romade Limited
Sterling Fragrances International
TLY Supplies Ltd
Velforms Limited
Warpaint Cosmetics (2014) Ltd
Zest Cosmetics Limited

April-June 2014 [49]
4 Corners Distribution Ltd
APC (UK) Limited
Amly Limited
Argan Liquid Gold Limited
Argan Vanity Ltd
Arosci Trading Limited
Base Pro Artists Ltd
Beever Haircare Ltd
Bes Hair Products Limited
Dermatx Ltd
Diverse Solution Ltd
Eden Perfumes Limited
Fragrance Group London Ltd
Gentille Limited
Global Couture (UK) Ltd
Greenfrog Soap Co Ltd
Greenwise Distribution Ltd
Harvey Pharma Ltd
Image Hub Limited
Jess Nails Limited
Juju Beauty Care Ltd
Kathleen Natural Limited
Kiddeo Limited
Thomas Kosmala Parfums Ltd
Le Pure Limited
Legacy Wholesalers Limited
Lionmark Limited
Maxibay Limited
NA Medical Care Ltd
NYDG UK Limited
Nabeel Perfumes International Ltd
Natur Life Ltd
Perezoso Limited
Pouty Lipzz Limited
Raynolds Ltd
Red Gold London Ltd
Scent Angels UK Ltd
Sinoeast XJ Ltd
Iryna Stewart Ltd
Top Beauty Limited
Trading Scents (2014) Limited
Trading Scents Group Limited
True Brit London Limited
True Scents Ltd
UK Heluns Industry Co., Ltd
UK Vimin Industry Co., Limited
Warpaint Cosmetics Group Ltd
White Space Beauty Limited
Wrimes Cosmetics Ltd

July-September 2014 [44]
Aeden UK Ltd
Aenea Cosmetics Ltd
Atlantic Beauty Store Limited
Azur Interiors Limited
BSB Fashion Limited
Charms Europe Ltd
Chief Cosmetics Ltd

Clean & Care Facilities Management
Company NBN Limited
Control Cosmetics Ltd
Cosmetic Traders Limited
DKB Essentials Ltd
David & Co. Traders Ltd
Discounted Cosmetics Limited
Fit Brands (UK) Ltd
Glow Beauty Shop Ltd
Herbal Hakeem Ltd
Ila Asia Limited
Innovaderma PLC
Jacob's Well Limited
Yasmin Karimi Ltd
Knight & Wilson Limited
Knight & Wilson Trading Ltd
Katherine Longhi Ltd
Lovely Distribution Co Ltd
Maverick Hair & Beauty Ltd
Meadow Farm Friends Ltd
Neo Elegance Ltd
Nyasa Organics Limited
Oakwood Williams Limited
Orveda Limited
Paiman Limited
Perfume Lab Limited
Prism Parfums Limited
Quality Check Ltd
Rejuvapen UK Ltd
Albert Roger & Partner France Ltd
Rosmetics Aesthetics Limited
Skindoc Formula Limited
Sulis Minerva Limited
Total Beauty Network (UK) Ltd
Uniqtrend Limited
Very British Baby International Ltd
Yejisu Innovation Ltd

October-December 2014 [33]
20seven Limited
4R Guest Supplies Limited
A Pony Called Steve Ltd
BS Supply Ltd
Crystal Nails No1 Ltd
Editions de Parfums Limited
Elite Capital Limited
Elite Salon Solutions Limited
Escentric Ltd
Etonigbo Limited
Europebro Wholesalers Ltd
Flowscent Limited
Generic Physics Limited
Glow Consumer Products UK Ltd
Humanity Cosmetics Limited
Lottie London Limited
Lyal Intertrading Ltd
M.S.S (Micro Scientific Services)
Mayfair Export London Limited
No.1 Nail Supply Limited
Nowdynamic Ltd.
Orange Balloon Ltd
Pandhy's UK Sweet Cosmetics Ltd.
Plant Me Botanics Ltd
Product World Limited
Pure Swiss Aesthetics Ltd
Samla Tribe Limited
Sandine Zartaux Holding Ltd
Siam Skin Ltd
Southsea Bathing Hut Limited
Vanilla Blanc Limited
Veridot Asset Dna Limited
Votary Limited

January 2015 [12]
Amassuna Limited
Belfast Beard Co Ltd
Elysian Design Limited
Fuzzique Limited
Hair from India Limited
Hive of Beauty Limited
Innon Vision Limited
One Green Lab Ltd
Ovis Liv Limited
RX Cosmetics Limited
Regima Zone Ltd
Whimsical Beard Co Ltd

February 2015 [18]
AIGC Limited
Candii Bath Limited
Daughter of The Soil Limited
EOB Distribution Ltd
Essentials4men Ltd
GroundedBodyScrub Limited
Iconic Beauty London Limited
James & Jake Ltd
Legends London Limited
Mega Mane Limited
Mitonia Co Ltd
Sara Post Ltd
Ris Healthcare Limited
SB Selected Beauty Ltd
Twelve Beauty Ltd
UK Elements of Beauty Ltd
Very Nature Limited
Warehouse.5 Limited

March 2015 [21]
Aneen Ventures Limited
Aurora Spa Health and Beauty Ltd
Beautiful World Limited
Bizi Bazzar Limited
Ferrara-Bardile Ltd
HABM Ltd
Heir & Grace Ltd
Iiuvo Limited
Kiki Body Limited
Latam HQ Health Ltd
Mebon Investment Limited
Moyou Ltd
My Beauty World Ltd
Optimavia Ltd
Sama Perfumes Ltd
Scent N Essence UK Ltd
Sias Corp Limited
Skin Matrix HD+ Cosmetology Ltd
Tarsago Ltd
UK Direct Imports Ltd
Varana UK Limited

April 2015 [18]
Allure Beauty Supplies Ltd
Amberhue Limited
Aqua Qualia Limited
Beautyge Fragrances Holdings Ltd
C Distribution UK Limited
Global Beauty Wholesale Ltd
Glute Plus Limited
HDDirect Limited
Marque of Brands Limited
Oasis Beauty Distribution Ltd
Olfacstory Parfums Limited
Pearson Cosmetics Limited

Petersham Ventures Ltd
Protective World Ltd
Albert Roger Benelux Limited
San & Amad General Trade Co Ltd
Slixir Ltd
Vilhelm Parfumerie Limited

May 2015 [13]
Azzy London Ltd
Collier & Wood Ltd
Eyeslices UK Limited
London Export Ltd
Luxe Associates Ltd
Alexandra de Markoff Limited
Mirimiri Limited
NC Import Limited
Phoenix Hair & Beauty (Ely) Ltd
Respect Male Grooming Ltd.
S & P Cosmetics Limited
Shyline Ltd
Wafson Ltd

June 2015 [10]
Ansor Supplies Ltd
Bedfordshire Beard Co. Limited
Bespoke Mr Ltd
Essence of Esther Ltd
Gelmoment Limited
My Pink Ltd
Rokka Imagine Ltd
Shebelle Limited
Simona Beauty Store Ltd
UK Fillers Ltd

July 2015 [20]
Active Tan Limited
Ameera London Limited
Beauty Cosmetics (Bristol) Ltd
Beauty Cosmetics (Nottingham) Ltd
Diamonds on Demand Ltd
Existo Limited
Ha-Derma Limited
Hairco Hair & Beauty Ltd
Carolina Herrera UK Ltd
Ijapan Ltd
Kor Cosmetics Ltd
L'Revolution Beauty Ltd
Lee Gallop Enterprise Ltd
Mr B Skincare Limited
Oilyspirit Ltd
Olo Edt Ltd
Purple Tree Skincare Limited
Rationale Skincare Limited
Splashes & Spills Ltd.
Wild Beauty Ltd

August 2015 [14]
Amor et Psyche Ltd
Bigben Healthcare Limited
Complexi-Light Ltd
Ekah Foundation C.I.C.
Fragrance London Limited
MGC Pharma (UK) Ltd
Melya & Co. Trading Ltd.
Nomad Care Ltd
Paradise Organics London Ltd
Parfum Club Ltd
STT Industries Ltd.
Sahney Siblings Limited
Silvercleanse Health & Beauty Ltd
Zaliant Skincare Limited

September 2015 [19]
Al Janan Fragrances Limited
Bush Oil Limited
ENS Europe Limited
Egyptian Magic Ltd
Philip Hansard Limited
Instant Effects Ltd
JF Malcolm Ltd
Modernist Fragrance Ltd.
NBS Distribution Ltd
Nail Polish Gel Colours Ltd
Natasha Denona Make Up Ltd.
Naturyl Glow Ltd
Okmarket24 Ltd
Online Motions Limited
Salt and Pamper Limited
Sopureoils Ltd
Spartzy Lifestyle Brands Ltd
Vereer Limited
Vision Trading Limited

October 2015 [20]
2M PH. Intl. Limited
Adams General Ltd
Affinity Fragrances Limited
Belensa Limited
Bellevue of London Ltd.
Chando-UK Ltd
Conatural Ltd
Dr. Gabriela Ltd
For All Dogkind Limited
Grandelash MD UK Ltd
Green Harmony Limited
Lava Jai Limited
Magnum Beauty International Ltd
Guy Morgan Apothecary Limited
Pak Beauty Ltd
Pococks Absolute Rose Ltd
SMCK Hair Care Products Ltd
Tibetan Cosmetics Ltd
Tir Chonaill London Ltd
Vancooler Ltd

November 2015 [20]
Alianaz Ltd.
Alwais Ltd
Buff Natural Body Care Ltd
Connessioni UK Limited
Diet Plan Unique Ltd
East Garden Ltd
Eleuthere Ltd
Green Jiva Ltd
Holistic Plant Technologies Ltd
Hugworld Cristalinas UK Ltd
Ileri Trading Limited
Janssen Cosmetics UK Ltd
Lilyz Cosmetics UK Ltd
Onna Export Import Ltd
J. Rudzitis Ltd
Ruxley Medical Aids Limited
Salon Supplies 365 Limited
Searching Plants Ltd
Spirit of Dubai Limited
Yellbird Limited

December 2015 [15]
African Garden Limited
Asadilari Limited
Beuti Limited
Chanson Worldwide Limited

Disley Limited
Emel Trade Ltd
Given By Nature Limited
Mayjoy The Perfumer Ltd
Oodiee Limited
Pandorra Ltd.
Perfume London Ltd
Revolution Beauty Limited
Silk Route Impex Limited
VR Consult Limited
Vortex Holding Limited

January 2016 [24]
AJ Metals Ltd.
Arlenne Ltd
Beauty Ideas Group Limited
Brand Evolution (Europe) Ltd
Cosmetics R Us 1 Limited
Esthermarie Limited
Exentrique Limited
GP Mediplus Ltd
Herba Skincare Limited
House of Vanity Limited
Imperial Bioscience Ltd
Interall Ltd
Love Little Prices Ltd
Lucas Haynes Limited
Makeup54 Ltd
Moroccan Argan Limited
Nukua Limited
Our-Scent Ltd
Perfumeprice.co.uk Ltd
Angela Pickering Limited
SGJ Perfumes Limited
TRS & Co (Europe) Limited
V@M Limited
Venus Beauty Limited

February 2016 [20]
Arna Group Ltd
Barnsley Card Ltd
Beautifull Planet Ltd
Best Choice FMCG Ltd
Chirp Body Ltd
Crane and Peach Limited
Eifelcorp Consumer Care Ltd
Green Breeze Ambient (UK) Ltd
Kingdom Scotland Limited
Leslie International Ltd
Mindful Soulful Limited
Myriad Skincare Limited
Natural Serenity Ltd
Rock Perfumes Ltd
SKN Rehab Limited
SYN-RG Trading Ltd
Salus Cutis Ltd
Swiss Pharma Dynamic Ltd
U 2 Shine Limited
Up Roar Ltd.

The Top UK Perfume and Cosmetics Wholesalers

March 2016 [18]
AJ Active Enterprises Ltd
BBA Products Limited
Cosimpex Ltd
Earth Aid Group Limited
GS Fragrances Limited
Global Luxury Beauty Ltd
Honor London Limited
Jo Loves (Wholesale) Limited
Korres International Limited
Laurens Cosmetics UK Limited
Legendbio Beauty Group Limited
Luscious Skincare Ltd
Mann & Noble Europe Limited
Mono Naturoils Ltd
Oh My Scent Limited
Oud Milano UK Limited
Pebbles Creative Ltd
Skin Health Solutions Ltd

April 2016 [19]
BLK Cosmetics Limited
Brighton Group Ltd
Califa Ltd
EBF Europe Ltd
Korebeauty Limited
Lins Bros Limited
Minx Lashes Ltd
Niko Pro Limited
Pinnacle Pharma Limited
Pur3 Health Limited
Rekze Laboratories Ltd
SMC Cosmetics (UK) Ltd
Sassy Hair & Beauty Supplies Ltd
Scent Edit Limited
Semy-Estoiles Limited
Strategy M Ltd
TWC Products Limited
Wildsmith Collection Limited
Younghair AB Ltd

May 2016 [23]
72 Hair Limited
Alsons Beauty Ltd.
American Cosmetics Limited
Beautyline Limited
Blossom Colour Limited
Business Angels Syndicate Ltd
Ere Perez UK Limited
Essence Cosmetics Limited
Florals of London Limited
Alexander Iris Solutions Ltd
Kendo Brands Limited
Korban Beauty Limited
Lash House Eyelash Extensions Supplies
MB Professional Beauty Ltd
Mayfair Gate Limited
Myroo Ltd
PLTradeGroup Limited
Procare Women Health Limited
Albert Roger Portugal Limited
Smart Skin Limited
Viib Limited
Vikenias UK Ltd
Wild Things Cosmetics Ltd

June 2016 [21]
Adible Limited
Alpha Auriga Limited
Aromeco Limited

Atlantis Research Limited
BBT Products Limited
Beauty Link Wholesale Ltd
Best Pure Natural Products Ltd
Hair Dressing Supplies Lincoln Ltd
Hemp Earth Ltd
Luscious Lashes International Ltd
Lushes Ltd
Ossulstone Hundred Limited
Perfumer Ltd
Pink Parasol Ltd
Prevura Ltd
Razias London Ltd
Revive Express Beauty Ltd
Sanchi Corp Limited
Sash Products Limited
Lauren Stone Limited
Wild Celia Ltd

July 2016 [23]
Asian Fashions Ltd
Beau Belle Brushes Ltd
Bullingberg Limited
Buy Perfumes London Limited
EOS Products Limited
Fox Group International Ltd
Galaxy Grooming Limited
Grooming Galaxy Limited
Hommage International Ltd
Kokolokahi Limited
Meddiamonds Ltd
Moyra UK Ltd
Muse and Rose Limited
Nizz Cosmetics Ltd
Omega Flax Limited
Pam Trading Limited
S & E Ventures Ltd
Skins Sexual Health Limited
Soap and Candle Co Ltd
Unigrand Group Limited
Valiscious Limited
Warpaint London PLC
ZS Beauty Ltd

August 2016 [24]
Abington Cosmetics Ltd
Adnoz Limited
Antian World Limited
Arahant Ltd
Aster & Bay Ltd.
Burton Blackmore International Ltd
Cosmetics Online Limited
Doers Skincare Limited
Five Elements Healthcare Ltd
GS7 IT Consultants Ltd
Hamon Concepts Limited
Indigo Direct Ltd
Ivee Group Ltd
Kailijumei Ltd
Lanko Naturals-UK (PVT) Ltd
Natural Hair Emporium Limited
Natural Spa Factory Limited
Paint It Orange Ltd
Prema Naturals Limited
Q River Limited
Scented Home Limited
Solution Cosmetic Ltd
Uppercut Deluxe Co Limited
XIP Professional Ltd

September 2016 [38]
CNI Services Limited
Canna Biology Distributing Ltd
Colwayland Co Ltd
Corley Capital Limited
Ecocare Organic Limited
Eurasia Property Limited
Glasgow Nails & Beauty Supplies Ltd
Good Beauty International Holding
Inga Permanent Make Up Limited
JZM International Limited
Kaxton Limited
L & L Sunlight Importers and Exporters
La Personal Products Ltd
Lavender Concept Ltd
Les Lilas Limited
Liaver Limited
London Health Sciences Ltd
Lore Originals Limited
Luxury Consulting by Bethan Williams
Miss Vivien Ltd
Nails & London Holdings Ltd
Olivia Kate Cosmetics Ltd
Orrwa Pharma Health & Beauty Ltd
Polish Cosmetics Distribution Centre UK
Reimiece Ltd
MV Roberts & Co (UK) Ltd
Rooster & Rooster Ltd.
Ruby Concepts Ltd
Scrubd Ltd
Sherhind Accessorize Limited
Shortt Investments2 Limited
Sweden Eco Limited
T A Trading Ltd
Treas Biotechnology UK Ltd
UK Vietnam Trade Ltd
Ved Healthcare Limited
Vesta London Beauty Ltd
Walk on Gold Limited

October 2016 [31]
A.R Cosmetics Limited
Adam and Eve Distribution Ltd
Ahwaz Ltd
Arizona Botaniq Limited
Art-Eclair Limited
Beautivate Ltd
Bellissimo Fashion Ltd
Brand Holdings Limited
Brooks Aesthetics Clinic Ltd
Butterflyy Productions Ltd
CP Parfums Ltd
Dr Shea Ltd
Dupeshop Ltd
Ecooner Cosmetics London Ltd
Fashion Fragrances & Cosmetics UK Ltd
Gel Labs Limited
Hair There & Everywhere Hair & Beauty
Ibeautheart Limited
Kamarino Limited
LMS Brands Ltd.
LW International Ltd
Marina Muda Ltd
Maryam Imports & Exports Ltd
Mounir's Ltd
Moyy Limited
Neora UK Limited
Nota Nota Limited
Pennies and Feathers Limited
Phyto Pharm Limited
Phyto Pharma Limited
Leonora Sanche Limited

November 2016 [29]
AHS Services Ltd
Ashmira Botanica Ltd
Cadden & Lee Limited
Cazza Professional Ltd
Cedron Ltd.
Disciple Skincare Limited
From Mini Acorns Ltd
Genetiq Lab Limited
Glamn Holding Ltd
Hairdye Direct Limited
Hazellbrook Limited
Heavenly Riches Limited
Here We Flo Ltd
J & W Distribution Limited
Juliajosh Limited
Magia BLV International Ltd
Mega Direct Limited
NMB Property Limited
Nailzee Ltd
National Supplement Beauty Solutions
Neo Cosmetics Limited
Profusion Cosmetics UK Ltd
Ring in Ring Ltd
Sandgroper Limited
Sun Spirit Skincare Limited
Sun Zapper UK Limited
Trimmz Ltd
Uni Supply Ltd
Zerocann Ltd

December 2016 [21]
Atkinson London 1799 Ltd
Ayursavvyveda Limited
Bali Secrets Ltd
Beauty Center Ltd
Bluesky Cosmetics Limited
Brand Euro Limited
Doyin Tradings UK Limited
Enimarkets Ltd
Haych Cosmetics Limited
Highbase Market Limited
Indigo Nails Online Shop Ltd.
Jedidiah Group Ltd
Kiara Sky Professional Nail Distribution
Lief Essentials Limited
Maskhouse Wholesale Limited
Mellor & Russell Direct Distribution Ltd
New Era Hair Ltd
Optic Eye Wear Ltd
Piggy Paint UK Ltd
Scented Sachets (London) Ltd.
ShopAndEnjoy111 Limited

January 2017 [28]
Aurum Argan Ltd
Bigteal Industries Limited
Biovate Limited
Botanik Beauty Limited
Busy Bee Personal Care Limited
CHT Supplies Limited
Carol Skins Ltd
Casa Cosmetics Ltd
Contour and More London Ltd
Dermanor Ltd.
Faceoff Limited
Hexbomb Ltd
Irum Cosmetics Ltd
JLE Trading Limited
Lukony Ltd
MSD Trading Services Limited

Mayfair Export UK Ltd
Miya Hair Limited
Organica Skincare Ltd
Shalohm Ltd
Shama Pharma Ltd
Sikania Ltd
Skin Enrich Limited
Skinsense Ltd
Skinvital Ltd
Sunrise Essential Oil Limited
Supreme Beard Ltd
Tiyati Ltd

February 2017 [47]
72 Hair Retail Limited
Amahla Limited
Aysthetics Limited
Beard Nature Limited
Beautifect Ltd
Beautx Ltd
Beauty at The Avenue Online Ltd
Bleach Makeup Limited
Bonroy International Limited
CC Dist UK Ltd
Chronicles Medical Consulting Ltd
Cosmetiques de France Ltd.
D'Zario UK Ltd
Dermafrance Ltd.
Droplet Cosmetics Limited
Ella Nur Ltd
Excellent Edges Ltd
Face Fodder Limited
Global Beautique Limited
Great British Bee Co Ltd
Ink Oil Limited
J K International Trading Ltd
Julio & Ejder Ltd
Kitoko Make Up Ltd
La Maison Hedonique Limited
Lifestyle International Ltd
Man & Diva's Ltd
Mlle Cosmetics Co Ltd
Mupe Ltd
Nut Dust Ltd
Paradoxx Ltd
Pharmafrance Ltd.
Photonic Limited
Pilaten EU Ltd
Pink Empire Limited
Posh Gift Ltd
Potions & Possibilities Ltd
SZ Beauty Limited
Salon Distribution Concepts Ltd
Secret Cosmetics Limited
Skinsider Cosmetics Ltd
Super Natural Apothecary Ltd.
Top Beauty Brands Ltd
Unified Commerce Limited
Viral Solutions General Trading Ltd
Vtessia Cosmetic Ltd
Wiltshire Beekeeper Ltd

March 2017 [51]
Ashley & Co UK Ltd
Bbeauty Lounge Limited
Beauty Brand (Europe) Ltd
Beauty Camp Profesional Ltd
BeautyEmpireUK Ltd
Bullet and Bone Limited
By Sarah Limited
Curl Coach Ltd

Dancing Unicorn Limited
Dermacure Aesthetics Limited
Elegance Gel UK Ltd
Esspire Limited
Eternal Hair & Beauty Limited
Evans Close Limited
Florence Verity Limited
Globe Intraworks Limited
Glow Investment Ltd
Gold Pillar Holding Ltd
Hermossa Limited
Hughes Evans Essentials Ltd
IR International Ltd
Innocent Alchemy Ltd
Isha Cosmetics Limited
Ladyology Limited
Laldhinio Limited
Lixir Skin Limited
Lovorika London Limited
Luban & Murr Ltd
Medipro Pharma Limited
NXSK UK Ltd
Nail Art Direct Ltd
Need4health Limited
Onlinexclusive Limited
Orveda UK Limited
Pixie Crypt Ltd
Prispens Limited
Pure Natural Therapy Ltd
Reetal Development Co Ltd
Republik Inc Limited
Rupitex Limited
Shared Beauty Secrets Spas Ltd
Sheabynature Ltd
Spa and Salon Solutions Ltd
Stylish & Luxurious Limited
UK Skinlabs Limited
Vasuda Beauty Limited
Vetivert & Co Ltd
Vlinder Cosmetics Ltd
Wrap N Pack Ltd
Zagorah Ltd
Zojo. The Gorgeousness Co Ltd

April 2017 [35]
3D Lifestyle Ltd
Apotheca London Skincare Ltd
Bambi & Co Ltd
Beard Zone Ltd
Budget Beauty Limited
Cancun Collection Limited
Cosmedi Limited
Cosmetica Natural Oils Ltd
Eco Twinkle Ltd
Eutek Group Limited
Finest Mineral Make Up Limited
Five Dot Botanics Limited
Fragrance Plus Limited
Glad Gent Ltd
Grautrans Limited
Hill and Dale Limited
Hotel Essentials Ltd
Ilys Organic Ltd
Lavish London Cosmetics Ltd.
Luxmeticgroup Limited
Make Up for Ever U.K. Limited
Mane Love Ltd
Moor Direct Ltd
Natural Vitale Limited
Nevitrade Ltd
Noa London Ltd
Perfectly Natural Limited

The Top UK Perfume and Cosmetics Wholesalers												dellam

Pherolec Global Ltd
Project 1 Skincare Ltd
Signature Fragrances London Ltd
Skinjam Cosmetics Limited
Slim Line Club UK Ltd
TJ Nail Supplies Ltd
UK Brand Holdings Ltd
UK Calluspeel Limited

May 2017 [47]
Al Sunnah Perfumes (Wholesale) Ltd
Angel Lash Limited
Aroma of Grace Ltd
Artifact Skin Co Ltd
Arvense Skin Care Ltd
Bath Bombs and Beyond Limited
Beached Limited
Beauty Africa Limited
Beauty Mastery Ltd.
Brand Evangelists for Beauty Ltd
CFBP Ltd
CFN 1 Limited
Carbon Theory Limited
Connected Beauty Limited
Cosmetic Bases Limited
Derma Organics by CFBP Ltd
Donovan Luxe Limited
Emma Danmark Ltd
Emma Group Ltd
Empire Worldwide Ltd
Fragrance Samples UK Limited
Golo Hair & Beauty Limited
Green Guru Enterprices Ltd.
Greenpol Distribution Ltd
Hamiltons of Canterbury Ltd
Herbaleva Ltd
Info Cosmetics Limited
Instant Beauty UK Limited
Ital Living Market Ltd
Jigu Corporation Limited
Karaama Fragrances Ltd
Maison de Maa Ltd
NS Brands International Ltd
Pretty Silhouette Limited
Pure Skincare London Ltd
Qing Ltd
RMD Global Wholesale Limited
Rawmans Ltd
Rexcel Trading Ltd
Leonora Sanche Cosmetics Ltd
Seed Fashion and Beauty Incubator Ltd
Silk Lounge Beauty Ltd
Top Brands Australia Limited
Un Air D'Antan Limited
Unicorn Magic Enterprises Ltd
Viridian Leaf Limited
Naseem Zeenah Natural Cosmetics Ltd

June 2017 [53]
Avee Ltd
Baltica Beauty Professional Ltd
Beauty Bash Limited
Bespoke Beauty Co Ltd
Beverly Beauty & Fragrances Ltd
Biogene Group Limited
Burly Cosmetics Ltd
Cleardot Group Ltd
Comfortz Ltd
Cosmetic Hooligans Ltd
Cuelyine Limited
Dabrimela Limited

Elegantes London Limited
Ellya UK Ltd
EmmaDK Ltd
Fruu Cosmetics Limited
HA Distribution Limited
Harmonious Brown Limited
Healtholozy UK Limited
Homsense Ltd
Honeystyle Limited
Ibeautify Ltd
Invicta Cosmetics Limited
King's Vegan Grooming Ltd
Kokoa UK Limited
Koutos Limited
L.A. Professional Cosmetic Labs Ltd.
Landermark Ltd
Lavy Sprays International Ltd
Lesimone Global Limited
MQS Group London Limited
MS Rarytas Ltd
Manas Organics Ltd
Manhattan Group Ltd.
Me Sentir Ltd.
Meviq Ltd
Moda Exportation Limited
My Perfumes London Ltd
Nevah Rose Ltd
Organic Land Global Ltd
Purity Derma Limited
Sana Jardin (UK) Limited
Scontimania Online SRL Limited
Soft and Curly Products Ltd
Supernova UK Pty Ltd
Tailord Chic Ltd
Tiarna Ltd
Torcall of Edinburgh Ltd
Unilux Trading Ltd
Winkies Limited
Wuyu Mother and Baby Ltd
Yorkshire Beard Co Ltd
Zahrat Alqurashi Ltd

July 2017 [45]
Alade Ltd
Ava Corporations Ltd
Beauty Consociare Ltd
Body Organics Limited
Bohdidharma Perfume UK Limited
Butterwhips Ltd
Damrick's White Bunny Ltd
Darklake Limited
Delmoss Ltd
Easybusiness24 Ltd
Elie Consumer Care Ltd
Elliott Nutrition Ltd
Emuology UK 2017 Limited
Felix Medical Group Ltd
Flynn Group of Companies Ltd
Glory Cosmetics Ltd
Hadley and Reed Ltd
Hemo Bioscience Ltd
JNVshop La Piazza Delle Idee Ltd
Julie's Natural Health Ltd
Kitchen Witch Aromatherapy Ltd
Lashflix Limited
Lime and Lead Global Ltd
Livoliv Cosmetics Ltd.
Loveco Ltd
Lyons Pride Limited
Make Up Madness Ltd
Mesostrata Limited
Nasser Waziri Ltd

Naturenk Ltd
Natures Merchant Ltd
Nouela Organics Ltd
Novumis Ltd
Pearl & Rocky Limited
Perfumes Logistics & Distribution
Lisa Preston Ltd
Regis Personal Care Ltd
Riley & Sons Ltd
Seba Trade Limited
Siwel Trading Ltd
Skin Chef Limited
Sparking-Jy International Trading Co.,
Storm of UK Limited
Tattva Ltd.
Virgovogue Ltd

August 2017 [44]
ASVR Bebidas Limited
Absolute Cosmetic Essentials Ltd
Acquaderm Ltd
Adem Oygur Ltd
Alizcare Limited
Allied Aerosols Limited
Aquabeauty Limited
BU Cosmetics Limited
Bad Mermaid Limited
Beauty Royale Ltd
Chemical Poetry Ltd
Chulo Naturals Ltd
Concept Healthcare Limited
Dr Sun Limited
Dream Girl Limited
Dudu-Osun Limited
Dug and Bitch Ltd
Eblouir Group Ltd
Equisalud Ltd
Ersag UK Limited
Good Pharma Dermatology Ltd
Grand Beaute Ltd
Green Merchandising Ltd
JML Cosmetics Limited
Janou Brand Limited
KM Cosmetics Distribution Ltd
Labapothecary Ltd.
Ladd Cosmetics Ltd
Lino Rose Ltd
Lulu Tanner Limited
MNM International UK Limited
Neolox Ltd
Niquel Ltd
Norpro Limited
Nurologie Ltd
Organic Professional Ltd
S Beauty Ltd
Sabeauti Ltd.
Sisi Cosmetics Ltd
Trending Scents Ltd.
VY Club Limited
Valentia Skincare Limited
Ve-Glam Limited
XY Skin Ltd

September 2017 [57]
Arowell Products Ltd
Barber & Salon Supplies Ltd
Bear Journal Limited
Beauty Kosmetika Ltd
Bedeaux Ltd
Benefit & Riley Healthcare Ltd
CZ Cosmetics Ltd.

Clarins & Felix Healthcare Ltd
Cleanux Chemicals Ltd
Color Studio Ltd
Conscience Clear Tan Limited
Constantine K Ltd
Coriungo Limited
Crown Cosmetics Limited
Crypt Doll Ltd
Diymonde Corporation Limited
Dooa Capital Limited
Elan Skincare Ltd
Eloise Group Ltd
European Essential Oils (UK) Ltd
Forte Organics Ltd
Garnier & Hemo Healthcare Ltd
Honey Corn Limited
IJN Pure Oils Ltd
JSProfessionnel Limited
Kityee Limited
Lamer & Ava Healthcare Ltd
Little Big Brands Ltd
C Looker Ltd
Louts Remit Beautiful International Group Co.,
Maraki International Limited
Millenium Fragrance Limited
Monarch Health & Beauty Ltd.
Muamko Uzuri Limited
Najah Ltd
Nars & Elliott Healthcare Ltd
Natural British Limited
Naya London Ltd
Nomalogic Ltd
Opal Naturals Ltd
Pixie Lott Paint Limited
Prima Makeup Ltd
Rektaz Ltd
Revlon & Elie Healthcare Ltd
Rimmel & Flynn Healthcare Ltd
Royce Health Sciences Ltd
Sansuri Hair & Beauty Supplies and Training
Serendipity (N.I.) Ltd
Shopti UK Limited
South West Aesthetics Ltd
Three Organics Ltd
Tioluxe Europe Limited
Tothun Group UK Ltd
True Hemp Ltd
UK Beauty Cosmetics International Group
We Two By Kelly Simpkin Ltd
Young Now Ltd

October 2017 [52]
Aamir Traders Ltd
Amalsons Ltd
Amiri Perfume Ltd
Available Beauty Ltd
B. Silki Naturally Ltd
Beatnut Butter Ltd
Cambridge Sprouts Limited
Cure Hair & Skin Care Ltd
Direct Trade Limited
Effective and Simple Ltd
Ethnoceuticals Limited
Evagray Limited
Foodprint Network Ltd
Gifts of Earth Ltd
HG-UK (Pty) Ltd
Haltrade UK Ltd
Hanana Traders Ltd
Imaage Ltd
Inshirah Enterprises Limited

JK Hair & Beauty Salon Supplies Ltd
Leigh Jones & Associates Ltd
Jufa Cosmetics Ltd
La Loire Ltd
Natascha Lacombe Cosmetics Ltd
Le-Vap Limited
Line21 Ltd.
Macial Ltd
Makeup Boutique Limited
Natcare Beauty Ltd
Nature-Solves Ltd
Newincco 2301 Limited
Pennystore Limited
Pro Esthe Ltd.
Profline Ltd
Project Cosmetics Limited
Puff & Petals Ltd.
Razzo Limited
Rebatchi Perfums Ltd
Rembrandt London Limited
SGHP Ltd
Sankofa Heritage Ltd
Scott Weeks Enterprises Ltd
Spa Pro Ltd
Sweet Lilli Ltd
Tassels UK Ltd
Thrillage Ltd.
Toppers Nails Limited
Two Daughters Limited
Vibrantz Cosmetics Ltd
Wake Up Beauty Ltd
Wild Source Apothecary Ltd
Yehmea Limited

November 2017 [58]
11:11 Limited
Amelgo Ltd
Ample Biotechnology UK Co. Ltd
Atarah Beauty Collection Ltd
B2B Beauty UK Limited
Belgravia London Ltd
Buly UK Limited
By Mia Cosmetics Ltd
C & A International Trading Ltd
C Beauty Agency Limited
Reevis Chan Ltd
Convent Venue Limited
Cosma Fragrances Limited
Cover Up Hairloss Ltd
Cozmetica UK Ltd
Diamond Smile NE Limited
Ether Cosmetics Ltd
Fashion Conspiracy Ltd
Flexi Beauty Care Ltd
Florence Health & Beauty Ltd
Fols for Men Ltd
French Beauty Expert Ltd
GoodNaturedSkincare Ltd
Goodsky Co., Ltd.
Hair and Cosmetics Wholesale Ltd
Hair for Men Products Ltd
Hansraj House Limited
Hemsley James Cosmetics Ltd
K. S. D Beauty Zone Ltd
Khushi Skincare Limited
Larmed Limited
Live Rich Academy Limited
London Outlet Store Limited
Lustra Beauty Limited
Luxuria Generation Limited
MTIstanbul Ltd
Mise N Ltd

Mob Cosmetics Limited
Moffat Perfume Co Ltd
Monat Global UK Ltd
Moore Cosmetics Ltd
Nextporter Ltd.
Nova Cellulis Ltd
Organic Stuff Limited
Parker & Moses Ltd
Perfect Lady Ltd
Pure & Sure Limited
Rewind Botanics Limited
Riviere Groupe (Europe) Ltd
SK Flawless Dipping Powder Ltd
Shea Touch Ltd
Shhh-Holistic Limited
Stella Tailor Ltd
Traderuk Limited
US Beauty Store Limited
Unac Salon Supplies Limited
Universe Cosmetics Limited
YSL Trading Ltd

December 2017 [51]
ASR Aesthetics Ltd
Amaffi London Limited
Aromabar (Scotland) Ltd
Beauty Spot Holdings Limited
Blk Oil Limited
Blossom Organics Limited
Boutique Fragrances Ltd
Bristol Consumer Health Ltd
Butterfly Cosmetics Limited
Calestio Ltd
Comets Intertrade Co Ltd
Cosnique Group Holdings Ltd
DNA Beauty Group Ltd.
Dream Skin Ltd
Eden's Legends Limited
Enhancing You Limited
Ensley and Ensley Limited
Euroluxe Enterprise UK Ltd
Five Star International Consulting
G.Q Homes Ltd
Garron Labs Private Limited
S K A Gibson Ltd
Has To Be Ltd
Herbal Essentials UK Limited
House of Oud Perfumes Limited
J.Cat Beauty UK Ltd
JJ Promotions Limited
K2Y Limited
KMZA Enterprises Ltd
Lienex Beauty London Ltd
Lush Lashes London Limited
Medivas Herbals Ltd
Millennium Nails Europe Ltd
Molecula Ltd
My SNS Academy UK Ltd
Nova Bleu Cosmetics Limited
One Flower Qinga Limited
Oudh Co Ltd
Pera Cosmetics Ltd
Perfume Outlet Ltd
Pommade Divine Skincare Ltd
Quality Brand MG Ltd
Radiant and Refined Limited
Regal Skincare Ltd
Reviron Limited
Shop Beauty Ltd
Spktra Limited
UK Cosmetic Formula Limited
Universal Beauty Products Europe Ltd

Uoma Beauty Group Limited
Wax Authority Limited

January 2018 [96]
Afthrone Ltd
Ak-Kur Furniture & Fitting Ltd
Al Masiya Cosmetic Ltd
All Naturals Beauty Limited
Aro-Matic (Scotland) Ltd
Ashymo Ltd
Aya Natural (UK) Limited
B & D Fragrance Limited Co Ltd
Balmonds Skincare Ltd
Bare Cosmetics Ltd
Beautonomy Limited
Beauty Complex Europe Ltd
Beauty Trinity UK Limited
Big Wholesale Co Ltd
Biotrade Cosmeceuticals Ltd
Black Gold Hair Limited
Bluebells Hair Boutique Ltd
Body Month Ltd
Boutique Parfum Limited
Brunucorp Ltd
Cadyle Ltd
Clink Street FX Ltd
Cosmetics Wholesale Limited
Cosmetics of London Chelsie Ltd
Crivalis Ltd
DYB Tarding Ltd
Deeco Supplies Limited
Deja Vu International Ltd
Dorian House Marketplace Ltd
E-MO Nails Ltd
Earthly Pleasures Ltd
El Sabbagh Trading Limited
Essence Room Ltd
Eurohandle Ltd
Facecharm Ltd
Fields Finesse Limited
Florence Consumer Products Ltd
Flowery Whiff Limited
Fragrance Express Limited
Fragrant Spa Limited
Franok Business Solutions Ltd
Frontrow International UK Ltd
Fysifarm Limited
Glamify Beauty Limited
Guilty Fashion Ltd
H & R Cosmetics Ltd
Haybae Cosmetics Ltd
Holistic Natural Wellbeing Co Ltd
Huskie London Ltd
Iconic Fragrances Ltd
Iras Trading Ltd
Margaret Jordan Cosmetics Ltd
Kalabash Limited
Kind Planet Co Ltd
Koha Beauty Co Ltd
Komodo Skincare Ltd
L'Amour Cosmetics London Ltd
Loles Cosmetics UK Limited
London Heartbeat Ltd
Look Lovable Ltd.
Lucerne Perfumes Ltd
M Cosmetics Distribution Ltd
Madison Steward Ltd
Mcaniis Ltd
Medical Technology Caraco (MYC) Ltd.
Medileen UK Ltd
NOP Cosmetics Ltd
Nanat Limited

Olfactive Thirty Eight Fragrances
Oud & Musk UK Ltd
Party Supplies and More Ltd
Plenaire Limited
Polcosmetics Ltd
Precision Brows and Lashes Ltd
Pro Bright Ltd
Pure Savvy Limited
R & B Hair Extensions Limited
Revoke Ltd.
Risa Lux Ltd
SA Plus Enterprise Ltd
SU Labs Limited
Shimmer and Shine Cosmetics Ltd
Shuei Trading UK Ltd
Sirra Limited
Solarius UK & Overseas Limited
South China Bio-Pharma Co Ltd.
Sun Light EU Trading Ltd
Swan Leigh Cosmetics Ltd
Trade Dream Ltd
Tradinguk55 Limited
Urhan Group Limited
VNS London Limited
Valhalla Perfume Limited
Vir Original Limited
Vogue Cosmetics Ltd
Zamantraders Limited

February 2018 [87]
Adraji Ltd
Aesthetic & Luxury Distribution Ltd
Alayna Cosmetics and Beauty Ltd
Asante Distributors Limited
Aube Laboratories Ltd
Ayaon Ltd
Barbers Warehouse Ltd
Beauty Cosmetics (Luton) Ltd
Biologico Cosmetics Limited
A & P Blickling Ltd
Bloom Remedies Ltd
Carr Greens Limited
Clickpoint Limited
Dea Disir Ltd
Dermaloch Limited
David Dinero Ltd
ED Trading & Consultancy Ltd
EL Companies Ltd
Eku Skin Care Ltd
Elinor-UK Ltd
Emita Europe Limited
Emma Prime Ltd
Endetrox Ltd.
Espoir Beauty Ltd
Esscenti Ltd
Exa World Ltd
Excess Beauty Ltd
Exoditi Limited
Farmers Pure Organics Ltd
Forever Young Cosmetics UK Ltd
Global One Wholesale Ltd
Glochina Trading UK Ltd.
Goldstone Perfumes Limited
Greenleaf Luton Limited
HQPS Ltd
Happy Beauty Life Ltd
Healthcare Wholesale Ltd
Hoff Beards Limited
Iberia Skin Brands Ltd
Infinityredox Holdings Limited
Joddor London Limited
Kathy Salon Equipment Limited

Ko. Essentials Ltd.
LTSC Ltd
Laguna Organa Ltd
Lahang Ltd
MGM UK Limited
Felicity McDonald Organics Ltd
Multi Imports Limited
Natural Beauty Import Limited
NaturallyClearSkin Limited
North One Limited
Oh So Locks Ltd
Oscar & Louis Limited
PL Distribution Ltd
Pavone Profumi SRL Ltd
Pizzaz Ventures Limited
Potion Dynamo Limited
Qiaochu Trading Co. Ltd
Rawly Processed Ltd.
Recruit Skincare Ltd
Renibo Ltd
Rexez Ltd
SA & A Ltd
SSB Ltd
Sangels Limited
Sassy N Trendy Cosmetics Ltd
Siam Botanicals UK Limited
Simply Squirrel Limited
Soapy J Limited
Somerset Perfumery Ltd
Spice International Trading Co Ltd
Stuff of Life Limited
TAC Perfumes & Cosmetics (UK) Ltd
Tauri Corporation Limited
Theodory Ltd
Think Be Nature Ltd
Tonic15 Ltd
Ukin Ltd
Valma Consumer Co Ltd
Ruth Venessa Services Ltd
VevBeautyCosmeticsTrading Ltd
Debra Jayne Walker Limited
Wonderland Sales Ltd
Worldwide International Retail Ltd
Yazmae Cosmetics Limited
Zivi Cosmetics Ltd

March 2018 [99]
A Essentials Limited
Angsana Ltd
Antiageing Haircare Specialists Ltd
Arabian Aroma Limited
Argan Care Ltd
Aromaclub Handmade Skincare Ltd
Aurum D Limited
Aviva Health Solutions Limited
BC (PVT) Ltd
Beauty Stable Ltd
Bedrock Trade Ltd
Beehive Cosmetics UK Limited
Blink Street Limited
Bloomtown Ltd
Boundless Beauty Ltd
CHM Holdings Ltd
Cherry Cherry Fashion Ltd
Chintys Ltd
Clearance Masters Ltd
Cosmetiqa Ltd
Dead Sea London Ltd
Enhance You Ltd
Evercore UK Limited
Face & Beauty Limited
Facil Haircare Ltd

Farmavita Ltd
Feel and Heal UK Limited
Fem Distribution Limited
France Eclavour Cosmetic Ltd
Geek's Cosmetics Ltd
General Shop Ltd
Golden Vanity Ltd
Great London Beauty Limited
Gridt Beauty Ltd
HBDeadSea-UK.Com Limited
Hekiti Cosmetics Ltd
Herb Stuff Limited
Jaden Cosmetics Limited
Jivesse Limited
Jonatho Ltd
Jouer Jouer Limited
Juni Cosmetics Limited
K3W Trading Limited
KBM London Limited
KSE Cosmetics Ltd
Kandahar Trading Limited
Khuba Limited
Konya Food Biotechnology Co., Ltd
LYF Cosmetics Limited
La Boutique du Discount Ltd.
Lady Smidgeton's Apothecary Ltd
Les Blanches Limited
Loop Beauty Limited
ME & II Limited
MM Product Trading UK Limited
Marcman Perfume Ltd
Melanative Ltd
Mepro Cosmetic Ltd
Mimm Organics Ltd
Miss U Cosmetics Limited
Mr Carters Essentials Limited
Narizaonline Ltd
Natural Jeanius Ltd
Natural Sheaness Ltd
Niya Cosmetics Ltd
Nocov Ltd
Noli Distribution Ltd
A W Oliver & Co Ltd
Oliver & Taylor Ltd
Pause Skincare Limited
Pinklady International Ltd
Procter & Procter Limited
RMD Global OYB Limited
RR Cosmeceuticals (UK) Ltd
Relaxa Trading Ltd
Reliance HBC UK Ltd
Reneebeauty Limited
Rishi Human Hair Extensions Wholesale
Rock Beauty Junkie Limited
Saltee Skincare Limited
Sfera London Limited
Sheacare Cosmetics Limited
Splendor Europe Ltd.
Stroppy Ltd
Sucre By Zoe Skincare Limited
Sun Jelly Ltd
Supply Zoom Ltd
Swipes Fragrance Ltd
Swiss Trading .UK. Ltd
Tawakkal Perfumes Ltd
Trade Giant Limited
Trollion Limited
True Mia Limited
True Skincare Limited
Ude Cosmetics Limited
Vida Skincare Ltd
WGTSS Ltd

Wonder and Wild Ltd
Zoeva UK Limited

April 2018 [83]
Afro Hair and Beauty International
Allure Cosmetics Ltd
Always 20 Limited
Be Savvy Ltd
Bodyhug Limited
CJ Cosmetics Ltd
Catalina Beauty Group Limited
Ciao Brow Henna Limited
Clever Skin Co Limited
Cont-Hemp-Orary Ltd
Cont-Hemp-Orary Skincare Ltd
Cornish Beard Co Ltd
Cosmetics Store Ltd
Cosmetics Wholsale Ltd
Cosmetolife Limited
Cutelovelee Limited
Dilmaherbals Limited
Dinair Airbrush Makeup Systems Ltd
Double Skies Limited
Dr.K Skinlab Ltd
Edward London Ltd
Eye Kandy Cosmetics Ltd
Fade The Itch Ltd
Fandealtastic Limited
Fatale Cosmetics Limited
Forever Heng UK Limited
Foreverbeyoung Ltd
Hairenvy Boutique Limited
Hava Traders Limited
Heavenly Body Ltd
Helia-D UK Ltd
Hydro Fresh Ltd
Indiggle Limited
Sarah Ireland Perfumes Ltd
Jia Bo Rui International Trade Ltd
Gabriel Kalevi Ltd
Kenzak Beauty and Jewellery Ltd
Klean Skincare Ltd
Kservices Group Ltd
La Bello Beauty Limited
Lagoon Soaps Limited
Leixaco Trading Ltd
Lilies of The Valley Cosmetics Ltd
Liolax Limited
Love Henna Brows Limited
MD-101 Ltd
Memoize Parfum Ltd
Mine of Goods Ltd
Mlaveau Cuban Origins Ltd
My London Trade Ltd
My Meghan Ltd
My Pure Life-Style Limited
N & L Cosmetic Limited
Nail Creation UK Distribution Ltd
Nakkali Limited
Ned London Limited
On & Off Beauty Ltd
Orca Distributor Ltd
Orgreen Naturals Ltd
Otterganics Ltd
Potteries Transport Services Ltd
Prismologie International Ltd
Pro Brands (UK) Ltd
Prostar Trending Online Ltd
Robh Scrub Limited
Roots Are Remedies Ltd
Skinkode Ltd
TPC Smith Limited

Smuccii Trading Ltd
Sofil Cosmetic Ltd
Solo JC Trade Ltd
Spice Fragrances Ltd
Sunscreen X Limited
Surrati Perfumes Limited
Thalasso Ltd
ULB Limited
Ultimate Henna Brows Ltd
WH Corporation (UK) PTE. Ltd
Wash Your Mouth Out Ltd
Wealden Aesthetics Limited
Xhorah Skincare Ltd
Yates-Lee and Burnett Limited
Yu Parfums Ltd

May 2018 [97]
A Beauty Story Ltd
AK Wholesale Limited
Amaxa Ltd
Anita Brows Cosmetics Limited
Attraxion Cosmetics Ltd.
B & F Ventures Ltd
Bare Kind Limited
Mahc Beau UK & Europe Ltd
Beautonic Skincare Ltd
Beauty Solutions Trading Ltd
Beauty The Divine Ltd
Beauty and Trade Ltd
Bioaqua -Biotechnology Ltd.
Blank Factory Limited
Blk Deer Co. Ltd
Bortlam Postpartum Restore Health Management (International) Chain Co.,
Bubbleworks Limited
California Glow Ltd
Charlize London Ltd
Cursed Cosmetics Ltd
Custom Tan UK Limited
DMK Distribution (NI) Ltd
Dead Pretty Official Ltd
Dimonauk Ltd
Drimex Limited
Esscential Ltd
Evanto Fragrance Limited
Express Online Superstore, London Ltd
Facemane Ltd
Faye Florais Global Holdings., Ltd
Fegoo Limited
Foramca Ltd
Gemini Beauty Products Ltd
Gentlemend Ltd
Glamrolls Limited
Green Essence Ltd
Guestproud Ltd
HD Cosmetics Ltd
Hempo Logical International Ltd
Hild International Group Ltd
Hubert & Emilie Ltd
Hudsonry Ltd
Ila Pothecary Limited
Infini Lab Ltd
International Traders House P.I.T.
Itala Group Ltd
Ivy Wild Ltd
Jardin de Parfums Ltd
Joyganics Ltd
Just Acrylics Ltd
Lamari London Ltd
Larisa Markus Limited
Look Fab Limited
Lotus Cosmetics Ltd

Luqs Womenswear Ltd
Luxuryscope London Limited
MQL International Ltd
Mamondo Fragrance and Beauty Ltd
Marksman Green Ltd
Medna Fashions Ltd
Modern Man Ltd
Mondor & Bache Ltd
Morgan Jost Ltd
Nature Scents Limited
Neopilina Moda Ltd
Niche Aromas Ltd
Njubien Ltd
Organic Cosmetic Products Ltd
Perfume Brands Limited
Pet Scentuary Ltd
Phi Advisory & Consulting Ltd
Phoenix Beauty Ltd
Purederma Ltd
Regista Fragrance Ltd
Resquire Health & Beauty Ltd
Rich Cosmetics Ltd
Robert Cosmetics Limited
Roz Cosmetics Ltd
SHH Logistics Ltd
Scence Ltd
Serengeti Skincare Limited
Shori Ltd
Skincare 18 Ltd
So Boujee Limited
Sophistique Beauty Ltd
Soybalm Ltd
Spaquashop Ltd
Speak Beauty Limited
St-Creation Ltd
TA-65 (UK) Wholesale Limited
Total Salon Supplies Limited
Tree of Life Cosmetics Ltd
Trichy Ltd
Unidus Limited
Venkh Retail Ltd
YSO Import-Export Limited
Zamoux Cosmetics Limited

June 2018 [98]

7th Heaven Scents Ltd
A Rebours Limited
A S Pacho Ltd
ACH Cosmetics Limited
Aga Cosmetics Ltd
Age Infinite Ltd
Al-Abideen Perfumes Ltd
All-Around Infinity Limited
Amor Beauty Cosmetics Ltd
Anandi Cosmetics Private Ltd
Asase Tree Ltd
Azik Group Ltd
Beauty Everich Ltd
Beautybaseuk Ltd
Bel Corporation Ltd
Mark Birch Hair Ltd
Bloom Artisan Brands Limited
CH General Traders Limited
Caarmi Ltd
Cheap Cosmetic Ltd
Cherie Cosmetics Limited
Corium Health Limited
Crane + Wilton Ltd
Cult Candy Limited
Chloe Davids Limited
Dermica Laboratoires UK Ltd
Doyle's Group Ltd

Duke of Charm Limited
Duo Beauty Products Limited
EB Stores Ltd
Earthkind Ltd
Effay Limited
Egotistic Hair & Beauty Ltd
Emilia's Handmade Bath and Body Ltd
Essential Oil Sell Ltd
Exotic Fragrance Ltd
Farah Organics Ltd
FayshCosmetics Ltd
Fourie Hair Limited
Fragrance de Maison Limited
Functional Skincare Ltd
Geeza Cosmetics Ltd
Gen Next Ltd
Glitterati Shop Ltd
Goodangels Ltd
Hydracol Pty Ltd
Iconic Perfumes Ltd
Infinity K Ltd
JWWJ Limited
K588 Limited
Kaniz International Limited
Kaniz Organics Limited
Kendra Cosmetics Limited
Kissess Lips of The Essence Ltd
Lanmix Enterperises Ltd
Lash Authority Ltd
Lashed London Limited
Le Parfum Ltd
Little Duckling Soaps Ltd
Lom Trade Limited
Lozano Skincare Ltd
M & H Cosmetic Limited
Mahogany Crownz Ltd
Maskologist Ltd
Meadow Skincare Limited
Megaco Limited
Mirtas Cosmetics Ltd
Miy Sofiyah Limited
Muchacho (London) Limited
N Organics Ltd
NABS Promotions Limited
Natrorg Ltd
Nice Smell Trade Ltd
Nicholas Fragrances Ltd
Noble Soap Limited
Noor Int'l Trading Limited
Onamex Ltd
Only Perfection Ltd
Organic Skincare Originals Ltd
PLBrands Limited
Planet Sparkle Ltd
Prescripteur Ltd
R & R Global Consumer Healthcare Ltd
Seigur Rose International Group Co., Ltd
Shine Shampoo Bars Ltd
Souvre UK Ltd
Spruce Vita Limited
Summerlilly Limited
Swiss Cosmetic Distribution Ltd
There-There Baby Ltd
Tobco Limited
Tommco Limited
Trade Anchor Limited
Valencia Cy Makeup Ltd
Vivora Limited
We Concept Ltd
Z Online Ltd
Zoee Cosmetics Co., Ltd

July 2018 [98]

9 Silk Gates Ltd
Adwa Impex Ltd
Afrocare Ltd
Al Amira Limited
Alumier Labs UK Limited
Aromatic Yogi Ltd
Asifall Ltd
Beautiful By Nature Ltd
Beauty By Aliyah Ltd
Beauty Queen Milano Ltd
Berry Inc Ltd
Biola Beauty Ltd
Birch & Hayer Ltd
Blue Rose Shop Ltd
Body Beauty Wholesale Exporters Ltd
Boost Balm Ltd
Brownie Beauty Products Cosmetics Ltd
Cheet Beauty Ltd
Clean Living Ltd
Cochabamba Parfums Limited
Colourscent Limited
Cor Cosmetics Limited
Cosmolovely Limited
Cxlture Cosmetics Ltd
DS Express Barbering Ltd
Deewin Stomatology Research Center Co.,
Dermura Skin Ltd
Diamond Brands Limited
Dream Glow Ltd
Earth Goddess Ltd
Elegant Boss Ltd
Envision International Co., Ltd
Evbioo Ltd
FHM Consulting Ltd
Fillers Pro Ltd
Forest Hive Ltd
Fox Cosmetics Ltd
Fragrance Souk Limited
Fragrance Weekly Ltd
GVM Long Life Formula UK Ltd
HT Cosmetics Ltd
Happy Carrot Skincare Ltd
Ilex Wood Ltd
Insta-Jell Cosmetics Ltd
K Co Cosmetics Ltd
Kizzle Beauty Ltd
Labo Nine Limited
Ladorisa Limited
Lashline Ltd
Lavish Lashes Ltd
Lax Group Co Ltd
Le Lissage UK Limited
Mabxclusive Limited
Majestic Company London Ltd
Masculin Limited
Mata Labs Cosmetics Ltd
Miracle8 Ltd
Modazi Ltd
Mr. Smith Products UK Ltd
Muse Make Up Ltd
N18 Ltd
Naeemah & Al Farhad Ltd
Naiga Naturals Ltd
Narges Beauty Limited
Naturally Untamed Ltd
New York 77 Ltd
Nika Cosmo Group Ltd
Nuke Manufacturing, Distribution & Investments
Paliano Ltd
Paris Elysees Holding Ltd.

Pheora Rucci Limited
QZE Limited
Real Cosmetics Ltd
Ru Si Lacquers Global Ltd.
S T K Brows Limited
SPTB Ltd
Sacha Cosmetics UK Ltd
Sambio Ltd
Soap Industry Limited
Someplace Nice Limited
Soul Cosmetics Limited
Standfast Solutions International Ltd
Style Cosmetics Limited
T4Colins Beautifician Ltd
TheGlobalTrading Ltd
Thiossane Ltd
Trelux Limited
UK Aimutaike Electronics Co., Ltd
UK Esthetics Ltd
Uchepeace Limited
Uni London Limited
United Nomads Limited
Valorem Distribution Ltd
Vilai Europe Trading Limited
Vivlai Europe Trading Limited
Whip Cosmetics Ltd
Wwinc. Ltd
Ibrahim Yusuf and Sons Ltd

August 2018 [124]
100% Vegan Skincare Limited
446-012 File Limited
Agoda Limited
Arrah Ltd
Beanies Beauty Lab Ltd
Beard Gang Ltd
Beard and Bones UK Limited
Beard of Attraction Ltd
Beauty Pod Limited
Best-Bio Ltd
Beyond Glamour Ltd
Bio Global Limited
Bioxane Ltd
Birmingham Fragrances Ltd
Bluesky Cosmetics UK HQ Ltd
C-Bombe Limited
Chaleur Ltd
Chinese Gentry Limited
Chit.Ka Ltd
Comglobal Limited
Consy Limited
Contrast Cosmetics Ltd.
Cosmetic Orb Ltd
Dermaperfetca Ltd
Dorothy Hair and Beauty Shop Ltd
Dufeal Your Best Beauty Ltd
Duron Ltd
East Cosmetics Limited
Eau de Parfum Limited
Eileen Group (UK) Ltd
Eleu Beauty Ltd
Eloise M Beauty Ltd
Esteem Royale Cosmetics Ltd
Evie Skincare Ltd
Exbrands Ltd
FG Traders Ltd
Fab Professional Hair Supplies Ltd
Farshety Ltd
GameelaCosmetics Ltd
Glow Jar Ltd
H2 World Health and Beauty Co Ltd
HBD International Limited

HE Products Ltd
Hair & Skin Care Ltd
Halal Beauty Co Ltd
Helen Gel Colour Ltd
Hemangini Limited
Heyvega Ltd
IDK Balms Ltd
Iattar Perfume Oils Ltd
International Integrated Solutions Co
Ish Products Ltd
Jax of London Ltd
Jerome Fashion Ltd
Joanna Naturals Limited
Kind2 Limited
Krizma Cosmetics Ltd
LMD Cosmetics Ltd
LPG Clinics Wholesale Ltd
Landional Ltd
Larouge Cosmetics Limited
Lefami Cosmetics Group Ltd
Lex Roris Ltd
Londonscentsuk Limited
Lovoir Ltd
Macden Beauty Ltd
Make It Up Limited
Manicure You Ltd
Medica Ltd
Monrone Health Ltd
NRS Cosmetics Ltd
Nacho Vidal Distribuciones Ltd
Rochelle Natty Business Group Ltd
Navya Innoveda Ltd
Nefil Ltd
Nekta Botanics Ltd
OhMyLashUK Ltd
Ohsho Ltd
Omaoli Limited
Orit Limited
Oya 9 Ltd
P & P Cosmetics Ltd
P.T & Co Ltd
Parfume-Mania Ltd
Peters Cosmet Ltd
Pota Nini Limited
Prestonelite Limited
Pure Body Skin Care Ltd
Pure Skincare Limited
RHI By ROC Ltd
Reminiscents of Didsbury Ltd
Renaissance Manyane Global Group Ltd
SS Wholesaler Limited
Salem Stores Ltd
Santa Code Limited
Saravio UK Ltd
Sasy N Savy Ltd
Scented LDN Limited
Seaside Investments Ltd
Secret Line Ltd
SeductiveDirect Ltd
Select & Bargain Ltd
Shave Algorithm Ltd
Simply Pure Skincare Ltd
Skin Sanity Limited
Skinlab Medical Ltd
Skintel Cosmetics Ltd
Smellycat Ltd
Sphere 7 Lab Ltd
Stolen Beauty Limited
Style4you Ltd
Tiggy Lashes Ltd
Timeless Temple Ltd
Timi's Cosmetics Ltd

Toggle Genetica Group Limited
Trine Oils Limited
Turning Tides Ltd
UK Cosmeticz International Ltd
UK Lemenic International Medical Group
W8T Ltd
Wheesht Ltd
YJX Group PLC
ZZ Traders Ltd
Zoe Balm Ltd

September 2018 [87]
Aabis Duty Free Limited
Jalali Agarwood Ltd
Albertina Dorosario Ltd
Alkaiser Perfumes Ltd
Aquapurity Ltd
Asia Nails and Beauty Supply Ltd
Aurum Essence Ltd
Beautessential Limited
Beauty Alliance International Ltd
Beauty and More 2000 Ltd
Bellissimo GmbH International Ltd
Black Candle Company of Northumberland
Blissible Ltd
Body of Work Beauty Ltd
Butter Park Ltd
Buy It Out Ltd
Steven Carey Hair & Beauty Ltd
Chic Clothing Limited
Alia Collyns Cosmetics Ltd
Complete Healing Limited
DealsRUsOnline Ltd
Dily Oka International Group Co., Ltd
Dunia Organic Ltd
Egg Pillow Limited
Elder & Co Limited
Electimuss Limited
Estela Dermocosmetics Ltd
Esthetica Pure Ltd
Eva Cosmetics Ltd
Evanesce Ltd
Flores Brand Works Limited
GCKK Ltd
Gabs Cosmetologist Limited
Green Ladies N.I Ltd
H.H.L.Brothers Limited
Hasanah Global Ltd
IBS Shopeye World Ltd
Isobel C Professional Cosmetics Ltd
Jak Beauty Ltd
Jayeed Perfumes Ltd
Kimibeauty Ltd
J Kobain London Ltd
J Kobain Ltd
L.P Cosmetics Ltd
Laogong Laopo Limited
Lazeeza Lashes Limited
Lbeautie Ltd
Leclair Cosmetics Limited
Leicala Natural Products Ltd
Liquor Lips Ltd
Lumine Beauty Ltd
Magpie's Ocean Ltd
Paul Marney & Co Ltd
Microskin Cosmeceuticals UK Ltd
Mintology Limited
Multitude Makeup Ltd
Nacho Vidal Distribuciones 2 Ltd
Olivoderm Cosmetics UK Limited
Organic Iway Ltd
OrganicBeautyshop Ltd

The Top UK Perfume and Cosmetics Wholesalers — dellam

Oudh Al Aasmah Perfume UK Ltd
P & Z Solutions Limited
Danica Payne Ltd
Pharmdex UK Ltd
Pink Lush Lips Ltd
Quelsa Ltd
RSJ Trading Limited
Refan Portadown Limited
Renski Limited
SFL Group Ltd
Saint Cosmetics Ltd
Salimaskinsolutions Ltd
Saroza Limited
Shop4stocks Limited
Sopure London Limited
Splash Cosmetics Ltd
TheGoodSkinCo Ltd
TheManeCo Ltd
Truthpaste Ltd
Tryon Products Limited
Valya Beauty Cosmetics Ltd
Web Store Group Limited
Wipes Direct Ltd
Wisp Care Products Limited
Woodwood Limited
Zed Beauty Ltd
Zjonline Ltd

October 2018 [109]

A Natural Treat Limited
AM Botanical Limited
AR Scents Limited
Adora Beauty Limited
Afex Skin Care Ltd
Altundag Ltd
Apsara Cosmetics Ltd
B.Me Skincare Ltd
Barbers House Ltd
Beauty Healthcare Ltd
Bemysoul Ltd
Binaya Solution Ltd
By Al Kindi Ltd
Cacti Cosmetics Ltd
Cannabinoid Oil Solutions Ltd
Churchill Motley Limited
Claracutis, Ltd
Clinibella Ltd
Colour Lux Cosmetics Ltd
Cosmelinks Consultancy Ltd
DC Salon Products Ltd
Dance on Tan Limited
Dazzle Dee Ltd
Divit Beauty Ltd
Dolly Custard Ltd
Emortal Maquillage Ltd
Esem International Ltd
Essex Beauty Palace Ltd
Eukes Global Limited
Ex'klusive Products Ltd
Express Hair and Beauty Supply Ltd
Feel Good Products Limited
Forderma Laboratory Ltd.
Fragrancekent (UK) Ltd
GDT Global Limited
Gattino Cosmetics Ltd
Gentel Works Ltd
Gift Presentp Ltd
Gordon-McCarthy Limited
Hair Contrast UK Limited
Headrocka Ltd
Health Future Limited
Hempia Limited

Herbalise Limited
Hothouse Holdings Limited
House of Kendra Ltd
Husaco Ltd
Icilda's Ltd
Indulge Therapeutics UK Ltd
InternationalBeautyLondon Ltd
JP Products and Services Ltd
Jas Etrading Ltd
Jennifer Klar Ltd
Land of Beauty Supplies Ltd
Leela Living Limited
Lovalova Ltd
Lyons Men's Grooming Ltd
Mahiri Africa Ltd
Maliboo Hair and Cosmetics Ltd
Man'd Skincare Ltd
Meet T Needs Limited
Mitvana and Biological Industries Ltd
Mooi-H Ltd
Mystique Swan Ltd
NM Beauty Industries Ltd
Natural Health Harmony Group Ltd
Nefert Ltd
OPA Botanicals Ltd
On-Top Skincare Limited
Orien Beauty & Selfcare Ltd
Otonix Limited
Peau Royale Limited
Perfumez Limited
Plenteous Ltd
Ploom (U.K.) Limited
Portobello Organics Ltd
Privilago Fashion Ltd
Purelonia Ltd
Real Skin Pickle Ltd
Roccotek Limited
JC Rosedale Co Ltd
Rosse Beau Ltd
Rub-a-Dub Scrub Ltd
Sage Apothecary Limited
Sahinler Limited
Saint and Sinner Cosmetics Ltd
Sheyton Ltd
Shuhui Limited
Soadperf Limited
Star Pearls Ltd
Sueno Cosmetics Ltd
Sweet Arabian Ltd
Tententen Limited
Tetra Hydro Cannabinoid Oils Global Ltd
Tina Trading Co Ltd
Toure Ltd
Trade Mall Limited
Triaton Ltd
Trulips Ltd
UK Irelia Co Ltd
Villainelle Ltd
Vivacy Laboratoires Ltd
Vyas International Ltd
Wharfedale Herbal Ltd
Wild Earth Botanicals Ltd
Wizard Brands Limited
Wizer Ltd
Zarahs World Ltd
Zimmerglobal Ltd

November 2018 [104]

305 Professionals Ltd
4symbols Ltd
876 Skin Beauty Limited
Adam Michaels Group Ltd

African Wild Organics Ltd
Albland Limited
Amour Pigments Ltd
Ark Inta Ltd
Asenov Traders Ltd
Avelena Ltd
Bayan Ltd
Bcara Ltd
Beauty Full Ltd
Beauty Queen Limited
Beautyzon Limited
Bemi Banks Cosmetics Ltd
Bendito Trading Limited
Bloom International Group Ltd
Bod Beauty Ltd
Botanika Group Ltd
Boujelle Ltd
Bracknell Gardens Ltd
Brazilian Kimberlite Clay Ltd
Cocobaba Ltd
Coslab Ltd
Cosmos Cosmetics Limited
DLG Partners Limited
Eabir Ltd
Eacho Green Ltd
Eden's Daughter Limited
Elleshouse Ltd
Ethereal Beauty Ltd
FFC International Limited
Fasa Capillago Limited
Ferana Ltd
Glitterfreaks Limited
Goldeivy London Lashes Ltd
Good By Nature Ltd
Guerison Skin Solutions Ltd
Hello Dame London Ltd
It Worx Cosmetics Limited
Ives Lab Ltd
Jaspmab Ltd
Jorum of Scotland Limited
K Wholesale Limited
K. V. Fair Trades Limited
KMC's Fabulous Cosmetics Ltd
Kehal Ltd
King of Sytle Ltd
Kozmar International Limited
Krish Shoppers Ltd
Kurlysue Limited
Layan Pharma Ltd
Lensmeuk Limited
Lese & Lista Ltd
Light Up Skincare Ltd
Loaded Cosmetics Limited
Lollipop Treats Ltd
Love Anousta Limited
Loveliness Limited
MDistributor Hair and Beauty Products
MEA Health and Wellness Ltd
MH Exports Limited
Marrouge Limited
Mediskin Pro Limited
Meilikki Ltd
Minxx Lashes Ltd
Miraculous UK Ltd
Miss Glamm Limited
My7heavens Ltd
Myrrh & Co. Limited
Nail Island Ltd
Naturity Cosmetics Ltd
Norm and Glo Limited
Oakhill Luxury Ltd
Omprus Limited

P & M Beauty Ltd
Photics Skincare Ltd
Plants Work Limited
Powered By Nature Cosmetics Ltd
Prime Skincare Ltd
Quanis Cosmetic Limited
Radiant Glow Beauty UK Ltd
Raisingthebaruk Ltd
Rapsodi Ltd
Revolax Ltd
Saveasy Ltd.
Scentric Ltd
Silk and Bubble Limited
Spring and Underworld Ltd
Step International Cosmetic Ltd
Style Factory Limited
Suave Cents Limited
Sweet Pea Soaps Co Ltd
Tanovation Ltd
Texthold Ltd
Think Beauty Online Limited
UK Ailise Biotechnology Trade Ltd
UK Deer Running Co., Ltd
Valerie Lady Co., Ltd
Villa Sauod Ltd
Wild Kynd Ltd
Wildmint Cosmetics Limited
Yaami's Fashion Beauty & Cosmetics UK

December 2018 [97]
Aeroeco Co Ltd
Aether Elements Ltd
Arewa Styles Limited
Argan Blossom Ltd
Azaleo Limited
Be Fairall Limited
Be Fast Innovation Services Ltd
Beauty & Skincare Essentials Ltd
Beauty Solutions Global Ltd
Bioline Ltd
Bisch Limited
Brands Gallery Ltd
C & P Neptune Ltd
CBD Bakes Ltd
Capital Import & Export Co. Ltd
Choize Ltd
Crete Online Ltd.
Delhicious Ltd
Design4nails Ltd
Directfrom Ltd
Dont Poke It Ltd
Dots for Spots Ltd
Dr. Twilight Ltd
Drugget Ltd
East To West Lifestyle Co Ltd
Ethical House Ltd
Evoiq International Ltd
FB Cosmetologist Limited
Floest Beauty Solutions Ltd
Flutter Cosmetics Limited
Fragrance World Ltd
Genten Skincare Ltd
Giva Solution Ltd
Global Hair Care Limited
Gulz Cosmetics Ltd
H07CNN Limited
Hedgerow Medicine Chest Ltd
Inspired by RJP Limited
Irregular Cosmetics Co Ltd
Jardins D'Eden Ltd
Jass Perfumes Limited
KD Cosmetics (Midlands) Ltd

KMY Group Ltd
Kandi Apple Limited
Kanj Wholesale Ltd
Kathy Sue-Ann's Ltd
Kayanna Ltd
Kerria, Limited
Kiara Beauty Ltd
L'Art & La Matiere Limited
LBB Skin Ltd
Laila Cosmetics Limited
Lam Cosmetics Ltd
Le Glamour UK Ltd
Les Laboratoires ILP UK Ltd
Loveve. Ltd
MWK Cosmetics (UK) Ltd
Man Mask Ltd
Mandragora Ltd
Margan Oil Ltd
Mast - Art Group Limited
Master Beauty Limited
Misawa Healthcare Ltd
Misspap X Bperfect Limited
Modern Innovations Limited Ltd
Moroccan Attlas Ltd
Moxxy Limited
NJ Apparel Ltd.
Niami1893 Ltd
Nutrics Ltd
Odeferus Limited
Onsen Secret UK Ltd
Oxmetics Ltd
PSR Wellness Limited
Pharmacare International Ltd
R & T Natural Cosmetics Ltd
R10 Labs Skincare Ltd
S & G Supplies Ltd
SK Network Ltd
Sang Real Tattoo Ltd
Simple Bargain Limited
Soak Rochford Ltd
Square Wholesale Ltd
Strdom Ltd
Trees of Beauty Ltd
Tyn y Ddol Enterprises Ltd
UK Natural Serenity Ltd
Urban Altar Ltd
VI Beauty Ltd
Vegan Republic Beauty Ltd
Vegan Republic Ltd
Vitaglow Ltd
Whimsical Beauty Ltd
World Links Europe Limited
World Wide Gifts Limited
Zarroug Limited
Zoe Lane Ltd

January 2019 [139]
11 Scent Limited
1CBDUK Ltd
AMS-Uhren Ambiente mit Style Ltd
Adorexo Ltd
Ahoaloe Cosmetics Limited
Almcells Bioscience Ltd.
Ank Innovation Limited
Antipodes Europe Limited
Arbar Ltd
Ascenttial Ltd
Asel Ltd
Atlas Global Trade Ltd
Axa Beauty World Limited
Ayhamco Limited
B Luxury Scents Ltd

Back To Eve Ltd
Belgrave Traders Ltd
Bespoke Hospitality Supplies Ltd
Bibishor Limited
Body Beauty & Hair Ltd
Botany Squared Limited
Box of Beauty Ltd
Boylondon Holdings Limited
Bragarlin Limited
Cannamplify Ltd
Caprise Limited
Ches Editions Ltd
Co Beauty Ltd
Coffeinium Germania Ltd
Colour Life Limited
Cosplus International Ltd
Coveti Limited
Croma-Pharma Limited
DLM Trade Limited
DSE Companies Limited
Dacre Skincare Limited
Deep Red Marketing International Ltd
Dojah Limited
Earthbreath Ltd
Ekoderma Ltd
Lisa Eldridge Beauty Ltd
Elitelashes Ltd
Emma Victoria Cosmetics Ltd
Erin Cosmetics Ltd
Essench Cosmetics Limited
Fin Perri Ltd
Fizz 'n' Bliss Ltd
Fleeks Hair & Beauty Limited
Flower Cosmetic Ltd
Freshly Whip'd Limited
G & G Skincare Ltd
Gajas Gift Limited
Glossy Center Limited
Gluedon Ltd
Green Mass Limited
Greenery Skincare Limited
Gxskin Limited
Hair Passion Limited
Hair Wardrobe Ltd
Health-Beauty Ltd
Hidden for Purpose Ltd
Icebox Brands EU Limited
Imamcom Ltd
In & Outbrands Ltd
Ismile Beauty Ltd
Ivy Nat Ltd
J26 Limited
Josie Rose Ltd
Just Do You Limited
Justins Essentials Ltd
K2 Supplies Ltd
Khali Min Limited
Kovet Kit Ltd
LGC Cosmetics Ltd
Estee Lauder (UK) International Group
Lavant Beauty and Personal Care Ltd
Libhairation Ltd
Liluna-Organics Ltd
London Bathers Limited
Lueno Cosmetics Limited
Luuann Limited
MH Products Limited
Madame Laveau Ltd
Mary-Jane's Beauty Ltd
Mink Company U.K Ltd
Mint Julip Ltd
Modern Man Project Ltd

Nanosafe Ltd.
Natural Blends of Nature Ltd
Natural Pal Limited
Neete Holdings Limited
New Aesthetic Ltd
Nu-E55ence Ltd
Official IV Ltd
Ombre Cosmetics Limited
Ombre Paris Limited
Onyx Clothing Ltd
Original Taste Ltd
Orikii Naturals Ltd
Outcome Zero Ltd
P P Oil UK Limited
Perfume Bodega Dist. Ltd
Plush Soap Ltd
Prezance Ltd
Raebeauty Ltd
Rich & Ruitz Perfume Industry Ltd
Riway International Group (Euro) Ltd
Riway International Group (UK) Ltd
Riway Ltd
Roxie Cosmetics Ltd
SHL Medical Limited
Salon Professional London Ltd
Same Cosmetics Limited
Serenityy Ltd
Shadi's Hairdresser Ltd
Sheasecrets Ltd
Shhuk Ltd
Sjonlineuk Ltd
Spree Trading Ltd
Sublime Cosmetics UK Ltd
Suvaz Linen UK Ltd
Tannovation Laboratories Ltd
Tebs Distribution Limited
Theglossfairy Ltd
Trading Corporation International Export and Import
Trinity General Trading Ltd
Truity Limited
Underground Girl London Ltd
Veels UK Limited
Vidology Group Ltd
Wat Cosmetics Ltd
Wild Violet X Limited
Worldwidegoodstraders Ltd
YWC (Yes We Can) Limited
Yurexroar Cosmetic Wholesale Ltd
Zealousco Limited
Zee Sales Limited
Zero Cosmetics UK Limited
Zyzven Naturals Cosmetics Ltd

February 2019 [105]
50shadez Ltd
ANGMG Ltd
Adonis Skin Ltd
Adoris UK Ltd
Africa's Best Artisans Limited
Aftershave Gaff Ltd
Aiweisier Limited
Al-Jazeera Perfumes Ltd
Alfa Parf UK Ltd
Alihair Ltd
Amaani Q Ltd
Apex Beard Co Ltd
Aroma Dead Sea Limited
Array of Scents Ltd
Arrogant Limited
Arthur Michel Cosmetics Distribution Ltd
Asaya Cosmeceuticals Limited
Autoscentsco Ltd
B.Cosmetics Ltd
Banafa for Oud and Perfume Ltd
Beauty Avenue Limited
Beauty Glow Wholesale Limited
Beauty Oasis Ltd
Beauty Science UK Ltd
Billionhaire Limited
Bubble-Bubble Ltd
Contemporary Cosmetic Enterprise Ltd
Cosmic Eyes Ltd
Crazy Smiles Group Ltd
D'val Ltd
Death Head Beard Co Ltd
Dermacosmeticsweb Ltd
Dos Osatos International Ltd
Dreamage Ltd.
Eleven Eleven Cosmetics Ltd
Expo Deal Ltd
Eye Love Beauty (Chester) Ltd
Ezili Botanicals Limited
Feelgoode Ltd
Feinkost & Getranke Ltd
Flo with It Ltd
France Parfums International Ltd
Simona Fridrich Limited
Gabriellas Beauty Ltd
Genixo Ltd
Glaci Natural Ltd
Gorillacare Ltd
Hairya Ltd
Imxpo Ltd
Jay Kay Wholesale Ltd
Kamila Health & Beauty Ltd
Kavali Cosmetics Limited
L'dreams Limited
LEM Beauty Ltd
LK Beauty Ltd
La Fumes Ltd
Lana's Beauty Box Ltd
Lavelle Store UK Ltd
Liza Organics Ltd
Lucy Beauty Products Ltd
Lux Aesthetics Hull Ltd
Luxurious Personal Care Ltd
Luxury Personal Care Ltd
MLM Cosmetics Ltd
MNF Commodities Ltd
Magpie Holdings Ltd
Meek and Mild Essentials Ltd
Mesoskinline (UK) Limited
Neonails Ltd
Nogender London Ltd
Nouvriet Boutros (UK) Ltd
Organic and Mineral Salons Ltd
Oxygen Skin Care - London Ltd
PSM Vision Limited
Preen Queen Limited
Prossentials Ltd
Pure Revolution Ltd
Quint Essence Lab Ltd
Rakhee LB Ltd
Republic Cosmetics UK Ltd
Retailwolfs Ltd
Reveal Naturals Ltd
Rhug Organic and Natural Ltd
Rose & Thorn Ltd
S.I Attar Ltd
Salon Theory Ltd
Selfish Cosmetics Ltd
Serenityhands Ltd
Shaw International Ltd
Smell Neutralizer Ltd
Solo Skin London Ltd
Stenko Ltd
Stonera Ltd
TLGrooming Limited
Taylor Grange Cosmetics Ltd
Thai Wellness Ltd
United Mart (UK) Limited
Velvet Bee Co Ltd
Velvet Vapours UK Limited
Very Essence Ltd
Vickie's Boutique Ltd
Victoire Limited
Vilasa Limited
Wow Facial Ltd
Zajil Limited

This page is intentionally left blank

Geographic Distribution by County

Co Antrim [30]
Apex Beard Co Ltd
Belfast Beard Co Ltd
Bendito Trading Limited
DMK Distribution (NI) Ltd
Elie Consumer Care Ltd
Elliott Nutrition Ltd
Essentials4men Ltd
Felix Medical Group Ltd
Forever Living Products Ireland Ltd
Hexbomb Ltd
Irregular Cosmetics Co Ltd
J & W Distribution Limited
Kityee Limited
Lahang Ltd
Lamer & Ava Healthcare Ltd
Larmed Limited
MJL Products Ltd
McCoey & Co. Limited
Mil locshlainte, All Natural Balms Ltd
Nars & Elliott Healthcare Ltd
Paradoxx Ltd
Regis Personal Care Ltd
Riley & Sons Ltd
Rimmel & Flynn Healthcare Ltd
Savvy & Shine Ltd
Serendipity (N.I.) Ltd
Shebelle Limited
Talza Limited
UK Vietnam Trade Ltd
Vita Liberata Limited

Co Armagh [8]
Angel Lash Limited
Ava Corporations Ltd
Beautifully Bliss Ltd
Cor Cosmetics Limited
E-MO Nails Ltd
Little Enterprises (NI) Ltd
Nomalogic Ltd
Refan Portadown Limited

Co Down [13]
Beauty School Limited
Bespoke Hospitality Supplies Ltd
Clarins & Felix Healthcare Ltd
Excellent Edges Ltd
Green Ladies N.I Ltd
He-Shi Enterprises Ltd
Hemo Bioscience Ltd
Hempia Limited
JS Marketing (N.I.) Limited
Lash House Eyelash Extensions Supplies
Mega Mane Limited
Revlon & Elie Healthcare Ltd
Snob Distribution Limited

Co Fermanagh
Age Infinite Ltd
Flynn Group of Companies Ltd
Genixo Ltd
Hazellbrook Limited

Co Londonderry [9]
Beautessential Limited
Conscience Clear Tan Limited
Fasa Capillago Limited
Garnier & Hemo Healthcare Ltd
Hydro Fresh Ltd
Julie's Natural Health Ltd
Mahogany Crownz Ltd
Quanis Cosmetic Limited
Zed Beauty Ltd

Co Tyrone [8]
Benefit & Riley Healthcare Ltd
Dr. Gabriela Ltd
Everyday Cosmetics Ltd
Labapothecary Ltd.
Lacomo Beauty Ltd
Revive Express Beauty Ltd
Salon Select (NI) Limited
Swift Retail Limited

Aberdeenshire [7]
Arizona Botaniq Limited
BM Beauty Ltd.
Droplet Cosmetics Limited
Dunia Organic Ltd
Flirties Products and Training Ltd
Halal Beauty Co Ltd
Smooth Image Beauty Limited

Angus
Asifall Ltd
Custom Tan UK Limited

Ayrshire [5]
Arnest International Limited
Indigo Nails Online Shop Ltd.
Mint Julip Ltd
Sanmex International Limited
Skin Sanity Limited

Dumfries-shire
Euro Healthcare Services Ltd
Eurocare Impex Services Ltd

Dumfries & Galloway [5]
Earth Aid Group Limited
Moffat Perfume Co Ltd
Organii Limited
Pravera Ltd
Yates-Lee and Burnett Limited

Dunbartonshire
Dance on Tan Limited
Warehouse.5 Limited

Fife
ABC Beauty Limited
Elder & Co Limited
Purelonia Ltd

Highland
Highland Soap Co. Limited
Wild Organics Limited

Inverness-shire
Alimacskincare Limited

Kirkcudbrightshire
Siam Skin Ltd

Lanarkshire [32]
A Pony Called Steve Ltd
Aro-Matic (Scotland) Ltd
Aromatic Yogi Ltd
Avee Ltd
B2B Beauty UK Limited
BeautyEmpireUK Ltd
Chando-UK Ltd
Dermafood Limited
Excess Beauty Ltd
Fabdoo Limited
Fizz 'n' Bliss Ltd
Genetiq Lab Limited
Jas Etrading Ltd
KMC's Fabulous Cosmetics Ltd
KMZA Enterprises Ltd
Man & Diva's Ltd
My Pink Ltd
Nature-Solves Ltd
Natures Merchant Ltd
Nicholas Fragrances Ltd
Nut Dust Ltd
Nutrics Ltd
Pixie Dust Products Limited
SGJ Perfumes Limited
Saint Cosmetics Ltd
Serious Skin Care Co Ltd.
Shuhui Limited
Smiles Glasgow Limited
Suvaz Linen UK Ltd
Tanovation Ltd
XSS Scotland Limited
XY Skin Ltd

Moray
Mary Jean Limited

Peebles-shire
Dug and Bitch Ltd

Perthshire
ABX Beauty Limited

Renfrewshire [7]
A.R Cosmetics Limited
Aromabar (Scotland) Ltd
Beauty Solutions Limited
Beauty Systems Group Ltd.
DHB (UK) Ltd.
MWK Cosmetics (UK) Ltd
Specialist Hair Products Ltd

Ross-shire
Earthbreath Ltd
SMC Cosmetics (UK) Ltd

Stirlingshire
Chintys Ltd
Gracefruit Limited
Indulge Therapeutics UK Ltd
JK Hair & Beauty Salon Supplies Ltd

The Top UK Perfume and Cosmetics Wholesalers

Bedfordshire [27]
Anar Naturals Limited
Argan Vanity Ltd
Barefaced Beauty Ltd
Best Pure Natural Products Ltd
Beyond Hair Ltd
Butterflyy Productions Ltd
Consy Limited
D'val Ltd
Dazzle Dee Ltd
Divine Natural Limited
Fair Pharm Limited
Fields Finesse Limited
Greenleaf Luton Limited
Hair Contrast UK Limited
Himalaya Enterprise Limited
Kenzak Beauty and Jewellery Ltd
Lilies of The Valley Cosmetics Ltd
Man Mask Ltd
Mehron Limited
Meller Design Solutions Ltd
OrganicBeautyshop Ltd
P & T PL Ltd
Salon Depot Ltd
Sasy N Savy Ltd
Soul Cosmetics Limited
Spartzy Lifestyle Brands Ltd
Wwinc. Ltd

Berkshire [57]
2M PH. Intl. Limited
Alianaz Ltd.
Alkaiser Perfumes Ltd
Anglo Indian Trading Limited
Beauty Senses Limited
Boost Balm Ltd
Brandaroma Limited
Calla Distribution Ltd
Cosmetic Bases Limited
Daughter of The Soil Limited
Dermura Skin Ltd
Duo Beauty Products Limited
Dynamic Skincare Ltd
Export Solutions (International) Ltd
F.D.D. International Limited
Fashion Conspiracy Ltd
Fragrance Sales Limited
Gemini Beauty Products Ltd
Green Merchandising Ltd
Guinot-Mary Cohr UK Limited
Haltrade UK Ltd
Heir & Grace Ltd
Hotel Essentials Ltd
Hydrea London Limited
Johnson & Johnson Limited
La Generale Limited
London International Inflammation Foundation
Lubatti Limited
MNM International UK Limited
Mesoskinline (UK) Limited
Mesostrata Limited
Sue Moxley Beauty Limited
Najah Ltd
Natcare Beauty Ltd
Ned London Limited
OhMyLashUK Ltd
P & M Beauty Ltd
Perfectly Natural Limited
Perfumer Ltd
Phyto Pharm Limited

Phyto Pharma Limited
Plan Target Limited
Regima Medic Ltd
Regima UK Ltd
Regima Zone Ltd
Regima@Dr H Ltd
Rejuvapen UK Ltd
Roccotek Limited
Rose Tree Enterprises Ltd.
SI & D (UK) Limited
Salon Success Limited
Seascape Island Management Ltd
Skincare Sanctuary Limited
Takasago (U.K.) Limited
True Skincare Limited
VIS International Corporation Ltd
Zero Cosmetics UK Limited

Buckinghamshire [48]
Aftershave Gaff Ltd
Amazon Healthcare Ltd
Askett & English Ltd
Autoscentsco Ltd
Avelena Ltd
Bulldog Skincare Limited
Calbrook Cosmetics UK Ltd
Cosmetic Orb Ltd
Tom Daxon Limited
Diverse Investment (London) Group
Doterra (Europe) Ltd
Enimarkets Ltd
Euroluxe Enterprise UK Ltd
Floest Beauty Solutions Ltd
Foodprint Network Ltd
Gojo Industries - Europe Ltd
Good Pharma Dermatology Ltd
Hair & Skin Care Ltd
Iconic Beauty London Limited
Joy Limited
King of Shaves Co Ltd
LEM Beauty Ltd
Natascha Lacombe Cosmetics Ltd
Larouge Cosmetics Limited
Loopy Hair & Beauty Ltd
Mellor & Russell Direct Distribution Ltd
Miss Vivien Ltd
Monat Global UK Ltd
NRS Cosmetics Ltd
Neete Holdings Limited
Orien Beauty & Selfcare Ltd
Prime Skincare Ltd
Albert Roger & Partner France Ltd
Albert Roger Benelux Limited
Albert Roger Limited
Albert Roger Portugal Limited
S & E Ventures Ltd
Same Cosmetics Limited
Saravio UK Ltd
Saveasy Ltd.
Silk Lounge Beauty Ltd
Surreal Health & Beauty Ltd
T A Trading Ltd
Unique Fragrances Limited
Warpaint Cosmetics (2014) Ltd
Warpaint Cosmetics Group Ltd
Warpaint London PLC
Winter Hill No.2 Limited

Cambridgeshire [30]
11:11 Limited
4T Medical Ltd

Biola Beauty Ltd
Butterwhips Ltd
Cacti Cosmetics Ltd
Cambridge Sprouts Limited
Clink Street FX Ltd
Contour and More London Ltd
Cutagen Ltd
Emma Victoria Cosmetics Ltd
Galactix Ltd
Good Skin Care Co Ltd
Gorillacare Ltd
Gridt Beauty Ltd
Hera Beauty Ltd
Highfields Health Limited
Liza Organics Ltd
Lush Lashes London Limited
Palmsextra Limited
Pearl & Rocky Limited
Pharmadose Limited
Phoenix Hair & Beauty (Ely) Ltd
RMD Global OYB Limited
RMD Global Wholesale Limited
SB Beauty Marketing Limited
Slim Line Club UK Ltd
Eve Taylor (London) Limited
Tibetan Cosmetics Ltd
Turning Tides Ltd
Vancooler Ltd

Carmarthenshire
DS Express Barbering Ltd
Wellbeing Skincare Limited

Cheshire [55]
Anne Marie Beauty Products (U.K.)
Ayursavvyveda Limited
B Luxury Scents Ltd
Balm Balm Limited
Barber & Salon Supplies Ltd
Beard Zone Ltd
Beauty at The Avenue Online Ltd
Carr Greens Limited
Chronicles Medical Consulting Ltd
Cosmetia UK Limited
Discounted Cosmetics Limited
Esscenti Ltd
Eye Love Beauty (Chester) Ltd
Florence Verity Limited
Fox Group International Ltd
GDT Global Limited
Gift Presentp Ltd
Gordon-McCarthy Limited
HD Cosmetics Ltd
Hair Cosmetics Limited
Hanfan (UK) Limited
Healthcare Wholesale Ltd
Heath Consumables Ltd
Heyvega Ltd
Hugworld Cristalinas UK Ltd
J S Trading (UK) Limited
JGR UK Distributions Limited
KDM Supplies Limited
Amelia Knight Holdings Ltd
Amelia Knight Limited
Kokoa UK Limited
L.A.Tanning Co Ltd
Laogong Laopo Limited
MGM UK Limited
MacKenzie Cosmetics Limited
Makki Cosmetics Limited
Niko Pro Limited

Pearson Cosmetics Limited
Perfume Supplies Limited
Pippa Beauty Limited
Prezance Ltd
Prism Parfums Limited
Resquire Health & Beauty Ltd
Retailwolfs Ltd
Revolax Ltd
Skin Care Co Ltd
Smart Nails (UK) Ltd
Spice International Trading Co Ltd
Lauren Stone Limited
Sundome Leisure Products Ltd
TLY Supplies Ltd
TheManeCo Ltd
UK Natural Serenity Ltd
Winchpharma (Consumer Healthcare) Ltd
Zurego Limited

Cleveland [11]
Additional Lengths Ltd
Aqolade Ltd
Collier & Wood Ltd
Create Images Ion Limited
Glam Wholesale Limited
H & R Cosmetics Ltd
Hair Wardrobe Ltd
KSE Cosmetics Ltd
Millennium Nails Europe Ltd
Oh So Locks Ltd
P.R. Professional Salon Supplies Ltd

Clwyd
Geek's Cosmetics Ltd

Co Derry
LMD Cosmetics Ltd

Co Durham [12]
Allure Cosmetics Ltd
Asabeauty Ltd
Brambles Farm Ltd
Casa Cosmetics Ltd
Cheet Beauty Ltd
Mitvana and Biological Industries Ltd
Pern Consumer Products Limited
Ray & Company (Hairdressers Sundries Men)
Razaq & Iqbal Limited
Skinjam Cosmetics Limited
TRS & Co (Europe) Limited
Winning Lines Limited

Cornwall [11]
ASR Aesthetics Ltd
Beautysugaring Limited
Bloom Remedies Ltd
Bloomtown Ltd
Cornish Beard Co Ltd
Fandealtastic Limited
C Looker Ltd
Nanat Limited
Photics Skincare Ltd
Scence Ltd
Skincare Cornwall Ltd

Cumbria [7]
20seven Limited
Dilecta Cosmetics Limited
H.H.L.Brothers Limited
It Worx Cosmetics Limited
Leclair Cosmetics Limited
Siwel Trading Ltd
Debra Jayne Walker Limited

Denbighshire
Flutter Cosmetics Limited
Hughes Evans Essentials Ltd
Polar Export Services Limited
Rhug Organic and Natural Ltd

Derbyshire [32]
Akoma International (UK) Ltd
Bad Mermaid Limited
Bigteal Industries Limited
Bouffe Limited
Brand Holdings Limited
CBD Bakes Ltd
Corley Capital Limited
Dermaenhance Ltd.
Divit Beauty Ltd
Dovedale Limited
Elleshouse Ltd
Esthermarie Limited
Faceoff Limited
Hair from India Limited
Indiggle Limited
Jess Nails Limited
KD Cosmetics (Midlands) Ltd
Mancave Limited
Medora of London Limited
Moyra UK Ltd
Neo Elegance Ltd
On-Top Skincare Limited
Perfume Addict (UK) Ltd
Planet Sparkle Ltd
Pure Thoughts Ltd
Sang Real Tattoo Ltd
Sun-Glo Limited
Swipes Fragrance Ltd
UK Cosmetic Formula Limited
UK MUA Limited
Valiscious Limited
Zaliant Skincare Limited

Devon [17]
Akwaaba Social Enterprises Ltd
Beard and Bones UK Limited
Buff Natural Body Care Ltd
Darklake Limited
FreshBreathOnline Limited
Rhona Gillmore Limited
Intercos UK Ltd
Lavant Beauty and Personal Care Ltd
Lola's Apothecary Ltd
Nature et Bien-Etre Limited
Nowdynamic Ltd.
P.H.A.B Wholesale Limited
PH Group UK Limited
Perfume Outlet Ltd
Prispens Limited
Red Hot Products Limited
Roxie Cosmetics Ltd

Dorset [23]
1962 Ltd
446-012 File Limited
Bubble-Bubble Ltd
Bush Oil Limited
Clinibella Ltd
Coslab Ltd
Crypt Doll Ltd
Cursed Cosmetics Ltd
Earth Goddess Ltd
Filberts Bees Limited
Livoliv Cosmetics Ltd.
Love Anousta Limited
Lush Ltd.
Make Up Madness Ltd
Mupe Ltd
Neal's Yard (Natural Remedies) Ltd
Neal's Yard Remedies (Home) Ltd
Neal's Yard Remedies (International) Ltd
Nov'max Keratin Limited
Pixie Crypt Ltd
Plant Me Botanics Ltd
Profile Hair & Skin Care Ltd
Sulis Minerva Limited

Essex [127]
1st Choice Nails Limited
A S Pacho Ltd
AHS Services Ltd
Aabis Duty Free Limited
Acti Laboratories UK Ltd
Adible Limited
Amiri Perfume Ltd
Annexa Solutions Limited
Ansor Supplies Ltd
Aromeco Limited
Asase Tree Ltd
Aurum Argan Ltd
Awobajo Brother's Limited
Beauty Forever Cosmetics Ltd
Beauty Forever Limited
Beauty Healthcare Ltd
Beauty The Divine Ltd
Belgrave Traders Ltd
Bella Rootz Limited
Bellissimo Fashion Ltd
Benefit Cosmetics Limited
Bodyhug Limited
CFN 1 Limited
Can Celebrity Brands Limited
Cosma Fragrances Limited
Cosmeceuticals Limited
Cyrano Limited
Earthkind Ltd
East Cosmetics Limited
Elegance By London Limited
Emel Trade Ltd
EnhanceColor Limited
Essex Beauty Palace Ltd
Evanto Fragrance Limited
Evoiq International Ltd
Exotic Fragrance Ltd
Eyelash Design Co Ltd
Ezili Botanicals Limited
F A Commodities Ltd
Fleuroma Limited
Fox Cosmetics Ltd
Fragrance Samples UK Limited
Gel Labs Limited
Global Couture (UK) Ltd
Global Essence UK Ltd

Golden Rose Limited
GroundedBodyScrub Limited
HG-UK (Pty) Ltd
Hair Ornaments UK Limited
Hairways (Hair & Beauty) Ltd
Hairways Direct Limited
Harley Street Fulfilment Co Ltd
Headissimo Limited
Healthcare Procurement Services Ltd
Herc Ltd.
Holistic Natural Wellbeing Co Ltd
Honeypie Minerals Limited
Imxpo Ltd
Jaydaw Limited
Kailijumei Ltd
Kamila Health & Beauty Ltd
Kiss Products UK Limited
Kizzle Beauty Ltd
Le Lissage UK Limited
Look Fab Limited
Lore Originals Limited
Manas Organics Ltd
Mark McDonald Consultancy Ltd
Minmar (1008) Limited
Mono Naturoils Ltd
Mr. Smith Products UK Ltd
Muse Make Up Ltd
My Meghan Ltd
Myriad Skincare Limited
Myridium Active.Com Limited
NC Import Limited
Nail Polish Gel Colours Ltd
Natural Sheaness Ltd
Nixsi Limited
Oasis Beauty Distribution Ltd
Oatany Ltd
One Beauty Ltd
Online Motions Limited
Onyx Clothing Ltd
Organica Skincare Ltd
Orikii Naturals Ltd
Oxygen Skin Care - London Ltd
PSM Vision Limited
Pennystore Limited
Perfumez Limited
Piggy Paint UK Ltd
Predator Trading Limited
Primoil Limited
Pure & Sure Limited
Pure Swiss Aesthetics Ltd
Rapsodi London Ltd
Rexez Ltd
Rita Roberts Cosmetics Ltd
Rock Beauty Junkie Limited
S.I Attar Ltd
SYN-RG Trading Ltd
Sai Darshan Limited
Searching Plants Ltd
Secret Cosmetics Limited
SeductiveDirect Ltd
Shaw International Ltd
Skinlab Medical Ltd
Southend Hair and Beauty Ltd
Spa Therapies Ltd
Style4you Ltd
Surrati Perfumes Limited
TA-65 (UK) Wholesale Limited
Total Beauty Ltd
Unique Cosmetics Limited
United Solutions (UK) Limited
Vickie's Boutique Ltd
Virgovogue Ltd

Vtessia Cosmetic Ltd
W-Healthy Aging Limited
White Space Beauty Limited
Wild Earth Botanicals Ltd
Wonderland Sales Ltd
Wuyu Mother and Baby Ltd
Zagorah Ltd
Zainab Limited
Zamoux Cosmetics Limited
Zjonline Ltd

Glamorgan [36]
3D Lifestyle Ltd
AK Wholesale Limited
Attraxion Cosmetics Ltd.
Beautifull Planet Ltd
Body Reform Limited
Bortlam Postpartum Restore Health Management (International) Chain Co.,
Brooks Aesthetics Clinic Ltd
Chinese Gentry Limited
Dr. Organic Limited
Ensley and Ensley Limited
Ethnoceuticals Limited
Exentrique Limited
Guestproud Ltd
H & B Supplies Limited
Inovair Limited
Konya Food Biotechnology Co., Ltd
LK Beauty Ltd
Lanko Naturals-UK (PVT) Ltd
Maison Danu (UK) Ltd
Maraki International Limited
Meilikki Ltd
Mimm Organics Ltd
Optima Consumer Health Limited
Pure Revolution Ltd
Ru Si Lacquers Global Ltd.
S & P Cosmetics Limited
Sloane Home Ltd
Solarius UK & Overseas Limited
Spruce Vita Limited
Sub Tropic Limited
Toggle Genetica Group Limited
Toppers Nails Limited
US Beauty Store Limited
Velvet Vapours UK Limited
Wat Cosmetics Ltd
World Links Europe Limited

Gloucestershire [16]
Alumier Labs UK Limited
Convent Venue Limited
DKH Retail Limited
Dolly Custard Ltd
Fizzy Peach Ltd
LTSC Ltd
Nouvriet Boutros (UK) Ltd
Nova Cellulis Ltd
Saint and Sinner Cosmetics Ltd
Seaside Investments Ltd
Shortt Investments2 Limited
Synlatex Limited
Temple Spirit Ltd
Ukab Limited
Woldscot Limited
Yes To Carrots UK Limited

Gwent
Maxibay Limited
Young Now Ltd

Gwynedd
Hedgerow Medicine Chest Ltd
Janiro Ltd
Thalasso Ltd

Hampshire [64]
Absolute Cosmetic Essentials Ltd
Aurum D Limited
Beauty By Aliyah Ltd
Brandcare Group Limited
Bubbleworks Limited
Cassolette & Co (Sales & Marketing)
Clinova Limited
Creative Colours International Ltd
Crystal Spring Consumer Division Ltd
Dojah Limited
Edge Nail & Beauty Limited
Effay Limited
Eleuthere Ltd
Emilia's Handmade Bath and Body Ltd
Etonigbo Limited
Eyeslices UK Limited
Fab Professional Hair Supplies Ltd
Feelgoode Ltd
GBBC Ltd
Glitterfreaks Limited
Harpar Grace International Ltd
Herb U.K. Limited
Incorporated Beauty Limited
International Hair Cosmetics Ltd
Joyganics Ltd
K.B. Salon Supplies Limited
Knight & Wilson Limited
Knight & Wilson Trading Ltd
Korban Beauty Limited
L'Anza Europe Limited
Lashed London Limited
Latam HQ Health Ltd
Charlie Locks Ltd
Markwins Beauty Brands International
Markwins Beauty Products Ltd
Mimi's Organics Ltd
Miya Hair Limited
Myego Ltd
Nature Scents Limited
Orange Balloon Ltd
Organic Professional Ltd
Danica Payne Ltd
Plants Work Limited
Pococks Absolute Rose Ltd
Protective World Ltd
Rawmans Ltd
Romade Limited
S T K Brows Limited
Salon Supplies Limited
Saroza Limited
Sci Check Limited
She Who Dares UK Ltd
Sikania Ltd
Smart Skin Limited
Southsea Bathing Hut Limited
Spa Voyage Limited
Spa and Salon Solutions Ltd
Standfast Solutions International Ltd
Uchepeace Limited
Uppercut Deluxe Co Limited
Use Natural Ltd
Wake Up Beauty Ltd
Wild Brands Limited
Wisp Care Products Limited

Herefordshire [6]
Aesthetic & Luxury Distribution Ltd
Botany Squared Limited
EOB Distribution Ltd
Radiant Glow Beauty UK Ltd
Sandaig Ltd
UK Elements of Beauty Ltd

Hertfordshire [94]
4R Guest Supplies Limited
AJS Marketing Limited
Adam and Eve Distribution Ltd
American Cosmetics Limited
Amor et Psyche Ltd
Antiageing Haircare Specialists Ltd
Asia Nails and Beauty Supply Ltd
B. Silki Naturally Ltd
Beauty Premier Limited
Beauty Royale Ltd
Beauty Wholesale Limited
Bedfordshire Beard Co. Limited
Berkeley Square Cosmetics Co Ltd
Brand Agency (London) Limited
Cancun Collection Limited
Concept Healthcare Limited
D & L Hair Products Limited
DC Salon Products Ltd
DNA Beauty Group Ltd.
Deity World Ltd
Ecobeauty Ltd
Lisa Eldridge Beauty Ltd
Face Lace Limited
Fragranceexpert Limited
Freestyle (Trade) Ltd.
Freestyle Trade (UK) Limited
Gaya Cosmetics Limited
Gaya Minerals Limited
Generic Physics Limited
Global Beautique Limited
Gold Class Hair Limited
Good Ventures Limited
Green Sprouts Limited
HBD International Limited
Hair There & Everywhere Hair & Beauty
Hairways 77 Limited
Holy Lama Naturals Ltd
Hommage International Ltd
House of Worth Limited
Huskie London Ltd
Incorporated Perfumery Distribution
International Trade Corporation Ltd
Ish Products Ltd
Jojoba Cosmetics Limited
Juju Beauty Care Ltd
Larisa Markus Limited
Le-Vap Limited
Lief Essentials Limited
Lipoid Kosmetik Ltd
Lottie London Limited
Lustra Beauty Limited
Luxurious Personal Care Ltd
MQL International Ltd
Mamado International Limited
Mane (UK) Limited
Manhattan Group Ltd.
Mashco Limited
Miluv Ltd
Moor Direct Ltd
Moore Cosmetics Ltd
Moyou Ltd
Nakkali Limited

Nevah Rose Ltd
North One Limited
Organic Cosmetic Products Ltd
Organic and Mineral Salons Ltd
Oud Milano UK Limited
Perfumes Logistics & Distribution
Pherolec Global Ltd
Plectra Polish Limited
Pouty Lipzz Limited
Pretty Silhouette Limited
Procare Women Health Limited
Protec Botanica Ltd
Protec Ingredia Limited
RDC (UK) Limited
Re:New Beauty Ltd
Reveal Naturals Ltd
Ris Healthcare Limited
S A Designer Parfums Limited
Sassy N Trendy Cosmetics Ltd
Scrubd Ltd
Shyline Ltd
Skincare 18 Ltd
Sunspa Europe Limited
Sunspa UK Limited
Transeur Export Finance Co. Ltd
Trollion Limited
UK Mineral Make-Up Limited
Universal Toiletries Corporation Ltd
Vyas International Limited
Wrimes Cosmetics Ltd
YSL Trading Ltd
Zieseniss Limited

Isles of Scilly
Innocent Alchemy Ltd

Kent [99]
Abington Cosmetics Ltd
Allure Beauty Supplies Ltd
Amassuna Limited
Aneen Ventures Limited
Apsara Cosmetics Ltd
Ark Inta Ltd
Ars Nova (UK) Limited
Aurora Spa Health and Beauty Ltd
Australian Bodycare U.K. Ltd
Azur Interiors Limited
BBA Products Limited
Back To Eve Ltd
Barbers House Ltd
Bare Kind Limited
Base Pro Artists Ltd
Beanies Beauty Lab Ltd
Beard Nature Limited
Beard of Attraction Ltd
Beauty & Skincare Essentials Ltd
Biogene Group Limited
Blank Factory Limited
Bodygold Limited
Chulo Naturals Ltd
Cosmedi Limited
Cosmetronic Global Limited
DSE Companies Limited
Dos Osatos International Ltd
Doyin Tradings UK Limited
Eden's Daughter Limited
Essential Bodycare Limited
Eurocosmetics Limited
Finders International Limited
First Choice Hair & Beauty Ltd
Gen Next Ltd

Gracy Hair and Makeup Ltd
H07CNN Limited
HBDeadSea-UK.Com Limited
HFC Prestige Products Limited
Honeystyle Limited
Ileri Trading Limited
Imaage Ltd
Imijo Ltd
Alexander Iris Solutions Ltd
Jakor Limited
Jia Bo Rui International Trade Ltd
K2 Supplies Ltd
Kent Cosmetics Limited
Kerria, Limited
Kiara Beauty Ltd
Kidlex Limited
Kind Planet Co Ltd
Koutos Limited
La Bello Beauty Limited
Lagoon Soaps Limited
Ken Lamacraft Marketing Ltd
Lotus Cosmetics Ltd
Luxe Associates Ltd
M.S.S (Micro Scientific Services)
MDistributor Hair and Beauty Products
MH Products Limited
MQS Group London Limited
Maringo Ltd
Meet T Needs Limited
Megaco Limited
Doris Michaels Cosmetics Ltd
Minx Lashes Ltd
Miracle8 Ltd
Mypure Limited
Naiga Naturals Ltd
Nail Perfection Limited
Natural Skincare Co Ltd.
Niki & Co Ltd
Northdown Cosmetics Limited
ORA Naturals Limited
Oakhill Luxury Ltd
P & Z Solutions Limited
Pispo Ltd
Plush Soap Ltd
Prescripteur Ltd
Purity Derma Limited
Razias London Ltd
Renski Limited
Revolution Beauty Limited
Rich 101 Ltd
Riway International Group (Euro) Ltd
Riway International Group (UK) Ltd
Riway Ltd
SA Plus Enterprise Ltd
Splash Cosmetics Ltd
Stolen Beauty Limited
Sunrise Essential Oil Limited
Tassels UK Ltd
Tobco Limited
Tommco Limited
True Brit London Limited
Trulips Ltd
Wisdom of Nature Limited
Worldwide International Retail Ltd
ZZ Traders Ltd

Lancashire [198]
11 Scent Limited
1CBDUK Ltd
Acorn Brokerage Limited
Adam Michaels Group Ltd
Argan Liquid Gold Limited

The Top UK Perfume and Cosmetics Wholesalers

Asel Ltd
Atlantis Research Limited
B & F Ventures Ltd
BKSL Limited
Batalveez Ltd
Be Savvy Ltd
Beautiful Body Limited
Beauty Fort Limited
Beauty Select Limited
Beauty Trinity UK Limited
Bemi Banks Cosmetics Ltd
Bespoke Beauty Co Ltd
Bespoke Mr Ltd
Big Wholesale Co Ltd
Bigben Healthcare Limited
Binaya Solution Ltd
Bits4hair Limited
Blissible Ltd
Branded Hair Limited
CRM Trading Limited
California Glow Ltd
Cedron Ltd.
Charms Europe Ltd
Cherry Cherry Fashion Ltd
Churchill Motley Limited
Clickpoint Limited
Code Beautiful Limited
Complete Healing Limited
Cool Blades Limited
Cosnique Group Holdings Ltd
County Sales Limited
Damrick's White Bunny Ltd
Dancing Unicorn Limited
David & Co. Traders Ltd
Dead Pretty Official Ltd
Deep Red Marketing International Ltd
Design Essentials Limited
Direct Salon Supplies Limited
Directfrom Ltd
Dont Poke It Ltd
Dreamweave Products Ltd
ESPA International (UK) Ltd
Eabir Ltd
Earth Mother Limited
Ekah Foundation C.I.C.
Ekoderma Ltd
Eleven Eleven Cosmetics Ltd
Enhance You Ltd
Enhancing You Limited
Essential Oils Direct Ltd
Esteem Royale Cosmetics Ltd
Euro Aromas Limited
FB Cosmetologist Limited
FFC International Limited
FG Traders Ltd
Flo with It Ltd
Forever Young Cosmetics UK Ltd
Fourie Hair Limited
Fragrance & Beauty Creations Ltd
Fragrance Acquisitions Limited
Fragrance World Ltd
Fragrance and Beauty Limited
Fragrance de Maison Limited
Gabs Cosmetologist Limited
Geeza Cosmetics Ltd
General Shop Ltd
Glamify Beauty Limited
Glendale Group Limited
Glendale S/S Limited
Global One Wholesale Ltd
Green Essence Ltd
Guerison Skin Solutions Ltd

Gymbar Limited
Hair Operating Products Ltd
Halal Cosmetics Co Ltd
Haych Cosmetics Limited
Healthpoint Limited
Hidden for Purpose Ltd
Highbase Market Limited
Home & Bodycare Limited
IDK Balms Ltd
In & Outbrands Ltd
Intermercantile Limited
Into Exports Limited
Janssen Cosmetics UK Ltd
Jardins D'Eden Ltd
Jigsaw International Holdings Ltd
Kanj Wholesale Ltd
Kendra Cosmetics Limited
Klean Skincare Ltd
Krizma Cosmetics Ltd
Landional Ltd
Joseph Lanzante Products Ltd
Lashflix Limited
Lava Jai Limited
Legacy Wholesalers Limited
Liluna-Organics Ltd
Love Henna Brows Limited
Love Little Prices Ltd
M Beauty Ltd
MM Product Trading UK Limited
MNF Commodities Ltd
Mahrosh Beauty Ltd
Make It Up Limited
Mama Mio Limited
Alexandra de Markoff Limited
Maryam Imports & Exports Ltd
Masculin Limited
Medivas Herbals Ltd
Meviq Ltd
Misspap X Bperfect Limited
Mitonia Co Ltd
Moda Exportation Limited
Multi Imports Limited
My SNS Academy UK Ltd
N.S.I. (U.K.) Limited
Neolox Ltd
New Era Hair Ltd
Niche Aromas Ltd
Nogender London Ltd
Nomad Care Ltd
North West Cosmetics Limited
Nuke Manufacturing, Distribution & Investments
A W Oliver & Co Ltd
Oliver & Taylor Ltd
Opal Naturals Ltd
Organic Skincare Originals Ltd
Orrwa Pharma Health & Beauty Ltd
Oscar & Louis Limited
PL Distribution Ltd
Pebbles Creative Ltd
Per-Scent Fine Limited
Per-Scent Group Limited
Per-Scent Limited
Perfect Lady Ltd
Perfume Essence Ltd
Peters Cosmet Ltd
Pink Cosmetics London Limited
Pink Parasol Ltd
Precision Brows and Lashes Ltd
Pro Esthe Ltd.
Project Cosmetics Limited
Prossentials Ltd

Puff & Petals Ltd.
Pure Skincare Limited
RSJ Trading Limited
Rainbow Cosmetics (Manchester) Ltd
Real Cosmetics Ltd
Reminiscents of Didsbury Ltd
Repechage Europe Limited
Ringley Trading Limited
Rock Perfumes Ltd
Rose & Thorn Ltd
Roz Cosmetics Ltd
J. Rudzitis Ltd
SES Wholesale Limited
SK Flawless Dipping Powder Ltd
SZ Beauty Limited
Salon Focus Ltd
Scent Factory Limited
Scent Global Ltd
Semy-Estoiles Limited
Serene House UK Limited
Shimmer and Shine Cosmetics Ltd
Silk and Bubble Limited
Simply Squirrel Limited
Soapy J Limited
Speak Beauty Limited
Stroppy Ltd
Sublyme Cosmetics Limited
Sueno Cosmetics Ltd
Supreme Beard Ltd
Sweet Pea Soaps Co Ltd
T.L.C. (Total Luxury Cosmetics) Ltd
Think Beauty Online Limited
Tradinguk55 Limited
Transformulas International Ltd
Transformulas Limited
Trending Scents Ltd.
UK Calluspeel Limited
Ultimate Henna Brows Ltd
Unilux Trading Ltd
VI Beauty Ltd
Vidology Group Ltd
Vir Original Limited
Vivatinell Limited
Vlinder Cosmetics Ltd
Wipes Direct Ltd
World Wide Gifts Limited
Yazmae Cosmetics Limited
Yu Parfums Ltd
Z & J Enterprises Limited
Zoe Balm Ltd

Leicestershire [50]
4M Cosmetics Limited
7th Heaven Scents Ltd
Acering Limited
Afex Skin Care Ltd
Alayna Cosmetics and Beauty Ltd
Amelgo Ltd
Beauty Camp Profesional Ltd
Body Organics Limited
Botanical Brands Ltd
Cherie Cosmetics Limited
Dermatx Ltd
Design4nails Ltd
Duron Ltd
Ebong and Brothers Ltd
Ella Nur Ltd
Exquisite Cosmetics Limited
Fragrance Souk Limited
GS7 IT Consultants Ltd
Headrocka Ltd
Ibeautheart Limited

Impulse Global Solutions Ltd
International Traders House P.I.T.
Irum Cosmetics Ltd
Kandi Apple Limited
La Fumes Ltd
MH Exports Limited
Madre Skincare Limited
Marcman Perfume Ltd
Miy Sofiyah Limited
Moroccan Golden Sands Ltd
Neo Cosmetics Limited
Njubien Ltd
Onlinexclusive Limited
Organic Land Global Ltd
Penny Price Aromatherapy Ltd
Pixie Lott Paint Limited
Pro Impressions (UK) Limited
Project 1 Skincare Ltd
Qing Ltd
Real Looks Limited
Revoke Ltd.
Royce Health Sciences Ltd
Select & Bargain Ltd
Shhuk Ltd
Shopti UK Limited
Smartway Pharma Limited
Star Qualities Ltd
Summerlilly Limited
Top Beauty Brands Ltd
UK Make Up Limited

Lincolnshire [13]

Cloud 19 Limited
Glute Plus Limited
Hair Dressing Supplies Lincoln Ltd
Olivia Kate Cosmetics Ltd
Original Taste Ltd
Pure Savvy Limited
Rooster & Rooster Ltd.
ShopAndEnjoy111 Limited
Soak Rochford Ltd
Solo JC Trade Ltd
Trade Dream Ltd
Traderuk Limited
Value for Money (Cleethorpes) Ltd

London [1325]

305 Professionals Ltd
4 Corners Distribution Ltd
50shadez Ltd
72 Hair Limited
72 Hair Retail Limited
9 Silk Gates Ltd
A & B Supply Co. Limited
A Beauty Story Ltd
A Natural Treat Limited
A Rebours Limited
AIGC Limited
AJ Active Enterprises Ltd
AMS-Uhren Ambiente mit Style Ltd
ANGMG Ltd
AR Scents Limited
Acqua di Parma Limited
Acquaderm Ltd
Active Skincare Limited
Adams General Ltd
Adem Oygur Ltd
Adonis Skin Ltd
Adoris UK Ltd
Adwa Impex Ltd
Aenea Cosmetics Ltd

Aeroeco Co Ltd
Aesthetic Brands (Distribution and Management)
Aesthetic Cosmetic Ltd
Aether Elements Ltd
Africa's Best Artisans Limited
African Wild Organics Ltd
Afro Hair and Beauty International
Afthrone Ltd
Aga Cosmetics Ltd
Ahoaloe Cosmetics Limited
Ahwaz Ltd
Aiweisier Limited
Al Amira Limited
Al Cosmetics Ltd
Al Masiya Cosmetic Ltd
Al-Jazeera Perfumes Ltd
Alade Ltd
Albertina Dorosario Ltd
Maddi Alexander Limited
Alfa Parf UK Ltd
All-Around Infinity Limited
Alliance SG Limited
Allied Warden Marketing Ltd
Almcells Bioscience Ltd.
Alpha Auriga Limited
Alton Trading Ltd
Altundag Ltd
Alwais Ltd
Always 20 Limited
Amaffi London Limited
Amalgamated Euro Products UK Ltd
Amaxa Ltd
Ameera London Limited
Amor Beauty Cosmetics Ltd
Anandi Cosmetics Private Ltd
Anatomicals London (England, The World, The Universe-Known and Unknown)
Anglia-Perfumery Ltd.
Angsana Ltd
Anita Brows Cosmetics Limited
Antipodes Europe Limited
Apex Trading Limited
Apotheca London Skincare Ltd
Aqua Qualia Limited
Aquabeauty Limited
Arabian Aroma Limited
Arbar Ltd
Elizabeth Arden (UK) Ltd
Arewa Styles Limited
Argan Blossom Ltd
Argan Care Ltd
W. S Argan Limited
Argan Secrets Limited
Arna Group Ltd
Aroma Actives Limited
Aroma of Grace Ltd
Aromaclub Handmade Skincare Ltd
Aromaderme UK Limited
Arowell Products Ltd
Arrah Ltd
Array of Scents Ltd
Arrogant Limited
Art-Eclair Limited
Arthur Michel Cosmetics Distribution Ltd
Artifact Skin Co Ltd
Arvense Skin Care Ltd
Asadilari Limited
Asaya Cosmeceuticals Limited
Asenov Traders Ltd
Ashley & Co UK Ltd
Ashymo Ltd

Asian Fashions Ltd
Atarah Beauty Collection Ltd
Atkinson London 1799 Ltd
Atlas Global Trade Ltd
Aube Laboratories Ltd
Aurelia Skincare (International) Ltd
Aurelia Skincare Limited
Aurum Essence Ltd
Available Beauty Ltd
Aveda Limited
Aviva Health Solutions Limited
Axa Beauty World Limited
Aya Natural (UK) Limited
Ayaon Ltd
Ayhamco Limited
Aysthetics Limited
Azaleo Limited
Azhar Academy Limited
Azzy London Ltd
B & O Natural Cosmetics Ltd
BC (PVT) Ltd
BM Supplier UK & Europe Ltd
BS Supply Ltd
BSB Global Limited
Bambi & Co Ltd
Banafa for Oud and Perfume Ltd
Basic Needs Ltd
Bcara Ltd
Beached Limited
Bear Journal Limited
Beard Gang Ltd
Beatnut Butter Ltd
Mahc Beau UK & Europe Ltd
Beaute Prestige International Ltd
Beautifect Ltd
Beautiful By Nature Ltd
Beautonic Skincare Ltd
Beautonomy Limited
Beauty Brand (Europe) Ltd
Beauty Center Ltd
Beauty Code Limited
Beauty Everich Ltd
Beauty Pod Limited
Beauty Queen Milano Ltd
Beauty Science UK Ltd
Beauty Solutions Global Ltd
Beauty Solutions Trading Ltd
Beauty Stable Ltd
Beauty Star Limited
Beauty and More 2000 Ltd
Beauty and Trade Ltd
Beautybaseuk Ltd
Beautyge Fragrances Holdings Ltd
Bedrock Trade Ltd
Beehive Cosmetics UK Limited
Bel Corporation Ltd
Belensa Limited
Belgravia London Ltd
Bellapierre Cosmetics Limited
Beltech Limited
Bemysoul Ltd
Berry Inc Ltd
Bessacarr Ltd
Beta Novis Limited
Better Nature International Ltd
Beuti Limited
Bioactivebeauty Ltd
Bioaqua -Biotechnology Ltd.
Bioeffect Limited
Bioline Ltd
Bion Corporation Limited
Bioxane Ltd

The Top UK Perfume and Cosmetics Wholesalers   dellam

Bisch Limited
Bleach Makeup Limited
A & P Blickling Ltd
Blink Street Limited
Blk Oil Limited
Bloom International Group Ltd
Blossom Colour Limited
Blossom Organics Limited
Blue Rose Shop Ltd
Bluesky Cosmetics UK HQ Ltd
Bod Beauty Ltd
Body Beauty & Hair Ltd
Body Beauty Wholesale Exporters Ltd
Body of Work Beauty Ltd
Bond Street Cosmetics Limited
Bonfit UK Limited
Bonitec Ltd
Bonroy International Limited
Botanik Beauty Limited
Botanika Group Ltd
Bottlemate UK Limited
Boujelle Ltd
Boutique Perfumes Limited
Box of Beauty Ltd
Boylondon Holdings Limited
Bracknell Gardens Ltd
Brain Burgeon Ltd
Brand Euro Limited
Brand Evolution (Europe) Ltd
Brands Gallery Ltd
Brands de Luxe Co Ltd
Brazilian Kimberlite Clay Ltd
Britexim Ltd
G & J Britton Consulting Ltd
Brownie Beauty Products Cosmetics Ltd
Brunucorp Ltd
Bullet and Bone Limited
Buly UK Limited
Busy Bee Personal Care Limited
Butter Park Ltd
Butterfly Cosmetics Limited
Buy It Out Ltd
By Al Kindi Ltd
C & A International Trading Ltd
C & P Neptune Ltd
C Distribution UK Limited
C-Bombe Limited
CC Dist UK Ltd
CFBP Ltd
CHK (UK) Ltd
CJ Cosmetics Ltd
CP Parfums Ltd
CZ Cosmetics Ltd.
Caarmi Ltd
Cadden & Lee Limited
Cadyle Ltd
Calestio Ltd
Califa Ltd
Canna Biology Distributing Ltd
Cannamplify Ltd
Capital Import & Export Co. Ltd
Carbon Theory Limited
Steven Carey Hair & Beauty Ltd
Carol Skins Ltd
Ayesha Carolina Limited
Catalina Beauty Group Limited
Caudalie UK Limited
Reevis Chan Ltd
Chanel Limited
Chanson Worldwide Limited
Sarah Chapman Ltd.
Charlize London Ltd

Chemical Poetry Ltd
Chic Clothing Limited
Chief Cosmetics Ltd
Chirp Body Ltd
Choice of Nature Limited
Clive Christian Perfume Ltd
Claracutis, Ltd
Clarendon of London Limited
Clarins (U.K.) Limited
Clean Living Ltd
Clearance Masters Ltd
Cleardot Group Ltd
Cochabamba Parfums Limited
Cocobaba Ltd
Colbico Limited
Coll Gen Limited
Collection 1212 Limited
Color Studio Ltd
Colour Life Limited
Colourscent Limited
Com4hospitality Ltd.
Comets Intertrade Co Ltd
Comglobal Limited
Company NBN Limited
Connected Beauty Limited
Connessioni UK Limited
Jasper Conran Perfumes Ltd
Constantine K Ltd
Cont-Hemp-Orary Skincare Ltd
Contrast Cosmetics Ltd.
Control Cosmetics Ltd
Cool Essentials Limited
Corium Health Limited
Elizabeth Cornelius Limited
Cosimpex Ltd
Cosmelinks Consultancy Ltd
Cosmetic Alchemy Ltd
Cosmetic Doctor at Work Ltd
Cosmetic Traders Limited
Cosmetics 4U Limited
Cosmetics Store Ltd
Cosmetics Wholesale Limited
Cosmetics of London Chelsie Ltd
Cosmetiques de France Ltd.
Cosmic Eyes Ltd
Cosmolab Limited
Cosmolovely Limited
Cosmos Cosmetics Limited
Cover Up Hairloss Ltd
Coveti Limited
Cowshed Products Limited
Crabtree & Evelyn (Overseas) Ltd
Crane + Wilton Ltd
Crane and Peach Limited
Crazy Smiles Group Ltd
Crete Online Ltd.
Crivalis Ltd
Croma-Pharma Limited
Crystal Nails No1 Ltd
Crystalnails4u Ltd
Cuelyine Limited
Cult Candy Limited
Cure Hair & Skin Care Ltd
Curl Coach Ltd
Cxlture Cosmetics Ltd
DLG Partners Limited
DLM Trade Limited
DYB Tarding Ltd
Dabrimela Limited
Daimon Barber Limited
Daisy Anai Limited
Danlab Ltd.

Chloe Davids Limited
Dea Disir Ltd
DealsRUsOnline Ltd
Dear Body Limited
Deciem UK Ltd.
Deeco Supplies Limited
Deewin Stomatology Research Center Co.,
Delmoss Ltd
Deltagamma Limited
Demert Brands EU Ltd
Deo Beauty Products Limited
Derma Organics by CFBP Ltd
Dermacure Aesthetics Limited
Dermafrance Ltd.
Dermaperfetca Ltd
Dermashack Limited
Diamond Brands Limited
Dily Oka International Group Co., Ltd
Dimonauk Ltd
David Dinero Ltd
Direct Trade Limited
Disciple Skincare Limited
Diva Deva UK Limited
Diverse Solution Ltd
Doers Skincare Limited
Donovan Luxe Limited
Dooa Capital Limited
Dorian House Marketplace Ltd
Dorothy Hair and Beauty Shop Ltd
Doyle's Group Ltd
Dr Shea Ltd
Dr. Twilight Ltd
Dr.K Skinlab Ltd
Dr.Lipp Ltd
Dream Girl Limited
Dream Glow Ltd
Dream Skin Ltd
Dreamage Ltd.
Drimex Limited
Drugget Ltd
Dudu-Osun Limited
Dufeal Your Best Beauty Ltd
Duke of Charm Limited
Dunstan and Burr Ltd
EB Stores Ltd
EBF Europe Ltd
EL Companies Ltd
ENS Europe Limited
EOS Products Limited
Earthly Pleasures Ltd
East End Cosmetics Limited
East Garden Ltd
East To West Lifestyle Co Ltd
Easybusiness24 Ltd
Eau de Parfum Limited
Eblouir Group Ltd
Eco Twinkle Ltd
Ecocare Organic Limited
Editions de Parfums Limited
Edward London Ltd
Effective and Simple Ltd
Egg Pillow Limited
Egotistic Hair & Beauty Ltd
Egyptian Magic Ltd
Eileen Group (UK) Ltd
Eku Skin Care Ltd
El Sabbagh Trading Limited
Elan Skincare Ltd
Electimuss Limited
Elegance Gel UK Ltd
Elegant Boss Ltd
Elegantes London Limited

Elemental Herbology Limited
Elequra Limited
Eleu Beauty Ltd
Elinor-UK Ltd
Elitelashes Ltd
Eloise Group Ltd
Eloise M Beauty Ltd
Elysian Design Limited
Emma Danmark Ltd
Emma Group Ltd
Emma Prime Ltd
EmmaDK Ltd
Emortal Maquillage Ltd
Empire Worldwide Ltd
Emuology UK 2017 Limited
Emvi Limited
Endetrox Ltd.
Envision International Co., Ltd
Erin Cosmetics Ltd
Thalia Erodotou Limited
Escentric Ltd
Esem International Ltd
Espoir Beauty Ltd
Esscential Ltd
Essence Pur Ltd.
Essence of Esther Ltd
Estela Dermocosmetics Ltd
Ether Cosmetics Ltd
Eukes Global Limited
Eurasia Property Limited
Euro Perfumes (UK) Ltd
Eurohandle Ltd
European Essential Oils (UK) Ltd
Eva Cosmetics Ltd
Evany Personal Care Limited
Evbioo Ltd
Evie Skincare Ltd
Evorin Pharma Limited
Ex'klusive Products Ltd
Exa World Ltd
Exbrands Ltd
Excelcia Limited
Existo Limited
Exoditi Limited
Expo Deal Ltd
Express Hair and Beauty Supply Ltd
Express Online Superstore, London Ltd
Eye Kandy Cosmetics Ltd
FB Beauty Ltd
FHM Consulting Ltd
FM Cosmetics UK Ltd
Face Boutique Limited
Facecharm Ltd
Facil Haircare Ltd
Farah Organics Ltd
Farmavita Ltd
Farshety Ltd
Fashion Fragrances & Cosmetics UK Ltd
Faye Florais Global Holdings., Ltd
Feel and Heal UK Limited
Ferana Ltd
Ferrara-Bardile Ltd
Fin Perri Ltd
Five Dot Botanics Limited
Fleeks Hair & Beauty Limited
Florals of London Limited
Flower Cosmetic Ltd
Fols for Men Ltd
Foramca Ltd
Forderma Laboratory Ltd.
Forest Hive Ltd
Forte Organics Ltd

Foundation Brands Ltd
Fragrance Express Limited
Fragrance Factory Limited
Fragrance Group London Ltd
Fragrance Weekly Ltd
Fragrancekent (UK) Ltd
Fragrant Spa Limited
France Eclavour Cosmetic Ltd
France Parfums International Ltd
Franok Business Solutions Ltd
Fresh Cosmetics Limited
From Mini Acorns Ltd
Frontrow International UK Ltd
Fruu Cosmetics Limited
Functional Skincare Ltd
Fushi Wellbeing Limited
Fuzzique Limited
Fysifarm Limited
G & G Skincare Ltd
G.Q Homes Ltd
GP Mediplus Ltd
GVM Long Life Formula UK Ltd
Gajas Gift Limited
Galaxy Grooming Limited
Gallya Deelya Ltd.
Louise Galvin Limited
Garda Service Ltd
Garron Labs Private Limited
Gattino Cosmetics Ltd
Gazelli International Limited
Gelmoment Limited
Gentel Works Ltd
Genten Skincare Ltd
Gentille Limited
Gentle Beauty Co Ltd
S K A Gibson Ltd
Giva Solution Ltd
Given By Nature Limited
Glad Gent Ltd
Glamn Holding Ltd
Glitterati Distributions Ltd
Global Luxury Beauty Ltd
Glochina Trading UK Ltd.
Glory Cosmetics Ltd
Glow Investment Ltd
Glow Jar Ltd
Gluedon Ltd
Gold Pillar Holding Ltd
Goldeivy London Lashes Ltd
Golden Vanity Ltd
Goldshore (UK) Limited
Good Beauty International Holding
Good By Nature Ltd
GoodNaturedSkincare Ltd
Goodsky Co., Ltd.
Gracetree Ltd
Grautrans Limited
Green & Dionisi Ltd
Green Breeze Ambient (UK) Ltd
Green Harmony Limited
Green Mass Limited
Greenery Skincare Limited
Grooming Galaxy Limited
Grossmith Limited
Gruhme UK Limited
Guerlain Limited
Guilty Fashion Ltd
Gulz Cosmetics Ltd
H2 World Health and Beauty Co Ltd
HA Distribution Limited
HCT Beauty Ltd
HCT Europe Limited

HE Products Ltd
HQPS Ltd
HSK Enterprises Ltd
HT Cosmetics Ltd
Ha-Derma Limited
Hair & Cosmetic Co Ltd
Hair Passion Limited
Hairco Hair & Beauty Ltd
Hairya Ltd
Hamon Concepts Limited
Hanana Traders Ltd
Philip Hansard Limited
Happy Carrot Skincare Ltd
David Hart (Santo) Limited
Haybae Cosmetics Ltd
Headlines (Hair & Beauty Supplies)
Health-Beauty Ltd
Heavenly Body Ltd
Heavenly Fragrance (UK) Ltd
Hekiti Cosmetics Ltd
Hello Dame London Ltd
Hemp Earth Ltd
Hempo Logical International Ltd
Herba Skincare Limited
Herbal Essentials UK Limited
Herbaleva Ltd
Herbalise Limited
Here We Flo Ltd
Hermossa Limited
Carolina Herrera UK Ltd
Hi Life Health and Beauty (UK) Ltd
Hild International Group Ltd
Hill and Dale Limited
Hisamitsu Pharmaceutical UK Ltd
Hisamitsu UK Limited
Hive of Beauty Limited
Holistic Plant Technologies Ltd
Holy Group Limited
Home Design 24 Ltd
Homsense Ltd
Honey Corn Limited
Honor London Limited
Horatio London Holdings Ltd
Hot (UK) Limited
House of Vanity Limited
Hubert & Emilie Ltd
Hudsonry Ltd
Humanity Cosmetics Limited
Hy-Brd Ltd
Hydracol Pty Ltd
I.S.O.D Limited
IBS Shopeye World Ltd
ID Skincare Limited
IJN Pure Oils Ltd
IR International Ltd
Iam By Nature Ltd.
Iam Finance Limited
Iattar Perfume Oils Ltd
Ibeautify Ltd
Iberia Skin Brands Ltd
Icebox Brands EU Limited
Icilda's Ltd
Iconic Fragrances Ltd
Iiuvo Limited
Ila Pothecary Limited
Imamcom Ltd
In Situ Cosmetics Ltd
Indigo Direct Ltd
Infini Lab Ltd
Infinityredox Holdings Limited
Info Cosmetics Limited
Inga Permanent Make Up Limited

The Top UK Perfume and Cosmetics Wholesalers

Innon Vision Limited
Innovaderma PLC
Insta-Jell Cosmetics Ltd
Instant Beauty UK Limited
Interall Ltd
International Integrated Solutions Co
Intertrade Group Ltd
Invicta Cosmetics Limited
Iras Trading Ltd
Sarah Ireland Perfumes Ltd
Ismile Beauty Ltd
Itala Group Ltd
Ivaxane UK Ltd
Ives Lab Ltd
Ivy Nat Ltd
J K International Trading Ltd
J's Luxury Perfumery Ltd
J.Cat Beauty UK Ltd
JF Malcolm Ltd
JMAR Op No 2 Ltd
JML Cosmetics Limited
JNVshop La Piazza Delle Idee Ltd
JSProfessionnel Limited
JWWJ Limited
JZM International Limited
Jak Beauty Ltd
Janou Brand Limited
Jardin de Parfums Ltd
Jaspmab Ltd
Jass Perfumes Limited
Jax of London Ltd
Jazzy Hair Limited
Jerome Fashion Ltd
Jeunvie Ltd
Jigu Corporation Limited
Jivesse Limited
Jo Loves (Wholesale) Limited
Joanna Naturals Limited
Joddor London Limited
Jolly Rogers Crew Limited
Jonatho Ltd
Leigh Jones & Associates Ltd
Margaret Jordan Cosmetics Ltd
Jouer Jouer Limited
Jufa Cosmetics Ltd
Juliajosh Limited
Julien Miguel Ltd
Julio & Ejder Ltd
Just Beautiful Skin Ltd
Just Cosmetics Ltd
Just Do You Limited
K. S. D Beauty Zone Ltd
K. V. Fair Trades Limited
K2Y Limited
K3W Trading Limited
K588 Limited
KBM London Limited
KM Cosmetics Distribution Ltd
KMY Group Ltd
Kalabash Limited
Karina Enterprise Ltd
Kathleen Natural Limited
Kathy Salon Equipment Limited
Kathy Sue-Ann's Ltd
Kayanna Ltd
Kazi Brothers Group Limited
Kehal Ltd
Kendo Brands Limited
Khali Min Limited
Khuba Limited
Kiddeo Limited
Kiki Body Limited

Kimibeauty Ltd
Kind2 Limited
King of Sytle Ltd
Kitoko Make Up Ltd
Jennifer Klar Ltd
Koha Beauty Co Ltd
Komodo Skincare Ltd
Kor Cosmetics Ltd
Korres International Limited
Kounga Ltd
Kozmar International Limited
Kurlysue Limited
L'Oreal (U.K.) Limited
LBB Skin Ltd
LVMH Fragrance Brands UK Ltd
La Boutique du Discount Ltd.
La Loire Ltd
La Maison Hedonique Limited
La Personal Products Ltd
La Prairie (UK) Limited
Lab Brands Limited
Labrayon Cosmetiques France UK Ltd
Lactura Ltd
Ladd Cosmetics Ltd
Lady Smidgeton's Apothecary Ltd
Lady T Limited
Ladyology Limited
Laguna Organa Ltd
Laila Cosmetics Limited
Lamari London Ltd
Lambsmead Limited
Lana's Beauty Box Ltd
Landermark Ltd
Erno Laszlo Group Ltd
Estee Lauder (UK) International Group
Estee Lauder Cosmetics Ltd
Laurelle London Ltd
Lavelle Store UK Ltd
Lavender Concept Ltd
Lavish Lashes Ltd
Lavish London Cosmetics Ltd.
Layan Pharma Ltd
Lazeeza Lashes Limited
Lbeautie Ltd
Le Labo UK Limited
Le Parfum Ltd
Le Pure Limited
Lee Gallop Enterprise Ltd
Lefami Cosmetics Group Ltd
Legendbio Beauty Group Limited
Legends London Limited
Leicala Natural Products Ltd
Leixaco Trading Ltd
Lensmeuk Limited
Les Blanches Limited
Les Laboratoires ILP UK Ltd
Les Lilas Limited
Les Petits Parfums Limited
Lex Roris Ltd
Liaver Limited
Libhairation Ltd
Lienex Beauty London Ltd
Light Up Skincare Ltd
Lime and Lead Global Ltd
Lino Rose Ltd
Liolax Limited
Lionmark Limited
Liplast Ltd
Lipstick and Black Coffee Ltd
Liquor Lips Ltd
Live Rich Academy Limited
Lixir Skin Limited

Lollipop Treats Ltd
Lom Trade Limited
London Bathers Limited
London Export Ltd
London Health Sciences Ltd
London Heartbeat Ltd
London Links Trading Limited
Londonscentsuk Limited
Katherine Longhi Ltd
Look Lovable Ltd.
Loop Beauty Limited
Lord & Berry Ltd
Louts Remit Beautiful International Group Co.,
Lovalova Ltd
Loveco Ltd
Loveliness Limited
Loveve. Ltd
Lovoir Ltd
Lozano Skincare Ltd
Luban & Murr Ltd
Lucas Haynes Limited
Lucerne Perfumes Ltd
Lucy Beauty Products Ltd
Lueno Cosmetics Limited
Lukony Ltd
Lumine Beauty Ltd
Lumos Products Limited
Luscious Lashes International Ltd
Lushes Ltd
Luxmeticgroup Limited
Luxury Consulting by Bethan Williams
Luxury Personal Care Ltd
Luxuryscope London Limited
Lyal Intertrading Ltd
Lyons Pride Limited
M & H Cosmetic Limited
M & M Cosmetics Limited
M & N Traders Limited
MB Professional Beauty Ltd
MD-101 Ltd
MGC Pharma (UK) Ltd
MLM Cosmetics Ltd
MSD Trading Services Limited
MTIstanbul Ltd
MYNC Brands Limited
Macks Ltd.
Madame Laveau Ltd
Madison Steward Ltd
Magia BLV International Ltd
Magnum Beauty International Ltd
Magpie Holdings Ltd
Mahiri Africa Ltd
Maison de Maa Ltd
Majestic Company London Ltd
Make Up for Ever U.K. Limited
Make-Up International Limited
Makeup Boutique Limited
Makeup54 Ltd
Maliboo Hair and Cosmetics Ltd
Mamondo Fragrance and Beauty Ltd
Mane Love Ltd
Manicure You Ltd
Mann & Noble Europe Limited
Margan Oil Ltd
Marina Muda Ltd
Paul Marney & Co Ltd
Marque of Brands Limited
Marrouge Limited
Mary Kay Cosmetics (U.K.) Ltd
Maskologist Ltd
Mast - Art Group Limited

Master Beauty Limited
Mata Labs Cosmetics Ltd
Maverick Hair & Beauty Ltd
Maximaliste Limited
Mayfair Export London Limited
Mayjoy The Perfumer Ltd
Felicity McDonald Organics Ltd
Me Sentir Ltd.
Meadow Skincare Limited
Meddiamonds Ltd
Meder Beauty International Ltd
Medical Technology Caraco (MYC) Ltd.
Medileen UK Ltd
Meek and Mild Essentials Ltd
Mega Direct Limited
Melanative Ltd
Memoize Parfum Ltd
Mepro Cosmetic Ltd
Linda Meredith Skin Care Ltd
Merumaya Limited
Metropolitan Beauty Ltd.
Mine of Goods Ltd
Mink Company U.K Ltd
Mintology Limited
Minxx Lashes Ltd
Miracle Herbs & Fruits Cosmetics Ltd
Miraculous UK Ltd
Mirtas Cosmetics Ltd
Misawa Healthcare Ltd
Mise N Ltd
Miss Glamm Limited
Mob Cosmetics Limited
Modazi Ltd
Modern Man Project Ltd
Modernist Fragrance Ltd.
Molecula Ltd
Monarch Health & Beauty Ltd.
Mondor & Bache Ltd
Monrone Health Ltd
Monshea Limited
Mooi-H Ltd
Guy Morgan Apothecary Limited
Moroccan Argan Limited
Moroccan Attlas Ltd
Moxxy Limited
Moyy Limited
Mr B Skincare Limited
Mr Carters Essentials Limited
Muamko Uzuri Limited
Muchacho (London) Limited
My Beauty World Ltd
My Pure Life-Style Limited
Jennifer Myers Limited
Mystique Swan Ltd
N & L Cosmetic Limited
N Organics Ltd
NB Beauty Limited
NBS Distribution Ltd
NM Beauty Industries Ltd
NMB Property Limited
NOP Cosmetics Ltd
NS Brands International Ltd
NXSK UK Ltd
NYDG UK Limited
Nacho Vidal Distribuciones 2 Ltd
Nacho Vidal Distribuciones Ltd
Naeemah & Al Farhad Ltd
Nalla Skincare Ltd
Nanosafe Ltd.
Narges Beauty Limited
Nasser Waziri Ltd
Nat & Co Limited

Natasha Denona Make Up Ltd.
Natrorg Ltd
Rochelle Natty Business Group Ltd
Natural Hair Emporium Limited
Natural Jeanius Ltd
Natural Serenity Ltd
Natural Skincare London Ltd
Naturally Untamed Ltd
Naturela Limited
Naturity Cosmetics Ltd
Naya London Ltd
Nectar International Limited
Nefil Ltd
Nekta Botanics Ltd
Neopilina Moda Ltd
Neora UK Limited
Neville Cut and Shave Limited
Nevitrade Ltd
New Aesthetic Ltd
Nice Smell Trade Ltd
Nicfead Cosmetics & Fragrance Ltd
Nika Cosmo Group Ltd
Niquel Ltd
Niya Cosmetics Ltd
Nizz Cosmetics Ltd
No.1 Nail Supply Limited
Noa London Ltd
Noble Soap Limited
Nocov Ltd
Noli Distribution Ltd
Nota Nota Limited
Nova Bleu Cosmetics Limited
Novmedic Limited
Novumis Ltd
Noyras Ltd
Nu-E55ence Ltd
Nukua Limited
Nurologie Ltd
Nyasa Organics Limited
Oakwood Williams Limited
Occo London Limited
Odeferus Limited
Official IV Ltd
Oh My Scent Limited
Oilyspirit Ltd
Olfacstory Parfums Limited
Olfactive Thirty Eight Fragrances
Olivoderm Cosmetics UK Limited
Olo Edt Ltd
Omaoli Limited
Omega Flax Limited
On & Off Beauty Ltd
Onamex Ltd
One Flower Qinga Limited
Only Perfection Ltd
Onna Export Import Ltd
Onsen Secret UK Ltd
Opatra Limited
Optimavia Ltd
Orca Distributor Ltd
Organic Colour Systems Limited
Organic Iway Ltd
Organic Stuff Limited
Orit Limited
Orveda Limited
Orveda UK Limited
Ossulstone Hundred Limited
Otonix Limited
Otterganics Ltd
Oud & Musk UK Ltd
Oudh Al Aasmah Perfume UK Ltd
Our Choice Gift Limited

Our-Scent Ltd
Outdoor Girl Limited
Oxmetics Ltd
Oya 9 Ltd
Ozone Perfumes and Cosmetics Ltd
P & P Cosmetics Ltd
P P Oil UK Limited
Paint It Orange Ltd
Pak Beauty Ltd
Pangaea Laser Ltd
Pareto Cosmedics Ltd
Parfume-Mania Ltd
Parfums Christian Dior (U.K.) Ltd
Paris Elysees Holding Ltd.
Parkside Nails Supplies Ltd
Patagonia Consult Limited
Pavone Profumi SRL Ltd
Peau Royale Limited
Pellitier & Perkins Limited
Pennies and Feathers Limited
Per Capelli Ltd
Pera Cosmetics Ltd
Perezoso Limited
Perricone MD Cosmeceuticals UK Ltd
Pharmacare International Ltd
Pharmaclinix Limited
Pharmafrance Ltd.
Pheora Rucci Limited
Phi Advisory & Consulting Ltd
Photonic Limited
Pilaten EU Ltd
Pink Empire Limited
Pink Lush Lips Ltd
Pinklady International Ltd
Pinnacle Pharma Limited
Pinoline Trading Co Ltd
Plane Luxuries Limited
Plenaire Limited
Ploom (U.K.) Limited
Polcosmetics Ltd
Pole Position (Licensing) Ltd
Polex Limited
Pommade Divine Skincare Ltd
Pota Nini Limited
Potion Dynamo Limited
Powered By Nature Cosmetics Ltd
Previa UK Ltd
Prevura Ltd
Prismologie International Ltd
Privilago Fashion Ltd
Profline Ltd
Puig UK Limited
Pur3 Health Limited
Pure Skincare London Ltd
Purederma Ltd
Purity Skincare Limited
Q River Limited
QZE Limited
R & R Global Consumer Healthcare Ltd
R & T Natural Cosmetics Ltd
REN Skincare Limited
RR Cosmeceuticals (UK) Ltd
Rabimed International Limited
Railworth Limited
Rapsodi Ltd
Rationale Skincare Limited
Rawly Processed Ltd.
Realine Beauty Limited
Red Gold London Ltd
Rederm Limited
Reetal Development Co Ltd
Regista Fragrance Ltd

The Top UK Perfume and Cosmetics Wholesalers

Rektaz Ltd
Rekze Laboratories Ltd
Relaxa Trading Ltd
Reliance HBC UK Ltd
Rembrandt London Limited
Ren Ltd
Renaissance Manyane Global Group Ltd
Reneebeauty Limited
Renibo Ltd
Republic Cosmetics UK Ltd
Republik Inc Limited
Reviron Limited
Rewind Botanics Limited
Rexcel Trading Ltd
Rich & Ruitz Perfume Industry Ltd
Rich Cosmetics Ltd
Riviere Groupe (Europe) Ltd
Robert Cosmetics Limited
Robh Scrub Limited
Rokka Imagine Ltd
Roots Are Remedies Ltd
Rosebud Perfume Co Ltd
Rosense (UK) Ltd
Rosse Beau Ltd
Rouge Bunny Rouge UK Limited
Ruby Concepts Ltd
Rupitex Limited
Jerome Russell Limited
S Beauty Ltd
SA & A Ltd
SFL Group Ltd
SGHP Ltd
SHH Logistics Ltd
SHL Medical Limited
SK Network Ltd
SKN Rehab Limited
SKN-RG Ltd
SPTB Ltd
SU Labs Limited
Sabeauti Ltd.
Sacha Cosmetics UK Ltd
Saffron Beauty Ltd
P.S. Sahney & Co Limited
Sahney Siblings Limited
Salem Stores Ltd
Salimaskinsolutions Ltd
Salon Professional London Ltd
Salon Theory Ltd
Salonpas UK Limited
Salus Cutis Ltd
Sana Jardin (UK) Limited
Sandgroper Limited
Sandine Zartaux Holding Ltd
Daniel Sandler Ltd
Sankofa Heritage Ltd
Santa Code Limited
Santini Trade Ltd.
Sawa Trading & Shipping Ltd
Scent Angels UK Ltd
Scent Edit Limited
Scented Home Limited
Scented LDN Limited
Scented Sachets (London) Ltd.
Scontimania Online SRL Limited
Scope Cosmetics Ltd
Scott Weeks Enterprises Ltd
Season of Beauty Limited
Sebaroyale Ltd
Secret Line Ltd
Seed Fashion and Beauty Incubator Ltd
Seigur Rose International Group Co., Ltd
Selective Fragrances Ltd
Selfcare Corporation Ltd
Selfish Cosmetics Ltd
Serenityhands Ltd
Serenityy Ltd
Seventa Image Ltd
Sfera London Limited
Shama Pharma Ltd
Sharp's Global Trading Limited
Shave Algorithm Ltd
Shay & Blue Ltd
Sheacare Cosmetics Limited
Sherhind Accessorize Limited
Shilcroft Limited
Shivax International Ltd
Shop4stocks Limited
Shure Enterprises (UK) Limited
Siam Botanicals UK Limited
Sias Corp Limited
Silvercleanse Health & Beauty Ltd
Simona Beauty Store Ltd
Simple Bargain Limited
Simple Beauty (UK) Limited
Simple Hair Limited
Sinoeast XJ Ltd
Sisley UK Limited
Sjonlineuk Ltd
Skin & Tonic London Ltd
Skin Enrich Limited
Skindoc Formula Limited
Skinkode Ltd
Skinsider Cosmetics Ltd
Skintel Cosmetics Ltd
Smellycat Ltd
TPC Smith Limited
Smuccii Trading Ltd
So Susan Limited
Soadperf Limited
Sofil Cosmetic Ltd
Soft and Curly Products Ltd
Solution Cosmetic Ltd
Someplace Nice Limited
Sophistique Beauty Ltd
Sopureoils Ltd
Soulful Beauty Ltd
South China Bio-Pharma Co Ltd.
Souvre UK Ltd
Soybalm Ltd
Space Brands Limited
Spaquashop Ltd
Sparking-Jy International Trading Co.,
Sphere 7 Lab Ltd
Spice Fragrances Ltd
Spktra Limited
Sportclinix Labs Ltd.
Spree Trading Ltd
Square Wholesale Ltd
St-Creation Ltd
Star Pearls Ltd
Steam Cream Limited
Step International Cosmetic Ltd
Iryna Stewart Ltd
Storm of UK Limited
Strategy M Ltd
Strdom Ltd
Strip Distribution Limited
Stuff of Life Limited
Style Factory Limited
Sublime Cosmetics UK Ltd
Sucre By Zoe Skincare Limited
Sun Zapper UK Limited
Sunscreen X Limited
Super Natural Apothecary Ltd.
Supernova UK Pty Ltd
Supply Zoom Ltd
Sur Trading Limited
Swan Leigh Cosmetics Ltd
Sweden Eco Limited
Sweet Arabian Ltd
Sweet Lilli Ltd
Swiss Arabian Perfumes (UK) Ltd
Swiss Cosmetic Distribution Ltd
Swiss Pharma Dynamic Ltd
Swiss Trading .UK. Ltd
TAC Perfumes & Cosmetics (UK) Ltd
TLC - Tender Loving Care UK Ltd
TWC Products Limited
Stella Tailor Ltd
Tailord Chic Ltd
Tannovation Laboratories Ltd
Tarsago Ltd
Tauri Corporation Limited
Tebs Distribution Limited
Tententen Limited
Texthold Ltd
Thai Wellness Ltd
Thalgo UK Limited
TheGoodSkinCo Ltd
Theodory Ltd
Think Be Nature Ltd
Thiossane Ltd
This Works Products Limited
Three Beauties of London Ltd
Three Organics Ltd
Tiarna Ltd
Tir Chonaill London Ltd
Tiyati Ltd
Tonic15 Ltd
Top Beauty Limited
Top Brands Australia Limited
Toure Ltd
Trade Giant Limited
Trade Mall Limited
Trading Corporation International Export and Import
Treas Biotechnology UK Ltd
Trees of Beauty Ltd
Triaton Ltd
Trichy Ltd
Trimmz Ltd
Trine Oils Limited
True Affinity Limited
True Mia Limited
True Scents Ltd
Truity Limited
Geo. F. Trumper (Perfumer and Products)
Tryon Products Limited
Twelve Beauty Ltd
Two Daughters Limited
Tyn y Ddol Enterprises Ltd
UK Ailise Biotechnology Trade Ltd
UK Aimutaike Electronics Co., Ltd
UK Beauty Cosmetics International Group
UK Brand Holdings Ltd
UK Deer Running Co., Ltd
UK Esthetics Ltd
UK Heluns Industry Co., Ltd
UK Irelia Co Ltd
UK Lemenic International Medical Group
UK Skinlabs Limited
UK Vimin Industry Co., Limited
ULB Limited
Ude Cosmetics Limited
Un Air D'Antan Limited
Unicorn Magic Enterprises Ltd

Unidus Limited
Unified Commerce Limited
Unineed Limited
United Mart (UK) Limited
United Nomads Limited
United Perfumes Limited
United Retail & Sourcing Ltd
Universal Attraction (London) Ltd
Universal Beauty Products Europe Ltd
Universal Design Promotion Ltd
Uoma Beauty Group Limited
Urhan Group Limited
VNS London Limited
VR Consult Limited
VY Club Limited
Valencia Cy Makeup Ltd
Valerie Lady Co., Ltd
Valhalla Perfume Limited
Valma Consumer Co Ltd
Valorem Capital One Ltd
Varana UK Limited
Veels UK Limited
Velforms Limited
Velvet Bee Co Ltd
Ruth Venessa Services Ltd
Venkh Retail Ltd
Very British Baby International Ltd
Very Nature Limited
Vesta London Beauty Ltd
VevBeautyCosmeticsTrading Ltd
Victoire Limited
Victoria Pharma London Ltd
Viib Limited
Vikenias UK Ltd
Vilai Europe Trading Limited
Vilhelm Parfumerie Limited
Villa Sauod Ltd
Viral Solutions General Trading Ltd
Vision Trading Limited
Vivacy Laboratoires Ltd
Vivlai Europe Trading Limited
Vogue Cosmetics Ltd
Vortex Holding Limited
Votary Limited
W8T Ltd
WGTSS Ltd
WH Corporation (UK) PTE. Ltd
We Concept Ltd
We Two By Kelly Simpkin Ltd
Werson International Ltd
West Three Trading Limited
Wharfedale Herbal Ltd
Whip Cosmetics Ltd
White Lotus Anti Aging Ltd
Wild Beauty Ltd
Wild Celia Ltd
Wild Kynd Ltd
Wild Things Cosmetics Ltd
Wildmint Cosmetics Limited
Wildsmith Collection Limited
Wish List Limited
Wizer Ltd
Wonderful Life PHBS Ltd
Worldwidegoodstraders Ltd
Wow Facial Ltd
Wrap N Pack Ltd
YJX Group PLC
YSO Import-Export Limited
YWC (Yes We Can) Limited
Yejisu Innovation Ltd
Younghair AB Ltd
Ibrahim Yusuf and Sons Ltd

Z Online Ltd
ZS Beauty Ltd
Zamantraders Limited
Zarvis London Limited
Naseem Zeenah Natural Cosmetics Ltd
Zimmerglobal Ltd
Zoe Lane Ltd
Zoee Cosmetics Co., Ltd
Zoeva UK Limited

Lothian [7]
AAA Edinburgh Ltd
Cazza Professional Ltd
Choize Ltd
Ivee Group Ltd
Land of Beauty Supplies Ltd
Lesimone Global Limited
Torcall of Edinburgh Ltd

Merseyside [26]
100% Vegan Skincare Limited
Beauty Bash Limited
Body Month Ltd
Bracey Overseas Ltd
C Beauty Agency Limited
Green World Spa Products Ltd
Husaco Ltd
Jayeed Perfumes Ltd
Koreesa Limited
LCB Trading (UK) Limited
LW International Ltd
Millennium Nails North West Ltd
Natrelle Limited
Nefert Ltd
Norm and Glo Limited
Perfume Brands Limited
Prestige Perfumes Limited
Salon Supplies 365 Limited
Smell Neutralizer Ltd
TJ Nail Supplies Ltd
UK Fillers Ltd
Veridot Asset Dna Limited
Wild Violet X Limited
Winkies Limited
Yurexroar Cosmetic Wholesale Ltd
Zojo. The Gorgeousness Co Ltd

Middlesex [202]
876 Skin Beauty Limited
AMF Distribution Limited
ASVR Bebidas Limited
Aamir Traders Ltd
Chris Adams Perfumes Ltd
Affinity Fragrances Limited
Afrocare Ltd
Al Janan Fragrances Limited
Alico Exports Limited
Almirall Limited
Alvor Limited
Anglia Enterprise (UK) Limited
Aqua Bleu Limited
Art Creative Limited
Asante Distributors Limited
Ascenttial Ltd
Beautiful World Limited
Beauty Africa Limited
Beauty Avenue Limited
Beauty Complex Europe Ltd
Beauty Full Ltd
Beauty Kosmetika Ltd
Beauty Magasin Ltd

Beautyzon Limited
Best Choice FMCG Ltd
Best-Bio Ltd
Beverly Beauty & Fragrances Ltd
Bibishor Limited
Bio Global Limited
Birch & Hayer Ltd
Mark Birch Hair Ltd
Black Pearl Beauty Limited
Blissworld Limited
Bluestar Enterprise Limited
Bohdidharma Perfume UK Limited
Boutique Parfum Limited
Andre Boyard Perfumes Limited
British American Solutions Ltd
Brodie and Stone PLC
Buy Perfumes London Limited
By Mia Cosmetics Ltd
CNI Services Limited
Cannabinoid Oil Solutions Ltd
Celeb Products Ltd
Cleanux Chemicals Ltd
Cosmetiqa Ltd
Crescent Soaps Ltd
Dazzlers & Toppers PTL Ltd
Deism IT Solutions Ltd
Deja Vu International Ltd
Delhicious Ltd
Denbond Pharmaceuticals Ltd
Dermica Laboratoires UK Ltd
Direct Supplies (2014) Limited
Disley Limited
Diymonde Corporation Limited
Dr Sun Limited
Eacho Green Ltd
Ecooner Cosmetics London Ltd
Eden Brands Limited
Eden Parfums Limited
Edenwest Limited
Elite Beauty (London) Limited
Ellya UK Ltd
Emita Europe Limited
Enfield Distribution Ltd
Essence Cosmetics Limited
Essential Oil Sell Ltd
Esspire Limited
Europebro Wholesalers Ltd
Face & Beauty Limited
Farmers Pure Organics Ltd
Finest Mineral Make Up Limited
Flores Brand Works Limited
Fragrance London Limited
Fragrance Plus Limited
Freshly Whip'd Limited
Simona Fridrich Limited
General Healthcare Limited
Glasgow Nails & Beauty Supplies Ltd
Gold 22 (UK) Limited
Golo Hair & Beauty Limited
Grand By Designs Limited
Great London Beauty Limited
Greenpol Distribution Ltd
Gxskin Limited
Hairganic Limited
Hairshine UK Ltd
Hampton Brands Limited
Has To Be Ltd
Herbline U.K. Limited
Honeypot Cosmetics (Wholesale) Ltd
House of Oud Perfumes Limited
Imperial Pharmaceuticals Ltd
InternationalBeautyLondon Ltd

The Top UK Perfume and Cosmetics Wholesalers

Jay Kay Wholesale Ltd
KMI Brands Limited
Kandahar Trading Limited
Kaniz International Limited
Kaniz Organics Limited
Yasmin Karimi Ltd
Karium Ltd
Kaxton Limited
Kovet Kit Ltd
Krish Shoppers Ltd
L'Amour Cosmetics London Ltd
L.P Cosmetics Ltd
La Beauty Labs Ltd.
Leela Living Limited
Lese & Lista Ltd
Lifestyle International Ltd
Linrose Care Ltd
London Ethnic Ltd
London Outlet Store Limited
Luxuria Generation Limited
Lyons Men's Grooming Ltd
M Cosmetics Distribution Ltd
ME & II Limited
Mad Beauty Limited
Malvina Skin Care Limited
Mayfair Export UK Ltd
Mcaniis Ltd
Medipro Pharma Limited
Medna Fashions Ltd
Millenium Fragrance Limited
Mounir's Ltd
My Perfumes London Ltd
My7heavens Ltd
NABS Promotions Limited
Nabeel Perfumes International Ltd
Natur Life Ltd
Navya Innoveda Ltd
Ombre Cosmetics Limited
Ombre Paris Limited
Original Additions (Beauty Products)
Oudh Co Ltd
P.T & Co Ltd
PSR Wellness Limited
Pampering Pattie International Ltd
Pandorra Ltd.
Perfume London Ltd
Phils (Wholesale) Limited
Phoenix Beauty Ltd
Pixie Porter Ltd
Pizzaz Ventures Limited
Portobello Organics Ltd
Pound Ring Ltd
Pro Brands (UK) Ltd
Product World Limited
RHI By ROC Ltd
Radiant and Refined Limited
Rashimex Trading Limited
Reliant Overseas UK Limited
Charlotte Rhys UK Limited
Risa Lux Ltd
SS Wholesaler Limited
Sai Enterprise Limited
Saltee Skincare Limited
Sambio Ltd
Sanay Ltd
Leonora Sanche Cosmetics Ltd
Leonora Sanche Limited
Sanchi Corp Limited
Sangels Limited
Sassy Hair & Beauty Supplies Ltd
Scent N Essence UK Ltd
Scentric Ltd

Shalohm Ltd
Shaneel Enterprises Limited
Sheasecrets Ltd
Shuei Trading UK Ltd
Signature Fragrances London Ltd
Sipro (UK) Ltd
Solo Skin London Ltd
Sopure London Limited
Spirit of Dubai Limited
Starcount Limited
Sterling Fragrances International
Stylish & Luxurious Limited
Tetra Hydro Cannabinoid Oils Global Ltd
TheGlobalTrading Ltd
Tioluxe Europe Limited
Trade Anchor Limited
Universe Cosmetics Limited
Ve-Glam Limited
Ved Healthcare Limited
Vedaway Ltd
Vegan Republic Beauty Ltd
Vegan Republic Ltd
Veramic Limited
Vereer Limited
Vetivert & Co Ltd
Vibrantz Cosmetics Ltd
Vittoria Ventures Limited
Vivora Limited
Walk on Gold Limited
Whimsical Beauty Ltd
Worth Worldwide Property Ltd
Ximtrade (UK) Ltd
Yaami's Fashion Beauty & Cosmetics UK
Yummy Home Ltd
Zaigul Wholesale Ltd

Midlothian [19]
Aster & Bay Ltd.
Biologico Cosmetics Limited
CHT Supplies Limited
Gentlemend Ltd
Grimas.co.uk Limited
HDDirect Limited
Innes McBeath Sourcing Ltd.
Jorum of Scotland Limited
Kingdom Scotland Limited
Korebeauty Limited
Laurens Cosmetics UK Limited
London Cosmetics Co Ltd
National Supplement Beauty Solutions
Sisi Cosmetics Ltd
Trade Smart Marketing Limited
Urban Altar Ltd
Vitaglow Ltd
Westfield House Distributors Ltd
Wheesht Ltd

Monmouthshire [12]
Atlantic Beauty Store Limited
B.Cosmetics Ltd
Beauty Alliance International Ltd
Cosmetics Wholsale Ltd
Elite Salon Solutions Limited
Gilmor Hair and Beauty (Newport) Ltd
Green Jiva Ltd
KPACA Limited
Sage Apothecary Limited
Salon Distribution Concepts Ltd
Serendipity Herbals Ltd
Urban Retreat Products Limited

Norfolk [13]
Azik Group Ltd
Cilko Ltd
Ellipsis Brands Limited
Evans Close Limited
Funky Skincare Limited
Gifts of Earth Ltd
Initiative (UK) Limited
Juni Cosmetics Limited
Kservices Group Ltd
Lemon Tree Beauty Limited
Martha & Daughter Limited
Oils4life Limited
Skin Chef Limited

Northamptonshire [30]
Abbliss Limited
Active Tan Limited
Adelphi Corporation Limited
Arbonne UK Limited
T L Brooks Limited
Dacre Skincare Limited
Dee Doo Limited
Eifelcorp Consumer Care Ltd
Excel (GS) Limited
Fade The Itch Ltd
Healtholozy UK Limited
Ilex Wood Ltd
Kirimi Limited
Luuann Limited
M & M Import Ltd
Mlle Cosmetics Co Ltd
Modern Man Ltd
NA Medical Care Ltd
Narizaonline Ltd
OPA Botanicals Ltd
Oodiee Limited
Plantain Essential Oils Ltd
Silk Route Impex Limited
Skin Health Solutions Ltd
Spring and Underworld Ltd
Ulric de Varens UK Limited
Very Essence Ltd
Villainelle Ltd
XL Marketing Ltd.
Yehmea Limited

Northumberland
Ersag UK Limited
Graham Hair and Beauty Limited

Nottinghamshire [41]
All Naturals Beauty Limited
Aquapurity Ltd
B & D Fragrance Limited Co Ltd
BLK Cosmetics Limited
Be Fast Innovation Services Ltd
Beauty Consociare Ltd
Beauty Expression (UK) Limited
Billionhaire Limited
Biotrade Cosmeceuticals Ltd
Boots International Limited
Caprise Limited
Dilmaherbals Limited
Dots for Spots Ltd
Eutek Group Limited
Foreverbeyoung Ltd
Globe Intraworks Limited
Hadley and Reed Ltd
Hair and Cosmetics Wholesale Ltd

Hemsley James Cosmetics Ltd
Ideal Beauty Products Limited
Ijapan Ltd
L'Art & La Matiere Limited
Lipolift Ltd
Loles Cosmetics UK Limited
Mabxclusive Limited
Natural Birthing Co Ltd
Natural British Limited
PLTradeGroup Limited
Pink Beauty Supplies (UK) Ltd.
Potions & Possibilities Ltd
Pure Body Skin Care Ltd
Refan UK Ltd
Reimiece Ltd
Rogia Romini Limited
Simlar 2 Limited
Skins Sexual Health Limited
Timeless Temple Ltd
Underground Girl London Ltd
Valya Beauty Cosmetics Ltd
Wash Your Mouth Out Ltd
Zee Sales Limited

Oxfordshire [22]
Bays International Limited
Denise Brown Limited
Cath Collins Devon Ltd
Leighton Denny Limited
Flores Distribution Limited
Fragrance and Gifts Limited
Camilla Hepper Sales Limited
Hundred Acres Apothecary Ltd
Ila Asia Limited
Life's Big Stuff Ltd
Line21 Ltd.
MS Rarytas Ltd
Mebon Investment Limited
Morgan Jost Ltd
Nail Art Direct Ltd
Naturally By Nature Ltd
Prema Naturals Limited
MV Roberts & Co (UK) Ltd
Samla Tribe Limited
Seba Trade Limited
Sun Light EU Trading Ltd
Watsoap.Com Limited

Pembrokeshire
Boundless Beauty Ltd

Powys
STT Industries Ltd.

Rhondda Cynon Taf
Oyemam Ltd

Rutland
Cosmetics Direct Limited
Direct Cosmetics Limited

Shropshire
L'Revolution Beauty Ltd
Melya & Co. Trading Ltd.
Polish Cosmetics Distribution Centre UK

Somerset [46]
A & R Salon Enterprises Ltd
Adorexo Ltd
Agenda Salon Concepts Limited
Allied Aerosols Limited
Allied Fragrances Limited
Ashmira Botanica Ltd
B.Me Skincare Ltd
BBT Products Limited
Bath Spa Skincare Limited
Bayan Ltd
Beau Belle Brushes Ltd
Beautynet Limited
Co Beauty Ltd
Designer Fragrances Limited
Double Skies Limited
E.J. Contracts Limited
Equisalud Ltd
Essential Beauty Supplies Ltd
Eternal Beauty (UK) Ltd
Firecrest Communications Ltd
Fish London Limited
Herbal Hakeem Ltd
Image Hub Limited
Jean Christian Perfumes Ltd
Jedidiah Group Ltd
King's Vegan Grooming Ltd
Lashline Ltd
Lovorika London Limited
Mary-Jane's Beauty Ltd
Meadow Farm Friends Ltd
Natural Spa Factory Limited
Perfume Lab Limited
Perfumeprice.co.uk Ltd
Pharma Medico Limited
Preen Queen Limited
Profusion Cosmetics UK Ltd
Rakhee LB Ltd
SSB Ltd
Silk Oil of Morocco UK Limited
Somerset Perfumery Ltd
Tothun Group UK Ltd
UK Cosmeticz International Ltd
Valentia Skincare Limited
Wild Source Apothecary Ltd
Wiv Global Limited
Wizard Brands Limited

Staffordshire [26]
Bluesky Products Limited
Colour Lux Cosmetics Ltd
Diva Cosmetics Limited
Essential Cosmetics Ltd
Glitterati Shop Ltd
Glow Consumer Products UK Ltd
Grandelash MD UK Ltd
Kissess Lips of The Essence Ltd
Little Duckling Soaps Ltd
MEA Health and Wellness Ltd
Magpie's Ocean Ltd
Nails & London Holdings Ltd
Nature's Dream Limited
Norpro Limited
Nouela Organics Ltd
Potteries Transport Services Ltd
Rub-a-Dub Scrub Ltd
Sasha Hair & Beauty Ltd
Sheyton Ltd
Skin Matrix HD+ Cosmetology Ltd
Skin Matrix Limited
Super Yacht Spa Ltd

Total Beauty Network (UK) Ltd
UK Direct Imports Ltd
Uni Supply Ltd
Woodwood Limited

Suffolk [12]
Beauty Without Cruelty Limited
Bes Hair Products Limited
Pazery Bouffard and Co Ltd
Cosmetica Natural Oils Ltd
Loaded Cosmetics Limited
Niroshini Skincare Limited
Respect Male Grooming Ltd.
Soap and Candle Co Ltd
There-There Baby Ltd
Thrifty Limited
Ultra Glow Cosmetics Limited
Web Store Group Limited

Surrey [157]
40075 Limited
A B International Limited
AM Botanical Limited
Adnoz Limited
Adora Beauty Limited
Aglory Merchant Enterprises Ltd
Agoda Limited
Ajmal Perfume (UK) Limited
Alihair Ltd
Alpha La Roche Limited
Amahla Limited
Antian World Limited
BU Cosmetics Limited
Bare Cosmetics Ltd
Be Fairall Limited
Beauty Buddy Limited
Beauty Link Wholesale Ltd
Beauty Mastery Ltd.
Beautyline Limited
Beegood Enterprises Limited
Bellevue of London Ltd.
Belsay Ltd
Bizi Bazzar Limited
Black Gold Hair Limited
Bluebells Hair Boutique Ltd
Boz Ego Ltd
Anthony Braden Limited
Anthony Braden Online Ltd.
Bragarlin Limited
Brand Evangelists for Beauty Ltd
Burly Cosmetics Ltd
Business Angels Syndicate Ltd
CBee (Europe) Limited
Calmer Solutions Limited
Chaleur Ltd
Ches Editions Ltd
Classic Beaute Limited
Colgate-Palmolive (U.K.) Ltd
Comedic Limited
Comfort Click Limited
Conatural Ltd
Contemporary Cosmetic Enterprise Ltd
Coriungo Limited
Cult 51 Ltd
Dermalogica (UK) Limited
Dermanor Ltd.
Direct Salon Limited
EJS Brand Management Limited
Ere Perez UK Limited
Essence Room Ltd
Evagray Limited

Evercore UK Limited
B.Fairall (UK) Limited
Feel Good Products Limited
Fillers Pro Ltd
Five Star International Consulting
Flexi Beauty Care Ltd
Foad Wax Limited
For All Dogkind Limited
Glorious Brands Ltd.
Kenneth Green Associates Ltd
Greenwise Distribution Ltd
Guess Her Secret Limited
HABM Ltd
Hair for Men Products Ltd
Harmonious Brown Limited
Herra Hair Care Limited
Hoff Beards Limited
Ilys Organic Ltd
Impressions Beauty Limited
Inspired Hair Supplies Limited
Instant Effects Ltd
Isha Cosmetics Limited
Istylists Limited
Jacob's Well Limited
Janson Limited
Jica Beauty Products Limited
Just The Product Ltd
Karaama Fragrances Ltd
Kenbar Beauty Products Limited
L & L Sunlight Importers and Exporters
Labo Nine Limited
Laldhinio Limited
Lam Cosmetics Ltd
Lanmix Enterperises Ltd
Lax Group Co Ltd
Liqwd Limited
London Beauty Limited
Lovely Distribution Co Ltd
Lulu Tanner Limited
Mayfair Gate Limited
Menco International Limited
Modern Innovations Limited Ltd
Motion Junkies Limited
My London Trade Ltd
Myrrh & Co. Limited
Natural Blends of Nature Ltd
Natural Health Harmony Group Ltd
Natural Vitale Limited
Neroli Limited
Suzanne Neville Fragrance Ltd
Nu Essence Limited
Orange Square Co Ltd.
Ovis Liv Limited
PLBrands Limited
Paliano Ltd
Pam Trading Limited
Paradise Organics London Ltd
Passion 4 Health International Ltd
Pause Skincare Limited
Perfume Holding UK Limited
Petersham Ventures Ltd
Pharmacare (Europe) Limited
Pharmdex UK Ltd
Posh Gift Ltd
Prestonelite Limited
Prostar Trending Online Ltd
Pure Products Limited
QOD UK Ltd
Real Skin Pickle Ltd
Ring in Ring Ltd
JC Rosedale Co Ltd
Ruxley Medical Aids Limited

SB Selected Beauty Ltd
Salon Ambition Limited
Santiago Distribution Limited
Sash Products Limited
Satya Life Ltd
Seadrift Trading Limited
Serengeti Skincare Limited
Shea Touch Ltd
Skinsense Ltd
South West Aesthetics Ltd
Stenko Ltd
Sun Jelly Ltd
TM Brands Limited
Tansi Packaging Solutions Ltd
Theglossfairy Ltd
Trading Scents (2014) Limited
Trading Scents Group Limited
Trading Scents Limited
Tree of Life Cosmetics Ltd
Ukin Ltd
Unigrand Group Limited
Uniqtrend Limited
Up Roar Ltd.
Valorem Distribution Ltd
Vanilla Blanc Limited
Wafson Ltd
Walking Pet Balloons (UK) Ltd
Warpaint Cosmetics Limited
Wonder and Wild Ltd
Xpoze International Limited
Zealousco Limited
Zerocann Ltd
Zivi Cosmetics Ltd
Zyzven Naturals Cosmetics Ltd

Sussex [91]
Adraji Ltd
Aeden UK Ltd
Amazingface Limited
Ambassadors Choice Limited
Amber House Limited
Amly Limited
Amour Pigments Ltd
Arahant Ltd
Aspects Beauty Co Ltd
Balmain Hair UK Ltd
Balmonds Skincare Ltd
Beaming White Ltd
Beauty Ideas Group Limited
Beauty Masks Limited
Beautypro Ltd
Bedeaux Ltd
Biodeb Beauty Ltd
Body Shop International Ltd
Bolm4 Limited
Brighton Group Ltd
Bullingberg Limited
By Sarah Limited
Capital (Hair and Beauty) Ltd
Comfortz Ltd
Cor Europe Limited
Dermacosmeticsweb Ltd
Dermamaitre Ltd.
Eden Perfumes Limited
Evanesce Ltd
Five Elements Healthcare Ltd
GCKK Ltd
Galenti Limited
GameelaCosmetics Ltd
Glamrolls Limited
Greenfrog Soap Co Ltd
Hahydra Technologies Ltd

Hamiltons of Canterbury Ltd
Helia-D UK Ltd
Imperial Bioscience Ltd
Infinity K Ltd
Ink Oil Limited
JJ Promotions Limited
James & Jake Ltd
Kokolokahi Limited
Thomas Kosmala Parfums Ltd
LIV Organic Co Ltd
Lanolips Limited
Leading National Training Ltd
Logical Content Ltd
London Skincare Co Ltd.
Marksman Green Ltd
Mlaveau Cuban Origins Ltd
Moderna Aesthetics Ltd
Nailzee Ltd
Natural Beauty Import Limited
Newincco 2301 Limited
Nextporter Ltd.
One Green Lab Ltd
Onya Limited
Outcome Zero Ltd
Pompadour Laboratories Limited
Quality Brand MG Ltd
Quality Check Ltd
Quint Essence Lab Ltd
Raynolds Ltd
Roja Dove Limited
Salon Connection (Wales) Ltd
Salt and Pamper Limited
Scent Retail Ltd
Shadi's Hairdresser Ltd
Shared Beauty Secrets Limited
Shared Beauty Secrets Spas Ltd
Shhh-Holistic Limited
Shine Shampoo Bars Ltd
Shop Beauty Ltd
Simply Nature Ltd.
Simply Pure Skincare Ltd
Sirra Limited
Spa Pro Ltd
Splendor Europe Ltd.
Square Spots Limited
Sun Spirit Skincare Limited
Tiggy Lashes Ltd
Truthpaste Ltd
Vida Aesthetics Ltd
Vida Skincare Ltd
Wealden Aesthetics Limited
Wellness Style Limited
Whitening World Ltd
Wholesale Hair Extensions Ltd
Daniele de Winter Monaco-UK Ltd

Tyne & Wear [21]
Ak-Kur Furniture & Fitting Ltd
Black Candle Company of Northumberland
Cont-Hemp-Orary Ltd
Diamond Smile NE Limited
French Beauty Expert Ltd
Hair North East Limited
Haircosmetics (Sunderland) Ltd
Health Future Limited
L.A. Professional Cosmetic Labs Ltd.
La Tips Limited
Lilyz Cosmetics UK Ltd
Maskhouse Wholesale Limited
Naturenk Ltd
Ohsho Ltd
Perfect Look & Health Ltd

Perfume World Limited
Qiaochu Trading Co. Ltd
Raisingthebaruk Ltd
Rishi Human Hair Extensions Wholesale
Sun Lounge Supplies Limited
Viridian Leaf Limited

Warwickshire [41]

ACH Cosmetics Limited
Arlenne Ltd
Aroma Dead Sea Limited
Arrow Hair & Beauty Supplies Ltd
Bains and Daughters Limited
Baltica Beauty Professional Ltd
Bath Bombs and Beyond Limited
Beauty Innovator 2012 Ltd.
Beauty Queen Limited
Bloom Artisan Brands Limited
Body Care Brand Development Ltd
Bristol Consumer Health Ltd
Burton Blackmore International Ltd
Eden's Legends Limited
Glow Beauty Shop Ltd
Goodangels Ltd
Goodscents Limited
Haircare of Sweden Ltd
Happy Beauty Life Ltd
Ivy Wild Ltd
JLE Trading Limited
Jaden Cosmetics Limited
Just Acrylics Ltd
Kavali Cosmetics Limited
Le Glamour UK Ltd
Le Keux Vintage Enterprises Ltd
Lins Bros Limited
Mindful Soulful Limited
NJ Apparel Ltd.
NaturallyClearSkin Limited
Okmarket24 Ltd
Ozprodz Limited
Paragon Enterprise Limited
Perfume Bodega Dist. Ltd
Procter & Procter Limited
RX Cosmetics Limited
Sahinler Limited
Shori Ltd
Tabitha JK Limited
U 2 Shine Limited
Venus Beauty Limited

West Midlands [128]

AJ Metals Ltd.
APC (UK) Limited
Actuate Services (GB) Ltd
Jalali Agarwood Ltd
Al-Abideen Perfumes Ltd
Albland Limited
Alizcare Limited
Allies Network Ltd
Alsons Beauty Ltd.
Amalsons Ltd
Ample Biotechnology UK Co. Ltd
Angel Remy Ltd
Asurex Limited
Attar Mist Ltd
BSB Fashion Limited
Bali Secrets Ltd
Barbers Warehouse Ltd
Bbeauty Lounge Cosmetics Ltd
Bbeauty Lounge Limited
Beautivate Ltd

Beautx Ltd
Beauty Cosmetics (Bristol) Ltd
Beauty Cosmetics (Luton) Ltd
Beauty Cosmetics (Nottingham) Ltd
Beauty Glow Wholesale Limited
Beiersdorf UK Ltd.
Birmingham Fragrances Ltd
Bluesky Cosmetics Limited
Boutique Fragrances Ltd
CH General Traders Limited
CM Hair & Beauty Supplies Ltd
Chit.Ka Ltd
Ciao Brow Henna Limited
City Beauty Supplies (UK) Ltd
Complexi-Light Ltd
Cosmetic Hooligans Ltd
Cosmetics Online Limited
Cosmetics R Us 1 Limited
Crown Cosmetics Limited
Cutelovelee Limited
DKB Essentials Ltd
DMG Wholesale Limited
Daly Beauty Limited
Death Head Beard Co Ltd
Dupeshop Ltd
Echo Hair Limited
Elite Capital Limited
Elko Electrical Ltd.
Essench Cosmetics Ltd
Esthetica Pure Ltd
Fit Brands (UK) Ltd
Florascent Duftmanufaktur Ltd
Florence Consumer Products Ltd
Flowscent Limited
Forever Heng UK Limited
G.P.B. Supplies Limited
GS Fragrances Limited
Gabriellas Beauty Ltd
Grand Beaute Ltd
Hairdye Direct Limited
Hairenvy Boutique Limited
Hansraj House Limited
Hasanah Global Ltd
Heavenly Riches Limited
Hemangini Limited
Iconic Perfumes Ltd
Inbeauting Ltd
Inshirah Enterprises Limited
JCB Skincare Limited
Jan Nails & Beauty Suppliers Ltd
K Co Cosmetics Ltd
K Wholesale Limited
Gabriel Kalevi Ltd
Kiara Sky Professional Nail Distribution
J Kobain London Ltd
J Kobain Ltd
L'dreams Limited
LYF Cosmetics Limited
Lescaro Health Limited
Lock Stock & Barrel Grooming Co Ltd
Luqs Womenswear Ltd
Luscious Skincare Ltd
MB Promotion Ltd.
Microskin Cosmeceuticals UK Ltd
Miss U Cosmetics Limited
Muse and Rose Limited
Nail & Beauty Link Limited
Nail Island Ltd
Naturyl Glow Ltd
Need4health Limited
Neolife International Ltd
Neonails Ltd

New Horizons (UK) Ltd
New York 77 Ltd
Niami1893 Ltd
Omprus Limited
Orgreen Naturals Ltd
PHB Franchise Limited
Paiman Limited
Parfum Club Ltd
Plenteous Ltd
Sara Post Ltd
Prima Makeup Ltd
Quelsa Ltd
R & B Hair Extensions Limited
Raebeauty Ltd
Rebatchi Perfums Ltd
S & G Supplies Ltd
SMCK Hair Care Products Ltd
SMCK Limited
Sama Perfumes Ltd
Sansuri Hair & Beauty Supplies and Training
Skinsmith Limited
Stonera Ltd
TLGrooming Limited
Tawakkal Perfumes Ltd
Taylor Grange Cosmetics Ltd
Three Pears Online Limited
Thrillage Ltd.
Timi's Cosmetics Ltd
Trinity General Trading Ltd
True Hemp Ltd
USA Hair Extensions Ltd
V@M Limited
Vasuda Beauty Limited
Vilasa Limited
Xhorah Skincare Ltd
Yellbird Limited

Wiltshire [26]

Arosci Trading Limited
Beyond Glamour Ltd
Blk Deer Co. Ltd
Bramley Products Ltd
Budget Beauty Limited
CHM Holdings Ltd
Fade Out Limited
Fairy Dust Limited
Fine Fragrances and Cosmetics Ltd
A.H. Francis Professional Beauty
Functional Fragrances Ltd
Great British Bee Co Ltd
Helen Gel Colour Ltd
Interparcos U.K. Limited
Lynch-Staunton Cosmetics Ltd
McCarthy Inter Africa Ltd
JO Nielsen Limited
Purple Tree Skincare Limited
Shahadah Ltd
Simply Untouched Ltd
Spa Skincare Limited
Teoxane UK Limited
Vivalis Beauty Limited
Vivalis Limited
Wiltshire Beekeeper Ltd
XIP Professional Ltd

Worcestershire [11]

Ank Innovation Limited
Beautytrade Limited
Cozmetica UK Ltd
Eternal Hair & Beauty Limited
Inside Trading (Beauty) Ltd

Jealous Cow Limited
Lavy Sprays International Ltd
Mirimiri Limited
Nails and Co (Midlands) Ltd
Rosmetics Aesthetics Limited
Skinnydip Skincare Limited

Yorkshire [149]
2B Enterprises Limited
4symbols Ltd
A Essentials Limited
Adel Professional Limited
African Garden Limited
Al Sunnah Perfumes (Wholesale) Ltd
Amaani Q Ltd
Amberhue Limited
Barnsley Card Ltd
Beauty Leisure Industry Supplies and Services
Beauty Oasis Ltd
Beauty Spot Holdings Limited
Beautywise Limited
Beever Haircare Ltd
Bellissimo GmbH International Ltd
Biovate Limited
Candii Bath Limited
Cheap Cosmetic Ltd
Clean & Care Facilities Management
Clever Skin Co Limited
Coffeinium Germania Ltd
Alia Collyns Cosmetics Ltd
Colwayland Co Ltd
Cosmetolife Limited
Cosplus International Ltd
D'Zario UK Ltd
Dead Sea London Ltd
Delights Beauty Co Ltd
Dermaloch Limited
Diamonds on Demand Ltd
Diet Plan Unique Ltd
Dinair Airbrush Makeup Systems Ltd
Drammock International Limited
ED Trading & Consultancy Ltd
Ethereal Beauty Ltd
Ethical House Ltd
Face Fodder Limited
Facemane Ltd
Fatale Cosmetics Limited
FayshCosmetics Ltd
Fegoo Limited
Feinkost & Getranke Ltd
Fem Distribution Limited

Florence Health & Beauty Ltd
Flowery Whiff Limited
Georgie Salon Supplies Limited
Glaci Natural Ltd
Global Beauty Wholesale Ltd
Global Hair Care Limited
Glossy Center Limited
Goldstone Perfumes Limited
Green Guru Enterprices Ltd.
H2K Limited
Hair Fantastic Retail Limited
Haresgraces Limited
Harvey Pharma Ltd
Hava Traders Limited
Herb Stuff Limited
Hothouse Holdings Limited
House of Kendra Ltd
I Love Cosmetics Limited
ID Aromatics Limited
Icon Consultancy Ltd
Inspired by RJP Limited
Isobel C Professional Cosmetics Ltd
Ital Living Market Ltd
J26 Limited
JP Products and Services Ltd
Josie Rose Ltd
Justins Essentials Ltd
Kamarino Limited
Khushi Skincare Limited
Kitchen Witch Aromatherapy Ltd
Ko. Essentials Ltd.
LGC Cosmetics Ltd
LMS Brands Ltd.
LPG Clinics Wholesale Ltd
Ladorisa Limited
Lash Authority Ltd
Leslie International Ltd
Little Big Brands Ltd
Lux Aesthetics Hull Ltd
Macden Beauty Ltd
Macial Ltd
Mainline Marketing U K. Ltd
Man'd Skincare Ltd
Mandragora Ltd
Medica Ltd
Mediskin Pro Limited
Multitude Makeup Ltd
Myroo Ltd
N18 Ltd
Nail Creation UK Distribution Ltd
Natural Pal Limited
Natural Touch Enterprises Ltd
Noor Int'l Trading Limited

Optic Eye Wear Ltd
Pandhy's UK Sweet Cosmetics Ltd.
Parker & Moses Ltd
Party Supplies and More Ltd
Pet Scentuary Ltd
Phyto Therapeutics Limited
Angela Pickering Limited
Portland House International Trading
Lisa Preston Ltd
Pricecheck Toiletries Limited
Pro Bright Ltd
Pure Natural Therapy Ltd
R10 Labs Skincare Ltd
RMG Hair Limited
Razzo Limited
Recruit Skincare Ltd
Regal Skincare Ltd
Rosdon Group Limited
San & Amad General Trade Co Ltd
Sculptola Ltd
Sheabynature Ltd
Skinmed Ltd
Skinvital Ltd
Slixir Ltd
So Boujee Limited
Soap Industry Limited
Splashes & Spills Ltd.
Stantondown Limited
Style Cosmetics Limited
Suave Cents Limited
Sweet Squared Limited
T4Colins Beautifician Ltd
Tattva Ltd.
Tina Trading Co Ltd
Total Salon Supplies Limited
Trelux Limited
Unac Salon Supplies Limited
Uni London Limited
Varama Limited
Vett Limited
Waterman Corporate Enterprises Ltd
Wax Authority Limited
Whimsical Beard Co Ltd
White Rose Aromatics Limited
Dennis Williams Limited
Yorkshire Beard Co Ltd
Yorkshire Beauty Supplies Ltd
Zahrat Alqurashi Ltd
Zajil Limited
Zarahs World Ltd
Zarroug Limited
Zest Cosmetics Limited
Zipco Limited

This page is intentionally left blank

Company Profiles

100% Vegan Skincare Limited
Incorporated: 14 August 2018
Registered Office: 3 Hall Lane, Bold, St Helens, Merseyside, WA9 4SN
Major Shareholder: Donna Pearson
Officers: Donna Pearson [1981] Director/Teacher

11 Scent Limited
Incorporated: 29 January 2019
Registered Office: 416 Clifton Drive North, Lytham St Annes, Lancs, FY8 2PN
Major Shareholder: Warren Michael Brooks
Officers: Warren Michael Brooks [1967] Director

11:11 Limited
Incorporated: 1 November 2017
Registered Office: 24 Sleford Close, Balsham, Cambridge, CB21 4DP
Shareholders: Heidi Gordon-Smith; Holly Anne Helt
Officers: Heidi Gordon-Smith [1981] Director; Holly Anne Helt [1964] Director [American]; Edward Alexander Sanson [1980] Director; Mark James Tanser [1968] Director

1962 Ltd
Incorporated: 3 January 2008
Net Worth: £2 *Total Assets:* £20,125
Registered Office: 18-20 High Street, Shaftesbury, Dorset, SP7 8JG
Major Shareholder: Christopher Johnson
Officers: Pauline Carol Knight, Secretary; Christopher Mark Johnson [1962] Director/Salesman

1CBDUK Ltd
Incorporated: 14 January 2019
Registered Office: Office 1, Quebec Building, Bury Street, Manchester, M3 7DU
Major Shareholder: Peter Benedetti
Officers: Peter Benedetti [1977] Director/Self Employed

1st Choice Nails Limited
Incorporated: 3 February 2014 *Employees:* 3
Net Worth Deficit: £1,455 *Total Assets:* £49,440
Registered Office: 3rd Floor, Crown House, 151 High Road, Loughton, Essex, IG10 4LG
Major Shareholder: Shuab Akhtar
Officers: Shuab Akhtar [1979] Director

20seven Limited
Incorporated: 29 December 2014
Net Worth Deficit: £689 *Total Assets:* £1,062
Registered Office: 158 Blackwell Road, Carlisle, Cumbria, CA2 4DL
Major Shareholder: Kim Reay
Officers: Kimberley Reay, Secretary; Kimberley Reay [1987] Director/Network Marketing; Lauren Reay [1993] Director/Student

2B Enterprises Limited
Incorporated: 5 January 2004 *Employees:* 3
Net Worth Deficit: £84,910 *Total Assets:* £4,905
Registered Office: 54 Moor Lane, Highburton, Huddersfield, W Yorks, HD8 0QS
Major Shareholder: Ian Elliot Smith
Officers: Michael John Bouguenon [1967] Director/Consultant [South African/British]; Victor Paul Bouguenon [1963] Director/Marketing [South African]; Ian Elliot Smith [1957] Director

2M PH. Intl. Limited
Incorporated: 20 October 2015
Net Worth: £9,574 *Total Assets:* £15,601
Registered Office: Bridge House, 2 Bridge Avenue, Maidenhead, Berks, SL6 1RR
Major Shareholder: Massimiliano Melano
Officers: Massimiliano Melano, Secretary; Massimiliano Melano [1966] Director/Entrepreneur [Italian]

305 Professionals Ltd
Incorporated: 29 November 2018
Registered Office: 71-75 Shelton Street, London, WC2H 9JQ
Shareholders: Aston Campbell; Jacqui McIntosh
Officers: Aston Campbell [1950] Director/Bus Driver [Jamaican]; Jacqui McIntosh [1965] Director/Hairdresser

3D Lifestyle Ltd
Incorporated: 5 April 2017
Registered Office: Companies House, Default Address, Cardiff, CF14 8LH
Major Shareholder: Waqar Ahmad
Officers: Waqar Ahmad [1969] Director/Business Professional [Canadian]

4 Corners Distribution Ltd
Incorporated: 2 June 2014
Net Worth Deficit: £140,409 *Total Assets:* £617,647
Registered Office: 702 Romford Road, London, E12 5AJ
Major Shareholder: Mohmad Shoeb Mangera
Officers: Mohmad Shoeb Managera [1976] Director

40075 Limited
Incorporated: 28 June 2013
Net Worth Deficit: £32,556 *Total Assets:* £32,600
Registered Office: 16 Watson Avenue, Sutton, Surrey, SM3 9RE
Major Shareholder: Elena Lebedeva
Officers: Elena Lebedeva, Secretary; Elena Lebedeva [1968] Director/Retailer Luxury Sector

446-012 File Limited
Incorporated: 30 August 2018
Registered Office: 12 Haviland Road, Ferndown Industrial Estate, Wimborne, Dorset, BH21 7RG
Major Shareholder: Linda Anousta
Officers: Gary David Elson [1958] Director/Accountants; Chris Paul Geaves [1963] Director/Accountant

4M Cosmetics Limited
Incorporated: 16 September 2013
Registered Office: Unit 21 Waterfield Way, Sketchley Meadows Industrial Estate, Hinckley, Leics, LE10 3ER
Officers: Stephen David Cook [1973] Director; Matthew James Pringle [1980] Director [New Zealander]

4R Guest Supplies Limited
Incorporated: 27 October 2014
Previous: Limrok Hotel Supplies Limited
Net Worth: £7,250 *Total Assets:* £50,312
Registered Office: 37 Beltona Gardens, Cheshunt, Waltham Cross, Herts, EN8 0PA
Major Shareholder: Reenal Rakesh Makwana
Officers: Rakesh Makwana, Secretary; Reenal Rakesh Makwana [1982] Director

4symbols Ltd
Incorporated: 20 November 2018
Registered Office: 555 Scott Hall Road, Leeds, LS7 2NF
Major Shareholder: Alina Khan
Officers: Alina Khan [1992] Director

4T Medical Ltd
Incorporated: 2 February 2012 *Employees:* 5
Net Worth: £224,624 *Total Assets:* £385,008
Registered Office: G12 Blenheim House, Cambridge Innovation Park, Denny End Road, Waterbeach, Cambs, CB25 9GL
Shareholder: Julien Telesphore Tordjmann
Officers: Julien Telesphore Tordjmann [1972] Director; Laure Rolande Elisabeth Tordjmann [1971] Director [Swiss]

50shadez Ltd
Incorporated: 12 February 2019
Registered Office: 14 Forest Business Park, Argall Avenue, London, E10 7FB
Major Shareholder: Shahid Shabbir
Officers: Shahid Shabbir [1974] Director/Businessman; Chandrikaben Karsan Vekaria [1975] Director

72 Hair Limited
Incorporated: 19 May 2016
Net Worth Deficit: £80,920 *Total Assets:* £163,840
Registered Office: 305 Regents Park Road, Finchley, London, N3 1DP
Officers: Gianni Gaetano Alberto Dionisi [1965] Director; Gary Michum Green [1962] Director; Matthew Jamie Green [1988] Director; Nicholas Luke Green [1988] Director

72 Hair Retail Limited
Incorporated: 10 February 2017
Registered Office: 305 Regents Park Road, Finchley, London, N3 1DP
Officers: Gianni Gaetano Alberto Dionisi [1965] Director; Gary Michum Green [1962] Director; Matthew Jamie Green [1988] Director; Nicholas Luke Green [1988] Director

7th Heaven Scents Ltd
Incorporated: 7 June 2018
Registered Office: 19 Saville Street, Leicester, LE5 4GT
Officers: Ebrahim Lambat [1983] Director/Retailer

876 Skin Beauty Limited
Incorporated: 29 November 2018
Registered Office: 203 Hertford Road, Enfield, Middlesex, EN3 5JH
Major Shareholder: Luckiva Malika Watson
Officers: Luckiva Malika Watson [1995] Director/Support Worker [Jamaican]

9 Silk Gates Ltd
Incorporated: 19 July 2018
Registered Office: 71-75 Shelton Street, Covent Garden, London, WC2H 9JQ
Officers: Hassan Akachab [1991] Director [Moroccan]

A & B Supply Co. Limited
Incorporated: 20 February 2013
Registered Office: 24 Mitre Bridge Industrial Estate, Mitre Way, London, W10 6AU
Officers: Joseph Cotton [1971] Director

A & R Salon Enterprises Limited
Incorporated: 6 August 2009 *Employees:* 1
Net Worth: £38,421 *Total Assets:* £45,583
Registered Office: Courthouse West, Thornfalcon, Taunton, Somerset, TA3 5NH
Major Shareholder: Alison Jean Cooney
Officers: Alison Jean Cooney, Secretary/Director; Alison Jean Cooney [1968] Director

A B International Limited
Incorporated: 1 March 1991 *Employees:* 3
Net Worth: £1,321,637 *Total Assets:* £1,420,556
Registered Office: Almac House, Church Lane, Bisley, Surrey, GU24 9DR
Shareholders: Rebecca Brown; David Brown
Officers: Rebecca Brown, Secretary; David Paul Brown [1966] Director; Rebecca Brown [1969] Director

A Beauty Story Ltd
Incorporated: 2 May 2018
Registered Office: 71-75 Shelton Street, Covent Garden, London, WC2H 9JQ
Major Shareholder: Arthur Mitroulas
Officers: Arthur Mitroulas [1974] Managing Director [Australian]

A Essentials Limited
Incorporated: 21 March 2018
Registered Office: c/o Allertons, 3 Queens Arcade, Leeds, LS1 6LF
Major Shareholder: Nicholas Nicola
Officers: Nicholas Nicola [1983] Director

A Natural Treat Limited
Incorporated: 21 October 2018
Registered Office: 67-68 Hatton Garden, London, EC1N 8JY
Major Shareholder: Leigh-Marie Alcide
Officers: Leigh-Marie Alcide [1984] Director/Entrepreneur

A Pony Called Steve Ltd
Incorporated: 24 November 2014
Net Worth Deficit: £13,238 *Total Assets:* £9,550
Registered Office: 20 Broompark Road, Glasgow, G72 0DR
Officers: Emma Louise Campbell [1984] Director/Beauty Wholesale; Aminah Morgan [1984] Director/Beauty Wholesale

A Rebours Limited
Incorporated: 7 June 2018
Registered Office: 11a Trafalgar Mews, London, E9 5JG
Major Shareholder: Xiaoxiao Yu
Officers: Xiaoxiao Yu [1986] Director [Chinese]

A S Pacho Ltd
Incorporated: 26 June 2018
Registered Office: 10 Lupin Crescent, Ilford, Essex, IG1 2JR
Major Shareholder: Andrzej Stanislaw Pachonski
Officers: Andrzej Stanislaw Pachonski [1981] Director/Sales [Romanian]

A.R Cosmetics Limited
Incorporated: 3 October 2016
Registered Office: 34 Roundhouse Circle, Renfrew, PA4 8FL
Officers: Rozina Saleem [1978] Director

AAA Edinburgh Ltd
Incorporated: 17 July 2008
Previous: PBM Design and Construction Limited
Net Worth: £31,093 *Total Assets:* £96,882
Registered Office: 6 Queen Margaret University Way, Old Craighall, Musselburgh, E Lothian, EH21 8SL
Major Shareholder: Elena Barns
Officers: Elena Barns [1958] Director/Accountant

Aabis Duty Free Limited
Incorporated: 25 September 2018
Registered Office: 14-18 Forest Road, Loughton, Essex, IG10 1DX
Shareholders: Hassan Shah; Amna Shah
Officers: Amna Shah [1969] Director; Hassan Shah [1995] Director

Aamir Traders Ltd
Incorporated: 31 October 2017
Registered Office: 27 Highview, Byron Way, Northolt, Middlesex, UB5 6BL
Major Shareholder: Mohammed Aamir
Officers: Mohammed Aamir, Secretary; Mohammed Aamir [1982] Director

Abbliss Limited
Incorporated: 18 March 2005
Net Worth: £1,910 *Total Assets:* £14,280
Registered Office: The Stables, Church Walk, Daventry, Northants, NN11 4BL
Shareholders: William Lawrence Jordan; Lynn Patricia Jordan
Officers: Lynn Patricia Jordan, Secretary; William Lawrence Jordan [1959] Director

ABC Beauty Limited
Incorporated: 6 April 2006 *Employees:* 2
Net Worth: £27,638 *Total Assets:* £71,140
Registered Office: Wymet House, 87 New Row, Dunfermline, Fife, KY12 7DZ
Shareholders: Lynne Bell; David Marshall Bell
Officers: David Marshall Bell [1957] Director/Account Manager

Abington Cosmetics Ltd
Incorporated: 22 August 2016
Registered Office: 244 Rydal Drive, Bexleyheath, Kent, DA7 5DG
Major Shareholder: Anders Wikner
Officers: Anders Wikner [1978] Director [Swedish]

Absolute Cosmetic Essentials Limited
Incorporated: 22 August 2017
Registered Office: 1 Absolute House, Mill Lane, Alton, Hants, GU34 2PX
Parent: Absolute Aromas Limited
Officers: Josias Cunningham [1985] Director; David Guy Tomlinson [1965] Director

ABX Beauty Limited
Incorporated: 18 November 2009
Net Worth: £5,010 *Total Assets:* £58,500
Registered Office: First Floor, Inchcape House, Inchcape Place, North Muirton Industrial Estate, Perth, PH1 3DU
Shareholder: Iain Robert Lamont
Officers: Angela Lamont [1963] Director/Manager; Iain Robert Lamont [1957] Director/Manager

Acering Limited
Incorporated: 9 May 1986 *Employees:* 6
Net Worth: £190,708 *Total Assets:* £547,190
Registered Office: 30 Nelson Street, Leicester, LE1 7BA
Parent: SRL International FZE
Officers: Paresh Kumar Kotecha, Secretary; Jayshyam Kotecha [1989] Director/Accountant; Kamal Vandravan Kotecha [1965] Director/Computer Programmer; Kashmira Kotecha [1962] Director; Liam Kotecha [2001] Director; Minal Kotecha [1969] Director; Paresh Kumar Kotecha [1960] Director/Pharmacist; Ravi Kotecha [1994] Director

ACH Cosmetics Limited
Incorporated: 14 June 2018
Registered Office: 296 Camp Hill Road, Nuneaton, Warwicks, CV10 0JN
Major Shareholder: Adam Charles Hart
Officers: Adam Charles Hart [1983] Director/Wholesaler

Acorn Brokerage Limited
Incorporated: 28 March 2011 *Employees:* 2
Net Worth: £6,320 *Total Assets:* £39,089
Registered Office: c/o Edwards Veeder (UK) Limited, Ground Floor, 4 Broadgate, Broadway Business Park, Chadderton, Oldham, Lancs, OL9 9XA
Officers: Jill McPake [1964] Director; Lawrence McPake [1948] Director/Consultant

Acqua di Parma Limited
Incorporated: 25 October 2013 *Employees:* 73
Net Worth: £1,362,530 *Total Assets:* £4,486,617
Registered Office: 6th Floor, UK House, 180 Oxford Street, London, W1D 1AB
Parent: Sofidiv UK Limited
Officers: Laura Luciana Burdese [1971] Director [Italian]; Stephane Paul Regis Euzen [1976] Director [French]; Loic Pierre Marie Henriot [1978] Director [French]; Guiseppe Andrea Violante [1974] Director [Italian]

Acquaderm Ltd
Incorporated: 31 August 2017
Total Assets: £100
Registered Office: 71-75 Shelton Street, Covent Garden, London, WC2H 9JQ
Major Shareholder: Ricardo Vieira Rego
Officers: Ricardo Vieira Rego [1980] Director/Manager [Brazilian]

Acti Laboratories UK Ltd
Incorporated: 17 March 2006 *Employees:* 14
Previous: Aesthetimeds Ltd
Net Worth: £1,944,587 *Total Assets:* £2,781,150
Registered Office: The Stables, Shipton Bridge Farm, Widdington, Saffron Walden, Essex, CB11 3SU
Shareholders: Christopher John Hillyard-Miller; James Hugo Hillyard-Miller
Officers: Christopher John Hillyard-Miller, Secretary; Christopher John Hillyard-Miller [1961] Director/Chemist; James Hugo Hillyard-Miller [1987] Director/Chemist

Active Skincare Limited
Incorporated: 25 November 2011
Net Worth: £164,716 *Total Assets:* £172,716
Registered Office: 45 Franche Court Road, London, SW17 0JX
Shareholders: Leyla Muna Cooper; Leyla Muna Cooper
Officers: Edward Cooper [1982] Director/Lawyer; Leyla Muna Cooper [1981] Director; James Harding Vowles [1972] Director

Active Tan Limited
Incorporated: 29 July 2015
Net Worth Deficit: £40,130 *Total Assets:* £7,410
Registered Office: 58 Fieldfare Close, Corby, Northants, NN18 8FF
Shareholders: James Collier; Louise Jane Beard
Officers: James Collier, Secretary; Louise Jane Beard [1968] Director/Trainer; James Collier [1972] Director

Actuate Services (GB) Ltd
Incorporated: 13 July 2012
Net Worth Deficit: £19,678 *Total Assets:* £17,152
Registered Office: c/o MNSK, 206 Robin Hood Lane, Hall Green, Birmingham, B28 0LG
Major Shareholder: Abdullah Khan
Officers: Abdullah Khan [1974] Director

Adam and Eve Distribution Ltd
Incorporated: 21 October 2016
Registered Office: Fairclough Hall Farm, Halls Green, Weston, Hitchin, Herts, SG4 7DP
Shareholders: David Simon Colborne; Karen Colborne
Officers: David Simon Colborne [1966] Director/Owner; Karen Colborne [1965] Director/Owner

Adam Michaels Group Ltd
Incorporated: 12 November 2018
Registered Office: 15 Drumhead Road, Chorley North Industrial Park, Chorley, Lancs, PR6 7BX
Officers: Soab Bhuta [1969] Director; Zuber Lulat [1979] Director; Shahid Malek [1970] Director; Nasim Akhtar Patel [1972] Director

Adams General Ltd
Incorporated: 30 October 2015
Net Worth: £247,370 *Total Assets:* £286,150
Registered Office: First Floor, 244 Edgware Road, London, W2 1DS
Major Shareholder: Hussain Ali Hussain Al-Bayati
Officers: Hussain Ali Hussain Al-Bayati [1973] Director/Business Executive [Iraqi]

Chris Adams Perfumes Ltd
Incorporated: 30 December 2009
Net Worth Deficit: £2,737 *Total Assets:* £632,440
Registered Office: Unit 3 Hounslow Business Park, Alice Way, Hounslow, Middlesex, TW3 3UD
Officers: Howaida Asgher Adam Ali, Secretary; Mustafa Asghar Adam Ali Ibrahim [1978] Executive Director [Kittitian]; Howaida Asgher Adam Ali [1981] Director

Additional Lengths Ltd
Incorporated: 26 January 2007
Net Worth: £1,498,650 *Total Assets:* £1,926,480
Registered Office: Maxwell's Corner, 1-3 Norton Road, Stockton on Tees, Cleveland, TS18 2BW
Major Shareholder: Victoria Lynch
Officers: Victoria Lynch [1977] Director

Adel Professional Limited
Incorporated: 13 September 2007 *Employees:* 61
Net Worth: £214,233 *Total Assets:* £2,708,869
Registered Office: Unit 4, 38-40 Roman Ridge Road, Sheffield, S9 1GB
Officers: Susan Kemp, Secretary; Derek John Kemp [1951] Director; Oliver Benjamin Kemp [1978] Director; Edward Ternie McDermott [1962] Director

Adelphi Corporation Limited
Incorporated: 21 December 1994 *Employees:* 17
Net Worth: £1,839,841 *Total Assets:* £1,977,184
Registered Office: Waterside House, Nene Park, Station Road, Irthlingborough, Wellingborough, Northants, NN9 5QF
Major Shareholder: Paul Garcia
Officers: Paul Garcia [1963] Director/Consultant

Adem Oygur Ltd
Incorporated: 22 August 2017
Registered Office: 291 Green Lanes, London, N13 4XS
Major Shareholder: Adem Oygur
Officers: Adem Oygur [1985] Director/Hairdresser

Adible Limited
Incorporated: 22 June 2016
Previous: Email Experts Limited
Net Worth Deficit: £11,866 *Total Assets:* £601
Registered Office: Cambridge House, 16 High Street, Saffron Walden, Essex, CB10 1AX
Major Shareholder: Jesse Jacob Rees
Officers: Stefan Cudby [1973] Director

Adnoz Limited
Incorporated: 8 August 2016
Registered Office: 11 Goldfinch Gardens, Guildford, Surrey, GU4 7DN
Major Shareholder: Siripan Chansevikul
Officers: Siripan Chansevikul [1982] Director/Marketing Consultant [Thai]

Adonis Skin Ltd
Incorporated: 21 February 2019
Registered Office: Unit 13, 2 Artichoke Hill, London, E1W 2DE
Shareholders: Sydwat Andrew Chiu-Mo Pitayanukul; Alex Lai
Officers: Sydwat Andrew Chiu-Mo Pitayanukul [1989] Director

Adora Beauty Limited
Incorporated: 4 October 2018
Registered Office: 58 Ashley Road, Hampton, Surrey, TW12 2HU
Major Shareholder: Adora Oleh
Officers: Adora Oleh [1977] Director

Adorexo Ltd
Incorporated: 14 January 2019
Registered Office: 38 Eastover, Langport, Somerset, TA10 9RX
Officers: Dr Corbey Michael Warner [1998] Company Secretary/Director

Adoris UK Ltd
Incorporated: 12 February 2019
Registered Office: 14a Thomas Hardy House, Commerce Road, London, N22 8EE
Officers: Sahra Mohamoud [1965] Director/Businesswoman

Adraji Ltd
Incorporated: 19 February 2018
Registered Office: Flat 21, Percival Mansion, Percival Terrace, Brighton, BN2 1FP
Shareholders: Majid Ali Talib Albusaidy; Majid Ali Talib Albusaidy
Officers: Majid Ali Talib Albusaidy [1969] Director [Kenyan]

Adwa Impex Ltd
Incorporated: 2 July 2018
Registered Office: 27 Old Gloucester Street, London, WC1N 3AX
Major Shareholder: Artur Szalka
Officers: Artur Szalka, Secretary; Artur Szalka [1986] Director [Hungarian]

Aeden UK Ltd
Incorporated: 18 August 2014
Previous: Flowlife Consulting Ltd
Net Worth Deficit: £2,170
Registered Office: 77 High Street, Littlehampton, W Sussex, BN17 5AG
Major Shareholder: Attila Istvan Kuti
Officers: Attila Istvan Kuti [1983] Director [Hungarian]

Aenea Cosmetics Ltd
Incorporated: 25 September 2014
Net Worth Deficit: £120,247 *Total Assets:* £33,753
Registered Office: First Floor, Thavies Inn House, Holborn Circus, London, EC1N 2HA
Parent: Aenea Group Holdings Ltd
Officers: Graham John Barrett [1954] Director

Aeroeco Company Limited
Incorporated: 11 December 2018
Registered Office: Suite 108, Chase Business Centre, 39-41 Chase Side, London, N14 5BP
Major Shareholder: Xiangyu Gao
Officers: Xiangyu Gao, Secretary; Xiangyu Gao [1981] Director/Merchant [Chinese]

Aesthetic & Luxury Distribution Ltd
Incorporated: 15 February 2018
Registered Office: Hunters Lodge, Ballards Drive, Colwall, Herefords, WR13 6QY
Major Shareholder: Stephen Andrew Bates
Officers: Stephen Andrew Bates [1978] Director/Entrepreneur

Aesthetic Brands (Distribution and Management) Limited
Incorporated: 15 June 2012
Net Worth: £150,175 *Total Assets:* £376,918
Registered Office: 3 Kensington Church Street, London, W8 4LB
Shareholders: Theo Fieldgrass; Natalie Kingsley-Fieldgrass
Officers: Theodore Fieldgrass, Secretary; Theo Fieldgrass [1981] Director/Healthcare Manager; Natalie Ursula Kingsley [1984] Director

Aesthetic Cosmetic Ltd
Incorporated: 3 July 2012
Net Worth: £104 *Total Assets:* £3,500
Registered Office: Suite E, 1-3 Canfield Place, London, NW6 3BT
Major Shareholder: Jonathan Spital
Officers: Jonathan Spital [1958] Director

Aether Elements Ltd
Incorporated: 7 December 2018
Registered Office: 374 Kings Road, Chelsea, London, SW3 5UZ
Major Shareholder: Emre Gurcan
Officers: Emre Gurcan [1982] Director

Afex Skin Care Ltd
Incorporated: 23 October 2018
Registered Office: Hawthorne House, 17a Hawthorne Drive, Leicester, LE5 6DL
Officers: Tristan Davison [1996] Director/Consultant; Julia Susan Tiffin [1996] Director/Consultant [South African]; Robert George Tiffin [1961] Director [South African]

Affinity Fragrances Limited
Incorporated: 26 October 2015 *Employees:* 11
Net Worth: £370,000 *Total Assets:* £6,106,000
Registered Office: Unit 16 Uxbridge Trade Park, Cowley Mill Road, Uxbridge, Middlesex, UB8 2DB
Shareholders: Jagdish Prabhudas Karia; Vishal Karia
Officers: Jagdish Prabhudas Karia [1958] Director; Mala Jagdish Karia [1962] Director; Vishal Karia [1989] Director

Africa's Best Artisans Limited
Incorporated: 27 February 2019
Registered Office: 152 Purves Road, London, NW10 5TG
Major Shareholder: Chinapa Aguh
Officers: Chinapa Aguh [1980] Director

African Garden Limited
Incorporated: 8 December 2015
Registered Office: Broad Oak Farm, Stopes Road, Stannington, Sheffield, S6 6BW
Major Shareholder: Andrew Nicholas Maskill
Officers: Andrew Nicholas Maskill [1953] Director/Marketing Consultant

African Wild Organics Ltd
Incorporated: 19 November 2018
Registered Office: 31 Grecian Crescent, Norwood, London, SE19 3HQ
Major Shareholder: Mufadzi Nkomo
Officers: Mufadzi Nkomo [1969] Director

Afro Hair and Beauty International Limited
Incorporated: 12 April 2018
Registered Office: 3 Greenwich High Road, London, SE10 8JL
Officers: Verna Angela McKenzie, Secretary; Verna Angela McKenzie [1961] Director/Event Organiser; Renford Smith [1952] Director/Electrician

Afrocare Ltd
Incorporated: 5 July 2018
Registered Office: 54 Westwood Avenue, Harrow, Middlesex, HA2 8NS
Major Shareholder: Mylene Larisa Kubanza
Officers: Mylene Larisa Kubanza [1996] Director [Romanian]

The Aftershave Gaff Ltd
Incorporated: 11 February 2019
Registered Office: 63 Arnison Avenue, High Wycombe, Bucks, HP13 6DB
Officers: Kishan Parmar [1990] Managing Director

Afthrone Ltd
Incorporated: 12 January 2018
Registered Office: 177 Munster Road, London, SW6 6BZ
Major Shareholder: Morakinyo Oreoluwa Omosebi
Officers: Morakinyo Oreoluwa Omosebi [1983] Director

Aga Cosmetics Ltd
Incorporated: 11 June 2018
Registered Office: Office 56, Mill Mead Business Centre, Mill Mead Road, Tottenham, London, N17 9QU
Officers: Agnieszka Adrjanowicz [1973] Sales Director [Polish]; Krzysztof Tadeusz Rejza [1974] Managing Director [Polish]

Jalali Agarwood Ltd
Incorporated: 17 September 2018
Registered Office: 12 Crompton Road, Tipton, W Midlands, DY4 8RY
Major Shareholder: Stephane Khan
Officers: Stephane Khan [1986] Director/Self Employed [French/Bangladeshi]

Age Infinite Ltd
Incorporated: 11 June 2018
Registered Office: 2 Mill Court, Mill Street, Enniskillen, Co Fermanagh, BT74 6FB
Major Shareholder: Mariusz Szczesny
Officers: Mariusz Szczesny [1975] Director [Polish]

Agenda Salon Concepts Limited
Incorporated: 20 May 2004 *Employees:* 9
Net Worth: £561,285 *Total Assets:* £970,994
Registered Office: 11 Laura Place, Bath, BA2 4BL
Parent: Agenda Marketing Holdings Limited
Officers: Gail Eggleton, Secretary; Christopher John Eggleton [1957] Director

Aglory Merchant Enterprises Limited
Incorporated: 29 September 2004
Net Worth: £197,908 *Total Assets:* £1,028,863
Registered Office: Doshi Accountants Ltd, 6th Floor, Amp House, Dingwall Road, Croydon, Surrey, CR0 2LX
Shareholders: Esther Ibidoja Adebola; Mohammed Kamoru Adebola
Officers: Esther Ibidoja Adebola, Secretary; Esther Ibidoja Adebola [1969] Director; Mohammed Kamoru Adebola [1961] Director [Dutch]

Agoda Limited
Incorporated: 9 August 2018
Registered Office: 334 Kingston Road, New Malden, Surrey, KT3 3RX
Major Shareholder: Weiyan Zhou
Officers: Weiyan Zhou [1972] Director

Ahoaloe Cosmetics Limited
Incorporated: 8 January 2019
Registered Office: Flat 3, 1 Telegraph Avenue, London, NW9 4BA
Major Shareholder: Gustavo Henrique Acorsi
Officers: Gustavo Henrique Acorsi [1981] Director/Business Executive [Italian]

AHS Services Ltd
Incorporated: 8 November 2016
Registered Office: 75 Crouch Avenue, Barking, Essex, IG11 0QY
Officers: Hamza Mehmood [1995] Director

Ahwaz Ltd
Incorporated: 10 October 2016
Net Worth Deficit: £2,054 *Total Assets:* £28,515
Registered Office: 20-22 Wenlock Road, London, N1 7GU
Major Shareholder: Fazel Hamidi
Officers: Fazel Hamidi [1988] Director

AIGC Limited
Incorporated: 3 February 2015
Net Worth: £143 *Total Assets:* £216
Registered Office: 6 Arthur Road, London, E6 6EF
Major Shareholder: Adnan Iqbal
Officers: Adnan Iqbal, Secretary; Adnan Iqbal [1970] Director [Pakistani]

Aiweisier Limited
Incorporated: 12 February 2019
Registered Office: Suite 108, Chase Business Centre, 39-41 Chase Side, London, N14 5BP
Major Shareholder: Lijun Zheng
Officers: Lijun Zheng, Secretary; Lijun Zheng [1969] Director/Merchant [Chinese]

AJ Active Enterprises Ltd
Incorporated: 9 March 2016
Net Worth: £5,078 *Total Assets:* £5,078
Registered Office: 71-75 Shelton Street, Covent Garden, London, WC2H 9JQ
Major Shareholder: Ali Bathawab
Officers: Ali Salem Bathawab [1962] Managing Director [Yemeni]

AJ Metals Ltd.
Incorporated: 5 January 2016 *Employees:* 3
Net Worth: £106,527 *Total Assets:* £117,527
Registered Office: 696 Yardley Wood Road, Billesley, Birmingham, B13 0HY
Major Shareholder: Ali Jawad
Officers: Ali Jawad [1975] Director [Pakistani]

Ajmal Perfume (UK) Limited
Incorporated: 8 May 1997
Registered Office: 1st Floor, Crosspoint House, 28 Stafford Road, Wallington, Surrey, SM6 9AA
Parent: Fabson Import Export Ltd
Officers: Abdulla Amiruddin Ajmal, Secretary; Mohammed Amiruddin Ajmal [1953] Director [Indian]; Mohammed Sirajuddin Ajmal [1958] Director [Indian]; Mohammed Fakhruddin Ajmal [1954] Director [Indian]

AJS Marketing Limited
Incorporated: 9 December 1999 *Employees:* 2
Net Worth Deficit: £32,514 *Total Assets:* £40,178
Registered Office: First Floor, Radius House, 51 Clarendon Road, Watford, Herts, WD17 1HP
Major Shareholder: Arif Jamal Syed
Officers: Arif Jamal Syed [1970] Director

AK Wholesale Limited
Incorporated: 2 May 2018
Registered Office: 10 Second Avenue, Merthyr Tydfil, CF47 9UB
Major Shareholder: Adam Kujawski
Officers: Adam Kujawski [1988] Director [Polish]

Ak-Kur Furniture & Fitting Ltd
Incorporated: 26 January 2018
Registered Office: 37e Lindisfarne Court, Bede Trading Estate, Jarrow, Tyne & Wear, NE32 3HG
Major Shareholder: Kenan Akkurt
Officers: Kenan Akkurt [1981] Director

Akoma International (UK) Limited
Incorporated: 4 September 2002 *Employees:* 4
Net Worth: £96,293 *Total Assets:* £348,160
Registered Office: Unit 9A Sawley Park, Nottingham Road, Derby, DE21 6AS
Major Shareholder: Augustus Wynn Klufio
Officers: Augustus Wynn Klufio [1970] Director/IT Consultant & Computing

Akwaaba Social Enterprises Limited
Incorporated: 28 January 2014
Net Worth Deficit: £16,035 *Total Assets:* £584
Registered Office: Ford House, Chawleigh, Chulmleigh, Devon, EX18 7JY
Officers: George Alan Bainborough [1950] Director; Sally Jane Elizabeth Bainborough [1952] Director

Al Amira Limited
Incorporated: 16 July 2018
Registered Office: 4th Floor, 54 Conduit Street, London, W1S 2YY
Major Shareholder: Mohamed Ahmed Mahmoud Ahmed
Officers: Mohamed Ahmed Mahmoud Ahmed [1983] Director [Egyptian]

Al Cosmetics Ltd
Incorporated: 21 February 2013
Net Worth Deficit: £179,370 *Total Assets:* £10,930
Registered Office: 127 Balaam Street, London, E13 8AF
Shareholders: Natallia Bahdanava; Yury Berahavoi; Yury Berahavoi
Officers: Yury Berahavoi [1965] Managing Director [Belarusian]

Al Janan Fragrances Limited
Incorporated: 10 September 2015
Registered Office: 44 Acacia Close, Stanmore, Middlesex, HA7 3JR
Major Shareholder: Janet Elizabeth Flemming
Officers: Janet Elizabeth Flemming [1964] Director/Legal Secretary; Aadam Howard-Flemming [1984] Director

Al Masiya Cosmetic Ltd
Incorporated: 23 January 2018
Registered Office: 432 Edgware Road, London, W2 1EG
Officers: Azal Al Bayati [1961] Director/Businessman

Al Sunnah Perfumes (Wholesale) Ltd
Incorporated: 19 May 2017
Registered Office: 1 Hadfield Road, Heckmondwike, W Yorks, WF16 9PN
Major Shareholder: Soieb Mulla
Officers: Soieb Mulla [1980] Director

Al-Abideen Perfumes Ltd
Incorporated: 13 June 2018
Registered Office: Unit 37 Hooryal Business Centre, Coventry Road, Small Heath, Birmingham, B10 0SW
Major Shareholder: Mickael Karim Jabeur
Officers: Mickael Karim Jabeur [1986] Director [French]

Al-Jazeera Perfumes Ltd
Incorporated: 1 February 2019
Registered Office: Amine El-Bacha, 61 Mill Lane, London, NW6 1NB
Major Shareholder: Amine El-Bacha
Officers: Amine El-Bacha [1972] Director/Self Employed

Alade Ltd
Incorporated: 21 July 2017
Registered Office: 86-90 Paul Street, London, EC2A 4NE
Officers: Riliwan Balogun [1989] Director

Alayna Cosmetics and Beauty Limited
Incorporated: 19 February 2018
Registered Office: 90 Sanvey Gate, Leicester, LE1 4BQ
Shareholder: Babar Abbas
Officers: Babar Abbas [1976] Director/Online Sale

Albertina Dorosario Ltd
Incorporated: 6 September 2018
Registered Office: 19 Rathborne East, 17-19 Maud Street, London, E16 1YS
Major Shareholder: Albertina Nambu Kimfumu
Officers: Princess Luila Clementina Kimfumu [1995] Director

Albland Limited
Incorporated: 13 November 2018
Registered Office: 568e Brighton Road, Birmingham, B12 8QN
Officers: Fatjon Qerimi [1991] Director/Plumber [Italian]

Maddi Alexander Limited
Incorporated: 22 June 2011
Net Worth Deficit: £61,683 *Total Assets:* £12,930
Registered Office: 71-75 Shelton Street, Covent Garden, London, WC2H 9JQ
Major Shareholder: Analisa Ariss
Officers: Analisa Ariss [1973] Director

Alfa Parf UK Ltd
Incorporated: 20 February 2019
Registered Office: 2nd Floor, Whitehall House, 41 Whitehall, London, SW1A 2BY
Major Shareholder: Roberto Franchina
Officers: Attilio Brambilla [1961] Director/Entrepreneur [Italian]

Alianaz Ltd.
Incorporated: 23 November 2015
Net Worth: £6,110 *Total Assets:* £7,010
Registered Office: 26 Pearce Road, Maidenhead, Berks, SL6 7LF
Officers: Nigar Sultana [1978] Director [Bangladeshi]

Alico Exports Limited
Incorporated: 15 August 1980
Net Worth Deficit: £30,780 *Total Assets:* £13,244
Registered Office: 1275 Greenford Road, Greenford, Middlesex, UB6 0HY
Major Shareholder: Marlene Yourdi
Officers: Marlene Yourdi [1959] Director

Alihair Ltd
Incorporated: 27 February 2019
Registered Office: The Coach House, 1 Howard Road, Reigate, Surrey, RH2 7JE
Major Shareholder: Yimin Lu
Officers: GA Ning Lay [1977] Director [Malaysian]; Yimin Lu [1936] Director [Chinese]

Alimacskincare Limited
Incorporated: 8 June 2012
Net Worth Deficit: £126,539 *Total Assets:* £3,868
Registered Office: 24 Station Square, Academy Street, Inverness, IV1 1LD
Shareholder: Alison McIntosh
Officers: Alison McIntosh [1967] Director

Alizcare Limited
Incorporated: 23 August 2017
Registered Office: 7 Chad Road, Birmingham, B15 3EN
Major Shareholder: Mussarat Khattak
Officers: Dr Mussarat Fawad Khattak [1971] Director/Doctor

Alkaiser Perfumes Ltd
Incorporated: 8 September 2018
Registered Office: Aramex House, Old Bath Road, Colnbrook, Slough, Berks, SL3 0NS
Shareholders: Yamen Muneer Albakour; Safaa Mohamed Ali Mohamed Ali Mohamed
Officers: Yamen Muneer Albakour [1979] Director/Manager [Syrian]

All Naturals Beauty Limited
Incorporated: 11 January 2018
Registered Office: Medicity D6 Building West, Thane Road, Nottingham, NG90 6BH
Major Shareholder: Julita Joanna Geary
Officers: Dr Julita Geary, Secretary; Dr Julita Joanna Geary [1973] Managing Director [Polish]

All-Around Infinity Limited
Incorporated: 20 June 2018
Registered Office: 27 Old Gloucester Street, London, WC1N 3AX
Major Shareholder: Szu-Yun Chang
Officers: Szu-Yun Chang [1982] Director/C.E.O [Taiwanese]

Alliance SG Limited
Incorporated: 9 August 2011
Net Worth: £100 Total Assets: £10,947
Registered Office: 135-137 Station Road, Chingford, London, E4 6AG
Shareholders: Criterion Properties Limited; Andrew Patrick
Officers: Andrew Patrick [1966] Director/Marketing Consultant

Allied Aerosols Limited
Incorporated: 14 August 2017
Net Worth: £2,790 Total Assets: £705,444
Registered Office: 4 King Square, Bridgwater, Somerset, TA6 3YF
Major Shareholder: Christopher Robinson
Officers: Christopher Robinson [1969] Director

Allied Fragrances Limited
Incorporated: 25 February 1998 Employees: 3
Net Worth: £828,712 Total Assets: £898,170
Registered Office: 4 King Square, Bridgwater, Somerset, TA6 3YF
Shareholders: Christopher Robinson; Robert Edward Robinson
Officers: Karen Robinson, Secretary; Christopher Robinson [1969] Director/Purchase Manager

Allied Warden Marketing Limited
Incorporated: 3 December 1998
Net Worth: £4,891 Total Assets: £5,579
Registered Office: c/o Temples, Kemp House, 152-160 City Road, London, EC1V 2NX
Major Shareholder: Marc Alexander Rene Mackie
Officers: Dr Marc Alexander Rene Mackie [1964] Director/Pharmacist [French]

Allies Network Ltd
Incorporated: 3 March 2014
Net Worth: £100 Total Assets: £100
Registered Office: 26 Clipston Road, Birmingham, B8 3HJ
Officers: Nura Ali Dhuhul [1986] Director; Dave Blakemore [1949] Company Secretary/Director; Quaye Botchway [1963] Director/Community Advice

Allure Beauty Supplies Ltd
Incorporated: 30 April 2015
Net Worth: £3,240 Total Assets: £18,370
Registered Office: 7 Sandpiper Close, Greenhithe, Kent, DA9 9RU
Major Shareholder: Sohail Rafiq
Officers: Sohail Rafiq [1991] Director [French]

Allure Cosmetics Ltd
Incorporated: 23 April 2018
Registered Office: Seaton Holme, Hall Walk, Peterlee, Co Durham, SR8 3BS
Officers: Sarah Ann Garside [1990] Director/Semi Permanent Makeup Technician

Almcells Bioscience Ltd.
Incorporated: 28 January 2019
Registered Office: Kemp House, 160 City Road, London, EC1V 2NX
Major Shareholder: Oleg Gorskov
Officers: Oleg Gorskov, Secretary; Oleg Gorskov [1967] Director/Manager [Czech]

Almirall Limited
Incorporated: 23 July 2007 Employees: 35
Net Worth: £8,029,066 Total Assets: £14,548,521
Registered Office: 1 George Street, Uxbridge, Middlesex, UB8 1QQ
Parent: Almirall S.A.
Officers: Alfredo Baron de Juan [1967] Senior Director [Spanish]

Alpha Auriga Limited
Incorporated: 10 June 2016
Registered Office: Top Floor, Trojan House, 34 Arcadia Avenue, London, N3 2JU
Parent: Brinkmeier Holding Limited
Officers: Olaf Brinkmeier [1976] Director/Established Merchant [German]; Dana Klaus [1976] Director/Established Merchant [German]

Alpha La Roche Limited
Incorporated: 31 January 2013
Net Worth Deficit: £6,290 Total Assets: £16,727
Registered Office: 1 The Green, Richmond, Surrey, TW9 1PL
Officers: Mel Shantonas [1959] Director

Alsons Beauty Ltd.
Incorporated: 10 May 2016
Net Worth Deficit: £13,344 Total Assets: £40,839
Registered Office: Unit G2, 353 Upper Balsall Heath Road, Birmingham, B12 9DR
Officers: Ali Mehdi Lalji [1986] Director; Kumail Hassan Lalji [1988] Director

Alton Trading Ltd
Incorporated: 6 February 2009
Net Worth: £9,300 Total Assets: £206,210
Registered Office: Regent House, 316 Beulah Hill, London, SE19 3HF
Major Shareholder: Anzhela Markova
Officers: Henry Alexander Rosas Morales [1987] Director/Consultant [Panamanian]

Altundag Ltd
Incorporated: 4 October 2018
Registered Office: 20-22 Wenlock Road, London, N1 7GU
Major Shareholder: Bilal Altundag
Officers: Bilal Altundag [1988] Director [Swedish]

Alumier Labs UK Limited
Incorporated: 11 July 2018
Registered Office: Unit 5 Draycott Business Centre, Draycott, Moreton in Marsh, Glos, GL56 9JY
Officers: Don Wessel Maree [1977] Managing Director

Alvor Limited
Incorporated: 24 November 1981
Net Worth: £1,823,836 Total Assets: £1,853,052
Registered Office: 4a Honeypot Business Centre, Parr Road, Stanmore, Middlesex, HA7 1NL
Shareholders: Muzafferali Lalji; Mohamed Lalji; Mustafa Lalji
Officers: Mustafa Lalji, Secretary; Muzafferali Lalji, Secretary/Sales Manager; Mohamed Lalji [1946] Director; Mustafa Lalji [1976] Director/Chartered Accountant; Muzafferali Lalji [1978] Director

Alwais Ltd
Incorporated: 16 November 2015
Net Worth: £5,237 Total Assets: £36,961
Registered Office: 1-2 Craven Road, London, W5 2UA
Major Shareholder: Farzad Rashad
Officers: Farzad Rashad [1992] Director/Retail/Wholesale

Always 20 Limited
Incorporated: 20 April 2018
Registered Office: 71-75 Shelton Street, London, WC2H 9JQ
Major Shareholder: Cheung Sai Mui
Officers: Cheung Sai Mui, Secretary; Cheung Sai Mui [1955] Director [Chinese]

AM Botanical Limited
Incorporated: 31 October 2018
Registered Office: Flat 2, 110 Mulgrave Road, Sutton, Surrey, SM2 6LZ
Shareholders: Alondra Del Rocio Michel Sanchez; Damien Leprince
Officers: Damien Leprince [1984] Director/IT Business Analyst [French]; Alondra Del Rocio Michel Sanchez [1988] Director/Skincare Manufacturer [Mexican]

Amaani Q Ltd
Incorporated: 25 February 2019
Registered Office: 39 Springwood Hall Gardens, Gledholt, Huddersfield, W Yorks, HD1 4HA
Major Shareholder: Azr Abdul Quaddus
Officers: Azr Abdul Quaddus [1962] Director

Amaffi London Limited
Incorporated: 27 December 2017
Registered Office: 3rd Floor, Fairgate House, 78 New Oxford Street, London, WC1A 1HB
Officers: Didier-Alexandre Ambroise [1982] Managing Director [American]; Michael Charles Smith [1947] Director

Amahla Limited
Incorporated: 8 February 2017
Net Worth: £12,782 *Total Assets:* £21,989
Registered Office: 14 Anderson Place, Bagshot, Surrey, GU19 5LX
Major Shareholder: Michele Elise Sarah Frost
Officers: Michele Frost, Secretary; Michele Elise Sarah Frost [1962] Director/Consultant

Amalgamated Euro Products UK Ltd
Incorporated: 6 March 2012
Net Worth: £95,100 *Total Assets:* £1,040,000
Registered Office: Unit 3 Rufus Business Centre, Ravensbury Terrace, London, SW18 4RL
Parent: Amalgamated Euro Products Canada Corporation
Officers: Mehrdad Mirzaee-Ghomi [1966] Managing Director

Amalsons Ltd
Incorporated: 16 October 2017
Registered Office: 24 Ash Tree Road, Birmingham, B30 2BJ
Officers: Usaamah El-Alaoui [1989] Director

Amassuna Limited
Incorporated: 26 January 2015
Net Worth: £6,500 *Total Assets:* £6,500
Registered Office: 62 Beddington Road, Orpington, Kent, BR5 2TF
Major Shareholder: Giorgio Stamerra
Officers: Giorgio Stamerra [1979] Director/Cosmetics Industry

Amaxa Ltd
Incorporated: 14 May 2018
Registered Office: 31 John Islip Street, London, SW1P 4FE
Major Shareholder: Jane Tkachenko
Officers: Gabriella Wheeler [1996] Director

Amazingface Limited
Incorporated: 28 August 2007
Net Worth Deficit: £31,667 *Total Assets:* £1,947
Registered Office: 66 South Street, Lancing, W Sussex, BN15 8AJ
Major Shareholder: Grace Jackaman
Officers: Grace Jackaman [1965] Director/Beauty Therapist

Amazon Healthcare Ltd
Incorporated: 30 October 2012
Net Worth Deficit: £5,392 *Total Assets:* £2,088
Registered Office: 37 Selwood Way, High Wycombe, Bucks, HP13 5XR
Major Shareholder: Uthayakumar Cumarasamy
Officers: Uthayakumar Cumarasamy [1952] Director

Ambassadors Choice Limited
Incorporated: 3 November 1987
Net Worth: £824,477 *Total Assets:* £1,729,580
Registered Office: MacDonald House, 1 Lowfield Way, Lowfield Heath, Crawley, W Sussex, RH11 0PW
Shareholders: Gordon Ian Sankey; Barry Howard Smart
Officers: Deborah Gould, Secretary; Gordon Ian Sankey [1959] Director; Stephen Robert Wescott [1959] Director

Amber House Limited
Incorporated: 20 December 2004 *Employees:* 10
Net Worth: £945,149 *Total Assets:* £1,598,140
Registered Office: The Old Dairy, Barcombe Mills Road, Lewes, E Sussex, BN8 5FF
Shareholders: John Charles Kingham; Catherine Mann Voogd Bergwerf; John Charles Kingham
Officers: Catherine Mann Voogd Bergwerf [1969] Director; John Charles Kingham [1956] Director/Salesman; Sophie Kingham [1987] Business Development Director; Corrina Lancaster [1980] Commercial Director

Amberhue Limited
Incorporated: 19 April 2015
Net Worth Deficit: £4,150 *Total Assets:* £12,220
Registered Office: Unit 4 Access 26, Chain Bar Road, Cleckheaton, W Yorks, BD19 3QF
Officers: Robert Lee Milner [1977] Director

Ameera London Limited
Incorporated: 29 July 2015
Net Worth: £16,577 *Total Assets:* £26,541
Registered Office: 10c Applegarth Road, London, W14 0HY
Major Shareholder: Nabil Abbaze
Officers: Nabil Abbaze [1986] Director/Health & Beauty

Amelgo Ltd
Incorporated: 9 November 2017
Registered Office: 109 Coleman Road, Leicester, LE5 4LE
Major Shareholder: Nadir Shkukani
Officers: Nadir Shkukani [1991] Director

American Cosmetics Limited
Incorporated: 19 May 2016
Registered Office: c/o SP Accounting, 3 George Street, Watford, Herts, WD18 0BX
Officers: Sadikally Gulamabbas Premji [1984] Director/Businessman [New Zealander]

AMF Distribution Limited
Incorporated: 16 August 2011
Net Worth: £27,130 *Total Assets:* £27,130
Registered Office: 30 Grove Farm Park, Northwood, Middlesex, HA6 2BQ
Shareholder: Aiman Raffiq
Officers: Mohamed Ali Roshanali Raffiq [1981] Director

The Top UK Perfume and Cosmetics Wholesalers   dellam

Amiri Perfume Ltd
Incorporated: 9 October 2017
Registered Office: 25 Brandon Close, Chafford Hundred, Grays, Essex, RM16 6QX
Major Shareholder: Faisal Al Dousari
Officers: Khaled Al Mansour, Secretary; Faisal Al Dousari [1982] Director/Businessman [Kuwaiti]

Amly Limited
Incorporated: 28 April 2014
Net Worth: £4,918 *Total Assets:* £29,807
Registered Office: Hawthbush Farm, Gun Hill, Heathfield, E Sussex, TN21 0JY
Shareholders: Lisa Frances O'Connor; Kerry Moore
Officers: Kerry Ann Moore [1962] Director; Lisa Frances O'Connor [1973] Director

Amor Beauty Cosmetics Ltd
Incorporated: 28 June 2018
Registered Office: Amor Beauty Cosmetics Ltd, 71-75 Shelton Street, Covent Garden, London, WC2H 9JQ
Major Shareholder: April Louise Jenner
Officers: April Louise Jenner [1991] Director

Amor et Psyche Ltd
Incorporated: 21 August 2015
Registered Office: The Burrow, 13 The Hawthorns, Maple Cross, Rickmansworth, Herts, WD3 9UH
Major Shareholder: Alexandra Lane
Officers: Alexandra Lane, Secretary; Alexandra Lane [1984] Director/Chandler

Amour Pigments Ltd
Incorporated: 23 November 2018
Registered Office: 2a-2b Coronation Buildings, Ham Road, Worthing, W Sussex, BN11 2NN
Major Shareholder: Mia Elizabeth Clark
Officers: Mia Elizabeth Clark [1996] Director/Businesswoman

Ample Biotechnology UK Co. Limited
Incorporated: 10 November 2017
Registered Office: Suite B, 8th Floor, Albany House, 31 Hurst Street, Birmingham, B5 4BD
Major Shareholder: Ka Wai Fung
Officers: Ka Wai Fung [1984] Director [Chinese]

AMS-Uhren Ambiente mit Style Ltd
Incorporated: 11 January 2019
Registered Office: 20-22 Wenlock Road, London, N1 7GU
Major Shareholder: Thanaphon Prayoonkham
Officers: Thanaphon Prayoonkham [1982] Director [Thai]

Anandi Cosmetics Private Ltd
Incorporated: 13 June 2018
Registered Office: 245 Sherrard Road, London, E12 6UG
Major Shareholder: Deniz Dirlik
Officers: Deniz Dirlik [1982] Director [Turkish]

Anar Naturals Limited
Incorporated: 19 April 2011
Net Worth: £5,030 *Total Assets:* £5,050
Registered Office: Unit R, Cradock Road, Luton, Beds, LU4 0JF
Officers: Amish Rajnikant Radia [1983] Director/Accountant

Anatomicals London (England, The World, The Universe-Known and Unknown) Ltd
Incorporated: 18 September 2006
Net Worth: £339,903 *Total Assets:* £400,702
Registered Office: Just Nominees Limited, Suite 3B2, Northside House, Mount Pleasent, Barnet, London, EN4 9EB
Shareholders: Gary Marshall; Paul Marshall
Officers: Gary Marshall [1965] Advertising Art Director; Paul Marshall [1961] Director/Advertising Copywriter

Aneen Ventures Limited
Incorporated: 2 March 2015
Net Worth Deficit: £11,036 *Total Assets:* £18,109
Registered Office: 47 London Road, Tunbridge Wells, Kent, TN4 0PB
Shareholders: Anastasiya Yovkova-Telang; Praveen Telang
Officers: Praveen Telang, Secretary; Anastasiya Yovkova Telang, Secretary; Praveen Telang [1977] Director [Indian]; Anastasiya Yovkova Telang [1980] Director [Bulgarian]

Angel Lash Limited
Incorporated: 2 May 2017
Net Worth Deficit: £4,920 *Total Assets:* £2,090
Registered Office: 37a Annahugh Road, Loughgall, Co Armagh, BT61 8PQ
Major Shareholder: Andrea Margaret Watters
Officers: Andrea Margaret Watters [1980] Director [Irish]

Angel Remy Ltd
Incorporated: 23 January 2014
Net Worth: £712,804 *Total Assets:* £1,134,498
Registered Office: Block B, Unit 13 Red Mill Trading Estate, Rigby Street, Wednesbury, W Midlands, WS10 0NP
Shareholder: Deborah Christine Morrison
Officers: Zak Berrow [1986] Director; Deborah Christine Morrison [1967] Director

Anglia Enterprise (UK) Limited
Incorporated: 2 October 2007
Previous: Anglia Vehicle Leasing Limited
Net Worth: £37,586 *Total Assets:* £2,887,935
Registered Office: Office 2.18, Harrow Business Centre, 429-433 Pinner Road, Harrow, Middlesex, HA1 4HN
Major Shareholder: Nishanthan Jothinathan
Officers: Nishanthan Jothinathan [1974] Director/Manager [Sri Lankan]

Anglia-Perfumery Ltd.
Incorporated: 16 December 2004
Net Worth Deficit: £2,183 *Total Assets:* £4,512
Registered Office: B508, Tower Bridge Business Complex, 100 Clements Road, London, SE16 4DG
Major Shareholder: Lothar Ruff
Officers: Lothar Ruff [1945] Director/Businessman [German]

Anglo Indian Trading Limited
Incorporated: 13 December 2011 *Employees:* 2
Net Worth: £65,634 *Total Assets:* £605,866
Registered Office: 1 Enterprise Court, Downmill Road, Bracknell, Berks, RG12 1QS
Officers: John Guy Hewitt [1971] Managing Director; Daryl John Sudworth [1967] Director

ANGMG Ltd
Incorporated: 11 February 2019
Registered Office: 39b Plumstead Common Road, London, SE18 3AS
Officers: Miguel Joao, Secretary; Miguel Joao [1985] Director [Angolan]

Angsana Ltd
Incorporated: 28 March 2018
Registered Office: Suite 6, 5 Percy Street, Fitzrovia, London, W1T 1DG
Major Shareholder: Oleg Uperenko
Officers: Oleg Uperenko [1974] Director [Latvian]

Anita Brows Cosmetics Limited
Incorporated: 3 May 2018
Registered Office: 50 Britten Close, Golders Green, London, NW11 7HQ
Shareholders: Adetola Anita Adetoye; Adedayo Dina
Officers: Adetola Anita Adetoye [1991] Director [Irish/Nigerian]; Adedayo Dina [1978] Director

Ank Innovation Limited
Incorporated: 30 January 2019
Registered Office: 48 Birmingham Road, Bromsgrove, Worcs, B61 0DD
Shareholders: Chan Va Lam; Yang Luo
Officers: Chan Va Lam [1966] Director [Portuguese]; Yang Luo [1983] Director [Chinese]

Anne Marie Beauty Products (U.K.) Limited
Incorporated: 20 December 1988
Net Worth Deficit: £26,850 *Total Assets:* £4,670
Registered Office: 1 Market Street, Disley, Cheshire, SK12 2AA
Major Shareholder: Anne-Marie Ovens
Officers: David Ovens, Secretary; Anne-Marie Ovens [1951] Director/Beautician

Annexa Solutions Limited
Incorporated: 9 December 2008 *Employees:* 4
Net Worth: £489,845 *Total Assets:* £652,176
Registered Office: Pinnacle House, 2-10 Rectory Road, Benfleet, Essex, SS7 2ND
Shareholders: Jelena Abramova; Roger Emanuell Green
Officers: Jelena Abromova, Secretary; Jelena Abramova [1976] Director; Roger Emanuell Green [1949] Director

Ansor Supplies Ltd
Incorporated: 16 June 2015
Net Worth: £3,461 *Total Assets:* £7,582
Registered Office: 9 Bown Close, Tilbury Town, Thurrock, Essex, RM18 8EH
Major Shareholder: Alexandra Soremi
Officers: Julius Onyedikachi, Secretary; Alexandra Soremi, Secretary; Alexandra Soremi [1992] Director/Business Executive [Austrian]

Antiageing Haircare Specialists Limited
Incorporated: 26 March 2018
Registered Office: 101 Hampermill Lane, Watford, Herts, WD19 4NX
Major Shareholder: Susan Barbara Maxwell Smith
Officers: Susan Barbara Maxwell Smith [1955] Director

Antian World Limited
Incorporated: 9 August 2016
Registered Office: 26 Old Palace Road, Guildford, Surrey, GU2 7TX
Major Shareholder: Feng Niu
Officers: Feng Niu [1980] Director [Chinese]

Antipodes Europe Limited
Incorporated: 2 January 2019
Registered Office: 49 Greek Street, London, W1D 4EG
Major Shareholder: Elizabeth Janet Barbalich
Officers: Paul David Beare, Secretary; Elizabeth Janet Barbalich [1968] Director [New Zealander]; Zoran John Barbalich [1961] Director [New Zealander]

APC (UK) Limited
Incorporated: 3 June 2014
Registered Office: 90 Stechford Lane, Birmingham, B8 2AN
Major Shareholder: Zahra Hussain
Officers: Ali Younis Ahmed [1973] Commercial Director; Zahra Hussain [1964] Director

Apex Beard Co Ltd
Incorporated: 21 February 2019
Registered Office: 35 Upper Malvern Park, Belfast, BT8 6TE
Major Shareholder: Ryan Michael Catherwood
Officers: Ryan Michael Catherwood [1987] Director/Fitness Trainer

Apex Trading Limited
Incorporated: 10 May 1999
Net Worth: £19,730 *Total Assets:* £273,796
Registered Office: 135 Colindeep Lane, London, NW9 6DD
Shareholder: Akbar Ali Bhanji
Officers: Akbar Ali Bhanji, Secretary; Akbar Ali Bhanji [1958] Director/Trader

Apotheca London Skincare Ltd
Incorporated: 10 April 2017
Registered Office: P O Box 74301, 37e Milner Square, London, N1P 3AG
Major Shareholder: Therese Catherine Rankin
Officers: Therese Catherine Rankin [1981] Director/Solicitor

Apsara Cosmetics Ltd
Incorporated: 15 October 2018
Registered Office: 56 Central Avenue, Welling, Kent, DA16 3BD
Shareholders: Jaspal Kaur; Jujhar Singh Chima
Officers: Jaspal Kaur [1963] Director

Aqolade Ltd
Incorporated: 10 January 2013
Net Worth: £13,038 *Total Assets:* £13,038
Registered Office: 21 Crosscliff, Hemlington, Middlesbrough, Cleveland, TS8 9JJ
Officers: Andreea Gabriela Shaw [1973] Director [Romanian]

Aqua Bleu Limited
Incorporated: 17 September 2002
Net Worth: £7,790 *Total Assets:* £19,860
Registered Office: 70-72 Victoria Road, Ruislip, Middlesex, HA4 0AH
Major Shareholder: Farzana Mitha
Officers: Firoz Akberali Mitha, Secretary; Farzana Mitha [1972] Director/Entrepreneur

Aqua Qualia Limited
Incorporated: 20 April 2015
Net Worth Deficit: £5,070 *Total Assets:* £35,150
Registered Office: 27 Old Gloucester Street, London, WC1N 3AX
Major Shareholder: Jacobus Nicolas Steyn Grobler
Officers: Jacobus Nicolas Steyn Grobler [1985] Director/Fragrance Specialist

Aquabeauty Limited
Incorporated: 3 August 2017
Registered Office: 8 Standard Road, London, NW10 6EU
Major Shareholder: Ningning Tao
Officers: Ningning Tao, Secretary; Ningning Tao [1987] Director [Chinese]

Aquapurity Ltd
Incorporated: 3 September 2018
Registered Office: 414 Perry Road, Nottingham, NG5 1GS
Major Shareholder: Bushra Farid
Officers: Bushra Farid [1981] Director/Self Employed

AR Scents Limited
Incorporated: 9 October 2018
Registered Office: 403 Hornsey Road, London, N19 4DX
Major Shareholder: Ashrafur Rahman
Officers: Ashrafur Rahman [1989] Director/Businessman

Arabian Aroma Limited
Incorporated: 5 March 2018
Registered Office: 59 Kempron Road, East Ham, London, E6 2LG
Shareholder: Senthur Pandian Narayanan
Officers: Senthur Pandian Narayanan [1976] Director

Arahant Ltd
Incorporated: 31 August 2016
Net Worth: £580 *Total Assets:* £697
Registered Office: 77 High Street, Littlehampton, W Sussex, BN17 5AG
Major Shareholder: Tibor Janos Szabo
Officers: Tibor Janos Szabo [1974] Director [Hungarian]

Arbar Ltd
Incorporated: 28 January 2019
Registered Office: 114 St Mary's Road, London, SE15 2DU
Major Shareholder: Rosemary MacGregor
Officers: Rosemary MacGregor [1989] Director

Arbonne UK Limited
Incorporated: 24 March 2006 *Employees:* 75
Net Worth Deficit: £1,251,507 *Total Assets:* £23,843,860
Registered Office: Unit 16 Basset Court, Loake Close, Grange Park, Northampton, NN4 5EZ
Officers: Bernadette Chala, Secretary; Victoria Mary Beckett [1963] Director; Bernadette Chala [1975] Director/SVP, General Counsel [American]; Cary Okawa [1966] Director/SVP, Corporate Controller [American]; Jean-David Schwartz [1974] Director [French]; Astrid Van Ruymbeke [1981] Director [French]

Elizabeth Arden (UK) Ltd
Incorporated: 12 December 2000 *Employees:* 517
Net Worth: £5,112,214 *Total Assets:* £14,282,117
Registered Office: Greater London House, Hampstead Road, London, NW1 7QX
Officers: Yossi Almani [1976] Director/VP, Corp & Securities Law [American]; Mitra O'Neil [1969] Director/EVP, General Counsel [American]; Michael Thomas Sheehan [1964] Director/SVP, Deputy Gen Counsel [American]

Arewa Styles Limited
Incorporated: 28 December 2018
Registered Office: 15 Hinksey Path, Abbeywood, London, SE2 9TB
Major Shareholder: Titilayo Olugunna
Officers: Titilayo Olugunna, Secretary; Titilayo Olugunna [1966] Director

Argan Blossom Ltd
Incorporated: 28 December 2018
Registered Office: 71-75 Shelton Street, Covent Garden, London, WC2H 9JQ
Shareholders: Soukaina Badri; James Elwen
Officers: James Elwen [1974] Director/Lawyer

Argan Care Ltd
Incorporated: 29 March 2018
Registered Office: 71-75 Shelton Street, Covent Garden, London, WC2H 9JQ
Major Shareholder: Tarik Sadni
Officers: Tarik Sadni [1984] Director/SEO Manager [Moroccan]

W. S Argan Limited
Incorporated: 28 May 2013
Net Worth Deficit: £11,201
Registered Office: 148 Elgin Avenue, London, W9 2NT
Major Shareholder: Adam Ladjadj
Officers: Adam Ladjadj [1985] Director/Merchant

Argan Liquid Gold Limited
Incorporated: 17 April 2014
Net Worth Deficit: £25,690 *Total Assets:* £13,810
Registered Office: 41a Bloom Street, Manchester, M1 3LY
Major Shareholder: May Hamid
Officers: May Hamid [1975] Director/Business Development

Argan Secrets Limited
Incorporated: 4 June 2007
Net Worth Deficit: £38,393 *Total Assets:* £3,125
Registered Office: 2 Links Drive, Totteridge, London, N20 8QN
Major Shareholder: Jeremy Lawton
Officers: Jeremy Lawton [1950] Managing Director

Argan Vanity Ltd
Incorporated: 28 April 2014 *Employees:* 1
Net Worth Deficit: £4,916 *Total Assets:* £3,684
Registered Office: 41 Montrose Avenue, Luton, Beds, LU3 1HP
Major Shareholder: Zahil Akram
Officers: Zahil Akram [1980] Director/IT

Arizona Botaniq Limited
Incorporated: 19 October 2016
Net Worth Deficit: £7,703 *Total Assets:* £200
Registered Office: 43 Gaitside Drive, Aberdeen, AB10 7BH
Major Shareholder: Arizona Arizona Brodie
Officers: Arizona Brodie [1992] Director

Ark Inta Ltd
Incorporated: 26 November 2018
Registered Office: 6 North House, Monks Orchard Road, Beckenham, Kent, BR3 3BW
Major Shareholder: Jonathan Ashvin Unimke
Officers: Vincentia Ifeanyi Opara, Secretary; Jonathan Ashvin Unimke [1983] Director/Salesman [Belgian]

Arlenne Ltd
Incorporated: 6 January 2016
Net Worth: £27,486 *Total Assets:* £51,536
Registered Office: 5 Fenside Avenue, Coventry, Warwicks, CV3 5NF
Shareholder: Santa Pozdnakova
Officers: Santa Kalnina [1989] Director [Latvian]

Arna Group Ltd
Incorporated: 25 February 2016
Registered Office: 18 Fiador Apartments, 21 Telegraph Avenue, London, SE10 0TH
Major Shareholder: Irina Rupina
Officers: Irina Rupina [1982] Director/Wholesale [Lithuanian]

Arnest International Limited
Incorporated: 6 June 2011 *Employees:* 6
Net Worth Deficit: £849,000 *Total Assets:* £4,206,000
Registered Office: 5 Riverside Way, Riverside Business Park, Irvine, N Ayrshire, KA11 5DJ
Parent: Barony Universal Products PLC
Officers: Eliot Swan, Secretary; Steven David Groden [1970] Director; Alexandre Matytsine [1958] Director [Russian]; Eliot Swan [1966] Finance Director

Aro-Matic (Scotland) Ltd
Incorporated: 16 January 2018
Registered Office: 6 Woodside Place, Glasgow, G3 7QF
Major Shareholder: Edward Barry Golrdberg
Officers: Edward Barry Goldberg [1958] Director/Consultant

Aroma Actives Limited
Incorporated: 31 October 2012
Net Worth: £267,000 *Total Assets:* £328,000
Registered Office: 4th Floor, Sedley Place, 361 Oxford Street, London, W1C 2JL
Parent: Aromatherapy Investments Limited
Officers: Frank Standish, Secretary; James Edward Higginson [1966] Director; Anna Teal [1978] Director; David Waller [1980] Director

Aroma Dead Sea Limited
Incorporated: 28 February 2019
Registered Office: 2 Llewellyn Road, Leamington Spa, Warwicks, CV31 2BJ
Officers: Evita Svampane [1980] Director/Lawyer [Latvian]

Aroma of Grace Ltd
Incorporated: 15 May 2017
Registered Office: First Floor, 85 Great Portland Street, London, W1W 7LT
Major Shareholder: Oluwakemi Mary Vincent
Officers: Oluwakemi Mary Vincent, Secretary; Oluwakemi Mary Vincent [1969] Director/Business Owner

Aromabar (Scotland) Ltd
Incorporated: 5 December 2017
Registered Office: Unit 9-11 Robertson Street, Barrhead, E Renfrewshire, G78 1QW
Shareholders: Alan Grant; Catherine Grant
Officers: Alan Grant [1963] Director; Catherine Grant [1964] Director

Aromaclub Handmade Skincare Ltd
Incorporated: 20 March 2018
Registered Office: 34 Atalanta Street, Fulham, London, SW6 6TR
Major Shareholder: Marie Ann Powell
Officers: Marie Ann Powell [1962] Director

Aromaderme UK Limited
Incorporated: 2 July 1996
Registered Office: One Fitzroy, 6 Mortimer Street, London, W1T 3JJ
Parent: Estee Lauder UK Holdings Limited
Officers: Edward Robert Hughes, Secretary; Sara Ellen Moss, Secretary [American]; Spencer Gary Smul, Secretary; Alison Claire Day [1971] Finance Director; Pedro Miguel Pons Ester [1969] Director/Corporate Controller [Spanish]

Aromatic Yogi Ltd
Incorporated: 2 July 2018
Registered Office: 10 McKay Grove, Bellshill, N Lanarks, ML4 3EB
Major Shareholder: Angela Claire Elliott
Officers: Angela Claire Elliott [1981] Director/Fitness Trainer

Aromeco Limited
Incorporated: 27 June 2016
Net Worth Deficit: £8,463 *Total Assets:* £371
Registered Office: 119 Rose Lane, Romford, Essex, RM6 5NR
Major Shareholder: Aleksandr Kaigorodcev
Officers: Aleksandr Kaigorodcev [1988] Director/Accountant [Lithuanian]

Arosci Trading Limited
Incorporated: 6 May 2014
Net Worth: £241 *Total Assets:* £66,661
Registered Office: Unit 3 Berwick Courtyard, Berwick St Leonard, Salisbury, Wilts, SP3 5UA
Major Shareholder: Nigel William McCarthy
Officers: Nigel William McCarthy [1955] Director

Arowell Products Ltd
Incorporated: 29 September 2017
Registered Office: 20-22 Wenlock Road, London, N1 7GU
Major Shareholder: Pritha Nikhilesh Deshpande
Officers: Pritha Nikhilesh Deshpande [1973] Director [Indian]

Arrah Ltd
Incorporated: 1 August 2018
Registered Office: 20-22 Wenlock Road, London, N1 7GU
Shareholders: Mohammed Haroon Asif; Rabail Ali
Officers: Rabail Ali [1986] Director; Mohammed Haroon Asif [1995] Director

Array of Scents Ltd
Incorporated: 6 February 2019
Registered Office: 88 Holland Road, London, E6 2EP
Major Shareholder: Shazia Mohamed
Officers: Shazia Mohamed [1992] Director

Arrogant Limited
Incorporated: 8 February 2019
Registered Office: 30 Clayponds Gardens, London, W5 4RE
Major Shareholder: Johann Gabriel Sarmes Daridon
Officers: Johann Gabriel Sarmes Daridon [1982] Director [French]

Arrow Hair & Beauty Supplies Limited
Incorporated: 29 January 1997 *Employees:* 15
Net Worth: £325,265 *Total Assets:* £355,627
Registered Office: Priory Farm, Studley, Warwicks, B80 7BB
Shareholder: Melvyn Alexander Speirs
Officers: Patricia Anne Mary Speirs, Secretary; Melvyn Alexander Speirs [1946] Director

Ars Nova (UK) Limited
Incorporated: 22 October 2001
Net Worth Deficit: £55,192 *Total Assets:* £1,528
Registered Office: 9 Cornes Close, Ashford, Kent, TN24 0LG
Shareholders: M'lle Nelly Hanaig Agossou; Monsieur Xavier Martin
Officers: Brian Leslie Ridpath, Secretary; Nelly Hanaig Agossou [1974] Director [French]

Art Creative Limited
Incorporated: 11 May 2012
Previous: Marketing Solutions London Limited
Net Worth: £25,332 *Total Assets:* £34,645
Registered Office: 67 Melbury Avenue, Norwood Green, Southall, Middlesex, UB2 4HT
Major Shareholder: Lakhwinder Singh Sekhon
Officers: Lakhwinder Singh Sekhon [1981] Director/Mortgage Advisor

Art-Eclair Limited
Incorporated: 31 October 2016
Registered Office: 25 Glenavon Road, London, E15 4DE
Major Shareholder: Sylwia Monika Brzeska
Officers: Sylwia Monika Brzeska [1979] Director/Beauty and Nails [Polish]

Arthur Michel Cosmetics Distribution Ltd
Incorporated: 21 February 2019
Registered Office: 70 Alkham Road, London, N16 6XF
Major Shareholder: Arthur Michel Besnard
Officers: Arthur Michel Besnard [1991] Director [French]

Artifact Skin Company Limited
Incorporated: 4 May 2017
Registered Office: 1st Floor, 2 Woodberry Grove, Finchley, London, N12 0DR
Major Shareholder: Elie Nehme
Officers: Elie Nehme [1977] Director/Owner of Cosmetics Company [Canadian]

Arvense Skin Care Ltd
Incorporated: 31 May 2017
Registered Office: 16 Pembridge Gardens, London, W2 4DU
Major Shareholder: Hannah Lamb
Officers: Hannah Lamb [1976] Director

Asabeauty Ltd
Incorporated: 25 July 2012 *Employees:* 6
Previous: Andranik Sargis Abarian Ltd
Net Worth: £84,616 *Total Assets:* £383,133
Registered Office: Stephenson House, Richard Street, Hetton-le-Hole, Co Durham, DH5 9HW
Shareholders: Andranik Abarian; Narine Safarian; Andranik Abarian
Officers: Andranik Abarian [1969] Director

Asadilari Limited
Incorporated: 21 December 2015
Registered Office: Unit 59 Cromwell Industrial Estate, Staffa Road, London, E10 7QZ
Major Shareholder: Hamed Asadi Lari
Officers: Hamed Asadi Lari [1990] Director [Iranian]

Asante Distributors Limited
Incorporated: 2 February 2018
Net Worth: £100 *Total Assets:* £100
Registered Office: 21 Jesmond Way, Stanmore, Harrow, Middlesex, HA7 4QR
Shareholders: Mahmoud Jiva Rayani; Ashwin Karsandas Padia; Kim Patrick Rawson
Officers: Ashwin Karsandas Padia [1958] Director [Kenyan]; Kim Patrick Rawson [1955] Director; Mahmoud Jiva Rayani [1952] Director/Wine Merchant

Asase Tree Ltd
Incorporated: 25 June 2018
Registered Office: 19 Sherwood House, Harlow, Essex, CM18 6NN
Major Shareholder: Isaiah Nimako
Officers: Isaiah Nimako [1977] Director/Media Production

Asaya Cosmeceuticals Limited
Incorporated: 11 February 2019
Registered Office: First Floor, 85 Great Portland Street, London, W1W 7LT
Major Shareholder: Natalie Echeverria
Officers: Natalie Echeverria [1970] Director

Ascenttial Ltd
Incorporated: 7 January 2019
Registered Office: 37 Beatty Road, Stanmore, Middlesex, HA7 4EU
Major Shareholder: Hiten Kalyanji
Officers: Hiten Kalyanji [1977] Director/Bank Manager

Asel Ltd
Incorporated: 8 January 2019
Registered Office: Unit 2, 130 Broughton Street, Manchester, M8 8AN
Major Shareholder: Zhong Wu Lin
Officers: Zhong Wu Lin [1974] Director

Asenov Traders Ltd
Incorporated: 9 November 2018
Registered Office: 47 Park Road, London, N15 3HR
Officers: Iliyan Asenov Asenov [1993] Director [Bulgarian]

Ashley & Co UK Ltd
Incorporated: 29 March 2017
Net Worth: £100 *Total Assets:* £100
Registered Office: 10 John Street, London, WC1N 2EB
Shareholders: Jeremy Patrick Scott; Jacquiline Louise Carolyn Ashley
Officers: Jacqueline Louise Carolyn Ashley [1976] Director [New Zealander]; Jeremy Patrick Scott [1975] Director [New Zealander]

Ashmira Botanica Ltd
Incorporated: 8 November 2016 *Employees:* 2
Net Worth Deficit: £49,540 *Total Assets:* £51,302
Registered Office: Unit 1d Blackdown Business Park, Sylvan Road, Wellington, Somerset, TA21 8ST
Major Shareholder: Tracey Anne Smith
Officers: Tracey Anne Smith [1966] Director/Wholesaler of Beauty Products

Ashymo Ltd
Incorporated: 15 January 2018
Registered Office: Flat 33, Attilburgh House, St Saviours Estate, London, SE1 3DL
Officers: Sherif Adebayo Olorunfemi [1986] Director/Hair Treatment [Nigerian]

Asia Nails and Beauty Supply Ltd
Incorporated: 19 September 2018
Registered Office: c/o Absolute Accountants Ltd, Suite K, 19-25 Salisbury Square, Hatfield, Herts, AL9 5BT
Major Shareholder: Thi Hong Nhung Nguyen
Officers: Thi Hong Nhung Nguyen [1989] Director [Vietnamese]

Asian Fashions Ltd
Incorporated: 6 July 2016
Registered Office: 905 Romford Road, London, E12 5JT
Officers: Abid Hussain [1967] Director/Businessman

Asifall Ltd
Incorporated: 13 July 2018
Registered Office: 171 High Street, Arbroath, Angus, DD11 1DY
Major Shareholder: Asif Asif Naseer
Officers: Naseer Naseer Asif [1979] Director

Askett & English Ltd
Incorporated: 9 February 2011
Net Worth: £50   Total Assets: £50
Registered Office: Mercury House, 19-21 Chapel Street, Marlow, Bucks, SL7 3HN
Major Shareholder: Matthew David Jeffs
Officers: Matthew David Jeffs [1962] Director

Aspects Beauty Company Limited
Incorporated: 21 December 1993   Employees: 212
Net Worth: £1,229,783   Total Assets: £5,913,270
Registered Office: Railview Lofts, 19c Commercial Road, Eastbourne, E Sussex, BN21 3XE
Officers: Andrew John Stanley Field, Secretary/Director; Jonathan Dunn [1957] Commercial Director; Andrew John Stanley Field [1962] Director; Andrew James Benjamin Jackson [1971] Business Analysis Director; James Leonard Thomas Jackson [1942] Managing Director; Jill Adrienne Jackson-Hill [1953] Managing Director; Geoffrey Howard Matthews [1953] Director/Corporate Financier; Janey Emma Pumphrey [1966] Brands and Business Strategy Director

ASR Aesthetics Ltd
Incorporated: 27 December 2017
Registered Office: Murdoch Suite No 6, Clinton Road, Redruth, Cornwall, TR15 2QE
Major Shareholder: Amber Thomas
Officers: Amber Thomas [1992] Director/Account Manager

Aster & Bay Ltd.
Incorporated: 31 August 2016
Net Worth: £4,500   Total Assets: £4,500
Registered Office: The Biscuit Factory, 4-6 Anderson Place, Edinburgh, EH6 5NP
Major Shareholder: Glen Hammond
Officers: Erin Hammond, Secretary; Glen Hammond [1983] Director/Owner

Asurex Limited
Incorporated: 20 March 2002   Employees: 7
Net Worth: £3,577,474   Total Assets: £4,027,577
Registered Office: Suite D, Astor House, 282 Lichfield Road, Four Oaks, Sutton Coldfield, W Midlands, B74 2UG
Shareholders: Pankaj Sodha; Naina Sodha
Officers: Naina Sodha, Secretary; Naina Sodha [1957] Director; Pankaj Sodha [1953] Director/Pharmacist

ASVR Bebidas Limited
Incorporated: 14 August 2017
Registered Office: 42-46 Station Road, Edgware, Middlesex, HA8 7AB
Major Shareholder: Sanjay Chandubhai Patel
Officers: Sanjay Chandubhai Patel, Secretary; Sanjay Chandubhai Patel [1965] Director/Trader

Atarah Beauty Collection Ltd
Incorporated: 15 November 2017
Registered Office: Flat 12, Sillitoe House, Colville Estate, London, N1 5NH
Shareholders: Letticia Donkor; Benedicta Korantemg
Officers: Letticia Donkor [1990] Director/Accountant; Benedicta Koranteng [1991] Director/Paralegal

Atkinson London 1799 Ltd
Incorporated: 2 December 2016   Employees: 5
Net Worth: £191,135   Total Assets: £856,114
Registered Office: 17 Grosvenor Street, Mayfair, London, W1K 4QG
Officers: Giovanni Borri [1943] Director [Italian]

Atlantic Beauty Store Limited
Incorporated: 22 July 2014
Net Worth: £6,519   Total Assets: £13,779
Registered Office: 71 Commercial Road, Newport, NP20 2PF
Major Shareholder: Djibi Jassey
Officers: Djibi Jassey [1977] Director/Businessman

Atlantis Research Limited
Incorporated: 8 June 2016
Registered Office: Richmond House, 29 Parkfield Avenue, Ashton on Ribble, Preston, Lancs, PR2 1JB
Major Shareholder: Andrew Croft
Officers: Andrew Croft [1966] Director/Consultant

Atlas Global Trade Ltd
Incorporated: 11 January 2019
Registered Office: 85 Great Portland Street, London, W1W 7LT
Major Shareholder: Theodoros Tsompanidis
Officers: Theodoros Tsompanidis [1965] Director [Greek]

Attar Mist Ltd
Incorporated: 7 March 2013
Net Worth Deficit: £11,730   Total Assets: £11,220
Registered Office: 35 Cofield Road, Sutton Coldfield, W Midlands, B73 5SD
Officers: Yasir Rafi [1976] Director/IT Manager; Humaira Yasir Rafi [1976] Director/Housewife

Attraxion Cosmetics Ltd.
Incorporated: 21 May 2018
Registered Office: 25 Pantbach Road, Cardiff, CF14 1TU
Officers: Kirsty Diane Denver [1989] Managing Director

Aube Laboratories Ltd
Incorporated: 8 February 2018
Registered Office: 27 Old Gloucester Street, London, WC1N 3AX
Parent: Swit Pharma SP Z O.O
Officers: Waldemar Siwak [1969] Director [Polish]

Aurelia Skincare (International) Limited
Incorporated: 15 March 2013
Net Worth: £65,530   Total Assets: £142,750
Registered Office: 100 Cambridge Grove, Hammersmith, London, W6 0LE
Officers: Laetitia Marie Edmee Jehanne Albertini Ep. Garnier [1980] Director/Chief Strategy Officer of The H&H Group [French]; Fei Luo [1964] Director/Chief Executive Officer of The H&H Group [Chinese]

Aurelia Skincare Limited
Incorporated: 20 March 2012
Net Worth: £811,410   Total Assets: £1,060,000
Registered Office: 100 Cambridge Grove, London, W6 0LE
Officers: Laetitia Marie Edmee Jehanne Albertini Ep. Garnier [1980] Director/Chief Strategy Officer of The H&H Group [French]; Fei Luo [1964] Director/Chief Executive Officer of The H&H Group [Chinese]

Aurora Spa Health and Beauty Limited
Incorporated: 2 March 2015
Net Worth Deficit: £11,120 *Total Assets:* £14,120
Registered Office: 30 Trosley Avenue, Gravesend, Kent, DA11 7QW
Shareholders: Stephen Rogerson; Atanaska Rogerson
Officers: Atanaska Rogerson, Secretary; Atanaska Rogerson [1981] Director [Bulgarian]; Stephen Rogerson [1973] Director

Aurum Argan Ltd
Incorporated: 25 January 2017
Net Worth Deficit: £13,843 *Total Assets:* £10,679
Registered Office: Broom House, 39-43 London Road, Hadleigh, Benfleet, Essex, SS7 2QL
Major Shareholder: Ali Rezaei
Officers: Ali Rezaei [1986] Director/Application Developer

Aurum D Limited
Incorporated: 15 March 2018
Registered Office: 7 Lynwood Court, Priestlands Place, Lymington, Hants, SO41 9GA
Major Shareholder: Diana Jenner
Officers: Diana Jenner [1982] Director

Aurum Essence Ltd
Incorporated: 11 September 2018
Registered Office: 143 Ashfield Street, London, E1 3EX
Major Shareholder: Kamal Hassan Shumon
Officers: Kamal Hassan Shumon [1996] Director

Australian Bodycare U.K. Limited
Incorporated: 13 February 1989 *Employees:* 8
Net Worth: £1,007,596 *Total Assets:* £1,727,205
Registered Office: Bodycare House, Danegate, Eridge Green, Tunbridge Wells, Kent, TN3 9JA
Parent: Ken Lamacraft Marketing Ltd
Officers: Kevin Michael Gambrill [1976] Director/Accountant; Fiona McMillan Peerless [1979] Director/Operations Manager

Autoscentsco Ltd
Incorporated: 13 February 2019
Registered Office: Violet House, Chapel Lane, Bledlow, Princes Risborough, Bucks, HP27 9QG
Shareholders: Charlie Barker; Michael Powers
Officers: Michael Powers, Secretary; Michael Powers [2001] Director/Self Employed

Ava Corporations Ltd
Incorporated: 7 July 2017
Registered Office: 14 Abbey Street, Armagh, BT61 7DX
Major Shareholder: Collin Grayson
Officers: Collin Grayson [1970] Director/Businessman

Available Beauty Ltd
Incorporated: 12 October 2017
Registered Office: 20-22 Wenlock Road, London, N1 7GU
Major Shareholder: Kevin Smith
Officers: Kevin Smith [1980] Director/Lettings Branch Manager

Aveda Limited
Incorporated: 23 March 1999
Registered Office: One Fitzroy, 6 Mortimer Street, London, W1T 3JJ
Parent: Estee Lauder UK Holdings Ltd.
Officers: Edward Robert Hughes, Secretary; Sara Ellen Moss, Secretary [American]; Spencer Gary Smul, Secretary; Alison Claire Day [1971] Finance Director; Barbara de Laere [1976] Director/Senior Vice President, Global General Manager [Belgian]; Philippe Michel Warnery [1970] Director/Corporate General Manager [French]

Avee Ltd
Incorporated: 30 June 2017
Registered Office: 272 Bath Street, Glasgow, G2 4JR
Major Shareholder: Arnesto Goncalves Segredo
Officers: Arnesto Goncalves Segredo [1965] Director/Engineer [Dutch]

Avelena Ltd
Incorporated: 16 November 2018
Registered Office: Unit 6 Premacto Business Estate, Queensmead Road, Loudwater, High Wycombe, Bucks, HP10 9XA
Major Shareholder: Georgina Avalina McLean
Officers: Georgina Avalina McLean [1985] Marketing Director

Aviva Health Solutions Limited
Incorporated: 16 March 2018
Registered Office: Kemp House, 160 City Road, London, EC1V 2NX
Major Shareholder: Ashley Crowne
Officers: Ashley Crowne [1968] Director

Awobajo Brother's Limited
Incorporated: 7 September 1999
Registered Office: 111 Rowdowns Road, Dagenham, Essex, RM9 6NH
Officers: Adewale Olukayode Awobajo, Secretary; Adewale Olukayode Awobajo [1972] Director/Manager; Jimmy Babajide Awobajo [1977] Director/Sales Assistant

Axa Beauty World Limited
Incorporated: 8 January 2019
Registered Office: 1146 High Road, London, N20 0RA
Parent: Milvio II Limited
Officers: Nadi Alkhouri, Secretary; Nadi Alkhouri [1980] Director/Businessman [Syrian]; Guiseppe Piccirillo [1954] Director/Businessman [Italian]

Aya Natural (UK) Limited
Incorporated: 22 January 2018
Registered Office: 20-22 Wenlock Road, London, N1 7GU
Major Shareholder: Graham Walton
Officers: Graham Walton [1968] Managing Director

Ayaon Ltd
Incorporated: 26 February 2018
Registered Office: 71-75 Shelton Street, London, WC2H 9JQ
Officers: Ayan Abokor [1981] Director [Dutch]

Ayhamco Limited
Incorporated: 2 January 2019
Registered Office: 115 Baker Street, London, W1U 7EX
Major Shareholder: Ayham Awad
Officers: Ayham Awad [1976] Director/General Manager [Australian]

Aysthetics Limited
Incorporated: 6 February 2017
Registered Office: c/o ADL, 37th Floor, Canada Square, London, E14 5AA
Parent: Nail Polish Express Ltd
Officers: Quang Minh Nguyen [1993] Director

Ayursavvyveda Limited
Incorporated: 9 December 2016
Net Worth Deficit: £7,400 *Total Assets:* £987,000
Registered Office: 97 Alderley Road, Wilmslow, Cheshire, SK9 1PT
Parent: Narkam Investments Ltd
Officers: Renu Misra [1976] Director

Azaleo Limited
Incorporated: 24 December 2018
Registered Office: First Floor, 85 Great Portland Street, London, W1W 7LT
Major Shareholder: Soraya Bakhtiar
Officers: Soraya Bakhtiar, Secretary; Soraya Bakhtiar [1989] Director/Founder [Swiss]

Azhar Academy Limited
Incorporated: 7 March 2000
Net Worth: £72,980 *Total Assets:* £283,220
Registered Office: Khudhail Industrial Complex, 54-68 Little Ilford Lane, Manor Park, London, E12 5QA
Officers: Muhammed Musaddiq Iqbal, Secretary; Bilal Mohammed Gangat [1971] Director; Ismail Gangat [1970] Director/Principal; Maksud Ahmed Gangat [1969] Director; Ebrahim Hasan Sader [1975] Director [South African]

Azik Group Ltd
Incorporated: 15 June 2018
Registered Office: 6 Dowsing Court, Norwich, NR7 0RW
Major Shareholder: Damian Wieslaw Azikiewicz
Officers: Damian Wieslaw Azikiewicz [1982] Director [Polish]

Azur Interiors Limited
Incorporated: 9 September 2014
Net Worth Deficit: £1,019 *Total Assets:* £868
Registered Office: 42a High Street, Broadstairs, Kent, CT10 1JT
Shareholders: Ines Pinder-White; Jonathan Charles Pinder-White; Jonathan Charles Pinder-White
Officers: Jonathan Charles Pinder-White [1963] Director; George Henry Rusiecki [1961] Director

Azzy London Ltd
Incorporated: 20 May 2015
Net Worth Deficit: £2,162 *Total Assets:* £3,230
Registered Office: The Lodge, Old Warren Farm, Camp Road, London, SW19 4UR
Shareholders: Brian Jason Hanover; Mary Gale Hanover
Officers: Brian Jason Hanover [1970] Financial Director; Mary Gale Hanover [1965] Director/Temporary Tattoos

B & D Fragrance Limited Company Ltd
Incorporated: 26 January 2018
Registered Office: 212 Abbotsford Drive, St Anns, Nottingham, NG3 1ND
Major Shareholder: Iyobo Osazuwa
Officers: Iyobo Osazuwa [1990] Director

B & F Ventures Ltd
Incorporated: 10 May 2018
Registered Office: 9 Bushell Place, Preston, Lancs, PR1 3TQ
Shareholders: Freya Alice Mayo; Bryony Letitia Watson
Officers: Freya Alice Mayo [1993] Director/Businesswoman; Bryony Letitia Watson [1993] Director/Businesswoman

B & O Natural Cosmetics Ltd
Incorporated: 9 September 2013
Net Worth: £8,597 *Total Assets:* £27,691
Registered Office: 20-22 Wenlock Road, London, N1 7GU
Shareholders: Barbara Toth; Oliver Csernatony
Officers: Oliver Csernatony [1972] Director [Hungarian]; Barbara Toth [1976] Director [Hungarian]

B Luxury Scents Ltd
Incorporated: 9 January 2019
Registered Office: 22 Everest Close, Great Sutton, Ellesmere Port, Cheshire, CH66 2RH
Major Shareholder: Luke Daniel Rochell
Officers: Luke Daniel Rochell [1989] Director/Security Guard

B. Silki Naturally Ltd
Incorporated: 18 October 2017
Registered Office: 62d Clifford Road, Barnet, Herts, EN5 5NY
Major Shareholder: Nancy Tanscia Smith
Officers: Nancy Tanscia Smith [1973] Director

B.Cosmetics Ltd
Incorporated: 4 February 2019
Registered Office: 1 Bailey Crescent, Newport, NP18 2BL
Major Shareholder: Rebecca Kate Bolton
Officers: Rebecca Kate Bolton [1995] Director/Beautician

B.Me Skincare Ltd
Incorporated: 12 October 2018
Registered Office: Meriton Foundry, Meriton Street, Bristol, BS2 0SZ
Major Shareholder: Veronika Korytakova
Officers: Veronika Korytakova [1981] Director/Administrator [Czech]

B2B Beauty UK Limited
Incorporated: 24 November 2017
Registered Office: 51 Greendyke Street, Glasgow, G1 5PX
Major Shareholder: Paul Wilson
Officers: Paul Wilson [1984] Director/Sales

Back To Eve Ltd
Incorporated: 23 January 2019
Registered Office: 32 Thorndon Close, Orpington, Kent, BR5 2SJ
Major Shareholder: Annabel Eve Gladstone Allen
Officers: Annabel Eve Gladstone Allen [1973] Director/Formulator

Bad Mermaid Limited
Incorporated: 7 August 2017
Registered Office: The Old Vicarage, Church Street, Baslow, Derbys, DE45 1RY
Major Shareholder: Zoe Lukic
Officers: Zoe Lukic, Secretary; Zoe Lukic [1994] Director/Business Owner

Bains and Daughters Limited
Incorporated: 6 November 2006
Registered Office: 449 Green Lane, Coventry, Warwicks, CV3 6EL
Major Shareholder: Gurdeep Singh Bains
Officers: Gurdeep Singh Bains [1963] Director

Bali Secrets Ltd
Incorporated: 15 December 2016
Registered Office: Colman House, Station Road, Knowle, Solihull, W Midlands, B93 0HL
Major Shareholder: Martin Leitner
Officers: Laurence John Collins [1972] Director/Accountant; Martin Leitner [1980] Director [Austrian]

Balm Balm Limited
Incorporated: 18 March 2011
Previous: Natura Distribution Limited
Net Worth Deficit: £2,282 *Total Assets:* £6
Registered Office: 1 Middlewich Road, Holmes Chapel, Crewe, Cheshire, CW4 7EA
Parent: Amarya Limited
Officers: Sonia Myung-Hee White [1973] Sales Director [German]

Balmain Hair UK Ltd
Incorporated: 26 February 2003 *Employees:* 22
Net Worth: £332,868 *Total Assets:* £489,471
Registered Office: Unit 4 North Crescent Industrial Park, Diplocks Way, Hailsham, E Sussex, BN27 3JF
Shareholder: Paul Stephen Reily
Officers: Paul Stephen Reilly, Secretary; Richard Guliker [1971] Director [Dutch]; Steward Anton Guliker [1969] Director [Dutch]; Paul Stephen Reilly [1954] Director/Sales & Marketing

Balmonds Skincare Ltd
Incorporated: 31 January 2018
Registered Office: Unit 7 Westergate Business Centre, Westergate Road, Brighton, BN2 4QN
Shareholders: Andrew Martin Gerrie; Alison Margaret Hawksley
Officers: Andrew Martin Gerrie [1963] Director

Baltica Beauty Professional Limited
Incorporated: 19 June 2017
Registered Office: 93 Dewis House, Riley Square, Coventry, Warwicks, CV2 1LW
Officers: Gita Grostina [1960] Director/Sales Woman [Latvian]

Bambi & Co Ltd
Incorporated: 24 April 2017
Registered Office: 20-22 Wenlock Road, London, N1 7GU
Shareholders: Mariam Ogunbambi; Rafiqat Ogunbambi
Officers: Mariam Ogunbambi [1988] Director/Project Manager; Rafiqat Ogunbambi [1992] Director/Administrative Assistant

Banafa for Oud and Perfume Ltd
Incorporated: 6 February 2019
Registered Office: 395 Seven Sisters Road, London, N15 6RD
Major Shareholder: Abdulla Abdulkhaliq Abdulla Banafa
Officers: Abdulla Abdulkhaliq Abdulla Banafa [1986] Director

Barber & Salon Supplies Ltd
Incorporated: 13 September 2017
Net Worth: £10,370 *Total Assets:* £48,140
Registered Office: 2c Rossbank Road, Rossmore Industrial Estate, Ellesmere Port, Cheshire, CH65 3AN
Shareholder: Nesat Durak
Officers: Nesat Durak [1977] Director [Turkish]

Barbers House Ltd
Incorporated: 12 October 2018
Registered Office: Flat 1, 26 Gordon Road, Margate, Kent, CT9 2DN
Major Shareholder: Attila Szucs
Officers: Attila Szucs [1983] Director/Printer [Slovak]

Barbers Warehouse Ltd
Incorporated: 14 February 2018
Registered Office: 6 Mill Street, Birmingham, B6 4BS
Major Shareholder: Kemal Ciftci
Officers: Kemal Ciftci [1974] Director

Bare Cosmetics Ltd
Incorporated: 15 January 2018
Registered Office: Suite 37, Dingwall Road, Croydon, Surrey, CR0 2LX
Major Shareholder: Leslie Hugh Wilson
Officers: Kimberley Jane Brown [1974] Director; Benjamin Piers Wilson [1981] Director

Bare Kind Limited
Incorporated: 8 May 2018
Registered Office: 6 Torrington Close, Mereworth, Maidstone, Kent, ME18 5LQ
Major Shareholder: Lucy Victoria Jeffrey
Officers: Lucy Victoria Jeffrey [1994] Director/Banker

Barefaced Beauty Ltd
Incorporated: 17 May 2005
Net Worth: £3,990 *Total Assets:* £58,020
Registered Office: Second Floor, 1 Church Square, Leighton Buzzard, Beds, LU7 1AE
Major Shareholder: Nadine Anderson
Officers: Nadine Anderson [1971] Director

Barnsley Card Ltd
Incorporated: 25 February 2016
Previous: Winchpharma (Consumer Products) Ltd
Net Worth Deficit: £64,810 *Total Assets:* £15,070
Registered Office: 15 Queen Square, Leeds, LS2 8AJ
Parent: Camden Kaylock Holdings Ltd
Officers: Nathan Joseph Winch [1990] Director

Base Pro Artists Ltd
Incorporated: 9 May 2014
Net Worth Deficit: £7,522 *Total Assets:* £26,184
Registered Office: Golford Place, Tenterden Road, Golford, Cranbrook, Kent, TN17 3PA
Major Shareholder: Natalie Cahill
Officers: Natalie Cahill, Secretary; Natalie Cahill [1987] Director/Makeup Artist

Basic Needs Ltd
Incorporated: 2 May 2013
Net Worth: £120,260 *Total Assets:* £279,540
Registered Office: Avery House, 8 Avery Hill Road, New Eltham, London, SE9 2BD
Shareholders: Terence William Barker; Christine Elizabeth Barker
Officers: Christine Elizabeth Barker [1946] Director; Terence William Barker [1948] Director

Batalveez Ltd
Incorporated: 8 August 2013
Net Worth Deficit: £6,252 *Total Assets:* £45,887
Registered Office: 83 Ducie Street, Manchester, M1 2JQ
Major Shareholder: Mubeen Haider
Officers: Mubeen Haider [1987] Director [Pakistani]

Bath Bombs and Beyond Limited
Incorporated: 5 May 2017
Registered Office: 58 Mulliner Street, Coventry, Warwicks, CV6 5EU
Shareholders: Aman Mann; Paris Robertson
Officers: Aman Mann, Secretary; Paris Robertson, Secretary; Aman Mann [1988] Director; Paris Robertson [1994] Director

Bath Spa Skincare Limited
Incorporated: 8 January 2010
Net Worth Deficit: £9,842 *Total Assets:* £10,523
Registered Office: 2 Westhall Road, Bath, BA1 3BQ
Officers: Sally Elizabeth Merrett [1969] Director

Bayan Ltd
Incorporated: 19 November 2018
Registered Office: Rayne Thatch, North Road, Leigh Woods, Bristol, BS8 3PJ
Major Shareholder: Enam Bagedo
Officers: Kyriakos Kyvelos, Secretary; Enam Bagedo [1972] Director

Bays International Limited
Incorporated: 1 June 2012 *Employees:* 12
Previous: Bays Distribution International Limited
Net Worth Deficit: £211,894 *Total Assets:* £367,917
Registered Office: 37a Oxford Road, Oxford, OX4 2EN
Major Shareholder: Sohail Ahmed
Officers: Uzma Sohail, Secretary; Sohail Ahmed [1968] Managing Director [Pakistani]; Ammar Sohail [1994] Director/Student [Pakistani]; Bashaar Sohail [1997] Director/Student [Pakistani]

BBA Products Limited
Incorporated: 31 March 2016
Net Worth Deficit: £256,587 *Total Assets:* £196,759
Registered Office: Westminster House, Denton Wharf, Mark Lane, Gravesend, Kent, DA12 2PL
Shareholders: Trevor Studd; Westminster Gulf Co. W.L.L
Officers: Kevin James Clifford [1963] Director; Trevor Studd [1973] Director [New Zealander]

Bbeauty Lounge Cosmetics Limited
Incorporated: 1 August 2008
Previous: Shoe Star Limited
Registered Office: Trilogy Suite, 9 Church Street, Wednesfield, Wolverhampton, W Midlands, WV11 1SR
Shareholders: Chad William Burgin; Gurjit Singh Chaggar
Officers: Chad William Burgin [1987] Director; Gurjit Singh Chaggar [1966] Director

Bbeauty Lounge Limited
Incorporated: 30 March 2017
Registered Office: Trilogy Suite, 9 Church Street, Wednesfield, Wolverhampton, W Midlands, WV11 1SR
Major Shareholder: Chad William Burgin
Officers: Chad William Burgin [1987] Director

BBT Products Limited
Incorporated: 13 June 2016
Net Worth Deficit: £4,773 *Total Assets:* £6,203
Registered Office: 1 Audley Grove, Bath, BA1 3BS
Major Shareholder: Paolo Francis Del-Greco
Officers: Paolo Francis Del-Greco [1982] Director/Accountant

BC (PVT) Ltd
Incorporated: 10 March 2018
Registered Office: Office 4, 219 Kensington High Street, Kensington, London, W8 6BD
Shareholders: Dimuth Prasanna Jagodaarachchi; Dilani Nirosha Jayanetti
Officers: Dilani Nirosha Jayanetti, Secretary; Dimuth Prasanna Jagodaarachchi [1970] Managing Director [Sri Lankan]; Dilani Nirosha Jayanetti [1972] Director [Sri Lankan]

The Bcara Ltd
Incorporated: 6 November 2018
Registered Office: 7 London Plane House, 10 Teasel Way, London, E15 3BY
Major Shareholder: Frisca Gobert
Officers: Frisca Gobert [1980] Managing Director [French]

Be Fairall Limited
Incorporated: 5 December 2018
Registered Office: 6th Floor, Amp House, Dingwall Road, Croydon, Surrey, CR0 2LX
Shareholders: Ghulam Mustafa; Adeel Rubani
Officers: Ghulam Mustafa [1979] Director/Businessman; Adeel Rubani [1982] Director/Businessman

Be Fast Innovation Services Limited
Incorporated: 14 December 2018
Registered Office: 13-15 Regent Street, Nottingham, NG1 5BS
Shareholders: Mark Curry; Samantha Murton
Officers: Mark Curry [1982] Creative Director; Samantha Murton [1972] Director/Brand Development

Be Savvy Ltd
Incorporated: 16 April 2018
Registered Office: 66 Seymour Grove, Manchester, M16 0LN
Shareholders: Muhammad Ijaz; Muhammad Aamir Naveed
Officers: Muhammad Ijaz [1977] Director; Muhammad Aamir Naveed [1978] Director [Pakistani]

Beached Limited
Incorporated: 2 May 2017
Net Worth: £228,200 *Total Assets:* £241,170
Registered Office: 11 Staple Inn, London, WC1V 7QH
Major Shareholder: Megan Katie Gallagher
Officers: Tracy Anne de Groose [1968] Director/Chair; Megan Katie Gallagher [1988] Director [British/Australian]; John Mark Swales [1956] Finance Director

Beaming White Ltd
Incorporated: 19 January 2011
Net Worth: £1,015 *Total Assets:* £1,015
Registered Office: 4 Magellan Terrace, Gatwick Road, Crawley, W Sussex, RH10 9PJ
Major Shareholder: Luis Lajous
Officers: Luis Lajous [1969] Director [Canadian]

Beanies Beauty Lab Ltd
Incorporated: 30 August 2018
Registered Office: 28 Granville Road, Gravesend, Kent, DA11 0JT
Major Shareholder: Sabina Dewsbury-Ennis
Officers: Sabina Dewsbury-Ennis [1988] Director/Laboratory Technician

Bear Journal Limited
Incorporated: 14 September 2017
Registered Office: 71-75 Shelton Street, Covent Garden, London, WC2H 9JQ
Shareholders: Gary Cunningham; Samuel Leetham; Saasha Burns
Officers: Samuel Leetham, Secretary; Saasha Burns [1989] Creative Director [Australian]; Samuel Leetham [1989] Director/Chief Executive Officer [Australian]

Beard and Bones UK Limited
Incorporated: 24 August 2018
Registered Office: 256 Old Laira Road, Plymouth, PL3 6AF
Shareholders: Daniel Thomas Henders; Jake Daniel Luke Grant-Jones
Officers: Jake Daniel Luke Grant-Jones [1996] Director/Businessman; Daniel Thomas Henders [1995] Director/Salesman

Beard Gang Ltd
Incorporated: 24 August 2018
Registered Office: Kemp House, 160 City Road, London, EC1V 2NX
Major Shareholder: Jagdeep Singh
Officers: Jagdeep Singh [1986] Director/Manager

Beard Nature Limited
Incorporated: 13 February 2017
Registered Office: 82a Delce Road, Rochester, Kent, ME1 2DH
Officers: Edgars Miezitis [1987] Director [Latvian]

The Beard of Attraction Ltd
Incorporated: 1 August 2018
Registered Office: 1 Coventry Close, Rochester, Kent, ME2 2QZ
Major Shareholder: Mustafa Eren Pertev
Officers: Mustafa Eren Pertev [1982] Director/Editor

Beard Zone Ltd
Incorporated: 6 April 2017
Net Worth Deficit: £1,790 *Total Assets:* £15,000
Registered Office: 9 Holt Street, Crewe, Cheshire, CW1 3AY
Major Shareholder: Roland Resch
Officers: Roland Resch [1984] Director [Hungarian]

Beatnut Butter Ltd
Incorporated: 25 October 2017
Registered Office: 20-22 Wenlock Road, London, N1 7GU
Major Shareholder: Hannelore Lemmerhofer
Officers: Markus Therre [1967] Director/Manager [German]

Beau Belle Brushes Ltd
Incorporated: 15 July 2016
Net Worth Deficit: £535 *Total Assets:* £9,144
Registered Office: 23 Gores Marsh Road, Bristol, BS3 2PF
Major Shareholder: Lauren Johns
Officers: Lauren Johns [1990] Managing Director

Mahc Beau UK & Europe Ltd
Incorporated: 1 May 2018
Registered Office: Flat 2, Fiske Court, Lansdowne Road, London, N17 0NA
Major Shareholder: Olumide Fred Abayomi Sanya
Officers: Olumide Fred Abayomi Sanya [1981] Director

Beaute Prestige International Ltd
Incorporated: 14 April 2000
Previous: Shiseido Group UK Limited
Net Worth: £600,000 *Total Assets:* £600,000
Registered Office: Third Floor, The Broadgate Tower, 20 Primrose Street, London, EC2A 2RS
Parent: Shiseido Company, Limited
Officers: Eric Henry [1955] Director [French]

Beautessential Limited
Incorporated: 20 September 2018
Registered Office: Unit 1 The Glassworks, Skeoge Industrial Estate, Londonderry, BT48 8SE
Shareholders: John Doherty; Colette Doherty; Lisa McDermott
Officers: Colette Doherty [1980] Director [Irish]; John Doherty [1987] Director [Irish]; Lisa McDermott [1980] Director [Irish]

Beautifect Ltd
Incorporated: 3 February 2017
Registered Office: 71-75 Shelton Street, Covent Garden, London, WC2H 9JQ
Major Shareholder: Tara Lalvani
Officers: Dr Tara Lalvani [1979] Director

Beautiful Body Limited
Incorporated: 17 November 2011
Net Worth: £477,946 *Total Assets:* £547,213
Registered Office: 20 Melbourne Avenue, Fleetwood, Lancs, FY7 8AY
Shareholder: Jessica Brookes
Officers: Jessica Brookes [1989] Director; Scott Stanley Remblance [1982] Director

Beautiful By Nature Ltd
Incorporated: 3 July 2018
Registered Office: 71-75 Shelton Street, Covent Garden, London, WC2H 9JQ
Shareholders: Stuart O'Malley; Laura Jones
Officers: Laura Jones [1985] Director; Stuart O'Malley [1983] Director

Beautiful World Limited
Incorporated: 19 March 2015
Registered Office: 14 Park View, Pinner, Middlesex, HA5 4LN
Officers: Gary Anthony Ince, Secretary; Neel Arora [1978] Director/Administrator; Kalpeshkumar Patel [1979] Director/Accountant

Beautifull Planet Ltd
Incorporated: 9 February 2016
Net Worth Deficit: £13,661 *Total Assets:* £849
Registered Office: 151 City Road, Cardiff, CF24 3BQ
Major Shareholder: Rafal Marcin Zochowski
Officers: Rafal Marcin Zochowski [1981] Director/General Manager [Polish]

Beautifully Bliss Ltd
Incorporated: 15 June 2009
Net Worth: £332 *Total Assets:* £24,380
Registered Office: 85 Markville, Portadown, Co Armagh, BT63 5SZ
Major Shareholder: Catriona McDonnell
Officers: Catriona McDonnell, Secretary; Catriona McDonnell [1983] Director/Beauty Distributors

Beautivate Ltd
Incorporated: 13 October 2016
Net Worth: £10,110 *Total Assets:* £145,995
Registered Office: 7 Highfield Road, Hall Green, Birmingham, B28 0EL
Officers: Fariza Javed [1978] Director/Self Employed

Beautonic Skincare Ltd
Incorporated: 16 May 2018
Registered Office: 20-22 Wenlock Road, London, N1 7GU
Shareholder: Ahmed Gobdon
Officers: Ahmed Gobdon [1995] Director/Self Employed

Beautonomy Limited
Incorporated: 19 January 2018
Registered Office: LABS, 136 High Holborn, London, WC1V 6PX
Shareholders: Thomas Arthur Salmon; Hans Henrik Werdelin; Prehype UK Ltd
Officers: Thomas Arthur Salmon [1984] Director

Beautx Ltd
Incorporated: 13 February 2017
Registered Office: Office AJ, 272 Kings Road, Tyseley, Birmingham, B11 2AB
Major Shareholder: Ehsen Ajaib
Officers: Ehsen Ajaib [1983] Director/Cosmetics

Beauty & Skincare Essentials Limited
Incorporated: 5 December 2018
Registered Office: Bodycare House, Unit 1 and 2 Sham Farm Business Units, Danegate, Eridge Green, Tunbridge Wells, Kent, TN3 9JA
Shareholders: Fiona McMillan Peerless; Kevin Michael Gambrill
Officers: Kevin Michael Gambrill [1976] Director/Financial Accountant; Fiona McMillan Peerless [1979] Director/Operations Manager

Beauty Africa Limited
Incorporated: 26 May 2017
Registered Office: Devonshire House, 582 Honeypot Lane, Stanmore, Middlesex, HA7 1JS
Shareholders: Anish Popat; Ashna Popat
Officers: Anish Popat [1971] Director; Ashna Popat [1976] Director

The Beauty Alliance International Limited
Incorporated: 21 September 2018
Registered Office: Unit 3 Heads of The Valley Industrial Estate, Rhymney, Tredegar, Blaenau Gwent, NP22 5RL
Major Shareholder: Mitchell Laurence Field
Officers: Mitchell Laurence Field [1952] Director

Beauty and More 2000 Ltd
Incorporated: 19 September 2018
Registered Office: Kemp House, 160 City Road, London, EC1V 2NX
Major Shareholder: Yaniv Yosef
Officers: Yaniv Yosef, Secretary; Yaniv Yosef [1982] Director/Businessman [Israeli]

Beauty and Trade Ltd
Incorporated: 1 May 2018
Registered Office: Flat 27, 1 Prescot Street, London, E1 8RJ
Shareholders: Quentin Fevre; Eden Frimpong
Officers: Quentin Fevre [1990] Director [French]; Eden Frimpong [1992] Director [French]

Beauty at The Avenue Online Limited
Incorporated: 13 February 2017
Net Worth Deficit: £1,891 *Total Assets:* £2,364
Registered Office: 22 Stephenson Street, Winnington, Northwich, Cheshire, CW8 4SQ
Officers: Carl Beesley [1975] Director/Selling Beauty Products

Beauty Avenue Limited
Incorporated: 4 February 2019
Registered Office: 93 Harrow View, Harrow, Middlesex, HA1 4SZ
Shareholders: Adrienn Papdi; Joshua Mwanje
Officers: Joshua Mwanje [1984] Sales Director; Adrienn Papdi [1989] Director

Beauty Bash Limited
Incorporated: 6 June 2017
Net Worth: £1 *Total Assets:* £4,377
Registered Office: 69 Shrewsbury Road, Wirral, Merseyside, CH43 6TE
Major Shareholder: Annie-Louise Carter
Officers: Annie-Louise Carter [1990] Director

Beauty Brand (Europe) Ltd
Incorporated: 9 March 2017
Registered Office: 44 Theydon Road, London, E5 9NA
Major Shareholder: Allan Grossman
Officers: Aaron Grossman [1954] Director

Beauty Buddy Limited
Incorporated: 25 May 2005 *Employees:* 2
Net Worth: £25,369 *Total Assets:* £35,472
Registered Office: The Little House, 88a West Street, Farnham, Surrey, GU9 7EP
Major Shareholder: Fiona Parkhouse
Officers: Fiona Parkhouse [1960] Director/Marketing Executive; Richard Parkhouse [1959] Director/Banker

Beauty By Aliyah Ltd
Incorporated: 26 July 2018
Registered Office: Flat 1, Hawke Street, Portsmouth, PO1 3EJ
Shareholders: Tonima Hussain; Mohammed Ali
Officers: Tonima Hussain [1998] Director/Telephonist

Beauty Camp Profesional Limited
Incorporated: 6 March 2017
Registered Office: 51 Harker Drive, Coalville, Leics, LE67 4GG
Major Shareholder: Florin Dumitrascu
Officers: Dumitrascu Florin [1981] Director/Transport Manager [Romanian]

The Beauty Center Ltd
Incorporated: 29 December 2016
Net Worth Deficit: £9,980 *Total Assets:* £9,810
Registered Office: 20 Wellington Avenue, London, N15 6AS
Officers: Baruch Geldzahler [1990] Director [Belgian]; Israel Geldzahler [1989] Director [Belgian]

Beauty Code Limited
Incorporated: 5 July 2010
Net Worth Deficit: £8,031 *Total Assets:* £222
Registered Office: 61 Clegg Street, London, E13 0HY
Major Shareholder: Huanhuan Li
Officers: Huanhuan Li [1982] Managing Director

Beauty Complex Europe Ltd
Incorporated: 23 January 2018
Registered Office: Unit 1 Chandani Bazzar, 29-33 Ealing Road, Wembley, Middlesex, HA0 4YA
Major Shareholder: Ampalam Jeyadeesan
Officers: Kandiah Ampalam Jeyadeesan [1969] Director

Beauty Consociare Ltd
Incorporated: 6 July 2017
Registered Office: 12 Bridgford Road, West Bridgford, Nottingham, NG2 6AB
Major Shareholder: Karen Lee-Thompson
Officers: Karen Lee-Thompson [1977] Director

Beauty Cosmetics (Bristol) Limited
Incorporated: 30 July 2015
Net Worth: £100 *Total Assets:* £100
Registered Office: 18-22 Stoney Lane, Yardley, Birmingham, B25 8YP
Major Shareholder: Adill Hussain
Officers: Adill Hussain [1985] Director

Beauty Cosmetics (Luton) Limited
Incorporated: 5 February 2018
Registered Office: 18-22 Stoney Lane, Yardley, Birmingham, B25 8YP
Major Shareholder: Adill Hussain
Officers: Adill Hussain [1985] Director

Beauty Cosmetics (Nottingham) Limited
Incorporated: 30 July 2015
Net Worth: £100 *Total Assets:* £100
Registered Office: 18-22 Stoney Lane, Yardley, Birmingham, B25 8YP
Major Shareholder: Adill Hussain
Officers: Adill Hussain [1985] Director

Beauty Everich Ltd
Incorporated: 18 June 2018
Registered Office: International House, 12 Constance Street, London, E16 2DQ
Officers: Chloe Severigny [1981] Director [Hong Kong]

Beauty Expression (UK) Limited
Incorporated: 29 January 2013
Net Worth Deficit: £2,126 *Total Assets:* £11,389
Registered Office: Centrefield, The Broadway Industrial Estate, Mansfield, Notts, NG18 2RL
Major Shareholder: Feliksas Rimkevicius
Officers: Silva Rimkeviciene [1970] Director/Beauty Products and Cosmetics [Lithuanian]; Feliksas Rimkevicius [1992] Director (Marketing) [Lithuanian]

Beauty Forever Cosmetics Limited
Incorporated: 7 December 2006
Net Worth: £19,350 *Total Assets:* £302,530
Registered Office: 66 Gelsthorpe Road, Collier Row, Romford, Essex, RM5 2LX
Major Shareholder: Ammer Iqbal
Officers: Ammer Iqbal [1971] Director

Beauty Forever Limited
Incorporated: 15 October 2009
Registered Office: 66 Gelsthorpe Road, Romford, Essex, RM5 2LX
Major Shareholder: Ammer Iqbal
Officers: Saira Ayyaz [1982] Director [Pakistani]; Ammer Iqbal [1971] Director

Beauty Fort Limited
Incorporated: 11 March 2008
Previous: Acid Computer Services Ltd
Net Worth: £40,330 *Total Assets:* £264,740
Registered Office: 22 Guinness Road Trading Estate, Guinness Road, Trafford Park, Manchester, M17 1SB
Parent: Brothorn Group Limited
Officers: Deane Brooks [1976] Director; Michael Hawthornthwaite [1985] Managing Director

Beauty Full Ltd
Incorporated: 21 November 2018
Registered Office: 157 Kenton Lane, Harrow, Middlesex, HA3 8TL
Major Shareholder: Dina Hiteshkumar Shukla
Officers: Dina Hiteshkumar Shukla [1965] Managing Director

Beauty Glow Wholesale Limited
Incorporated: 22 February 2019
Registered Office: 39 Bhullar Way, Oldbury, W Midlands, B69 2GJ
Major Shareholder: Jafeer Hussain
Officers: Charu Bhatia [1983] Director

Beauty Healthcare Ltd
Incorporated: 29 October 2018
Registered Office: 321-323 High Road, Romford, Essex, RM6 6AX
Major Shareholder: Hassan Iqbal
Officers: Hassan Iqbal [1987] Director/Business Executive [Pakistani]

Beauty Ideas Group Limited
Incorporated: 27 January 2016
Net Worth: £3,620 *Total Assets:* £60,620
Registered Office: 5 Glynde Place, Horsham, W Sussex, RH12 1NZ
Major Shareholder: Cornelia Erika Wittke-Kothe
Officers: Cornelia Erika Gabriele Wittke [1972] Director [German]

Beauty Innovator 2012 Ltd.
Incorporated: 6 August 2012
Net Worth: £33,896 *Total Assets:* £367,704
Registered Office: 43 Bayton Road, Exhall, Coventry, Warwicks, CV7 9EF
Officers: Geoffrey Peter Morris, Secretary; Geoffrey Peter Morris [1962] Director; Timothy David Stooks [1974] Finance Director

Beauty Kosmetika Ltd
Incorporated: 27 September 2017
Registered Office: 1 Northolt Avenue, South Ruislip, Hillingdon, Middlesex, HA4 6SS
Shareholders: Ashok Virpal Shah; Robson Goncalves Lopes
Officers: Robson Goncalves Lopes [1965] Director; Ashok Virpal Shah [1952] Director

Beauty Leisure Industry Supplies and Services Limited
Incorporated: 4 July 1996 *Employees:* 22
Net Worth: £740,206 *Total Assets:* £2,186,087
Registered Office: Woodland House, Clayton Wood Close, West Park, Leeds, LS16 6QE
Major Shareholder: Christopher John Wilson
Officers: Christopher John Wilson, Secretary/Director; Dale Mangham [1972] Director; Mark John Tillotson [1984] Operations Director; Christopher John Wilson [1963] Director

Beauty Link Wholesale Ltd
Incorporated: 10 June 2016
Net Worth: £23,413 *Total Assets:* £89,494
Registered Office: Linden End, Linden Gardens, Leatherhead, Surrey, KT22 7HB
Shareholders: Denise Rosedam; Robert Raymond Rosedam
Officers: Denise Rosedam [1981] Director; Robert Raymond Rosedam [1980] Director/Electrician

Beauty Magasin Ltd
Incorporated: 12 December 2013
Net Worth: £414,703 *Total Assets:* £3,814,213
Registered Office: 337 Athlon Road, Wembley, Middlesex, HA0 1EF
Major Shareholder: Gaumish Patel
Officers: Gaumish Patel [1981] Director [American]

Beauty Masks Limited
Incorporated: 8 September 2006
Previous: Hair We Go UK Ltd
Net Worth Deficit: £17,899 *Total Assets:* £5,924
Registered Office: Carlton House, 1 Commerce Way, Lancing, W Sussex, BN15 8TA
Parent: A & C Group Limited
Officers: Charlie Claude Barbagelata, Secretary [French]; Charlie Claude Barbagelata [1946] Managing Director [French]; Angela Mary Eileen Barbagelata-Fabes [1952] Sales Director

Beauty Mastery Ltd.
Incorporated: 2 May 2017
Registered Office: 54 Downing Street, Farnham, Surrey, GU9 7PH
Major Shareholder: Samantha Robyn Pooley
Officers: Samantha Robyn Pooley [1977] Director/Educator [South African]

Beauty Oasis Ltd
Incorporated: 19 February 2019
Registered Office: 12 Spring Bank Place, Bradford, W Yorks, BD8 7BX
Major Shareholder: Taher Tokatly
Officers: Taher Tokatly [1971] Director [Dominican]

The Beauty Pod Limited
Incorporated: 31 August 2018
Registered Office: 9 Radcliffe Place, London, SW10 9DB
Major Shareholder: Natalia Blaskovicova
Officers: Natalia Blaskovicova [1983] Director [Slovak]

Beauty Premier Limited
Incorporated: 13 February 2006
Net Worth: £270,972 *Total Assets:* £977,466
Registered Office: Unit C, Penfold Trading Estate, Imperial Way, Watford, Herts, WD24 4YY
Officers: Isaac Cohen, Secretary; Avishai Partouche [1981] Director/Salesman [French]; Uriya Partoush [1980] Director [Israeli]

Beauty Queen Limited
Incorporated: 22 November 2018
Registered Office: 1 & 2 Mercia Village, Torwood Close, Westwood Business Park, Coventry, Warwicks, CV4 8HX
Major Shareholder: Jasbir Kaur Bassi
Officers: Jasbir Kaur Bassi [1974] Director

Beauty Queen Milano Ltd
Incorporated: 13 July 2018
Registered Office: 1 Salter House, Aldrington Road, London, SW16 1TX
Major Shareholder: Ihssane Bouybayoune
Officers: Dr Ihssane Bouybayoune [1987] Director/Neuroscientist [Italian]

Beauty Royale Ltd
Incorporated: 18 August 2017
Registered Office: 99 Cassiobury Park Avenue, Watford, Herts, WD18 7LH
Major Shareholder: Yalda Attai
Officers: Yalda Attai, Secretary; Yalda Attai [1981] Director [Australian]

The Beauty School Limited
Incorporated: 11 July 2007
Net Worth: £153,860 *Total Assets:* £363,492
Registered Office: 11-14 Newry Street, Warrenpoint, Newry, Co Down, BT34 3JZ
Shareholders: John Robert Feehan; Elizabeth Mary Feehan
Officers: John Robert Feehan, Secretary; Elizabeth Mary Feehan [1961] Director/Lecturer [Irish]; John Robert Feehan [1962] Director/Accountant

Beauty Science UK Ltd
Incorporated: 6 February 2019
Registered Office: 71-75 Shelton Street, London, WC2H 9JQ
Officers: Antonia Jane Hawke [1963] Director

Beauty Select Limited
Incorporated: 23 August 2006
Net Worth: £220,562 *Total Assets:* £245,976
Registered Office: Manor House, 35 St Thomas's Road, Chorley, Lancs, PR7 1HP
Major Shareholder: James Ian Duckworth
Officers: Christine Judith Duckworth, Secretary; Christine Judith Duckworth [1958] Director/Beauty Consultant; James Ian Duckworth [1957] Director/Management Consultant

Beauty Senses Limited
Incorporated: 2 October 2008 *Employees:* 3
Net Worth: £38,694 *Total Assets:* £145,472
Registered Office: 27 Broad Street, Wokingham, Berks, RG40 1AU
Major Shareholder: Andrew Graham Browne
Officers: Andrew Graham Browne [1973] Director/Importer; Richard Squires [1974] Managing Director

Beauty Solutions Global Ltd
Incorporated: 13 December 2018
Registered Office: 20-22 Wenlock Road, London, N1 7GU
Officers: Sara Louise Dhillon [1975] Managing Director

Beauty Solutions Limited
Incorporated: 26 February 2001
Net Worth: £10,519 *Total Assets:* £13,070
Registered Office: Unit 3 Newmains Avenue, Inchinnan Business Park, Renfrew, PA4 9RR
Officers: Brian Aitken, Secretary/Accountant; Brian Aitken [1954] Director/Accountant; General Patrick Hegarty [1940] Director/Sales Executive

Beauty Solutions Trading Ltd
Incorporated: 17 May 2018
Registered Office: 20-22 Wenlock Road, London, N1 7GU
Major Shareholder: Anna Marie Van Rosenveldt
Officers: Anna Marie Van Rosenveldt [1977] Managing Director

Beauty Spot Holdings Limited
Incorporated: 11 December 2017
Registered Office: 1 Park View Court, St Pauls Road, Shipley, W Yorks, BD18 3DZ
Shareholders: Michael Ogden; Rosemary Sarah Ogden
Officers: Michael Ogden [1980] Director; Rosemary Sarah Ogden [1980] Director/Solicitor

Beauty Stable Ltd
Incorporated: 28 March 2018
Registered Office: 20-22 Wenlock Road, London, N1 7GU
Shareholders: Donna Coleman; Marva Dione Williams; Samantha Miranda Jameson
Officers: Donna Coleman [1968] Director; Samantha Miranda Jameson [1976] Creative Director; Marva Dione Williams [1972] Director

Beauty Star Limited
Incorporated: 18 April 1995 *Employees:* 10
Net Worth: £5,319,521 *Total Assets:* £6,241,957
Registered Office: 71 Goldhawk Road, London, W12 8EG
Officers: Harinder Paul Singh, Secretary/Director; Harinder Paul Singh [1955] Director; Ranjit Kaur Singh [1954] Director

Beauty Systems Group Ltd.
Incorporated: 26 February 2001
Registered Office: Unit 3 Newmains Avenue, Inchinnan Business Park, Renfrew, PA4 9RR
Shareholder: Gerard Patrick Hegarty
Officers: Brian Aitken, Secretary/Accountant; Brian Aitken [1954] Director/Accountant; General Patrick Hegarty [1940] Director/Sales Executive

Beauty The Divine Ltd
Incorporated: 3 May 2018
Registered Office: 51a East Street, Barking, Essex, IG11 8EN
Major Shareholder: Mohammad Moazzem Hossain
Officers: Mohammad Moazzem Hossain [1985] Director/Manager

Beauty Trinity UK Limited
Incorporated: 24 January 2018
Registered Office: Halifax House, Bridge Street, Manchester, M3 2GX
Major Shareholder: Sarah Maskell
Officers: Sarah Maskell, Secretary; Sarah Maskell [1982] Director/Artist

Beauty Wholesale Limited
Incorporated: 8 June 1999 *Employees:* 29
Net Worth: £1,738,514 *Total Assets:* £9,373,346
Registered Office: 3 George Street, Watford, Herts, WD18 0BX
Parent: KMS Holdings Limited
Officers: Gulam Nasser [1965] Director

Beauty Without Cruelty Limited
Incorporated: 9 October 2003
Registered Office: Unit 10 Gamma Terrace, West Road, Ransomes Europark, Ipswich, Suffolk, IP3 9SX
Major Shareholder: Louise Mary Green
Officers: Cathleen Lockwood, Secretary; Louise Mary Green [1961] Director

Beautybaseuk Ltd
Incorporated: 4 June 2018
Registered Office: 32 Barnes Avenue, London, SW13 9AB
Major Shareholder: Uzma Tahir
Officers: Uzma Tahir [1978] Director/Housewife

BeautyEmpireUK Ltd
Incorporated: 31 March 2017
Net Worth Deficit: £1,210 *Total Assets:* £4,250
Registered Office: 64 Arduthie Road, Glasgow, G51 4TS
Officers: Rafal Targosz [1983] Director [Polish]

Beautyge Fragrances Holdings Ltd
Incorporated: 10 April 2015
Net Worth Deficit: £31,550,000 *Total Assets:* £28,000
Registered Office: Greater London House, Hampstead Road, London, NW1 7QX
Parent: Revlon, Inc.
Officers: Yossi Almani [1976] Director/Attorney [Israeli]; Paul Gregory Devin [1971] Director/UK General Manager; Michael Thomas Sheehan [1964] Director/Attorney [American]

Beautyline Limited
Incorporated: 4 May 2016
Net Worth Deficit: £2,963
Registered Office: 87 Lambert Avenue, Richmond, Surrey, TW9 4QT
Major Shareholder: Ivona Marcelja Paravic
Officers: Vibor Paravic, Secretary; Ivona Marcelja Paravic [1982] Director/Doctor

Beautynet Limited
Incorporated: 30 August 2007 *Employees:* 2
Net Worth: £2,757,018 *Total Assets:* £8,885,306
Registered Office: Newminster House, 27-29 Baldwin Street, Bristol, BS1 1LT
Shareholders: Jack Edward de Glanville; Liam Giles de Glanville
Officers: Holly Elizabeth de Glanville, Secretary; Jack Edward de Glanville [1982] Director; Liam Giles de Glanville [1976] Managing Director

Beautypro Ltd
Incorporated: 26 August 2010
Net Worth: £501,470 *Total Assets:* £1,750,000
Registered Office: Unit 20 Silveroaks Farm, Hawkhurst Lane, Waldron, Heathfield, E Sussex, TN21 0RS
Shareholders: Ibrahim Ansari; David George Herdman
Officers: Ibrahim Ansari [1976] Director; David George Herdman [1982] Director

Beautysugaring Limited
Incorporated: 18 April 2011
Net Worth Deficit: £9,985 *Total Assets:* £12,181
Registered Office: La Corbiere, Highway Lane, Mount Ambrose, Redruth, Cornwall, TR15 1SE
Major Shareholder: Anu Theresa Kaija Schneider
Officers: Anu Schneider [1977] Director/Beauty Therapist [German]

Beautytrade Limited
Incorporated: 10 April 2000 *Employees:* 2
Net Worth: £45,478 *Total Assets:* £64,941
Registered Office: Woodcote Manor, Kidderminster Road, Dodford, Bromsgrove, Worcs, B61 9DY
Shareholder: William Paul Taylor
Officers: William Paul Taylor, Secretary/Manager; Shirley Jean Taylor [1959] Director/Distribution; William Paul Taylor [1957] Director

Beautywise Limited
Incorporated: 14 May 1992
Registered Office: Tower House, Westfield Industrial Estate, Kirk Lane, Yeadon, Leeds, LS19 7LX
Officers: Susan Mottram, Secretary; Paul Mottram [1948] Managing Director

Beautyzon Limited
Incorporated: 16 November 2018
Registered Office: 4 Fairacres, Ruislip, Middlesex, HA4 8AN
Major Shareholder: Shelina Bhanji
Officers: Shelina Bhanji [1969] Director

Bedeaux Ltd
Incorporated: 27 September 2017
Registered Office: Kingfisher House, Hurstwood Lane, Haywards Heath, W Sussex, RH17 7QX
Major Shareholder: Amanda Beadle
Officers: Amanda Beadle [1964] Director/Accountant

Bedfordshire Beard Co. Limited
Incorporated: 22 June 2015 *Employees:* 2
Net Worth: £4,985 *Total Assets:* £8,947
Registered Office: Invision House, Wilbury Way, Hitchin, Herts, SG4 0TY
Shareholders: Caitlin Welsh; Tom Andrew Dowie
Officers: Tom Andrew Dowie [1990] Director; Caitlin Welsh [1991] Director

Bedrock Trade Ltd
Incorporated: 19 March 2018
Registered Office: 71-75 Shelton Street, Covent Garden, London, WC2H 9JQ
Major Shareholder: Andrea Faure Rolland
Officers: Andrea Faure Rolland, Secretary; Andrea Faure Rolland [1977] Director [Italian]

Beegood Enterprises Limited
Incorporated: 25 February 2013 *Employees:* 4
Net Worth: £42,178 *Total Assets:* £105,829
Registered Office: Ping CA, P O Box 1077, Camberley, Surrey, GU15 9QH
Officers: Hilary Ann Andrews [1961] Director; Simon Rafe Cavill [1960] Director; John Colin LooSeniore [1948] Director [Australian]; David John Parker [1965] Director

Beehive Cosmetics UK Limited
Incorporated: 22 March 2018
Registered Office: 20-22 Wenlock Road, London, N1 7GU
Major Shareholder: Md Sadiqur Rahman Khan
Officers: MD Sadiqur Rahman Khan [1982] Director/Operations Manager

Beever Haircare Ltd
Incorporated: 4 June 2014 *Employees:* 4
Net Worth: £827 *Total Assets:* £89,948
Registered Office: Unit 1 Castlefields Road, Bingley, W Yorks, BD16 2AF
Officers: Paul Martin Hammond, Secretary; Stephen Colin Beever [1964] Director/Hairdresser

Beiersdorf UK Ltd.
Incorporated: 20 May 1949 *Employees:* 217
Net Worth: £40,264,000 *Total Assets:* £103,750,000
Registered Office: Trinity Central, Trinity Park, Bickenhill Lane, Birmingham, B37 7ES
Parent: Beiersdorf AG
Officers: Patrick Albrecht [1970] Marketing Director [German]; Lynette Amanda Brown [1977] HR Director; Thomas Ingelfinger [1960] Director/Member Executive Board [German]; James Edward Livesey [1976] Finance Director; Andreas Ostermayr [1970] Director/General Manager [German]; Paul Bryan Price [1964] Director; Andrew Thomas Rawle [1976] Pharmacy Director; Thomas Riedner [1976] Supply Chain Director [German]

Bel Corporation Ltd
Incorporated: 1 June 2018
Registered Office: Upper Floor, 27 Colonnade, London, WC1N 1JA
Major Shareholder: Zlatina Belova
Officers: Zlatina Belova [1992] Director/Chief Executive [Bulgarian]

Belensa Limited
Incorporated: 29 October 2015
Net Worth: £366 *Total Assets:* £76,831
Registered Office: Office 32, 19-21 Crawford Street, London, W1H 1PJ
Shareholders: Patricia Kotek; Laurent Didier Perrin
Officers: Patricia Kotek [1971] Director [Swiss]

Belfast Beard Company Ltd
Incorporated: 9 January 2015
Net Worth: £6,830 *Total Assets:* £10,180
Registered Office: Unit 13 Ledcom Industrial Estate, Bank Road, Larne, Co Antrim, BT40 3AW
Shareholder: Laura Henshaw
Officers: Adam Henshaw, Secretary; Laura Henshaw [1985] Director/Barber

Belgrave Traders Ltd
Incorporated: 21 January 2019
Registered Office: c/o Ally De Maurice, 1 George Williams Way, Colchester, Essex, CO1 2JS
Major Shareholder: Shaenaze Toofail
Officers: Shaenaze Toofail [1976] Director

Belgravia London Ltd
Incorporated: 16 November 2017
Registered Office: 62 Camden Road, London, NW1 9DR
Shareholders: Laith Radi Mohammad Mahafza; Kheiry Kheiry
Officers: Kheiry Kheiry [1962] Director

Bella Rootz Limited
Incorporated: 8 August 2013
Registered Office: 4 York House, Langston Road, Loughton, Essex, IG10 3TQ
Officers: Kasim Learbuch Butt [1985] Director

Bellapierre Cosmetics Limited
Incorporated: 29 September 2006 *Employees:* 8
Net Worth: £1,273,161 *Total Assets:* £1,797,884
Registered Office: Churchill House, 137-139 Brent Street, London, NW4 4DJ
Shareholders: Guy Scetbon; David Orencyr
Officers: Guy Scetbon, Secretary/Director [Italian]; David Orencyr [1978] Director [American]; Guy Scetbon [1980] Director [Italian]

Bellevue of London Ltd.
Incorporated: 28 October 2015
Net Worth Deficit: £14,409 *Total Assets:* £9,174
Registered Office: 28 Cumnor Road, Sutton, Surrey, SM2 5DW
Major Shareholder: Ricardo Reza Krishna Menon Singh
Officers: Irena Singh [1969] Director [Slovenian]; Ricardo Reza Krishna Menon Singh [1967] Director

Bellissimo Fashion Ltd
Incorporated: 17 October 2016
Registered Office: Unit 2 Greenstead Road, Colchester, Essex, CO1 2SJ
Major Shareholder: Yuen Yan Law
Officers: Yuen Yan Law [1982] Director

Bellissimo GmbH International Ltd
Incorporated: 10 September 2018
Registered Office: 122 Woodhall Road, Bradford, BD3 7BT
Officers: Sanjay Mitra, Secretary; Sanjay Mitra [1993] Director

Belsay Ltd
Incorporated: 22 May 2000 *Employees:* 1
Net Worth: £132,179 *Total Assets:* £809,873
Registered Office: Suite 7, Claremont House, 22-24 Claremont Road, Surbiton, Surrey, KT6 4QU
Major Shareholder: Constantine Leo Borissoff
Officers: Liudmila Borissova, Secretary; Constantine Leo Borissoff [1958] Director/Sales Manager

Beltech Limited
Incorporated: 16 October 1998
Net Worth: £37,200 *Total Assets:* £45,170
Registered Office: 9 Chapel Place, Rivington Street, London, EC2A 3DQ
Officers: Philip Caraly [1983] Director [Italian]

Bemi Banks Cosmetics Ltd
Incorporated: 30 November 2018
Registered Office: 364 Stockport Road, Manchester, M13 0LE
Major Shareholder: Olamide Rachael Ige
Officers: Olamide Rachael Ige [1996] Director/Student

Bemysoul Ltd
Incorporated: 15 October 2018
Registered Office: 5 Cloves Crescent, Poplar, London, E14 2BG
Shareholders: Sira Sidibe; Charlene Charles
Officers: Charlene Charles [1995] Director/Shop Assistant [French]; Sira Sidibe [1995] Director/Shop Assistant [French]

Bendito Trading Limited
Incorporated: 26 November 2018
Registered Office: 54 Greystown Avenue, Belfast, BT9 6UJ
Major Shareholder: Anne Catherine Clarke
Officers: Anne Catherine Clarke [1961] Director

Benefit & Riley Healthcare Ltd
Incorporated: 15 September 2017
Registered Office: 1 Torrent Complex, 9 Hillview Avenue, Dungannon, Co Tyrone, BT70 3DL
Parent: Riley & Sons Ltd
Officers: Charlotte Riley [1974] Director/Businesswoman

Benefit Cosmetics Limited
Incorporated: 9 February 2000 *Employees:* 523
Net Worth: £50,226,812 *Total Assets:* £73,419,360
Registered Office: Marconi Building, New Street, Chelmsford, Essex, CM1 1PH
Parent: LVMH Moet Hennessy Louis Vuitton
Officers: Hugues Philippe Dusseaux [1954] Director/President [French]; Sarah Anne Harbon [1975] Sales Director; Andrea Dawn Lansbury [1964] Director; Jean Andre Rougeot [1958] Managing Director [French]

The Berkeley Square Cosmetics Company Limited
Incorporated: 10 July 1995 *Employees:* 2
Net Worth Deficit: £705,906 *Total Assets:* £390,669
Registered Office: Unit 13 Watford Metro Centre, Dwight Road, Watford, Herts, WD18 9SB
Parent: Calamander Investments Limited
Officers: Mohamed Ameen Kalla, Secretary; Aiyub Abdullah Ahmed [1954] Sales Director

Berry Inc Ltd
Incorporated: 30 July 2018
Registered Office: Kemp House, 160 City Road, London, EC1V 2NX
Major Shareholder: Evbi O'Sullivan
Officers: Evbi O'Sullivan, Secretary; Evbi O'Sullivan [1972] Director/Consultant

Bes Hair Products Limited
Incorporated: 16 April 2014 *Employees:* 1
Net Worth Deficit: £11,077 *Total Assets:* £2,974
Registered Office: 89 High Street, Hadleigh, Ipswich, Suffolk, IP7 5EA
Shareholders: Nicholas John Maser; Tara Louise Maser
Officers: Nicholas John Maser [1975] Art Director; Tara Louise Maser [1987] Director/Personal Assistant

The Bespoke Beauty Company Ltd
Incorporated: 2 June 2017
Registered Office: 1st Floor, Cloister House, New Bailey Street, Salford, M3 5FS
Shareholders: Andre Frenkel; Mom Ltd
Officers: Andre Frenkel [1952] Director [Swiss]; Oliver McMahon [1974] Director

Bespoke Hospitality Supplies Ltd
Incorporated: 25 January 2019
Registered Office: 43 Rowallon, Warrenpoint, Co Down, BT34 3TR
Major Shareholder: Damian Caldwell
Officers: Damian Caldwell, Secretary; Damian Caldwell [1967] Director/Hospitality Sales [Irish]

Bespoke Mr Ltd
Incorporated: 25 June 2015
Net Worth Deficit: £531 *Total Assets:* £1
Registered Office: 83 Ducie Street, Manchester, M1 2JQ
Major Shareholder: Maria Rouvali
Officers: Maria Rouvali [1975] Director [Greek]

Bessacarr Ltd
Incorporated: 11 March 2010
Net Worth: £241 *Total Assets:* £1,431
Registered Office: 20 Burnham Court, Moscow Road, London, W2 4SW
Officers: Andrew James McDermott, Secretary; Andrew James McDermott [1949] Director

Best Choice FMCG Ltd
Incorporated: 17 February 2016
Net Worth: £27,120 *Total Assets:* £29,130
Registered Office: Elizabeth House, 54-58 High Street, Edgware, Middlesex, HA8 7EJ
Major Shareholder: Basir Sangerwal
Officers: Basir Sangerwal [1980] Director

Best Pure Natural Products Limited
Incorporated: 14 June 2016
Registered Office: Staple House, 5 Eleanors Cross, Dunstable, Beds, LU6 1SU
Major Shareholder: Katarzyna Kynska
Officers: Katarzyna Krynska [1979] Director

Best-Bio Ltd
Incorporated: 20 August 2018
Registered Office: 3 Hornbeam Road, Hayes, Middlesex, UB4 9ED
Major Shareholder: Awad Kazem Abbas
Officers: Awad Kazem Abbas [1955] Director/Businessman

Beta Novis Limited
Incorporated: 11 February 2011
Net Worth Deficit: £313,030 *Total Assets:* £2,790,000
Registered Office: 17 Grosvenor Street, Mayfair, London, W1K 4QG
Major Shareholder: Daniele Teresio Andrea Bernini
Officers: Sani George Aweida [1959] Director/Accountant

Better Nature International Ltd
Incorporated: 25 November 2009
Net Worth: £5,800 *Total Assets:* £24,030
Registered Office: Third Floor, 207 Regent Street, London, W1B 3HH
Major Shareholder: Deyi Zhang-Cribbin
Officers: Colin Alexander, Secretary; Deyi Zhang-Cribbin, Secretary; Deyi Zhang-Cribbin [1977] Director [Chinese]

Beuti Limited
Incorporated: 4 December 2015 *Employees:* 3
Total Assets: £19,243
Registered Office: Ground Floor, 2 Woodberry Grove, London, N12 0DR
Shareholders: Joanna Aalam; Leila Marie Aalam
Officers: Joanna Aalam [1961] Director; Leila Marie Aalam [1981] Director

Beverly Beauty & Fragrances Ltd
Incorporated: 28 June 2017
Registered Office: 231 Greenford Road, Greenford, Middlesex, UB6 8QZ
Officers: Gaganmeet Singh [1986] Director [Indian]

Beyond Glamour Ltd
Incorporated: 15 August 2018
Registered Office: 2 St Johns Close, Pewsey, Wilts, SN9 5BJ
Major Shareholder: Elisabeth Jane Williams
Officers: Elisabeth Jane Williams [1965] Director/Management Consultant

Beyond Hair Ltd
Incorporated: 8 August 2011
Net Worth Deficit: £79,840 *Total Assets:* £78,230
Registered Office: 51 Cardiff Road, Luton, Beds, LU1 1PP
Major Shareholder: Jemel Henry
Officers: Jemel Henry [1987] Director/Entrepreneur

Bibishor Limited
Incorporated: 30 January 2019
Registered Office: 24b Bessborough Road, Harrow, Middlesex, HA1 3DL
Major Shareholder: Vasile Slevoaca
Officers: Vasile Slevoaca [1991] Director [Romanian]

The Big Wholesale Company Ltd
Incorporated: 9 January 2018
Registered Office: Almel House, Derby Street, Manchester, M8 8AT
Major Shareholder: Howard Jameson
Officers: Omar Hussain [1986] Sales Director; Howard Jameson [1977] Director; Khalid Wahab [1980] Director

Bigben Healthcare Limited
Incorporated: 12 August 2015
Registered Office: Foerster Chambers, Fernhills House, Todd Street, Bury, Lancs, BL9 5BJ
Officers: Jimmy Taylor [1960] Director/Businessman

Bigteal Industries Limited
Incorporated: 24 January 2017
Net Worth: £192 *Total Assets:* £1,508
Registered Office: Unit 14 Victoria Centre, Royal Way, Pride Park, Derby, DE24 8AN
Shareholders: Daniel Berrecloth; Martyn Simon Frost
Officers: Daniel Berrecloth [1988] Director; Martyn Simon Frost [1962] Director

Billionhaire Limited
Incorporated: 25 February 2019
Registered Office: Unit 8 Lenton Business Centre, Lenton Boulevard, Nottingham, NG7 2BY
Shareholders: Rochelle Simpson; Chanel Richards
Officers: Rochelle Simpson [2001] Director/Businesswoman

Binaya Solution Ltd
Incorporated: 9 October 2018
Registered Office: 22 Grosvenor Street, Rochdale, Lancs, OL11 2SU
Officers: Juniore Ghislaine Nkouele, Secretary; Juniore Ghislaine Nkouele [1991] Director/Chef [French]

Bio Global Limited
Incorporated: 8 August 2018
Registered Office: 3 Hornbeam Road, Hayes, Middlesex, UB4 9ED
Major Shareholder: Mohaned Awad Abbas
Officers: Mohaned Awad Abbas [1992] Director/Businessman; Ross Generald Wilkins [1990] Director/Self Employed

Bioactivebeauty Ltd
Incorporated: 17 April 2008 *Employees:* 1
Net Worth: £751 *Total Assets:* £42,822
Registered Office: Suite 1, 3rd Floor, 11-12 St James's Square, London, SW1Y 4LB
Major Shareholder: Kathy Jane Taylor-Brewin
Officers: Katherine Jane Taylor-Brewin, Secretary; Katherine Jane Taylor-Brewin [1959] Director/Cosmetic Distributor

Bioaqua -Biotechnology Ltd.
Incorporated: 22 May 2018
Registered Office: 120 High Road, London, N2 9ED
Officers: Janos Zsolt [1987] Director [Hungarian]

Biodeb Beauty Ltd
Incorporated: 27 September 2013
Net Worth: £10,248 *Total Assets:* £72,032
Registered Office: 49 Station Road, Polegate, E Sussex, BN26 6EA
Major Shareholder: Rasidat Abiola
Officers: Rasidat Ajisafe Abiola [1969] Director [Nigerian]

Bioeffect Limited
Incorporated: 6 September 2010 *Employees:* 8
Previous: Sif Cosmetics Ltd.
Net Worth Deficit: £223,590 *Total Assets:* £670,724
Registered Office: Suite 215, 2nd Floor, 1-2 Broadgate Circle, London, EC2M 2QS
Officers: Frosti Olafsson [1982] Director [Icelander]

Biogene Group Limited
Incorporated: 22 June 2017
Registered Office: 280a High Street, Orpington, Kent, BR6 0ND
Shareholders: Santoshi Vasantha Govindarajula; Swarna Jyothi Sriperambuduru
Officers: Santoshi Vasantha Govindarajula, Secretary; Divakar Sriperambuduru, Secretary; Santoshi Vasantha Govindarajula [1985] Director/IT Consultant [Indian]; Divakar Sriperambuduru [1974] Director/Businessman

Biola Beauty Ltd
Incorporated: 26 July 2018
Registered Office: 200 Apollo Avenue, Peterborough, Cambs, PE2 8LA
Major Shareholder: Aleksandra Chodera
Officers: Aleksandra Chodera [1988] Director/Team Leader [Polish]

Bioline Ltd
Incorporated: 13 December 2018
Registered Office: 85 Great Portland Street, London, W1W 7LT
Officers: Sergii Bondarenko [1985] Director [Ukrainian]

Biologico Cosmetics Limited
Incorporated: 14 February 2018
Registered Office: 3rd Floor, Citypoint, 65 Haymarket Terrace, Edinburgh, EH12 5HD
Major Shareholder: Craig McKay
Officers: Craig McKay [1983] Director

Bion Corporation Limited
Incorporated: 18 January 2012
Net Worth: £28,838 *Total Assets:* £119,860
Registered Office: Ground Floor, Solar House, 282 Chase Road, Southgate, London, N14 6NZ
Major Shareholder: Shiv Sahni
Officers: Ritu Sahni, Secretary; Shiv Sahni [1972] Director/Owner [Indian]

Biotrade Cosmeceuticals Ltd
Incorporated: 12 January 2018
Registered Office: H5 Ash Tree Court, Nottingham Business Park, Nottingham, NG8 6PY
Shareholders: Nikolay Naydenov; Evgeniya Naydenova
Officers: Raya Kardzhieva, Secretary; Raya Kardzhieva [1985] Director [Bulgarian]

Biovate Limited
Incorporated: 4 January 2017
Registered Office: Fanshawe House, Pioneer Business Park, Amy Johnson Way, York, YO30 4TN
Major Shareholder: Sami Safadi
Officers: Sami Safadi [1975] Director [Jordanian]

Bioxane Ltd
Incorporated: 21 August 2018
Registered Office: Kemp House, 160 City Road, London, EC1V 2NX
Major Shareholder: Ahmed Mahmoud
Officers: Dr Ahmed Mahmoud, Secretary; Dr Ahmed Mahmoud [1979] Director/Manager [Egyptian]

Birch & Hayer Ltd
Incorporated: 23 July 2018
Registered Office: Suite 47, The Wenta Business Centre, Electric Avenue, Innova Park, Enfield, Middlesex, EN3 7XU
Major Shareholder: Manjit Kaur
Officers: Manjit Kaur [1977] Director

Mark Birch Hair Ltd
Incorporated: 25 June 2018
Registered Office: 12 Tulip Way, West Drayton, Middlesex, UB7 7ED
Major Shareholder: Mark William Birch
Officers: Tuija Maarit Anneli Lindstrom [1970] Director/Chief Executive [Finnish]

Birmingham Fragrances Ltd
Incorporated: 30 August 2018
Registered Office: G10, Crown House, 123 Hagley Road, Birmingham, B16 8LD
Major Shareholder: Mohammed Salamathullah
Officers: Mohammed Salamathullah [1963] Director [Indian]

Bisch Limited
Incorporated: 20 December 2018
Registered Office: Flat 99, Stratosphere Tower, 55 Great Eastern Road, London, E15 1DS
Shareholder: Kostiantyn Stotyka
Officers: Anna Zoumaras [1975] Director/Manager

Bits4hair Limited
Incorporated: 13 January 2006
Net Worth: £13,480 *Total Assets:* £168,920
Registered Office: 33 Gibfield Park Avenue, Atherton, Manchester, M46 0SY
Major Shareholder: Philip John Naylor
Officers: Gail Dawn Naylor, Secretary; Philip John Naylor [1959] Director

Bizi Bazzar Limited
Incorporated: 5 March 2015
Net Worth Deficit: £8,560 *Total Assets:* £9,940
Registered Office: 108 Church Hill Road, Cheam, Sutton, Surrey, SM3 8NA
Parent: Bunty Enterprises Limited
Officers: Kauser Perveen Malik [1961] Director/Social Worker

BKSL Limited
Incorporated: 17 November 2006
Net Worth: £1 *Total Assets:* £360,921
Registered Office: Churchill Point, Lake Edge Green, Trafford Park Road, Manchester, M17 1BL
Parent: Cartoon (Holdings) Limited
Officers: Vipul Jayantilal Vadera, Secretary; Sanjay Jayantilal Vadera [1967] Director

The Black Candle Company of Northumberland Limited
Incorporated: 1 September 2018
Registered Office: Courtyard, Blagdon Estate, Seaton Burn, Newcastle upon Tyne, NE13 6DB
Shareholders: Angela Walton; Samantha Louise Walton; Douglas Thomas Walton
Officers: Angela Walton [1964] Director; Douglas Thomas Walton [1963] Director; Samantha Louise Walton [1990] Director

Black Gold Hair Limited
Incorporated: 12 January 2018
Registered Office: 42 Penrith Road, New Malden, Surrey, KT3 3QS
Major Shareholder: Shil Hwan Chung
Officers: Shil Hwan Chung [1971] Director [South Korean]

Black Pearl Beauty Limited
Incorporated: 1 August 2013
Net Worth: £50,308 *Total Assets:* £50,453
Registered Office: 95 Stag Lane, Edgware, Middlesex, HA8 5LJ
Major Shareholder: Hassan Uddin Ahmed
Officers: Hassan Uddin Ahmed [1985] Director/Hair and Beauty Products [Pakistani]

Blank Factory Limited
Incorporated: 14 May 2018
Registered Office: Flat 7, 19 Royal Road, Ramsgate, Kent, CT11 9LE
Shareholders: Alexander Peter Verier; Frederick Augustus Fenton Sharpe
Officers: Frederick Augustus Fenton Sharpe [1996] Director; Alexander Peter Verier [1993] Director

Bleach Makeup Limited
Incorporated: 13 February 2017 *Employees:* 3
Net Worth: £66 *Total Assets:* £133,338
Registered Office: Unit 1 Hunters Building, 110 Curtain Road, London, EC2A 3AH
Shareholders: Louise Teasdale; Alexandra Brownsell; Samantha Teasdale; Bleach Group Limited
Officers: Alexandra Brownsell [1987] Director; Samantha Campbell [1983] Director; Louise Teasdale [1983] Director

A & P Blickling Ltd
Incorporated: 22 February 2018
Registered Office: 27 Old Gloucester Street, London, WC1N 3AX
Officers: Patrik Blickling [1983] Director/Businessman [Slovak]; Ana Eugenia Calero de Blickling [1974] Director/Businesswoman [Nicaraguan]

Blink Street Limited
Incorporated: 16 March 2018
Registered Office: 24 Lime Kiln Wharf, 94 Three Colt Street, London, E14 8AP
Officers: Ira Blinkovskaja [1982] Sales Director [Swedish]

Blissible Ltd
Incorporated: 11 September 2018
Registered Office: 26 Harswell Close, Orrell, Wigan, Lancs, WN5 8RG
Major Shareholder: Melissa Ruane
Officers: Melissa Ruane, Secretary; Melissa Ruane [1974] Director

Blissworld Limited
Incorporated: 9 February 2000 *Employees:* 34
Net Worth Deficit: £70,151 *Total Assets:* £1,818,324
Registered Office: The Lodge, 92 Uxbridge Road, Harrow Weald, Middlesex, HA3 6DQ
Parent: Steiner UK Limited
Officers: Robert Boehm, Secretary; Marc Magliacano [1974] Director/Investor [American]; Robert Barry John Schaverien [1964] Managing Director

BLK Cosmetics Limited
Incorporated: 26 April 2016
Net Worth Deficit: £7,310 *Total Assets:* £19,800
Registered Office: 1 Fisher Lane, Bingham, Nottingham, NG13 8BQ
Major Shareholder: Robyn Black
Officers: Robyn Black [1986] Director; Dean Holland [1984] Director

Blk Deer Co. Ltd
Incorporated: 17 May 2018
Registered Office: Unit 3 Westbury Industrial Estate, Station Road, Westbury, Wilts, BA13 4HR
Major Shareholder: Sheung Wah Chow
Officers: Sheung Wah Chow [1983] Director [Hong Kong]

Blk Oil Limited
Incorporated: 28 December 2017
Registered Office: 172a Broadhurst Gardens, London, NW6 3BH
Major Shareholder: Sabrina Forde
Officers: Sabrina Forde [1977] Director/Buyer

Bloom Artisan Brands Limited
Incorporated: 25 June 2018
Registered Office: 17 Abbey Hill, Kenilworth, Warwicks, CV8 1LU
Shareholders: Gemma Flanagan; Reza Arya
Officers: Reza Arya [1973] Director/Plastic Surgeon; Gemma Flanagan [1979] Commercial Director

Bloom International Group Ltd
Incorporated: 26 November 2018
Registered Office: 20-22 Wenlock Road, London, N1 7GU
Major Shareholder: Basil Saad Abdulwahab Nader
Officers: Basil Saad Abdulwahab Nader [1965] Director

Bloom Remedies Ltd
Incorporated: 23 February 2018
Registered Office: 32 Pendarves Road, Penzance, Cornwall, TR18 2AJ
Shareholders: Stephen Richard Hall; Marie Elizabeth Hall
Officers: Marie Elizabeth Hall [1974] Director; Stephen Richard Hall [1970] Director

Bloomtown Ltd
Incorporated: 8 March 2018
Registered Office: Bloomtown Ltd, Unit 3 Empire Way, Tregoniggie Industrial Estate, Falmouth, Cornwall, TR11 4RX
Shareholders: Medwin John Culmer; Preyanka Jayanti Clark Prakash
Officers: Preyanka Jayanti Clark Prakash [1982] Director [American]; Medwin John Culmer [1977] Managing Director

Blossom Colour Limited
Incorporated: 9 May 2016
Net Worth: £16,580 *Total Assets:* £102,550
Registered Office: Kemp House, 160 City Road, London, EC1V 2NX
Shareholders: Mark Saragossi; Simon Sandler-Vallance
Officers: Nicola Saragossi, Secretary; Simon Sandler-Vallance [1969] Director/Local Government Officer; Mark Saragossi [1957] Director/Chartered Accountant; Nicola Saragossi [1959] Managing Director

Blossom Organics Limited
Incorporated: 28 December 2017
Registered Office: 3 Steels Lane, London, E1 0DP
Major Shareholder: Rabia Fiaz
Officers: Rabia Fiaz [1996] Director/Student

Blue Rose Shop Ltd
Incorporated: 17 July 2018
Registered Office: 262 Norbury Avenue, London, SW16 3RL
Officers: Adam Walentynowicz [1993] Director/Manager [Polish]

Bluebells Hair Boutique Limited
Incorporated: 31 January 2018
Registered Office: 69 Shepherds Way, South Croydon, Surrey, CR2 8HS
Officers: Ebun Oliver-Wallace [1984] Director/Health Care

Bluesky Cosmetics Limited
Incorporated: 13 December 2016
Registered Office: Trilogy Suite, 9 Church Street, Wednesfield, Wolverhampton, W Midlands, WV11 1SR
Major Shareholder: Chad William Burgin
Officers: Chad William Burgin [1987] Director

Bluesky Cosmetics UK HQ Limited
Incorporated: 25 August 2018
Registered Office: Fisher Phillips, Summit House, 170 Finchley Road, London, NW3 6BP
Shareholders: Honghua Ye; Deal Pot Limited
Officers: Jemma Robinson [1986] Director; Honghua Ye [1979] Director [Chinese]

Bluesky Products Limited
Incorporated: 5 December 2012
Net Worth Deficit: £151,251 *Total Assets:* £64,123
Registered Office: St Thomas House, 83 Wolverhampton Road, Cannock, Staffs, WS11 1AR
Major Shareholder: Chad William Burgin
Officers: Chad William Burgin [1987] Director

Bluestar Enterprise Limited
Incorporated: 27 September 2010
Net Worth: £1,260,832 *Total Assets:* £14,963,473
Registered Office: Unit 4 Imperial Park, Stonefield Way, South Ruislip, Middlesex, HA4 0JW
Major Shareholder: Manisha Thakrar
Officers: Nayan Thakrar [1960] Director

BM Beauty Ltd.
Incorporated: 13 January 2011 *Employees:* 1
Net Worth Deficit: £74,112 *Total Assets:* £63,268
Registered Office: 19 Bon Accord Crescent, Aberdeen, AB11 6DE
Major Shareholder: Laura Anne Nicholson
Officers: Laura Anne Nicholson [1976] Director

BM Supplier UK & Europe Ltd
Incorporated: 14 March 2014
Net Worth Deficit: £24,150 *Total Assets:* £24,270
Registered Office: 1 College Yard, 56 Winchester Avenue, London, NW6 7UA
Major Shareholder: Taliane Bernardinelli
Officers: Taliane Bernardinelli [1987] Director [Italian]

Bod Beauty Ltd
Incorporated: 7 November 2018
Registered Office: 112 Firs Avenue, London, N11 3NQ
Major Shareholder: Pejman Safaie
Officers: Pejman Safaie [1972] Managing Director [Iranian]

Body Beauty & Hair Ltd
Incorporated: 21 January 2019
Registered Office: 64 Sherbourn Court, 180-186 Cromwell Road, London, SW5 0ST
Major Shareholder: Leila Al Arnab
Officers: Leila Al Arnab [1975] Director/Businesswoman [Tunisian]

Body Beauty Wholesale Exporters Ltd
Incorporated: 27 July 2018
Registered Office: 71-75 Shelton Street, London, WC2H 9JQ
Major Shareholder: Van Geel Matthews
Officers: Van Geel Matthews [1985] Director of Operations [Dutch]

Body Care Brand Development Ltd
Incorporated: 22 January 2013
Net Worth: £16,330 *Total Assets:* £133,550
Registered Office: 145-177 Foleshill Road, Coventry, Warwicks, CV1 4LF
Major Shareholder: Hamzah Islam
Officers: Hamzah Islam, Secretary; Hamzah Islam [1980] Director

Body Month Ltd
Incorporated: 22 January 2018
Registered Office: Apartment 160, 6 Royal Quay, Liverpool, L3 4EX
Officers: Emeka Okafor, Secretary; Emeka Okafor [1993] Director [Nigerian]

Body of Work Beauty Ltd
Incorporated: 24 September 2018
Registered Office: 64 Jenkins Road, London, E13 8NP
Major Shareholder: Nicole Fisher
Officers: Nicole Fisher [1995] Director/Manager

Body Organics Limited
Incorporated: 3 July 2017
Registered Office: 24 Pollard Road, Leicester, LE3 1RB
Major Shareholder: Viola Ogbunude
Officers: Viola Ogbunude [1986] Director/Accountant [Nigerian]

Body Reform Limited
Incorporated: 28 June 2006
Net Worth: £20,001 *Total Assets:* £20,001
Registered Office: 96a Cardiff Road, Llandaff, Cardiff, CF5 2DT
Major Shareholder: Klaus Georg Ueber
Officers: Klaus Georg Ueber, Secretary; Klaus Georg Ueber [1947] Director

The Body Shop International Limited
Incorporated: 1 November 1976 *Employees:* 5,870
Previous: The Body Shop International PLC
Net Worth: £272,000,000 *Total Assets:* £502,000,000
Registered Office: Watersmead, Littlehampton, W Sussex, BN17 6LS
Officers: Peter O'Byrne, Secretary; Robert Claus Chatwin [1970] Director/Executive/Chartered Accountant; Itamar Gaino Filho [1976] Director/Attorney [Brazilian]

Bodygold Limited
Incorporated: 20 January 1995 *Employees:* 1
Net Worth: £25,972 *Total Assets:* £29,598
Registered Office: Aroma House, Kingsnorth Industrial Estate, Ashford, Kent, TN23 6LN
Major Shareholder: Cheryll Lynn Hollis
Officers: Louise Marie Spragg, Secretary; Cheryll Lynn Hollis [1952] Director

Bodyhug Limited
Incorporated: 24 April 2018
Registered Office: 4 Green Lane, Canvey Island, Essex, SS8 0ET
Officers: Adebanji Olufaderin Jawo [1971] Director; Florence Taiwo Jawo [1973] Director/Accountant

Bohdidharma Perfume UK Limited
Incorporated: 11 July 2017
Registered Office: 2 Marrilyne Avenue, Enfield, Middlesex, EN3 6EG
Major Shareholder: John Mensah Nash
Officers: John Mensah Nash [1952] Director/Manager

Bolm4 Limited
Incorporated: 5 April 2008
Net Worth Deficit: £3,000 *Total Assets:* £8,480
Registered Office: 49 Station Road, Polegate, E Sussex, BN26 6EA
Officers: Budimir Jokovic [1958] Director/Sales Representative

Bond Street Cosmetics Limited
Incorporated: 26 January 1999 *Employees:* 3
Net Worth: £159,318 *Total Assets:* £268,401
Registered Office: 5th Floor, 89 New Bond Street, London, W1S 1DA
Officers: Raymond Philip Carroll, Secretary; Raymond Philip Carroll [1955] Director/Accountant [Irish]; Jonathan James Osborne [1957] Director/Accountant; Barry Douglas Wade [1943] Director/Sales Manager

Bonfit UK Limited
Incorporated: 24 May 2012 *Employees:* 1
Net Worth Deficit: £117,515 *Total Assets:* £170,524
Registered Office: 140 Buckingham Palace Road, London, SW1W 9SA
Major Shareholder: Paul Anthony Krok
Officers: Paul Anthony Krok [1966] Director/Company President [American]

Bonitec Ltd
Incorporated: 21 September 2010
Registered Office: Kemp House, 160 City Road, London, EC1V 2NX
Major Shareholder: Leonid Gubin
Officers: Leonid Gubin [1949] Director/Manager [Spanish]

Bonroy International Limited
Incorporated: 24 February 2017
Registered Office: Kemp House, 160 City Road, London, EC1V 2NX
Shareholders: Ning Lu; Yuezhu Wei
Officers: Ning Lu [1993] Director/Marketing; Yuezhu Wei [1990] Director/IT [Chinese]

Boost Balm Ltd
Incorporated: 6 July 2018
Registered Office: Unit 1, 65 Alexandra Road, Slough, SL1 2NQ
Officers: Shareezma Shishani Binti Mohamed Hanif, Secretary; Shareezma Shishani Binti Mohamed Hanif [1990] Managing Director [Malaysian]; Sameer Mahmood Yahya [1990] Director

Boots International Limited
Incorporated: 11 July 2000
Net Worth: £43,343,000 *Total Assets:* £74,912,000
Registered Office: 1 Thane Road West, Nottingham, NG2 3AA
Parent: Alliance Boots Holdings Limited
Officers: Andrew Richard Thompson, Secretary; Rosemary Frances Counsell [1963] Director/Chief Financial Officer; Anne Louise Murphy [1967] Director

Bortlam Postpartum Restore Health Management (International) Chain Co., Ltd
Incorporated: 9 May 2018
Registered Office: 9 Pantygraigwen Road, Pontypridd, Mid Glamorgan, CF37 2RR
Major Shareholder: Yongman Zhuo
Officers: Yongman Zhuo [1984] Director [Chinese]

Botanical Brands Ltd
Incorporated: 6 November 2012
Net Worth: £3,619 *Total Assets:* £35,851
Registered Office: Business Partners, Unit 19 The Manor, Main Street, Tur Langton, Leicester, LE8 0PJ
Major Shareholder: Kim Jennifer Allan
Officers: Kim Jennifer Allan [1969] Sales Director

Botanik Beauty Limited
Incorporated: 25 January 2017
Registered Office: The Beauty Crop Limited, Suite 2, 5 Percy Street, London, W1T 1DG
Parent: The Beauty Crop Limited
Officers: Ning Chiann Cheah [1983] Director

Botanika Group Ltd
Incorporated: 19 November 2018
Registered Office: Flat 63, Youngs Court, London, SW11 5JE
Major Shareholder: Noman Khan
Officers: Noman Khan [1988] Director/Entrepreneur [Pakistani]

Botany Squared Limited
Incorporated: 23 January 2019
Registered Office: 61 Bridge Street, Kington, Herefords, HR5 3DJ
Major Shareholder: Meeri Moilanen
Officers: Meeri Moilanen [1987] Director [Finnish]

Bottlemate UK Limited
Incorporated: 23 August 2013
Net Worth Deficit: £42,112 *Total Assets:* £85,125
Registered Office: 1st Floor, 6 Gerrard Street, London, W1D 5PG
Major Shareholder: Ming-Lang Chuang
Officers: Yu-Hui Cheng [1967] Director [Taiwanese]

Pazery Bouffard and Company Limited
Incorporated: 29 March 1928
Net Worth: £100 *Total Assets:* £100
Registered Office: 4 Michaels Mount, Little Bealings, Woodbridge, Suffolk, IP13 6LS
Major Shareholder: Laure Pazery Guerci
Officers: Laure Pazery Guerci [1966] Director/Operations Manager

Bouffe Limited
Incorporated: 21 August 2013
Net Worth Deficit: £80,888 *Total Assets:* £43,778
Registered Office: Reabrook Building, Rawdon Road, Moira, Swadlincote, Derbys, DE12 6DA
Shareholder: Angela Tant
Officers: Anthony William Brealey [1957] Director; Angela Tant [1961] Director; Malcolm Peter Watkins [1954] Director

Boujelle Ltd
Incorporated: 22 November 2018
Registered Office: 53 Buckingham Road, London, HA8 6LY
Officers: Sharna Dempster [1987] Director/Nail Technician

Boundless Beauty Ltd
Incorporated: 28 March 2018
Registered Office: Farmhouse, Keeston, Haverfordwest, Pembrokeshire, SA62 6EE
Major Shareholder: Tymeika Marie Lunt
Officers: Tymeika Marie Lunt [1985] Director

Boutique Fragrances Ltd
Incorporated: 28 December 2017
Registered Office: 21 Treaford Lane, Birmingham, B8 2UF
Major Shareholder: Zain Matloob
Officers: Zain Matloob [1998] Director

Boutique Parfum Limited
Incorporated: 24 January 2018
Registered Office: 55 Ellerdine Road, Hounslow, Middlesex, TW3 2PN
Officers: Rodica-Maria Cireasa [1978] Director/Businesswoman [Romanian]

Boutique Perfumes Limited
Incorporated: 8 September 2004
Net Worth Deficit: £7,136 *Total Assets:* £4,912
Registered Office: New Burlington House, 1075 Finchley Road, London, NW11 0PU
Shareholders: Kenneth Charles Green; Susan Esther Green
Officers: Philip John Stokes, Secretary; Kenneth Charles Green [1945] Director; Susan Esther Green [1946] Director/Public Relations; Philip John Stokes [1956] Director/Company Secretary

Box of Beauty Ltd
Incorporated: 9 January 2019
Registered Office: 27 Old Gloucester Street, London, WC1N 3AX
Major Shareholder: Mirza Baig
Officers: Mirza Baig, Secretary; Mirza Baig [1984] Director [Pakistani]

Andre Boyard Perfumes Limited
Incorporated: 25 September 2002
Net Worth Deficit: £124,150 *Total Assets:* £49,878
Registered Office: Equity House, 128-136 High Street, Edgware, Middlesex, HA8 7TT
Shareholders: Constantine Leo Borissoff; Ameet Chandubhai Rughani; Constantine Leo Borissoff; Ameet Chandubhai Rughani
Officers: Constantine Leo Borissoff [1958] Director/Executive; Ameet Chandubhai Rughani [1963] Director

Boylondon Holdings Limited
Incorporated: 30 January 2019
Registered Office: 3rd Floor, 120 Baker Street, London, W1U 6TU
Major Shareholder: Jin A Kim
Officers: Eun Joo Lee [1961] Director/Dress Designer [South Korean]

Boz Ego Ltd
Incorporated: 8 April 2013
Registered Office: Flat 3, 2 Christ Church Road, Surbiton, Surrey, KT5 8JJ
Officers: Qian Wang [1985] Director [Chinese]

Bracey Overseas Ltd
Incorporated: 9 January 2012
Net Worth: £181,932 *Total Assets:* £358,034
Registered Office: Granite Building, 6 Stanley Street, Liverpool, L1 6AF
Major Shareholder: Daniel Bracey
Officers: Daniel Bracey [1974] Director/Manager

Bracknell Gardens Ltd
Incorporated: 6 November 2018
Registered Office: 4 Bracknell Gardens, London, NW3 7EB
Major Shareholder: Erika Tan
Officers: Erika Tan [1949] Director

Anthony Braden Limited
Incorporated: 25 June 2004 *Employees:* 1
Net Worth Deficit: £162,950 *Total Assets:* £9,641
Registered Office: Milverton, The Highlands, East Horsley, Leatherhead, Surrey, KT24 5BG
Major Shareholder: Stephen John Clennell
Officers: Susan Lynn Knappman, Secretary; Stephen John Clennell [1944] Director

Anthony Braden Online Ltd.
Incorporated: 21 January 2000
Net Worth Deficit: £278,438 *Total Assets:* £629
Registered Office: Milverton, The Highlands, East Horsley, Leatherhead, Surrey, KT24 5BG
Major Shareholder: Stephen John Clennell
Officers: Susan Lynn Knapman, Secretary; Stephen John Clennell [1944] Sales Director; Susan Lynn Knapman [1946] Director/Business Manager

Bragarlin Limited
Incorporated: 28 January 2019
Registered Office: 57 Sutherland Road, Croydon, Surrey, CR0 3QH
Major Shareholder: Brian Linnegar
Officers: Brian Linnegar [1965] Director

Brain Burgeon Ltd
Incorporated: 21 March 2014
Registered Office: Lower Ground Floor, 40 Bloomsbury Way, London, WC1A 2SE
Major Shareholder: Adrian Meszaros
Officers: Adrian Meszaros [1986] Director [Hungarian]

Brambles Farm Ltd
Incorporated: 7 September 2007 *Employees:* 15
Net Worth: £74,579 *Total Assets:* £360,142
Registered Office: 43 Coniscliffe Road, Darlington, Co Durham, DL3 7EH
Shareholders: Christopher John Stroud; Jayne Elizabeth Wilkins
Officers: Jayne Elizabeth Wilkins, Secretary/Sales Manager; Christopher John Stroud [1962] Director/Sales Manager; Jacqueline Lander Stroud [1962] Director; Jayne Elizabeth Wilkins [1970] Director/Sales Manager; Shaun Michael Wilkins [1969] Director/Consultant

Bramley Products Ltd
Incorporated: 8 October 2012 *Employees:* 2
Net Worth: £232,535 *Total Assets:* £280,976
Registered Office: The Beckford Arms, Fonthill Gifford, Tisbury, Salisbury, Wilts, SP3 6PX
Shareholders: Chloe Liz Warwick Luxton; Daniel Richard Brod
Officers: Daniel Richard Brod [1970] Director; Chloe Liz Warwick Luxton [1977] Director

Brand Agency (London) Limited
Incorporated: 10 September 2009 *Employees:* 26
Net Worth Deficit: £609,605 *Total Assets:* £6,557,248
Registered Office: Batchworth House, Batchworth Place, Church Street, Rickmansworth, Herts, WD3 1JE
Parent: PBS Brand Agency Limited
Officers: Charlotte Knight [1979] Director

Brand Euro Limited
Incorporated: 14 December 2016
Registered Office: Ground Floor, Unit 6, 7-8 Devenant Street, London, E1 5NB
Major Shareholder: Mohommad Abdullah
Officers: Mohommad Abdullah [1979] Director [Bangladeshi]

Brand Evangelists for Beauty Limited
Incorporated: 24 May 2017 *Employees:* 4
Net Worth Deficit: £248,445 *Total Assets:* £5,802
Registered Office: Nightingale House, 46-48 East Street, Epsom, Surrey, KT17 1HQ
Shareholders: Unilever Ventures General Partner Limited; John Mills Limited
Officers: Mark Curry [1982] Director; Olivier Gilbert Garel [1968] Director [French]; Rachel Susan Harris [1969] Director; Colette Newberry [1986] Director

Brand Evolution (Europe) Limited
Incorporated: 13 January 2016
Registered Office: 24a Aldermans Hill, Palmers Green, London, N13 4PN
Shareholders: Alexandros Panayioti Theofanous; Anna Theofanous
Officers: Anna Theofanous, Secretary; Alexandros Panayioti Theofanous [1981] Director; Anna Theofanous [1978] Director

Brand Holdings Limited
Incorporated: 27 October 2016
Net Worth: £3,675 *Total Assets:* £43,678
Registered Office: 17 Derwent Rise, Spondon, Derby, DE21 7PB
Officers: Jay Bond [1980] Director; Trevor Bond [1956] Director

Brandaroma Limited
Incorporated: 27 March 2006 *Employees:* 5
Net Worth: £162,192 *Total Assets:* £395,594
Registered Office: 102 Buckingham Avenue, Slough, SL1 4PF
Officers: Daniel Connors [1959] Director/Business Executive [American]

Brandcare Group Limited
Incorporated: 5 December 2008 *Employees:* 6
Net Worth: £91,569 *Total Assets:* £528,874
Registered Office: Fleming Court, Leigh Road, Eastleigh, Southampton, SO50 9PD
Shareholders: Lionel Philip Rampton; Susan Nanette Rampton
Officers: Susan Nanette Rampton, Secretary; Lionel Philip Rampton [1953] Director/Manager

Branded Hair Limited
Incorporated: 18 December 2007
Previous: Therapi (N W) Limited
Net Worth Deficit: £2,030 *Total Assets:* £7,190
Registered Office: 33 Gibfield Park Avenue, Gibfield Park, Atherton, Manchester, M46 0SY
Major Shareholder: Philip John Naylor
Officers: Gail Dawn Naylor, Secretary; Philip John Naylor [1959] Director

Brands de Luxe Company Ltd
Incorporated: 18 February 2008 *Employees:* 1
Net Worth: £44,446 *Total Assets:* £271,623
Registered Office: Elscot House, Arcadia Avenue, London, N3 2JU
Major Shareholder: Carlos Enrique Butron
Officers: Carlos Enrique Butron [1951] Director/Businessman [Italian]

Brands Gallery Ltd
Incorporated: 7 December 2018
Registered Office: 20-22 Wenlock Road, London, N1 7GU
Shareholders: Firoz Ibrahim Pagarkar; Ahmed Mohammed Al Riyami
Officers: Firoz Ibrahim Pagarkar, Secretary; Ahmed Mohammed Al Riyami [1990] Director [Omani]; Firoz Ibrahim Pagarkar [1972] Director [Indian]

Brazilian Kimberlite Clay Ltd
Incorporated: 13 November 2018
Registered Office: 13 Newbury Road, London, E4 9JH
Major Shareholder: Bianca Tavares Veloso
Officers: Bianca Tavares Veloso [1978] Director [Portuguese]

The Brighton Group Ltd
Incorporated: 12 April 2016 *Employees:* 3
Net Worth: £84,969 *Total Assets:* £198,261
Registered Office: Innovation Centre, Highfield Drive, St Leonards on Sea, E Sussex, TN38 9UH
Parent: Aleva UK LLC
Officers: Paul Chessell [1977] Director

Bristol Consumer Health Ltd
Incorporated: 7 December 2017
Registered Office: 2 Heath Green Way, Coventry, Warwicks, CV4 8GU
Officers: Magda Andrews, Secretary; Maged Andrawes [1970] Director [Egyptian]; Magda Andrews [1972] Director [Egyptian]

Britexim Ltd
Incorporated: 1 August 2013
Registered Office: 122 Park Avenue North, London, NW10 1JD
Officers: Claudiu Iulian Olaru [1976] Director/Catering [Romanian]

British American Solutions Ltd
Incorporated: 11 January 2012
Previous: Mike & Mason Limited
Registered Office: The Charter Building, Charter Place, Uxbridge, Middlesex, UB8 1JG
Major Shareholder: Ahmad Fayazdastjerdi
Officers: Ahmad Fayazdastjerdi [1950] Director/Consultant [Iranian]; Hossein Nikroodaryani [1976] Director/General Manager - Asia [Iranian]

G & J Britton Consulting Ltd
Incorporated: 23 September 2011
Previous: PHC (UK) Limited
Net Worth Deficit: £157,186
Registered Office: 304 Fulham Road, Chelsea, London, SW10 9ER
Major Shareholder: Viktor Glosz
Officers: Viktor Glosz, Secretary; Viktor Glosz [1982] Director

Brodie and Stone PLC
Incorporated: 7 November 1944
Net Worth: £102,878 *Total Assets:* £104,987
Registered Office: 64 Woodcock Hill, Harrow, Middlesex, HA3 0JF
Major Shareholder: Michael Eggerton
Officers: Daniel Mitchell, Secretary; Michael Stephen Eggerton [1953] Director; Daniel Derek Mitchell [1975] Finance Director

Brooks Aesthetics Clinic Ltd
Incorporated: 3 October 2016
Previous: Chillipepa Limited
Registered Office: Brook House, Tynant Road, Creigiau, Cardiff, CF72 8FG
Shareholders: Brian. Dean Lee; Margaret Joan Lee
Officers: Brian. Dean Lee, Secretary; Brian. Dean Lee [1949] Director; Margaret Joan Lee [1951] Director

T L Brooks Limited
Incorporated: 31 July 2009
Net Worth: £73,899 *Total Assets:* £146,975
Registered Office: Horton House, Alderton, Towcester, Northants, NN12 7LN
Shareholders: Thomas Lloyd Brooks; Anna Brooks
Officers: Thomas Lloyd Brooks [1945] Director

Denise Brown Limited
Incorporated: 9 May 2001 *Employees:* 1
Net Worth: £522 *Total Assets:* £13,807
Registered Office: Suite 312, Cromwell Business Centre, Cromwell Park, 15 Banbury Road, Chipping Norton, Oxon, OX7 5SR
Major Shareholder: Denise Whichello
Officers: Garry Whichello, Secretary/Administrator; Denise Whichello [1956] Director/Aromatherapy Supplies; Garry Whichello [1954] Director/Administrator

Brownie Beauty Products Cosmetics Ltd
Incorporated: 17 July 2018
Registered Office: 17 New Ash Close, London, N2 8DQ
Major Shareholder: Georgina Carnegie
Officers: Tricia Williams, Secretary; Georgina Carnegie [1973] Sales Director

Brunucorp Ltd
Incorporated: 22 January 2018
Registered Office: Dept 1766, 196 High Road, London, N22 8HH
Major Shareholder: Bruno Abele
Officers: Bruno Abele [1993] Director/Businessman [Latvian]

BS Supply Ltd
Incorporated: 9 October 2014 *Employees:* 5
Net Worth: £195,382 *Total Assets:* £624,305
Registered Office: 1 Kings Avenue, London, N21 3NA
Shareholders: Barrie Kyriaco Kangellaris; Katerina Kyriacou
Officers: Barrie Kyriaco Kangellaris [1982] Director; Katerina Kyriacou [1986] Director

BSB Fashion Limited
Incorporated: 23 July 2014
Net Worth Deficit: £53,687 *Total Assets:* £3,899
Registered Office: Trilogy Suite, 9 Church Street, Wednesfield, Wolverhampton, W Midlands, WV11 1SR
Major Shareholder: Sharnjit Singh
Officers: Sharnjit Singh [1990] Director

BSB Global Limited
Incorporated: 17 February 2012
Net Worth: £214,100 *Total Assets:* £453,180
Registered Office: 4 Old Park Lane, London, W1K 1QW
Major Shareholder: Winston James Hayes
Officers: Winston James Hayes [1977] Director/Manager

BU Cosmetics Limited
Incorporated: 21 August 2017
Registered Office: 3 Julian Close, Woking, Surrey, GU21 3HD
Officers: Tanya Advani [1991] Director

Bubble-Bubble Ltd
Incorporated: 4 February 2019
Registered Office: Suite 18, Equity Chambers, 249 High Street North, Poole, Dorset, BH15 1DX
Major Shareholder: Aleksandra Ewa Krakowska
Officers: Aleksandra Ewa Krakowska [1995] Director [Polish]

Bubbleworks Limited
Incorporated: 21 May 2018
Registered Office: Claremont South Hill, Droxford, Southampton, SO32 3PB
Major Shareholder: Brett Eric Lockyer
Officers: Dr Brett Eric Lockyer [1975] Director/Chairman

Budget Beauty Limited
Incorporated: 27 April 2017
Registered Office: 64 College Road, Trowbridge, Wilts, BA14 0ET
Major Shareholder: Shahibul Ambia Choudhury
Officers: Shahibul Ambia Choudhury [1977] Director/Businessman

Buff Natural Body Care Ltd
Incorporated: 9 November 2015 *Employees:* 1
Net Worth Deficit: £5,716 *Total Assets:* £7,017
Registered Office: 67 Beverley Gardens, Ashburton, Newton Abbot, Devon, TQ13 7BN
Major Shareholder: Joanna Kate Woolvett
Officers: Joanna Kate Woolvett [1973] Director/Aromatherapy Products

Bulldog Skincare Limited
Incorporated: 22 February 2006 *Employees:* 16
Previous: The Little Wing Trading Company Limited
Net Worth: £3,714,442 *Total Assets:* £9,546,162
Registered Office: Sword House, Totteridge Road, High Wycombe, Bucks, HP13 6DG
Parent: Bulldog Skincare Holdings Limited
Officers: David Paul Hatfield [1960] Director/Executive Officer [American]; Colin Anthony Hutchison [1958] Director/Chief Operating Officer; Rod Ryan Little [1969] Director/Chief Financial Officer [American]

Bullet and Bone Limited
Incorporated: 28 March 2017
Net Worth Deficit: £13,439 *Total Assets:* £40,310
Registered Office: c/o Bennett Brooks & Co Limited, Suite 345, 50 Eastcastle Street, London, W1W 8EA
Shareholders: Paul Wilson; Ian Murphy
Officers: Paul Wilson, Secretary; Ian Murphy [1971] Director/Entrepreneur; Paul Wilson [1976] Director/Finance

Bullingberg Limited
Incorporated: 8 July 2016
Net Worth Deficit: £42,075 *Total Assets:* £19,508
Registered Office: The Old Casino, 28 Fourth Avenue, Hove, E Sussex, BN3 2PJ
Major Shareholder: Yousaf Sekander
Officers: Yousaf Sekander, Secretary; Yousaf Mohammed Sekander [1985] Director

Buly UK Limited
Incorporated: 13 November 2017
Registered Office: 20-22 Wenlock Road, London, N1 7GU
Major Shareholder: Ramdane Touhami
Officers: Ramdane Touhami [1974] Director [French]

Burly Cosmetics Ltd
Incorporated: 12 June 2017
Registered Office: 50 Firs Close, Mitcham, Surrey, CR4 1AY
Shareholders: Abid Shoaib; Yasir Khan
Officers: Abid Shoaib [1985] Director/Doctor

Burton Blackmore International Limited
Incorporated: 2 August 2016 *Employees:* 2
Net Worth Deficit: £14,295
Registered Office: The Apex, Sheriffs Orchard, Coventry, Warwicks, CV1 3PP
Officers: Glen Junior Francis [1959] Director/Manager; Charmayne Johnson-Francis [1983] Director/Manager

Bush Oil Limited
Incorporated: 14 September 2015
Net Worth Deficit: £1,575 *Total Assets:* £425
Registered Office: Park View, 75 Glenville Road, Walkford, Christchurch, Dorset, BH23 5PX
Officers: Nina Mellissa Frape [1979] Director/Sales; Andrew Murray McLean Silcock [1980] Director/Sales

Business Angels Syndicate Ltd
Incorporated: 17 May 2016
Net Worth: £1,618 *Total Assets:* £1,618
Registered Office: 62 Elmbank Avenue, Egham, Surrey, TW20 0TJ
Shareholders: Karolina Izabela Cisar; Konrad Tadeusz Sieracki
Officers: Karolina Izabela Cisar [1980] Director [Polish]; Konrad Tadeusz Sieracki [1982] Director [Polish]

Busy Bee Personal Care Limited
Incorporated: 6 January 2017
Registered Office: 3rd Floor, 207 Regent Street, London, W1B 3HH
Major Shareholder: Takashi Yukimoto
Officers: Takashi Yukimoto [1972] Director [Japanese]

Butter Park Ltd
Incorporated: 28 September 2018
Registered Office: 71-75 Shelton Street, Covent Garden, London, WC2H 9JQ
Major Shareholder: Charesa Gayle
Officers: Charesa Gayle, Secretary; Charesa Gayle [1987] Director/Recruitment Manager

Butterfly Cosmetics Limited
Incorporated: 21 December 2017
Registered Office: Flat 1, 4 Compayne Gardens, London, NW6 3DH
Major Shareholder: Aurelia-Elena Afloarei
Officers: Aurelia-Elena Alfloarei [1984] Director/Sales [Romanian]

Butterflyy Productions Ltd
Incorporated: 1 October 2016
Net Worth: £400 *Total Assets:* £400
Registered Office: 58 New Bedford Road, Luton, Beds, LU1 1SH
Officers: Candice Amanda Lee [1980] Director

Butterwhips Ltd
Incorporated: 28 July 2017
Net Worth Deficit: £1,630 *Total Assets:* £358,000
Registered Office: 19 Maule Close, Eynesbury, St Neots, Cambs, PE19 2HJ
Shareholders: Alexander James Usher; Victoria May Usher
Officers: Alexander James Usher [1975] Director; Victoria May Usher [1973] Creative Director

Buy It Out Ltd
Incorporated: 3 September 2018
Registered Office: 27 Old Gloucester Street, London, WC1N 3AX
Major Shareholder: Karolis Luksas
Officers: Karolis Luksas, Secretary; Karolis Luksas [1986] Director/Manager [Lithuanian]

Buy Perfumes London Limited
Incorporated: 4 July 2016
Net Worth Deficit: £4,474 *Total Assets:* £1,021
Registered Office: 11 Balmoral Drive, Hayes, Middlesex, UB4 0DA
Major Shareholder: Gayathri Thayakaran
Officers: Gayathri Thayakaran, Secretary; Gayathri Thayakaran [1989] Director/Web Administrator

By Al Kindi Ltd
Incorporated: 26 October 2018
Registered Office: 11 High Street Wanstead, London, E11 1QF
Shareholders: Ferdous Ahmed Ali; Esaa Rahman Chaudary
Officers: Ferdous Ahmed Ali [1991] Director; Esaa Rahman Chaudary [1990] Director

By Mia Cosmetics Ltd
Incorporated: 28 November 2017
Registered Office: 16 Yeomans Way, Enfield, Middlesex, EN3 5AP
Officers: Selim Kefli, Secretary; Selim Kefli [1984] Director/Trader [Turkish]

By Sarah Limited
Incorporated: 7 March 2017
Net Worth Deficit: £16,270 *Total Assets:* £15,020
Registered Office: The Studio, South Downs Cottage, Midhurst, W Sussex, GU29 0HD
Shareholders: Lauren Murrell; Sarah Murrell
Officers: Lauren Murrell [1988] Director/Solicitor; Sarah Murrell [1986] Director/Consultant

C & A International Trading Ltd
Incorporated: 23 November 2017
Registered Office: 71-75 Shelton Street, Covent Garden, London, WC2H 9JQ
Major Shareholder: Siu Kuen Michelle Lam
Officers: Siu Kuen Michelle Lam [1982] Director/Sales Manager

C & P Neptune Ltd
Incorporated: 24 December 2018
Registered Office: 71-75 Shelton Street, Covent Garden, London, WC2H 9JQ
Major Shareholder: Suzanne Jamin
Officers: Salim Aitmokhtar [1965] Director [French]

C Beauty Agency Limited
Incorporated: 28 November 2017
Registered Office: 90 Grosvenor Road, Wavertree, Liverpool, L15 0HB
Major Shareholder: Clodagh Bell
Officers: Clodagh Bell [1994] Director

C Distribution UK Limited
Incorporated: 30 April 2015 *Employees:* 2
Net Worth Deficit: £258,449 *Total Assets:* £628,745
Registered Office: Unit 5e Atlas Business Centre, Oxgate Lane, London, NW2 7HJ
Shareholder: Shahar Yuval
Officers: Amnon Yuval [1957] Director [Israeli]

C-Bombe Limited
Incorporated: 23 August 2018
Registered Office: 88 Crawford Street, London, W1H 2EJ
Officers: Julian Gregory [1984] Director; Oliver David Sacha Mammon [1988] Director; Daniella Harriet Posner [1986] Commercial Director; Nathan Simon Wogman [1986] Sales Director

Caarmi Ltd
Incorporated: 1 June 2018
Registered Office: Flat 45, Kingston House East, Prince's Gate, London, SW7 1LP
Major Shareholder: Rhea Maria Papanicolaou
Officers: Rhea Maria Papanicolaou [1984] Director [Greek]

Cacti Cosmetics Ltd
Incorporated: 4 October 2018
Registered Office: 16a Star Road, Peterborough, Cambs, PE1 5HP
Major Shareholder: Bethany Amber D'Inverno
Officers: Bethany Amber D'Inverno [1996] Director

Cadden & Lee Limited
Incorporated: 30 November 2016
Net Worth: £2,632 *Total Assets:* £2,632
Registered Office: 3rd Floor, 86-90 Paul Street, London, EC2A 4NE
Major Shareholder: Yae Sel Lee
Officers: Andrew Cadden [1985] Director; Yae Sel Lee [1989] Director [South Korean]

Cadyle Ltd
Incorporated: 2 January 2018
Registered Office: 80 Walm Lane, London, NW2 4RA
Officers: Adina Rusu [1987] Director/Sales Manager [Romanian]

Calbrook Cosmetics UK Ltd
Incorporated: 6 November 2006
Registered Office: Unit 36 Goulds Close, Bletchley, Milton Keynes, Bucks, MK1 1EQ
Major Shareholder: Izabelle Barbara Hammon
Officers: Izabelle Barbara Hammon [1961] Director [South African]

Calestio Ltd
Incorporated: 19 December 2017
Registered Office: Craven House, 40-44 Uxbridge Road, London, W5 2BS
Officers: Valts Vavere [1980] Director/Market Psychologist [Latvian]

Califa Ltd
Incorporated: 18 April 2016
Net Worth Deficit: £13,930 Total Assets: £477,000
Registered Office: 71-75 Shelton Street, Covent Garden, London, WC2H 9JQ
Major Shareholder: Chris Wilson
Officers: Chris Wilson [1969] Director/Entrepreneur

California Glow Ltd
Incorporated: 25 May 2018
Registered Office: Smile Enhance Academy, 95 Manchester Road, Bolton, Lancs, BL4 8QJ
Major Shareholder: Rebecca Moorfield
Officers: Rebecca Moorfield [1989] Director

Calla Distribution Ltd
Incorporated: 18 April 2012
Net Worth: £13,160 Total Assets: £51,380
Registered Office: 1 Basingstoke Road, Kingsclere, Newbury, Berks, RG20 5NN
Major Shareholder: Lynne Denise Baker
Officers: Lynne Denise Baker [1963] Director/Beauty Therapist

Calmer Solutions Limited
Incorporated: 21 November 2003 Employees: 2
Net Worth: £5,348 Total Assets: £16,916
Registered Office: Hadresham, Woolborough Lane, Outwood, Surrey, RH1 5QR
Shareholder: Hannah Claire Buck
Officers: Hannah Claire Buck, Secretary/Director; Hannah Claire Buck [1971] Director; Paul David Hewett [1962] Director; Victoria Lynne Hewett [1961] Director

Cambridge Sprouts Limited
Incorporated: 2 October 2017
Registered Office: 7 Yeoman Drive, Cambridge, CB3 0GY
Shareholders: Liangshen Wei; Yun Krystal Chen
Officers: Dr Yun Krystal Chen [1983] Director/Market Access Consultant [Chinese]; Dr Liangshen Wei [1984] Director/Business Manager [Chinese]

Can Celebrity Brands Limited
Incorporated: 1 August 2012
Net Worth Deficit: £38,368 Total Assets: £411
Registered Office: Livermore House, High Street, Dunmow, Essex, CM6 1AW
Parent: CAN International Limited
Officers: Stephen Gould [1960] Director; Claire Powell [1965] Director/Public Relations Consultant

Cancun Collection Limited
Incorporated: 3 April 2017
Net Worth Deficit: £26,879 Total Assets: £43,659
Registered Office: 1 Greenacres, Bushey Heath, Herts, WD23 1RF
Officers: Abraham Albert Sheena [1936] Director; Claudia Martine Hannah Sheena [1971] Director/Chartered Accountant

Candii Bath Limited
Incorporated: 20 February 2015
Registered Office: Flat 35, 81a Halifax Road, Huddersfield, W Yorks, HD3 3BR
Officers: Ingrid Fields [1972] Director/Entrepreneur

Canna Biology Distributing Ltd
Incorporated: 5 September 2016
Registered Office: Lower Ground Floor, Carlyle House, 235-237 Vauxhall Bridge Road, London, SW1V 1EJ
Shareholder: Lionel Edmond Rene Schwenke
Officers: Lionel Edmond Rene Schwenke, Secretary; Jonathan Taylor Phillips [1955] Director [Canadian]; Lionel Edmond Rene Schwenke [1975] Director [French]

Cannabinoid Oil Solutions Limited
Incorporated: 15 October 2018
Registered Office: 66 Hindes Road, Harrow, Middlesex, HA1 1SL
Major Shareholder: Brian Francis McKay
Officers: Brian Francis McKay [1974] Director/Artist

Cannamplify Ltd
Incorporated: 30 January 2019
Registered Office: 71-75 Shelton Street, Covent Garden, London, WC2H 9JQ
Shareholders: Jeffrey Stewart Jones; Shaan Mahrotri
Officers: Shaan Mahrotri, Secretary; Jeffrey Stewart Jones [1969] Director; Shaan Mahrotri [1975] Director

Capital (Hair and Beauty) Limited
Incorporated: 11 March 1954 Employees: 430
Net Worth: £22,084,154 Total Assets: £29,652,584
Registered Office: Capital (Hair & Beauty) Ltd, Crowhurst Corner, Crowhurst Road, Brighton, BN1 8AP
Shareholder: Peter Ross Vans Agnew
Officers: Peter Ross Vans Agnew, Secretary; David John Harrison [1963] Director; Harry Anthony Sleet [1968] Director/Chartered Accountant; Hamish Michael Vans Agnew [1958] Director; Peter Ross Vans Agnew [1960] Managing Director; Rachel Generaldine Vans Agnew [1966] Director; Sally Jane Vans Agnew [1966] Director

Capital Import & Export Co. Ltd
Incorporated: 7 December 2018
Registered Office: 2a St George Wharf, London, SW8 2LE
Major Shareholder: Guillermo Ramon Rodriguez Sone
Officers: Guillermo Ramon Rodriguez Sone [1963] Director/Manager [Dominican]

Caprise Limited
Incorporated: 22 January 2019
Registered Office: 32 Nottingham South & Wilford Industrial Estate, Nottingham, NG11 7EP
Officers: Dongyang Wang [1980] Director

Carbon Theory Limited
Incorporated: 10 May 2017
Net Worth: £5,700 Total Assets: £81,620
Registered Office: 13a Wallace Road, London, N1 2PG
Officers: Philip William Taylor [1979] Director/Founder

Steven Carey Hair & Beauty Limited
Incorporated: 28 September 2018
Registered Office: Suite A, 4-6 Canfield Place, London, NW6 3BT
Shareholders: Steven David Carey; Veronica Louise Saunders
Officers: Steven David Carey [1957] Director; Veronica Louise Saunders [1959] Director

Carol Skins Ltd
Incorporated: 19 January 2017
Registered Office: 2 Drury Close, London, SW15 5FD
Major Shareholder: Yang Chen
Officers: Yang Chen [1987] Director [Chinese]

Ayesha Carolina Limited
Incorporated: 4 February 2011
Net Worth Deficit: £1,340 *Total Assets:* £428,000
Registered Office: Flat 13, Beresford House, Rubens Place, London, SW4 7RB
Officers: Anthony Horcliptes, Secretary; Anthony Horcliptes [1981] Director; Ayesha Moonla Horcliptes [1964] Director/Makeup Artist

Carr Greens Limited
Incorporated: 19 February 2018
Registered Office: 107 Higher Lane, Lymm, Cheshire, WA13 0BZ
Major Shareholder: Andrew Harris
Officers: Dr Andrew Harris [1977] Director/Surgeon; Joseph Rydell [1978] Director/Engineer

Casa Cosmetics Ltd
Incorporated: 16 January 2017
Net Worth: £12,472 *Total Assets:* £27,319
Registered Office: 3a Gresley Road, South West Industrial Estate, Peterlee, Co Durham, SR8 2LU
Officers: Harun Tayfun Ergun [1993] Director [German]

Cassolette & Co (Sales & Marketing) Limited
Incorporated: 15 April 1998
Net Worth Deficit: £75,190 *Total Assets:* £14,774
Registered Office: Alum House, 5 Alum Chine Road, Bournemouth, BH4 8DT
Major Shareholder: Fay Robertson
Officers: Brian Warren, Secretary; Fay Robertson [1948] Director

Catalina Beauty Group Limited
Incorporated: 28 April 2018
Registered Office: Fifth Floor, 3 Gower Street, London, WC1E 6HA
Major Shareholder: Siyang Ye
Officers: Siyang Ye, Secretary; Siyang Ye [1988] Director [Chinese]

Caudalie UK Limited
Incorporated: 8 January 2002 *Employees:* 31
Net Worth: £720,199 *Total Assets:* £1,188,945
Registered Office: 1st Floor, 26 Eastcastle Street, London, W1W 8DQ
Officers: Stephane Michel Enouf [1966] Director [French]; Jean-Christophe Samyn [1971] UK Director [French]

Cazza Professional Ltd
Incorporated: 9 November 2016
Net Worth Deficit: £595
Registered Office: Flat 5, 34 Main Street, Bathgate, W Lothian, EH48 4HW
Officers: Sebastian Kulwicki [1985] Director/Cazza Professional [Polish]

CBD Bakes Ltd
Incorporated: 3 December 2018
Registered Office: 64 Main Street, Netherseal, Swadlincote, Derbys, DE12 8DA
Major Shareholder: Carol Patricia Dorricott
Officers: Carol Patricia Dorricott [1954] Director

CBee (Europe) Limited
Incorporated: 23 January 2007 *Employees:* 44
Net Worth: £2,539,023 *Total Assets:* £12,713,475
Registered Office: Eton House, 18-24 Paradise Road, Richmond, Surrey, TW9 1SE
Parent: Burt's Bees International Holdings, Inc
Officers: Charlotte Marie Bailey, Secretary; Todd Lawrence Brock [1966] Director/VP/General Manager [American]; Ajaz Ahmad Khan [1962] Director/General Manager; Giles Addis Malone [1966] Director/Accountant [Irish]

CC Dist UK Ltd
Incorporated: 7 February 2017
Net Worth: £9,900 *Total Assets:* £140,521
Registered Office: 57 Ocean Wharf, 60 Westferry Road, London, E14 8JS
Major Shareholder: Fatih Mehmet Sutcu
Officers: Fatih Mehmet Sutcu [1978] Director [Turkish]

Cedron Ltd.
Incorporated: 1 November 2016
Net Worth: £1,000 *Total Assets:* £1,000
Registered Office: Flat 20, Cranford Court, 82 Plymouth Grove, Manchester, M13 9LW
Officers: Ali Asghar Cheraghi [1964] Director

Celeb Products Ltd
Incorporated: 1 August 2012
Net Worth Deficit: £16,443 *Total Assets:* £550
Registered Office: 44 Curthwaite Gardens, Enfield, Middlesex, EN2 7LN
Major Shareholder: Ali Mustafa
Officers: Ali Mustafa [1973] Director

CFBP Ltd
Incorporated: 11 May 2017
Registered Office: Flat 47, Lord Kensington House, 5 Radnor Terrace, Kensington, London, W14 8BU
Major Shareholder: Adaaku Iwuajoku
Officers: Adaaku Iwuajoku [1992] Director/Entrepreneur

CFN 1 Limited
Incorporated: 10 May 2017
Net Worth Deficit: £24,784 *Total Assets:* £37,806
Registered Office: Dickens House, Guithavon Street, Witham, Essex, CM8 1BJ
Major Shareholder: Jason Nevada Westwood
Officers: Jason Nevada Westwood [1968] Director

CH General Traders Limited
Incorporated: 11 June 2018
Registered Office: 6 Astley Close, Tipton, W Midlands, DY4 0LT
Officers: Caesar Hosseini [1975] Director [Iranian]

Chaleur Ltd
Incorporated: 1 August 2018
Registered Office: Forth House, Beech Drive, Kingswood, Tadworth, Surrey, KT20 6PJ
Major Shareholder: Joseph Daniel Manning
Officers: Joseph Daniel Manning [1990] Director

Reevis Chan Ltd
Incorporated: 2 November 2017
Registered Office: 74 Springfield Gardens, London, NW9 0SA
Major Shareholder: Reena Channa
Officers: Reena Channa [1982] Director

Chando-UK Ltd
Incorporated: 27 October 2015
Net Worth Deficit: £54,581 *Total Assets:* £1,783
Registered Office: The Basement, 17 Belmont Crescent, Glasgow, G12 8EU
Major Shareholder: Delysia Kaur Grewal
Officers: Delysia Kaur Grewal [1986] Director/Sales Person

Chanel Limited
Incorporated: 6 February 1925 *Employees:* 20,197
Net Worth: £2,818,455,808 *Total Assets:* £6,879,171,584
Registered Office: 5 Barlow Place, London, W1J 6DG
Officers: Paul Stuart Gaff, Secretary; Paul Alain Abecassis [1950] Director/Banker [Swiss]; Philippe Bernard Blondiaux [1965] Director/Chief Financial Officer [French]; Richard Maurice Collasse [1953] Director/President [French]; John Stephen Galantic [1961] Director/President [American/Swiss]; Bertrand Henry Gros [1950] Director/Lawyer [Swiss]; Suzanne Elizabeth Heywood [1969] Managing Director; Baroness Martha Lane Fox [1973] Director/Entrepreneur; Olivier Nicolay [1957] Director [French]; Bruno Andre Jean Pavlovsky [1962] Director/President [French]; Vincent Graham Shaw [1958] Director/President

Chanson Worldwide Limited
Incorporated: 8 December 2015
Registered Office: Unit G25, Waterfront Studios, 1 Dock Road, London, E16 1AH
Major Shareholder: Liangmei Chen
Officers: Liangmei Chen [1987] Director [Chinese]

Sarah Chapman Ltd.
Incorporated: 3 February 2005 *Employees:* 21
Net Worth: £1,640,985 *Total Assets:* £3,027,642
Registered Office: 2nd Floor, 59 Markham Street, Chelsea, London, SW3 3NR
Major Shareholder: Sarah Chapman
Officers: Heather Darnell, Secretary; Sarah Chapman [1970] Director/Beauty Consultant; Heather Rodgers Durrell [1971] Finance Director

Charlize London Ltd
Incorporated: 24 May 2018
Registered Office: 20-22 Wenlock Road, London, N1 7GU
Major Shareholder: Pedram Memarian
Officers: Roxanne Memarian, Secretary; Pedram Memarian [1987] Director/Businessman; Roxanne Memarian [1990] Director/Businesswoman

Charms Europe Ltd
Incorporated: 29 September 2014
Net Worth: £1,548 *Total Assets:* £2,713
Registered Office: 239 Ribbleton Lane, Preston, Lancs, PR1 5EA
Shareholder: Jacek Budner
Officers: Jacek Budner [1966] Director [Polish]; Weronika Dudzik [1981] Director [Polish]

Cheap Cosmetic Ltd
Incorporated: 27 June 2018
Registered Office: 108 Percy Street, Goole, E Yorks, DN14 5SE
Major Shareholder: Branislav Findrik
Officers: Branislav Findrik, Secretary; Branislav Findrik [1974] Director [Slovak]

Cheet Beauty Ltd
Incorporated: 16 July 2018
Registered Office: 20 Station Street, Waterhouses, Co Durham, DH7 9AS
Major Shareholder: Mary Elizabeth Fuller
Officers: Mary Elizabeth Fuller [1996] Director

Chemical Poetry Ltd
Incorporated: 18 August 2017
Registered Office: 56 Nelson Gardens, London, E2 7AA
Major Shareholder: Keren Bester
Officers: Keren Bester, Secretary; Keren Bester [1980] Founder Director [Australian]

Cherie Cosmetics Limited
Incorporated: 4 June 2018
Registered Office: Unit B15 Troon Way Business Centre, Humberstone Lane, Leicester, LE4 9HA
Officers: Manoj Gupta [1982] Director

Cherry Cherry Fashion Ltd
Incorporated: 7 March 2018
Registered Office: 1 Bent Street, Manchester, M8 8NF
Shareholders: Sim Hui Toa; Shaoyan Lin
Officers: Sim Hui Toa, Secretary; Shaoyan Yan Lin [1981] Director/Manager; Sim Hui Toa [1974] Director/Operations Manager

Ches Editions Ltd
Incorporated: 30 January 2019
Registered Office: 124 High Street, Hampton Hill, Hampton, Surrey, TW12 1NS
Major Shareholder: Francesca Barrow
Officers: Francesca Barrow [1989] Director

Chic Clothing Limited
Incorporated: 17 September 2018
Registered Office: 71-75 Shelton Street, London, WC2H 9JQ
Shareholders: Stacy Salisha Ibiks-Ibikunle; Candy Ria Ramjohn
Officers: Stacy Salisha Ibiks-Ibikunle [1981] Director [Trinidadian]; Candy Ria Ramjohn [1984] Director [Trinidadian]

Chief Cosmetics Ltd
Incorporated: 23 July 2014
Net Worth Deficit: £26,940 *Total Assets:* £11,591
Registered Office: Unit 517, Crown House, Business Centre, London, NW10 7PN
Officers: Fiona Rhoden [1969] Director/Health & Beauty

Chinese Gentry Limited
Incorporated: 8 August 2018
Registered Office: 9 Pantygraigwen Road, Pontypridd, Mid Glamorgan, CF37 2RR
Shareholders: Lili Ge; Xuepei Liu
Officers: Lili GE [1988] Director [Chinese]

Chintys Ltd
Incorporated: 28 March 2018
Registered Office: 50 Clarinda Avenue, Camelon, Falkirk, Stirlingshire, FK1 4LZ
Shareholders: Chantelle Curran; Kenny Sawers
Officers: Chantelle Curran [1988] Director/Nail Supplier; Kenny Sawers [1985] Director/Nail Supplier [South African]

Chirp Body Ltd
Incorporated: 23 February 2016
Net Worth Deficit: £7,540 *Total Assets:* £13,970
Registered Office: Niddry Lodge, 51 Holland Street, London, W8 7JB
Shareholders: Ryan Alexander Carstairs; Krystyna Marszalek
Officers: Ryan Carstairs [1989] Director; Krystyna Marszalek [1989] Director [Polish]

Chit.Ka Ltd
Incorporated: 6 August 2018
Registered Office: 27 Cole Bank Road, Hall Green, Birmingham, B28 8EZ
Major Shareholder: Henna Irum Amin Sajawal
Officers: Henna Irum Amin Sajawal [1992] Director/Telephonist

CHK (UK) Ltd
Incorporated: 3 May 2012
Net Worth Deficit: £12,038 Total Assets: £100,294
Registered Office: 299a Bethnal Green Road, London, E2 6AH
Shareholder: Guy Trieu
Officers: Guy Trieu [1977] Director/Importer

CHM Holdings Ltd
Incorporated: 9 March 2018
Registered Office: Lynes House, Bishops Cannings, Devizes, Wilts, SN10 2LD
Major Shareholder: Charles McCloy
Officers: Charles McCloy [1991] Director/Chartered Surveyor

Choice of Nature Limited
Incorporated: 18 April 1996 Employees: 1
Net Worth: £9,940 Total Assets: £47,776
Registered Office: Regent House, 316 Beulah Hill, London, SE19 3HF
Parent: Gapardis Health & Beauty Inc
Officers: Michael Maurice Farah [1959] Director

Choize Ltd
Incorporated: 7 December 2018
Registered Office: 56 Almondvale South, Livingston, W Lothian, EH54 6NB
Shareholders: Khajahussain Kizhakkepurath Mohiyudeen; Rafeeque Olikkathodi
Officers: Khajahussain Kizhakkepurath Mohiyudeen [1985] Managing Director [Indian]; Rafeeque Olikkathodi [1981] Director

Clive Christian Perfume Limited
Incorporated: 1 April 1998 Employees: 23
Net Worth: £188,776 Total Assets: £7,538,419
Registered Office: 4th Floor, Yalding House, Great Portland Street, London, W1W 6AJ
Major Shareholder: Brian Souter
Officers: Yvonne Johnson, Secretary; Clive Christian [1951] Managing Director; Andrew James MacFie [1956] Director; Amy Elizabeth Nelson-Bennett [1969] Director/Chief Executive Officer [American]; Ahmad Salam [1960] Director; Rahan Ahmad Shaheen [1967] Director

Chronicles Medical Consulting Ltd
Incorporated: 23 February 2017
Net Worth Deficit: £880 Total Assets: £120
Registered Office: c/o Pelican Pharmacy, 344 Manchester Road, West Timperley, Altrincham, Cheshire, WA14 5NH
Officers: Gary Kai Wai Chan, Secretary; Gary Kai Wai Chan [1979] Director

CHT Supplies Limited
Incorporated: 4 January 2017 Employees: 2
Net Worth: £422 Total Assets: £10,999
Registered Office: 9 Blackford Hill Grove, Edinburgh, EH9 3HA
Shareholder: Colin Harvey Thomson
Officers: Colin Harvey Thomson [1968] Director; Karen King Thomson [1966] Director

Chulo Naturals Ltd
Incorporated: 31 August 2017
Registered Office: 119 Twydall Lane, Gillingham, Kent, ME8 6JU
Major Shareholder: Claire Ann Hulott
Officers: Claire Ann Hulott [1965] Director/Manufacture and Wholesale of Skincare Products

Churchill Motley Limited
Incorporated: 4 October 2018
Registered Office: Churchill Point, Lake Edge Green, Trafford Park Road, Manchester, M17 1BL
Parent: Per-Scent Acquisitions Limited
Officers: Sanjay Jayantilal Vadera [1967] Director; Vipul Jayantilal Vadera [1972] Director

Ciao Brow Henna Limited
Incorporated: 26 April 2018
Registered Office: 95 New Road, Willenhall, W Midlands, WV13 2BG
Shareholders: Karon Holmes; Paul Bird
Officers: Paul Bird, Secretary; Paul Bird [1962] Director/Beautician; Karon Holmes [1962] Director/Beautician

Cilko Ltd
Incorporated: 4 November 2008
Registered Office: Hayhow & Co, 19 King Street, Kings Lynn, Norfolk, PE30 1HB
Major Shareholder: Joanne Elizabeth Darbost
Officers: Joanne Elizabeth Darbost [1965] Director

City Beauty Supplies (UK) Ltd
Incorporated: 15 August 2013
Net Worth: £21,578 Total Assets: £78,872
Registered Office: 59-61 Summer Lane, Birmingham, B19 3TH
Major Shareholder: Mohammed Shamas Shabir
Officers: Mohammed Shamas Shabir [1994] Director/Entrepreneur

CJ Cosmetics Ltd
Incorporated: 3 April 2018
Registered Office: 20-22 Wenlock Road, London, N1 7GU
Major Shareholder: Joe Fletcher
Officers: Joe Fletcher [1990] Director/Engineer

Claracutis, Ltd
Incorporated: 25 October 2018
Registered Office: Flat 14 Merryfield Court, 411 Battersea Park, London, SW11 5BF
Shareholders: Django Marecaux; Michael Pui Hing Lau
Officers: Dr Michael Lau, Secretary; Dr Michael Pui Hing Lau [1948] Director/Medical Doctor [American]; Django Marecaux [1979] Director/Business Professional [French]

Clarendon of London Limited
Incorporated: 14 April 2008
Net Worth Deficit: £24,910 Total Assets: £7,440
Registered Office: 343 City Road, London, EC1V 1LR
Officers: Livingston Anthony White [1962] Director/Businessman

Clarins & Felix Healthcare Ltd
Incorporated: 22 September 2017
Registered Office: Lot 28, 17-21 Hunter's Mill, Downpatrick, Co Down, BT30 6BL
Parent: Felix Medical Group Ltd
Officers: Dr Karren Brady [1976] Director/Businessman

Clarins (U.K.) Limited
Incorporated: 14 August 1981 Employees: 2,004
Net Worth: £31,618,822 Total Assets: £69,669,808
Registered Office: 10 Cavendish Place, London, W1G 9DN
Officers: Deborah Ann Lewis [1964] Director; Alison Mary Surridge [1966] Director

Classic Beaute Limited
Incorporated: 6 August 1996 Employees: 16
Net Worth: £718,586 Total Assets: £3,061,265
Registered Office: Hill House, Monument Hill, Weybridge, Surrey, KT13 8RX
Shareholders: Kenneth Charles Green; Susan Esther Green
Officers: Philip John Stokes, Secretary; Fabien Georges Jacques Callens [1969] Marketing Director [French]; Kenneth Charles Green [1945] Director; Susan Esther Green [1946] Director/Public Relations; Jonathan Richard Lee [1965] Commercial Director; Fleur Nyman [1971] Sales Director; Pamela Roy-Jones [1947] Retail Director; Brian John Stanton [1978] Managing Director [New Zealander]; Philip John Stokes [1956] Director/Company Secretary

Clean & Care Facilities Management Limited
Incorporated: 18 July 2014
Net Worth Deficit: £5,620 Total Assets: £56,410
Registered Office: 13a South Hawksworth Street, Ilkley, W Yorks, LS29 9DX
Officers: Mark Judkowski [1959] Director

Clean Living Ltd
Incorporated: 5 July 2018
Registered Office: 3 Garratt Terrace, London, SW17 0QE
Major Shareholder: Bethany Plumley-Korab
Officers: Bethany Plumley-Korab [1994] Director/Retailer

Cleanux Chemicals Ltd
Incorporated: 11 September 2017
Registered Office: 20 Whitebutts Road, Ruislip, Middlesex, HA4 0NB
Officers: Himanshu Patel, Secretary; Himanshu Patel [1966] Director

Clearance Masters Ltd
Incorporated: 15 March 2018
Registered Office: 71-75 Shelton Street, Covent Garden, London, WC2H 9JQ
Major Shareholder: Ales Kminek
Officers: Ales Kminek, Secretary; Ales Kminek [1973] Managing Director [Czech]

Cleardot Group Ltd
Incorporated: 30 June 2017
Registered Office: Cleardot Group Ltd, 7 Davies Lane, London, E11 3DR
Major Shareholder: Teodor Boev
Officers: Teodor Boev [1982] Director [Bulgarian]

Clever Skin Co Limited
Incorporated: 11 April 2018
Registered Office: 5a Railway Road, Ilkley, W Yorks, LS29 8HQ
Major Shareholder: Claire Janine Hurst
Officers: Claire Janine Hurst [1973] Director

Clickpoint Limited
Incorporated: 12 February 2018
Registered Office: 59 Tamworth Street, Oldham, Lancs, OL9 7QY
Officers: Nicusor Constantin Dobre [1993] Director/Work [Romanian]

Clinibella Ltd
Incorporated: 30 October 2018
Registered Office: Lytchett House, 13 Freeland Park, Wareham Road, Lytchett Matravers, Poole, Dorset, BH16 6FA
Major Shareholder: Dori Baruch
Officers: Dori Baruch [1981] Director [Israeli]

Clink Street FX Ltd
Incorporated: 8 January 2018
Registered Office: 28 Mill Hill, Weston Colville, Cambridge, CB21 5NY
Shareholders: Jane Wheeler; Stephen Wheeler
Officers: Jane Wheeler [1958] Director; Steven Wheeler [1958] Director

Clinova Limited
Incorporated: 23 May 2006 Employees: 9
Net Worth: £314,029 Total Assets: £955,018
Registered Office: International House, Southampton International Business Park, George Curl Way, Southampton, SO18 2RZ
Shareholders: Arsalan Karim; Charles Ebubedike
Officers: Charles Ebubedike, Secretary; Charles Ebubedike [1981] Director; Arsalan Karim [1980] Director

Cloud 19 Limited
Incorporated: 5 February 2010
Net Worth Deficit: £32,090 Total Assets: £100,000
Registered Office: 16 Manor Street, Ruskington, Sleaford, Lincs, NG34 9ER
Shareholders: Elizabeth Ann Hughes; John William Hughes
Officers: Elizabeth Ann Hughes [1969] Director/Administrator; John William Hughes [1967] Director/IT Consultant

CM Hair & Beauty Supplies Limited
Incorporated: 9 January 2013
Net Worth: £14,519 Total Assets: £136,561
Registered Office: 206-208 Walsall Wood Road, Walsall, W Midlands, WS9 8HB
Major Shareholder: Mark Allsop
Officers: Mark Allsop [1981] Director/Graphic Designer; Craig Johnson [1978] Director/Accountant

CNI Services Limited
Incorporated: 17 September 2016
Net Worth: £103,540 Total Assets: £106,950
Registered Office: 21 High Road, Cowley, Uxbridge, Middlesex, UB8 2HL
Officers: Sarmin Sultana Sathi [1988] Director/Businesswoman [Bangladeshi]

Co Beauty Ltd
Incorporated: 21 January 2019
Registered Office: 12 Jenny Lane, Bristol, BS10 6WH
Major Shareholder: Sophie Nicole Laker
Officers: Sophie Nicole Laker [1980] Director

Cochabamba Parfums Limited
Incorporated: 9 July 2018
Registered Office: 80-83 Long Lane, London, EC1A 9ET
Shareholders: Bridget Emma Plant; Rebecca Louise Brown
Officers: Rebecca Louise Brown [1979] Director; Bridget Emma Plant [1979] Director

Cocobaba Ltd
Incorporated: 5 November 2018
Registered Office: 20-22 Wenlock Road, London, N1 7GU
Officers: Andrew David Block [1978] Director

Code Beautiful Limited
Incorporated: 11 September 2012 Employees: 2
Net Worth: £120,247 Total Assets: £182,853
Registered Office: Piccadilly House, 49 Piccadilly, Manchester, M1 2AP
Major Shareholder: Sarah Jane Cross
Officers: Sarah Jane Cross [1978] Director

Coffeinium Germania Ltd
Incorporated: 10 January 2019
Registered Office: The Picasso Building, Caldervale Road, Wakefield, W Yorks, WF1 5PF
Officers: Sascha Behrendt [1983] Director/Computer Programmer [German]

Colbico Limited
Incorporated: 12 January 2010
Net Worth: £82,345 *Total Assets:* £126,836
Registered Office: Albert House, 256-260 Old Street, London, EC1V 9DD
Shareholders: Alderville Investissements SARL; Roger Stephane Dhelens; Dominique Ibanez
Officers: Roger Stephane Dhelens [1964] Director/Consultant [French]; Dominique Ibanez [1960] Director/Consultant [French]

Colgate-Palmolive (U.K.) Limited
Incorporated: 7 January 1922
Net Worth: £32,711,000 *Total Assets:* £92,973,000
Registered Office: Guildford Business Park, Middleton Road, Guildford, Surrey, GU2 8JZ
Parent: Colgate-Palmolive Company
Officers: Christopher Robert Burniston [1980] Associate Legal Director; Philip Durocher [1964] Managing Director [Canadian/American]; Charalabos Klados [1967] Director/Division General Counsel [German]; Dean Pratt [1965] Finance Director

Coll Gen Limited
Incorporated: 27 September 2012
Net Worth Deficit: £19,675 *Total Assets:* £34,488
Registered Office: 590 Kingston Road, London, SW20 8DN
Major Shareholder: Piotr Marian Romanowicz
Officers: Piotr Marian Romanowicz [1973] Director [Polish]

Collection 1212 Limited
Incorporated: 15 October 2003 *Employees:* 1
Previous: Sahara Traders (UK) Limited
Net Worth Deficit: £368 *Total Assets:* £30,130
Registered Office: 925 Finchley Road, London, NW11 7PE
Major Shareholder: Ananya Kaur Banga
Officers: Rajinder Singh Banga [1962] Director/Entrepreneur

Collier & Wood Ltd
Incorporated: 21 May 2015
Registered Office: Advanced House, Wesley Square, Hartlepool, Cleveland, TS24 8BX
Shareholders: John Wood; Robert Matthew Collier
Officers: Robert Collier [1980] Director; John Paul Wood [1954] Director

Cath Collins Devon Ltd
Incorporated: 21 April 2010
Net Worth Deficit: £36,920 *Total Assets:* £57,970
Registered Office: 5 The Chambers, Vineyard, Abingdon on Thames, Oxon, OX14 3PX
Major Shareholder: Alice Bedi
Officers: Alice Bedi [1978] Director

Alia Collyns Cosmetics Ltd
Incorporated: 13 September 2018
Registered Office: Acc Office, Manor House, Moorhouse Lane, Kirklees, Birkenshaw, W Yorks, BD11 2AY
Officers: Alia Elmamoun [1994] Director/Company Owner [New Zealander]

Color Studio Ltd
Incorporated: 7 September 2017
Registered Office: 71-75 Shelton Street, London, WC2H 9JQ
Major Shareholder: Ozair Mateen
Officers: Ozair Mateen, Secretary; Ozair Mateen [1985] Director [Pakistani]

Colour Life Limited
Incorporated: 15 January 2019
Registered Office: 71 Newington Green Road, London, N1 4QU
Major Shareholder: Mustafa Halit Niksarli
Officers: Mustafa Halit Niksarli [1958] Sales Director

Colour Lux Cosmetics Ltd
Incorporated: 26 October 2018
Registered Office: 8 Ernest Egerton Close, Stoke on Trent, Staffs, ST6 5XE
Major Shareholder: Syeda Asma Zaidi
Officers: Syeda Asma Zaidi [1985] Director

Colourscent Limited
Incorporated: 9 July 2018
Registered Office: 27 Old Gloucester Street, London, WC1N 3AX
Shareholders: Lay Shuan Wee; Pang Ngan Chiang
Officers: Pang Ngan Chiang [1970] Director; Lay Shuan Wee [1971] Director

Colwayland Company Limited
Incorporated: 11 September 2016
Registered Office: 3 Laurence Grove, Selby, N Yorks, YO8 8DS
Shareholder: Tomasz Kuliberda
Officers: Paulina Kalinowska, Secretary; Tomasz Kuliberda [1974] Director [Polish]

Com4hospitality Ltd.
Incorporated: 14 May 2009
Net Worth Deficit: £169,804 *Total Assets:* £328,589
Registered Office: 483 Green Lanes, London, N13 4BS
Major Shareholder: Stefan Ruprecht
Officers: Stefan Ruprecht [1962] Director/Businessman [German]

Comedic Limited
Incorporated: 21 February 1983 *Employees:* 24
Net Worth: £4,736,399 *Total Assets:* £6,675,613
Registered Office: Unit B, 32a Eveline Road, Mitcham, Surrey, CR4 3LE
Shareholder: William Spencer Mendes
Officers: Jeronimo Cirilo Mendes, Secretary; Anastasia Leonara Mendes [1947] Director/Manageress; Jeronimo Cirilo Mendes [1940] Director; Sharon Lillian Mendes [1969] Director/Manageress; William Spencer Mendes [1966] Director

Comets Intertrade Company Limited
Incorporated: 21 December 2017
Registered Office: 71-75 Shelton Street, Covent Garden, London, WC2H 9JQ
Shareholders: Chantarach Piboonswasdi; Saritratch Piboonswasdi
Officers: Chantarach Piboonswasdi [1994] Director [Thai]

Comfort Click Limited
Incorporated: 7 November 2005 *Employees:* 1
Net Worth: £387,605 *Total Assets:* £1,507,888
Registered Office: 106 Lower Addiscombe Road, Croydon, Surrey, CR0 6AD
Shareholders: CC Group Services Limited; Minesh Rasiklal Pattni; Chetan Vinodrai Shukla; Vivek Vinodrai Shukla
Officers: Minesh Rasiklal Pattni [1972] Director

Comfortz Ltd
Incorporated: 5 June 2017
Registered Office: 30 Turnpike Place, Crawley, W Sussex, RH11 7UA
Major Shareholder: Balqees Nazir
Officers: Balqees Nazir [1978] Director/Businesswomen [Pakistani]

Comglobal Limited
Incorporated: 1 August 2018
Registered Office: Unit 27 Cygnus Business Centre, Dalmeyer Road, Willesden, London, NW10 2XA
Officers: Dhanush Patel [1997] Director; Lalji Premji Vekaria [1965] Director

Company NBN Limited
Incorporated: 6 August 2014
Net Worth Deficit: £4,060,000 *Total Assets:* £3,300,000
Registered Office: Devonshire House, 1 Devonshire Street, London, W1W 5DR
Parent: Pinnacle Brands Pty Limited
Officers: Luke Phillips [1982] Director [Australian]; Mark Thompson [1969] Director [Irish]

Complete Healing Limited
Incorporated: 13 September 2018
Registered Office: 13 Bay Street, Blackburn, Lancs, BB1 5NJ
Major Shareholder: Nasir Ahmed
Officers: Nasir Ahmed [1979] Director

Complexi-Light Ltd
Incorporated: 6 August 2015
Net Worth: £7,200 *Total Assets:* £7,200
Registered Office: 14 Riverside Close, Cheswick Green, Solihull, W Midlands, B90 4LB
Officers: Dr Anita Ghag [1986] Director/Lecturer; Opreet Ghag [1983] Director/Pharmacist

Conatural Ltd
Incorporated: 26 October 2015
Registered Office: 115 London Road, Morden, Surrey, SM4 5HP
Major Shareholder: Myra Husain Qureshi
Officers: Myra Husain Qureshi [1983] Director/Entrepreneur

Concept Healthcare Limited
Incorporated: 29 August 2017
Registered Office: Flat 26, Mayfair Court, Observer Drive, Rickmansworth Road, Watford, Herts, WD18 7GA
Major Shareholder: Snehal Kavlanekar
Officers: Snehal Kavlanekar [1978] Director [Indian]

Connected Beauty Limited
Incorporated: 26 May 2017
Registered Office: Accountancy House, 90 Walworth Road, London, SE1 6SW
Major Shareholder: Mehboob Abdulla
Officers: Mehboob Abdulla [1956] Director

Connessioni UK Limited
Incorporated: 17 November 2015
Net Worth Deficit: £82,580 *Total Assets:* £60,790
Registered Office: 3rd Floor, 207 Regent Street, London, W1B 3HH
Shareholders: Syed Muhammad Amir Ali Jafri; Almas Tariq
Officers: Dr Syed Muhammad Amir Ali Jafri [1966] Director [Italian]; Almas Tariq [1980] Director [Italian]

Jasper Conran Perfumes Limited
Incorporated: 7 February 2000
Net Worth: £39,280 *Total Assets:* £104,270
Registered Office: 1-7 Rostrevor Mews, Fulham, London, SW6 5AZ
Officers: Robert Michael Litler, Secretary; Jasper Alexander Thirlby Conran [1959] Director/Designer

Conscience Clear Tan Limited
Incorporated: 20 September 2017
Registered Office: 8 Queen Street, Londonderry, BT48 7EF
Shareholder: Ronan Stewart
Officers: Connor Grant [1988] Director [Irish]; Ronan Stewart [1981] Director [Irish]

Constantine K Ltd
Incorporated: 20 September 2017
Registered Office: 807 Green Lanes, London, N21 2SG
Officers: Constantinos Kyriacos [1988] Director/Business Analyst

Consy Limited
Incorporated: 2 August 2018
Registered Office: 5 Darlington Close, Sandy, Beds, SG19 1RW
Officers: Malin Sara Andersson [1992] Director/Cosmetics [Swedish]

Cont-Hemp-Orary Ltd
Incorporated: 11 April 2018
Registered Office: 9 Park Place East, Sunderland, Tyne & Wear, SR2 8EE
Shareholders: Scott Grainger; Antonio Dos Santos Carvalho Silva
Officers: Scott Grainger [1971] Director/Chemist

Cont-Hemp-Orary Skincare Ltd
Incorporated: 16 April 2018
Registered Office: 20-22 Wenlock Road, London, N1 7GU
Major Shareholder: Scott Grainger
Officers: Scott Grainger [1971] Director/Chemist

Contemporary Cosmetic Enterprise Ltd
Incorporated: 25 February 2019
Registered Office: 24 Sheen Road, Richmond, Surrey, TW9 1YT
Major Shareholder: Ali Javidmehr
Officers: Ali Javidmehr [1976] Managing Director [Iranian]

Contour and More London Limited
Incorporated: 23 January 2017
Net Worth: £4,080 *Total Assets:* £12,749
Registered Office: P O Box 314, St Neots, Cambs, PE19 9FX
Shareholders: Callum Morgan; Jasmine Golding
Officers: Jasmine Golding [1996] Director/Cosmetics Designer; Callum Morgan [1991] Director/Export Sales

Contrast Cosmetics Ltd.
Incorporated: 3 August 2018
Registered Office: 27 Old Gloucester Street, London, WC1N 3AX
Major Shareholder: Matthias Thans
Officers: Matthias Thans, Secretary; Matthias Thans [1997] Director/Sales [Belgian]

Control Cosmetics Ltd
Incorporated: 5 August 2014
Net Worth: £2,885 *Total Assets:* £28,283
Registered Office: 85 Great Portland Street, London, W1W 7LT
Shareholders: Jaroslaw Starczewski; Daniel Bogusz
Officers: Daniel Bogusz [1983] Director [Polish]; Jaroslaw Starczewski [1974] Director [Polish]

The Convent Venue Limited
Incorporated: 20 November 2017
Registered Office: 34 Field Fare, Abbeydale, Gloucester, GL4 4WF
Officers: Matthew John [1978] Director/Film Producer

Cool Blades Limited
Incorporated: 1 February 2011 Employees: 10
Net Worth: £212,477 Total Assets: £683,778
Registered Office: Unit 5 Wyre Court, Bracewell Avenue, Poulton-le-Fylde, Lancs, FY6 8JF
Shareholder: Julie Bannister
Officers: Brian Peter Bannister [1961] Director; Julie Bannister [1964] Director; Rupert Harry Alwyn Hughes [1966] Director

Cool Essentials Limited
Incorporated: 23 June 2000
Net Worth Deficit: £12,320 Total Assets: £7,910
Registered Office: 10 Uxbridge Street, Kensington, London, W8 7SY
Officers: Moray Frank St John Hughes, Secretary; Gisele Mir [1956] Director/Cosmetic Scientist and Lawyer

Cor Cosmetics Limited
Incorporated: 18 July 2018
Registered Office: 76 Forkhill Road, Newry, Co Armagh, BT35 8QY
Major Shareholder: Chimene O'Reilly
Officers: Chimene O'Reilly [1983] Director [Irish]

Cor Europe Limited
Incorporated: 16 April 2009
Net Worth: £4,391 Total Assets: £15,602
Registered Office: 67 Church Road, Hove, E Sussex, BN3 2BD
Major Shareholder: Taras Andrew Nadvirny
Officers: Taras Andrew Nadvirny [1968] Director

Corium Health Limited
Incorporated: 29 June 2018
Registered Office: Kemp House, 160 City Road, London, EC1V 2NX
Shareholder: David Raymond Robinson
Officers: Mark Clifford Butterfield, Secretary; Mark Clifford Butterfield [1955] Director/Accountant; Clifford Jean-Marie Giles [1967] Director [Australian]; David Raymond Robinson [1971] Director [Australian]

Coriungo Limited
Incorporated: 15 September 2017
Registered Office: 1 Golden Court, Richmond, Surrey, TW9 1EU
Officers: Pieter-Jan Beyls [1987] Director [Belgian]

Corley Capital Limited
Incorporated: 8 September 2016
Previous: Bodi Care Limited
Net Worth: £13,214 Total Assets: £40,666
Registered Office: Mingary Cottage, Smalley Mill Road, Horsley, Derby, DE21 5BL
Shareholders: Chloe Lewtas Corley; Benjamin David Corley
Officers: Benjamin David Corley [1991] Director; Chloe Lewtas Corley [1992] Director

Elizabeth Cornelius Limited
Incorporated: 18 May 2009
Net Worth Deficit: £25,620 Total Assets: £5,480
Registered Office: Kemp House, 152 City Road, London, EC1V 2NX
Major Shareholder: Elizabeth Wyllie Hawthorne
Officers: Elizabeth Wyllie Hawthorne [1958] Managing Director

Cornish Beard Company Limited
Incorporated: 3 April 2018
Registered Office: 13 Hendra Vean, Truro, Cornwall, TR1 3TT
Major Shareholder: Daniel David Crispin Osmond
Officers: Daniel David Crispin Osmond [1980] Director/Designer

Cosimpex Ltd
Incorporated: 11 March 2016
Net Worth: £257,418 Total Assets: £1,087,888
Registered Office: 152 City Road, London, EC1V 2NX
Major Shareholder: Ahmet Hamdi Parlak
Officers: Ahmet Hamdi Parlak [1971] Director [Turkish]

Coslab Ltd
Incorporated: 26 November 2018
Registered Office: Suite 18, Equity Chambers, 249 High Street North, Poole, Dorset, BH15 1DX
Major Shareholder: Anna Maria Molenda-Skowronek
Officers: Anna Maria Molenda-Skowronek [1969] Director [Polish]

Cosma Fragrances Limited
Incorporated: 6 November 2017
Registered Office: 3rd Floor, 210 South Street, Romford, Essex, RM1 1TG
Shareholders: Laurent Richard Mauger; Christine Louise Gunningham
Officers: Christine Louise Gunningham [1978] Director/Financial Manager [South African]; Laurent Richard Mauger [1969] Director [South African]

Cosmeceuticals Limited
Incorporated: 19 February 2007 Employees: 31
Net Worth: £1,194,967 Total Assets: £3,084,327
Registered Office: The Pavillion, Josselin Road, Basildon, Essex, SS13 1QB
Parent: Adonia Medical Group Ltd
Officers: Ronald Thomas Sullivan, Secretary; Patrick James Bowler [1950] Director/Cosmetic Doctor; Ronald Thomas Sullivan [1953] Finance Director; Paul William Wilkinson [1965] Director

Cosmedi Limited
Incorporated: 25 April 2017
Net Worth: £1,067 Total Assets: £35,337
Registered Office: Shearway Business Park, Shearway Road, Folkestone, Kent, CT19 4RH
Shareholder: Jurgita Daukante
Officers: Jurgita Daukante, Secretary; Jurgita Daukante [1982] Director/Manager [Lithuanian]

Cosmelinks Consultancy Ltd
Incorporated: 3 October 2018
Registered Office: 27 Old Gloucester Street, London, WC1N 3AX
Major Shareholder: Yun Zuo
Officers: Yun Zuo [1982] Director [Chinese]

Cosmetia UK Limited
Incorporated: 22 January 2004 Employees: 1
Net Worth: £6,630 Total Assets: £15,689
Registered Office: 93a Chester Road, Northwich, Cheshire, CW8 1HH
Officers: Elizabeth Willis Cottrell, Secretary; David Anthony Cottrell [1946] Director/Nursery & Babywear Wholesaler

Cosmetic Alchemy Ltd
Incorporated: 25 July 2013
Previous: Cosmetic Pros Ltd
Net Worth: £51,586 *Total Assets:* £52,768
Registered Office: B508 Tower Bridge Business Complex, 100 Clements Road, London, SE16 4DG
Major Shareholder: Scott Alan Wasserman
Officers: Scott Wasserman [1962] Director [American]

Cosmetic Bases Limited
Incorporated: 31 May 2017
Registered Office: Bell House, Ashford Hill, Thatcham, Berks, RG19 8BB
Shareholders: Mark Richard Brimicombe; Mark Richard Brimicombe
Officers: Dawn Rachel Brimicombe [1964] Director; Mark Richard Brimicombe [1968] Director

Cosmetic Doctor at Work Limited
Incorporated: 21 July 2004 *Employees:* 28
Net Worth: £10,833,401 *Total Assets:* £12,198,167
Registered Office: 9 Wimpole Street, London, W1G 9SG
Shareholders: Melissa Emily Francis John; Jean Louis Sebagh
Officers: Melissa Emily Francis John [1963] Director; Jean-Louis Sebagh [1954] Director/Cosmetic Surgeon [French]

Cosmetic Hooligans Ltd
Incorporated: 29 June 2017
Registered Office: 153 Caledonia Road, Wolverhampton, W Midlands, WV2 1JA
Officers: Patrycja Kalkowska [1995] Director/Cosmetic Production [Polish]

Cosmetic Orb Ltd
Incorporated: 3 August 2018
Registered Office: 18 Bergamot Gardens, Walnut Tree, Milton Keynes, Bucks, MK7 7NG
Major Shareholder: Arooj Arif
Officers: Dr Arooj Arif [1991] Director/Trade [Pakistani]

Cosmetic Traders Limited
Incorporated: 23 September 2014 *Employees:* 3
Previous: Sentire Parfums Limited
Net Worth: £18,113 *Total Assets:* £343,109
Registered Office: 20-21 Jockey's Fields, London, WC1R 4BW
Shareholder: Jason Paul Collison
Officers: Luke Henry James Granger [1980] Director

Cosmetica Natural Oils Ltd
Incorporated: 26 April 2017
Net Worth: £36,590 *Total Assets:* £223,780
Registered Office: 249 Rosehill Road, Ipswich, Suffolk, IP3 8HG
Major Shareholder: Andrew Knowles
Officers: Andrew Knowles [1990] Director

Cosmetics 4U Limited
Incorporated: 30 October 2012
Net Worth Deficit: £2,446 *Total Assets:* £5,237
Registered Office: 4 Coburg Road, London, N22 6UJ
Major Shareholder: Miroslaw Roman Pietruszka
Officers: Miroslaw Roman Pietruszka [1962] Director/Trader [Polish]

Cosmetics Direct Limited
Incorporated: 7 December 2000
Registered Office: Long Row, Oakham, Rutland, LE15 6LN
Shareholders: William Francis Doody; Sylvia Doody
Officers: Sylvia Doody, Secretary; William Francis Doody [1942] Director/Cosmetics Wholesaler

Cosmetics of London Chelsie Ltd
Incorporated: 4 January 2018
Registered Office: 16 Wilkinson Road, London, E16 3RJ
Major Shareholder: Chelsie Benjamin-Drysdale
Officers: Chelsie Benjamin-Drysdale [1992] Director/Beautician

Cosmetics Online Limited
Incorporated: 23 August 2016
Registered Office: 174 Dudley Road, Wolverhampton, W Midlands, WV2 3DR
Major Shareholder: Anuj Paudel
Officers: Anuj Paudel [1994] Director/Accountant

Cosmetics R Us 1 Limited
Incorporated: 12 January 2016
Net Worth: £44,571 *Total Assets:* £385,572
Registered Office: 35 Broad Street, Wolverhampton, W Midlands, WV1 1HZ
Major Shareholder: Ajmal Yakoob
Officers: Ajmal Yakoob [1981] Director

The Cosmetics Store Ltd
Incorporated: 11 April 2018
Registered Office: Kemp House, 160 City Road, London, EC1V 2NX
Officers: Rukshana Begum [1993] Director/Administrator

Cosmetics Wholesale Limited
Incorporated: 16 January 2018
Registered Office: 85 Great Portland Street, London, W1W 7LT
Officers: Guillaume Groleau [1975] Director [French]

Cosmetics Wholsale Ltd
Incorporated: 23 April 2018
Registered Office: 2nd Floor Flat, 39 Frogmore, Abergavenny, Monmouthshire, NP7 5AN
Major Shareholder: Edgars Rudgalvis
Officers: Edgars Rudgalvis [1984] Director/Manager [Latvian]

Cosmetiqa Ltd
Incorporated: 5 March 2018
Registered Office: 42 Granville Road, Uxbridge, Middlesex, UB10 9AE
Major Shareholder: Claudia Liliana Cucicea
Officers: Claudia Liliana Cucicea [1987] Director [Romanian]

Cosmetiques de France Ltd.
Incorporated: 2 February 2017
Registered Office: A52 Ambassador Building, 5 New Union Square, London, SW11 7BN
Major Shareholder: Arnaud Marie Alfred Deroulede
Officers: Arnaud Marie Alfred Deroulede [1961] Director/Cosmetic Consultant [French]

Cosmetolife Limited
Incorporated: 25 April 2018
Registered Office: 93 Westbourne Road, Marsh, Huddersfield, W Yorks, HD1 4LG
Shareholders: Parvin Kaur Jaswan Singh; Jagdeesh Singh
Officers: Parvin Kaur Jaswan Singh [1980] Director/Legal Advisor [Malaysian]; Jagdeesh Singh [1975] Director/Business Consultant [Malaysian]

Cosmetronic Global Limited
Incorporated: 18 October 2010
Net Worth Deficit: £14,948 *Total Assets:* £203,124
Registered Office: 117 Dartford Road, Dartford, Kent, DA1 3EN
Major Shareholder: Simon Derry Grogan
Officers: Simon Derry Grogan [1963] Director

Cosmic Eyes Ltd
Incorporated: 5 February 2019
Registered Office: Kemp House, 160 City Road, London, EC1V 2NX
Officers: Mohamed Hegab, Secretary; Clarise Klue [1984] Director [South African]

Cosmolab Limited
Incorporated: 20 November 2009
Previous: Philanthropic Brands Limited
Net Worth Deficit: £335,420 *Total Assets:* £1,140
Registered Office: 8 Grosvenor Place, London, SW1X 7SH
Major Shareholder: George Christopher Hammer
Officers: George Christopher Hammer [1950] Director

Cosmolovely Limited
Incorporated: 13 July 2018
Registered Office: Suite 23, Fifth Floor, 63-66 Hatton Garden, London, EC1N 8LE
Major Shareholder: Ibrahima Diop
Officers: Ibrahima Diop [1995] Director [French]

Cosmos Cosmetics Limited
Incorporated: 30 November 2018
Registered Office: 71-75 Shelton Street, Covent Garden, London, WC2H 9JQ
Shareholders: Alptekin Aydin; Funda Hocaoglu
Officers: Funda Hocaoglu, Secretary; Alptekin Aydin [1973] Director; Funda Hocaoglu [1973] Director [Turkish]

Cosnique Group Holdings Ltd
Incorporated: 28 December 2017
Registered Office: 14 Croftlands Road, Manchester, M22 9YF
Major Shareholder: Bing You
Officers: Bing You [1982] Director [Chinese]

Cosplus International Ltd
Incorporated: 2 January 2019
Registered Office: 70 Solly Street, Sheffield, S1 4BP
Major Shareholder: Keya Li
Officers: Keya Li [1991] Director/Student [Chinese]

County Sales Limited
Incorporated: 2 November 2000 *Employees:* 6
Net Worth: £762,798 *Total Assets:* £1,530,087
Registered Office: Unit 1 Kestrel Court, Bridgewater Close, Network 65 Business Park, Burnley, Lancs, BB11 5NA
Shareholders: Duncan Andrew Jackson; Phillip James Collins; Julie Jackson
Officers: Phillip James Collins, Secretary; Phillip James Collins [1971] Finance Director; Duncan Andrew Jackson [1963] Director

Cover Up Hairloss Ltd
Incorporated: 10 November 2017
Registered Office: 71-75 Shelton Street, London, WC2H 9JQ
Major Shareholder: Andrew Bayliss
Officers: Andrew Bayliss [1967] Director

Coveti Limited
Incorporated: 3 January 2019
Registered Office: Crown House, 27 Old Gloucester Street, London, WC1N 3AX
Officers: Heba Khamis Jumaa Shenain Alfzari [1980] Director [Emirati]

Cowshed Products Limited
Incorporated: 1 November 1999 *Employees:* 245
Net Worth: £3,982,862 *Total Assets:* £12,586,555
Registered Office: 72-74 Dean Street, London, W1D 3SG
Parent: Soho House Limited
Officers: Nicholas Keith Arthur Jones [1963] Director; Peter Jonathan McPhee [1975] Director [American]

Cozmetica UK Ltd
Incorporated: 29 November 2017
Registered Office: Suite 1 & 2 Business Centre, Hagley Golf & Country Club, Wassell Grove Lane, Hagley, Worcs, DY9 9JW
Shareholders: Luke George William Wellings; Lloyd Wayne Baker; Cassie Louise Brown
Officers: Luke George William Wellings [1988] Commercial Director

CP Parfums Ltd
Incorporated: 13 October 2016
Net Worth Deficit: £1,925 *Total Assets:* £209,429
Registered Office: Lynton House, 7-12 Tavistock Square, London, WC1H 9LT
Shareholder: Valorem Capital One Ltd
Officers: David Adrian Crisp [1958] Director

Crabtree & Evelyn (Overseas) Limited
Incorporated: 2 July 1979 *Employees:* 228
Net Worth Deficit: £5,595,938 *Total Assets:* £47,446,560
Registered Office: 15 Bonhill Street, London, EC2P 2EA
Shareholders: Hon Keong Chin; Mui Leng Loh; Susan Mei Wan Low; Pun Hoi Yu
Officers: David Lawrence Stern [1963] Director [American]; Xin Yu [1977] Director [Australian]; Lei Zhao [1980] Director [Chinese]

Crane + Wilton Ltd
Incorporated: 7 June 2018
Registered Office: Suite 6, 8 Melior Street, London, SE1 3QP
Major Shareholder: Christina Marie Wilton
Officers: Christina Marie Wilton [1967] Director/Business Executive

Crane and Peach Limited
Incorporated: 22 February 2016
Net Worth: £28,416 *Total Assets:* £152,363
Registered Office: International House, 24 Holborn Viaduct, London, EC1A 2BN
Shareholders: Victoria Kai Wai Martin; Joyce Zi Yan Tay
Officers: Victoria Kai Wai Martin [1983] Director; Joyce Zi Yan Tay [1984] Director [Singaporean]

Crazy Smiles Group Ltd
Incorporated: 14 February 2019
Registered Office: 71-75 Shelton Street, London, WC2H 9JQ
Shareholders: German Antonio Soares; Raffaele Croce
Officers: Raffaele Croce, Secretary; German Antonio Soares, Secretary; Raffaele Croce [1977] Director/IT Engineer; German Antonio Soares [1985] Director/Business Development [Italian]

Create Images Ion Limited
Incorporated: 13 November 1996
Net Worth: £1,560,000 *Total Assets:* £1,850,000
Registered Office: 24 Brenda Road, Hartlepool, Cleveland, TS25 1QE
Shareholders: Christine Cesarano; Gerardo Cesarano
Officers: Christine Cesarano, Secretary; Christine Cesarano [1947] Director/Administrator; Gerardo Cesarano [1946] Director [Italian]

Creative Colours International Ltd
Incorporated: 28 November 2008
Net Worth: £101,910 *Total Assets:* £205,480
Registered Office: Wessex House, Upper Market Street, Eastleigh, Hants, SO50 9FD
Shareholders: Simon James Tarling; Elspeth Tarling
Officers: Elspeth Tarling [1966] Director; Simon James Tarling [1967] Sales Director

Crescent Soaps Ltd
Incorporated: 23 January 2012
Net Worth Deficit: £13,634 *Total Assets:* £2,865
Registered Office: 50 Forty Avenue, Wembley, Middlesex, HA9 8LQ
Shareholders: Adnan Ishtiaq Khan; Reema Adnan Khan
Officers: Adnan Ishtiaq Khan, Secretary; Reema Adnan Khan [1976] Director

Crete Online Ltd.
Incorporated: 21 December 2018
Registered Office: Office 32, 19-21 Crawford Street, London, W1H 1PJ
Major Shareholder: Henricus Simon Roozendaal
Officers: Henricus Simon Roozendaal [1975] Director [Dutch]

Crivalis Ltd
Incorporated: 4 January 2018
Registered Office: 208 Footscray Road, London, SE9 2EL
Major Shareholder: Anco Maurizio Accordi
Officers: Daniela Bailo [1982] Director [Italian]

CRM Trading Limited
Incorporated: 22 June 1982
Net Worth: £3,860,000 *Total Assets:* £33,690,000
Registered Office: 1st Floor, Cloister House, New Bailey Street, Salford, M3 5FS
Parent: CRM Hdgs Limited
Officers: Matthew Pettit, Secretary; Simon Tennant Barker [1956] Finance Director; Charles Rodney Mathers [1956] Director [New Zealander]

Croma-Pharma Limited
Incorporated: 25 January 2019
Registered Office: Suite 1, 3rd Floor, 11-12 St James's Square, London, SW1Y 4LB
Officers: Andreas Prinz [1975] Director [Austrian]; Gerhard Prinz [1940] Director [Austrian]; Martin Schoeller [1981] Director [Austrian]

Crown Cosmetics Limited
Incorporated: 4 September 2017
Registered Office: 4 Wensleydale Road, Birmingham, B42 1PP

Crypt Doll Ltd
Incorporated: 27 September 2017
Registered Office: 5 Thornford Road, Yetminster, Sherborne, Dorset, DT9 6LW
Major Shareholder: Charlotte Elena Martin
Officers: Charlotte Elena Martin [1994] Managing Director

Crystal Nails No1 Ltd
Incorporated: 17 November 2014 *Employees:* 3
Net Worth: £1,229 *Total Assets:* £2,072
Registered Office: 3 London Wall Buildings, London, EC2M 5PD
Major Shareholder: Annamaria Farkas
Officers: Kerry Samantha Moores, Secretary; Annamaria Farkas [1978] Director [Hungarian]

Crystal Spring Consumer Division Limited
Incorporated: 2 April 1993
Net Worth: £218,170 *Total Assets:* £540,940
Registered Office: Unit 7 Avenger Close, Chandler's Ford, Eastleigh, Hants, SO53 4DQ
Shareholders: Thomas James Laird; Sally Kate Laird; Stuart Wilson Laird
Officers: Stuart Wilson Laird, Secretary; Sally Kate Laird [1957] Director/Company Secretary; Stuart Wilson Laird [1953] Director; Thomas James Laird [1984] Director

Crystalnails4u Ltd
Incorporated: 5 May 2010
Net Worth: £22,400 *Total Assets:* £208,360
Registered Office: 3 London Wall Buildings, London, EC2M 5PD
Major Shareholder: Annamaria Farkas
Officers: Annamaria Farkas [1978] Director [Hungarian]

Cuelyine Limited
Incorporated: 14 June 2017
Registered Office: Chase Business Centre, 39-41 Chase Side, London, N14 5BP
Major Shareholder: Cui Ding
Officers: Cui Ding [1989] Director [Chinese]

Cult 51 Ltd
Incorporated: 18 April 2013
Net Worth: £111,450 *Total Assets:* £272,270
Registered Office: Mulberry House, 9 Stoatley Rise, Haslemere, Surrey, GU27 1AF
Major Shareholder: Richard John Mears
Officers: Richard John Mears [1964] Director

Cult Candy Limited
Incorporated: 23 June 2018
Registered Office: Crown House, Old Gloucester Street, London, WC1N 3AX
Shareholders: Paul Scott; Angela Adams
Officers: Paul Scott, Secretary; Angela Adams [1975] Director/Designer; Paul Scott [1968] Director

Cure Hair & Skin Care Ltd
Incorporated: 13 October 2017
Registered Office: 71 Cedars Road, London, SW4 0PW
Major Shareholder: Alice Afflick-Mensah
Officers: Alice Afflick-Mensah [1988] Director

The Curl Coach Ltd
Incorporated: 10 March 2017
Registered Office: First Floor, 71 Sydenham Road, London, SE26 5EZ
Major Shareholder: Folake Kassim
Officers: Folake Kassim [1978] Director/Entrepreneur

Cursed Cosmetics Ltd
Incorporated: 29 May 2018
Registered Office: 5 Thornford Road, Yetminster, Sherborne, Dorset, DT9 6LW
Major Shareholder: Charlotte Elena Martin
Officers: Charlotte Elena Martin [1994] Managing Director

Custom Tan UK Limited
Incorporated: 3 May 2018
Registered Office: Langdale, 48 Main Street, Longforgan, Dundee, DD2 5EU
Major Shareholder: Yvonne Nellie Murrie
Officers: Yvonne Nellie Murrie [1983] Director

Cutagen Ltd
Incorporated: 22 October 2012
Net Worth: £12,535   *Total Assets:* £94,297
Registered Office: 3 Willow Lane, Great Cambourne, Cambridge, CB23 6AB
Major Shareholder: Rizwana Kausar Alvi
Officers: Doctor Rizwana Kausar Alvi [1971] Director/Research Scientist; Doctor Faizan Ahmad Awan [1981] Director/General Practitioner

Cutelovelee Limited
Incorporated: 25 April 2018
Registered Office: 339 High Street, West Bromwich, W Midlands, B70 9QG
Major Shareholder: Leanna Natasha Campbell
Officers: Leanna Natasha Campbell [1990] Director

Cxlture Cosmetics Ltd
Incorporated: 2 July 2018
Registered Office: 147 Davenport Road, London, SE6 2AT
Major Shareholder: Obatarhe Avwunu
Officers: Obatarhe Avwunu [1995] Director/Administrator [Nigerian]

Cyrano Limited
Incorporated: 15 April 1998
Net Worth: £2,170,000   *Total Assets:* £4,070,000
Registered Office: 24 Finch Drive, Springwood Industrial Estate, Braintree, Essex, CM7 2SF
Officers: Simon John Adlington, Secretary; Mark Justin Adlington [1963] Director/Leisure Industry Consultants; Simon John Adlington [1961] Director

CZ Cosmetics Ltd.
Incorporated: 30 September 2017
Registered Office: Suite 108, 15 Ingestre Place, London, W1F 0DU
Shareholder: Feilin Zhu
Officers: Luoyi Cha [1985] Director [Chinese]; Feilin Zhu [1988] Director/General Manager [Chinese]

D & L Hair Products Limited
Incorporated: 20 May 2010
Net Worth Deficit: £377,012   *Total Assets:* £71,969
Registered Office: 39 Deacons Hill Road, Elstree, Borehamwood, Herts, WD6 3HZ
Officers: David Alan Rose, Secretary; David Alan Rose [1953] Director/Chartered Accountant; Jonathan Russell Rose [1982] Director/Broker; Lorraine Sandra Rose [1956] Director/Hairdresser

D'val Ltd
Incorporated: 11 February 2019
Registered Office: Flat 1, 1 Icknield Street, Dunstable, Beds, LU6 3AD
Major Shareholder: Demet Hodzheva
Officers: Demet Hodzheva [1995] Director/Manager [Bulgarian]

D'Zario UK Ltd
Incorporated: 10 February 2017
Registered Office: 203 Manningham Lane, Bradford, BD8 7HP
Officers: Ahmer Afaq [1977] Director [Indian]

Dabrimela Limited
Incorporated: 13 June 2017
Registered Office: Flat 116, Totteridge House, 15 Yelverton Road, London, SW11 3QH
Officers: Abdella Omer Abdella [1989] Director

Dacre Skincare Limited
Incorporated: 9 January 2019
Registered Office: 63 Broad Green, Wellingborough, Northants, NN8 4LQ
Major Shareholder: Alexandra May Howard Roberts
Officers: Alexandra May Howard Roberts [1985] Director

The Daimon Barber Limited
Incorporated: 7 March 2014
Net Worth Deficit: £359,770   *Total Assets:* £100,510
Registered Office: 71-75 Shelton Street, London, WC2H 9JQ
Shareholders: Leo Neelands; Stephen Michael Crosby
Officers: Stephen Michael Crosby [1971] Director; Leo Neelands [1976] Director/Visual Effects Artist

Daisy Anai Limited
Incorporated: 19 February 2014
Registered Office: 43 Waterhall Avenue, London, E4 6NA
Officers: Chantelle Kimberley Azille [1985] Director/Skincare

Daly Beauty Limited
Incorporated: 30 January 2009
Net Worth: £2,147   *Total Assets:* £5,540
Registered Office: 48 Hylton Street, Birmingham, B18 6HN
Shareholders: Claire Shread; Helen Elizabeth Daly
Officers: Helen Elizabeth Daly [1969] Director/TV Actress; Claire Shread [1967] Director

Damrick's White Bunny Ltd
Incorporated: 6 July 2017
Registered Office: 1 Deyne Street, Salford, M6 5WT
Shareholders: Derrick Andrew Schultz; Damien Paul Richmond Sleath
Officers: Derrick Andrew Schultz [1990] Director of Operations [American]; Damien Paul Richmond Sleath [1980] Director of Research & Development

Dance on Tan Limited
Incorporated: 26 October 2018
Registered Office: 11 Alexander Street, Clydebank, W Dunbartonshire, G81 1SQ
Major Shareholder: Marie Claire McKell
Officers: Marie Claire McKell [1981] Director

The Dancing Unicorn Limited
Incorporated: 24 March 2017
Registered Office: 19 Kilmaine Avenue, Blackley, Manchester, M9 7FZ
Officers: Kelly Collinson [1989] Director/Beautician

Danlab Ltd.
Incorporated: 20 June 2007
Net Worth: £48,744   *Total Assets:* £64,371
Registered Office: 483 Green Lanes, London, N13 4BS
Shareholders: Kim Wium-Andersen; Olav Francois-Friis
Officers: Olav Francois-Friis [1968] Director/Businessman [Danish]; Kim Wium-Andersen [1969] Director/Businessman [Danish]

Darklake Limited
Incorporated: 7 July 2017
Net Worth: £783,777 *Total Assets:* £2,107,982
Registered Office: 28 Darklake View, Estover, Plymouth, PL6 7TL
Officers: Lee Paul Harper, Secretary; Lee Paul Harper [1974] Director

Daughter of The Soil Limited
Incorporated: 5 February 2015
Net Worth Deficit: £183,090 *Total Assets:* £79,490
Registered Office: Castle Hill House, 12 Castle Hill Road, Castle Hill, Windsor, Berks, SL4 1PD
Shareholders: Helen Lawuo-Meena; Elibariki Robert Magembe; Maria Kaitamalya Magembe
Officers: Maria Magembe, Secretary; Hellen Lawuo-Meena [1977] Director/Project Manager; Elibariki Robert Magembe [1979] Managing Director [New Zealander]; Maria Kaitamalya Magembe [1980] Director/Business Change Project Manager

David & Co. Traders Ltd
Incorporated: 7 July 2014
Net Worth Deficit: £3,040
Registered Office: 10 Kent Street, Burnley, Lancs, BB12 0DJ
Major Shareholder: Ubaid Ur Rehman
Officers: Ubaid Ur Rehman [1976] Director

Chloe Davids Limited
Incorporated: 27 June 2018
Registered Office: 38 Cumberland House, Erebus Drive, London, SE28 0GE
Major Shareholder: Chloe Davids
Officers: Chloe Davids [1982] Director

Tom Daxon Limited
Incorporated: 7 January 2010 *Employees:* 2
Net Worth: £124,642 *Total Assets:* £141,944
Registered Office: 19 North Park, Gerrards Cross, Bucks, SL9 8JS
Major Shareholder: Dale Daxon Bowers
Officers: Dale Daxon Bowers [1953] Director; Thomas Jay Daxon Bowers [1987] Director

Dazzle Dee Ltd
Incorporated: 24 October 2018
Registered Office: 17b Bridge Street, Leighton Buzzard, Beds, LU7 1AH
Shareholders: Diana Zaki; Sara Iskander
Officers: Sara Iskander [1988] Director [Egyptian]; Diana Zaki [1984] Director [Egyptian]

Dazzlers & Toppers PTL Ltd
Incorporated: 14 August 2008 *Employees:* 1
Net Worth: £32,482 *Total Assets:* £38,723
Registered Office: Harrow Business Centre, 429-433 Pinner Road, North Harrow, Middlesex, HA1 4HN
Officers: Vikas Rishi [1957] Director/Businessman [Indian]

DC Salon Products Ltd
Incorporated: 17 October 2018
Registered Office: Unit 36 Silk Mill Industrial Estate, Brook Street, Tring, Herts, HP23 5EF
Shareholders: Zoe Carnell; Sabrina Dolan
Officers: Zoe Carnell [1975] Director/Consultant; Sabrina Dolan [1963] Director/Consultant

Dea Disir Ltd
Incorporated: 19 February 2018
Registered Office: International House, 142 Cromwell Road, Kensington, London, SW7 4EF
Major Shareholder: Nicholas Masters
Officers: Nicholas Masters [1987] Director

Dead Pretty Official Ltd
Incorporated: 10 May 2018
Registered Office: 1193 Rochdale Road, Manchester, M9 7FP
Major Shareholder: Shanna McCormick
Officers: Shanna McCormick [1983] Director/Project Manager

Dead Sea London Ltd
Incorporated: 1 March 2018
Registered Office: 36 Melrose Street, Bradford, BD7 3EW
Shareholder: Munawar Ahmad
Officers: Faiza Ahmad [1977] Director/Sales; Munawar Ahmad [1986] Director/Accountant

DealsRUsOnline Ltd
Incorporated: 14 September 2018
Registered Office: 71-75 Shelton Street, London, WC2H 9JQ
Officers: Alpan Shah [1972] Director

Dear Body Limited
Incorporated: 13 August 2008
Registered Office: Suite LG01, Chancery House, Chancery Lane, London, WC2A 1QU
Major Shareholder: Haiyan Zhang
Officers: Haiyan Zhang [1976] Director [Chinese]

Death Head Beard Company Ltd
Incorporated: 1 February 2019
Registered Office: 146 Gracemere Crescent, Hall Green, Birmingham, B28 0UD
Major Shareholder: Calumn John McCann
Officers: Calumn John McCann [1987] Director

Deciem UK Ltd.
Incorporated: 25 January 2013 *Employees:* 21
Net Worth Deficit: £264,714 *Total Assets:* £6,176,499
Registered Office: 59 Redchurch Street, London, E2 7DJ
Parent: Deciem Beauty Group Inc
Officers: Nicola Leanne Kilner [1989] Director/Executive

Dee Doo Limited
Incorporated: 11 June 2004
Net Worth Deficit: £52,441 *Total Assets:* £13,766
Registered Office: Unit E, Edison Courtyard, Brunel Road, Earlstrees Industrial Estate, Corby, Northants, NN17 4LS
Shareholders: Simon Timothy Rhodes; Suzan Rhodes
Officers: Simon Timothy Rhodes, Secretary; Simon Timothy Rhodes [1969] Director; Suzan Rhodes [1965] Director

Deeco Supplies Limited
Incorporated: 26 January 2018
Registered Office: Kemp House, 160 City Road, London, EC1V 2NX
Officers: David Dean [1962] Director

Deep Red Marketing International Ltd
Incorporated: 28 January 2019
Registered Office: 85a Lightfoot Lane, Fulwood, Preston, Lancs, PR2 3LS
Shareholders: Barbara Bantleman; Lutero Silva Mariano
Officers: Lutero Silva Mariano, Secretary; Barbara Bantleman [1967] Director

Deewin Stomatology Research Center Co., Ltd
Incorporated: 4 July 2018
Registered Office: Fourth Floor, 3 Gower Street, London, WC1E 6HA
Major Shareholder: Fei Wang
Officers: Fei Wang [1990] Director [Chinese]

Deism IT Solutions Ltd
Incorporated: 28 November 2013
Net Worth: £7,741 *Total Assets:* £78,408
Registered Office: Flat 6, Lancaster House, Borough Road, Isleworth, Middlesex, TW7 5FJ
Officers: Abhishek Haritash [1984] Director [Indian]; Mokshika Sharma [1981] Director [Indian]

Deity World Ltd
Incorporated: 23 February 2011
Registered Office: 9 Ash Hill Close, Bushey, Herts, WD23 1BW
Major Shareholder: Anthony Waites
Officers: Anthony Waites [1961] Director; Redwood Wilson [1966] Director/Accountant

Deja Vu International Ltd
Incorporated: 12 January 2018
Registered Office: 31 Nibthwaite Road, Harrow, Middlesex, HA1 1TB
Major Shareholder: Marius Valentino Gurska
Officers: Marius Valentino Gurska [1979] Director/Wholesale of Perfume and Cosmetics [Romanian]

Delhicious Ltd
Incorporated: 4 December 2018
Registered Office: 20 Lyon Park Avenue, Wembley, Middlesex, HA0 4DR
Major Shareholder: Zara Saleem
Officers: Zara Saleem [1988] Director

Delights Beauty Company Limited
Incorporated: 16 April 1997
Registered Office: Tower House, Westfield Industrial Estate, Kirk Lane, Yeadon, Leeds, LS19 7LX
Shareholder: Paul Mottram
Officers: Paul Mottram, Secretary/Director; Paul Mottram [1948] Director; Ian Colin Stewart [1949] Director

Delmoss Ltd
Incorporated: 17 July 2017
Registered Office: 36a Greenham Crescent, London, E4 8YQ
Parent: Delmoss
Officers: Oludamola Ikusika [1988] Director

Deltagamma Limited
Incorporated: 21 February 2012
Net Worth Deficit: £6,299 *Total Assets:* £1,027
Registered Office: 248 Hydethorpe Road, London, SW12 0JH
Major Shareholder: Yaw Owusu Asante
Officers: Nana Asante, Secretary; Yaw Asante [1965] Director/Registered Nurse

Demert Brands EU Ltd
Incorporated: 28 November 2013
Registered Office: B508 Tower Bridge Business Complex, 100 Clements Road, London, SE16 4DG
Major Shareholder: Rocky Pagliarulo
Officers: Rocky Pagliarulo [1955] Director [American]

Denbond Pharmaceuticals Limited
Incorporated: 5 July 1976
Net Worth: £160,623 *Total Assets:* £290,359
Registered Office: 4th Floor, Amba House, 15 College Road, Harrow, Middlesex, HA1 1BA
Shareholders: Rekha Ashok Rajani; Ashokkumar Haridas Rajani
Officers: Rekha Ashok Rajani, Secretary; Ashokkumar Haridas Rajani [1946] Director/Pharmacist; Rekha Ashok Rajani [1950] Director

Leighton Denny Limited
Incorporated: 9 May 2003 *Employees:* 3
Net Worth: £1,521 *Total Assets:* £74,994
Registered Office: The Coach House, Greys Green Business Centre, Henley on Thames, Oxon, RG9 4QG
Shareholders: Leighton Denny; Mitchell Lawrence Field; George Christopher Hammer
Officers: Leighton Denny [1974] Director/Nail Specialist; Mitchell Lawrence Field [1952] Sales Director; George Christopher Hammer [1950] Director

Deo Beauty Products Limited
Incorporated: 14 September 1999
Net Worth: £1,283 *Total Assets:* £29,449
Registered Office: 6 Ritherdon Road, London, SW17 8QD
Shareholders: Jai Indar Ragbir; Sergio Ragbir
Officers: Donatina Grandta Ragbir, Secretary; Jai Indar Ragbir [1948] Director/Businessman; Sergio Ragbir [1983] Director/Businessman

Derma Organics by CFBP Ltd
Incorporated: 11 May 2017
Registered Office: Flat 47, Lord Kensington House, 5 Radnor Terrace, Kensington, London, W14 8BU
Major Shareholder: Adaaku Iwuajoku
Officers: Adaaku Iwuajoku [1992] Director/Entrepreneur

Dermacosmeticsweb Ltd
Incorporated: 8 February 2019
Registered Office: 98 Western Road, Hove, E Sussex, BN3 1FA
Major Shareholder: Janet Dymott
Officers: Janet Dymott [1949] Director

Dermacure Aesthetics Limited
Incorporated: 7 March 2017
Registered Office: Ray Cochrane School Basement, 118 Bakers Street, London, W1U 6TT
Officers: Eleonora Androva [1986] Director [Bulgarian]; Xubin Yuan [1974] Business Director

Dermaenhance Ltd.
Incorporated: 19 April 2012
Net Worth Deficit: £15,900 *Total Assets:* £6,130
Registered Office: 5 Shop Lane, Nether Heage, Belper, Derbys, DE56 2AR
Major Shareholder: Keith James Massie
Officers: Keith James Massie [1961] Director; Nicola Eleanor Paulson [1972] Director/Admin Worker; Judith Ann Taylor [1943] Director/Supply of Moisturising Cream

Dermafood Limited
Incorporated: 21 November 2011
Net Worth Deficit: £5,568 *Total Assets:* £191
Registered Office: 53 Bothwell Street, Glasgow, G2 6TS
Major Shareholder: Teodora Georgieva Caldwell
Officers: Teodora Georgieva Caldwell [1969] Director

Dermafrance Ltd.
Incorporated: 3 February 2017
Registered Office: A52 Ambassador Building, 5 New Union Square, London, SW11 7BN
Major Shareholder: Isabelle Marie Francoise Deroulede
Officers: Isabelle Marie Francoise Deroulede [1964] Director/Healthcare Consultant [French]

Dermaloch Limited
Incorporated: 22 February 2018
Registered Office: 30 Moor Lane, Carleton, Pontefract, W Yorks, WF8 3RX
Major Shareholder: Gary Sheard
Officers: Dr Gary Sheard [1954] Managing Director

Dermalogica (UK) Limited
Incorporated: 1 June 1988 *Employees:* 342
Net Worth: £19,056,980 *Total Assets:* £24,956,168
Registered Office: The Manser Building, Thorncroft Manor, Thorncroft Drive, Dorking Road, Leatherhead, Surrey, KT22 8JB
Parent: Unilever Overseas Holdings Limited
Officers: James Oliver Earley, Secretary; Richard Clive Hazell, Secretary; Pamela Dickson [1968] Finance Director; Stuart Colin Parkinson Hill [1979] Director/CFO Dermalogica; Glenn Derrick Poy [1957] Director/General Manager [Canadian]; Anthony Colin Rudd [1975] Finance Director

Dermamaitre Ltd.
Incorporated: 10 October 2012
Registered Office: Curzon House, Cavendish Place, Brighton, BN1 2HS
Shareholders: Gabriella Bethany Tamsin Harman; Michelle Lorraine Angela Harman
Officers: Gabriella Bethany Tamsin Harman [1991] Director/Company Management & Product Development

Dermanor Ltd.
Incorporated: 27 January 2017
Net Worth: £2 *Total Assets:* £2
Registered Office: 60 Brick Farm Close, Kew, Richmond, Surrey, TW9 4EG

Dermaperfetca Ltd
Incorporated: 7 August 2018
Registered Office: Appt 1, 7 Cumberland Road, London, E13 8LH
Major Shareholder: Wagma Ismail
Officers: Dr Wagma Ismail [1981] Director/Doctor [Pakistani]

Dermashack Limited
Incorporated: 24 July 2013
Net Worth Deficit: £7,305 *Total Assets:* £18,513
Registered Office: 1 Arc Court, 1 Friern Barnet Road, London, N11 1PT
Shareholders: Ruth Shimuli Owino; Ruth Owino; Ben Robertson Bomford
Officers: Ben Robertson Bomford [1987] Director/Product Development Manager; Ruth Owino [1956] Director/Property Manager

Dermatx Ltd
Incorporated: 30 May 2014 *Employees:* 1
Net Worth: £71,784 *Total Assets:* £105,315
Registered Office: 47 Bridgewater Drive, Great Glen, Leicester, LE8 9DX
Major Shareholder: Kamlesh Patel
Officers: Kamlesh Patel [1962] Director/Landlord

Dermica Laboratoires UK Ltd
Incorporated: 26 June 2018
Registered Office: 54a Cowley Mill Road, Uxbridge, Middlesex, UB8 2QE
Officers: Khaled Mouloud Haj Mohamed [1964] Director/Doctor [Syrian]

Dermura Skin Ltd
Incorporated: 26 July 2018
Registered Office: 113 Altwood Road, Maidenhead, Berks, SL6 4QD
Shareholders: Laura Janet Stafford; Allie Jolly
Officers: Allie Jolly [1993] Director; Laura Janet Stafford [1993] Director

Design Essentials Limited
Incorporated: 21 December 2011
Registered Office: The Chapel, 378-380 Deansgate, Manchester, M3 4LY
Officers: Cornell McBride Jr [1965] Director/Business Manager [American]; Cornell McBride Sr [1943] Director/Business Manager [American]

Design4nails Ltd
Incorporated: 17 December 2018
Registered Office: 67 Pindar Road, Leicester, LE3 9RN
Shareholders: Katarzyna Gaj Komincz; Piotr Komincz
Officers: Katarzyna Gaj Komincz [1986] Director [Polish]; Piotr Komincz [1981] Director [Polish]

Designer Fragrances Limited
Incorporated: 21 May 2001
Net Worth: £915,180 *Total Assets:* £1,230,000
Registered Office: 202c Burcott Road, Bristol, BS11 8AP
Major Shareholder: Carol Ann Coleman
Officers: Carol Ann Coleman, Secretary; Carol Ann Coleman [1948] Director; Thomas Martin Coleman [1986] Director

DHB (UK) Ltd.
Incorporated: 10 April 2000
Net Worth: £44,860 *Total Assets:* £75,690
Registered Office: 9 Glasgow Road, Paisley, Renfrewshire, PA1 3QS
Shareholders: David Geoffrey Naylor; Sandra Naylor
Officers: Sandra Gardner Naylor, Secretary; David Geoffrey Naylor [1951] Sales Director

Diamond Brands Limited
Incorporated: 25 July 2018
Registered Office: 55 Whitlock Drive, London, SW19 6SJ
Shareholders: Orlin Nikolov Dimov; Tyanko Martinov Patev
Officers: Orlin Nikolov Dimov [1989] Director [Bulgarian]

Diamond Smile NE Limited
Incorporated: 29 November 2017
Registered Office: 5 The Riverside, Hebburn, Tyne & Wear, NE31 1BG
Officers: Jack Paul Nichol [1993] Director

Diamonds on Demand Ltd
Incorporated: 10 July 2015
Net Worth: £8,510 *Total Assets:* £15,840
Registered Office: 9 Morwick Grove, Scholes, Leeds, LS15 4DS
Major Shareholder: Natalie Jayne Bootle
Officers: Natalie Jayne Bootle [1978] Director/Beautician

Diet Plan Unique Ltd
Incorporated: 17 November 2015
Net Worth Deficit: £3,006 Total Assets: £2,645
Registered Office: 2 Wellfield Close, Ridgeway, Sheffield, S12 3XN
Officers: Nicola Anne Laycock, Secretary; Joe Laycock [1984] Director

Dilecta Cosmetics Limited
Incorporated: 15 March 2013
Registered Office: Primrose Bank, Catterlen, Penrith, Cumbria, CA11 0BQ
Officers: Steven Smith [1977] Director/Laboratory Manager

Dilmaherbals Limited
Incorporated: 30 April 2018
Registered Office: 39 Belfry Way, Edwalton, Nottingham, NG12 4FA
Major Shareholder: Gaurav Gupta
Officers: Gaurav Gupta [1990] Director/Pharmacist

Dily Oka International Group Co., Ltd
Incorporated: 4 September 2018
Registered Office: Unit G25, Waterfront Studios, 1 Dock Road, London, E16 1AH
Major Shareholder: Fuwei Qian
Officers: Fuwei Qian Qian [1993] Director [Chinese]

Dimonauk Ltd
Incorporated: 21 May 2018
Registered Office: Flat 2, 115 Blegborough Road, London, SW16 6DL
Major Shareholder: Monika Sopyte
Officers: Monika Sopyte [1988] Director/Buying and Marketing Assisting [Lithuanian]

Dinair Airbrush Makeup Systems Limited
Incorporated: 3 April 2018
Registered Office: 311 Shoreham Street, Sheffield, S2 4FA
Shareholders: Dina Ousley; George Lampman
Officers: George Lampman [1952] Director [American]; Dina Ousley [1946] Director [American]

David Dinero Ltd
Incorporated: 7 February 2018
Registered Office: 71-75 Shelton Street, Covent Garden, London, WC2H 9JQ
Major Shareholder: David Alawode
Officers: David Alawode, Secretary; David Alawode [1993] Director/Student [Nigerian]

Direct Cosmetics Limited
Incorporated: 5 September 1977 Employees: 14
Net Worth: £1,988,822 Total Assets: £2,367,745
Registered Office: Long Row, Oakham, Rutland, LE15 6LN
Shareholder: William Francis Doody
Officers: William Francis Doody, Secretary; Sylvia Doody [1943] Director/Cosmetics Retailer; William Francis Doody [1942] Director/Cosmetics Retailer

Direct Salon Limited
Incorporated: 21 May 2003
Net Worth Deficit: £27,048 Total Assets: £59,198
Registered Office: 600 Purley Way, Croydon, Surrey, CR0 4RF
Shareholder: Sharon Mason
Officers: Sharon Mason, Secretary; Sharon Mason [1965] Director; Lloyd McLeary [1960] Director

Direct Salon Supplies Limited
Incorporated: 23 May 2005 Employees: 4
Net Worth: £115,387 Total Assets: £215,564
Registered Office: Unit 5a, Fox Industrial Estate, Holyoake Avenue, Bispham, Blackpool, Lancs, FY2 0QX
Shareholders: Carl Cohen; Frederick Russell Bedson
Officers: Frederick Russell Bedson, Secretary; Carl Cohen [1960] Director

Direct Supplies (2014) Limited
Incorporated: 31 March 2014 Employees: 2
Net Worth: £2,263,064 Total Assets: £7,294,925
Registered Office: 166 College Road, Harrow, Middlesex, HA1 1RA
Parent: Direct Supplies (2014) Group Limited
Officers: Samuel Bazini [1963] Director; Sara Lisa Bazini [1964] Director

Direct Trade Limited
Incorporated: 24 October 2017
Registered Office: First Floor, 85 Great Portland Street, London, W1W 7LT
Major Shareholder: Huihui Qiao
Officers: Slawomir Leszek Maj [1984] Director/Accounts Manager [Polish]; Huihui Qiao [1983] Director [Chinese]

Directfrom Ltd
Incorporated: 5 December 2018
Registered Office: 3 Stanley Close, Longridge, Preston, Lancs, PR3 3SE
Major Shareholder: Chris McGowan
Officers: Chris McGowan [1972] Director/Businessman

Disciple Skincare Limited
Incorporated: 22 November 2016
Net Worth: £328 Total Assets: £328
Registered Office: A31 Ugli Campus, 56 Wood Lane, London, W12 7SB
Major Shareholder: Charlotte Rebecca Ferguson-Quilter
Officers: Charlotte Rebecca Ferguson-Quilter [1983] Director/Founder; Colin Pyle [1981] Director [Canadian]

Discounted Cosmetics Limited
Incorporated: 5 September 2014 Employees: 2
Net Worth: £357 Total Assets: £60,291
Registered Office: 7-9 Macon Court, Crewe, Cheshire, CW1 6EA
Shareholders: Caroline Price; David Skeffington
Officers: Caroline Price [1989] Director; David Skeffington [1985] Director

Disley Limited
Incorporated: 30 December 2015
Net Worth: £6,354 Total Assets: £8,487
Registered Office: 96A The Green, Southall, Middlesex, UB2 4BG
Major Shareholder: Asif Qadir
Officers: Asif Qadir [1988] Director [Pakistani]

Diva Cosmetics Limited
Incorporated: 26 January 2000
Net Worth: £100 Total Assets: £100
Registered Office: Unit 1 Leekbrook Way, Leek, Staffs, ST13 7AP
Officers: Patrick John McDermott [1957] Director

Diva Deva UK Limited
Incorporated: 27 February 2008
Net Worth Deficit: £117,840 *Total Assets:* £6,500
Registered Office: Connect House, 133-137 Alexandra Road, Wimbledon, London, SW19 7JY
Major Shareholder: Aniela Meyer
Officers: Timmothy Meyer, Secretary; Aniela Meyer [1960] Director/Textile Designer

The Diverse Investment (London) Group Limited
Incorporated: 3 November 2010 *Employees:* 1
Net Worth: £352,016 *Total Assets:* £1,133,366
Registered Office: Thames House, Bourne End Business Park, Cores End Road, Bourne End, Bucks, SL8 5AS
Shareholder: Active Cleaning Contractors Limited
Officers: James Joseph Manning [1965] Director

Diverse Solution Ltd
Incorporated: 15 April 2014
Net Worth: £11,790 *Total Assets:* £25,140
Registered Office: 4th Floor, 101 Whitechapel High Street, London, E1 7RA
Major Shareholder: Sharmin Nahar
Officers: Sharmin Nahar [1986] Director/Business Executive [Bangladeshi]

Divine Natural Limited
Incorporated: 17 June 2010
Net Worth Deficit: £21,064 *Total Assets:* £4,047
Registered Office: 5 Benson Close, Luton, Beds, LU3 3QW
Shareholder: Donna Carrington
Officers: Donna Carrington [1965] Director/Beauty Therapist; John Andrew Carrington [1965] Director/Shipping Operative

Divit Beauty Ltd
Incorporated: 19 October 2018
Registered Office: 30 East Street, Derby, DE1 2AF
Major Shareholder: Hetal Chiragkumar Patel
Officers: Hetal Chiragkumar Patel [1978] Director

Diymonde Corporation Limited
Incorporated: 12 September 2017
Registered Office: 46 Syon Lane, Isleworth, Middlesex, TW7 5NQ
Major Shareholder: Baiba Rozenberga
Officers: Baiba Rozenberga, Secretary; Baiba Rozenberga [1984] Director [Latvian]

DKB Essentials Ltd
Incorporated: 18 September 2014
Net Worth Deficit: £22,477 *Total Assets:* £5,509
Registered Office: 1 Whitton Street, Wednesbury, W Midlands, WS10 8BA
Officers: Razna Devi, Secretary; Devinder Kumar [1969] Director

DKH Retail Limited
Incorporated: 2 November 2009
Net Worth: £275,530,000 *Total Assets:* £473,450,000
Registered Office: Unit 60 The Runnings, Cheltenham, Glos, GL51 9NW
Parent: Superdry PLC
Officers: Edward Peter Barker [1972] Director; Simon Callander [1967] Director/Group General Counsel and Company Secretary; Euan Angus Sutherland [1969] Director

DLG Partners Limited
Incorporated: 6 November 2018
Registered Office: 71-75 Shelton Street, London, WC2H 9JQ
Shareholder: Charles Desmond Desforges
Officers: Edouard-Henri Olivier Desforges, Secretary; Dr Charles Desmond Desforges [1940] Director/Scientist; Edouard-Henri Olivier Desforges [1985] Research & Development Director; John Peregrine Lycett-Green [1978] Director/Botanist

DLM Trade Limited
Incorporated: 7 January 2019
Registered Office: 236 Brunswick Park Road, London, N11 1EX
Major Shareholder: Zvezdana Manev
Officers: Zvezdana Manev [1966] Director/Accountant [Serbian]

DMG Wholesale Limited
Incorporated: 21 January 2013
Net Worth: £1,170,000 *Total Assets:* £3,020,000
Registered Office: Unit 5-7 Tintagel Way, Aldridge, Walsall, W Midlands, WS9 8ER
Officers: Dale Gibson [1969] Director; Daniel Mark O'Connor [1981] Finance Director

DMK Distribution (NI) Ltd
Incorporated: 10 May 2018
Registered Office: 585 Lisburn Road, Belfast, BT9 7GS
Shareholder: Jenna Mulholland
Officers: Jenna Mulholland [1987] Director; Mark Mulholland [1985] Director

DNA Beauty Group Ltd.
Incorporated: 18 December 2017
Registered Office: Amertrans Park, Bushey Mill Lane, Watford, Herts, WD24 7JG
Officers: Dilesh Bhogilal Mehta [1960] Director

Doers Skincare Limited
Incorporated: 18 August 2016
Registered Office: 24a Aldermans Hill, Palmers Green, London, N13 4PN
Shareholders: Giangiacomo Postir; Zacharias Charalambous
Officers: Zacharias Charalambous [1981] Director/MD Cosmetics; Giangiacomo Postir [1980] Director/Consultant [Italian]

Dojah Limited
Incorporated: 14 January 2019
Registered Office: 5 Westbourne Crescent, Southampton, SO17 1EA
Major Shareholder: George Johnson
Officers: George Johnson [1990] Director/Entrepreneur

Dolly Custard Ltd
Incorporated: 9 October 2018
Registered Office: Springhill Barn, Upper Slaughter, Cheltenham, Glos, GL54 2JH
Shareholders: Terasa Christine Pilcher; Colin Pilcher
Officers: Colin Pilcher [1961] Operations Director; Terasa Christine Pilcher [1960] Artistic Creative Director

Donovan Luxe Limited
Incorporated: 2 May 2017
Registered Office: 167 Peckham Rye, London, SE15 3HZ
Major Shareholder: Michael Charles Donovan
Officers: Michael Charles Donovan [1963] Director/Public Relations Consultant

Dont Poke It Ltd
Incorporated: 3 December 2018
Registered Office: 34 Bartlett Street, Manchester, M11 2EU
Major Shareholder: Donna Marie Melia
Officers: Donna Marie Melia [1982] Director

Dooa Capital Limited
Incorporated: 27 September 2017
Registered Office: 61 North Acton Road, Park Royal, London, NW10 6PH
Shareholder: Ravinder Singh Dooa
Officers: Ravinder Singh Dooa [1978] Director; Jasvinder Singh Dooa [1976] Director

Dorian House Marketplace Ltd
Incorporated: 15 January 2018
Registered Office: Kemp House, 160 City Road, London, EC1V 2NX
Major Shareholder: Enrique Extremera Junquera
Officers: Enrique Extremera Junquera [1989] Managing Director [Spanish]

Dorothy Hair and Beauty Shop Ltd
Incorporated: 13 August 2018
Registered Office: Flat 2, 5 Woodside Avenue, South Norwood, London, SE25 5DW
Major Shareholder: Leticia Owusu Dickson
Officers: Leticia Dorothy Owusu-Dickson [1958] Director/Store Assistant [Dutch]

Dos Osatos International Ltd
Incorporated: 12 February 2019
Registered Office: 57 Ockley Court, 183 Main Road, Sidcup, Kent, DA14 6TB
Major Shareholder: Paris Osato
Officers: Paris Osato, Secretary; Paris Osato [1987] Director [Nigerian]

Doterra (Europe) Ltd
Incorporated: 6 April 2009 *Employees:* 20
Net Worth: £8,433,477 *Total Assets:* £22,412,516
Registered Office: Altius House, 1 North Fourth Street, Milton Keynes, Bucks, MK9 1DG
Officers: Gregory Paul Cook [1969] Director/Sales [American]; Kirk Lincoln Jowers [1967] Director/Business Executive [American]; Murray Moyle Smith [1966] Director/Business Executive [American/Canadian]; David Stirling [1963] Director [American]

Dots for Spots Ltd
Incorporated: 14 December 2018
Registered Office: Abbot House, Park Terrace, Nottingham, NG1 5DN
Major Shareholder: Sarah Louise O'Connor
Officers: Sarah Louise O'Connor [1986] Director

Double Skies Limited
Incorporated: 24 April 2018
Registered Office: 2 Fennel Drive, Bradley Stoke, Bristol, BS32 0BX
Major Shareholder: Wing Hang Lau
Officers: Wing Hang Lau [1954] Director

Dovedale Limited
Incorporated: 1 October 1986
Net Worth: £55,703 *Total Assets:* £61,365
Registered Office: 20 Coxon Street, Spondon, Derby, DE21 7JG
Major Shareholder: Rafael Cohen
Officers: Rafael Cohen, Secretary; Oren Cohen [1982] Director/Software Sales; Rafael Cohen [1952] Director [Israeli]

Doyin Tradings UK Limited
Incorporated: 1 December 2016
Net Worth: £2,534 *Total Assets:* £26,917
Registered Office: 10 Belvedere Business Park, Crabtree Manorway South, Belvedere, Kent, DA17 6AH
Officers: Adebayo Adepegba Oniyide [1959] Director

Doyle's Group Ltd
Incorporated: 29 June 2018
Registered Office: 71-75 Shelton Street, London, WC2H 9JQ
Major Shareholder: Pascal Kempson
Officers: Pascal Kempson [1996] Director

Dr Shea Ltd
Incorporated: 4 October 2016
Net Worth Deficit: £278 *Total Assets:* £492
Registered Office: 27 Old Gloucester Street, London, WC1N 3AX
Major Shareholder: Michael Blake
Officers: Michael Blake [1975] Director/Self Employed

Dr Sun Limited
Incorporated: 24 August 2017
Registered Office: 409 Harlington Road, Uxbridge, Middlesex, UB8 3JG
Officers: Zuhaib Babar Syed [1988] Director [Pakistani]

Dr. Gabriela Ltd
Incorporated: 5 October 2015
Registered Office: 1 Church Street, Fintona, Co Tyrone, BT78 2BR
Officers: Grzegorz Gabriel Mercik [1989] Director [Polish]

Dr. Organic Limited
Incorporated: 28 June 2007 *Employees:* 46
Net Worth: £17,220,000 *Total Assets:* £26,357,000
Registered Office: Dr Organic Limited, Valley Way, Swansea Enterprise Park, Swansea, SA6 8QP
Parent: NBTY (2015) Limited
Officers: Nicholas John Heywood Collins [1962] Director/Chief Strategy & Product Supply Officer International; Stephen Kelsey Ford [1968] Finance Director; Matthew James Richard Harvey [1980] Director/Chartered Accountant; Michael Henryk Lightowlers [1972] Managing Director; Stephen Ronald Price [1964] Group Export Director

Dr. Twilight Ltd
Incorporated: 21 December 2018
Registered Office: 71-75 Shelton Street, London, WC2H 9JQ
Shareholders: Connor Qiu; Maleeha Zafar
Officers: Dr Connor Qiu [1994] Director/Doctor; Dr Maleeha Zafar [1989] Director/Doctor [German]

Dr.K Skinlab Ltd
Incorporated: 26 April 2018
Registered Office: 71-75 Shelton Street, London, WC2H 9JQ
Shareholders: Dr.K Gruppen AB; UK Skinlabs Limited
Officers: Nima Habib [1989] Director/Sales Manager [Swedish]

Dr.Lipp Ltd
Incorporated: 9 June 2004 *Employees:* 2
Net Worth: £336,324 *Total Assets:* £370,097
Registered Office: Bond House, 19-20, Woodstock Street, London, W1C 2AN
Parent: Pontine Holding AS
Officers: Isobel Jane Taylor, Secretary; Pontine Cecilie Alexandra Paus [1973] Director/Designer [Norwegian]

Drammock International Limited
Incorporated: 26 October 1993 *Employees:* 16
Net Worth: £642,828 *Total Assets:* £1,765,066
Registered Office: Tower House, Westfield Industrial Estate, Kirk Lane, Yeadon, Leeds, LS19 7LX
Officers: Susan Mottram, Secretary/Office Manager; Alan David Ingram [1973] Director/Manager; Paul Mottram [1948] Director/Exporter of Beauty Products; Susan Mottram [1947] Director/Office Manager; Paul Richard Schofield [1974] Director/Salesman

Dream Girl Limited
Incorporated: 22 August 2017
Registered Office: 55 North Acton Road, Park Royal, Brent, London, NW10 6PH
Shareholders: Jasvinder Singh Dooa; Ravinder Singh Dooa
Officers: Jasvinder Singh Dooa [1976] Director; Ravinder Singh Dooa [1978] Director

Dream Glow Ltd
Incorporated: 27 July 2018
Registered Office: Suite S7, Rays House, North Circular Road, London, NW10 7XP
Shareholders: Akbarali Bhanji; Nikhar Jivani
Officers: Akbarali Bhanji [1958] Director; Nikhar Jivani [1993] Director

Dream Skin Ltd
Incorporated: 15 December 2017
Registered Office: 20-22 Wenlock Road, London, N1 7GU
Major Shareholder: Michelle Russell
Officers: Michelle Russell [1987] Director

Dreamage Ltd.
Incorporated: 4 February 2019
Registered Office: 71-75 Shelton Street, Covent Garden, London, WC2H 9JQ
Major Shareholder: Jinqi Zhang
Officers: Jinqi Zhang [1994] Director [Chinese]

Dreamweave Products Ltd
Incorporated: 24 January 2012
Net Worth: £577,620 *Total Assets:* £832,350
Registered Office: 11 Dalton Court, Commercial Road, Darwen, Lancs, BB3 0DG
Shareholders: Steven Mather; Elaine Mather
Officers: Elaine Mather [1965] Director/Cosmetics Manufacturer; Steven Mather [1965] Director/Cosmetics Manufacturer

Drimex Limited
Incorporated: 2 May 2018
Registered Office: 2nd-3rd Floor, 37a Great Cumberland Place, London, W1H 7TD
Officers: Djamel Benallal [1970] Director [French]

Droplet Cosmetics Limited
Incorporated: 10 February 2017
Net Worth: £296 *Total Assets:* £15,132
Registered Office: 18 Braecroft Avenue, Westhill, Aberdeenshire, AB32 6RF
Shareholders: Aref Ghaffarzadeh Artloui Kochak; Andrey Prosenko
Officers: Aref Ghaffarzadeh Artloui Kochak [1969] Director [Iranian]; Andrey Prosenko [1984] Director [Azerbaijani]

Drugget Ltd
Incorporated: 4 December 2018
Registered Office: 71-75 Shelton Street, Covent Garden, London, WC2H 9JQ
Major Shareholder: Ham Mukama Yorachi
Officers: Juliet Namubiru, Secretary; Ham Mukama Yorachi [1991] Director

DS Express Barbering Ltd
Incorporated: 13 July 2018
Registered Office: 9 Tan Y Fan, Ammanford, Carmarthenshire, SA18 3SG
Officers: Riza Eruncak [1986] Director

DSE Companies Limited
Incorporated: 18 January 2019
Registered Office: 48 Longfield Avenue, Longfield, Dartford, Kent, DA3 7LA
Shareholders: Dexter Coleman-Mitchell; Samuel Kenneth Liam Fathers
Officers: Dexter Coleman-Mitchell [1991] Commercial Director

Dudu-Osun Limited
Incorporated: 23 August 2017
Registered Office: 100 New Bridge Street, London, EC4V 6JA
Shareholders: Abiola Ogunrinde; Oladipo Demilade Ogunrinde
Officers: Abiola Ogunrinde [1951] Director/Manufacturer [Nigerian]; Oladipo Demilade Ogunrinde [1992] Director/Manufacturer [Nigerian]

Dufeal Your Best Beauty Ltd
Incorporated: 22 August 2018
Registered Office: Kemp House, 152-160 City Road, London, EC1V 2NX
Shareholder: Tolive Dufeal
Officers: Tolive Dufeal, Secretary; Tolive Dufeal [1980] Director/Beautician

Dug and Bitch Ltd
Incorporated: 3 August 2017
Registered Office: Pipersknowe, Traquair, Innerleithen, Peebles-shire, EH44 6PL
Major Shareholder: Neil Ian Robson
Officers: Neil Ian Robson [1970] Director

Duke of Charm Limited
Incorporated: 1 June 2018
Registered Office: Kemp House, 160 City Road, London, EC1V 2NX
Major Shareholder: Chakomba Shamwana
Officers: Chakomba Shamwana, Secretary; Chakomba Shamwana [1986] Director/Recruitment Consultant [Zambian]

Dunia Organic Ltd
Incorporated: 14 September 2018
Registered Office: 81 Spencer Court, Froghall Terrace, Aberdeen, AB24 3PG
Major Shareholder: Klaudia Rubaszewska
Officers: Klaudia Rubaszewska [1991] Director/Dental Nurse [Polish]

Dunstan and Burr Ltd
Incorporated: 7 February 2014
Net Worth Deficit: £8,792 *Total Assets:* £4,828
Registered Office: Brookscity, 6th Floor, New Baltic House, 65 Fenchurch Street, London, EC3M 4BE
Major Shareholder: Chloe Lee
Officers: Chloe Lee [1988] Director

Duo Beauty Products Limited
Incorporated: 4 June 2018
Registered Office: 9 MacKenzie Street, Slough, SL1 1XQ
Shareholders: Kahinaat Raja; Aarzu Raja
Officers: Aarzu Raja [1998] Director/Student; Kahinaat Raja [1998] Director/Student

Dupeshop Ltd
Incorporated: 10 October 2016
Registered Office: 50-54 St Pauls Square, Birmingham, B3 1QS
Shareholders: Laghu Bhardwaj; Amir Awan
Officers: Amir Awan [1993] Director; Laghu Bhardwaj [1994] Director

Duron Ltd
Incorporated: 22 August 2018
Registered Office: 17 Glenfield Road, Leicester, LE3 6AT
Major Shareholder: Rudolfs Freimanis
Officers: Rudolfs Freimanis, Secretary; Rudolfs Freimanis [1996] Director [Latvian]

DYB Tarding Ltd
Incorporated: 5 January 2018
Registered Office: 1c Bergholt Crescent, London, N16 5JE
Major Shareholder: David Braun
Officers: David Braun, Secretary; David Braun [1992] Director/Sales

Dynamic Skincare Ltd
Incorporated: 30 July 2007
Previous: Organic@Heart Ltd
Net Worth: £87,482 *Total Assets:* £124,536
Registered Office: 5 Addington Gardens, Woodley, Reading, Berks, RG5 3EW
Major Shareholder: Sally Robinson
Officers: Sally Anne Robinson [1965] Director

E-MO Nails Ltd
Incorporated: 10 January 2018
Registered Office: 23 Edencrieve, Newry, Co Armagh, BT35 8UE
Shareholder: Monika Selim
Officers: Erol Selim [1977] Director [Irish]; Monika Selim [1985] Director/Nail Technician [Polish]

E.J. Contracts Limited
Incorporated: 7 February 1995 *Employees:* 3
Net Worth: £374,996 *Total Assets:* £419,125
Registered Office: Unit D, Poplar Way East, Cabot Park, Avonmouth, Bristol, BS11 0DD
Parent: Elemis Limited
Officers: Daniel Michael Chambers, Secretary; Michael Stephan Haringman, Secretary; Oriele Anne Dunbar [1965] Director [Canadian]; Noella Gabriel [1956] Director [Irish]; Michael Stephan Haringman [1944] Director/Solicitor; Sean Harrington [1966] Director; Christopher Vieth [1965] Director [American]

Eabir Ltd
Incorporated: 5 November 2018
Registered Office: 16 Arlington Road, Stretford, Manchester, M32 9HJ
Major Shareholder: Ambreen Abdul
Officers: Ambreen Abdul [1989] Director [French]

Eacho Green Ltd
Incorporated: 16 November 2018
Registered Office: 107 Church Road, Hayes, Middlesex, UB3 2LE
Major Shareholder: Duraiz Hussain Butt
Officers: Duraiz Hussain Butt [1988] Director [Belgian]

Earth Aid Group Limited
Incorporated: 18 March 2016
Net Worth: £80 *Total Assets:* £100
Registered Office: Earth Aid Group Limited, Conchieton Business Centre, Kirkcudbright, Dumfries & Galloway, DG6 4TA
Major Shareholder: Graeme Paul Hume
Officers: Graeme Paul Hume [1953] Director

Earth Goddess Ltd
Incorporated: 19 July 2018
Registered Office: 60 Martins Hill Lane, Burton, Christchurch, Dorset, BH23 7JE
Major Shareholder: Hannah Christian Cutler
Officers: Hannah Christian Cutler [1984] Director/Manufacturer

Earth Mother Limited
Incorporated: 5 July 2000 *Employees:* 2
Net Worth Deficit: £59,392 *Total Assets:* £21,264
Registered Office: 66 Bridge Street, Ramsbottom, Bury, Lancs, BL0 9AG
Shareholders: Joanna Helen Kelly-Morris; Rachel Elizabeth Kelly
Officers: Joanna Helen Kelly-Morris, Secretary; Rachel Elizabeth Kelly [1972] Director; Joanna Helen Kelly-Morris [1975] Director

Earthbreath Ltd
Incorporated: 15 January 2019
Registered Office: Cairn Mount, Contin, Strathpeffer, Ross-shire, IV14 9ES
Major Shareholder: Renars Bumanis
Officers: Renars Bumanis [1978] Director [Latvian]; Erlands Luika [1978] Director [Latvian]

Earthkind Ltd
Incorporated: 11 June 2018
Registered Office: 53 King George VI Avenue, East Tilbury, Tilbury, Essex, RM18 8SL
Major Shareholder: Claire Yerlett
Officers: Claire Yerlett [1986] Director/Housewife

Earthly Pleasures Ltd
Incorporated: 30 January 2018
Registered Office: 207 Regent Street, London, W1B 3HH
Major Shareholder: Olaitan Oluwaseun Kadri
Officers: Olaitan Oluwaseun Kadri [1979] Director

East Cosmetics Limited
Incorporated: 1 August 2018
Registered Office: Office 89, 321-323 High Road, Chadwell Heath, Essex, RM6 6AX
Shareholders: Natalie Johnson; Shackeema Donna-Kay Brown; Parisimo Campbell
Officers: Shackeema Donna-Kay Brown [1990] Director [Jamaican]; Parisimo Campbell [1978] Director; Natalie Johnson [1985] Director [Canadian]

East End Cosmetics Limited
Incorporated: 26 June 2003 *Employees:* 4
Net Worth: £116,196 *Total Assets:* £897,837
Registered Office: 131 Middlesex Street, London, E1 7JF
Shareholders: Akbar Bhanji; Shabir Ali Bhanji
Officers: Shabir Ali Bhanji, Secretary; Akbar Ali Bhanji [1958] Director/Shop Proprietor; Shabir Ali Bhanji [1960] Director

East Garden Ltd
Incorporated: 19 November 2015
Net Worth: £1,232 *Total Assets:* £1,515
Registered Office: Kemp House, 152 City Road, London, EC1V 2NX
Major Shareholder: Michal Strzalkowski
Officers: Michal Strzalkowski [1965] Director [Polish]

The East To West Lifestyle Company Ltd
Incorporated: 11 December 2018
Registered Office: Coach House, Ealing Green, London, W5 5ER
Major Shareholder: Sherry Adhami
Officers: Sherry Adhami [1981] Director

Easybusiness24 Ltd
Incorporated: 24 July 2017
Registered Office: 2a St George Wharf, London, SW8 2LE
Shareholders: Francesco Palestini; Antonio Ricciardo
Officers: Francesco Palestini [1976] Director/Quantity Surveyor [Italian]; Antonio Ricciardo [1971] Director/Leader [Italian]

Eau de Parfum Limited
Incorporated: 29 August 2018
Registered Office: c/o Sidikies Accountants, 1 Sun Street, London, EC2A 2EP
Shareholder: Adam Joosub
Officers: Adam Joosub [1975] Director [Grenadian]; Asif Taiyab Sunka [1976] Director

EB Stores Ltd
Incorporated: 14 June 2018
Registered Office: 98 Hodder Drive, London, UB6 8LL
Major Shareholder: Elisabeta Bacala
Officers: Elisabeta Bacala [1981] Director [Romanian]

EBF Europe Ltd
Incorporated: 28 April 2016
Net Worth Deficit: £239,610 *Total Assets:* £17,850
Registered Office: 98 Chingford Mount Road, South Chingford, London, E4 9AA
Shareholder: Eric Scott Buterbaugh
Officers: Eric Scott Buterbaugh [1960] Director/Florist/Perfumer [American]

Eblouir Group Ltd
Incorporated: 30 August 2017
Registered Office: 70 Laxfield Court, Pownall Road, London, E8 4PT
Officers: Vu-Hoang Le [1985] Director [French]; Shubi Zhang [1988] Director [Chinese]

Ebong and Brothers Ltd
Incorporated: 10 January 2011
Net Worth: £26,000 *Total Assets:* £26,000
Registered Office: 10 Matthew Arnold Court, Loughborough, Leics, LE11 5JS
Officers: Dr Fidelis Sameh Ebong [1975] Director/Research [Swedish]

Echo Hair Limited
Incorporated: 15 May 2013
Net Worth: £1,120 *Total Assets:* £361,599
Registered Office: 18 Dollman Street, Birmingham, B7 4RP
Major Shareholder: Shengli Li
Officers: Shengli Li [1978] Director [Chinese]

Eco Twinkle Ltd
Incorporated: 12 April 2017
Registered Office: 27 Old Gloucester Street, London, WC1N 3AX
Major Shareholder: Zoe Disco
Officers: Zoe Disco [1979] Director/Business Owner

Ecobeauty Ltd
Incorporated: 11 September 2006
Net Worth: £32,361 *Total Assets:* £60,711
Registered Office: Ground Floor, Unit 501 Centennial Park, Centennial Avenue, Elstree, Borehamwood, Herts, WD6 3FG
Major Shareholder: Denise Zucker
Officers: Denise Zucker, Secretary [Swiss]; Denise Zucker [1959] Director/Consultant [Swiss]

Ecocare Organic Limited
Incorporated: 8 September 2016
Net Worth Deficit: £15,537 *Total Assets:* £24,715
Registered Office: 10 John Street, London, WC1N 2EB
Officers: Callan Joel Taylor [1986] Director [Australian]

Ecooner Cosmetics London Ltd
Incorporated: 1 October 2016
Net Worth Deficit: £1,454 *Total Assets:* £53,593
Registered Office: Flat 30, Trident House, 76 Station Road, Hayes, Middlesex, UB3 4FP
Major Shareholder: Xiaomei Yu
Officers: Xiaomei Yu [1987] Director [Chinese]

ED Trading & Consultancy Limited
Incorporated: 27 February 2018
Registered Office: 371 Harehills Lane, Leeds, LS9 6AP
Major Shareholder: Abdullah Foqaha
Officers: Abdullah Harbi Foqaha [1981] Director [Jordanian]

Eden Brands Limited
Incorporated: 11 March 2013
Previous: Eden Parfums Limited
Registered Office: Unit 4 Imperial Park Business Centre, Stonefield Way, Ruislip, Middlesex, HA4 0JW
Major Shareholder: Manisha Thakrar
Officers: Nayan Thakrar [1960] Director

Eden Parfums Limited
Incorporated: 27 August 2013
Net Worth Deficit: £138,490 *Total Assets:* £3,450,000
Registered Office: Unit 4 Imperial Park Business Centre, Stonefield Way, Ruislip, Middlesex, HA4 0JW
Major Shareholder: Manisha Thakrar
Officers: Manisha Thakrar, Secretary; Nayan Thakrar [1960] Director

Eden Perfumes Limited
Incorporated: 22 April 2014
Net Worth Deficit: £6,920 *Total Assets:* £178,380
Registered Office: 26 Gardner Street, Brighton, BN1 1UP
Shareholder: Francisco Javier Moya Soria
Officers: Aida Berliavsky Harshundia [1957] Director [Spanish]; Francisco-Javier Moya Soria [1957] Director [Spanish]; Antoun Yousif Shidiak [1985] Director

Eden's Daughter Limited
Incorporated: 7 November 2018
Registered Office: 3 Syndale Cottages, Ospringe, Faversham, Kent, ME13 0RJ
Major Shareholder: Natalie Da Costa
Officers: Natalie Da Costa [1985] Director

Eden's Legends Limited
Incorporated: 14 December 2017
Registered Office: Bank Gallery, 13 High Street, Kenilworth, Warwicks, CV8 1LY
Officers: Donniece Greene-Smith [1966] Director [American]; Matthew Nathaniel Smith [1969] Director

Edenwest Limited
Incorporated: 20 November 1989
Net Worth Deficit: £163,205 *Total Assets:* £1,480,743
Registered Office: Unit 4 Imperial Park, Stonefield Way, Ruislip, Middlesex, HA4 0JW
Shareholder: Shivani Thakrar
Officers: Manisha Thakrar, Secretary; Nayan Thakrar [1960] Director

The Edge Nail & Beauty Limited
Incorporated: 21 November 2005
Net Worth: £758,313 *Total Assets:* £836,626
Registered Office: Unit C1, Antura Bond Close, Kingsland Business Park, Basingstoke, Hants, RG24 8PZ
Major Shareholder: Alistair Robin Murray Wood
Officers: Alistair Robin Murray Wood [1954] Director/Cosmetic & Beauty Wholesaler

Editions de Parfums Limited
Incorporated: 4 December 2014 *Employees:* 12
Net Worth Deficit: £4,500,581 *Total Assets:* £19,562,614
Registered Office: One Fitzroy, 6 Mortimer Street, London, W1T 3JJ
Parent: The Estee Lauder Companies Inc.
Officers: Ana Elena Morales Arce, Secretary; Spencer Gary Smul, Secretary; Alison Claire Day [1971] Finance Director; Pierre Frederic Serge Louis Jacques Malle [1962] Director/Founder, Editions de Parfums LLC [French]; Philippe Michel Warnery [1970] Director/Corporate General Manager [French]

Edward London Ltd
Incorporated: 3 April 2018
Registered Office: 20-22 Wenlock Road, London, N1 7GU
Major Shareholder: Philip Moreau
Officers: Philip Moreau [1958] Director/Independent [Belgian]

Effay Limited
Incorporated: 20 June 2018
Registered Office: 229a Portswood Road, Southampton, SO17 2NF
Major Shareholder: Farah Amin
Officers: Farah Amin [1991] Director/Business Executive

Effective and Simple Ltd
Incorporated: 11 October 2017
Registered Office: 20-22 Wenlock Road, London, N1 7GU
Major Shareholder: Michael Simpson
Officers: Michael Simpson [1973] Director

Egg Pillow Limited
Incorporated: 5 September 2018
Registered Office: 34 Cadet Drive, London, SE1 5RU
Major Shareholder: Zhe Lin
Officers: Zhe Lin [1990] Director [Chinese]; Chung Nam Jason Tai [1994] Director [Hong Kong]

Egotistic Hair & Beauty Ltd
Incorporated: 4 June 2018
Registered Office: 71-75 Shelton Street, Covent Garden, London, WC2H 9JQ
Major Shareholder: Empress-Shera Williams
Officers: Empress-Shera Williams [1974] Director/Entrepreneur

Egyptian Magic Ltd
Incorporated: 10 September 2015
Net Worth: £29,206 *Total Assets:* £67,673
Registered Office: 10 Courtyard Apartments, 3 Avantgarde Place, London, E1 6GU
Parent: Egyptian Magic Skin Cream LLC
Officers: Lord Pharaoh Imhotep Amonra [1945] Director [American]; Christian Forrest Stroud [1982] Director [American]

Eifelcorp Consumer Care Ltd
Incorporated: 3 February 2016
Registered Office: 161 St Andrews Road, Northampton, NN2 6HL
Officers: Williams Aspinall [1972] Director/Businessman; Trang Huyen Thi Le [1987] Director/Businesswoman [Vietnamese]

Eileen Group (UK) Ltd
Incorporated: 15 August 2018
Registered Office: 27 Old Gloucester Street, London, WC1N 3AX
Officers: Yu Ping Ho [1989] Director/Sales & Marketing [Hong Kong]

EJS Brand Management Limited
Incorporated: 10 January 2013
Net Worth: £571 *Total Assets:* £43,990
Registered Office: Fides House, 10 Chertsey Road, Woking, Surrey, GU21 5AB
Major Shareholder: Eilidh Janet Smith
Officers: Eilidh Janet Smith [1982] Director/Sales & Marketing

Ekah Foundation C.I.C.
Incorporated: 19 August 2015
Registered Office: Vidya Matha UK, 331 Burnley Road, Rushbed, Rossendale, Lancs, BB4 8LA
Officers: Anand Ennis-Cole [1965] Director; Ramana Ennis-Cole [1974] Director/Teacher; Kishin Uttam-Chandani [1941] Director

Ekoderma Ltd
Incorporated: 29 January 2019
Registered Office: 384 Downall Green Road, Ashton in Makerfield, Wigan, Lancs, WN4 0LZ
Major Shareholder: Stephanie Murray
Officers: Stephanie Murray [1992] Director/Manager

Eku Skin Care Ltd
Incorporated: 21 February 2018
Registered Office: 160 City Road, London, EC1V 2NX
Shareholders: Delphine Emenyonu; Douglas Pollyn
Officers: Delphine Emenyonu [1986] Commercial Director; Douglas Apabara Pollyn [1984] Director [Nigerian]

EL Companies Ltd
Incorporated: 27 February 2018
Registered Office: Suite 1, 5 Percy Street, Fitzrovia, London, W1T 1DG
Officers: Elmarie Ibanez [1966] Director [South African]

El Sabbagh Trading Limited
Incorporated: 31 January 2018
Registered Office: 449 Edgware Road, London, W2 1TH
Shareholder: Ziad El Sabbagh
Officers: Abd Al Halem El Sabbagh [1974] Director/Businessman [Lebanese]; Ziad El Sabbagh [1972] Director/Businessman [Lebanese]

Elan Skincare Ltd
Incorporated: 18 September 2017
Registered Office: 73 Dairsie Road, London, SE9 1XN
Major Shareholder: Joanna Wiktoria Silva
Officers: Rafael Dos Santos Silva, Secretary; Joanna Wiktoria Silva [1978] Director

Elder & Co Limited
Incorporated: 20 September 2018
Registered Office: 55 Beechwood Drive, Glenrothes, Fife, KY7 6GE
Major Shareholder: Connor Jake Elder
Officers: Connor Jake Elder [1996] Director

Lisa Eldridge Beauty Ltd
Incorporated: 22 January 2019
Registered Office: 42 Lytton Road, Barnet, Herts, EN5 5BY
Major Shareholder: Lisa Eldridge
Officers: Lisa Eldridge [1966] Director

Electimuss Limited
Incorporated: 26 September 2018
Registered Office: 20-21 Jockey's Fields, London, WC1R 4BW
Shareholders: Jason Paul Collison; Luke Henry James Granger; Al Arbash United Group for General Trading & Contracting Company W.L.L
Officers: Jason Paul Collison [1973] Director [Australian]; Luke Henry James Granger [1980] Director

Elegance By London Limited
Incorporated: 26 November 2010 *Employees:* 7
Net Worth: £902,299 *Total Assets:* £1,941,905
Registered Office: 27 Hornsby Square, Southfields Business Park, Basildon, Essex, SS15 6SD
Shareholder: Vikas Goyal
Officers: Neha Goyal [1985] Director; Vikas Goyal [1987] Director

Elegance Gel UK Ltd
Incorporated: 24 March 2017
Net Worth: £3,170 *Total Assets:* £42,890
Registered Office: Flat 5 Hillsborough Court, Mortimer Crescent, Kilburn, London, NW6 5NR
Major Shareholder: Diksha Kumar
Officers: Diksha Kumar [1993] Director [Italian]

Elegant Boss Ltd
Incorporated: 6 July 2018
Registered Office: 98 Ponsonby House, Bishops Way, Bethnal Green, London, E2 9HS
Major Shareholder: Phillip Johnson
Officers: Phillip Johnson [1966] Director/Security Controller [German]

Elegantes London Limited
Incorporated: 12 June 2017
Registered Office: 21 Bedford Square, London, WC1B 3HH
Major Shareholder: Dagmar Smit
Officers: Dagmar Smit [1965] CEO & Director [Czech]; Thomas Smit [1953] Director/Group Company Chairman & CEO [Dutch]

Elemental Herbology Limited
Incorporated: 12 December 2002 *Employees:* 9
Net Worth: £273,996 *Total Assets:* £488,013
Registered Office: Studio D, Tay Building, 2a Wrentham Avenue, London, NW10 3HA
Officers: Carolyne Ann Beck [1973] Commercial Director; Kim Hurd [1962] Director; Miles Stanley Clewley Johnson [1963] Director; William Rollason [1960] Director

Elequra Limited
Incorporated: 21 October 2011
Previous: Elethea Limited
Net Worth Deficit: £481,290 *Total Assets:* £111,570
Registered Office: Suite 316, 28 Old Brompton Road, London, SW7 3SS
Major Shareholder: Nausheen Qureshi
Officers: Nausheen Qureshi [1983] Director/Businesswoman

Eleu Beauty Ltd
Incorporated: 22 August 2018
Registered Office: 16 William Cobbett House, 1 Scarsdale Place, London, W8 5SY
Shareholders: Qin Zhou; Hairong Qiu; Zhaohui Zhu
Officers: Qin Zhou [1979] Director

Eleuthere Ltd
Incorporated: 12 November 2015
Registered Office: Unit 3 Lake Farm House, Allington Lane, Fair Oak, Eastleigh, Hants, SO50 7DD
Major Shareholder: Julio Marcel Brugos Eleuterio
Officers: Julio Marcel Brugos Eleuterio [1976] Director [Spanish]

Eleven Eleven Cosmetics Ltd
Incorporated: 4 February 2019
Registered Office: 189 Varley Street, Manchester, M40 7EJ
Major Shareholder: Rowan Louise Sear
Officers: Rowan Louise Sear [1992] Director/Administrator

Elie Consumer Care Ltd
Incorporated: 4 July 2017
Registered Office: 54 Elmwood Avenue, Belfast, BT9 6AZ
Major Shareholder: Mary Stephen
Officers: Trang Huyen Thi Le [1987] Director/Businesswoman [Vietnamese]; Mary Stephen [1972] Director/Businesswoman

Elinor-UK Ltd
Incorporated: 19 February 2018
Registered Office: 1st Floor, 2 Woodberry Grove, Finchley, London, N12 0DR
Major Shareholder: Vladislav Mihaylov Indzhov
Officers: Vladislav Mihaylov Indzhov, Secretary; Vladislav Mihaylov Indzhov [1986] Director [Bulgarian]

Elite Beauty (London) Limited
Incorporated: 22 February 2011
Net Worth Deficit: £2,180 *Total Assets:* £27,370
Registered Office: 225 Kenton Lane, Harrow, Middlesex, HA3 8RP
Major Shareholder: Mahanbir Singh Kalsi
Officers: Kuldip Kaur Sokhi [1942] Director

Elite Capital Limited
Incorporated: 28 November 2014 *Employees:* 7
Net Worth Deficit: £8,890 *Total Assets:* £318,958
Registered Office: Studio 4, Clarks Courtyard, 145 Granville Street, Birmingham, B1 1SB
Major Shareholder: Anh Thi Phuong Nguyen
Officers: Anh Nguyen [1990] Director [Vietnamese]

Elite Salon Solutions Limited
Incorporated: 17 December 2014
Net Worth Deficit: £8,677 *Total Assets:* £46,523
Registered Office: 5 Blaen Y Pant Avenue, Newport, NP20 5PU
Shareholders: Claire Louise McCarthy; Timothy Patrick McCarthy
Officers: Claire Louise McCarthy [1968] Managing Director; Timothy Patrick McCarthy [1969] Director

Elitelashes Ltd
Incorporated: 22 January 2019
Registered Office: 20-22 Wenlock Road, London, N1 7GU
Major Shareholder: Natalia Samyshkina
Officers: Natalia Samyshkina [1980] Director [Portuguese]

Elko Electrical Ltd.
Incorporated: 1 October 2003
Net Worth: £341,672 *Total Assets:* £393,944
Registered Office: 148 Ralph Road, Shirley, Solihull, W Midlands, B90 3JZ
Major Shareholder: Christopher Dawson
Officers: Christopher Dawson [1985] Director/Electrician; Ruth Elizabeth Floyd [1986] Director

Ella Nur Ltd
Incorporated: 15 February 2017
Net Worth Deficit: £3,480 *Total Assets:* £18,370
Registered Office: 67 Hartington Road, Leicester, LE2 0GQ
Major Shareholder: Sara Liyakat Nurmahomed
Officers: Umar Liyakat Nurmahomed [1990] Director/Business Executive

Elleshouse Ltd
Incorporated: 27 November 2018
Registered Office: 152 St Thomas Road, Derby, DE23 8SX
Major Shareholder: Adeeba Hussain
Officers: Adeeba Hussain [1993] Director/Accountant

Elliott Nutrition Ltd
Incorporated: 24 July 2017
Registered Office: NI647055: Companies House, Default Address, 2nd Floor The Linenhall 32-38 Linenhall Street, Belfast, BT2 8BG
Major Shareholder: Laura Ashley
Officers: Prof Laura Ashley [1978] Director/Professor

Ellipsis Brands Limited
Incorporated: 7 June 2013 *Employees:* 5
Previous: F & M Cosmetics Limited
Net Worth: £219,323 *Total Assets:* £456,789
Registered Office: Suite 7, Station Court, Station Lane, Hethersett, Norfolk, NR9 3AY
Major Shareholder: Frederick Peter Furber
Officers: Julia Cavanagh, Secretary; Edward Richard Alexander Furber [1957] Director; Frederick Peter Furber [1987] Director

Ellya UK Ltd
Incorporated: 9 June 2017
Registered Office: 102 Wembley Park Drive, Wembley Park, Middlesex, HA9 8HP
Major Shareholder: Penda Soumano
Officers: Penda Soumano [1984] Director [French]

Eloise Group Ltd
Incorporated: 15 September 2017
Registered Office: 20-22 Wenlock Road, London, N1 7GU
Major Shareholder: Ding Yuan
Officers: Oliver Felstead [1981] Director; Ding Yuan [1985] Director [Chinese]

Eloise M Beauty Ltd
Incorporated: 13 August 2018
Registered Office: 38 Layard Square, London, SE16 2JE
Major Shareholder: Eloise Megan O'Rourke
Officers: Eloise Megan O'Rourke [1999] Director

Elysian Design Limited
Incorporated: 8 January 2015 *Employees:* 2
Net Worth: £58,737 *Total Assets:* £134,524
Registered Office: 122 Brunswick Road, London, E10 6RS
Major Shareholder: Madeline Lucy Griffiths
Officers: Madeline Lucy Griffiths [1984] Director/Designer

Emel Trade Ltd
Incorporated: 4 December 2015
Net Worth: £3,910 *Total Assets:* £5,400
Registered Office: Unit 2 Christy Court, Basildon, Essex, SS15 6TL
Shareholders: Emel Kuntes; Emel Kuntes
Officers: Emel Kuntes [1980] Director/Businesswomen [Turkish]

Emilia's Handmade Bath and Body Ltd
Incorporated: 18 June 2018
Registered Office: 41 Mountbatten Avenue, Romsey, Hants, SO51 8DX
Major Shareholder: Emilia Sophia Mary Primrose Head
Officers: Emilia Sophia Mary Primrose Head [1999] Director

Emita Europe Limited
Incorporated: 23 February 2018
Registered Office: 54 Hillbury Avenue, Harrow, Middlesex, HA3 8EW
Major Shareholder: Dilip Kumar Poddar
Officers: George Myrants, Secretary; Dilip Kumar Poddar [1957] Director [Indian]

Emma Danmark Ltd
Incorporated: 31 May 2017
Registered Office: Emma Danmark Ltd, 20-22 Wenlock Road, London, N1 7GU
Major Shareholder: Tommy Henning Hansen
Officers: Tommy Henning Hansen [1973] Director [Danish]

Emma Group Ltd
Incorporated: 31 May 2017
Registered Office: 20-22 Wenlock Road, London, N1 7GU
Officers: Tommy Henning Hansen [1973] Director/Entrepreneur [Danish]

Emma Prime Ltd
Incorporated: 14 February 2018
Registered Office: 20-22 Wenlock Road, London, N1 7GU
Major Shareholder: Tommy Henning Hansen
Officers: Tommy Henning Hansen [1973] Director/Entrepreneur [Danish]

Emma Victoria Cosmetics Ltd
Incorporated: 7 January 2019
Registered Office: Emma Victoria Cosmetics, P O Box 1380, Cambridge, CB1 0HH
Shareholders: Wesley Timothy Sukdao; Emma Victoria Yates
Officers: Wesley Timothy Sukdao [1986] Director/Consultant [South African]; Dr Emma Victoria Yates [1988] Director/Chemist [British/American]

EmmaDK Ltd
Incorporated: 23 June 2017
Registered Office: 20-22 Wenlock Road, London, N1 7GU
Major Shareholder: Tommy Henning Hansen
Officers: Tommy Henning Hansen [1973] Director/Entrepreneur [Danish]

Emortal Maquillage Ltd
Incorporated: 8 October 2018
Registered Office: Kemp House, 160 City Road, London, EC1V 2NX
Officers: Emily Hein [1997] Director

Empire Worldwide Ltd
Incorporated: 24 May 2017
Registered Office: 27 Old Gloucester Street, London, WC1N 3AX
Major Shareholder: Ivan Spina
Officers: Ivan Spina [1986] Director/Consultant [Italian]

Emuology UK 2017 Limited
Incorporated: 14 July 2017
Registered Office: 71-75 Shelton Street, Covent Garden, London, WC2H 9JQ
Major Shareholder: Harold Reid Rankin
Officers: Harold Reid Rankin [1953] Director/Manager

Emvi Limited
Incorporated: 4 March 1998
Net Worth Deficit: £6,210,000
Registered Office: Farringdon Street, London, EC4A 4AB
Major Shareholder: Vibhaker Devshi Jatania
Officers: Vibhaker Devshi Jatania [1955] Director

Endetrox Ltd.
Incorporated: 15 February 2018
Registered Office: 4 Ryhope Road, London, N11 1BX
Major Shareholder: Laszlo Horvath
Officers: Laszlo Horvath [1986] Director [Hungarian]

Enfield Distribution Ltd
Incorporated: 10 May 2012 *Employees:* 17
Net Worth: £388,348 *Total Assets:* £667,438
Registered Office: The Business Centre, 758 Great Cambridge Road, Enfield, Middlesex, EN1 3RN
Shareholders: Rakesh Dhirajlal Dasani; Sunny Nalin Rach
Officers: Rakesh Dhirajlal Dasani [1984] Director; Sunny Nalin Rach [1985] Director

Enhance You Ltd
Incorporated: 14 March 2018
Registered Office: 72 Gartside Street, Manchester, M3 3EL
Major Shareholder: Michael Clapcott
Officers: Michael Clapcott [1985] Director/Business Consultant

EnhanceColor Limited
Incorporated: 5 January 2009
Previous: Enhance Color Limited
Net Worth: £76,478 *Total Assets:* £207,826
Registered Office: 5 Waltham Close, Hutton, Brentwood, Essex, CM13 1YE
Major Shareholder: Marc Bernard Alexander Ward
Officers: Marc Bernard Alexander Ward [1965] Director

Enhancing You Limited
Incorporated: 1 December 2017
Registered Office: 19 Adamson House, Towers Business Park, Didsbury, Manchester, M20 2YY
Shareholder: Michael Clapcott
Officers: Michael Clapcott [1985] Director/Business Consultant

Enimarkets Ltd
Incorporated: 23 December 2016
Net Worth Deficit: £5,695
Registered Office: 10 Bilbrook Lane, Furzton, Milton Keynes, Bucks, MK4 1LW
Major Shareholder: Kofi Asiama Osei
Officers: Edward Akosah, Secretary; Kofi Asiama Osei [1986] Director; Hannah Serwaah [1984] Finance Director [Ghanaian]

ENS Europe Limited
Incorporated: 2 September 2015
Registered Office: 71-75 Shelton Street, Covent Garden, London, WC2H 9JQ
Major Shareholder: Jun Han Park
Officers: Jun Han Park [1972] Director/ENS Korea [Australian]

Ensley and Ensley Limited
Incorporated: 18 December 2017
Registered Office: 41 Newborough Avenue, Llanishen, Cardiff, CF14 5BZ
Officers: Sonia Rosalind Evelyn [1963] Director/Minister

Envision International Co., Ltd
Incorporated: 9 July 2018
Registered Office: Fourth Floor, 3 Gower Street, London, WC1E 6HA
Major Shareholder: Ying Wu
Officers: Ying Wu [1986] Director [Australian]

EOB Distribution Ltd
Incorporated: 26 February 2015
Net Worth: £6,211 *Total Assets:* £53,717
Registered Office: The Beeches, Brampton Abbotts, Ross on Wye, Herefords, HR9 7JD
Shareholders: Michael Andre O'Brien; Sascha Moerl
Officers: Sascha Moerl [1977] Director [German]; Michael Andre O'Brien [1953] Director

EOS Products Limited
Incorporated: 6 July 2016 *Employees:* 5
Net Worth: £133,406 *Total Assets:* £1,667,435
Registered Office: Unit 305, 2-6 Boundary Row, London, SE1 8HP
Shareholders: Sanjiv Mehra; Jonathan Teller
Officers: Sanjiv Mehra [1962] Director/Executive [American]; Jonathan Teller [1968] Director/Executive [American]

Equisalud Ltd
Incorporated: 24 August 2017
Registered Office: 14 Whittock Square, Bristol, BS14 8DA
Major Shareholder: Jose Maria Hernandez
Officers: Jose Maria Hernandez Garcia [1959] Director [Spanish]

Ere Perez UK Limited
Incorporated: 12 May 2016
Net Worth: £2,051 *Total Assets:* £17,550
Registered Office: 36 Titsey Road, Oxted, Surrey, RH8 0DF
Major Shareholder: Sophie Elizabeth Cross
Officers: Sophie Elizabeth Cross [1971] Director/Sales Manager

Erin Cosmetics Ltd
Incorporated: 16 January 2019
Registered Office: c/o FKGB, Second Floor, 201 Haverstock Hill, London, NW3 4QG
Major Shareholder: Maayan Aptik
Officers: Maayan Aptik [1982] Director/Customer Service Manager [Israeli]

Thalia Erodotou Limited
Incorporated: 24 September 2010
Net Worth Deficit: £9,922 *Total Assets:* £35,201
Registered Office: 484 Green Lanes, Palmers Green, London, N13 5PA
Shareholders: Thalia Erodotou; Nicholas Erodotou
Officers: Nicholas Erodotou [1977] Director; Thalia Erodotou [1978] Director/Beautician

Ersag UK Limited
Incorporated: 8 August 2017
Net Worth Deficit: £224,540
Registered Office: SME CofE Business Centre, Main Street, Ponteland, Northumberland, NE20 9NH
Major Shareholder: Mustafa Nejat Kilci
Officers: Mustafa Nejat Kilci [1966] Director

Escentric Ltd
Incorporated: 27 October 2014
Registered Office: 15 Studios, Charlton Kings Road, London, NW5 2SB
Parent: Holdme Company Limited
Officers: Paul Douglas White [1959] Director/Designer

Esem International Ltd
Incorporated: 2 October 2018
Registered Office: 2nd Floor, 255-259 Commercial Road, London, E1 2BT
Major Shareholder: Kazi Mohammed Ashiqur Rahman
Officers: Kazi Mohammed Ashiqur Rahman [1989] Director

ESPA International (UK) Limited
Incorporated: 21 August 1992 *Employees:* 195
Net Worth: £11,894,000 *Total Assets:* £14,837,000
Registered Office: 5th Floor, Voyager House, Chicago Avenue, Manchester Airport, Manchester, M90 3DQ
Parent: El Spa Holdings (UK) Limited
Officers: John Andrew Gallemore [1969] Director; Paul Jonathan Gedman [1981] Director

Espoir Beauty Ltd
Incorporated: 26 February 2018
Registered Office: 7 The Belvedere, Chelsea Harbour, London, SW10 0XA
Shareholder: Lara Melkonian
Officers: Lara Melkonian [1993] Director/Cosmetic Sales; Polly Monckton [1993] Director/Cosmetic Sales

Esscenti Ltd
Incorporated: 21 February 2018
Registered Office: The Old Workshop, 12b Kennerleys Lane, Wilmslow, Cheshire, SK9 5EQ
Major Shareholder: Michael Draper
Officers: Michael Draper [1953] Director

Esscential Ltd
Incorporated: 18 May 2018
Registered Office: 17 Bendish Road, East Ham, London, E6 1JH
Major Shareholder: Shazia Mohamed
Officers: Shazia Mohamed [1992] Director

Essence Cosmetics Limited
Incorporated: 9 May 2016 *Employees:* 1
Net Worth: £10,374 *Total Assets:* £49,994
Registered Office: 284 Station Road, Harrow, Middlesex, HA1 2EA
Major Shareholder: Walid Brahim Abed Bouit
Officers: Walid Brahim Abed Bouit [1984] Director

The Essence of Esther Ltd
Incorporated: 23 June 2015
Net Worth Deficit: £9,649 *Total Assets:* £42
Registered Office: 71-75 Shelton Street, Covent Garden, London, WC2H 9JQ
Major Shareholder: Marie-Claude Kacy
Officers: Marie-Claude Kacy [1979] Director [French]

Essence Pur Ltd.
Incorporated: 4 January 2005
Registered Office: 483 Green Lanes, London, N13 4BS
Major Shareholder: Claudia Anna Luise Kasparides
Officers: Johanna Broich, Secretary; Claudia Anna Luise Kasparides [1952] Director [German]

Essence Room Ltd
Incorporated: 26 January 2018
Registered Office: 36 Phipps Bridge Road, Mitcham, Surrey, CR4 3PG
Major Shareholder: Nathan Jerome Gray
Officers: Nathan Jerome Gray [1987] Director [British/Australian]

Essench Cosmetics Ltd
Incorporated: 28 January 2019
Registered Office: 25 Hemlingford Road, Kingshurst, Birmingham, B37 6DJ
Major Shareholder: Christina French
Officers: Christina French [1982] Director/Electrician; Jennifer O'Neill [1984] Director

Essential Beauty Supplies Limited
Incorporated: 7 October 1997 *Employees:* 4
Net Worth: £74,716 *Total Assets:* £264,446
Registered Office: Unit 18a Bagley Road, Wellington, Somerset, TA21 9PZ
Shareholder: Steven Michael Wright
Officers: Steven Michael Wright [1960] Director/Wholesaler of Beauty Products

Essential Bodycare Limited
Incorporated: 24 January 2002
Registered Office: Bodycare House, Danegate Eridge Green, Tunbridge Wells, Kent, TN3 9JA
Parent: Australian Bodycare UK Ltd
Officers: Kevin Michael Gambrill [1976] Director/Accountant; Fiona McMillan Peerless [1979] Director/Operations Manager

Essential Cosmetics Ltd
Incorporated: 10 October 2013
Net Worth Deficit: £5,220 *Total Assets:* £13,680
Registered Office: 6 Marsh Parade, Newcastle, Staffs, ST5 1DU
Shareholders: Andrew John Higley; Ayman Alfi
Officers: Ayman Alfi [1980] Director [Saudi Arabian]; Andrew John Higley [1990] Director

Essential Oil Sell Ltd
Incorporated: 28 June 2018
Registered Office: 36c Stafford Road, Ruislip, Middlesex, HA4 6PJ
Major Shareholder: Emil Genadiev Iliev
Officers: Emil Genadiev Iliev [1987] Director/Engineer

Essential Oils Direct Ltd
Incorporated: 13 April 2001
Net Worth: £9,250 *Total Assets:* £117,050
Registered Office: Unit 13 Parkside Industrial Estate, Edge Lane Street, Royton, Oldham, Lancs, OL2 6DS
Shareholders: David Freer; Mary Elizabeth Freer
Officers: Mary Elizabeth Freer, Secretary; David Freer [1969] Director/Manager

Essentials4men Ltd
Incorporated: 6 February 2015
Net Worth Deficit: £9,870 *Total Assets:* £6,990
Registered Office: 50 Bedford Street, Belfast, BT2 7FW
Officers: Wesley David Knox [1976] Director

Essex Beauty Palace Ltd
Incorporated: 3 October 2018
Registered Office: 12 Southchurch Road, Southend on Sea, Essex, SS1 2NE
Major Shareholder: Mohammad Zohair Govani
Officers: Mohammad Zohair Govani [1986] Director/Businessman

Esspire Limited
Incorporated: 30 March 2017
Registered Office: 23 Lyndon Avenue, Pinner, Middlesex, HA5 4QF
Major Shareholder: Michael Pearce
Officers: Michael Pearce [1995] Director

Esteem Royale Cosmetics Limited
Incorporated: 6 August 2018
Registered Office: 19 Bulbridge Drive, Worsley, Salford, M28 3YB
Shareholders: Idowu Okheren Ejere; Odion Belinda Ejere
Officers: Odion Belinda Ejere, Secretary; Idowu Okheren Ejere [1983] Director/Chief Product Officer [Nigerian]

Estela Dermocosmetics Ltd
Incorporated: 27 September 2018
Registered Office: 71-75 Shelton Street, Covent Garden, London, WC2H 9JQ
Major Shareholder: Ersin Akif Adil
Officers: Ersin Akif Adil [1982] Director [Bulgarian]

Esthermarie Limited
Incorporated: 18 January 2016
Registered Office: 7 Stanton Road, Ashbourne, Derbys, DE6 1SH
Major Shareholder: Esther Marie Woolley
Officers: Esther Marie Woolley [1970] Director/Makeup Artist

Esthetica Pure Ltd
Incorporated: 5 September 2018
Registered Office: 795 Chester Road, Erdington, Birmingham, B24 0BX
Officers: Syed Naseer Ahmed [1952] Director; Syed Salmaan Ahmed [1980] Director; Dr Mabroor Ahmed Bhatty [1958] Director/Plastic Surgeon; Nicola Susan Bhatty [1964] Director/Housewife

Eternal Beauty (UK) Ltd
Incorporated: 5 April 2013
Net Worth: £52,850 *Total Assets:* £68,854
Registered Office: Poplar Cottage, Wick St Lawrence, Weston-Super-Mare, Somerset, BS22 9NY
Officers: Ben England [1983] Director; Sheila Heather King [1961] Director

Eternal Hair & Beauty Limited
Incorporated: 6 March 2017
Registered Office: 164 Bromsgrove Road, Redditch, Worcs, B97 4SP
Major Shareholder: Zakrina Afzak
Officers: Zakrina Afzal, Secretary; Zakrina Afzal [1984] Director/Health & Beauty

Ether Cosmetics Ltd
Incorporated: 9 November 2017
Registered Office: 16 Francis House, Colville Estate, London, N1 5PX
Major Shareholder: Akin Gursoy
Officers: Akin Gursoy [1991] Director/Owner

Ethereal Beauty Ltd
Incorporated: 5 November 2018
Registered Office: Flat 84, High Street, Bentley, Doncaster, S Yorks, DN5 0AT
Major Shareholder: Fay Rochelle Walker
Officers: Fay Rochelle Walker [1986] Director

Ethical House Ltd
Incorporated: 3 December 2018
Registered Office: 34 Navigation Way, Victoria Dock, Hull, HU9 1SW
Major Shareholder: Faith Elizabeth Hanson
Officers: Faith Elizabeth Hanson [1991] Director and Company Secretary

Ethnoceuticals Limited
Incorporated: 5 October 2017
Registered Office: Companies House, Default Address, Cardiff, CF14 8LH
Officers: Hannah George [1987] Director

Etonigbo Limited
Incorporated: 31 October 2014
Net Worth Deficit: £96 *Total Assets:* £259
Registered Office: 43 Abercrombie Gardens, Southampton, SO16 8FQ
Major Shareholder: Jacinthe Manga Zinga
Officers: Jacinthe Manga Zinga [1982] Director/Self Employed [French]

Eukes Global Limited
Incorporated: 29 October 2018
Registered Office: 71-75 Shelton Street, London, WC2H 9JQ
Major Shareholder: Ankit Patel
Officers: Ankit Patel, Secretary; Ankit Patel [1989] Director [Indian]

Eurasia Property Limited
Incorporated: 15 September 2016
Net Worth: £49,470 *Total Assets:* £69,880
Registered Office: Kemp House, 160 City Road, London, EC1V 2NX
Officers: Narinji Atwal [1988] Director/Investor

Euro Aromas Limited
Incorporated: 10 October 2002
Net Worth: £69,850 *Total Assets:* £406,260
Registered Office: 29 Nugent Road, Bolton, Lancs, BL3 3DE
Shareholders: Javid Ibrahim Munshi; Khalid Munshi
Officers: Javid Ibrahim Munshi [1961] Director/Sales Advisor [Indian]; Khalid Munshi [1985] Director

Euro Healthcare Services Limited
Incorporated: 10 December 1993
Net Worth: £85,848 *Total Assets:* £155,279
Registered Office: 166 Irish Street, Dumfries, DG1 2NJ
Major Shareholder: John David Murray
Officers: Dominique Claire Carr [1982] Director/Teacher; Darren Clarke Murray [1986] Director; John David Murray [1954] Director; Jonathan Conrad Murray [1985] Director; Linda Murray [1952] Director/Teacher

Euro Perfumes (UK) Ltd
Incorporated: 16 January 2012 Employees: 3
Net Worth: £40,653 Total Assets: £323,725
Registered Office: 925 Finchley Road, London, NW11 7PE
Major Shareholder: Ruchi Vyas
Officers: Ruchi Vyas [1966] Director

Eurocare Impex Services Limited
Incorporated: 16 July 1992 Employees: 4
Net Worth Deficit: £48,746 Total Assets: £65,350
Registered Office: 166 Irish Street, Dumfries, DG1 2NJ
Shareholder: John David Murray
Officers: Linda Murray, Secretary; Dominique Claire Carr [1982] Director/Teacher; Darren Clarke Murray [1986] Director; John David Murray [1954] Director/Salesman; Jonathan Conrad Murray [1985] Director; Linda Murray [1952] Director/Teacher

Eurocosmetics Limited
Incorporated: 29 March 1990 Employees: 6
Net Worth: £143,890 Total Assets: £392,636
Registered Office: Hillhurst House, Hillhurst Farm, Saltwood Stone Street, Hythe, Kent, CT21 4HU
Parent: Sothys International SAS
Officers: Monsieur Frederic Mas, Secretary; Monsieur Christian Mas [1972] Director [French]; Monsieur Frederic Mas [1974] Director/Secretary [French]

Eurohandle Ltd
Incorporated: 17 January 2018
Registered Office: 20-22 Wenlock Road, London, N1 7GU
Officers: Tommy Henning Hansen [1973] Director [Danish]

Euroluxe Enterprise UK Ltd
Incorporated: 21 December 2017
Registered Office: Suite 44, Midshire Business Park, Smeaton Close, Aylesbury, Bucks, HP19 8HL
Major Shareholder: Nishanthan Jothinathan
Officers: Nishanthan Jothinathan [1974] Director [Sri Lankan]

European Essential Oils (UK) Limited
Incorporated: 26 September 2017
Registered Office: 3a Horseshoe Close, London, NW2 7JJ
Major Shareholder: Michael John Quentin Steele
Officers: Michael John Quentin Steele [1945] Director

Europebro Wholesalers Ltd
Incorporated: 17 November 2014
Net Worth: £5,006 Total Assets: £20,414
Registered Office: 41 Gainsborough Tower, Academy Gardens, Northolt, Middlesex, UB5 5PF
Major Shareholder: Daniel Coumarakichenane
Officers: Daniel Coumarakichenane [1971] Director [French]

Eutek Group Limited
Incorporated: 26 April 2017
Net Worth: £2,630 Total Assets: £237,510
Registered Office: 18 St Peters Street, Nottingham, NG7 3FF
Major Shareholder: Diu Hien Vu
Officers: Diu Hien Vu [1983] Director [Vietnamese]

Eva Cosmetics Ltd
Incorporated: 26 September 2018
Registered Office: 262 High Street North, London, E12 6SB
Major Shareholder: Sundas Shaheen
Officers: Sundas Shaheen [1994] Director/Businesswoman

Evagray Limited
Incorporated: 10 October 2017
Registered Office: 41 Oak Tree Close, Virginia Water, Surrey, GU25 4JG
Major Shareholder: Paula Jane Ribeiro Kerr
Officers: Paula Jane Ribeiro Kerr [1975] Director [South African]

Evanesce Ltd
Incorporated: 7 September 2018
Registered Office: Unit 20 Silveroaks Farm, Hawkhurst Lane, Waldron, Heathfield, E Sussex, TN21 0RS
Shareholders: Ibrahim Ansari; Christopher Woodhead; David George Herdman
Officers: Ibrahim Ansari [1976] Director; David George Herdman [1982] Director; Christopher Woodhead [1958] Director

Evans Close Limited
Incorporated: 30 March 2017
Net Worth Deficit: £231,360 Total Assets: £251,020
Registered Office: 3rd Floor, Office 3, Keystone Innovation Centre, Croxton Road, Thetford, Norfolk, IP24 1JD
Officers: Simon Jonathan Mitchell [1965] Director

Evanto Fragrance Limited
Incorporated: 4 May 2018
Registered Office: Flat 29, Westside Apartments, 69 Roden Street, Ilford, Essex, IG1 2AQ
Major Shareholder: Mohammed Ashfaq Ahmed
Officers: Mohammed Ashfaq Ahmed [1986] Director [Bangladeshi]

Evany Personal Care Limited
Incorporated: 15 November 2001
Registered Office: 15 Appold Street, London, EC2A 2HB
Shareholder: Mardijaty Joenoes
Officers: Kusmijaty Joenoes [1951] Product Development Director [Indonesian]; Mardijaty Joenoes [1953] Marketing Director [Indonesian]

Evbioo Ltd
Incorporated: 24 July 2018
Registered Office: Kemp House, 160 City Road, London, EC1V 2NX
Major Shareholder: Evbi O'Sullivan
Officers: Evbi O'Sullivan, Secretary; Evbi O'Sullivan [1972] Director/Consultant

Evercore UK Limited
Incorporated: 14 March 2018
Registered Office: 1a Claremont Avenue, New Malden, Surrey, KT3 6QL
Major Shareholder: Arif Selim Alkaya
Officers: Arif Selim Alkaya [1966] Director/Businessman [Turkish]

Everyday Cosmetics Ltd
Incorporated: 3 March 2011
Net Worth: £5,620 Total Assets: £10,330
Registered Office: 15e Molesworth Street, Cookstown, Co Tyrone, BT80 8NX
Major Shareholder: Assumpta O'Neill
Officers: Assumpta O'Neill [1941] Director/Marketing [Irish]

Evie Skincare Ltd
Incorporated: 16 August 2018
Registered Office: 4 Hurrell Drive, Harrow, London, HA2 6DY
Major Shareholder: Eva Barbara Appiah-Brantuo
Officers: Eva Barbara Appiah-Brantuo [1985] Director

Evoiq International Ltd
Incorporated: 7 December 2018
Registered Office: c/o Talat Qazi Consulting, 58b Ilford Lane, Ilford, Essex, IG1 2JZ
Parent: Evoiq
Officers: Mona Mahmoud Saad Salama [1983] Director [Egyptian]

Evorin Pharma Limited
Incorporated: 30 January 2014
Net Worth: £1,000 *Total Assets:* £1,000
Registered Office: 3 Gower Street, London, WC1E 6HA
Shareholders: Ibrahim Abdelrazik Albayoomi Fouda; Ahmed Sami
Officers: Ahmed Sami, Secretary; Ibrahim Abdelrazik Albayoomi Fouda [1978] Director [Egyptian]

Ex'klusive Products Ltd
Incorporated: 15 October 2018
Registered Office: 20-22 Wenlock Road, London, N1 7GU
Major Shareholder: Nokuthula Pambano Ndebele
Officers: Nokuthula Pambano Ndebele [1980] Director/Nurse Manager [Zimbabwean]

Exa World Ltd
Incorporated: 14 February 2018
Registered Office: 71-75 Shelton Street, Covent Garden, London, WC2H 9JQ
Major Shareholder: Mashal Al Busaidi
Officers: Mashal Al Busaidi [1976] Director [Omani]

Exbrands Ltd
Incorporated: 31 August 2018
Registered Office: 71-75 Shelton Street, London, WC2H 9JQ
Major Shareholder: Sage Sebastian
Officers: Sage Sebastian, Secretary; Sage Sebastian [1978] Director/IT Consultant

Excel (GS) Limited
Incorporated: 18 August 1999 *Employees:* 16
Net Worth: £361,943 *Total Assets:* £607,348
Registered Office: The Stables, Church Walk, Daventry, Northants, NN11 4BL
Shareholders: Paul Andrew Malone; John Anthony Malone
Officers: John Anthony Malone [1952] Director; Paul Andrew Malone [1974] Director

Excelcia Limited
Incorporated: 1 December 2011
Net Worth: £66,130 *Total Assets:* £248,890
Registered Office: 7 Sunbeam Road, Park Royal, London, NW10 6JP
Major Shareholder: Syed Hassan Haider Rizvi
Officers: Syed Hassan Haider Rizvi [1977] Director/Chemical Engineer

Excellent Edges Ltd
Incorporated: 20 February 2017
Net Worth Deficit: £4,920 *Total Assets:* £2,090
Registered Office: 29 Springmount Road, Ballygowan, Co Down, BT23 6NF
Major Shareholder: Noel David King Irvine
Officers: Noel David King Irvine [1955] Director

Excess Beauty Ltd
Incorporated: 16 February 2018
Registered Office: 272 Bath Street, Glasgow, G2 4JR
Major Shareholder: Muqbil Shinan Akbarali
Officers: Muqbil Shinan Akbarali [2000] Director [Indian]

Exentrique Limited
Incorporated: 7 January 2016
Net Worth Deficit: £10,391 *Total Assets:* £6,206
Registered Office: 24 The Shires, Marshfield, Cardiff, CF3 2AX
Major Shareholder: Danika Lili Woods
Officers: Danika Lili Woods [1997] Director/Marketing

Existo Limited
Incorporated: 15 July 2015
Net Worth Deficit: £128,422 *Total Assets:* £120,933
Registered Office: 21 Eastcastle Street, London, W1W 8DD
Major Shareholder: James Watson Trimming
Officers: James Watson Trimming [1971] Director/Wholesale Cosmetic

Exoditi Limited
Incorporated: 20 February 2018
Registered Office: 71-75 Shelton Street, Covent Garden, London, WC2H 9JQ
Major Shareholder: Jamie Baugh
Officers: Jamie Baugh [1998] Director/Chief Executive Officer

Exotic Fragrance Ltd
Incorporated: 13 June 2018
Registered Office: 86 Castleton Road, Ilford, Essex, IG3 9QS
Major Shareholder: Mohammed Faisal Ishaq
Officers: Mohammed Faisal Ishaq [1997] Director

Expo Deal Ltd
Incorporated: 13 February 2019
Registered Office: Kemp House, 152-160 City Road, London, EC1V 2NX
Major Shareholder: Md Kamal Uddin
Officers: MD Kamal Uddin [1976] Managing Director

Export Solutions (International) Limited
Incorporated: 17 October 2000 *Employees:* 2
Net Worth Deficit: £47,777 *Total Assets:* £299,669
Registered Office: Suite 1, Bulldog House, London Road, Twyford, Berks, RG10 9EU
Shareholder: Philip John Woodall
Officers: Catherine Elizabeth Woodall, Secretary; Dr Bahaa Tharwat Naium [1961] Director [Egyptian]; Philip John Woodall [1950] Director/Export Manager

Express Hair and Beauty Supply Ltd
Incorporated: 18 October 2018
Registered Office: 71-75 Shelton Street, Covent Garden, London, WC2H 9JQ
Major Shareholder: Monica Deng
Officers: Monica Deng [1976] Director

Express Online Superstore, London Ltd
Incorporated: 1 May 2018
Registered Office: 249a East India Dock Road, Poplar, London, E14 0EG
Officers: MD Yosuf Kamal Chowdhary [1990] Director [Bangladeshi]

Exquisite Cosmetics Limited
Incorporated: 1 June 1977
Net Worth: £183,433 *Total Assets:* £237,027
Registered Office: The Barracks, Barwell, Leics, LE9 8EF
Major Shareholder: Christopher Roy Baxter
Officers: Christopher Roy Baxter, Secretary; Christopher Roy Baxter [1959] Director; Jack Lawrence Baxter [1987] Director

Eye Kandy Cosmetics Ltd
Incorporated: 11 April 2018
Registered Office: Kemp House, 160 City Road, London, EC1V 2NX
Major Shareholder: Dhiraj Gogna
Officers: Dhiraj Gogna, Secretary; Dhiraj Gogna [1979] Director/Manager [New Zealander]

Eye Love Beauty (Chester) Ltd
Incorporated: 19 February 2019
Registered Office: Military House, 24 Castle Street, Chester, CH1 2DS
Major Shareholder: Kathryn Elizabeth Johnson
Officers: Kathryn Elizabeth Johnson [1981] Director/Beautician

The Eyelash Design Company Limited
Incorporated: 16 August 2006
Net Worth: £1,030,000 *Total Assets:* £1,350,000
Registered Office: 38d Chigwell Lane, Loughton, Essex, IG10 3NY
Parent: Fuller Brook Limited
Officers: Beverly Alison Piper [1961] Director/Beauty Therapist; Roland Piper [1960] Director/Manager

Eyeslices UK Limited
Incorporated: 22 May 2015
Net Worth Deficit: £5,741 *Total Assets:* £14,568
Registered Office: Flat 8, Guardian Court, 47 Westwood Road, Southampton, SO17 1WH
Parent: I-Slices Manufacturing
Officers: Kerryne Krause-Neufeldt [1973] Director/Business Owner [South African]; Tobias Neufeldt [1966] Technical Director [German]; Valecia Eunice Zelkin [1945] Director/Retired

Ezili Botanicals Limited
Incorporated: 4 February 2019
Registered Office: 10 Heather Glen, Romford, Essex, RM1 4SR
Major Shareholder: Amanda Michaela Joyce Brown
Officers: Amanda Michaela Joyce Brown [1990] Director

F A Commodities Ltd
Incorporated: 25 June 2003
Net Worth: £1,530,000 *Total Assets:* £7,020,000
Registered Office: Abacus House, 14-18 Forest Road, Loughton, Essex, IG10 1DX
Shareholders: Fatima Shah; Amna Shah
Officers: Fatima Shah, Secretary; Amna Shah [1969] Director; Fatima Shah [1973] Director

F.D.D. International Limited
Incorporated: 21 February 1992
Net Worth: £8,140,000 *Total Assets:* £14,650,000
Registered Office: Unit F, Ascot Business Park, Lyndhurst Road, Ascot, Berks, SL5 9FE
Major Shareholder: David Thomas Clark
Officers: Nicola Sheehan, Secretary; Stuart John Catton [1977] Sales Director; Daniel John Clark [1971] Director/Logistics Manager; David Thomas Clark [1946] Director; Nadia Ann Peacock [1976] Sales Director; Nicola Sheehan [1969] Finance Director; Daniel Jon Silvester [1975] Commercial Director

Fab Professional Hair Supplies Limited
Incorporated: 30 August 2018
Registered Office: 323 Holdenhurst Road, Bournemouth, BH8 8BT
Major Shareholder: Dougal Jonathan Matthews
Officers: Dougal Jonathan Matthews [1972] Managing Director

Fabdoo Limited
Incorporated: 14 June 2006
Net Worth: £36,039 *Total Assets:* £105,180
Registered Office: Unit B3, 30 Glenwood Place, Glenwood Business Park, Glasgow, G45 9UH
Major Shareholder: Irene Fergusson
Officers: Kenneth Fergusson, Secretary; Irene Fergusson [1960] Director/Administrator; Kenneth Fergusson [1956] Director/Salesman

Face & Beauty Limited
Incorporated: 14 March 2018
Registered Office: 3 Kotecha House, 297 Pinner Road, Harrow, Middlesex, HA1 4HF
Major Shareholder: Ahmad Mokhtar Bakhtar
Officers: Ahmad Mokhtar Bakhtar, Secretary; Ahmad Mokhtar Bakhtar [1983] Director

Face Boutique Limited
Incorporated: 23 September 2004
Registered Office: Office 296, 56 Gloucester Road, London, SW7 4UB
Officers: Sarah Vorbach [1966] Director

Face Fodder Limited
Incorporated: 9 February 2017
Net Worth Deficit: £1,813 *Total Assets:* £4,018
Registered Office: 17 Tower Close, Pontefract, W Yorks, WF8 4SS
Major Shareholder: Casey Casey Lam
Officers: Casey Mon-Ye Banks [1986] Director

Face Lace Limited
Incorporated: 5 August 2011
Net Worth Deficit: £20,136 *Total Assets:* £60,130
Registered Office: 34a Watling Street, Radlett, Herts, WD7 7NN
Major Shareholder: Phyllis Haxby
Officers: Phyllis Haxby [1958] Director/Makeup Artist

Facecharm Ltd
Incorporated: 24 January 2018
Registered Office: 20-22 Wenlock Road, London, N1 7GU
Shareholders: Anita Katarzyna Folaron; Michal Jan Bedkowski
Officers: Anita Katarzyna Folaron [1966] Director/Entrepreneur [Polish]

Facemane Ltd
Incorporated: 25 May 2018
Registered Office: The Pentagon, 3365 Century Way, Thorpe Park, Leeds, LS15 8ZB
Shareholders: David Bradley Jones; Joshua Luke Daniels
Officers: David Bradley Jones [1983] Director

Faceoff Limited
Incorporated: 16 January 2017
Registered Office: Woodeaves, Doles Lane, Clifton, Ashbourne, Derbys, DE6 2DH
Major Shareholder: Ryan Forrest
Officers: Ryan Forrest [1977] Director/Marketing Consultant

Facil Haircare Ltd
Incorporated: 23 March 2018
Registered Office: 25 Keith Connor Close, Heath Road, London, SW8 3DD
Major Shareholder: Patrick Drmola
Officers: Patrick Drmola [1993] Director/Credit Analyst

Fade Out Limited
Incorporated: 10 October 2011
Net Worth Deficit: £41,098 Total Assets: £568,135
Registered Office: Newbury House, Aintree Avenue, White Horse Business Park, Trowbridge, Wilts, BA14 0XB
Parent: Lynch-Staunton Cosmetics Holdings Limited
Officers: Graham Murray Lynch-Staunton [1969] Director; Susan Angela Lynch-Staunton [1967] Sales Director

Fade The Itch Ltd
Incorporated: 4 April 2018
Registered Office: 20 Woodland Avenue, Overstone, Northampton, NN6 0AJ
Officers: Stephen Whiting [1956] Director and Company Secretary

Fair Pharm Limited
Incorporated: 20 March 2002
Net Worth: £240,830 Total Assets: £492,289
Registered Office: 103 Church Lane, Bedford, MK41 0PW
Major Shareholder: Hitesh Vanmali Patel
Officers: Bina Hitesh Patel, Secretary; Bina Hitesh Patel [1970] Director/Clerical; Hitesh Vanmali Patel [1962] Director/Pharmacist

B.Fairall (UK) Limited
Incorporated: 7 July 2005
Net Worth: £822,700 Total Assets: £1,290,000
Registered Office: Doshi Accountants Ltd, 6th Floor, Amp House, Dingwall Road, Croydon, Surrey, CR0 2LX
Shareholders: Fidahusein Gulamali Asharia; Moshin Janmohamed
Officers: Fidahusein Gulamali Asharia, Secretary; Fidahusein Gulamali Asharia [1953] Director; Moshin Janmohamed [1961] Director

Fairy Dust Limited
Incorporated: 29 April 2009
Net Worth Deficit: £28,010 Total Assets: £16,250
Registered Office: 28 Brunel Way, Box, Corsham, Wilts, SN13 8LR
Major Shareholder: Benjamin Seymour Biscoe
Officers: Benjamin Seymour Biscoe [1964] Director

Fandealtastic Limited
Incorporated: 13 April 2018
Registered Office: Apartment 24362, Chynoweth House, Trevissome Park, Truro, Cornwall, TR4 8UN
Officers: Taranjot Kaur [1988] Director; Omkar Singh [1986] Director [Indian]

Farah Organics Ltd
Incorporated: 15 June 2018
Registered Office: Berkeley Square House, Berkeley Square, London, W1J 6BD
Major Shareholder: Reem Fakhroo
Officers: Reem Fakhroo, Secretary; Reem Fakhroo [1969] Business Director [Qatari]

Farmavita Ltd
Incorporated: 6 March 2018
Registered Office: 20-22 Wenlock Road, London, N1 7GU
Major Shareholder: Giedrius Grebliunas
Officers: Giedrius Grebliunas [1970] Director/College [Lithuanian]

Farmers Pure Organics Ltd
Incorporated: 12 February 2018
Registered Office: 27 Medway Parade, Perivale, Greenford, Middlesex, UB6 8HP
Officers: Milena Marinova Abdulhafiz [1966] Director [Bulgarian]

Farshety Ltd
Incorporated: 16 August 2018
Registered Office: 27 Old Gloucester Street, London, WC1N 3AX
Major Shareholder: Islam Samy Abdelhamid Abdelhamid
Officers: Islam Samy Abdelhamid Abdelhamid, Secretary; Islam Samy Abdelhamid Abdelhamid [1975] Managing Director [Egyptian]

Fasa Capillago Limited
Incorporated: 27 November 2018
Registered Office: 87 Gortree Road, Londonderry, BT47 3LL
Officers: Dr Terence McIvor [1970] Director [Irish]

Fashion Conspiracy Ltd
Incorporated: 13 November 2017
Registered Office: 23 Raven Drive, Maidenhead, Berks, SL6 8AE
Officers: Asiye Suleyman [1971] Director/Entrepreneur

Fashion Fragrances & Cosmetics UK Ltd
Incorporated: 14 October 2016 Employees: 15
Net Worth Deficit: £310,301 Total Assets: £959,217
Registered Office: 1st Floor, Sackville House, 143-149 Fenchurch Street, London, EC3M 6BN
Major Shareholder: Leslie Bayly Ledes
Officers: Leslie Bayly Ledes [1963] Director/President [American]

Fatale Cosmetics Limited
Incorporated: 13 April 2018
Registered Office: Unit 3 Wellington Mills, Elland, W Yorks, HX5 9AS
Shareholder: Simon Prato-Scarlett
Officers: Bethany Jane Rose Davies [1982] Director; Simon Prato-Scarlett [1981] Director; Clare Louise Quartrmaine [1976] Director; Jonathan Simon Shaw [1967] Director

Faye Florais Global Holdings., Ltd
Incorporated: 3 May 2018
Registered Office: Unit G25, Waterfront Studios, 1 Dock Road, London, E16 1AH
Major Shareholder: Jingwen Liu
Officers: Jingwen Liu [1982] Director [Chinese]

FayshCosmetics Ltd
Incorporated: 11 June 2018
Registered Office: 33 Gibraltar Road, Halifax, W Yorks, HX1 4HE
Major Shareholder: Shabana Ali
Officers: Shabana Ali [1995] Director/Full Time Mother

FB Beauty Ltd
Incorporated: 5 August 2009 Employees: 26
Net Worth Deficit: £15,794,580 Total Assets: £8,184,772
Registered Office: Third Floor, 49 Carnaby Street, London, W1F 9PY
Officers: Benjamin Clive Tubb, Secretary; Benjamin Clive Tubb [1972] Managing Director; Alan Robert Wormser [1958] Director [American]; David Lewis Wormser [1953] Director [American]

FB Cosmetologist Limited
Incorporated: 28 December 2018
Registered Office: 4 Grosvenor Road, Manchester, M16 8JP
Major Shareholder: Fabia Batin
Officers: Fabia Batin [1997] Director/Cosmetologist

Feel and Heal UK Limited
Incorporated: 22 March 2018
Registered Office: 71-75 Shelton Street, London, WC2H 9JQ
Officers: Thanveer Ahammed Puthyia Purayil [1978] Director [Indian]

Feel Good Products Limited
Incorporated: 18 October 2018
Registered Office: 21 Aspen House, 10 Forest Road, Richmond, Surrey, TW9 3BY
Major Shareholder: Ankit Gaur
Officers: Dr. Ankit Gaur [1984] Director/Lecturer [Indian]

Feelgoode Ltd
Incorporated: 7 February 2019
Registered Office: Flat 9, Haven Court, Marine Road, Bournemouth, BH6 3NX
Major Shareholder: Kristie Victoria Goode
Officers: Kristie Victoria Goode [1988] Director/Nurse

Fegoo Limited
Incorporated: 11 May 2018
Registered Office: Hudson House, Reeth, Richmond, N Yorks, DL11 6TB
Major Shareholder: Samuel Thomas Johnson
Officers: Samuel Thomas Johnson [1987] Director

Feinkost & Getranke Ltd
Incorporated: 6 February 2019
Registered Office: The Picasso Building, Caldervale Road, Wakefield, W Yorks, WF1 5PF
Major Shareholder: Sascha Behrendt
Officers: Sascha Behrendt [1983] Director/Computer Programmer [German]

Felix Medical Group Ltd
Incorporated: 17 July 2017
Registered Office: NI646902: Companies House, Default Address, 2nd Floor The Linenhall 32-38 Linenhall Street, Belfast, BT2 8BG
Major Shareholder: Karren Brady
Officers: Dr Karren Brady [1976] Director/Businesswoman

Fem Distribution Limited
Incorporated: 13 March 2018
Registered Office: 1 Park View Court, St Pauls Road, Shipley, W Yorks, BD18 3DZ
Major Shareholder: Florence Kynaston
Officers: Florence Kynaston [1946] Director/Retailer

Ferana Ltd
Incorporated: 16 November 2018
Registered Office: Lower Ground Floor, 40 Bloomsbury Way, London, WC1A 2SE
Major Shareholder: Tony, Ryan Andriatsiferana
Officers: Tony Andriatsiferana [1998] Director [French]

Ferrara-Bardile Ltd
Incorporated: 30 March 2015
Net Worth: £4,000 *Total Assets:* £4,000
Registered Office: 75 Alfriston Road, London, SW11 6NR
Major Shareholder: Maria Anna Ferrara-Bardile
Officers: Maria Anna Ferrara-Bardile Muller [1972] Director/Entrepreneur

FFC International Limited
Incorporated: 26 November 2018
Registered Office: Lyndon House, 79 Bury Road, Tottington, Bury, Lancs, BL8 3EU
Major Shareholder: Andrew William Barlow
Officers: Andrew William Barlow [1986] Director/Chief Executive

FG Traders Ltd
Incorporated: 16 August 2018
Registered Office: 88 Rochdale Road, Bury, Lancs, BL9 7AY
Officers: Gergo Ficzu, Secretary; Gergo Ficzu [1996] Director/Self Employed [Slovak]

FHM Consulting Ltd
Incorporated: 20 July 2018
Registered Office: 162 Quadrangle Tower, Cambridge Square, London, W2 2PL
Major Shareholder: Gabriel-Lucian Cucu
Officers: Gabriel-Lucian Cucu [1992] Director [Romanian]

Fields Finesse Limited
Incorporated: 8 January 2018
Registered Office: 96 Fourth Avenue, Luton, Beds, LU3 3BU
Officers: Chelsea Duggan [1988] Director/Interpreter

Filberts Bees Limited
Incorporated: 26 September 2002
Net Worth Deficit: £2,120 *Total Assets:* £65,260
Registered Office: Unit 10 Melstock Farm, Higher Bockhampton, Dorchester, DT2 8QJ
Shareholders: Philada Rose Rogers; Mark Adam Rogers
Officers: Kathleen Hobbs, Secretary; Mark Adam Rogers [1982] Director; Philada Rose Rogers [1955] Director

Fillers Pro Ltd
Incorporated: 26 July 2018
Registered Office: 4 High Beech, South Croydon, Surrey, CR2 7QB
Shareholders: Olga Kozenevska; Aleksandr Kozenevski
Officers: Aleksandr Kozenevska, Secretary; Olga Kozenevska [1973] Director [Lithuanian]; Aleksandr Kozenevski [1982] Director/Company Owner [Lithuanian]

Fin Perri Ltd
Incorporated: 17 January 2019
Registered Office: 71-75 Shelton Street, Covent Garden, London, WC2H 9JQ
Shareholder: Jamal Muse
Officers: Sarah Muddei [1987] Director [Italian]; Jamal Muse [1988] Director

Finders International Limited
Incorporated: 24 October 1990 *Employees:* 32
Net Worth: £788,482 *Total Assets:* £1,401,710
Registered Office: Winchet Hill, Goudhurst, Kent, TN17 1JY
Shareholders: Robert Czik; Janet Czik
Officers: Janet Czik, Secretary; Katherine Bunyan [1979] Marketing Director; Janet Czik [1951] Director at Finders; Rebecca Czik [1981] Director; Robert Czik [1946] Managing Director

Fine Fragrances and Cosmetics Limited
Incorporated: 2 December 1985
Net Worth: £52,486 *Total Assets:* £90,392
Registered Office: Newbury House, Aintree Avenue, White Horse Business Park, Trowbridge, Wilts, BA14 0XB
Parent: Lynch-Staunton Limited
Officers: Graham Murray Lynch Staunton [1969] Managing Director; Susan Angela Lynch Staunton [1967] UK Sales Director

Finest Mineral Make Up Limited
Incorporated: 5 April 2017
Registered Office: 1st Floor, Healthaid House, Marlborough Hill, Harrow, Middlesex, HA1 1UD
Officers: Cristina de Fries, Secretary; Cristina de Fries [1986] Director [Romanian]

Firecrest Communications Limited
Incorporated: 13 November 2002 *Employees:* 3
Net Worth Deficit: £53,078 *Total Assets:* £178,957
Registered Office: Unit 4 Landmark House, Wirrall Park Road, Glastonbury, Somerset, BA6 9FR
Shareholders: Clifford John Wilson; Celina Soheila Fashandi
Officers: Celina Soheila Fashandi, Secretary/Consultant Director [Canadian]; Celina Sohelia Fashandi [1959] Director [Canadian]; Clifford John Wilson [1965] Director

First Choice Hair & Beauty Limited
Incorporated: 12 August 2004 *Employees:* 3
Net Worth: £8,300 *Total Assets:* £36,795
Registered Office: B9 St Georges Business Park, Castle Road, Sittingbourne, Kent, ME10 3TB
Shareholder: Jacqueline Ann Heasman
Officers: Jacqueline Ann Heasman, Secretary; Jacqueline Ann Heasman [1962] Director/SEDC; Nigel John Heasman [1962] Director/Wholesaler

Fish London Limited
Incorporated: 28 September 2006
Net Worth: £423,041 *Total Assets:* £687,770
Registered Office: Swallowfield House, Station Road, Wellington, Somerset, TA21 8NL
Parent: Swallowfield PLC
Officers: Matthew Gazzard, Secretary; Jane Fletcher [1967] Director/Sales and Marketing; Matthew Gazzard [1971] Director; Timothy James Perman [1962] Director

Fit Brands (UK) Ltd
Incorporated: 1 August 2014
Net Worth Deficit: £48,700 *Total Assets:* £153,990
Registered Office: Colmore Plaza, 20 Colmore Circus, Queensway, Birmingham, B4 6AT
Major Shareholder: Akhtar Ali Tahir
Officers: Akhtar Ali Tahir [1983] Director [Pakistani]

Five Dot Botanics Limited
Incorporated: 26 April 2017
Net Worth Deficit: £16,540 *Total Assets:* £50,000
Registered Office: 71-75 Shelton Street, London, WC2H 9JQ
Shareholders: Zaffrin Aysha O'Sullivan; Brian Zaffrin O'Sullivan
Officers: Dr Brian O'Sullivan [1976] Director/Finance [Irish]; Zaffrin Aysha O'Sullivan [1978] Director/Solicitor

Five Elements Healthcare Limited
Incorporated: 30 August 2016
Registered Office: Fox Wood, 44 Spinney Walk, Barnham, Bognor Regis, W Sussex, PO22 0HT
Major Shareholder: Eve Natasha Goodison
Officers: Eve Natasha Goodison [1974] Director/Entrepreneur

Five Star International Consulting Limited
Incorporated: 6 December 2017
Registered Office: Unit 97 Kingspark Business Centre, 152-178 Kingston Road, New Malden, Surrey, KT3 3ST
Major Shareholder: Paolo Urbano
Officers: Noella Soo Eom [1984] Director; Dr Paolo Urbano [1950] Director [Italian]

Fizz 'n' Bliss Ltd
Incorporated: 3 January 2019
Registered Office: 56 Wellmeadow Road, Pollokshaws, Glasgow, G43 1JZ
Shareholders: Mary Mollison; Steven Mollison
Officers: Mary Mollison [1967] Director/Biomedical Support Worker

Fizzy Peach Ltd
Incorporated: 16 May 2011 *Employees:* 4
Net Worth: £45,065 *Total Assets:* £162,214
Registered Office: Unit 3 The Elliott Centre, 20 Elliott Road, Love Lane Industrial Estate, Cirencester, Glos, GL7 1YS
Officers: Joanne Claire Prangell, Secretary; Meik Bayley [1975] Sales Director; Joanne Claire Prangell [1981] Director/Retailer

Fleeks Hair & Beauty Limited
Incorporated: 9 January 2019
Registered Office: 130 Old Street, London, EC1V 9BD
Officers: Paula Rachel Brown [1984] Director/Self Employed

Fleuroma Limited
Incorporated: 14 December 1993 *Employees:* 3
Net Worth: £78,301 *Total Assets:* £180,449
Registered Office: Blue Chip Business Centre, The Old Exchange, Mill Lane, Dunmow, Essex, CM6 1BG
Major Shareholder: Edward William Satchell
Officers: Amanda Latchford, Secretary; Amanda Latchford [1964] Director; Edward William Satchell [1935] Managing Director

Flexi Beauty Care Ltd
Incorporated: 1 November 2017
Registered Office: 19 Merrilands Road, Worcester Park, Surrey, KT4 8NU
Major Shareholder: Amirthalinkam Ajitkumar
Officers: Amirthalinkam Ajitkumar [1975] Director

Flirties Products and Training Ltd
Incorporated: 5 April 2012
Net Worth: £136,780 *Total Assets:* £261,110
Registered Office: Unit 2 Tarlair Way, Tarlair Business Park, Macduff, Aberdeenshire, AB44 1RU
Major Shareholder: Britta Krueger
Officers: Britta Krueger [1970] Director [German]

Flo with It Ltd
Incorporated: 5 February 2019
Registered Office: 27 Stottfield, Royton, Oldham, Lancs, OL2 5EJ
Shareholders: Sinead Ingham; Sarah Deegan
Officers: Sinead Ingham [1990] Director/Machinist [Irish]

Floest Beauty Solutions Ltd
Incorporated: 19 December 2018
Registered Office: 38 Helford Place, Fishermead, Milton Keynes, Bucks, MK6 2DQ
Shareholders: Tamunoiyewuna Esther Iyalla; Florentine Akouvi Nana
Officers: Tamunoiyewuna Esther Iyalla [1986] Director [Nigerian]; Florentine Akouvi Nana [1972] Director

Florals of London Limited
Incorporated: 19 May 2016
Net Worth: £1,000 *Total Assets:* £1,000
Registered Office: 33/2 Gloucester Street, London, SW1V 2DB
Shareholder: Gualtiero Gualtieri
Officers: Gualtiero Gualtieri [1957] Director [Italian]

Florascent Duftmanufaktur Ltd
Incorporated: 20 June 2005
Registered Office: c/o Adrian Andruzko, Appt 99, Westside 2, 20 Suffolk Street, Queensway, Birmingham, B1 1LY
Major Shareholder: Roland Tentunian
Officers: Adrian Andruzko, Secretary; Roland Tentunian [1962] Director/Perfumer [German]

Florence Consumer Products Limited
Incorporated: 4 January 2018
Registered Office: 2 Wheeleys Road, Edgbaston, Birmingham, B15 2LD
Major Shareholder: Parisa Mirbod
Officers: Parisa Mirbod [1981] Director

Florence Health & Beauty Limited
Incorporated: 21 November 2017
Registered Office: 3 Shining Bank, Sheffield, S13 9DJ
Shareholders: Muthana Obeed; Fatima Aloum
Officers: Fatima Aloum [1982] Director [Syrian]; Muthana Obeed [1976] Director [Iraqi]

Florence Verity Limited
Incorporated: 14 March 2017
Registered Office: Tishon House, Warrington Road, High Legh, Knutsford, Cheshire, WA16 0RT
Major Shareholder: Florence Verity Alice Webster
Officers: Florence Verity Alice Webster [1991] Director

Flores Brand Works Limited
Incorporated: 29 September 2018
Registered Office: Suite 4, Stanmore Towers, 8-14 Church Road, Stanmore, Middlesex, HA7 4AW
Shareholders: Karine Fleury-Richards; Loredana Angela Fiori
Officers: Loredana Angela Fiori [1963] Director; Karine Fleury-Richards [1975] Director [French]

Flores Distribution Limited
Incorporated: 9 March 2005
Net Worth Deficit: £56,630 *Total Assets:* £5,240
Registered Office: 10 Cumberland Road, Oxford, OX4 2DA
Major Shareholder: Lumka Mngxitama
Officers: Lumka Mngxitama, Secretary; Annette Mngxitama [1950] Director; Lumka Mngxitama [1976] Director

Flower Cosmetic Ltd
Incorporated: 25 January 2019
Registered Office: Unit 13 & 13a Ashley House, Ashley Road, London, N17 9LZ
Major Shareholder: Mustafa Cicek
Officers: Mustafa Cicek [1976] Director/Hairdresser [Turkish]

Flowery Whiff Limited
Incorporated: 3 January 2018
Registered Office: 6 Victoria Street, Scarborough, N Yorks, YO12 7SS
Shareholders: Carolyn Popple; Alex Popple
Officers: Alex Popple [1996] Director of Marketing; Carolyn Popple [1963] Director of Manufacturing

Flowscent Limited
Incorporated: 29 December 2014
Net Worth: £61,142 *Total Assets:* £268,856
Registered Office: 17 Stanley Avenue, Shirley, Solihull, W Midlands, B90 3NJ
Shareholders: Kuldeep Viren Bhatt; Mona Viren Bhatt
Officers: Kuldeep Viren Bhatt [1989] Director; Mona Viren Bhatt [1966] Director; Viren Natwarlal Bhatt [1965] Director

Flutter Cosmetics Limited
Incorporated: 31 December 2018
Registered Office: 51 Ffordd Aberkinsey, Rhyl, Denbighshire, LL18 4FB
Shareholders: Kayley Louise Martin; Curtis Saul Breeze
Officers: Curtis Saul Breeze [1992] Director; Kayley Louise Martin [1994] Director

Flynn Group of Companies Ltd
Incorporated: 17 July 2017
Registered Office: 18 Queen Street, Enniskillen, Co Fermanagh, BT74 7DB
Major Shareholder: Michael Bronson
Officers: Michael Bronson [1975] Director/Businessman

FM Cosmetics UK Ltd
Incorporated: 24 April 2007
Net Worth: £405,090 *Total Assets:* £1,720,000
Registered Office: 490-492 Neasden Lane North, London, NW10 0DG
Shareholder: Anita Sieniuc
Officers: Anita Sieniuc, Secretary [Polish]; Anita Sieniuc [1978] Director/Building Engineer [Polish]; Karol Sieniuc [1958] Director/Electrician [Polish]

Foad Wax Limited
Incorporated: 20 June 2011
Net Worth: £360 *Total Assets:* £1,516
Registered Office: 27a Washington Road, Worcester Park, Surrey, KT4 8JG
Shareholders: Patrick Neil Foad; Leonie Rachel Foad
Officers: LeOne Rachel Foad [1986] Director; Patt Foad [1985] Director

Fols for Men Ltd
Incorporated: 3 November 2017
Registered Office: Flat 4, 45 Gloucester Square, London, W2 2TQ
Major Shareholder: Pedro Lopes Dias Moorcraft
Officers: Pedro Lopes Dias Moorcraft [1992] Director/Manager

Foodprint Network Ltd
Incorporated: 26 October 2017
Registered Office: Business Enterprise Hub, The University of Buckingham, Hunter Street, Buckingham, MK18 1EG
Major Shareholder: Yiwei Li
Officers: Yiwei Li [1986] Director/CEO of Foodprint Network Ltd [Chinese]

For All Dogkind Limited
Incorporated: 28 October 2015 *Employees:* 1
Net Worth Deficit: £9,290 *Total Assets:* £39,108
Registered Office: 99 Horton Hill, Epsom, Surrey, KT19 8SY
Shareholders: Laura Jane Redstone; Emily Louise Butcher; Joanna Claire Butcher
Officers: Emily Louise Butcher [1979] Director/Marketing; Joanna Claire Butcher [1978] Director/Product; Laura Jane Redstone [1986] Director/Sales

Foramca Ltd
Incorporated: 31 May 2018
Registered Office: 20-22 Wenlock Road, London, N1 7GU
Major Shareholder: Gyorgy Ugrin
Officers: Gyorgy Ugrin [1976] Director/Manager [Hungarian]

Forderma Laboratory Ltd.
Incorporated: 23 October 2018
Registered Office: Flat 107, 25 Indescon Square, London, E14 9DG
Major Shareholder: Ching-Peng Wei
Officers: Ching-Peng Wei [1971] Director [Taiwanese]

Forest Hive Ltd
Incorporated: 9 July 2018
Registered Office: First Floor, 85 Great Portland Street, London, W1W 7LT
Major Shareholder: Martyna Helena Plewka
Officers: Luciana Carvalho Se [1989] Director/Businesswoman [Portuguese/Brazilian]; Martyna Helena Plewka [1991] Director/Entrepreneur [Polish]

Forever Heng UK Limited
Incorporated: 17 April 2018
Registered Office: 29 Oxley Moor Road, Wolverhampton, W Midlands, WV10 6TT
Officers: Harvinder Bahia [1985] Director

Forever Living Products Ireland Limited
Incorporated: 23 December 2002 *Employees:* 24
Net Worth: £770,739 *Total Assets:* £1,546,694
Registered Office: 50 Bedford Street, Belfast, BT2 7FW
Shareholders: Rex Maughan; Ruth Maughan
Officers: Gregg Elliott Maughan [1968] Director/President [American]; Rex Maughan [1936] Director [American]

Forever Young Cosmetics UK Limited
Incorporated: 27 February 2018
Registered Office: 1 Bolton Road, Darwen, Lancs, BB3 1DF
Major Shareholder: Bill Stanford
Officers: Bill Stanford [1961] Director

Foreverbeyoung Ltd
Incorporated: 16 April 2018
Registered Office: 172 Newgate Lane, Mansfield, Notts, NG18 2QA
Officers: Dan Zhao [1974] Director

Forte Organics Ltd
Incorporated: 1 September 2017
Registered Office: 70 Jermyn Street, Mayfair, London, SW1Y 6NY
Major Shareholder: Irene Alisea Forte
Officers: Irene Alisea Forte [1988] Group Project Director at Rocco Forte

Foundation Brands Ltd
Incorporated: 3 August 2012
Net Worth Deficit: £56,600 *Total Assets:* £1,150,000
Registered Office: Unit 3 Rufus Business Centre, Ravensbury Terrace, London, SW18 4RL
Major Shareholder: Mehrdad Mirzaee Ghomi
Officers: Mehrdad Mirzaee Ghomi, Secretary; Mehrdad Mirzaee Ghomi [1966] Director/Operations Manager

Fourie Hair Limited
Incorporated: 4 June 2018
Registered Office: 51 Dargai Street, Manchester, M11 4PW
Officers: Stephan Fourie [1996] Director/Trader

Fox Cosmetics Ltd
Incorporated: 3 July 2018
Registered Office: 21 East Street, Barking, Essex, IG11 8ER
Major Shareholder: Fahim Ali Chaudhry
Officers: Fahim Ali Chaudhry [1990] Director

Fox Group International Ltd
Incorporated: 4 July 2016 *Employees:* 9
Net Worth: £829,140 *Total Assets:* £1,831,570
Registered Office: 8a Cinnabar Court, Daresbury Park, Daresbury, Warrington, Cheshire, WA4 4GE
Shareholders: Michael Foxley; Michael Foxley
Officers: Michael Foxley, Secretary; Michael Foxley [1983] Director; Victoria Quinn [1986] Director

Fragrance & Beauty Creations Limited
Incorporated: 12 September 2006
Net Worth: £435,150 *Total Assets:* £1,250,000
Registered Office: Churchill Point, Lake Edge Green, Trafford Park Road, Manchester, M17 1BL
Shareholder: Sanjay Jayantilal Vadera
Officers: Sanjay Jayantilal Vadera, Secretary/Director; Mark Ian Earnshaw [1964] Director; Sanjay Jayantilal Vadera [1967] Director

Fragrance Acquisitions Limited
Incorporated: 14 February 2005
Net Worth: £50,520,000 *Total Assets:* £62,100,000
Registered Office: Churchill Point, Lake Edge Green, Trafford Park Road, Trafford Park, Manchester, M17 1BL
Officers: Sanjay Jayantilal Vadera, Secretary/Director; Sanjay Jayantilal Vadera [1967] Director; Vipul Jayantilal Vadera [1972] Director

Fragrance and Beauty Limited
Incorporated: 2 September 2005
Net Worth: £2,540,000 *Total Assets:* £4,210,000
Registered Office: Churchill Point, Lake Edge Green, Trafford Park Road, Trafford Park, Manchester, M17 1BL
Shareholders: Vipul Jayantilal Vadera; Mark Ian Earnshaw; Sanjay Jayantilal Vadera
Officers: Sanjay Jayantilal Vadera, Secretary; Mark Ian Earnshaw [1964] Director; Sanjay Jayantilal Vadera [1967] Director; Vipul Jayantilal Vadera [1972] Director

Fragrance and Gifts Limited
Incorporated: 10 October 1997
Net Worth Deficit: £144,745 *Total Assets:* £3,289
Registered Office: 6 Newbury Street, Wantage, Oxon, OX12 8BS
Major Shareholder: Roger William Soper
Officers: Anita Anne Hodgess, Secretary; Roger William Soper [1952] Director

Fragrance de Maison Limited
Incorporated: 7 June 2018
Registered Office: 74 Lowercroft Road, Skelmersdale, Lancs, WN8 6TZ
Officers: John Hutchison [1975] Director/Self Employed

Fragrance Express Limited
Incorporated: 11 January 2018
Registered Office: Level 3, 207 Regent Street, London, W1B 3HH
Major Shareholder: Waseem Sarwar
Officers: Waseem Sarwar, Secretary; Waseem Sarwar [1987] Director/Accounts Administration

Fragrance Factory Limited
Incorporated: 29 June 1995 *Employees:* 26
Net Worth: £2,972,245 *Total Assets:* £5,415,582
Registered Office: 7 Blenheim Court, 62 Brewery Road, London, N7 9NY
Shareholders: Georges Pharand; Howard Shaughnessy
Officers: Halldora Halldorsdottir Adler [1948] Director/Company Secretary [Icelander]; Jeremy David Adler [1951] Director; Georges Pharand [1961] Director/Chairman; Howard Shaughnessy [1963] Managing Director

Fragrance Group London Ltd
Incorporated: 5 June 2014 *Employees:* 4
Previous: Fragrance Dynamics Limited
Net Worth: £728,649 *Total Assets:* £3,702,898
Registered Office: 84 Eccleston Square, London, SW1V 1PX
Major Shareholder: Steven Ferguson
Officers: Anna Ferguson [1990] Director; Richard James Smith [1959] Director; Paul Yacoubian [1960] Director

Fragrance London Limited
Incorporated: 8 August 2015
Net Worth: £10,105 *Total Assets:* £57,222
Registered Office: 123 Ascot Gardens, Southall, Middlesex, UB1 2SE
Shareholders: Rajesh Rameshbhai Patel; Bhavesh Rajesh Patel
Officers: Bhavesh Rajesh Patel [1992] Director; Rajesh Rameshbhai Patel [1966] Director

Fragrance Plus Limited
Incorporated: 4 April 2017
Net Worth: £3,750 *Total Assets:* £21,720
Registered Office: 35 Hertford House, Taywood Road, Northolt, Middlesex, UB5 6GD
Shareholders: Rinku Ramesh Radia; Shaini Harman Jasraj Unadkat
Officers: Rinku Ramesh Radia [1973] Sales Director; Shaini Harman Jasraj Unadkat [1976] Director

Fragrance Sales Limited
Incorporated: 10 December 2007 *Employees:* 2
Net Worth: £385,996 *Total Assets:* £1,205,000
Registered Office: Griffins Court, 24-32 London Road, Newbury, Berks, RG14 1JX
Major Shareholder: Claire Linda Dovey
Officers: Claire Linda Dovey [1974] Director/Beauty

Fragrance Samples UK Limited
Incorporated: 16 May 2017
Net Worth: £27,900 *Total Assets:* £59,930
Registered Office: The Lodge, Beacon End Farmhouse, London Road, Stanway, Colchester, Essex, CO3 0NQ
Major Shareholder: Greg Jonathan Hartill
Officers: Debbie Hartill [1973] Director; Greg Jonathan Hartill [1976] Director

Fragrance Souk Limited
Incorporated: 9 July 2018
Registered Office: 81 London Road, Leicester, LE2 0PF
Officers: Ali Irfan [1972] Director/Businessman [Pakistani]

Fragrance Weekly Ltd
Incorporated: 26 July 2018
Registered Office: Basement Front, 34a Marylands Road, London, W9 2DX
Major Shareholder: Abdennour Boukernous
Officers: Abdennour Boukernous [1985] Director [French]

Fragrance World Ltd
Incorporated: 21 December 2018
Registered Office: Swan Centre, Higher Swan Lane, Bolton, Lancs, BL3 3AQ
Major Shareholder: Mohammed Jahangir
Officers: Mohammed Jahangir [1976] Director

Fragranceexpert Limited
Incorporated: 21 November 2006
Net Worth: £1,240,000 *Total Assets:* £1,570,000
Registered Office: Amertrans Park, Bushey Mill Lane, Watford, Herts, WD24 7JG
Parent: Shaneel Enterprises Ltd
Officers: Krishna Murthy Panthula, Secretary/Accountant; Dilesh Bhogilal Mehta [1960] Director; Hitesh Bhogilal Mehta [1956] Director

Fragrancekent (UK) Ltd
Incorporated: 23 October 2018
Registered Office: 107 Dunholme Road, London, N9 9QT
Major Shareholder: Michael Phillips
Officers: Michael Phillips [1983] Director/Internet Marketer

Fragrant Spa Limited
Incorporated: 24 January 2018
Registered Office: Basement, 146 Ladbroke Grove, London, W10 5NE
Major Shareholder: Xiangrong Liu
Officers: Xiangrong Liu [1982] Director [Chinese]

France Eclavour Cosmetic Ltd
Incorporated: 7 March 2018
Registered Office: Flat 32, Adventures Court, 12 Newport Avenue, London, E14 2DN
Major Shareholder: Lingzhi Chen
Officers: Lingzhi Chen [1989] Director/Businessman [Chinese]

France Parfums International Limited
Incorporated: 4 February 2019
Registered Office: First Floor, 85 Great Portland Street, London, W1W 7LT
Major Shareholder: Bruno Diaouga O'Reilly
Officers: Bruno Diaouga Oreilly, Secretary; Bruno Diaouga Oreilly [1974] Director [French]

A.H. Francis Professional Beauty Limited
Incorporated: 29 July 1998
Net Worth: £100,139 *Total Assets:* £125,440
Registered Office: 111 Exeter Street, Salisbury, Wilts, SP1 2SF
Major Shareholder: Alsion Helen Francis
Officers: Alison Helen Francis, Secretary; Alison Helen Francis [1962] Director/Beautician

Franok Business Solutions Limited
Incorporated: 8 January 2018
Registered Office: 329 Lilian Penson Hall, Talbot Square, London, W2 1TT
Major Shareholder: Maryam Bakari
Officers: Maryam Bakari [1980] Director

Freestyle (Trade) Ltd.
Incorporated: 19 April 2001
Net Worth: £2,409 *Total Assets:* £454,271
Registered Office: 41 High Street, Royston, Herts, SG8 9AW
Major Shareholder: Richard Campbell-Davys
Officers: Richard Campbell [1947] Director/Commodity Trader

Freestyle Trade (UK) Limited
Incorporated: 28 September 2006
Registered Office: 41 High Street, Royston, Herts, SG8 9AW
Major Shareholder: Richard Campbell-Davys
Officers: Richard Campbell [1947] Director/Manager; Lydia Campbell Davys [1983] Director/Trainee Surveyor

French Beauty Expert Ltd
Incorporated: 21 November 2017
Registered Office: Suite 2b, North Sands Business, Liberty Way, Sunderland, Tyne & Wear, SR6 0QA
Shareholder: Peter Fisher
Officers: Peter Fisher [1962] Director/Accountant

Fresh Cosmetics Limited
Incorporated: 24 January 2003 *Employees:* 29
Net Worth Deficit: £3,380,389 *Total Assets:* £3,775,909
Registered Office: 6th Floor, UK House, 180 Oxford Street, London, W1D 1AB
Parent: LVMH Moet Hennessy Louis Vuitton
Officers: Anne-Veronique Bruel [1963] Director [French]; Gael Charfi [1974] Director/C.O.O [French]; Stephanie Marie-Pierre David Roy [1971] Director [French]; Loic Pierre Marie Henriot [1978] Business Director [French]

FreshBreathOnline Limited
Incorporated: 16 January 2001
Net Worth: £8,980 *Total Assets:* £60,150
Registered Office: 1-5 Market Square, Ilfracombe, Devon, EX34 9AU
Shareholders: Joanne Alexandra Smith; Phillip John Smith
Officers: Joanne Alexandra Smith, Secretary/Administrator; Philip John Smith [1966] Director

Freshly Whip'd Limited
Incorporated: 21 January 2019
Registered Office: 1 Heron Mead, Enfield, Middlesex, EN3 6FD
Major Shareholder: Nneoma Chibudibia Okeke
Officers: Dr Nneoma Chibudibia Okeke [1992] Director and Company Secretary

Simona Fridrich Limited
Incorporated: 15 February 2019
Registered Office: 134 Canterbury Road, Harrow, Middlesex, HA1 4PB
Major Shareholder: Simona-Codruta Munteanu
Officers: Simona-Codruta Munteanu [1985] Director [Romanian]

From Mini Acorns Ltd
Incorporated: 23 November 2016
Net Worth: £3,071 *Total Assets:* £3,071
Registered Office: Kemp House, 160 City Road, London, EC1V 2NX
Shareholder: Margery Nicholson
Officers: Margery Nicholson [1958] Director/Finance; Sherine Nicholson [1984] Director/Product Developer

Frontrow International UK Ltd
Incorporated: 29 January 2018
Registered Office: Basement Level, 137 Earls Court Road, London, SW5 9RH
Major Shareholder: Adielmofranches Fornoles
Officers: Adielmofranches Fornoles [1983] Director [Filipino]

Fruu Cosmetics Limited
Incorporated: 1 June 2017
Registered Office: Kemp House, 160 City Road, London, EC1V 2NX
Major Shareholder: Terence Tsz-Hong Chung
Officers: Dr Terence Tsz-Hong Chung [1985] Founder and Director; Kelly Yee [1990] Director/Operations Manager

Functional Fragrances Ltd
Incorporated: 5 January 2011 *Employees:* 7
Net Worth Deficit: £937,727 *Total Assets:* £545,940
Registered Office: Windover House, St Ann Street, Salisbury, Wilts, SP1 2DR
Major Shareholder: Catherine Lara Morgan
Officers: Catherine Lara Morgan [1967] Director

Functional Skincare Ltd
Incorporated: 14 June 2018
Registered Office: 41 Hugh Street, Victoria, London, SW1V 1QJ
Shareholders: Mike Alexander Mockford; Jennifer Mockford; Stephen Mockford
Officers: Jennifer Mockford [1988] Marketing Director; Mike Alexander Mockford [1992] Sales Director; Stephen Mockford [1963] Commercial Director

Funky Skincare Limited
Incorporated: 14 August 2013
Net Worth Deficit: £12,731 *Total Assets:* £7,337
Registered Office: 15 Bradbury House, Kinghorn Road, Norwich, NR2 3PT
Shareholder: Sarah Louise Gare
Officers: Sarah Louise Gare [1985] Director

Fushi Wellbeing Limited
Incorporated: 17 April 2008
Net Worth: £30,380 *Total Assets:* £509,340
Registered Office: Unit 9 Roslin Square, Roslin Road, London, W3 8DH
Shareholders: Raj Pattni Jansari; Rannesh Jansari
Officers: Rannesh Jansari, Director of Business Development; Rannesh Jansari [1973] Director

Fuzzique Limited
Incorporated: 5 January 2015
Net Worth Deficit: £76,450 *Total Assets:* £12,330
Registered Office: 71-75 Shelton Street, Covent Garden, London, WC2H 9JQ
Major Shareholder: Akhil Sonchhatla
Officers: Akhil Sonchhatla [1978] Director

Fysifarm Limited
Incorporated: 16 January 2018
Registered Office: 27 Old Gloucester Street, London, WC1N 3AX
Major Shareholder: Nikolaos Chalvatzis
Officers: Panagiotis Laskaris [1966] Director [Greek]

G & G Skincare Ltd
Incorporated: 2 January 2019
Registered Office: Venthams Ltd, 51 Lincoln's Inn Fields, London, WC2A 3NA
Shareholders: Benjamin Gibbs; Mark Girven
Officers: Benjamin Gibbs [1980] Director/Sales; Mark Girven [1988] Director/Sales

G.P.B. Supplies Limited
Incorporated: 21 January 2002
Net Worth: £128,420 *Total Assets:* £342,850
Registered Office: Unit 6 Ash Court, Crystal Drive, Smethwick, W Midlands, B66 1QG
Major Shareholder: George Patrick Badcham
Officers: Richard Bernardo Green, Secretary; George Patrick Badcham [1953] Director

G.Q Homes Ltd
Incorporated: 8 December 2017
Registered Office: 20-22 Wenlock Road, London, N1 7GU
Major Shareholder: Giao Quynh Nguyen
Officers: Giao Quynh Nguyen [1969] Director

Gabriellas Beauty Ltd
Incorporated: 8 February 2019
Registered Office: Flat 5, 13b Parkway Road, Dudley, W Midlands, DY1 2QA
Major Shareholder: Maria Gabriela Patroiu
Officers: Maria Gabriela Patroiu [1975] Director/General Manager [Romanian]

Gabs Cosmetologist Limited
Incorporated: 13 September 2018
Registered Office: Flat 4, 50 Osborne Road, Manchester, M19 2DY
Major Shareholder: Gabriela Szczubelek
Officers: Gabriela Szczubelek [1963] Director/Cosmetologist [Polish]

Gajas Gift Limited
Incorporated: 3 January 2019
Registered Office: Flat 5, 6-10 Exmouth Market, City Mansions, London, EC1R 4PY
Shareholders: Linda Prigarska; Gija Mezare
Officers: Gija Mezare [1991] Director [Latvian]; Linda Prigarska [1988] Director [Latvian]

Galactix Ltd
Incorporated: 12 November 1998
Net Worth: £351,390 *Total Assets:* £375,000
Registered Office: c/o Ideal Hair & Beauty Supplies Ltd, Vicarage Farm Road, Peterborough, Cambs, PE1 5TP
Major Shareholder: Malcolm Arnold Ralph
Officers: Malcolm Arnold Ralph [1964] Director/Sales Negotiator

Galaxy Grooming Limited
Incorporated: 28 July 2016
Registered Office: Lower Ground Floor, 40 Bloomsbury Way, London, WC1A 2SE
Major Shareholder: Jason Rockyie Bissessur
Officers: Jason Rockyie Bissessur [1984] Director/Brand Consultant; Letecia Malagayo Bissessur [1955] Director/Care Professional

Galenti Limited
Incorporated: 25 March 2013
Registered Office: Dirleton House, Lewes Road, Forest Row, E Sussex, RH18 5AA
Major Shareholder: Julie Mary Aitchison
Officers: Julie Mary Aitchison [1956] Director/Sales P.A

Gallya Deelya Ltd.
Incorporated: 9 November 2011
Net Worth Deficit: £941 *Total Assets:* £560
Registered Office: 104 Stepney Green Court, Stepney Green, London, E1 3LN
Shareholder: Louise Cng Gylsen
Officers: Louise Cng Gylsen [1968] Director

Louise Galvin Limited
Incorporated: 25 June 2002 *Employees:* 1
Net Worth Deficit: £64,066 *Total Assets:* £75,554
Registered Office: 73 Cornhill, London, EC3V 3QQ
Major Shareholder: Charles Henry Rowland Bracken
Officers: Samantha Hughes, Secretary; Louise Galvin [1967] Director

GameelaCosmetics Ltd
Incorporated: 20 August 2018
Registered Office: 24 Farhalls Crescent, Horsham, W Sussex, RH12 4DA
Major Shareholder: Yasmin Elharrak
Officers: Yasmin Elharrak [1984] Director/Teacher

Garda Service Ltd
Incorporated: 5 April 2011
Net Worth: £16,120 *Total Assets:* £20,920
Registered Office: International House, 24 Holborn Viaduct, London, EC1A 2BN
Major Shareholder: Luigi Testolin
Officers: Luigi Testolin [1962] Director/Trader [Italian]

Garnier & Hemo Healthcare Ltd
Incorporated: 14 September 2017
Registered Office: 14 Whitehouse Road, Londonderry, BT48 0NE
Parent: Hemo Bioscience Ltd
Officers: Dr David Leppinen [1968] Director/Businessman

Garron Labs Private Limited
Incorporated: 13 December 2017
Registered Office: 27 Old Gloucester Street, London, WC1N 3AX
Shareholders: Gundecha Ashish Mohanlal; Oswal Hiteshkumar Popatlal; Oswal Rajesh Popatlal; Bhandari Rahul Maniklal; Zanvar Gopal Laxminarayan
Officers: Zanvar Gopal Laxminarayan [1978] Director/Businessman [Indian]; Sharma Vivek [1970] Director/Businessman [Indian]

Gattino Cosmetics Ltd
Incorporated: 25 October 2018
Registered Office: 20-22 Wenlock Road, London, N1 7GU
Major Shareholder: Taylor Phillipa McIntosh
Officers: Taylor Phillipa McIntosh [1996] Director/Make-Up Artist

Gaya Cosmetics Limited
Incorporated: 21 February 2014
Net Worth Deficit: £25,442 *Total Assets:* £108,414
Registered Office: 103 High Street, Waltham Cross, Herts, EN8 7AN
Major Shareholder: Shahar Gamliel
Officers: Shahar Gamliel [1984] Director/Retailer [Israeli]

Gaya Minerals Limited
Incorporated: 19 August 2011
Net Worth Deficit: £86,763 *Total Assets:* £51
Registered Office: 103 High Street, Waltham Cross, Herts, EN8 7AN
Shareholders: Gilad Gamliel; Shahar Gamliel
Officers: Gilad Avi Gamliel [1975] Director/Wholesaler of Minerals and Cosmetics [Israeli]; Shahar Gamliel [1984] Director/Wholesaler of Minerals & Cosmetics [Israeli]

Gazelli International Limited
Incorporated: 17 October 2007 *Employees:* 17
Net Worth: £4,017,960 *Total Assets:* £14,576,240
Registered Office: 15 Bury Walk, London, SW3 6QD
Major Shareholder: Jamila Askarova
Officers: Jamila Askarova [1983] Creative Director [Azerbaijani]

GBBC Ltd
Incorporated: 31 May 2013
Previous: EBK Skincare Ltd
Net Worth Deficit: £6,040 *Total Assets:* £13,633
Registered Office: 80 High Street, Winchester, Hants, SO23 9AT
Major Shareholder: Benjamin Douglas Swift
Officers: Benjamin Swift [1979] Director

GCKK Ltd
Incorporated: 26 September 2018
Registered Office: Kent House, Kent Street, Sedlescombe, Battle, E Sussex, TN33 0SG
Major Shareholder: Guy Dominic Cornelius
Officers: Guy Dominic Cornelius [1987] Director

GDT Global Limited
Incorporated: 14 October 2018
Registered Office: 7 St Petersgate, Stockport, Cheshire, SK1 1EB
Major Shareholder: Christopher David Longden
Officers: Christopher David Longden [1983] Sales Director

Geek's Cosmetics Ltd
Incorporated: 7 March 2018
Registered Office: Geek's Barbers, 40 Brook Street, Wrexham, Clwyd, LL13 7LL
Major Shareholder: Mark Lloyd Jones
Officers: Mark Lloyd Jones [1987] Director

Geeza Cosmetics Ltd
Incorporated: 25 June 2018
Registered Office: 83 Ducie Street, Manchester, M1 2JQ
Shareholders: Hamze Ismail; Beau Heaven
Officers: Beau Heaven [1992] Director; Hamze Ismail [1997] Director

Gel Labs Limited
Incorporated: 10 October 2016
Registered Office: 75 Springfield Road, Chelmsford, Essex, CM2 6JB
Shareholders: Chin-Ying Huang; Shih-Chien Wang
Officers: Shih-Chieh Wang [1975] Director

Gelmoment Limited
Incorporated: 25 June 2015
Net Worth Deficit: £5,558 *Total Assets:* £26,389
Registered Office: First Floor, Winston House, 349 Regents Park Road, London, N3 1DH
Major Shareholder: Dov Grossnass
Officers: Dov Grossnass [1971] Director

Gemini Beauty Products Ltd
Incorporated: 3 May 2018
Registered Office: First Floor, 9 MacKenzie Street, Slough, SL1 1XQ
Shareholders: Kahinaat Raja; Aarzu Raja
Officers: Aarzu Raja [1998] Director/Student; Kahinaat Raja [1998] Director/Student

Gen Next Ltd
Incorporated: 21 June 2018
Registered Office: 8 Jackdaw Way, Halling, Rochester, Kent, ME2 1FL
Major Shareholder: Amit Ashok Jain
Officers: Amit Jain, Secretary; Amit Ashok Jain [1980] Director

General Healthcare Limited
Incorporated: 4 July 1986 *Employees:* 6
Net Worth: £380,379 *Total Assets:* £2,525,929
Registered Office: 111 Blyth Road, Hayes, Middlesex, UB3 1DB
Major Shareholder: Antoinette Kseib
Officers: Anthony Adel Kseib [1981] Director/Marketing Manager; Antoinette Kseib [1956] Director

General Shop Ltd
Incorporated: 8 March 2018
Registered Office: Trafalgar Mill Business Exchange, Trafalgar Street, Burnley, Lancs, BB11 1TQ
Officers: John Green [1970] Director/Business Executive [Russian]

Generic Physics Limited
Incorporated: 31 December 2014
Registered Office: 17 Wenham Place, Hatfield, Herts, AL10 0DD
Major Shareholder: Hermann Yedoh
Officers: Dr Hermann Yedoh [1975] Director/Pharmacist [French]

Genetiq Lab Limited
Incorporated: 11 November 2016
Registered Office: 53 Carolside Avenue, Clarkston, Glasgow, G76 7AD
Major Shareholder: Colin Smith
Officers: Colin Smith [1988] Director/Accountant

Genixo Ltd
Incorporated: 11 February 2019
Registered Office: 2 Mill Street, Enniskillen, Co Fermanagh, BT74 6FB
Shareholders: Mariusz Szczesny; Dorota Kwasniewska; Krzysztof Zielinski
Officers: Dorota Kwasniewska [1985] Director [Polish]; Mariusz Szczesny [1975] Director [Polish]; Krzysztof Zielinski [1972] Director [Polish]

Gentel Works Ltd
Incorporated: 22 October 2018
Registered Office: 27 Old Gloucester Street, London, WC1N 3AX
Major Shareholder: Georgios Drakakis-Kastrinakis
Officers: Georgios Drakakis-Kastrinakis, Secretary; Georgios Drakakis-Kastrinakis [1971] Director/Businessman [Greek]

Genten Skincare Ltd
Incorporated: 31 December 2018
Registered Office: Flat 84, Ivor Court, Gloucester Place, London, NW1 6BP
Shareholders: Ayaka Fujiwara; Jie Yang
Officers: Ayaka Fujiwara [1988] Director/Investment Specialist [Japanese]

Gentille Limited
Incorporated: 9 June 2014
Net Worth: £33,588 *Total Assets:* £341,933
Registered Office: Office 204, 24-26 Arcadia Avenue, London, N3 2JU
Major Shareholder: Afsaneh Zandi Goharrizi
Officers: Afsaneh Zandi Goharrizi [1968] Director [Iranian]

Gentle Beauty Co Ltd
Incorporated: 15 November 2001
Net Worth: £247,714 *Total Assets:* £358,498
Registered Office: 10 Thornsett Road, London, SW18 4EN
Major Shareholder: Paul Williams
Officers: Shobha Rani Angadi, Secretary; Paul Williams [1947] Director

Gentlemend Ltd
Incorporated: 21 May 2018
Registered Office: 12e Baileyfield Road, Edinburgh, EH15 1DL
Major Shareholder: Kieran Cooke
Officers: Kieran Cooke [1988] Director/Teacher

Georgie Salon Supplies Limited
Incorporated: 30 March 2009
Net Worth: £19,120 *Total Assets:* £199,880
Registered Office: Unit CO2, Magna 34 Business Park, Temple Street, Rotherham, S Yorks, S60 1FG
Shareholders: Georgina Darbyshire; Stewart William Bell
Officers: Georgina Darbyshire, Secretary; Stewart William Bell [1959] Director; Georgina Darbyshire [1965] Director

S K A Gibson Ltd
Incorporated: 12 December 2017
Registered Office: Apartment 204, 8 Wren Mews, London, SE11 6BA
Major Shareholder: Shennell Shenika Gibson
Officers: Shennell Shenika Gibson [1992] Director/Self Employed

Gift Presentp Ltd
Incorporated: 11 October 2018
Registered Office: 56 The Avenue, Sale, Cheshire, M33 4QA
Major Shareholder: Mohammed Altoumi
Officers: Mohammed Altoumi [1996] Director [Libyan]

Gifts of Earth Ltd
Incorporated: 25 October 2017
Registered Office: 11 Primrose Crescent, Norwich, NR7 0SE
Officers: Simona Whyte [1987] Director [Slovak]

Rhona Gillmore Limited
Incorporated: 7 November 1991
Net Worth: £4,487 *Total Assets:* £17,525
Registered Office: 21 Angel Hill, Tiverton, Devon, EX16 6PE
Major Shareholder: Pamela Noelle Alers-Hankey
Officers: Pamela Noelle Alers-Hankey, Secretary/Retailer; Pamela Noelle Alers-Hankey [1948] Director/Retailer; Ryan Samuel Gormley [1972] Director/Stock Controller [Canadian]

Gilmor Hair and Beauty (Newport) Limited
Incorporated: 9 September 2013 *Employees:* 12
Net Worth: £8,391 *Total Assets:* £291,872
Registered Office: 1b Enterprise Way, Newport, NP20 2AQ
Shareholders: Angela Jayne Hancock; Mark Andrew Hancock
Officers: Angela Jayne Hancock [1966] Director; Mark Andrew Hancock [1963] Director; Thomas Andrew Hancock [1988] Director

Giva Solution Ltd
Incorporated: 7 December 2018
Registered Office: 20 Nicoll Road, Harlesden, London, NW10 9AB
Officers: Sir Joseph Marc Raymond, Secretary; Sir Joseph Marc Raymond [1991] Director [French]

Given By Nature Limited
Incorporated: 17 December 2015
Net Worth Deficit: £1,442 *Total Assets:* £4,473
Registered Office: 14 New Oak Road, London, N2 8LN
Shareholders: Kinga Stojek; Jolanta Szydlowska
Officers: Kinga Stojek [1973] Director/Pharmacy Manager [Polish]; Jolanta Szydlowska [1974] Director/Ecologist [Polish]

Glaci Natural Ltd
Incorporated: 13 February 2019
Registered Office: Wharfedale, 7 Wharfedale Grove, Leeds, LS7 2LQ
Major Shareholder: Glaci Braga Silva
Officers: Glaci Braga Silva [1960] Director/Chemistry [Brazilian]

Glad Gent Ltd
Incorporated: 28 April 2017
Registered Office: 87 Fernleigh Road, London, N21 3AJ
Major Shareholder: Jonathan Wolfgang Draper
Officers: Jonathan Wolfgang Draper [1972] Director

Glam Wholesale Limited
Incorporated: 23 April 2013
Net Worth: £100 *Total Assets:* £4,182
Registered Office: Unit 22 Orde Wingate Way, Primrose Hill Industrial Estate, Stockton on Tees, Cleveland, TS19 0GA
Major Shareholder: Shaun Robert Thwaites
Officers: Shaun Robert Thwaites [1977] Director

Glamify Beauty Limited
Incorporated: 24 January 2018
Registered Office: Crown House, Plantation Road, Burscough Industrial Estate, Ormskirk, Lancs, L40 8JT
Major Shareholder: Andrew Cook
Officers: Andrew Cook [1984] Commercial Director

Glamn Holding Ltd
Incorporated: 8 November 2016
Net Worth Deficit: £38,103 *Total Assets:* £2,306
Registered Office: Craven House, 40-44 Uxbridge Road, Ealing, London, W5 2BS
Parent: Sanco Holding Ltd
Officers: Victoria Paier [1990] Director [Austrian]

Glamrolls Limited
Incorporated: 1 May 2018
Registered Office: 16 Fernwood Rise, Brighton, BN1 5EP
Officers: Sophie Stanbury [1975] Director/Interior Designer

Glasgow Nails & Beauty Supplies Limited
Incorporated: 7 September 2016
Net Worth Deficit: £22,386 *Total Assets:* £108,579
Registered Office: Suite 66, The Wenta Business Centre, Electric Avenue, Enfield, Middlesex, EN3 7XU
Officers: Son Dang Ngoc [1962] Director/Businessman [Slovak]

Glendale Group Limited
Incorporated: 24 March 1988
Net Worth: £50,100 *Total Assets:* £110,100
Registered Office: 1st Floor, Cloister House, New Bailey Street, Salford, M3 5FS
Parent: Glendale Holdings Limited
Officers: Matthew Pettit, Secretary; Simon Tennant Barker [1956] Finance Director; Charles Rodney Mathers [1956] Director/Wholesaler [New Zealander]

Glendale S/S Limited
Incorporated: 9 August 1979
Net Worth: £2,180,000 *Total Assets:* £7,720,000
Registered Office: 1st Floor, Cloister House, New Bailey Street, Salford, M3 5FS
Parent: Glendale Group Limited
Officers: Matthew Pettit, Secretary; Simon Tennant Barker [1956] Finance Director; Charles Rodney Mathers [1956] Director [New Zealander]

Glitterati Distributions Limited
Incorporated: 14 December 2006
Net Worth Deficit: £34,877 Total Assets: £112,684
Registered Office: 24a Aldermans Hill, Palmers Green, London, N13 4PN
Shareholders: Alexandros Panayioti Theofanous; Anna Theofanous
Officers: Anna Theofanous, Secretary/Beautician; Alexandros Panayioti Theofanous [1981] Director; Anna Theofanous [1978] Director/Beautician

The Glitterati Shop Ltd
Incorporated: 28 June 2018
Registered Office: 76 Burnthill Lane, Rugeley, Staffs, WS15 2HY
Shareholders: Robert John Standley; Jasmin Danielle Burgess
Officers: Jasmin Danielle Burgess [1994] Director/Nurse; Robert John Standley [1991] Marketing Director

Glitterfreaks Limited
Incorporated: 2 November 2018
Registered Office: c/o Bulpitt Crocker Taxation Limited, Burlington House, Old Christchurch Road, Bournemouth, BH1 2HZ
Major Shareholder: Kristin Lee Williams
Officers: Scott Alexander Le ROI [1977] Director; Kristin Lee Williams [1979] Director

Global Beautique Limited
Incorporated: 3 February 2017
Registered Office: Unit 2 Capital Business Park, Manor Way, Borehamwood, Herts, WD6 1GW
Major Shareholder: Karen Millie-James
Officers: Mark James Felstein, Secretary; Karen Millie-James [1954] Director

Global Beauty Wholesale Ltd
Incorporated: 22 April 2015
Net Worth: £48,840 Total Assets: £190,710
Registered Office: Network House, Stubs Beck Lane, West 26 Industrial Estate, Cleckheaton, W Yorks, BD19 4TT
Major Shareholder: Iltaf Bahadur
Officers: Iltaf Bahadur [1980] Director

Global Couture (UK) Ltd
Incorporated: 12 June 2014
Net Worth: £147,313 Total Assets: £241,117
Registered Office: Units 24-25 Yardley Business Park, Luckyn Lane, Basildon, Essex, SS14 3GL
Major Shareholder: Christopher Diaper
Officers: Christopher Diaper [1961] Director; John Edward Diaper [1965] Director

Global Essence UK Ltd
Incorporated: 9 March 2001 Employees: 10
Net Worth: £1,185,023 Total Assets: £4,834,465
Registered Office: Unit 1 Parklands Business Centre, Stortford Road, Leaden Roding, Dunmow, Essex, CM6 1GF
Major Shareholder: Katrina Anne Neale
Officers: Deborah Joan Mockford, Secretary; Deborah Joan Mockford [1959] Director/Commodities Trader; Katrina Anne Neale [1960] Director/Importer; Alan Edward York [1960] Director/Import Export

Global Hair Care Limited
Incorporated: 13 December 2018
Registered Office: 24 Occupation Road, Lindley, Huddersfield, W Yorks, HD3 3BD
Shareholders: John Birrel Abel; Simon William Abel; Christopher Torlop
Officers: John Birrel Abel [1943] Managing Director; Simon William Abel [1967] Operations Director; Christopher Torlop [1954] Sales Director

Global Luxury Beauty Ltd
Incorporated: 1 March 2016 Employees: 10
Previous: Chantrey Green Limited
Net Worth Deficit: £144,753 Total Assets: £404,122
Registered Office: 2nd Floor, 11 Argyll Street, London, W1F 7TH
Major Shareholder: Francis John Elliot Walker
Officers: Francis John Elliot Walker [1977] Director

Global One Wholesale Ltd
Incorporated: 27 February 2018
Registered Office: 4th Floor, Unit 4A & 4b, Mill No 3, Higher Swan Lane, Bolton, Lancs, BL3 3BJ
Officers: Moeiyed Daremi [1979] Director [Iranian]

Globe Intraworks Limited
Incorporated: 7 March 2017
Net Worth: £16,204 Total Assets: £21,559
Registered Office: H5 Ash Tree Court, Nottingham Business Park, Nottingham, NG8 6PY
Major Shareholder: Seitaro Sunami
Officers: Seitaro Sunami [1977] Director/Business Consultant [Japanese]

Glochina Trading UK Ltd.
Incorporated: 26 February 2018
Registered Office: 6th Floor, 52 Grosvenor Gardens, London, SW1W 0AU
Major Shareholder: Sisi Chen
Officers: Sisi Chen [1990] Managing Director [Chinese]

Glorious Brands Ltd.
Incorporated: 25 May 2010 Employees: 43
Net Worth: £3,491,625 Total Assets: £6,115,543
Registered Office: Allen House, 1 Westmead Road, Sutton, Surrey, SM1 4LA
Shareholders: Philip St John Moores; Tracy Jane Moores
Officers: John George Demaine [1961] Commercial Director; Philip St John Moores [1958] Director; Tracy Jane Moores [1965] Director

Glory Cosmetics Ltd
Incorporated: 5 July 2017
Registered Office: 26 Westbury Road, London, E7 8BU
Major Shareholder: Rashid Qassim
Officers: Rashid Qassim, Secretary; Shamshad Begum [1979] Director

Glossy Center Limited
Incorporated: 22 January 2019
Registered Office: 119 De Grey Street, Hull, HU5 2RU
Major Shareholder: Aneta Jarosz
Officers: Aneta Jarosz [1989] Director [Polish]

Glow Beauty Shop Ltd
Incorporated: 30 August 2014
Net Worth Deficit: £3,350 Total Assets: £47,460
Registered Office: 1 & 2 Mercia Village, Torwood Close, Westwood Business Park, Coventry, Warwicks, CV4 8HX
Major Shareholder: Salman Asad
Officers: Salman Asad [1976] Director

Glow Consumer Products UK Limited
Incorporated: 6 October 2014 *Employees:* 3
Net Worth: £771,233 *Total Assets:* £1,854,338
Registered Office: 6 Marsh Parade, Newcastle, Staffs, ST5 1DU
Shareholders: Ian David Andrews; Glow International Investments Pty Ltd
Officers: Ian David Andrews [1957] Director; Gregory Owen Coulter [1958] Finance Director [Australian]; Anthony George Jenkins [1959] Marketing Director [Australian]

Glow Investment Ltd
Incorporated: 25 March 2017
Registered Office: 71-75 Shelton Street, Covent Garden, London, WC2H 9JQ
Major Shareholder: Isaac Abednego Sackey
Officers: Isaac Abednego Sackey, Secretary; Isaac Abednego Sackey [1980] Director/Radiographer [Ghanaian]

The Glow Jar Ltd
Incorporated: 17 August 2018
Registered Office: Flat 12, Wetherby House, 20-21 Wetherby Gardens, London, SW5 0JP
Shareholders: Kunal Bhagat; Elena Petrov
Officers: Kunal Bhagat [1976] Director

Gluedon Ltd
Incorporated: 16 January 2019
Registered Office: 27 Old Gloucester Street, London, WC1N 3AX
Officers: Antonio Siano [1973] Director/Entrepreneur [Italian]

Glute Plus Limited
Incorporated: 9 April 2015
Net Worth: £6,910 *Total Assets:* £6,910
Registered Office: 82 Church Lane, Scunthorpe, N Lincs, DN15 7AF
Shareholder: Shuhel Ahmed
Officers: Shuhel Ahmed [1989] Director

Gojo Industries - Europe Limited
Incorporated: 22 February 1990 *Employees:* 385
Net Worth: £8,726,525 *Total Assets:* £60,227,816
Registered Office: Unit 5 & 6 Stratus Park, Brinklow, Milton Keynes, Bucks, MK10 0DA
Officers: Mark Steven Lerner, Secretary [American]; Timothy Dye [1965] Commercial Director [American]; Joseph Samuel Kanfer [1947] Director/President [American]; Mark Steven Lerner [1949] Director/Secretary & Treasurer [American]; Scott Levin [1952] Director [American]

Gold 22 (UK) Limited
Incorporated: 3 March 2009
Net Worth Deficit: £22,090 *Total Assets:* £254,300
Registered Office: 15a Alperton Lane, Perivale, Greenford, Middlesex, UB6 8DH
Officers: Manoj Navnitlal Gandhi, Secretary/Director; Anoj Navnitlal Gandhi [1960] Director; Manoj Navnitlal Gandhi [1957] Director; Amarjeet Singh Gulati [1968] Director

Gold Class Hair Limited
Incorporated: 7 January 2014
Net Worth Deficit: £29,270 *Total Assets:* £610,730
Registered Office: 52 Bluebridge Road, Brookmans Park, Hatfield, Herts, AL9 7SA
Shareholder: Inanch Emir
Officers: Cahit Joe Emir [1973] Director; Inanch Emir [1973] Director/Hairdresser

Gold Pillar Holding Ltd
Incorporated: 16 March 2017
Registered Office: Level 18, 40 Bank Street, Canary Wharf, London, E14 5NR
Major Shareholder: Deoclides Jandir Pian
Officers: Deoclides Jandir Pian [1969] Director [Italian]

Goldeivy London Lashes Ltd
Incorporated: 9 November 2018
Registered Office: 71-75 Shelton Street, London, WC2H 9JQ
Major Shareholder: EMI France
Officers: Mark France [1971] Director

Golden Rose Limited
Incorporated: 26 April 2004
Net Worth: £31,930 *Total Assets:* £63,280
Registered Office: 11 South Walk, Basildon, Essex, SS14 1BZ
Major Shareholder: Mohammed Ahmed Majid
Officers: Mohammed Ahmed Majid [1967] Director

Golden Vanity Ltd
Incorporated: 26 March 2018
Registered Office: 71-75 Shelton Street, London, WC2H 9JQ
Major Shareholder: Bruna Rossana Pina
Officers: Bruna Rossana Pina [1998] Director [Portuguese]

Goldshore (UK) Limited
Incorporated: 24 June 2005
Net Worth Deficit: £5,693 *Total Assets:* £668
Registered Office: 8 Wimpole Street, London, W1G 9SP
Major Shareholder: Philippe Henri Prive
Officers: Gael Vanessa Prive [1980] Director [French]; Philippe Henri Prive [1954] Director [French]

Goldstone Perfumes Limited
Incorporated: 6 February 2018
Registered Office: 6 Herbert Road, Sheffield, S7 1RL
Major Shareholder: Mohammed Rafiq Khan
Officers: Mohammed Rafiq Khan [1962] Director

Golo Hair & Beauty Limited
Incorporated: 30 May 2017
Registered Office: 111a High Street, Wealdstone, Harrow, Middlesex, HA3 5DL
Major Shareholder: Shabbir Gulamali Dungersi
Officers: Shabbir Gulamali Dungersi [1960] Director

Good Beauty International Holding Limited
Incorporated: 23 September 2016
Registered Office: 309 Winston House, 2 Dollis Park, Finchley Central, London, N3 1HF
Shareholders: Yiu Chun Wong; Ho Yin Cheung; Man Keung Lam
Officers: Yiu Chun Wong [1988] Director/Businesswoman [Chinese]

Good By Nature Ltd
Incorporated: 8 November 2018
Registered Office: Flat 9, Tiggap House, 20 Cable Walk, London, SE10 0TP
Shareholders: Tara Louise O'Malley; Julian Ruiz
Officers: Tara Louise O'Malley [1993] Director/Editor

Good Pharma Dermatology Limited
Incorporated: 29 August 2017
Registered Office: 12 Caledon Road, Beaconsfield, Bucks, HP9 2BX
Shareholders: John O'Shea; Jason Humphries
Officers: Jason Humphries [1969] Director/Entrepreneur; Dr John O'Shea [1977] Director/Entrepreneur [Irish]

Good Skin Care Company Limited
Incorporated: 5 February 2014
Registered Office: Enterprise House, 38 Tyndall Court, Commerce Road, Lynchwood, Peterborough, Cambs, PE2 6LR
Officers: Christopher Mark Taylor, Secretary; Alan Leslie Taylor [1952] Director; Christopher Mark Taylor [1963] Director; Raymond Neil Taylor [1957] Director; Evelyn May Taylor [1932] Director

Good Ventures Limited
Incorporated: 19 November 2007
Net Worth: £82,520 *Total Assets:* £385,620
Registered Office: Studio 20, Alexander Road, London Colney, St Albans, Herts, AL2 1JG
Major Shareholder: Laura Francesca Rudoe
Officers: Laura Francesca Rudoe [1977] Director/Finance

Goodangels Ltd
Incorporated: 28 June 2018
Registered Office: 173 Blackwatch Road, Radford, Coventry, Warwicks, CV6 3GU
Officers: Thembelihle Ncube Goremucheche [1981] Director/Support Worker [Zimbabwean]

GoodNaturedSkincare Ltd
Incorporated: 23 November 2017
Registered Office: 20-22 Wenlock Road, London, N1 7GU
Major Shareholder: Mazel Caryl John
Officers: Mazel Caryl John [1984] Director/Owner

Goodscents Limited
Incorporated: 19 September 2013
Net Worth Deficit: £5,311 *Total Assets:* £13,151
Registered Office: 1 Loverock Crescent, Hilmorton, Rugby, Warwicks, CV21 4AH
Shareholders: Adrian Paul Evans; Barbara Jean Evans
Officers: Claire Evans-Hare, Secretary; Adrian Paul Evans [1951] Director; Barbara Jean Evans [1948] Director

Goodsky Co., Ltd.
Incorporated: 28 November 2017
Registered Office: Fourth Floor, 3 Gower Street, London, WC1E 6HA
Major Shareholder: Dier Weng
Officers: Dier Weng [1982] Director [Chinese]

Gordon-McCarthy Limited
Incorporated: 18 October 2018
Registered Office: Englesea House, Barthomley Road, Crewe, Cheshire, CW1 5UF
Shareholders: John Nigel St. Ledger McCarthy; The Fayrefield Group Limited
Officers: Philip Austin, Secretary; Nicholas Anthony Hilton [1953] Director; John Nigel St. Ledger McCarthy [1956] Director; Ashley Weaver [1966] Director

Gorillacare Ltd
Incorporated: 7 February 2019
Registered Office: 4 Station Road, St Neots, Cambs, PE19 1QF
Major Shareholder: Julia Ida Jakobsson
Officers: Julia Ida Jakobsson [1982] Director/Support Specialist [Swedish]

GP Mediplus Ltd
Incorporated: 11 January 2016
Net Worth: £897 *Total Assets:* £896
Registered Office: 20-22 Wenlock Road, London, N1 7GU
Shareholders: Georghios Petropoulakis; Goldman Capital Group Ltd
Officers: Michalakis Nestor Megas [1946] Director/Accountant [Cypriot]; Georghios Petropoulakis [1957] Director/Entrepreneur [Cypriot]

Gracefruit Limited
Incorporated: 8 March 2010 *Employees:* 13
Net Worth: £60,159 *Total Assets:* £164,023
Registered Office: 146 Glasgow Road, Longcroft, Stirlingshire, FK4 1QL
Shareholders: Elizabeth Carnahan; Paul Carnahan
Officers: Elizabeth Carnahan [1967] Director; Paul Carnahan [1968] Director/Journalist

Gracetree Ltd
Incorporated: 1 March 2010 *Employees:* 2
Net Worth: £16,614 *Total Assets:* £84,566
Registered Office: 4 Old Park Lane, Mayfair, London, W1K 1QW
Major Shareholder: Antonia Burrell
Officers: Antonia Burrell [1972] Managing Director

Gracy Hair and Makeup Ltd
Incorporated: 22 November 2011
Net Worth: £31,334 *Total Assets:* £36,605
Registered Office: 6 Paper Mill Lane, Dartford, Kent, DA1 5BF
Officers: Ijeoma Grace Ofoegbu [1981] Director

Graham Hair and Beauty Limited
Incorporated: 2 May 1986 *Employees:* 13
Net Worth: £667,790 *Total Assets:* £956,989
Registered Office: MacGregor House, Station Road, Seaton Delaval, Northumberland, NE25 0PT
Major Shareholder: Graham Millis Janaway
Officers: Patricia Bennett, Secretary; Graham Millis Janaway [1944] Director/Hairdressing Wholesaler

Grand Beaute Ltd
Incorporated: 22 August 2017
Registered Office: 28 Limestone Close, Aldridge, Walsall, W Midlands, WS9 0DN
Major Shareholder: Tanyaradzwa Fidelity Chikosi
Officers: Tanyaradzwa Fidelity Chikosi [1985] Director [Zimbabwean]

Grand By Designs Limited
Incorporated: 12 May 2005
Registered Office: 68 Sandymount Avenue, Stanmore, Middlesex, HA7 4TY
Shareholders: Dennis Grandison; John Lloyd Grandison
Officers: Andrea Rosario Gborie, Secretary; Dennis N/A Grandison [1963] Director/Engineer; Shenston N/A Grandison [1940] Director/Engineer

Grandelash MD UK Ltd
Incorporated: 3 October 2015
Registered Office: 5 Woodland Way, Burntwood, Staffs, WS7 4UP
Shareholders: Maria-Victoria Adriana Gomez; Monique Julia Gomez
Officers: Maria-Victoria Victoria Gomez [1961] Director; Monique Julia Gomez [1970] Director

Grautrans Limited
Incorporated: 19 April 2017
Net Worth: £10,000 Total Assets: £15,870
Registered Office: 27 Old Gloucester Street, London, WC1N 3AX
Major Shareholder: Itsumi Tanaka
Officers: Itsumi Tanaka [1980] Director/Business Consultant [Japanese]

The Great British Bee Company Ltd
Incorporated: 24 February 2017
Registered Office: 26 Victoria Road, Devizes, Wilts, SN10 1ET
Officers: Ben Swift [1979] Director

Great London Beauty Limited
Incorporated: 7 March 2018
Registered Office: 15a Alperton Lane, Greenford, Middlesex, UB6 8DH
Shareholders: Aseem Thukral; Sunny Anooj Gandhi
Officers: Sunny Anooj Gandhi, Secretary; Sunny Anooj Gandhi [1993] Director; Aseem Thukral [1979] Director [American]

Green & Dionisi Ltd
Incorporated: 22 June 2009
Net Worth: £81,770 Total Assets: £202,800
Registered Office: 305 Regents Park Road, Finchley, London, N3 1DP
Shareholders: Gary Michum Green; Gianni Gaetano Alberto Dionisi
Officers: Gianni Gaetano Alberto Dionisi [1965] Director; Gary Michum Green [1962] Director

Kenneth Green Associates Limited
Incorporated: 30 September 1992 Employees: 310
Net Worth: £26,602,820 Total Assets: £42,828,352
Registered Office: Hill House, Monument Hill, Weybridge, Surrey, KT13 8RX
Shareholders: Susan Esther Green; Kenneth Charles Green
Officers: Philip John Stokes, Secretary; Kenneth Charles Green [1945] Director/Business Consultant; Brian John Stanton [1978] Managing Director [New Zealander]; Philip John Stokes [1956] Finance Director

Green Breeze Ambient (UK) Ltd
Incorporated: 27 February 2016
Registered Office: 27 Old Gloucester Street, London, WC1N 3AX
Major Shareholder: Sio Peng Lam
Officers: Chan Va Lam [1966] Director [Portuguese]; Sio Peng Lam [1968] Director [Portuguese]

Green Essence Ltd
Incorporated: 30 May 2018
Registered Office: 7 Kings Avenue, Manchester, M8 5AS
Major Shareholder: Damian Makowski
Officers: Damian Makowski [1985] Director [Polish]

Green Guru Enterprices Ltd.
Incorporated: 9 May 2017
Registered Office: Dept 302, 43 Owston Road, Carcroft, Doncaster, S Yorks, DN6 8DA
Shareholders: Godwyn Joseph Orlando Roy Rollocks; Evert Charles Boom
Officers: Evert Charles Boom [1963] Director/Chief Operating Officer [Dutch]; Godwyn Joseph Orlando Roy Rollocks [1965] Director/Chief Executive Officer [Dutch]

Green Harmony Limited
Incorporated: 16 October 2015
Net Worth Deficit: £21,977 Total Assets: £9,939
Registered Office: 88 Crawford Street, London, W1H 2EJ
Shareholders: Daniela Skopalova; Martin Brian Kirsop
Officers: Martin Brian Kirsop [1967] Director; Daniela Skopalova [1969] Director

Green Jiva Ltd
Incorporated: 26 November 2015
Previous: Lilitu Ltd
Registered Office: 99 Heol Senni, Foxglove Meadows, Bettws, Newport, NP20 7GB
Shareholders: Jessica Grace Element; Andrew Christopher Hunter
Officers: Jessica Grace Element [1981] Director/R&D Software Technician; Andrew Christopher Hunter [1975] Director/R&D Software Technician

Green Ladies N.I Ltd
Incorporated: 19 September 2018
Registered Office: 48 Crawfordstown Road, Downpatrick, Co Down, BT30 8QA
Major Shareholder: Tracy Megoran
Officers: Tracy Megoran [1982] Director/Entrepreneur

Green Mass Limited
Incorporated: 14 January 2019
Registered Office: Flat 32, Adventures Court, 12 Newport Avenue, London, E14 2DN
Major Shareholder: Chunxiang Yang
Officers: Chunxiang Yang [1980] Director/Businessman [Chinese]

Green Merchandising Ltd
Incorporated: 31 August 2017
Registered Office: 2 Ditton Park Road, Slough, SL3 7JA
Major Shareholder: Durrenaz Eram
Officers: Durrenaz Eram [1974] Director

Green Sprouts Limited
Incorporated: 5 March 2012
Net Worth: £17,710 Total Assets: £36,480
Registered Office: 26 Church Street, Bishop's Stortford, Herts, CM23 2LY
Major Shareholder: Joanne Burke
Officers: Joanne Burke [1968] Director/Marketing Manager

Green World Spa Products Limited
Incorporated: 19 April 2012
Previous: NCH Supplies Limited
Net Worth: £7,400 Total Assets: £51,910
Registered Office: 7 Dover Road, Southport, Merseyside, PR8 4TF
Shareholders: John Wonta; Neil Paul Halsall
Officers: Neil Paul Halsall [1960] Director/Executive Sales Manager; John Wonta [1963] Director

Greenery Skincare Limited
Incorporated: 18 January 2019
Registered Office: 71-75 Shelton Street, London, WC2H 9JQ
Shareholders: Rhodri Andrew Ferrier; Simon Joseph Duffy
Officers: Rhodri Andrew Ferrier, Secretary; Simon Joseph Duffy [1976] Director; Rhodri Andrew Ferrier [1978] Director

The Greenfrog Soap Company Limited
Incorporated: 12 June 2014
Net Worth: £42,387 Total Assets: £86,916
Registered Office: 22 Stoneham Road, Hove, E Sussex, BN3 5HJ
Shareholders: Nicholas Bridger; Julie Bridger
Officers: Julie Bridger [1971] Director [French]; Nicholas Bridger [1970] Director

Greenleaf Luton Limited
Incorporated: 6 February 2018
Registered Office: Windsor House, 9-15 Adelaide Street, Luton, Beds, LU1 5BJ
Major Shareholder: Nazmul Hasan
Officers: Nazmul Hasan [1966] Director

Greenpol Distribution Ltd
Incorporated: 11 May 2017
Registered Office: 36 Fairlawn Close, Feltham, Middlesex, TW13 6LJ
Major Shareholder: Wojciech Pawel Olesiejuk
Officers: Wojciech Pawel Olesiejuk [1982] Director [Polish]

Greenwise Distribution Ltd
Incorporated: 14 May 2014
Net Worth Deficit: £50,073 *Total Assets:* £29,200
Registered Office: Unit 5 Progress Business Park, Progress Way, Croydon, Surrey, CR0 4XD
Major Shareholder: Chirag Pramod Patel
Officers: Ashita Patel, Secretary; Chirag Pramod Patel [1968] Director

Gridt Beauty Ltd
Incorporated: 22 March 2018
Registered Office: East Wing, Stuart House, St Johns Street, Peterborough, Cambs, PE1 5DD
Major Shareholder: Oludamilola Davies
Officers: Oludamilola Davies [1989] Director/Project Support Officer [Nigerian]

Grimas.co.uk Limited
Incorporated: 3 March 2014
Net Worth: £53,769 *Total Assets:* £70,477
Registered Office: 24 Pennywell Road, Edinburgh, EH4 4HD
Shareholders: Gerardus Johannes Van Huizen; Rutgerus Martines Maria Assendeleft
Officers: Rutgerus Martines Maria Assendelft, Secretary; Nicholas Safdar, Secretary; Rutgerus Martines Maria Assendelft [1952] Director [Dutch]; Gerardus Johannes Van Huizen [1978] Director [Dutch]

Grooming Galaxy Limited
Incorporated: 28 July 2016
Registered Office: Lower Ground Floor, 40 Bloomsbury Way, London, WC1A 2SE
Major Shareholder: Jason Rockyie Bissessur
Officers: Jason Rockyie Bissessur [1984] Director/Brand Consultant

Grossmith Limited
Incorporated: 23 February 2009
Net Worth Deficit: £436,710 *Total Assets:* £129,720
Registered Office: 6 Deanery Street, London, W1K 1BA
Parent: J Grossmith & Son Ltd
Officers: Amanda Brooke, Secretary; Amanda Jane Brooke [1955] Director; Simon Peter Brooke [1952] Director/Chartered Surveyor

GroundedBodyScrub Limited
Incorporated: 25 February 2015
Net Worth: £77,801 *Total Assets:* £171,097
Registered Office: Grounded Body Scrub Ltd, Unit 12a, Progress Road, Leigh on Sea, Essex, SS9 5PR
Shareholders: Tasha Harris; Lloyd Alexander Hazell
Officers: Tasha Harris, Secretary; Lloyd Hazell, Secretary; Tasha Harris [1990] Director/Businesswoman; Lloyd Hazell [1989] Director/Music Producer

Gruhme UK Limited
Incorporated: 5 February 2013
Net Worth Deficit: £31,340 *Total Assets:* £21,070
Registered Office: International House, 142 Cromwell Road, Kensington, London, SW7 4EF
Major Shareholder: Robert Spencer Hallmark
Officers: Robert Spencer Hallmark [1981] Director

GS Fragrances Limited
Incorporated: 3 March 2016
Net Worth: £1,420 *Total Assets:* £1,530
Registered Office: 75 Whitley Court Road, Quinton, Birmingham, B32 1EZ
Major Shareholder: Gurmukh Singh Guru
Officers: Gurmukh Singh Guru [1995] Director/Entrepreneur

GS7 IT Consultants Ltd
Incorporated: 19 August 2016
Registered Office: 547 Melton Road, Leicester, LE4 7SJ
Major Shareholder: Pranav Mehta
Officers: Pranavkumar Satishchandra Mehta, Secretary; Pranavkumar Satishchandra Mehta [1979] Director/Self Employed

Guerison Skin Solutions Ltd
Incorporated: 12 November 2018
Registered Office: 14 Turnberry, Bolton, Lancs, BL3 4XJ
Shareholders: Mohammad Aadam Dad; Beverley Ann Higham
Officers: Mohammad Aadam Dad [1999] Director; Beverley Ann Higham [1964] Director/Lecturer

Guerlain Limited
Incorporated: 8 August 1936 *Employees:* 244
Net Worth: £2,395,421 *Total Assets:* £7,892,760
Registered Office: 6th Floor, United Kingdom House, 180 Oxford Street, London, W1D 1AB
Parent: LVMH Moet Hennessy Louis Vuitton
Officers: Loic Pierre Marie Henriot, Secretary; Stephane Auge [1972] International Director [French]; Laurent Boillot [1964] Director [French]; Loic Pierre Marie Henriot [1978] Director [French]; Brian John Stanton [1978] Director [New Zealander]

Guess Her Secret Limited
Incorporated: 13 June 2012
Net Worth: £8,184 *Total Assets:* £30,916
Registered Office: Doshi Accountants Ltd, 6th Floor, Amp House, Dingwall Road, Croydon, Surrey, CR0 2LX
Major Shareholder: Choi Yung Hung
Officers: Choi Yung Hung [1975] Director

Guestproud Ltd
Incorporated: 11 May 2018
Registered Office: c/o Applingua Ltd, 210 The Creative Quarter, Morgan Arcade, Cardiff, CF10 1AF
Major Shareholder: Robert John Michael Lo Bue
Officers: Robert John Michael Lo Bue [1986] Director [British/Italian]

Guilty Fashion Ltd
Incorporated: 9 January 2018
Registered Office: Flat 4, Hortensia Road, London, SW10 0FU
Major Shareholder: Jose Maria Soares Bento
Officers: Jose Maria Soares Bento [1957] Director [Portuguese]

Guinot-Mary Cohr UK Limited
Incorporated: 2 October 1972 *Employees:* 73
Net Worth: £7,594,280 *Total Assets:* £9,200,507
Registered Office: The Clock House, High Street, Ascot, Berks, SL5 7HU
Parent: Guinot SAS
Officers: Frederic Charo, Secretary; Christopher Derek Gillam [1955] Director; Dr. Jean Daniel Dominique Mondin [1947] Director/Company President [French]

Gulz Cosmetics Ltd
Incorporated: 3 December 2018
Registered Office: 11 High Street, Wanstead, London, E11 1QF
Major Shareholder: Somia Javed
Officers: Somia Javed [1993] Director [French]

GVM Long Life Formula UK Ltd
Incorporated: 2 July 2018
Registered Office: 37-38 Long Acre, London, WC2E 9JT
Officers: Lucia Magnani [1960] Director [Italian]; Carlo Giuseppe Montenovesi [1953] Director [Italian]; Luca Vegetti [1982] Director [Italian]

Gxskin Limited
Incorporated: 28 January 2019
Registered Office: Thistledown House, 6 Periwood Crescent, Perivale, Greenford, Middlesex, UB6 7FL
Major Shareholder: Gawan Ghabat
Officers: Gawan Ghabat [1993] Director/Aesthetic Practitioner [Dutch]

Gymbar Limited
Incorporated: 7 February 2013
Registered Office: 34 Charlotte Street, Manchester, M1 4FD
Officers: Mario Pavlou [1970] Director

H & B Supplies Limited
Incorporated: 6 May 1998 *Employees:* 43
Net Worth: £6,999,259 *Total Assets:* £13,055,914
Registered Office: Unit D1-D4 Capital Point, Capital Business Park, Parkway, Cardiff, CF3 2PY
Shareholders: Alun John Glasson; Susanne Elizabeth Glasson
Officers: Alun John Glasson, Secretary/Director; Alun John Glasson [1961] Director; James Bernard Glasson [1971] Director; Susanne Elizabeth Glasson [1961] Director

H & R Cosmetics Ltd
Incorporated: 2 January 2018
Registered Office: 46 Arkley Crescent, Hartlepool, Cleveland, TS24 9HE
Officers: Malik Ahsan Raza [1978] Director/Owner [Pakistani]

H.H.L.Brothers Limited
Incorporated: 14 September 2018
Registered Office: 16 Stephen Street, Barrow in Furness, Cumbria, LA14 1BY
Major Shareholder: Shenglong Liu
Officers: Shenglong Liu [1989] Director [Chinese]

H07CNN Limited
Incorporated: 27 December 2018
Registered Office: 12 Darenth Mill Lane, Dartford, Kent, DA2 7BF
Major Shareholder: Henrietta Nartey
Officers: Henrietta Nartey [1984] Director [Ghanaian]

H2 World Health and Beauty Company Ltd
Incorporated: 8 August 2018
Registered Office: 85 Great Portland Street, London, W1W 7LT
Major Shareholder: David Marsalek
Officers: David Marsalek [1981] Director [Czech]

H2K Limited
Incorporated: 29 September 2000 *Employees:* 5
Net Worth: £323,110 *Total Assets:* £389,800
Registered Office: 31 Montpellier Parade, Harrogate, N Yorks, HG1 2TG
Major Shareholder: Hazel Christine Barry
Officers: Christine Barrett, Secretary; Hazel Christine Barry [1975] Managing Director

HA Distribution Limited
Incorporated: 16 June 2017
Registered Office: 27 Belltrees Grove, London, SW16 2HZ
Shareholders: Haris Tariq Butt; Annam Tariq Butt
Officers: Annam Tariq Butt [1988] Director; Haris Tariq Butt [1993] Director

Ha-Derma Limited
Incorporated: 10 July 2015 *Employees:* 3
Net Worth: £328 *Total Assets:* £700,619
Registered Office: 215 Hampstead House, 176 Finchley Road, London, NW3 6BT
Shareholders: Iveta Vinklerova; Hana Te Reo
Officers: Hana Te Reo [1976] Director [Czech]; Iveta Vinklerova [1978] Director [Slovak]

HABM Ltd
Incorporated: 17 March 2015
Net Worth: £10,988 *Total Assets:* £116,597
Registered Office: Warren Place, Birch Vale, Cobham, Surrey, KT11 2PX
Major Shareholder: Mike Escott
Officers: Mike Escott [1954] Director/Sales

Hadley and Reed Ltd
Incorporated: 6 July 2017
Registered Office: 2 Lawrence Avenue, Eastwood, Nottingham, NG16 3LD
Officers: Emma Louise Maxfield Skermer [1983] Director; Craig John Taylor [1975] Director

Hahydra Technologies Ltd
Incorporated: 25 April 2013
Registered Office: 77 High Street, Littlehampton, W Sussex, BN17 5AG
Major Shareholder: Istvan Novak
Officers: Istvan Novak [1976] Director [Hungarian]

The Hair & Cosmetic Company Limited
Incorporated: 22 October 2004 *Employees:* 1
Net Worth Deficit: £44,328 *Total Assets:* £3,323
Registered Office: Accountancy House, 90 Walworth Road, London, SE1 6SW
Major Shareholder: Mehboob Mohammed Hussein Abdulla
Officers: Mehboob Mohammed Hussein Abdulla [1956] Director

Hair & Skin Care Ltd
Incorporated: 10 August 2018
Registered Office: 51 Olympic Crescent, Brooklands, Milton Keynes, Bucks, MK10 7LE
Major Shareholder: Tahir Qayyum
Officers: Tahir Qayyum [1981] Director

Hair and Cosmetics Wholesale Ltd
Incorporated: 24 November 2017
Registered Office: 27 Brushfield Street, Nottingham, NG7 5LL
Major Shareholder: Ami Kalpitkumar Patel
Officers: Ami Kalpitkumar Patel [1980] Director [Indian]

Hair Contrast UK Limited
Incorporated: 17 October 2018
Registered Office: 28 West Street, Dunstable, Beds, LU6 1TA
Shareholder: Jon Walker
Officers: Tracey Walker, Secretary; Jon Walker [1967] Director

Hair Cosmetics Limited
Incorporated: 7 October 1971
Net Worth: £273,770 *Total Assets:* £368,340
Registered Office: 107-109 Cross Street, Sale, Cheshire, M33 7JN
Shareholders: Alan Butler Ward; Jonathan Mark Ward
Officers: Jonathan Mark Ward, Secretary; Alan Butler Ward [1938] Managing Director; Jonathan Mark Ward [1968] Director/Manager

Hair Dressing Supplies Lincoln Ltd
Incorporated: 6 June 2016 *Employees:* 16
Net Worth: £60,774 *Total Assets:* £452,800
Registered Office: 12 Crofton Drive, Allenby Trading Estate, Lincoln, LN3 4NR
Major Shareholder: Michael Brian Jones
Officers: Michael Brian Jones [1985] Director

Hair Fantastic Retail Limited
Incorporated: 24 February 2012
Net Worth Deficit: £7,930 *Total Assets:* £38,530
Registered Office: Sidings House, Sidings Court, Lakeside, Doncaster, S Yorks, DN4 5NU
Shareholders: Christopher John Mather; Deborah Tracy Denise Mather
Officers: Christopher John Mather [1957] Director; Deborah Tracy Denise Mather [1967] Director

Hair for Men Products Ltd
Incorporated: 21 November 2017
Registered Office: Unit 007 Basepoint Business Centre, 377-399 London Road, Camberley, Surrey, GU15 3HL
Officers: Colin Perkins [1982] Director

Hair from India Limited
Incorporated: 28 January 2015
Net Worth: £467 *Total Assets:* £18,551
Registered Office: 30 Market Place, Belper, Derbys, DE56 1FZ
Major Shareholder: Stephen Milward
Officers: Stephen Milward [1969] Director/Building Contractor

Hair North East Limited
Incorporated: 6 October 2009 *Employees:* 6
Net Worth: £3,767 *Total Assets:* £195,220
Registered Office: Bainbridge House, 379 Stamfordham Road, Westerhope, Newcastle upon Tyne, NE5 2LH
Shareholders: Thomas Wilson; Jacqueline Hilda Wilson
Officers: Jacqueline Hilda Wilson [1966] Director; Thomas Wilson [1965] Director

Hair Operating Products Limited
Incorporated: 24 April 2007 *Employees:* 2
Net Worth: £19,674 *Total Assets:* £31,211
Registered Office: 9 Wheatcroft Avenue, Fence, Burnley, Lancs, BB12 9QL
Shareholders: Darren Helliwell; Janet Elizabeth Helliwell
Officers: Janet Elizabeth Helliwell, Secretary; Darren Helliwell [1969] Sales Director; Janet Elizabeth Helliwell [1968] Director/Office Manager

Hair Ornaments UK Limited
Incorporated: 21 April 2008
Net Worth: £373,346 *Total Assets:* £788,598
Registered Office: 10 Thames Road, Barking, Essex, IG11 0HZ
Major Shareholder: Abdul Majeed
Officers: Abdul Majeed, Secretary; Abdul Majeed [1965] Director/Businessman

Hair Passion Limited
Incorporated: 29 January 2019
Registered Office: 1146 High Road, London, N20 0RA
Major Shareholder: Giuseppe Piccirilo
Officers: Giuseppe Piccirilo [1954] Director [Italian]

Hair There & Everywhere Hair & Beauty Ltd
Incorporated: 1 October 2016
Net Worth: £1,007 *Total Assets:* £33,779
Registered Office: 11 Shanklin Close, Cheshunt, Waltham Cross, Herts, EN7 6HF
Officers: Giovanna Vincenza Lanza [1969] Director

The Hair Wardrobe Ltd
Incorporated: 21 January 2019
Registered Office: 25 Orde Wingate Way, Stockton on Tees, Cleveland, TS19 0GA
Officers: Sarah Birch [1986] Director

Haircare of Sweden Ltd
Incorporated: 25 February 2009
Net Worth: £10,740 *Total Assets:* £99,880
Registered Office: Unit 2, 3a Wellington Road, Bidford on Avon, Warwicks, B50 4JH
Major Shareholder: Jan Edward Ernstberger
Officers: Steven Francis Langley, Secretary; Jan Edward Ernstberger [1947] Director/Chief Executive [Swedish]

Hairco Hair & Beauty Ltd
Incorporated: 23 July 2015
Net Worth: £1,262 *Total Assets:* £33,601
Registered Office: 35 Grafton Way, London, W1T 5DB
Major Shareholder: Christopher Nicholas Nicolaou
Officers: Christopher Nicholas Nicolaou [1983] Director

Haircosmetics (Sunderland) Limited
Incorporated: 31 January 2012
Net Worth: £6,407 *Total Assets:* £105,421
Registered Office: Queens Court Business Centre, Carrmere Road, Leechmere Industrial Estate, Sunderland, Tyne & Wear, SR2 9TW
Parent: Aston and Fincher Limited
Officers: Oliver James Markham Fincher [1970] Director/Wholesale; David St. John Winnington [1967] Director

Hairdye Direct Limited
Incorporated: 21 November 2016
Registered Office: 132 High Street, Walsall, W Midlands, WS3 2DG
Major Shareholder: Craig Johnson
Officers: Craig Johnson [1978] Director/Accountant

Hairenvy Boutique Limited
Incorporated: 10 April 2018
Registered Office: 71 Tempest Street, Wolverhampton, W Midlands, WV2 1AA
Major Shareholder: Serena Asaggar
Officers: Serena Asaggar [1984] Managing Director

Hairganic Limited
Incorporated: 6 June 2009
Registered Office: 509 Whitton Avenue West, Greenford, Middlesex, UB6 0DY
Officers: Colin Powell [1968] Director

Hairshine UK Ltd
Incorporated: 23 September 2008
Net Worth: £1,951 *Total Assets:* £41,111
Registered Office: 1 Northolt Avenue, South Ruislip, Hillingdon, Middlesex, HA4 6SS
Major Shareholder: Robson Gongalves Lopes
Officers: Adriana Miniguini Falaguasta Lopes, Secretary; Robson Goncalves Lopes [1965] Director/Commercial Manager

Hairways (Hair & Beauty) Limited
Incorporated: 25 February 1985 *Employees:* 64
Net Worth: £2,206,635 *Total Assets:* £2,952,589
Registered Office: Units 24-25 Yardley Business Park, Luckyn Lane, Pipps Hill, Basildon, Essex, SS14 3GL
Major Shareholder: Christopher Diaper
Officers: Christopher Diaper, Secretary; Christopher Diaper [1961] Director; John Edward Diaper [1965] Executive Director; Julie Diaper [1962] Director

Hairways 77 Limited
Incorporated: 19 May 2003
Net Worth: £127,756 *Total Assets:* £200,438
Registered Office: Bridge House, 25 Fiddlebridge Lane, Hatfield, Herts, AL10 0SP
Major Shareholder: Roger Malcolm Blow
Officers: Nicholas Alexander Blow, Secretary; Nicholas Alexander Blow [1968] Director; Roger Malcolm Blow [1945] Director; Angela Victoria Carman [1971] Director

Hairways Direct Limited
Incorporated: 24 November 2000
Net Worth: £100 *Total Assets:* £100
Registered Office: Units 24 & 25 Yardley Business Park, Luckyn Lane, Pipps Hill, Basildon, Essex, SS14 3GL
Major Shareholder: Christopher Diaper
Officers: Christopher Diaper, Secretary; Christopher Diaper [1961] Director; John Edward Diaper [1965] Director

Hairya Ltd
Incorporated: 11 February 2019
Registered Office: 20-22 Wenlock Road, London, N1 7GU
Major Shareholder: Stefano Robba
Officers: Dr Stefano Robba [1969] Director/Business Development Consultant [Italian]

Halal Beauty Company Ltd
Incorporated: 29 August 2018
Registered Office: 1 Holburn Road, Aberdeen, AB10 6EY
Shareholders: Chas Shiekh; Rajia Khatun
Officers: Rajia Khatun [1978] Property Director

The Halal Cosmetics Company Limited
Incorporated: 5 February 2013
Net Worth: £2,100 *Total Assets:* £12,190
Registered Office: Unit E2, Tower Business Park, Blackburn Interchange, Darwen, Lancs, BB3 0DG
Shareholders: JH Nisiac Limited; Salma Chaudhry
Officers: Salma Chaudhry [1967] Director

Haltrade UK Ltd
Incorporated: 2 October 2017
Registered Office: Unit 19 Observatory Mall, Deen, High Street, Slough, Berks, SL1 1LE
Shareholders: Zahid Sharif Butt; Tengku Rozidar
Officers: Zahid Sharif Butt [1976] Director; Maximiliana Theresia Henrica Hendrickx-Butt [1982] Director and Company Secretary [Dutch]; Tengku Rozidar [1968] Director [Malaysian]

Hamiltons of Canterbury Limited
Incorporated: 24 May 2017
Registered Office: 49 The Drive, Hove, E Sussex, BN3 3JE
Major Shareholder: Max Richard Leslie Burton
Officers: Max Richard Leslie Burton, Secretary; Max Richard Leslie Burton [1950] Director

Hamon Concepts Limited
Incorporated: 31 August 2016
Net Worth: £10 *Total Assets:* £7,022
Registered Office: 85 Great Portland Street, London, W1W 7LT
Officers: Corentin Jacques Octave Hamon [1984] Director/Founder/Owner [French]

Hampton Brands Limited
Incorporated: 19 March 2008
Net Worth: £230,000 *Total Assets:* £1,090,000
Registered Office: 169 Waverley Avenue, Twickenham, Middlesex, TW2 6DJ
Major Shareholder: Sujith Nayanapriya Wijesena
Officers: Samangi Sudarshani Somapala, Secretary; Sujith Nayanapriya Wijesena [1968] Director

Hanana Traders Ltd
Incorporated: 24 October 2017
Registered Office: 3 Willingdon Road, London, N22 6SG
Officers: Mohammad Shawood Rujbally [1967] Director [Mauritian]

Hanfan (UK) Limited
Incorporated: 28 November 2006
Net Worth: £3,239 *Total Assets:* £42,412
Registered Office: 136 Northenden Road, Sale, Cheshire, M33 3HE
Officers: Ying Lu, Secretary; Sheng Li Zou [1967] Director

Philip Hansard Limited
Incorporated: 16 September 2015
Net Worth: £1,406 *Total Assets:* £4,133
Registered Office: Philip Hansard Limited, 86-90 Paul Street, London, EC2A 4NE
Officers: Jonas Survila [1986] Director/Sales [Estonian]

Hansraj House Limited
Incorporated: 22 November 2017
Registered Office: Manley Chartered Accountants, 696 Yardley Wood Road, Birmingham, B13 0HY
Major Shareholder: Ali Jawad
Officers: Ali Jawad [1975] Director [Pakistani]

Happy Beauty Life Ltd
Incorporated: 15 February 2018
Registered Office: 24 Spring Pool, Warwick, CV34 4UR
Major Shareholder: Zuheir Elsheikh
Officers: Zuheir Elsheikh [1966] Director

Happy Carrot Skincare Ltd
Incorporated: 31 July 2018
Registered Office: 71-75 Shelton Street, Covent Garden, London, WC2H 9JQ
Major Shareholder: Victoria Carpenter
Officers: Victoria Carpenter [1979] Director/Teacher

Haresgraces Limited
Incorporated: 10 November 1993 Employees: 3
Previous: Perfume Heaven Limited
Net Worth: £698 Total Assets: £43,361
Registered Office: 9 Carlton, Elloughton, E Yorks, HU15 1FF
Shareholder: Sharon Muriel Taylor
Officers: Sharon Muriel Taylor, Secretary; Abigail Deborah Marie Taylor [1988] Director; Brittany Dominique Taylor [1992] Director; Sharon Muriel Taylor [1962] Director/Retailer

The Harley Street Fulfilment Company Limited
Incorporated: 14 August 2012 Employees: 2
Net Worth Deficit: £3,105 Total Assets: £113,792
Registered Office: 14a Burnham Business Park, Springfield Road, Burnham on Crouch, Essex, CM0 8TE
Shareholders: Anne Theresa Gray; Colin Gray
Officers: Anne Theresa Gray [1956] Director/Manager

Harmonious Brown Limited
Incorporated: 12 June 2017
Registered Office: Suite 115, Challenge House Business Centre, 616 Mitcham Road, Croydon, Surrey, CR0 3AA
Major Shareholder: Chantelle Brown
Officers: Chantelle Brown [1987] Creative Director

Harpar Grace International Ltd
Incorporated: 8 April 2013 Employees: 8
Net Worth: £205,839 Total Assets: £519,252
Registered Office: Highland House, Mayflower Close, Chandler's Ford, Hants, SO53 4AR
Major Shareholder: Alana Marie Chalmers
Officers: Alana Marie Chalmers [1982] Director; Cheryl Lynn Martin [1980] Commercial Director

David Hart (Santo) Limited
Incorporated: 11 February 2003 Employees: 2
Net Worth: £298,167 Total Assets: £498,006
Registered Office: 213 St John Street, London, EC1V 4LY
Parent: Allwarehouse and Logistics Limited
Officers: Jagdeesh Singh Cheema [1977] Director/Pharmacist; Kirandeep Singh Cheema [1985] Director

Harvey Pharma Ltd
Incorporated: 10 June 2014
Net Worth: £496,890 Total Assets: £855,370
Registered Office: Unit 6 Carbrook Business Park, Dunlop Street, Sheffield, S9 2HR
Shareholders: Jeremiah Nguru Kiiru; Mercy Wambui Nguru
Officers: Mercy Wambui Nguru, Secretary; Jeremiah Nguru Kiiru [1972] Director/Pharmacist

Has To Be Ltd
Incorporated: 19 December 2017
Registered Office: 131 Ashford Road, Feltham, Middlesex, TW13 4RU
Major Shareholder: Hasan Akar
Officers: Hasan Akar [1994] Director

Hasanah Global Ltd
Incorporated: 25 September 2018
Registered Office: 39 Gladys Road, Birmingham, B25 8BX
Shareholders: Muhammad Umair Yasir; Mohammad Shahid Ullah
Officers: Mohammad Shahid Ullah [1977] Director; Muhammad Umair Yasir [1987] Director [Pakistani]

Hava Traders Limited
Incorporated: 24 April 2018
Registered Office: 1a Hawthorn Avenue, Batley, W Yorks, WF17 7BT
Officers: Hava Dervisevic [1971] Director

Haybae Cosmetics Ltd
Incorporated: 4 January 2018
Registered Office: 20-22 Wenlock Road, London, N1 7GU
Major Shareholder: Mikhaila Antoinette Russell
Officers: Mikhaila Antoinette Russell [1986] Director/Sales Broker

Haych Cosmetics Limited
Incorporated: 2 December 2016
Net Worth Deficit: £8,585 Total Assets: £45,429
Registered Office: Unit 5 Meadowcroft Mill, Bury Road, Bamford, Rochdale, Lancs, OL11 4AU
Major Shareholder: Joy Elizabeth Howieson
Officers: Kenneth Howieson, Secretary; Joy Elizabeth Howieson [1990] Director

Hazellbrook Limited
Incorporated: 25 November 2016
Net Worth Deficit: £765 Total Assets: £5,410
Registered Office: c/o Peter Fivey, 153 Churchill Road, Drumreask, Derrygonnelly, Co Fermanagh, BT93 6HL
Shareholders: Peter Fivey; Brendan McLoughlin
Officers: Peter Fivey [1974] Director [Irish]; Brendan McLoughlin [1975] Director [Irish]

HBD International Limited
Incorporated: 23 August 2018
Registered Office: Northside House, Mount Pleasant, Barnet, Herts, EN4 9EE
Major Shareholder: Paul Mason
Officers: Ian Randall, Secretary; Daniel Luke Mason [1979] Director; Paul Mason [1943] Director

HBDeadSea-UK.Com Limited
Incorporated: 9 March 2018
Registered Office: 6 Belvedere Business Park, Crabtree Manorway South, Belvedere, Kent, DA17 6AH
Major Shareholder: Joel Monger
Officers: Joel Monger, Secretary; Joel Monger [1958] Managing Director

HCT Beauty Ltd
Incorporated: 23 March 2012
Net Worth: £145,520 Total Assets: £145,520
Registered Office: Pepys House, 84-86 The Chase, Clapham, London, SW4 0NF
Parent: HCT Europe Limited
Officers: Richard Flook, Secretary; Richard Flook [1960] Director

HCT Europe Limited
Incorporated: 30 November 1987
Net Worth: £9,660,000 Total Assets: £24,520,000
Registered Office: Pepys Court, 84-86 The Chase, Clapham, London, SW4 0NF
Major Shareholder: Clare Rose Thorpe
Officers: Richard Flook, Secretary; Mohammed Mohsin Asaria [1974] Director; Richard Flook [1960] Director

HD Cosmetics Ltd
Incorporated: 16 May 2018
Registered Office: 17 Lawton Road, Alsager, Cheshire, ST7 2AA
Shareholders: Daniel Grimes; Haylee Davies
Officers: Haylee Davies [1992] Director; Daniel Grimes [1990] Director

HDDirect Limited
Incorporated: 28 April 2015
Net Worth: £4,211 Total Assets: £15,000
Registered Office: 36 Bridge Street, Newbridge, Edinburgh, EH28 8SH
Officers: Andrew Clelland [1965] Director

HE Products Ltd
Incorporated: 13 August 2018
Registered Office: 71-75 Shelton Street, London, WC2H 9JQ
Officers: Oleur Rashid, Secretary; Nadir Choudhury [1971] Director; Oleur Rashid [1975] Director; Abeda Sheikh [1970] Director

He-Shi Enterprises Ltd
Incorporated: 6 December 2006
Net Worth: £469,761 Total Assets: £804,458
Registered Office: 6a Ballykeigle Road, Comber, Co Down, BT23 5SD
Shareholder: Hilary McMuray
Officers: Hilary Hanna McMurray, Secretary; Colin Coffey [1958] Director; Shelley Martin [1981] Director/Beauty Products; Hilary Hanna McMurray [1957] Director/Beauty Products; William James McMurray [1953] Director/Beauty Products; Marette Mooney [1976] Sales & Marketing Director [Irish]

Headissimo Limited
Incorporated: 12 September 1975
Previous: European Banking Nominees Limited
Registered Office: 153 Eastern Esplanade, Canvey Island, Essex, SS8 7HY
Major Shareholder: Stefanie Seyda
Officers: Paul Rudolf Bastin [1965] Director/Securities Officer; Marc Ulrich Goeke [1966] Director [German]; Stefanie Seyda [1968] Director [German]

Headlines (Hair & Beauty Supplies) Limited
Incorporated: 4 December 1990 Employees: 5
Net Worth: £2,570,768 Total Assets: £3,299,255
Registered Office: Unit 4 Space Business Centre, Abbey Road, Park Royal, London, NW10 7SU
Major Shareholder: David Arnold Stennett
Officers: Orlean Stennett, Secretary; David Arnold Stennett [1960] Sales Director

Headrocka Ltd
Incorporated: 26 October 2018
Registered Office: 72 Heyworth Road, Leicester, LE3 2DB
Major Shareholder: Nathan Busby
Officers: Nathan Busby [1987] Director

Health Future Limited
Incorporated: 29 October 2018
Registered Office: 23 Thirlington Close, Newcastle upon Tyne, NE5 4BN
Officers: Yahya Muftah Abdulhamid, Secretary; Yahya Muftah Abdulhamid [1998] Director/Businessman

Health-Beauty Ltd
Incorporated: 7 January 2019
Registered Office: 2 Norwich Road, London, E7 9JH
Major Shareholder: Jahidul Hoque
Officers: Jahidul Hoque [1993] Director

Healthcare Procurement Services Ltd
Incorporated: 20 May 2004 Employees: 1
Net Worth: £361,804 Total Assets: £411,847
Registered Office: Suite 310F, Sterling House, Langston Road, Loughton, Essex, IG10 3TS
Major Shareholder: David John Tipp
Officers: Christopher James Pace [1956] Director

Healthcare Wholesale Ltd
Incorporated: 23 February 2018
Registered Office: Suite M, No 2 The Courtyard, Earl Road, Stanley Green, Cheadle Hulme, Cheadle, Cheshire, SK8 6GN
Parent: Pharmacy Care Plus Limited
Officers: Dr Robert George Andrew [1961] Director; Michael Niblock [1981] Director; Dr Devendra Shah [1967] Director

Healtholozy UK Limited
Incorporated: 7 June 2017
Registered Office: 4 New Street, Daventry, Northants, NN11 4BU
Major Shareholder: Hafiz Ahmed
Officers: Hafiz Ahmed, Secretary; Hafiz Ahmed [1979] Director

Healthpoint Limited
Incorporated: 22 February 1996 Employees: 17
Net Worth: £3,472,170 Total Assets: £6,661,664
Registered Office: 11 Darwin Court, Blackpool Technology Park, Blackpool, Lancs, FY2 0JN
Shareholder: Robin Neil Womersley
Officers: Amanda Parkinson [1983] Director; Michael Ryan [1965] Finance Director; Robert William Waling [1956] Director; Robin Neil Womersley [1971] Director

The Heath Consumables Ltd
Incorporated: 2 February 2010
Net Worth Deficit: £9,237 Total Assets: £13,905
Registered Office: 28 School Road, Handforth, Wilmslow, Cheshire, SK9 3EZ
Officers: Hayley Rebecca Powell [1974] Director/Businesswoman

Heavenly Body Ltd
Incorporated: 27 April 2018
Registered Office: 104 Ashley Crescent, London, SW11 5QY
Shareholders: Selina Esho; Leanne Davis
Officers: Selina Esho, Secretary; Leanne Davis [1982] Director; Selina Esho [1982] Director

Heavenly Fragrance (UK) Limited
Incorporated: 12 August 2010
Registered Office: Dalton House, 60 Windsor Avenue, London, SW19 2RR
Major Shareholder: Titty Pappachen Thomas
Officers: Titty Pappachen Thomas [1974] Director/Engineer [Indian]

Heavenly Riches Limited
Incorporated: 1 November 2016
Net Worth Deficit: £24,040 Total Assets: £27,120
Registered Office: East End Towers, Upper Thomas Street, Birmingham, B6 5AD
Shareholders: Helen Rafie; Paul Deep Wouhra
Officers: Helen Rafie [1983] Director [Iranian]

Hedgerow Medicine Chest Ltd
Incorporated: 20 December 2018
Registered Office: 43 Water Street, Llanllechid, Gwynedd, LL57 3EU
Major Shareholder: Margaret Doherty
Officers: Margaret Doherty [1964] Director/Natural Cosmetic Formulation

Heir & Grace Ltd
Incorporated: 9 March 2015
Net Worth Deficit: £15,100 *Total Assets:* £4,500
Registered Office: 33 Clifton Rise, Windsor, Berks, SL4 5SX
Shareholders: Mark Edward Evans; Anna Evans
Officers: Mark Edward Evans [1984] Director/Marketing

Hekiti Cosmetics Ltd
Incorporated: 5 March 2018
Registered Office: 75D Landor Road, London, SW9 9RT
Major Shareholder: Jess Castillian
Officers: Jessica Castillian [1991] Director [French]; James Kirkman [1994] Director

Helen Gel Colour Ltd
Incorporated: 16 August 2018
Registered Office: 9 Were Close, Warminster, Wilts, BA12 8TB
Major Shareholder: Xeng Su Lui
Officers: Xeng Su Lui [1966] Director/Nail Technician

Helia-D UK Ltd
Incorporated: 11 April 2018
Registered Office: 77 High Street, Littlehampton, W Sussex, BN17 5AG
Major Shareholder: Peter Miklos Budahazy
Officers: Peter Miklos Budahazy [1961] Director [Hungarian]

Hello Dame London Ltd
Incorporated: 13 November 2018
Registered Office: 71-75 Shelton Street, London, WC2H 9JQ
Major Shareholder: Zoe St Pierre
Officers: Zoe St Pierre [1967] Director

Hemangini Limited
Incorporated: 23 August 2018
Registered Office: First Floor, Black Country House, Rounds Green Road, Oldbury, W Midlands, B69 2DG
Major Shareholder: Hemangini Mali
Officers: Hemangini Mali [1972] Director

Hemo Bioscience Ltd
Incorporated: 6 July 2017
Registered Office: 6 St Colman's Park, Newry, Co Down, BT34 2BX
Major Shareholder: David Leppinen
Officers: Dr David Leppinen [1968] Director/Businessman

Hemp Earth Ltd
Incorporated: 3 June 2016
Registered Office: 3rd Floor, 207 Regent Street, London, W1B 3HH
Shareholders: Richard McDonald Hawker; Nina Leora Wainman
Officers: Richard McDonald Hawker [1988] Director [New Zealander]; Nina Leora Wainman [1987] Director [South African]

Hempia Limited
Incorporated: 24 October 2018
Registered Office: 3 Milfort Green, Banbridge, Co Down, BT32 4NX
Major Shareholder: Ilja Matvejevs
Officers: Ilja Matvejevs, Secretary; Ilja Matvejevs [1986] Director/Compliance Identification Officer [Latvian]

Hempo Logical International Ltd
Incorporated: 3 May 2018
Registered Office: Kemp House, 160 City Road, London, EC1V 2NX
Major Shareholder: Peter Launsky
Officers: Peter Launsky [1971] Director [Austrian]

Hemsley James Cosmetics Limited
Incorporated: 28 November 2017
Registered Office: 69 Debdale Way, Mansfield Woodhouse, Mansfield, Notts, NG19 7NR
Major Shareholder: Joe Daniel Hemsley
Officers: Michael Elliott [1970] Director; Joe Daniel Hemsley [1993] Director

Camilla Hepper Sales Limited
Incorporated: 31 January 1989
Registered Office: 4 St Mary's Arcade, Wallingford, Oxon, OX10 0EY
Officers: Richard Montague Rowse [1948] Director

Hera Beauty Ltd
Incorporated: 5 April 2011 *Employees:* 5
Net Worth: £10,314 *Total Assets:* £56,358
Registered Office: 4 Fairweather Court, Peterborough, Cambs, PE1 5UN
Shareholders: Kathryn Ruth Kennedy; Andrew Martin Kennedy
Officers: Kathryn Ruth Kennedy, Secretary; Andrew Martin Kennedy [1980] Director [Irish]

Herb Stuff Limited
Incorporated: 26 March 2018
Registered Office: 4 Mannville Terrace, Bradford, BD7 1BA
Shareholder: Navid Hanif
Officers: Navid Hanif [1984] Director

Herb U.K. Limited
Incorporated: 7 March 1990 *Employees:* 57
Net Worth: £1,407,075 *Total Assets:* £2,917,670
Registered Office: 310 Ampress Lane, Ampress Park, Lymington, Hants, SO41 8JX
Parent: Herb U.K. (Holdings) Limited
Officers: Ian Bishop [1967] Director; Mark D'Arcy [1975] Director; Raoul John Perfitt [1966] Managing Director

Herba Skincare Limited
Incorporated: 11 January 2016 *Employees:* 1
Net Worth Deficit: £4,289 *Total Assets:* £2,679
Registered Office: AJP Business Centre, 152-154 Coles Green Road, London, NW2 7HD
Officers: Peter De-Bique [1968] Director/Chartered Surveyor

Herbal Essentials UK Limited
Incorporated: 8 December 2017
Registered Office: 6th Floor, One London Wall, London, EC2Y 5EB
Officers: Abbas Rahimtoola [1966] Director; Aly Rahimtoola [1970] Director

Herbal Hakeem Ltd
Incorporated: 13 August 2014
Net Worth Deficit: £83 *Total Assets:* £316
Registered Office: Tanglewood, Pill Road, Abbots Leigh, Bristol, BS8 3RF
Shareholders: Naeem Ghafoor; Smara Ghafoor
Officers: Naeem Ghafoor [1965] Director; Smara Ghafoor [1967] Director/Manager

Herbaleva Ltd
Incorporated: 16 May 2017
Registered Office: Flat D, 290 Dollis Hill Lane, London, NW2 6HH
Major Shareholder: Abdelrahman Traboulssi Barake
Officers: Abdelrahman Traboulssi Barake, Secretary; Abdelrahman Traboulssi Barake [1968] Director [Swedish]

Herbalise Limited
Incorporated: 23 October 2018
Registered Office: 71-75 Shelton Street, London, WC2H 9JQ
Major Shareholder: Yolande Maria Nadine Newton
Officers: Yolande Maria Nadine Newton [1982] Director

Herbline U.K. Limited
Incorporated: 17 September 2008
Registered Office: 54 Hillbury Avenue, Harrow, Middlesex, HA3 8EW
Officers: George Myrants, Secretary; Arjun Khanna [1974] Director [Indian]

Herc Ltd.
Incorporated: 4 February 2006
Net Worth Deficit: £20,790 *Total Assets:* £97,450
Registered Office: Lewis House, Great Chesterford Court, Great Chesterford, Essex, CB10 1PF
Major Shareholder: Arun Dev Kumar
Officers: Narinder Kumar, Secretary; Dr Ajay Kumar [1981] Director/Doctor; Narinder Kumar [1961] Director/Manager

Here We Flo Ltd
Incorporated: 11 November 2016
Net Worth Deficit: £6,650 *Total Assets:* £41,030
Registered Office: 9 Perseverance Works, Kingsland Road, London, E2 8DD
Parent: Sustainable Ethical Enterprises Limited
Officers: Susan Charlene Allen [1985] Operations Director; Tara Chandra [1987] Managing Director [American]

Hermossa Limited
Incorporated: 10 March 2017
Net Worth Deficit: £187,100 *Total Assets:* £1,030
Registered Office: 208-210 Tooting High Street, London, SW17 0SG
Shareholders: Luiza Gobiec; Krystian Wlazlo
Officers: Luiza Gobiec [1989] Director [Polish]; Sylwia Gobiec [1981] Director [Polish]; Krystian Wlazlo [1980] Director [Polish]

Herra Hair Care Limited
Incorporated: 26 January 2010
Net Worth Deficit: £26,190 *Total Assets:* £1,070
Registered Office: Unit 1 Heath Buildings, 5 High Street, Oxshott, Leatherhead, Surrey, KT22 0JP
Shareholders: James Edward Davis; Dragon Gulf FZE
Officers: Stephen Strange, Secretary; James Edward Davis [1979] Director

Carolina Herrera UK Ltd
Incorporated: 9 July 2015
Net Worth Deficit: £971,000 *Total Assets:* £1,260,000
Registered Office: Fifth Floor, Russell Square House, 10-12 Russell Square, London, WC1B 5EH
Officers: Giuseppe Gabrielle Celio [1964] Director/Chief Operating Officer [American]

Hexbomb Ltd
Incorporated: 4 January 2017
Net Worth: £2,188 *Total Assets:* £8,053
Registered Office: 5-9 Donegall Street, Belfast, BT1 2FF
Major Shareholder: Maria Harte
Officers: Maria Harte [1979] Director

Heyvega Ltd
Incorporated: 9 August 2018
Registered Office: 19 Waterloo Road, Northwich, Cheshire, CW8 1EJ
Major Shareholder: Michelle Morris
Officers: Michelle Morris [1973] Director/Lecturer

HFC Prestige Products Limited
Incorporated: 24 November 1967 *Employees:* 307
Previous: P & G Prestige Products Limited
Net Worth: £33,084,000 *Total Assets:* £106,194,000
Registered Office: Bradfield Road, Eureka Science Park, Ashford, Kent, TN25 4AQ
Officers: Emma Walters, Secretary; Vengadan Swaminathan [1977] Director; Emma Morag Dorothy Walters [1974] Director/Financial Controller

HG-UK (Pty) Ltd
Incorporated: 4 October 2017
Registered Office: 20-22 Broomfield House, Lanswood Park, Broomfield Road, Elmstead, Colchester, Essex, CO7 7FD
Shareholders: Susan Mortimer; Athena Williams
Officers: Susan Mortimer [1971] Director; Athena Williams [1959] Director

Hi Life Health and Beauty (UK) Limited
Incorporated: 17 December 2009
Net Worth Deficit: £38,141 *Total Assets:* £1,968
Registered Office: Devonshire House, 1 Devonshire Street, London, W1W 5DR
Major Shareholder: Peter Nicholas
Officers: Peter Nicholas [1967] Director [Australian]

Hidden for Purpose Ltd
Incorporated: 18 January 2019
Registered Office: 8 Barmouth Street, Beswick, Manchester, M11 3BZ
Officers: Russell Ndhlovu [1984] Director [Malawian]; Shinel Walcott [1993] Director

Highbase Market Limited
Incorporated: 13 December 2016
Registered Office: c/o Whiteside & Davies, 158 Cromwell Road, Salford, M6 6DE
Officers: Jacob Fischer, Secretary; Jacob Fischer [1979] Director [American]

Highfields Health Limited
Incorporated: 22 June 2009
Net Worth: £9,300 *Total Assets:* £121,850
Registered Office: Highfield House, 90 West Drive, Highfields, Caldecote, Cambs, CB23 7NY
Officers: Neville Duncan Hawkins [1962] Director; Dr Olutumininu Olufolabomi Hawkins [1961] Director

The Highland Soap Co. Limited
Incorporated: 17 July 2006 *Employees:* 23
Net Worth: £205,939 *Total Assets:* £294,882
Registered Office: The Highland Soap Co Ltd, Spean Bridge, Highland, PH34 4EP
Major Shareholder: Archibald Sven MacDonald
Officers: Angus Francis MacDonald [1962] Director; Archibald Sven MacDonald [1990] Director; Emma Parton [1973] Director

Hild International Group Ltd
Incorporated: 14 May 2018
Registered Office: Level 18, 40 Bank Street, Canary Wharf, London, E14 5NR
Major Shareholder: Antoinette Sabiketi Lesdos
Officers: Dr Denis Bernard Charles Jean Lesdos [1956] Director/Pharmacist Doctor [French]; Antoinette Sabiketi Lesdos [1964] Director/Beauty Specialist [French]

Hill and Dale Limited
Incorporated: 27 April 2017
Registered Office: Unit 5-6, 388 Green Street, London, E13 9AP
Major Shareholder: Mahmudul Hasan
Officers: Mahmudul Hasan [1964] Director

Himalaya Enterprise Limited
Incorporated: 9 March 2009
Registered Office: 448 Poynters Road, Luton, Beds, LU4 0TW
Major Shareholder: Nitinkumar Kumar Kapadiya
Officers: Nitinkumar Kumar Kapadiya [1986] Director [Indian]

Hisamitsu Pharmaceutical UK Limited
Incorporated: 9 January 2002
Net Worth: £1 *Total Assets:* £1
Registered Office: 5 Chancery Lane, London, WC2A 1LG
Parent: Hisamitsu Pharmaceutical Co Inc
Officers: Yoshio Hiyama, Secretary; Yoshio Hiyama [1974] Director [Japanese]; Yuichi Isobe [1971] President and Managing Director [Japanese]

Hisamitsu UK Limited
Incorporated: 9 January 2002 *Employees:* 4
Net Worth: £835,534 *Total Assets:* £941,929
Registered Office: 5 Chancery Lane, London, WC2A 1LG
Parent: Hisamitsu Pharmaceutical Co., Inc.
Officers: Yoshio Hiyama, Secretary; Yoshio Hiyama [1974] Director [Japanese]; Yuichi Isobe [1971] President and Managing Director [Japanese]

Hive of Beauty Limited
Incorporated: 19 January 2015 *Employees:* 9
Net Worth: £351,672 *Total Assets:* £3,096,592
Registered Office: 1 Queens Grove Studios, London, NW8 6EP
Officers: Brian Aitken, Secretary; Brian Aitken [1954] Director/Accountant; Sheena Johnston Cunniffe [1972] Director/Commercial Manager; Colette Frances MacDonough [1967] Director; Stephen James MacDonough [1962] Director; Stephen McLaughlin [1974] Director/Accountant

Hoff Beards Limited
Incorporated: 20 February 2018
Registered Office: 14 Tolworth Rise South, Tolworth, Surrey, KT5 9NN
Major Shareholder: Adam Reddyhoff
Officers: Adam Reddyhoff [1992] Director

The Holistic Natural Wellbeing Company Limited
Incorporated: 18 January 2018
Registered Office: Rockalls Cottage, Polstead, Colchester, Essex, CO6 5AT
Major Shareholder: Engela Elizabeth van der Berg
Officers: Engela Elizabeth Van Der Berg [1974] Director/Skincare Formulator [South African]

Holistic Plant Technologies Ltd
Incorporated: 5 November 2015
Net Worth Deficit: £18,970 *Total Assets:* £35,000
Registered Office: Office 228, The Legacy Business Centre, 2a Ruckholt Road, London, E10 5NP
Major Shareholder: Tomasz Kwiecinski
Officers: Tomasz Kwiecinski [1985] Director/Coach [Polish]

Holy Group Limited
Incorporated: 27 September 2012
Previous: Online Assistance Limited
Net Worth: £403,698 *Total Assets:* £4,405,821
Registered Office: 3rd Floor, 23-24 Margaret Street, Fitzrovia, London, W1W 8RU
Major Shareholder: Vijay Pal Gandhi
Officers: Vijay Pal Gandhi [1984] Director/IT Enabled Services & Retail Sector [Indian]

Holy Lama Naturals Ltd
Incorporated: 10 September 2010
Previous: Herbosys Limited
Net Worth: £19,046 *Total Assets:* £62,100
Registered Office: 11 Sycamore Avenue, Hatfield, Herts, AL10 8LZ
Shareholders: Gouri Kubair; Anirudha Surendra Kubair
Officers: Gouri Kubair, Secretary; Anirudha Kubair [1976] Director/IT Consultant; Gouri Kubair [1980] Director/Chartered Accountant

Home & Bodycare Limited
Incorporated: 24 May 2005
Net Worth: £161,790 *Total Assets:* £707,810
Registered Office: 2 Brighton Range, Manchester, M18 7LP
Shareholders: Asad Mahmood; Masarat Mahmood
Officers: Masarat Mahmood, Secretary; Asad Mahmood [1973] Director

Home Design 24 Ltd
Incorporated: 23 October 2012
Previous: Cosmetic Technology Ltd
Net Worth Deficit: £2,435 *Total Assets:* £5,750
Registered Office: 43 Wimbledon Hill Road, London, SW19 7NA
Shareholder: Marcin Trytko
Officers: Marcin Trytko [1977] Director/General Manager [Polish]

Hommage International Ltd
Incorporated: 6 July 2016
Net Worth: £124,578 *Total Assets:* £415,737
Registered Office: 40a Manor Road, Potters Bar, Herts, EN6 1DQ
Parent: Oasis International Investments Ltd.
Officers: Umair Nisar, Secretary; Vivian James Watts [1988] Director/Financial Analyst

Homsense Ltd
Incorporated: 9 June 2017
Registered Office: 23 Raith Avenue, London, N14 7DU
Officers: Sherife Gokay [1964] Director

Honey Corn Limited
Incorporated: 28 September 2017
Registered Office: 71-75 Shelton Street, London, WC2H 9JQ
Major Shareholder: Ayesha Ibrahim
Officers: Mona Fofana [1954] Director; Ayesha Ibrahim [1976] Director

Honeypie Minerals Limited
Incorporated: 2 October 2012
Net Worth: £505 *Total Assets:* £5,152
Registered Office: 41 Southwell Road, Benfleet, Essex, SS7 1JB
Major Shareholder: Claudia Keogh
Officers: Claudia Keogh [1990] Managing Director

Honeypot Cosmetics (Wholesale) Limited
Incorporated: 12 June 2007
Net Worth: £7,227 *Total Assets:* £316,093
Registered Office: Unit 4A Honeypot Business Centre, Parr Road, Stanmore, Middlesex, HA7 1NL
Parent: Alvor Ltd
Officers: Mustafa Lalji, Secretary/Accountant; Mohamed Lalji [1946] Director; Mustafa Lalji [1976] Director/Accountant; Muzafferali Lalji [1978] Director

Honeystyle Limited
Incorporated: 8 June 2017
Registered Office: 73 Glimpsing Green, Erith, Kent, DA18 4HB
Major Shareholder: Oyinlola Omowunmi Fatunke
Officers: Oyinlola Omowunmi Fatunke [1970] Director/Entrepreneur/Business Management Professional

Honor London Limited
Incorporated: 10 March 2016
Net Worth Deficit: £14,870 *Total Assets:* £1,430
Registered Office: 27 Arterberry Road, London, SW20 8AF
Major Shareholder: Kate Wright
Officers: Kate Wright [1964] Director

Horatio London Holdings Limited
Incorporated: 25 January 2007
Previous: Simplestartuk Limited
Registered Office: 255 Hainault Road, London, E11 1EU
Officers: David Carter, Secretary; David Carter [1964] Director/Businessman; Larisa Carter [1976] Director/Consultant [Russian]

Hot (UK) Limited
Incorporated: 16 November 1994 *Employees:* 48
Net Worth: £23,798,748 *Total Assets:* £57,816,000
Registered Office: 100 New Bridge Street, London, EC4V 6JA
Parent: Helen of Troy Limited
Officers: Brian Lee Grass [1970] Director [American]; Tessa Nathene Judge [1983] Director/General Counsel [American]; Roelof Zeijpveld [1954] Director [Dutch]

Hotel Essentials Ltd
Incorporated: 25 April 2017
Net Worth: £3,180 *Total Assets:* £3,180
Registered Office: 81 Beecham Road, Reading, Berks, RG30 2RB
Shareholders: Daniel Robson; Alexander Sadlier
Officers: Daniel Robson [1991] Director; Alexander Sadlier [1991] Director

Hothouse Holdings Limited
Incorporated: 2 October 2018
Registered Office: Needle, Grove House, Mansion Gate Drive, Leeds, LS7 4DN
Shareholder: Melanie Brownlow
Officers: Melanie Brownlow [1967] Managing Director; Dean Garth Cook [1968] Director/Chairman

House of Kendra Ltd
Incorporated: 8 October 2018
Registered Office: 256 Newsome Road, Huddersfield, W Yorks, HD4 6NA
Shareholders: Tracey Allen; Anthony Lee Collins
Officers: Anthony Lee Collins [1971] Director

House of Oud Perfumes Limited
Incorporated: 27 December 2017
Registered Office: Congress House, 14 Lyon Road, Harrow, Middlesex, HA1 2EN
Major Shareholder: Hamza Mursaleen
Officers: Hamza Mursaleen [1993] Director/Manager

House of Vanity Limited
Incorporated: 7 January 2016
Registered Office: 30 Alexandra Park Road, London, N10 2AB
Major Shareholder: Kayleigh O'Donovan
Officers: Kayleigh O'Donovan [1988] Director

House of Worth Limited
Incorporated: 19 February 1999
Net Worth: £253,630 *Total Assets:* £255,450
Registered Office: Amertrans Park, Bushey Mill Lane, Watford, Herts, WD24 7JG
Parent: Shaneel Enterprises Ltd
Officers: Hitesh Bhogilal Mehta, Secretary; Dilesh Bhogilal Mehta [1960] Director; Hitesh Bhogilal Mehta [1956] Director/Secretary

HQPS Ltd
Incorporated: 27 February 2018
Registered Office: Kemp House, 160 City Road, London, EC1V 2NX
Shareholder: Linda Wilson
Officers: Howard Hayes, Secretary; Howard Hayes [1955] Director; Linda Wilson [1963] Director

HSK Enterprises Ltd
Incorporated: 22 December 2009
Net Worth Deficit: £16,690 *Total Assets:* £47,000
Registered Office: 925 Finchley Road, London, NW11 7PE
Major Shareholder: Hartej Singh Kahai
Officers: Hartej Singh Kahai, Secretary; Hartej Singh Kahai [1990] Director/Student

HT Cosmetics Ltd
Incorporated: 23 July 2018
Registered Office: Suite 512, Dephna House, 2 Portal Way, London, W3 6RT
Shareholders: Vladimir Aleixo Martins; Taise Joana Feltrin
Officers: Vladimir Aleixo Martins [1978] Director [Brazilian]

Hubert & Emilie Ltd
Incorporated: 30 May 2018
Registered Office: Flat 10, Selworthy House, Battersea Church Road, London, SW11 3NG
Major Shareholder: Theresa Lydie Furaha
Officers: Theresa Lydie Furaha [1987] Director/Teaching Assistant [Congolese]

Hudsonry Ltd
Incorporated: 8 May 2018
Registered Office: 20-22 Wenlock Road, London, N1 7GU
Major Shareholder: Kyio Scarlett-Hudson
Officers: Kyio Scarlett-Hudson [1994] Director/Sealing and Packing Assistant

Hughes Evans Essentials Ltd
Incorporated: 9 March 2017
Net Worth Deficit: £1,064 *Total Assets:* £2,642
Registered Office: Unit 32 Llys Edmund Prys, St Asaph Business Park, St Asaph, Denbighshire, LL17 0JA
Shareholders: Russell Paul Hughes; Richard Graham Evans
Officers: Richard Graham Evans [1992] Director/Hairdresser; Russell Paul Hughes [1966] Director/Hairdresser

Hugworld Cristalinas UK Limited
Incorporated: 30 November 2015
Net Worth Deficit: £519,492 *Total Assets:* £354,414
Registered Office: Hyde Park House, Cartwright Street, Hyde, Cheshire, SK14 4EH
Parent: Hugworld International Distributions S.L.
Officers: Michael Lewis Bentley [1975] Director; Alfonso Perez Perez [1975] Director [Spanish]

Humanity Cosmetics Limited
Incorporated: 18 November 2014
Net Worth Deficit: £648 *Total Assets:* £24,045
Registered Office: 1st Floor, 2 Woodberry Grove, Finchley, London, N12 0DR
Shareholders: Gerald Floyd; Christopher Reid
Officers: Christopher Reid, Secretary; Genenrald Floyd [1973] Director/Technologist; Christopher Reid [1982] Director/Designer [Irish]

Hundred Acres Apothecary Limited
Incorporated: 14 March 2013 *Employees:* 3
Net Worth Deficit: £56,853 *Total Assets:* £22,895
Registered Office: c/o Bronsens Ltd, Albion Street, Chipping Norton, Oxon, OX7 5BH
Shareholders: Sam Murray Pearman; Georgina Elizabeth Pearman
Officers: Georgina Pearman [1973] Director; Sam Pearman [1978] Director

Husaco Ltd
Incorporated: 2 October 2018
Registered Office: 42 Moorland Road, Maghull, Merseyside, L31 5JN
Shareholder: Leanne Leguen
Officers: Laura Jane Leguen [1989] Director/IT Consultant

Huskie London Ltd
Incorporated: 15 January 2018
Registered Office: 37 Grantham Green, Borehamwood, Herts, WD6 2JQ
Major Shareholder: Michael Chiedozie Ozumba
Officers: Michael Chiefozie Ozumba [1994] Director/Retailer

Hy-Brd Ltd
Incorporated: 31 January 2011
Net Worth: £13,670 *Total Assets:* £24,410
Registered Office: Tkc Miracles House, 93 Camberwell Station Road, London, SE5 9JJ
Major Shareholder: Archbishop Climate Irungu
Officers: Climate Irungu [1975] Director/Minister of Religion

Hydracol Pty Ltd
Incorporated: 20 June 2018
Registered Office: 71-75 Shelton Street, Covent Garden, London, WC2H 9JQ
Major Shareholder: Emma Grojnowski
Officers: Emma Grojnowski, Secretary; Emma Grojnowski [1972] Director [Australian]

Hydrea London Limited
Incorporated: 10 August 2009
Registered Office: Unit 11 Slough Interchange Industrial Estate, Whittenham Close, Slough, Berks, SL2 5EP
Major Shareholder: Diamantis Bersos
Officers: Diamantis Bersos, Secretary; Diamantis Bersos [1962] Director

Hydro Fresh Ltd
Incorporated: 9 April 2018
Registered Office: 87 Gortree Road, Drumahoe, Co Londonderry, BT47 3LL
Officers: Zita Bertha, Secretary; Dr Terence McIvor [1970] Director [Irish]

I Love Cosmetics Limited
Incorporated: 23 December 2003 *Employees:* 9
Net Worth: £31,572 *Total Assets:* £2,083,616
Registered Office: 5 Acorn Business Park, Woodseats Close, Sheffield, S8 0TB
Officers: David Thomas Kearns, Secretary; James Nathan Brown [1977] Director/Product Design and Development; David Thomas Kearns [1968] Director; Graham Royle [1959] Director

I.S.O.D Limited
Incorporated: 22 June 2011 *Employees:* 13
Net Worth: £3,782,381 *Total Assets:* £5,140,190
Registered Office: Enterprise House, 2 The Crest, Hendon, London, NW4 2HN
Officers: Ofer Hai [1979] Director [Israeli]; Sasi Shiri [1978] Director [Israeli]

Iam By Nature Ltd.
Incorporated: 30 August 2002
Net Worth Deficit: £567,927 *Total Assets:* £210,488
Registered Office: Vox Studios, Unit W112, 1-45 Durham Street, London, SE11 5JH
Shareholder: Mai Abdulatif Aljadawi
Officers: Mai Abdulatif Aljadawi [1976] Director [Saudi Arabian]

Iam Finance Limited
Incorporated: 31 October 2008 *Employees:* 10
Net Worth: £2,821,666 *Total Assets:* £7,646,464
Registered Office: 24 Bedford Row, London, WC1R 4TQ
Major Shareholder: Lajwanti Lakhwani
Officers: Johnny Mohan Lakhwani [1981] Director/Manager [Danish]

Iattar Perfume Oils Ltd
Incorporated: 3 August 2018
Registered Office: 2 Morning Lane, London, E9 6NA
Major Shareholder: Zahura Khanum
Officers: Zahura Khanum [1982] Director

Ibeautheart Limited
Incorporated: 20 October 2016
Net Worth: £100 *Total Assets:* £100
Registered Office: 23 Purley Road, Leicester, LE4 6PB
Shareholder: Deep Jayprakash Dashani Dashani
Officers: Deep Jayprakash Dashani Dashani [1986] Director; Priya Ramesh Savani [1988] Director

Ibeautify Ltd
Incorporated: 1 June 2017
Registered Office: 516 Oxo Tower Wharf, South Bank, London, SE1 9GY
Major Shareholder: Jeannette Lahai-Taylor
Officers: Dr Jeannette Lahai-Taylor [1971] Director/Aesthetic & Surgical Doctor

Iberia Skin Brands Ltd
Incorporated: 19 February 2018
Registered Office: 20-22 Wenlock Road, London, N1 7GU
Major Shareholder: Nitin Jain
Officers: Nitin Jain [1976] Director [Indian]; Agata Kieda [1990] Director [Polish]; Ridhima Sharma [1985] Director

IBS Shopeye World Ltd
Incorporated: 17 September 2018
Registered Office: 71-75 Shelton Street, Covent Garden, London, WC2H 9JQ
Major Shareholder: Igor Bublic
Officers: Igor Bublic [1969] Director [Croatian]

Icebox Brands EU Limited
Incorporated: 29 January 2019
Registered Office: Third Floor, 207 Regent Street, London, W1B 3HH
Major Shareholder: Sean Omara
Officers: Sean Omara, Secretary; Sean Omara [1977] Director [American]

Icilda's Ltd
Incorporated: 22 October 2018
Registered Office: 71-75 Shelton Street, London, WC2H 9JQ
Major Shareholder: Diane Hutchinson
Officers: Diane Hutchinson, Secretary; Diane Hutchinson [1972] Director

The Icon Consultancy Ltd
Incorporated: 25 April 1997 *Employees:* 46
Previous: American Crew U.K. Limited
Net Worth: £4,362,605 *Total Assets:* £5,290,676
Registered Office: Unit 2 Green Park, Coal Road, Leeds, LS14 1FB
Parent: Sweet Squared Limited
Officers: James Alan Nordstrom [1957] Director [American]; Samantha Jane Sweet [1969] Director; Samuel Whitney Sweet [1972] Director [American]

Iconic Beauty London Limited
Incorporated: 20 February 2015
Registered Office: 22 St John Street, Newport Pagnell, Bucks, MK16 8HJ
Major Shareholder: Joan Albert Roger Jara
Officers: Joan Albert Roger Jara [1965] Director [Spanish]

Iconic Fragrances Ltd
Incorporated: 29 January 2018
Registered Office: Kemp House, 160 City Road, London, EC1V 2NX
Officers: Desmond Campbell [1961] Director/Perfumer

Iconic Perfumes Ltd
Incorporated: 1 June 2018
Registered Office: 62 Ash Road, Birmingham, B8 1DJ
Major Shareholder: Muhammad Bilal
Officers: Muhammad Bilal [1998] Director

ID Aromatics Limited
Incorporated: 10 March 1989 *Employees:* 5
Net Worth Deficit: £2,132 *Total Assets:* £29,595
Registered Office: 12 New Station Street, Leeds, LS1 5DL
Major Shareholder: Antony Alaric Rodgers
Officers: Antony Alaric Rodgers [1963] Director

ID Skincare Limited
Incorporated: 14 January 2011
Net Worth: £35,130 *Total Assets:* £177,990
Registered Office: 47 Oakleigh Park South, London, N20 9JR
Shareholders: Ian Andrew Rapley; Donna Glazer
Officers: Ian Rapley, Secretary; Donna Glazer [1967] Director/Skin Therapist; Ian Andrew Rapley [1963] Director/Accountant

Ideal Beauty Products Limited
Incorporated: 4 August 2009
Registered Office: Cliff House, South Well Road, Lowdham, Gonalston, Notts, NG14 7DR
Major Shareholder: Isobel Hibbitt
Officers: Melanie Hibbitt, Secretary; Mark Hassan [1960] Director/Buyer

IDK Balms Ltd
Incorporated: 25 August 2018
Registered Office: 16 Hartley Grove, Orrell, Wigan, Lancs, WN5 0DJ
Shareholders: Steven Woodcock; Cameron Tye
Officers: Steven Woodcock [1991] Director/Mechanical Engineer

Iiuvo Limited
Incorporated: 10 March 2015
Net Worth Deficit: £54,231 *Total Assets:* £76,759
Registered Office: First Floor, Thavies Inn House, 3-4 Holborn Circus, London, EC1N 2HA
Shareholders: Leo William Gibbon; Oluwafikayo Olutomi Oladipupo Ahmed
Officers: Oluwafikayo Olutomi Oladipupo Ahmed [1989] Creative Director; Leo William Gibbon [1990] Sales Director; Richard Singh [1988] Director; Jonathan Wood [1984] Director

Ijapan Ltd
Incorporated: 20 July 2015
Net Worth Deficit: £41,750 *Total Assets:* £158,100
Registered Office: Unit 14 North Nottinghamshire Business Centre, 32-34 Rosemary Street, Mansfield, Notts, NG18 1QL
Major Shareholder: Ruihuan Huang
Officers: Ruihuan Huang [1991] Director

IJN Pure Oils Ltd
Incorporated: 4 September 2017
Registered Office: Suite 16, Exhibition House, Addison Bridge Place, London, W14 8XP
Major Shareholder: Iman Jafer Naji
Officers: Iman Jafer Naji [1961] Director

Ila Asia Limited
Incorporated: 5 August 2014
Previous: Ila Only Limited
Net Worth: £28,720 *Total Assets:* £232,060
Registered Office: Gate Farm, Park Road, Kiddington, Oxon, OX20 1DB
Parent: Ila-Spa Ltd
Officers: John William Leicester [1950] Director/Accountant; Theresa Yeh [1978] Director [Taiwanese]

Ila Pothecary Limited
Incorporated: 17 May 2018
Registered Office: 37 Chapel Street, London, SW1X 7DD
Officers: Efstratios Chatzigiannis [1960] Director/Financier; John William Leicester [1950] Director/Chief Executive

Ileri Trading Limited
Incorporated: 13 November 2015
Net Worth: £1,548 *Total Assets:* £5,032
Registered Office: 74 Westmoreland Avenue, Welling, Kent, DA16 2QD
Major Shareholder: Nasir Ileri
Officers: Nasir Ileri [1985] Director/Cosmetic Salesman [Turkish]

The Ilex Wood Ltd
Incorporated: 2 July 2018
Registered Office: 80 Queen Street, Weedon, Northampton, NN7 4RA
Major Shareholder: Holly Anna Coulton
Officers: Holly Anna Coulton [1985] Director

Ilys Organic Ltd
Incorporated: 18 April 2017
Registered Office: 46 Nova Road, Croydon, Surrey, CR0 2TL
Major Shareholder: Ghazele Alalouch
Officers: Ghazele Alalouch [1982] Director [French]

Imaage Ltd
Incorporated: 4 October 2017
Registered Office: Flat 13, Carl Ekman House, Tooley Street, Gravesend, Kent, DA11 9PN
Major Shareholder: Roberta Regine Mayasi
Officers: Roberta Mayasi, Secretary; Roberta Regine Mayasi [1986] Director

Image Hub Limited
Incorporated: 2 June 2014 *Employees:* 1
Net Worth Deficit: £24,600 *Total Assets:* £15,937
Registered Office: Old Town Hall, Fore Street, Wellington, Somerset, TA21 8LS
Major Shareholder: Alfred Handley
Officers: Alfred Handley [1962] Director/Marketing Consultant; Juliet Anne Handley [1965] Director/Development Officer

Imamcom Ltd
Incorporated: 24 January 2019
Registered Office: 3 Gower Street, London, WC1E 6HA
Major Shareholder: Mohamed Said Moustafa Ahmed Imam
Officers: Dr Mohamed Said Moustafa Ahmed Imam [1980] Director/Pharmacist [Egyptian]

Imijo Ltd
Incorporated: 13 April 2009
Net Worth: £1,010 *Total Assets:* £89,790
Registered Office: 76 St Johns Road, Tunbridge Wells, Kent, TN4 9PH
Officers: Stephen McDonald Laurie, Secretary; Stephen McDonald Laurie [1970] Director/Salesman

Imperial Bioscience Ltd
Incorporated: 7 January 2016 *Employees:* 3
Net Worth Deficit: £59,870 *Total Assets:* £18,581
Registered Office: Mocatta House, Trafalgar Place, Brighton, BN1 4DU
Major Shareholder: Muhammet Avcil
Officers: Dr Muhammet Avcil [1984] Director

Imperial Pharmaceuticals Limited
Incorporated: 14 August 1996
Net Worth: £21,340,000 *Total Assets:* £43,300,000
Registered Office: Unit 4 Imperial Park, Stonefield Way, South Ruislip, Middlesex, HA4 0JW
Shareholder: Manisha Thakrar
Officers: Manisha Thakrar, Secretary; Nayan Thakrar [1960] Director; Shivani Thakrar [1987] Director/Dentist

Impressions Beauty Limited
Incorporated: 31 July 2007
Net Worth Deficit: £4,020 *Total Assets:* £2,910
Registered Office: 6 Hermitage Road, St Johns, Woking, Surrey, GU21 8TB
Shareholders: Gary Sarah Gill; Renuka Sujanani
Officers: Gary Joseph Lawlor, Secretary; Renuka Sujanani [1967] Director/Businesswoman

Impulse Global Solutions Limited
Incorporated: 20 June 2012 *Employees:* 3
Net Worth Deficit: £112,462 *Total Assets:* £535,033
Registered Office: 5 Armston Road, Quorn, Loughborough, Leics, LE12 8QP
Officers: Marie Helen Dawkins, Secretary; Marie Helen Dawkins [1957] Director/Executive; Steven Dawkins [1956] Executive Director; Siobhan Sear-Mayes [1961] Director

Imxpo Ltd
Incorporated: 22 February 2019
Registered Office: Bargain Booze, 81 High Road, Pitsea, Basildon, Essex, SS13 3BB
Major Shareholder: Md Tanjil Islam
Officers: MD Tanjil Islam [1989] Director [Bangladeshi]

In & Outbrands Ltd
Incorporated: 14 January 2019
Registered Office: 3 Oakley Road, Rawtenstall, Lancs, BB4 6RB
Shareholders: Philippa Kay; Katie Grime
Officers: Katie Grime [1987] Director; Philippa Kay [1988] Director

In Situ Cosmetics Ltd
Incorporated: 16 June 2011
Net Worth: £37,626 *Total Assets:* £41,432
Registered Office: 20-22 Wenlock Road, London, N1 7GU
Major Shareholder: Maria Salichou
Officers: Dr Maria Salichou [1983] Founder and Director [Greek]

Inbeauting Ltd
Incorporated: 7 May 2013
Net Worth: £15,530 *Total Assets:* £601,347
Registered Office: 57 Himley Close, Bilston, W Midlands, WV14 0LJ
Major Shareholder: Qiong Hu
Officers: Qiong Hu [1981] Director [Chinese]

Incorporated Beauty Limited
Incorporated: 16 April 2010 *Employees:* 2
Previous: Bargain Beauty UK Limited
Net Worth: £681 *Total Assets:* £27,066
Registered Office: Fleming Court, Leigh Road, Eastleigh, Southampton, SO50 9PD
Shareholders: Kerry Chambers; Stewart Chambers
Officers: Kerry Chambers [1962] Director; Stewart Chambers [1948] Director

Incorporated Perfumery Distribution Limited
Incorporated: 11 August 1994 Employees: 5
Net Worth: £106,762 Total Assets: £429,567
Registered Office: 5 Beaumont Gate, Shenley Hill, Radlett, Herts, WD7 7AR
Major Shareholder: Michele Perris
Officers: Ian Laird [1957] Managing Director; Gian-Luca Perris [1969] Director/Manager [Italian]; Michele Perris [1941] Director/Executive [Italian]

Indiggle Limited
Incorporated: 18 April 2018
Registered Office: 20 Bells End Road, Walton on Trent, Swadlincote, Derbys, DE12 8ND
Officers: Huaqing Lin [1994] Director [Chinese]; Zhentao Lin [1991] Director [Chinese]

Indigo Direct Ltd
Incorporated: 18 August 2016
Net Worth Deficit: £24,479 Total Assets: £12,688
Registered Office: Office 39, 78 Golders Green Road, London, NW11 8LN
Major Shareholder: Daniel Z Ilic
Officers: Daniel Z Ilic [1980] Director [American]

Indigo Nails Online Shop Ltd.
Incorporated: 19 December 2016 Employees: 2
Net Worth Deficit: £17,540 Total Assets: £8,029
Registered Office: 52 Main Street, Ayr, KA8 8EF
Major Shareholder: Dawid Soldanski
Officers: Dawid Soldanski [1992] Director/IT [Polish]; Monika Terlecka [1983] Director/Nail Technician [Polish]

Indulge Therapeutics UK Ltd
Incorporated: 24 October 2018
Registered Office: 42 Victoria Road, Grangemouth, Stirlingshire, FK3 9JN
Major Shareholder: Ross Miller
Officers: Ross Miller [1984] Director/Self Employed

Infini Lab Ltd
Incorporated: 31 May 2018
Registered Office: 20-22 Wenlock Road, London, N1 7GU
Major Shareholder: Raphael Richardson
Officers: Raphael Richardson [1981] Director

Infinity K Ltd
Incorporated: 21 June 2018
Registered Office: Redington Court, 69 Church Road, Hove, E Sussex, BN3 2BB
Major Shareholder: Alexander James Dalley
Officers: Alexander James Dalley [1989] Director

Infinityredox Holdings Limited
Incorporated: 19 February 2018
Registered Office: Kemp House, 160 City Road, London, EC1V 2NX
Major Shareholder: Angelo Li Volsi
Officers: Angelo Li Volsi, Secretary; Angelo Li Volsi [1970] Director/Entrepreneur [Italian]

Info Cosmetics Limited
Incorporated: 3 May 2017
Registered Office: Kemp House, 160 City Road, London, EC1V 2NX
Major Shareholder: Jayne Dudfield
Officers: Jayne Dudfield [1955] Director; Malcolm Tullett [1954] Director

Inga Permanent Make Up Limited
Incorporated: 21 September 2016 Employees: 2
Net Worth: £3,182 Total Assets: £9,816
Registered Office: 9 Bickels Yard, Bermondsey Street, London, SE1 3HA
Shareholder: Inga Marcinkeviciene
Officers: Inga Marcinkeviciene [1980] Director [Lithuanian]; Darius Marcinkevicius [1979] Director [Lithuanian]

Initiative (UK) Limited
Incorporated: 26 June 2007
Net Worth Deficit: £21,045 Total Assets: £54,329
Registered Office: 3-4 Spar Road, Vulcan Road Estate, Norwich, NR6 6BY
Shareholder: Linda Denise Carman
Officers: Susan Maria Barker, Secretary; Susan Maria Barker [1960] Director; Linda Denise Carman [1966] Director

Ink Oil Limited
Incorporated: 9 February 2017
Net Worth: £1 Total Assets: £10,001
Registered Office: 8 Surrey Street, Brighton, BN1 3PA
Major Shareholder: Brian Gerald Clifford Roe
Officers: Conor Barry [1990] Director/Senior Strategist [Irish]; Robin Ivan Gadsby [1972] Director/Chief Executive Officer; Brian Generald Clifford Roe [1965] Director/Web Designer

Innes McBeath Sourcing Ltd.
Incorporated: 12 November 2008
Net Worth: £359,732 Total Assets: £856,872
Registered Office: 12 Polwarth Terrace, Edinburgh, EH11 1ND
Shareholders: Innes Archibald Wilson McBeath; Susan Valerie McBeath
Officers: Innes Archibald Wilson McBeath [1963] Director; Susan Valerie McBeath [1966] Director

Innocent Alchemy Ltd
Incorporated: 28 March 2017
Registered Office: Fairlawn, St Mary's, Isles of Scilly, TR21 0NS
Major Shareholder: Alison Nicholson
Officers: Alison Nicholson [1978] Director

Innon Vision Limited
Incorporated: 20 January 2015
Net Worth Deficit: £7,474 Total Assets: £3,559
Registered Office: Dawson House, 5 Jewry Street, London, EC3N 2EX
Officers: Maria Plomarteli [1959] Director [Greek]

Innovaderma PLC
Incorporated: 19 September 2014
Net Worth: £9,610,000 Total Assets: £12,810,000
Registered Office: 27 Old Gloucester Street, London, WC1N 3AX
Officers: Ross Martin Hilton Andrews [1960] Director; Joseph John Bayer [1957] Director [Australian]; Kieran Winston Callan [1960] Director [Australian]; Haris Altaf Chaudhry [1972] Director [Australian]; Rodney David Turner [1961] Director [Australian]

Inovair Limited
Incorporated: 4 September 2002
Net Worth Deficit: £167,903 Total Assets: £45,422
Registered Office: Companies House, Default Address, Cardiff, CF14 8LH
Major Shareholder: Hubert Willem Maat
Officers: Hubert Willem Maat [1965] Director [Dutch]

Inshirah Enterprises Limited
Incorporated: 26 October 2017
Registered Office: 30 Churchill Drive, Stourbridge, W Midlands, DY8 4JR
Officers: Saira Akram Mughal [1981] Director/Wholesale

Inside Trading (Beauty) Limited
Incorporated: 28 February 2013 *Employees:* 5
Net Worth: £49,410 *Total Assets:* £298,546
Registered Office: Bank Street Business Centre, 6 Bank Street, Malvern, Worcs, WR14 2JN
Shareholders: David Paul Thompson; Marian Claire Edgecombe
Officers: Marian Claire Edgecombe [1963] Managing Director; David Paul Thompson [1963] Sales Director

Inspired by RJP Limited
Incorporated: 5 December 2018
Registered Office: 35 St Peters Road, Balby, Doncaster, S Yorks, DN4 0SZ
Officers: Richard John Pinder [1983] Director/Warehouse Operative

Inspired Hair Supplies Limited
Incorporated: 6 December 2012 *Employees:* 1
Net Worth: £11,691 *Total Assets:* £23,174
Registered Office: Berkeley House, 86 High Street, Carshalton, Surrey, SM5 3AE
Major Shareholder: Mark Tillyer
Officers: Mark Tillyer [1985] Director

Insta-Jell Cosmetics Ltd
Incorporated: 18 July 2018
Registered Office: 32 Coalstore Court, 5 Candle Street, London, E1 4RS
Major Shareholder: Kim Marguerite Husbands
Officers: Kim Marguerite Husbands [1967] Director/Cosmetic Packaging Solutions

Instant Beauty UK Limited
Incorporated: 3 May 2017
Net Worth Deficit: £11,724 *Total Assets:* £142,476
Registered Office: 46 Garrick Avenue, London, NW11 9AS
Major Shareholder: Kfir Yizhaq Atias
Officers: Kfir Yizhaq Atias [1980] Director; Parveen Kaur Purewal [1979] Managing Director

Instant Effects Ltd
Incorporated: 10 September 2015
Net Worth: £121,320 *Total Assets:* £185,100
Registered Office: Mulberry House, 9 Stoatley Rise, Haslemere, Surrey, GU27 1AF
Major Shareholder: Richard John Mears
Officers: Richard John Mears [1964] Director

Interall Ltd
Incorporated: 12 January 2016
Net Worth: £100 *Total Assets:* £100
Registered Office: 49 Charnwood Road, London, SE25 6NT
Major Shareholder: Claudiu Pal
Officers: Claudiu Ionut Pal [1983] Director/Sales [Romanian]

Intercos UK Ltd
Incorporated: 30 November 1987 *Employees:* 4
Net Worth: £2,277,465 *Total Assets:* £3,172,919
Registered Office: 15a Silver Street, Barnstaple, Devon, EX32 8HR
Officers: Pauline Ann Bromell, Secretary; Dario Ferrari [1943] Director [Italian]; Thomas Anthony Rossiter [1947] Director

Intermercantile Limited
Incorporated: 6 October 2000
Net Worth Deficit: £181,960
Registered Office: 7th Floor, Boulton House, 17-21 Chorlton Street, Manchester, M1 3HY
Major Shareholder: Joshua Rowe
Officers: Michael Rowe, Secretary; Joshua Rowe [1948] Director

International Hair Cosmetics Limited
Incorporated: 24 January 1996
Net Worth: £1,970,000 *Total Assets:* £5,100,000
Registered Office: 3 Acorn Business Centre, Northarbour Road, Cosham, Portsmouth, PO6 3TH
Shareholders: Eric John Bailey; Jennifer Bailey
Officers: Eric Bailey, Secretary; Douglas John Bailey [1978] Director; Eric John Bailey [1949] Director; Tristan Richard Pattison [1980] Director/General Manager [British/Canadian]; Nicola Summer [1971] Director/Chemist [Italian]

International Integrated Solutions Company Ltd
Incorporated: 17 August 2018
Registered Office: 3 Gower Street, London, WC1E 6HA
Shareholders: Khaldoon Mansour; Yousef Kadro
Officers: Yousef Kadro [1984] Director [Syrian]; Khaldoon Mansour [1982] Director [Syrian]

International Trade Corporation Limited
Incorporated: 8 January 1991
Net Worth: £3,580,000 *Total Assets:* £4,610,000
Registered Office: Northside House, Mount Pleasant, Barnet, Herts, EN4 9EE
Shareholders: Roy Henry Presswell; June Linda Presswell
Officers: June Linda Presswell, Secretary; Joanne Sarah Hurst [1972] Director; James Stephen Presswell [1978] Director; June Linda Presswell [1950] Director; Roy Henry Presswell [1948] Director/Cosmetic & Toiletries Distributor

International Traders House P.I.T. Limited
Incorporated: 16 May 2018
Registered Office: 81 Ratcliffe Road, Loughborough, Leics, LE11 1LG
Major Shareholder: Damian Andrzej Bajer
Officers: Damian Andrzej Bajer [1988] Director/Trader [Polish]

InternationalBeautyLondon Limited
Incorporated: 30 October 2018
Registered Office: 63 Dudley Road, Southall, Middlesex, UB2 5AS
Officers: Muhammad Aqeel [1982] Director/Cosmetics [Italian]

Interparcos U.K. Limited
Incorporated: 4 April 2009
Net Worth: £133,671 *Total Assets:* £349,125
Registered Office: Crown Chambers, Bridge Street, Salisbury, Wilts, SP1 2LZ
Officers: Christophe de La Poeze [1965] Director [French]

Intertrade Group Ltd
Incorporated: 18 September 2001 *Employees:* 17
Previous: Intertrade Holding Ltd
Net Worth: £51,938 *Total Assets:* £3,482,766
Registered Office: 5th Floor, North Side, 7-10 Chandos Street, London, W1G 9DQ
Major Shareholder: Celso Fadelli
Officers: Massimo Della Bruna [1966] Director [Italian]; Celso Fadelli [1959] Director [Italian]

Into Exports Limited
Incorporated: 23 December 2011
Net Worth: £57,182 Total Assets: £60,082
Registered Office: Unit 10 Hanson Close Industrial Estate, Hanson Park, Hanson Close, Middleton, Manchester, M24 2QZ
Officers: George Kofi Dei-Danquah [1974] Director/Wholesaler & Distributor; Rizwan Zeb [1981] Director

Invicta Cosmetics Limited
Incorporated: 19 June 2017
Registered Office: c/o Grand Consultancy, 60 Millmead Business Center, Mill Mead Road, London, N17 9QU
Officers: Gokhan Kara [1990] Director/Hairdresser [Turkish]

IR International Ltd
Incorporated: 6 March 2017
Net Worth Deficit: £2,139 Total Assets: £2,026
Registered Office: Office 1 & 2, 203 The Vale, London, W3 7QS
Major Shareholder: Ridha Al-Dalawi
Officers: Koubi Mhamead [1967] Director

Iras Trading Ltd
Incorporated: 5 January 2018
Registered Office: Kemp House, 160 City Road, London, EC1V 2NX
Major Shareholder: Mohamed Inshaf Mohamed Thahir
Officers: Mohamed Shiraz Mohamed Thahir [1979] Director; Mohamed Inshaf Mohamed Thahir [1987] Managing Director [Sri Lankan]

Sarah Ireland Perfumes Ltd
Incorporated: 4 April 2018
Registered Office: Crown House, 27 Old Gloucester Street, London, WC1N 3AX
Major Shareholder: Sarah Louise Ireland
Officers: Sarah Louise Ireland [1981] Director/Perfumer

Alexander Iris Solutions Limited
Incorporated: 5 May 2016
Registered Office: 31 Beulah Road, Tunbridge Wells, Kent, TN1 2NS
Officers: Jonathan Hodge, Secretary; Jonathan Hodge [1970] Managing Director

Irregular Cosmetics Company Ltd
Incorporated: 7 December 2018
Registered Office: 32 Meadow View, Newtownabbey, Co Antrim, BT37 0US
Officers: George Philip Holtom [1965] Director; Leslie John Morrow [1965] Director; Rachel Lesley Morrow [1994] Director; Angie Frances Morton [1963] Director

Irum Cosmetics Ltd
Incorporated: 24 January 2017
Net Worth: £3,501 Total Assets: £3,501
Registered Office: 19 Lockerbie Avenue, Leicester, LE4 7NL
Major Shareholder: Naeem Ismail
Officers: Naeem Ismail [1990] Director

Ish Products Ltd
Incorporated: 6 August 2018
Registered Office: Staff Quarter, 6 Watford Hilton, 35 Elton Way, Watford, Herts, WD25 8HA
Major Shareholder: Ishawu Osumanu
Officers: Ishawu Osumanu [1987] Director [Ghanaian]

Isha Cosmetics Limited
Incorporated: 16 March 2017
Net Worth Deficit: £1,530 Total Assets: £330,000
Registered Office: 39 Cabrera Avenue, Virginia Water, Surrey, GU25 4HA
Major Shareholder: Isha Panesar
Officers: Isha Panesar [1988] Director

Ismile Beauty Ltd
Incorporated: 21 January 2019
Registered Office: 89 Vicars Moor Lane, London, N21 1BL
Major Shareholder: Sheree Carissa Watt
Officers: Sheree Carissa Watt [1983] Director

Isobel C Professional Cosmetics Limited
Incorporated: 12 September 2018
Registered Office: 9 Husthwaite Road, Brough, E Yorks, HU15 1TF
Major Shareholder: Erlinda Muis
Officers: Erlinda Muis [1976] Director [Malaysian]

Istylists Limited
Incorporated: 21 September 2010
Registered Office: 6 Hurst Way, Pyrford, Woking, Surrey, GU22 8PH
Major Shareholder: Stephen James Bown
Officers: Stephen James Bown [1976] Director/Office Worker

It Worx Cosmetics Limited
Incorporated: 1 November 2018
Registered Office: Maple House, Great Strickland, Penrith, Cumbria, CA10 3DJ
Major Shareholder: Samantha Louise Sharp
Officers: Samantha Louise Sharp [1988] Marketing Director; Helen Marie Willison-Holt [1966] Sales Director

Ital Living Market Ltd
Incorporated: 10 May 2017
Registered Office: 1 Ormonde Drive, Allerton, Bradford, BD15 7SZ
Major Shareholder: Leon Cogan
Officers: Leon Cogan [1987] Director

Itala Group Ltd
Incorporated: 16 May 2018
Registered Office: 27 Old Gloucester Street, London, WC1N 3AX
Officers: Silvia Musiani, Secretary; Andrea Ghiaroni [1968] Director/President [Italian]; Silvia Musiani [1969] Director [Italian]

Ivaxane UK Ltd
Incorporated: 12 May 2009
Registered Office: Unit 6425, 59 Station Road, London, NW10 4UX
Major Shareholder: Ana Lucia Rosa
Officers: Ana Lucia Rosa [1980] Director/Operational Manager [Brazilian]

Ivee Group Ltd
Incorporated: 1 August 2016
Registered Office: P O Box 28143, 29 Badger Brook, Broxburn, W Lothian, EH52 5TB
Shareholders: Katarzyna Drywa; Michal Drywa
Officers: Katarzyna Drywa [1988] Managing Director [Polish]; Michal Drywa [1982] Managing Director [Polish]

Ives Lab Ltd
Incorporated: 14 November 2018
Registered Office: 20-22 Wenlock Road, London, N1 7GU
Shareholders: Kumar Dayaram Datwani; Vijay Wadhwani
Officers: Kumar Dayaram Datwani [1950] Director [Indian]; Vijay Wadhwani [1945] Director/Businessman [Hong Kong]

Ivy Nat Ltd
Incorporated: 25 January 2019
Registered Office: 207 Regent Street, London, W1B 3HH
Officers: Chinedu Enemuo [1979] Director

Ivy Wild Ltd
Incorporated: 16 May 2018
Registered Office: Ground Floor, Warwick House, Banbury Road, Southam, Warwicks, CV47 2PT
Major Shareholder: Sherine Walrond
Officers: Sherine Walrond [1991] Director

J & W Distribution Limited
Incorporated: 2 November 2016 *Employees:* 2
Net Worth Deficit: £7,836 *Total Assets:* £6,643
Registered Office: 118 Greenwood Hill, Belfast, BT8 7WF
Shareholder: Jorge Jorge Minguez
Officers: Jorge Minguez Gonzalez [1977] Director [Spanish]; Eric Wee Shou Keong [1977] Director [Malaysian]

J K International Trading Ltd
Incorporated: 2 February 2017
Net Worth Deficit: £49,038 *Total Assets:* £112,389
Registered Office: Flat 9, Horatio House, Horatio Street, London, E2 7SD
Major Shareholder: Jabir Ahmed Chowdhury
Officers: Jahangir Kabir Choudhury [1976] Director/Business Manager [Indian]; Jabir Ahmed Chowdhury [1982] Director/Business Manager

J S Trading (UK) Limited
Incorporated: 31 January 2003
Net Worth Deficit: £13,882
Registered Office: Eden Point, Three Acres Lane, Cheadle Hulme, Cheadle, Cheshire, SK8 6RL
Major Shareholder: Janet Sudnik
Officers: Jonathan Sudnik, Secretary/Student; Janet Sudnik [1959] Director

J's Luxury Perfumery Ltd
Incorporated: 24 June 2013
Net Worth: £8,400 *Total Assets:* £8,400
Registered Office: 1 Rochdale Road, London, SE2 0XE
Officers: Jennifer Kelly [1970] Director

J.Cat Beauty UK Ltd
Incorporated: 22 December 2017
Registered Office: Winnington House, 2 Woodberry Grove, London, N12 0DR
Major Shareholder: Jinyoung Victor Chang
Officers: Jinyoung Victor Chang [1970] Director [American]

J26 Limited
Incorporated: 30 January 2019
Registered Office: 17 Marley Place, Leeds, LS11 8QW
Major Shareholder: Sandra Pagiryte
Officers: Sandra Pagiryte [1994] Director [Lithuanian]

Jacob's Well Limited
Incorporated: 22 September 2014
Net Worth: £1,174 *Total Assets:* £189,362
Registered Office: Unit 9 Romans Business Park, East Street, Farnham, Surrey, GU9 7SX
Major Shareholder: Zhongshi Jia
Officers: Zhongshi Jia [1982] Director/Manager

Jaden Cosmetics Limited
Incorporated: 26 March 2018
Registered Office: Unit 5 Woodbarn Farm, Ansley, Nuneaton, Warwicks, CV10 0QP
Major Shareholder: Richard Arthurs
Officers: Richard Arthurs [1972] Director/Commodities Trader

Jak Beauty Ltd
Incorporated: 27 September 2018
Registered Office: 154 Higham Hill Road, London, E17 6EJ
Major Shareholder: Jawed Akhtar
Officers: Jawed Akhtar [1957] Director

Jakor Limited
Incorporated: 29 January 2007
Net Worth Deficit: £945 *Total Assets:* £12,054
Registered Office: 29-31 Tufton Street, Ashford, Kent, TN23 1QN
Major Shareholder: Adam Kinnear
Officers: Martin Brown, Secretary; Adam Kinnear [1975] Director [Australian]

James & Jake Ltd
Incorporated: 4 February 2015
Net Worth Deficit: £21,480 *Total Assets:* £1,000
Registered Office: 1 Wells Close, Horsham, W Sussex, RH12 1US
Shareholders: James Matthew Hood; Sarah Louise Hood
Officers: James Hood [1980] Director; Sarah Louise Hood [1983] Director

Jan Nails & Beauty Suppliers Ltd
Incorporated: 13 November 2013
Net Worth: £72,220 *Total Assets:* £171,474
Registered Office: Unit F, 3 Eyre Street, Springhill Industrial Park, Birmingham, B18 7AA
Major Shareholder: Tung Phuoc Nguyen
Officers: Phuoc Tung Nguyen [1966] Director

Janiro Ltd
Incorporated: 3 October 2011
Net Worth Deficit: £25,390 *Total Assets:* £26,710
Registered Office: 26 Windsor House, 26 Mostyn Avenue, Llandudno, Gwynedd, LL30 1YY
Shareholders: Robert James Lyons; Nicole Wong
Officers: Robert James Lyons [1966] Director; Nicole Wong [1976] Director [Malaysian]

Janou Brand Limited
Incorporated: 14 August 2017
Registered Office: 71-75 Shelton Street, Covent Garden, London, WC2H 9JQ
Shareholders: Sean Jean Fall; Surat Samavi Aziz Khan
Officers: Sean Jean Fall [1987] Director [Senegalese]; Surat Samavi Aziz Khan [1992] Director [Swedish]

Janson Limited
Incorporated: 24 May 2002 *Employees:* 13
Net Worth: £1,772,266 *Total Assets:* £4,234,088
Registered Office: Unit 19 Mitcham Industrial Estate, Streatham Road, Mitcham, Surrey, CR4 2AP
Shareholders: Khairunnisha Janmohamed; Riyaz Janmohamed
Officers: Riyaz Janmohamed, Secretary; Khairunnisha Janmohamed [1944] Director; Riyaz Janmohamed [1973] Director

Janssen Cosmetics UK Ltd
Incorporated: 13 November 2015
Net Worth: £4,609 *Total Assets:* £8,695
Registered Office: Suite 2, 112-114 Market Street, Hindley, Wigan, Lancs, WN2 3AY
Major Shareholder: Krestyna Batty
Officers: Krestyna Batty, Secretary; Krestyna Batty [1963] Director

Jardin de Parfums Ltd
Incorporated: 24 May 2018
Registered Office: 71-75 Shelton Street, London, WC2H 9JQ
Major Shareholder: Firas Al-Assadi
Officers: Firas Al-Assadi [1976] Director [Dominican]

Jardins D'Eden Ltd
Incorporated: 27 December 2018
Registered Office: 2nd Floor, Hanover House, 30 Charlotte Street, Manchester, M1 4EX
Major Shareholder: Zeina Nazer
Officers: Zeina Nazer, Secretary; Zeina Nazer [1975] Director

Jas Etrading Ltd
Incorporated: 18 October 2018
Registered Office: 40 Clarendon Place, Glasgow, G20 7PZ
Major Shareholder: Yun Feng
Officers: Yun Feng [1985] Director/Manager [Chinese]

Jaspmab Ltd
Incorporated: 19 November 2018
Registered Office: 71-75 Shelton Street, London, WC2H 9JQ
Officers: Jean-Baptiste Guerin [1980] Director [French]

Jass Perfumes Limited
Incorporated: 18 December 2018
Registered Office: 59 Kempton Road, London, E6 2LG
Major Shareholder: Senthurpandian Narayanan
Officers: Senthur Pandian Narayanan [1976] Director/Businessman

Jax of London Ltd
Incorporated: 15 August 2018
Registered Office: 71-75 Shelton Street, London, WC2H 9JQ
Major Shareholder: Mark Ford
Officers: Mark Ford [1967] Director

Jay Kay Wholesale Ltd
Incorporated: 14 February 2019
Registered Office: 71 Longmead Road, Hayes, Middlesex, UB3 2HF
Major Shareholder: Muhammad Haroon Tanveer
Officers: Muhammad Haroon Tanveer [1978] Director/Manager

Jaydaw Limited
Incorporated: 9 May 2013
Net Worth: £105,457 *Total Assets:* £126,224
Registered Office: Second Floor, De Burgh House, Market Road, Wickford, Essex, SS12 0FD
Major Shareholder: Davide Bianco
Officers: Robert John Mason [1983] Director

Jayeed Perfumes Ltd
Incorporated: 3 September 2018
Registered Office: 22 Longstone Walk, Liverpool, L7 3PP
Major Shareholder: Osman Jibril
Officers: Osman Jibril [1992] Director

Jazzy Hair Limited
Incorporated: 23 February 2000
Net Worth Deficit: £58,840 *Total Assets:* £23,810
Registered Office: c/o 6 Ritherdon Road, London, SW17 8QD
Shareholders: Ajitkumar Patel; Vijanti Ajitkumar Patel
Officers: Vijanti Ajitkumar Patel, Secretary/Businesswoman; Ajitkumar Patel [1958] Director/Businessman; Vijanti Ajitkumar Patel [1959] Director/Businesswoman

JCB Skincare Limited
Incorporated: 2 March 2012
Registered Office: 3 The Corngreaves, Birmingham, B34 6TR
Major Shareholder: Singapaulo Daniel
Officers: Singa Paulo Daniel [1982] Director [Angolan]

Jealous Cow Limited
Incorporated: 1 April 2011
Net Worth: £3,897 *Total Assets:* £21,784
Registered Office: 77 Mill Street, Kidderminster, Worcs, DY11 6XJ
Shareholders: Rebecca Charlotte Cross; Samantha Alexandra Biddle
Officers: Samantha Alexandra Biddle [1971] Director; Rebecca Charlotte Cross [1979] Director

Jean Christian Perfumes Limited
Incorporated: 12 September 1997
Net Worth: £143,800 *Total Assets:* £289,970
Registered Office: 202c Burcott Road, Avonmouth, Bristol, BS11 8AP
Major Shareholder: Carol Ann Coleman
Officers: Carol Ann Coleman, Secretary; Carol Ann Coleman [1948] Managing Director; Thomas Martin Coleman [1986] Director

Jedidiah Group Ltd
Incorporated: 28 December 2016
Net Worth: £95 *Total Assets:* £9,254
Registered Office: Flat 16, Great Western Court, Frome Road, Radstock, Somerset, BA3 3FZ
Officers: Justina Kwakye, Secretary; Ibrahim Ahmed Ibrahim [1979] Director

Jerome Fashion Ltd
Incorporated: 14 August 2018
Registered Office: 247 Elgine Avenue, London, W9 1NJ
Major Shareholder: Jerome Lapeyre
Officers: Jerome Lapeyre [1965] Director/Design [French]

Jess Nails Limited
Incorporated: 14 April 2014
Net Worth: £2,970 *Total Assets:* £3,000
Registered Office: Unit 1 Beech Works, Wreakes Lane, Dronfield, Derbys, S18 1PN
Major Shareholder: Kathryn Rachel Cavan
Officers: Kathryn Rachel Cavan [1963] Director

Jeunvie Ltd
Incorporated: 8 February 2013
Net Worth Deficit: £51,200 *Total Assets:* £2,309
Registered Office: 20-22 Wenlock Road, London, N1 7GU
Officers: Maria Delray [1965] Director/Therapist; Jeffrey Wayne Mollett [1967] Director/Businessman; Donya Shadeh Shirazi [1999] Director/Student; Hanaha-Mae Shirazi [2001] Director/Student; Melodie Lily Shirazi [1996] Director/Student

The Top UK Perfume and Cosmetics Wholesalers

JF Malcolm Ltd
Incorporated: 4 September 2015
Net Worth Deficit: £3,227 Total Assets: £214,013
Registered Office: International House, 24 Holborn Viaduct, London, EC1A 2BN
Major Shareholder: Rafal Duda
Officers: Rafal Duda [1964] Director/Manager [Polish]

JGR UK Distributions Limited
Incorporated: 3 December 2003 Employees: 9
Net Worth: £164,170 Total Assets: £308,944
Registered Office: Automation House, Newton Road, Lowton, Warrington, Cheshire, WA3 2AP
Officers: Eddie Patrick Renda [1956] Director; Arthur Sutcliffe [1947] Director

Jia Bo Rui International Trade Limited
Incorporated: 30 April 2018
Registered Office: 28 Cottall Avenue, Chatham, Kent, ME4 6HG
Major Shareholder: Ruizi Jiang
Officers: Ruizi Jiang [1985] Director/Self Employed [Chinese]

Jica Beauty Products Limited
Incorporated: 21 April 1978
Net Worth: £519,600 Total Assets: £528,220
Registered Office: 37 Oakdene Road, Peasmarsh, Guildford, Surrey, GU3 1ND
Major Shareholder: Caroline Frances Kentish
Officers: Caroline Frances Kentish, Secretary; Caroline Frances Kentish [1964] Director

Jigsaw International Holdings Limited
Incorporated: 20 December 2001
Previous: Jigsaw European Holdings Limited
Net Worth Deficit: £155,390 Total Assets: £2,050
Registered Office: 6 Dallas Court, Salford, M50 2GF
Major Shareholder: Dipak Maganlal Thakrar
Officers: Dipak Maganlal Thakrar [1966] Director

Jigu Corporation Limited
Incorporated: 2 May 2017
Net Worth Deficit: £2,470 Total Assets: £445,000
Registered Office: 1st & 2nd Floors Flat, 42 Overstone Road, London, W6 0AB
Shareholders: Ainhoa Llorente Coto; Lic. Anabel Leibovic Farrar
Officers: Anabel Leibovic Farrar [1982] Director [Argentinian]; Dr. Ainhoa Llorente Coto [1971] Director [Spanish]

Jivesse Limited
Incorporated: 6 March 2018
Registered Office: 20-22 Wenlock Road, London, N1 7GU
Major Shareholder: Mitesh Soma
Officers: Mitesh Soma [1976] Director

JJ Promotions Limited
Incorporated: 5 December 2017
Registered Office: 4 Darleydale, Crawley, W Sussex, RH11 8QS
Officers: Muhterem Yakin [1971] Director/C.S.M [Turkish]

JK Hair & Beauty Salon Supplies Ltd
Incorporated: 9 October 2017
Registered Office: 25 Munro Avenue, Stirling, FK9 5QZ
Major Shareholder: Zhanna Koc
Officers: Zhanna Koc [1979] Director

JLE Trading Limited
Incorporated: 13 January 2017
Net Worth: £38 Total Assets: £617
Registered Office: 4 Arden Mews, Station Road, Wilmcote, Stratford upon Avon, Warwicks, CV37 9UG
Major Shareholder: James Lewis Eborall
Officers: James Lewis Eborall [1984] Director

JMAR Op No 2 Ltd
Incorporated: 12 June 2013 Employees: 1
Net Worth: £189,669 Total Assets: £353,818
Registered Office: 20-22 Wenlock Road, London, N1 7GU
Shareholders: Abraham Kayrouz; Julia Marinkovich
Officers: Abraham Kayrouz, Secretary; Abraham Kayrouz [1979] Director/Accountant [Australian]; Julia Katherine Marinkovich [1980] Director/Media [Australian]

JML Cosmetics Limited
Incorporated: 23 August 2017
Net Worth: £199,466 Total Assets: £202,716
Registered Office: 610 Chiswick High Road, Chiswick Green, London, W4 5RU
Parent: John Mills Limited
Officers: Kenneth John Daly [1971] Director

JNVshop La Piazza Delle Idee Ltd
Incorporated: 12 July 2017
Registered Office: 24 Churchill Road, London, NW2 5EA
Shareholders: Jeanith Calvo Villecco; Carmine Villecco
Officers: Carmine Villecco [1975] Director/Chef [Italian]; Jeanith Calvo Villecco [1969] Director [Filipino]

Jo Loves (Wholesale) Limited
Incorporated: 23 March 2016 Employees: 2
Net Worth Deficit: £9,890 Total Assets: £37,463
Registered Office: Suite 4, Queripel House, 1 Duke of York Square, London, SW3 4LY
Shareholders: Gary John Willcox; Joanne Lesley Willcox
Officers: Gary John Willcox [1960] Director; Joanne Lesley Willcox [1963] Director

Joanna Naturals Limited
Incorporated: 30 August 2018
Registered Office: 71-75 Shelton Street, London, WC2H 9JQ
Major Shareholder: Joanne Linda Manchester
Officers: Joanne Linda Manchester [1973] Director/Aromatherapist & Natural Skincare Formulator

Joddor London Limited
Incorporated: 20 February 2018
Registered Office: Office 118, 4 Montpelier Street, London, SW7 1EE
Major Shareholder: Soumia El-Bouziani
Officers: Soumia El - Bouziani [1975] Director

Johnson & Johnson Limited
Incorporated: 8 October 1987 Employees: 307
Net Worth: £80,768,000 Total Assets: £204,111,008
Registered Office: Foundation Park, Roxborough Way, Maidenhead, Berks, SL6 3UG
Parent: Johnson & Johnson Management Ltd
Officers: Luc Huys [1967] Managing Director [Belgian]; Graham Rice [1968] Finance Director; Christopher Ronald Thorne [1959] Director/Accountant

Jojoba Cosmetics Limited
Incorporated: 3 August 2009
Net Worth Deficit: £45,833 Total Assets: £79,294
Registered Office: 3 Leeming Road, Borehamwood, Herts, WD6 4EB
Officers: Michael Byers [1986] Director/Entrepreneur

Jolly Rogers Crew Limited
Incorporated: 15 January 2013
Registered Office: Flat 5, 43-49 Gunnersbury Lane, London, W3 8ED
Shareholder: Mariusz Banas
Officers: Mariusz Banas [1977] Director [Polish]

Jonatho Ltd
Incorporated: 28 March 2018
Registered Office: 71-75 Shelton Street, Covent Garden, London, WC2H 9JQ
Major Shareholder: Johannes Joore
Officers: Johannes Joore, Secretary; Johannes Joore [1970] Director [Dutch]

Leigh Jones & Associates Ltd
Incorporated: 31 October 2017
Registered Office: Kemp House, 160 City Road, London, EC1V 2NX
Major Shareholder: David Jones
Officers: David Jones, Secretary; David Leigh Jones [1958] Director; Sonia Margaret Jones [1957] Director

Margaret Jordan Cosmetics Limited
Incorporated: 23 January 2018
Registered Office: Kemp House, City Road, London, EC1V 2NX
Officers: Margaret Jordan [1988] Director/Cosmetics

Jorum of Scotland Limited
Incorporated: 29 November 2018
Registered Office: 3-8 Rodney Street, Edinburgh, EH7 4EN
Major Shareholder: Euan David McCall
Officers: Euan David McCall [1989] Director/Perfumer, Entrepreneur

Josie Rose Ltd
Incorporated: 15 January 2019
Registered Office: 19 East Parade, Harrogate, N Yorks, HG1 5LF
Shareholders: Adrian John Daniels; Anna Lily Daniels
Officers: Adrian John Daniels [1980] Director [British/Australian]; Anna Lily Daniels [1982] Director [British/Australian]

Jouer Jouer Limited
Incorporated: 20 March 2018
Registered Office: 54 Pelton Road, Greenwich, London, SE10 9AH
Major Shareholder: Carlos Davies
Officers: Carlos Davies, Secretary; Carlos Davies [1993] Director/Finance Analyst

Joy Limited
Incorporated: 13 December 2005 Employees: 15
Net Worth: £2,547,644 Total Assets: £6,390,251
Registered Office: 1 Holly Court, Tring Road, Wendover, Aylesbury, Bucks, HP22 6PE
Shareholder: Leslie Georgie Spears
Officers: Rachel Maher, Secretary; Reginald Keith Chandler [1947] Director; Rachel Claire Maher [1966] Director; Margaret Jean Plastow [1966] Director/Chartered Accountant; Georgina Louise Ramsay [1989] Sales & Marketing Director; Leslie George Spears [1937] Director; Stephen Robert Way [1939] Director

Joyganics Ltd
Incorporated: 22 May 2018
Registered Office: 24 Pettys Brook Road, Chineham, Basingstoke, Hants, RG24 8RW
Major Shareholder: Tobi Mistura Browne-Marke
Officers: Tobi Mistura Browne-Marke [1993] Director [Nigerian]

JP Products and Services Limited
Incorporated: 29 October 2018
Registered Office: 10 Park Stone Rise, Shelf, Halifax, W Yorks, HX3 7NL
Major Shareholder: Jake Alexander Poucher
Officers: Jake Alexander Poucher [1993] Director/Financial Consultant

JS Marketing (N.I.) Limited
Incorporated: 11 May 2000 Employees: 7
Net Worth: £622,872 Total Assets: £875,495
Registered Office: 134a Head Road, Ballymartin, Newry, Co Down, BT34 4PX
Shareholder: Paul Shields
Officers: Paul Shields, Secretary; Paul Shields [1970] Director [Irish]; Sinead Mary Shields [1971] Director [Irish]

JSProfessionnel Limited
Incorporated: 28 September 2017
Registered Office: 39 Stanhope Gardens, Kensington, London, SW7 5QY
Major Shareholder: Jasjinder Singh Jhally
Officers: Jasjinder Singh Jhally [1956] Director [Australian]

Jufa Cosmetics Ltd
Incorporated: 2 October 2017
Registered Office: 20-22 Wenlock Road, London, N1 7GU
Shareholders: Dobrin Dobrev Dobrev; Dobrin Dobrev Dobrev
Officers: Dobrin Dobrev Dobrev [1969] Director [Bulgarian]

Juju Beauty Care Ltd
Incorporated: 8 April 2014
Registered Office: 4 Garnett Drive, Bricket Wood, St Albans, Herts, AL2 3QN
Major Shareholder: Everoy Johnson
Officers: Jurema Mendes Hopkins [1965] Director [Brazilian]

Juliajosh Limited
Incorporated: 1 November 2016
Net Worth Deficit: £260 Total Assets: £2,393
Registered Office: Kemp House, 160 City Road, London, EC1V 2NX
Shareholders: Saji Mathew; Susan Saji Mathew
Officers: Saji Mathew, Secretary; Saji Mathew [1970] Director; Susan Saji Mathew [1971] Director

Julie's Natural Health Ltd
Incorporated: 10 July 2017
Registered Office: 3F River House Business Centre, Castle Lane, Coleraine, Co Londonderry, BT51 3DR
Major Shareholder: Thomas Jones
Officers: Prof Thomas Jones [1966] Director

Julien Miguel Ltd
Incorporated: 8 March 2010
Net Worth: £1 *Total Assets:* £4,345
Registered Office: Unit 8-12, 117-119 Denmark Road, London, SE5 9LB
Parent: Alliance UK Ltd
Officers: Alcinda Camacho Jardim Fernandes, Secretary; Alcinda Camacho Jardim Fernandes [1971] Finance Director [Portuguese]; Emanuel Pedro Andrade Fernandes [1968] Managing Director [Portuguese]

Julio & Ejder Ltd
Incorporated: 25 February 2017 *Employees:* 2
Net Worth: £869 *Total Assets:* £1,073
Registered Office: 180e Du Cane Road, London, W12 0TX
Shareholder: Julio Lemos
Officers: Antonio Julio Nogueira Gomes de Lemos [1974] Director/Cook [Portuguese]

Juni Cosmetics Limited
Incorporated: 23 March 2018
Registered Office: Lovewell Blake LLP, The Gables, Old Market Street, Thetford, Norfolk, IP24 2EN
Shareholders: Madeleine White; Suzanne White; Kevin White
Officers: Kevin White [1964] Director; Madeleine White [1997] Director/Make Up Artist; Suzanne White [1962] Director

Just Acrylics Ltd
Incorporated: 26 May 2018
Registered Office: 115-116 Spon End, Coventry, Warwicks, CV1 3HF
Major Shareholder: Nicola Helena Salmon
Officers: Nicola Helena Salmon [1979] Director [Jamaican]

Just Beautiful Skin Ltd
Incorporated: 28 February 2013
Registered Office: Dept 1942, 601 International House, 223 Regent Street, London, W1B 2QD
Officers: MD Ferrozzi Abd Majid [1982] Director/Entrepreneur [Bruneian]; Iram Nadia Xeynah Kassam [1982] Director; Zainas Sadeken Mohd Sanusi [1983] Director [Bruneian]

Just Cosmetics Ltd
Incorporated: 18 December 2013
Registered Office: 101a Brockley Grove, London, SE4 1DZ
Officers: Justine Elizabeth Jenkins [1970] Director

Just Do You Limited
Incorporated: 21 January 2019
Registered Office: 126D Friern Road, London, SE22 0AY
Shareholders: Stephanie-Grace Amoakohene; Elizabeth Ellen Adade
Officers: Stephanie-Grace Amoakohene [2002] Director

Just The Product Ltd
Incorporated: 5 December 2011
Registered Office: Bompy Hollow, The Fairway, Godalming, Surrey, GU7 1PG
Parent: Paul Weigall
Officers: Richard Kentish, Secretary; Paul Jonathan Stewart Weigall [1962] Sales Director

Justins Essentials Ltd
Incorporated: 2 January 2019
Registered Office: 21 Forge Close, Huntington, York, YO32 9LX
Major Shareholder: Madalin Iustin Grigore
Officers: Madalin Iustin Grigore [1983] Director/Electrical Engineer [Romanian]

JWWJ Limited
Incorporated: 20 June 2018
Registered Office: Studio 2, 16A Chapel Market, London, N1 9EZ
Major Shareholder: Jonathan Ward
Officers: Jonathan Ward [1973] Director/Designer

JZM International Limited
Incorporated: 21 September 2016
Net Worth: £355 *Total Assets:* £1,055
Registered Office: Flat 11, 63 Fairthorn Road, London, SE7 7FX
Major Shareholder: Yujuan Li
Officers: Yujuan Li [1987] Director [Chinese]

K Co Cosmetics Ltd
Incorporated: 20 July 2018
Registered Office: 22 Antringham Gardens, Edgbaston, Birmingham, B15 3QL
Major Shareholder: Kathleen Westwood
Officers: Kathleen Westwood [1952] Director/Beautician

K Wholesale Limited
Incorporated: 21 November 2018
Registered Office: Flat 192, iLand Apartment, 41 Essex Street, Birmingham, B5 4TU
Major Shareholder: Qian Cheng
Officers: Qian Cheng [1988] Director [Chinese]

K. S. D Beauty Zone Ltd
Incorporated: 3 November 2017
Registered Office: Flat 28 Webheath, Netherwood Street, London, NW6 2JR
Major Shareholder: Yanyan Liu
Officers: Lady Yanyan Liu [1987] Director [Chinese]

K. V. Fair Trades Limited
Incorporated: 13 November 2018
Registered Office: 2 Exon Street, Walworth, London, SE17 2JW
Officers: Ketija Vitola [1979] Director [Latvian]

K.B. Salon Supplies Limited
Incorporated: 4 March 2004
Net Worth: £2,670,000 *Total Assets:* £5,880,000
Registered Office: Salon Supplies, Bond Street, Southampton, SO14 5QA
Parent: Marblesea Ltd
Officers: Ian Martin Campbell Aherne, Secretary; Ian Martin Campbell Aherne [1980] Director/Accountant; Keith Boothroyde [1947] Director; Anthony Reginald Webb [1954] Director

K2 Supplies Ltd
Incorporated: 8 January 2019
Registered Office: 22 Phoenix Court, Black Eagle Drive, Northfleet, Kent, DA11 9AQ
Officers: Ankit Patel [1985] Director

K2Y Limited
Incorporated: 4 December 2017
Registered Office: 71-75 Shelton Street, Covent Garden, London, WC2H 9JQ
Major Shareholder: Raghbir Sanghera
Officers: Raghbir Sanghera, Secretary; Raghbir Sanghera [1968] Director/Accountant

K3W Trading Limited
Incorporated: 26 March 2018
Registered Office: Kemp House, 160 City Road, London, EC1V 2NX
Major Shareholder: Edna Agyeman Woname
Officers: Edna Woname, Secretary; Edna Agyeman Woname [1974] Director/Development Coordinator

K588 Limited
Incorporated: 5 June 2018
Registered Office: 3rd Floor, Paternoster House, 65 St Paul's Churchyard, London, EC4M 8AB
Shareholders: Charles James Anthony Bradshaw; Robert Michael Calcraft
Officers: Charles James Anthony Bradshaw [1975] Director; Robert Michael Calcraft [1964] Director/Consultant

Kailijumei Ltd
Incorporated: 30 August 2016
Net Worth: £662 *Total Assets:* £662
Registered Office: Suite A, 1 New Road, Grays, Essex, RM17 6NG
Major Shareholder: Cezary Bielawski
Officers: Cezary Bielawski [1974] Director/Manager [Polish]

Kalabash Limited
Incorporated: 4 January 2018
Registered Office: First Floor, 85 Great Portland Street, London, W1W 7LT
Major Shareholder: Sharron Jenkins
Officers: Sharron Jenkins [1963] Director/Business Owner

Gabriel Kalevi Ltd
Incorporated: 17 April 2018
Registered Office: 17 Steepwood Croft, Birmingham, B30 1AR
Major Shareholder: Gabrial Kalvei
Officers: Sir Gabrial Kalvei, Secretary; Sir Gabrial Kalvei [1988] Director

Kamarino Limited
Incorporated: 1 October 2016
Net Worth: £12,545 *Total Assets:* £16,146
Registered Office: Hussains Hall, 38 Devonshire Street, Keighley, W Yorks, BD21 2AU
Major Shareholder: Giuseppe Marino
Officers: Giuseppe Marino [1963] Director [Italian]

Kamila Health & Beauty Ltd
Incorporated: 18 February 2019
Registered Office: 16 Melford Avenue, Barking, Essex, IG11 9HT
Major Shareholder: Nazir Miah
Officers: Nazir Miah [1990] Managing Director

Kandahar Trading Limited
Incorporated: 5 March 2018
Registered Office: 152 Oldfield Lane South, Greenford, Middlesex, UB6 9JX
Major Shareholder: Obidullah Yousfzai
Officers: Obidullah Yousfzai, Secretary; Obidullah Yousfzai [1953] Director

Kandi Apple Limited
Incorporated: 4 December 2018
Registered Office: 27 Manor Road, Loughborough, Leics, LE11 2LU
Officers: Kelly Mitchell [1987] Director/Beauty Therapist

Kaniz International Limited
Incorporated: 12 June 2018
Registered Office: Mamado House, 8 Parr Road, Stanmore, Middlesex, HA7 1NP
Officers: Kumail Nasser [1996] Director

Kaniz Organics Limited
Incorporated: 11 June 2018
Registered Office: Mamado House, 8 Parr Road, Stanmore, Middlesex, HA7 1NP
Major Shareholder: Kumail Nasser
Officers: George Myrants, Secretary; Kumail Nasser [1996] Director

Kanj Wholesale Ltd
Incorporated: 12 December 2018
Registered Office: 5 Chamber House Farm, Rochdale Road East, Heywood, Lancs, OL10 1SD
Major Shareholder: Antonio Lloyd Rizzelli
Officers: Antonio Lloyd Rizzelli [1993] Director/Sales Person [Italian]

Karaama Fragrances Ltd
Incorporated: 16 May 2017
Registered Office: Omega Accountants, 54 Lower Addiscombe Road, Croydon, Surrey, CR0 6AA
Major Shareholder: Runu Miah
Officers: Runu Miah [1973] Director

Yasmin Karimi Ltd
Incorporated: 5 August 2014
Net Worth Deficit: £49,058 *Total Assets:* £21,416
Registered Office: Victoria House, 18 Dalston Gardens, Stanmore, Middlesex, HA7 1BU
Major Shareholder: Yasmin Akhtar
Officers: Yasmin Akhtar [1986] Director/Beauty

Karina Enterprise Ltd
Incorporated: 11 August 2011
Net Worth: £2,326 *Total Assets:* £2,890
Registered Office: 34 Metcalfe Court, John Harrison Way, London, SE10 0BY
Major Shareholder: Ismael Kallon
Officers: Ismael Kallon [1980] Director/Staff Nurse

Karium Ltd
Incorporated: 14 August 1990 *Employees:* 61
Previous: Godrej Consumer Products (UK) Limited
Net Worth: £14,725,599 *Total Assets:* £29,025,880
Registered Office: Falcon House, 115-123 Staines Road, Hounslow, Middlesex, TW3 3LL
Parent: JZ Consumer Brands Limited
Officers: Benjamin David Hammersley, Secretary; Lee Graham Gelderd [1974] Managing Director; Jock Green-Armytage [1945] Director; Benjamin David Hammersley [1970] Finance Director; Alexander James MacGillivray Langmuir [1985] Director; Richard Reverdy Otley [1974] Director/Chairman [British Virgin Islander]; Miguel Rueda Hernando [1967] Director [Spanish]; Martin Stephen Northcote Wright [1968] Director

Kathleen Natural Limited
Incorporated: 17 April 2014
Net Worth: £24,050 *Total Assets:* £36,890
Registered Office: 20-22 Wenlock Road, London, N1 7GU
Major Shareholder: Mei Man Chu
Officers: Kang Wing Ken Chow, Secretary; Mei Man Chu [1968] Director/Businessman [Hong Kong]

Kathy Salon Equipment Limited
Incorporated: 15 February 2018
Registered Office: 89 Umfreville Road, Harringay, London, N4 1RZ
Major Shareholder: Katherine Deal
Officers: Katherine Deal, Secretary; Katherine Deal [1985] Director/Salon Equipment Supply

Kathy Sue-Ann's Ltd
Incorporated: 14 December 2018
Registered Office: Kemp House, 160 City Road, London, EC1V 2NX
Major Shareholder: Kathy Drummond
Officers: Kathy Drummond, Secretary; Kathy Drummond [1987] Director/Paediatric Nurse

Kavali Cosmetics Limited
Incorporated: 11 February 2019
Registered Office: The Apex, 2 Sheriffs Orchard, Coventry, Warwicks, CV1 3PP
Officers: Kathleen Marie Ali [1990] Director

Kaxton Limited
Incorporated: 20 September 2016
Net Worth Deficit: £99 *Total Assets:* £1
Registered Office: Trinity House, Heather Park Drive, Wembley, Middlesex, HA0 1SU
Major Shareholder: Usha Manu
Officers: Usha Manu [1992] Director [Portuguese]

Kayanna Ltd
Incorporated: 11 December 2018
Registered Office: 25b Hargrave Park, London, N19 5JP
Officers: Albert Marie Hanitra Rakoto, Secretary; Albert Marie Hanitra Rakoto [1989] Director [French]

Kazi Brothers Group Limited
Incorporated: 4 November 2010
Previous: Kazi Brothers Wholesale Limited
Net Worth Deficit: £230,183 *Total Assets:* £245,675
Registered Office: Unit 56 Pedley Street, off Vallance Road, London, E1 5BW
Shareholder: Kazi Mohammed Abidur Rahman
Officers: Kazi MD Luthfur Rahman, Secretary; Kazi Mohammed Abidur Rahman [1994] Director

KBM London Limited
Incorporated: 5 March 2018
Registered Office: 135-137 Station Road, Chingford, London, E4 6AG
Major Shareholder: Kathleen Baird-Murray
Officers: Kathleen Baird-Murray [1968] Director/Freelance Writer

KD Cosmetics (Midlands) Ltd
Incorporated: 12 December 2018
Registered Office: 20 Burns Street, Ilkeston, Derbys, DE7 8AA
Major Shareholder: Darren James Heatherington
Officers: Darren James Heatherington [1967] Director/Manager

KDM Supplies Limited
Incorporated: 14 March 2002
Net Worth: £40,760 *Total Assets:* £123,800
Registered Office: The Annexe, Walton Lodge, Hillcliffe Road, Walton, Warrington, Cheshire, WA4 6NU
Shareholder: Andrew Robert Bush
Officers: Andrew Robert Bush, Secretary/Sales Manager; Andrew Robert Bush [1960] Director/Sales Manager; Beverley Anne Bush [1962] Director/Administration Manager

Kehal Ltd
Incorporated: 2 November 2018
Registered Office: Premier Business Centre, 47-49 Park Royal Road, London, NW10 7LQ
Major Shareholder: Abdulazeez Althefeeri
Officers: Abdulazeez Althefeeri [1979] Director [Kuwaiti]

Kenbar Beauty Products Limited
Incorporated: 21 October 1992
Net Worth Deficit: £110,050 *Total Assets:* £11,000
Registered Office: 37 Oakdene Road, Peasmarsh, Guildford, Surrey, GU3 1ND
Major Shareholder: Caroline Frances Kentish
Officers: Caroline Frances Kentish, Secretary; Caroline Frances Kentish [1964] Director

Kendo Brands Limited
Incorporated: 26 May 2016 *Employees:* 148
Net Worth: £550,310 *Total Assets:* £5,347,231
Registered Office: 6th Floor, UK House, 180 Oxford Street, London, W1D 1AB
Parent: LVMH Moet Hennessy Louis Vuitton
Officers: Christine Cassidy [1968] Director; Karen Sue Cate [1964] Director [American]; David Suliteanu [1953] Director [American]

Kendra Cosmetics Limited
Incorporated: 13 June 2018
Registered Office: 10 Robert Lewis Court, Wigan, Lancs, WN5 9NL
Major Shareholder: Tracey Allen
Officers: Tracey Allen [1983] Director/Project Manager

Kent Cosmetics Limited
Incorporated: 9 November 1979
Net Worth: £772,400 *Total Assets:* £1,620,000
Registered Office: Kent House, Ashford Road, Harrietsham, Maidstone, Kent, ME17 1BW
Parent: Northdown Cosmetics Ltd
Officers: Hazel Jean Young, Secretary; Alan John Jenner [1959] Director/Sales and Marketing; David James Jenner [1964] Director/Works Manager; Hazel Jean Young [1957] Director/Administrator

Kenzak Beauty and Jewellery Ltd
Incorporated: 24 April 2018
Registered Office: 10 Needham Road, Luton, Beds, LU4 9HD
Major Shareholder: Tbarak Hawash
Officers: Tbarak Hawash [1991] Director/Teacher

Kerria, Limited
Incorporated: 21 December 2018
Registered Office: 22 Mount Ephraim, Tunbridge Wells, Kent, TN4 8AS
Shareholders: Kamel Mecheri; Keiko Mecheri
Officers: Kamel Mecheri [1959] Director/Business Owner [American/French]; Keiko Mecheri [1969] Director/Business Owner [American/Japanese]

Khali Min Limited
Incorporated: 17 January 2019
Registered Office: 32 Cubitt Street, London, WC1X 0LR
Shareholders: Anna Vanessa Karlo; Jehan Marei
Officers: Anna Vanessa Karlo [1980] Director/Founder [American]; Jehan Marei [1977] Director/Founder [Egyptian]

Khuba Limited
Incorporated: 7 March 2018
Registered Office: c/o PSB Accountants, Townsend Lane, London, NW9 8TZ
Officers: Fiona Jane Chandler-Day [1964] Director

Khushi Skincare Limited
Incorporated: 21 November 2017
Registered Office: 6 Sycamore Court, Leeds, LS8 2NY
Major Shareholder: Surinder Kaur Rall
Officers: Surinder Kaur Rall [1985] Director/Manager

Kiara Beauty Ltd
Incorporated: 13 December 2018
Registered Office: 145 Okehampton Crescent, Welling, Kent, DA16 1DH
Major Shareholder: Yashara Rukshani Thalgaswatta
Officers: Yashara Rukshani Thalgaswatta [1990] Director [Sri Lankan]

Kiara Sky Professional Nail Distribution Limited
Incorporated: 12 December 2016
Net Worth: £114,428 *Total Assets:* £406,750
Registered Office: Kiara Sky Professional Nails Europe, 105 Soho Hill, Birmingham, B19 1AY
Shareholders: Van Tuan Phan; Thi Huong Thao Nguyen
Officers: Van Tuan Phan [1983] Director

Kiddeo Limited
Incorporated: 1 May 2014
Net Worth Deficit: £31,510 *Total Assets:* £3,000
Registered Office: Unit 34, 67-68 Hatton Garden, London, EC1N 8JY
Major Shareholder: Maggie Oyewole
Officers: Maggie Oyewole [1980] Director/Manufacturer

Kidlex Limited
Incorporated: 30 June 1982 *Employees:* 6
Net Worth: £906,353 *Total Assets:* £1,155,463
Registered Office: 83 High Street, West Wickham, Kent, BR4 0LS
Major Shareholder: Paul Mendoza
Officers: Teresa Jones [1972] Sales Director; Paul Mendoza [1961] Stores and Sales Director

Kiki Body Limited
Incorporated: 19 March 2015
Net Worth Deficit: £1,879 *Total Assets:* £2,314
Registered Office: 37 Church Way, London, N20 0JZ
Major Shareholder: Katerina Androulla Protopapas
Officers: Katerina Androulla Protopapas [1982] Director

Kimibeauty Ltd
Incorporated: 27 September 2018
Registered Office: 20-22 Wenlock Road, London, N1 7GU
Major Shareholder: Kimberley Anne England
Officers: Kimberley Anne England [1982] Director

The Kind Planet Company Limited
Incorporated: 30 January 2018
Registered Office: Cassidy's Chartered Accountants Ltd, South Stour Offices, Roman Road, Mersham, Kent, TN25 7HS
Shareholders: Kevin Francis Godlington; Britt Godlington
Officers: Britt Godlington [1986] Director/Accountant [American]; Kevin Francis Godlington [1975] Director

Kind2 Limited
Incorporated: 13 August 2018
Registered Office: 70 Colebrooke Row, London, N1 8AA
Shareholders: Susan Gai Campbell; Richard Douglas Bellingham
Officers: Richard Douglas Bellingham [1968] Finance Director; Susan Gai Campbell [1966] Director/CEO & Founder

The King of Shaves Company Limited
Incorporated: 27 February 2008
Net Worth Deficit: £2,982,000 *Total Assets:* £2,190,000
Registered Office: 10 Penn Road, Beaconsfield, Bucks, HP9 2LH
Parent: The King of Shaves Holding Company Limited
Officers: Andrew Steven Hill [1968] Director; Douglas Richard John King [1967] Director/Fund Manager; William Ashley King [1965] Director

The King of Sytle Ltd
Incorporated: 5 November 2018
Registered Office: 20-22 Wenlock Road, London, N1 7GU
Major Shareholder: Metish Kachra
Officers: Metish Kachra [1978] Director

King's Vegan Grooming Ltd
Incorporated: 7 June 2017
Net Worth: £1 *Total Assets:* £1
Registered Office: Leigh Court Business Centre, Pill Road, Abbots Leigh, Bristol, BS8 3RA
Major Shareholder: Blue Robert John O'Connor
Officers: Blue Robert John O'Connor [1987] Director/International Trade Researcher

Kingdom Scotland Limited
Incorporated: 26 February 2016
Net Worth: £2,070 *Total Assets:* £17,190
Registered Office: 15 Young Street, Edinburgh, EH2 4HU
Officers: Imogen Russon-Taylor [1970] Director

Kirimi Limited
Incorporated: 17 September 2008
Net Worth: £8,500 *Total Assets:* £15,690
Registered Office: Peterbridge House, The Lakes, Northampton, NN4 7HB
Shareholders: Francis Dominic Gilchrist; Robin Hugh Maxted
Officers: Donna Juliette Maxted [1979] Director; Robin Hugh Maxted [1955] Director

Kiss Products UK Limited
Incorporated: 17 July 1997
Net Worth: £168,733 *Total Assets:* £388,868
Registered Office: Unit 9, 97-101 Peregrine Road, Hainault Business Park, Ilford, Essex, IG6 3XH
Major Shareholder: Akbar Choudry
Officers: Elizabeth Choudhry, Secretary; Akbar Choudhry [1962] Director; Elizabeth Choudhry [1973] Director

Kissess Lips of The Essence Ltd
Incorporated: 18 June 2018
Registered Office: Flat 6, New Street, Stoke on Trent, Staffs, ST6 4GX
Major Shareholder: Fiona Katherine Douglas
Officers: Fiona Katherine Douglas [1990] Director/Carer

The Kitchen Witch Aromatherapy Limited
Incorporated: 12 July 2017
Registered Office: 12 Cromwell Heights, Cromwell Street, Leeds, LS9 7SQ
Major Shareholder: Michelle Haigh
Officers: Michelle Haigh [1987] Director/Manager

Kitoko Make Up Ltd
Incorporated: 10 February 2017
Registered Office: Flat 7, Oakley House, Hotspur Street, London, SE11 6BT
Officers: Bibish Mbemba Nseko Mayala [1977] Director/Beautician [Congolese]; Nella Mayitane Muabinga [1980] Director/Beautician

Kityee Limited
Incorporated: 5 September 2017
Registered Office: Apartment 51, 71 Dublin Road, Belfast, BT2 7HG
Officers: Rachel Kit Yee Tang, Secretary; Rachel Kit Yee Tang [1995] Director/Makeup Artist

Kizzle Beauty Ltd
Incorporated: 17 July 2018
Registered Office: 48 Springfield Court, Forsythia Close, Ilford, Essex, IG1 2BN
Major Shareholder: Ekhoaye Aigbogun
Officers: Ekhoaye Aigbogun [1987] Creative Director [Nigerian]

Jennifer Klar Ltd
Incorporated: 23 October 2018
Registered Office: 92a Dunsmure Road, London, N16 5JY
Major Shareholder: Moses Breuer
Officers: Moses Breuer [1999] Director

Klean Skincare Ltd
Incorporated: 6 April 2018
Registered Office: 13 Lorton Close, Middleton, Manchester, M24 4NB
Shareholder: Ewelina Barbara Forma
Officers: Ewelina Barbara Forma [1985] Director/Store Assistant [Polish]

KM Cosmetics Distribution Limited
Incorporated: 21 August 2017
Registered Office: 71-75 Shelton Street, Covent Garden, London, WC2H 9JQ
Major Shareholder: Fatima Mohamed Sharif Abdulrahman
Officers: Fatima Mohamed Sharif Abdulrahman [1986] Director

KMC's Fabulous Cosmetics Ltd
Incorporated: 9 November 2018
Registered Office: 58 Food Street, Motherwell, N Lanarks, ML1 3TA
Major Shareholder: Kelly Marie Caulfield
Officers: Kelly Marie Caulfield [1987] Director/Beauty

KMI Brands Limited
Incorporated: 24 August 2001 *Employees:* 32
Net Worth: £4,664,000 *Total Assets:* £12,905,000
Registered Office: Floor 1, Harlequin House, 7 High Street, Teddington, Middlesex, TW11 8EE
Parent: Knowledge & Merchandising Inc Limited
Officers: Charlotte Amy Lee, Secretary; Hiten Jackis Dayal [1958] Director; Lorna Mitchell [1975] Product and Brand Director; Rachel Lisa Parsonage [1974] Managing Director

KMY Group Ltd
Incorporated: 6 December 2018
Registered Office: 59 Devons Road, London, E3 3DW
Major Shareholder: Karolis Mykolaitis
Officers: Karolis Mykolaitis [1994] Director/Manager [Lithuanian]

KMZA Enterprises Ltd
Incorporated: 4 December 2017
Registered Office: 272 Bath Street, Glasgow, G2 4JR
Major Shareholder: Khurram Iqbal
Officers: Khurram Iqbal [1980] Director/Technical Analyst

Knight & Wilson Limited
Incorporated: 1 July 2014
Net Worth: £1,297 *Total Assets:* £46,892
Registered Office: 3 Acorn Business Centre, Northarbour Road, Portsmouth, PO6 3TH
Shareholders: Scott Lee Limited; Eric John Bailey
Officers: Rachel Barnes, Secretary; Douglas John Bailey [1978] Director; Eric John Bailey [1949] Director; Lee Steven Bannister [1976] Director

Knight & Wilson Trading Limited
Incorporated: 15 August 2014 *Employees:* 2
Net Worth: £858,479 *Total Assets:* £2,254,243
Registered Office: 3 Acorn Business Centre, Northarbour Road, Portsmouth, PO6 3TH
Parent: Knight & Wilson Limited
Officers: Rachel Barnes, Secretary; Douglas John Bailey [1978] Director; Eric John Bailey [1949] Director; Lee Steven Bannister [1976] Director

Amelia Knight Holdings Limited
Incorporated: 5 December 2013 *Employees:* 301
Net Worth: £4,078,868 *Total Assets:* £16,228,597
Registered Office: The Pavilions, Knutsford Business Park, Mobberley Road, Knutsford, Cheshire, WA16 8ZR
Shareholder: David Brinley Salmon
Officers: Lynn Salmon, Secretary; Daniel Edward Salmon [1974] Group Operations Director; David Brinley Salmon [1950] Director/Chairman; Lynn Salmon [1951] Administrative Director; Mark Winston Salmon [1980] Technical Director; Paul James Salmon [1975] Marketing Director; Tiffany Lynn Salmon [1987] Design Director

Amelia Knight Limited
Incorporated: 29 December 1995 *Employees:* 46
Net Worth: £2,621,278 *Total Assets:* £11,315,489
Registered Office: The Pavilions, Mobberley Road, Knutsford Business Park, Knutsford, Cheshire, WA16 8ZR
Parent: Amelia Knight Holdings Limited
Officers: Lynn Salmon, Secretary/Administrative Director; Daniel Edward Salmon [1974] Group Operations Director; David Brinley Salmon [1950] Director/Chairman; Lynn Salmon [1951] Administrative Director; Mark Winston Salmon [1980] Technical Director; Paul James Salmon [1975] Logistics Director; Tiffany Lynn Salmon [1987] Design Director

Ko. Essentials Ltd.
Incorporated: 26 February 2018
Registered Office: 161 Tinshill Lane, Leeds, LS16 6EE
Major Shareholder: Megan Landreth-Smith
Officers: Christine Gilland Robinson [1984] Director/Entrepreneur; Joseph Landreth-Smith [1990] Director/Entrepreneur; Megan Landreth-Smith [1991] Director/Entrepreneur; Naomi Joy Partridge [1984] Director/Entrepreneur; Thomas Michael Partridge [1981] Director/Entrepreneur

J Kobain London Ltd
Incorporated: 5 September 2018
Registered Office: c/o Rus & Co, 1192 Stratford Road, Hall Green, Birmingham, B28 8AB
Major Shareholder: Yousaf Khan
Officers: Yousaf Khan [1972] Director

J Kobain Ltd
Incorporated: 5 September 2018
Registered Office: c/o Rus & Co, 1192 Stratford Road, Hall Green, Birmingham, B28 8AB
Major Shareholder: Yousaf Khan
Officers: Yousaf Khan [1972] Director

The Koha Beauty Company Limited
Incorporated: 23 January 2018
Registered Office: Kemp House, 160 City Road, London, EC1V 2NX
Major Shareholder: Zayaahn Hartley
Officers: Zayaahn Hartley [1983] Director/Founder [Belgian]

Kokoa UK Limited
Incorporated: 13 June 2017
Registered Office: 13 The Downs, Altrincham, Cheshire, WA14 2QD
Major Shareholder: Catherine Akobeng
Officers: Catherine Akobeng [1993] Director/Chief Executive Officer (CEO) & Founder

Kokolokahi Limited
Incorporated: 21 July 2016
Registered Office: 7-9 The Avenue, Eastbourne, E Sussex, BN21 3YA
Major Shareholder: Clare Louise Steadman
Officers: Clare Louise Steadman [1975] Director

Komodo Skincare Ltd
Incorporated: 26 January 2018
Registered Office: International House, 24 Holborn Viaduct, London, EC1A 2BN
Officers: Matthew Wallace-Jones [1987] Director

Konya Food Biotechnology Co., Limited
Incorporated: 12 March 2018
Registered Office: Companies House, Default Address, Cardiff, CF14 8LH
Major Shareholder: Shuangxing Yan
Officers: Shuangxing Yan [1983] Director [Chinese]

Kor Cosmetics Ltd
Incorporated: 8 July 2015
Registered Office: 55 Loveday Road, London, W13 9JT
Major Shareholder: Malgorzata Ollendorff
Officers: Malgorzata Ollendorff [1979] Director/Distribution [Polish]

Korban Beauty Limited
Incorporated: 4 May 2016
Net Worth Deficit: £1,397 *Total Assets:* £5,193
Registered Office: Flat 1, 267a Holdenhurst Road, Bournemouth, BH8 8BZ
Officers: Rogerio Fernando Balbo [1973] Director [Italian]

Korebeauty Limited
Incorporated: 15 April 2016 *Employees:* 1
Net Worth Deficit: £6,042 *Total Assets:* £23,955
Registered Office: 7 Howe Street, Edinburgh, EH3 6TE
Shareholders: Taekyung Gilbert; Christopher Gilbert
Officers: Christopher Gilbert [1975] Director; Taekung Gilbert [1980] Director

Koreesa Limited
Incorporated: 28 December 2007
Net Worth: £1,523 *Total Assets:* £57,233
Registered Office: 19b The Matchworks, 140 Speke Road, Garston, Liverpool, L19 2RF
Shareholders: Lisa Armitage-Adams; Sonia Armitage-Adams
Officers: Sonia Elizabeth Armitage-Adams, Secretary; Lisa Ann Armitage-Adams [1972] Director; Sonia Armitage-Adams [1966] Director

Korres International Limited
Incorporated: 11 March 2016
Registered Office: New Bridge Street House, 30-34 New Bridge Street, London, EC4V 6BJ
Parent: Korres Anonimi Etairia Fysika Proionta SA
Officers: George Tenediotis, Secretary; Sophia Spilotopoulou [1967] Director/Manager [Greek]; Dimitrios Vidakis [1962] Director/Manager [Greek]

Thomas Kosmala Parfums Ltd
Incorporated: 17 April 2014
Net Worth Deficit: £15,363 *Total Assets:* £39,284
Registered Office: Suites 2 & 3, Marine Trade Centre, Lockside, Brighton Marina Village, Brighton, BN2 5HA
Shareholders: Andrew Roger Moss; Tomasz Kosmala
Officers: Tomasz Kosmala [1981] Director/Perfumer [Polish]

Kounga Ltd
Incorporated: 3 March 2008
Previous: Nukua Limited
Net Worth: £176,010 *Total Assets:* £236,100
Registered Office: 75 St Josephs Vale, London, SE3 0XG
Shareholders: Javier Martinez de San Vicente; Jessy Alexandra Maguhn Elie
Officers: Jessy Alexandra Maguhn Elie [1980] Director/Auditor [Venezuelan]; Javier Martinez de San Vicente [1978] Director/Banker [Spanish]

Koutos Limited
Incorporated: 20 June 2017
Registered Office: The Coach House, Timber Close, Chislehurst, Kent, BR7 5PA
Major Shareholder: Luke John Fairbrass
Officers: Jack Craig Fairbrass [1987] Director

Kovet Kit Ltd
Incorporated: 7 January 2019
Registered Office: 5 Otter Way, Yiewsley, West Drayton, Middlesex, UB7 8FA
Major Shareholder: Chananchida Kongnurat
Officers: Chananchida Kongnurat [1994] Director/Designer [Thai]

Kozmar International Limited
Incorporated: 5 November 2018
Registered Office: 32 Willoughby Road, Hornsey, London, N8 0JG
Major Shareholder: Huseyin Sert
Officers: Huseyin Sert [1984] Director [Turkish]

KPACA Limited
Incorporated: 10 July 2013 *Employees:* 32
Net Worth: £1,359,289 *Total Assets:* £2,496,459
Registered Office: Cedar House, Hazell Drive, Newport, NP10 8FY
Major Shareholder: Salaheddine Nizam Osseiran
Officers: Bengt Algot Dahl [1949] Managing Director [Swedish]; Salaheddine Nizam Osseiran [1955] Director [Lebanese]; Charles William Tuke [1967] Director

Krish Shoppers Ltd
Incorporated: 23 November 2018
Registered Office: 27 Central Road, Wembley, Middlesex, HA0 2LQ
Officers: Vaishaliben Shah [1982] Director [Indian]

Krizma Cosmetics Ltd
Incorporated: 30 August 2018
Registered Office: 51 Turton Heights, Bolton, Lancs, BL2 3DU
Major Shareholder: Samantha Jane Prendergast
Officers: Samantha Jane Prendergast [1974] Managing Director

KSE Cosmetics Ltd
Incorporated: 29 March 2018
Registered Office: 136 Low Lane, Middlesbrough, Cleveland, TS5 8EE
Major Shareholder: Kassi Emadi
Officers: Kassi Emadi [1993] Managing Director

Kservices Group Ltd
Incorporated: 18 April 2018
Registered Office: 125 King Street, Great Yarmouth, Norfolk, NR30 2PQ
Officers: Zeferino Pinho Leite Da Costa [1972] Managing Director [Portuguese]

Kurlysue Limited
Incorporated: 6 November 2018
Registered Office: Flat 18, 85 Cobourg Road, Camberwell, London, SE5 0HU
Major Shareholder: Coline Casandra Benjamin
Officers: Coline Casandra Benjamin [1986] Director/Nurse [Jamaican]

L & L Sunlight Importers and Exporters Limited
Incorporated: 30 September 2016
Net Worth Deficit: £179 Total Assets: £1
Registered Office: 6th Floor, Amp House, Dingwall Road, Croydon, Surrey, CR0 2LX
Major Shareholder: Lucy Dolapo Esdale
Officers: Lucy Dolapo Esdale [1971] Director

L'Amour Cosmetics London Limited
Incorporated: 5 January 2018
Registered Office: c/o Charterwells, Old Brewery House, 189 Stanmore Hill, Stanmore, Middlesex, HA7 3HA
Shareholders: David Krishna Mallipal; Chhayaben Patel; Nilam Patel
Officers: David Krishna Mallipal [1985] Director; Chhayaben Patel [1985] Director; Nilam Patel [1989] Director

L'Anza Europe Limited
Incorporated: 18 June 1991 Employees: 28
Net Worth: £141,145 Total Assets: £917,748
Registered Office: 800 Wellworthy Road, Lymington, Hants, SO41 8JY
Shareholder: David John Rippon
Officers: Paul Anthony Hetherington [1967] Sales Director; Elizabeth Katharine Hornigold [1977] Operations Director; Hilton Hornigold [1974] Director; Dominic Anton Patten [1974] Director; Victoria Jane Patten [1975] Marketing Director; David John Rippon [1947] Director/Merchant Banker

L'Art & La Matiere Limited
Incorporated: 13 December 2018
Registered Office: H5 Ash Tree Court, Nottingham Business Park, Nottingham, NG8 6PY
Officers: Jessica Stephanie Sardo [1985] Director of SpA [French]

L'dreams Limited
Incorporated: 26 February 2019
Registered Office: 82 Stratford Road, Sparkhill, Birmingham, B11 1AN
Major Shareholder: Riyad Elmizeb
Officers: Riyad Elmizeb [2000] Director [French]

L'Oreal (U.K.) Limited
Incorporated: 24 December 1932 Employees: 4,846
Net Worth: £220,012,000 Total Assets: £561,248,000
Registered Office: 255 Hammersmith Road, London, W6 8AZ
Officers: Mark Andrew Chesson, Secretary; Stephan Jean Paul Marie Bezy [1963] Director [French]; Yannick Chalme [1958] Director/Group General Counsel [French]; Vianney Marie Hugues Derville [1967] Director [French]; Vismay Sharma [1971] Managing Director [Indian]; Geoffrey Christopher Skingsley [1958] Director/Chairman

L'Revolution Beauty Ltd
Incorporated: 2 July 2015
Net Worth Deficit: £3,122 Total Assets: £11,393
Registered Office: 36 St Lawrence Close, Wellington, Telford, Salop, TF1 3GB
Major Shareholder: Konstantins Lagutins
Officers: Konstantins Lagutins [1984] Director [Latvian]

L.A. Professional Cosmetic Labs Ltd.
Incorporated: 21 June 2017
Registered Office: 14 Royle Street, Sunderland, Tyne & Wear, SR2 9RJ
Major Shareholder: David Harding
Officers: David Harding [1991] Director

L.A.Tanning Company Ltd
Incorporated: 3 June 2011 Employees: 7
Net Worth Deficit: £122,355 Total Assets: £85,286
Registered Office: 62 Buxton Road, Heavily, Stockport, Cheshire, SK2 6NB
Shareholders: Daniel Moynihan; Carl Moynihan
Officers: Carl Michael Moynihan [1955] Director; Daniel Michael Moynihan [1974] Director

L.P Cosmetics Ltd
Incorporated: 11 September 2018
Registered Office: Flat 47, Phoenix Court, Chertsey Road, Feltham, Middlesex, TW13 4RN
Major Shareholder: Akil Porter
Officers: Akil Porter [1989] Director/Marketing Manager [American]

La Beauty Labs Ltd.
Incorporated: 22 August 2013
Previous: RPN Investment Ltd
Net Worth Deficit: £48,306 Total Assets: £9,807
Registered Office: Unit 23 Wadsworth Business Centre, 21 Wadsworth Road, Perivale, Greenford, Middlesex, UB6 7LQ
Major Shareholder: Patrycja Jolanta Nowak
Officers: Patrycja Jolanta Nowak [1986] Director [Polish]

La Bello Beauty Limited
Incorporated: 30 April 2018
Registered Office: 56 Milton Road, Belvedere, Kent, DA17 5BA
Officers: Adeyosola Adeyoyin Odufuwa [1988] Director; Sukurat Omolara Raji [1994] Director

La Boutique du Discount Ltd.
Incorporated: 28 March 2018
Registered Office: c/o MK-Consult, 16 Upper Woburn Place, London, WC1H 0BS
Officers: Nicolas Urban [1985] Director [French]

La Fumes Ltd
Incorporated: 4 February 2019
Registered Office: 42 Gwendolen Road, Leicester, LE5 5FE
Major Shareholder: Naeem Inayat Mohmad Umarji
Officers: Naeem Inayat Mohmad Umarji [1981] Director

La Generale Limited
Incorporated: 24 May 2011
Registered Office: 12 Brudenell, Windsor, Berks, SL4 4UR
Officers: Antoinette Kseib, Secretary; Anthony Kseib [1981] Director; Antoinette Kseib [1956] Director

La Loire Ltd
Incorporated: 31 October 2017
Registered Office: 71-75 Shelton Street, Covent Garden, London, WC2H 9JQ
Major Shareholder: Yin Yin Wu
Officers: Yin Yin Wu, Secretary [Chinese]; Yin Yin Wu [1982] Director [Chinese]

La Maison Hedonique Limited
Incorporated: 7 February 2017
Registered Office: 27 Old Gloucester Street, London, WC1N 3AX
Major Shareholder: Lucy Oldham
Officers: Lucy Oldham [1970] Director/Actor

La Personal Products Ltd
Incorporated: 20 September 2016
Net Worth: £65,240 *Total Assets:* £69,150
Registered Office: Grand Union House, 20 Kentish Town Road, Camden, London, NW1 9NX
Major Shareholder: Lucy Read
Officers: Richard Atherton, Secretary; Lucy Read [1974] Director

La Prairie (UK) Limited
Incorporated: 24 August 2011 *Employees:* 107
Net Worth: £1,978,000 *Total Assets:* £4,370,000
Registered Office: 4th Floor, High Holborn House, 52-54 High Holborn, London, WC1V 6RL
Parent: La Prairie Group AG
Officers: Craig Hunter McKinney, Secretary; Phillipe Despax [1969] Director/General Manager [French]; Patrick Nicolas Edouard Jacques Rasquinet [1967] Chief Executive Director [Belgian]

La Tips Limited
Incorporated: 24 June 2013
Net Worth: £590 *Total Assets:* £6,003
Registered Office: 22 Berkley Avenue, Blaydon on Tyne, Tyne & Wear, NE21 5NN
Shareholder: Andrew Arthur Lowdon
Officers: Andrew Lowdon [1978] Director; Antonia Lowdon [1985] Director

Lab Brands Limited
Incorporated: 12 June 2012 *Employees:* 5
Previous: Prontaguerra Ltd.
Net Worth: £132,490 *Total Assets:* £427,203
Registered Office: 9 Warwick Gardens, London, W14 8PH
Officers: Defaf Alamri [1982] Director; Philippe Hostalery [1961] Director [French]; Wolfram Langer [1950] Director [German]; Steven Lorn Schapera [1960] Director [Australian]; Antonio Della Virgiliana Varano [1957] Director [Australian]

Labapothecary Ltd.
Incorporated: 14 August 2017
Registered Office: 175 Ballygawley Road, Dungannon, Co Tyrone, BT70 1RX
Officers: Eoin Quinn [1987] Director [Irish]

Labo Nine Limited
Incorporated: 4 July 2018
Registered Office: 1 Park Road, Hampton Wick, Kingston upon Thames, Surrey, KT1 4AS
Major Shareholder: Dhani Besso-Pianetto
Officers: Dhani Besso-Pianetto [1979] Director; Philip Moser [1981] Director

Labrayon Cosmetiques France UK Ltd
Incorporated: 22 August 2013
Net Worth: £40 *Total Assets:* £50
Registered Office: 20-22 Wenlock Road, London, N1 7GU
Major Shareholder: Rev Rafal Krzysztof Pstrucha
Officers: Robert Jozef Cembala [1976] Director [Polish]

Natascha Lacombe Cosmetics Ltd
Incorporated: 25 October 2017
Registered Office: Rassler Wood Lodge, Henley Road, Medmenham, Marlow, Bucks, SL7 2EN
Shareholder: James Pond
Officers: James Pond [1986] Director/Finance

Lacomo Beauty Ltd
Incorporated: 1 February 2012
Net Worth Deficit: £49,720 *Total Assets:* £4,310
Registered Office: The Rectory, 32 Rash Road, Omagh, Co Tyrone, BT78 5NJ
Shareholders: Helen McCrumlish; Paschal McCrumlish
Officers: Helen McCrumlish [1984] Director [Irish]; Paschal McCrumlish [1969] Director/Secretary [Irish]

Lactura Ltd
Incorporated: 9 February 2012
Registered Office: 61C Carlisle Mansions, Carlisle Place, London, SW1P 1HZ
Shareholder: Jelena Soldatova
Officers: Jelena Soldatova [1986] Director/Cosmetics [Lithuanian]; Tatjana Soldatova [1981] Director/Cosmetics [Lithuanian]

Ladd Cosmetics Ltd
Incorporated: 31 August 2017
Registered Office: 27 Old Gloucester Street, London, WC1N 3AX
Major Shareholder: Mark Barton
Officers: Mark Barton [1986] Director/Office Administrator

Ladorisa Limited
Incorporated: 9 July 2018
Registered Office: 2 Hall Road, Armley, Leeds, LS12 1XB
Shareholders: Doris Balafama Uche-Amadi; Prince Uche Amadi
Officers: Prince Uche Amadi [1982] Director/Student [Nigerian]; Doris Balafama Uche-Amadi [1990] Director/Businesswoman [Nigerian]

Lady Smidgeton's Apothecary Ltd
Incorporated: 13 March 2018
Registered Office: 3 Galway House, Radnor Street, London, EC1V 3SL
Major Shareholder: Kirsty Patricia Fisher McRoberts
Officers: Kirsty Patricia Fisher McRoberts [1993] Director

Lady T Limited
Incorporated: 10 January 1994 Employees: 1
Net Worth Deficit: £310,646 Total Assets: £2,966
Registered Office: 86 Genesta Road, Plumstead, London, SE18 3EU
Shareholders: Adebola Ogebule; Margaret Ogebule
Officers: Emmanuel Adebisi Kujore, Secretary; Elizabeth O Ogebule, Secretary; Daniel Kujore [1998] Director/Student; Alice Adebola Ogebule [1985] Director/Student; Olubunmi Omotunde Ogebule [1961] Director; Omolade Margaret Ogebule [1983] Director/IT Instructor

Ladyology Limited
Incorporated: 31 March 2017
Registered Office: 92 Dollis Hill Lane, London, NW2 6JD
Major Shareholder: Shuqi Zhang
Officers: Shuqi Zhang [1984] Director [Chinese]

Lagoon Soaps Limited
Incorporated: 3 April 2018
Registered Office: 90 Ivy Street, Rainham, Gillingham, Kent, ME8 8BH
Major Shareholder: Laura Deanne Jones
Officers: Laura Deanne Jones [1983] Director/Soap Maker

Laguna Organa Ltd
Incorporated: 2 February 2018
Registered Office: 20-22 Wenlock Road, London, N1 7GU
Major Shareholder: Adrienn Gomori
Officers: Adrienn Gomori [1976] Director [Hungarian]

Lahang Ltd
Incorporated: 5 February 2018
Registered Office: 25 Sandhurst Drive, Belfast, BT9 5AY
Major Shareholder: Tuan Tran
Officers: Tuan Tran [1988] Director/Business Manager [Vietnamese]

Laila Cosmetics Limited
Incorporated: 10 December 2018
Registered Office: Third Floor, 207 Regent Street, London, W1B 3HH
Major Shareholder: Ali Taha
Officers: Ali Taha [1980] Director

Laldhinio Limited
Incorporated: 21 March 2017
Net Worth Deficit: £5,079 Total Assets: £11,571
Registered Office: Hunters Lodge, 20 Godstone Road, Oxted, Surrey, RH8 9JT
Major Shareholder: Lara Harwell
Officers: Lara Harwell [1980] Director

Lam Cosmetics Ltd
Incorporated: 31 December 2018
Registered Office: The Minnow, 104 Thames Street, Weybridge, Surrey, KT13 8NG
Major Shareholder: Adrian-Marcel Lazar
Officers: Adrian-Marcel Lazar [1980] Director [Romanian]

Ken Lamacraft Marketing Limited
Incorporated: 9 February 1995 Employees: 6
Net Worth: £2,376,211 Total Assets: £2,409,120
Registered Office: Bodycare House, Danegate Eridge Green, Tunbridge Wells, Kent, TN3 9JA
Parent: Beauty and Skincare Essentials Limited
Officers: Kevin Michael Gambrill [1976] Director/Accountant; Fiona McMillan Peerless [1979] Director/Operations Manager

Lamari London Ltd
Incorporated: 29 May 2018
Registered Office: 3 Derrycombe House, Great Western Road, London, W2 5UF
Major Shareholder: Ibrahim Lamrani
Officers: Ibrahim Lamrani [1997] Director/Student

Lambsmead Limited
Incorporated: 5 July 1976 Employees: 20
Net Worth: £257,433 Total Assets: £350,601
Registered Office: 222 Upper Richmond Road West, London, SW14 8AH
Officers: Ivor Deitsch, Secretary; Ivor Deitsch [1939] Director/Pharmacist; Lancelot Piers Duncan Deitsch [1971] Director; Sandra Estelle Deitsch [1942] Director; Sebastian Richard Oliver Deitsch [1969] Director

Lamer & Ava Healthcare Ltd
Incorporated: 14 September 2017
Registered Office: Unit 8d, Office 10, Kilroot Business Park, Carrickfergus, Co Antrim, BT38 7PR
Parent: Ava Corporations Ltd
Officers: Collin Grayson [1970] Director/Businessman

Lana's Beauty Box Ltd
Incorporated: 27 February 2019
Registered Office: 22 Mead Court, Buck Lane, Kingsbury, London, NW9 0XN
Major Shareholder: Judith Miranda Cudjoe
Officers: Judith Miranda Cudjoe [1987] Director/Makeup Artist

Land of Beauty Supplies Ltd
Incorporated: 3 October 2018
Registered Office: 17 Hopetoun Street, Bathgate, W Lothian, EH48 4PA
Major Shareholder: Perveen Javed
Officers: Perveen Javed [1961] Director

Landermark Ltd
Incorporated: 6 June 2017
Registered Office: 71-75 Shelton Street, Covent Garden, London, WC2H 9JQ
Major Shareholder: Saber Alaghbari
Officers: Saber Alaghbari [1984] Director [Yemeni]

Landional Ltd
Incorporated: 2 August 2018
Registered Office: 59 Whetstone Hill Lane, Oldham, Lancs, OL1 4NB
Major Shareholder: Ion Muyizere
Officers: Aline Mukacyubahiro [1980] Director/Management Consultant [Rwandan]

Lanko Naturals-UK (PVT) Ltd
Incorporated: 19 August 2016
Net Worth Deficit: £9,004 Total Assets: £3,491
Registered Office: 17 Forest Oak Close, Cardiff, CF23 6QN
Major Shareholder: Ranjith Jayasinghe
Officers: Dilshani Buddhika Jayasinghe [1985] Director/Biomedical Scientist; Dilshara Rashmika Jayasinghe [1987] Director/Quality Assurance Engineer; Ranjith Jayasinghe [1955] Director/Occupational Therapist

Lanmix Enterperises Ltd
Incorporated: 22 June 2018
Registered Office: 8 Wood Croft Flats, 10 Chepstow Road, Croydon, Surrey, CR0 5JA
Major Shareholder: Lucie Anais Nathalie Mixeras
Officers: Lucie Anais Nathalie Mixeras [1987] Director/Beautician [French]

Lanolips Limited
Incorporated: 3 October 2013
Net Worth: £18,409 *Total Assets:* £203,042
Registered Office: 3 Newhouse Business Centre, Old Crawley Road, Horsham, W Sussex, RH12 4RU
Major Shareholder: Kirsten Carrioll
Officers: Kirsten Carriol [1972] Director/Cosmetics Manufacturer [Australian]

Joseph Lanzante Products Limited
Incorporated: 5 October 2012
Net Worth Deficit: £6,250 *Total Assets:* £38,010
Registered Office: 8 King Street, Clitheroe, Lancs, BB7 2EP
Shareholder: Giuseppe Lanzante
Officers: Giuseppe Lanzante [1958] Director; Kuldeep Randhawa [1973] Director

Laogong Laopo Limited
Incorporated: 19 September 2018
Registered Office: 95 Briony Avenue, Hale, Altrincham, Cheshire, WA15 8PZ
Major Shareholder: Fey Tsang
Officers: Fey Tsang [1989] Director

Larisa Markus Limited
Incorporated: 14 May 2018
Registered Office: 54 Brighton Road, Watford, Herts, WD24 5HW
Major Shareholder: Olga Novokhatska
Officers: Olga Novokhatska [1986] Director/General Manager [Ukrainian]

Larmed Limited
Incorporated: 29 November 2017
Registered Office: Forsyth House, Cromac Square, Belfast, BT2 8LA
Parent: Supraherbal Limited
Officers: Andrew Ross [1956] Director/Manager [American]

Larouge Cosmetics Limited
Incorporated: 23 August 2018
Registered Office: 16 Morley Crescent, Old Farm Park, Milton Keynes, Bucks, MK7 8PA
Officers: Anna Abel [1978] Director

Lash Authority Ltd
Incorporated: 22 June 2018
Registered Office: 2 Green Park, Coal Road, Leeds, LS14 1FB
Major Shareholder: Samuel Sweet
Officers: Julia Moran, Secretary; Julia Moran [1964] Director; James Alan Nordstrom [1957] Director [American]; Samantha Sweet [1969] Director; Samuel Sweet [1972] Managing Director [American]; Fiona Wallace [1958] Director

Lash House Eyelash Extensions Supplies Ltd
Incorporated: 23 May 2016 *Employees:* 1
Net Worth: £12,959 *Total Assets:* £25,156
Registered Office: 22 Woodcroft Park, Holywood, Co Down, BT18 0PS
Major Shareholder: Angela McStravick
Officers: Angela McStravick [1979] Director [Irish]; Steven Russel Taylor [1980] Director [British/Australian]

Lashed London Limited
Incorporated: 22 June 2018
Registered Office: Unit 24 Highcroft Industrial Estate, Enterprise Road, Horndean, Waterlooville, Hants, PO8 0BT
Major Shareholder: Cherrelle Bell
Officers: Cherrelle Bell [1991] Director

Lashflix Limited
Incorporated: 10 July 2017
Registered Office: 30 Milford Road, Bolton, Lancs, BL3 3DH
Officers: Shahida Nessa [1985] Managing Director; Grzegorz Wu-Kosinski [1983] Director [Polish]

Lashline Ltd
Incorporated: 25 July 2018
Registered Office: 4 The Leaze, Yate, Bristol, BS37 5XJ
Major Shareholder: Paige Any Hodkinson
Officers: Paige Any Hodkinson [1996] Director

Erno Laszlo Group Ltd
Incorporated: 25 January 2011 *Employees:* 4
Net Worth Deficit: £169,842 *Total Assets:* £626,104
Registered Office: 5th Floor, 89 New Bond Street, London, W1S 1DA
Officers: Hans Allegaert [1973] Director [Belgian]; Charles James Denton [1965] Director; Avery Tuchman [1971] Director/Chief Financial Officer [American]; Hanxi Zhao [1972] Director [Chinese]

Latam HQ Health Ltd
Incorporated: 13 March 2015
Net Worth Deficit: £126,880 *Total Assets:* £68,770
Registered Office: 24 Howard Close, Fleet, Hants, GU51 3ER
Major Shareholder: Harold John Christopher Paul
Officers: Harold John Christopher Paul [1967] Director/Businessman; Simon John Christopher Paul [1941] Director/Consultant

Estee Lauder (UK) International Group Ltd.
Incorporated: 9 January 2019
Registered Office: Flat 32, Adventures Court, 12 Newport Avenue, London, E14 2DN
Shareholders: Yang Lyu; Bin Wu
Officers: Yang Lyu [1982] Director/Businessman [Chinese]

Estee Lauder Cosmetics Limited
Incorporated: 16 May 1960 *Employees:* 9,723
Net Worth: £503,360,992 *Total Assets:* £789,843,008
Registered Office: One Fitzroy, 6 Mortimer Street, London, W1T 3JJ
Parent: Estee Lauder UK Holdings Limited
Officers: Steffi Kipperman Bogart, Secretary; Raniero de Stasio, Secretary; Edward Robert Hughes, Secretary; Sara Ellen Moss, Secretary [American]; Charles Edward Reese, Secretary; Spencer Gary Smul, Assistant Secretary; Agnieszka Trzesicka, Secretary; Agata Wieczorek, Secretary; Alison Claire Day [1971] Finance Director; Marc Cedric Yann Prouve [1960] Director/Business Executive [French]; Tracey Thomas Travis [1962] Director/Executive Vice President and CFO [American]; Philippe Michel Warnery [1970] Director/Corporate General Manager [French]

Laurelle London Ltd
Incorporated: 9 March 2007 *Employees:* 29
Net Worth: £1,238,956 *Total Assets:* £3,104,143
Registered Office: 207 Regent Street, London, W1B 3HH
Major Shareholder: Oliver McMahon
Officers: Susan Eileen McMahon, Secretary; Oliver McMahon [1974] Director

Laurens Cosmetics UK Limited
Incorporated: 15 March 2016
Net Worth: £419 Total Assets: £5,261
Registered Office: 142/12 St Stephen Street, Edinburgh, EH3 5AA
Officers: Maria Leal, Secretary; Maria Eugenia Leal Herrera [1976] Director [Venezuelan]; Pedro Jose Riera Sucre [1976] Director [Venezuelan]

Lava Jai Limited
Incorporated: 29 October 2015
Registered Office: 54 Lauderdale Street, Preston, Lancs, PR1 8JL
Major Shareholder: Amita Limbachia
Officers: Amita Limbachia, Secretary; Amita Limbachia [1975] Managing Director

Lavant Beauty and Personal Care Ltd
Incorporated: 25 January 2019
Registered Office: 20a Magdalen Road, Exeter, EX2 4TD
Shareholders: Andrew Maidment; Alexander Ivan Buirski
Officers: Alexander Ivan Buirski [1978] Director/Consultant; Rawya Roumieh Catto [1983] Director/Chemist [French]; Andrew Maidment [1982] Marketing Director; Mariam Kamel Mohanna [1988] Director/Engineer [Lebanese]

Lavelle Store UK Ltd
Incorporated: 21 February 2019
Registered Office: 71-75 Shelton Street, Covent Garden, London, WC2H 9JQ
Major Shareholder: Rany Begum
Officers: Rany Begum [1997] Director/Secretary

The Lavender Concept Ltd
Incorporated: 5 September 2016
Registered Office: 1st Floor, 2 Woodberry Grove, Finchley, London, N12 0DR
Major Shareholder: Abeer Makki
Officers: Abeer Makki [1974] Director/Senior Specialist

Lavish Lashes Ltd
Incorporated: 22 July 2018
Registered Office: 71-75 Shelton Street, London, WC2H 9JQ
Major Shareholder: Iman Shakera Shakelle French
Officers: Iman Shakera Shakelle French, Secretary; Iman Shakera Shakelle French [1998] Director/Sales Specialist

Lavish London Cosmetics Ltd.
Incorporated: 27 April 2017
Registered Office: Lavish London Cosmetics Limited, 27 Old Gloucester Street, London, WC1N 3AX
Major Shareholder: Princess Curtis-Broni
Officers: Princess Curtis-Broni [1994] Director

Lavy Sprays International Ltd
Incorporated: 1 June 2017
Registered Office: The Cottage, Lower Fields, Tewkesbury Road, Eckington, Worcs, WR10 3DE
Parent: Optimum Life Ltd
Officers: David Anthony Molyneux [1944] Director/Retired

Lax Group Company Limited
Incorporated: 13 July 2018
Registered Office: 67c St James's Road, Croydon, Surrey, CR0 2US
Major Shareholder: Manoj Ojha
Officers: Manoj Ojha [1989] Director/Businessman [Nepalese]

Layan Pharma Ltd
Incorporated: 29 November 2018
Registered Office: 152-160 City Road, London, EC1V 2NX
Shareholders: Ahmed Badawy; Osama Abdelhamid
Officers: Abduallah Alradhi, Secretary; Mohammad Alrashdi, Secretary; Osama Abdelhamid [1984] Director/Chief Operations Officer (COO) [Egyptian]; Ahmed Badawy [1981] Director/Chief Executive Officer (CEO) [Egyptian]

Lazeeza Lashes Limited
Incorporated: 3 September 2018
Registered Office: 2 Harvey Terrace, Credon Road, London, E13 9BH
Major Shareholder: Nancy Boctor
Officers: Nancy Boctor [1996] Director/Beautician

LBB Skin Ltd
Incorporated: 6 December 2018
Registered Office: 134 Putney Bridge Road, London, SW15 2NQ
Major Shareholder: Nnenna Onuba
Officers: Nnenna Onuba [1980] Director

Lbeautie Ltd
Incorporated: 4 September 2018
Registered Office: 20-22 Wenlock Road, London, N1 7GU
Major Shareholder: Lilah Mansour
Officers: Lilah Mansour [1986] Director

LCB Trading (UK) Limited
Incorporated: 30 November 2012
Registered Office: 19 Bingle Way, Liverpool, L12 7AD
Major Shareholder: Qian Lu
Officers: Qian Lu [1988] Director/Investor [Chinese]

Le Glamour UK Ltd
Incorporated: 17 December 2018
Registered Office: Suite 1, 21-23 Clifton Road, Rugby, Warwicks, CV21 3PY
Shareholders: Beata Zdanowska; Adam Meller
Officers: Beata Zdanowska [1979] Director [Polish]

Le Keux Vintage Enterprises Limited
Incorporated: 2 May 2012
Net Worth Deficit: £74,238 Total Assets: £50,392
Registered Office: 4 Lime Avenue, Leamington Spa, Warwicks, CV32 7DA
Major Shareholder: Lynsey Lekeux
Officers: Melanie Armsden [1987] Director; Lynsey Lekeux [1983] Director

Le Labo UK Limited
Incorporated: 12 August 2009 Employees: 33
Net Worth: £1,894,721 Total Assets: £5,038,555
Registered Office: One Fitzroy, 6 Mortimer Street, London, W1T 3JJ
Parent: The Estee Lauder Companies Inc.,
Officers: Spencer Gary Smul, Secretary; Alison Claire Day [1971] Finance Director; Sara Ellen Moss [1946] Director/Lawyer [American]; Tracey Thomas Travis [1962] Director/Executive Vice President and CFO [American]; Philippe Michel Warnery [1970] Director/Corporate General Manager [French]

Le Lissage UK Limited
Incorporated: 26 July 2018
Registered Office: 9 Great Chesterford Court, London Road, Great Chesterford, Essex, CB10 1PF
Shareholders: Ralitsa Hristova Vasilovska; Simon Paul Blagden
Officers: Simon Paul Blagden [1962] Director; Ralitsa Hristova Vasilovska [1987] Director

Le Parfum Ltd
Incorporated: 14 June 2018
Registered Office: 71-75 Shelton Street, London, WC2H 9JQ
Major Shareholder: Djamel Benrejdal
Officers: Djamel Benrejdal, Secretary; Djamel Benrejdal [1967] Director

Le Pure Limited
Incorporated: 12 June 2014
Net Worth Deficit: £2,105 Total Assets: £3,089
Registered Office: Bourner Bullock, Sovereign House, 212-224 Shaftesbury Avenue, London, WC2H 8HQ
Major Shareholder: Julia Atzesberger
Officers: Julia Atzesberger [1974] Director/Sales - Skin Care Products [Austrian]

Le-Vap Limited
Incorporated: 6 October 2017
Registered Office: 20 Daneland, Barnet, Herts, EN4 8PY
Major Shareholder: Syed Umair Naseer
Officers: Syed Umair Naseer [1973] Director/Engineer

Leading National Training Ltd
Incorporated: 17 December 2007
Net Worth Deficit: £3,950 Total Assets: £451
Registered Office: Edenderry, Lowfield Road, Haywards Heath, W Sussex, RH16 4DW
Major Shareholder: Tatiana Shapovalova-Peters
Officers: Olga Anatolievna Shapovalova, Secretary; Philip David Peters [1955] Director/Business Consultant; Tatiana Shapovalova-Peters [1971] Director/Management Consultant

Leclair Cosmetics Limited
Incorporated: 5 September 2018
Registered Office: 13 Fairholme, Sedbergh, Cumbria, LA10 5AY
Major Shareholder: Clare Elizabeth Townley
Officers: Clare Elizabeth Townley [1972] Director/Beautician

Lee Gallop Enterprise Ltd
Incorporated: 3 July 2015
Registered Office: Unit G25, Waterfront Studios, 1 Dock Road, London, E16 1AH
Officers: Teng Li [1987] Director/Businessman [Chinese]

Leela Living Limited
Incorporated: 5 October 2018
Registered Office: 35-37 Lowlands Road, Harrow on the Hill, Middlesex, HA1 3AW
Shareholders: Akash Mehta; Nikita Mehta
Officers: Akash Mehta [1994] Director; Nikita Mehta [1991] Director

Lefami Cosmetics Group Ltd
Incorporated: 1 August 2018
Registered Office: Suite 6, 5 Percy Street, Fitzrovia, London, W1T 1DG
Officers: Teresa Anne Elizabeth Brewster [1993] Director [Seychellois]

Legacy Wholesalers Limited
Incorporated: 9 April 2014
Net Worth Deficit: £39,859 Total Assets: £595,000
Registered Office: Lord House, 51 Lord Street, Manchester, M3 1HE
Officers: Bachan Singh Arora [1973] Director

Legendbio Beauty Group Limited
Incorporated: 29 March 2016
Registered Office: 27 Old Gloucester Street, London, WC1N 3AX
Major Shareholder: Jianhua Liu
Officers: Jianhua Liu [1964] Business Director

The Legends London Limited
Incorporated: 23 February 2015
Net Worth: £5,290 Total Assets: £17,340
Registered Office: 12 Lamb's Conduit Passage, London, WC1R 4RH
Major Shareholder: Adrianna Kravitz
Officers: Adrianna Kravitz [1978] Director/International Trade/Logistics Specialist

Leicala Natural Products Ltd
Incorporated: 13 September 2018
Registered Office: 320 City Road, London, EC1V 2NZ
Shareholders: Caroline Maurwen Henry-Ledgister; Leighton Wellesley Ledgister; Latoya Lovitta Francis
Officers: Latoya Lovitta Francis [1988] Director/Entrepreneur [British/Caymanian]; Caroline Maurwen Henry-Ledgister [1976] Director/Teacher; Leighton Wellesley Ledgister [1978] Director/Teacher

Leixaco Trading Ltd
Incorporated: 30 April 2018
Registered Office: 28C Strathblaine Road, Wandsworth, London, SW11 1RJ
Major Shareholder: Loic Guy Bernard Simon
Officers: Loic Guy Bernard Simon [1988] Director [French]

LEM Beauty Ltd
Incorporated: 26 February 2019
Registered Office: The Stable Yard, Vicarage Road, Stony Stratford, Milton Keynes, Bucks, MK11 1BN
Major Shareholder: Lydia Elise Millen-Gordon
Officers: Lydia Elise Millen-Gordon [1988] Director

The Lemon Tree Beauty Limited
Incorporated: 6 May 2003
Net Worth: £27,980 Total Assets: £528,236
Registered Office: Woburn Court, 8 Guildhall Hill, Norwich, NR2 1JG
Major Shareholder: Arnold Raetz
Officers: Isolde Raetz, Secretary/Banker [German]; Arnold Raetz [1965] Director [German]

Lensmeuk Limited
Incorporated: 12 November 2018
Registered Office: 154 Trentham Court, Victoria Road, London, W3 6BF
Major Shareholder: Atyan Al-Rwasheda
Officers: Atyan Al-Rwasheda [1991] Director [Jordanian]

Les Blanches Limited
Incorporated: 21 March 2018
Registered Office: Lawford House, 4 Albert Place, London, N3 1QB
Shareholders: Ermela Tagliente Halilaj; Ermela Tagliente Halilaj
Officers: Ermela Tagliente Halilaj [1994] Director [Italian]

Les Laboratoires ILP UK Ltd
Incorporated: 20 December 2018
Registered Office: 20-22 Wenlock Road, London, N1 7GU
Major Shareholder: Kazi-Tani Sonia
Officers: Kazi-Tani Sonia [1982] Director [French]

Les Lilas Limited
Incorporated: 2 September 2016
Registered Office: Kemp House, 160 City Road, London, EC1V 2NX
Officers: Ihor Halaziuk [1962] Director/Retail Trader [Ukrainian]

Les Petits Parfums Limited
Incorporated: 20 April 2009
Net Worth: £10,030 *Total Assets:* £70,480
Registered Office: Symal House, 423 Edgware Road, London, NW9 0HU
Major Shareholder: Helene Schleider
Officers: Helene Schleider [1963] Director [Belgian]

Lescaro Health Limited
Incorporated: 26 March 2010
Net Worth: £23,330 *Total Assets:* £108,300
Registered Office: 11 Wrens Court, 46 South Parade, Sutton Coldfield, W Midlands, B72 1QY
Shareholders: Andrew Ian Williams; Leslie Glyndon Henry Williams
Officers: Andrew Ian Williams [1966] Director; Leslie Glyndon Henry Williams [1944] Director

Lese & Lista Ltd
Incorporated: 19 November 2018
Registered Office: 2nd Floor, College House, 17 King Edwards Road, Ruislip, Middlesex, HA4 7AE
Major Shareholder: Randy Lindo Cornwall
Officers: Randy Cornwall, Secretary; Randy Lindo Cornwall [1977] Director/Entrepreneur

Lesimone Global Limited
Incorporated: 15 June 2017
Registered Office: 24 Wellview Lane, Livingston, W Lothian, EH54 9HU
Major Shareholder: Simon Richmond Wallace
Officers: Simon Richmond Wallace [1965] Director

Leslie International Ltd
Incorporated: 2 February 2016
Net Worth Deficit: £27,048 *Total Assets:* £186,288
Registered Office: 1st Floor, Kingsway Chambers, Kingsway Arcade, Dewsbury, W Yorks, WF13 1DU
Shareholders: Adnan Shaukat; Rizwan Shaukat
Officers: Adnan Shaukat [1971] Director/Business Executive [Pakistani]; Rizwan Shaukat [1966] Director/Business Executive [Pakistani]

Lex Roris Ltd
Incorporated: 15 August 2018
Registered Office: Lex Roris LMT, P O Box 72396, London, SW18 9PW
Shareholders: Alexis Rosalia von Pfefer; Carlos Augusto Romero
Officers: Alexis Rosalia Von Pfefer [1988] Director

LGC Cosmetics Ltd
Incorporated: 23 January 2019
Registered Office: 38a Parish Ghyll Road, Ilkley, W Yorks, LS29 9NE
Major Shareholder: Leah Georgia Connolley
Officers: Leah Georgia Connolley [1997] Director/Administrator

Liaver Limited
Incorporated: 13 September 2016
Net Worth Deficit: £16,396 *Total Assets:* £389
Registered Office: Kemp House, 152 City Road, London, EC1V 2NX
Major Shareholder: Lianne Bruney
Officers: Lianne Bruney [1981] Director

Libhairation Ltd
Incorporated: 21 January 2019
Registered Office: 20-22 Wenlock Road, London, N1 7GU
Major Shareholder: Kimberleen Duncan-Lajewski
Officers: Kimberleen Duncan-Lajewski [1985] Director/General Sales Advisor

Lief Essentials Limited
Incorporated: 1 December 2016
Registered Office: 1 Beauchamp Court, 10 Victors Way, Barnet, Herts, EN5 5TZ
Major Shareholder: Wayne Clark
Officers: Wayne Clark [1977] Director

Lienex Beauty London Ltd
Incorporated: 4 December 2017
Registered Office: 83 Stewart Road, London, E15 2BA
Officers: Habibur Rahman [1989] Director [Bangladeshi]

Life's Big Stuff Ltd
Incorporated: 10 January 2011
Registered Office: 1 Crown Road, Wheatley, Oxford, OX33 1UH
Major Shareholder: Katherine Mary Gannon Bedford
Officers: Katherine Mary Bedford [1961] Director

Lifestyle International Limited
Incorporated: 13 February 2017 *Employees:* 1
Net Worth: £3,496 *Total Assets:* £7,230
Registered Office: 2 Sigma Business Centre, 7 Havelock Place, Harrow, Middlesex, HA1 1LJ
Major Shareholder: Samita Jain
Officers: Ashish Kumar Jain [1984] Director/Businessman; Samita Jain [1985] Director

Light Up Skincare Ltd
Incorporated: 29 November 2018
Registered Office: 3 Chichester Road, London, N9 9DL
Major Shareholder: Silva Gashi
Officers: Silva Gashi [1990] Director

Lilies of The Valley Cosmetics Limited
Incorporated: 18 April 2018
Registered Office: 16 Winchfield, Caddington, Luton, Beds, LU1 4NE
Major Shareholder: Chrissi Tomiwa Oluwadare
Officers: Dr Chrissi Tomiwa Oluwadare [1990] Director

Liluna-Organics Ltd
Incorporated: 28 January 2019
Registered Office: 76c Davyhulme Road, Urmston, Manchester, M41 7DN
Major Shareholder: Marlena Anna Gendis
Officers: Marlena Anna Gendis [1977] Director/Natural Therapist [Polish]

Lilyz Cosmetics UK Ltd
Incorporated: 6 November 2015
Net Worth Deficit: £25,431 *Total Assets:* £146,204
Registered Office: 321J Mayoral Way, Team Valley Trading Estate, Gateshead, Tyne & Wear, NE11 0RT
Major Shareholder: Lily Zhan
Officers: Lily Zhan [1972] Director

Lime and Lead Global Ltd
Incorporated: 26 July 2017
Registered Office: 27 Old Gloucester Street, London, WC1N 3AX
Officers: Taoufiq Boukri [1981] Director/Business Executive [South Korean]; Ioana Francisca Vasilescu [1976] Director/Administrator [Romanian]

Line21 Ltd.
Incorporated: 20 October 2017
Registered Office: 21 Hardwick Hill, Banbury, Oxon, OX16 2DA
Major Shareholder: Chloe Ellen Smith
Officers: Chloe Ellen Smith [1993] Director/Buyer

Lino Rose Ltd
Incorporated: 11 August 2017
Net Worth: £1,288 *Total Assets:* £1,288
Registered Office: 20 The Drive, London, EN5 4JQ
Major Shareholder: Vania Pavlova
Officers: Vania Pavlova [1976] Director [Bulgarian]

Linrose Care Ltd
Incorporated: 7 October 2011
Previous: Linrose Bodycare Ltd
Net Worth Deficit: £6,170 *Total Assets:* £4,865
Registered Office: 52 Barmouth Avenue, Perivale, Middlesex, UB6 8JT
Major Shareholder: Salahadeen Kadier
Officers: Salahadeen Kadier [1958] Director

Lins Bros Limited
Incorporated: 25 April 2016
Registered Office: The Business Resource Network, 53 Whateleys Drive, Kenilworth, Warwicks, CV8 2GY
Major Shareholder: Yujuan Yang
Officers: Yujuan Yang [1994] Director [Chinese]

Liolax Limited
Incorporated: 6 April 2018
Registered Office: 71-75 Shelton Street, Covent Garden, London, WC2H 9JQ
Major Shareholder: Karolina Urszula Radziszewska
Officers: Karolina Urszula Radziszewska, Secretary; Karolina Urszula Radziszewska [1989] Director [Polish]

Lionmark Limited
Incorporated: 23 May 2014
Registered Office: 925 Finchley Road, London, NW11 7PE
Major Shareholder: Rajinder Singh Banga
Officers: Ramtin Siaghi, Secretary; Rajinder Singh Banga [1962] Director

Liplast Ltd
Incorporated: 21 June 2011
Registered Office: 88a Derwent Road, Palmers Green, London, N13 4PX
Major Shareholder: Elsa Jane Yule
Officers: Elsa Jane Yule [1952] Director/Retired [American]

Lipoid Kosmetik Ltd
Incorporated: 2 July 1982 *Employees:* 3
Net Worth: £160,793 *Total Assets:* £236,532
Registered Office: Unit 10 Delta Court, Manor Way, Borehamwood, Herts, WD6 1FJ
Shareholder: Protec Ingredia Limited
Officers: Alan Edward Eastwood [1955] Director; Andreas Gilg [1967] Director [Swiss]; Daniel Reuben Straus [1972] Director/Business Manager

Lipolift Ltd
Incorporated: 29 January 2013
Net Worth: £53,660 *Total Assets:* £119,390
Registered Office: 32 Main Street, Lambley, Nottingham, NG4 4PN
Major Shareholder: Tammy Marie Hollis
Officers: Tammy Marie Hollis [1978] Director

Lipstick and Black Coffee Ltd
Incorporated: 18 October 2012
Registered Office: 33 Wolfe Crescent, London, SE7 8TS
Major Shareholder: Irene Eyo-Ephraim
Officers: Irene Eyo-Ephraim [1987] Director/Entrepreneur

Liquor Lips Ltd
Incorporated: 19 September 2018
Registered Office: 64 Jenkins Road, London, E13 8NP
Major Shareholder: Nicole Fisher
Officers: Nicole Fisher [1995] Director/Manager

Liqwd Limited
Incorporated: 25 March 2013
Net Worth Deficit: £14,210 *Total Assets:* £108,810
Registered Office: Ibex House, Baker Street, Weybridge, Surrey, KT13 8AH
Major Shareholder: Balazs Csaba Cserna
Officers: James Beecher, Secretary; Dean Vegas Christal [1964] Director/Cosmetic Manufacturer [American]; Klaus Went [1950] Director [Austrian]

Little Big Brands Ltd
Incorporated: 19 September 2017
Registered Office: Harrogate Business Centre, Hookstone Avenue, Harrogate, N Yorks, HG2 8ER
Officers: Jenna Collins [1985] Director/Educator

Little Duckling Soaps Ltd
Incorporated: 21 June 2018
Registered Office: 32 Regent Street, Penkhull, Stoke on Trent, Staffs, ST4 5HG
Major Shareholder: Sarah Louise Grand
Officers: Sarah Louise Grand [1980] Director

Little Enterprises (NI) Ltd
Incorporated: 20 February 2004 *Employees:* 2
Net Worth: £1,102 *Total Assets:* £49,472
Registered Office: 12 Beechfield Manor, Belfast Road, Dollingstown, Co Armagh, BT66 7GR
Shareholders: Ian Little; Faye Little
Officers: Ian Little [1974] Director/Business Consultant

LIV Organic Company Limited
Incorporated: 5 September 2013
Net Worth Deficit: £45,379 *Total Assets:* £6,373
Registered Office: Hova House, 1 Hova Villas, Hove, E Sussex, BN3 3DH
Major Shareholder: Agnes Donazy
Officers: Agnes Donazy [1968] Director [Hungarian]

Live Rich Academy Limited
Incorporated: 15 November 2017
Registered Office: Lynton House, 7-12 Tavistock Square, London, WC1H 9BQ
Major Shareholder: Charalampos Daniilidis
Officers: Charalampos Daniilidis, Secretary; Charalampos Daniilidis [1973] Director/High School [Greek]

Livoliv Cosmetics Ltd.
Incorporated: 21 July 2017
Registered Office: 160 Lake Road, Hamworthy, Poole, Dorset, BH15 4LW
Shareholder: Susan Sue Curran
Officers: Liam Curran [1973] Director [Irish]; Susan Marie Curran [1970] Director

Lixir Skin Limited
Incorporated: 22 March 2017
Net Worth Deficit: £20,271 *Total Assets:* £121,550
Registered Office: Palladium House, 1-4 Argyll Street, London, W1F 7LD
Shareholders: Colette Marguerite Louise Haydon; Walter John Haydon
Officers: Colette Marguerite Louise Haydon [1959] Director/Cosmetic Scientist; Dr James Henri Haydon [1987] Director; Roxanne Louise Haydon [1989] Director; Walter John Haydon [1960] Director

Liza Organics Ltd
Incorporated: 22 February 2019
Registered Office: 2 Rayson Way, Cambridge, CB5 8NP
Shareholders: Sadat Yoonus Nalakath; Moniza Rahman
Officers: Sadat Yoonus Nalakath, Secretary; Sadat Yoonus Nalakath [1975] Director/Manager; Moniza Rahman [1975] Director/Compliance Specialist

LK Beauty Ltd
Incorporated: 13 February 2019
Registered Office: 25 Penderyn Close, Merthyr Tydfil, Mid Glamorgan, CF48 1AS
Major Shareholder: Libby Kate Oleary
Officers: Libby Kate Oleary [2001] Director/CEO/Owner/Beautician

LMD Cosmetics Ltd
Incorporated: 22 August 2018
Registered Office: 4 Union Road, Magherafelt, Co Derry, BT45 5DF
Shareholders: Linda Jane Stinson; Louise McDonnell
Officers: Louise McDonnell [1991] Director [Irish]; Linda Jane Stinson [1983] Director

LMS Brands Ltd.
Incorporated: 28 October 2016
Registered Office: 19 Meadow Lane, Wakefield, W Yorks, WF2 0HB
Shareholder: Kaushik Dutta
Officers: Jigar Daru, Secretary; Kaushik Dutta [1980] Director

Loaded Cosmetics Limited
Incorporated: 30 November 2018
Registered Office: 24 Gipping Place, Bury Road, Stowmarket, Suffolk, IP14 1JW
Major Shareholder: Lucy Victoria Evans
Officers: Lucy Victoria Evans [1995] Director/Accounts Manager

Lock Stock & Barrel Grooming Company Ltd
Incorporated: 18 July 2005
Net Worth: £267,700 *Total Assets:* £376,770
Registered Office: A1 OYO Business Park, 187 Park Lane, Birmingham, B35 6AN
Major Shareholder: Ben Alan Snowdon
Officers: Mary Lorraine Archer [1974] Director/Manager [Irish]; Caroline Ann McGuire [1975] Director; Ben Alan Snowdon [1983] Director/Manager

Charlie Locks Ltd
Incorporated: 7 August 1992
Net Worth Deficit: £92,620 *Total Assets:* £33,468
Registered Office: Unit A1, Belmore Hill Court, Belmore Lane, Owslebury, Hants, SO21 1JW
Major Shareholder: Julie Raines
Officers: Julie Raines, Secretary; Julie Raines [1962] Director/Company Secretary; Mark Andrew Raines [1963] Director

Logical Content Ltd
Incorporated: 13 April 2007
Net Worth: £22,290 *Total Assets:* £124,980
Registered Office: The Design Studio, Mayes Farm, Grinstead Lane, East Grinstead, W Sussex, RH19 4HP
Officers: Susan Moore, Secretary; Susan Moore [1950] Finance Director; Terence Frederick Moore [1954] Director; William Moore [1984] Director

Lola's Apothecary Ltd
Incorporated: 11 November 2011
Net Worth Deficit: £44,520 *Total Assets:* £26,210
Registered Office: Colleton Manor, Colleton, Chulmleigh, Devon, EX18 7JS
Major Shareholder: Dominic Beavis Blake Phillips
Officers: Dominic Beavis Blake Phillips [1988] Director/Accountant; Grania Tiffany Phillips [1953] Director/Farmer; Simon Blake Phillips [1949] Director/Farmer

Loles Cosmetics UK Limited
Incorporated: 22 January 2018
Registered Office: c/o Atkinson Evans Limited, The Old Drill Hall, 10 Arnot Hill Road, Arnold, Nottingham, NG5 6LJ
Major Shareholder: Ian Iger
Officers: Ian Iger [1958] Director

Lollipop Treats Ltd
Incorporated: 16 November 2018
Registered Office: 20-22 Wenlock Road, London, N1 7GU
Major Shareholder: Lorraine Amanda Thomas
Officers: Lorraine Amanda Thomas [1978] Director/Nail Technician

Lom Trade Limited
Incorporated: 18 June 2018
Registered Office: Basement Front, 34a Marylands Road, London, W9 2DX
Officers: Abdennour Boukernous [1985] Director [French]

London Bathers Limited
Incorporated: 30 January 2019
Registered Office: 85 Higham Road, London, N17 6NL
Major Shareholder: Christopher Long
Officers: Christopher Long [1972] Director [New Zealander]

London Beauty Limited
Incorporated: 2 January 2014
Registered Office: 17 Lych Way, Woking, Surrey, GU21 4QG
Shareholders: Stuart John Catton; Cheryl Su Yin Catton
Officers: Neville Catton, Secretary; Cheryl Catton [1979] Director/Human Resource Manager; Stuart John Catton [1977] Director/International Sales Manager

The London Cosmetics Company Limited
Incorporated: 15 June 1994
Net Worth: £160,311 *Total Assets:* £220,311
Registered Office: Exchange Tower, 19 Canning Street, Edinburgh, EH3 8EH
Shareholder: Syed Hasan Rizvi
Officers: Farhana Hasan [1944] Director/Accounts; Syed Rizwan Hasan Rizvi [1975] Director/Business Executive; Syed Hasan Rizvi [1942] Director/Sales Representative

London Ethnic Ltd
Incorporated: 26 September 2011
Net Worth Deficit: £193,138 *Total Assets:* £992
Registered Office: 57 Kingsley Avenue, Hounslow, Middlesex, TW3 4AE
Major Shareholder: Saumen Kar
Officers: Saumen Kar [1975] Director/Fashion Retailer

London Export Ltd
Incorporated: 21 May 2015
Net Worth: £6,851 *Total Assets:* £11,417
Registered Office: 104 Woodgrange Road, London, E7 0EW
Major Shareholder: Shirin Ayesha Siddiqua
Officers: Shirin Ayesha Siddiqua [1974] Director/Private Service [Bangladeshi]

London Health Sciences Ltd
Incorporated: 15 September 2016
Net Worth Deficit: £6,735
Registered Office: 20-22 Wenlock Road, London, N1 7GU
Major Shareholder: Kaya Duman
Officers: Kaya Duman [1977] Director [Turkish]

London Heartbeat Ltd
Incorporated: 2 January 2018
Registered Office: 56 Warren Street, Fitzrovia, London, W1T 5NP
Major Shareholder: Ahmer Afaq
Officers: Ahmer Afaq [1977] Director [Indian]

London International Inflammation Foundation Limited
Incorporated: 24 September 2013
Registered Office: 5 Theale Lakes Business Park, Moulden Way, Sulhamstead, Reading, Berks, RG7 4GB
Officers: Daniel James Faucitt [1982] Director; Dr Charmaine Jooste [1965] Director/Doctor [South African]

London Links Trading Limited
Incorporated: 19 July 2013
Net Worth Deficit: £46,755 *Total Assets:* £243,386
Registered Office: Unit 2, 5 Baldwin Street, London, EC1V 9NU
Major Shareholder: Bahaa Tharwat Saad Naoum
Officers: Haidy Adel Labib Hanna [1981] Director [Egyptian]; Dr Bahaa Tharwat Saad Naoum [1961] Director [Egyptian]; Philip John Woodhall [1950] Director

London Outlet Store Limited
Incorporated: 20 November 2017
Registered Office: 2nd Floor, College House, 17 King Edwards Road, Ruislip, Middlesex, HA4 7AE
Major Shareholder: Baneen Fatima Moosa
Officers: Baneen Fatima Moosa [1994] Director [Pakistani]

The London Skincare Company Ltd.
Incorporated: 12 April 2013
Net Worth Deficit: £164,560 *Total Assets:* £54,400
Registered Office: 4 Sudley Road, Bognor Regis, W Sussex, PO21 1EU
Major Shareholder: Catkin Bodmer
Officers: David John Carl Bodmer, Secretary; Catkin Bodmer [1963] Director/Skincare

Londonscentsuk Limited
Incorporated: 10 August 2018
Registered Office: 71-75 Shelton Street, London, WC2H 9JQ
Shareholders: Anish Patel; Havan Patel
Officers: Anish Patel [1989] Director/Accountant; Havan Patel [1988] Director/Accountant

Katherine Longhi Ltd
Incorporated: 23 September 2014
Net Worth Deficit: £346 *Total Assets:* £1,187
Registered Office: Suite 933, Point West, 116 Cromwell Road, London, SW7 4XL
Major Shareholder: Katherine Longhi
Officers: Katherine Longhi [1980] Director/Entrepreneur

Look Fab Limited
Incorporated: 31 May 2018
Registered Office: 143 Victoria Ave, Southend-on-Sea, Essex, SS2 6EL
Major Shareholder: Hilda Aldina Chimanayi
Officers: Hilda Aldina Chimanayi [1975] Director/Owner [Zambian]

Look Lovable Ltd.
Incorporated: 17 January 2018
Registered Office: 175a Brownhill Road, London, SE6 2BQ
Officers: Jessica Raynsford [1994] Director/Part-Time

C Looker Ltd
Incorporated: 19 September 2017
Registered Office: The Old School, The Stennack, St Ives, Cornwall, TR26 1QU
Major Shareholder: Carmen Corinna Looker
Officers: Carmen Corinna Looker [1970] Director [German]

Loop Beauty Limited
Incorporated: 6 March 2018
Registered Office: 130 Old Street, London, EC1V 9BD
Officers: Ariel Roberts [1986] Director [American]

Loopy Hair & Beauty Ltd
Incorporated: 22 June 2010
Net Worth: £51,268 *Total Assets:* £58,981
Registered Office: 24 Bourton Road, Buckingham, MK18 1BE
Major Shareholder: Wioletta Pazdanska
Officers: Wioletta Pazdanska, Secretary; Wioletta Pazdanska [1978] Sales Director [Polish]

Lord & Berry Ltd
Incorporated: 25 February 2014
Net Worth Deficit: £39,650 *Total Assets:* £144,600
Registered Office: 88 Crawford Street, London, W1H 2EJ
Major Shareholder: Pablo Blayer
Officers: Paolo Blayer [1960] Director [Italian]

Lore Originals Limited
Incorporated: 13 September 2016
Registered Office: 47 Butt Road, Colchester, Essex, CO3 3BZ
Major Shareholder: Sarah Dawn Brass
Officers: Cameron James Amos [1976] Director; Sarah Dawn Brass [1970] Director/Salon Owner

Lottie London Limited
Incorporated: 4 November 2014 *Employees:* 26
Net Worth: £188,605 *Total Assets:* £4,227,193
Registered Office: Batchworth House, Batchworth Place, Church Street, Rickmansworth, Herts, WD3 1JE
Parent: PBS Brand Agency Limited
Officers: Charlotte Knight [1979] Director

Lotus Cosmetics Ltd
Incorporated: 22 May 2018
Registered Office: 4 Goldcrest Walk, Whitstable, Kent, CT5 4TL
Major Shareholder: Caroline Lyons
Officers: Caroline Lyons [1972] Director

Louts Remit Beautiful International Group Co., Limited
Incorporated: 18 September 2017
Registered Office: Unit G25, Waterfront Studios, 1 Dock Road, London, E16 1AH
Major Shareholder: Zongqiong Chen
Officers: Zongqiong Chen [1977] Director [Chinese]

Lovalova Ltd
Incorporated: 12 October 2018
Registered Office: 71-75 Shelton Street, London, WC2H 9JQ
Major Shareholder: Iuliana Onofriescu
Officers: Iuliana Onofriescu [1991] Director/Administrator [Romanian]

Love Anousta Limited
Incorporated: 2 November 2018
Registered Office: 12 Haviland Road, Ferndown Industrial Estate, Wimborne, Dorset, BH21 7RG
Major Shareholder: Linda Anousta
Officers: Linda Anousta [1958] Director/Manager

Love Henna Brows Limited
Incorporated: 4 April 2018
Registered Office: 2 The Keep, Bolton, Lancs, BL1 5NG
Shareholders: Bernadette Ann Mulligan; Naomi Clara Katy Bardusco-Marlow; Rhianna Dawn Frend-Bullock
Officers: Naomi Clara Katy Bardusco-Marlow [1984] Director; Rhianna Dawn Frend-Bullock [1983] Director; Bernadette Ann Mulligan [1967] Director

Love Little Prices Ltd
Incorporated: 27 January 2016
Registered Office: Unit 1 Orchard Trading Estate, Langley Road South, Salford, M6 6SD
Major Shareholder: Wojciech Strzelecki
Officers: Wojciech Strzelecki [1967] Director [Polish]

Loveco Ltd
Incorporated: 25 July 2017
Registered Office: 35 Broughton Court, Broughton Road, London, W13 8QN
Officers: Predrag Gnjatovic [1971] Director/Project Manager [Croatian]; Atsuko Ogawa Gnjatovic [1977] Director/Chemist [Japanese]

Loveliness Limited
Incorporated: 20 November 2018
Registered Office: Flat 3, Warspite House, Cahir Street, London, E14 3QU
Officers: Inesa Antonova [1963] Director [Latvian]

The Lovely Distribution Company Limited
Incorporated: 8 July 2014
Net Worth: £2,563,273 *Total Assets:* £5,183,221
Registered Office: Unit 3 Woking8, Forsyth Road, Woking, Surrey, GU21 5SB
Shareholders: Charles Rodney Mathers; Andre Frenkel
Officers: Andre Frenkel [1952] Director [Swiss]

Loveve. Ltd
Incorporated: 11 December 2018
Registered Office: 1 Topsfield Close, Crouch End, London, N8 8DW
Major Shareholder: Evelyn Isabel Blackman
Officers: Evelyn Isabel Blackman [1974] Director/Manufacturer

Lovoir Ltd
Incorporated: 7 August 2018
Registered Office: 71-75 Shelton Street, Covent Garden, London, WC2H 9JQ
Major Shareholder: Teresa Maree Sime
Officers: Teresa Maree Sime [1990] Director [New Zealander]

Lovorika London Limited
Incorporated: 15 March 2017
Net Worth Deficit: £2,260 *Total Assets:* £766,000
Registered Office: 40 St James Buildings, St James Street, Taunton, Somerset, TA1 1JR
Shareholders: Daphna Anducich-Rowe; Jason Rowe
Officers: Daphna Anducich - Rowe [1975] Director [American]; Jason Rowe [1969] Director

Lozano Skincare Ltd
Incorporated: 22 June 2018
Registered Office: Kemp House, 160 City Road, London, EC1V 2NX
Officers: Matthew Kelly [1982] Director/Marketing; Paul Stimpson [1986] Director/Designer

LPG Clinics Wholesale Ltd
Incorporated: 16 August 2018
Registered Office: 16 Hall Lane, Kirkburton, Huddersfield, W Yorks, HD8 0QW
Major Shareholder: Lyam Pearson Gill
Officers: Lyam Pearson Gill [1989] Director

LTSC Ltd
Incorporated: 6 February 2018
Registered Office: 40 Albert Place, Cheltenham, Glos, GL52 2JX
Shareholders: Leigh Thompson; Steven Crumblehulme
Officers: Steven John Crumblehulme [1980] Director/Reflexologist; Leigh Thompson [1976] Director/Contractor

Luban & Murr Ltd
Incorporated: 28 March 2017
Registered Office: 20-22 Wenlock Road, London, N1 7GU
Major Shareholder: Saed Mohamed Jama
Officers: Saed Mohamed Jama [1975] Director/Entrepreneur

Lubatti Limited
Incorporated: 22 September 2008
Net Worth Deficit: £557,000 *Total Assets:* £140,000
Registered Office: Venture House, 2 Arlington Square, Bracknell, Berks, RG12 1WA
Parent: Venture Life Group PLC
Officers: Giuseppe Gioffre, Secretary; Sharon Mary Collins [1974] Director; Jeremy Anthony Philip Randall [1964] Director/Management Consultant

Lucas Haynes Limited
Incorporated: 22 January 2016
Registered Office: 71-75 Shelton Street, Covent Garden, London, WC2H 9JQ
Officers: Weijun Zhou [1980] Director/Business Owner [Chinese]

Lucerne Perfumes Ltd
Incorporated: 24 January 2018
Registered Office: International House, 24 Holborn Viaduct, London, EC1A 2BN
Major Shareholder: Ali Alzaabi
Officers: Ali Alzaabi [1995] Director/Businessman [Emirati]

Lucy Beauty Products Ltd
Incorporated: 4 February 2019
Registered Office: 20-22 Wenlock Road, London, N1 7GU
Major Shareholder: Alyssa Daphiny Fernandes Hill
Officers: Alyssa Daphiny Fernandes Hill [2000] Director/Manager [American]

Lueno Cosmetics Limited
Incorporated: 22 January 2019
Registered Office: 71-75 Shelton Street, London, WC2H 9JQ
Major Shareholder: Samuel Wood
Officers: Samuel Wood [1996] Managing Director

Lukony Ltd
Incorporated: 13 January 2017 *Employees:* 2
Net Worth: £4,731 *Total Assets:* £514,939
Registered Office: c/o Gannons Solicitors, 20-21 Jockey's Fields, London, WC1R 4BW
Shareholders: Luke Henry James Granger; Antony Charles Kazer
Officers: Antony Charles Kazer [1960] Sales Director

Lulu Tanner Limited
Incorporated: 7 August 2017
Registered Office: 147 Melfort Road, Thornton Heath, Surrey, CR7 7RU
Major Shareholder: Xun Xun
Officers: Xun Xun [1990] Director [Chinese]

Lumine Beauty Ltd
Incorporated: 13 September 2018
Registered Office: 50 Haines House, The Residence, 10 Charles Clowes Walk, London, SW11 7AH
Major Shareholder: Aie Chen
Officers: Aie Chen [1973] Director [Chinese]

Lumos Products Limited
Incorporated: 16 September 2002
Net Worth Deficit: £3,488 *Total Assets:* £10,264
Registered Office: 8 Southfields Road, London, SW18 1QN
Officers: Antonia Brann, Secretary; Nicholas Stephen Brann [1961] Director/Finance Consultant

Luqs Womenswear Ltd
Incorporated: 17 May 2018
Registered Office: 143 St Saviours Road, Birmingham, B8 1HW
Major Shareholder: Mohammed Luqman Qasim
Officers: Mohammed Luqman Qasim [1999] Director

Luscious Lashes International Ltd
Incorporated: 30 June 2016
Net Worth: £12,620 *Total Assets:* £19,800
Registered Office: Kemp House, 160 City Road, London, EC1V 2NX
Major Shareholder: Clifford Neil Altree
Officers: Clifford Neil Altree, Secretary; Clifford Neil Altree [1966] Director

Luscious Skincare Ltd
Incorporated: 11 March 2016
Net Worth Deficit: £5,900 *Total Assets:* £3,960
Registered Office: 17 Cornmill Grove, Perton, Wolverhampton, W Midlands, WV6 7XU
Major Shareholder: Dana Marie Cooper
Officers: Dana Marie Cooper [1984] Director/Distributor

Lush Lashes London Limited
Incorporated: 12 December 2017
Registered Office: 12b High Street, Spaldwick, Cambs, PE28 0TD
Shareholder: Emma Sentance
Officers: Danielle Sampson [1983] Director/Beauty Therapist; Emma Sentance [1976] Director/Eyelash Technician

Lush Ltd.
Incorporated: 17 June 1994 *Employees:* 282
Net Worth: £59,083,000 *Total Assets:* £133,899,000
Registered Office: 29 High Street, Poole, Dorset, BH15 1AB
Parent: Lush Cosmetics Limited
Officers: Karl Joseph Bygrave, Secretary; Rowena Jaqueline Bird [1959] Director/Retail Consultant; Karl Joseph Bygrave [1962] Director/Manager; Jack Constantine [1984] Director; Margaret Joan Constantine [1953] Director/Inventor; Mark Constantine [1952] Director; Hilary Anita Jones [1962] Director; Simon George Nicholls [1963] Director

Lushes Ltd
Incorporated: 13 June 2016
Registered Office: 225 Marsh Wall, London, E14 9FW
Shareholders: Younes Ghouini; Soumia Ghouini; Kaouther Ghouini; Marwa Ghouini
Officers: Soumia Ghouini [1991] Director

Lustra Beauty Limited
Incorporated: 23 November 2017
Registered Office: Davis Bonley, Northside House, Mount Pleasant, Barnet, Herts, EN4 9EE
Shareholders: June Linda Presswell; Roy Henry Presswell
Officers: Joanne Sarah Hurst [1972] Director; James Stephen Presswell [1978] Director; June Linda Presswell [1950] Director; Roy Henry Presswell [1948] Director

Luuann Limited
Incorporated: 29 January 2019
Registered Office: 4 Wimpole, Wellingborough, Northants, NN8 3TQ
Shareholders: Andrzej Boron; Lukasz Ogrodnik
Officers: Andrzej Boron [1990] Director [Polish]; Lukasz Ogrodnik [1991] Director [Polish]

Lux Aesthetics Hull Ltd
Incorporated: 11 February 2019
Registered Office: 100 Shinewater Park, Kingswood, Hull, HU7 3DN
Shareholders: Savannah Pearson; Stephen John Goodfellow
Officers: Savannah Pearson [1993] Director

Luxe Associates Ltd
Incorporated: 16 May 2015
Net Worth: £1,520 *Total Assets:* £12,670
Registered Office: 1 Warwick Road, Tunbridge Wells, Kent, TN1 1YL
Officers: Terence Pearce [1967] Director

Luxmeticgroup Limited
Incorporated: 27 April 2017
Registered Office: 10-11 Heathfield Terrace, London, W4 4JE
Major Shareholder: Saeid Kargozar
Officers: Saeid Kargozar [1984] Director

Luxuria Generation Limited
Incorporated: 21 November 2017
Registered Office: 30 Rosebank Avenue, Wembley, Middlesex, HA0 2TW
Major Shareholder: Hazza Al Meqbali
Officers: Hazza Al Meqbali [1985] Director/Purchasing Manager [Emirati]; Amine Berdai [1992] Director/Sales Manager [Moroccan]

Luxurious Personal Care Ltd
Incorporated: 19 February 2019
Registered Office: 55 High Street, Hoddesdon, Herts, EN11 8TQ
Major Shareholder: James Shipton
Officers: James Shipton, Secretary; Bradley John Shipton [1995] Director; James Shipton [1993] Director

Luxury Consulting by Bethan Williams Limited
Incorporated: 26 September 2016
Net Worth Deficit: £2,531 *Total Assets:* £112
Registered Office: 32c Belsize Park, London, NW3 4DX
Major Shareholder: Bethan Williams
Officers: Bethan Williams [1966] Director

Luxury Personal Care Ltd
Incorporated: 15 February 2019
Registered Office: Kemp House, 160 City Road, London, EC1V 2NX
Major Shareholder: James Shipton
Officers: James Shipton, Secretary; Brad Shipton [1995] Director/Buyer; James Shipton [1993] Director/Buyer

Luxuryscope London Limited
Incorporated: 3 May 2018
Registered Office: Roxburghe House, 273-287 Regent Street, London, W1B 2HA
Shareholders: Signe Kurup Stenbaek; Carola Margarete Weymouth
Officers: Signe Kurup Stenbaek [1959] Director [Danish]; Carola Margarete Weymouth [1968] Director [German]

LVMH Fragrance Brands UK Limited
Incorporated: 27 September 1968 *Employees:* 130
Net Worth: £1,246,564 *Total Assets:* £5,940,969
Registered Office: 6th Floor, United Kingdom House, 180 Oxford Street, London, W1D 1AB
Parent: LVMH Moet Hennessy Louis Vuitton
Officers: Loic Pierre Marie Henriot, Secretary; Loic Pierre Marie Henriot [1978] Director [French]; Guillemette Norlain [1971] Director/General Manager [French]; Romain Spitzer [1971] Director [French]

LW International Ltd
Incorporated: 21 October 2016
Net Worth: £89,226 *Total Assets:* £275,056
Registered Office: 42 Station Road, Ainsdale, Southport, Merseyside, PR8 3HW
Major Shareholder: Steven Bolger
Officers: Steven Bolger [1960] Director/Manager

Lyal Intertrading Ltd
Incorporated: 10 November 2014
Net Worth Deficit: £201 *Total Assets:* £39,044
Registered Office: 2nd Floor, 13 John Prince's Street, London, W1G 0JR
Officers: Jan Harm Snyman [1968] Director/Consultant [South African]

LYF Cosmetics Limited
Incorporated: 29 March 2018
Registered Office: Innovation, Birmingham Campus, Faraday Wharf, Holt Street, Birmingham, B7 4BB
Major Shareholder: Madiha Khusar
Officers: Madiha Khusar [1996] Director

Lynch-Staunton Cosmetics Limited
Incorporated: 6 August 1985
Registered Office: Newbury House, Aintree Avenue, White Horse Business Park, Trowbridge, Wilts, BA14 0XB
Parent: Lynch-Staunton Cosmetics Holdings Limited
Officers: Graham Murray Lynch Staunton [1969] Director; Susan Angela Lynch-Staunton [1967] UK Sales Director

Lyons Men's Grooming Ltd
Incorporated: 10 October 2018
Registered Office: 143 Ringway, Southall, Middlesex, UB2 5ST
Major Shareholder: Jeffred Lyons
Officers: Jeffred Lyons [1991] Director/Self Employed

Lyons Pride Limited
Incorporated: 25 July 2017
Registered Office: 45 Peckham High Street, London, SE15 5EB
Officers: Ifeoluwa Abiola Ademola, Secretary; Ifeoluwa Abiola Ademola [1981] Director/Trader [Nigerian]

M & H Cosmetic Limited
Incorporated: 4 June 2018
Registered Office: 292-294 Fulham Road, London, SW10 9EW
Officers: Matthias Hecht [1983] Director [German]

M & M Cosmetics Limited
Incorporated: 14 September 1994 *Employees:* 6
Net Worth: £823,997 *Total Assets:* £1,120,525
Registered Office: 183-189 The Vale, London, W3 7RW
Parent: Investcape Ltd
Officers: Aiyub Abdullah Ahmed, Secretary; Mohamed Ameen Kalla [1971] Director

M & M Import Ltd
Incorporated: 15 July 2009
Net Worth: £12,330 *Total Assets:* £411,410
Registered Office: 33 Willmott Road, Rushden, Northants, NN10 0YU
Shareholder: Maria Madalena Lemes Da Silva
Officers: Marco Aurelio Alves Conceicao [1977] Director/Sales Manager [Brazilian]; Maria Madalena Lemes Da Silva [1972] Director [Spanish]

M & N Traders Limited
Incorporated: 20 November 1995 Employees: 14
Net Worth: £3,687,437 Total Assets: £5,473,454
Registered Office: 925 Finchley Road, London, NW11 7PE
Shareholders: Narinder Singh Kohli; Manjinder Kaur Kohli
Officers: Narinder Singh Kohli, Secretary [Indian]; Manjinder Kaur Kohli [1964] Director

M Beauty Ltd
Incorporated: 19 June 2006 Employees: 13
Net Worth: £355,692 Total Assets: £1,741,423
Registered Office: 5th Floor, Voyager House, Chicago Avenue, Manchester Airport, Manchester, M90 3DQ
Parent: Thehut.Com Limited
Officers: James Patrick Pochin, Secretary; John Andrew Gallemore [1969] Director/Accountant; James Patrick Pochin [1976] Legal Director

M Cosmetics Distribution Ltd
Incorporated: 4 January 2018
Registered Office: 211 Station Road, Harrow, Middlesex, HA1 2TP
Officers: Sukhdeep Singh Mason [1963] Director/Manager

M.S.S (Micro Scientific Services) Limited
Incorporated: 22 December 2014
Net Worth Deficit: £2,600 Total Assets: £3,610
Registered Office: 179 White Horse Hill, Chislehurst, Kent, BR7 6DH
Major Shareholder: Beata Marta Wojciechowska
Officers: Beata Marta Wojciechowska [1961] Director [Polish]

Mabxclusive Limited
Incorporated: 12 July 2018
Registered Office: H5 Ash Tree Court, Nottingham Business Park, Nottingham, NG8 6PY
Major Shareholder: Habeeb Anifowoshe
Officers: Habeeb Anifowoshe [1985] Director/Entrepreneur [Nigerian]; Adebukola Balogun [1987] Director/Entrepreneur [Nigerian]

Macden Beauty Ltd
Incorporated: 1 August 2018
Registered Office: 1 Victoria Court, Bank Square, Morley, Leeds, LS27 9SE
Shareholders: Thomas Richard Macpherson Le Maire; Matthew Robert Denby
Officers: Matthew Robert Denby [1988] Director; Thomas Richard Macpherson Le Maire [1982] Director

Macial Ltd
Incorporated: 24 October 2017
Registered Office: 34 Twine Street, Hunslet, Leeds, LS10 1GN
Major Shareholder: Matthew Dowell
Officers: Matt Dowell [1992] Director

MacKenzie Cosmetics Limited
Incorporated: 6 August 2003
Net Worth: £37,690 Total Assets: £44,870
Registered Office: Eden Point, Three Acres Lane, Cheadle Hulme, Cheadle, Cheshire, SK8 6RL
Major Shareholder: Mali MacKenzie
Officers: Mali MacKenzie, Secretary; Mali MacKenzie [1945] Director

Macks Ltd.
Incorporated: 15 December 2000 Employees: 8
Net Worth: £4,627,030 Total Assets: £6,780,867
Registered Office: 24 Bedford Row, London, WC1R 4TQ
Officers: Kishore Kumar Mohan Lakhwani [1974] Director [Danish]

Mad Beauty Limited
Incorporated: 3 September 1998 Employees: 10
Net Worth: £152,349 Total Assets: £749,824
Registered Office: Unit 3, 1st Floor, North Cavendish House, 369-391 Burnt Oak Broadway, Edgware, Middlesex, HA8 5AW
Shareholders: Trevor Ian Cash; Julia Cash
Officers: Julia Cash, Secretary; Julia Cash [1963] Director/Beauty Therapist; Trevor Ian Cash [1958] Director/Marketing Manager; Tao Xiong [1973] Director of Business Development [Hong Kong]

Madame Laveau Ltd
Incorporated: 2 January 2019
Registered Office: 164 Andrewes House, Barbican, London, EC2Y 8BA
Major Shareholder: Lonnee Eileen Hamilton
Officers: Lonnee Eileen Hamilton [1962] Director [American]

Madison Steward Ltd
Incorporated: 17 January 2018
Registered Office: International House, 12 Constance Street, London, E16 2DQ
Officers: Bernahrd Trixl [1986] Director [Austrian]

Madre Skincare Limited
Incorporated: 13 April 2011
Net Worth Deficit: £1,270 Total Assets: £2,030
Registered Office: 98 Averil Road, Leicester, LE5 2DB
Major Shareholder: Ravinder Kandohla
Officers: Ravinder Kandohla [1976] Director

Magia BLV International Ltd
Incorporated: 9 November 2016
Registered Office: 71-75 Shelton Street, Covent Garden, London, WC2H 9JQ
Major Shareholder: Giorgio Calapa
Officers: Giorgio Calapa [1977] Director/Business Analyst [Italian]

Magnum Beauty International Limited
Incorporated: 20 October 2015
Previous: The London Wholesale Cosmetics Company Ltd
Registered Office: 85 Great Portland Street, London, W1W 7LT
Major Shareholder: Muhammadali Kassamali
Officers: Muhammadali Kassamali [1986] Director/Businessman

Magpie Holdings Ltd
Incorporated: 13 February 2019
Registered Office: Kemp House, 160 City Road, London, EC1V 2NX
Major Shareholder: Phillip Smith
Officers: Phillip Smith, Secretary; Phillip Smith [1975] Director

Magpie's Ocean Ltd
Incorporated: 19 September 2018
Registered Office: 34 Wain Street, Stoke on Trent, Staffs, ST6 4ES
Shareholders: Samantha Ophelia Chinnery; Eleanor Lunaria Hetherington
Officers: Samantha Ophelia Chinnery [1980] Director/Manufacturer; Eleanor Lunaria Hetherington [1992] Director/Manufacturer

Mahiri Africa Ltd
Incorporated: 14 October 2018
Registered Office: 361a High Street North, Manor Park, London, E12 6PQ
Major Shareholder: Osman Sheikhali
Officers: Abdirahman Mohamed [1980] Director/Businessman [Somali]; Osman Sheikhali [1982] Director/Businessman

Mahogany Crownz Ltd
Incorporated: 15 June 2018
Registered Office: 72 Blackthorn Manor, Londonderry, BT47 5ST
Major Shareholder: Dikeledi Nkele Mushapho
Officers: Dikeledi Nkele Mushapho [1996] Director/Chemist

Mahrosh Beauty Ltd
Incorporated: 3 June 2010
Net Worth: £82,830 *Total Assets:* £376,800
Registered Office: 38 Hulme High Street, Manchester, M15 5JP
Major Shareholder: Shahzad Ahmad
Officers: Saima Nourine, Secretary; Shahzad Ahmad [1977] Director/Software Engineer

Mainline Marketing U K. Limited
Incorporated: 11 July 1983
Net Worth: £1,954,854 *Total Assets:* £2,132,736
Registered Office: Coleford House, 300 Coleford Road, Sheffield, S9 5PH
Officers: Peter Rutter, Secretary; James Alistair Rutter [1972] Director; Peter Rutter [1944] Director; Robert Edward Rutter [1975] Director; Vivien Grace Rutter [1948] Director

Maison Danu (UK) Ltd
Incorporated: 13 November 2006
Previous: La Vie D'Anu Limited
Net Worth Deficit: £455,198
Registered Office: Companies House, Default Address, Cardiff, CF14 8LH
Major Shareholder: Elizabeth Catherine Horgan-Novarro
Officers: Elizabeth Catherine Horgan-Novarro [1965] Director [Irish]

Maison de Maa Ltd
Incorporated: 17 May 2017
Registered Office: Flat 5, 9-11 Cromwell Lodge, London, SW7 2JA
Major Shareholder: Abdulmalek Almasmoum
Officers: Abdulmalek Almasmoum [1992] Director [Syrian]

Majestic Company London Limited
Incorporated: 4 July 2018
Registered Office: Ground Floor, Anchorage House, 2 Clove Crescent, East India Dock, London, E14 2BE
Major Shareholder: Hamza Mursaleen
Officers: Hamza Mursaleen [1993] Director/Manager

Make It Up Limited
Incorporated: 8 August 2018
Registered Office: Myrtle Grove Mill, Bacup Road, Rossendale, Lancs, BB4 7JJ
Major Shareholder: Anastasia Catherine Alexandra Kenyon
Officers: Anastasia Catherine Alexandra Kenyon [1992] Director

Make Up for Ever U.K. Limited
Incorporated: 5 April 2017
Registered Office: LVMH Perfumes and Cosmetics, 6th Floor, UK House, 180 Oxford Street, London, W1D 1AB
Parent: LVMH Moet Hennessy Louis Vuitton S.E.
Officers: Melanie Delphine Constance Bois Sevestre [1976] Director [French]; Aline Burelier [1979] Director [French]; Loic Pierre Marie Henriot [1978] Director [French]; Rachel Gina Marouani [1971] Director [French]

Make Up Madness Ltd
Incorporated: 20 July 2017
Registered Office: 29 King Street, Portland, Dorset, DT5 1NH
Major Shareholder: Jessica O'Connor
Officers: Jessica O'Connor, Secretary; Jessica O'Connor [1982] Director/Beautician

Make-Up International Limited
Incorporated: 19 January 1983
Net Worth: £44,161 *Total Assets:* £84,227
Registered Office: 9a Burroughs Gardens, London, NW4 4AU
Officers: Mei-Ting Jessica Chow [1981] Director/Administration Manager

Makeup Boutique Limited
Incorporated: 27 October 2017
Registered Office: 20-22 Wenlock Road, London, N1 7GU
Major Shareholder: Florin Stratulat
Officers: Florin Stratulat [1989] Director [Romanian]

Makeup54 Ltd
Incorporated: 26 January 2016
Net Worth: £1 *Total Assets:* £1
Registered Office: 20-22 Wenlock Road, London, N1 7GU
Officers: Anna Priadka [1985] Director

Makki Cosmetics Limited
Incorporated: 29 March 2011
Net Worth: £375,960 *Total Assets:* £507,280
Registered Office: 125 Northenden Road, Sale, Cheshire, M33 3HF
Major Shareholder: Mansour Nassif Makki
Officers: Mansour Nassif Makki [1968] Director

Maliboo Hair and Cosmetics Ltd
Incorporated: 2 October 2018
Registered Office: Flat 17, Poppy Court, 73 Childers Street, London, SE8 5JR
Major Shareholder: Malika Robinson
Officers: Malika Robinson, Secretary; Malika Robinson [1998] Director/Hair Stylist [Jamaican]

Malvina Skin Care Limited
Incorporated: 16 April 2012 *Employees:* 1
Net Worth Deficit: £49,844 *Total Assets:* £5,144
Registered Office: Unit 3, 1st Floor, North Cavendish House, 369-391 Burnt Oak Broadway, Edgware, Middlesex, HA8 5AW
Major Shareholder: Malvina Fraser
Officers: Malvina Fraser [1958] Director

Mama Mio Limited
Incorporated: 6 October 2004 *Employees:* 10
Net Worth: £383,000 *Total Assets:* £503,000
Registered Office: 5th Floor, Voyager House, Chicago Avenue, Manchester Airport, Manchester, M90 3DQ
Parent: Ensco 818 Ltd
Officers: James Patrick Pochin, Secretary; John Andrew Gallemore [1969] Director; Paul Jonathan Gedman [1981] Director/Retailer

Mamado International Limited
Incorporated: 12 June 2007 *Employees:* 3
Net Worth Deficit: £72,688 *Total Assets:* £128,274
Registered Office: 3 George Street, Watford, Herts, WD18 0BX
Parent: KMS Holdings Limited
Officers: Gulam Nasser [1965] Director

Mamondo Fragrance and Beauty Ltd
Incorporated: 17 May 2018
Registered Office: 19 Artisan Mews, Warfield Road, London, NW10 5GL
Officers: Oussama Lagbaj [1989] Director [French]

Man & Diva's Ltd
Incorporated: 21 February 2017
Net Worth: £4,992 *Total Assets:* £17,708
Registered Office: 33 Harris Close, Newton Mearns, Glasgow, G77 6TU
Officers: Tarun Khadiya [1980] Director/Online Trading [Indian]

Man Mask Ltd
Incorporated: 12 December 2018
Registered Office: 1 Park Farm Court, Clapham, Bedford, MK41 6EF
Shareholders: Benjamin Gibbs; Mark Girven
Officers: Benjamin Gibbs [1980] Director/Sales; Mark Girven [1988] Director/Sales

Man'd Skincare Ltd
Incorporated: 30 October 2018
Registered Office: 5 The Mount, Swinton, Malton, N Yorks, YO17 6SN
Major Shareholder: Tommy Bernard Leach
Officers: Tommy Bernard Leach [1991] Managing Director

Manas Organics Ltd
Incorporated: 27 June 2017
Registered Office: 58 Derwent Road, Colchester, Essex, CO4 9RU
Major Shareholder: Jo Danbury
Officers: Jo Danbury, Secretary; Jo Danbury [1988] Director/Chief Executive Officer

Mancave Limited
Incorporated: 11 December 2009 *Employees:* 3
Net Worth: £459,401 *Total Assets:* £806,737
Registered Office: Chartwell House, 1 Brunel Parkway, Pride Park, Derby, DE24 8HR
Shareholders: Mark Antony Grogan; Sarah Elizabeth Grogan
Officers: Alexander Joseph Grogan [1992] Director; Mark Anthony Grogan [1964] Director; Sarah Elizabeth Grogan [1967] Director/Administrator; Brian William McGlynn [1957] Director; Damian Richard Stroud [1966] Director

Mandragora Ltd
Incorporated: 12 December 2018
Registered Office: 13 Barkston Grove, York, YO26 5AU
Officers: Mariangela Lopardi [1984] Director/Dealer [Italian]; Daniele Pica [1977] Director/Dealer [Italian]

Mane (UK) Limited
Incorporated: 29 November 1983
Net Worth: £171,241 *Total Assets:* £574,895
Registered Office: 4 Grenville Avenue, Broxbourne, Herts, EN10 7DH
Major Shareholder: William Neagle Cathcart
Officers: William Neagle Cathcart [1953] Director

Mane Love Ltd
Incorporated: 6 April 2017
Registered Office: 12 Constance Street, London, E16 2DQ
Officers: Amir Thomas [1984] Director

The Manhattan Group Ltd.
Incorporated: 19 June 2017
Registered Office: The White House, 5 Staines Green, Hertford, SG14 2LN
Major Shareholder: Zarina Zarina Morris
Officers: Zarina Zarina Morris [1989] Director

Manicure You Ltd
Incorporated: 16 August 2018
Registered Office: 12 Gladstone Road, London, W4 5HE
Shareholder: Nicola Jade Soremekun
Officers: Nicola Jade Soremekun [1987] Director/Legal Adviser

Mann & Noble Europe Limited
Incorporated: 9 March 2016
Net Worth: £104 *Total Assets:* £6,398
Registered Office: 1 Vincent Square, Westminster, London, SW1P 2PN
Parent: Mann & Noble International Pty Ltd
Officers: Robert Llewellyn Harris [1970] Director

Maraki International Limited
Incorporated: 11 September 2017
Registered Office: Companies House, Default Address, Cardiff, CF14 8LH
Major Shareholder: Jamila Jangaria
Officers: Jamila Jangaria, Secretary; Jamila Jangaria [1979] Managing Director

Marcman Perfume Ltd
Incorporated: 20 March 2018
Registered Office: 19 Kirkby Road, Barwell, Leics, LE9 8FP
Shareholders: Krisztian Pintea; Beatrix Stangerean
Officers: Krisztian Pintea [1984] Director [Hungarian]; Beatrix Stangerean [1988] Director [Hungarian]

Margan Oil Ltd
Incorporated: 4 December 2018
Registered Office: 295 Holloway Road, London, N7 8HS
Major Shareholder: Mohammed Slaoui
Officers: Mohammed Slaoui [1998] Director [Moroccan]

Marina Muda Ltd
Incorporated: 24 October 2016
Registered Office: 4 Monmouth Road, London, W2 5SB
Major Shareholder: Ezam Mat-Ali
Officers: Ezam Mat-Ali [1972] Director

Maringo Ltd
Incorporated: 22 March 2011
Previous: Pure and Natural Brands Ltd
Net Worth Deficit: £439,040 *Total Assets:* £7,520
Registered Office: Bulleign Barn, Smallhythe Road, Tenterden, Kent, TN30 7NQ
Major Shareholder: Seonaid MacDonald
Officers: Andrew Reginald Rushworth Dixon [1960] Director/Retailer; Seonaid MacDonald [1961] Director/Business Management

Alexandra de Markoff Limited
Incorporated: 27 May 2015
Net Worth: £153 *Total Assets:* £12,180
Registered Office: 416b Clifton Drive North, Lytham St Annes, Lancs, FY8 2PN
Major Shareholder: Warren Brooks
Officers: Warren Brooks [1966] Director

Marksman Green Ltd
Incorporated: 31 May 2018
Registered Office: 105 Shirley Drive, Hove, E Sussex, BN3 6UE
Major Shareholder: Andrew Miles Pollard
Officers: Andrew Miles Pollard [1988] Director

Markwins Beauty Brands International Limited
Incorporated: 9 February 2000 *Employees:* 34
Previous: Markwins International Corporation Limited
Net Worth Deficit: £2,830,521 *Total Assets:* £40,203,952
Registered Office: 4 Elmwood, Crockford Lane, Chineham Business Park, Chineham, Basingstoke, Hants, RG24 8WG
Shareholders: Sung Tsei Chen; Lina Chen
Officers: John Phillip Stephenson, Secretary; Lina Chen [1958] Director [American]; Sung Tsei Chen [1958] Director [American]; Giancarlo di Majo [1962] Managing Director [Italian]; John Phillip Stephenson [1959] Director [American]

Markwins Beauty Products Limited
Incorporated: 21 April 2004
Net Worth: £21,771 *Total Assets:* £21,771
Registered Office: 4 Elmwood, Crockford Lane, Chineham Business Park, Basingstoke, Hants, RG24 8WG
Parent: Markwins Beauty Brands International Limited
Officers: Lina Chen [1958] Director/Chief Administrator [American]; Sung Tsei Chen [1958] Director [American]; John Phillip Stephenson [1959] Director/Executive [American]

Paul Marney & Co Ltd
Incorporated: 6 September 2018
Registered Office: 71-75 Shelton Street, London, WC2H 9JQ
Major Shareholder: Paul Mihoc
Officers: Paul Mihoc, Secretary; Paul Mihoc [1995] Director/Hotel Employee [Italian]

Marque of Brands Limited
Incorporated: 7 April 2015 *Employees:* 1
Net Worth: £8,731 *Total Assets:* £158,067
Registered Office: 24 Chiswell Street, London, EC1Y 4YX
Major Shareholder: Justin,Cameron Campbell
Officers: Cameron Campbell, Secretary; Cameron Campbell [1979] Director/Manager [Australian]

Marrouge Limited
Incorporated: 22 November 2018
Registered Office: 19 Rosary Gardens, London, SW7 4NJ
Shareholders: Syndele Douazi; Drena Gashi
Officers: Syndele Douazi [1992] Director [French]; Drena Gashi [1984] Director [American]

Martha & Daughter Limited
Incorporated: 13 May 2005
Net Worth Deficit: £38,575 *Total Assets:* £3,811
Registered Office: Park Farm, Gunton Park, Hanworth, Norwich, NR11 7HL
Major Shareholder: Sally Martha Martin
Officers: Sally Martha Martin, Secretary; Amy Martin [1992] Director; Sally Martha Martin [1947] Director

Mary Jean Limited
Incorporated: 25 November 2008
Net Worth Deficit: £7,579 *Total Assets:* £832
Registered Office: Whincroft Braehead, Orton, Fochabers, Moray, IV32 7QH
Shareholders: Leslie Thomas Quinn; Elizabeth Quinn
Officers: Elizabeth Quinn [1954] Director; Leslie Thomas Quinn [1972] Director

Mary Kay Cosmetics (U.K.) Limited
Incorporated: 25 November 1992 *Employees:* 26
Net Worth Deficit: £14,058,308 *Total Assets:* £1,615,294
Registered Office: 163 Eversholt Street, London, NW1 1BU
Parent: Mary Kay Inc
Officers: Tara Ann Eustace [1970] Director/Businesswoman [American]; Cheryl Elaine Monroe [1970] Director/Vice President Controller & Treasurer [American]

Mary-Jane's Beauty Ltd
Incorporated: 10 January 2019
Registered Office: 5 Furze Close, Bridgwater, Somerset, TA6 7AN
Parent: Mary-Jane's Coffee Limited
Officers: Jane Antoniou [1949] Director

Maryam Imports & Exports Ltd
Incorporated: 31 October 2016
Net Worth: £333 *Total Assets:* £49,521
Registered Office: Suite 125, 1 Evolution Park, Haslingden Road, Blackburn, Lancs, BB1 2FD
Officers: Bilal Hussain [1990] Director/Airline Pilot; Jamal Hussain [1992] Managing Director; Omar Saleh Hussain [1995] Director/Airline Pilot; Asif Inam [1970] Director [Pakistani]

Masculin Limited
Incorporated: 30 July 2018
Registered Office: 4 Princes Road, Walton-le-Dale, Preston, Lancs, PR5 4HH
Major Shareholder: Olvera Maitigere Simango
Officers: Olvera Maitigere Simango [1996] Director/Chemist [Zimbabwean]

Mashco Limited
Incorporated: 21 March 1997 *Employees:* 15
Net Worth: £5,641,555 *Total Assets:* £6,896,520
Registered Office: 17 Colonial Way, Watford, Herts, WD24 4PT
Major Shareholder: Jayant Kumar Gokaldas Mashru
Officers: Alka Jayant Mashru, Secretary; Alka Jayant Mashru [1960] Director/Secretary; Jayant Kumar Gokaldas Mashru [1958] Director

Maskhouse Wholesale Limited
Incorporated: 5 December 2016
Net Worth: £4,324 *Total Assets:* £210,033
Registered Office: B3 Kingfisher House, Kingsway, Team Valley Trading Estate, Gateshead, Tyne & Wear, NE11 0JQ
Officers: Kaman Lee [1978] Director

Maskologist Ltd
Incorporated: 5 June 2018
Registered Office: Kemp House, 160 City Road, London, EC1V 2NX
Major Shareholder: Sam Nouri
Officers: Sam Nouri, Secretary; Sam Nouri [1993] Director [Iranian]

Mast - Art Group Limited
Incorporated: 13 December 2018
Registered Office: 17 Green Lanes, London, N16 9BS
Shareholder: Umran Aysan
Officers: Umran Aysan [1976] Director [Turkish]

Master Beauty Limited
Incorporated: 6 December 2018
Registered Office: Flat 2, Green Street, Upton Park, London, E13 9AP
Major Shareholder: Anjlee Virendra Panchal
Officers: Anjlee Virendra Panchal [1982] Director

Mata Labs Cosmetics Ltd
Incorporated: 4 July 2018
Registered Office: 17 Mead Plat, Stonebridge, London, NW10 0PD
Major Shareholder: Mata Marielle Mumvadi
Officers: Mata Marielle Mumvadi [1998] Director/Artist

Maverick Hair & Beauty Ltd
Incorporated: 11 September 2014 *Employees:* 4
Net Worth: £40,868 *Total Assets:* £141,711
Registered Office: Unit 5 Hale House, 296a Green Lanes, Palmers Green, London, N13 5TP
Major Shareholder: Paul Anthony Ward
Officers: Jose Martinez [1968] Director/Management Consultant [Spanish]; Paul Anthony Ward [1964] Managing Director

Maxibay Limited
Incorporated: 8 April 2014
Net Worth: £13,540 *Total Assets:* £13,670
Registered Office: 14 Victoria Way, Undy, Caldicot, Gwent, NP26 3NW
Major Shareholder: Tian Tian Owen
Officers: Tiantian Owen [1970] Director/Sales

Maximaliste Limited
Incorporated: 29 October 2009 *Employees:* 2
Net Worth: £61,294 *Total Assets:* £368,988
Registered Office: 64 New Cavendish Street, London, W1G 8TB
Shareholders: Andre Baradat; Giovanni Pisu
Officers: Andre Baradat [1968] Director [French]; Giovanni Pisu [1968] Director [Italian]

Mayfair Export London Limited
Incorporated: 26 November 2014
Net Worth: £29,487 *Total Assets:* £57,690
Registered Office: 1008 Falcon Wharf, 34 Lombard Road, London, SW11 3RY
Officers: Hanna Dzhansyz [1974] Director

Mayfair Export UK Ltd
Incorporated: 10 January 2017
Net Worth: £198 *Total Assets:* £771
Registered Office: 2nd Floor, College House, 17 King Edwards Road, Ruislip, Middlesex, HA4 7AE
Shareholders: Vinod Ratnani; Prakash Narayandas Keswani
Officers: Prakash Narayandas Keswani [1963] Director [Indian]; Vinod Ratnani [1972] Director [Indian]

Mayfair Gate Limited
Incorporated: 19 May 2016
Net Worth Deficit: £26,290 *Total Assets:* £107,270
Registered Office: Suite 12, Link House, 140 The Broadway, Tolworth, Surbiton, Surrey, KT6 7HT
Major Shareholder: Haitham Sabeeh Ali Al-Jumaili
Officers: Haitham Sabeeh Ali Al-Jumaili [1968] Director [Iraqi]

Mayjoy The Perfumer Ltd
Incorporated: 17 December 2015
Net Worth Deficit: £11,033 *Total Assets:* £9,045
Registered Office: 71-75 Shelton Street, Covent Garden, London, WC2H 9JQ
Major Shareholder: Gianmauro Lombardi
Officers: Gianmauro Lombardi [1978] Director [Italian]

MB Professional Beauty Ltd
Incorporated: 9 May 2016
Registered Office: 71-75 Shelton Street, Covent Garden, London, WC2H 9JQ
Major Shareholder: Mariam Mahroos
Officers: Mariam Mahroos [1989] Director [Canadian]

MB Promotion Ltd.
Incorporated: 19 August 2005
Net Worth Deficit: £26,941 *Total Assets:* £79,002
Registered Office: 69 Great Hampton Street, Birmingham, B18 6EW
Officers: Maya Belihart [1975] Director [German]

Mcaniis Ltd
Incorporated: 18 January 2018
Registered Office: 48 Solway Close, Hounslow, Middlesex, TW4 7DH
Major Shareholder: Muhammad Kashif Anis
Officers: Muhammad Kashif Anis [1976] Director

McCarthy Inter Africa Ltd
Incorporated: 29 January 2013
Net Worth Deficit: £208,070 *Total Assets:* £56,004
Registered Office: Unit 3 Berwick Courtyard, Berwick St Leonard, Salisbury, Wilts, SP3 5UA
Shareholder: Nigel William McCarthy
Officers: Nigel William McCarthy [1955] Director

McCoey & Co. Limited
Incorporated: 27 June 1952 *Employees:* 10
Net Worth: £294,734 *Total Assets:* £495,320
Registered Office: 2 Balmoral Road, Belfast, BT12 6QA
Parent: Alan Howard (Stockport) Limited
Officers: Anthony James Littler [1976] Director; Jonathan Mark Littler [1973] Director

Mark McDonald Consultancy Limited
Incorporated: 20 February 2014
Net Worth: £215,870 *Total Assets:* £472,960
Registered Office: 3c Sopwith Crescent, Hurricane Way, Wickford, Essex, SS11 8YU
Major Shareholder: Mark Andrew McDonald
Officers: Mark Andrew McDonald [1968] Director/Distributor

Felicity McDonald Organics Limited
Incorporated: 2 February 2018
Registered Office: 3rd Floor, 86-90 Paul Street, London, EC2A 4NE
Officers: Felicity McDonald-Bing [1987] Director/Pilates Teacher; Julian Vickers [1992] Director/Musician

MD-101 Ltd
Incorporated: 3 April 2018
Registered Office: 16 Morville Street, Bow, London, E3 2GX
Shareholder: Mohammed Dinar Saddiqur Rahman
Officers: Mohammed Dinar Saddiqur Rahman [1995] Director/Entrepreneur

MDistributor Hair and Beauty Products Ltd
Incorporated: 8 November 2018
Registered Office: Unit 50 Thomas Way, Lakesview Business Park, Canterbury, Kent, CT3 4JJ
Shareholders: Dalis Guisel Rother; Marco Antonio Alves de Sousa
Officers: Marco Antonio Alves de Sousa [1983] Director; Dalis Guisel Rother [1970] Director

ME & II Limited
Incorporated: 6 March 2018
Registered Office: Chartwell House, 292-294 Hale Lane, Edgware, Middlesex, HA8 8NP
Shareholders: Hayley Barbara Berrick; Irene Susan Deutsch
Officers: Hayley Barbara Berrick [1966] Director; Irene Susan Deutsch [1958] Director

Me Sentir Ltd.
Incorporated: 12 June 2017
Registered Office: 3-5 Upper Dock Walk, Royal Docks, Royal Albert Wharf, London, E16 2QJ
Major Shareholder: Albert Mensah
Officers: Albert Mensah [1990] Director/Managing; Ebenezer Mensah [1994] Second Assistant Director; Gabriel Mensah [1992] Assistant Director

MEA Health and Wellness Ltd
Incorporated: 23 November 2018
Registered Office: 2 Holdiford Road, Milford, Stafford, ST17 0UX
Major Shareholder: Thomas David Harley
Officers: Thomas David Harley [1980] Director

Meadow Farm Friends Ltd
Incorporated: 14 July 2014
Registered Office: Meadow Cottage, 23 Church Road, Sparkford, Somerset, BA22 7JN
Major Shareholder: Verity Kate Bracher
Officers: Verity Kate Bracher [1975] Director

Meadow Skincare Limited
Incorporated: 20 June 2018
Registered Office: Hyde Park House, 5 Manfred Road, London, SW15 2RS
Shareholders: Wendy Louise Lane; Kelly Louise Spinks
Officers: Wendy Louise Lane [1975] Director; Kelly Louise Spinks [1979] Director

Mebon Investment Limited
Incorporated: 16 March 2015
Registered Office: Hanover House, 24 Homeland Way, Henley on Thames, Oxon, RG9 1SN
Officers: Etienne Lennuyeux Vergier, Secretary; Alan Worster Ashby [1938] Director

Meddiamonds Ltd
Incorporated: 29 July 2016
Net Worth Deficit: £232 *Total Assets:* £1,964
Registered Office: 20-22 Wenlock Road, London, N1 7GU
Major Shareholder: Magdalena Sledzianowska
Officers: Magdalena Sledzianowska [1990] Director/Business Consultant [Polish]

Meder Beauty International Ltd
Incorporated: 6 February 2014
Net Worth: £116,040 *Total Assets:* £313,850
Registered Office: Unit 3 Central Business Centre, Iron Bridge Close, London, NW10 0UR
Major Shareholder: Tiina Orasmae
Officers: Tiina Orasmae [1972] Director [Estonian]

Medica Ltd
Incorporated: 25 August 2018
Registered Office: 53 Sheepridge Road, Huddersfield, W Yorks, HD2 1HD
Shareholders: Riyadh Alallaq; Ahmed Alallaq
Officers: Dr Ahmed Alallaq [1975] Director/Financial Adviser [Iraqi]; Dr Riyadh Alallaq [1970] Director [Iraqi]

Medical Technology Caraco (MYC) Ltd.
Incorporated: 18 January 2018
Registered Office: 71-75 Shelton Street, Covent Garden, London, WC2H 9JQ
Shareholders: Raheleh Honari Sharif; Ahmad Sharifian; Hamid Chenary
Officers: Akram Chenary, Secretary; Azam Chenary [1984] Director [Iranian]; Hamid Chenary [1968] Director [Iranian]; Raheleh Honari Sharif [1979] Director [Iranian]; Ahmad Sharifian [1982] Director [Iranian]

Medileen UK Ltd
Incorporated: 12 January 2018
Registered Office: 3rd Floor, 86-90 Paul Street, London, EC2A 4NE
Major Shareholder: Ruethairat Trakulchang
Officers: Ruethairat Trakulchang [1990] Director [Thai]; Irene Tsang [1993] Director/Operations Manager

Medipro Pharma Limited
Incorporated: 23 March 2017 *Employees:* 3
Net Worth Deficit: £914 *Total Assets:* £120,062
Registered Office: c/o Saashiv & Co, Pentax House, South Hill Avenue, South Harrow, Middlesex, HA2 0DU
Shareholders: Anoop Shah; Rupeshkumar Dinubhai Patel; Tushar Vinodchandra Shah
Officers: Rupeshkumar Dinubhai Patel [1974] Director/Accountant; Anoop Shashikant Shah [1966] Director/Pharmacist; Tushar Vinodchandra Shah [1978] Director

Mediskin Pro Limited
Incorporated: 27 November 2018
Registered Office: 29 Harrogate Road, Leeds, LS7 3PD
Shareholder: Lucy Katherine Hall
Officers: Lucy Katherine Hall [1984] Director

Medivas Herbals Ltd
Incorporated: 19 December 2017
Registered Office: 354a Hollinwood Avenue, Manchester, M40 0JB
Shareholders: Farhan Iqbal; Faizaan Ahmed Munir
Officers: Faizaan Ahmed Munir [1995] Director/Self Employed

Medna Fashions Ltd
Incorporated: 1 May 2018
Registered Office: 229 Beaconsfield Road, Enfield, Middlesex, EN3 6AY
Shareholder: Edna Mantey Aggrey
Officers: Edna Mantey Aggrey [1999] Director/Student [Dutch]

Medora of London Limited
Incorporated: 8 March 2000
Net Worth: £4,200 *Total Assets:* £4,200
Registered Office: 209a Upper Dale Road, Derby, DE23 8BS
Parent: Momoessa Capital Management Limited
Officers: Farhana Hasan [1944] Director

Meek and Mild Essentials Ltd
Incorporated: 21 February 2019
Registered Office: Kemp House, 160 City Road, London, EC1V 2NX
Major Shareholder: Samara Allan
Officers: Samara Allan, Secretary; Samara Allan [1990] Director

Meet T Needs Limited
Incorporated: 23 October 2018
Registered Office: 8 Jackdaw Way, Halling, Rochester, Kent, ME2 1FL
Officers: Binal Jain [1979] Director/Physiotherapist

Mega Direct Limited
Incorporated: 21 November 2016
Registered Office: 5 Thorney Hedge Road, London, W4 5SB
Major Shareholder: Velibor Barzut
Officers: Velibor Barzut [1962] Director/Consultant

Mega Mane Limited
Incorporated: 10 February 2015
Net Worth: £12,908 *Total Assets:* £13,714
Registered Office: 81 Newry Street, Banbridge, Co Down, BT32 3EA
Major Shareholder: Simon Raymond Shaw
Officers: Simon Raymond Shaw [1971] Director

Megaco Limited
Incorporated: 20 June 2018
Registered Office: 60-64 Canterbury Street, Gillingham, Kent, ME7 5UJ
Shareholder: Megan Head
Officers: Megan Head [1995] Director; Tobias Head [1997] Director

Mehron Limited
Incorporated: 5 June 2013
Registered Office: Spinney Hill House, Sharnbrook Road, Souldrop, Bedford, MK44 1EX
Officers: Martin Melik [1950] Director [American]; Stephen Anthony Rawlinson [1953] Director

Meilikki Ltd
Incorporated: 21 November 2018
Registered Office: 3 Wernlys Road, Pen-Y-Fai, Bridgend, CF31 4NS
Major Shareholder: Steve Davies
Officers: Steve Davies [1970] Director

Melanative Ltd
Incorporated: 5 March 2018
Registered Office: 67 Anerley Vale, London, SE19 2BG
Officers: Leo Chin [1983] Director/Clothing & Beauty Retailer

Meller Design Solutions Limited
Incorporated: 28 March 2006 *Employees:* 36
Net Worth: £4,879,533 *Total Assets:* £11,733,302
Registered Office: Unit H, Bedford Business Centre, Mile Road, Bedford, MK42 9TW
Shareholders: David Robert Meller; Michael Joseph Meller
Officers: Jeremy Curtis, Secretary; John Christopher McGrath [1969] Director/Accountant

Mellor & Russell Direct Distribution Ltd
Incorporated: 13 December 2016 *Employees:* 1
Net Worth Deficit: £1,771 *Total Assets:* £740,158
Registered Office: Gloucester House, 399 Silbury Boulevard, Milton Keynes, Bucks, MK9 2AH
Parent: Rubella Cosmetics AD
Officers: Andrew Charles William Poole [1963] Finance Director; Svetoslav Uzunov [1972] Director [Bulgarian]

Melya & Co. Trading Ltd.
Incorporated: 11 August 2015 *Employees:* 1
Net Worth: £19,507 *Total Assets:* £73,173
Registered Office: 5-7 Beatrice Street, Oswestry, Salop, SY11 1QE
Shareholders: Peter David Thorley; Melya Margaret Thorley; Peter David Thorley
Officers: Peter Thorley, Secretary; Melya Margaret Thorley [1957] Director/Supply & Development of Artist & Cosmetic Products [Canadian]

Memoize Parfum Ltd
Incorporated: 17 April 2018
Registered Office: c/o Gorrie Whitson Limited, 1st Floor, Cromwell House, 14 Fulwood Place, London, WC1V 6HZ
Major Shareholder: Holly Elizabeth Marion Hutchinson
Officers: Holly Elizabeth Marion Hutchinson [1988] Director

Menco International Limited
Incorporated: 22 May 2008 *Employees:* 2
Net Worth: £185,041 *Total Assets:* £362,197
Registered Office: Woodhurst House, Warren Drive, Tadworth, Surrey, KT20 6PY
Shareholder: Eva Octaviana Mendes
Officers: Eva Octaviana Mendes [1973] Director [Indian]; William Spencer Mendes [1966] Director

Mepro Cosmetic Ltd
Incorporated: 10 March 2018
Registered Office: 20-22 Wenlock Road, London, N1 7GU
Major Shareholder: Di Cai
Officers: Di Cai [1988] Director [Chinese]; Ding Yuan [1985] Director [Chinese]

Linda Meredith Skin Care Limited
Incorporated: 10 November 2003 *Employees:* 6
Net Worth Deficit: £163,909 *Total Assets:* £380,824
Registered Office: 30 City Road, London, EC1Y 2AB
Shareholders: Dominic Benjamin Mason; Linda Meredith
Officers: Dominic Benjamin Mason, Secretary; Dominic Benjamin Mason [1984] Director; Linda Meredith [1953] Director/Therapist

Merumaya Limited
Incorporated: 29 March 2010 *Employees:* 1
Net Worth Deficit: £106,390 *Total Assets:* £281,102
Registered Office: 15 Peel Street, London, W8 7PA
Major Shareholder: Maleka Dattu
Officers: Maleka Dattu, Secretary; Maleka Dattu [1962] Director

Mesoskinline (UK) Limited
Incorporated: 6 February 2019
Registered Office: 99 Oxford Road, Wokingham, Berks, RG41 2YL
Shareholders: Keith James Rogers; Vanessa Stella Randall Rogers
Officers: Keith James Rogers [1950] Director; Vanessa Stella Randall Rogers [1947] Director

Mesostrata Limited
Incorporated: 6 July 2017
Registered Office: Unit 2 Lake End Court, Taplow Road, Maidenhead, Berks, SL6 0JQ
Major Shareholder: Daniel Smith
Officers: Irina Dumbrell [1955] Director [Russian]; Daniel Smith [1970] Marketing Director

Metropolitan Beauty Ltd.
Incorporated: 4 March 2011
Net Worth: £192,469 *Total Assets:* £351,262
Registered Office: 483 Green Lanes, London, N13 4BS
Major Shareholder: Agnieszka Duelli
Officers: Agnieszka Duelli [1970] Director/Businesswoman [German]

Meviq Ltd
Incorporated: 5 June 2017
Registered Office: Tameside Centre for Enterprise, Old Street, Ashton under Lyne, Lancs, OL6 7SF
Officers: Iqraa Baig [1998] Director; Mehvish Baig [1996] Director

MGC Pharma (UK) Ltd
Incorporated: 26 August 2015 *Employees:* 4
Net Worth: £137,770 *Total Assets:* £2,896,542
Registered Office: Central Working, Ecclestone Yards, 25 Ecclestone Place, London, SW1W 9NF
Officers: Anthony Neville Chisholm Eastman [1974] Director/Chartered Accountant [Australian]; Brett Anthony Mitchell [1971] Director [Australian]; Nativ Segev [1978] Director [Israeli]; Roby Reuven Zomer [1980] Managing Director [Israeli]

MGM UK Limited
Incorporated: 26 February 2018
Registered Office: 86 Greenings Court, Warrington, Cheshire, WA2 7GH
Shareholders: Irina Ursu; Marian Gabriel Musat
Officers: Marian Gabriel Musat [1982] Director/Retail [Romanian]; Irina Ursu [1985] Director/Retail [Romanian]

MH Exports Limited
Incorporated: 23 November 2018
Registered Office: 96 Uplands Road, Oadby, Leicester, LE2 4NQ
Major Shareholder: Mohammed Anwarul Hoque
Officers: Mohammed Anwarul Hoque [1961] Director

MH Products Limited
Incorporated: 22 January 2019
Registered Office: 76 Buckland Road, Maidstone, Kent, ME16 0SD
Major Shareholder: Anthony Robert Mann
Officers: Robert William Cooper [1978] Director; Anthony Robert Mann [1964] Director and Company Secretary

Doris Michaels Cosmetics Ltd
Incorporated: 18 November 2003 *Employees:* 1
Net Worth: £118,791 *Total Assets:* £148,860
Registered Office: 2 Exeter House, Beaufort Court, Sir Thomas Longley Road, Rochester, Kent, ME2 4FE
Major Shareholder: Doris Mary Edema Michaels
Officers: Doris Mary Edema Michaels, Secretary; Doris Mary Edema Michaels [1963] Director/Sales Executive

Microskin Cosmeceuticals UK Ltd
Incorporated: 5 September 2018
Registered Office: 795 Chester Road, Erdington, Birmingham, B24 0BX
Officers: Syed Naseer Ahmed [1952] Director; Syed Salmaan Ahmed [1980] Director; Dr Mabroor Ahmed Bhatty [1958] Director/Plastic Surgeon; Nicola Susan Bhatty [1964] Director/Housewife

Mil locshlainte, All Natural Balms Ltd
Incorporated: 29 November 2010
Net Worth Deficit: £2,207 *Total Assets:* £7,978
Registered Office: 15 Fairhead Road, Ballycastle, Co Antrim, BT54 6RD
Shareholders: Reamann Gearoid Mathers; Sinead Mathers
Officers: Reamann Gearoid Mathers [1969] Director [Irish]; Sinead Mathers [1971] Director [Irish]

Millenium Fragrance Limited
Incorporated: 26 September 2017
Registered Office: Unit 1 Rooks Corner, Roxeth Green Avenue, South Harrow, Middlesex, HA2 0GP
Major Shareholder: Sunil Desai
Officers: Sunil Desai [1973] Director

Millennium Nails Europe Limited
Incorporated: 18 December 2017
Registered Office: Unit E, Ascot Drive, Lustrum Trade Park, Stockton on Tees, Cleveland, TS18 2QQ
Shareholders: Alan Steven Carter; Yvonne Carter
Officers: Alan Steven Carter [1993] Director; Yvonne Carter [1954] Director

Millennium Nails North West Limited
Incorporated: 22 February 2005
Net Worth: £19,878 *Total Assets:* £30,539
Registered Office: 300 St Marys Road, Garston, Liverpool, L19 0NQ
Major Shareholder: Justine Chew
Officers: James Peter Chew, Secretary; Justine Chew [1972] Director/Manager

Miluv Ltd
Incorporated: 27 September 2012 *Employees:* 1
Net Worth Deficit: £3,630 *Total Assets:* £6,359
Registered Office: Meridien House, 69-71 Clarendon Road, Watford, Herts, WD17 1DS
Major Shareholder: Alan Bassin
Officers: Alan Bassin [1978] Director/Merchant [Slovenian]

Mimi's Organics Ltd
Incorporated: 22 April 2013
Net Worth Deficit: £32,790 *Total Assets:* £1,510
Registered Office: 22a Park Parade, Havant, Hants, PO9 5AD
Major Shareholder: Rumbidzai Serima-Fowler
Officers: Rumbidzai Serima-Fowler [1967] Managing Director [Zimbabwean]

Mimm Organics Ltd
Incorporated: 23 March 2018
Registered Office: Prospect Cottage, North Road, Cowbridge, Vale of Glamorgan, CF71 7DF
Major Shareholder: Miriam Holcombe
Officers: Miriam Holcombe [1971] Director

Mindful Soulful Limited
Incorporated: 19 February 2016 *Employees:* 1
Previous: La Buena Vida Limited
Net Worth: £12,873 *Total Assets:* £32,023
Registered Office: Fulford House, Newbold Terrace, Leamington Spa, Warwicks, CV32 4EA
Major Shareholder: Danielle Lamb
Officers: Danielle Lamb [1983] Director

The Mine of Goods Ltd
Incorporated: 23 April 2018
Registered Office: Kemp House, 160 City Road, London, EC1V 2NX
Officers: Ionut Bogdan Banica [1985] Director/Artist [Romanian]

The Mink Company U.K Ltd
Incorporated: 18 January 2019
Registered Office: 20-22 Wenlock Road, London, N1 7GU
Major Shareholder: Saphora Bint Zayd-Aziz
Officers: Saphora Bint Zayd-Aziz [1986] Director

Minmar (1008) Limited
Incorporated: 11 July 2002
Previous: Skinbrands Limited
Registered Office: The Pavilion, Josselin Road, Burnt Mills Industrial Estate, Basildon, Essex, SS13 1QB
Parent: Adonia Medical Group Ltd
Officers: Paul William Wilkinson [1965] Director

Mint Julip Ltd
Incorporated: 21 January 2019
Registered Office: XL Business Solutions, Catcraig Quarry, Craigie, Kilmarnock, E Ayrshire, KA1 5NB
Major Shareholder: Sheila Joyce Steele
Officers: Sheila Joyce Steele [1950] Director

Mintology Limited
Incorporated: 3 September 2018
Registered Office: 71-75 Shelton Street, London, WC2H 9JQ
Shareholders: Rhodri Andrew Ferrier; Simon Joseph Duffy
Officers: Rhodri Andrew Ferrier, Secretary; Simon Joseph Duffy [1976] Director; Rhodri Andrew Ferrier [1978] Director

Minx Lashes Ltd
Incorporated: 4 April 2016
Registered Office: 5a Alexandra Crescent, Bromley, Kent, BR1 4ET
Major Shareholder: Mimi Barakat Milolaoluwa Alabi
Officers: Mimi Barakat Milolaoluwa Alabi [1996] Director

Minxx Lashes Ltd
Incorporated: 26 November 2018
Registered Office: 31 Whitwell Road, London, E13 8BP
Major Shareholder: Salma Novella
Officers: Salma Novella [1998] Director/Retail

Miracle Herbs & Fruits Cosmetics Limited
Incorporated: 10 January 2008
Registered Office: 14 Lovage Approach, Beckton, London, E6 5UL
Major Shareholder: Jennifer Uchenna Orji
Officers: Jennifer Uchenna Orji [1968] Director/Consultant

Miracle8 Ltd
Incorporated: 20 July 2018
Registered Office: Byre House, The Parrock, Gravesend, Kent, DA12 1NU
Officers: Malkiat Kooner, Secretary; Malkiat Kooner [1964] Director

Miraculous UK Ltd
Incorporated: 5 November 2018
Registered Office: Lower Ground Floor, 40 Bloomsbury Way, London, WC1A 2SE
Major Shareholder: Athanasios Pollalis
Officers: Athanasios Pollalis [1976] Director

Mirimiri Limited
Incorporated: 5 May 2015
Net Worth Deficit: £847 *Total Assets:* £2,537
Registered Office: First Floor, Shaw House, 110-114 Barnards Green Road, Malvern, Worcs, WR14 3ND
Officers: Michael Anthony Sheriff [1962] Director

Mirtas Cosmetics Ltd
Incorporated: 27 June 2018
Registered Office: 20-22 Wenlock Road, London, N1 7GU
Major Shareholder: Mirka Lotta Irene Tahvanainen
Officers: Mirka Lotta Irene Tahvanainen [1984] Director [Finnish]

Misawa Healthcare Ltd
Incorporated: 18 December 2018
Registered Office: 27 Old Gloucester Street, London, WC1N 3AX
Major Shareholder: Mehdi Gharibavi
Officers: Mehdi Gharibavi [1987] Director/Manufacturer and Trader [Iranian]

Mise N Ltd
Incorporated: 20 November 2017
Registered Office: 20-22 Wenlock Road, London, N1 7GU
Major Shareholder: Nelly Wanjiru Mwangi
Officers: Nelly Wanjiru Mwangi [1961] Director/Student

Miss Glamm Limited
Incorporated: 26 November 2018
Registered Office: 27 Old Gloucester Street, London, WC1N 3AX
Major Shareholder: Abu Sayeed Jamil
Officers: Abu Sayeed Jamil [1986] Director [Indian]

Miss U Cosmetics Limited
Incorporated: 15 March 2018
Registered Office: Apartment 6, 68 Rhayader Road, Birmingham, B31 1TX
Officers: Yu Dong [1983] Director

Miss Vivien Ltd
Incorporated: 28 September 2016 *Employees:* 2
Net Worth Deficit: £1,883 *Total Assets:* £2,731
Registered Office: 22 St John Street, Newport Pagnell, Bucks, MK16 8HJ
Shareholders: Viviana Torres; Joan Albert Roger Jara
Officers: Joan Albert Roger Jara [1965] Director [Spanish]; Viviana Torres [1973] Director [Spanish]

Misspap X Bperfect Limited
Incorporated: 14 December 2018
Registered Office: Crown House, Plantation Road, Burscough Industrial Estate, Ormskirk, Lancs, L40 8JT
Shareholders: Ashley Fareed Ali; BMD Holdings Ltd
Officers: Ashley Fareed Ali [1984] Director

Mitonia Company Limited
Incorporated: 24 February 2015
Net Worth Deficit: £10,040 *Total Assets:* £16,350
Registered Office: 10 Borough Road, Darwen, Lancs, BB3 1PL
Major Shareholder: Michael Jackson
Officers: Michael Jackson [1960] Director

Mitvana and Biological Industries Ltd
Incorporated: 18 October 2018
Registered Office: The Oak Centre, Whinfield Drive, Aycliffe Business Park, Newton Aycliffe, Co Durham, DL5 6AU
Shareholders: Gary John Stainsby; Ryan John Stainsby
Officers: Gary John Stainsby [1969] Director; Ryan John Stainsby [1996] Director

Miy Sofiyah Limited
Incorporated: 13 June 2018
Registered Office: Miy Sofiyah, 32 Poplar Road, Loughborough, Leics, LE11 2JT
Officers: Nasir Uddin [1990] Director

Miya Hair Limited
Incorporated: 19 January 2017
Net Worth Deficit: £130 *Total Assets:* £8,721
Registered Office: 7a Bell Street, Romsey, Hants, SO51 8GY
Major Shareholder: Nicola Sargent
Officers: Nicola Sargent [1978] Director

MJL Products Ltd
Incorporated: 5 September 2012
Net Worth Deficit: £36,973 *Total Assets:* £5,934
Registered Office: 663 Lisburn Road, Belfast, BT9 7GT
Major Shareholder: James Toland
Officers: James Toland, Secretary; James Toland [1966] Director

Mlaveau Cuban Origins Ltd
Incorporated: 30 April 2018
Registered Office: 61 Poynings Road, Ifield, Crawley, W Sussex, RH11 0TL
Officers: Mayelin Solorzano Cruz [1974] Director/Passenger Service Agent

Mlle Cosmetics Company Ltd
Incorporated: 10 February 2017
Registered Office: 226 Abington Avenue, Northampton, NN1 4PR
Major Shareholder: Reynell Daniel
Officers: Reynell Daniel [1979] Director [Saint Lucian]

MLM Cosmetics Ltd
Incorporated: 21 February 2019
Registered Office: 20-22 Wenlock Road, London, N1 7GU
Major Shareholder: Robert Kaczan
Officers: Robert Kaczan [1982] Managing Director [Polish]

MM Product Trading UK Limited
Incorporated: 11 March 2018
Registered Office: 58 Egerton Road, Ashton on Ribble, Preston, Lancs, PR2 1AL
Officers: Mohamad Member [1995] Director

MNF Commodities Ltd
Incorporated: 14 February 2019
Registered Office: 11 Lakeside Avenue, Ashton under Lyne, Lancs, OL7 9HJ
Shareholder: Tabbita Sardar
Officers: Roksana Baig [1976] Director/Businesslady; Tabbita Sardar [1985] Director/Beauty & Health Care

MNM International UK Limited
Incorporated: 2 August 2017
Registered Office: c/o James Cowper Kreston, 8th Floor, South Reading Bridge House, George Street, Reading, Berks, RG1 8LS
Major Shareholder: Vasudev Ghanshamdas Adnani
Officers: Prathna Vasudev Adnani [1970] Director [Indian]; Vasudev Ghanshamdas Adnani [1967] Director [Indian]; Philip John Woodall [1950] Director

Mob Cosmetics Limited
Incorporated: 23 November 2017
Registered Office: 135-137 Station Road, Chingford, London, E4 6AG
Major Shareholder: Andrew Patrick
Officers: Andrew Patrick [1966] Director/Marketing Consultant

Moda Exportation Limited
Incorporated: 30 June 2017
Registered Office: 4 Chapel Close, Pilling, Preston, Lancs, PR3 6HF
Major Shareholder: Marlus Filipe Machado Dos Santos
Officers: Marlus Filipe Machado Dos Santos [1987] Director [Brazilian]

Modazi Ltd
Incorporated: 4 July 2018
Registered Office: 229-231 Kingsland Road, London, E2 8AN
Major Shareholder: Ertugrul Salich Oglou
Officers: Ertugrul Salich Oglou [1994] Director/Businessman [Greek]

Modern Innovations Limited Ltd
Incorporated: 6 December 2018
Registered Office: 1 Purley Road, Croydon, Surrey, CR8 6EZ
Major Shareholder: Yasser Kamaleldin Ahmed Mostafa
Officers: Dalia Abdelhamid Husien Saleh, Secretary; Yasser Kamaleldin Ahmed Mostafa [1961] Director/GM [Egyptian]

Modern Man Ltd
Incorporated: 29 May 2018
Registered Office: 7 Wood Lane, Hartwell, Northampton, NN7 2HG
Officers: Toby Roger Beesley [1995] Director/Farmer; Matthew Michael Johnson [1995] Director/Mechanical Engineer

The Modern Man Project Ltd
Incorporated: 14 January 2019
Registered Office: 544 Bonham Carter House, 52-54 Gower Street, London, WC1E 6EB
Major Shareholder: Richard Hudson
Officers: Richard Hudson [1985] Director/Nurse

Moderna Aesthetics Ltd
Incorporated: 20 January 2011
Net Worth: £1,888 *Total Assets:* £2,172
Registered Office: 4 Magellan Terrace, Gatwick Road, Crawley, W Sussex, RH10 9PJ
Major Shareholder: Luis Lajous
Officers: Luis Lajous [1969] Director [Canadian]

Modernist Fragrance Ltd.
Incorporated: 22 September 2015
Net Worth Deficit: £20,022 *Total Assets:* £15,598
Registered Office: 3rd Floor, 207 Regent Street, London, W1B 3HH
Major Shareholder: John Albert Charles Evans
Officers: John Albert Charles Evans [1964] Managing Director

The Moffat Perfume Company Limited
Incorporated: 30 November 2017
Registered Office: 8 Frenchland Drive, Moffat, Dumfries & Galloway, DG10 9LN
Major Shareholder: Victoria Jane Barr
Officers: Victoria Jane Barr [1966] Managing Director

Molecula Ltd
Incorporated: 5 December 2017
Registered Office: 20-22 Wenlock Road, London, N1 7GU
Major Shareholder: Martina Dragicevic
Officers: Danijel Palic, Secretary; Martina Dragicevic [1975] Director [Croatian]

Monarch Health & Beauty Ltd.
Incorporated: 12 September 2017
Registered Office: 27 Old Gloucester Street, London, WC1N 3AX
Shareholder: Javier Biurrarena Basulto
Officers: Javier Biurrarena Basulto [1976] Director/Sales [Spanish]

Monat Global UK Ltd
Incorporated: 14 November 2017
Registered Office: The Pinnacle, 170 Midsummer Boulevard, Milton Keynes, Bucks, MK9 1BP
Shareholders: Luis Urdaneta; Rayner Urdaneta
Officers: Thomas Joseph Hoolihan [1956] Director/Chief Legal Officer [American]; Stuart Alexander Macmillan [1961] Director/Company President [Canadian]; Francisco Javier Urdaneta [1989] Director [American]; Rayner Urdaneta [1981] Director [American]; Luis Emiro Urdaneta Fuenmayor [1961] Director/Chairman [Venezuelan]

Mondor & Bache Ltd
Incorporated: 14 May 2018
Registered Office: 20-22 Wenlock Road, London, N1 7GU
Shareholders: Geoffray Mondor; Estelle Bache
Officers: Estelle Bache [1990] Director/Artist [French]; Geoffray Mondor [1990] Director/Artist [French]

Mono Naturoils Ltd
Incorporated: 29 March 2016
Net Worth Deficit: £3,240 Total Assets: £4,660
Registered Office: Cobweb Cottage, Weaverhead Close, Thaxted, Essex, CM6 2PP
Shareholders: Tracy Michelle Goodson; Kevin Joseph Goodson
Officers: Kevin Joseph Goodson [1974] Art Director; Tracy Goodson [1975] Creative Director [Canadian]

Monrone Health Ltd
Incorporated: 10 August 2018
Registered Office: Kemp House, 160 City Road, London, EC1V 2NX
Shareholders: Dilafruz Rakhmonova; Mohamed Saadeldin
Officers: Dilafruz Rakhmonova, Secretary; Dr Mohamed Saadeldin, Secretary; Dilafruz Rakhmonova [1985] Director/Businesswoman [Uzbek]

Monshea Limited
Incorporated: 27 July 2011
Net Worth Deficit: £11,070 Total Assets: £1,659
Registered Office: 5-208 Thamesside Studios, Harrington Way, London, SE18 5NR
Major Shareholder: Monigho Griffin
Officers: Monigho Griffin [1967] Director/Wholesaler/Retailer/Assessor

Mooi-H Ltd
Incorporated: 25 October 2018
Registered Office: 71-75 Shelton Street, Covent Garden, London, WC2H 9JQ
Major Shareholder: Ssu-Ying Huang
Officers: Ssu-Ying Huang [1990] Director/Trader [Chinese]

Moor Direct Ltd
Incorporated: 6 April 2017
Registered Office: 54 Clarendon Road, Watford, Herts, WD17 1DU
Officers: Vita Prodniece, Secretary; Jose Pachacama [1960] Director/Investor; Jose Pachacama [1960] Director/Investor; Vita Prodniece [1968] Director/Investor [Latvian]

Moore Cosmetics Ltd
Incorporated: 27 November 2017
Registered Office: 10 Appletree Gardens, Barnet, Herts, EN4 9TQ
Major Shareholder: Mellissa Alleyne
Officers: Mellissa Alleyne, Secretary; Mellissa Alleyne [1985] Director/Manager

Guy Morgan Apothecary Limited
Incorporated: 27 October 2015
Registered Office: 1 Wellington Mansions, Shacklewell Road, London, N16 7TP
Shareholder: Guy Morgan
Officers: Guy Morgan [1990] Director/Owner

Morgan Jost Ltd
Incorporated: 21 May 2018
Registered Office: 31 Harpsden Road, Henley on Thames, Oxon, RG9 1EE
Officers: Charlotte Jost [1989] Director; Georgina Morgan [1991] Director

Moroccan Argan Limited
Incorporated: 26 January 2016
Registered Office: 11 Tower Court, MacKennal Street, St Johns Wood, London, NW8 7DL
Officers: Hamza El Houdaigui, Secretary; Hamza El Houdaigui [1989] Director

Moroccan Attlas Ltd
Incorporated: 11 December 2018
Registered Office: 71-75 Shelton Street, London, WC2H 9JQ
Major Shareholder: Zakaria Hajij
Officers: Zakaria Hajij [1991] Director [Moroccan]

Moroccan Golden Sands Ltd
Incorporated: 4 March 2013
Net Worth Deficit: £6,434
Registered Office: 63 Oxon Way, Leicester, LE5 4TU
Shareholder: Samir Bounia
Officers: Kersti Janno Bounia, Secretary; Samir Bounia [1970] Director/General Manager [Moroccan]

Motion Junkies Limited
Incorporated: 19 October 2010
Net Worth Deficit: £6,471 Total Assets: £678
Registered Office: 5 Beddington Grove, Wallington, Surrey, SM6 8LB
Major Shareholder: Arthur David Bales
Officers: Arthur David Bales [1972] Director [South African]

Mounir's Ltd
Incorporated: 6 October 2016
Net Worth Deficit: £12,667 Total Assets: £378
Registered Office: 71 Brookside Road, Hayes, Middlesex, UB4 0PL
Officers: Sherif Ibrahim [1994] Director

Sue Moxley Beauty Limited
Incorporated: 29 November 2012
Net Worth: £13,049 Total Assets: £13,049
Registered Office: Unit 37 Space Business Centre, Molly Millars Lane, Wokingham, Berks, RG41 2PQ
Officers: Andrew Graham Browne [1973] Director; Susan Anne Moxley [1960] Director/Beauty Expert; David Andrew Petherbridge [1961] Director; David Van Day [1956] Director/Entertainer

Moxxy Limited
Incorporated: 5 December 2018
Registered Office: 6 Fernlea House, 151 Hanger Lane, London, W5 1EF
Major Shareholder: Salman Wafiullah
Officers: Salman Wafiullah [1979] Director/Entrepreneur

Moyou Ltd
Incorporated: 26 March 2015
Net Worth Deficit: £2,520 Total Assets: £10,430
Registered Office: Kenwood House, 77a Shenley Road, Borehamwood, Herts, WD6 1AG
Major Shareholder: Ilana Kohavi
Officers: Ilana Kohavi [1983] Director

Moyra UK Ltd
Incorporated: 28 July 2016 Employees: 1
Net Worth: £2,661 Total Assets: £16,751
Registered Office: 14 Melbourne Business Court, Pride Park, Derby, DE24 8LZ
Shareholders: Cheryl Dawn Ogden; Stephen Ogden
Officers: Cheryl Dawn Ogden [1968] Director

Moyy Limited
Incorporated: 3 October 2016
Registered Office: 91 Lichfield Grove, London, N3 2JL
Major Shareholder: Andrew James Smith
Officers: Andrew James Smith [1980] Director/Landlord

MQL International Ltd
Incorporated: 15 May 2018
Registered Office: Queensway House, Queens Way, Hatfield, Herts, AL10 0LW
Major Shareholder: Xiurong Zeng
Officers: Xiurong Zeng [1974] Director [Chinese]

MQS Group London Limited
Incorporated: 30 June 2017
Registered Office: 72 Burch Road, Northfleet, Gravesend, Kent, DA11 9NE
Officers: Dr. Mahmood Qasim Majeed [1989] Director [Iraqi]

Mr B Skincare Limited
Incorporated: 20 July 2015
Registered Office: Kemp House, 152 City Road, London, EC1V 2NX
Shareholders: Jason Carl Bottomley; Jonathan James Briscoe
Officers: Jonathan Peter Chapman, Secretary; Jason Carl Bottomley [1981] Director/Business Development Manager

Mr Carters Essentials Limited
Incorporated: 20 March 2018
Registered Office: Kemp House, 160 City Road, London, EC1V 2NX
Major Shareholder: Jonathan Remington Hamilton
Officers: Jonathan Remington Hamilton [1986] Director

Mr. Smith Products UK Ltd
Incorporated: 20 July 2018
Registered Office: Aylmers Farm, Lower Sheering Road, Old Harlow, Essex, CM17 0NE
Shareholders: Freda Rossidis; David Justin Rossidis
Officers: Freda Rossidis [1957] Director [Greek]

MS Rarytas Ltd
Incorporated: 6 June 2017
Registered Office: 12 Sunnyside, Oxford, OX4 2NW
Shareholders: Maciej Blachut; Stanislaw Wolski
Officers: Maciej Blachut [1974] Director [Polish]; Stanislaw Wolski [1974] Director [Polish]

MSD Trading Services Limited
Incorporated: 17 January 2017
Net Worth Deficit: £1,800 *Total Assets:* £1,700
Registered Office: Kemp House, 160 City Road, London, EC1V 2NX
Major Shareholder: Ali Selman
Officers: Ali Selman, Secretary; Ali Selman [1983] Director

MTIstanbul Ltd
Incorporated: 23 November 2017
Registered Office: 59-60 The Market Square, London, N9 0TZ
Officers: Abdulkadir Akan [1988] Director/Marketing Consultant [Turkish]

Muamko Uzuri Limited
Incorporated: 22 September 2017
Registered Office: 1b Harcourt Road, London, SE4 2AJ
Major Shareholder: Asmara Mitchell
Officers: Asmara Mitchell [1990] Director

Muchacho (London) Limited
Incorporated: 22 June 2018
Registered Office: 1 Archer Mews, London, SW9 9BU
Major Shareholder: James Webster Gordon
Officers: James Webster Gordon [1980] Managing Director

Multi Imports Limited
Incorporated: 2 February 2018
Registered Office: 32 Wilton Road, Crumpsall, Manchester, M8 4WQ
Major Shareholder: Abid Mehmood
Officers: Abid Mehmood [1977] Director/Imports & Exports

Multitude Makeup Ltd
Incorporated: 3 September 2018
Registered Office: 4 Dunelm Crescent, Moorends, Doncaster, S Yorks, DN8 4PT
Shareholders: Natasha Amy Wainwright; Lee Moran
Officers: Lee Moran [1985] Director/Mechanic; Natasha Amy Wainwright [1991] Director/Consultant

Mupe Ltd
Incorporated: 15 February 2017
Net Worth Deficit: £603 *Total Assets:* £6,244
Registered Office: 20 Vespasian Way, Dorchester, DT1 2RD
Major Shareholder: George William Foot
Officers: George William Foot [1989] Managing Director; Stephen Karl Foot [1963] Director

Muse and Rose Limited
Incorporated: 7 July 2016
Registered Office: Studio 4, Clarks Courtyard, 145 Granville Street, Birmingham, B1 1SB
Major Shareholder: Anh Thi Phuong Nguyen
Officers: Anh Thi Phuong Nguyen [1990] Business Director [Vietnamese]

Muse Make Up Ltd
Incorporated: 27 July 2018
Registered Office: Suite 1, Bowden Terminal, Luckyn Lane, Basildon, Essex, SS14 3AX
Major Shareholder: Cristina de Fries
Officers: Cristina de Fries [1986] Director [Romanian]

MWK Cosmetics (UK) Ltd
Incorporated: 31 December 2018
Registered Office: 2/2, 37 Morar Drive, Paisley, Renfrewshire, PA2 9BG
Major Shareholder: Francis Nderitu Gatongi
Officers: Francis Nderitu Gatongi [1965] Managing Director

My Beauty World Ltd
Incorporated: 11 March 2015
Net Worth: £3,340 *Total Assets:* £20,190
Registered Office: 20-22 Wenlock Road, London, N1 7GU
Major Shareholder: Tina Sogaard
Officers: Tina Sogaard [1967] Director/Consultant [Danish]

My London Trade Ltd
Incorporated: 24 April 2018
Registered Office: 6 Elmstead Gardens, Worcester Park, Surrey, KT4 7BD
Major Shareholder: Mignon Yang
Officers: Mignon Yang [1973] Director [South Korean]

My Meghan Ltd
Incorporated: 17 April 2018
Registered Office: 1 Brewery House, Brook Street, Wivenhoe, Colchester, Essex, CO7 9DS
Major Shareholder: Clive Vincent Drake
Officers: Clive Vincent Drake [1958] Director

My Perfumes London Ltd
Incorporated: 15 June 2017
Registered Office: 111 Park Lane, Hayes, Middlesex, UB4 8AF
Major Shareholder: Alefiyah Zoher Anverali Husseinbhai
Officers: Alefiyah Zoher Anverali Husseinbhai [1984] Director

My Pink Ltd
Incorporated: 8 June 2015
Net Worth: £4,631 *Total Assets:* £27,435
Registered Office: 85a Bonnyton Drive, Eaglesham, Glasgow, G76 0LS
Major Shareholder: Jamie Miller
Officers: Jamie Miller, Secretary; Jamie Miller [1981] Director

My Pure Life-Style Limited
Incorporated: 6 April 2018
Registered Office: Flat 52, Shore House, 8 Heather Close, London, SW8 3BX
Officers: Kristelle Audrey Assi [1988] Director [French]

My SNS Academy UK Ltd
Incorporated: 18 December 2017
Registered Office: Unit 2 Bridge Court, Liverpool New Road, Little Hoole, Preston, Lancs, PR4 5BF
Major Shareholder: Gregory Thomas Kirby
Officers: Gregory Thomas Kirby [1971] Director/Accountant

My7heavens Ltd
Incorporated: 9 November 2018
Registered Office: 2nd Floor, College House, 17 King Edwards Road, Ruislip, Middlesex, HA4 7AE
Major Shareholder: Selma de Fatima Goncalves Pacheco
Officers: Selma de Fatima Goncalves Pacheco, Secretary; Selma de Fatima Goncalves Pacheco [1987] Director/Store Manager [Portuguese]

Myego Ltd
Incorporated: 14 June 2006 *Employees:* 3
Net Worth Deficit: £25,909 *Total Assets:* £34,875
Registered Office: 6 Waterloo Road, Lymington, Hants, SO41 9AU
Officers: Frances Marian Sandhu, Secretary; Mohammad Dehghani [1971] Director; Ben David Sandhu [1987] Director

Jennifer Myers Limited
Incorporated: 18 August 2005
Net Worth Deficit: £52,436 *Total Assets:* £8,921
Registered Office: 1 The Court Building, Market Street, London, SE18 6FU
Major Shareholder: Jennifer Wedderburn
Officers: Jennifer Wedderburn [1966] Director/Entrepreneur

MYNC Brands Limited
Incorporated: 19 March 2012 *Employees:* 1
Net Worth Deficit: £19,250 *Total Assets:* £22,365
Registered Office: 925 Finchley Road, London, NW11 7PE
Major Shareholder: Ajay Vyas
Officers: Ajay Vyas [1962] Director [Indian]

Mypure Limited
Incorporated: 27 February 2004
Registered Office: 13 Bryony Drive, Kingsnorth, Ashford, Kent, TN23 3RE
Major Shareholder: Simon Peter Golding
Officers: Lara Smith, Secretary; Paul David Smith [1964] Director/Online Retailer

Myriad Skincare Limited
Incorporated: 23 February 2016
Net Worth Deficit: £2,780 *Total Assets:* £3,770
Registered Office: 44 Church Street, Bocking, Braintree, Essex, CM7 5JY
Major Shareholder: Nicholas Andrew Hawkins
Officers: Nicholas Andrew Hawkins [1967] Director

Myridium Active.Com Limited
Incorporated: 1 August 2000 *Employees:* 2
Net Worth: £23,244 *Total Assets:* £83,357
Registered Office: Blue House Farm Office, Brentwood Road, West Horndon, Essex, CM13 3LX
Major Shareholder: Colin Meredith Barthelmy
Officers: Colin Meredith Barthelmy, Secretary; Colin Meredith Barthelmy [1961] Director; Kim Diane Barthelmy [1958] Director

Myroo Ltd
Incorporated: 12 May 2016
Net Worth: £11,510 *Total Assets:* £14,070
Registered Office: Myroo Skincare, 12 Grasmere Crescent, Harrogate, N Yorks, HG2 0ED
Shareholders: Philip Alexander Dunseath; Rachael Dunseath
Officers: Philip Alexander Dunseath [1971] Director; Rachael Dunseath [1975] Director/Skincare Industry Consultant

Myrrh & Co. Limited
Incorporated: 26 November 2018
Registered Office: 8 Almond Way, Mitcham, Surrey, CR4 1LN
Major Shareholder: Priscilla Grant
Officers: Priscilla Grant [1993] Director/Analyst

Mystique Swan Ltd
Incorporated: 25 October 2018
Registered Office: 71-75 Shelton Street, Covent Garden, London, WC2H 9JQ
Major Shareholder: Jotinder Singh Sidhu
Officers: Jotinder Singh Sidhu [1986] Director/Marketing Consultant [Indian]

N & L Cosmetic Limited
Incorporated: 3 April 2018
Registered Office: 319 Scott Ellis Gardens, London, NW8 9RU
Officers: Noel Ladebat [1978] Sales Director [French]

N Organics Ltd
Incorporated: 18 June 2018
Registered Office: 33b Wimbledon Park Road, London, SW18 5SJ
Major Shareholder: Nazia Choudhury
Officers: Nazia Choudhury [1992] Director/Teacher

N.S.I. (U.K.) Limited
Incorporated: 21 February 1992 *Employees:* 22
Net Worth: £4,563,523 *Total Assets:* £5,145,631
Registered Office: James Nasmyth Way, Eccles, Manchester, M30 0SF
Major Shareholder: Jason Andrew Shaw
Officers: Diane Shaw, Secretary; Marie Littlewood [1963] Director/General Manager; Diane Shaw [1966] Director; Jason Andrew Shaw [1961] Director

N18 Ltd
Incorporated: 2 July 2018
Registered Office: c/o Saba Services, Sorby House, 42 Spital Hill, Sheffield, S4 7LG
Officers: Seham Mousa [1987] Director

NA Medical Care Ltd
Incorporated: 3 April 2014
Net Worth Deficit: £67,599 *Total Assets:* £124
Registered Office: Cottingham House, Number 1 Rothwell Road, Kettering, Northants, NN16 8UZ
Shareholder: Najib Ayoub
Officers: Dr Najib Ayoub [1978] Director/Plastic Surgeon [Lebanese]; Ecaterina Voica [1984] Director/Claims Inspector [Romanian]

Nabeel Perfumes International Limited
Incorporated: 7 May 2014
Registered Office: Unit 3 Hounslow Business Park, Alice Way, Hounslow, Middlesex, TW3 3UD
Officers: Howaida Ali [1981] Director/Businesswomen; Asghar Adam Ali Ibrahim [1953] Director/Businessman [Yemeni]

NABS Promotions Limited
Incorporated: 5 June 2018
Registered Office: 20 Wescott Way, Uxbridge, Middlesex, UB8 2RE
Major Shareholder: Nabeela Wahid Osman
Officers: Nabeela Wahid Osman [1996] Director/Salesman

Nacho Vidal Distribuciones 2 Limited
Incorporated: 13 September 2018
Registered Office: 18 Soho Square, London, W1D 3QL
Major Shareholder: Olga Jorda Brase
Officers: Olga Jorda Brase [1960] Director/Salesman [Spanish]

Nacho Vidal Distribuciones Limited
Incorporated: 22 August 2018
Registered Office: 18 Soho Square, London, W1D 3QL
Major Shareholder: Ignacio Jorda Gonzalez
Officers: Ignacio Jorda Gonzalez [1973] Sales Director [Spanish]

Naeemah & Al Farhad Ltd
Incorporated: 26 July 2018
Registered Office: 101e St Georges Square, London, SW1V 3QP
Officers: Mohammed Abdul Batin [1986] Director

Naiga Naturals Ltd
Incorporated: 9 July 2018
Registered Office: 103 Brook Street, Erith, Kent, DA8 1JJ
Major Shareholder: Naiga Mary Kibuuka
Officers: Nassaka Stella Kibuuka [1993] Director/Dental Nurse

The Nail & Beauty Link Limited
Incorporated: 7 March 2011
Net Worth: £153,780 *Total Assets:* £213,870
Registered Office: 8 Selborne Road, Handsworth Wood, Birmingham, B20 2DW
Shareholders: Van Tuan Phan; Thi-Huong Thao Nguyen
Officers: Thi-Huong Thao Nguyen [1983] Director/Self Employed; Van Tuan Phan [1983] Director

Nail Art Direct Ltd
Incorporated: 8 March 2017
Registered Office: Rectory Cottage, Little Marsh, Marsh Gibbon, Bicester, Oxon, OX27 0AP
Parent: Coolcarz UK Ltd
Officers: Edward Turner [1971] Director

Nail Creation UK Distribution Limited
Incorporated: 17 April 2018
Registered Office: 36 Barnsley Road, Wakefield, W Yorks, WF1 5NW
Officers: Victoria Vickers [1974] Director; Darren Wragg [1972] Director

Nail Island Ltd
Incorporated: 16 November 2018
Registered Office: Apartment 2, Hobnail House, Shropshire Way, West Bromwich, W Midlands, B71 1BT
Major Shareholder: Anna Nowacka
Officers: Anna Nowacka [1986] Director [Polish]

Nail Perfection Limited
Incorporated: 29 November 2011
Net Worth: £42,680 *Total Assets:* £68,280
Registered Office: Unit 15 Canal Industrial Park, Canal Road, Gravesend, Kent, DA12 2PA
Shareholders: Gerardo James Cientanni; Maria Cientanni; Maria Cientanni
Officers: Gerardo James Cientanni [1984] Director; Maria Cientanni [1971] Director; Theresa Louise Cientanni [1988] Director; Ashley Howard Smith [1973] Director

Nail Polish Gel Colours Limited
Incorporated: 10 September 2015
Previous: Gel Nail Polish Limited
Registered Office: 3rd Floor, Crown House, 151 High Road, Loughton, Essex, IG10 4LG
Major Shareholder: Shuab Akhtar
Officers: Shuab Akhtar [1979] Director

Nails & London Holdings Limited
Incorporated: 5 September 2016
Previous: The Hand & Foot Spa Holdings Ltd
Registered Office: Baldwins (Tamworth) Ltd, Ventura Park Road, Tamworth, Staffs, B78 3HL
Major Shareholder: Donna Lesley Haar-Jorgensen
Officers: Donna Lesley Haar-Jorgensen [1962] Director/Business Executive

Nails and Co (Midlands) Limited
Incorporated: 3 January 2008
Net Worth Deficit: £88,994 *Total Assets:* £64,107
Registered Office: 77 Mill Street, Kidderminster, Worcs, DY11 6XJ
Major Shareholder: Rebecca Cross
Officers: Rebecca Charlotte Cross, Secretary; Rebecca Charlotte Cross [1979] Director

Nailzee Ltd
Incorporated: 3 November 2016
Registered Office: 168 Church Road, Hove, E Sussex, BN3 2DL
Major Shareholder: Alison Louise Jerrard
Officers: Alison Louise Jerrard [1967] Director/Housewife

Najah Ltd
Incorporated: 6 September 2017
Registered Office: Flat 7, Ludlow Road, Salisbury Court, Maidenhead, Berks, SL6 2RS
Shareholders: Sarah Hamdoune; Imad Bouklata
Officers: Sarah Hamdoune [1994] Director [Moroccan]

Nakkali Limited
Incorporated: 9 April 2018
Registered Office: 8 Ellesbrough Close, South Oxhey, Watford, Herts, WD19 6TH
Major Shareholder: Rakhi Shrestha Dali
Officers: Rakhi Shrestha Dali [1975] Director/Service

Nalla Skincare Ltd
Incorporated: 7 June 2013
Net Worth Deficit: £3,724 *Total Assets:* £1,023
Registered Office: 56 Wisden House, Meadow Road, London, SW8 1LT
Major Shareholder: Jade Castello
Officers: Jade Castello [1984] Director/Cosmetics

Nanat Limited
Incorporated: 15 January 2018
Registered Office: Penventinnie Barn, Penventinnie Lane, Truro, Cornwall, TR4 9EG
Shareholders: Kate Richards; Edward Richards
Officers: Edward Richards [1986] Director/Teacher; Kate Richards [1985] Director/Teacher

Nanosafe Ltd.
Incorporated: 30 January 2019
Registered Office: 17 Green Lanes, London, N16 9BS
Shareholders: Harika Pekinel; Mehmet Tanturk
Officers: Harika Pekinel [1970] Director; Mehmet Tanturk [1965] Director [Turkish]

Narges Beauty Limited
Incorporated: 25 July 2018
Registered Office: 11 Sale Place, London, W2 1PX
Major Shareholder: Neda Sarah Ghenai
Officers: Neda Sarah Ghenai [1988] Director [French]

Narizaonline Ltd
Incorporated: 9 March 2018
Registered Office: 3 Dave Bowen Close, Northampton, NN5 4US
Officers: Virgil Nicolae Narita [1988] Director [Romanian]

Nars & Elliott Healthcare Ltd
Incorporated: 22 September 2017
Registered Office: Unit 41 Antrim Business Park, 25 Randalstown Road, Antrim, BT41 4LD
Parent: Elliott Nutrition Ltd
Officers: Prof Laura Ashley [1978] Director/Businesswoman

Nasser Waziri Ltd
Incorporated: 28 July 2017
Registered Office: 85 Great Portland Street, London, W1W 7LT
Officers: Waziri Nasser [1978] Director/Business Consultant [German]

Nat & Co Limited
Incorporated: 2 May 2012
Net Worth Deficit: £11,075 *Total Assets:* £33,468
Registered Office: 15 Northfields Prospect, London, SW18 1PE
Major Shareholder: Ernesto Franz
Officers: Ernesto Franz [1951] Director/Business Consultant [Italian]; Andrea Mognol [1966] Director [Italian]

Natasha Denona Make Up Ltd.
Incorporated: 4 September 2015
Registered Office: Turnberry House, 1404-1410 High Road, Whetstone, London, N20 9BH
Shareholders: Yosi Cohen; Yaron Adi
Officers: Yaron Adi [1967] Director [Israeli]; Yosi Cohen [1962] Director [Israeli]

Natcare Beauty Ltd
Incorporated: 17 October 2017
Registered Office: 18a Bridge Street, Maidenhead, Berks, SL6 8BJ
Officers: Natalia Szyzka [1994] Director [Polish]

National Supplement Beauty Solutions Limited
Incorporated: 1 November 2016
Net Worth Deficit: £20,709 *Total Assets:* £297,906
Registered Office: Hudson House Business Centre, 8 Albany Street, Edinburgh, EH1 3QB
Officers: Molly Rita Roselie [1964] Director/Lawyer [Seychellois]

Natrelle Limited
Incorporated: 28 November 2002
Net Worth Deficit: £127,611 *Total Assets:* £12,450
Registered Office: Waella, Wallrake, Heswall, Wirral, Merseyside, CH60 8PG
Shareholders: Lynette Ann Armitage; Paul William Tunstall
Officers: Lynette Anne Armitage, Secretary; Lynette Anne Armitage [1949] Director; Paul William Tunstall [1964] Director

Natrorg Ltd
Incorporated: 18 June 2018
Registered Office: Kemp House, 160 City Road, London, EC1V 2NX
Officers: Faiza Farah [1989] Director [Danish]

Rochelle Natty Business Group Ltd
Incorporated: 28 August 2018
Registered Office: First Floor, 85 Great Portland Street, London, W1W 7LT
Major Shareholder: Rochelle Natty
Officers: Rochelle Natty [1991] Director [Jamaican]

Natur Life Ltd
Incorporated: 2 April 2014 *Employees:* 2
Net Worth: £53,241 *Total Assets:* £94,174
Registered Office: 156a Burnt Oak Broadway, Edgware, Middlesex, HA8 0AX
Shareholders: Stavros Moutrikas; Georgios Zachariou
Officers: Stavros Moutrikas [1987] Director/General Merchant [Greek]; Georgios Zachariou [1962] Director/General Merchant [Greek]

Natural Beauty Import Limited
Incorporated: 26 February 2018
Registered Office: 46 St Andrews Drive, Seaford, E Sussex, BN25 2SD
Officers: Elena Craig [1967] Managing Director

Natural Birthing Company Ltd
Incorporated: 26 October 2011 *Employees:* 1
Net Worth: £22,138 *Total Assets:* £59,947
Registered Office: Unit 50 Ransom Hall South, Ransomwood Business Park, Mansfield, Notts, NG21 0HJ
Shareholder: Jane Mary Mason
Officers: Jane Mary Mason [1967] Director; John Lawrence Radford [1965] Director; Barry Keith Tong [1977] Director

Natural Blends of Nature Ltd
Incorporated: 31 January 2019
Registered Office: 44 Blackhorse Lane, Croydon, Surrey, CR0 6RS
Major Shareholder: Paulette Rose Blye
Officers: Paulette Rose Blye [1970] Director/Manager

Natural British Limited
Incorporated: 15 September 2017
Net Worth Deficit: £51,736 *Total Assets:* £23,236
Registered Office: Unit 4 Premier Court, Kings Mill Way, Mansfield, Notts, NG18 5ER
Major Shareholder: Mark Ryan
Officers: Mark Ryan [1965] Director

Natural Hair Emporium Limited
Incorporated: 17 August 2016
Registered Office: P O Box 53182, London, E18 9BZ
Major Shareholder: Karen Duberry
Officers: Karen Helena Duberry [1968] Director/IT Consultant

Natural Health Harmony Group Ltd
Incorporated: 17 October 2018
Registered Office: 212 St James's Road, Croydon, Surrey, CR0 2BW
Major Shareholder: Nathan Walker
Officers: Nathan Walker [1980] Director/Entrepreneur

Natural Jeanius Ltd
Incorporated: 8 March 2018
Registered Office: Kemp House, 160 City Road, London, EC1V 2NX
Officers: Jennifer Jean Njoku [1968] Director

Natural Pal Limited
Incorporated: 11 January 2019
Registered Office: 3 Lee Terrace, Scholes, Holmfirth, W Yorks, HD9 1UB
Shareholders: Hollie Moss; Bryde Grace Town
Officers: Hollie Moss [1987] Director/Marketing Consultant; Bryde Grace Town [1991] Director/IT Consultant

Natural Serenity Ltd
Incorporated: 9 February 2016
Net Worth Deficit: £21,056 *Total Assets:* £148,315
Registered Office: 12 Townshend Court, Shannon Place, London, NW8 7DP
Shareholders: Halleh Mortazavi; Vahid Tayefi Nasrabadi
Officers: Dr Vahid Tayefi Nasrabadi [1970] Director/Principal Consultant

Natural Sheaness Ltd
Incorporated: 30 March 2018
Registered Office: 122 Hurstbourne Gardens, Barking, Essex, IG11 9UT
Major Shareholder: Crystal Dale Browne
Officers: Crystal Dale Browne [1990] Director/Podiatrist

The Natural Skincare Company Ltd.
Incorporated: 6 October 2003
Net Worth: £3,162 *Total Assets:* £19,448
Registered Office: Oxford House, 15-17 Mount Ephraim Road, Tunbridge Wells, Kent, TN1 1EN
Major Shareholder: Amanda Jane McGillivray
Officers: Adrian John McGillivray, Secretary; Amanda Jane McGillivray [1958] Managing Director

Natural Skincare London Limited
Incorporated: 25 March 2011
Net Worth Deficit: £50,600 *Total Assets:* £7,210
Registered Office: 9 Summerfield Road, Ealing, London, W5 1ND
Major Shareholder: Elaine Chi Kit Leung
Officers: Elaine Chi Kit Leung [1960] Director

Natural Spa Factory Limited
Incorporated: 4 August 2016
Registered Office: Unit 1 Foxcote Avenue, Bath Business Park, Peasedown St John, Bath, BA2 8SF
Shareholder: Emma Webber
Officers: Jeremy Smith, Secretary; Emma Kate Webber [1971] Director/Owner

Natural Touch Enterprises Ltd
Incorporated: 14 June 2010
Registered Office: 9 St Margarets Road, Bradford, W Yorks, BD7 3AE
Officers: Mohammed Shafique [1970] Director

Natural Vitale Limited
Incorporated: 10 April 2017
Registered Office: 205 Mersham Road, Thornton Heath, Surrey, CR7 8NU
Major Shareholder: Caroline Susannah Townsend
Officers: Caroline Susannah Townsend [1976] Managing Director

Naturally By Nature Ltd
Incorporated: 13 April 2010
Net Worth Deficit: £10,820 *Total Assets:* £8,030
Registered Office: 65 Andersey Way, Abingdon, Oxon, OX14 5NW
Major Shareholder: Dennis Hazleton
Officers: John Philip Ormrod, Secretary; John Philip Ormrod [1947] Director/Chartered Accountant

Naturally Untamed Ltd
Incorporated: 3 July 2018
Registered Office: 17 Avondale Road, London, E17 8JG
Major Shareholder: Zoe Power
Officers: Zoe Power [1996] Director/Manufacturer

NaturallyClearSkin Limited
Incorporated: 2 February 2018
Registered Office: 118 Parade, Leamington Spa, Warwicks, CV32 4AQ
Officers: David Grayham Clayton-Wright [1965] Director/Business Person

Nature et Bien-Etre Limited
Incorporated: 13 December 2001
Net Worth Deficit: £55,711 *Total Assets:* £1,488
Registered Office: Cary Chambers, 1 Palk Street, Torquay, Devon, TQ2 5EL
Shareholder: Catherine Guillard
Officers: Teddy Guillard, Secretary; Catherine Guillard [1961] Director [French]

Nature Scents Limited
Incorporated: 30 May 2018
Registered Office: Suite 560, 5 Charter House, Portsmouth, PO1 2SN
Officers: Ariana Fernanda Paranhos Quida [1984] Director/Manager [Spanish]

Nature's Dream Limited
Incorporated: 25 November 1999 *Employees:* 14
Net Worth: £897,669 *Total Assets:* £1,845,800
Registered Office: Overton Farm, Overton, Hollington, Stoke on Trent, Staffs, ST10 4HW
Parent: The Brand Cloud (Holdings) Limited
Officers: Nigel de Lisle Stubley [1960] Director; Peter Lewis Whitehurst [1969] Director; Colin Vincent Wright [1962] Non-Executive Director Chairman

Nature-Solves Ltd
Incorporated: 27 October 2017
Registered Office: 272 Bath Street, Glasgow, G2 4JR
Shareholders: William Graham Hogg; Eunice Hogg
Officers: William Hogg, Secretary; Eunice Hogg [1958] Director/Housewife; William Graham Hogg [1957] Director/Project Manager

Naturela Limited
Incorporated: 15 January 2013
Net Worth: £2,390 Total Assets: £69,585
Registered Office: Flat 2a, 32 Devonshire Close, London, W1G 7BE
Major Shareholder: Onur Ozkol
Officers: Onur Ozkol [1983] Director/Import/Exports, Marketing and Film Production [Turkish]

Naturenk Ltd
Incorporated: 27 July 2017
Registered Office: 7 Bankside, The Watermark, Gateshead, Tyne & Wear, NE11 9SY
Shareholders: Halit Sepin; Bulent Hepurker
Officers: Bulent Hepurker [1961] Director

Natures Merchant Ltd
Incorporated: 18 July 2017
Registered Office: 35 Dirleton Avenue, Cambuslang, Glasgow, G72 8ZB
Major Shareholder: Graeme Todd
Officers: Graeme Todd [1986] Director

Naturity Cosmetics Ltd
Incorporated: 19 November 2018
Registered Office: Flat 16, Brook House, Gunnersbury Lane, London, W3 8HS
Major Shareholder: Mariapia Crovara
Officers: Mariapia Crovara [1987] Director [Italian]

Naturyl Glow Ltd
Incorporated: 16 September 2015
Net Worth: £2,977 Total Assets: £2,977
Registered Office: Naturyl Glow, P O Box 16964, Birmingham, B25 9HF
Shareholders: Aisha Iqbal; Ishtiaq Ahmed Khan
Officers: Aisha Iqbal [1984] Director/Founder; Ishtiaq Ahmed Khan [1982] Director/Founder; Mohammed Abdul-Quddus Khan [1990] Director/Self Employed

Navya Innoveda Ltd
Incorporated: 29 August 2018
Registered Office: 20 Egerton Close, Pinner, Middlesex, HA5 2LP
Major Shareholder: Aryanish Patel
Officers: Aryanish Patel [1973] Director/Entrepreneur [Indian]

Naya London Ltd
Incorporated: 20 September 2017
Registered Office: 15-17 Caledonian Road, London, N1 9DX
Major Shareholder: Vanessa Pinho Fernandes
Officers: Vanessa Pinho Fernandes [1987] Managing Director [Portuguese]

NB Beauty Limited
Incorporated: 29 March 2012
Net Worth: £265,980 Total Assets: £265,980
Registered Office: Pepys Court, 84-86 The Chase, Clapham, London, SW4 0NF
Parent: HCT Europe Limited
Officers: Richard Flook, Secretary; Richard Flook [1960] Director

NBS Distribution Ltd
Incorporated: 17 September 2015 Employees: 4
Net Worth: £70,845 Total Assets: £787,000
Registered Office: 452-458 New Cross Road, London, SE14 6TY
Major Shareholder: Thanh Binh Duong
Officers: Thanh Binh Duong [1976] Director

NC Import Limited
Incorporated: 20 May 2015
Net Worth: £2,873 Total Assets: £31,228
Registered Office: Chitral, Unit 2-2a Wyatts Green Road, Swallows Cross, Doddinghurst, Brentwood, Essex, CM15 0SS
Major Shareholder: Frederick Leonard Cook
Officers: Frederick Leonard Cook [1986] Director

Neal's Yard (Natural Remedies) Limited
Incorporated: 11 November 1981
Net Worth: £6,890,000 Total Assets: £24,280,000
Registered Office: Peacemarsh, Gillingham, Dorset, SP8 4EU
Officers: Elizabeth York, Secretary; Denise Anne Bonner [1955] Director; Anabel Kindersley [1971] Director; Barnabas Guy Kindersley [1970] Director; Peter David Kindersley [1941] Director/Publisher and Farmer; Alexander Ian Leach [1981] Sales Director; Timothy Alan Baylor Leach [1964] Director; Stephen Henry Tobitt [1965] Director/Chief Operating Officer; Susan Jane Winter [1960] Director/Product Development Manager

Neal's Yard Remedies (Home) Limited
Incorporated: 24 February 2009
Net Worth: £3,150,000 Total Assets: £5,570,000
Registered Office: Peacemarsh, Gillingham, Dorset, SP8 4EU
Officers: Elizabeth York, Secretary; Barnabas Guy Kindersley [1970] Director; Peter David Kindersley [1941] Director/Publisher and Farmer

Neal's Yard Remedies (International) Ltd
Incorporated: 6 June 2008
Net Worth: £11,700 Total Assets: £11,700
Registered Office: 1 Peacemarsh, Gillingham, Dorset, SP8 4EU
Officers: Elizabeth York, Secretary; Barnabas Guy Kindersley [1970] Director; Peter David Kindersley [1941] Director/Publisher and Farmer

Nectar International Limited
Incorporated: 11 May 2001
Net Worth: £184,891 Total Assets: £304,139
Registered Office: 52 Berkeley Square, London, W1J 5BT
Officers: Robert Peter Smith, Secretary/Consultant; Mhd Anas Al Kasmi [1973] Director/Marketing [Syrian]; Robert Peter Smith [1939] Director; William Banks Waring [1950] Director

Ned London Limited
Incorporated: 3 April 2018
Registered Office: 8 Hartland Road, Reading, Berks, RG2 8BN
Major Shareholder: Catalin-Leonard Popa
Officers: Catalin-Leonard Popa [1986] Director/Recruitment [Romanian]

Need4health Limited
Incorporated: 6 March 2017
Net Worth Deficit: £2,450 Total Assets: £6,380
Registered Office: Redstone House, 7 Langley Road, Birmingham, B10 0TN
Shareholders: Nassar Mahmood Hussain; Zeeshan Haroon Khanani
Officers: Nassar Mahmood Hussain [1971] Director; Zeeshan Haroon Khanani [1973] Director

Neete Holdings Limited
Incorporated: 25 January 2019
Registered Office: Unit K, Haybrook Barn, Brooklands Park, Milton Keynes, Bucks, MK16 0HU
Shareholders: Nilam Holmes; Peter James Holmes
Officers: Peter James Holmes, Secretary; Nilam Holmes [1971] Director; Peter James Holmes [1980] Director

Nefert Ltd
Incorporated: 17 October 2018
Registered Office: Unit 7, 2 Commerce Way, Liverpool, L8 7BL
Major Shareholder: Desiree Talleu Kouma
Officers: Desiree Talleu Kouma [1968] Director/Retailer [French]

Nefil Ltd
Incorporated: 14 August 2018
Registered Office: 20-22 Wenlock Road, London, N1 7GU
Major Shareholder: Filippo Costantino
Officers: Filippo Costantino [1991] Director/Catering [Italian]

Nekta Botanics Ltd
Incorporated: 30 August 2018
Registered Office: 20-22 Wenlock Road, London, N1 7GU
Shareholder: Minesh Bachoo Pankhania
Officers: Minesh Bachoo Pankhania [1978] Director

Neo Cosmetics Limited
Incorporated: 7 November 2016
Net Worth Deficit: £1,875 *Total Assets:* £1,125
Registered Office: 67 Moulton Road, Leicester, LE5 1BS
Shareholder: Yassin Bhadurali Mamade
Officers: Yassin Bhadurali Mamade [1988] Director [Portuguese]

Neo Elegance Ltd
Incorporated: 15 August 2014
Net Worth: £62,041 *Total Assets:* £146,986
Registered Office: Unit 2 Keys Road, Nixs Hill Industrial Estate, Alfreton, Derbys, DE55 7FQ
Major Shareholder: Farrah Allarakha
Officers: Farrah Allarakha [1989] Managing Director

Neolife International Ltd
Incorporated: 18 March 1994 *Employees:* 1
Previous: GNLD International Ltd
Net Worth: £49,833 *Total Assets:* £146,835
Registered Office: Old Bank Chambers, 582-586 Kingsbury Road, Erdington, Birmingham, B24 9ND
Officers: Rok Podlesnik, Secretary; Hakan Bjorklund [1959] Director/Vice President of Operations Northern Europe [Swedish]

Neolox Ltd
Incorporated: 10 August 2017
Registered Office: 2 Northumberland Close, Manchester, M16 9BG
Shareholders: Marcus Nelson; Jacqueline Nelson
Officers: Jacqueline Nelson [1964] Director/Administrator; Marcus Nelson [1992] Director/Administrator

Neonails Ltd
Incorporated: 11 February 2019
Registered Office: Flat 3, 375 City Road, Birmingham, B17 8LD
Major Shareholder: Milada Simonova
Officers: Milada Simonova [1994] Director/Hairdresser [Czech]

Neopilina Moda Ltd
Incorporated: 4 May 2018
Registered Office: 27 Old Gloucester Street, London, WC1N 3AX
Officers: Moulay Driss Khayati [1969] Director [Moroccan]

Neora UK Limited
Incorporated: 3 October 2016
Previous: Nerium International UK Limited
Registered Office: 100 New Bridge Street, London, EC4V 6JA
Major Shareholder: Jeffrey Alan Olson
Officers: Steven Corby Bright [1977] Finance Director [American]; Steven Mark Nicholls [1966] Director [American]

Neroli Limited
Incorporated: 15 May 2013
Net Worth: £1,661 *Total Assets:* £279,957
Registered Office: 35 Middle Farm Place, Effingham, Leatherhead, Surrey, KT24 5LA
Shareholders: Jerome Muscat; Terri Muscat
Officers: Jerome Peter Muscat [1968] Director/Chief Executive; Terri Muscat [1969] Director/Skincare Company

Nevah Rose Ltd
Incorporated: 15 June 2017
Registered Office: 22 Barley Ponds Road, Ware, Herts, SG12 7EZ
Shareholders: Neeta Deshpande; Tovah Sutherland
Officers: Tovah Sutherland [1987] Managing Director

Neville Cut and Shave Limited
Incorporated: 14 August 2013
Registered Office: 72-74 Dean Street, London, W1D 3SG
Parent: Soho House Limited
Officers: Nicholas Keith Arthur Jones [1963] Director; Peter Jonathan McPhee [1975] Director [American]

Suzanne Neville Fragrance Limited
Incorporated: 28 November 2009
Net Worth: £18,908 *Total Assets:* £22,246
Registered Office: Winterfold House, Barhatch Lane, Cranleigh, Surrey, GU6 7NH
Officers: Jane Hampton, Secretary; Anthony Michael Hampton [1947] Director

Nevitrade Ltd
Incorporated: 7 April 2017
Registered Office: 78 York Street, London, W1H 1DP
Officers: Alexey Bizyukov [1973] Director/Consultant [Russian]

New Aesthetic Ltd
Incorporated: 24 January 2019
Registered Office: 20-22 Wenlock Road, London, N1 7GU
Major Shareholder: Manuela Antonini
Officers: Manuela Antonini [1964] Director/Massage Therapist Project Manager [Italian]

New Era Hair Ltd
Incorporated: 14 December 2016
Net Worth: £26,830 *Total Assets:* £476,007
Registered Office: 29 Roundhouse Court, Barnes Wallis Way, Buckshaw Village, Chorley, Lancs, PR7 7JN
Shareholders: Eddie Patrick Renda; Alison Marianne Renda
Officers: Alison Marianne Renda [1965] Director; Eddie Patrick Renda [1956] Director

New Horizons (UK) Ltd
Incorporated: 9 August 2012
Net Worth: £213,168 *Total Assets:* £413,513
Registered Office: 2nd Floor, Quayside Tower, 252-260 Broad Street, Birmingham, B1 2HF
Major Shareholder: Asmat Ullah
Officers: Asmat Ullah [1975] Director/Businessman [Pakistani]

New York 77 Ltd
Incorporated: 25 July 2018
Registered Office: 80 Cape Hill, Smethwick, W Midlands, B66 4PB
Major Shareholder: Mushtaq Hussain
Officers: Mushtaq Hussain [1977] Director/Businessman

Newincco 2301 Limited
Incorporated: 6 October 2017
Registered Office: 3rd Floor, Portland Building, 25 High Street, Crawley, W Sussex, RH10 1BG
Major Shareholder: Catherine Neal
Officers: Catherine Neal [1971] Director

Nextporter Ltd.
Incorporated: 15 November 2017
Registered Office: 2nd Floor, Crown House, 37 High Street, East Grinstead, W Sussex, RH19 3AF
Major Shareholder: Marcela Zahatlanova
Officers: Marcela Zahatlanova [1980] Director [Slovak]

Niami1893 Ltd
Incorporated: 28 December 2018
Registered Office: 29 Oxley Moor Road, Wolverhampton, W Midlands, WV10 6TT
Major Shareholder: Harvinder Bahia
Officers: Harvinder Bahia [1985] Commercial Director

Nice Smell Trade Ltd
Incorporated: 18 June 2018
Registered Office: Flat 49, Coniston Court, Kendal Street, London, W2 2AN
Officers: Badar Din Benanbar [1996] Director/Businessman [Italian]

Nicfead Cosmetics & Fragrance Ltd
Incorporated: 18 December 2013
Net Worth Deficit: £1,165 *Total Assets:* £747
Registered Office: Kemp House, 152 City Road, London, EC1V 2NX
Major Shareholder: Oluwafemi Samuel Adesanya
Officers: Oluwafemi Samuel Adesanya [1981] Director [Nigerian]

Niche Aromas Ltd
Incorporated: 18 May 2018
Registered Office: 86 Burnley Road, Padiham, Burnley, Lancs, BB12 8QN
Major Shareholder: Clare Elizabeth Francis
Officers: Clare Elizabeth Francis, Secretary; Clare Elizabeth Francis [1968] Director

Nicholas Fragrances Ltd
Incorporated: 25 June 2018
Registered Office: 91 Alexander Street, Airdrie, N Lanarks, ML6 0BD
Major Shareholder: Paul Nicholas
Officers: Paul Nicholas [1985] Director

JO Nielsen Limited
Incorporated: 4 August 2003
Net Worth: £7,823 *Total Assets:* £22,028
Registered Office: Units 16-18 Mills Way, Amesbury, Salisbury, Wilts, SP4 7SD
Officers: Johanna Claire Krogh McCann [1978] Director/Manager

Nika Cosmo Group Ltd
Incorporated: 16 July 2018
Registered Office: Kemp House, 160 City Road, London, EC1V 2NX
Officers: Vladimir Nikolov [1977] Director [Bulgarian]; Zdravka Nikolova [1979] Director [Bulgarian]

Niki & Co Ltd
Incorporated: 30 September 2011
Registered Office: 24 Apex Close, Beckenham, Kent, BR3 5TU
Officers: Ledwina Bruckschlogl [1974] Managing Director [German]; Mark Phillips [1970] Director

Niko Pro Limited
Incorporated: 27 April 2016
Net Worth: £86,559 *Total Assets:* £138,066
Registered Office: 31 Wellington Road, Nantwich, Cheshire, CW5 7ED
Major Shareholder: Charlotte Emily Miskell
Officers: Charlotte Emily Miskell [1987] Managing Director

Niquel Ltd
Incorporated: 23 August 2017
Registered Office: 20-22 Wenlock Road, London, N1 7GU
Major Shareholder: Latoya Nekoya Stainrod
Officers: Latoya Nekoya Stainrod [1986] Director/Advisor [Jamaican]

Niroshini Skincare Limited
Incorporated: 3 March 2014
Registered Office: 66 Bloomfield Street, Ipswich, Suffolk, IP4 5JH
Major Shareholder: Melissa Niroshini Day
Officers: Melissa Niroshini Day [1985] Director

Nixsi Limited
Incorporated: 11 June 2010
Net Worth: £8,562 *Total Assets:* £8,562
Registered Office: Gilbert House, 406 Roding Lane South, Woodford Green, Essex, IG8 8EY
Officers: Dr Shadab Din [1988] Director

Niya Cosmetics Ltd
Incorporated: 19 March 2018
Registered Office: Office 4, 219 Kensington High Street, Kensington, London, W8 6BD
Shareholders: Hamzah Yusuf; Hussna Tariq
Officers: Hussna Tariq [1994] Director/Quality Assurance Analyst; Hamzah Yusuf [1993] Director/Sales Development

Nizz Cosmetics Ltd
Incorporated: 27 July 2016
Net Worth: £1,422 *Total Assets:* £2,228
Registered Office: Green Man Skills Zone, 225 Coldharbour Lane, London, SW9 8RR
Major Shareholder: Charlene Laville
Officers: Charlene Laville [1982] Director

NJ Apparel Ltd.
Incorporated: 12 December 2018
Registered Office: 3 Gerard Court, Cawston, Rugby, Warwicks, CV22 7GS
Major Shareholder: Narianne Nirpal Kaur Junday
Officers: Narianne Nirpal Kaur Junday [1990] Director

Njubien Ltd
Incorporated: 21 May 2018
Registered Office: 16 Maplin Road, Leicester, LE5 1SA
Major Shareholder: Chantelle Roberts
Officers: Chantelle Roberts [1991] Director/Analyst

NM Beauty Industries Ltd
Incorporated: 8 October 2018
Registered Office: 32 Seymour Place, London, W1H 7NR
Major Shareholder: Natalia Mizejewska
Officers: Natalia Mizejewska [1985] Director/Founder and CEO [Polish]

NMB Property Limited
Incorporated: 4 November 2016
Net Worth: £7,765 *Total Assets:* £16,441
Registered Office: 161 Forest Road, London, E17 6HE
Officers: Nevzat Hakan Mehmet [1976] Director

No.1 Nail Supply Limited
Incorporated: 30 December 2014
Net Worth: £402,450 *Total Assets:* £694,950
Registered Office: 12 The Village, London, SE7 8UD
Major Shareholder: Lam Van Trinh
Officers: Hang Thi Nguyen, Secretary; Lam Van Trinh [1981] Director/Businessman

Noa London Ltd
Incorporated: 7 April 2017
Registered Office: 20-22 Wenlock Road, London, N1 7GU
Major Shareholder: Norville Stephenson
Officers: Norville Stephenson [1991] Director/Cosmetics Operations Coordinator

Noble Soap Limited
Incorporated: 22 June 2018
Registered Office: Suite 101, Hanovia House, 30 Eastman Road, Acton, London, W3 7YG
Major Shareholder: Lama Andoura
Officers: Lama Andoura [1988] Director/Owner [Syrian]

Nocov Ltd
Incorporated: 6 March 2018
Registered Office: Kemp House, 160 City Road, London, EC1V 2NX
Officers: Muhammad Zukermi Bin Edi [1991] Director [Malaysian]

Nogender London Ltd
Incorporated: 11 February 2019
Registered Office: 9 Lea Green Close, Oldham, Lancs, OL4 2TF
Major Shareholder: Paula Hunston
Officers: Paula Hunston [1983] Director

Noli Distribution Ltd
Incorporated: 5 March 2018
Registered Office: 3rd Floor, 86-90 Paul Street, London, EC2A 4NE
Major Shareholder: Lassina Karamoko Toure
Officers: Lassina Karamoko Toure [1972] Director [Ivorian]

Nomad Care Ltd
Incorporated: 17 August 2015
Net Worth Deficit: £1,612 *Total Assets:* £8,992
Registered Office: 300 Platt Lane, Manchester, M14 7BZ
Shareholders: Muhammed Ige; Muhammed Ige
Officers: Ibrahim Hussein, Secretary; Mohamed Ahmed Ige [1978] Director

Nomalogic Ltd
Incorporated: 6 September 2017
Registered Office: 23 Rose Cottages, Portadown, Co Armagh, BT62 1RU
Major Shareholder: Marcin Henryk Nowakowski
Officers: Wiktor Sopel, Secretary; Marcin Henryk Nowakowski [1976] Director [Polish]; Wiktor Sopel [1983] Director [Polish]

Noor Int'l Trading Limited
Incorporated: 26 June 2018
Registered Office: 23 Lichfield Mount, Bradford, BD2 1NX
Major Shareholder: Raza Al-Tamimi
Officers: Raza Al-Tamimi [1993] Director/Civil Engineer [Norwegian]

NOP Cosmetics Ltd
Incorporated: 23 January 2018
Registered Office: 71-75 Shelton Street, Covent Garden, London, WC2H 9JQ
Major Shareholder: Dorel Vadaniuc
Officers: Iuliana Onofriescu [1991] Director [Romanian]; Dorel Vadaniuc [1992] Director [Romanian]

Norm and Glo Limited
Incorporated: 26 November 2018
Registered Office: 92 Littledale Road, Wallasey, Merseyside, CH44 8EQ
Major Shareholder: Nadine Inez Isaacs
Officers: Nadine Inez Isaacs [1969] Director

Norpro Limited
Incorporated: 10 August 2017
Registered Office: 138 Hassell Street, Newcastle-under-Lyme, Staffs, ST5 1BB
Shareholders: Norah Procter; Garry Procter
Officers: Dorris Procter [1997] Director

North One Limited
Incorporated: 9 February 2018
Registered Office: 34a Watling Street, Radlett, Herts, WD7 7NN
Major Shareholder: Paul Zimbler
Officers: Paul Zimbler [1972] Director

North West Cosmetics Limited
Incorporated: 30 December 1996 *Employees:* 6
Net Worth: £17,656 *Total Assets:* £320,155
Registered Office: 165 Cheetham Hill Road, Manchester, M8 8LG
Shareholders: Linda Bamford; Amanda Ramsbottom
Officers: Linda Bamford, Secretary; Amanda Ramsbottom [1962] Financial Director

Northdown Cosmetics Limited
Incorporated: 21 November 1974
Net Worth: £692,360 *Total Assets:* £781,720
Registered Office: Kent House, Ashford Road, Harrietsham, Maidstone, Kent, ME17 1BW
Shareholders: Alan John Jenner; Hazel Jean Young; David James Jenner
Officers: Hazel Jean Young, Secretary; Alan John Jenner [1959] Director/Sales and Marketing; David James Jenner [1964] Director/Works Manager; Hazel Jean Young [1957] Director/Administrator

Nota Nota Limited
Incorporated: 21 October 2016
Registered Office: 3rd Floor, 14 Hanover Street, London, W1S 1YH
Major Shareholder: Abdullah Bahabri
Officers: Abdullah Bahabri, Secretary; Abdullah Bahabri [1986] Director/Founder [Saudi Arabian]

Nouela Organics Ltd
Incorporated: 31 July 2017
Registered Office: 4 Middlesmoor, Tamworth, Staffs, B77 4PL
Major Shareholder: Victoria Elizabeth Probert
Officers: Victoria Elizabeth Probert [1991] Director/Merchandiser

Nouvriet Boutros (UK) Ltd
Incorporated: 21 February 2019
Registered Office: CCOB, Badminton Road, Chipping Sodbury, S Glos, BS37 6LL
Shareholders: Gary Vincent Pope; Nouvriet Boutros
Officers: Nouvriet Boutros [1965] Director [American]; Gary Vincent Pope [1962] Director

Nov'max Keratin Limited
Incorporated: 17 January 2011
Net Worth: £93,136 *Total Assets:* £119,915
Registered Office: 2 Havelock Road, Poole, Dorset, BH12 1LA
Shareholders: Esther Suzannah Juliani; Emerson Diones Juliani
Officers: Emerson Diones Juliani [1980] Director; Esther Suzannah Juliani [1987] Director

Nova Bleu Cosmetics Limited
Incorporated: 13 December 2017
Registered Office: 5 Mansion Close, London, SW9 8QJ
Officers: Yaa Boatemaa Manson [1975] Director/Sales Assistant

Nova Cellulis Ltd
Incorporated: 28 November 2017
Registered Office: 97 Hewlett Road, Cheltenham, Glos, GL52 6BB
Major Shareholder: Jen Williams
Officers: Jen Williams [1976] Director/Make Up Supplier and Demonstrator

Novmedic Limited
Incorporated: 17 December 2009
Registered Office: 42 Church Street, Edmonton, London, N9 9DU
Officers: Elias Demetroudi [1962] Director/Businessman

Novumis Ltd
Incorporated: 6 July 2017
Registered Office: 71-75 Shelton Street, Covent Garden, London, WC2H 9JQ
Shareholders: Balazs Imre Lendvay; Hajnalka Lendvayne Szantai-Kis
Officers: Hajnalka Lendvayne Szantai-Kis [1973] Director/Housewife [Hungarian]

Nowdynamic Ltd.
Incorporated: 25 November 2014
Registered Office: Candlelight Cottage, Ackrells Hill, Littlehempston, Totnes, Devon, TQ9 6LX
Shareholders: Keith Adrian Taylor; Charlotte Noel Taylor
Officers: Charlotte Noel Taylor [1968] Director; Keith Adrian Taylor [1965] Director

Noyras Ltd
Incorporated: 14 February 2013
Previous: Botanique Ltd
Net Worth: £2,670 *Total Assets:* £13,140
Registered Office: Grand Union House, 20 Kentish Town Road, London, NW1 9NX
Major Shareholder: Grzegorz Skwarek
Officers: Grzegorz Skwarek [1975] Director [Polish]

NRS Cosmetics Ltd
Incorporated: 10 August 2018
Registered Office: 55a High Street, Marlow, Bucks, SL7 1BA
Major Shareholder: Natasha Jasmine Shergill
Officers: Natasha Jasmine Shergill, Secretary; Natasha Jasmine Shergill [1998] Director/Make Up Artist and Cosmetic Designer

NS Brands International Ltd
Incorporated: 24 May 2017
Registered Office: Flat 16, 39-40 Queens Gate, London, SW7 5HR
Major Shareholder: Nahid Sultana
Officers: Nahid Sultana [1976] Director

Nu Essence Limited
Incorporated: 18 March 2013
Net Worth: £100,290 *Total Assets:* £109,720
Registered Office: 3 The Coach House Stables, Tilburstow Hill Road, South Godstone, Surrey, RH9 8LY
Major Shareholder: Jane Vanessa Rieman
Officers: Jane Vanessa Rieman [1950] Sales Director

Nu-E55ence Ltd
Incorporated: 8 January 2019
Registered Office: 20-22 Wenlock Road, London, N1 7GU
Officers: Charmaine Cameron [1983] Director

Nuke Manufacturing, Distribution & Investments Limited
Incorporated: 12 July 2018
Registered Office: Suite 209, 131 Friargate, City House, Preston, Lancs, PR1 2EF
Major Shareholder: Dan Povey
Officers: Dan Povey [1993] Director

Nukua Limited
Incorporated: 4 January 2016
Net Worth: £28,176 *Total Assets:* £46,201
Registered Office: 12 Ravenswood Court, Stanley Road, London, W3 8GQ
Shareholders: Solmantex Ltd; Mplus2 Ltd
Officers: Javier Martinez de San Vicente [1978] Director/Banker [Spanish]; Alvaro Montenegro Leon [1980] Director/Architect [Venezuelan]

Nurologie Ltd
Incorporated: 24 August 2017
Registered Office: 20-22 Wenlock Road, London, N1 7GU
Major Shareholder: Marian Mohamud
Officers: Marian Mohamud [1989] Director/Medical Project Manager [Swedish]

Nut Dust Ltd
Incorporated: 20 February 2017
Net Worth Deficit: £3,280 *Total Assets:* £8,620
Registered Office: 46 Kingslynne Drive, Kings Park, Glasgow, G44 4JA
Shareholders: Lorraine Clark; Julie Molloy
Officers: James Corner, Secretary; Andrew Clark [1976] Director/Teacher; James Corner [1976] Director/Accountant; Julie Molloy [1976] Director

Nutrics Ltd
Incorporated: 31 December 2018
Registered Office: 272 Bath Street, Glasgow, G2 4JR
Major Shareholder: Vlada Griskevica
Officers: Vlada Griskevica, Secretary; Vlada Griskevica [1982] Director [Latvian]

NXSK UK Ltd
Incorporated: 16 March 2017
Registered Office: Kemp House, 160 City Road, London, EC1V 2NX
Officers: Naim Hamade, Secretary; Naim Hamade [1994] Director/CEO & Founder [Portuguese]

The Nyasa Organics Limited
Incorporated: 3 July 2014
Net Worth Deficit: £245,737 *Total Assets:* £85,481
Registered Office: Ground Floor, 31 Kentish Town Road, London, NW1 8NL
Shareholders: Katerina Athanasi; Maria Hristova Grigorova
Officers: Katerina Athanasi [1966] Director; Maria Hristova Grigorova [1963] Director

NYDG UK Limited
Incorporated: 17 June 2014
Net Worth Deficit: £20,197 *Total Assets:* £61,058
Registered Office: 4 Prince Albert Road, London, NW1 7SN
Shareholders: David Anthony Colbert; Jean-Pierre Aime Van Laere
Officers: David Anthony Colbert [1957] Director [American]; Jean-Pierre Aime Van Laere [1955] Director [American]

Oakhill Luxury Ltd
Incorporated: 12 November 2018
Registered Office: Fairview House, Nightingale Lane, Ide Hill, Sevenoaks, Kent, TN14 6BX
Major Shareholder: Franco Mignemi
Officers: Claudia Contesotto [1966] Director [British/Italian]

Oakwood Williams Limited
Incorporated: 11 September 2014
Net Worth Deficit: £7,656
Registered Office: 71-75 Shelton Street, Covent Garden, London, WC2H 9JQ
Major Shareholder: Elizabeth Dosu
Officers: John Jnr Dosu [1999] Director/E-Commerce [Irish]

Oasis Beauty Distribution Ltd
Incorporated: 15 April 2015
Registered Office: 2 Oyster Park, Greenstead Road, Colchester, Essex, CO1 2SJ
Major Shareholder: Yuen Yan Law
Officers: Yuen Yan Law [1982] Director

Oatany Ltd
Incorporated: 8 April 2013
Registered Office: 28 Fenman Gardens, Ilford, Essex, IG3 9QE
Officers: Ashleigh Shantelle Grimes [1986] Director

Occo London Limited
Incorporated: 12 June 2008
Net Worth: £1,242 *Total Assets:* £1,242
Registered Office: 27 Old Gloucester Street, London, WC1N 3AX
Officers: Alexander Stewart Penkul, Secretary; Anna Laurie Doyle [1970] Director [French]; Alexander Stewart Penkul [1965] Director

Odeferus Limited
Incorporated: 20 December 2018
Registered Office: 71-75 Shelton Street, London, WC2H 9JQ
Officers: Faizan Ahmed [1993] Director [Pakistani]; AMR Shaltoot [1972] Director [Egyptian]

Official IV Ltd
Incorporated: 22 January 2019
Registered Office: Kemp House, 160 City Road, London, EC1V 2NX
Major Shareholder: Ivan Vasilj
Officers: Andrej Vasilj, Secretary; Ivan Vasilj [1999] Director [Croatian]

Oh My Scent Limited
Incorporated: 18 March 2016
Net Worth: £1,272,568 *Total Assets:* £1,276,984
Registered Office: Hill Dickinson LLP, The Broadgate Tower, 20 Primrose Street, London, EC2A 2EW
Shareholders: Jean-Laurent Marcel Carmine Dupont; Nathalie Vinciguerra
Officers: Alexandre Matthieu Valdemar Casin [1973] Director [French]; Jean-Laurent Marcel Carmine Dupont [1976] Director/Business Consultant [French]; Jean-Louis Vinciguerra [1944] Director [French]; Nathalie Vinciguerra [1965] Director/Fragrance Developer [French]; Philip Von Wulffen [1972] Director [German]

Oh So Locks Ltd
Incorporated: 20 February 2018
Registered Office: 11 Oxford Road, Middlesbrough, Cleveland, TS5 5DY
Major Shareholder: Mica Frances Coleman
Officers: Mica Frances Coleman [1996] Director/Beautician [British/Jamaican]

OhMyLashUK Ltd
Incorporated: 1 August 2018
Registered Office: 20 St Davids Close, Maidenhead, Berks, SL6 3BB
Shareholders: Natalie Bridgette Cairns; Francesca Julie Cairns
Officers: Natalie Bridgette Cairns [1990] Director

Ohsho Ltd
Incorporated: 23 August 2018
Registered Office: Grainger Suite, Regent Centre, Gosforth, Newcastle upon Tyne, NE3 3PF
Major Shareholder: Paul John Richardson
Officers: Paul John Richardson [1964] Director/Entrepreneur

Oils4life Limited
Incorporated: 30 January 2003
Net Worth: £46,050 *Total Assets:* £116,610
Registered Office: Holistic House, Unit 9 Enterprise Court, Gapton Hall Road, Great Yarmouth, Norfolk, NR31 0ND
Major Shareholder: Rachael Farrow
Officers: Rachael Farrow [1973] Director

Oilyspirit Ltd
Incorporated: 29 July 2015
Net Worth Deficit: £8,603 *Total Assets:* £10
Registered Office: 18 Wingford Road, London, SW2 4DS
Major Shareholder: Janis Damoison
Officers: Janis Damoison [1982] Director [French]

Okmarket24 Ltd
Incorporated: 4 September 2015
Net Worth Deficit: £3,551 *Total Assets:* £1,862
Registered Office: 2 Sheriffs Orchard, Coventry, Warwicks, CV1 3PP
Major Shareholder: Jerzy Antoni Baryliszyn
Officers: Jerzy Baryliszyn [1971] Director/Entrepreneur [Polish]

Olfacstory Parfums Limited
Incorporated: 22 April 2015
Net Worth: £358 *Total Assets:* £380
Registered Office: Office D5, Floor 3, 44 Broadway, London, E15 1XH
Major Shareholder: Marius Catalin Neagu
Officers: Marius Catalin Neagu [1986] Director/Sales [Romanian]

Olfactive Thirty Eight Fragrances Limited
Incorporated: 10 January 2018
Registered Office: Kemp House, 160 City Road, London, EC1V 2NX
Officers: Johnathon Brown, Secretary; Christopher Bennett [1984] Director/Owner; Johnathon Brown [1983] Director/Owner

A W Oliver & Co Ltd
Incorporated: 14 March 2018
Registered Office: 5 Oram Street, Bury, Lancs, BL9 6EN
Major Shareholder: Andrew William Oliver
Officers: Andrew William Oliver [1980] Director

Oliver & Taylor Ltd
Incorporated: 19 March 2018
Registered Office: 37 John Heywood Street, Manchester, M11 4EL
Major Shareholder: Andrew Oliver
Officers: Andrew Oliver [1980] Director/Perfumer

Olivia Kate Cosmetics Ltd
Incorporated: 8 September 2016
Net Worth Deficit: £18 *Total Assets:* £4,607
Registered Office: 5 Beresford Crescent, Skegness, Lincs, PE25 3JJ
Major Shareholder: Christopher Carter
Officers: Christopher Carter [1979] Director/Sales Agent

Olivoderm Cosmetics UK Limited
Incorporated: 19 September 2018
Registered Office: Kemp House, 160 City Road, London, EC1V 2NX
Shareholders: Stamatia Gkenou; Dimitrios Mastoras
Officers: Stamatia Gkenou [1956] Director/Entrepreneur [Greek]; Dimitrios Mastoras [1992] Director/Entrepreneur [Greek]

Olo Edt Ltd
Incorporated: 8 July 2015
Registered Office: Flat 14, 1 Bessborough Road, London, SW15 4AB
Major Shareholder: Romain Grosjean
Officers: Romain Grosjean [1970] Director/Tennis Coach [French]

Omaoli Limited
Incorporated: 21 August 2018
Registered Office: 71-75 Shelton Street, Covent Garden, London, WC2H 9JQ
Shareholders: Stuart O'Malley; Laura Jones
Officers: Laura Jones [1985] Director; Stuart O'Malley [1983] Director

Ombre Cosmetics Limited
Incorporated: 7 January 2019
Registered Office: 1st Floor, The Barn House, 38 Meadow Way, Ruislip, Middlesex, HA4 8SY
Major Shareholder: Sunny Malhotra
Officers: Sunny Malhotra [1975] Director

Ombre Paris Limited
Incorporated: 7 January 2019
Registered Office: 1st Floor, The Barn House, 38 Meadow Way, Ruislip, Middlesex, HA4 8SY
Major Shareholder: Sunny Malhotra
Officers: Sunny Malhotra [1975] Director

Omega Flax Limited
Incorporated: 29 July 2016
Net Worth: £767 *Total Assets:* £97,558
Registered Office: 85 Great Portland Street, London, W1W 7LT
Officers: Dastan Koshbakov [1984] Director [Kyrgyzstani]

Omprus Limited
Incorporated: 12 November 2018
Registered Office: 338 Bristol Road, Birmingham, B5 7SN
Major Shareholder: Mohammed Fakhir Hashim Yassin
Officers: Mohammed Fakhir Hashim Yassin [1996] Director/Self Employed

On & Off Beauty Ltd
Incorporated: 24 April 2018
Registered Office: Unit 1 Broadbent Close, London, N6 5JW
Shareholders: Arnaud Allard; Paul Rogers
Officers: Arnaud Allard [1978] Director/Freelance [French]; Paul Rogers [1991] Director

On-Top Skincare Limited
Incorporated: 26 October 2018
Registered Office: Lockwood House, Trent Lane, Derby, DE72 2BT
Shareholders: David Fuher; Lee Samuel Stafford
Officers: David Fuher [1968] Director; Lawrence Marc Howlett [1983] Marketing Director; Lee Samuel Stafford [1987] Director

Onamex Ltd
Incorporated: 18 June 2018
Registered Office: 27 Old Gloucester Street, London, WC1N 3AX
Major Shareholder: Onuoha Prince Alison
Officers: Imeh Godwin, Secretary; Onwuka Uchenna Sandra, Secretary; Onuoha Prince Alison [1984] Director/Businessman [Nigerian]

One Beauty Ltd
Incorporated: 15 November 2006
Net Worth Deficit: £27,940 *Total Assets:* £59,450
Registered Office: 72 Hainault Road, Romford, Essex, RM5 3AL
Shareholder: Nicholas James Mark White
Officers: Priti White, Secretary; Nicholas James Mark White [1964] Director/Consultant; Priti White [1972] Director/Consultant

One Flower Qinga Limited
Incorporated: 7 December 2017
Registered Office: Fourth Floor, 3 Gower Street, London, WC1E 6HA
Shareholders: Qihang Li; Mengchen Qu
Officers: Qihang Li [1992] Director [Chinese]

One Green Lab Ltd
Incorporated: 12 January 2015
Net Worth: £40,801 *Total Assets:* £48,653
Registered Office: 77 High Street, Littlehampton, W Sussex, BN17 5AG
Shareholders: Peter Laszlo Takacs; Zsanett Kolonics
Officers: Peter Laszlo Takacs [1974] Director [Hungarian]

Online Motions Limited
Incorporated: 21 September 2015
Net Worth Deficit: £8,560 *Total Assets:* £6,510
Registered Office: 23 Mafeking Avenue, Ilford, Essex, IG2 7AW
Officers: Arushka Devi Sooree Bedacee [1985] Business Director [Mauritian]; Avinash Nagamah [1981] Business Director [Mauritian]

Onlinexclusive Limited
Incorporated: 31 March 2017
Registered Office: 1 Darley Street, Leicester, LE2 0GB
Major Shareholder: Afzal Boodi
Officers: Afzal Boodi [1975] Director/Sales

Only Perfection Ltd
Incorporated: 15 June 2018
Registered Office: Kemp House, 160 City Road, London, EC1V 2NX
Officers: Mellisa Simon-Cort, Secretary; Mellisa Simon-Cort [1979] Director/Entrepreneur

Onna Export Import Ltd
Incorporated: 2 November 2015
Registered Office: Fifth Floor, 3 Gower Street, London, WC1E 6HA
Major Shareholder: Arslan Ridvan
Officers: Arslan Ridvan, Secretary; Arslan Ridvan [1970] Director/Merchant [German]

Onsen Secret UK Ltd
Incorporated: 14 December 2018
Registered Office: 20-22 Wenlock Road, London, N1 7GU
Major Shareholder: Doron Santo
Officers: Doron Santo [1978] Director [American]

Onya Limited
Incorporated: 15 April 2013
Registered Office: Dirleton House, Lewes Road, Forest Row, E Sussex, RH18 5AA
Major Shareholder: Julie Mary Aitchison
Officers: Julie Mary Aitchison [1956] Director/Sales Administration

Onyx Clothing Ltd
Incorporated: 23 January 2019
Registered Office: Flat 270, Sunset Court, Navestock Crescent, Woodford Green, Essex, IG8 7BE
Major Shareholder: Jessica Matondo David
Officers: Jessica Matondo David [1993] Director/Designer

Oodiee Limited
Incorporated: 4 December 2015
Registered Office: 5 Giffard Court, Millbrook Close, Northampton, NN5 5JF
Major Shareholder: Jeanne Williams
Officers: Karen Victoria Harwood [1982] Director; Victoria Louise Tydeman [1966] Director

OPA Botanicals Ltd
Incorporated: 9 October 2018
Registered Office: Opa Botanicals Ltd, P O Box 1544, Northampton, NN1 9JE
Major Shareholder: Daniel Marc Martin-De Lapa
Officers: Daniel Marc Martin-De Lapa [1992] Director/Salesman

Opal Naturals Ltd
Incorporated: 27 September 2017
Registered Office: 334 Slade Lane, Manchester, M19 2BL
Major Shareholder: Aroona Naheed Ali
Officers: Aroona Naheed Ali, Secretary; Aroona Naheed Ali [1971] Director/Sales

Opatra Limited
Incorporated: 10 March 2010
Net Worth: £18,410 *Total Assets:* £225,560
Registered Office: Dalton House, Windsor Avenue, London, SW19 2RR
Major Shareholder: Efraim Salhov
Officers: Efraim Salhov [1979] Director [Israeli]

Optic Eye Wear Ltd
Incorporated: 19 December 2016
Net Worth: £46,670 *Total Assets:* £234,020
Registered Office: 17 The Triangle, Huddersfield, W Yorks, HD1 4RN
Major Shareholder: Amjad Ali
Officers: Amjad Ali [1972] Director

Optima Consumer Health Limited
Incorporated: 24 January 2011 *Employees:* 30
Net Worth: £15,204,000 *Total Assets:* £16,419,000
Registered Office: Dr Organic Group Limited, Alberto Road, Valley Way, Swansea, SA6 8RG
Parent: Organic Group Ltd
Officers: Nicholas John Heywood Collins [1962] Director/Chief Strategy & Product Supply Officer International; Stephen Kelsey Ford [1968] Finance Director; Matthew James Richard Harvey [1980] Director/Chartered Accountant; Michael Henryk Lightowlers [1972] Managing Director; Stephen Ronald Price [1964] Group Export Director

Optimavia Ltd
Incorporated: 23 March 2015
Previous: Face Lab Limited
Registered Office: Kemp House, 152-160 City Road, London, EC1V 2NX
Major Shareholder: Mariusz Lucjan Raszewski
Officers: Mariusz Lucjan Raszewski [1978] Director [Polish]

ORA Naturals Limited
Incorporated: 6 December 2011
Net Worth Deficit: £63,121 *Total Assets:* £18,214
Registered Office: 72 Wickham Way, Beckenham, Kent, BR3 3AF
Shareholder: Natasha Rebecca Anne King
Officers: Natasha Rebecca Anne King [1981] Sales Director

Orange Balloon Ltd
Incorporated: 24 October 2014
Net Worth Deficit: £12,171 *Total Assets:* £31,189
Registered Office: Station House, North Street, Havant, Hants, PO9 1QU
Major Shareholder: Sarah Jane Penney
Officers: Sarah Jane Penney, Secretary; Sarah Jane Penney [1970] Director

The Orange Square Company Ltd.
Incorporated: 20 March 1991 *Employees:* 143
Net Worth: £4,034,576 *Total Assets:* £7,251,013
Registered Office: Peregrine House, 26-28 Paradise Road, Richmond upon Thames, Surrey, TW9 1SE
Major Shareholder: Christopher Michael Hawksley
Officers: Jayne Elizabeth Fox [1958] Director; Christopher Michael Hawksley [1955] Managing Director

Orca Distributor Ltd
Incorporated: 11 April 2018
Registered Office: 32 Greenview Drive, London, SW20 9DS
Major Shareholder: Mai Phan McArdle
Officers: Mai Phan McArdle [1987] Director

Organic and Mineral Salons Limited
Incorporated: 25 February 2019
Registered Office: 1 Brookmans Avenue, Brookmans Park, Hatfield, Herts, AL9 7QH
Officers: Daniel Field, Secretary; Daniel Field [1958] Director/Hairdresser

Organic Colour Systems Limited
Incorporated: 25 November 1994
Net Worth: £22,712 *Total Assets:* £474,815
Registered Office: 64 Baker Street, London, W1U 7GB
Parent: Herb U.K. (Holdings) Limited
Officers: Raoul John Perfitt, Secretary/Operations Director; Ian Bishop [1967] Director; Mark D'Arcy [1975] Operations Director; Raoul John Perfitt [1966] Operations Director

Organic Cosmetic Products Ltd
Incorporated: 8 May 2018
Registered Office: 54 Brighton Road, Watford, Herts, WD24 5HW
Major Shareholder: Zeynab Abiyeva
Officers: Zeynab Abiyeva [1977] Director/General Manager [Azerbaijani]

Organic Iway Ltd
Incorporated: 18 September 2018
Registered Office: 27 Old Gloucester Street, London, WC1N 3AX
Major Shareholder: Constantin Eduard Hristudor
Officers: Constantin Eduard Hristudor, Secretary; Constantin Eduard Hristudor [1985] Director/Engineer [Romanian]

Organic Land Global Ltd
Incorporated: 29 June 2017
Registered Office: 111 Kingsway Road, Leicester, LE5 5TU
Shareholder: Mohammed Abdussalam
Officers: Mohammed Abdussalam [1982] Managing Director [Libyan]; Aiman Ahmed Mohamed Qhatit [1980] Director [Libyan]

Organic Professional Ltd
Incorporated: 8 August 2017
Registered Office: 63 Elm Grove, Southsea, Hants, PO5 1JF
Major Shareholder: Marcin Prus
Officers: Marcin Prus [1975] Managing Director [Polish]

Organic Skincare Originals Ltd
Incorporated: 18 June 2018
Registered Office: 115 Whitby Avenue, Ingol, Preston, Lancs, PR2 3ZP
Officers: Megan Kaytie McHugh [1992] Director

Organic Stuff Limited
Incorporated: 7 November 2017
Registered Office: International House, 24 Holborn Viaduct, London, EC1A 2BN
Shareholder: Irma Luotiene
Officers: Irma Luotiene [1968] Director [Lithuanian]

Organica Skincare Ltd
Incorporated: 12 January 2017
Net Worth: £1,000 *Total Assets:* £1,000
Registered Office: 76-80 Baddow Road, Chelmsford, Essex, CM2 7PJ
Shareholders: Lubna Sengul; Mavesh Malik
Officers: Mavesh Malik [1984] Director/Sales Manager; Lubna Sengul [1978] Director

OrganicBeautyshop Ltd
Incorporated: 3 September 2018
Registered Office: 1 Waldeck Road, Luton, Beds, LU1 1HG
Major Shareholder: Mohammed Rezine
Officers: Mohammed Rezine [1983] Director/Beautician [French]

Organii Limited
Incorporated: 19 November 2012
Net Worth: £15,653 *Total Assets:* £48,517
Registered Office: Conchieton Business Centre, Twynholm, Kirkcudbright, Dumfries & Galloway, DG6 4TA
Officers: Graeme Paul Hume [1953] Director

Orgreen Naturals Ltd
Incorporated: 18 April 2018
Registered Office: 11 Burnside Gardens, Walsall, W Midlands, WS5 3LB
Major Shareholder: Rozina Qaiser
Officers: Rozina Qaiser, Secretary; Rozina Qaiser [1970] Director/Self Employed

Orien Beauty & Selfcare Limited
Incorporated: 8 October 2018
Registered Office: 3 Shirwell Crescent, Furzton, Milton Keynes, Bucks, MK4 1GA
Parent: Orien Trade LLC
Officers: Madis Marius Vahtre [1978] Director/Chief Executive Officer [Estonian]

Original Additions (Beauty Products) Limited
Incorporated: 5 April 2004 *Employees:* 96
Net Worth: £23,715,480 *Total Assets:* £27,130,652
Registered Office: Ventura House, Bullsbrook Road, Hayes, Middlesex, UB4 0UJ
Parent: Original Additions Topco Limited
Officers: James Rogers [1966] Director [American]; James Stammer [1974] Director/President [American]; Mark Alexander Wood [1973] Director

Original Taste Ltd
Incorporated: 14 January 2019
Registered Office: 55 Harrington Street, Cleethorpes, N E Lincs, DN35 7BD
Major Shareholder: Gatis Straume
Officers: Gatis Straume [1994] Director [Latvian]

Orikii Naturals Ltd
Incorporated: 7 January 2019
Registered Office: 28 Felipe Road, Chafford Hundred, Grays, Essex, RM16 6NE
Major Shareholder: Olubunmi Oyetoun Johnson
Officers: Olubunmi Oyetoun Johnson [1968] Director

Orit Limited
Incorporated: 6 August 2018
Registered Office: 71-75 Shelton Street, Covent Garden, London, WC2H 9JQ
Major Shareholder: Mohammed Malim
Officers: Mohammed Malim, Secretary; Mohammed Malim [1976] Director [French]

Orrwa Pharma Health & Beauty Limited
Incorporated: 8 September 2016
Previous: Worrela International Limited
Net Worth: £1 *Total Assets:* £1
Registered Office: 104a North Road, Manchester, M11 4LD
Officers: Aran Jaff [1983] Director/Businessman

Orveda Limited
Incorporated: 9 September 2014 *Employees:* 1
Previous: Orveda Holdings Limited
Net Worth Deficit: £1,345,022 *Total Assets:* £1,012,170
Registered Office: 3rd Floor, 1-5 Wandsworth Road, London, SW8 2LN
Major Shareholder: Youcef Nabi
Officers: Youcef Nabi [1968] Director [French]; Nicolas Ngoc Vu [1974] Director [French]

Orveda UK Limited
Incorporated: 2 March 2017 *Employees:* 1
Net Worth Deficit: £26,158 *Total Assets:* £104,514
Registered Office: 3rd Floor, 1-5 Wandsworth Road, London, SW8 2LN
Officers: Youcef Nabi [1968] Director [French]

Oscar & Louis Limited
Incorporated: 12 February 2018
Registered Office: Oscar & Louis, First Floor, Swan Buildings, Swan Street, Manchester, M4 5JW
Major Shareholder: Aaron Levin
Officers: Deborah Lester, Secretary; Aaron Levin [1990] Director

Ossulstone Hundred Limited
Incorporated: 24 June 2016
Net Worth: £124 *Total Assets:* £124
Registered Office: 36 Rectory Square, London, E1 3NG
Officers: Edmund Anthony Prendergast [1960] Director/Retail Consultant

Otonix Limited
Incorporated: 23 October 2018
Registered Office: Suite 163, No 2 Lansdowne Row, Mayfair, London, W1J 6HL
Shareholders: Belinda Aloisio; Seanne Grasso
Officers: Philip Evangelou, Secretary; Belinda Aloisio [1982] Director [Australian]; Sadaf Ataei Khoshro [1983] Director; Philip Evangelou [1983] Director [Australian]; Seanne Grasso [1969] Director

Otterganics Ltd
Incorporated: 12 April 2018
Registered Office: Kemp House, 160 City Road, London, EC1V 2NX
Major Shareholder: Chimezie Ezirim
Officers: Chimezie Ezirim [1985] Director

The Oud & Musk UK Ltd
Incorporated: 5 January 2018
Registered Office: 56 Warren Street, Fitzrovia, London, W1T 5NP
Major Shareholder: Ahmer Afaq
Officers: Ahmer Afaq [1977] Director [Indian]

Oud Milano UK Limited
Incorporated: 3 March 2016 *Employees:* 2
Net Worth Deficit: £204,538 *Total Assets:* £836,276
Registered Office: 62 Wilbury Way, Hitchin, Herts, SG4 0TY
Shareholder: Anas Abdulsamad Alqurashi
Officers: Abdulsamad Qawas, Secretary; Gamal Mahmoud El-Hawary [1964] Managing Director [Irish/Egyptian]; Ibrahim Musali [1977] Director [Saudi Arabian]; Abdulsamad Qawas [1990] Director [Saudi Arabian]

Oudh Al Aasmah Perfume UK Ltd
Incorporated: 3 September 2018
Registered Office: 10 Nursery Terrace, 4 Epsom Road, London, E10 6ES
Major Shareholder: Mohammed Rashid Khan
Officers: Mohammed Rashid Khan [1984] Director [Indian]

Oudh Company Limited
Incorporated: 27 December 2017
Registered Office: Congress House, 14 Lyon Road, Harrow, Middlesex, HA1 2EN
Major Shareholder: Hamza Mursaleen
Officers: Hamza Mursaleen [1993] Director/Manager

Our Choice Gift Limited
Incorporated: 11 April 2011
Net Worth Deficit: £49,020 *Total Assets:* £41,980
Registered Office: 128 Whitechapel Road, London, E1 1JE
Major Shareholder: Mohammed Nizam Uddin
Officers: Mohammed Nizam Uddin, Secretary; Mohammed Nizam Uddin [1969] Director

Our-Scent Ltd
Incorporated: 12 January 2016 *Employees:* 1
Previous: Scent-Citi Ltd
Net Worth: £4,411 *Total Assets:* £5,469
Registered Office: 403 Hornsey Road, London, N19 4DX
Major Shareholder: Ashadur Rahman
Officers: Ashadur Rahman [1990] Director/Businessman

Outcome Zero Ltd
Incorporated: 30 January 2019
Registered Office: 30 New Road, Brighton, BN1 1BN
Shareholders: Geneva Tayne; Bradley George Tayne
Officers: Bradley George Tayne [1989] Managing Director; Geneva Tayne [1990] Managing Director

Outdoor Girl Limited
Incorporated: 7 March 2011
Net Worth: £4,715 *Total Assets:* £96,931
Registered Office: 2nd Floor, 314 Regents Park Road, London, N3 2JX
Major Shareholder: Neil Rodol
Officers: Neil Rodol, Secretary; Neil Rodol [1962] Director

Ovis Liv Limited
Incorporated: 23 January 2015
Net Worth Deficit: £45,810 *Total Assets:* £17,580
Registered Office: 96 Wodeland Avenue, Guildford, Surrey, GU2 4LD
Major Shareholder: Wanjun Zhang
Officers: Wanjun Zhang [1991] Director [Chinese]

Oxmetics Ltd
Incorporated: 3 December 2018
Registered Office: International House, 12 Constance Street, London, E16 2DQ
Shareholders: Cordelia Petra Nadine Rampley; Assia Kasdi
Officers: Dr Assia Kasdi [1988] Director/Scientist [French]; Dr Cordelia Petra Nadine Rampley [1989] Director/Scientist

Oxygen Skin Care - London Ltd
Incorporated: 12 February 2019
Registered Office: 53 Dale Close, Stanway, Colchester, Essex, CO3 0FQ
Shareholders: Flora Pitsiali; Charalambos Vassiliou
Officers: Charalambos Vassiliou, Secretary; Flora Pitsiali [1985] Director; Charalambos Vassiliou [1983] Director

Oya 9 Ltd
Incorporated: 24 August 2018
Registered Office: 71-75 Shelton Street, London, WC2H 9JQ
Major Shareholder: Andrea Lawrence
Officers: Andrea Lawrence [1964] Director

Oyemam Ltd
Incorporated: 19 February 2009
Registered Office: 71 Worcester Court, Tonyrefail, Porth, Rhondda Cynon Taf, CF39 8JU
Shareholders: Pearl Florence Hamre; Kjetil Hamre
Officers: Kjetil Hamre [1969] Director/Manager [Norwegian]; Pearl Florence Hamre [1968] Director/Manager [Norwegian]

Ozone Perfumes and Cosmetics Limited
Incorporated: 10 November 2011
Net Worth Deficit: £1,608 Total Assets: £199
Registered Office: 85 Great Portland Street, London, W1W 7LT
Major Shareholder: Sachin Arvind Bhavsar
Officers: Sachin Bhavsar [1976] Director [Indian]

Ozprodz Limited
Incorporated: 10 June 2009
Net Worth: £474,800 Total Assets: £571,420
Registered Office: Unit C1, Little Heath Industrial Estate, Old Church Road, Coventry, Warwicks, CV6 7ND
Shareholders: Nigel Alan Glaister; Laurence Edward Raymond Green
Officers: Laurence Edward Raymond Green, Secretary; Laurence Edward Raymond Green [1958] Director; Alan Stuart Maxwell [1971] Director/Business Development Manager

P & M Beauty Ltd
Incorporated: 7 November 2018
Registered Office: Willows, Cherry Tree Road, Farnham Royal, Slough, Berks, SL2 3EF
Shareholders: Roshni Shah; Sudhir Punja Shah
Officers: Pooja Shah [1988] Director/Accountant; Sudhir Punja Shah [1956] Director

P & P Cosmetics Ltd
Incorporated: 30 August 2018
Registered Office: Suite D, 10 Leyton Studios, 15 Argall Avenue, Leyton, London, E10 7QE
Shareholders: James Daniel Tharratt; Rhydian Ross Tharratt
Officers: James Daniel Tharratt [1979] Director

P & T PL Ltd
Incorporated: 27 January 2014
Net Worth Deficit: £27,110 Total Assets: £21,100
Registered Office: 24 Strathmore Avenue, Luton, Beds, LU1 3NZ
Major Shareholder: Tomasz Walkowiak
Officers: Tomasz Walkowiak [1978] Director/Manager [Polish]

P & Z Solutions Limited
Incorporated: 11 September 2018
Registered Office: 87 Fens Way, Swanley, Kent, BR8 7SW
Major Shareholder: Zdravka Stefanova
Officers: Zdravka Stefanova [1989] Director [Bulgarian]

P P Oil UK Limited
Incorporated: 15 January 2019
Registered Office: Flat 26, Arrandene Apartment, Silverworks Close, Colindale, London, NW9 0FA
Shareholders: Prince Shah; Jinali Meisheri
Officers: Jinali Meisheri [1985] Director; Prince Shah [1987] Director/Businessman [Indian]

P.H.A.B Wholesale Limited
Incorporated: 20 June 2002 Employees: 20
Net Worth: £234,469 Total Assets: £563,563
Registered Office: Unit 27 Trade City, Apple Lane, Sowton, Exeter, Devon, EX2 5GL
Shareholders: Grant Northover; Jane Northover
Officers: Jane Northover, Secretary; Grant Northover [1964] Director/Wholesaler; Jane Northover [1966] Director/Company Secretary

P.R. Professional Salon Supplies Limited
Incorporated: 23 October 2007 Employees: 4
Net Worth: £170,496 Total Assets: £329,774
Registered Office: 24 Brenda Road, Hartlepool, Cleveland, TS25 1QE
Shareholders: Peter Cesarano; Robert Michael Pailor; Mark Cesarano
Officers: Robert Michael Pailor, Secretary; Gerardo Cesarano [1946] Director [Italian]; Mark Cesarano [1975] Director; Peter Cesarano [1979] Director/Manager; Robert Michael Pailor [1980] Director/General Manager

P.T & Co Ltd
Incorporated: 20 August 2018
Registered Office: Suite 66, The Wenta Business Centre, Electric Avenue, Enfield, Middlesex, EN3 7XU
Major Shareholder: Paul Anh Hoang
Officers: Paul Anh Hoang [1990] Director/Businessman

Paiman Limited
Incorporated: 22 August 2014 Employees: 1
Net Worth: £102 Total Assets: £15,999
Registered Office: 76 Thomas Crescent, Smethwick, W Midlands, B66 3LF
Major Shareholder: Abdul Wadood Shirzad
Officers: Abdul Wadood Shirzad [1971] Director [Dutch]

Paint It Orange Ltd
Incorporated: 4 August 2016
Registered Office: Lynton House, 7-12 Tavistock Square, London, WC1H 9BQ
Major Shareholder: Jale Demirchi
Officers: Jale Demirchi [1988] Director [Bulgarian]

Pak Beauty Ltd
Incorporated: 21 October 2015
Registered Office: Unit 14 The Aylesham Centre, Rye Lane, London, SE15 5EW
Major Shareholder: Jabir Hussain Sarwar
Officers: Jabir Hussain Sarwar [1972] Director

Paliano Ltd
Incorporated: 23 July 2018
Registered Office: Flat 1, Whitewood House, 41 Hook Road, Surbiton, Surrey, KT6 5AA
Major Shareholder: Giulio Marchetti
Officers: Lauren Viegas Marchetti, Secretary; Giulio Marchetti [1981] Director [Italian/Brazilian]

Palmsextra Limited
Incorporated: 16 April 2003
Net Worth Deficit: £287,183 Total Assets: £90,603
Registered Office: 7 Holkham Road, Orton Southgate, Peterborough, Cambs, PE2 6TE
Officers: Linda Jean Reeve, Secretary; Kathryn Jane Darwin [1979] Director; Alison Suzanne Reeve [1982] Director; Linda Jean Reeve [1946] Director/Administrator; Robert George Reeve [1949] Managing Director

Pam Trading Limited
Incorporated: 13 July 2016
Net Worth Deficit: £12,250 Total Assets: £3,260
Registered Office: 5 The Square, Bagshot, Surrey, GU19 5AX
Officers: Paul Andrew Milner [1965] Director

Pampering Pattie International Limited
Incorporated: 1 October 2007
Net Worth: £23,248 Total Assets: £32,643
Registered Office: 23 Orford Court, Marsh Lane, Stanmore, Middlesex, HA7 4TQ
Major Shareholder: Lawrence Freeman
Officers: Karen Lisa Freeman, Secretary; Lawrence Freeman [1943] Director

Pandhy's UK Sweet Cosmetics Ltd.
Incorporated: 28 October 2014
Net Worth Deficit: £18,150 Total Assets: £16,670
Registered Office: 311 Shoreham Street, Sheffield, S2 4FA
Shareholders: Eva Borbiro Gertrud; Gabor Laszlo Simon
Officers: Gertrud Eva Borbiro [1967] Director [Hungarian]

Pandorra Ltd.
Incorporated: 14 December 2015
Net Worth Deficit: £2,299
Registered Office: Tally Accountants Ltd, Top Floor, College House, 17 King Edwards Road, Ruislip, Middlesex, HA4 7AE
Major Shareholder: Daniel Wilhelm
Officers: Daniel Wilhelm, Secretary; Daniel Wilhelm [1974] Managing Director [German]

Pangaea Laser Ltd
Incorporated: 17 September 2013
Registered Office: 35 Ballards Lane, London, N3 1XW
Shareholders: Hasan Ercan; Elliot James Isaacs
Officers: Hasan Ercan [1985] Director [Turkish]; Elliot James Isaacs [1971] Director

Paradise Organics London Ltd
Incorporated: 25 August 2015 Employees: 2
Net Worth Deficit: £18,613 Total Assets: £10,806
Registered Office: 3 Longmeadow Villas, Ifield Road, Charlwood, Horley, Surrey, RH6 0DJ
Shareholders: Ali Moussazadeh; Ali Moussazadeh
Officers: Ali Moussazadeh [1950] Director

Paradoxx Ltd
Incorporated: 13 February 2017
Net Worth Deficit: £1,019 Total Assets: £3,280
Registered Office: 3rd Floor, 1 Edward Street, Belfast, BT1 2LR
Major Shareholder: Yolanda Cooper
Officers: Claire Andrews [1987] Marketing Director; Yolanda Cooper [1985] Director; Sean Martin Curran [1969] Director [Irish]; Hilary Dart [1955] Director/Self Employed Consultant; Audrey Osborne [1984] Director/Investor [American]; Colin Reid [1957] Director

Paragon Enterprise Limited
Incorporated: 9 February 2009 Employees: 5
Net Worth Deficit: £3,600 Total Assets: £47,812
Registered Office: 1 & 2 Mercia Village, Torwood Close, Westwood Business Park, Coventry, Warwicks, CV4 8HX
Parent: Glow Beauty Shop Ltd
Officers: Asad Salman, Secretary; Salman Asad [1976] Director

Pareto Cosmedics Ltd
Incorporated: 30 April 2013
Previous: Busymint Ltd
Net Worth: £67,912 Total Assets: £103,849
Registered Office: 100 Chepstow Road, London, W2 5QP
Officers: John Robert Dalton [1983] Director [Australian]; Alison Halliwell [1974] Director/Importer

The Parfum Club Ltd
Incorporated: 12 August 2015
Net Worth Deficit: £4,866 Total Assets: £9,163
Registered Office: 195 Sutton Road, Walsall, W Midlands, WS5 3AW
Shareholders: Jeremy Patrick Bridgman; Claudia Virginia Olmos; Mark Edward Bridgman
Officers: Jeremy Patrick Bridgman [1958] Director/College Dean; Mark Edward Bridgman [1988] Director; Claudia Virginia Olmos [1964] Director/College Lecturer [Italian]

Parfume-Mania Ltd
Incorporated: 1 August 2018
Registered Office: 71-75 Shelton Street, Covent Garden, London, WC2H 9JQ
Major Shareholder: Tamas Vegh
Officers: Tamas Vegh, Secretary; Tamas Vegh [1979] Director/Self Employed [Hungarian]

Parfums Christian Dior (U.K.) Limited
Incorporated: 26 May 1971 Employees: 1,166
Net Worth: £7,907,075 Total Assets: £45,344,508
Registered Office: 6th Floor, United Kingdom House, 180 Oxford Street, London, W1D 1AB
Parent: LVMH Moet Hennessy Louis Vuitton
Officers: Loic Pierre Marie Henriot, Secretary; Bruno Angibeau [1960] Director [French]; Margaret Attwooll [1961] Director; Hugues Philippe Dusseaux [1954] Director/President [French]; Christiane Freund [1975] Director [German]; Loic Pierre Marie Henriot [1978] Director [French]; Claude Marie Joseph Martinez [1957] Director [French]; Bertrand Albert Francois Tefra [1969] Director [French]

Paris Elysees Holding Ltd.
Incorporated: 5 July 2018
Registered Office: c/o Downton Investment, 16 Upper Woburn Place, London, WC1H 0BS
Officers: Jean-Luc Seban [1957] Director [French]

Parker & Moses Ltd
Incorporated: 23 November 2017
Registered Office: Park House, Wilmington Street, Leeds, LS7 2BP
Major Shareholder: Ilyas Mohammed Salim
Officers: Ilyas Mohammed Salim [1988] Director/Businessman

Parkside Nails Supplies Ltd
Incorporated: 30 September 2003
Net Worth: £66,355 Total Assets: £936,757
Registered Office: Warehouse 6, Compass West Estate, 33 West Road, Tottenham, London, N17 0XL
Officers: Xuyen Thi Tran, Secretary; Son Thanh Tran [1971] Managing Director

Party Supplies and More Ltd
Incorporated: 22 January 2018
Registered Office: 53 Aireville Terrace, Ilkley, W Yorks, LS29 7LD
Major Shareholder: Lee McGowan
Officers: Lee McGowan [1989] Director

Passion 4 Health International Limited
Incorporated: 29 October 1997
Net Worth Deficit: £836,490 *Total Assets:* £304,832
Registered Office: Unit C, The Forum, Hanworth Lane, Chertsey, Surrey, KT16 9JX
Shareholder: Nadeem Dean Pasha
Officers: Seema Pasha, Secretary; Nadeem Pasha [1966] Managing Director

Patagonia Consult Limited
Incorporated: 11 December 2009
Net Worth: £36,816 *Total Assets:* £146,187
Registered Office: Office 34, 15 Falcon Road, London, SW11 2PJ
Major Shareholder: Marc Lee
Officers: Marc Geoffrey Lee [1957] Director/Accountant

Pause Skincare Limited
Incorporated: 8 March 2018
Registered Office: c/o Squirrels Wood, Reigate Road, Leatherhead, Surrey, KT22 8QY
Officers: Andrea Jean Feeney [1969] Director; Nicholas John Feeney [1972] Director

Pavone Profumi SRL Ltd
Incorporated: 20 February 2018
Registered Office: 20-22 Wenlock Road, London, N1 7GU
Major Shareholder: Dorin Eliodor Paun
Officers: Dorin Eliodor Paun [1969] Director [Romanian]

Danica Payne Ltd
Incorporated: 18 September 2018
Registered Office: Wessex House, Upper Market Street, Eastleigh, Hants, SO50 9FD
Major Shareholder: Danica Payne
Officers: Danica Payne [1993] Director

Pearl & Rocky Limited
Incorporated: 14 July 2017
Registered Office: Unit 2 Fordham House, Fordham, Ely, Cambs, CB7 5LL
Shareholders: Guy James Roger Westcott; Eleanor Howard Crowe
Officers: Eleanor Howard Crowe [1980] Director; Guy James Roger Westcott [1968] Director

Pearson Cosmetics Limited
Incorporated: 10 April 2015
Net Worth Deficit: £69,150 *Total Assets:* £314,940
Registered Office: Thorn House, Road One, Winsford Industrial Estate, Winsford, Cheshire, CW7 3PZ
Major Shareholder: Michael Norman Pearson
Officers: Michael Norman Pearson [1953] Managing Director

Peau Royale Limited
Incorporated: 4 October 2018
Registered Office: Suite D, 30 Goldsworthy Gardens, London, SE16 2TB
Major Shareholder: Zerthun Feltamo
Officers: Zerthun Feltamo [1983] Director/Self Employed [Ethiopian]

Pebbles Creative Ltd
Incorporated: 7 March 2016
Net Worth: £12,280 *Total Assets:* £129,130
Registered Office: 1st Floor, Cloister House, New Bailey Street, Salford, M3 5FS
Major Shareholder: Atul Thakrar
Officers: Atul Thakrar [1967] Managing Director

Pellitier & Perkins Limited
Incorporated: 26 March 2009 *Employees:* 2
Previous: Ribbonbill Services Limited
Net Worth: £590 *Total Assets:* £612,536
Registered Office: Charles House, 108-110 Finchley Road, London, NW3 5JJ
Shareholders: Yardena Landman; Peter Benedict Stone
Officers: Michelle Paradisgarten [1953] Director/Administrator Executive; Laura Maria Stan [1978] Director [Romanian]

Pennies and Feathers Limited
Incorporated: 24 October 2016
Net Worth Deficit: £15,415
Registered Office: First Floor, 85 Great Portland Street, London, W1W 7LT
Major Shareholder: Jessica Hurley
Officers: Jessica Hurley [1989] Director/Hair and Makeup Artist

Penny Price Aromatherapy Ltd
Incorporated: 21 May 2003
Net Worth: £260,240 *Total Assets:* £340,260
Registered Office: D3, Radius Court, Maple Way, Hinckley, Leics, LE10 3BE
Shareholders: Penelope Anne Stephen; Revd Dr Robert Stephen
Officers: Revd Dr Robert Stephen, Secretary; Penelope Anne Stephen [1957] Director/Aromatherapist; Revd Dr Robert Stephen [1963] Director/Teacher

Pennystore Limited
Incorporated: 10 October 2017
Registered Office: 36 Windsor Road, Ilford, Essex, IG1 1HQ
Officers: Rajinder Jassi [1978] Director/Businessman [Indian]

Per Capelli Ltd
Incorporated: 17 January 2014 *Employees:* 4
Net Worth: £22,065 *Total Assets:* £76,324
Registered Office: First Floor Office, 34 Great Queen Street, London, WC2B 5AA
Shareholders: Gokmen Kaymakam; Altug Erdal Mehmet; Yucem Salih
Officers: Gokmen Kaymakam [1979] Director; Altug Erdal Mehmet [1975] Director; Yucem Salih [1984] Director/Salesman

Per-Scent Fine Limited
Incorporated: 28 May 2003
Net Worth: £183,020 *Total Assets:* £3,830,000
Registered Office: Churchill Point, Lake Edge Green, Trafford Park, Manchester, M17 1BL
Officers: Sanjay Jayantilal Vadera, Secretary/Managing Director; Sanjay Jayantilal Vadera [1967] Managing Director; Vipul Jayantilal Vadera [1972] Director

Per-Scent Group Limited
Incorporated: 16 December 1994
Net Worth: £4,340,000 *Total Assets:* £8,250,000
Registered Office: Churchill Point, Lake Edge Green, Trafford Park Road, Manchester, M17 1BL
Parent: Fragrance Acquisitions Ltd
Officers: Sanjay Jayantilal Vadera, Secretary; Sanjay Jayantilal Vadera [1967] Managing Director; Vipul Jayantilal Vadera [1972] Director

Per-Scent Limited
Incorporated: 29 September 2004
Net Worth: £57,220,000 *Total Assets:* £68,810,000
Registered Office: Churchill Point, Lake Edge Green, Trafford Park Road, Manchester, M17 1BL
Parent: Per-Scent Group Ltd
Officers: Sanjay Jayantilal Vadera, Secretary; Sanjay Jayantilal Vadera [1967] Director; Vipul Jayantilal Vadera [1972] Director

Pera Cosmetics Ltd
Incorporated: 13 December 2017
Registered Office: c/o FMA Accountants Ltd, Building 3, Chiswick Business Park, 566 Chiswick High Road, Chiswick, London, W4 5YA
Major Shareholder: Dogan Yener
Officers: Dogan Yener [1980] Managing Director [Turkish]

Perezoso Limited
Incorporated: 2 June 2014
Net Worth: £1,090 *Total Assets:* £11,695
Registered Office: First Floor, 85 Great Portland Street, London, W1W 7LT
Major Shareholder: Katarzyna Rutka
Officers: Katarzyna Rutka [1988] Director/Manager [Polish]

The Perfect Lady Ltd
Incorporated: 22 November 2017
Registered Office: 45 Preston New Road, Blackburn, BB2 6AE
Major Shareholder: Farzeen Jalal
Officers: Farzeen Jalal, Secretary; Farzeen Jalal [2000] Director

Perfect Look & Health Ltd
Incorporated: 2 July 2008
Net Worth: £23,760 *Total Assets:* £51,190
Registered Office: Collagen House, 2 Duchess Street, Whitley Bay, Tyne & Wear, NE26 3PW
Shareholder: Stephen Maurice Mack
Officers: Kimberley Mack, Secretary; Kimberley Mack [1958] Director/Administration; Stephen Mack [1955] Director/Sales

Perfectly Natural Limited
Incorporated: 19 April 2017
Registered Office: 3 Clonmel Way, Burnham, Slough, SL1 7DA
Shareholders: Slavka Hayden; Andrew Gavin Hayden
Officers: Andrew Gavin Hayden [1982] Director/Sales; Slavka Hayden [1985] Director/Marketing Executive [Slovak]

Perfume Addict (UK) Ltd
Incorporated: 16 March 2010 *Employees:* 4
Net Worth: £511,999 *Total Assets:* £639,829
Registered Office: 85-87 Saltergate, Chesterfield, Derbys, S40 1JS
Shareholders: Brett Heaps; Jane Belshaw
Officers: Brett Heaps, Secretary; Jane Belshaw [1975] Director; Brett Heaps [1987] Managing Director

Perfume Bodega Dist. Ltd
Incorporated: 9 January 2019
Registered Office: Stall 12, Coventry Retail Market, Queen Victoria Road, Coventry, Warwicks, CV1 3HT
Major Shareholder: Maxine Ann Milton
Officers: Maxine Ann Milton [1968] Director/Accounts Manager

Perfume Brands Limited
Incorporated: 31 May 2018
Registered Office: Tiptrans (Perfume Brands), Suite 7913, 2e Parkinson Road, Liverpool, L9 1DL
Major Shareholder: Zed Tereq Sefi
Officers: Zed Tereq Sefi [1979] Director/Online Retail

Perfume Essence Ltd
Incorporated: 22 January 2013
Net Worth: £25,272 *Total Assets:* £179,342
Registered Office: 334 Slade Lane, Manchester, M19 2BL
Major Shareholder: Chanchal Soni
Officers: Chanchal Soni [1965] Director

Perfume Holding UK Limited
Incorporated: 26 April 2010
Previous: MSB Perfume Holdings Limited
Net Worth: £105,606 *Total Assets:* £1,271,499
Registered Office: Sundial House, High Street, Horsell, Woking, Surrey, GU21 4SU
Officers: Giovanni Borri [1943] Director [Italian]; Leonardo Cullura [1965] Director [Italian]

The Perfume Lab Limited
Incorporated: 23 September 2014
Net Worth: £1,244 *Total Assets:* £86,498
Registered Office: 3 The Coach House, 24 Station Road, Shirehampton, Bristol, BS11 9TX

Perfume London Ltd
Incorporated: 11 December 2015
Net Worth: £18,342 *Total Assets:* £1,182,925
Registered Office: Unit 17 Barrett Industrial Park, Park Avenue, Southall, Middlesex, UB1 3AF
Major Shareholder: Amrit Giri
Officers: Amrit Giri [1993] Director

Perfume Outlet Ltd
Incorporated: 13 December 2017
Registered Office: Office 1, 5 Mill Street, Bideford, Devon, EX39 2JT
Major Shareholder: Timothy Ahlbeck
Officers: Lord Timothy Ahlbeck [1983] Managing Director; Timothy Skelding [1983] Operations Director

Perfume Supplies Limited
Incorporated: 10 March 2004
Net Worth: £472,120 *Total Assets:* £1,080,000
Registered Office: Garrison House, Sutton Garrison, Byrons Lane, Macclesfield, Cheshire, SK11 7JW
Officers: Katherine Jowle, Secretary; Katherine Jowle [1964] Director

Perfume World Limited
Incorporated: 10 May 2000 *Employees:* 1
Net Worth: £62,811 *Total Assets:* £108,056
Registered Office: 86 Polwarth Road, Brunton Park, Newcastle upon Tyne, NE3 5NE
Parent: B & S International BV
Officers: Francis Malcolm Turnbull, Secretary; Minke Petra Bijma [1968] Director [Dutch]; Gerrit Van Laar [1954] Director [Dutch]

Perfumeprice.co.uk Ltd
Incorporated: 22 January 2016
Registered Office: 9 High Street, Wellington, Somerset, TA21 8QT
Shareholders: Alexander James Elliman; Maryna Elliman
Officers: Alexander James Elliman [1973] Director; Maryna Elliman [1984] Director [Ukrainian]

The Perfumer Ltd
Incorporated: 3 June 2016
Registered Office: 52 Kendal Drive, Slough, Berks, SL2 5JA
Major Shareholder: Saheel Haroon Akhtar
Officers: Soumiya El Battari, Secretary; Saheel Haroon Akhtar [1979] Director

Perfumes Logistics & Distribution Limited
Incorporated: 21 July 2017
Registered Office: 103 High Street, Waltham Cross, Herts, EN8 7AN
Shareholders: David Jacob; Rahel Jacob-Karol
Officers: David Jacob [1962] Director [Israeli]; Rahel Jacob-Karol [1963] Director/Home Maker [Israeli]

Perfumez Limited
Incorporated: 10 October 2018
Registered Office: 18 Roneo Corner, Hornchurch, Essex, RM12 4TN
Major Shareholder: Amani Omar
Officers: Amani Omar [1976] Director/Marketing Executive

Pern Consumer Products Limited
Incorporated: 21 February 2007
Net Worth: £1,370,000 *Total Assets:* £1,770,000
Registered Office: Quantum House, Hobson Industrial Estate, Burnopfield, Co Durham, NE16 6EA
Officers: Amanda Miller, Secretary; David John Bryant [1967] Director/Chief Business Officer; Richard John Paling [1970] Director/Group Financial Controller; David Alan Sanson [1959] Quality Director

Perricone MD Cosmeceuticals UK Limited
Incorporated: 14 January 2008 *Employees:* 20
Net Worth Deficit: £351,038 *Total Assets:* £8,062,350
Registered Office: rear Mezzanine, 16-18 Berners Street, London, W1T 3LN
Officers: Ronald Lee Fugate [1957] Director/Chief Executive Officer [American]; Tracey Mann [1966] Director/Chief International Officer; Susan Vandegrift [1964] Director [American]

Pet Scentuary Ltd
Incorporated: 24 May 2018
Registered Office: Stephen R Allen & Co, Unit 11 Priory Park, Hessle, E Yorks, HU13 9PB
Shareholders: Derek Long; Susan Mary Long
Officers: Derek Long [1952] Director/Wholesaler; Susan Mary Long [1956] Director/Operations Manager

Peters Cosmet Ltd
Incorporated: 3 August 2018
Registered Office: 7 Kings Avenue, Manchester, M8 5AS
Major Shareholder: Janusz Jan Burdak
Officers: Janusz Jan Burdak [1971] Director/Manager [Polish]; Beata Krolikowska [1974] Director [Polish]; Elzbieta Malgorzata Schutz [1967] Director [Polish]

Petersham Ventures Ltd
Incorporated: 16 April 2015
Net Worth: £100 *Total Assets:* £100
Registered Office: 115 London Road, Morden, Surrey, SM4 5HP
Shareholders: Zeeshan Tayyeb; Omur Turan
Officers: Zeeshan Tayyeb [1976] Director/Entrepreneur; Omur Turan [1976] Director/Entrepreneur

PH Group UK Limited
Incorporated: 5 July 2000 *Employees:* 16
Net Worth: £566,230 *Total Assets:* £875,982
Registered Office: 28 Darklake View, Estover, Plymouth, PL6 7TL
Parent: Darklake Limited
Officers: Carol Ann Harper, Secretary; Carol Ann Harper [1949] Director/Secretary; Lee Paul Harper [1974] Managing Director; Paul Dennis Harper [1948] Director; Tony Stephen Tremain [1984] Director

Pharma Medico Limited
Incorporated: 31 January 2013 *Employees:* 6
Net Worth Deficit: £55,704 *Total Assets:* £1,265,051
Registered Office: First Floor, 10 Temple Back, Bristol, BS1 6FL
Parent: Pharma Medico UK Limited
Officers: Geoffrey Stuart Cleall-Harding [1950] Director/Accountant; Christopher John Keeble [1961] Director

Pharmacare (Europe) Limited
Incorporated: 24 October 2007 *Employees:* 36
Net Worth Deficit: £2,150,795 *Total Assets:* £6,085,796
Registered Office: The Old Rectory, Church Street, Weybridge, Surrey, KT13 8DE
Major Shareholder: Toby Rowley Browne
Officers: Toby Rowley Browne, Secretary/Director [Australian]; Toby Rowley Browne [1953] Director [Australian]; Anthony John Robertson [1973] Director [Australian]

Pharmacare International Ltd
Incorporated: 28 December 2018
Registered Office: 96-98 Baker Street, London, W1U 6TJ
Major Shareholder: Sanaa Al-Hadethee
Officers: Sanaa Al-Hadethee [1964] Director

Pharmaclinix Limited
Incorporated: 24 January 2005
Net Worth: £191,481 *Total Assets:* £260,287
Registered Office: Unit 3 Issigonis House, Cowley Road, London, W3 7UN
Shareholders: Shashi Kiran Gossain; Jagdeep Balram Gossain
Officers: Dr. Jagdeep Balram Gossain [1958] Director/Manager-Research & Development; Shashi Kiran Gossain [1958] Director/Pharmacist; Shiv Nandan Gossain [1989] Director; Sarita Pindoria [1986] Director; Vanita Rattan [1983] Director

Pharmadose Limited
Incorporated: 1 December 2010 *Employees:* 13
Net Worth: £254,573 *Total Assets:* £3,458,054
Registered Office: Unit 14 Dodson Way, Fen Gate, Peterborough, Cambs, PE1 5XJ
Shareholders: Svikrut Patel; Amita Patel; Divyeshkumar Patel
Officers: Divyesh Kumar Patel [1976] Director/Pharmacy Technician; Krishan Janak Patel [1989] Director/Financial Analyst; Svikrut Patel [1980] Director

Pharmafrance Ltd.
Incorporated: 3 February 2017 *Employees:* 1
Net Worth Deficit: £359 *Total Assets:* £1
Registered Office: A52 Ambassador Building, 5 New Union Square, London, SW11 7BN
Major Shareholder: Capucine Marie Camille Deroulede
Officers: Capucine Marie Camille Deroulede [1993] Director/Student [French]

Pharmdex UK Ltd
Incorporated: 25 September 2018
Registered Office: 14 Gainsborough Road, New Malden, Surrey, KT3 5NU
Major Shareholder: Geon Lee
Officers: Geon Lee [1982] Director [South Korean]

PHB Franchise Limited
Incorporated: 6 June 2011
Net Worth Deficit: £30,466 *Total Assets:* £14,439
Registered Office: Unit 21 Mucklow Hill, Halesowen, W Midlands, B62 8TP
Shareholders: Sally Ann Gibbins; John Peter Francis Tierney; Rose Anna Brown
Officers: Sally Ann Gibbins [1964] Director/Businesswoman; John Peter Francis Tierney [1988] Director/Businessman

Pheora Rucci Limited
Incorporated: 4 July 2018
Registered Office: B06, Railton House, 10 Craven Hill, London, W2 3DT
Major Shareholder: Twamanguluka Ndayaamena Nambili
Officers: Twamanguluka Ndayaamena Nambili [1990] Director/Entrepreneur [Namibian]

Pherolec Global Ltd
Incorporated: 6 April 2017
Net Worth Deficit: £2,860 *Total Assets:* £1,380
Registered Office: Suite 2, Old Town Court, Queensway, Hemel Hempstead, Herts, HP2 5HD
Major Shareholder: Julia Ferdek-Guzik
Officers: Julia Ferdek-Guzik [1988] Director [Polish]

Phi Advisory & Consulting Ltd
Incorporated: 1 May 2018
Registered Office: Kemp House, 160 City Road, London, EC1V 2NX
Major Shareholder: Stephane Cherif
Officers: Stephane Cherif, Secretary

Phils (Wholesale) Limited
Incorporated: 2 September 1963 *Employees:* 3
Net Worth: £2,594,309 *Total Assets:* £2,670,200
Registered Office: 484 Honeypot Lane, Stanmore, Middlesex, HA7 1JR
Major Shareholder: Mark Leonard Davis
Officers: Mark Leonard Davis, Secretary; Mark Leonard Davis [1964] Managing Director; Sylvia Davis [1943] Director

Phoenix Beauty Ltd
Incorporated: 30 May 2018
Registered Office: 2nd Floor, College House, 17 King Edwards Road, Ruislip, Middlesex, HA4 7AE
Shareholder: Margaret Shiers
Officers: Amy Buckley [1986] Marketing Director; Margaret Shiers [1962] Sales Director

Phoenix Hair & Beauty (Ely) Limited
Incorporated: 6 May 2015 *Employees:* 10
Net Worth: £43,803 *Total Assets:* £475,143
Registered Office: Unit 6 Norman Business Park, Thorby Avenue, March, Cambs, PE15 0AR
Major Shareholder: Sandra May Summerlee
Officers: Mishah Summerlee [1988] Director; Sandra May Summerlee [1963] Director; Tegan Summerlee [1995] Director

Photics Skincare Ltd
Incorporated: 20 November 2018
Registered Office: 25 Eliot Drive, St Germans, Saltash, Cornwall, PL12 5NL
Major Shareholder: Anisoara Huettemann
Officers: Anisoara Huettemann [1991] Director [German]; Nathan Paul Smith [1993] Director/Designer

Photonic Limited
Incorporated: 6 February 2017 *Employees:* 2
Net Worth: £2,753 *Total Assets:* £133,659
Registered Office: 35 Crowden Way, London, SE28 8HE
Shareholders: Binrui Zhang; Binrui Zhang
Officers: Binrui Zhang [1993] Director [Chinese]

Phyto Pharm Limited
Incorporated: 12 October 2016
Registered Office: 5 Jupiter House, Calleva Park, Aldermaston, Reading, Berks, RG7 8NN
Major Shareholder: Laura Catherine Dewar
Officers: Laura Dewar [1957] Director

Phyto Pharma Limited
Incorporated: 13 October 2016
Registered Office: 5 Jupiter House, Calleva Park, Aldermaston, Reading, Berks, RG7 8NN
Major Shareholder: Laura Catherine Dewar
Officers: Laura Catherine Dewar [1957] Director

Phyto Therapeutics Limited
Incorporated: 4 September 1995
Net Worth: £1,010,000 *Total Assets:* £1,150,000
Registered Office: 337 Baslow Road, Totley, Sheffield, S17 4AD
Major Shareholder: Kathryn Rachel Cavan
Officers: Kathryn Rachel Cavan, Secretary/Beauty Therapist; Kathryn Rachel Cavan [1963] Director/Beauty Therapist

Angela Pickering Limited
Incorporated: 7 January 2016
Net Worth: £18,224 *Total Assets:* £27,848
Registered Office: 23 Calverley Drive, Leeds, LS13 3LN
Major Shareholder: Angela Pickering
Officers: Angela Pickering [1957] Director

Piggy Paint UK Ltd
Incorporated: 8 December 2016
Net Worth Deficit: £13,391 *Total Assets:* £12,375
Registered Office: Unit 12 Stafford Industrial Estate, Hillman Close, Romford, Essex, RM11 2SJ
Officers: Mark William Phillips [1977] Director; Natalie Rebecca Phillips [1952] Director; Georgina Smedley [1973] Director; Jason Kenneth Smedley [1970] Director

Pilaten EU Ltd
Incorporated: 10 February 2017
Net Worth: £100 *Total Assets:* £100
Registered Office: 120 High Road, East Finchley, London, N2 9ED
Major Shareholder: Lionel Farjon
Officers: Lionel Farjon [1987] Managing Director [Canadian]

Pink Beauty Supplies (UK) Ltd.
Incorporated: 22 June 2005
Net Worth Deficit: £239,910 *Total Assets:* £36,520
Registered Office: 35 Sherwood Street, Warsop, Mansfield, Notts, NG20 0JR
Shareholders: Tony Chien Feng Chan; Pailin Chan
Officers: Tony Chien Feng Chan, Secretary; Tony Chien Feng Chan [1973] Director/Importer

Pink Cosmetics London Limited
Incorporated: 5 August 2009 *Employees:* 4
Net Worth: £474,917 *Total Assets:* £621,593
Registered Office: 76 Manchester Road, Denton, Manchester, M35 3PS
Shareholders: Patricia Anne Helsby; John Douglas Ratcliffe
Officers: Patricia Anne Helsby, Secretary; Patricia Anne Helsby [1947] Director; John Douglas Ratcliffe [1946] Sales Director

Pink Empire Limited
Incorporated: 3 February 2017
Net Worth Deficit: £6,230
Registered Office: Premier Business Centre, Unit M7, 47-49 Park Royal Road, London, NW10 7LQ
Shareholders: Qassem Al-Kitabi; Subhi Sultan
Officers: Qassem Al-Kitabi [1980] Director [Jordanian]; Subhi Sultan [1986] Director [Jordanian]

Pink Lush Lips Ltd
Incorporated: 25 September 2018
Registered Office: 20-22 Wenlock Road, London, N1 7GU
Major Shareholder: Crystal Paris Jadine Bryan
Officers: Crystal Paris Jadine Bryan [1991] Director/Train Dispatcher

Pink Parasol Ltd
Incorporated: 11 June 2016
Registered Office: 6th Floor, Cardinall House, 20 St Mary's Parsonage, Manchester, M3 2LG
Major Shareholder: Atul Thakrar
Officers: Atul Thakrar [1967] Managing Director

Pinklady International Ltd
Incorporated: 26 March 2018
Registered Office: Kemp House, 160 City Road, London, EC1V 2NX
Officers: Norzaidah Abdul Razak [1986] 2nd Director [Malaysian]; Heidi Shafiq Haidzir [1986] Director [Malaysian]

Pinnacle Pharma Limited
Incorporated: 5 April 2016
Registered Office: Palladium House, 1-4 Argyll Street, London, W1F 7LD
Officers: Alan Jeremy Bloom [1962] Director; Malcolm Yesner [1957] Director [Australian]

Pinoline Trading Company Ltd
Incorporated: 22 June 2012
Net Worth Deficit: £2,073 *Total Assets:* £19,787
Registered Office: 249 Fordwych Road, London, NW2 3LY
Major Shareholder: Hussein Darwiche
Officers: Hussein Darwiche [1970] Director [Lebanese]

Pippa Beauty Limited
Incorporated: 18 February 2005
Net Worth Deficit: £16,130 *Total Assets:* £106,730
Registered Office: 1a The Moorings, Dane Road Industrial Estate, Sale, Cheshire, M33 7BH
Major Shareholder: Simon Charles Wheeler Moorehead
Officers: Simon Charles Wheeler Moorehead, Secretary; Simon Charles Wheeler Moorehead [1962] Director/Chartered Accountant

Pispo Ltd
Incorporated: 3 January 2012
Net Worth: £17,300 *Total Assets:* £207,170
Registered Office: Unit 9 London Road, West Kingsdown, Sevenoaks, Kent, TN15 6ES
Major Shareholder: Cristina Racca
Officers: Cristina Racca [1978] Director [Italian]

Pixie Crypt Ltd
Incorporated: 24 March 2017
Registered Office: 5 Thornford Road, Yetminster, Sherborne, Dorset, DT9 6LW
Major Shareholder: Charlotte Elena Martin
Officers: Charlotte Elena Martin [1994] Managing Director

Pixie Dust Products Limited
Incorporated: 24 August 2011
Net Worth: £15,398 *Total Assets:* £1,322,901
Registered Office: 38 Queen Street, Glasgow, G1 3DX
Shareholder: Laura Weir
Officers: Angela Davidson, Secretary; John Paul Weir [1967] Director/Sales Executive; Laura Weir [1975] Director

Pixie Lott Paint Limited
Incorporated: 18 September 2017
Registered Office: 5 Armston Road, Quorn, Loughborough, Leics, LE12 8QP
Major Shareholder: David James Sear-Mayes
Officers: David James Sear-Mayes [1961] Director

Pixie Porter Ltd
Incorporated: 11 March 2014
Registered Office: Flat 136, Trident Point, 19 Pinner Road, Harrow, Middlesex, HA1 4FW
Officers: Amina Ahmed Butt, Secretary; Amina Ahmed Butt [1984] Director/Administrative Officer

Pizzaz Ventures Limited
Incorporated: 21 February 2018
Registered Office: 71a Gordon Avenue, Stanmore, Middlesex, HA7 3QR
Officers: Alisha Ahluwalia, Secretary; Hardaman Bamby Ahluwalia [1968] Director

PL Distribution Ltd
Incorporated: 27 February 2018
Registered Office: 53b Crossgate House, Irwin Street, Denton, Manchester, M34 2AX
Major Shareholder: Patricia Corry
Officers: Patricia Corry [1965] Director

Plan Target Limited
Incorporated: 9 March 2005
Previous: Plan Target Vision Limited
Net Worth Deficit: £146,015 *Total Assets:* £176,186
Registered Office: Bray Business Centre, Weir Bank, Bray, Maidenhead, Berks, SL6 2ED
Officers: Bipin Patel, Secretary/IFA; Bhash Valambia [1969] Director/Business Consultant

Plane Luxuries Limited
Incorporated: 15 April 2011
Registered Office: 226 Upper Richmond Road, London, SW15 6TG
Major Shareholder: Louise Kirkby
Officers: Louise Kirkby [1983] Director/Barrister

Planet Sparkle Ltd
Incorporated: 8 June 2018
Registered Office: 31 High Street, Chapel-en-le-Frith, High Peak, Derbys, SK23 9SS
Shareholders: Lauren Kate Holmes; Julie Kay Holmes; Jennifer Lea Bamford Holmes
Officers: Lauren Kate Holmes [1988] Director/Retail Manager

Plant Me Botanics Ltd
Incorporated: 15 October 2014
Registered Office: 2 Higher Barn, Crossways, Dorchester, DT2 8BT
Officers: Sandra Paddon, Secretary; Paul Berrow [1952] Director

Plantain Essential Oils Ltd
Incorporated: 6 March 2008 Employees: 1
Net Worth: £683 Total Assets: £69,976
Registered Office: Stable Cottage, Kislingbury Grange, Rothersthorpe Road, Kislingbury, Northants, NN7 4AB
Major Shareholder: Tracy Ann Turner
Officers: Tracy Ann Turner [1963] Director

Plants Work Limited
Incorporated: 29 November 2018
Registered Office: 14 Slington House, Rankine Road, Basingstoke, Hants, RG24 8PH
Major Shareholder: Olufemi Odutola
Officers: Olufemi Odutola [1960] Director [Nigerian]

PLBrands Limited
Incorporated: 7 June 2018
Registered Office: 10 The Crescent, Farnham, Surrey, GU9 0LE
Major Shareholder: Sarah Louise Evans
Officers: Sarah Louise Evans [1971] Director/Chief Executive

Plectra Polish Limited
Incorporated: 9 October 2012
Net Worth Deficit: £11,550 Total Assets: £9,084
Registered Office: The Old Vicarage, Vicarage Lane, Ugley, Bishop's Stortford, Herts, CM22 6HU
Major Shareholder: Hannah Elisabeth Igbon-Woods
Officers: Hannah Igbon-Woods [1978] Director/Financial Controller

Plenaire Limited
Incorporated: 26 January 2018
Registered Office: 4 Bovingdon Road, London, SW6 2AP
Parent: Shalohm Ltd
Officers: Namrata Nayyar-Kamdar [1976] Director [Indian]

Plenteous Ltd
Incorporated: 4 October 2018
Registered Office: Edgbaston Studio, 7 Raglan Road, Birmingham, B5 7RA
Major Shareholder: Okpoti George Jeremy Oddoye
Officers: Okpoti George Jeremy Oddoye [1995] Director/Student [British/Ghanaian]

Ploom (U.K.) Limited
Incorporated: 12 October 2018
Registered Office: Kemp House, 160 City Road, London, EC1V 2NX
Shareholders: Steve Wishart; Alia Samai Barros Silva
Officers: Steve Wishart, Secretary; Alia Samai Barros Silva [1988] Director/Founder [Brazilian]

PLTradeGroup Limited
Incorporated: 26 May 2016
Net Worth: £88 Total Assets: £4,000
Registered Office: Flat 2, 7-9 Herbert Road, Nottingham, NG5 1BS
Major Shareholder: Mikolaj Anusiewicz
Officers: Mikolaj Anusiewicz [1985] Director [Polish]

Plush Soap Ltd
Incorporated: 8 January 2019
Registered Office: 13 Brewer Street, Maidstone, Kent, ME14 1RU
Shareholders: Timothy William Licence; Wendy Patricia Licence
Officers: Timothy William Licence [1988] Director/Retailer; Wendy Patricia Licence [1957] Director/Local Government Officer

Pococks Absolute Rose Ltd
Incorporated: 19 October 2015
Net Worth Deficit: £2,867 Total Assets: £22,869
Registered Office: 2 Hickory Drive, Winchester, Hants, SO22 6NJ
Major Shareholder: Stewart Pocock
Officers: Rebecca Ann Pocock [1959] Director/Rose Grower; Stewart James Pocock [1964] Director/Rose Grower

Polar Export Services Limited
Incorporated: 7 December 1988
Net Worth Deficit: £73,780 Total Assets: £38,540
Registered Office: 40 Weaverton Drive, Rhyl, Denbighshire, LL18 4LB
Major Shareholder: Peter Walter Harrison
Officers: Alan Harrison, Secretary; Peter Walter Harrison [1954] Director

Polcosmetics Ltd
Incorporated: 25 January 2018
Registered Office: 1st Floor, Gibson House, 800 High Road, London, N17 0DH
Major Shareholder: Rafal Klosinski
Officers: Rafal Klosinski [1973] Director

Pole Position (Licensing) Limited
Incorporated: 15 December 2005
Net Worth Deficit: £262,230 Total Assets: £752,000
Registered Office: 1st Floor, Puerorum House, 26 Great Queen Street, London, WC2B 5BB
Major Shareholder: Simon Gook
Officers: Simon Gook [1964] Director

Polex Limited
Incorporated: 17 September 1958
Net Worth: £1,636,613 Total Assets: £1,760,319
Registered Office: 23-25 Sherbrooke Road, London, SW6 7QJ
Shareholder: Martin Klocek
Officers: Peter Adonis Klocek, Secretary; Henry Stanislaw Klocek [1952] Director; Mark Henryk Klocek [1979] Director; Martin Klocek [1975] Director; Peter Adonis Klocek [1964] Director

Polish Cosmetics Distribution Centre UK Limited
Incorporated: 19 September 2016
Net Worth Deficit: £4,339 Total Assets: £24,073
Registered Office: 50 Smithfield Road, Market Drayton, Salop, TF9 1EN
Major Shareholder: Wojciech Hoja
Officers: Wojciech Hoja [1988] Director [Polish]

Pommade Divine Skincare Limited
Incorporated: 13 December 2017
Registered Office: 38 Turner Street, London, E1 2AS
Major Shareholder: Nicholas James Richmond
Officers: Anna Maria Adelaide Richmond [1984] Director/Entrepreneur

Pompadour Laboratories Limited
Incorporated: 29 December 1947
Registered Office: Capital Hair & Beauty, Crowhurst Road, Brighton, BN1 8AP
Parent: Capital (Hair & Beauty) Ltd
Officers: Hamish Michael Vans Agnew [1958] Director; Peter Ross Vans Agnew [1960] Managing Director

Portland House International Trading Limited
Incorporated: 16 November 2010 *Employees:* 5
Net Worth Deficit: £448,774 *Total Assets:* £6,800
Registered Office: P O Box 978, Sidings Court, Lakeside, Doncaster, S Yorks, DN4 5NU
Parent: Portland Holdings & Investements Limited
Officers: Sally Kathryn Summers, Secretary; Helen Mary Arjomandkhah [1962] Director; Nardair Arjomandkhah [1989] Director; Samir Arjomandkhah [1991] Director

Portobello Organics Ltd
Incorporated: 15 October 2018
Registered Office: 66 Hindes Road, Harrow, Middlesex, HA1 1SL
Major Shareholder: Brian Francis McKay
Officers: Brian Francis McKay [1974] Director/Artist

Posh Gift Ltd
Incorporated: 9 February 2017
Net Worth Deficit: £4,500 *Total Assets:* £1,000
Registered Office: 1 Times Square, High Street, Sutton, Surrey, SM1 1LF
Major Shareholder: Seefat Mustafa
Officers: Seefat Mustafa [1993] Director/Business Manager [Bangladeshi]

Sara Post Ltd
Incorporated: 27 February 2015
Net Worth: £1,520 *Total Assets:* £12,790
Registered Office: 10 Bissell Street, Birmingham, B5 7HP
Major Shareholder: Soran Rashid
Officers: Soran Rashid [1974] Director

Pota Nini Limited
Incorporated: 28 August 2018
Registered Office: K-Hair Studio, Mandarin Wharf, 70-76 De Beauvoir Crescent, London, N1 5SB
Major Shareholder: Keiichiro Hirano
Officers: Keiichiro Hirano [1973] Director/Hair Stylist [Japanese]

Potion Dynamo Limited
Incorporated: 9 February 2018
Registered Office: 127 Cambridge Street, London, SW1V 4PZ
Shareholders: Elise Bari Kandrac; Martin Kandrac
Officers: Elise Bari Kandrac [1970] Director

Potions & Possibilities Limited
Incorporated: 2 February 2017
Registered Office: 10 Kindlewood Drive, Toton, Nottingham, NG9 6NE
Major Shareholder: Lu Wang
Officers: Lu Wang, Secretary; Lu Wang [1977] Director [Chinese]

Potteries Transport Services Ltd
Incorporated: 23 April 2018
Registered Office: 73 Heath Avenue, Newcastle-under-Lyme, Staffs, ST5 9NU
Major Shareholder: Andrew Pickerill
Officers: Andrew Pickerill [1986] Director/Salesman

Pound Ring Ltd
Incorporated: 21 June 2012
Net Worth Deficit: £101,587 *Total Assets:* £131,003
Registered Office: 226-228 Northolt Road, Harrow, Middlesex, HA2 8DU
Officers: Ragini Sabesan [1976] Director/Businesswoman

Pouty Lipzz Limited
Incorporated: 24 April 2014
Net Worth Deficit: £20,470 *Total Assets:* £47,010
Registered Office: Northside House, Mount Pleasant, Barnet, Herts, EN4 9EE
Major Shareholder: Roy Henry Presswell
Officers: Joanne Sarah Hurst [1972] Director; James Stephen Presswell [1978] Director; June Linda Presswell [1950] Director; Roy Henry Presswell [1948] Director

Powered By Nature Cosmetics Limited
Incorporated: 27 November 2018
Registered Office: 59 Gainsborough Road, London, N12 8AA
Major Shareholder: Bianca Jane Sobell
Officers: Bianca Jane Sobell [1984] Managing Director

Pravera Ltd
Incorporated: 20 March 2001 *Employees:* 14
Net Worth: £166,337 *Total Assets:* £544,179
Registered Office: Conchieton Business Centre, Kirkcudbright, Dumfries & Galloway, DG6 4TA
Officers: Graeme Paul Hume [1953] Director

Precision Brows and Lashes Limited
Incorporated: 26 January 2018
Registered Office: 27 Maldon Drive, Eccles, Manchester, M30 9LU
Major Shareholder: Alix Sobowale
Officers: Alix Sobowale [1986] Business Director

Predator Trading Limited
Incorporated: 5 November 2008 *Employees:* 2
Net Worth: £175,947 *Total Assets:* £248,210
Registered Office: The Mall, Dolphin Approach, Romford, Essex, RM1 3EE
Shareholders: Deep Gupta; Meetu Gupta
Officers: Deep Gupta [1979] Director/Sales

Preen Queen Limited
Incorporated: 26 February 2019
Registered Office: 24 Chatsworth Road, Fishponds, Bristol, BS16 3QR
Major Shareholder: Henaa Malik
Officers: Henaa Malik [1990] Director/Adjudicator

Prema Naturals Limited
Incorporated: 31 August 2016
Net Worth Deficit: £2,752
Registered Office: 2 Hinksey Court, Church Way, Oxford, OX2 9SX
Major Shareholder: Dalia Monassebian
Officers: Bijan Monassebian [1939] Director/Entrepreneur [American]; Dalia Monassebian [1976] Director/Entrepreneur [American]

The Prescripteur Ltd
Incorporated: 29 June 2018
Registered Office: Unit 3 Merchant, Evegate Business Park, Ashford, Kent, TN25 6SX
Major Shareholder: Sara Khaldi
Officers: Sara Khaldi [1983] Director [Moroccan]

Prestige Perfumes Limited
Incorporated: 6 March 2012
Net Worth: £46,769 *Total Assets:* £437,347
Registered Office: 4102 Queens Dock Commercial Centre, Norfolk Street, Liverpool, L1 0BG
Major Shareholder: George Quintard
Officers: George George Quintard [1953] Director

The Top UK Perfume and Cosmetics Wholesalers

Lisa Preston Ltd
Incorporated: 3 July 2017
Registered Office: 10 Firshill Avenue, Sheffield, S4 7AA
Major Shareholder: Trieu Hai Preston
Officers: Trieu Hai Preston [1983] Director/Businesswoman [Vietnamese]

Prestonelite Limited
Incorporated: 1 August 2018
Registered Office: 102b St James's Road, Croydon, Surrey, CR0 2UJ
Officers: Jack Preston [1991] Director/Trader

Pretty Silhouette Limited
Incorporated: 5 May 2017
Registered Office: 110 Baldwins Lane, Croxley Green, Rickmansworth, Herts, WD3 3LJ
Shareholders: Jessica Harris; Cheryl Simpson; Victoria Wareham
Officers: Victoria Wareham, Secretary; Jessica Harris [1978] Director; Cheryl Simpson [1969] Director; Victoria Wareham [1980] Director

Previa UK Ltd
Incorporated: 31 January 2014
Net Worth: £46,774 *Total Assets:* £72,853
Registered Office: Kemp House, 152 City Road, London, EC1V 2NX
Major Shareholder: Dan Tomsa
Officers: Tatiana Tomsa, Secretary; Dan Tomsa [1981] Director [Romanian]

Prevura Ltd
Incorporated: 27 June 2016
Registered Office: 71-75 Shelton Street, Covent Garden, London, WC2H 9JQ
Officers: Ahmed Garhy [1976] Director [Egyptian]

Prezance Ltd
Incorporated: 4 January 2019
Registered Office: 111a Reddish Road, Stockport, Cheshire, SK5 7HP
Shareholders: Wayne Arthur Sutherland; Julie McGovern
Officers: Julie McGovern [1971] Director/Owner; Wayne Arthur Sutherland [1970] Director/Owner

Pricecheck Toiletries Limited
Incorporated: 22 March 1978 *Employees:* 123
Net Worth: £12,630,976 *Total Assets:* £23,155,352
Registered Office: Pricecheck Toiletries Ltd, Old Colliery Way, Beighton, Sheffield, S20 1DJ
Shareholders: Mark Andrew Lythe; Deborah Harrison
Officers: Mark Andrew Lythe, Secretary; Barry John Corker [1972] Director; Deborah Harrison [1970] Sales Director; Jonathan Edward Harrison [1963] Director; Amanda Jane Lythe [1965] Director; Mark Andrew Lythe [1967] Director; Lee Philip Walker [1975] Finance Director

Prima Makeup Ltd
Incorporated: 28 September 2017
Registered Office: 2 The Newhouse Stuart Works, High Street, Wordsley, Stourbridge, W Midlands, DY8 4FB
Major Shareholder: Emma Jane Moss
Officers: Simon Moss, Secretary; Emma Jane Moss [1983] Director; Simon Moss [1983] Director

Prime Skincare Ltd
Incorporated: 15 November 2018
Registered Office: 63 Plantation Road, Amersham, Bucks, HP6 6HW
Major Shareholder: Prian Perry Dattani
Officers: Ashitkumar Dattani [1960] Director; Jennica Gillian Dattani [1997] Director; Prian Perry Dattani [1995] Director

Primoil Limited
Incorporated: 30 March 1999
Net Worth: £398,162 *Total Assets:* £407,787
Registered Office: Second Floor, De Burgh House, Market Road, Wickford, Essex, SS12 0FD
Major Shareholder: Alain Claude Henri Muraour
Officers: Deborah O'Boyle [1968] Director

Prism Parfums Limited
Incorporated: 6 August 2014
Net Worth Deficit: £14,520 *Total Assets:* £395,430
Registered Office: 1a The Moorings, Dane Road Industrial Estate, Sale, Cheshire, M33 7BH
Shareholders: Simon Charles Wheeler Moorehead; Ian Clayton Smith
Officers: Simon Charles Wheeler Moorehead, Secretary; Ian Clayton Smith [1954] Director; Simon Charles Wheeler Moorehead [1962] Director/Chartered Accountant

Prismologie International Ltd
Incorporated: 17 April 2018
Registered Office: Leytonstone House, 3 Hanbury Drive, Leytonstone, London, E11 1GA
Shareholders: Intisar Salem Ali Alsabah; Fatima Mubarak Jaber Alsabah
Officers: Fatima Mubarak Jaber Alsabah [1986] Director [Kuwaiti]; Intisar Salem Ali Alsabah [1964] Director [Kuwaiti]

Prispens Limited
Incorporated: 4 March 2017
Net Worth Deficit: £16,150 *Total Assets:* £6,390
Registered Office: 16 Park Street, Crediton, Devon, EX17 3EQ
Shareholders: Jane Harding-Smolik; Jakub Harding-Smolik
Officers: Jakub Harding-Smolik [1981] Director [Czech]; Jane Harding-Smolik [1985] Director

Privilago Fashion Ltd
Incorporated: 1 October 2018
Registered Office: 67 Farmilo Road, London, E17 8JL
Shareholders: Claudiu Victorian Pascovski; Daiana Mihaela Sinca
Officers: Claudiu Victorian Pascovski [1989] Director [Romanian]; Daiana Mihaela Sinca [1990] Director [Romanian]

Pro Brands (UK) Ltd
Incorporated: 3 April 2018
Registered Office: 2 Melcombe Gardens, Harrow, Middlesex, HA3 9RH
Major Shareholder: Daniel Horea
Officers: Daniel Horea [1991] Director/Business Manager [Romanian]

Pro Bright Ltd
Incorporated: 8 January 2018
Registered Office: 25 Walkley Road, Sheffield, S6 2XL
Major Shareholder: Robert Newark Newark
Officers: Robert Newark Newark [1989] Director

Pro Esthe Ltd.
Incorporated: 13 October 2017
Registered Office: Enterprise House, 2 Pass Street, Oldham, Lancs, OL9 6HZ
Officers: Pavel Uhliar [1972] Director [Slovak]

Pro Impressions (UK) Limited
Incorporated: 1 May 2002
Registered Office: 29-31 Cannock Street, Troon Industrial Area, Leicester, LE4 9HR
Major Shareholder: Rajendra Naranbhai Mistry
Officers: Rajendra Naranbhai Mistry, Secretary/Director; Rajendra Naranbhai Mistry [1964] Director

Procare Women Health Limited
Incorporated: 16 May 2016
Net Worth: £632 *Total Assets:* £1,548
Registered Office: 271 High Street, Berkhamsted, Herts, HP4 1AA
Shareholders: Yann Gaslain; Vincent Cheney
Officers: Vincent Cheney [1955] Director/Business Partner International [French]

Procter & Procter Limited
Incorporated: 23 March 2018
Registered Office: The Apex, 2 Sheriffs Orchard, Coventry, Warwicks, CV1 3PP
Major Shareholder: Doris Andrew Procter
Officers: Doris Andrew Procter [1977] Director/Pharmacist

Product World Limited
Incorporated: 24 October 2014
Registered Office: 3 Gressenham Court, Aran Drive, Stanmore, Middlesex, HA7 4LZ
Major Shareholder: Steven Silver
Officers: Jill Silver [1957] Director/Teacher; Steven Silver [1951] Director/Wholesaler

Profile Hair & Skin Care Limited
Incorporated: 23 December 2011 *Employees:* 18
Net Worth: £37,875 *Total Assets:* £744,844
Registered Office: James House, 40 Lagland Street, Poole, Dorset, BH15 1QG
Officers: Dianne Kelleher, Secretary; Timothy Anthony Kelleher [1953] Director

Profline Ltd
Incorporated: 16 October 2017
Registered Office: Kemp House, 152-160 City Road, London, EC1V 2NX
Major Shareholder: Iuliia Agafonova
Officers: Iuliia Agafonova [1980] Director

Profusion Cosmetics UK Ltd
Incorporated: 2 November 2016 *Employees:* 3
Net Worth Deficit: £158,584 *Total Assets:* £638,398
Registered Office: St Brandon's House, 27-29 Great George Street, Bristol, BS1 5QT
Major Shareholder: Efon Wang
Officers: Efon Wang, Secretary; Efon Wang [1981] Director/Business Owner [American]

Project 1 Skincare Ltd
Incorporated: 3 April 2017
Registered Office: 58 Aldfield Green, Hamilton, Leicester, LE5 1BP
Shareholders: Aly Walji; Rizwan Ladak; Imtiyaz Alwany
Officers: Imtiyaz Alwany [1983] Director/Accountant; Rizwan Ladak [1982] Director/Chartered Accountant; Aly Walji [1982] Director/Banking

Project Cosmetics Limited
Incorporated: 16 October 2017
Registered Office: Meadowcroft Mill, Bury Road, Rochdale, Lancs, OL11 4AU
Major Shareholder: Joy Elizabeth Howieson
Officers: Joy Howieson, Secretary; Joy Elizabeth Howieson [1990] Director/Cosmetics Manufacturer and Retailer

Prossentials Ltd
Incorporated: 15 February 2019
Registered Office: 50 Badger Street, Bury, Lancs, BL9 6AD
Major Shareholder: Kiera Louise Harrison
Officers: Kiera Louise Harrison [1989] Director/Businesswoman

Prostar Trending Online Ltd
Incorporated: 10 April 2018
Registered Office: 9A-B Twin Bridges Estate, Selsdon Road, South Croydon, Surrey, CR2 6PL
Major Shareholder: Ajaz-Ahmad Hussain
Officers: Ajaz-Ahmad Hussain [1973] Director

Protec Botanica Ltd
Incorporated: 16 June 2011 *Employees:* 6
Net Worth Deficit: £306,365 *Total Assets:* £295,602
Registered Office: Unit 10 Delta Court, Manor Way, Borehamwood, Herts, WD6 1FJ
Parent: London Pharma & Chemicals Group Ltd
Officers: Kevin Mark Cousins [1969] Sales Director; Alan Edward Eastwood [1955] Director; Dean Austin Lockton [1975] Director; Daniel Reuben Straus [1972] Director/Business Manager

Protec Ingredia Limited
Incorporated: 4 February 2011 *Employees:* 12
Net Worth: £1,490,587 *Total Assets:* £2,895,331
Registered Office: Unit 10 Delta Court, Manor Way, Borehamwood, Herts, WD6 1FJ
Parent: London Pharma & Chemicals Group Ltd
Officers: Kevin Mark Cousins [1969] Sales Director; Alan Edward Eastwood [1955] Director; Daniel Reuben Straus [1972] Director/Business Manager

Protective World Ltd
Incorporated: 16 April 2015
Net Worth: £120 *Total Assets:* £120
Registered Office: 40 Norwich Road, Bournemouth, BH2 5QZ
Shareholder: Sandor Szucs
Officers: Monika Dome [1980] Director/Economist [Hungarian]; Sandor Szucs [1981] Director/Service [Hungarian]

PSM Vision Limited
Incorporated: 5 February 2019
Registered Office: 4 Hamleton Terrace, Dagenham, Essex, RM9 4HJ
Major Shareholder: Purvi Dave
Officers: Purvi Dave [1986] Director

PSR Wellness Limited
Incorporated: 10 December 2018
Registered Office: 10 Hall Farm Close, Stanmore, Middlesex, HA7 4JT
Shareholders: Nikunj Harishankar Panchal; Ashvin Govindji Shah
Officers: Nikunj Harishankar Panchal [1975] Director

Puff & Petals Ltd.
Incorporated: 25 October 2017
Registered Office: 14 Kilburn Avenue, Manchester, M9 6SW
Major Shareholder: Wendy Shima
Officers: Wendy Shima [1990] Director/HR Personnel

Puig UK Limited
Incorporated: 20 December 1972 Employees: 157
Net Worth: £4,089,000 Total Assets: £48,891,000
Registered Office: Fifth Floor, Russell Square House, 10-12 Russell Square, London, WC1B 5EH
Officers: Joan Albiol [1967] Director [Spanish]; Javier Bach Kutschruetter [1969] Director [Spanish]; Pilar Trabal Ogazon [1963] Director/VP Europe [Spanish]

Pur3 Health Limited
Incorporated: 28 April 2016
Net Worth Deficit: £7,910 Total Assets: £6,630
Registered Office: 133 The Broadway, Mill Hill, London, NW7 4RN
Officers: Parag Pramod Nawathe [1974] Director/IT Consultant; Prajakta Parag Nawathe [1980] Director/Physiotherapist

Pure & Sure Limited
Incorporated: 27 November 2017
Registered Office: 20 Merlin Grove, Ilford, Essex, IG6 2QX
Officers: Samir Monga [1980] Managing Director

The Pure Body Skin Care Ltd
Incorporated: 9 August 2018
Registered Office: H5 Ash Tree Court, Nottingham Business Park, Nottingham, NG8 6PY
Officers: Neil Aragon [1978] Director/Operations [American]

Pure Natural Therapy Ltd
Incorporated: 4 March 2017
Net Worth Deficit: £3,170 Total Assets: £984,000
Registered Office: 1 Bridge Cottages, Birstwith, Harrogate, N Yorks, HG3 2NP
Major Shareholder: Gabrielle Lydia Palmer
Officers: Gabrielle Lydia Palmer [1976] Director/Owner

Pure Products Limited
Incorporated: 26 January 2004
Previous: BEA Imports Limited
Net Worth Deficit: £17,060 Total Assets: £22,410
Registered Office: Eagle House, Cranleigh Close, South Croydon, Surrey, CR2 9LH
Shareholders: Kelly McManigan; Rory Fergus McManigan
Officers: Rory Fergus McManigan [1966] Director/Importer

Pure Revolution Ltd
Incorporated: 18 February 2019
Registered Office: 64 The Hawthorns, Cardiff, CF23 7AQ
Major Shareholder: Mohamed Saraj Ali
Officers: Mohamed Saraj Ali [1972] Director

Pure Savvy Limited
Incorporated: 19 January 2018
Registered Office: 2 Darnes Close, Bourne, Lincs, PE10 9GP
Shareholders: Stephanie Jane Kelby; Stephen Anthony Kelby
Officers: Stephanie Jane Kelby [1971] Director; Stephen Anthony Kelby [1971] Director

Pure Skincare Limited
Incorporated: 7 August 2018
Registered Office: Richmond House, 29 Parkfield Avenue, Ashton on Ribble, Preston, Lancs, PR2 1JB
Major Shareholder: Andrew Croft
Officers: Andrew Croft [1966] Director/Consultant

Pure Skincare London Ltd
Incorporated: 2 May 2017
Registered Office: Kemp House, 152-160 City Road, London, EC1V 2NX
Major Shareholder: Karim Oualnan
Officers: Karim Oualnan, Secretary; Karim Oualnan [1990] Director/Lawyer

Pure Swiss Aesthetics Ltd
Incorporated: 11 December 2014 Employees: 1
Net Worth Deficit: £281,561 Total Assets: £33,162
Registered Office: Corporation House, Hackmans Lane, Purleigh, Chelmsford, Essex, CM3 6RH
Major Shareholder: Teresa Da Graca
Officers: Teresa Paula Da Graca [1968] Director [Swiss/Portuguese]

Pure Thoughts Ltd
Incorporated: 7 February 2012 Employees: 2
Net Worth: £48,460 Total Assets: £76,362
Registered Office: 12 Darley Abbey Mills, Darley Abbey, Derby, DE22 1DZ
Shareholders: Leanna Marie Doolin; Michael Edward Houlden
Officers: Leanna Marie Doolin [1976] Director; Michael Edward Houlden [1981] Director

Purederma Ltd
Incorporated: 17 May 2018
Registered Office: Devon House, 40-42 Upper Street, London, N1 0PL
Officers: Alastair Danzig [1992] Director/Health Accounts Manager

Purelonia Ltd
Incorporated: 17 October 2018
Registered Office: 6 Pitdinnie Road, Cairneyhill, Fife, KY12 8RE
Shareholders: Mark Goodridge; Simon George Cormack
Officers: Simon George Cormack [1981] Director; Mark Goodridge [1978] Director

Purity Derma Limited
Incorporated: 1 June 2017
Registered Office: 31 Gwydor Road, Beckenham, Kent, BR3 4DT
Major Shareholder: Phillip Duncan Boyd
Officers: Phillip Boyd, Secretary; Phillip Duncan Boyd [1977] Director

Purity Skincare Limited
Incorporated: 12 April 2006
Net Worth Deficit: £512,160 Total Assets: £36,520
Registered Office: 4th Floor, Tuition House, 27-37 St Georges Road, Wimbledon, London, SW19 4EU
Major Shareholder: Paisley Arnold
Officers: Paisley Arnold [1965] Director/Investment Banker

Purple Tree Skincare Limited
Incorporated: 14 July 2015
Net Worth: £14,616 Total Assets: £57,545
Registered Office: Newbury House, Aintree Avenue, Trowbridge, Wilts, BA14 0XB
Officers: Susan Angela Lynch Staunton [1967] UK Sales Director; Graham Murray Lynch-Staunton [1969] Director

Q River Limited
Incorporated: 4 August 2016
Net Worth: £668,418 Total Assets: £787,788
Registered Office: Grove Park Studios, 188-192 Sutton Court Road, London, W4 3HR
Shareholder: Rajiv Chandra
Officers: Anuradha Chandra [1965] Director [Indian]; Rajiv Chandra [1964] Managing Director; David Cowell [1959] Director; Natasha Margaret Kaplinsky [1972] Director/Journalist; Catherine Stopp [1977] Director

Qiaochu Trading Co. Ltd
Incorporated: 15 February 2018
Registered Office: 8 St Marys Place, Newcastle upon Tyne, NE1 7PG
Major Shareholder: Jiefeng Chen
Officers: Jiefeng Chen [1987] Director [Chinese]

Qing Ltd
Incorporated: 16 May 2017
Registered Office: Park House, 37 Clarence Street, Leicester, LE1 3RW
Major Shareholder: Yu Pan
Officers: Yu Pan [1976] Director [Chinese]

QOD UK Ltd
Incorporated: 6 January 2012 Employees: 1
Net Worth: £3,774 Total Assets: £10,322
Registered Office: 17a Taunton Lane, Old Coulsdon, Surrey, CR5 1SG
Officers: John Kenneth Priestman [1950] Director/Motor Mechanic

Quality Brand MG Ltd
Incorporated: 14 December 2017
Registered Office: 15a High Street, Westham, Pevensey, E Sussex, BN24 5LR
Major Shareholder: Marin Angelov Popov
Officers: Marin Angelov Popov [1968] Director [Bulgarian]

Quality Check Ltd
Incorporated: 8 September 2014
Net Worth Deficit: £1,874 Total Assets: £140
Registered Office: 4 Martello Road, Eastbourne, E Sussex, BN22 7SU
Shareholders: Valerija Brezovar; Maks Rozman
Officers: Valerija Brezovar [1988] Director/Chemical Engineer [Slovenian]; Maks Rozman [1972] Director/Business Consultant [Slovenian]

Quanis Cosmetic Limited
Incorporated: 27 November 2018
Registered Office: 87 Gortree Road, Londonderry, BT47 3LL
Officers: Dr Terence McIvor [1970] Director [Irish]

Quelsa Ltd
Incorporated: 14 September 2018
Registered Office: Suite 52, 51 Pinfold Street, Birmingham, B2 4AY
Shareholders: Susana Gonzalez Antonete; Raquel Corral Casero
Officers: Raquel Corral Casero [1989] Director/Financial Consultant [Spanish]; Susana Gonzalez Antonete [1984] Director/Consultant [Spanish]

The Quint Essence Lab Ltd
Incorporated: 13 February 2019
Registered Office: Hova House, 1 Hova Villas, Hove, E Sussex, BN3 3DH
Shareholders: Agnes Renata Majoros; Attila Varro
Officers: Agnes Renata Majoros [1978] Director [Hungarian]; Attila Varro [1959] Director [Hungarian]

QZE Limited
Incorporated: 24 July 2018
Registered Office: 276-244 Crondall Street, London, N1 6JF
Major Shareholder: Dimitar Petkov
Officers: Dimitar Petkov, Secretary; Dimitar Petkov [1989] Director [Bulgarian]

R & B Hair Extensions Limited
Incorporated: 31 January 2018
Registered Office: 12 Newells Drive, Tipton, W Midlands, DY4 0LD
Officers: Dean Fisher [1985] Director/Hair and Beauty; Imogen Gooby [1990] Director/Hair and Beauty

R & R Global Consumer Healthcare Limited
Incorporated: 22 June 2018
Registered Office: 71-75 Shelton Street, Covent Garden, London, WC2H 9JQ
Major Shareholder: Erik Lambert
Officers: Erik Lambert [1986] Director/Owner [Swedish]

R & T Natural Cosmetics Limited
Incorporated: 31 December 2018
Registered Office: Kemp House, 160 City Road, London, EC1V 2NX
Major Shareholder: Rose Etim-Ibom
Officers: Rose Etim-Ibom, Secretary; Rose Etim-Ibom [1973] Director/Teacher; Tracy Ibom [2002] Director/Student

R10 Labs Skincare Ltd
Incorporated: 4 December 2018
Registered Office: Crown House, 94 Armley Road, Leeds, LS12 2EJ
Major Shareholder: Khalid Bulbul
Officers: Khalid Bulbul [1987] Director

Rabimed International Limited
Incorporated: 29 July 2002
Net Worth Deficit: £5,004 Total Assets: £3,001
Registered Office: Unit 61 Battersea Business Centre, 99-109 Lavender Hill, London, SW11 5QL
Officers: Dr Nolitha Mji [1965] Director/Gynaecologist [South African]

Radiant and Refined Limited
Incorporated: 28 December 2017
Registered Office: 35 Uppingham Avenue, Stanmore, Middlesex, HA7 2JF
Major Shareholder: Rabiya Saleem
Officers: Rabiya Saleem [1997] Director

Radiant Glow Beauty UK Ltd
Incorporated: 12 November 2018
Registered Office: 61 Bridge Street, Kington, Herefords, HR5 3DJ
Major Shareholder: Abiodun Olusesan
Officers: Abiodun Olusesan [1965] Commercial Director

Raebeauty Ltd
Incorporated: 25 January 2019
Registered Office: Rae Beauty, 94 Dimmingsdale Bank, Quinton, Birmingham, B32 1ST
Major Shareholder: Talitha Rachel Delcena Macpherson Guy
Officers: Talitha Rachel Delcena Macpherson Guy [1995] Director/Administrator

Railworth Limited
Incorporated: 8 August 1977 *Employees:* 5
Net Worth: £153,186 *Total Assets:* £356,827
Registered Office: Unit 13 Space Business Park, Abbey Road, London, NW10 7SU
Officers: Ahmed Jhamaney, Secretary; Mohammed Abu Bakr [1952] Director/Shop Manager [Indian]; Salman Alfarsi [1959] Director/Shop Manager

Rainbow Cosmetics (Manchester) Limited
Incorporated: 11 January 2002 *Employees:* 53
Net Worth: £575,604 *Total Assets:* £17,311,892
Registered Office: 61 Stanley Road, Whitefield, Manchester, M45 8GZ
Parent: Rainbow Cosmetics (Holdings) Ltd
Officers: Heather Sharman, Secretary; Heather Sharman [1957] Director/Company Secretary; John William Sharman [1955] Director; Stephen John Sharman [1980] Director

Raisingthebaruk Ltd
Incorporated: 21 November 2018
Registered Office: 9 Park Place East, Sunderland, Tyne & Wear, SR2 8EE
Major Shareholder: Scott Grainger
Officers: Scott Grainger [1971] Director/Chemist

Rakhee LB Ltd
Incorporated: 18 February 2019
Registered Office: 147 Filton Avenue, Horfield, Bristol, BS7 0AT
Major Shareholder: Rakhee Boodoo-Lumbus
Officers: Rakhee Boodoo-Lumbus [1975] Director/Nurse [Mauritian]

Rapsodi London Ltd
Incorporated: 26 May 2011
Net Worth: £11,300 *Total Assets:* £92,330
Registered Office: Unit 12 Breach Road, Grays, Essex, RM20 3NR
Major Shareholder: Saleem Ullah
Officers: Saleem Ullah [1986] Director [Pakistani]

Rapsodi Ltd
Incorporated: 9 November 2018
Registered Office: Unit 1, Alder's Mall, North End, Croydon, London, CR9 1SB
Officers: Aslihan Akyildiz [1984] Managing Director [Turkish]

Rashimex Trading Limited
Incorporated: 7 September 2012
Registered Office: 3 Richmond Court, Forty Avenue, Wembley, Middlesex, HA9 8LL
Major Shareholder: Boris Rashkov
Officers: Boris Rashkov [1972] Director/Business Consultant and Trader [Bulgarian]

Rationale Skincare Limited
Incorporated: 28 July 2015
Registered Office: 10 John Street, London, WC1N 2EB
Officers: Richard Parker [1960] Director [Australian]

Rawly Processed Ltd.
Incorporated: 28 February 2018
Registered Office: Flat 6, Troutbeck, Albany Street, London, NW1 4EG
Major Shareholder: Roxanne Pedersen
Officers: Roxanne Pedersen [1994] Director/Digital Marketer [Danish]

Rawmans Ltd
Incorporated: 30 May 2017
Registered Office: 8 Festing Grove, Portsmouth, PO4 9QA
Major Shareholder: Farjana Lisa Rahman
Officers: Farjana Lisa Rahman [1993] Director

Ray & Company (Hairdressers Sundries Men) Limited
Incorporated: 15 November 1946
Net Worth: £1,230,000 *Total Assets:* £2,020,000
Registered Office: Trade Hair Supplies, Lingfield Way, Yarm Road Business Park, Darlington, Co Durham, DL1 4PZ
Officers: Virginia Ann Sliufko, Secretary; Christopher Harry Sliufko [1987] Director; Olivia Mary Sliufko [1982] Director; Paul Anthony Garth Sliufko [1954] Director; Thomas Guy Sliufko [1985] Director/Manager

Raynolds Ltd
Incorporated: 9 April 2014
Net Worth Deficit: £3,080 *Total Assets:* £1,600
Registered Office: c/o Evla, 30 Worthing Road, Horsham, W Sussex, RH12 1SL
Shareholders: Attila Revesz; Adrienn Prepok
Officers: Adrienn Prepok [1981] Director [Hungarian]; Attila Revesz [1980] Director [Hungarian]

Razaq & Iqbal Limited
Incorporated: 8 May 1996
Net Worth: £134,019 *Total Assets:* £134,033
Registered Office: 9 Foxcover Distribution Park, Admiralty Way, Seaham, Co Durham, SR7 7DN
Shareholders: Jawid Iqbal; Mohammed Razaq
Officers: Mohammed Razaq, Secretary/Businessman; Jawid Iqbal [1963] Director/Businessman; Mohammed Razaq [1964] Director/Businessman

Razias London Ltd
Incorporated: 15 June 2016
Net Worth Deficit: £30,680 *Total Assets:* £9,450
Registered Office: Cranford House, 24a Longley Road, Rainham, Gillingham, Kent, ME8 7RU
Officers: Razia Malik [1964] Director

Razzo Limited
Incorporated: 30 October 2017
Registered Office: c/o UHY Hacker Young, 6 Broadfield Court, Broadfield Way, Sheffield, S8 0XF
Major Shareholder: Mohamad Zedki
Officers: Mohamad Zedki [1986] Director

RDC (UK) Limited
Incorporated: 14 November 1988
Net Worth: £170,810 *Total Assets:* £191,950
Registered Office: 209 Crescent Road, Barnet, Herts, EN4 8SB
Major Shareholder: David Alexander Lee
Officers: David Alexander Lee [1975] Director

Re:New Beauty Ltd
Incorporated: 23 November 1998 *Employees:* 16
Previous: Bio Sculpture G.B. Limited
Net Worth: £3,526,584 *Total Assets:* £4,029,690
Registered Office: 6 Park Industrial Estate, Frogmore, St Albans, Herts, AL2 2DR
Shareholders: Richard Lipsitz; Kerri Lipsitz
Officers: David Melvin Lipsitz [1954] Director/Dental Surgeon; Richard Lipsitz [1986] Director

Real Cosmetics Ltd
Incorporated: 25 July 2018
Registered Office: Sedulo, 62-66 Deansgate, Manchester, M3 2EN
Major Shareholder: Samsara Hussain
Officers: Samsara Hussain [1992] Director

Real Looks Limited
Incorporated: 26 June 2002
Net Worth: £4,944 *Total Assets:* £46,399
Registered Office: 21 New Walk, Leicester, LE1 6TE
Major Shareholder: Harishkumar Pravinchandra Patel
Officers: Harishkumar Pravinchandra Patel [1965] Director

Real Skin Pickle Ltd
Incorporated: 24 October 2018
Registered Office: Flat 14, 39 Kingston Road, New Malden, Surrey, KT3 3PE
Major Shareholder: Marzia Rahmani
Officers: Marzia Rahmani [1978] Director

Realine Beauty Limited
Incorporated: 4 March 2013
Net Worth Deficit: £56,450 *Total Assets:* £10,710
Registered Office: Suite 530, 405 Kings Road, Chelsea, London, SW10 0BB
Major Shareholder: Robin Paul Capstick
Officers: Robin Paul Capstick [1966] Director/Entrepreneur

Rebatchi Perfums Ltd
Incorporated: 25 October 2017
Registered Office: Unit 23 Horyaal Business Centre, 363 Coventry Road, Birmingham, B10 0SW
Major Shareholder: Mohamed-Lamine Rebatchi
Officers: Mohamed-Lamine Rebatchi [1991] Director [French]

Recruit Skincare Ltd
Incorporated: 6 February 2018
Registered Office: 5 The Mount, High Street, Swinton, Malton, N Yorks, YO17 6SN
Major Shareholder: Tommy Bernard Leach
Officers: Tommy Bernard Leach [1991] Director

Red Gold London Ltd
Incorporated: 13 May 2014
Previous: Red Gold Roses Limited
Registered Office: 88-90 Hatton Garden, London, EC1N 8PN
Major Shareholder: Vassilena Buhova
Officers: Vassilena Buhova, Secretary; Vassilena Buhova [1988] Director [Bulgarian]

Red Hot Products Limited
Incorporated: 27 February 2009 *Employees:* 15
Net Worth: £840,943 *Total Assets:* £2,045,250
Registered Office: Unit 1 Jacks Way, Hill Barton Business Park, Exeter, Devon, EX5 1FG
Shareholders: Grant Northover; Brenda Berrell
Officers: Grant Northover [1954] Director

Rederm Limited
Incorporated: 25 January 2013 *Employees:* 5
Net Worth Deficit: £665,488 *Total Assets:* £466,808
Registered Office: 368 Forest Road, London, E17 5JF
Parent: Institute Hyalual GmbH
Officers: Iryna Stewart [1971] Director/Doctor

Reetal Development Company Ltd
Incorporated: 29 March 2017
Registered Office: 63 Grosvenor Street, Mayfair, London, W1K 3JG
Officers: Husam Ali, Secretary; Husam Ali [1962] Director

Refan Portadown Limited
Incorporated: 10 September 2018
Registered Office: 61 Eglish Road, Portadown, Craigavon, Co Armagh, BT62 1NL
Major Shareholder: Wayne Mulligan
Officers: Wayne Mulligan [1979] Director

Refan UK Ltd
Incorporated: 3 February 2014 *Employees:* 2
Net Worth Deficit: £32,818 *Total Assets:* £4,148
Registered Office: 76 Portland Road, Long Eaton, Nottingham, NG10 3FN
Officers: Sergey Ludzhev [1971] Director/Self Employed [Bulgarian]; Dian Pentchev Rakadjiev [1976] Director/Manager

Regal Skincare Ltd
Incorporated: 11 December 2017
Registered Office: 9 Stonecliffe Close, Leeds, LS12 5BJ
Officers: Dobri Todorov Petkov [1970] Director [Bulgarian]

Regima Medic Ltd
Incorporated: 21 September 2010
Net Worth Deficit: £7,548 *Total Assets:* £11,033
Registered Office: Unit 9A Southview Park, Marsack Street, Caversham, Reading, Berks, RG4 5AP
Shareholders: Daniel James Faucitt; Peter Andrew Faucitt; Jacqueline Faucitt
Officers: Daniel James Faucitt [1982] Director; Jacqueline Faucitt [1957] Director; Peter Andrew Faucitt [1952] Director

Regima UK Ltd
Incorporated: 26 January 2010
Net Worth Deficit: £27,829 *Total Assets:* £685,726
Registered Office: Unit 9 Southview Park, Caversham, Reading, Berks, RG4 5AF
Major Shareholder: Daniel Faucitt
Officers: Daniel James Faucitt [1982] Director; Jacqueline Faucitt [1957] Director; Peter Andrew Faucitt [1952] Director

Regima Zone Ltd
Incorporated: 30 January 2015 *Employees:* 3
Net Worth Deficit: £136,331 *Total Assets:* £75,336
Registered Office: Unit 9 Southview Park, Caversham, Reading, Berks, RG4 5AF
Major Shareholder: Daniel James Faucitt
Officers: Daniel James Faucitt [1982] Director; Jacqueline Faucitt [1957] Director; Laura Kay Puttick [1991] Director

Regima@Dr H Ltd
Incorporated: 3 October 2006
Net Worth Deficit: £732,419 *Total Assets:* £179,661
Registered Office: Unit 9 Southview Park, Caversham, Reading, Berks, RG4 5AF
Major Shareholder: Daniel Faucitt
Officers: Daniel James Faucitt [1982] Director

Regis Personal Care Ltd
Incorporated: 24 July 2017
Registered Office: Unit 16, Building 10, Central Park, Mallusk, Newtownabbey, Co Antrim, BT36 4FS
Major Shareholder: Richard Walsh
Officers: Dr Richard Walsh [1967] Director/Doctor

Regista Fragrance Ltd
Incorporated: 24 May 2018
Registered Office: 71-75 Shelton Street, London, WC2H 9JQ
Major Shareholder: Pascal Kempson
Officers: Pascal Kempson [1996] Director

Reimiece Ltd
Incorporated: 21 September 2016
Registered Office: 7 Hedderley Walk, Nottingham, NG3 1NX
Major Shareholder: Samantha Elaine Hayes
Officers: Samantha Elaine Hayes [1974] Director & Founder

Rejuvapen UK Ltd
Incorporated: 4 July 2014
Net Worth Deficit: £13,954 Total Assets: £14,042
Registered Office: 16a Huntercombe Lane North, Taplow, Maidenhead, Berks, SL6 0LG
Major Shareholder: Paul Haydn Evans
Officers: Paul Haydn Evans [1961] Director/Consultant

Rektaz Ltd
Incorporated: 29 September 2017
Registered Office: 10 Acorn Close, Chingford, London, E4 9DA
Major Shareholder: Md Zahir Islam
Officers: MD Zahir Islam, Secretary; MD Zahir Islam [1980] Director

Rekze Laboratories Ltd
Incorporated: 21 April 2016
Net Worth Deficit: £527 Total Assets: £8,433
Registered Office: 2nd Floor, Beaumont House, 1b Lambton Road, London, SW20 0LW
Major Shareholder: Virgil Sorin Chiriac
Officers: Virgil Sorin Chiriac [1985] Director/Consultant [Romanian]

Relaxa Trading Ltd
Incorporated: 10 March 2018
Registered Office: 2nd Floor, A Block, 284 Chase Road, London, N14 6HF
Major Shareholder: Doruk Otcu
Officers: Doruk Otcu [1991] Director [Turkish]

Reliance HBC UK Ltd
Incorporated: 22 March 2018
Registered Office: 64 Stoneycroft Close, London, SE12 0SL
Major Shareholder: Ikechukwu Nebeolisa
Officers: Ujunwa Nebeolisa, Secretary; Ikechukwu Nebeolisa [1963] Director; Ujunwa Comfort Nebeolisa [1967] Director/Nurse

Reliant Overseas UK Limited
Incorporated: 29 February 2012
Registered Office: 33 Frobisher Crescent, Staines upon Thames, Middlesex, TW19 7DU
Major Shareholder: Viral Pravinkumar Parikh
Officers: Viral Parikh [1985] Director [Indian]

Rembrandt London Limited
Incorporated: 9 October 2017
Registered Office: 3-4 Sentinel Square, London, NW4 2EL
Officers: Melanie Nicholls [1972] Director

Reminiscents of Didsbury Ltd
Incorporated: 28 August 2018
Registered Office: 1 Victoria Avenue, Didsbury, Manchester, M20 2GY
Shareholders: Lucy Walsh; Richard William Walsh
Officers: Lucy Anne Walsh, Secretary; Richard William Walsh [1969] Director

Ren Ltd
Incorporated: 13 March 1997 Employees: 56
Net Worth: £3,812,000 Total Assets: £6,821,000
Registered Office: Union House, 182-194 Union Street, London, SE1 0LH
Parent: Unilever U.K. Holdings Limited
Officers: James Oliver Earley, Secretary; Richard Clive Hazell, Secretary; Sophia Platts, Secretary; Pamela Dickson [1968] Finance Director; Lucy Elizabeth Howell Hovey [1983] Director/Accountant; Arnaud Maurice Jean Meysselle [1971] Director [French]; Vasiliki Petrou [1967] Director/SVP Prestige

REN Skincare Limited
Incorporated: 19 March 2013
Registered Office: Union House, 182-194 Union Street, London, SE1 0LH
Parent: Ren Limited
Officers: Lucy Elizabeth Howell Hovey [1983] Director/Accountant; Arnaud Maurice Jean Meysselle [1971] Director [French]; Vasiliki Petrou [1967] Director/SVP Prestige

Renaissance Manyane Global Group Ltd
Incorporated: 23 August 2018
Registered Office: Kemp House, 160 City Road, London, EC1V 2NX
Major Shareholder: Joseph Kambani Banda
Officers: Sisanda Mxonywa, Secretary; Joseph Kambani Banda [1990] Director/Businessman [Zambian]; Sisanda Mxonywa [1991] Director/Businesswoman [South African]

Reneebeauty Limited
Incorporated: 21 March 2018
Registered Office: 204 Hercules House, Botanic Square, London, E14 0LH
Major Shareholder: Zhen Ren
Officers: Zhen Ren [1988] Director/Entrepreneur [Chinese]

Renibo Ltd
Incorporated: 7 February 2018
Registered Office: Kemp House, 160 City Road, London, EC1V 2NX
Major Shareholder: Lazar Trajchev
Officers: Lazar Trajchev [1978] Director/Lawyer [Macedonian]

Renski Limited
Incorporated: 3 September 2018
Registered Office: 30 Homefield Road, Bromley, Kent, BR1 3AL
Major Shareholder: Jessica Renaud
Officers: Jessica Renaud [1993] Director/Administrator

Repechage Europe Limited
Incorporated: 30 July 1996
Net Worth Deficit: £53,332 Total Assets: £103,051
Registered Office: Forest Mill, Burnley Road East, Water, Rossendale, Lancs, BB4 9PY
Parent: Repechage Holdings Ltd
Officers: Valerie Cooper, Secretary; David Sarfati [1945] Director [American]; Shiri Sarfati [1979] Director Co Communications [American]

Republic Cosmetics UK Ltd
Incorporated: 27 February 2019
Registered Office: 71-75 Shelton Street, Covent Garden, London, WC2H 9JQ
Major Shareholder: Bijal Patel
Officers: Bijal Patel [1983] Director; Chandu Patel [1953] Director; Kamini Patel [1959] Director

Republik Inc Limited
Incorporated: 23 March 2017
Net Worth: £131,530 *Total Assets:* £141,730
Registered Office: 43 Manchester Street, London, W1U 7LP
Shareholders: David Edward Conway; Kevinn Cayuti Hirsch; Alexander Gregory Theodorou
Officers: Kevinn Cayuti Hirsch [1984] Director/Designer [French]; Alexander Gregory Theodorou [1975] Director/Designer

Respect Male Grooming Ltd.
Incorporated: 7 May 2015
Net Worth Deficit: £468 *Total Assets:* £833
Registered Office: 7 Laureate Paddocks, Newmarket, Suffolk, CB8 0AP
Major Shareholder: Joseph Telfer
Officers: Joseph Telfer [1986] Director/Cosmetics

Resquire Health & Beauty Ltd
Incorporated: 17 May 2018
Registered Office: 53 Dorset Avenue, Cheadle Hulme, Cheadle, Cheshire, SK8 5QR
Major Shareholder: Thomas White
Officers: Thomas White [1986] Director/Cosmetic Executive

Retailwolfs Ltd
Incorporated: 21 February 2019
Registered Office: Carpenter Court, 1 Maple Road, Bramhall, Stockport, Cheshire, SK7 2DH
Shareholders: Mohammad Hariri; Jonas Svensson
Officers: Mohammad Hariri [1986] Director [Swedish]

Reveal Naturals Ltd
Incorporated: 5 February 2019
Registered Office: Flat 1, 30 Windsor Drive, Barnet, Herts, EN4 8UE
Major Shareholder: Osama Abuhammad
Officers: Osama Abuhammad [1978] Director and Company Secretary [Canadian]

Reviron Limited
Incorporated: 15 December 2017
Registered Office: 26 Bloemfontein Avenue, London, W12 7BL
Major Shareholder: Sylvain Reviron
Officers: Sylvain Reviron [1980] Director [French]

Revive Express Beauty Ltd
Incorporated: 10 June 2016
Net Worth Deficit: £66,950 *Total Assets:* £102,130
Registered Office: 16 Charlemont Street, Moy, Co Tyrone, BT71 7SL
Major Shareholder: Una McGurk
Officers: Una McGurk [1968] Director; Martin O'Hart [1977] Director [Irish]

Revlon & Elie Healthcare Ltd
Incorporated: 14 September 2017
Registered Office: Unit 2 Block B, Scrabo Business Park, Jubilee Road, Newtownards, Co Down, BT23 4YH
Parent: Elie Consumer Care Ltd
Officers: Mary Stephen [1972] Director/Businesswoman

Revoke Ltd.
Incorporated: 16 January 2018
Registered Office: 1 Falconer Crescent, Leicester, LE3 6QS
Major Shareholder: Sheree Anne Gamble
Officers: Sheree Anne Gamble [1993] Director/Online Sales

Revolax Ltd
Incorporated: 1 November 2018
Registered Office: 8a Cinnabar Court, Daresbury Park, Daresbury, Warrington, Cheshire, WA4 4GE
Parent: Fox Group Global Limited
Officers: Michael Foxley [1983] Director; Victoria Quinn [1986] Director

Revolution Beauty Limited
Incorporated: 14 December 2015 *Employees:* 84
Previous: Tam Beauty (Distribution) Ltd
Net Worth: £11,975,247 *Total Assets:* £49,814,564
Registered Office: 2-3 Sheet Glass Road, Cullet Drive, Queenborough, Kent, ME11 5JS
Shareholders: Thomas Donald Allsworth; Adam Nicholas Minto
Officers: Thomas Donald Allsworth [1965] Director; Adam Nicholas Minto [1970] Director

Rewind Botanics Limited
Incorporated: 21 November 2017
Registered Office: 82 Brockley Rise, London, SE23 1LN
Officers: Vivien Leung, Secretary; Vivien Leung [1985] Director

Rexcel Trading Ltd
Incorporated: 31 May 2017
Registered Office: 71-75 Shelton Street, Covent Garden, London, WC2H 9JQ
Major Shareholder: Md Saiful Alam Bhuiyan
Officers: MD Saiful Alam Bhuiyan [1987] Director [Bangladeshi]

Rexez Ltd
Incorporated: 13 February 2018
Registered Office: 60 Stour Road, Dagenham, Essex, RM10 7JB
Officers: Motwakil Abdalla [1980] Director/Import Clerk

RHI By ROC Ltd
Incorporated: 31 August 2018
Registered Office: 35 Montrose Road, Harrow, Middlesex, HA3 7DY
Major Shareholder: Rochelle Marie Buncombe
Officers: Rochelle Marie Buncombe [1990] Director/Manager

Rhug Organic and Natural Limited
Incorporated: 6 February 2019
Registered Office: Rhug Estate Office, Rhug, Corwen, Denbighshire, LL21 0EH
Major Shareholder: Robert Vaughan Newborough
Officers: Lord Robert Vaughan Newborough [1949] Director

Charlotte Rhys UK Limited
Incorporated: 25 July 2011 *Employees:* 3
Net Worth Deficit: £47,550 *Total Assets:* £4,136
Registered Office: 79a High Street, Teddington, Middlesex, TW11 8HG
Officers: Carolyn Vivienne Beggin [1960] Director/Doctor; Shaun McDermott [1960] Director; Janet Mary Spyropoulos [1943] Director

Rich & Ruitz Perfume Industry Ltd
Incorporated: 8 January 2019
Registered Office: 702 Romford Road, London, E12 5AJ
Major Shareholder: Mohammed Emadur Rahman
Officers: Mohammed Emadur Rahman, Secretary; Mohammed Emadur Rahman [1984] Director [American]

The Top UK Perfume and Cosmetics Wholesalers   dellam

Rich 101 Ltd
Incorporated: 13 October 2009
Net Worth Deficit: £651 Total Assets: £3,452
Registered Office: 29 Mead Road, Willesborough, Ashford, Kent, TN24 0BS
Major Shareholder: David Victor Giles
Officers: David Victor Giles [1962] Director/Accountant

Rich Cosmetics Ltd
Incorporated: 25 May 2018
Registered Office: 49 Lealand Road, London, N15 6JS
Officers: Joseph Kadish Barzesky [1974] Director/Administrator [Israeli]

Riley & Sons Ltd
Incorporated: 17 July 2017
Registered Office: 57 High Street, Ballymena, Co Antrim, BT43 6DT
Major Shareholder: Charlotte Riley
Officers: Charlotte Riley [1974] Director/Businesswoman

Rimmel & Flynn Healthcare Ltd
Incorporated: 15 September 2017
Registered Office: Unit 41 Antrim Business Park, Enkalon Industrial Estate, Antrim, BT41 4LD
Parent: Flynn Group of Companies Ltd
Officers: Michael Bronson [1975] Director/Businessman

Ring in Ring Ltd
Incorporated: 9 November 2016
Registered Office: 3 Acres Gardens, Tadworth, Surrey, KT20 5LP
Major Shareholder: Behzad Gharehbaghi
Officers: Behzad Gharehbaghi [1971] Director [Iranian]

Ringley Trading Limited
Incorporated: 10 November 2010
Registered Office: 61 Stanley Road, Whitefield, Manchester, M45 8GZ
Officers: John William Sharman [1955] Director

Ris Healthcare Limited
Incorporated: 5 February 2015
Registered Office: 10 Prospect Place, Welwyn, Herts, AL6 9EW
Shareholders: Charles Stephen Unwin; Stephen Ronald Unwin
Officers: Charles Stephen Unwin [1978] Director; Stephen Ronald Unwin [1953] Director

Risa Lux Ltd
Incorporated: 17 January 2018
Registered Office: 41 Swan House, Enfield, Middlesex, EN3 4DD
Major Shareholder: Jacqueline Evans
Officers: Jacqueline Evans [1985] Director

Rishi Human Hair Extensions Wholesale Ltd
Incorporated: 19 March 2018
Registered Office: 3 Graingerville South, Westgate Road, Newcastle upon Tyne, NE4 6UH
Major Shareholder: Rishanthini Subramaniyam
Officers: Rishanthini Subramaniyam [1994] Director [Sri Lankan]

Riviere Groupe (Europe) Limited
Incorporated: 7 November 2017
Registered Office: 370 Neasden Lane North, London, NW10 0BT
Shareholders: Hing Yu Wong; Hiang Sim Chiu
Officers: Hiang Sim Chiu [1961] Director [Chinese]; Hing Yu Wong [1954] Director

Riway International Group (Euro) Ltd
Incorporated: 15 January 2019
Registered Office: Pik K Chau, 3 Cross Street, Chatham, Kent, ME4 4LT
Officers: Pik Keung Chau, Secretary; Pik Keung Chau [1960] Director/Manager

Riway International Group (UK) Ltd
Incorporated: 15 January 2019
Registered Office: Pik K Chau, 3 Cross Street, Chatham, Kent, ME4 4LT
Officers: Pik Keung Chau, Secretary; Pik Keung Chau [1960] Director/Manager

Riway Ltd
Incorporated: 17 January 2019
Registered Office: Pik K Chau, 3 Cross Street, Chatham, Kent, ME4 4LT
Officers: Pik Keung Chau, Secretary; Pik Keung Chau [1960] Director/Manager

RMD Global OYB Limited
Incorporated: 21 March 2018
Registered Office: Unit 12 Dodson Way, Peterborough, Cambs, PE1 5XJ
Parent: Sharf Holdings Limited
Officers: Roei Sharf [1989] Director [French]

RMD Global Wholesale Limited
Incorporated: 26 May 2017
Registered Office: 12 Dodson Way, Peterborough, Cambs, PE1 5XJ
Parent: RMD Global Holdings Limited
Officers: Roei Sharf [1989] Director [French]

RMG Hair Limited
Incorporated: 26 October 2006
Net Worth: £30,787 Total Assets: £70,651
Registered Office: Sanderson House, Station Road, Horsforth, Leeds, LS18 5NT
Shareholder: Martin Andrew Rae
Officers: Martin Andrew Rae, Secretary; Gavin Paul Rae [1968] Director; Martin Andrew Rae [1966] Director

Robert Cosmetics Limited
Incorporated: 14 May 2018
Registered Office: Flat 7, 194 Finchley Road, London, NW3 6BX
Officers: Julien Jean Maxime Robert [1979] Director [French]

MV Roberts & Co (UK) Ltd
Incorporated: 22 September 2016 Employees: 1
Net Worth: £10,019 Total Assets: £29,318
Registered Office: Commerce House, Telford Road, Bicester, Oxon, OX26 4LD
Shareholder: Michael Vann Roberts
Officers: Michael Vann Roberts [1948] Director [American]; Lawrence Philip Trout [1959] Director

Rita Roberts Cosmetics Limited
Incorporated: 4 March 2002
Net Worth: £2,550 Total Assets: £3,140
Registered Office: Grove Farm, Grove Hill, Langham, Colchester, Essex, CO4 5PJ
Major Shareholder: Gerald Robert Glancey
Officers: Dr Generall Robert Glancey, Secretary/Doctor; Rita Yvonne Upchurch, Secretary; Dr Generall Robert Glancey [1958] Director/Doctor; Liudmilla Pentcheva Glancey [1967] Director/Doctor; Rita Yvonne Upchurch [1932] Director/Consultant

Robh Scrub Limited
Incorporated: 3 April 2018
Registered Office: 37 Toynbee Street, London, E1 7NE
Officers: Badhol Umor Robh [1992] Director/Sales

Roccotek Limited
Incorporated: 19 October 2018
Registered Office: 17 Providence House, Providence Place, Maidenhead, Berks, SL6 8BF
Shareholder: Justin Oliver Hall
Officers: Justin Oliver Hall [1973] Director/Owner [South African]

Rock Beauty Junkie Limited
Incorporated: 6 March 2018
Registered Office: Third Floor Offices, 191 South Street, Romford, Essex, RM1 1QA
Major Shareholder: Heather Martin
Officers: Heather Martin [1986] Managing Director

Rock Perfumes Ltd
Incorporated: 4 February 2016
Registered Office: 10 Park Place, Manchester, M4 4EY
Major Shareholder: Atul Thakrar
Officers: Atul Thakrar [1967] Managing Director

Albert Roger & Partner France Limited
Incorporated: 23 September 2014 *Employees:* 2
Net Worth: £53,288 *Total Assets:* £707,857
Registered Office: 22 St John Street, Newport Pagnell, Bucks, MK16 8HJ
Shareholders: Guillaume Sylvain Samuel Bakouch; Joan Albert Roger Jara
Officers: Guillaume Sylvain Samuel Bakouch [1979] Director/Managing Partner [French]; Joan Albert Roger Jara [1965] Director [Spanish]

Albert Roger Benelux Limited
Incorporated: 17 April 2015
Net Worth Deficit: £28 *Total Assets:* £10,904
Registered Office: 22 St John Street, Newport Pagnell, Bucks, MK16 8HJ
Officers: Gerardus Van Den Eijnden, Secretary; Joan Albert Roger Jara [1965] Managing Director [Spanish]

Albert Roger Limited
Incorporated: 2 December 2013 *Employees:* 4
Net Worth: £156,851 *Total Assets:* £3,059,196
Registered Office: 22 St John Street, Newport Pagnell, Bucks, MK16 8HJ
Major Shareholder: Joan Albert Roger Jara
Officers: Joan Albert Roger Jara [1965] Director/Chief Executive Officer [Spanish]

Albert Roger Portugal Limited
Incorporated: 24 May 2016 *Employees:* 1
Net Worth: £12,640 *Total Assets:* £87,977
Registered Office: 22 St John Street, Newport Pagnell, Milton Keynes, Bucks, MK16 8HJ
Officers: Joan Albert Roger Jara [1965] Director [Spanish]

Roja Dove Limited
Incorporated: 29 September 2004
Net Worth: £1,580,000 *Total Assets:* £3,070,000
Registered Office: 41 New England Street, New England Quarter, Brighton, BN1 4GQ
Parent: Roja Parfums Holdings Limited
Officers: Peter John Causer [1947] Director; Roger John Dove [1956] Director; Jamie Robert Kelly [1977] Director

Rokka Imagine Ltd
Incorporated: 25 June 2015
Net Worth Deficit: £34,900 *Total Assets:* £7,580
Registered Office: Brookscity, 6th Floor, New Baltic House, 65 Fenchurch Street, London, EC3M 4BE
Major Shareholder: Lisa Lee
Officers: Lisa Lee [1957] Director

Romade Limited
Incorporated: 14 January 2014 *Employees:* 2
Net Worth: £138 *Total Assets:* £17,333
Registered Office: 3 Graduate Court, Tudor Crescent, Portsmouth, PO6 2BZ
Major Shareholder: Radu Mihai Ghircoias
Officers: Radu Mihai Ghircoias [1981] Director/Self Employed [Romanian]

Rogia Romini Limited
Incorporated: 31 January 2013
Previous: Pharmajoint Limited
Registered Office: 23 Arnos Grove, Nuthall, Nottingham, NG16 1QA
Major Shareholder: Ramin Nooraldin Moosa
Officers: Ramin Nooraldin Moosa [1965] Director

Rooster & Rooster Ltd.
Incorporated: 26 September 2016
Registered Office: 139a Hawthorn Bank, Spalding, Lincs, PE11 2UN
Shareholder: Steven Antony Rawlins
Officers: Wei Li [1969] Director/Owner [Chinese]; Steven Antony Rawlins [1957] Director/Owner

Roots Are Remedies Ltd
Incorporated: 16 April 2018
Registered Office: 5 Firgrove Court, Adenmore Road, London, SE6 4BN
Major Shareholder: Jelisa Cole-Burke
Officers: Jelisa Cole-Burke [1994] Director/Lecturer

Rosdon Group Limited
Incorporated: 8 March 2012
Previous: Cougar Products Ltd
Net Worth: £342,450 *Total Assets:* £641,530
Registered Office: 5 Commondale Way, Bradford, W Yorks, BD4 6SF
Major Shareholder: Paula Diane Dunne
Officers: Paula Diane Dunne [1967] Director

Rose & Thorn Ltd
Incorporated: 4 February 2019
Registered Office: 42 Edenbridge Drive, Radcliffe, Manchester, M26 1GN
Major Shareholder: Jade Anike Quinn
Officers: Jade Anike Quinn [1986] Director/Businesswoman

Rose Tree Enterprises Ltd.
Incorporated: 25 November 2013
Net Worth: £7,315 *Total Assets:* £12,099
Registered Office: 3 Heron Way, Aldermaston, Reading, Berks, RG7 4UU
Major Shareholder: Olga Jane Rumble
Officers: Olga Jane Rumble [1970] Director/OJR Consulting

The Rosebud Perfume Company Limited
Incorporated: 11 May 2009 *Employees:* 1
Net Worth: £170,275 *Total Assets:* £212,681
Registered Office: 36 Melbury Court, Kensington High Street, London, W8 6NH
Major Shareholder: Fenella Kayser
Officers: Oliver Kayser, Secretary; Fenella Kayser [1973] Director/Entrepreneur

JC Rosedale Co. Ltd.
Incorporated: 10 October 2018
Registered Office: JC Rosedale Co Ltd, Park House, Park Terrace, Worcester Park, Surrey, KT4 7JZ
Major Shareholder: Covey Son
Officers: Covey Son [1994] Director [American]

Rosense (UK) Ltd
Incorporated: 8 December 2010
Net Worth Deficit: £87,246 *Total Assets:* £1,785
Registered Office: 33 Singleton Scarp, London, N12 7AR
Shareholder: Niyazi Alpaslan Karabulut
Officers: Niyazi Alpaslan Karabulut, Secretary; Niyazi Alpaslan Karabulut [1966] Director/Accountant

Rosmetics Aesthetics Limited
Incorporated: 18 September 2014
Net Worth: £112,033 *Total Assets:* £287,071
Registered Office: 53 Worcester Road, Bromsgrove, Worcs, B61 7DN
Major Shareholder: Rosaline Bown
Officers: Rosaline Bown [1956] Director/Facial Aesthetic Practitioner

Rosse Beau Ltd
Incorporated: 26 October 2018
Registered Office: Kemp House, 160 City Road, London, EC1V 2NX
Shareholder: Hannah Johnson
Officers: Hannah Johnson, Secretary; Hannah Johnson [1983] Director/Management Consultant; Everton Small [1966] Director/Tradesman

Rouge Bunny Rouge UK Limited
Incorporated: 2 February 2005 *Employees:* 12
Net Worth Deficit: £6,262,551 *Total Assets:* £1,196,487
Registered Office: 3rd Floor, 207 Regent Street, London, W1B 3HH
Major Shareholder: Arkadii Degtev
Officers: Karina Romanova [1978] Director/Manager [Russian]

Roxie Cosmetics Ltd
Incorporated: 15 January 2019
Registered Office: Unit 26 Mary Seacole Road, Plymouth, PL1 3JY
Shareholders: Dawid Pawel Skwiot; Roksana Ewa Sliwinska-Skwiot
Officers: Dawid Pawel Skwiot [1988] Director [Polish]; Roksana Ewa Sliwinska-Skwiot [1986] Director [Polish]

Royce Health Sciences Ltd
Incorporated: 21 September 2017
Registered Office: 58 Aldfield Green, Hamilton, Leicester, LE5 1BP
Shareholders: Sinnan Fazwani; Rizwan Ladak
Officers: Sinnan Fazwani [1993] Director [Pakistani]; Rizwan Ladak [1982] Director

Roz Cosmetics Ltd
Incorporated: 8 May 2018
Registered Office: 18 Borrowdale Drive, Rochdale, Lancs, OL11 3JZ
Major Shareholder: Peshran Khder
Officers: Peshran Khder [1982] Director/Manager

RR Cosmeceuticals (UK) Ltd
Incorporated: 7 March 2018
Registered Office: 925 Finchley Road, London, NW11 7PE
Major Shareholder: Mohd Rodzi Bin Abdul Rahman
Officers: Mohd Rodzi Bin Abdul Rahman [1972] Director [Malaysian]; Nor Faiz Bin Ahmad Helimi [1978] Director [Malaysian]

RSJ Trading Limited
Incorporated: 20 September 2018
Registered Office: 7 Alton Close, Bury, Lancs, BL9 8BN
Shareholders: Rosalie Byrne; Andrew Byrne
Officers: Rosalie Byrne [1977] Director [Filipino]

Ru Si Lacquers Global Ltd.
Incorporated: 3 July 2018
Registered Office: Companies House, Default Address, Cardiff, CF14 8LH
Officers: Vidya Bhushan Goyal [1955] Director/Self Employed; Rushikesh Vishwanath Nashte [1995] Director/Businessman [Indian]

Rub-a-Dub Scrub Ltd
Incorporated: 1 October 2018
Registered Office: 4 Brempton Croft, Hilderstone, Stone, Staffs, ST15 8XL
Major Shareholder: Audrey Alaine Burton
Officers: Audrey Alaine Burton [1976] Managing Director [American]

Ruby Concepts Ltd
Incorporated: 22 September 2016
Net Worth: £847 *Total Assets:* £8,218
Registered Office: 52 Booth Court, Thurston Road, London, SE13 7GU
Officers: Bemigho Jennifer Onemokpe [1979] Director/Trade and Services

J. Rudzitis Ltd
Incorporated: 23 November 2015
Net Worth Deficit: £8,818 *Total Assets:* £4,224
Registered Office: 132-134 Great Ancoats Street, Manchester, M4 6DE
Officers: Artis Kaposts [1985] Director/IT Programmer [Latvian]

Rupitex Limited
Incorporated: 28 March 2017
Net Worth Deficit: £7,750
Registered Office: Suite 81, 22 Notting Hill Gate, London, W11 3JE
Major Shareholder: Darius Saulenas
Officers: Darius Saulenas [1983] Director/Chief Executive Officer [Lithuanian]

Jerome Russell Limited
Incorporated: 10 October 2011 *Employees:* 6
Net Worth: £1,189,593 *Total Assets:* £2,265,709
Registered Office: 1 Queens Grove Studios, Queens Grove, London, NW8 6EP
Officers: Brian Aitken [1954] Director; Sheena Johnston Cunniffe [1972] Director/Commercial Manager; Colette Frances MacDonough [1967] Director; Stephen James MacDonough [1962] Director; Stephen McLaughlin [1974] Director/Accountant

Ruxley Medical Aids Limited
Incorporated: 17 November 2015
Net Worth Deficit: £697 *Total Assets:* £10
Registered Office: 2 Ruxley Lane, Ewell, Surrey, KT19 0JA
Shareholder: Purgent Vinubhai Patel
Officers: Purgent Vinubhai Patel [1954] Director/Pharmacist

RX Cosmetics Limited
Incorporated: 20 January 2015 Employees: 4
Net Worth: £116,599 Total Assets: £273,527
Registered Office: 3 Russell Street, Leamington Spa, Warwicks, CV32 5QA
Major Shareholder: Mary Angela Teague
Officers: Mary Angela Teague [1955] Director

S & E Ventures Ltd
Incorporated: 7 July 2016
Net Worth: £2,113 Total Assets: £5,430
Registered Office: 5 Aidan Close, Aylesbury, Bucks, HP21 9XQ
Shareholders: Emma Louise Merrett; Sophie Westbrooke
Officers: Emma Louise Merrett [1987] Director/Executive; Sophie Westbrooke [1989] Director/Executive

S & G Supplies Ltd
Incorporated: 10 December 2018
Registered Office: 82 Glendower Road, Perry Barr, Birmingham, B42 1SR
Major Shareholder: Waqar Rehman
Officers: Waqar Rehman [1983] Director

S & P Cosmetics Limited
Incorporated: 18 May 2015 Employees: 2
Net Worth Deficit: £7,539 Total Assets: £1,066
Registered Office: Office 14-15-16, Neptune Court, Vanguard Way, Cardiff, CF24 5PJ
Officers: Victoria Louise Patterson [1984] Director; Gareth Edward Shears [1978] Director/Financial Planner

S A Designer Parfums Limited
Incorporated: 11 April 2001
Net Worth: £9,480,000 Total Assets: £38,090,000
Registered Office: Amertrans Park, Bushey Mill Lane, Watford, Herts, WD24 7JG
Parent: Shaneel Enterprises Ltd
Officers: Hitesh Bhogilal Mehta, Secretary; Dilesh Bhogilal Mehta [1960] Director; Hitesh Bhogilal Mehta [1956] Director

S Beauty Ltd
Incorporated: 2 August 2017
Registered Office: 103a Bishops Way, London, E2 9HL
Major Shareholder: Kyjar Khan
Officers: Kyjar Khan [1992] Director

S T K Brows Limited
Incorporated: 19 July 2018
Registered Office: Unit 24 Highcroft Industrial Estate, Enterprise Road, Horndean, Waterlooville, Hants, PO8 0BT
Major Shareholder: Jamielee Akosua Yeboaa
Officers: Jamielee Akosua Yeboaa [1991] Director

S.I Attar Ltd
Incorporated: 1 February 2019
Registered Office: 637e High Road, Ilford, Essex, IG3 8RG
Major Shareholder: Shariful Islam
Officers: Shariful Islam [1993] Director [Bangladeshi]

SA & A Ltd
Incorporated: 15 February 2018
Registered Office: Office 4, 219 Kensington High Street, Kensington, London, W8 6BD
Major Shareholder: Salem Hesham Mohamed Salem
Officers: Salem Hesham Mohamed Salem [1989] Director/Businessman [Yemeni]

SA Plus Enterprise Ltd
Incorporated: 18 January 2018
Registered Office: Unit 3 Merchant, Evegate Business Park, Ashford, Kent, TN25 6SX
Major Shareholder: Sandra Frimpong
Officers: Sandra Frimpong [1992] Director [Ghanaian]

Sabeauti Ltd.
Incorporated: 16 August 2017
Registered Office: Office 32, 19-21 Crawford Street, London, W1H 1PJ
Shareholders: Afsana Jowkar; Saeed Yakoobi
Officers: Afsana Jowkar, Secretary; Afsana Jowkar [1976] Director [Pakistani]; Saeed Yakoobi [1984] Director [Indian]

Sacha Cosmetics UK Ltd
Incorporated: 20 July 2018
Registered Office: 20-22 Wenlock Road, London, N1 7GU
Major Shareholder: Gerard Lindon Alibocas
Officers: Gerard Lindon Alibocas [1967] Director/Entrepreneur

Saffron Beauty Ltd
Incorporated: 30 March 2007
Net Worth: £83,470 Total Assets: £125,610
Registered Office: 152 Forest Road, London, E17 6JQ
Major Shareholder: Basharat Ali
Officers: Zariat Bi, Secretary; Basharit Ali [1971] Director

The Sage Apothecary Limited
Incorporated: 19 October 2018
Registered Office: Westward House, Llanishen, Chepstow, Monmouthshire, NP16 6QS
Major Shareholder: Abigail Louise Jackson Burks
Officers: Abigail Louise Jackson Burks [1975] Director [British/New Zealander]

Sahinler Limited
Incorporated: 24 October 2018
Registered Office: 37 Park Road, Leamington Spa, Warwicks, CV32 6LG
Major Shareholder: Hasan Sahin
Officers: Hasan Sahin [1994] Director/General Manager [Turkish]

P.S. Sahney & Co Limited
Incorporated: 3 November 1983
Net Worth: £2,210,000 Total Assets: £4,480,000
Registered Office: Unit 2 Manhattan Business Park, Westgate, Ealing, London, W5 1UP
Shareholders: Pritpal Singh Sahney; Jasbir Kaur Sahney; Jasprit Kaur Sahney
Officers: Jasbir Kaur Sahney, Secretary; Jasbir Kaur Sahney [1948] Director/Housewife; Jasprit Kaur Sahney [1975] Director

Sahney Siblings Limited
Incorporated: 5 August 2015
Net Worth: £6,344 Total Assets: £14,743
Registered Office: 2b Manhattan Business Park, Westgate, Ealing, London, W5 1UP
Shareholders: Gursharn Singh Sahney; Jasprit Kaur Sahney
Officers: Gursharn Singh Sahney [1980] Director; Jasprit Kaur Sahney [1975] Director

Sai Darshan Limited
Incorporated: 11 August 2005
Net Worth Deficit: £29,030 *Total Assets:* £1,670
Registered Office: 904 Lemonade Building, 3 Arboretum Place, Barking, Essex, IG11 7PX
Shareholder: Darshan Hanumanth Kumar
Officers: Shruthi Mysore Jagadishwara, Secretary; Dr Darshan Hanumanth Kumar [1977] Director/Doctor; Shruthi Mysore Jagadishwara [1983] Director/IT Professional

Sai Enterprise Limited
Incorporated: 15 May 2002
Net Worth: £211,150 *Total Assets:* £456,430
Registered Office: 15a Alperton Lane, Perivale, Greenford, Middlesex, UB6 8DH
Shareholder: Manoj Navnitlal Gandhi
Officers: Manoj Navnitlal Gandhi, Secretary/Manager; Anoj Navnitlal Gandhi [1960] Director/Beauty Products-Cosmetics Wholesaling; Manoj Navnitlal Gandhi [1957] Director/Manager

Saint and Sinner Cosmetics Ltd
Incorporated: 29 October 2018
Registered Office: 2 Kingsway, Quedgeley, Gloucester, GL2 2FJ
Major Shareholder: April Louise Jenner
Officers: April Louise Jenner [1991] Director

Saint Cosmetics Ltd
Incorporated: 13 September 2018
Registered Office: 17 Canniesburn Drive, Bearsden, Glasgow, G61 1RX
Major Shareholder: Nicole Campbell
Officers: Chiara Fionda, Secretary; Nicole Campbell [1996] Director

Salem Stores Ltd
Incorporated: 22 August 2018
Registered Office: 20-22 Wenlock Road, London, N1 7GU
Major Shareholder: Nathan Salem
Officers: Nathan Salem [1999] Director

Salimaskinsolutions Ltd
Incorporated: 11 September 2018
Registered Office: 44 Hunt Close, London, W11 4JU
Major Shareholder: Abubakar Haji Ali
Officers: Abubakar Haji Ali [1980] Director/Businessman [Somali]

Salon Ambition Limited
Incorporated: 18 November 2004
Net Worth Deficit: £13,771 *Total Assets:* £21,482
Registered Office: 65 Manor Road, Walton on Thames, Surrey, KT12 2NX
Shareholder: Simon Nicholas Webb
Officers: Robert Webb, Secretary; Robert Webb [1937] Director/Accountant; Simon Nicholas Webb [1965] Director/Publisher

Salon Connection (Wales) Limited
Incorporated: 18 July 2006
Net Worth: £551,820 *Total Assets:* £1,731,733
Registered Office: Crowhurst Corner, Crowhurst Road, Brighton, BN1 8AP
Shareholders: Christopher Henry Hughes; Elizabeth Ann Hughes
Officers: Harry Anthony Sleet [1968] Director/Chartered Accountant; Peter Ross Vans Agnew [1960] Managing Director

Salon Depot Ltd
Incorporated: 8 March 2012
Net Worth: £1,550 *Total Assets:* £111,940
Registered Office: 28 West Street, Dunstable, Beds, LU6 1TA
Shareholders: Jonathan Walker; Tracey Susan Walker
Officers: Tracey Walker, Secretary; Jonathan Walker [1967] Director

Salon Distribution Concepts Limited
Incorporated: 14 February 2017
Net Worth: £2,321 *Total Assets:* £50,475
Registered Office: c/o UHY Hacker Young, Lanyon House, Mission Court, Newport, NP20 2DW
Shareholders: Christopher Eggleton; Bradley Niner; Mark Andrew Hancock
Officers: Christopher Eggleton [1957] Director; Mark Andrew Hancock [1963] Director; Bradley Niner [1970] Director

Salon Focus Ltd
Incorporated: 21 January 2003
Net Worth: £8,240 *Total Assets:* £359,980
Registered Office: 33 Gibfield Park Avenue, Gibfield Park, Atherton, Manchester, M46 0SY
Major Shareholder: Philip John Naylor
Officers: Gail Dawn Naylor, Secretary; Phillip John Naylor [1959] Director

Salon Professional London Ltd
Incorporated: 8 January 2019
Registered Office: Kemp House, 160 City Road, London, EC1V 2NX
Officers: Mustapha Khatib [1985] Director/Owner [Lebanese]

Salon Select (NI) Limited
Incorporated: 16 August 2011
Net Worth: £69,547 *Total Assets:* £234,891
Registered Office: 58 Main Street, Strabane, Co Tyrone, BT82 8AX
Major Shareholder: Alan Chadwick
Officers: Denise Chadwick, Secretary; Alan Chadwick [1959] Director [Irish]; Denise Chadwick [1961] Director [Irish]

Salon Success Limited
Incorporated: 22 November 1985 *Employees:* 126
Net Worth: £14,198,714 *Total Assets:* £16,843,722
Registered Office: Ground Floor, Inspired, Easthampstead Road, Bracknell, Berks, RG12 1YQ
Parent: Sally UK Holdings Limited
Officers: Nina Azemoudeh, Secretary; Olivier Badezet [1969] Managing Director (Senior VP) [French]; Simon Andrew Tickler [1971] Managing Director; Heidi Van Ocken [1968] Director [Belgian]

Salon Supplies 365 Limited
Incorporated: 16 November 2015
Net Worth: £19,525 *Total Assets:* £55,194
Registered Office: 10 Mapleton Close, Prenton, Birkenhead, Merseyside, CH43 3EZ
Shareholders: Ramon Carl Ygartua; Amy Louise Hughes
Officers: Amy Louise Hughes [1987] Director/Self Employed; Geoffrey William Edward Hughes [1950] Director/Retired; Patricia Anne Hughes [1957] Director/Sales Assistant; Ramon Carl Ygartua [1984] Director/Business Analyst

Salon Supplies Limited
Incorporated: 25 June 2004
Registered Office: Bond Street, Shamrock Quay, Northam, Southampton, SO14 5QA
Major Shareholder: Keith Boothroyde
Officers: Ian Martin Campbell Aherne, Secretary; Keith Boothroyde [1947] Director

Salon Theory Ltd
Incorporated: 14 February 2019
Registered Office: c/o Kandi London, Studio B04, Tripod, Lambeth Town Hall, Brixton Hill, London, SW2 1RW
Major Shareholder: Dong Young Hwang
Officers: Dong Young Hwang [1990] Director

Salonpas UK Limited
Incorporated: 9 January 2002
Net Worth: £1 *Total Assets:* £1
Registered Office: 5 Chancery Lane, London, WC2A 1LG
Parent: Hisamitsu Pharmaceutical Co., Inc.
Officers: Yoshio Hiyama, Secretary; Yoshio Hiyama [1974] Director [Japanese]; Yuichi Isobe [1971] President and Managing Director [Japanese]

Salt and Pamper Limited
Incorporated: 5 September 2015
Net Worth Deficit: £764 *Total Assets:* £340
Registered Office: 2 Faulkners Farm Cottages, Edenbridge Road, Hartfield, E Sussex, TN7 4JL
Shareholders: Mark Graham Westoll; Caroline Mary Westoll
Officers: Caroline Mary Westoll [1976] Director; Mark Graham Westoll [1972] Director

Saltee Skincare Limited
Incorporated: 29 March 2018
Registered Office: Winton House, Village Road, Denham, Uxbridge, Middlesex, UB9 5BH
Shareholders: Samuel James Ivo Richardson; Patrick Daniel McGuirk
Officers: Patrick Daniel McGuirk [1975] Director; Samuel James Ivo Richardson [1975] Director

Salus Cutis Ltd
Incorporated: 18 February 2016
Registered Office: c/o Italian Accountants Limited, Office 3.2, Central House, 1 Ballards Lane, Finchley Central, London, N3 1LQ
Parent: Clusternanotech Ltd
Officers: Bruno Cantarelli [1955] Director/Entrepreneur [Italian]; Nataliya Cantarelli [1995] Director/Entrepreneur [Russian]

Sama Perfumes Ltd
Incorporated: 17 March 2015
Net Worth: £10,410 *Total Assets:* £87,790
Registered Office: 57 Mead Crescent, Birmingham, B9 5UU
Major Shareholder: Syed Yakub Ali
Officers: Syed Yakub Ali, Secretary; Syed Yakub Ali [1978] Director/Self Employed

Sambio Ltd
Incorporated: 30 July 2018
Registered Office: 31-33 College Road, Harrow, Middlesex, HA1 1EJ
Shareholders: Diana Iaghanashvili; Giorgi Sulkhanishvili
Officers: Diana Iaghanashvili, Secretary; Diana Iaghanashvili [1983] Director/Accountant; Giorgi Sulkhanishvili [1964] Director/Consultant [Georgian]

Same Cosmetics Limited
Incorporated: 31 January 2019
Registered Office: Maple House, Northern Heights, Bourne End, Bucks, SL8 5LE
Major Shareholder: Sarah Louise Ashcroft
Officers: Sarah Louise Ashcroft [1994] Director/Influencer

Samla Tribe Limited
Incorporated: 10 October 2014
Net Worth: £127 *Total Assets:* £127
Registered Office: 59 The Broadway, Didcot, Oxon, OX11 8AJ
Shareholders: Alexander Leonard Pearce; Joshua Laitphlang-Williams
Officers: Alexander Leonard Pearce, Secretary; Joshua Laitphlang-Williams [1993] Creative Director; Alexander Leonard Pearce [1993] Managing Director

San & Amad General Trade Company Ltd
Incorporated: 13 April 2015
Net Worth: £23,962 *Total Assets:* £270,471
Registered Office: 10-11 Shaw Lane Industrial Estate, Ogden Road, Doncaster, S Yorks, DN2 4SE
Major Shareholder: Aihd Omar
Officers: Aihd Omar [1984] Director

Sana Jardin (UK) Limited
Incorporated: 28 June 2017
Registered Office: 21-27 Lambs Conduit Street, London, WC1N 3GS
Parent: Sana Jardin Limited
Officers: Amy Christiansen Sl-Ahmed [1974] Director [American]

Sanay Ltd
Incorporated: 12 February 2013
Net Worth: £142 *Total Assets:* £3,212
Registered Office: Devonshire House, 582 Honeypot Lane, Stanmore, Middlesex, HA7 1JS
Major Shareholder: Neel Rameshchandra Shah
Officers: Neel Rameshchandra Shah [1974] Director

Leonora Sanche Cosmetics Limited
Incorporated: 15 May 2017
Registered Office: c/o Tally Accountants Ltd, Top Floor, College House, 17 King Edwards Road, Ruislip, Middlesex, HA4 7AE
Shareholders: Jalil Ahmed Chaudhri; Nila Leonor Simon-Sanchez
Officers: Jalil Ahmed Chaudhri [1970] Director; Nila Leonor Simon-Sanchez [1974] Director

Leonora Sanche Limited
Incorporated: 12 October 2016
Registered Office: Top Floor, College House, 17 King Edwards Road, Ruislip, Middlesex, HA4 7AE
Major Shareholder: Nila Leonor Simon-Sanchez
Officers: Jalil Ahmed Chaudhri [1970] Director/Entrepreneur; Nila Leonor Simon-Sanchez [1974] Director

Sanchi Corp Limited
Incorporated: 13 June 2016
Net Worth: £3,324 *Total Assets:* £6,697
Registered Office: 4 Fernleigh Court, Headstone Lane, Hatch End, Middlesex, HA2 6NA
Major Shareholder: Hardik Mehta
Officers: Hardik Mehta [1979] Director/Businessman

Sandaig Ltd
Incorporated: 20 February 1985 *Employees:* 4
Net Worth: £25,126 *Total Assets:* £455,633
Registered Office: West Lodge, Rainbow Street, Leominster, Herefords, HR6 8DQ
Shareholders: Johnathan Noel Sellers; Janet Susan Sellers
Officers: Janet Susan Sellers, Secretary; Janet Susan Sellers [1945] Director/Accounts Clerk; Jonathan Noel Sellers [1944] Director; James Meenan Sharp [1970] Director; Melanie Joy Sharp [1975] Director/Salesperson

Sandgroper Limited
Incorporated: 25 November 2016
Registered Office: 2h Weld Works Mews, London, SW2 5AX
Major Shareholder: Neil Jonathon Chambers
Officers: Neil Jonathon Chambers [1972] Director/Accountant [Australian]

Sandine Zartaux Holding Ltd
Incorporated: 25 November 2014
Net Worth Deficit: £3,722 *Total Assets:* £3,544
Registered Office: 27 Old Gloucester Street, London, WC1N 3AX
Major Shareholder: Kyriaki Zartaloudi
Officers: Kyriaki Zartaloudi [1973] Director/Trader [Greek]

Daniel Sandler Ltd
Incorporated: 2 February 2005
Net Worth: £609,630 *Total Assets:* £917,310
Registered Office: Office 7, 35-37 Ludgate Hill, London, EC4M 7JN
Shareholders: Nicola Saragossi; Daniel Sandler-Vallance
Officers: Nicola Saragossi, Secretary; Daniel Sandler-Vallance [1965] Director; Nicola Saragossi [1959] Director

Sang Real Tattoo Ltd
Incorporated: 14 December 2018
Registered Office: 77 Ashbourne Road, Derby, DE22 3FW
Major Shareholder: Jordan Croke
Officers: Jordan Croke [1990] Director; Haley Mackintosh [1991] Director

Sangels Limited
Incorporated: 21 February 2018
Registered Office: 2nd Floor, College House, 17 King Edwards Road, Ruislip, Middlesex, HA4 7AE
Major Shareholder: Satu Pietarinen
Officers: Satu Pietarinen [1968] Director [Finnish]

Sankofa Heritage Ltd
Incorporated: 3 October 2017
Registered Office: 24 Anderson Heights, 1260 London Road, Norbury, London, SW16 4EH
Major Shareholder: Rebecca Bonsu-Stewart
Officers: Rebecca Bonsu-Stewart [1973] Director/Teacher [Ghanaian]

Sanmex International Limited
Incorporated: 22 June 1982
Net Worth: £4,070,000 *Total Assets:* £6,230,000
Registered Office: 5 Riverside Way, Riverside Business Park, Irvine, N Ayrshire, KA11 5DJ
Parent: Barony Universal Products PLC
Officers: Eliot Swan, Secretary; Andrei Borshchev [1971] Director [Russian]; Steven David Groden [1970] Director/Sales & Marketing; Victor Lobashkov [1974] Director [Russian]; Alexandre Matytsine [1958] Director [Russian]; Eliot Swan [1966] Director; Eric Kevin Woolfson [1960] Commercial Director

Sansuri Hair & Beauty Supplies and Training Ltd
Incorporated: 1 September 2017
Registered Office: Unit C1, Hamstead Industrial Estate, Austin Way, Hamstead Industrial Estate, Birmingham, B42 1DU
Major Shareholder: Narinder Kaur Chaggar
Officers: Jasvir Singh Chaggar [1980] Director; Narinder Kaur Chaggar [1984] Director

Santa Code Limited
Incorporated: 28 August 2018
Registered Office: 2 Sutherland Court, Marylands Road, London, W9 2DT
Officers: Giorgio Codeghini [1982] Director/Businessman; Giselle Almeida Codeghini [1986] Director/Businesswoman

Santiago Distribution Limited
Incorporated: 4 July 2005
Net Worth Deficit: £33,906 *Total Assets:* £10,223
Registered Office: Linden End, Linden Gardens, Leatherhead, Surrey, KT22 7HB
Shareholders: Michael Charles Olney; Dawn Patricia Olney
Officers: Dawn Patricia Olney, Secretary; Michael Charles Olney [1943] Director

Santini Trade Ltd.
Incorporated: 10 October 2012
Net Worth: £10,000 *Total Assets:* £11,923
Registered Office: 72 Great Suffolk Street, London, SE1 0BL
Major Shareholder: Daniel Santini
Officers: Daniel Santini [1978] Director/Manager [Czech]

Saravio UK Ltd
Incorporated: 25 August 2018
Registered Office: No 16 Gillfield Close, High Wycombe, Bucks, HP11 1TS
Shareholder: Chaminda Thushara Gigurawa Gamage
Officers: Upamali Manohari Wijeratne, Secretary; Chaminda Thushara Gigurawa Gamage [1976] Director [Sri Lankan]; Shigeru Hamada [1956] Director [Japanese]; Kuniyoshi Kaseda [1971] Director [Japanese]

Saroza Limited
Incorporated: 24 September 2018
Registered Office: 1 Copper Street, Southsea, Hants, PO5 3BJ
Major Shareholder: Stephanie Samer Fahem
Officers: Stephanie Samer Fahem [1995] Director/Entrepreneur [French]

Sash Products Limited
Incorporated: 6 June 2016
Net Worth Deficit: £486 *Total Assets:* £1,198
Registered Office: 24 Douglas Road, Esher, Surrey, KT10 8BB
Major Shareholder: Kumarini Maria Goonesekera
Officers: Kumarini Maria Goonesekera [1982] Director

Sasha Hair & Beauty Ltd
Incorporated: 2 March 2011
Net Worth: £19,280 *Total Assets:* £143,140
Registered Office: 58-60 Wetmore Road, Burton on Trent, Staffs, DE14 1SN
Major Shareholder: Adam Timbrell
Officers: Adam Timbrell, Secretary; Adam Timbrell [1969] Director/Sales

Sassy Hair & Beauty Supplies Ltd
Incorporated: 6 April 2016
Registered Office: 26 Sycamore Road, Northolt, Middlesex, UB5 5BG
Officers: Karema Henderson [1979] Director/Hairstylist

Sassy N Trendy Cosmetics Ltd
Incorporated: 6 February 2018
Registered Office: 191 St Albans Road, Watford, Herts, WD24 5BH
Shareholders: Casha Catherine Muguiyi; Casha Muguiyi
Officers: Casha Catherine Muguiyi [1969] Director/Support Worker

Sasy N Savy Ltd
Incorporated: 2 August 2018
Registered Office: Grove House, 1 Grove Place, Bedford, MK40 3JJ
Major Shareholder: Samea Maakrun
Officers: Samea Maakrun [1974] Managing Director [Australian]

Satya Life Ltd
Incorporated: 24 March 2003 *Employees:* 2
Previous: Exclusive Spa Brands (Europe) Ltd
Net Worth: £20,398 *Total Assets:* £116,272
Registered Office: 1st Floor, 21 Victoria Road, Surbiton, Surrey, KT6 4JZ
Major Shareholder: Claudia Agha
Officers: Sandra Agha, Secretary; Claudia Agha [1974] Director/Marketing Consultant

Saveasy Ltd.
Incorporated: 5 November 2018
Registered Office: P O Box 6357, 72 Melrose Avenue, Bletchley, Milton Keynes, Bucks, MK1 9GU
Major Shareholder: Kestutis Streimikis
Officers: Kestutis Streimikis [1986] Director [Lithuanian]

Savvy & Shine Ltd
Incorporated: 18 October 2010 *Employees:* 4
Net Worth Deficit: £32,332 *Total Assets:* £129,745
Registered Office: 6 Doagh Road, Ballyclare, Co Antrim, BT39 9BG
Shareholders: Thomas Maxwell; Joanna Maxwell
Officers: Joanna Maxwell [1979] Director; Tom Maxwell [1972] Director

Sawa Trading & Shipping Limited
Incorporated: 13 December 2011
Net Worth: £24,624 *Total Assets:* £487,344
Registered Office: 1a Crown Lane, London, SW16 3DJ
Officers: Nancy Bennett [1948] Director/Businesswoman

SB Beauty Marketing Limited
Incorporated: 2 May 2000
Net Worth: £6,840 *Total Assets:* £76,240
Registered Office: 36 Commerce Road, Lynch Wood, Peterborough, Cambs, PE2 6LR
Major Shareholder: Graham Michael Smith
Officers: Steven Anthony Barker [1965] Director; Graham Michael Smith [1946] Managing Director

SB Selected Beauty Ltd
Incorporated: 20 February 2015 *Employees:* 2
Net Worth: £363,317 *Total Assets:* £504,916
Registered Office: Linden End, Linden Gardens, Leatherhead, Surrey, KT22 7HB
Major Shareholder: Stephen Barter
Officers: Patricia Jane Woods, Secretary; Stephen Barter [1961] Director

Scence Ltd
Incorporated: 17 May 2018
Registered Office: Meaderville House, Wheal Buller, Redruth, Cornwall, TR16 6ST
Major Shareholder: Krista Louise Taylor
Officers: Krista Louise Taylor [1967] Director

Scent Angels UK Ltd
Incorporated: 23 June 2014
Registered Office: 20-22 Wenlock Road, London, N1 7GU
Officers: Jasmine Pagayon [1971] Director

The Scent Edit Limited
Incorporated: 19 April 2016
Registered Office: Lower Ground, Castlewood House, 77-91 New Oxford Street, London, WC1A 1DG
Major Shareholder: Sarah Elizabeth McCubbin
Officers: Sarah Elizabeth McCubbin [1975] Director

The Scent Factory Limited
Incorporated: 28 December 2000
Net Worth: £24,159 *Total Assets:* £320,085
Registered Office: Second Floor, 168 Cheetham Hill Round, Manchester, M8 8LQ
Shareholders: The Finance Corporation Limited; Arfan Tahir
Officers: Arfan Tahir, Secretary; Arfan Tahir [1973] Director

Scent Global Ltd
Incorporated: 20 May 2009
Previous: Rock Beauty Ltd
Net Worth: £345,000 *Total Assets:* £26,120,000
Registered Office: 1st Floor, Cloister House, New Bailey Street, Salford, M3 5FS
Major Shareholder: Atul Thakrar
Officers: Atul Thakrar [1967] Director

Scent N Essence UK Ltd
Incorporated: 5 March 2015 *Employees:* 2
Net Worth: £103,356 *Total Assets:* £182,741
Registered Office: 122 Wellington Road North, Hounslow, Middlesex, TW4 7AA
Shareholders: Sanjay Khatri; Rekha Khatri
Officers: Rekha Khatri, Secretary; Sanjay Khatri [1975] Director/Consultant

Scent Retail Ltd
Incorporated: 7 January 2009 *Employees:* 1
Net Worth: £693 *Total Assets:* £18,970
Registered Office: 303 Goring Road, Goring by Sea, Worthing, W Sussex, BN12 4NX
Major Shareholder: Simon Antony Pitzus
Officers: Phil Mair, Secretary; Simon Antony Pitzus [1977] Director

Scented Home Limited
Incorporated: 9 August 2016
Net Worth Deficit: £225 *Total Assets:* £7,649
Registered Office: 51 Craven Park Road, London, N15 6AH
Major Shareholder: Dora Matyas
Officers: Dora Matyas [1994] Director/Business Person

Scented LDN Limited
Incorporated: 24 August 2018
Registered Office: 18 Brixton Water Lane, London, SW2 1PB
Major Shareholder: Daniel Wilson
Officers: Daniel Wilson [1986] Director/Self Employed

Scented Sachets (London) Ltd.
Incorporated: 8 December 2016
Registered Office: 207 Regent Street, London, W1B 3HH
Shareholder: Peter Oxley
Officers: Peter Oxley [1958] Director [Irish]

Scentric Ltd
Incorporated: 15 November 2018
Registered Office: 32 Egerton Road, Twickenham, Middlesex, TW2 7SP
Major Shareholder: Ravi Kumar
Officers: Ravi Kumar [1987] Director

Sci Check Limited
Incorporated: 9 February 2009
Net Worth: £1,230,000 *Total Assets:* £2,210,000
Registered Office: The French Quarter, 114 High Street, Southampton, SO14 2AA
Shareholders: Charlotte Frances Rigby; Lauren Victoria Rigby; Sophie Alexandra Rigby
Officers: Lauren Victoria Rigby, Secretary; Charlotte Frances Rigby [1986] Sales Director; Lauren Victoria Rigby [1988] Director; Sophie Alexandra Rigby [1990] Director/Student

Scontimania Online SRL Limited
Incorporated: 6 June 2017
Registered Office: 27 Old Gloucester Street, London, WC1N 3AX
Major Shareholder: de Franco Marco
Officers: De Franco Marco [1984] Director/Employed [Italian]

Scope Cosmetics Ltd
Incorporated: 25 July 2013
Net Worth: £5,379 *Total Assets:* £7,241
Registered Office: Kemp House, 152-160 City Road, London, EC1V 2NX
Major Shareholder: Scott Alan Wasserman
Officers: Scott Wasserman [1962] Director [American]

Scott Weeks Enterprises Ltd
Incorporated: 16 October 2017
Registered Office: 12a Leopold Road, Wimbledon, London, SW19 7BD
Officers: Katherine Amelia Rose Scott-Weeks [1992] Director

Scrubd Ltd
Incorporated: 27 September 2016
Net Worth Deficit: £194,993 *Total Assets:* £53,046
Registered Office: Suite 5a, 21 Victoria Street, St Albans, Herts, AL1 3JJ
Major Shareholder: Mark Helvadjian
Officers: Mark Helvadjian, Secretary; Charles Ian Osborn Davies [1974] Director; Mark Helvadjian [1978] Director

Sculptola Ltd
Incorporated: 5 September 2013
Previous: Proteinology Ltd
Net Worth Deficit: £3,422 *Total Assets:* £1,578
Registered Office: 5 Acorn Business Park, Woodseats Close, Sheffield, S8 0TB
Major Shareholder: Nicola Rachel Royle
Officers: Graham Royle, Secretary; Graham Royle [1959] Director; Nicola Rachel Royle [1990] Director

Seadrift Trading Limited
Incorporated: 5 September 2012 *Employees:* 1
Net Worth: £1,071 *Total Assets:* £33,670
Registered Office: Ditton House, 59 Fleece Road, Long Ditton, Surbiton, Surrey, KT6 5JR
Major Shareholder: Jose Martinez
Officers: Jose Martinez [1968] Director/Consultant [Spanish]

Searching Plants Ltd
Incorporated: 24 November 2015
Registered Office: 583 Cranbrook Road, Ilford, Essex, IG2 6JZ
Shareholders: Guy Vingrovski; Bana Bandali
Officers: Bana Bandali [1965] Director [Israeli]; Guy Vingrovski [1970] Director [Israeli]

Seascape Island Management Limited
Incorporated: 7 September 2012
Net Worth Deficit: £459,073 *Total Assets:* £256,211
Registered Office: Ground Floor, Belmont Place, Belmont Road, Maidenhead, Berks, SL6 6TB
Shareholders: Tracey Dixon; Alexander Stuart MacTavish
Officers: Tracey Dixon [1966] Director/Cabin Crew; Alexander Stuart MacTavish [1957] Director

Seaside Investments Ltd
Incorporated: 15 August 2018
Registered Office: 57 Lansdown Road, Stroud, Glos, GL5 1BN
Shareholder: Naliandra Naidu
Officers: Naliandra Naidu [1965] Director [South African]

Season of Beauty Limited
Incorporated: 23 November 2005
Net Worth: £18,456 *Total Assets:* £206,683
Registered Office: 1 Kings Avenue, Winchmore Hill, London, N21 3NA
Major Shareholder: Michael Pavlou
Officers: Antigone Georgiou, Secretary; Antigone Georgiou [1979] Director/Businesswoman [Greek]

Seba Trade Limited
Incorporated: 19 July 2017
Net Worth Deficit: £1,190 *Total Assets:* £4,480
Registered Office: 20 Southdale Road, Oxford, OX2 7SD
Major Shareholder: Zekeriye Cil
Officers: Zekeriye Cil [1981] Director [Turkish]

Sebaroyale Ltd
Incorporated: 4 January 2011
Registered Office: 102 Gleneagle Road, London, SW16 6AF
Major Shareholder: Clara Odularu
Officers: Clara Odularu, Secretary; Clara Odularu [1971] Director

Secret Cosmetics Limited
Incorporated: 20 February 2017
Registered Office: Mill Haven, Mill Road, Aveley, South Ockendon, Essex, RM15 4SR
Parent: Kings Wardrobe

Secret Line Ltd
Incorporated: 16 August 2018
Registered Office: 27 Old Gloucester Street, London, WC1N 3AX
Major Shareholder: Walid Kenawy
Officers: Walid Kenawy, Secretary; Walid Kenawy [1972] Director [Egyptian]; Aneta Smolen-Kenawy [1976] Director [Polish]

SeductiveDirect Ltd
Incorporated: 2 August 2018
Registered Office: 49 Nelson Gardens, Braintree, Essex, CM7 9TG
Major Shareholder: Stela Stefanova Doncheva-Zabileva
Officers: Stela Stefanova Doncheva-Zabileva [1980] Director [Bulgarian]

Seed Fashion and Beauty Incubator Ltd
Incorporated: 9 May 2017
Registered Office: c/o Flat E24, 28 Guildhouse Street, London, SW1P 1ET
Officers: Nabila Riaz [1966] Director

Seigur Rose International Group Co., Ltd
Incorporated: 4 June 2018
Registered Office: Unit G25, Waterfront Studios, 1 Dock Road, London, E16 1AH
Major Shareholder: Genming Fang
Officers: Genming Fang [1969] Director [Chinese]

Select & Bargain Ltd
Incorporated: 31 August 2018
Registered Office: 69 Wintersdale Road, Leicester, LE5 2GS
Shareholders: Osman Imtiaz Mussa Mahomed; Mohammed Shakil Rashid
Officers: Osman Imtiaz Mussa Mahomed [1997] Director/Self Employed; Mohammed Shakil Rashid [1996] Director/Student

Selective Fragrances Ltd
Incorporated: 16 April 2013
Net Worth Deficit: £56,774 Total Assets: £100
Registered Office: Second Floor, 201 Haverstock Hill, London, NW3 4QG
Major Shareholder: Ben Gurt
Officers: Ben Gurt [1975] Director [French]

Selfcare Corporation Ltd
Incorporated: 8 August 2012
Net Worth: £100 Total Assets: £100
Registered Office: 10 John Street, London, WC1N 2EB
Major Shareholder: Sonia Amoroso
Officers: Sonia Amoroso [1970] Director [Australian]

Selfish Cosmetics Ltd
Incorporated: 7 February 2019
Registered Office: 189 Melrose Avenue, London, NW2 4NA
Major Shareholder: Nikki Beverley Antwi
Officers: Nikki Beverley Antwi [1993] Director

Semy-Estoiles Limited
Incorporated: 21 April 2016
Registered Office: 396 Wilmslow Road, Manchester, M20 3BN
Major Shareholder: Patricia Mary Ann Stibbs
Officers: Charlotte Joan Mary Stibbs [1998] Director; Patricia Mary Ann Stibbs [1958] Director; Timothy Paul Charles Stibbs [1947] Director

Serendipity (N.I.) Ltd
Incorporated: 21 September 2017
Registered Office: Unit 21 Carrick Enterprise Park, Meadowbank Road, Carrickfergus, Co Antrim, BT38 8YF
Shareholders: Jennifer Murray; Janet Stewart
Officers: Jennifer Murray [1973] Director; Janet Stewart [1976] Director

Serendipity Herbals Ltd
Incorporated: 31 May 2000
Net Worth: £11,317 Total Assets: £49,369
Registered Office: Croes Carn Einion Farm, Rhiwderin, Newport, NP10 8RR
Major Shareholder: Julie Carolyn Preston
Officers: Julie Carolyn Preston [1959] Director

Serene House UK Limited
Incorporated: 2 March 2010 Employees: 1
Net Worth: £57,985 Total Assets: £87,844
Registered Office: 1 City Road East, Manchester, M15 4PN
Shareholders: Howard David Cohen; Valerie Ann Cohen
Officers: Howard David Cohen [1954] Director; Valerie Ann Cohen [1957] Director/Teacher

Serengeti Skincare Limited
Incorporated: 17 May 2018
Registered Office: Flat 46, Field House, 40 Schoolgate Drive, Morden, Surrey, SM4 5DJ
Major Shareholder: Gail Anne Vlahakis
Officers: Gail Anne Vlahakis [1981] Director

Serenityhands Ltd
Incorporated: 27 February 2019
Registered Office: 19 High Road Leytonstone, London, E11 4RB
Major Shareholder: Sereta O'Donovan
Officers: Sereta Odonovan [1982] Director/Support Worker

Serenityy Ltd
Incorporated: 31 January 2019
Registered Office: 36 Osward Place, London, N9 7EF
Major Shareholder: Ander Anneka Sheila Ramsay-Peters
Officers: Ander Anneka Sheila Ramsay-Peters [1996] Director/Entrepreneur

The Serious Skin Care Company Ltd.
Incorporated: 12 September 1997
Net Worth: £7,953 Total Assets: £22,465
Registered Office: Blue Square House, 272 Bath Street, Glasgow, G2 4JR
Major Shareholder: James Anthony McPeake
Officers: James Anthony McPeake [1963] Director/Skin Care

SES Wholesale Limited
Incorporated: 6 April 2010 Employees: 1
Net Worth: £662,826 Total Assets: £758,422
Registered Office: 61 Stanley Road, Whitefield, Manchester, M45 8GZ
Major Shareholder: John William Sharman
Officers: John William Sharman [1955] Director

Seventa Image Ltd
Incorporated: 16 November 2010
Registered Office: 2nd Floor, 48 Poland Street, London, W1F 7ND
Major Shareholder: Juan Antonio Lopez Alvarez
Officers: Jill Allen [1956] Director/Financial Management Consultant; Jeffrey Euen-Gow [1971] Director/Business Manager [Australian]; Juan Antonio Lopez Alvarez [1973] Director/Business Manager [Spanish]

Sfera London Limited
Incorporated: 20 March 2018
Registered Office: Kemp House, 152-160 City Road, London, EC1V 2NX
Shareholder: Sadia Adris
Officers: Sadia Adris [1975] Director

SFL Group Ltd
Incorporated: 24 September 2018
Registered Office: Kemp House, 160 City Road, London, EC1V 2NX
Officers: Nazila Malik [1978] Director

SGHP Ltd
Incorporated: 30 October 2017
Registered Office: Kemp House, 152-160 City Road, London, EC1V 2NX
Major Shareholder: Sabrina Sonia Hernandez Guaitolini
Officers: Sabrina Sonia Hernandez Guaitolini [1986] Director [Spanish]

SGJ Perfumes Limited
Incorporated: 26 January 2016
Net Worth: £4,201 *Total Assets:* £19,084
Registered Office: 4 Middlerigg Road, Cumbernauld, N Lanarks, G68 9DP
Major Shareholder: Anup Bodane
Officers: Anup Bodane [1978] Director/Self Employed

Shadi's Hairdresser Ltd
Incorporated: 29 January 2019
Registered Office: 89 Boundary Road, Hove, E Sussex, BN3 7GA
Major Shareholder: Shadi Asmar
Officers: Shadi Asmar [1983] Director [Syrian]

Shahadah Ltd
Incorporated: 19 January 2012
Net Worth Deficit: £13,501 *Total Assets:* £118,201
Registered Office: Ratford Bridge Farm House, Ratford, Calne, Wilts, SN11 9JX
Shareholder: Ala Uddin
Officers: Suraiya Uddin, Secretary; Ala Uddin [1967] Director; Suraiya Uddin [1993] Director

Shalohm Ltd
Incorporated: 20 January 2017
Net Worth Deficit: £105,894 *Total Assets:* £10,587
Registered Office: 68 St Margarets Road, Edgware, Middlesex, HA8 9UU
Major Shareholder: Namrata Nayyar-Kamdar
Officers: Jeffrey Dale Thomas, Secretary; Namrata Nayyar-Kamdar [1976] Director [Indian]

Shama Pharma Ltd
Incorporated: 24 January 2017
Net Worth: £2,715 *Total Assets:* £5,253
Registered Office: 3 Iveagh Terrace, London, NW10 7DJ
Major Shareholder: Shikar Kerim
Officers: Shikar Kerim [1993] Director/Pharmacist

Shaneel Enterprises Limited
Incorporated: 30 September 1987
Net Worth: £55,740,000 *Total Assets:* £92,480,000
Registered Office: 78 Wembley Park Drive, Wembley, Middlesex, HA9 8HE
Officers: Chetna Dilesh Mehta, Secretary; Dilesh Bhogilal Mehta [1960] Director/Businessman Wholesaler; Hitesh Bhogilal Mehta [1956] Director/Pharmacist

Shared Beauty Secrets Limited
Incorporated: 21 January 2009 *Employees:* 8
Net Worth: £5,754 *Total Assets:* £204,414
Registered Office: 7-9 The Avenue, Eastbourne, E Sussex, BN21 3YA
Major Shareholder: Clare Louise Steadman
Officers: Clare Louise Steadman [1975] Director/Beauty Manager

Shared Beauty Secrets Spas Limited
Incorporated: 21 March 2017
Registered Office: 7-9 The Avenue, Eastbourne, E Sussex, BN21 3YA
Major Shareholder: Clare Louise Steadman
Officers: Clare Louise Steadman [1975] Director

Sharp's Global Trading Limited
Incorporated: 25 March 1993 *Employees:* 5
Net Worth: £1,440,711 *Total Assets:* £1,852,485
Registered Office: 6 Ritherdon Road, London, SW17 8QD
Shareholders: Ajitkumar Patel; Vijanti Ajitkumar Patel
Officers: Vijanti Ajitkumar Patel, Secretary/Businesswoman; Ajitkumar Patel [1958] Director/Businessman; Vijanti Ajit Patel [1959] Director/Secretary

Shave Algorithm Ltd
Incorporated: 15 August 2018
Registered Office: 71-75 Shelton Street, London, WC2H 9JQ
Major Shareholder: Dariusz Paprzycki
Officers: Dariusz Paprzycki [1970] Director [Polish]

Shaw International Ltd
Incorporated: 21 February 2019
Registered Office: 8c Cameron Road, Ilford, Essex, IG3 8LA
Major Shareholder: Adam Shaw
Officers: Adam Shaw, Secretary; Adam Shaw [1980] Director

Shay & Blue Ltd
Incorporated: 15 May 2012 *Employees:* 6
Net Worth: £648,121 *Total Assets:* £1,151,545
Registered Office: 80 York Street, London, W1H 1QW
Major Shareholder: Dominic Marc John Devetta
Officers: Dominic Marc John Devetta [1969] Director/Entrepreneur

She Who Dares UK Ltd
Incorporated: 26 July 2010
Registered Office: 1000 Lakeside North Harbour, Western Road, Portsmouth, PO6 3EZ
Major Shareholder: Simon James Dolan
Officers: Simon James Dolan [1969] Director

Shea Touch Ltd
Incorporated: 14 November 2017
Registered Office: 7 Johnson Road, Croydon, Surrey, CR0 2JS
Major Shareholder: Oyindamola Sukurat Olusanya
Officers: Oyindamola Sukurat Olusanya [1992] Director/Marketing Consultant

Sheabynature Ltd
Incorporated: 14 March 2017
Net Worth Deficit: £7,000 *Total Assets:* £4,000
Registered Office: 4 Victorian Crescent, Doncaster, S Yorks, DN2 5BW
Major Shareholder: Chinwe Mercy Russell
Officers: Chinwe Mercy Russell [1970] Director

Sheacare Cosmetics Limited
Incorporated: 7 March 2018
Registered Office: The Hawthorns, Bampton Road, Lewisham, London, SE23 2BG
Officers: Felix Robinson [1972] Director/Owner

Sheasecrets Ltd
Incorporated: 4 January 2019
Registered Office: 40 Boston Manor Road, Brentford, Middlesex, TW8 9JU
Major Shareholder: Cerise Leatham-Leacock
Officers: Cerise Leatham-Leacock [1986] Director/Customer Services

Shebelle Limited
Incorporated: 1 June 2015
Net Worth Deficit: £143,250 *Total Assets:* £5,840
Registered Office: 3rd Floor, Arnott House, 12-16 Bridge Street, Belfast, BT1 1LU
Major Shareholder: Einna Mildred Harrison-Mellon
Officers: Einna Mildred Harrison-Mellon [1977] Managing Director

Sherhind Accessorize Limited
Incorporated: 2 September 2016
Net Worth: £36,584 *Total Assets:* £46,144
Registered Office: 117 Whitechapel Road, London, E1 1DT
Major Shareholder: Mollah Md Hamim Yasin
Officers: Mollah MD Hamim Yasin, Secretary; Mollah MD Hamim Yasin [1983] Director [Bangladeshi]

Sheyton Ltd
Incorporated: 9 October 2018
Registered Office: Flat 12, Scotts House, Marsh Street, Stafford, ST16 3BQ
Major Shareholder: Matthew Omari Burris
Officers: Matthew Omari Burris [1990] Director

SHH Logistics Ltd
Incorporated: 22 May 2018
Registered Office: 71-75 Shelton Street, London, WC2H 9JQ
Shareholder: Alan Belshaw
Officers: Alan Belshaw, Secretary; Alan Belshaw [1981] Director

Shhh-Holistic Limited
Incorporated: 6 November 2017
Registered Office: The Old Library, Height Street, Wadhurst, E Sussex, TN5 6AP
Officers: Shelly Murphy [1976] Director/Therapist

Shhuk Ltd
Incorporated: 25 January 2019
Registered Office: Suite 1, Elizabethan House, Leicester Road, Lutterworth, Leics, LE17 4NJ
Shareholders: Richard Alexander Taylor; Katarzyna Monika Sherwood; Richard George Carey
Officers: Richard George Carey [1965] Director; Katarzyna Monika Sherwood [1989] Director/Nurse [Polish]; Richard Alexander Taylor [1965] Director

Shilcroft Limited
Incorporated: 2 November 1977
Net Worth: £513,760 *Total Assets:* £810,280
Registered Office: 32 High Road, East Finchley, London, N2 9PJ
Shareholder: Jaichand Hemraj Shah
Officers: Pradip Kumar Mohanlal Shah, Secretary; Jaichand Hemraj Shah [1946] Director/Pharmacist; Pradip Kumar Mohanlal Shah [1953] Director/Accountant

Shimmer and Shine Cosmetics Limited
Incorporated: 8 January 2018
Registered Office: 6 Weymouth Road, Blackpool, Lancs, FY3 9RN
Officers: Stephanie Mary Palmer [1978] Director

Shine Shampoo Bars Ltd
Incorporated: 13 June 2018
Registered Office: 61 Carlton Road, Seaford, E Sussex, BN25 2LS
Major Shareholder: Jonathan Jacob Harries
Officers: Jonathan Jacob Harries [1969] Director/Hairdresser

Shivax International Ltd
Incorporated: 17 March 2010
Net Worth: £10,200 *Total Assets:* £36,060
Registered Office: 6th Floor, 2-4 Maddox Street, London, W1B 2QD
Shareholders: Enzo Di Maio; Diomira Lorenzini
Officers: Enzo di Maio [1954] Director/Doctor [Italian]; Letizia di Maio [1991] Director/Entrepreneur [Italian]

SHL Medical Limited
Incorporated: 11 January 2019
Registered Office: 31 Woodvale Way, London, NW11 8SF
Major Shareholder: Salma Eldamarawy
Officers: Salma Eldamarawy [1997] Director [Egyptian]; Mohamed Islam Ibrahim [1978] Director

Shop Beauty Ltd
Incorporated: 13 December 2017
Registered Office: 12 Romany Close, Portslade, Brighton, BN41 2BA
Officers: Lee Teoh [1980] Director

Shop4stocks Limited
Incorporated: 20 September 2018
Registered Office: 71-75 Shelton Street, London, WC2H 9JQ
Major Shareholder: Bartlomiej Mikulski
Officers: Bartlomiej Mikulski, Secretary; Bartlomiej Mikulski [1981] Director [Polish]

ShopAndEnjoy111 Limited
Incorporated: 14 December 2016
Registered Office: 96 Hainton Avenue, Grimsby, N E Lincs, DN32 9LQ
Officers: Juris Zlidne [1991] Director [Latvian]

Shopti UK Limited
Incorporated: 23 September 2017
Registered Office: 107 Windrush Drive, Oadby, Leicester, LE2 4GL
Major Shareholder: Safiul Islam
Officers: Safiul Islam [1966] Director/Manager

Shori Ltd
Incorporated: 18 May 2018
Registered Office: 57 Ely Street, Stratford upon Avon, Warwicks, CV37 6LN
Shareholders: Adam Krzysztof Osak; Sebastian Rafal Kubaczka
Officers: Sebastian Rafal Kubaczka [1979] Director [Polish]; Adam Krzysztof Osak [1975] Director [Polish]

Shortt Investments2 Limited
Incorporated: 11 September 2016
Net Worth Deficit: £1,088 *Total Assets:* £40,474
Registered Office: The Orchards, Post Office Lane, Cleeve Hill, Cheltenham, Glos, GL52 3PS
Major Shareholder: Stephen Peter Shortt
Officers: Stephen Peter Shortt [1971] Director

Shuei Trading UK Ltd
Incorporated: 8 January 2018
Registered Office: 1 York Road, Hounslow, Middlesex, TW3 1LA
Major Shareholder: Kar Lam Cheung
Officers: Kar Lam Cheung [1980] Director

Shuhui Limited
Incorporated: 24 October 2018
Registered Office: 3/3, 4 Firpark Close, Glasgow, G31 2HQ
Major Shareholder: Junhui Wang
Officers: Junhui Wang [1989] Director [Chinese]

Shure Enterprises (UK) Limited
Incorporated: 10 March 2005
Net Worth: £956,040 *Total Assets:* £2,540,000
Registered Office: Accountancy House, 90 Walworth Road, London, SE1 6SW
Major Shareholder: Rajesh Patel
Officers: Celeste Marie Fontyn, Secretary; Pauline Audrey Harding [1940] Director/Receptionist

Shyline Ltd
Incorporated: 27 May 2015
Net Worth Deficit: £24,349 *Total Assets:* £9,236
Registered Office: 129 St Albans Road, Watford, Herts, WD17 1RA
Major Shareholder: Abdul Itani
Officers: Abdul Itani [1974] Director/Cosmetics

SI & D (UK) Limited
Incorporated: 3 February 2006 *Employees:* 2
Net Worth: £37,590 *Total Assets:* £114,559
Registered Office: 2nd Floor, Aquis House, 49-51 Blagrave Street, Reading, Berks, RG1 1PL
Officers: Nadine Ismiel-Nash, Secretary; Sue Ismiel [1958] Director [Australian]; Nadine Ismiel-Nash [1978] Director Product Development Manager [Australian]

Siam Botanicals UK Limited
Incorporated: 19 February 2018
Registered Office: 7 Torriano Mews, London, NW5 2RZ
Major Shareholder: Justin James Algie
Officers: Justin James Algie [1962] Director

Siam Skin Ltd
Incorporated: 17 October 2014
Net Worth: £1,000 *Total Assets:* £1,000
Registered Office: Unit 1 Conchieton Business Centre, Kirkcudbright, DG6 4TA
Officers: Graeme Paul Hume [1953] Managing Director

Sias Corp Limited
Incorporated: 17 March 2015
Registered Office: Suite 28, Space House, Space Business Park, Abbey Road, London, NW10 7SU
Major Shareholder: Iffat Ali Shah
Officers: Iffat Shah, Secretary; Iffat Shah [1974] Director/Entrepreneur

Signature Fragrances London Limited
Incorporated: 19 April 2017
Registered Office: Audit House, 260 Field End Road, Eastcote, Middlesex, HA4 9LT
Officers: Hamza Mursaleen [1993] Director/Manager

Sikania Ltd
Incorporated: 26 January 2017
Net Worth: £357 *Total Assets:* £1,447
Registered Office: 50 Mayfield Road, Gosport, Hants, PO12 1RA
Major Shareholder: Consolazione Ranno
Officers: Consolazione Ranno [1979] Director/Chemist [Italian]

Silk and Bubble Limited
Incorporated: 15 November 2018
Registered Office: Suite 125, The Innovation Centre, 1 Evolution Park, Haslingden Road, Blackburn, Lancs, BB1 2FD
Major Shareholder: Jamal Hussain
Officers: Jamal Hussain [1992] Managing Director

Silk Lounge Beauty Ltd
Incorporated: 15 May 2017
Registered Office: 1st & 2nd Floor Offices, 1 The Highway, Beaconsfield, Bucks, HP9 1QD
Shareholders: Paul Lennie Sweetland; Carolina Aliling Sweetland
Officers: Carolina Aliling Sweetland [1979] Director

Silk Oil of Morocco UK Limited
Incorporated: 17 December 2012
Net Worth Deficit: £20,210 *Total Assets:* £78,850
Registered Office: 30-31 St James Place, Mangotsfield, Bristol, BS16 9JB
Shareholders: Anthony Ricketts; Christina Ricketts
Officers: Louis Ricketts, Secretary; Anthony Ricketts [1957] Director/Engineer; Christina Ricketts [1959] Director

Silk Route Impex Limited
Incorporated: 16 December 2015
Net Worth Deficit: £25,372 *Total Assets:* £41,983
Registered Office: 12 Roman Close, Wootton, Northampton, NN4 6JQ
Major Shareholder: Fakhreddin Saifaddin Hussain Hussain
Officers: Fakhreddin Saifaddin Hussain Hussain [1974] Director [Yemeni]

Silvercleanse Health & Beauty Limited
Incorporated: 25 August 2015
Net Worth: £11,740 *Total Assets:* £22,962
Registered Office: 71-75 Shelton Street, Covent Garden, London, WC2H 9JQ
Major Shareholder: Helen Doherty
Officers: Helen Doherty, Secretary; Helen Doherty [1966] Director

Simlar 2 Limited
Incorporated: 23 February 2000 *Employees:* 9
Net Worth: £1,122,380 *Total Assets:* £1,208,327
Registered Office: Unit Bb Derby Road Trade Centre, Derby Road, Sandiacre, Nottingham, NG10 5HU
Shareholder: Peter Damien Allen
Officers: Peter Damien Allen, Secretary/Director; Carol Ann Allen [1951] Managing Director; Peter Damien Allen [1953] Director; Caroline Beverly Rix [1968] Director

Simona Beauty Store Ltd
Incorporated: 16 June 2015
Net Worth Deficit: £9,491 *Total Assets:* £686
Registered Office: c/o JSA Partners Accountants, 41 Skylines Village, Limeharbour, London, E14 9TS
Major Shareholder: Monika Sinko
Officers: Monika Sinko [1979] Director [Hungarian]

Simple Bargain Limited
Incorporated: 12 December 2018
Registered Office: Dept 2116, 196 High Road, Wood Green, London, N22 8HH
Major Shareholder: Giorgio Venzo
Officers: Giorgio Venzo [1978] Director/Entrepreneur [Italian]

Simple Beauty (UK) Limited
Incorporated: 24 October 2006
Net Worth Deficit: £450,210 *Total Assets:* £77,410
Registered Office: 66 Prescot Street, London, E1 8NN
Officers: Frixos Haralambus [1949] Director

Simple Hair Limited
Incorporated: 19 September 2013
Net Worth: £98,250 *Total Assets:* £627,080
Registered Office: 66 Moyser Road, London, SW16 6SQ
Major Shareholder: Rizwan Shan
Officers: Rizwan Shan [1977] Director

Simply Nature Ltd.
Incorporated: 14 March 2000 *Employees:* 8
Net Worth: £83,162 *Total Assets:* £206,373
Registered Office: Unit 11 Old Factory Buildings, Battenhurst Road, Stonegate, Wadhurst, E Sussex, TN5 7DU
Major Shareholder: Christopher John Liebe Moore
Officers: Christopher John Liebe Moore [1971] Managing Director

Simply Pure Skincare Ltd
Incorporated: 17 August 2018
Registered Office: 9 Kitsmead, Copthorne, Crawley, W Sussex, RH10 3PN
Major Shareholder: Kirsty Justine Scott
Officers: Kirsty Justine Scott [1969] Director

Simply Squirrel Limited
Incorporated: 5 February 2018
Registered Office: 28 Eaton Avenue, Matrix Office Park, Buckshaw Village, Chorley, Lancs, PR7 7NA
Shareholders: James Howard Gartside; Bernice Marie McWilliams
Officers: James Howard Gartside [1969] Director

Simply Untouched Ltd
Incorporated: 21 November 2013
Registered Office: The Beeches, Old Castle Road, Salisbury, Wilts, SP1 3SF
Major Shareholder: Ian Roger Douglas
Officers: Ian Roger Douglas [1944] Director

Sinoeast XJ Ltd
Incorporated: 23 May 2014
Registered Office: Chase Business Centre, 39-41 Chase Side, London, N14 5BP
Major Shareholder: Jian Xu
Officers: Jian Xu, Secretary; Jian Xu [1984] Director/Merchant [Chinese]

Sipro (UK) Ltd
Incorporated: 1 July 2013
Net Worth Deficit: £567 *Total Assets:* £1,002
Registered Office: Pentax House, South Hill Avenue, South Harrow, Middlesex, HA2 0DU
Shareholders: Abdullah Soltan Talib; Noraini Binti Soltan Talib
Officers: Abdul Rahman Soltan Talib [1966] Director [Malaysian]; Abdullah Soltan Talib [1953] Director [Malaysian]; Noraini Binti Soltan Talib [1961] Director [Malaysian]

Sirra Limited
Incorporated: 30 January 2018
Registered Office: Flat 27, Fairways, Dyke Road, Brighton, BN1 5AB
Major Shareholder: Ehab Mohammed Abdulwali Said Musareg
Officers: Ehab Mohammed Abdulwali Said Musareg [1980] Director

Sisi Cosmetics Ltd
Incorporated: 7 August 2017
Registered Office: 6/2 Wardlaw Place, Edinburgh, EH11 1UB
Major Shareholder: Stellah Linda Chonzi
Officers: Stellah Linda Chonzi [1994] Director/Entrepreneur

Sisley UK Limited
Incorporated: 27 January 1998 *Employees:* 246
Net Worth: £85,850 *Total Assets:* £3,333,470
Registered Office: 92 Golborne Road, London, W10 5PS
Shareholder: Isabelle D'Ornano
Officers: Christine D'Ornano, Secretary/Director [French]; Philippe D'Ornano [1964] Director [French]; Christine D'Ornano [1973] Director [French]; Alexandre Jean Le Vaillant de Chaudenay [1970] Director [French]

Siwel Trading Ltd
Incorporated: 25 July 2017
Registered Office: Siwel House, Cuddy Lonning, Wigton, Cumbria, CA7 0AA
Major Shareholder: Lewis Jarman
Officers: Lewis Jarman [1987] Director

Sjonlineuk Ltd
Incorporated: 9 January 2019
Registered Office: 82 Selsdon Road, London, E13 9BY
Major Shareholder: Shazia Jan
Officers: Shazia Jan [1983] Managing Director

SK Flawless Dipping Powder Ltd
Incorporated: 3 November 2017
Registered Office: Unit 2a Liverpool New Road, Little Hoole, Preston, Lancs, PR4 5BF
Major Shareholder: Gregory Thomas Kirby
Officers: Gregory Thomas Kirby [1971] Director

SK Network Ltd
Incorporated: 3 December 2018
Registered Office: 20-22 Wenlock Road, London, N1 7GU
Major Shareholder: Salma Karolia
Officers: Salma Karolia [1982] Director/Self Employed

Skin & Tonic London Ltd
Incorporated: 23 July 2013 *Employees:* 4
Net Worth Deficit: £68,720 *Total Assets:* £15,963
Registered Office: Unit J, 9c Queen's Yard, White Post Lane, London, E9 5EN
Shareholders: Joshua Wade; Sarah Hancock; Sarah Hancock; Joshua Wade
Officers: Brian Arthur Basham [1943] Director; Nicholas James Corkill [1983] Director/Member; Sarah Hancock [1982] Director/Founder of Skin & Tonic Skincare; Joshua Wade [1983] Director/Co Founder Skin & Tonic Skincare

The Skin Care Company Limited
Incorporated: 12 October 1993
Net Worth: £19,548 *Total Assets:* £30,109
Registered Office: 10 Nicholas Street, Chester, CH1 2NX
Shareholders: Barrie Christie Collins; Rebecca Laura Collins
Officers: Barrie Christie Collins, Secretary; Barrie Christie Collins [1936] Director; Rebecca Laura Collins [1944] Director

Skin Chef Limited
Incorporated: 20 July 2017
Registered Office: 7 Station Road, Coltishal, Norfolk, NR12 7JJ
Major Shareholder: Nikita Hoskin
Officers: Nikita Hoskin, Secretary; Nikita Hoskin [1988] Director

Skin Enrich Limited
Incorporated: 24 January 2017
Registered Office: Kemp House, 160 City Road, London, EC1V 2NX
Major Shareholder: George Goode
Officers: George Goode [1972] Director/Accountant

Skin Health Solutions Ltd
Incorporated: 22 March 2016 *Employees:* 3
Net Worth: £29,891 *Total Assets:* £94,711
Registered Office: Upton Lodge Buildings, Astrop Road, Middleton Cheney, Northants, OX17 2PJ
Major Shareholder: Emma Coates
Officers: Emma Coates [1964] Director/Skincare

Skin Matrix HD+ Cosmetology Limited
Incorporated: 3 March 2015 *Employees:* 1
Net Worth Deficit: £35,841 *Total Assets:* £29,668
Registered Office: c/o DPC, Vernon Road, Stoke on Trent, Staffs, ST4 2QY
Shareholders: Dominic Francis John Cheetham; Skin Matrix Investments Limited
Officers: Dominic Francis John Cheetham [1966] Director; Heather Dorigo [1966] Managing Director

Skin Matrix Limited
Incorporated: 2 June 2010 *Employees:* 4
Net Worth Deficit: £28,052 *Total Assets:* £108,001
Registered Office: c/o D P C, Vernon Road, Stoke on Trent, Staffs, ST4 2QY
Parent: Skin Matrix Investments Limited
Officers: Heather Dorigo, Secretary; Heather Dorigo [1966] Managing Director

Skin Sanity Limited
Incorporated: 14 August 2018
Registered Office: Ebor House, 7 Bentinck Crescent, Troon, S Ayrshire, KA10 6JN
Shareholders: Nicola Waring Willis; Ian Matthews
Officers: Ian Matthews, Secretary; Ian Matthews [1967] Director; Dr Nicola Waring Willis [1963] Director/Doctor

Skincare 18 Ltd
Incorporated: 18 May 2018
Registered Office: 24 Caractacus Green, Watford, Herts, WD18 6JU
Major Shareholder: Zala Markovic Ho
Officers: Zala Markovic Ho [1981] Director [Slovenian]

Skincare Cornwall Ltd
Incorporated: 31 January 2008
Net Worth: £11,950 *Total Assets:* £14,800
Registered Office: Honey Cosmetics, Mullion Meadows, Helston, Cornwall, TR12 7HB
Major Shareholder: Yarden Collins
Officers: Peter John Collins [1970] Director/Manager, Tourism Industry; Yarden Collins [1970] Director/Shop Manageress [Israeli]

The Skincare Sanctuary Limited
Incorporated: 21 May 1997 *Employees:* 22
Net Worth: £765,187 *Total Assets:* £2,899,590
Registered Office: 57 Victoria Street, Windsor, Berks, SL4 1EH
Shareholder: Andrew John Bagley
Officers: Cliff Lewis Powell, Secretary/Director; Andrew John Bagley [1967] Director; Sarah Edwina Bagley [1964] Director; Joseph John Keech [1984] Director; Cliff Lewis Powell [1969] Director

Skindoc Formula Limited
Incorporated: 26 September 2014
Net Worth Deficit: £106,030 *Total Assets:* £169,000
Registered Office: First Floor, 85 Great Portland Street, London, W1W 7LT
Major Shareholder: Dirk Kremer
Officers: Dirk Dr. Kremer [1970] Director/Medical Doctor [German]

Skinjam Cosmetics Limited
Incorporated: 7 April 2017
Registered Office: Victoria Building, 14 Elwin Lane, Darlington, Co Durham, DL1 5RX
Major Shareholder: Stephanie Sharman
Officers: Stephanie Sharman [1984] Director

Skinkode Ltd
Incorporated: 3 April 2018
Registered Office: 71-75 Shelton Street, London, WC2H 9JQ
Major Shareholder: Yi Jia
Officers: Yi Jia [1991] Director

Skinlab Medical Ltd
Incorporated: 6 August 2018
Registered Office: 12 Mendoza Close, Hornchurch, Essex, RM11 2RP
Major Shareholder: Malgorzata Gouzd
Officers: Magdalena Gouzd [1981] Director/Beautician [Polish]; Malgorzata Gouzd [1960] Director/Beautician [Polish]

Skinmed Ltd
Incorporated: 23 August 2001
Net Worth: £311,310 *Total Assets:* £388,090
Registered Office: Whitestacks Cottage, Havikil Lane, Scotton, Knaresborough, N Yorks, HG5 9HN
Major Shareholder: Peter Daryl Roberts
Officers: Carole Roberts, Secretary; Peter Daryl Roberts [1962] Director/Sales Manager

Skinnydip Skincare Limited
Incorporated: 16 January 2010
Net Worth Deficit: £37,175 *Total Assets:* £1,830
Registered Office: 6 Link Way, Howsell Road, Malvern Link, Worcs, WR14 1UQ
Major Shareholder: Emma Chetwynd Jarvis
Officers: Emma Chetwynd Jarvis [1978] Director/Beautician

Skins Sexual Health Limited
Incorporated: 20 July 2016
Registered Office: Unit 5 Brunel Business Park, Jessops Close, Northern Road Industrial Estate, Newark, Notts, NG24 2AG
Shareholders: Jonathan Richard Bowles; Jane Margaret Bowles
Officers: Jane Margaret Bowles [1963] Director; Jonathan Richard Bowles [1966] Director

Skinsense Ltd
Incorporated: 12 January 2017
Net Worth Deficit: £69,573 *Total Assets:* £883,611
Registered Office: 41 Holmethorpe Avenue, Redhill, Surrey, RH1 2NB
Parent: Graphters Ltd
Officers: Richard Milliner, Secretary; Abigail Claire Cleeve [1971] Director; Roland Kohl [1955] Director [Austrian]

Skinsider Cosmetics Ltd
Incorporated: 17 February 2017
Net Worth Deficit: £65,293 *Total Assets:* £43,170
Registered Office: Gunnery House, Gunnery 6, 9-11 Gunnery Terrace, London, SE18 6SW
Shareholders: Karolina Intek; Krzysztof Intek
Officers: Karolina Intek [1982] Director/Founder [Polish]; Krzysztof Intek [1981] Director [Polish]

The Skinsmith Limited
Incorporated: 20 February 2006 *Employees:* 4
Net Worth: £149,590 *Total Assets:* £186,819
Registered Office: 6 Yew Tree Road, Edgbaston, Birmingham, B15 2LX
Major Shareholder: Tracy Jayne Jordan
Officers: Tracey Jayne Jordan, Secretary; Marcus Andrew Jordan [1959] Director/Surveyor; Tracy Jayne Jordan [1963] Director

Skintel Cosmetics Ltd
Incorporated: 8 August 2018
Registered Office: 13 Harraden Road, Blackheath, London, SE3 8BZ
Shareholders: Nicholas Chitty; Adam Beese
Officers: Adam Beese [1998] Director/Student; Nicholas Chitty [1998] Director/Student

Skinvital Ltd
Incorporated: 18 January 2017
Registered Office: Whitestacks House, Havikil Lane, Scotton, Knaresborough, N Yorks, HG5 9HN
Shareholders: Peter Daryl Roberts; Carole Roberts
Officers: Carole Roberts, Secretary; Peter Daryl Roberts [1962] Managing Director

SKN Rehab Limited
Incorporated: 16 February 2016 *Employees:* 3
Net Worth Deficit: £27,403 *Total Assets:* £38,948
Registered Office: SKN Rehab, Suite RB 2.57, Citypoint, 1 Ropemaker Street, London, EC2Y 9AW
Shareholders: Julia Alison Fenton; Lucy Hilson; Kerstina Joanne Morris
Officers: Julia Alison Fenton [1978] Director; Lucy Hilson [1981] Director; Kerstina Joanne Morris [1970] Director

SKN-RG Ltd
Incorporated: 30 August 2011 *Employees:* 2
Previous: B2 Beauty Ltd
Net Worth Deficit: £113,994 *Total Assets:* £42,945
Registered Office: Winnington House, 2 Woodberry Grove, North Finchley, London, N12 0DR
Major Shareholder: Deborah Annette Scott
Officers: Deborah Annette Scott, Secretary; Deborah Annette Scott [1971] Director; Robert Scott [1973] Director

Slim Line Club UK Ltd
Incorporated: 27 April 2017
Net Worth: £1,520 *Total Assets:* £9,610
Registered Office: 107 Pandora Drive, Peterborough, Cambs, PE2 8HD
Major Shareholder: Risto Pop-Pecev
Officers: Risto Pop-Pecev [1975] Director [Bulgarian]

Slixir Ltd
Incorporated: 9 April 2015
Net Worth Deficit: £21,830 *Total Assets:* £33,560
Registered Office: 2nd Floor, 1 Horsefair, Wetherby, W Yorks, LS22 6JG
Major Shareholder: Helen Gilmore
Officers: Helen Gilmore [1976] Director/Cosmetics Development

Sloane Home Ltd
Incorporated: 14 November 2013
Net Worth Deficit: £3,650 *Total Assets:* £37,320
Registered Office: The Rectory, Llandow, Cowbridge, Vale of Glamorgan, CF71 7NT
Major Shareholder: Leanne Peta Johns
Officers: Leanne Peta Johns [1971] Director

Smart Nails (UK) Ltd
Incorporated: 17 May 2007
Net Worth Deficit: £17,353 *Total Assets:* £1,841
Registered Office: Heron House, 39-41 Higher Bents Lane, Bredbury, Stockport, Cheshire, SK6 1EE
Major Shareholder: Paul Barry Cummings
Officers: Rebecca Jane Cummings, Secretary; Paul Barry Cummings [1971] Director/Manager

Smart Skin Limited
Incorporated: 23 May 2016
Net Worth Deficit: £13,526 *Total Assets:* £18,481
Registered Office: 339 Charminster Road, Bournemouth, BH8 9QR
Shareholders: Marta Janina Kozlowska; Bartlomiej Dominik Czaplinski
Officers: Marta Janina Kozlowska [1984] Director [Polish]

Smartway Pharma Limited
Incorporated: 15 October 2012
Net Worth Deficit: £35,030 *Total Assets:* £426
Registered Office: The Old Mill, 9 Soar Lane, Leicester, LE3 5DE
Parent: Smartway PW Holdings Limited
Officers: Hitendra Patel [1966] Director

SMC Cosmetics (UK) Ltd
Incorporated: 4 April 2016 *Employees:* 1
Net Worth: £14,409 *Total Assets:* £168,522
Registered Office: Unit 2 Inverbreakie Steading, Invergordon, Ross-shire, IV18 0LP
Shareholders: Andrew James Pearson; Michael Norman Pearson
Officers: Derek Munro [1964] Director; Roy Robinson Munro [1965] Director; Andrew James Pearson [1980] Managing Director; Michael Norman Pearson [1953] Director/Chairman; Calvin Wang [1974] Director [Taiwanese]

SMCK Hair Care Products Limited
Incorporated: 23 October 2015
Net Worth Deficit: £172,892 *Total Assets:* £187,100
Registered Office: 87 Hewell Road, Barnt Green, Birmingham, B45 8NL
Major Shareholder: Sam McKnight
Officers: Brian Fox, Secretary; Samuel McKnight [1955] Director/Hairstylist

SMCK Limited
Incorporated: 3 June 2009
Net Worth: £130,719 *Total Assets:* £181,800
Registered Office: 87 Hewell Road, Barnt Green, Birmingham, B45 8NL
Major Shareholder: Samuel McKnight
Officers: Samuel McKnight [1955] Director/Hairdresser

Smell Neutralizer Ltd
Incorporated: 11 February 2019
Registered Office: 38 Brownmoor Park, Crosby, Liverpool, L23 0TN
Officers: Sean Doherty [1999] Director/Financial Advisor; Joe Winstanley [2000] Director/Software Engineer

Smellycat Ltd
Incorporated: 10 August 2018
Registered Office: 20-22 Wenlock Road, London, N1 7GU
Major Shareholder: Zubair Farooq
Officers: Zubair Farooq [1989] Director

Smiles Glasgow Limited
Incorporated: 1 February 2013
Net Worth Deficit: £1,180 *Total Assets:* £13,980
Registered Office: 223 Hope Street, Glasgow, G2 2UW
Officers: Ruchika Jain [1986] Director; Vikram Jain [1981] Director

TPC Smith Limited
Incorporated: 11 April 2018
Registered Office: 78 York Street, London, W1H 1DP
Major Shareholder: Thomas Smith
Officers: Thomas Smith [1978] Director [French]

Smooth Image Beauty Limited
Incorporated: 21 May 2008
Net Worth Deficit: £10,094 *Total Assets:* £28,961
Registered Office: Toadhall, Muchalls, Stonehaven, Aberdeenshire, AB39 3RQ
Major Shareholder: Angela June Wilken
Officers: Alastair Gow, Secretary; Angela June Wilken [1963] Director/Therapist

Smuccii Trading Ltd
Incorporated: 18 April 2018
Registered Office: Apartment 50, Foundry House, Lockington Road, London, SW8 4BE
Major Shareholder: Jing Sun
Officers: Jing Sun [1987] Director [Chinese]

Snob Distribution Limited
Incorporated: 30 October 2009
Net Worth Deficit: £12,200 *Total Assets:* £16,470
Registered Office: 22 Fortfield, Dromore, Co Down, BT25 1DD
Major Shareholder: Oonagh Boman
Officers: Oonagh Boman [1967] Director

So Boujee Limited
Incorporated: 31 May 2018
Registered Office: 42 Spital Hill, Sheffield, S4 7LG
Major Shareholder: Saleban Xassan Libane
Officers: Idil Xassan Libane [1995] Director/Student [Dutch]; Saleban Xassan Libane [1994] Director/Student [Dutch]; Hafssa Zarrai [1995] Director/Student

So Susan Limited
Incorporated: 6 August 2012 *Employees:* 1
Net Worth: £680,022 *Total Assets:* £1,561,556
Registered Office: Kemp House, 160 City Road, London, EC1V 2NX
Major Shareholder: Adrian Lee Jin Jia
Officers: Adrian Jin Jia Lee [1987] Director [Malaysian]

Soadperf Limited
Incorporated: 29 October 2018
Registered Office: 19b Petley Road, London, W6 9SU
Major Shareholder: Soad El Arras
Officers: Soad El Arras [1973] Director [French]

Soak Rochford Ltd
Incorporated: 12 December 2018
Registered Office: 10 Tongue End, Spalding, Lincs, PE11 3JJ
Major Shareholder: Jason Robert Rochford
Officers: Jason Robert Rochford [1989] Director

The Soap and Candle Company Ltd
Incorporated: 12 July 2016
Registered Office: South East Lodge, Rede Road, Whepstead, Bury St Edmunds, Suffolk, IP29 4ST
Shareholder: Paul McCaffrey
Officers: Josephine Anne McCaffrey [1965] Director; Paul David McCaffrey [1959] Director

The Soap Industry Limited
Incorporated: 20 July 2018
Registered Office: 2 Northorpe Rise, Bridlington, E Yorks, YO16 7QN
Major Shareholder: Casey Whip
Officers: Casey Whip [1995] Director

Soapy J Limited
Incorporated: 21 February 2018
Registered Office: Soapy J, Afflecks, 2nd Floor, 52 Church Street, Manchester, M4 1PW
Major Shareholder: Andrew Jackson
Officers: Andrew Jackson [1984] Director

Sofil Cosmetic Ltd
Incorporated: 23 April 2018
Registered Office: 20-22 Wenlock Road, London, N1 7GU
Major Shareholder: Sofiane Abdelaziz Louriki
Officers: Sofiane Abdelaziz Louriki [1984] Director [French]

Soft and Curly Products Ltd
Incorporated: 20 June 2017
Registered Office: 107e Vassall Road, London, SW9 6NJ
Major Shareholder: Dola Alika Akinola
Officers: Dola Alika Akinola [1981] Director/Project Accountant

Solarius UK & Overseas Limited
Incorporated: 15 January 2018
Registered Office: The Gate Business Centre, Keppoch Street, Cardiff, CF24 3JW
Shareholder: Tamer Mohamed Hassan Elzokrod
Officers: Tamer Aly Emam Aly Elkaramany [1975] Director [Egyptian]; Tamer Mohamed Hassan Elzokrod [1976] Director/Pharmacist [Egyptian]

Solo JC Trade Ltd
Incorporated: 5 April 2018
Registered Office: 162 Hainton Avenue, Grimsby, N E Lincs, DN32 9LQ
Officers: Janis Ceicans [1982] Director [Latvian]

Solo Skin London Ltd
Incorporated: 19 February 2019
Registered Office: 257 Park Avenue, Southall, Middlesex, UB1 3AP
Major Shareholder: Nazma Bashir
Officers: Nazma Bashir [1989] Director

Solution Cosmetic Ltd
Incorporated: 18 August 2016
Net Worth Deficit: £551 *Total Assets:* £14,228
Registered Office: Top Floor, Trojan House, 34 Arcadia Avenue, London, N3 2JU
Major Shareholder: Manuela Farmbauer
Officers: Christian Farmbauer, Secretary; Manuela Farmbauer [1973] Director/Established Merchant [German]

Someplace Nice Limited
Incorporated: 30 July 2018
Registered Office: 63 Whitmore Gardens, London, NW10 5HE
Major Shareholder: Paul Marc Gerrard
Officers: Paul Marc Gerrard [1971] Managing Director

Somerset Perfumery Ltd
Incorporated: 14 February 2018
Registered Office: Unit 21 The Beckery, Glastonbury, Somerset, BA6 9NX
Shareholders: Jan Brian Kusmirek; Shirley May Routley
Officers: Jan Brian Kusmirek [1946] Director; Shirley May Routley [1961] Director

Sophistique Beauty Ltd
Incorporated: 10 May 2018
Registered Office: Kemp House, 160 City Road, London, EC1V 2NX
Officers: Hebo Shire [1987] Director

Sopure London Limited
Incorporated: 11 September 2018
Registered Office: 21a Empire Road, Perivale, Greenford, Middlesex, UB6 7EH
Shareholders: Ahmed Ali Hamdan; Ali Hamdan
Officers: Ahmed Ali Hamdan [1980] Director; Ali Hamdan [1995] Director

Sopureoils Ltd
Incorporated: 5 September 2015
Net Worth Deficit: £5,513 *Total Assets:* £3,421
Registered Office: 28 Alric Avenue, Harlesden, London, NW10 8RB
Shareholders: Claudete Esprit; Selina Zina Jalloh
Officers: Claudette Esprit [1972] Director/Driving Instructor; Selina Zina Jalloh [1975] Director/Tax Advisor

Soul Cosmetics Limited
Incorporated: 12 July 2018
Registered Office: 217 Beechwood Road, Luton, Beds, LU4 9RZ
Major Shareholder: Khadijah Abdullahi
Officers: Khadijah Abdullahi [1999] Director/Student [Nigerian]

Soulful Beauty Ltd
Incorporated: 19 February 2010 *Employees:* 3
Net Worth: £188 *Total Assets:* £751,122
Registered Office: Unit 5 NCR Business Centre, Great Central Way, London, NW10 0AB
Major Shareholder: Liban Mahdi
Officers: Liban Mahdi [1984] Director/Businessman [Swedish]

South China Bio-Pharma Co Ltd.
Incorporated: 9 January 2018
Registered Office: 7-11 Minerva Road, Park Royal, London, NW10 6HJ
Major Shareholder: Xiaofeng Zhang
Officers: Xiaofeng Zhang [1973] Director [Chinese]

South West Aesthetics Ltd
Incorporated: 19 September 2017
Registered Office: Suite 128, Pegaxis House, 61 Victoria Road, Surbiton, Surrey, KT6 4JX
Shareholders: Chafic Kaedbey; Kamel Malek Jonblat
Officers: Kamel Malek Jonblat [1973] Managing Director [Lebanese]; Dr Chafic Kaedbey [1974] Director of Product Development and Operations [Lebanese]

Southend Hair and Beauty Limited
Incorporated: 7 February 2013
Net Worth Deficit: £44,621 *Total Assets:* £98,709
Registered Office: 119 High Street, Southend on Sea, Essex, SS1 1LH
Shareholder: Mohammed Ahmed Majid
Officers: Mohammad Maisam Govani [1988] Director; Mohammed Ahmed Majid [1967] Director

Southsea Bathing Hut Limited
Incorporated: 19 December 2014
Registered Office: 2c Albert Road, Southsea, Hants, PO5 2SH
Major Shareholder: Samantha Elisabeth Mary Worsey
Officers: Samantha Elisabeth Mary Worsey [1980] Director of Southsea Bathing Hut

Souvre UK Ltd
Incorporated: 22 June 2018
Registered Office: Unit 5 Windsor Park Industrial Estate, 50 Windsor Avenue, London, SW19 2TJ
Major Shareholder: Waldemar Leszek Smolinski
Officers: Malgorzata Alina Zawada [1974] Director/Manager [Polish]; Radoslaw Zuchlinski [1986] Director/Manager [Polish]

Soybalm Ltd
Incorporated: 25 May 2018
Registered Office: Suite 23, Fifth Floor, 63-66 Hatton Garden, London, EC1N 8LE
Major Shareholder: Michelle Gooden-Jones
Officers: Michelle Gooden-Jones [1994] Director/Civil Servant

Spa and Salon Solutions Ltd
Incorporated: 13 March 2017
Net Worth Deficit: £18,160 *Total Assets:* £6,790
Registered Office: Unit 3 Compass Point, Ensign Way, Hamble, Hants, SO31 4RA
Major Shareholder: Karen Rae Ellithorne
Officers: Karen Rae Ellithorne [1971] Director/Distribution Cosmetic Brands [South African]; Edward Philip Woods [1964] Marketing Director

Spa Pro Ltd
Incorporated: 5 October 2017
Registered Office: 33 Holland Mews, Hove, E Sussex, BN3 1JG
Shareholders: Aidan Conlin; Michael Shawn Conlin
Officers: Jacqueline Anne Edwards, Secretary; Aidan Conlin [1975] Director; Michael Shawn Conlin [1969] Director

Spa Skincare Limited
Incorporated: 2 November 2012
Net Worth: £100 *Total Assets:* £100
Registered Office: Wessex House, Challeymead Business Park, Bradford Road, Melksham, Wilts, SN12 8BU
Shareholders: David Neil Owen; Susan Margaret Auld
Officers: Susan Margaret Auld [1962] Director; David Neil Owen [1974] Director

Spa Therapies Ltd
Incorporated: 16 July 2013
Net Worth Deficit: £46,534 *Total Assets:* £79,606
Registered Office: Unit 10 Curtis Farm, High Road, Fobbing, Stanford-le-Hope, Essex, SS17 9JJ
Shareholders: Tracey Marie Sargeant; David John Sargeant
Officers: David John Sargeant [1970] Director; Tracey Marie Sargeant [1970] Director

Spa Voyage Limited
Incorporated: 4 February 2003
Net Worth Deficit: £53,896 *Total Assets:* £58,922
Registered Office: The Dormer House, Hunts Common, Hartley Wintney, Hook, Hants, RG27 8AA
Shareholder: Sarah Anne Strang
Officers: Anthony Hayden Noble, Secretary/Director; Anthony Hayden Noble [1945] Director; Sarah Anne Strang [1979] Managing Director

Space Brands Limited
Incorporated: 1 February 2012
Net Worth: £5,680,000 *Total Assets:* £18,000,000
Registered Office: 5th Floor, Shropshire House, 11-20 Capper Street, London, WC1E 6JA
Parent: Space NK Limited
Officers: Paula Levitan, Secretary; Christopher Garek [1956] Director [American]; Diane Kim [1969] Director [American]; Tom Macknay [1963] Director

Spaquashop Ltd
Incorporated: 29 May 2018
Registered Office: 27 Old Gloucester Street, London, WC1N 3AX
Major Shareholder: Nader Hamandi
Officers: Nader Hamandi, Secretary; Nader Hamandi [1977] Director/Commercial Photographer [Lebanese]

Sparking-Jy International Trading Co., Ltd
Incorporated: 21 July 2017
Registered Office: 8 Standard Road, London, NW10 6EU
Major Shareholder: Yan Lei
Officers: Yan Lei, Secretary; Yan Lei [1988] Director [Chinese]

Spartzy Lifestyle Brands Ltd
Incorporated: 3 September 2015
Previous: Revespor Brands International Ltd
Net Worth Deficit: £20,870 *Total Assets:* £2,940
Registered Office: 66 Coltsfoot Green, Luton, Beds, LU4 0XW
Shareholder: Tapati Ranjitkumar Dutta
Officers: Kaushik Dutta [1980] Director/Businessman; Tapati Ranjitkumar Dutta [1955] Director [Indian]

Speak Beauty Limited
Incorporated: 17 May 2018
Registered Office: 10 Ladyhill View, Worsley, Manchester, M28 7LH
Shareholders: Philip Crombleholme; Lisa Crombleholme
Officers: Lisa Crombleholme [1979] Director; Philip Crombleholme [1973] Director

Specialist Hair Products Limited
Incorporated: 26 February 2001
Registered Office: Unit 3 Newmains Avenue, Inchinnan Business Park, Renfrew, PA4 9RR
Officers: Brian Aitken, Secretary/Accountant; Brian Aitken [1954] Director/Accountant; Generald Patrick Hegarty [1940] Director/Sales Executive

Sphere 7 Lab Ltd
Incorporated: 13 August 2018
Registered Office: Unit 10, Studio 20, Elizabeth Industrial Estate, Juno Way, London, SE14 5RW
Major Shareholder: Maxamillion Henry
Officers: Maxamillion Henry [1983] Director

Spice Fragrances Ltd
Incorporated: 3 April 2018
Registered Office: 134 Haldane Road, London, E6 3JP
Officers: Syed Mohammed Imran Haider [1980] Director/Perfume Distribution

Spice International Trading Company Limited
Incorporated: 27 February 2018
Registered Office: 9 Mullion Drive, Altrincham, Cheshire, WA15 6SL
Officers: Karthikeyan Subramanian [1977] Director

The Spirit of Dubai Limited
Incorporated: 18 November 2015
Net Worth Deficit: £805,907 *Total Assets:* £1,109,323
Registered Office: Unit 3 Hounslow Business Park, Alice Way, Hounslow, Middlesex, TW3 3UD
Officers: Mustafa Asgher Adam Ali Ibrahim [1978] Executive Director [Kittitian]; Howaida Asgher Adam Ali [1981] Director/Businesswomen; Asghar Adam Ali Ibrahim [1953] Director/Businessman [Yemeni]

Spktra Limited
Incorporated: 5 December 2017
Registered Office: Flat 30, Charles Rowan House, Margery Street, London, WC1X 0EH
Shareholders: Sumai Bertrand; Guy Jonathan Kazumba Tshinkanka
Officers: Sumai Bertrand [1994] Director [French]; Guy Jonathan Kazumba Tshinkanka [1992] Director [Belgian]

Splash Cosmetics Ltd
Incorporated: 27 September 2018
Registered Office: 15 Beach Road, Westgate-on-Sea, Kent, CT8 8AD
Shareholders: Hannah Wild; Fredrick Wild
Officers: Fredrick Wild [1992] Director; Hannah Wild [1992] Director

Splashes & Spills Ltd.
Incorporated: 7 July 2015
Net Worth: £20,950 *Total Assets:* £94,290
Registered Office: Unit 31 The Ringway Centre, Beck Road, Huddersfield, W Yorks, HD1 5DG
Shareholder: Adnan Rasool
Officers: Adal Rasool [1991] Director; Mohammed Adnan Rasool [1987] Director

Splendor Europe Ltd.
Incorporated: 14 March 2018
Registered Office: 77 High Street, Littlehampton, W Sussex, BN17 5AG
Major Shareholder: Pal Schlick
Officers: Pal Schlick [1955] Director [Hungarian]

Sportclinix Labs Ltd.
Incorporated: 25 April 2013
Net Worth Deficit: £47,280 *Total Assets:* £32,410
Registered Office: Unit 3 Issigonis House, Cowley Road, London, W3 7UN
Shareholder: Jagdeep Balram Gossain
Officers: Jagdeep Balram Gossain [1958] Director/Retired Doctor; Shashi Kiran Gossain [1958] Director

Spree Trading Ltd
Incorporated: 15 January 2019
Registered Office: Kemp House, 160 City Road, London, EC1V 2NX
Officers: Jaafar Shawwa [1973] Director/Businessman; Rabie Shawwa [1978] Director/Businessman

Spring and Underworld Ltd
Incorporated: 14 November 2018
Registered Office: 519 Kettering Road North, Northampton, NN3 7BE
Shareholders: Christina Charalambous; Francis Robertson-Marriott
Officers: Christina Charalambous [1994] Director/Administrator; Francis Robertson-Marriott [1995] Director/Salesman

Spruce Vita Limited
Incorporated: 13 June 2018
Registered Office: 64 Coleridge Crescent, Killay, Swansea, SA2 7ER
Officers: Dr Sudhakar Pitchaimuthu [1979] Director/Physicist [Indian]; Sudhakar Ramanan [1979] Director/Enterprise Architect

SPTB Ltd
Incorporated: 4 July 2018
Registered Office: 20-22 Wenlock Road, London, N1 7GU
Major Shareholder: Youness Tanani
Officers: Souad Haissoubi, Secretary; Dr Youness Tanani [1980] Director/Education [Moroccan]

Square Spots Limited
Incorporated: 30 November 2000
Net Worth Deficit: £4,004
Registered Office: Little Monkhurst, Sandy Cross, Heathfield, E Sussex, TN21 8QR
Shareholders: John Charles Kingham; John Charles Kingham
Officers: Catherine Mann Voogd Bergwerf [1969] Director/Marketing Manager; John Charles Kingham [1956] Director/Salesman

Square Wholesale Ltd
Incorporated: 3 December 2018
Registered Office: 965 Romford Road, London, E12 5JR
Major Shareholder: Mahmud Ur Rasul
Officers: Mahmud Ur Rasul [1968] Director [Spanish]

SS Wholesaler Limited
Incorporated: 13 August 2018
Registered Office: 212 Worton Road, Isleworth, Middlesex, TW7 6EF
Major Shareholder: Ahmad Gharib
Officers: Ahmad Gharib [1992] Managing Director

SSB Ltd
Incorporated: 28 February 2018
Registered Office: 11 Holroyd House, Somerset Terrace, Bristol, BS3 4LQ
Major Shareholder: Suaad Ahmed
Officers: Suaad Ahmed [1984] Director/Entrepreneur [Dutch]

St-Creation Ltd
Incorporated: 25 May 2018
Registered Office: 71-75 Shelton Street, Covent Garden, London, WC2H 9JQ
Major Shareholder: Stefan Nowosz
Officers: Stefan Nowosz [1962] Director/Care Assistant [Polish]

Standfast Solutions International Ltd
Incorporated: 19 July 2018
Registered Office: 22 Bow Field, Hook, Hants, RG27 9SA
Major Shareholder: Brian Grant
Officers: Brian Grant [1977] Managing Director [British/New Zealander]

Stantondown Limited
Incorporated: 2 February 1984 *Employees:* 13
Net Worth: £593,894 *Total Assets:* £686,153
Registered Office: Shafton Lane, Leeds, LS11 9QY
Officers: Lee Jason Smith, Secretary; Lee Jason Smith [1967] Director/Production Manager; Stewart Leslie Smith [1965] Director/Production Manager; Terence Smith [1937] Director/General Manager

Star Pearls Ltd
Incorporated: 19 October 2018
Registered Office: 30 Portland Place, London, W1B 1LZ
Shareholders: David Flax; Rachel Flax; Nathan Flax
Officers: Jonathan Flax [1958] Director

Star Qualities Ltd
Incorporated: 1 June 2011 *Employees:* 4
Net Worth: £1,137,466 *Total Assets:* £1,879,699
Registered Office: Blackthorn House, Rolleston Road, Skeffington, Leicester, LE7 9YD
Major Shareholder: Leslie George Spears
Officers: Rachel Maher, Secretary; Reginald Keith Chandler [1947] Director; Vanessa Tracey Doherty [1969] Director; Rachel Claire Maher [1966] Director; Sharon Virginia Robbins [1958] Director; Elizabeth Jane Spears [1968] Director; Leslie George Spears [1937] Director/Chairman; Stephen Robert Way [1939] Director

Starcount Limited
Incorporated: 29 December 2000
Registered Office: 78 Wembley Park Drive, Wembley, Middlesex, HA9 8HB
Major Shareholder: Lawrence Hili
Officers: Lawrence Hili [1955] Director/Businessman [Maltese]

Steam Cream Limited
Incorporated: 8 August 2008
Net Worth Deficit: £1,968,560 *Total Assets:* £294,140
Registered Office: 2nd Floor, Heathmans House, 19 Heathmans Road, London, SW6 4TJ
Parent: International Brands Management and Services Corporation Ltd
Officers: Andrew Tone [1973] Director [Canadian]

Stenko Ltd
Incorporated: 5 February 2019
Registered Office: 22 Hughes Walk, Croydon, Surrey, CR0 2TR
Major Shareholder: Kwame Owusu Agyeman Mensa-Bonsu
Officers: Kwame Owusu Agyeman Mensa-Bonsu [1974] Director/Chartered Secretary

Step International Cosmetic Ltd
Incorporated: 5 November 2018
Registered Office: No 7 Imperial Wharf, London, SW2 2EX
Major Shareholder: Behzad Rostaminia
Officers: Behzad Rostaminia [1975] Director [Iranian]

Sterling Fragrances International Limited
Incorporated: 18 February 2014
Net Worth: £22,920 *Total Assets:* £1,780,000
Registered Office: 7 Poplar Road, Denham, Uxbridge, Middlesex, UB9 4AN
Shareholders: Husainy Fakhruddin; Mohammed Hussain Fakhruddin; Asgar Fakhruddin
Officers: Asgar Fakhruddin [1968] Director/Businessman [Indian]; Husainy Fakhruddin [1955] Director/Businessman [Indian]; Mohammed Husain Fakhruddin [1959] Director/Businessman [Indian]

Iryna Stewart Ltd
Incorporated: 19 May 2014 *Employees:* 1
Net Worth: £4,999 *Total Assets:* £9,358
Registered Office: 368 Forest Road, London, E17 5JF
Shareholders: Anastasiya Kryvenko; Christopher O'Kelly; Iryna Stewart
Officers: Iryna Stewart [1971] Director

The Top UK Perfume and Cosmetics Wholesalers												dellam

Stolen Beauty Limited
Incorporated: 17 August 2018
Registered Office: 7 Winston Drive, Biggin Hill, Westerham, Kent, TN16 3EP
Major Shareholder: Brandon Luan Garrard
Officers: Kirsty Jade Garrard [1989] Director/Cosmetic Designer

Lauren Stone Limited
Incorporated: 7 June 2016
Net Worth Deficit: £34,607 *Total Assets:* £39,728
Registered Office: McLintock Chartered Accountants, 2 Hilliards Court, Chester Business Park, Chester, CH4 9PX
Major Shareholder: Lauren Belinda Simon
Officers: Lauren Belinda Simon [1972] Director

Stonera Ltd
Incorporated: 22 February 2019
Registered Office: 19 George Road, Selly Oak, Birmingham, B29 6AH
Major Shareholder: Oluwatimilehin Marian McEwen
Officers: Oluwatimilehin Marian McEwen [1996] Director/Student

Storm of UK Limited
Incorporated: 11 July 2017
Registered Office: Kemp House, 160 City Road, London, EC1V 2NX
Officers: Thi Bao Tram Do [1982] Director [Vietnamese]; Claire Fritz [1985] Director/Manager

Strategy M Ltd
Incorporated: 13 April 2016 *Employees:* 2
Net Worth Deficit: £32,891 *Total Assets:* £18,426
Registered Office: Unit 10a Great Central Way, Central Business Center, London, NW10 0UR
Major Shareholder: Tiina Orasmae
Officers: Tiina Orasmae [1972] Director [Estonian]

Strdom Ltd
Incorporated: 10 December 2018
Registered Office: 71-75 Shelton Street, Covent Garden, London, WC2H 9JQ
Major Shareholder: Robert Lee-Roy Monan
Officers: Robert Lee-Roy Monan [1977] Director/Bus Driver

Strip Distribution Limited
Incorporated: 16 February 2007
Net Worth: £2,950,000 *Total Assets:* £3,660,000
Registered Office: 12 Northfields Prospect, Putney Bridge Road, London, SW18 1PE
Shareholders: Danielle Michelle Featherstone; Maria Louise Featherstone
Officers: Marie Featherstone, Secretary/Housewife; Danielle Michelle Featherstone [1974] Director; Maria Louise Featherstone [1973] Director; Gareth Price [1979] Director

Stroppy Ltd
Incorporated: 27 March 2018
Registered Office: 7 Crag Avenue, Bury, Lancs, BL9 5NZ
Shareholders: Hannah Elizabeth Vaughan; Marcia Harvey
Officers: Marcia Harvey [1976] Director/Online Retailer; Hannah Elizabeth Vaughan [1981] Director/Online Retailer

STT Industries Ltd.
Incorporated: 12 August 2015
Net Worth: £1,920 *Total Assets:* £1,920
Registered Office: Gwerncynydd Fach, Nantmel, Llandrindod Wells, Powys, LD1 6EW
Major Shareholder: Samuel Thomas Tolhurst
Officers: Samuel Thomas Tolhurst [1989] Director/Wholesale/Distribution of Recreational Products

Stuff of Life Limited
Incorporated: 1 February 2018
Registered Office: 208 Revelstoke Road, London, SW18 5NW
Major Shareholder: Sophie Helen Hooper
Officers: Sophie Helen Hooper [1967] Director

Style Cosmetics Limited
Incorporated: 24 July 2018
Registered Office: The Stylebar, 861 Ecclesall Road, Sheffield, S11 8TH
Shareholder: Cherise Hatfield
Officers: Cherise Hatfield [1986] Director

The Style Factory Limited
Incorporated: 26 November 2018
Registered Office: The Courtyard, Unit 2 Park Royal Road, Lower Park Trading Estate, London, W3 6XA
Shareholders: Ljubomir Radanovic; Zeljko Babic; Ratko Vukasinovic
Officers: Zeljko Babic [1979] Director; Ljubomir Radanovic [1977] Director; Ratko Vukasinovic [1974] Director

Style4you Ltd
Incorporated: 3 August 2018
Registered Office: 39 Brockenhurst Way, Bicknacre, Chelmsford, Essex, CM3 4XN
Major Shareholder: Shuhui Suo
Officers: Shuhui Suo [1984] Director/General Manager [Chinese]

Stylish & Luxurious Limited
Incorporated: 13 March 2017
Registered Office: 78 Lindsay Drive, Harrow, Middlesex, HA3 0TL
Officers: Nasmin Keshavji [1986] Director

SU Labs Limited
Incorporated: 25 January 2018
Registered Office: Flat 2, Elm Court, Admiral Walk, London, W9 3TZ
Major Shareholder: Su Yeon Sylvia Wong
Officers: Su Yeon Sylvia Wong [1992] Director

Suave Cents Limited
Incorporated: 6 November 2018
Registered Office: 4 Broom Terrace, Rotherham, S Yorks, S60 2TF
Officers: Fasil Khan [1986] Director

Sub Tropic Limited
Incorporated: 21 August 1995
Registered Office: 27 Connaught Street, Port Talbot, W Glamorgan, SA13 1ET
Officers: John Allan Simonson, Secretary; James Alexander Simonson [1989] Director/Student; John Allan Simonson [1939] Director/Consultant

Sublime Cosmetics UK Ltd
Incorporated: 7 January 2019
Registered Office: 27 Old Gloucester Street, London, WC1N 3AX
Major Shareholder: Elizabeth Olusesan
Officers: Elizabeth Olusesan [1975] Director

Sublyme Cosmetics Limited
Incorporated: 19 April 2013 *Employees:* 2
Net Worth: £194,454 *Total Assets:* £507,341
Registered Office: Parkside House, 167 Chorley New Road, Bolton, Lancs, BL1 4RA
Shareholders: Idris Mussa Bapu; Habib Patel
Officers: Idris Mussa Bapu [1975] Commercial Director; Habib Patel [1975] Finance Director

Sucre By Zoe Skincare Limited
Incorporated: 10 March 2018
Registered Office: 112 Middleton Avenue, Chingford, London, E4 8EE
Major Shareholder: Zoe Pyneeandy
Officers: Zoe Pyneeandy, Secretary; Zoe Pyneeandy [1992] Director

Sueno Cosmetics Ltd
Incorporated: 12 October 2018
Registered Office: 20 Constable Street, Manchester, M18 8QE
Officers: Lukasz Chomicki [1991] Director/Businessman [Polish]; Przemyslaw Marcin Szynkaruk [1987] Director/Businessman [Polish]; Krzysztof Jaroslaw Ustaszewski [1982] Director/Businessman [Polish]

Sulis Minerva Limited
Incorporated: 29 July 2014
Registered Office: 26 High East Street, Dorchester, DT1 1EZ
Shareholders: Scott James Duncan; Dean Giles Newton
Officers: Scott James Duncan [1975] Director; Dean Giles Newton [1966] Director

Summerlilly Limited
Incorporated: 26 June 2018
Registered Office: 9 Belmont Drive, Coalville, Leics, LE67 3LQ
Shareholders: Rebecca Nicholson; Andrew Lidwell
Officers: Rebecca Nicholson [1973] Director

Sun Jelly Ltd
Incorporated: 27 March 2018
Registered Office: 5 White Hart Lane, Wood Street Village, Guildford, Surrey, GU3 3DZ
Major Shareholder: Claudia Alice Swain
Officers: Claudia Alice Swain [1990] Director

Sun Light EU Trading Ltd
Incorporated: 29 January 2018
Registered Office: 1 Jubilee Way, Bicester, Oxon, OX26 6PN
Major Shareholder: Lei Zheng
Officers: Lei Zheng [1986] Director [Chinese]

Sun Lounge Supplies Limited
Incorporated: 26 January 2005 *Employees:* 1
Net Worth Deficit: £10,310 *Total Assets:* £22,699
Registered Office: Unit 1 Helsman House, Norham Road North, North Shields, Tyne & Wear, NE29 8RZ
Shareholders: Laura Wiszniewski; Mark Henrik Wiszniewski
Officers: Laura Wiszniewski, Company Secretary; Mark Henrik Wiszniewski [1972] Managing Director

Sun Spirit Skincare Limited
Incorporated: 18 November 2016
Registered Office: 30 Mackie Avenue, Brighton, BN1 8RA
Major Shareholder: Joseph Furini
Officers: Joseph Furini [1991] Director/Managerial

Sun Zapper UK Limited
Incorporated: 23 November 2016
Registered Office: 2h Weld Works Mews, London, SW2 5AX
Major Shareholder: Neil Jonathon Chambers
Officers: Neil Jonathon Chambers [1972] Director/Accountant [Australian]

Sun-Glo Limited
Incorporated: 29 April 2002
Net Worth Deficit: £48,680 *Total Assets:* £143,411
Registered Office: 20 Coxon Street, Spondon, Derby, DE21 7JG
Shareholders: Attilio Foa; Jacob Richard Fadlun
Officers: Attilio Foa, Secretary [Italian]; Attilio Foa [1961] Director [Italian]

Sundome Leisure Products Limited
Incorporated: 7 March 2002
Net Worth: £496 *Total Assets:* £60,769
Registered Office: 26 Berrycroft Lane, Romiley, Stockport, Cheshire, SK6 3AU
Officers: Jane Gillian Fletcher [1968] Director

Sunrise Essential Oil Limited
Incorporated: 31 January 2017
Registered Office: 3b-3c Lincoln Road, Erith, Kent, DA8 2DX
Shareholder: Sunil Kumar
Officers: Sunil Kumar [1985] Director [Indian]; Yashara Rukshani Talgaswatta [1990] Director/Teacher [Sri Lankan]

Sunscreen X Limited
Incorporated: 30 April 2018
Registered Office: 1 Inverforth Road, London, N11 1SY
Officers: Phillipe Anthony Moutousamy [1985] Director/Consultant

Sunspa Europe Limited
Incorporated: 14 June 2010
Net Worth Deficit: £23,164 *Total Assets:* £445
Registered Office: 87a High Street, The Old Town, Hemel Hempstead, Herts, HP1 3AH
Shareholders: Carl Stuart French; Paul Nicolaisen
Officers: Carl Stuart French [1947] Director; Paul Nicolaisen [1975] Director [Danish]

Sunspa UK Limited
Incorporated: 29 September 2006 *Employees:* 1
Net Worth Deficit: £27,347 *Total Assets:* £5,824
Registered Office: 87a High Street, The Old Town, Hemel Hempstead, Herts, HP1 3AH
Shareholder: Carl Stuart French
Officers: Carl Stuart French, Secretary; Carl Stuart French [1947] Director

Super Natural Apothecary Ltd.
Incorporated: 7 February 2017
Registered Office: 62 White Hart Lane, London, SW13 0PZ
Shareholders: Theodore Nicholas Bambacas; Anna Allington; Manveer Jandu
Officers: Anna Allington [1975] Director; Theodore Nicholas Bambacas [1968] Director [Australian]; Manveer Jandu [1985] Director

Super Yacht Spa Ltd
Incorporated: 17 December 2012
Net Worth: £7,512 *Total Assets:* £17,139
Registered Office: 570 Etruria Road, Newcastle-under-Lyme, Staffs, ST5 0SU
Major Shareholder: Ruth Amelia Lueck
Officers: Ruth Amelia Lueck [1979] Director

Supernova UK Pty Ltd
Incorporated: 14 June 2017
Registered Office: Suite 1, 3rd Floor, 11-12 St James's Square, London, SW1Y 4LB
Officers: Alexander Generald Ostrowski [1979] Director [German]

Supply Zoom Ltd
Incorporated: 11 March 2018
Registered Office: 2nd Floor, 124 Whitechapel Road, London, E1 1JE
Officers: MD Mushfiq Raihan [1980] Director [Bangladeshi]

Supreme Beard Ltd
Incorporated: 23 January 2017
Net Worth Deficit: £1,138
Registered Office: 150 St Pauls Road, Preston, Lancs, PR1 1PU
Major Shareholder: Wasim Patel
Officers: Wasim Patel, Secretary; Wasim Patel [1993] Director/Healthcare Assistant

Sur Trading Limited
Incorporated: 18 January 2013
Registered Office: 24 Lyndhurst Gardens, London, N3 1TB
Shareholders: Nir Kadosh; Shay Avi Kadosh
Officers: Nir Kadosh [1979] Director/Chief Executive Officer [Israeli]

Surrati Perfumes Limited
Incorporated: 20 April 2018
Registered Office: 57 Exeter Gardens, Ilford, Essex, IG1 3LB
Major Shareholder: Hava Dawood
Officers: Hava Dawood [1986] Director

Surreal Health & Beauty Limited
Incorporated: 7 May 2013
Net Worth: £100 *Total Assets:* £4,100
Registered Office: 14b South Park Drive, Gerrards Cross, Bucks, SL9 8JH
Officers: Catriona Jane Barber, Secretary; Leslie Christopher Barber [1957] Director

Suvaz Linen UK Ltd
Incorporated: 9 January 2019
Registered Office: Unit 10, 67 Tradeston Street, Glasgow, G5 8BL
Major Shareholder: Ramzia Toor
Officers: Ramzia Toor [1983] Director/Businesswoman [Pakistani]

Swan Leigh Cosmetics Ltd
Incorporated: 31 January 2018
Registered Office: 20-22 Wenlock Road, London, N1 7GU
Officers: James Morrison [1968] Director

Sweden Eco Limited
Incorporated: 6 September 2016
Net Worth: £326 *Total Assets:* £326
Registered Office: Kemp House, 160 City Road, London, EC1V 2NX
Major Shareholder: Adam Reis
Officers: Kayleigh Alexandra Toyra [1987] Director

Sweet Arabian Ltd
Incorporated: 9 October 2018
Registered Office: 20-22 Wenlock Road, London, N1 7GU
Shareholder: Bogdan Stefanidis-Vlad
Officers: Bogdan Stefanidis-Vlad [1987] Director/Marketing Specialist [Romanian]

Sweet Lilli Ltd
Incorporated: 5 October 2017
Registered Office: Suite 11, Penhurst House, 352-356 Battersea Park Road, London, SW11 3BY
Shareholders: Zuzana Muchova; Alex Pieter
Officers: Zuzana Muchova [1978] Director [Czech]; Alex Pieter [1972] Director [Czech]

Sweet Pea Soaps Company Ltd
Incorporated: 27 November 2018
Registered Office: Flat 11, Eden Court, 38 Wilbraham Road, Manchester, M14 7SA
Shareholders: Nadia Clark; Rejwana Hossain
Officers: Nadia Clark [1991] Director; Rejwana Hossain [1984] Director

Sweet Squared Limited
Incorporated: 9 August 2006
Net Worth: £7,800,000 *Total Assets:* £13,230,000
Registered Office: Unit 2 Green Park, Coal Road, Leeds, LS14 1FB
Major Shareholder: Samuel Sweet
Officers: Samuel Sweet, Secretary/Director [American]; James Alan Nordstrom [1957] Director/Executive [American]; Samantha Sweet [1969] Director; Samuel Sweet [1972] Director [American]

Swift Retail Limited
Incorporated: 24 July 2008 *Employees:* 17
Net Worth: £142,363 *Total Assets:* £299,541
Registered Office: 1 Knockcarra Grove, Omagh, Co Tyrone, BT79 7UR
Shareholders: Ryan Swift; Catherine Swift
Officers: Catherine Swift [1979] Director/Hairdresser [Irish]; Ryan Swift [1977] Director/Retailer [Irish]

Swipes Fragrance Ltd
Incorporated: 8 March 2018
Registered Office: Fairfield House, 25 The Common, Quarndon, Derby, DE22 5LD
Major Shareholder: Garry McBride
Officers: Garry McBride [1953] Director

Swiss Arabian Perfumes (UK) Ltd
Incorporated: 27 January 2012
Net Worth Deficit: £129,693 *Total Assets:* £2,807
Registered Office: 506 Kingsbury Road, London, NW9 9HE
Officers: Nabeel Hussein Adam Ali [1969] Director [Yemeni]

Swiss Cosmetic Distribution Limited
Incorporated: 21 June 2018
Registered Office: c/o Kaiser Nouman Nathan LLP, Unit 4, 17 Plumbers Row, London, E1 1EQ
Major Shareholder: Elena Vasileva
Officers: Elena Vasileva [1983] Director [Russian]

Swiss Pharma Dynamic Ltd
Incorporated: 18 February 2016
Registered Office: 27 Old Gloucester Street, London, WC1N 3AX
Major Shareholder: Kiriaki Zartaloudi
Officers: Kyriaki Zartaloudi [1973] Director [Greek]

Swiss Trading .UK. Ltd
Incorporated: 11 March 2018
Registered Office: 20-22 Wenlock Road, London, N1 7GU
Major Shareholder: Imran Choudhry
Officers: Imran Choudhry [1973] Director/Businessman

SYN-RG Trading Ltd
Incorporated: 26 February 2016
Registered Office: 18 Mafeking Avenue, Ilford, Essex, IG2 7AW
Shareholder: Birpal Singh Virdee
Officers: Dipen Patel [1988] Director/Pharmacist; Birpal Singh Virdee [1988] Director/Pharmacist

Synlatex Limited
Incorporated: 7 May 1985 *Employees:* 160
Net Worth: £12,402,876 *Total Assets:* £16,274,429
Registered Office: Studio 19, The Brewery Quarter, Unit H2, High Street, Cheltenham, Glos, GL50 3FF
Parent: SLG Allstars Limited
Officers: Lucy Jane Beresford [1980] Sales Director; Richard Mark Buckland [1977] Director; Timothy Cound [1963] Manufacturing Director; Miles Spencer Maitland Dunkley [1967] Managing Director; Susan Hutchings [1966] Director; Lisa Topping [1974] Manufacturing Sales Director

SZ Beauty Limited
Incorporated: 22 February 2017
Net Worth Deficit: £9,480 *Total Assets:* £34,720
Registered Office: 2nd Floor, Parkgates, Bury New Road, Prestwich, Manchester, M25 0TL
Shareholders: Naftoli Kahn; Sorah Zelda Kahn
Officers: Naftoli Kahn [1979] Director [Danish]; Sarah Zelda Kahn [1982] Director

T A Trading Ltd
Incorporated: 23 September 2016
Net Worth: £467 *Total Assets:* £712
Registered Office: Verna House, 9 Bicester Road, Aylesbury, Bucks, HP19 9AG
Major Shareholder: Alan Green
Officers: Alan Green [1959] Director/Salesman

T.L.C. (Total Luxury Cosmetics) Ltd
Incorporated: 3 January 2013 *Employees:* 3
Net Worth: £4,681 *Total Assets:* £868,089
Registered Office: Unit 8 Queen Street, Great Harwood, Blackburn, BB6 7AX
Major Shareholder: Clare Elizabeth Francis
Officers: Clare Elizabeth Francis, Secretary; Clare Elizabeth Francis [1968] Director

T4Colins Beautifician Ltd
Incorporated: 5 July 2018
Registered Office: 36 Eldon Court, Sheffield, S1 4GY
Major Shareholder: Tinu Amy Collins
Officers: Tinu Amy Collins [1991] Director/Cosmetologist

TA-65 (UK) Wholesale Limited
Incorporated: 24 May 2018
Registered Office: Old Rectory, North End Road, Little Yeldham, Halstead, Essex, CO9 4LE
Major Shareholder: David Christopher Heather
Officers: David Christopher Heather [1962] Director

Tabitha JK Limited
Incorporated: 16 December 2011
Net Worth Deficit: £12,124 *Total Assets:* £68,375
Registered Office: 3 Coventry Innovation Village, Cheetah Road, Coventry, Warwicks, CV1 2TL
Shareholders: Dennes Johannes James-Kraan; Tabitha Heather James-Kraan
Officers: Dennes Johannes James Kraan [1973] Director [Dutch]; Tabitha Heather James Kraan [1969] Director

TAC Perfumes & Cosmetics (UK) Ltd
Incorporated: 12 February 2018
Registered Office: Kemp House, 160 City Road, London, EC1V 2NX
Shareholders: Khandoker Choudhury; Tasbirul Ahmed Choudhury
Officers: Khandoker Choudhury, Secretary; Tasbirul Choudhury, Secretary; Khandoker Choudhury [1976] Director [Bangladeshi]; Tasbirul Ahmed Choudhury [1966] Managing Director [Bangladeshi]

Stella Tailor Ltd
Incorporated: 13 November 2017
Registered Office: 12 Bulwer Street, London, W12 8AP
Shareholder: Amir Ali Bazazi
Officers: Amir Ali Bazazi [1992] Director; Seulgi Lee [1990] Director [Korean]

Tailord Chic Ltd
Incorporated: 1 June 2017
Registered Office: 145 Wigan House, Warwick Grove, London, E5 9JD
Officers: Dionne Llewellyn [1978] Director

Takasago (U.K.) Limited
Incorporated: 19 April 1990 *Employees:* 7
Net Worth: £95,477 *Total Assets:* £403,593
Registered Office: Ground Floor, Scammell House, 9 High Street, Ascot, Berks, SL5 7JF
Officers: Pascal Dalle-Molle [1962] Director/Vice President Finance [French]; Motonobu Sekine [1966] Director [Japanese]

Talza Limited
Incorporated: 26 February 1987
Net Worth: £3,561,620 *Total Assets:* £3,582,667
Registered Office: Victoria House, Gloucester Street, Belfast, BT1 4LS
Parent: Clarins (UK) Limited
Officers: Deborah Ann Lewis [1964] Director; Alison Mary Surridge [1966] Director

Tannovation Laboratories Ltd
Incorporated: 7 January 2019
Registered Office: 20-22 Wenlock Road, London, N1 7GU
Major Shareholder: Karen Wood
Officers: Karen Wood [1977] Director

Tanovation Ltd
Incorporated: 6 November 2018
Registered Office: The Lodge, Blair Road, Crossford, Carluke, S Lanarks, ML8 5QR
Major Shareholder: Joyce Baillie Carslaw
Officers: Robyn Maryanne Baillie, Secretary; Joyce Baillie Carslaw [1965] Director/Beautician

Tansi Packaging Solutions Limited
Incorporated: 10 May 2010 *Employees:* 2
Net Worth Deficit: £187,149 *Total Assets:* £1,452,988
Registered Office: 5 Watchetts Lake Close, Camberley, Surrey, GU15 2PG
Major Shareholder: Benilda Grace Navamani
Officers: Sheila Grace Clarence [1957] Director; James Benjamin Jose [1953] Managing Director

Tarsago Ltd
Incorporated: 27 March 2015
Net Worth Deficit: £185,040 *Total Assets:* £251,820
Registered Office: 71-75 Shelton Street, Covent Garden, London, WC2H 9JQ
Officers: Ada Aurelia Saffell [1976] Business Development Director [Polish]

Tassels UK Ltd
Incorporated: 10 October 2017
Net Worth: £1 *Total Assets:* £19,342
Registered Office: 113 Hengist Road, Erith, Kent, DA8 1EZ
Officers: Ayodele Oyetunji, Secretary; Omolade Olayemi Oyetunji [1976] Director/Business Analyst

Tattva Ltd.
Incorporated: 6 July 2017
Registered Office: 63 Stafford Road, Sheffield, S2 2SF
Officers: Ganesh Singh Basera [1985] Sales Director [Indian]; Simona Vilnerova [1990] Director [Slovak]

Tauri Corporation Limited
Incorporated: 6 February 2018
Registered Office: 66 Hartslock Drive, London, SE2 9UU
Major Shareholder: Dorinda Eno-Young Faniku
Officers: Dorinda Eno-Young Faniku [1994] Director/Beautician [Austrian]

Tawakkal Perfumes Ltd
Incorporated: 15 March 2018
Registered Office: 28 Colonial Road, Birmingham, B9 5NG
Major Shareholder: Gulzar Hussain
Officers: Gulzar Hussain [1976] Director/Manager

Eve Taylor (London) Limited
Incorporated: 29 July 1968 *Employees:* 21
Net Worth: £632,366 *Total Assets:* £1,049,308
Registered Office: Unit 1 Mallard Business Centre, Bretton, Peterborough, Cambs, PE3 8YR
Shareholders: Raymond Neil Taylor; Alan Leslie Taylor; Christopher Mark Taylor
Officers: Evelyn May Taylor OBE, Secretary; Alan Leslie Taylor [1952] Director/Export Manager; Christopher Mark Taylor [1963] Marketing Director; Evelyn May Taylor OBE [1932] Director

Taylor Grange Cosmetics Limited
Incorporated: 6 February 2019
Registered Office: 2 Water Court, Water Street, Birmingham, B3 1HP
Shareholders: Rakesh Singh Doal; Samuel Ginda
Officers: Rakesh Singh Doal [1969] Director; Samuel Ginda [1983] Director

Tebs Distribution Limited
Incorporated: 9 January 2019
Registered Office: 71-75 Shelton Street, Covent Garden, London, WC2H 9JQ
Officers: Rowan Thomas Bailey [1990] Director; Adam Edgerley [1988] Director

Temple Spirit Ltd
Incorporated: 6 August 2010
Previous: Asana Lifestyle Limited
Net Worth Deficit: £54,240 *Total Assets:* £14,020
Registered Office: The Old School House, 3a Leckhampton Road, Cheltenham, Glos, GL53 0AX
Major Shareholder: Diane Susan Davies
Officers: Diane Susan Davies [1963] Director; Wyndham Glyn Davies [1946] Director

Tententen Limited
Incorporated: 30 October 2018
Registered Office: 141 Hartington Road, London, SW8 2EY
Shareholders: Robi Miles Dutta; Adam de Cruz
Officers: Adam de Cruz [1971] Managing Director; Robi Miles Dutta [1970] Managing Director

Teoxane UK Limited
Incorporated: 27 October 2005 *Employees:* 19
Previous: Lifestyle Aesthetics Limited
Net Worth: £1,966,430 *Total Assets:* £3,792,919
Registered Office: 54-55 Shrivenham Hundred Business Park, Majors Road, Watchfield, Swindon, Wilts, SN6 8TY
Parent: Teoxane SA
Officers: Sandra Fishlock [1967] Director/Product Specialist

Tetra Hydro Cannabinoid Oils Global Ltd
Incorporated: 17 October 2018
Registered Office: 66 Hindes Road, Harrow, Middlesex, HA1 1SL
Major Shareholder: Brian Francis McKay
Officers: Brian Francis McKay [1974] Director/Artist

Texthold Ltd
Incorporated: 21 November 2018
Registered Office: 71-75 Shelton Street, London, WC2H 9JQ
Major Shareholder: Esther Frand
Officers: Esther Frand [1991] Director/Teacher

Thai Wellness Ltd
Incorporated: 6 February 2019
Registered Office: 71-75 Shelton Street, London, WC2H 9JQ
Major Shareholder: Supadtra Brams
Officers: Supadtra Brams, Secretary; Supadtra Brams [1992] Director/Massage Therapist [Thai]

Thalasso Ltd
Incorporated: 5 April 2018
Registered Office: Cambrian View, Geraint Road, Criccieth, Gwynedd, LL52 0HR
Shareholder: Daniel James Burr
Officers: Sarah Jane Burr [1975] Director/Business Owner

Thalgo UK Limited
Incorporated: 16 September 1985 *Employees:* 14
Net Worth: £196,116 *Total Assets:* £988,818
Registered Office: 9 St Annes Street, London, E14 7PF
Officers: Michel Gras, Secretary; Jean-Claude Sirop [1941] Director/President CEO [French]

TheGlobalTrading Ltd
Incorporated: 11 July 2018
Registered Office: Unit 5 Martinbridge, 240-242 Lincoln Road, Enfield, Middlesex, EN1 1SP
Major Shareholder: Kai Pan
Officers: Kai Pan [1977] Director

Theglossfairy Ltd
Incorporated: 22 January 2019
Registered Office: 81 Campion Close, Croydon, Surrey, CR0 5SN
Officers: Abigail Dankyi [1997] Director/Finance Administration

TheGoodSkinCompany Ltd
Incorporated: 18 September 2018
Registered Office: 71-75 Shelton Street, London, WC2H 9JQ
Major Shareholder: Stephen Mockford
Officers: Mike Mockford [1992] Sales Director

TheManeCompany Ltd
Incorporated: 26 September 2018
Registered Office: 14 Portland Road, Great Sankey, Warrington, Cheshire, WA5 8DR
Major Shareholder: Sean Antony Cosgrave
Officers: Sean Antony Cosgrave [1988] Director

Theodory Ltd
Incorporated: 13 February 2018
Registered Office: 71-75 Shelton Street, Covent Garden, London, WC2H 9JQ
Major Shareholder: Teodora Csizmadia
Officers: Teodora Csizmadia [1984] Director [Hungarian]

There-There Baby Ltd
Incorporated: 11 June 2018
Registered Office: 7 Beaconsfield Road, Woodbridge, Suffolk, IP12 1EQ
Officers: Hannah Newman [1981] Director

Think Be Nature Ltd
Incorporated: 13 February 2018
Registered Office: 4th Floor, 18 St Cross Street, London, EC1N 8UN
Major Shareholder: Elzbieta Monika Rzepkowska
Officers: Elzbieta Monika Rzepkowska [1971] Director [Polish]

Think Beauty Online Limited
Incorporated: 19 November 2018
Registered Office: 5 Turing Close, Manchester, M11 2EP
Officers: Keith Wearing [1977] Director

Thiossane Ltd
Incorporated: 5 July 2018
Registered Office: Flat 2, Gouldy House, 82a Whitechapel High Street, London, E1 7QX
Shareholders: Ibrahima Sall; Ali Maher
Officers: Ali Maher [1991] Sales Director [French]; Ibrahima Sall [1987] Director [French]

This Works Products Limited
Incorporated: 10 July 2009 *Employees:* 32
Net Worth: £1,561,455 *Total Assets:* £7,457,314
Registered Office: MacKrell Turner Garrett, Savoy Hill House, Savoy Hill, London, WC2R 0BU
Parent: TWP UK Holdings Limited
Officers: Richard Gersten [1966] Director/Partner [American]; Anna Devi Persaud [1970] Director; Katherine Phillips [1948] Director/Journalist

Three Beauties of London Limited
Incorporated: 15 May 2000
Registered Office: 9 Perseverance Works, Kingsland Road, London, E2 8DD
Shareholders: Dyran Lambert Dharmaraj; Rajaram Dharmaraj
Officers: Dyran Lambert Dharmaraj, Secretary; Dyran Lambert Dharmaraj [1970] Director [Singaporean]; Rajaram Dharmaraj [1946] Director/General Manager [Singaporean]

Three Organics Ltd
Incorporated: 12 September 2017
Registered Office: 71-75 Shelton Street, Covent Garden, London, WC2H 9JQ
Major Shareholder: Hameed Alam
Officers: Roszella Ibrahim, Secretary; Hameed Alam [1967] Director/Finance Manager; Sagira Hussain [1968] Director/Teacher

Three Pears Online Limited
Incorporated: 12 August 1997
Previous: Three Pears Internet Limited
Net Worth Deficit: £618,144 *Total Assets:* £5,585
Registered Office: Unit 6 Station Road Industrial Estate, Station Road, Rowley Regis, Warley, W Midlands, B65 0JY
Shareholders: Three Pears Holdings Ltd; Three Pears Holdings Limited
Officers: Karen Elizabeth Tonks, Secretary; Edward Stanley Dunn [1969] Director

Thrifty Limited
Incorporated: 22 April 2013
Registered Office: 98 Swallow Road, Ipswich, Suffolk, IP2 0TS
Major Shareholder: Karl Wright
Officers: Karl Wright, Secretary; Karl Wright [1957] Director; Sam Wright [1997] Director

Thrillage Ltd.
Incorporated: 30 October 2017
Registered Office: 64 Farm Street, Birmingham, B19 2UE
Shareholders: Abdisamad Madey Nurey; Mascuud Yusuf Abdi Alasow
Officers: Mascuud Yusuf Abdi Alasow [1996] Director/Student [Finnish]; Abdisamad Madey Nurey [1996] Director/Student

Tiarna Ltd
Incorporated: 29 June 2017
Registered Office: 46 Kings Arms Court, 301 East Acton Lane, London, W3 7QN
Major Shareholder: Lisa Robyn Lamb
Officers: Lisa Robyn Lamb [1983] Director [American]

Tibetan Cosmetics Ltd
Incorporated: 8 October 2015
Net Worth Deficit: £18,622 *Total Assets:* £38,592
Registered Office: 9 Windsor Close, St Ives, Cambs, PE27 3DW
Officers: Edyta Katarzyna Wojcik [1972] Director [Polish]; Michal Piotr Wojcik [1973] Director [Polish]

Tiggy Lashes Ltd
Incorporated: 15 August 2018
Registered Office: Basement, 256 Eastern Road, Brighton, BN2 5TA
Shareholders: Claudia Rosa Bish; Jack Peter Greig
Officers: Claudia Rosa Bish [1995] Director

Timeless Temple Ltd
Incorporated: 31 August 2018
Registered Office: 8 New Row, Woodborough, Nottingham, NG14 6DT
Shareholder: Lucy Giacone
Officers: Gianfranco Giacone [1964] Director/Head Stylist; Lucy Giacone [1988] Business Director

Timi's Cosmetics Ltd
Incorporated: 29 August 2018
Registered Office: 15 Orslow Walk, Wolverhampton, W Midlands, WV10 0UE
Major Shareholder: Ibukunoluwa Oluwatimileyin Ojolo
Officers: Ibukunoluwa Oluwatimileyin Ojolo [1998] Director [Nigerian]

Tina Trading Company Ltd
Incorporated: 5 October 2018
Registered Office: 99 Childers Street, Doncaster, S Yorks, DN4 5BZ
Major Shareholder: Aihd Omar
Officers: Aihd Omar [1984] Director

Tioluxe Europe Limited
Incorporated: 12 September 2017
Registered Office: Scottish Provident House, 76-80 College Road, Harrow, Middlesex, HA1 1BQ
Major Shareholder: Lilaram Bharvani Rajan
Officers: Kannuswamy Venguswamy [1967] Director/Sales Marketing [Singaporean]

Tir Chonaill London Ltd
Incorporated: 28 October 2015
Net Worth: £7,359   Total Assets: £9,908
Registered Office: 32 Palmerston Crescent, Palmers Green, London, N13 4JN
Major Shareholder: Sean Oconghaile
Officers: Sean O' Conghaile [1956] Director/Manager

Tiyati Ltd
Incorporated: 18 January 2017
Net Worth: £8,396   Total Assets: £84,470
Registered Office: 590 Kingston Road, London, SW20 8DN
Officers: Katarzyna Wiktoria Gut [1982] Director [Polish]

TJ Nail Supplies Ltd
Incorporated: 27 April 2017
Registered Office: 48-52 Penny Lane, Mossley Hill, Liverpool, L18 1DG
Major Shareholder: Toan Ngoc Dang
Officers: Toan Ngoc Dang [1973] Director; John Quoc Tran [1984] Director

TLC - Tender Loving Care UK Limited
Incorporated: 20 January 1998
Net Worth Deficit: £346,690   Total Assets: £366,340
Registered Office: 73 Cornhill, London, EC3V 3QQ
Shareholders: Mordechai Lubezky; Tamir Lubezky; Dotan Lubezky
Officers: Tamir Lubezky [1972] Director [Israeli]

TLGrooming Limited
Incorporated: 27 February 2019
Registered Office: 105 Bell Barn Road, Birmingham, B15 2GL
Major Shareholder: Ayodeji Adedeji Ojuroye
Officers: Ayodeji Adedeji Ojuroye [1986] Director/Operations Manager

TLY Supplies Ltd
Incorporated: 17 March 2014
Net Worth: £18,620   Total Assets: £188,002
Registered Office: 29 Granby Road, Saighton, Chester, CH3 6FD
Shareholders: Andrew Sean Wray; Xiao Yan Wray
Officers: Andrew Sean Wray [1978] Director/Buying; Xiao Yan Wray [1974] Sales Director

TM Brands Limited
Incorporated: 21 September 2010
Net Worth: £1,734   Total Assets: £9,434
Registered Office: 12 Floyer Close, Richmond, Surrey, TW10 6HS
Major Shareholder: Stoyan Hristov
Officers: Zlatka Bimbelova, Secretary; Stoyan Hristov [1981] Director [Bulgarian]

Tobco Limited
Incorporated: 20 June 2018
Registered Office: 60-64 Canterbury Street, Gillingham, Kent, ME7 5UJ
Shareholder: Megan Head
Officers: Megan Head [1995] Director; Tobias Head [1997] Director

Toggle Genetica Group Limited
Incorporated: 15 August 2018
Registered Office: 16 Wyndham Arcade, Cardiff, CF10 1FJ
Major Shareholder: Kiera Ricci
Officers: Kiera Ricci [1989] Director

Tommco Limited
Incorporated: 20 June 2018
Registered Office: 60-64 Canterbury Street, Gillingham, Kent, ME7 5UJ
Officers: Megan Head [1995] Director; Moira Head [1967] Director

Tonic15 Ltd
Incorporated: 16 February 2018
Registered Office: Huckletree, Mediaworks, 191 Wood Lane, London, W12 7FP
Officers: Hyojin Kwon [1984] Director/Founder [South Korean]

Top Beauty Brands Ltd
Incorporated: 6 February 2017
Net Worth Deficit: £6,870
Registered Office: 50a Hinckley Road, Leicester, LE3 0RB
Shareholder: Stanislaw Pawelek
Officers: Damian Wieslaw Azikiewicz [1982] Director [Polish]; Stanislaw Pawelek [1977] Director [Polish]

Top Beauty Limited
Incorporated: 5 June 2014
Net Worth: £169,170   Total Assets: £857,337
Registered Office: Flat 107, 25 Indescon Square, London, E14 9DG
Parent: Nyso Development Limited
Officers: Shun Ding [1977] Director/Merchant [Chinese]

Top Brands Australia Limited
Incorporated: 24 May 2017
Registered Office: Devon Mansions, 166 Tooley Street, London, SE1 2XH
Major Shareholder: Peter Mulholland
Officers: Peter Mulholland [1985] Director/Founder & CEO [Australian]

Toppers Nails Limited
Incorporated: 11 October 2017
Registered Office: Meadowview, Llancadle, Barry, Vale of Glamorgan, CF62 3AQ
Major Shareholder: Michaela Weaver
Officers: Jeffrey Parker [1963] Director; Michaela Weaver [1965] Director

Torcall of Edinburgh Ltd
Incorporated: 12 June 2017
Registered Office: The Lodge, 6 Blegbie, Humbie, E Lothian, EH36 5PN
Major Shareholder: Joshua Curquejo
Officers: Joshua Curquejo, Secretary; Joshua Curquejo [1985] Director

Total Beauty Ltd
Incorporated: 4 January 2013
Net Worth: £639   Total Assets: £12,912
Registered Office: 29 Dale Close, South Ockendon, Essex, RM15 5DR
Major Shareholder: Fatimo Dawodu
Officers: Fatimo Dawodu [1970] Director

Total Beauty Network (UK) Limited
Incorporated: 25 September 2014
Net Worth: £4,254 *Total Assets:* £159,913
Registered Office: c/o Howsons, Winton House, Stoke Road, Stoke on Trent, Staffs, ST4 2RW
Parent: S & T Rechtman Pty Ltd
Officers: Anthony Rechtman [1971] Director [Australian]

Total Salon Supplies Limited
Incorporated: 10 May 2018
Registered Office: Unit 10 Accent Business Centre, Barkerend Road, Bradford, W Yorks, BD3 9BD
Parent: The 360 Hut Limited
Officers: Mohammed Monir Uddin [1982] Director

Tothun Group UK Ltd
Incorporated: 6 September 2017
Registered Office: 377A Filton Avenue, Horfield, Bristol, BS7 0LH
Major Shareholder: Yi Lu
Officers: Yi Lu [1982] Director/Manager [Chinese]

Toure Ltd
Incorporated: 30 October 2018
Registered Office: 71-75 Shelton Street, London, WC2H 9JQ
Major Shareholder: Djibril Fode Toure
Officers: Djibril Fode Toure, Secretary; Djibril Fode Toure [1989] Director [French]

Trade Anchor Limited
Incorporated: 19 June 2018
Registered Office: 2nd Floor, College House, 17 King Edwards Road, Ruislip, Middlesex, HA4 7AE
Major Shareholder: Surinder Baugh
Officers: Surinder Baugh [1966] Director

Trade Dream Ltd
Incorporated: 3 January 2018
Registered Office: 173 Victor Street, Grimsby, N E Lincs, DN32 7QB
Officers: Eriks Margis [1994] Director [Latvian]

Trade Giant Limited
Incorporated: 20 March 2018
Registered Office: Kemp House, 160 City Road, London, EC1V 2NX
Shareholders: Salman Omar; Abm Kamran Sarkar
Officers: Salman Omar, Secretary; Salman Omar [1987] Director [Bangladeshi]; Abm Kamran Sarkar [1987] Director [Bangladeshi]

Trade Mall Limited
Incorporated: 29 October 2018
Registered Office: Room 2C05, South Bank Techno Park, 90 London Road, London, SE1 6LN
Major Shareholder: Beibei Li
Officers: Beibei Li [1988] Director [Chinese]

Trade Smart Marketing Limited
Incorporated: 7 July 1983
Net Worth: £544,902 *Total Assets:* £1,537,017
Registered Office: 1 Rutland Court, Edinburgh, EH3 8EY
Parent: Thomas Brown & Sons (Funeral Directors) Limited
Officers: John Chapman Dalley, Secretary; Henry Patrick Fleming Cairney [1952] Director/Customer Services Manager; James Watson [1951] Director/Health & Safety Adviser

Traderuk Limited
Incorporated: 3 November 2017
Registered Office: 225 Willingham Street, Grimsby, N E Lincs, DN32 9PX
Major Shareholder: Armands Ramma
Officers: Armands Ramma [1983] Director [Latvian]

Trading Corporation International Export and Import Ltd
Incorporated: 21 January 2019
Registered Office: 20-22 Wenlock Road, London, N1 7GU
Shareholders: Jose Maria Lopes; Antonio Ferreira de Souza
Officers: Vanda Cristina Fonseca Rodrigues de Souza, Secretary; Noelia Pereira Zumba Lopes, Secretary; Antonio Ferreira de Souza [1970] Director [Portuguese]; Jose Maria Lopes [1957] Director [Brazilian]

Trading Scents (2014) Limited
Incorporated: 14 April 2014
Net Worth: £3,246,614 *Total Assets:* £5,596,729
Registered Office: 2 Park Court, Pyrford Road, West Byfleet, Surrey, KT14 6SD
Shareholders: Eoin Alan MacLeod; Trading Scents Group Limited
Officers: Eoin Alan MacLeod [1962] Director

Trading Scents Group Limited
Incorporated: 14 April 2014
Net Worth: £4,554,895 *Total Assets:* £6,196,438
Registered Office: 2 Park Court, Pyrford Road, West Byfleet, Surrey, KT14 6SD
Major Shareholder: Eoin Alan MacLeod
Officers: Eoin Alan MacLeod [1962] Director

Trading Scents Limited
Incorporated: 31 July 1992
Net Worth: £2,857,008 *Total Assets:* £3,090,783
Registered Office: 2 Park Court, Pyrford Road, West Byfleet, Surrey, KT14 6SD
Parent: Trading Scents (2014) Limited
Officers: Eoin Alan MacLeod [1962] Director

Tradinguk55 Limited
Incorporated: 4 January 2018
Registered Office: 61 Queens Road, Blackburn, BB1 1QF
Major Shareholder: Abdul-Qadeer Hayat
Officers: Dr Abdul-Qadeer Hayat [1956] Director/Consultant [Norwegian]

Transeur Export Finance Co. Limited
Incorporated: 16 July 1979 *Employees:* 7
Net Worth: £615,197 *Total Assets:* £1,200,660
Registered Office: Overseas House, 66-68 High Road, Bushey Heath, Herts, WD23 1GG
Shareholders: Gobind Hemandas Nandwani; Sajni Gobind Nandwani
Officers: Bhagwan Philip Nandwani, Secretary/Director; Bhagwan Philip Nandwani [1963] Director; Gobind Hemandas Nandwani [1931] Director/Merchant; Sajni Gobind Nandwani [1936] Director/Married Woman [Maltese]

Transformulas International Limited
Incorporated: 20 March 2002 *Employees:* 8
Net Worth: £237,836 *Total Assets:* £565,540
Registered Office: 39 Thorpe Lane, Austerlands, Oldham, Lancs, OL4 3QW
Major Shareholder: Rosalind Annette Whyers
Officers: Rosalind Annette Whyers [1963] Director

Transformulas Limited
Incorporated: 10 August 2005
Registered Office: 39 Thorpe Lane, Austerlands, Oldham, Lancs, OL4 3QW
Major Shareholder: Rosalind Annette Whyers
Officers: Rosalind Annette Whyers [1963] Director

Treas Biotechnology UK Ltd
Incorporated: 16 September 2016
Registered Office: International House, 24 Holborn Viaduct, London, EC1A 2BN
Major Shareholder: Dong Zhou
Officers: Dong Zhou [1975] Director [Chinese]

Tree of Life Cosmetics Ltd
Incorporated: 14 May 2018
Registered Office: 28 Cranwell Court, Wickham Road, Croydon, Surrey, CR0 8BB
Major Shareholder: Helen Adetokunbo Adesina
Officers: Helen Adetokunbo Adesina [1989] Director

Trees of Beauty Ltd
Incorporated: 20 December 2018
Registered Office: 71-75 Shelton Street, London, WC2H 9JQ
Major Shareholder: Cendesse Zidi
Officers: Cendesse Zidi [1979] Director/Manager [French]

Trelux Limited
Incorporated: 30 July 2018
Registered Office: 25 Beckhill Approach, Leeds, LS7 2RF
Major Shareholder: Linda Ndhlovu
Officers: Linda Ndhlovu [1981] Director [Zimbabwean]

Trending Scents Ltd.
Incorporated: 21 August 2017
Registered Office: 172 Shearbrow, Blackburn, Lancs, BB1 8DZ
Major Shareholder: Mohsin Munshi
Officers: Mohsin Munshi [1978] Director/IT Manager

Triaton Ltd
Incorporated: 31 October 2018
Registered Office: Office 50044, 5 Percy Street, Fitzrovia, London, W1T 1DG
Major Shareholder: Dmitry Veligura
Officers: Dmitry Veligura [1968] Director [Russian]

Trichy Ltd
Incorporated: 21 May 2018
Registered Office: 638 Holloway Road, London, N19 3NU
Major Shareholder: Jaspreet Kaur
Officers: Jaspreet Kaur [1987] Director/Sales [Indian]

Trimmz Ltd
Incorporated: 8 November 2016
Registered Office: 20-22 Wenlock Road, London, N1 7GU
Major Shareholder: Nicholas Cumberbatch
Officers: Nicholas Cumberbatch [1985] Director

Trine Oils Limited
Incorporated: 10 August 2018
Registered Office: 130 Old Street, London, EC1V 9BD
Officers: Shanti Doon-Pandit [1966] Director/Sales Consultant

Trinity General Trading Limited
Incorporated: 22 January 2019
Registered Office: 100 Durley Dean Road, Birmingham, B29 6RX
Major Shareholder: Robel Fessaha
Officers: Robel Fessaha [1988] Director/Chartered Accountant

Trollion Limited
Incorporated: 14 March 2018
Registered Office: 43 Altham Gardens, Watford, Herts, WD19 6HJ
Shareholders: Iqueg Ltd; Mohamed Zahid Govani
Officers: Mohamed Zahid Govani, Secretary; Mohamed Zahid Govani [1972] Director/Manager [Swedish]; Shafiq Govani [1976] Director/Businessman [Swedish]

TRS & Co (Europe) Limited
Incorporated: 22 January 2016 *Employees:* 6
Net Worth: £9,841 *Total Assets:* £291,791
Registered Office: Unit 15 IES Centre, Horndale Avenue, Aycliffe Business Park, Newton Aycliffe, Co Durham, DL5 6DS
Shareholders: Howard Vern Funk; Jane Debra Wild
Officers: Howard Funk [1962] Commercial Director [American]; Jane Debra Wild [1962] Commercial Director

True Affinity Limited
Incorporated: 12 April 2005
Net Worth Deficit: £16,600 *Total Assets:* £177,000
Registered Office: Prospect House, 2 Athenaeum Road, London, N20 9AE
Shareholders: Martin Paul Cracknell; Wendy Stallard
Officers: Martin Paul Cracknell [1961] Director

True Brit London Limited
Incorporated: 27 June 2014
Net Worth Deficit: £4,387 *Total Assets:* £102,716
Registered Office: Endiva House, Murray Road, St Paul's Cray, Orpington, Kent, BR5 3QY
Major Shareholder: Kathryn Rachel Cavan
Officers: Kathryn Rachel Cavan [1963] Director

True Hemp Ltd
Incorporated: 5 September 2017
Registered Office: 163 Heath Street, Birmingham, B18 4DA
Officers: Marlon Stefan Housen-Lewis [1989] Director; Michael Anthony Housen-Lewis [1989] Director; Nathan Alexander Rowe [1991] Director/Self Employed [British/Jamaican]

True Mia Limited
Incorporated: 20 March 2018
Registered Office: 4 Storth Oaks Mead, London, BR7 5FN
Major Shareholder: Jasmine Catherine Williams
Officers: Jasmine Catherine Williams, Secretary; Jasmine Catherine Williams [1980] Director

True Scents Ltd
Incorporated: 15 April 2014
Net Worth Deficit: £3,805 *Total Assets:* £344
Registered Office: 176 Church Road, London, NW10 9NP
Officers: Latifah Bilal-Beccan [1969] Director

True Skincare Limited
Incorporated: 6 March 2018
Registered Office: 7 Heronsbrook, Buckhurst Road, Ascot, Berks, SL5 7QD
Major Shareholder: Emma Louise Thornton
Officers: Emma Thornton, Secretary; Christine Ruth Thornton [1961] Director; Emma Louise Thornton [1990] Director/Marketing Manager

Truity Limited
Incorporated: 18 January 2019
Registered Office: 71-75 Shelton Street, London, WC2H 9JQ
Shareholders: Rhodri Andrew Ferrier; Simon Joseph Duffy
Officers: Rhodri Andrew Ferrier, Secretary; Simon Joseph Duffy [1976] Director; Rhodri Andrew Ferrier [1978] Director

Trulips Ltd
Incorporated: 26 October 2018
Registered Office: Flat 8, Sergeant Court, Station Road, Sidcup, Kent, DA15 7AY
Major Shareholder: Kaushal Pindoria
Officers: Kaushal Pindoria [1987] Director

Geo. F. Trumper (Perfumer and Products) Limited
Incorporated: 27 January 1923 *Employees:* 18
Net Worth: £1,307,793 *Total Assets:* £1,759,021
Registered Office: 166 Fairbridge Road, London, N19 3HT
Major Shareholder: Paulette Bersch
Officers: Paulette Bersch, Secretary; Paulette Bersch [1949] Director; Sebastian Cherchi Bersch [1980] Director/Manager

Truthpaste Ltd
Incorporated: 25 September 2018
Registered Office: Unit 13, 1 Ellen Street, Portslade, Brighton, BN41 1EU
Major Shareholder: Marisa Battrick
Officers: Marisa Battrick [1988] Director

Tryon Products Limited
Incorporated: 26 September 2018
Registered Office: 60 High Street, Wimbledon, London, SW19 5EE
Major Shareholder: Alan Wasfy
Officers: Alan Wasfy [1983] Director [Irish]

Turning Tides Ltd
Incorporated: 2 August 2018
Registered Office: 1 Cromwell Way, Market Deeping, Peterborough, PE6 8BX
Major Shareholder: Jason Fullman
Officers: Jason Fullman [1972] Director

TWC Products Limited
Incorporated: 8 April 2016 *Employees:* 2
Net Worth Deficit: £59,570 *Total Assets:* £854,136
Registered Office: St Bride's House, 10 Salisbury Square, London, EC4Y 8EH
Officers: Lars Soren Sorensen [1956] Director [Danish]

Twelve Beauty Ltd
Incorporated: 9 February 2015
Net Worth: £20,890 *Total Assets:* £55,560
Registered Office: 12 Wyndham House, 24 Bryanston Square, London, W1H 2DS
Major Shareholder: Pedro Juan Catala Moncho
Officers: Pedro Juan Catala Moncho [1974] Director/Pharmacist [Spanish]

Two Daughters Limited
Incorporated: 24 October 2017
Registered Office: 9 South Park Crescent, Hither Green, London, SE6 1JJ
Major Shareholder: Martin Nwike
Officers: Martin Nwike, Secretary; Martin Nwike [1985] Director/Entrepreneur

Tyn y Ddol Enterprises Ltd
Incorporated: 14 December 2018
Registered Office: 20-22 Wenlock Road, London, N1 7GU
Shareholders: Andrew John Fleming; Karen Marion Fleming
Officers: Andrew John Fleming [1963] Director/Buyer/Retailer; Karen Marion Fleming [1965] Director/Learning and Development Professional

U 2 Shine Limited
Incorporated: 11 February 2016
Net Worth Deficit: £5,537 *Total Assets:* £722
Registered Office: 15 Monksfield Close, Coventry, Warwicks, CV4 9XW
Major Shareholder: Shahana Iqtidar
Officers: Shahana Iqtidar [1979] Director

Uchepeace Limited
Incorporated: 9 July 2018
Registered Office: 3 Sycamore Road, Sycamore, Southampton, SO16 6BP
Major Shareholder: Uche Peace Abiakweh
Officers: Uche Peace Abiakweh [1978] Director/Health Assistance

Ude Cosmetics Limited
Incorporated: 6 March 2018
Registered Office: 106 Chandler Way, London, SE15 6GW
Major Shareholder: Ada Nwafor
Officers: Ada Nwafor [1985] Director [Nigerian]

UK Ailise Biotechnology Trade Limited
Incorporated: 6 November 2018
Registered Office: Unit G25, Waterfront Studios, 1 Dock Road, London, E16 1AH
Major Shareholder: Aibing Wang
Officers: Aibing Wang [1969] Director [Chinese]

UK Aimutaike Electronics Co., Ltd
Incorporated: 20 July 2018
Registered Office: c/o Nice Accounting, 2nd Floor, 36 Gerrard Street, London, W1D 5QA
Major Shareholder: Haiying Zheng
Officers: Li Zhang [1977] Director [Chinese]

UK Beauty Cosmetics International Group Ltd
Incorporated: 26 September 2017
Registered Office: Unit G25, Waterfront Studios, 1 Dock Road, London, E16 1AH
Major Shareholder: Weihong Liu
Officers: Weihong Liu [1974] Director [Chinese]

UK Brand Holdings Ltd
Incorporated: 28 April 2017
Registered Office: Ground Floor, 2 Woodberry Grove, London, N12 0DR
Shareholder: Rebecca Roach
Officers: Thomas Coleman [1986] Director; John Roach [1952] Commercial Director

UK Calluspeel Limited
Incorporated: 24 April 2017
Registered Office: Hambleton Hall Barn, Mill Lane, Hambleton, Poulton-le-Fylde, Lancs, FY6 9DE
Shareholders: Christine Duckworth; James Ian Duckworth
Officers: Christine Duckworth, Secretary; Christine Duckworth [1958] Director/Beauty Therapist; James Ian Duckworth [1957] Director/Management Consultant

UK Cosmetic Formula Limited
Incorporated: 8 December 2017
Registered Office: 20 Bells End Road, Walton on Trent, Swadlincote, Derbys, DE12 8ND
Major Shareholder: Wei Guo
Officers: Wei Guo [1980] Director [Chinese]

UK Cosmeticz International Ltd
Incorporated: 6 August 2018
Registered Office: 6 Rowberrow Way, Bristol, BS48 4PX
Major Shareholder: Md Masum Ahmed
Officers: MD Masum Ahmed, Secretary; MD Masum Ahmed [1983] Director [Bangladeshi]

UK Deer Running Co., Ltd
Incorporated: 29 November 2018
Registered Office: Unit G25, Waterfront Studios, 1 Dock Road, London, E16 1AH
Major Shareholder: Tingting He
Officers: Tingting HE [1982] Director [Chinese]

UK Direct Imports Ltd
Incorporated: 9 March 2015
Net Worth: £11,553 *Total Assets:* £50,516
Registered Office: 68 Whitfield Road, Stoke on Trent, Staffs, ST6 8AH
Major Shareholder: Paul Dean
Officers: Paul Dean [1964] Director

UK Elements of Beauty Ltd
Incorporated: 16 February 2015
Net Worth: £240 *Total Assets:* £735
Registered Office: The Beeches, Brampton Abbotts, Ross on Wye, Herefords, HR9 7JD
Shareholders: Alison Margaret O'Brien; Michael Andre O'Brien
Officers: Mike O'Brien [1953] Director

UK Esthetics Ltd
Incorporated: 30 July 2018
Registered Office: Flat 3, 118 Southwood Road, London, SE9 3QN
Major Shareholder: Gelena Dudo
Officers: Gelena Dudo [1960] Director [Lithuanian]

UK Fillers Ltd
Incorporated: 19 June 2015
Previous: Act 'n Achieve Ltd
Net Worth Deficit: £3,615 *Total Assets:* £4,295
Registered Office: 5 Church Road South, Woolton, Liverpool, L25 7RJ
Officers: Jody Lee Latham [1983] Director/Actor

UK Heluns Industry Co., Limited
Incorporated: 29 April 2014
Registered Office: Unit G25, Waterfront Studios, 1 Dock Road, London, E16 1AH
Major Shareholder: Fangyu Cao
Officers: Fangyu Cao [1976] Director [Chinese]

UK Irelia Company Ltd
Incorporated: 29 October 2018
Registered Office: Suite 108, Chase Business Centre, 39-41 Chase Side, London, N14 5BP
Major Shareholder: Guangwei Shi
Officers: Guangwei Shi, Secretary; Guangwei Shi [1996] Director/Merchant [Chinese]

UK Lemenic International Medical Group Limited
Incorporated: 1 August 2018
Registered Office: Suite 1, 3rd Floor, 11-12 St James's Square, London, SW1Y 4LB
Major Shareholder: Lei Zhang
Officers: Lei Zhang [1986] Director [Chinese]

UK Make Up Limited
Incorporated: 19 July 2011
Net Worth Deficit: £28,274 *Total Assets:* £426
Registered Office: 10 Evington Valley Road, Leicester, LE5 5LJ
Major Shareholder: Gulam Ahmed Mohamed
Officers: Gulam Ahmed Mohamed [1965] Director

UK Mineral Make-Up Limited
Incorporated: 7 July 2005
Net Worth Deficit: £28,129 *Total Assets:* £38,891
Registered Office: 5 Ducketts Wharf, South Street, Bishop's Stortford, Herts, CM23 3AR
Major Shareholder: Kathleen Anne Costello
Officers: Kathleen Anne Costello [1953] Director/Training

UK MUA Limited
Incorporated: 22 June 2012
Registered Office: 11 Market Street, Whaley Bridge, High Peak, Derbys, SK23 7AA
Shareholder: Liz Armstrong
Officers: Liz Armstrong [1973] Director; Vicky Holmes [1974] Director

UK Natural Serenity Ltd
Incorporated: 7 December 2018
Registered Office: 37 Pendle Gardens, Culcheth, Warrington, Cheshire, WA3 4LU
Major Shareholder: Elham Farahi
Officers: Dr Elham Farahi [1977] Managing Director

UK Skinlabs Limited
Incorporated: 9 March 2017
Registered Office: Kemp House, 160 City Road, London, EC1V 2NX
Major Shareholder: Nima Habib Pourian
Officers: Nima Habib Pourian [1989] Director/Business Owner [Swedish]

UK Vietnam Trade Ltd
Incorporated: 22 September 2016
Net Worth Deficit: £33,213 *Total Assets:* £24,377
Registered Office: 1a Lisavon Parade, Belfast, BT4 1LE
Shareholders: Christopher John Ward; Stephen Paul Ward
Officers: Christopher John Ward [1987] Director/Export; Stephen Paul Ward [1990] Director/Export

UK Vimin Industry Co., Limited
Incorporated: 4 April 2014
Registered Office: Unit G25, Waterfront Studios, 1 Dock Road, London, E16 1AH
Major Shareholder: Min Liu
Officers: Min Liu [1981] Director [Chinese]

Ukab Limited
Incorporated: 24 January 2003
Net Worth Deficit: £29,381 *Total Assets:* £40,115
Registered Office: Gowran House, 56 Broad Street, Chipping Sodbury, Glos, BS37 6AG
Major Shareholder: Huw Noel Davies
Officers: Angela Mary Davies, Secretary; Helena Colette Davies [1984] Director; Huw Noel Davies [1951] Director/Sales

Ukin Ltd
Incorporated: 26 February 2018
Registered Office: 98 Gravel Hill, Croydon, Surrey, CR0 5BE
Major Shareholder: Kayleigh Patel
Officers: Kayleigh Patel [1987] Director/Marketing Manager

ULB Limited
Incorporated: 23 April 2018
Registered Office: 45 Dewalden House, Allitsen Road, London, NW8 7BA
Shareholders: Mateusz Kacper Balcerek; Jedrzej Michal Pytel
Officers: Mateusz Kacper Balcerek [1996] Director/Manager [Polish]; Jedrzej Michal Pytel [1998] Director [Polish]

Ulric de Varens UK Limited
Incorporated: 19 May 2003
Net Worth Deficit: £25,411 *Total Assets:* £354
Registered Office: Radbourne House, Butchers Lane, Pattishall, Northants, NN12 8ND
Parent: Ulric de Varens SA
Officers: Yves Perrin, Secretary; Ulric Viellard [1947] Director/President [French]

Ultimate Henna Brows Ltd
Incorporated: 4 April 2018
Registered Office: Beckett House, Sovereign Court, Wyrefields, Poulton Industrial Estate, Poulton-le-Fylde, Lancs, FY6 8JX
Shareholders: Bernadette Ann Mulligan; Naomi Clara Katy Bardusco-Marlow; Rhianna Dawn Frend-Bullock
Officers: Naomi Clara Katy Bardusco-Marlow [1984] Director; Rhianna Dawn Frend-Bullock [1983] Director; Bernadette Ann Mulligan [1967] Director

Ultra Glow Cosmetics Limited
Incorporated: 21 January 1992
Net Worth: £287,182 *Total Assets:* £354,418
Registered Office: Unit 10 Gamma Terrace, West Road, Ransomes Europark, Ipswich, Suffolk, IP3 9SX
Major Shareholder: Louise Mary Green
Officers: Cathleen Lockwood, Secretary; Louise Mary Green [1961] Director

Un Air D'Antan Limited
Incorporated: 11 May 2017
Registered Office: 9 Harley House, Brunswick Place, London, NW1 4PR
Shareholders: Sophie Christine Laporte; Julien Philippe Noel Henry Laporte
Officers: Julien Philippe Noel Henry Laporte [1974] Director [French]; Sophie Christine Laporte [1977] Director [French]

Unac Salon Supplies Limited
Incorporated: 21 November 2017
Registered Office: Milanos Hair Design, Commercial Street, Batley, W Yorks, WF17 5EF
Officers: Khidir Salim Babakir [1986] Director/Shop Assistant; Hasan Mahmud [1976] Director/Businessman

Underground Girl London Limited
Incorporated: 8 January 2019
Registered Office: Quantum House, 3-5 College Street, Nottingham, NG1 5AQ
Shareholders: John Lloyd Naake; Nikhil Bhatia
Officers: Nikhil Bhatia [1977] Director [Indian]; John Lloyd Naake [1977] Director

Uni London Limited
Incorporated: 24 July 2018
Registered Office: 36 Manor Road, Beverley, E Yorks, HU17 7BL
Major Shareholder: Shehed Abdulmajeed Waleed Al-Hity
Officers: Shehed Abdulmajeed Waleed Al-Hity [1989] Director/Online Brand Manager [Iraqi]

Uni Supply Ltd
Incorporated: 1 November 2016
Net Worth Deficit: £1,331 *Total Assets:* £28,408
Registered Office: 17 Ridware House, Hobs Road, Lichfield, Staffs, WS13 6SY
Officers: Min Sun [1973] Director/Secretary

Unicorn Magic Enterprises Limited
Incorporated: 31 May 2017
Registered Office: 27a Nevern Square, London, SW5 9TH
Officers: Margo Marrone [1966] Director; Roksana Marrone [1998] Director/Fashion

Unidus Limited
Incorporated: 23 May 2018
Registered Office: 27 Old Gloucester Street, London, WC1N 3AX
Major Shareholder: Virendra K Chawla
Officers: Virendra K Chawla, Secretary; Virendra K Chawla [1942] Director [American]

Unified Commerce Limited
Incorporated: 1 February 2017
Registered Office: 71-75 Shelton Street, Covent Garden, London, WC2H 9JQ
Major Shareholder: Saba Kalia
Officers: Saba Kalia [1981] Director

Unigrand Group Limited
Incorporated: 25 July 2016
Net Worth: £195,716 *Total Assets:* £197,451
Registered Office: Suite 215a, Peel House, 34-44 London Road, Morden, Surrey, SM4 5BT
Major Shareholder: Hui Chen
Officers: Hui Chen [1982] Director [Chinese]

Unilux Trading Ltd
Incorporated: 6 June 2017
Registered Office: 1st Floor, Cloister House, New Bailey Street, Salford, M3 5FS
Officers: Matthew Pettit [1972] Director/Company Secretary

Unineed Limited
Incorporated: 25 March 2011
Net Worth: £155,140 *Total Assets:* £362,090
Registered Office: Ground Floor, 2 Woodberry Grove, North Finchley, London, N12 0DR
Major Shareholder: Chaofeng Wang
Officers: Chaofeng Wang [1988] Director/Manager [Chinese]

Uniqtrend Limited
Incorporated: 8 July 2014
Registered Office: Flat 5, 24 Barclay Road, Croydon, Surrey, CR0 1JN
Officers: Joyce Djagblorkor Adjei [1986] Director/Consultant [Ghanaian]

Unique Cosmetics Limited
Incorporated: 11 August 1997
Net Worth: £165,670 Total Assets: £1,040,000
Registered Office: Unit 41 Oakwood Hill Industrial Estate, Loughton, Essex, IG10 3TZ
Shareholders: Asad Ali Shah; Asif Haidra Ali Shah
Officers: Asad Ali Shah, Secretary/Student; Asad Ali Shah [1972] Sales Director; Asif Haidra Ali Shah [1967] Director

Unique Fragrances Limited
Incorporated: 20 March 2009
Net Worth Deficit: £17,982 Total Assets: £368
Registered Office: Units B & C, Orbital Forty Six, The Ridgeway Trading Estate, Iver, Bucks, SL0 9HW
Shareholders: Samuel Bazini; Eoin Alan MacLeod
Officers: Eoin Alan MacLeod, Secretary; Samuel Bazini [1963] Director; Eoin Alan MacLeod [1962] Director

United Mart (UK) Limited
Incorporated: 12 February 2019
Registered Office: Room 2C05, South Bank Techno Park, 90 London Road, London, SE1 6LN
Major Shareholder: Lingling Wan
Officers: Lingling Wan [1982] Director [Chinese]

United Nomads Limited
Incorporated: 25 July 2018
Registered Office: Flat 2.1, 4a Rupert Court, London, W1D 6DY
Major Shareholder: Artem Del Castillo
Officers: Artem Del Castillo [1982] Director/Manager

United Perfumes Limited
Incorporated: 3 August 2007 Employees: 23
Net Worth: £714,395 Total Assets: £2,147,091
Registered Office: 1 New Quebec Street, London, W1H 7DD
Officers: Christopher Yu, Secretary; Frederic Jean Laurent Delafon [1974] Managing Director [French]; Christopher Yu [1975] Director/Solicitor

United Retail & Sourcing Limited
Incorporated: 9 December 2008 Employees: 18
Net Worth: £5,453,786 Total Assets: £11,414,928
Registered Office: 2nd Floor, 10 Hills Place, London, W1F 7SD
Parent: United Clothing Limited
Officers: Miranda Auty [1982] Director; Alev Mehmet Duru [1971] Director

United Solutions (UK) Limited
Incorporated: 1 March 2007
Net Worth Deficit: £46,540 Total Assets: £9,180
Registered Office: 21 Stoke Avenue, Ilford, Essex, IG6 3ED
Shareholders: Mojammel Hoque Khan; Mojammel Hoque Khan
Officers: Mojammel Hoque Khan [1969] Director/Entrepreneur [Swedish]

Universal Attraction (London) Ltd
Incorporated: 2 April 2004
Net Worth: £150,740 Total Assets: £152,240
Registered Office: Acre House, 11-15 William Road, London, NW1 3ER
Parent: Lisap (UK) Limited
Officers: Marilyn Anne Bieber, Secretary; Kenneth George Selwyn Bieber [1944] Director/Salesman

Universal Beauty Products Europe Ltd
Incorporated: 7 December 2017
Registered Office: c/o Laytons LLP, 5th Floor, 2 More London Riverside, London, SE1 2AP
Major Shareholder: Yong Chin Park
Officers: Yong Chin Park [1965] Executive Director [American]

Universal Design Promotion Ltd
Incorporated: 7 January 2008
Net Worth: £426,240 Total Assets: £945,380
Registered Office: Lower Ground Floor, Carlyle House, 235-237 Vauxhall Bridge Road, London, SW1V 1AU
Major Shareholder: Marc Malka
Officers: Marc Malka [1957] Executive Director [French]

Universal Toiletries Corporation Limited
Incorporated: 27 October 1999 Employees: 7
Net Worth: £779,298 Total Assets: £1,933,357
Registered Office: Unit 7 Bermer Place, Imperial Way, Watford, Herts, WD24 4AY
Major Shareholder: Dinesh Shah
Officers: Mahendra Kanabar, Secretary; Dinesh Chhabildas Shah [1958] Director; Jayshree Dinesh Shah [1963] Director; Karan Shah [1988] Director

Universe Cosmetics Limited
Incorporated: 8 November 2017
Registered Office: 75 Longford Avenue, Feltham, Middlesex, TW14 9TH
Major Shareholder: Areej Majed Ali Barakat
Officers: Areej Majed Ali Barakat [1980] Director/Housewife

Uoma Beauty Group Limited
Incorporated: 22 December 2017
Registered Office: 27 Old Gloucester Street, London, WC1N 3AX
Officers: Sharon Chuter [1987] Director [Australian]

Up Roar Ltd.
Incorporated: 15 February 2016 Employees: 2
Net Worth Deficit: £55,138 Total Assets: £6,404
Registered Office: 12 Gorselands Close, West Byfleet, Surrey, KT14 6PU
Shareholders: Robin Nicholas Coleman; Robin Rhys Wilkins
Officers: Robin Nicholas Coleman [1971] Director/Operation Manager; Robin Rhys Wilkins [1976] Director/Sales Manager

Uppercut Deluxe Co Limited
Incorporated: 18 August 2016
Net Worth: £117,773 Total Assets: £763,275
Registered Office: Unit 2, M3 Trade Park, Manor Way, Eastleigh, Hants, SO50 9YA
Shareholders: Benjamin Alastair MacKay; Benjamin Alastair MacKay
Officers: Luke Richard Campbell, Secretary; Luke Richard Campbell [1985] Director [Australian]; Benjamin Alastair MacKay [1978] Director [Australian]; Kieran Elizabeth Purcell [1986] Director [Australian]; Samuel Scott Weiss [1954] Director [Australian]

Urban Altar Ltd
Incorporated: 27 December 2018
Registered Office: 9/3 Westfield Street, Edinburgh, EH11 2RB
Major Shareholder: Evan Taylor
Officers: Evan Taylor [1982] Director/Manager

Urban Retreat Products Limited
Incorporated: 9 March 2007
Net Worth Deficit: £12,676 *Total Assets:* £98
Registered Office: Cedar House, Hazell Drive, Newport, NP10 8FY
Parent: Urban Retreat Ventures Limited
Officers: George Christopher Hammer [1950] Director

Urhan Group Limited
Incorporated: 15 January 2018
Registered Office: 17 Green Lanes, London, N16 9BS
Major Shareholder: Harun Resit Urhan
Officers: Harun Resit Urhan [1981] Director [Turkish]

US Beauty Store Limited
Incorporated: 21 November 2017
Registered Office: Companies House, Default Address, Cardiff, CF14 8LH
Major Shareholder: Felipe Fermin
Officers: Felipe Fermin [1973] Director [American]

USA Hair Extensions Ltd
Incorporated: 9 January 2009
Net Worth Deficit: £11,433 *Total Assets:* £55,995
Registered Office: 29 Avondale Road, Whitmore Reans, Wolverhampton, W Midlands, WV6 0AL
Major Shareholder: Mark Lynch
Officers: Mark Lynch [1963] Director

Use Natural Ltd
Incorporated: 2 November 2009
Registered Office: Wessex House, Upper Market Street, Eastleigh, Hants, SO50 9FD
Shareholder: Daniela Popov
Officers: Viktor Popov, Secretary; Daniela Popov [1969] Director/Entrepreneur

V@M Limited
Incorporated: 13 January 2016
Net Worth Deficit: £596 *Total Assets:* £189
Registered Office: 118 High Street, Erdington, Birmingham, B23 6BG
Major Shareholder: Vadims Babkins
Officers: Babkins Vadims [1986] Director [Latvian]

Valencia Cy Makeup Ltd
Incorporated: 8 June 2018
Registered Office: 29a West Ella Road, London, NW10 9PT
Major Shareholder: Masota Muzongo
Officers: Masota Muzongo [1979] Director/Manager [Belgian]

Valentia Skincare Limited
Incorporated: 18 August 2017
Registered Office: First Floor, 10 Temple Back, Bristol, BS1 6FL
Major Shareholder: Lucas Abel Morea
Officers: Lucas Abel Morea [1981] Director [Argentinian]; Rohit Nair [1984] Director [Indian]

Valerie Lady Co., Ltd
Incorporated: 21 November 2018
Registered Office: Suite 108, Chase Business Centre, 39-41 Chase Side, London, N14 5BP
Major Shareholder: Jun Zhang
Officers: Jun Zhang, Secretary; Jun Zhang [1978] Director/Merchant [Chinese]

Valhalla Perfume Limited
Incorporated: 31 January 2018
Registered Office: Kemp House, 160 City Road, London, EC1V 2NX
Major Shareholder: Kwame Opoku Michael Boadi
Officers: Kwame Opoku Michael Boadi [1969] Director/Perfumer

Valiscious Limited
Incorporated: 5 July 2016
Net Worth: £100 *Total Assets:* £100
Registered Office: 37 Chatsworth Road, Chesterfield, Derbys, S40 2AH
Major Shareholder: Kayleigh Valeisa
Officers: Kayleigh Valeisa [1981] Director

Valma Consumer Company Limited
Incorporated: 21 February 2018
Registered Office: 71-75 Shelton Street, London, WC2H 9JQ
Officers: Vijairahul Janakiraman [1986] Director/Analyst [Indian]; Giovanni Meggiorini [1992] Director/Financial Analyst [Italian]

Valorem Capital One Ltd
Incorporated: 7 January 2010 *Employees:* 10
Net Worth: £1,586,808 *Total Assets:* £2,749,421
Registered Office: Lynton House, 7-12 Tavistock Square, London, WC1H 9LT
Shareholders: David Adrian Crisp; David Victor Garofalo
Officers: David Adrian Crisp, Secretary; David Adrian Crisp [1958] Director; David Victor Garofalo [1969] Director [Italian]

Valorem Distribution Ltd
Incorporated: 31 July 2018
Registered Office: 16 West Way, Carshalton, Surrey, SM5 4EW
Parent: Valorem Holdings Ltd
Officers: David Adrian Crisp [1958] Director

Value for Money (Cleethorpes) Limited
Incorporated: 30 January 2001
Registered Office: 31 Abbey Road, Grimsby, N E Lincs, DN32 0HQ
Shareholder: Thomas Malcolm Ellis
Officers: Thomas Malcolm Ellis [1965] Director; Jane Elizabeth Tumber [1968] Director

Valya Beauty Cosmetics Ltd
Incorporated: 10 September 2018
Registered Office: 85 Victoria Street, Long Eaton, Nottingham, NG10 3ET
Major Shareholder: Valentyna Kryvenko
Officers: Valentyna Kryvenko [1967] Director [Ukrainian]

Vancooler Ltd
Incorporated: 13 October 2015
Previous: KJ Cosmetix Limited
Net Worth: £1,000 *Total Assets:* £1,000
Registered Office: Unit 86 Culley Court, Orton Southgate, Peterborough, Cambs, PE2 6WA
Major Shareholder: Bartlomiej Kuba
Officers: Bratlomiej Kuba [1985] Director/Trade and Distribution of Cosmetic Articles [Polish]

Vanilla Blanc Limited
Incorporated: 30 October 2014
Net Worth: £12,110 *Total Assets:* £24,570
Registered Office: 6 Saxon Close, Surbiton, Surrey, KT6 6BP
Major Shareholder: Haydar Jalil Haji
Officers: Haydar Jalil Haji [1978] Director

Varama Limited
Incorporated: 22 May 2009
Net Worth: £5,330   Total Assets: £32,930
Registered Office: 2 Woodside Mews, Clayton Wood Close, Leeds, LS16 6QE
Major Shareholder: Vanessa Davies
Officers: Vanessa Davies [1963] Director

Varana UK Limited
Incorporated: 20 March 2015
Net Worth Deficit: £2,500,000   Total Assets: £2,260,000
Registered Office: 14 Dover Street, London, W1S 4LW
Shareholders: Ravi Prasad; Sujata, Keshvan Guha
Officers: Sujata Keshvan Guha [1961] Director/Businesswoman [Indian]; Ravi Prasad [1960] Director/Businessman [Indian]

Vasuda Beauty Limited
Incorporated: 27 March 2017
Registered Office: 88 Richmond Hill, Oldbury, W Midlands, B68 9TH
Shareholders: Jagdish Kaur; Mandeep Hayer
Officers: Mandeep Hayer [1989] Director; Jagdish Kaur [1993] Director

Ve-Glam Limited
Incorporated: 16 August 2017
Registered Office: 42 Pinner Hill Road, Pinner, Middlesex, HA5 3SB
Major Shareholder: Hansa Kava
Officers: Hansa Kava [1962] Director

Ved Healthcare Limited
Incorporated: 5 September 2016
Net Worth: £39,140   Total Assets: £99,010
Registered Office: 69 Moore Court, Station Grove, Wembley, Middlesex, HA0 4AF
Major Shareholder: Kanjikumar Mandanka
Officers: Kanjikumar Mandanka [1984] Director

Vedaway Ltd
Incorporated: 1 June 2010
Net Worth Deficit: £617   Total Assets: £139
Registered Office: 430 Legacy Centre, Hampton Road West, Feltham, Middlesex, TW13 6DH
Major Shareholder: Abdul Noor Ahmed
Officers: Abdul Noor Ahmed [1970] Director

Veels UK Limited
Incorporated: 7 January 2019
Registered Office: Kemp House, 160 City Road, London, EC1V 2NX
Major Shareholder: Mohd Shukri Ismail
Officers: Mohd Shukri Ismail [1978] Director [Malaysian]

Vegan Republic Beauty Ltd
Incorporated: 14 December 2018
Registered Office: 64 Woodcock Hill, Kenton, Middlesex, HA3 0JF
Parent: FD Secretarial Ltd

Vegan Republic Ltd
Incorporated: 14 December 2018
Registered Office: 64 Woodcock Hill, Kenton, Middlesex, HA3 0JF
Parent: FD Secretarial Ltd

Velforms Limited
Incorporated: 10 March 2014
Previous: GBCShop Limited
Registered Office: 40 Slocum Close, London, SE28 8LQ
Major Shareholder: Khosrow Arshia
Officers: Khosrow Arshia [1967] Director/Manager [Dutch]

Velvet Bee Company Ltd
Incorporated: 12 February 2019
Registered Office: Studio C7, 17 Lyon Road, London, SW19 2RL
Parent: The Hin Group Recruitment Limited
Officers: Thomas Hin, Secretary; Thomas Hin [1988] Director/Corporate Secretary

Velvet Vapours UK Limited
Incorporated: 5 February 2019
Registered Office: 144 Hanover Street, Swansea, SA1 6BN
Officers: Mohammad Amir Hussein [1993] Director/Pharmacist

Ruth Venessa Services Ltd
Incorporated: 16 February 2018
Registered Office: 12 Tant Avenue, London, E16 1JF
Major Shareholder: Venessa Dompreh
Officers: Venessa Dompreh [1996] Director/Self Employed

Venkh Retail Ltd
Incorporated: 25 May 2018
Registered Office: 71-75 Shelton Street, London, WC2H 9JQ
Major Shareholder: Oluwatoyin Badiru
Officers: Oluwatoyin Badiru [1986] Director

Venus Beauty Limited
Incorporated: 5 January 2016
Net Worth: £2,347   Total Assets: £12,078
Registered Office: Innovation Centre, Gallows Hill, Warwick, CV34 6UW
Major Shareholder: Tatiana Nadeena
Officers: Tatiana Nadeena [1976] Director [Russian]

Veramic Limited
Incorporated: 24 April 2012
Net Worth: £5,210   Total Assets: £57,765
Registered Office: Unit B2, Livingstone Court, 55 Peel Road, Harrow, Middlesex, HA3 7QT
Major Shareholder: Dimitris Kalogiannidis
Officers: Dr Dimitris Kalogiannidis [1981] Director/Doctor [Greek]; Irene Kalogiannidis [1984] Director/Interior Designer [Greek]

Vereer Limited
Incorporated: 4 September 2015   Employees: 1
Net Worth: £164,391   Total Assets: £1,452,182
Registered Office: 68 Darby Crescent, Sunbury on Thames, Middlesex, TW16 5LA
Major Shareholder: Zhou Wang
Officers: Zhou Wang, Secretary; Doctor Zhou Wang [1973] Director/Consultant [Chinese]

Veridot Asset Dna Limited
Incorporated: 17 December 2014
Registered Office: 367 Clipsley Lane, Haydock, St Helens, Merseyside, WA11 0SG
Shareholder: Nirmalaben Jayantilal Patel
Officers: Mrs Nirmalaben Jayantilal Patel, Secretary; Mr Jayantilal Dullabhbhai Patel [1954] Director; Mrs Nirmalaben Jayantilal Patel [1955] Director

Very British Baby International Limited
Incorporated: 22 July 2014
Net Worth Deficit: £55,160 *Total Assets:* £27,001
Registered Office: 20-22 Wenlock Road, London, N1 7GU
Major Shareholder: Mindy Eileen Rothstein
Officers: James Robert King [1977] Director/Self Employed; Mindy Eileen Rothstein [1956] Director/Self Employed [American]

The Very Essence Ltd
Incorporated: 4 February 2019
Registered Office: York Cottage, Easton Lane, Bozeat, Northants, NN29 7NN
Major Shareholder: Lisa Jane Burke
Officers: Anthony Michael Burke [1958] Director; Gemma Leanne Burke [1992] Director; Lisa Jane Burke [1968] Director

The Very Nature Limited
Incorporated: 11 February 2015
Registered Office: 32 Blakehall Crescent, London, E11 3RH
Major Shareholder: Martin Julian Goodman
Officers: Martin Julian Goodman, Secretary; Martin Julian Goodman [1953] Director/Accountant

Vesta London Beauty Ltd
Incorporated: 15 September 2016
Registered Office: 155 Queens Road, London, E17 8PJ
Major Shareholder: Vesta Boateng
Officers: Vesta Boateng [1992] Director/Quality Administrator

Vetivert & Co Ltd
Incorporated: 9 March 2017
Registered Office: 156 Mandeville Road, Enfield, Middlesex, EN3 6SG
Major Shareholder: Aanuoluwa Oduyemi
Officers: Aanuoluwa Oduyemi [1989] Director/Student [Nigerian]

Vett Limited
Incorporated: 28 May 2002
Registered Office: 1 Top Farm Court, Top Street, Bawtry, Doncaster, S Yorks, DN10 6TF
Major Shareholder: William Francis Alan de Fries
Officers: William Francis Alan de Fries [1953] Director

VevBeautyCosmeticsTrading Ltd
Incorporated: 12 February 2018
Registered Office: 20-22 Wenlock Road, London, N1 7GU
Major Shareholder: Zmary Malikzada
Officers: Zmary Malikzada [1972] Director/Sales

VI Beauty Ltd
Incorporated: 3 December 2018
Registered Office: Apartment 405, 275 Deansgate, Manchester, M3 4EW
Major Shareholder: Loyce Mwale
Officers: Loyce Mwale [1981] Director/Makeup Artist [Zambian]

Vibrantz Cosmetics Ltd
Incorporated: 3 October 2017
Registered Office: Vista Business Centre, 50 Salisbury Road, Hounslow, Middlesex, TW4 6JQ
Major Shareholder: Qaiser Mushtaq
Officers: Suleman Mehmood [1985] Director/IT Consultant; Qaiser Mushtaq [1981] Director

Vickie's Boutique Ltd
Incorporated: 18 February 2019
Registered Office: 30 Station Lane, Hornchurch, Essex, RM12 6NJ
Major Shareholder: Tinko Trifonov
Officers: Tinko Trifonov [1955] Director [Bulgarian]

Victoire Limited
Incorporated: 27 February 2019
Registered Office: Suite 23, Fifth Floor, 63-66 Hatton Garden, London, EC1N 8LE
Major Shareholder: Ireneusz Frackowiak
Officers: Ireneusz Frackowiak [1984] Director [Polish]

Victoria Pharma London Ltd
Incorporated: 27 May 2005
Previous: Osom Limited
Net Worth: £2 *Total Assets:* £2
Registered Office: 407 Britannia House, 1-11 Glenthorne Road, London, W6 0LH
Major Shareholder: Peter Hajnal
Officers: Peter Hajnal [1953] Director [Hungarian]

Vida Aesthetics Ltd
Incorporated: 24 January 2013
Previous: Vida Health & Beauty Limited
Net Worth Deficit: £32,923 *Total Assets:* £75,999
Registered Office: C1 Windsor Place, Faraday Road, Crawley, W Sussex, RH10 9TF
Shareholders: Michael Peter Ellis; Eduardo Emilio
Officers: Michael Peter Ellis [1958] Director; Eduardo Goncalves Emilio [1964] Director [Portuguese]

Vida Skincare Ltd
Incorporated: 7 March 2018
Registered Office: C1 Windsor Place, Faraday Road, Crawley, W Sussex, RH10 9TF
Major Shareholder: Michael Peter Ellis
Officers: Michael Peter Ellis [1958] Director; Eduardo Emilio [1964] Director [Portuguese]

Vidology Group Ltd
Incorporated: 7 January 2019
Registered Office: 3 Hawthorne Road, Bolton, Lancs, BL3 5RE
Major Shareholder: Vijay Kumar Solanki
Officers: Vijay Kumar Solanki [1970] Director/Businessman

Viib Limited
Incorporated: 12 May 2016
Net Worth: £3,850 *Total Assets:* £135,990
Registered Office: 3rd Floor, 86-90 Paul Street, London, EC2A 4NE
Major Shareholder: Victor Francis
Officers: Victor Francis, Secretary; Victor Francis [1977] Director/Manager

Vikenias UK Ltd
Incorporated: 4 May 2016 *Employees:* 1
Net Worth: £1,618 *Total Assets:* £122,013
Registered Office: New Bridge Street House, 30-34 New Bridge Street, London, EC4V 6BJ
Major Shareholder: Adriana Cuadros Gonzalez
Officers: Francisco Javier Jimenez Sanchez [1959] Director/Manager [Spanish]

Vilai Europe Trading Limited
Incorporated: 23 July 2018
Registered Office: 71-75 Shelton Street, London, WC2H 9JQ
Parent: EIK Consulting Limited
Officers: Chen Liu [1987] Director/Consultant [Chinese]

Vilasa Limited
Incorporated: 28 February 2019
Registered Office: 34 Stirling Road, Sutton Coldfield, W Midlands, B73 6PS
Shareholders: Lynne Leon; Jody Leon
Officers: Jody Leon [1983] Director; Lynne Leon [1987] Director

Vilhelm Parfumerie Limited
Incorporated: 10 April 2015
Net Worth Deficit: £140,580 Total Assets: £1,170
Registered Office: 10 John Street, London, WC1N 2EB
Officers: Jan Gustav Vilhelm Ahlgren [1978] Director [American]

Villa Sauod Ltd
Incorporated: 1 November 2018
Registered Office: Premier Business Centre, 47-49 Park Royal Road, London, NW10 7LQ
Major Shareholder: Abdulazeez Althefeeri
Officers: Abdulazeez Althefeeri [1979] Director [Kuwaiti]

Villainelle Ltd
Incorporated: 11 October 2018
Registered Office: Sapphire House, Crown Way, Rushden, Northants, NN10 6FB
Major Shareholder: Leyla Mai
Officers: Leyla Mai [2002] Director/Student

Vir Original Limited
Incorporated: 12 January 2018
Registered Office: 6 Moorfield Close, Penwortham, Preston, Lancs, PR1 0NW
Officers: Michael Richard Morgan [1991] Director

Viral Solutions General Trading Ltd
Incorporated: 15 February 2017
Registered Office: 27 Old Gloucester Street, London, WC1N 3AX
Major Shareholder: Ivan , Beng Hock Ong
Officers: Ivan Ong [1987] Director [Singaporean]

Virgovogue Ltd
Incorporated: 31 July 2017
Registered Office: 52 Water Lane, Purfleet, Essex, RM19 1GS
Major Shareholder: Yetunde Lawal
Officers: Yetunde Lawal [1968] Director/Trader [Nigerian]

Viridian Leaf Limited
Incorporated: 18 May 2017
Registered Office: 169 Regent Farm Road, Newcastle upon Tyne, NE3 3HE
Major Shareholder: Divya Namdeo
Officers: Divya Namdeo [1969] Director

VIS International Corporation Limited
Incorporated: 18 February 2009
Net Worth: £9,000 Total Assets: £9,000
Registered Office: 36 Fernbank Road, Ascot, Berks, SL5 8HD
Shareholder: Xifei Huang
Officers: Xifei Huang, Secretary; Xianlin Li [1943] Director/Self Employed [Chinese]

Vision Trading Limited
Incorporated: 21 September 2015 Employees: 1
Previous: Gabrini London Limited
Net Worth: £8,386 Total Assets: £21,556
Registered Office: 4 Pegamoid Road, London, N18 2NG
Major Shareholder: Mehmet Keskin
Officers: Mehmet Keskin [1980] Director/Businessman

Vita Liberata Limited
Incorporated: 23 May 2003 Employees: 46
Net Worth: £2,258,780 Total Assets: £8,235,086
Registered Office: 181a Templepatrick Road, Ballyclare, Co Antrim, BT39 0RA
Officers: Alyson Hogg, Secretary; Jeffery Alan Bedard [1961] Director [American]; Andrew Stansfield Goldman [1985] Director [American]; Stephen Hallenbeck [1986] Director [American]; Alison Hogg [1963] Director; David Frederick Solomon [1966] Director [American]

Vitaglow Ltd
Incorporated: 7 December 2018
Registered Office: 53/1 Stenhouse Gardens, Edinburgh, EH11 3LS
Major Shareholder: Esther Dangata
Officers: Esther Dangata [1965] Director

Vittoria Ventures Limited
Incorporated: 14 February 2013
Net Worth Deficit: £31,050 Total Assets: £10,320
Registered Office: 8 Wolsey Mansions, Main Avenue, Moor Park, Northwood, Middlesex, HA6 2HL
Major Shareholder: Brunello Acampora
Officers: Brunello Acampora [1966] Director [Italian]

Vivacy Laboratoires Ltd
Incorporated: 30 October 2018
Registered Office: 1st Floor, 14 Berkeley Street, London, W1J 8DX
Major Shareholder: Waldemar Stanislaw Kita
Officers: Gregory John Connor, Secretary; Gregory John Connor [1965] Director/Attorney at Law [Swiss]; Waldemar Stanislaw Kita [1954] Director/President of Vivacy [French]

Vivalis Beauty Limited
Incorporated: 9 January 1987 Employees: 15
Previous: Vivalis Trading Limited
Net Worth: £37,685 Total Assets: £2,140,637
Registered Office: Newbury House, Aintree Avenue, White Horse Business Park, Trowbridge, Wilts, BA14 0XB
Parent: Lynch-Staunton Cosmetics Holdings Limited
Officers: Graham Murray Lynch Staunton [1969] Director; Susan Angela Lynch-Staunton [1967] UK Sales Director

Vivalis Limited
Incorporated: 22 November 1979
Registered Office: Newbury House, Aintree Avenue, White Horse Business Park, Trowbridge, Wilts, BA14 0XB
Parent: Lynch-Staunton Cosmetics Holdings Limited
Officers: Graham Murray Lynch Staunton [1969] Director; Susan Angela Lynch Staunton [1967] UK Sales Director

Vivatinell Limited
Incorporated: 2 October 2008 Employees: 5
Net Worth Deficit: £193,578 Total Assets: £545,860
Registered Office: Unit 138 Bradley Hall Trading Estate, Bradley Lane, Standish, Wigan, Lancs, WN6 0XQ
Shareholders: Altug Barut; Ozgur Goknel
Officers: Altug Barut [1963] Director [Turkish]; Ozgur Goknel [1968] Director [Turkish]

Vivlai Europe Trading Limited
Incorporated: 9 July 2018
Registered Office: 71-75 Shelton Street, London, WC2H 9JQ
Parent: EIK Consulting Limited
Officers: Chen Liu [1987] Director/Consultant [Chinese]

Vivora Limited
Incorporated: 12 June 2018
Registered Office: Mamado House, 8 Parr Road, Stanmore, Middlesex, HA7 1NP
Officers: Kumail Nasser [1996] Director

Vlinder Cosmetics Ltd
Incorporated: 16 March 2017
Registered Office: 53 Timberbottom, Bolton, Lancs, BL2 3DQ
Shareholders: John Byrne; Louise Byrne
Officers: John Robert Byrne [1957] Director; Louise Clair Byrne [1988] Director

VNS London Limited
Incorporated: 10 January 2018
Registered Office: Flat 3, 34 Redcliffe Gardens, London, SW10 9HA
Shareholders: Serra Akyol; Vedat Akyol
Officers: Serra Akyol [1988] Director [Turkish]; Vedat Akyol [1954] Director [Turkish]

Vogue Cosmetics Ltd
Incorporated: 16 January 2018
Registered Office: 20-22 Wenlock Road, London, N1 7GU
Major Shareholder: Umar Hussain
Officers: Umar Hussain [1989] Director

Vortex Holding Limited
Incorporated: 10 December 2015
Registered Office: 843 Finchley Road, London, NW11 8NA
Major Shareholder: Farzin Abedini Abkhare
Officers: Farzin Abedini Abkhare [1969] Director/Self Employed Business Owner [Iranian]

Votary Limited
Incorporated: 15 October 2014
Previous: Simpson and Semler Limited
Net Worth: £18,222   *Total Assets:* £77,187
Registered Office: Vincent's Yard, 23 Alphabet Mews, London, SW9 0FN
Shareholders: Charlotte Semler-West; Arabella Preston
Officers: Arabella Charlotte Preston [1979] Director; Charlotte Semler-West [1970] Director [Danish]

VR Consult Limited
Incorporated: 7 December 2015
Previous: VR Marketing Limited
Net Worth: £45   *Total Assets:* £45
Registered Office: 26 Warwick Gardens, Haringey, London, N4 1JG
Shareholder: Kwaku Korankye Kyei
Officers: Kwaku Korankye Kyei [1983] Director/Engineer; Sarah Frances Nicholas [1987] Director/PR Consultant

Vtessia Cosmetic Ltd
Incorporated: 17 February 2017
Registered Office: Krypton Consulting Ltd, Navigation House, Unit 6 Town Quay Wharf, Abbey Road, Barking, Essex, IG11 7BZ
Major Shareholder: Vicktesha Cunningham
Officers: Vicktesha Cunningham [1989] Director/Nursing

VY Club Limited
Incorporated: 23 August 2017
Registered Office: Kemp House, 160 City Road, London, EC1V 2NX
Major Shareholder: Gerard Brandon
Officers: Gerard Brandon, Secretary; Dagmara Brandon [1973] Director [Polish]; Gerard Brandon [1961] Director [Irish]

Vyas International Ltd
Incorporated: 1 October 2018
Registered Office: 40 New House Park, St Albans, Herts, AL1 1UJ
Major Shareholder: Harishkumar Natvarlal Vyas
Officers: Harishkumar Natvarlal Vyas [1960] Director

W-Healthy Aging Limited
Incorporated: 25 November 2013   *Employees:* 1
Net Worth: £6,896   *Total Assets:* £37,497
Registered Office: Finance House, 9 The Square, Notley Green, Great Notley, Braintree, Essex, CM77 7WT
Major Shareholder: Orianne Christine Occelli
Officers: Orianne Christine Occelli [1980] Director [French]

W8T Ltd
Incorporated: 3 August 2018
Registered Office: Kemp House, 160 City Road, London, EC1V 2NX
Major Shareholder: Michal Arkadiusz Krawczyk
Officers: Michal Arkadiusz Krawczyk, Secretary; Michal Arkadiusz Krawczyk [1981] Director/Owner [Polish]

Wafson Ltd
Incorporated: 1 May 2015   *Employees:* 2
Net Worth Deficit: £6,949   *Total Assets:* £4,148
Registered Office: 20 Crown Road, Virginia Water, Surrey, GU25 4HT
Shareholder: Albert Joan Roger Jara
Officers: Guillermo Jose Arias-Ferrari Saramago [1990] Director [Spanish]; Joan Albert Roger Jara [1965] Director [Spanish]

Wake Up Beauty Ltd
Incorporated: 26 October 2017
Registered Office: Unit 320 Victory Business Centre, Somers Road North, Portsmouth, PO1 1PJ
Officers: Sylwia Krystyna Pietka [1974] Director [Polish]

Walk on Gold Limited
Incorporated: 2 September 2016
Registered Office: 5a Parr Road, Stanmore, Middlesex, HA7 1NP
Major Shareholder: Abdulla Mahmoud Ahmed Al Qaissieh
Officers: Abdulla Mahmoud Ahmed Al Qaissieh [1970] Director [Emirati]

Debra Jayne Walker Limited
Incorporated: 21 February 2018
Registered Office: 20 Greenways Drive, Kendal, Cumbria, LA8 0EL
Major Shareholder: Debra Jayne Walker
Officers: Debra Jayne Walker [1961] Director

Walking Pet Balloons (UK) Limited
Incorporated: 5 February 2008
Previous: Bargain Links Limited
Net Worth Deficit: £31,070   *Total Assets:* £8,590
Registered Office: 14 Ravensbury Avenue, Morden, Surrey, SM4 6ET
Shareholders: Nicholas Alan Smith; Nicholas William Smith
Officers: Nicholas Alan Smith, Secretary; Nicholas Alan Smith [1965] Director; Nicholas William Smith [1990] Director

Warehouse.5 Limited
Incorporated: 23 February 2015   *Employees:* 2
Net Worth: £2,252   *Total Assets:* £14,634
Registered Office: 53 High Street, Dumbarton, G82 1LS
Shareholder: William Ross Tevendale
Officers: Gayle Tevendale [1971] Director/Wholesale Distribution; William Ross Tevendale [1955] Director/Wholesale Distribution

Warpaint Cosmetics (2014) Limited
Incorporated: 31 March 2014 *Employees:* 46
Net Worth: £7,565,552 *Total Assets:* £15,663,241
Registered Office: Units B & C, Orbital Forty Six, The Ridgeway Trading Estate, Iver, Bucks, SL0 9HW
Parent: Warpaint Cosmetics Group Limited
Officers: Samuel Bazini [1963] Director; Eoin Alan MacLeod [1962] Director

Warpaint Cosmetics Group Limited
Incorporated: 14 April 2014 *Employees:* 2
Net Worth: £15,147,238 *Total Assets:* £18,742,896
Registered Office: Units B & C, Orbital Forty Six, The Ridgeway Trading Estate, Iver, Bucks, SL0 9HW
Parent: Warpaint London PLC
Officers: Samuel Bazini [1963] Director; Eoin Alan MacLeod [1962] Director

Warpaint Cosmetics Limited
Incorporated: 14 May 1998
Net Worth: £1,090,000 *Total Assets:* £5,170,000
Registered Office: 2 Park Court, Pyrford Road, West Byfleet, Surrey, KT14 6SD
Parent: Jonhenlon Limited
Officers: Samuel Bazini [1963] Director; Eoin Alan MacLeod [1962] Director

Warpaint London PLC
Incorporated: 4 July 2016 *Employees:* 52
Net Worth: £40,424,000 *Total Assets:* £48,258,000
Registered Office: Units B & C, Orbital Forty Six, The Ridgeway Trading Estate, Iver, Bucks, SL0 9HW
Officers: Sally Ann Craig, Secretary; Samuel Bazini [1963] Director; Sally Ann Craig [1960] Company Secretary/Director; Clive Richard Garston [1945] Director/Solicitor; Paul George Hagon [1963] Director; Eoin Alan MacLeod [1962] Director; Neil Rodol [1962] Director; Keith John Sadler [1958] Director

Wash Your Mouth Out Ltd
Incorporated: 28 April 2018
Registered Office: 57 Nottingham Road, Ravenshead, Nottingham, NG15 9HG
Shareholders: Robert Philip Roberts; Michelle Chyntia
Officers: Michelle Chyntia [1990] Director [Indonesian]; Robert Philip Roberts [1968] Director

Wat Cosmetics Ltd
Incorporated: 18 January 2019
Registered Office: 36 Parcau Avenue, Bridgend, CF31 4SY
Major Shareholder: Mollie Rebecca Watkins
Officers: Mollie Rebecca Watkins [1996] Director/Student

Waterman Corporate Enterprises Limited
Incorporated: 10 July 2012
Net Worth: £43,246 *Total Assets:* £514,087
Registered Office: Unit 12F-12G, Lidget Lane Industrial Estate, Albion Drive, Thurnscoe, Rotherham, S Yorks, S63 0BA
Major Shareholder: Matt Luca Waterman
Officers: Gail Marie Waterman [1972] Director/Chief Financial Officer (CFO); Matt Luca Waterman [1974] Managing Director/CEO

Watsoap.Com Limited
Incorporated: 13 February 2007 *Employees:* 7
Net Worth: £43,787 *Total Assets:* £189,709
Registered Office: 41 Cornmarket Street, Oxford, OX1 3HA
Shareholders: Ruth Watson; Jane Fairrie Comyn
Officers: Ruth Watson, Secretary; Jane Fairrie Comyn [1954] Director; Ruth Watson [1954] Director

Wax Authority Limited
Incorporated: 19 December 2017
Registered Office: 2 Green Park, Coal Road, Leeds, LS14 1FB
Major Shareholder: Samuel Sweet
Officers: James Alan Nordstrom [1957] Director [American]; Samantha Sweet [1969] Director; Samuel Sweet [1972] Managing Director [American]; Fiona Wallace [1958] Director

We Concept Ltd
Incorporated: 11 June 2018
Registered Office: Office 4, 219 Kensington High Street, Kensington, London, W8 6BD
Shareholders: Tule Park; Didier Rene Serge Magne
Officers: Didier Rene Serge Magne [1968] Director/Entrepreneur [French]; Tule Park [1969] Director/Entrepreneur [French]

We Two By Kelly Simpkin Ltd
Incorporated: 26 September 2017
Registered Office: Harben House, Harben Parade, Finchley Road, London, NW3 6LH
Major Shareholder: Kelly Elizabeth Simpkin
Officers: Kelly Elizabeth Simpkin [1981] Director

Wealden Aesthetics Limited
Incorporated: 19 April 2018
Registered Office: 10 Batchelor Crescent, Crowborough, E Sussex, TN6 2TY
Officers: Clair Turner [1983] Director

Web Store Group Limited
Incorporated: 18 September 2018
Registered Office: 1st Floor, 112c High Street, Hadleigh, Ipswich, Suffolk, IP7 5EL
Officers: Jens Gadegaard [1963] Director [Danish]

Wellbeing Skincare Limited
Incorporated: 3 September 2009
Net Worth Deficit: £291 *Total Assets:* £21,194
Registered Office: Gors Farm, Llanpumsaint, Carmarthen, SA33 6LE
Major Shareholder: Ieuan Arwel Nicholas
Officers: Ieuan Arwel Nicholas [1971] Director

Wellness Style Limited
Incorporated: 4 February 2013
Net Worth Deficit: £81,325 *Total Assets:* £108
Registered Office: 49 Station Road, Polegate, E Sussex, BN26 6EA
Major Shareholder: Krzysztof Karlinski
Officers: Krzysztof Karlinski [1965] Director/Manager [Polish]

Werson International Ltd
Incorporated: 21 March 2013
Net Worth Deficit: £245,280 *Total Assets:* £60,382
Registered Office: Berkeley Square House, Berkeley Square, London, W1J 6BD
Major Shareholder: Xintong Fan
Officers: Xintong Fan [1988] Director/Manager [Chinese]

West Three Trading Limited
Incorporated: 2 September 2002
Net Worth: £28,064 *Total Assets:* £87,562
Registered Office: 352 Fulham Road, London, SW10 9UH
Shareholders: Zoran Trajkovic; Jelena Trajkovic
Officers: Aleskandra Trajkovic, Secretary; Jelena Trajkovic [1960] Director/Trader [Serbian]; Zoran Trajkovic [1952] Director/Trader [Serbian]

Westfield House Distributors Limited
Incorporated: 27 August 2010
Net Worth: £2,716 *Total Assets:* £42,696
Registered Office: 4th Floor, 115 George Street, Edinburgh, EH2 4JN
Shareholders: Marion Cadwell; Ian Cadwell
Officers: Ian Cadwell [1962] Director; Kris Cadwell [1989] Director; Marion Cadwell [1962] Director

WGTSS Ltd
Incorporated: 13 March 2018
Registered Office: 71-75 Shelton Street, London, WC2H 9JQ
Major Shareholder: Abderrahmane Ifsasse
Officers: Abderrahmane Ifsasse [1966] Director

WH Corporation (UK) PTE. Ltd
Incorporated: 24 April 2018
Registered Office: Herkes Courtney Wong Limited, 3rd Floor, 19 Gerrard Street, London, W1D 6JG
Officers: Mingli Lai [1975] Director [Chinese]

Wharfedale Herbal Ltd
Incorporated: 24 October 2018
Registered Office: 20-22 Wenlock Road, London, N1 7GU
Shareholder: Nicholas Godfrey Holdsworth
Officers: Nicholas Godfrey Holdsworth [1961] Managing Director

Wheesht Ltd
Incorporated: 29 August 2018
Registered Office: Summit House, 4-5 Mitchell Street, Edinburgh, EH6 7BD
Major Shareholder: Kelly Ford
Officers: Kelly Ford [1978] Director

The Whimsical Beard Co Ltd
Incorporated: 12 January 2015
Registered Office: 3a Delph Wood Close, Bingley, W Yorks, BD16 3LQ
Major Shareholder: Mark Barton
Officers: Mark Barton [1986] Director/Retail

Whimsical Beauty Ltd
Incorporated: 27 December 2018
Registered Office: 2 Mill Ridge, Edgware, Middlesex, HA8 7PE
Major Shareholder: Theviya Naveenan
Officers: Pratheesh Puvanagopan, Secretary; Theviya Naveenan [1989] Director

Whip Cosmetics Ltd
Incorporated: 16 July 2018
Registered Office: 23c Gironde Road, London, SW6 7DY
Shareholders: Joanna Linda Banks; Natasha Louise Boxall
Officers: Joanna Linda Banks [1991] Director; Natasha Louise Boxall [1989] Director

White Lotus Anti Aging Ltd
Incorporated: 16 November 2010 *Employees:* 2
Net Worth: £5 *Total Assets:* £111,573
Registered Office: 483 Green Lanes, London, N13 4BS
Shareholders: Kamila Kingston; Anthony Kingston
Officers: Kamila Kingston, Secretary; Kamila Kingston [1978] Director/Acupuncture

White Rose Aromatics Limited
Incorporated: 28 April 1993
Net Worth: £8,170 *Total Assets:* £175,420
Registered Office: 10 Bank Walk, Baildon, Shipley, W Yorks, BD17 5HH
Shareholder: David Antony Peberdy
Officers: Suzanne Margaret Peberdy, Secretary; David Anthony Peberdy [1946] Director/Sales Executive; Suzanne Margaret Peberdy [1947] Director/Special Needs Assistant

White Space Beauty Limited
Incorporated: 15 April 2014
Registered Office: 35 Theydon Park Road, Theydon Bois, Essex, CM16 7LR
Shareholders: Kevin Lee Anderson; Steven Paul Anderson
Officers: Kevin Anderson [1970] Director

Whitening World Ltd
Incorporated: 26 January 2011
Net Worth: £65,376 *Total Assets:* £65,376
Registered Office: 4 Magellan Terrace, Gatwick Road, Crawley, W Sussex, RH10 9PJ
Major Shareholder: Luis Lajous
Officers: Luis Lajous [1969] Director [Canadian]

Wholesale Hair Extensions Ltd
Incorporated: 20 November 2012
Registered Office: The Old Casino, 28 Fourth Avenue, Hove, E Sussex, BN3 2PJ
Shareholders: Ian Anton Mitchell; Sonja Silmbrod
Officers: Ian Anton Mitchell [1980] Director; Sonja Silmbrod [1977] Director [Austrian]

Wild Beauty Ltd
Incorporated: 8 July 2015
Previous: Yelena Cosmetics Ltd
Net Worth Deficit: £353 *Total Assets:* £100
Registered Office: 120b Cavendish Drive, London, E11 1DJ
Major Shareholder: Jelena Serebrjakova
Officers: Jelena Serebrjakova [1988] Director/Business Analyst [Latvian]

Wild Brands Limited
Incorporated: 13 November 2008
Net Worth: £2,000 *Total Assets:* £152,000
Registered Office: The Dormer House, Hunts Common, Hartley Wintney, Hook, Hants, RG27 8AA
Shareholders: Sarah Anne Strang; Anthony Hayden Noble
Officers: Anthony Hayden Noble, Secretary; Anthony Hayden Noble [1945] Director; Sarah Anne Strang [1979] Director

Wild Celia Ltd
Incorporated: 17 June 2016
Net Worth Deficit: £583 *Total Assets:* £35,326
Registered Office: 27b Castellain Road, London, W9 1EY
Major Shareholder: Cecilia Du Preez
Officers: Cecilia Gertruida Magdalena Du Preez [1980] Director

Wild Earth Botanicals Ltd
Incorporated: 8 October 2018
Registered Office: 3 Hillside Mews, Chelmsford, Essex, CM2 9DH
Shareholders: Christopher Allen Leverett; John Paul Bannocks
Officers: John Paul Bannocks [1985] Director/Policeman; Christopher Allen Leverett [1984] Director/Retailer

The Top UK Perfume and Cosmetics Wholesalers					dellam

Wild Kynd Ltd
Incorporated: 20 November 2018
Registered Office: Kemp House, 160 City Road, London, EC1V 2NX
Shareholders: Helena Janicka; William Bellamy
Officers: William Bellamy [1989] Director/Owner; Helena Janicka [1990] Director/Owner

Wild Organics Limited
Incorporated: 7 October 2008
Net Worth: £1,000 *Total Assets:* £1,000
Registered Office: Office 5, 10 Harbour Terrace, Wick, Highland, KW1 5HB
Officers: Alan Grant MacKenzie [1952] Director/Designer/Furnisher

Wild Source Apothecary Ltd
Incorporated: 17 October 2017
Registered Office: 3 Warwick Avenue, Easton, Bristol, BS5 0YD
Officers: Kate Roath [1991] Director

Wild Things Cosmetics Ltd
Incorporated: 18 May 2016
Registered Office: 50a Waveney Avenue, London, SE15 3UE
Shareholder: Madeleine Jones
Officers: Natalie Lukaitis [1985] Director/Cosmetics Founder [Australian]

Wild Violet X Limited
Incorporated: 8 January 2019
Registered Office: 54 Shallmarsh Road, Wirral, Merseyside, CH63 2JZ
Major Shareholder: Jake Thomas Saunders
Officers: Jake Thomas Saunders [1992] Director/Videographer

Wildmint Cosmetics Limited
Incorporated: 2 November 2018
Registered Office: 71-75 Shelton Street, Covent Garden, London, WC2H 9JQ
Major Shareholder: Freddie Peter Trimble
Officers: Freddie Peter Trimble [1992] Director

The Wildsmith Collection Limited
Incorporated: 8 April 2016 *Employees:* 2
Net Worth Deficit: £620,581 *Total Assets:* £373,484
Registered Office: St Bride's House, 10 Salisbury Square, London, EC4Y 8EH
Officers: Lars Soren Sorensen [1956] Director [Danish]

Dennis Williams Limited
Incorporated: 22 December 1955 *Employees:* 96
Net Worth: £2,445,041 *Total Assets:* £6,319,750
Registered Office: 9 Kingsmark Freeway, Euroway Trading Estate, Bradford, W Yorks, BD12 7HW
Major Shareholder: Pamela Briony Lees
Officers: Pamela Briony Lees, Secretary; Anthony Richard Lees [1946] Director; Arron Richard Lees [1982] Operations Director; Pamela Briony Lees [1959] Managing Director

The Wiltshire Beekeeper Ltd
Incorporated: 27 February 2017
Registered Office: 26 Victoria Road, Devizes, Wilts, SN10 1ET
Officers: Ben Swift [1979] Director

Winchpharma (Consumer Healthcare) Ltd
Incorporated: 28 August 2012
Net Worth Deficit: £121 *Total Assets:* £2,538
Registered Office: c/o Byotrol PLC, Building 303, Thornton Science Park, Pool Lane, Chester, CH2 4NU
Parent: Byotrol PLC
Officers: Denise Yvonne Keenan, Secretary; Dr Thomas Trevor Francis [1950] Director; David Thomas Traynor [1965] Director

Winkies Limited
Incorporated: 19 June 2017
Registered Office: 50a Oxton Road, Birkenhead, Wirral, Merseyside, CH41 2TW
Major Shareholder: Laura McArdle
Officers: Dr Laura McArdle [1985] Director

Winning Lines Limited
Incorporated: 9 May 1994 *Employees:* 6
Net Worth: £806,155 *Total Assets:* £971,312
Registered Office: Prospect Road, Crook, Co Durham, DL15 8JL
Major Shareholder: Harry Forrester Williams
Officers: Rita Williams, Secretary; Harry Forrester Williams [1940] Director/Company Buyer

Winter Hill No.2 Limited
Incorporated: 16 January 1978
Net Worth: £250,000 *Total Assets:* £250,000
Registered Office: Denham Place, Village Road, Denham, Bucks, UB9 5BL
Officers: Vibhaker Devshi Jatania, Secretary; Mitesh Devshi Jatania [1965] Director; Pravin Chandra Devshi Jatania [1950] Director; Vibhaker Devshi Jatania [1955] Director

Daniele de Winter Monaco-UK Ltd
Incorporated: 13 August 2013
Previous: Daniele de Winter UK Limited
Net Worth: £7,000 *Total Assets:* £7,000
Registered Office: West Dean Manor The Lane, Westdean, Seaford, E Sussex, BN25 4AL
Officers: Lady Daniele Sylvie Valentine Michaela-Josephine de Winter [1963] Director

Wipes Direct Ltd
Incorporated: 7 September 2018
Registered Office: 18 Juneberry Avenue, Worsley, Manchester, M28 7GX
Major Shareholder: Andrew Stuart Abraham
Officers: Andrew Stuart Abraham [1977] Managing Director

Wisdom of Nature Limited
Incorporated: 24 November 2003
Registered Office: Unit E, Foster Road, Ashford Business Park, Sevington, Ashford, Kent, TN24 0SH
Parent: Natural Distribution (Holdings) Limited
Officers: Marcos David Pozo Caballero [1973] Business Development Director [Spanish]

Wish List Limited
Incorporated: 23 June 2009
Net Worth: £19,950 *Total Assets:* £164,220
Registered Office: 8 Rodborough Road, London, NW11 8RY
Major Shareholder: David Jacob Gilbert
Officers: David Jacob Gilbert [1970] Director/Management

Wisp Care Products Limited
Incorporated: 17 September 2018
Registered Office: 16 Staunton Avenue, Hayling Island, Hants, PO11 0EN
Shareholders: John Harold Charles Geden; Debbie Mulkern
Officers: John Harold Charles Geden [1966] Director; Debbie Mulkern [1969] Director

Wiv Global Limited
Incorporated: 10 March 2009 Employees: 2
Net Worth: £117,759 Total Assets: £356,481
Registered Office: Rubis House, Friarn Street, Bridgwater, Somerset, TA6 3LH
Major Shareholder: Ermila Ranpium Perera Jayasuriya Curtis
Officers: Ermila Curtis [1979] Director/Founder and Owner

Wizard Brands Limited
Incorporated: 2 October 2018
Registered Office: St Matthew's House, Quays Office Park, Conference Avenue, Portishead, Bristol, BS20 7LZ
Major Shareholder: Daniel John Scott
Officers: Daniel John Scott [1977] Director

Wizer Ltd
Incorporated: 23 October 2018
Registered Office: 71-75 Shelton Street, London, WC2H 9JQ
Major Shareholder: Lior Salman
Officers: Lior Salman, Secretary; Lior Salman [1978] Director [Hungarian]

Woldscot Limited
Incorporated: 19 August 2009
Net Worth Deficit: £32,210 Total Assets: £6,410
Registered Office: The Grange Lodge, Broadwell Hill, Broadwell, Moreton in Marsh, Glos, GL56 0UQ
Parent: Holistic Village Ltd
Officers: Diane Susan Davies [1963] Director; Wyndham Glyn Davies [1946] Director

Wonder and Wild Ltd
Incorporated: 16 March 2018
Registered Office: 10 D'Abernon Drive, Stoke D'Abernon, Cobham, Surrey, KT11 3JD
Shareholders: Lucy Mary Hey; Oliver Felstead
Officers: Oliver Felstead [1981] Director; Lucy Mary Hey [1982] Director

Wonderful Life PHBS Ltd
Incorporated: 25 July 2013 Employees: 10
Net Worth: £141,150 Total Assets: £517,031
Registered Office: 4 Green Lane Business Park, 238 Green Lanes, New Eltham, London, SE9 3TL
Shareholders: Zaine Damion Brookes; Ali Nail
Officers: Zaine Damion Brookes [1982] Director; Ali Nail [1964] Director/Secretary

Wonderland Sales Ltd
Incorporated: 1 February 2018
Registered Office: 56 Galleons Drive, Barking, Essex, IG11 0GU
Major Shareholder: Mihaela Dragan
Officers: Mihaela Dragan [1990] Director/Accounts Manager [Romanian]

Woodwood Limited
Incorporated: 3 September 2018
Registered Office: 6 Wedgwood Avenue, Stone, Staffs, ST15 0XR
Major Shareholder: Geraldine Sproston
Officers: Generaldine Sproston [1966] Director

World Links Europe Limited
Incorporated: 3 December 2018
Registered Office: 10 Plasnewydd Road, Cardiff, CF24 3EN
Shareholders: Stephen John Wiley Carr; Mai Kurisaka
Officers: Stephen John Wiley Carr [1982] Director/Lecturer; Mai Kurisaka [1987] Director/Businesswoman [Japanese]

World Wide Gifts Limited
Incorporated: 31 December 2018
Registered Office: Alps Accountancy, Business First Business Centre, Davyfield Road, Centurion Park, Blackburn, Lancs, BB1 2QY
Major Shareholder: Samantha Teasdale
Officers: Samantha Teasdale [1984] Director/Secretary

Worldwide International Retail Limited
Incorporated: 21 February 2018
Registered Office: Flat 2, Nightingale House, St Bartholomews Lane, Rochester, Kent, ME1 1RD
Officers: Daniel Paul Keogh, Secretary; Daniel Paul Keogh [1991] Director/Entrepreneur

Worldwidegoodstraders Ltd
Incorporated: 28 January 2019
Registered Office: 71-75 Shelton Street, London, WC2H 9JQ
Major Shareholder: Simon Smith
Officers: Simon Smith, Secretary; Simon Smith [1967] Director/Manager

Worth Worldwide Property Limited
Incorporated: 1 April 2011
Net Worth: £446,018 Total Assets: £613,412
Registered Office: 78 Wembley Park Drive, Wembley, Middlesex, HA9 8HB
Major Shareholder: Lawrence Hili
Officers: Lawrence Hili [1955] Director/Businessman [Maltese]; Jignesh Pravinkumar Mehta [1978] Director/Production Planner

Wow Facial Ltd
Incorporated: 19 February 2019
Registered Office: Flat 4, 31 Charles Road, London, W13 0ND
Major Shareholder: Claire Elizabeth Williams
Officers: Claire Elizabeth Williams [1976] Managing Director

Wrap N Pack Ltd
Incorporated: 21 March 2017
Net Worth Deficit: £6,560 Total Assets: £9,880
Registered Office: Flat 26, Dilton Gardens, London, SW15 4BY
Major Shareholder: Maliha Shahid-Humayun
Officers: Shafqat Ullah Humayun [1986] Director [Pakistani]; Maliha Shahid - Humayun [1989] Director [German]

Wrimes Cosmetics Ltd
Incorporated: 12 May 2014
Net Worth: £498,210 Total Assets: £1,250,000
Registered Office: Unit 1 Access Business Park, Gunnels Wood Road, Stevenage, Herts, SG1 2GR
Shareholders: Lewis Drew Ames; Lee Steven Wright
Officers: Lewis Drew Ames [1989] Director; Lee Steven Wright [1990] Director

Wuyu Mother and Baby Ltd
Incorporated: 8 June 2017
Registered Office: 32 Sherwood Close, Langdon Hills, Basildon, Essex, SS16 6JQ
Major Shareholder: Kudzai Sibanda
Officers: Kudzai Sibanda [1987] Director/Founder

The Top UK Perfume and Cosmetics Wholesalers

Wwinc. Ltd
Incorporated: 31 July 2018
Registered Office: 1 Muirfield, Great Denham, Bedford, MK40 4FB
Major Shareholder: Nitasha Buldeo
Officers: Dr Nitasha Buldeo, Secretary; Dr Nitasha Buldeo [1976] Director

Xhorah Skincare Ltd
Incorporated: 26 April 2018
Registered Office: 24-26 Regents Place, Birmingham, B1 3NJ
Major Shareholder: Tanya Weir
Officers: Tanya Weir [1986] Director

Ximtrade (UK) Ltd
Incorporated: 11 July 2013
Net Worth Deficit: £12,847 *Total Assets:* £40,258
Registered Office: 65 Langland Crescent, Stanmore, Middlesex, HA7 1NF
Major Shareholder: Sunil Galaiya
Officers: Harsha Galaiya, Secretary; Sunil Galaiya [1960] Director/Businessman

XIP Professional Ltd
Incorporated: 9 August 2016
Net Worth Deficit: £13,630
Registered Office: Crown Chambers, Bridge Street, Salisbury, Wilts, SP1 2LZ
Officers: Evert Gerhardus Helena Mechtildis Ilbrink [1980] Director [Dutch]; Dirk Willibrord Kersten [1978] Director [Dutch]

XL Marketing Ltd.
Incorporated: 2 March 2009
Net Worth: £38,391 *Total Assets:* £73,668
Registered Office: 6 Rixon Close, Weston Favell, Northampton, NN3 3PF
Officers: Stuart Thomas Gortley Knowles [1965] Director/Marketing Consultant

Xpoze International Limited
Incorporated: 14 June 2005
Net Worth: £1,812 *Total Assets:* £1,812
Registered Office: 2a Hillcrest Road, Purley, Surrey, CR8 2JE
Major Shareholder: Rasiah Parimelalagan
Officers: Rasiah Parimelalagan [1948] Director/Chemical Engineer

XSS Scotland Limited
Incorporated: 13 November 2007
Registered Office: 6 Balruddery Place, Bishopbriggs, Glasgow, G64 1JB
Shareholder: Brian Aitken
Officers: Brian Aitken, Secretary; Brian Aitken [1954] Director/Accountant; Sandra Aitken [1957] Director/Teacher

XY Skin Ltd
Incorporated: 22 August 2017
Registered Office: 3/2, 11 Bannatyne Avenue, Glasgow, G31 2UD
Officers: David Andrew McEwan [1984] Director [British/Filipino]

Yaami's Fashion Beauty & Cosmetics UK Ltd
Incorporated: 26 November 2018
Registered Office: 48 Clifford Road, Hounslow, Middlesex, TW4 7LT
Major Shareholder: Mayurika Chintankumar Pandya
Officers: Rushisagar Rameshbhai Patel [1990] Director/Businessman [Indian]

Yates-Lee and Burnett Limited
Incorporated: 27 April 2018
Registered Office: 9 Croft Manor, Eaglesfield, Lockerbie, Dumfries & Galloway, DG11 3PZ
Shareholders: Gemma Cluness Yates-Lee; Lynn Burnett
Officers: Lynn Burnett [1972] Director; Gemma Cluness Yates-Lee [1981] Director

Yazmae Cosmetics Limited
Incorporated: 7 February 2018
Registered Office: 2 Fairfield Drive, Ormskirk, Lancs, L39 1RL
Shareholders: Jamie Charnock; Steven Yates
Officers: Jamie Charnock [1997] Director; Steven Yates [1997] Director

Yehmea Limited
Incorporated: 25 October 2017
Net Worth: £100 *Total Assets:* £100
Registered Office: 19 Grasmere Green, Wellingborough, Northants, NN8 3EH
Major Shareholder: Olufunmilayo Sabi
Officers: Olu Sabi [1971] Director

Yejisu Innovation Ltd
Incorporated: 21 July 2014
Registered Office: 82 Felixstowe Road, Abbey Wood, London, SE2 9QH
Officers: John Kweku Mensah, Secretary; Oladele Agbedeyi [1976] Director/Accountant; Olutoyin Adebimpe Ogunbanjo [1956] Director/Health Trainer [Nigerian]; Sarah Oludamilola Peace [1986] Director/Project Manager [Nigerian]; Dr. Olufemi Olukayode Shode [1953] Director/Lecturer; Dr Oluyemisi Olabisi Shode [1954] Director/Chemist

Yellbird Limited
Incorporated: 25 November 2015
Net Worth: £4,500 *Total Assets:* £4,500
Registered Office: 172 Howley Grange Road, Halesowen, W Midlands, B62 0JD
Officers: Arasti Afrasiabi [1976] Director/Civil Structural Engineer [German]; Arnold Lobah [1977] Director/Businessman [German]

Yes To Carrots UK Limited
Incorporated: 7 May 2013 *Employees:* 3
Net Worth: £83,174 *Total Assets:* £167,483
Registered Office: Carrick House, Lypiatt Road, Cheltenham, Glos, GL50 2QJ
Officers: Ingrid Karine Jackel [1969] Director [French]

YJX Group PLC
Incorporated: 30 August 2018
Registered Office: 12 New Fetter Lane, London, EC4A 1JP
Major Shareholder: Geoffrey Stanton Morrow
Officers: Richard James Carter [1980] Director/Accountant; Geoffrey Stanton Morrow [1942] Director

Yorkshire Beard Company Ltd
Incorporated: 12 June 2017
Registered Office: 90 Larch Hill Crescent, Bradford, BD6 1DS
Officers: James David Ludbrook [1985] Managing Director

Yorkshire Beauty Supplies Limited
Incorporated: 14 April 2009
Net Worth: £3,282 *Total Assets:* £6,827
Registered Office: 146 Bawtry Road, Bramley, Rotherham, S Yorks, S66 2TS
Major Shareholder: Julie Marie Bowes
Officers: Julie Marie Bowes [1979] Director/Beauty Therapist

Young Now Ltd
Incorporated: 22 September 2017
Registered Office: Welsh ICE, Britannia House, Caerphilly Business Park, Vann Road, Caerphilly, Gwent, CF83 3GG
Major Shareholder: Paulina Chilarska
Officers: Dr Paulina Chilarska [1986] Director/Chief Executive [Polish]

Younghair AB Ltd
Incorporated: 19 April 2016
Net Worth: £44,560 *Total Assets:* £139,790
Registered Office: 20-22 Wenlock Road, London, N1 7GU
Major Shareholder: Gary Alan Young
Officers: Gary Alan Young [1960] Director/Internet Marketing

YSL Trading Ltd
Incorporated: 7 November 2017
Registered Office: 26 Benbow Close, St Albans, Herts, AL1 5SA
Major Shareholder: Aron Wertheimer
Officers: Aron Wertheimer [1970] Director [Austrian]

YSO Import-Export Limited
Incorporated: 30 May 2018
Registered Office: 125 Aspen Gardens, London, W6 9JF
Officers: Omar Yahya Al Magbouli [1968] Director [Yemeni]; Ahmed Hussein Ali [1996] Director/Accounts Manager [Somali]; Mohamad Hussein Ali [1994] Director/Company Secretary [Somali]

Yu Parfums Ltd
Incorporated: 16 April 2018
Registered Office: Per Scent Ltd, Churchill Point, Lake Edge Green, Trafford Park, Manchester, M17 1BL
Shareholders: CPL Aromas Limited; Per-Scent Limited
Officers: Christopher Pickthall [1968] Director; Nicholas Pickthall [1976] Director; Sanjay Jayantilal Vadera [1967] Director; Vipul Jayantilal Vadera [1972] Director

Yummy Home Ltd
Incorporated: 17 August 2000
Registered Office: 2 Moat Lodge, London Road, Harrow, Middlesex, HA1 3LU
Officers: Amina Sadiq, Secretary/Businesswoman; Amina Sadiq [1970] Director/Businesswoman; Nabila Sadiq [1968] Director/Businesswoman; Naseem Sadiq [1974] Director/Recruitment Consultant

Yurexroar Cosmetic Wholesale Ltd
Incorporated: 2 January 2019
Registered Office: 107 Admiral Street, Liverpool, L8 8BW
Officers: Shrin Agha [1985] Director/Wholesale of Cosmetics

Ibrahim Yusuf and Sons Ltd
Incorporated: 30 July 2018
Registered Office: 63a Kilburn Park Road, London, NW6 5LA
Shareholder: Ibrahim Ibrahim Yusuf
Officers: Aziza Yusuf [1972] Director/Businesswoman; Ibrahim Ibrahim Yusuf [1961] Director/Businessman; Ibrahim Junior Yusuf Jnr [1992] Director/Businessman

YWC (Yes We Can) Limited
Incorporated: 15 January 2019
Registered Office: 1146 High Road, Whetstone, London, N20 0RA
Major Shareholder: Guido Bottazzi
Officers: Guido Bottazzi [1961] Commercial Director [Italian]

Z & J Enterprises Limited
Incorporated: 14 August 2013
Net Worth Deficit: £67,239 *Total Assets:* £123,104
Registered Office: 291 Chaple House Road, Nelson, Lancs, BB9 0QU
Major Shareholder: Junaid Iqbal
Officers: Junaid Iqbal, Secretary; Junaid Iqbal [1966] Director/Self Employed [Pakistani]; Zeba Rafiq [1962] Director/Self Employed [Pakistani]

Z Online Ltd
Incorporated: 20 June 2018
Registered Office: 82 Selsdon Road, London, E13 9BY
Officers: Zahra Jan [1992] Director

Zagorah Ltd
Incorporated: 16 March 2017
Registered Office: 329 Ley Street, Ilford, Essex, IG1 4AA
Shareholders: Fabrizio Di Gianvincenzo; Elena Di Gianvincenzo
Officers: Fabrizio di Gianvincenzo [1979] Director/Manager [Italian]

Zahrat Alqurashi Ltd
Incorporated: 13 June 2017
Registered Office: 11-13 Ellesmere Road, Sheffield, S4 7JA
Officers: Qasem Qasem Mohammed Al-Ahmadi [1960] Director [Yemeni]; Gamal Ali Hussein Al-Esaei [1962] Director

Zaigul Wholesale Ltd
Incorporated: 15 May 2009
Registered Office: 20 Second Avenue, Wembley, Middlesex, HA9 8QF
Major Shareholder: Masuma Shabbir Dungersi
Officers: Masuma Shabbir Dungersi [1968] Director/Domestic Engineer

Zainab Limited
Incorporated: 28 April 2000
Net Worth: £1,420,000 *Total Assets:* £4,600,000
Registered Office: Unit 41 Oakwoodhill Industrial Estate, Loughton, Essex, IG10 3TZ
Shareholders: Shah Investment Partnership; Asad Ali Shah; Asif Haidra Ali Shah
Officers: Asad Ali Shah, Secretary/Sales Manager; Asad Ali Shah [1972] Director/Sales Manager; Asif Haidra Ali Shah [1967] Director

Zajil Limited
Incorporated: 20 February 2019
Registered Office: 252 Bowling Back Lane, Bradford, W Yorks, BD4 8SY
Major Shareholder: Hisham Ahmad Kelendar
Officers: Hisham Ahmad Kelendar [1981] Director/Doctor [Kuwaiti]

Zaliant Skincare Limited
Incorporated: 8 August 2015
Registered Office: 45 West Street, Swadlincote, Derbys, DE11 9DN
Major Shareholder: Terjinder Singh Purewal
Officers: Terjinder-Deep Singh Purewal [1988] Director/Business Consultant

Zamantraders Limited
Incorporated: 5 January 2018
Registered Office: 2 Townshend Estate, London, NW8 6JP
Officers: Arif Zaman [1959] Director

Zamoux Cosmetics Limited
Incorporated: 10 May 2018
Registered Office: 61 Tallow Close, Dagenham, Essex, RM9 6EF
Major Shareholder: Oziomachukwu Chikaodili Emelife
Officers: Emeka Augustine Emelife [1975] Director; Oziomachukwu Chikaodili Emelife [1976] Director/Chief Executive

Zarahs World Ltd
Incorporated: 23 October 2018
Registered Office: 1b Albion Street, Wakefield, W Yorks, WF1 3LR
Major Shareholder: Moheen Shakoor
Officers: Moheen Shakoor [1996] Director

Zarroug Limited
Incorporated: 7 December 2018
Registered Office: 32 Roger Drive, Sandal, Wakefield, W Yorks, WF2 7NE
Major Shareholder: Osman Hamza Osman Zarroug
Officers: Osman Hamza Osman Zarroug [1988] Director/Pharmacist

Zarvis London Limited
Incorporated: 18 September 2008
Registered Office: Flat 729, 28 Old Brompton Road, London, SW7 3SS
Officers: Lufric Demetrius Jasper Jagger [1972] Director/Production Consultant

Zealousco Limited
Incorporated: 18 January 2019
Registered Office: 10b Park Hill Road, Wallington, Surrey, SM6 0SB
Major Shareholder: Sasha Nicole Desouza-Willock
Officers: Sasha Nicole Desouza-Willock [1999] Director

Zed Beauty Ltd
Incorporated: 24 September 2018
Registered Office: 26 Moneysallin Road, Kilrea, Coleraine, Co Londonderry, BT51 5TQ
Major Shareholder: Louise Mary Donaghy
Officers: Louise Mary Donaghy [1983] Brand Director

Zee Sales Limited
Incorporated: 3 January 2019
Registered Office: 104 Wheatacre Road, Nottingham, NG11 8LN
Major Shareholder: Immaculata Ngozika Jordan
Officers: Immaculata Ngozika Jordan [1990] Director/Retailer [Nigerian]

Naseem Zeenah Natural Cosmetics Ltd
Incorporated: 8 May 2017
Registered Office: 34a Dean Road, London, NW2 5AE
Major Shareholder: Amina Farah
Officers: Amina Farah [1957] Managing Director

Zero Cosmetics UK Limited
Incorporated: 28 January 2019
Registered Office: 5 Theale Lakes Business Park, Moulden Way, Sulhamstead, Reading, Berks, RG7 4GB
Officers: Zakir Maqsood Hussain [1985] Director [Pakistani]; Zarlasht Jafar [1999] Director [Pakistani]; Nabila Maqsood Hussain [1963] Director [Pakistani]

Zerocann Ltd
Incorporated: 9 November 2016
Registered Office: 46 Nova Road, Croydon, Surrey, CR0 2TL
Major Shareholder: Michal Takac
Officers: Michal Takac [1979] Director [Czech]

Zest Cosmetics Limited
Incorporated: 6 February 2014
Net Worth: £46,360 *Total Assets:* £90,910
Registered Office: Crown Chambers, Princes Street, Harrogate, N Yorks, HG1 1NJ
Major Shareholder: James Fewtrell
Officers: James Fewtrell [1965] Director

Zieseniss Limited
Incorporated: 18 October 2001
Previous: Bio Sculpture (London) Limited
Net Worth: £70,300 *Total Assets:* £122,910
Registered Office: 1a Nelson Avenue, St Albans, Herts, AL1 5SE
Shareholders: Naomi Zieseniss; Anthony Mark Zieseniss
Officers: Anthony Mark Zieseniss, Secretary; Naomi Zieseniss [1956] Director

Zimmerglobal Ltd
Incorporated: 4 October 2018
Registered Office: 17/2 George Lowe Court, London, W2 5TA
Major Shareholder: Desmond George
Officers: Desmond George [1972] Director

Zipco Limited
Incorporated: 23 September 1999
Net Worth: £6,647 *Total Assets:* £8,017
Registered Office: 69 Sandmoor Lane, Leeds, LS17 7EA
Major Shareholder: Steven Martin Shonn
Officers: Steven Martin Shonn, Secretary/Director; Richard Lee Shonn [1977] Director; Steven Martin Shonn [1951] Director/Consultant

Zivi Cosmetics Ltd
Incorporated: 12 February 2018
Registered Office: 10 The Crescent, Farnham, Surrey, GU9 0LE
Major Shareholder: Paul Brian Johnson
Officers: Paul Brian Johnson [1972] Director

Zjonline Ltd
Incorporated: 24 September 2018
Registered Office: 2 Baden Powell Close, Dagenham, Essex, RM9 6XN
Major Shareholder: Zahra Jan
Officers: Zahra Jan [1992] Director

Zoe Balm Ltd
Incorporated: 16 August 2018
Registered Office: 27 Cleggswood Avenue, Littleborough, Lancs, OL15 0DF
Major Shareholder: Catherine Grace Marcroft
Officers: Catherine Grace Marcroft [1992] Director/Cosmetic Manufacturing and Sales

Zoe Lane Ltd
Incorporated: 12 December 2018
Registered Office: 590 Kingston Road, London, SW20 8DN
Major Shareholder: Waclaw Deren
Officers: Waclaw Deren [1965] Director [Polish]

Zoee Cosmetics Co., Ltd
Incorporated: 5 June 2018
Registered Office: Unit G25, Waterfront Studios, 1 Dock Road, London, E16 1AH
Major Shareholder: Xue An
Officers: Xue [1990] Director [Chinese]

Zoeva UK Limited
Incorporated: 27 March 2018
Registered Office: Suite 1, 3rd Floor, 11-12 St James's Square, London, SW1Y 4LB
Major Shareholder: Zoe Wolfram
Officers: Varvara Boikou [1982] Director of Business Development [Greek]; Zoe Wolfram [1980] Managing Director [Greek]

Zojo. The Gorgeousness Company Ltd
Incorporated: 28 March 2017
Registered Office: Sovereign House, Port Causeway, Wirral, Merseyside, CH62 4TP
Major Shareholder: Marta Joanna Ravensdale
Officers: Marta Joanna Ravensdale [1976] Director/Corporate Lawyer [Polish]

ZS Beauty Ltd
Incorporated: 13 July 2016
Net Worth: £263,590 *Total Assets:* £287,080
Registered Office: c/o Atoz Creatives Ltd, Aviation House, 125 Kingsway, London, WC2B 6NH
Officers: Zoe Elizabeth Sugg [1990] Director

Zurego Limited
Incorporated: 26 May 2011 *Employees:* 2
Net Worth Deficit: £28,709 *Total Assets:* £112,314
Registered Office: Alpha House, Greek Street, Stockport, Cheshire, SK3 8AB
Shareholders: Nicholas John Thompson; Cathryn Margaret Thompson
Officers: Cathryn Margaret Thompson [1968] Director; Nicholas John Thompson [1968] Managing Director

Zyzven Naturals Cosmetics Ltd
Incorporated: 7 January 2019
Registered Office: 12 Mayday Road, Thornton Heath, Surrey, CR7 7HL
Shareholder: Shawnafi Dynesen
Officers: Shawnafi Dynesen [1979] Director/Entrepreneur [Swedish]

ZZ Traders Ltd
Incorporated: 25 August 2018
Registered Office: 51 Isles Quarry Road, Borough Green, Sevenoaks, Kent, TN15 8FP
Major Shareholder: Maryam Adil
Officers: Maryam Adil [1985] Director

Index of Directorships

Aalam, Joanna
Beuti Limited

Aalam, Leila Marie
Beuti Limited

Aamir, Mohammed
Aamir Traders Ltd

Abarian, Andranik
Asabeauty Ltd

Abbas, Awad Kazem
Best-Bio Ltd

Abbas, Babar
Alayna Cosmetics and Beauty Ltd

Abbas, Mohaned Awad
Bio Global Limited

Abbaze, Nabil
Ameera London Limited

Abd Majid, MD Ferrozzi
Just Beautiful Skin Ltd

Abdalla, Motwakil
Rexez Ltd

Abdelhamid, Islam Samy Abdelhamid
Farshety Ltd

Abdelhamid, Osama
Layan Pharma Ltd

Abdul Rahman, Mohd Rodzi Bin
RR Cosmeceuticals (UK) Ltd

Abdul Razak, Norzaidah
Pinklady International Ltd

Abdul, Ambreen
Eabir Ltd

Abdulhafiz, Milena Marinova
Farmers Pure Organics Ltd

Abdulhamid, Yahya Muftah
Health Future Limited

Abdulla, Mehboob
Connected Beauty Limited

Abdullah, Mohommad
Brand Euro Limited

Abdullahi, Khadijah
Soul Cosmetics Limited

Abdulrahman, Fatima Mohamed Sharif
KM Cosmetics Distribution Ltd

Abdussalam, Mohammed
Organic Land Global Ltd

Abecassis, Paul Alain
Chanel Limited

Abel, Anna
Larouge Cosmetics Limited

Abel, John Birrel
Global Hair Care Limited

Abel, Simon William
Global Hair Care Limited

Abele, Bruno
Brunucorp Ltd

Abiakweh, Uche Peace
Uchepeace Limited

Abiola, Rasidat Ajisafe
Biodeb Beauty Ltd

Abiyeva, Zeynab
Organic Cosmetic Products Ltd

Abkhare, Farzin Abedini
Vortex Holding Limited

Abokor, Ayan
Ayaon Ltd

Abraham, Andrew Stuart
Wipes Direct Ltd

Abramova, Jelena
Annexa Solutions Limited

Abu Bakr, Mohammed
Railworth Limited

Abuhammad, Osama
Reveal Naturals Ltd

Acampora, Brunello
Vittoria Ventures Limited

Acorsi, Gustavo Henrique
Ahoaloe Cosmetics Limited

Adam Ali Ibrahim, Mustafa Asghar
Chris Adams Perfumes Ltd

Asgher Adam Ali, Howaida
Chris Adams Perfumes Ltd

Adams, Angela
Cult Candy Limited

Adebola, Esther Ibidoja
Aglory Merchant Enterprises Ltd

Adebola, Mohammed Kamoru
Aglory Merchant Enterprises Ltd

Ademola, Ifeoluwa Abiola
Lyons Pride Limited

Adesanya, Oluwafemi Samuel
Nicfead Cosmetics & Fragrance Ltd

Adesina, Helen Adetokunbo
Tree of Life Cosmetics Ltd

Adetoye, Adetola Anita
Anita Brows Cosmetics Limited

Adi, Yaron
Natasha Denona Make Up Ltd.

Adil, Ersin Akif
Estela Dermocosmetics Ltd

Adil, Maryam
ZZ Traders Ltd

Adjei, Joyce Djagblorkor
Uniqtrend Limited

Adler, Halldora Halldorsdottir
Fragrance Factory Limited

Adler, Jeremy David
Fragrance Factory Limited

Adlington, Mark Justin
Cyrano Limited

Adlington, Simon John
Cyrano Limited

Adnani, Prathna Vasudev
MNM International UK Limited

Adnani, Vasudev Ghanshamdas
MNM International UK Limited

Adris, Sadia
Sfera London Limited

Adrjanowicz, Agnieszka
Aga Cosmetics Ltd

Advani, Tanya
BU Cosmetics Limited

Afaq, Ahmer
D'Zario UK Ltd
London Heartbeat Ltd

Afflick-Mensah, Alice
Cure Hair & Skin Care Ltd

Afrasiabi, Arasti
Yellbird Limited

Parmar, Kishan
The Aftershave Gaff Ltd

Afzal, Zakrina
Eternal Hair & Beauty Limited

Agafonova, Iuliia
Profline Ltd

Khan, Stephane
Jalali Agarwood Ltd

Agbedeyi, Oladele
Yejisu Innovation Ltd

Aggrey, Edna Mantey
Medna Fashions Ltd

Agha, Claudia
Satya Life Ltd

Agha, Shrin
Yurexroar Cosmetic Wholesale Ltd

Agossou, Nelly Hanaig
Ars Nova (UK) Limited

Aguh, Chinapa
Africa's Best Artisans Limited

Aherne, Ian Martin Campbell
K.B. Salon Supplies Limited

Ahlbeck, Timothy, Lord
Perfume Outlet Ltd

Ahlgren, Jan Gustav Vilhelm
Vilhelm Parfumerie Limited

Ahluwalia, Hardaman Bamby
Pizzaz Ventures Limited

Ahmad, Faiza
Dead Sea London Ltd

Ahmad, Munawar
Dead Sea London Ltd

Ahmad, Shahzad
Mahrosh Beauty Ltd

Ahmad, Waqar
3D Lifestyle Ltd

Ahmed Butt, Amina
Pixie Porter Ltd

Ahmed Mostafa, Yasser Kamaleldin
Modern Innovations Limited Ltd

Ahmed, Abdul Noor
Vedaway Ltd

Ahmed, Ali Younis
APC (UK) Limited

Ahmed, Faizan
Odeferus Limited

Ahmed, Hafiz
Healtholozy UK Limited

Ahmed, Hassan Uddin
Black Pearl Beauty Limited

Ahmed, MD Masum
UK Cosmeticz International Ltd

Ahmed, Mohamed Ahmed Mahmoud
Al Amira Limited

Ahmed, Mohammed Ashfaq
Evanto Fragrance Limited

Ahmed, Nasir
Complete Healing Limited

Ahmed, Oluwafikayo Olutomi Oladipupo
Iiuvo Limited

Ahmed, Shuhel
Glute Plus Limited

Ahmed, Sohail
Bays International Limited

Ahmed, Suaad
SSB Ltd

Ahmed, Syed Naseer
Esthetica Pure Ltd
Microskin Cosmeceuticals UK Ltd

Ahmed, Syed Salmaan
Esthetica Pure Ltd
Microskin Cosmeceuticals UK Ltd

Aigbogun, Ekhoaye
Kizzle Beauty Ltd

Aitchison, Julie Mary
Galenti Limited
Onya Limited

Aitken, Brian
Beauty Solutions Limited
Beauty Systems Group Ltd.
Hive of Beauty Limited
Specialist Hair Products Ltd
XSS Scotland Limited

Aitken, Sandra
XSS Scotland Limited

Aitmokhtar, Salim
C & P Neptune Ltd

Ajaib, Ehsen
Beautx Ltd

Ajitkumar, Amirthalinkam
Flexi Beauty Care Ltd

Ajmal, Mohammed Amiruddin
Ajmal Perfume (UK) Limited

Ajmal, Mohammed Fakhruddin
Ajmal Perfume (UK) Limited

Ajmal, Mohammed Sirajuddin
Ajmal Perfume (UK) Limited

Akachab, Hassan
9 Silk Gates Ltd

Akan, Abdulkadir
MTIstanbul Ltd

Akar, Hasan
Has To Be Ltd

Akbarali, Muqbil Shinan
Excess Beauty Ltd

Akhtar, Jawed
Jak Beauty Ltd

Akhtar, Shuab
1st Choice Nails Limited
Nail Polish Gel Colours Ltd

Akinola, Dola Alika
Soft and Curly Products Ltd

Akkurt, Kenan
Ak-Kur Furniture & Fitting Ltd

Akobeng, Catherine
Kokoa UK Limited

Akram, Zahil
Argan Vanity Ltd

Akyildiz, Aslihan
Rapsodi Ltd

Akyol, Serra
VNS London Limited

Akyol, Vedat
VNS London Limited

Al Arnab, Leila
Body Beauty & Hair Ltd

Al Bayati, Azal
Al Masiya Cosmetic Ltd

Al Busaidi, Mashal
Exa World Ltd

Al Dousari, Faisal
Amiri Perfume Ltd

Al Kasmi, Mhd Anas
Nectar International Limited

Al Magbouli, Omar Yahya
YSO Import-Export Limited

Al Meqbali, Hazza
Luxuria Generation Limited

Al Qaissieh, Abdulla Mahmoud Ahmed
Walk on Gold Limited

Al Riyami, Ahmed Mohammed
Brands Gallery Ltd

Al-Ahmadi, Qasem Qasem Mohammed
Zahrat Alqurashi Ltd

Al-Assadi, Firas
Jardin de Parfums Ltd

Al-Bayati, Hussain Ali Hussain
Adams General Ltd

Al-Esaei, Gamal Ali Hussein
Zahrat Alqurashi Ltd

Al-Hadethee, Sanaa
Pharmacare International Ltd

Al-Jumaili, Haitham Sabeeh Ali
Mayfair Gate Limited

Al-Kitabi, Qassem
Pink Empire Limited

Al-Rwasheda, Atyan
Lensmeuk Limited

Al-Tamimi, Raza
Noor Int'l Trading Limited

Alabi, Mimi Barakat Milolaoluwa
Minx Lashes Ltd

Alaghbari, Saber
Landermark Ltd

Alallaq, Ahmed, Dr
Medica Ltd

Alallaq, Riyadh, Dr
Medica Ltd

Alalouch, Ghazele
Ilys Organic Ltd

Alam Bhuiyan, MD Saiful
Rexcel Trading Ltd

Alam, Hameed
Three Organics Ltd

Alamri, Defaf
Lab Brands Limited

Alasow, Mascuud Yusuf Abdi
Thrillage Ltd.

Albakour, Yamen Muneer
Alkaiser Perfumes Ltd

Albertini Ep. Garnier, Laetitia Marie Edmee Jehanne
Aurelia Skincare (International) Ltd
Aurelia Skincare Limited

Albiol, Joan
Puig UK Limited

Albrecht, Patrick
Beiersdorf UK Ltd.

Albusaidy, Majid Ali Talib
Adraji Ltd

Alcide, Leigh-Marie
A Natural Treat Limited

Ariss, Analisa
Maddi Alexander Limited

Alfarsi, Salman
Railworth Limited

Alfi, Ayman
Essential Cosmetics Ltd

Alfloarei, Aurelia-Elena
Butterfly Cosmetics Limited

Alfzari, Heba Khamis Jumaa Shenain
Coveti Limited

Algie, Justin James
Siam Botanicals UK Limited

Ali Dhuhul, Nura
Allies Network Ltd

Ali, Abubakar Haji
Salimaskinsolutions Ltd

Ali, Ahmed Hussein
YSO Import-Export Limited

Ali, Amjad
Optic Eye Wear Ltd

Ali, Aroona Naheed
Opal Naturals Ltd

Ali, Ashley Fareed
Misspap X Bperfect Limited

Ali, Basharit
Saffron Beauty Ltd

Ali, Ferdous Ahmed
By Al Kindi Ltd

Ali, Howaida
Nabeel Perfumes International Ltd

Ali, Husam
Reetal Development Co Ltd

Ali, Kathleen Marie
Kavali Cosmetics Limited

Ali, Mohamad Hussein
YSO Import-Export Limited

Ali, Mohamed Saraj
Pure Revolution Ltd

Ali, Nabeel Hussein Adam
Swiss Arabian Perfumes (UK) Ltd

Ali, Rabail
Arrah Ltd

Ali, Shabana
FayshCosmetics Ltd

Ali, Syed Yakub
Sama Perfumes Ltd

Alibocas, Gerard Lindon
Sacha Cosmetics UK Ltd

Aljadawi, Mai Abdulatif
Iam By Nature Ltd.

Alkaya, Arif Selim
Evercore UK Limited

Alkhouri, Nadi
Axa Beauty World Limited

Allan, Kim Jennifer
Botanical Brands Ltd

Allan, Samara
Meek and Mild Essentials Ltd

Allarakha, Farrah
Neo Elegance Ltd

Allard, Arnaud
On & Off Beauty Ltd

Allen, Annabel Eve Gladstone
Back To Eve Ltd

Allen, Carol Ann
Simlar 2 Limited

Allen, Jill
Seventa Image Ltd

Allen, Peter Damien
Simlar 2 Limited

Allen, Susan Charlene
Here We Flo Ltd

Allen, Tracey
Kendra Cosmetics Limited

Alleyne, Mellissa
Moore Cosmetics Ltd

Allington, Anna
Super Natural Apothecary Ltd.

Allsop, Mark
CM Hair & Beauty Supplies Ltd

Allsworth, Thomas Donald
Revolution Beauty Limited

Almani, Yossi
Beautyge Fragrances Holdings Ltd

Almasmoum, Abdulmalek
Maison de Maa Ltd

Aloisio, Belinda
Otonix Limited

Aloum, Fatima
Florence Health & Beauty Ltd

Alsabah, Fatima Mubarak Jaber
Prismologie International Ltd

Alsabah, Intisar Salem Ali
Prismologie International Ltd

Althefeeri, Abdulazeez
Kehal Ltd
Villa Sauod Ltd

Altoumi, Mohammed
Gift Presentp Ltd

Altree, Clifford Neil
Luscious Lashes International Ltd

Altundag, Bilal
Altundag Ltd

Alves Conceicao, Marco Aurelio
M & M Import Ltd

Alves de Sousa, Marco Antonio
MDistributor Hair and Beauty Products

Alvi, Rizwana Kausar, Doctor
Cutagen Ltd

Alwany, Imtiyaz
Project 1 Skincare Ltd

Alzaabi, Ali
Lucerne Perfumes Ltd

Amadi, Prince Uche
Ladorisa Limited

Ambroise, Didier-Alexandre
Amaffi London Limited

Ames, Lewis Drew
Wrimes Cosmetics Ltd

Amin, Farah
Effay Limited

Amoakohene, Stephanie-Grace
Just Do You Limited

Amoroso, Sonia
Selfcare Corporation Ltd

Amos, Cameron James
Lore Originals Limited

An, Xue
Zoee Cosmetics Co., Ltd

Anderson, Kevin
White Space Beauty Limited

Anderson, Nadine
Barefaced Beauty Ltd

Andersson, Malin Sara
Consy Limited

Andoura, Lama
Noble Soap Limited

Andrawes, Maged
Bristol Consumer Health Ltd

Andrew, Robert George, Dr
Healthcare Wholesale Ltd

Andrews, Claire
Paradoxx Ltd

Andrews, Hilary Ann
Beegood Enterprises Limited

Andrews, Ian David
Glow Consumer Products UK Ltd

Andrews, Magda
Bristol Consumer Health Ltd

Andrews, Ross Martin Hilton
Innovaderma PLC

Andriatsiferana, Tony
Ferana Ltd

Androva, Eleonora
Dermacure Aesthetics Limited

Anducich - Rowe, Daphna
Lovorika London Limited

Angibeau, Bruno
Parfums Christian Dior (U.K.) Ltd

Anifowoshe, Habeeb
Mabxclusive Limited

Anis, Muhammad Kashif
Mcaniis Ltd

Anousta, Linda
Love Anousta Limited

Ansari, Ibrahim
Beautypro Ltd
Evanesce Ltd

Antonini, Manuela
New Aesthetic Ltd

Antoniou, Jane
Mary-Jane's Beauty Ltd

Antonova, Inesa
Loveliness Limited

Antwi, Nikki Beverley
Selfish Cosmetics Ltd

Anusiewicz, Mikolaj
PLTradeGroup Limited

Appiah-Brantuo, Eva Barbara
Evie Skincare Ltd

Aptik, Maayan
Erin Cosmetics Ltd

Aqeel, Muhammad
InternationalBeautyLondon Ltd

Archer, Mary Lorraine
Lock Stock & Barrel Grooming Co Ltd

Sheehan, Michael Thomas
Elizabeth Arden (UK) Ltd

Almani, Yossi
Elizabeth Arden (UK) Ltd

O'Neil, Mitra
Elizabeth Arden (UK) Ltd

Ladjadj, Adam
W. S Argan Limited

Arias-Ferrari Saramago, Guillermo Jose
Wafson Ltd

Arif, Arooj, Dr
Cosmetic Orb Ltd

Arjomandkhah, Helen Mary
Portland House International Trading

Arjomandkhah, Nardair
Portland House International Trading

Arjomandkhah, Samir
Portland House International Trading

Armitage, Lynette Anne
Natrelle Limited

Armitage-Adams, Lisa Ann
Koreesa Limited

Armitage-Adams, Sonia
Koreesa Limited

Armsden, Melanie
Le Keux Vintage Enterprises Ltd

Armstrong, Liz
UK MUA Limited

Arnold, Paisley
Purity Skincare Limited

Arora, Bachan Singh
Legacy Wholesalers Limited

Arora, Neel
Beautiful World Limited

Arshia, Khosrow
Velforms Limited

Arthurs, Richard
Jaden Cosmetics Limited

Arya, Reza
Bloom Artisan Brands Limited

Asad, Salman
Glow Beauty Shop Ltd
Paragon Enterprise Limited

Asadi Lari, Hamed
Asadilari Limited

Asaggar, Serena
Hairenvy Boutique Limited

Asante, Yaw
Deltagamma Limited

Asaria, Mohammed Mohsin
HCT Europe Limited

Asenov, Iliyan Asenov
Asenov Traders Ltd

Ashby, Alan Worster
Mebon Investment Limited

Ashcroft, Sarah Louise
Same Cosmetics Limited

Ashley, Jacqueline Louise Carolyn
Ashley & Co UK Ltd

Ashley, Laura, Prof
Elliott Nutrition Ltd
Nars & Elliott Healthcare Ltd

Asif, Mohammed Haroon
Arrah Ltd

Asif, Naseer Naseer
Asifall Ltd

Askarova, Jamila
Gazelli International Limited

Asmar, Shadi
Shadi's Hairdresser Ltd

Aspinall, Williams
Eifelcorp Consumer Care Ltd

Assendelft, Rutgerus Martines Maria
Grimas.co.uk Limited

Assi, Kristelle Audrey
My Pure Life-Style Limited

Ataei Khoshro, Sadaf
Otonix Limited

Atias, Kfir Yizhaq
Instant Beauty UK Limited

Attai, Yalda
Beauty Royale Ltd

Attwooll, Margaret
Parfums Christian Dior (U.K.) Ltd

Atwal, Narinji
Eurasia Property Limited

Atzesberger, Julia
Le Pure Limited

Auge, Stephane
Guerlain Limited

Auld, Susan Margaret
Spa Skincare Limited

Auty, Miranda
United Retail & Sourcing Ltd

Avcil, Dr Muhammet
Imperial Bioscience Ltd

Avwunu, Obatarhe
Cxlture Cosmetics Ltd

Awad, Ayham
Ayhamco Limited

Awan, Amir
Dupeshop Ltd

Awan, Faizan Ahmad, Doctor
Cutagen Ltd

Aweida, Sani George
Beta Novis Limited

Awobajo, Adewale Olukayode
Awobajo Brother's Limited

Awobajo, Jimmy Babajide
Awobajo Brother's Limited

Aydin, Alptekin
Cosmos Cosmetics Limited

Ayoub, Najib, Dr
NA Medical Care Ltd

Aysan, Umran
Mast - Art Group Limited

Ayyaz, Saira
Beauty Forever Limited

Azikiewicz, Damian Wieslaw
Azik Group Ltd
Top Beauty Brands Ltd

Azille, Chantelle Kimberley
Daisy Anai Limited

Babakir, Khidir Salim
Unac Salon Supplies Limited

Bacala, Elisabeta
EB Stores Ltd

Bach Kutschruetter, Javier
Puig UK Limited

Bache, Estelle
Mondor & Bache Ltd

Badawy, Ahmed
Layan Pharma Ltd

Badcham, George Patrick
G.P.B. Supplies Limited

Badezet, Olivier
Salon Success Limited

Badiru, Oluwatoyin
Venkh Retail Ltd

Bagedo, Enam
Bayan Ltd

Bahabri, Abdullah
Nota Nota Limited

Bahadur, Iltaf
Global Beauty Wholesale Ltd

Bahia, Harvinder
Forever Heng UK Limited
Niami1893 Ltd

Baig, Iqraa
Meviq Ltd

Baig, Mehvish
Meviq Ltd

Baig, Mirza
Box of Beauty Ltd

Baig, Roksana
MNF Commodities Ltd

Bailey, Douglas John
International Hair Cosmetics Ltd
Knight & Wilson Limited
Knight & Wilson Trading Ltd

Bailey, Eric John
International Hair Cosmetics Ltd
Knight & Wilson Limited
Knight & Wilson Trading Ltd

Bailey, Rowan Thomas
Tebs Distribution Limited

Bailo, Daniela
Crivalis Ltd

Bainborough, George Alan
Akwaaba Social Enterprises Ltd

Bainborough, Sally Jane Elizabeth
Akwaaba Social Enterprises Ltd

Bains, Gurdeep Singh
Bains and Daughters Limited

Baird-Murray, Kathleen
KBM London Limited

Bajer, Damian Andrzej
International Traders House P.I.T.

Bakari, Maryam
Franok Business Solutions Ltd

Baker, Lynne Denise
Calla Distribution Ltd

Bakhtar, Ahmad Mokhtar
Face & Beauty Limited

Bakhtiar, Soraya
Azaleo Limited

Balbo, Rogerio Fernando
Korban Beauty Limited

Balcerek, Mateusz Kacper
ULB Limited

Bales, Arthur David
Motion Junkies Limited

Balogun, Adebukola
Mabxclusive Limited

Balogun, Riliwan
Alade Ltd

Bambacas, Theodore Nicholas
Super Natural Apothecary Ltd.

Banafa, Abdulla Abdulkhaliq Abdulla
Banafa for Oud and Perfume Ltd

Banas, Mariusz
Jolly Rogers Crew Limited

Banda, Joseph Kambani
Renaissance Manyane Global Group Ltd

Bandali, Bana
Searching Plants Ltd

Banga, Rajinder Singh
Collection 1212 Limited
Lionmark Limited

Banks, Casey Mon-Ye
Face Fodder Limited

Banks, Joanna Linda
Whip Cosmetics Ltd

Bannister, Brian Peter
Cool Blades Limited

Bannister, Julie
Cool Blades Limited

Bannister, Lee Steven
Knight & Wilson Limited
Knight & Wilson Trading Ltd

Bannocks, John Paul
Wild Earth Botanicals Ltd

Bantleman, Barbara
Deep Red Marketing International Ltd

Bapu, Idris Mussa
Sublyme Cosmetics Limited

Baradat, Andre
Maximaliste Limited

Barbagelata, Charlie Claude
Beauty Masks Limited

Barbagelata-Fabes, Angela Mary Eileen
Beauty Masks Limited

Barbalich, Elizabeth Janet
Antipodes Europe Limited

Barbalich, Zoran John
Antipodes Europe Limited

Barber, Leslie Christopher
Surreal Health & Beauty Ltd

Bardusco-Marlow, Naomi Clara Katy
Love Henna Brows Limited
Ultimate Henna Brows Ltd

Barker, Christine Elizabeth
Basic Needs Ltd

Barker, Edward Peter
DKH Retail Limited

Barker, Simon Tennant
CRM Trading Limited
Glendale Group Limited
Glendale S/S Limited

Barker, Steven Anthony
SB Beauty Marketing Limited

Barker, Susan Maria
Initiative (UK) Limited

Barker, Terence William
Basic Needs Ltd

Barlow, Andrew William
FFC International Limited

Barns, Elena
AAA Edinburgh Ltd

Baron de Juan, Alfredo
Almirall Limited

Barrett, Graham John
Aenea Cosmetics Ltd

Barros Silva, Alia Samai
Ploom (U.K.) Limited

Barrow, Francesca
Ches Editions Ltd

Barry, Conor
Ink Oil Limited

Barry, Hazel Christine
H2K Limited

Barter, Stephen
SB Selected Beauty Ltd

Barthelmy, Colin Meredith
Myridium Active.Com Limited

Barthelmy, Kim Diane
Myridium Active.Com Limited

Barton, Mark
Ladd Cosmetics Ltd

Baruch, Dori
Clinibella Ltd

Barut, Altug
Vivatinell Limited

Baryliszyn, Jerzy
Okmarket24 Ltd

Barzesky, Joseph Kadish
Rich Cosmetics Ltd

Barzut, Velibor
Mega Direct Limited

Basera, Ganesh Singh
Tattva Ltd.

Basham, Brian Arthur
Skin & Tonic London Ltd

Bashir, Nazma
Solo Skin London Ltd

Bassi, Jasbir Kaur
Beauty Queen Limited

Bassin, Alan
Miluv Ltd

Bastin, Paul Rudolf
Headissimo Limited

Bates, Stephen Andrew
Aesthetic & Luxury Distribution Ltd

Bathawab, Ali Salem
AJ Active Enterprises Ltd

Batin, Fabia
FB Cosmetologist Limited

Batin, Mohammed Abdul
Naeemah & Al Farhad Ltd

Battrick, Marisa
Truthpaste Ltd

Batty, Krestyna
Janssen Cosmetics UK Ltd

Baugh, Jamie
Exoditi Limited

Baugh, Surinder
Trade Anchor Limited

Baxter, Christopher Roy
Exquisite Cosmetics Limited

Baxter, Jack Lawrence
Exquisite Cosmetics Limited

Bayer, Joseph John
Innovaderma PLC

Bayley, Meik
Fizzy Peach Ltd

Bayliss, Andrew
Cover Up Hairloss Ltd

Bazini, Samuel
Direct Supplies (2014) Limited
Unique Fragrances Limited
Warpaint Cosmetics (2014) Ltd
Warpaint Cosmetics Group Ltd
Warpaint Cosmetics Limited
Warpaint London PLC

Bazini, Sara Lisa
Direct Supplies (2014) Limited

Gobert, Frisca
The Bcara Ltd

Beadle, Amanda
Bedeaux Ltd

Beard, Louise Jane
Active Tan Limited

Pertev, Mustafa Eren
The Beard of Attraction Ltd

Sanya, Olumide Fred Abayomi
Mahc Beau UK & Europe Ltd

Field, Mitchell Laurence
The Beauty Alliance International

Geldzahler, Israel
The Beauty Center Ltd

Geldzahler, Baruch
The Beauty Center Ltd

Blaskovicova, Natalia
The Beauty Pod Limited

Feehan, Elizabeth Mary
The Beauty School Limited

Feehan, John Robert
The Beauty School Limited

Beck, Carolyne Ann
Elemental Herbology Limited

Beckett, Victoria Mary
Arbonne UK Limited

Bedacee, Arushka Devi Sooree
Online Motions Limited

Bedard, Jeffery Alan
Vita Liberata Limited

Bedford, Katherine Mary
Life's Big Stuff Ltd

Beese, Adam
Skintel Cosmetics Ltd

Beesley, Carl
Beauty at The Avenue Online Ltd

Beesley, Toby Roger
Modern Man Ltd

Beever, Stephen Colin
Beever Haircare Ltd

Begum, Rany
Lavelle Store UK Ltd

Begum, Shamshad
Glory Cosmetics Ltd

Behrendt, Sascha
Coffeinium Germania Ltd
Feinkost & Getranke Ltd

Belihart, Maya
MB Promotion Ltd.

Bell, Cherrelle
Lashed London Limited

Bell, Clodagh
C Beauty Agency Limited

Bell, David Marshall
ABC Beauty Limited

Bell, Stewart William
Georgie Salon Supplies Limited

Bellamy, William
Wild Kynd Ltd

Bellingham, Richard Douglas
Kind2 Limited

Belova, Zlatina
Bel Corporation Ltd

Belshaw, Alan
SHH Logistics Ltd

Belshaw, Jane
Perfume Addict (UK) Ltd

Benallal, Djamel
Drimex Limited

Benanbar, Badar Din
Nice Smell Trade Ltd

Benedetti, Peter
1CBDUK Ltd

Benjamin, Coline Casandra
Kurlysue Limited

Benjamin-Drysdale, Chelsie
Cosmetics of London Chelsie Ltd

Bennett, Christopher
Olfactive Thirty Eight Fragrances

Bennett, Nancy
Sawa Trading & Shipping Ltd

Benrejdal, Djamel
Le Parfum Ltd

Bentley, Michael Lewis
Hugworld Cristalinas UK Ltd

Berahavoi, Yury
AI Cosmetics Ltd

Berdai, Amine
Luxuria Generation Limited

Beresford, Lucy Jane
Synlatex Limited

Bergwerf, Catherine Mann Voogd
Amber House Limited
Square Spots Limited

Ahmed, Aiyub Abdullah
The Berkeley Square Cosmetics Co Ltd

Berliavsky Harshundia, Aida
Eden Perfumes Limited

Bernardinelli, Taliane
BM Supplier UK & Europe Ltd

Berrecloth, Daniel
Bigteal Industries Limited

Berrick, Hayley Barbara
ME & II Limited

Berrow, Paul
Plant Me Botanics Ltd

Berrow, Zak
Angel Remy Ltd

Bersos, Diamantis
Hydrea London Limited

Bertrand, Sumai
Spktra Limited

Besnard, Arthur Michel
Arthur Michel Cosmetics Distribution Ltd

Frenkel, Andre
The Bespoke Beauty Co Ltd

McMahon, Oliver
The Bespoke Beauty Co Ltd

Besso-Pianetto, Dhani
Labo Nine Limited

Bester, Keren
Chemical Poetry Ltd

Beyls, Pieter-Jan
Coriungo Limited

Bezy, Stephan Jean Paul Marie
L'Oreal (U.K.) Limited

Bhanji, Akbar Ali
Apex Trading Limited
East End Cosmetics Limited

Bhanji, Akbarali
Dream Glow Ltd

Bhanji, Shabir Ali
East End Cosmetics Limited

Bhanji, Shelina
Beautyzon Limited

Bhardwaj, Laghu
Dupeshop Ltd

Bhatia, Charu
Beauty Glow Wholesale Limited

Bhatia, Nikhil
Underground Girl London Ltd

Bhatt, Kuldeep Viren
Flowscent Limited

Bhatt, Mona Viren
Flowscent Limited

Bhatt, Viren Natwarlal
Flowscent Limited

Bhatty, Mabroor Ahmed, Dr
Esthetica Pure Ltd
Microskin Cosmeceuticals UK Ltd

Bhatty, Nicola Susan
Esthetica Pure Ltd
Microskin Cosmeceuticals UK Ltd

Bhavsar, Sachin
Ozone Perfumes and Cosmetics Ltd

Bhuta, Soab
Adam Michaels Group Ltd

Biddle, Samantha Alexandra
Jealous Cow Limited

Bieber, Kenneth George Selwyn
Universal Attraction (London) Ltd

Bielawski, Cezary
Kailijumei Ltd

Wahab, Khalid
The Big Wholesale Co Ltd

Jameson, Howard
The Big Wholesale Co Ltd

Hussain, Omar
The Big Wholesale Co Ltd

Bijma, Minke Petra
Perfume World Limited

Bilal, Muhammad
Iconic Perfumes Ltd

Bilal-Beccan, Latifah
True Scents Ltd

Lindstrom, Tuija Maarit Anneli
Mark Birch Hair Ltd

Bird, Paul
Ciao Brow Henna Limited

Bird, Rowena Jaqueline
Lush Ltd.

Biscoe, Benjamin Seymour
Fairy Dust Limited

Bish, Claudia Rosa
Tiggy Lashes Ltd

Bishop, Ian
Herb U.K. Limited
Organic Colour Systems Limited

Bissessur, Jason Rockyie
Galaxy Grooming Limited
Grooming Galaxy Limited

Bissessur, Letecia Malagayo
Galaxy Grooming Limited

Biurrarena Basulto, Javier
Monarch Health & Beauty Ltd.

Bizyukov, Alexey
Nevitrade Ltd

Bjorklund, Hakan
Neolife International Ltd

Blachut, Maciej
MS Rarytas Ltd

Walton, Angela
The Black Candle Company of Northumberland

Walton, Douglas Thomas
The Black Candle Company of Northumberland

Walton, Samantha Louise
The Black Candle Company of Northumberland

Black, Robyn
BLK Cosmetics Limited

Blackman, Evelyn Isabel
Loveve. Ltd

Blagden, Simon Paul
Le Lissage UK Limited

Blake, Michael
Dr Shea Ltd

Blakemore, Dave
Allies Network Ltd

Blayer, Paolo
Lord & Berry Ltd

Blickling, Patrik
A & P Blickling Ltd

Calero de Blickling, Ana Eugenia
A & P Blickling Ltd

Blinkovskaja, Ira
Blink Street Limited

Block, Andrew David
Cocobaba Ltd

Blondiaux, Philippe Bernard
Chanel Limited

Bloom, Alan Jeremy
Pinnacle Pharma Limited

Blow, Nicholas Alexander
Hairways 77 Limited

Blow, Roger Malcolm
Hairways 77 Limited

Blye, Paulette Rose
Natural Blends of Nature Ltd

Boadi, Kwame Opoku Michael
Valhalla Perfume Limited

Boateng, Vesta
Vesta London Beauty Ltd

Boctor, Nancy
Lazeeza Lashes Limited

Bodane, Anup
SGJ Perfumes Limited

Chatwin, Robert Claus
The Body Shop International Ltd

Filho, Itamar Gaino
The Body Shop International Ltd

Boev, Teodor
Cleardot Group Ltd

Bogusz, Daniel
Control Cosmetics Ltd

Boikou, Varvara
Zoeva UK Limited

Boillot, Laurent
Guerlain Limited

Bois Sevestre, Melanie Delphine Constance
Make Up for Ever U.K. Limited

Bolger, Steven
LW International Ltd

Bolton, Rebecca Kate
B.Cosmetics Ltd

Boman, Oonagh
Snob Distribution Limited

Bomford, Ben Robertson
Dermashack Limited

Bond, Jay
Brand Holdings Limited

Bond, Trevor
Brand Holdings Limited

Bondarenko, Sergii
Bioline Ltd

Bonner, Denise Anne
Neal's Yard (Natural Remedies) Ltd

Bonsu-Stewart, Rebecca
Sankofa Heritage Ltd

Boodi, Afzal
Onlinexclusive Limited

Boodoo-Lumbus, Rakhee
Rakhee LB Ltd

Boom, Evert Charles
Green Guru Enterprices Ltd.

Boothroyde, Keith
K.B. Salon Supplies Limited
Salon Supplies Limited

Bootle, Natalie Jayne
Diamonds on Demand Ltd

Borbiro, Gertrud Eva
Pandhy's UK Sweet Cosmetics Ltd.

Borissoff, Constantine Leo
Belsay Ltd

Boron, Andrzej
Luuann Limited

Borri, Giovanni
Atkinson London 1799 Ltd
Perfume Holding UK Limited

Borshchev, Andrei
Sanmex International Limited

Botchway, Quaye
Allies Network Ltd

Bottazzi, Guido
YWC (Yes We Can) Limited

Bottomley, Jason Carl
Mr B Skincare Limited

Guerci, Laure Pazery
Pazery Bouffard and Co Ltd

Bouguenon, Michael John
2B Enterprises Limited

Bouguenon, Victor Paul
2B Enterprises Limited

Bouit, Walid Brahim Abed
Essence Cosmetics Limited

Boukernous, Abdennour
Fragrance Weekly Ltd
Lom Trade Limited

Boukri, Taoufiq
Lime and Lead Global Ltd

Bounia, Samir
Moroccan Golden Sands Ltd

Boutros, Nouvriet
Nouvriet Boutros (UK) Ltd

Bouybayoune, Ihssane, Dr
Beauty Queen Milano Ltd

Bowes, Julie Marie
Yorkshire Beauty Supplies Ltd

Bowler, Patrick James
Cosmeceuticals Limited

Bowles, Jane Margaret
Skins Sexual Health Limited

Bowles, Jonathan Richard
Skins Sexual Health Limited

Bown, Rosaline
Rosmetics Aesthetics Limited

Bown, Stephen James
Istylists Limited

Boxall, Natasha Louise
Whip Cosmetics Ltd

Borissoff, Constantine Leo
Andre Boyard Perfumes Limited

Rughani, Ameet Chandubhai
Andre Boyard Perfumes Limited

Boyd, Phillip Duncan
Purity Derma Limited

Bracey, Daniel
Bracey Overseas Ltd

Bracher, Verity Kate
Meadow Farm Friends Ltd

Clennell, Stephen John
Anthony Braden Limited
Anthony Braden Online Ltd.

Knapman, Susan Lynn
Anthony Braden Online Ltd.

Bradshaw, Charles James Anthony
K588 Limited

Brady, Karren, Dr
Clarins & Felix Healthcare Ltd
Felix Medical Group Ltd

Brambilla, Attilio
Alfa Parf UK Ltd

Brams, Supadtra
Thai Wellness Ltd

Brandon, Dagmara
VY Club Limited

Brandon, Gerard
VY Club Limited

Brann, Nicholas Stephen
Lumos Products Limited

Brass, Sarah Dawn
Lore Originals Limited

Braun, David
DYB Tarding Ltd

Brealey, Anthony William
Bouffe Limited

Breeze, Curtis Saul
Flutter Cosmetics Limited

Brewster, Teresa Anne Elizabeth
Lefami Cosmetics Group Ltd

Brezovar, Valerija
Quality Check Ltd

Bright, Steven Corby
Neora UK Limited

Chessell, Paul
The Brighton Group Ltd

Brimicombe, Dawn Rachel
Cosmetic Bases Limited

Brimicombe, Mark Richard
Cosmetic Bases Limited

Brinkmeier, Olaf
Alpha Auriga Limited

Glosz, Viktor
G & J Britton Consulting Ltd

Brock, Todd Lawrence
CBee (Europe) Limited

Brod, Daniel Richard
Bramley Products Ltd

Brodie, Arizona
Arizona Botaniq Limited

Bronson, Michael
Flynn Group of Companies Ltd
Rimmel & Flynn Healthcare Ltd

Brooke, Amanda Jane
Grossmith Limited

Brooke, Simon Peter
Grossmith Limited

Brookes, Jessica
Beautiful Body Limited

Brookes, Zaine Damion
Wonderful Life PHBS Ltd

Brooks, Thomas Lloyd
T L Brooks Limited

Brooks, Deane
Beauty Fort Limited

Brooks, Warren Michael
11 Scent Limited

Whichello, Denise
Denise Brown Limited

Whichello, Garry
Denise Brown Limited

Brown, Amanda Michaela Joyce
Ezili Botanicals Limited

Brown, Chantelle
Harmonious Brown Limited

Brown, David Paul
A B International Limited

Brown, James Nathan
I Love Cosmetics Limited

Brown, Johnathon
Olfactive Thirty Eight Fragrances

Brown, Kimberley Jane
Bare Cosmetics Ltd

Brown, Lynette Amanda
Beiersdorf UK Ltd.

Brown, Paula Rachel
Fleeks Hair & Beauty Limited

Brown, Rebecca Louise
Cochabamba Parfums Limited

Brown, Rebecca
A B International Limited

Brown, Shackeema Donna-Kay
East Cosmetics Limited

Browne, Andrew Graham
Beauty Senses Limited

Browne, Crystal Dale
Natural Sheaness Ltd

Browne, Toby Rowley
Pharmacare (Europe) Limited

Browne-Marke, Tobi Mistura
Joyganics Ltd

Brownlow, Melanie
Hothouse Holdings Limited

Brownsell, Alexandra
Bleach Makeup Limited

Bruckschlogl, Ledwina
Niki & Co Ltd

Bruel, Anne-Veronique
Fresh Cosmetics Limited

Bruney, Lianne
Liaver Limited

Bryan, Crystal Paris Jadine
Pink Lush Lips Ltd

Bryant, David John
Pern Consumer Products Limited

Brzeska, Sylwia Monika
Art-Eclair Limited

Bublic, Igor
IBS Shopeye World Ltd

Buck, Hannah Claire
Calmer Solutions Limited

Buckland, Richard Mark
Synlatex Limited

Buckley, Amy
Phoenix Beauty Ltd

Budahazy, Peter Miklos
Helia-D UK Ltd

Budner, Jacek
Charms Europe Ltd

Buhova, Vassilena
Red Gold London Ltd

Buirski, Alexander Ivan
Lavant Beauty and Personal Care Ltd

Bulbul, Khalid
R10 Labs Skincare Ltd

Buldeo, Nitasha, Dr
Wwinc. Ltd

Bumanis, Renars
Earthbreath Ltd

Buncombe, Rochelle Marie
RHI By ROC Ltd

Bunyan, Katherine
Finders International Limited

Burdak, Janusz Jan
Peters Cosmet Ltd

Burdese, Laura Luciana
Acqua di Parma Limited

Burelier, Aline
Make Up for Ever U.K. Limited

Burgin, Chad William
Bbeauty Lounge Cosmetics Ltd
Bbeauty Lounge Limited
Bluesky Cosmetics Limited
Bluesky Products Limited

Burke, Joanne
Green Sprouts Limited

Burnett, Lynn
Yates-Lee and Burnett Limited

Burniston, Christopher Robert
Colgate-Palmolive (U.K.) Ltd

Burns, Saasha
Bear Journal Limited

Burr, Sarah Jane
Thalasso Ltd

Burrell, Antonia
Gracetree Ltd

Burris, Matthew Omari
Sheyton Ltd

Burton, Audrey Alaine
Rub-a-Dub Scrub Ltd

Burton, Max Richard Leslie
Hamiltons of Canterbury Ltd

Busby, Nathan
Headrocka Ltd

Bush, Andrew Robert
KDM Supplies Limited

Bush, Beverley Anne
KDM Supplies Limited

Butcher, Emily Louise
For All Dogkind Limited

Butcher, Joanna Claire
For All Dogkind Limited

Buterbaugh, Eric Scott
EBF Europe Ltd

Butron, Carlos Enrique
Brands de Luxe Co Ltd

Butt, Annam Tariq
HA Distribution Limited

Butt, Duraiz Hussain
Eacho Green Ltd

Butt, Haris Tariq
HA Distribution Limited

Butt, Kasim Learbuch
Bella Rootz Limited

Butt, Zahid Sharif
Haltrade UK Ltd

Butterfield, Mark Clifford
Corium Health Limited

Byers, Michael
Jojoba Cosmetics Limited

Bygrave, Karl Joseph
Lush Ltd.

Byrne, John Robert
Vlinder Cosmetics Ltd

Byrne, Louise Clair
Vlinder Cosmetics Ltd

Byrne, Rosalie
RSJ Trading Limited

Cadden, Andrew
Cadden & Lee Limited

Cadwell, Ian
Westfield House Distributors Ltd

Cadwell, Kris
Westfield House Distributors Ltd

Cadwell, Marion
Westfield House Distributors Ltd

Cahill, Natalie
Base Pro Artists Ltd

Cai, Di
Mepro Cosmetic Ltd

Cairney, Henry Patrick Fleming
Trade Smart Marketing Limited

Cairns, Natalie Bridgette
OhMyLashUK Ltd

Calapa, Giorgio
Magia BLV International Ltd

Calcraft, Robert Michael
K588 Limited

Caldwell, Damian
Bespoke Hospitality Supplies Ltd

Caldwell, Teodora Georgieva
Dermafood Limited

Callan, Kieran Winston
Innovaderma PLC

Callander, Simon
DKH Retail Limited

Callens, Fabien Georges Jacques
Classic Beaute Limited

Camacho Jardim Fernandes, Alcinda
Julien Miguel Ltd

Cameron, Charmaine
Nu-E55ence Ltd

Campbell Davys, Lydia
Freestyle Trade (UK) Limited

Campbell, Aston
305 Professionals Ltd

Campbell, Cameron
Marque of Brands Limited

Campbell, Desmond
Iconic Fragrances Ltd

Campbell, Emma Louise
A Pony Called Steve Ltd

Campbell, Leanna Natasha
Cutelovelee Limited

Campbell, Luke Richard
Uppercut Deluxe Co Limited

Campbell, Nicole
Saint Cosmetics Ltd

Campbell, Parisimo
East Cosmetics Limited

Campbell, Richard
Freestyle (Trade) Ltd.
Freestyle Trade (UK) Limited

Campbell, Samantha
Bleach Makeup Limited

Campbell, Susan Gai
Kind2 Limited

Cantarelli, Bruno
Salus Cutis Ltd

Cantarelli, Nataliya
Salus Cutis Ltd

Cao, Fangyu
UK Heluns Industry Co., Ltd

Capstick, Robin Paul
Realine Beauty Limited

Caraly, Philip
Beltech Limited

Carey, Steven David
Steven Carey Hair & Beauty Ltd

Saunders, Veronica Louise
Steven Carey Hair & Beauty Ltd

Carey, Richard George
Shhuk Ltd

Carman, Angela Victoria
Hairways 77 Limited

Carman, Linda Denise
Initiative (UK) Limited

Carnahan, Elizabeth
Gracefruit Limited

Carnahan, Paul
Gracefruit Limited

Carnegie, Georgina
Brownie Beauty Products Cosmetics Ltd

Carnell, Zoe
DC Salon Products Ltd

Horcliptes, Anthony
Ayesha Carolina Limited

Horcliptes, Ayesha Moonla
Ayesha Carolina Limited

Carpenter, Victoria
Happy Carrot Skincare Ltd

Carr, Dominique Claire
Euro Healthcare Services Ltd
Eurocare Impex Services Ltd

Carr, Stephen John Wiley
World Links Europe Limited

Carrington, Donna
Divine Natural Limited

Carrington, John Andrew
Divine Natural Limited

Carriol, Kirsten
Lanolips Limited

Carroll, Raymond Philip
Bond Street Cosmetics Limited

Carslaw, Joyce Baillie
Tanovation Ltd

Carstairs, Ryan
Chirp Body Ltd

Carter, Alan Steven
Millennium Nails Europe Ltd

Carter, Annie-Louise
Beauty Bash Limited

Carter, Christopher
Olivia Kate Cosmetics Ltd

Carter, David
Horatio London Holdings Ltd

Carter, Larisa
Horatio London Holdings Ltd

Carter, Richard James
YJX Group PLC

Carter, Yvonne
Millennium Nails Europe Ltd

Carvalho Se, Luciana
Forest Hive Ltd

Cash, Julia
Mad Beauty Limited

Cash, Trevor Ian
Mad Beauty Limited

Casin, Alexandre Matthieu Valdemar
Oh My Scent Limited

Cassidy, Christine
Kendo Brands Limited

Castello, Jade
Nalla Skincare Ltd

Castillian, Jessica
Hekiti Cosmetics Ltd

Catala Moncho, Pedro Juan
Twelve Beauty Ltd

Cate, Karen Sue
Kendo Brands Limited

Cathcart, William Neagle
Mane (UK) Limited

Catherwood, Ryan Michael
Apex Beard Co Ltd

Catto, Rawya Roumieh
Lavant Beauty and Personal Care Ltd

Catton, Cheryl
London Beauty Limited

Catton, Stuart John
F.D.D. International Limited
London Beauty Limited

Caulfield, Kelly Marie
KMC's Fabulous Cosmetics Ltd

Causer, Peter John
Roja Dove Limited

Cavan, Kathryn Rachel
Jess Nails Limited
Phyto Therapeutics Limited
True Brit London Limited

Cavill, Simon Rafe
Beegood Enterprises Limited

Ceicans, Janis
Solo JC Trade Ltd

Cembala, Robert Jozef
Labrayon Cosmetiques France UK Ltd

Cesarano, Christine
Create Images Ion Limited

Cesarano, Gerardo
Create Images Ion Limited
P.R. Professional Salon Supplies Ltd

Cesarano, Mark
P.R. Professional Salon Supplies Ltd

Cesarano, Peter
P.R. Professional Salon Supplies Ltd

Cha, Luoyi
CZ Cosmetics Ltd.

Chadwick, Alan
Salon Select (NI) Limited

Chadwick, Denise
Salon Select (NI) Limited

Chaggar, Gurjit Singh
Bbeauty Lounge Cosmetics Ltd

Chaggar, Jasvir Singh
Sansuri Hair & Beauty Supplies and Training

Chaggar, Narinder Kaur
Sansuri Hair & Beauty Supplies and Training

Chala, Bernadette
Arbonne UK Limited

Chalme, Yannick
L'Oreal (U.K.) Limited

Chalmers, Alana Marie
Harpar Grace International Ltd

Chambers, Kerry
Incorporated Beauty Limited

Chambers, Neil Jonathon
Sandgroper Limited
Sun Zapper UK Limited

Chambers, Stewart
Incorporated Beauty Limited

Channa, Reena
Reevis Chan Ltd

Chan, Gary Kai Wai
Chronicles Medical Consulting Ltd

Chan, Tony Chien Feng
Pink Beauty Supplies (UK) Ltd.

Chandler, Reginald Keith
Joy Limited
Star Qualities Ltd

Chandler-Day, Fiona Jane
Khuba Limited

Chandra, Anuradha
Q River Limited

Chandra, Rajiv
Q River Limited

Chandra, Tara
Here We Flo Ltd

Chang, Jinyoung Victor
J.Cat Beauty UK Ltd

Chang, Szu-Yun
All-Around Infinity Limited

Chansevikul, Siripan
Adnoz Limited

Chapman, Sarah
Sarah Chapman Ltd.

Durrell, Heather Rodgers
Sarah Chapman Ltd.

Charalambous, Christina
Spring and Underworld Ltd

Charalambous, Zacharias
Doers Skincare Limited

Charfi, Gael
Fresh Cosmetics Limited

Charles, Charlene
Bemysoul Ltd

Charnock, Jamie
Yazmae Cosmetics Limited

Chatzigiannis, Efstratios
Ila Pothecary Limited

Chau, Pik Keung
Riway International Group (Euro) Ltd
Riway International Group (UK) Ltd
Riway Ltd

Chaudary, Esaa Rahman
By Al Kindi Ltd

Chaudhry, Fahim Ali
Fox Cosmetics Ltd

Chaudhry, Haris Altaf
Innovaderma PLC

Chawla, Virendra K
Unidus Limited

Cheah, Ning Chiann
Botanik Beauty Limited

Cheetham, Dominic Francis John
Skin Matrix HD+ Cosmetology Ltd

Chen, Aie
Lumine Beauty Ltd

Chen, Hui
Unigrand Group Limited

Chen, Jiefeng
Qiaochu Trading Co. Ltd

Chen, Liangmei
Chanson Worldwide Limited

Chen, Lina
Markwins Beauty Brands International
Markwins Beauty Products Ltd

Chen, Lingzhi
France Eclavour Cosmetic Ltd

Chen, Sisi
Glochina Trading UK Ltd.

Chen, Sung Tsei
Markwins Beauty Brands International
Markwins Beauty Products Ltd

Chen, Yang
Carol Skins Ltd

Chen, Yun Krystal, Dr
Cambridge Sprouts Limited

Chen, Zongqiong
Louts Remit Beautiful International Group Co.,

Chenary, Azam
Medical Technology Caraco (MYC) Ltd.

Chenary, Hamid
Medical Technology Caraco (MYC) Ltd.

Cheney, Vincent
Procare Women Health Limited

Cheng, Qian
K Wholesale Limited

Cheng, Yu-Hui
Bottlemate UK Limited

Cheraghi, Ali Asghar
Cedron Ltd.

Chetwynd Jarvis, Emma
Skinnydip Skincare Limited

Cheung, Kar Lam
Shuei Trading UK Ltd

Chew, Justine
Millennium Nails North West Ltd

Chiang, Pang Ngan
Colourscent Limited

Chikosi, Tanyaradzwa Fidelity
Grand Beaute Ltd

Chilarska, Paulina, Dr
Young Now Ltd

Chimanayi, Hilda Aldina
Look Fab Limited

Chin, Leo
Melanative Ltd

Chinnery, Samantha Ophelia
Magpie's Ocean Ltd

Chiriac, Virgil Sorin
Rekze Laboratories Ltd

Chitty, Nicholas
Skintel Cosmetics Ltd

Chiu, Hiang Sim
Riviere Groupe (Europe) Ltd

Chodera, Aleksandra
Biola Beauty Ltd

Chomicki, Lukasz
Sueno Cosmetics Ltd

Chonzi, Stellah Linda
Sisi Cosmetics Ltd

Choudhry, Akbar
Kiss Products UK Limited

Choudhry, Elizabeth
Kiss Products UK Limited

Choudhry, Imran
Swiss Trading .UK. Ltd

Choudhury, Jahangir Kabir
J K International Trading Ltd

Choudhury, Khandoker
TAC Perfumes & Cosmetics (UK) Ltd

Choudhury, Nadir
HE Products Ltd

Choudhury, Nazia
N Organics Ltd

Choudhury, Shahibul Ambia
Budget Beauty Limited

Choudhury, Tasbirul Ahmed
TAC Perfumes & Cosmetics (UK) Ltd

Chow, Mei-Ting Jessica
Make-Up International Limited

Chow, Sheung Wah
Blk Deer Co. Ltd

Chowdhary, MD Yosuf Kamal
Express Online Superstore, London Ltd

Chowdhury, Jabir Ahmed
J K International Trading Ltd

Christal, Dean Vegas
Liqwd Limited

Christian, Clive
Clive Christian Perfume Ltd

Salam, Ahmad
Clive Christian Perfume Ltd

Shaheen, Rahan Ahmad
Clive Christian Perfume Ltd

MacFie, Andrew James
Clive Christian Perfume Ltd

Nelson-Bennett, Amy Elizabeth
Clive Christian Perfume Ltd

Chu, Mei Manager
Kathleen Natural Limited

Chung, Shil Hwan
Black Gold Hair Limited

Chung, Terence Tsz-Hong, Dr
Fruu Cosmetics Limited

Chuter, Sharon
Uoma Beauty Group Limited

Chyntia, Michelle
Wash Your Mouth Out Ltd

Cicek, Mustafa
Flower Cosmetic Ltd

Cientanni, Gerardo James
Nail Perfection Limited

Cientanni, Maria
Nail Perfection Limited

Cientanni, Theresa Louise
Nail Perfection Limited

Ciftci, Kemal
Barbers Warehouse Ltd

Cil, Zekeriye
Seba Trade Limited

Cireasa, Rodica-Maria
Boutique Parfum Limited

Cisar, Karolina Izabela
Business Angels Syndicate Ltd

Clapcott, Michael
Enhance You Ltd
Enhancing You Limited

Clarence, Sheila Grace
Tansi Packaging Solutions Ltd

Clark Prakash, Preyanka Jayanti
Bloomtown Ltd

Clark, Andrew
Nut Dust Ltd

Clark, Daniel John
F.D.D. International Limited

Clark, David Thomas
F.D.D. International Limited

Clark, Mia Elizabeth
Amour Pigments Ltd

Clark, Nadia
Sweet Pea Soaps Co Ltd

Clark, Wayne
Lief Essentials Limited

Clarke, Anne Catherine
Bendito Trading Limited

Clayton Smith, Ian
Prism Parfums Limited

Clayton-Wright, David Grayham
NaturallyClearSkin Limited

Cleall-Harding, Geoffrey Stuart
Pharma Medico Limited

Cleeve, Abigail Claire
Skinsense Ltd

Clelland, Andrew
HDDirect Limited

Clifford, Kevin James
BBA Products Limited

Coates, Emma
Skin Health Solutions Ltd

Codeghini, Giorgio
Santa Code Limited

Codeghini, Giselle Almeida
Santa Code Limited

Coffey, Colin
He-Shi Enterprises Ltd

Cogan, Leon
Ital Living Market Ltd

Cohen, Carl
Direct Salon Supplies Limited

Cohen, Howard David
Serene House UK Limited

Cohen, Oren
Dovedale Limited

Cohen, Rafael
Dovedale Limited

Cohen, Valerie Ann
Serene House UK Limited

Cohen, Yosi
Natasha Denona Make Up Ltd.

Colbert, David Anthony
NYDG UK Limited

Colborne, David Simon
Adam and Eve Distribution Ltd

Colborne, Karen
Adam and Eve Distribution Ltd

Cole-Burke, Jelisa
Roots Are Remedies Ltd

Coleman, Carol Ann
Designer Fragrances Limited
Jean Christian Perfumes Ltd

Coleman, Donna
Beauty Stable Ltd

Coleman, Mica Frances
Oh So Locks Ltd

Coleman, Robin Nicholas
Up Roar Ltd.

Coleman, Thomas Martin
Designer Fragrances Limited
Jean Christian Perfumes Ltd

Coleman, Thomas
UK Brand Holdings Ltd

Coleman-Mitchell, Dexter
DSE Companies Limited

Collasse, Richard Maurice
Chanel Limited

Collier, James
Active Tan Limited

Collier, Robert
Collier & Wood Ltd

Bedi, Alice
Cath Collins Devon Ltd

Collins, Anthony Lee
House of Kendra Ltd

Collins, Jenna
Little Big Brands Ltd

Collins, Laurence John
Bali Secrets Ltd

Collins, Nicholas John Heywood
Dr. Organic Limited
Optima Consumer Health Limited

Collins, Peter John
Skincare Cornwall Ltd

Collins, Phillip James
County Sales Limited

Collins, Sharon Mary
Lubatti Limited

Collins, Tinu Amy
T4Colins Beautifician Ltd

Collins, Yarden
Skincare Cornwall Ltd

Collison, Jason Paul
Electimuss Limited

Elmamoun, Alia
Alia Collyns Cosmetics Ltd

Comyn, Jane Fairrie
Watsoap.Com Limited

Conlin, Aidan
Spa Pro Ltd

Conlin, Michael Shawn
Spa Pro Ltd

Connolley, Leah Georgia
LGC Cosmetics Ltd

Connor, Gregory John
Vivacy Laboratoires Ltd

Connors, Daniel
Brandaroma Limited

Conran, Jasper Alexander Thirlby
Jasper Conran Perfumes Limited

Constantine, Jack
Lush Ltd.

Constantine, Margaret Joan
Lush Ltd.

Constantine, Mark
Lush Ltd.

Contesotto, Claudia
Oakhill Luxury Ltd

John, Matthew
The Convent Venue Limited

Cook, Andrew
Glamify Beauty Limited

Cook, Dean Garth
Hothouse Holdings Limited

Cook, Frederick Leonard
NC Import Limited

Cook, Gregory Paul
Doterra (Europe) Ltd

Cook, Stephen David
4M Cosmetics Limited

Cooke, Kieran
Gentlemend Ltd

Cooney, Alison Jean
A & R Salon Enterprises Ltd

Cooper, Dana Marie
Luscious Skincare Ltd

Cooper, Edward
Active Skincare Limited

Cooper, Leyla Muna
Active Skincare Limited

Cooper, Robert William
MH Products Limited

Cooper, Yolanda
Paradoxx Ltd

Corker, Barry John
Pricecheck Toiletries Limited

Corkill, Nicholas James
Skin & Tonic London Ltd

Corley, Benjamin David
Corley Capital Limited

Corley, Chloe Lewtas
Corley Capital Limited

Cormack, Simon George
Purelonia Ltd

Hawthorne, Elizabeth Wyllie
Elizabeth Cornelius Limited

Cornelius, Guy Dominic
GCKK Ltd

Corner, James
Nut Dust Ltd

Cornwall, Randy Lindo
Lese & Lista Ltd

Corral Casero, Raquel
Quelsa Ltd

Corry, Patricia
PL Distribution Ltd

Cosgrave, Sean Antony
TheManeCo Ltd

Begum, Rukshana
The Cosmetics Store Ltd

Costantino, Filippo
Nefil Ltd

Costello, Kathleen Anne
UK Mineral Make-Up Limited

Cotton, Joseph
A & B Supply Co. Limited

Cottrell, David Anthony
Cosmetia UK Limited

Coulter, Gregory Owen
Glow Consumer Products UK Ltd

Coumarakichenane, Daniel
Europebro Wholesalers Ltd

Cound, Timothy
Synlatex Limited

Counsell, Rosemary Frances
Boots International Limited

Cousins, Kevin Mark
Protec Botanica Ltd
Protec Ingredia Limited

Cowell, David
Q River Limited

Cracknell, Martin Paul
True Affinity Limited

Craig, Elena
Natural Beauty Import Limited

Craig, Sally Ann
Warpaint London PLC

Crisp, David Adrian
CP Parfums Ltd
Valorem Capital One Ltd
Valorem Distribution Ltd

Croce, Raffaele
Crazy Smiles Group Ltd

Croft, Andrew
Atlantis Research Limited
Pure Skincare Limited

Croke, Jordan
Sang Real Tattoo Ltd

Crombleholme, Lisa
Speak Beauty Limited

Crombleholme, Philip
Speak Beauty Limited

Cross, Rebecca Charlotte
Jealous Cow Limited
Nails and Co (Midlands) Ltd

Cross, Sarah Jane
Code Beautiful Limited

Cross, Sophie Elizabeth
Ere Perez UK Limited

Crovara, Mariapia
Naturity Cosmetics Ltd

Crowe, Eleanor Howard
Pearl & Rocky Limited

Crowne, Ashley
Aviva Health Solutions Limited

Crumblehulme, Steven John
LTSC Ltd

Cruz, Mayelin Solorzano
Mlaveau Cuban Origins Ltd

Csernatony, Oliver
B & O Natural Cosmetics Ltd

Csizmadia, Teodora
Theodory Ltd

Cucicea, Claudia Liliana
Cosmetiqa Ltd

Cucu, Gabriel-Lucian
FHM Consulting Ltd

Cudby, Stefan
Adible Limited

Cudjoe, Judith Miranda
Lana's Beauty Box Ltd

Cullura, Leonardo
Perfume Holding UK Limited

Culmer, Medwin John
Bloomtown Ltd

Cumarasamy, Uthayakumar
Amazon Healthcare Ltd

Cumberbatch, Nicholas
Trimmz Ltd

Cummings, Paul Barry
Smart Nails (UK) Ltd

Cunniffe, Sheena Johnston
Hive of Beauty Limited

Cunningham, Josias
Absolute Cosmetic Essentials Ltd

Cunningham, Vicktesha
Vtessia Cosmetic Ltd

Kassim, Folake
The Curl Coach Ltd

Curquejo, Joshua
Torcall of Edinburgh Ltd

Curran, Chantelle
Chintys Ltd

Curran, Liam
Livoliv Cosmetics Ltd.

Curran, Sean Martin
Paradoxx Ltd

Curran, Susan Marie
Livoliv Cosmetics Ltd.

Curry, Mark
Be Fast Innovation Services Ltd
Brand Evangelists for Beauty Ltd

Curtis, Ermila
Wiv Global Limited

Curtis-Broni, Princess
Lavish London Cosmetics Ltd.

Cutler, Hannah Christian
Earth Goddess Ltd

Czik, Janet
Finders International Limited

Czik, Rebecca
Finders International Limited

Czik, Robert
Finders International Limited

D'arcy, Mark
Herb U.K. Limited
Organic Colour Systems Limited

D'inverno, Bethany Amber
Cacti Cosmetics Ltd

D'ornano, Christine
Sisley UK Limited

D'ornano, Philippe
Sisley UK Limited

Da Costa, Natalie
Eden's Daughter Limited

Da Graca, Teresa Paula
Pure Swiss Aesthetics Ltd

Da Silva, Maria Madalena Lemes
M & M Import Ltd

Dad, Mohammad Aadam
Guerison Skin Solutions Ltd

Dahl, Bengt Algot
KPACA Limited

Crosby, Stephen Michael
The Daimon Barber Limited

Neelands, Leo
The Daimon Barber Limited

Dalle-Molle, Pascal
Takasago (U.K.) Limited

Dalley, Alexander James
Infinity K Ltd

Dalton, John Robert
Pareto Cosmedics Ltd

Daly, Helen Elizabeth
Daly Beauty Limited

Daly, Kenneth John
JML Cosmetics Limited

Damoison, Janis
Oilyspirit Ltd

Danbury, Jo
Manas Organics Ltd

Collinson, Kelly
The Dancing Unicorn Limited

Dang Ngoc, Son
Glasgow Nails & Beauty Supplies Ltd

Dang, Toan Ngoc
TJ Nail Supplies Ltd

Dangata, Esther
Vitaglow Ltd

Daniel, Reynell
Mlle Cosmetics Co Ltd

Daniel, Singa Paulo
JCB Skincare Limited

Daniels, Adrian John
Josie Rose Ltd

Daniels, Anna Lily
Josie Rose Ltd

Daniilidis, Charalampos
Live Rich Academy Limited

Dankyi, Abigail
Theglossfairy Ltd

Danzig, Alastair
Purederma Ltd

Darbost, Joanne Elizabeth
Cilko Ltd

Darbyshire, Georgina
Georgie Salon Supplies Limited

Daremi, Moeiyed
Global One Wholesale Ltd

Daridon, Johann Gabriel Sarmes
Arrogant Limited

Dart, Hilary
Paradoxx Ltd

Darwiche, Hussein
Pinoline Trading Co Ltd

Darwin, Kathryn Jane
Palmsextra Limited

Dasani, Rakesh Dhirajlal
Enfield Distribution Ltd

Dashani, Deep Jayprakash Dashani
Ibeautheart Limited

Dattani, Ashitkumar
Prime Skincare Ltd

Dattani, Jennica Gillian
Prime Skincare Ltd

Dattani, Prian Perry
Prime Skincare Ltd

Dattu, Maleka
Merumaya Limited

Datwani, Kumar Dayaram
Ives Lab Ltd

Daukante, Jurgita
Cosmedi Limited

Dave, Purvi
PSM Vision Limited

David Roy, Stephanie Marie-Pierre
Fresh Cosmetics Limited

David, Jessica Matondo
Onyx Clothing Ltd

Davids, Chloe
Chloe Davids Limited

Davies, Bethany Jane Rose
Fatale Cosmetics Limited

Davies, Carlos
Jouer Jouer Limited

Davies, Charles Ian Osborn
Scrubd Ltd

Davies, Diane Susan
Temple Spirit Ltd
Woldscot Limited

Davies, Haylee
HD Cosmetics Ltd

Davies, Helena Colette
Ukab Limited

Davies, Huw Noel
Ukab Limited

Davies, Oludamilola
Gridt Beauty Ltd

Davies, Steve
Meilikki Ltd

Davies, Vanessa
Varama Limited

Davies, Wyndham Glyn
Temple Spirit Ltd
Woldscot Limited

Davis, James Edward
Herra Hair Care Limited

Davis, Leanne
Heavenly Body Ltd

Davis, Mark Leonard
Phils (Wholesale) Limited

Davis, Sylvia
Phils (Wholesale) Limited

Davison, Tristan
Afex Skin Care Ltd

Dawkins, Marie Helen
Impulse Global Solutions Ltd

Dawkins, Steven
Impulse Global Solutions Ltd

Dawodu, Fatimo
Total Beauty Ltd

Dawood, Hava
Surrati Perfumes Limited

Dawson, Christopher
Elko Electrical Ltd.

Bowers, Dale Daxon
Tom Daxon Limited

Bowers, Thomas Jay Daxon
Tom Daxon Limited

Day, Alison Claire
Aromaderme UK Limited
Aveda Limited
Editions de Parfums Limited
Le Labo UK Limited

Day, Melissa Niroshini
Niroshini Skincare Limited

Dayal, Hiten Jackis
KMI Brands Limited

De Cruz, Adam
Tententen Limited

De Fries, Cristina
Finest Mineral Make Up Limited
Muse Make Up Ltd

De Fries, William Francis Alan
Vett Limited

De Glanville, Jack Edward
Beautynet Limited

De Glanville, Liam Giles
Beautynet Limited

De Groose, Tracy Anne
Beached Limited

De La Poeze, Christophe
Interparcos U.K. Limited

De Laere, Barbara
Aveda Limited

De-Bique, Peter
Herba Skincare Limited

Deal, Katherine
Kathy Salon Equipment Limited

Dean, David
Deeco Supplies Limited

Dean, Paul
UK Direct Imports Ltd

Dehghani, Mohammad
Myego Ltd

Dei-Danquah, George Kofi
Into Exports Limited

Deitsch, Ivor
Lambsmead Limited

Deitsch, Lancelot Piers Duncan
Lambsmead Limited

Deitsch, Sandra Estelle
Lambsmead Limited

Deitsch, Sebastian Richard Oliver
Lambsmead Limited

Del Castillo, Artem
United Nomads Limited

Del-Greco, Paolo Francis
BBT Products Limited

Delafon, Frederic Jean Laurent
United Perfumes Limited

Della Bruna, Massimo
Intertrade Group Ltd

Delray, Maria
Jeunvie Ltd

Demaine, John George
Glorious Brands Ltd.

Demetroudi, Elias
Novmedic Limited

Demirchi, Jale
Paint It Orange Ltd

Dempster, Sharna
Boujelle Ltd

Denby, Matthew Robert
Macden Beauty Ltd

Deng, Monica
Express Hair and Beauty Supply Ltd

Field, Mitchell Lawrence
Leighton Denny Limited

Denny, Leighton
Leighton Denny Limited

Hammer, George Christopher
Leighton Denny Limited

Denver, Kirsty Diane
Attraxion Cosmetics Ltd.

Deren, Waclaw
Zoe Lane Ltd

Deroulede, Arnaud Marie Alfred
Cosmetiques de France Ltd.

Deroulede, Capucine Marie Camille
Pharmafrance Ltd.

Deroulede, Isabelle Marie Francoise
Dermafrance Ltd.

Derville, Vianney Marie Hugues
L'Oreal (U.K.) Limited

Dervisevic, Hava
Hava Traders Limited

Desai, Sunil
Millenium Fragrance Limited

Desforges, Charles Desmond, Dr
DLG Partners Limited

Desforges, Edouard-Henri Olivier
DLG Partners Limited

Deshpande, Pritha Nikhilesh
Arowell Products Ltd

Desouza-Willock, Sasha Nicole
Zealousco Limited

Despax, Phillipe
La Prairie (UK) Limited

Deutsch, Irene Susan
ME & II Limited

Devetta, Dominic Marc John
Shay & Blue Ltd

Devin, Paul Gregory
Beautyge Fragrances Holdings Ltd

Dewar, Laura Catherine
Phyto Pharma Limited

Dewar, Laura
Phyto Pharm Limited

Dewsbury-Ennis, Sabina
Beanies Beauty Lab Ltd

Dharmaraj, Dyran Lambert
Three Beauties of London Ltd

Dharmaraj, Rajaram
Three Beauties of London Ltd

Dhelens, Roger Stephane
Colbico Limited

Dhillon, Sara Louise
Beauty Solutions Global Ltd

Di Gianvincenzo, Fabrizio
Zagorah Ltd

Di Maio, Enzo
Shivax International Ltd

Di Maio, Letizia
Shivax International Ltd

Di Majo, Giancarlo
Markwins Beauty Brands International

Diaper, Christopher
Global Couture (UK) Ltd
Hairways (Hair & Beauty) Ltd
Hairways Direct Limited

Diaper, John Edward
Global Couture (UK) Ltd
Hairways (Hair & Beauty) Ltd
Hairways Direct Limited

Diaper, Julie
Hairways (Hair & Beauty) Ltd

Dickson, Pamela
Dermalogica (UK) Limited
Ren Ltd

Dimov, Orlin Nikolov
Diamond Brands Limited

Din, Shadab, Dr
Nixsi Limited

Dina, Adedayo
Anita Brows Cosmetics Limited

Alawode, David
David Dinero Ltd

Ding, Cui
Cuelyine Limited

Ding, Shun
Top Beauty Limited

Dionisi, Gianni Gaetano Alberto
72 Hair Limited
72 Hair Retail Limited
Green & Dionisi Ltd

Diop, Ibrahima
Cosmolovely Limited

Dirlik, Deniz
Anandi Cosmetics Private Ltd

Disco, Zoe
Eco Twinkle Ltd

Manning, James Joseph
The Diverse Investment (London) Group

Dixon, Andrew Reginald Rushworth
Maringo Ltd

Dixon, Tracey
Seascape Island Management Ltd

Do, Thi Bao Tram
Storm of UK Limited

Doal, Rakesh Singh
Taylor Grange Cosmetics Ltd

Dobre, Nicusor Constantin
Clickpoint Limited

Dobrev, Dobrin Dobrev
Jufa Cosmetics Ltd

Doherty, Colette
Beautessential Limited

Doherty, Helen
Silvercleanse Health & Beauty Ltd

Doherty, John
Beautessential Limited

Doherty, Margaret
Hedgerow Medicine Chest Ltd

Doherty, Sean
Smell Neutralizer Ltd

Doherty, Vanessa Tracey
Star Qualities Ltd

Dolan, Sabrina
DC Salon Products Ltd

Dolan, Simon James
She Who Dares UK Ltd

Dome, Monika
Protective World Ltd

Donaghy, Louise Mary
Zed Beauty Ltd

Donazy, Agnes
LIV Organic Co Ltd

Doncheva-Zabileva, Stela Stefanova
SeductiveDirect Ltd

Dong, Yu
Miss U Cosmetics Limited

Donkor, Letticia
Atarah Beauty Collection Ltd

Donovan, Michael Charles
Donovan Luxe Limited

Dooa, Jasvinder Singh
Dream Girl Limited

Dooa, Ravinder Singh
Dooa Capital Limited
Dream Girl Limited

Doody, Sylvia
Direct Cosmetics Limited

Doody, William Francis
Cosmetics Direct Limited
Direct Cosmetics Limited

Doolin, Leanna Marie
Pure Thoughts Ltd

Doon-Pandit, Shanti
Trine Oils Limited

Dorigo, Heather
Skin Matrix HD+ Cosmetology Ltd
Skin Matrix Limited

Dorricott, Carol Patricia
CBD Bakes Ltd

Dosu, John Jnr
Oakwood Williams Limited

Douazi, Syndele
Marrouge Limited

Douglas, Fiona Katherine
Kissess Lips of The Essence Ltd

Douglas, Ian Roger
Simply Untouched Ltd

Dove, Roger John
Roja Dove Limited

Dovey, Claire Linda
Fragrance Sales Limited

Dowell, Matt
Macial Ltd

Dowie, Tom Andrew
Bedfordshire Beard Co. Limited

Doyle, Anna Laurie
Occo London Limited

Dr. Kremer, Dirk
Skindoc Formula Limited

Dragan, Mihaela
Wonderland Sales Ltd

Dragicevic, Martina
Molecula Ltd

Drakakis-Kastrinakis, Georgios
Gentel Works Ltd

Drake, Clive Vincent
My Meghan Ltd

Draper, Jonathan Wolfgang
Glad Gent Ltd

Draper, Michael
Esscenti Ltd

Drmola, Patrick
Facil Haircare Ltd

Drummond, Kathy
Kathy Sue-Ann's Ltd

Drywa, Katarzyna
Ivee Group Ltd

Drywa, Michal
Ivee Group Ltd

Du Preez, Cecilia Gertruida Magdalena
Wild Celia Ltd

Duberry, Karen Helena
Natural Hair Emporium Limited

Duckworth, Christine Judith
Beauty Select Limited

Duckworth, Christine
UK Calluspeel Limited

Duckworth, James Ian
Beauty Select Limited
UK Calluspeel Limited

Duda, Rafal
JF Malcolm Ltd

Dudfield, Jayne
Info Cosmetics Limited

Dudo, Gelena
UK Esthetics Ltd

Dudzik, Weronika
Charms Europe Ltd

Duelli, Agnieszka
Metropolitan Beauty Ltd.

Dufeal, Tolive
Dufeal Your Best Beauty Ltd

Duffy, Simon Joseph
Greenery Skincare Limited
Mintology Limited
Truity Limited

Duggan, Chelsea
Fields Finesse Limited

Duman, Kaya
London Health Sciences Ltd

Dumbrell, Irina
Mesostrata Limited

Dunbar, Oriele Anne
E.J. Contracts Limited

Duncan, Scott James
Sulis Minerva Limited

Duncan-Lajewski, Kimberleen
Libhairation Ltd

Dungersi, Masuma Shabbir
Zaigul Wholesale Ltd

Dungersi, Shabbir Gulamali
Golo Hair & Beauty Limited

Dunkley, Miles Spencer Maitland
Synlatex Limited

Dunn, Edward Stanley
Three Pears Online Limited

Dunn, Jonathan
Aspects Beauty Co Ltd

Dunne, Paula Diane
Rosdon Group Limited

Dunseath, Philip Alexander
Myroo Ltd

Dunseath, Rachael
Myroo Ltd

Duong, Thanh Binh
NBS Distribution Ltd

Dupont, Jean-Laurent Marcel Carmine
Oh My Scent Limited

Durak, Nesat
Barber & Salon Supplies Ltd

Durocher, Philip
Colgate-Palmolive (U.K.) Ltd

Duru, Alev Mehmet
United Retail & Sourcing Ltd

Dusseaux, Hugues Philippe
Benefit Cosmetics Limited
Parfums Christian Dior (U.K.) Ltd

Dutta, Kaushik
LMS Brands Ltd.
Spartzy Lifestyle Brands Ltd

Dutta, Robi Miles
Tententen Limited

Dutta, Tapati Ranjitkumar
Spartzy Lifestyle Brands Ltd

Dye, Timothy
Gojo Industries - Europe Ltd

Dymott, Janet
Dermacosmeticsweb Ltd

Dynesen, Shawnafi
Zyzven Naturals Cosmetics Ltd

Dzhansyz, Hanna
Mayfair Export London Limited

Earnshaw, Mark Ian
Fragrance & Beauty Creations Ltd
Fragrance and Beauty Limited

Adhami, Sherry
The East To West Lifestyle Co Ltd

Eastman, Anthony Neville Chisholm
MGC Pharma (UK) Ltd

Eastwood, Alan Edward
Lipoid Kosmetik Ltd
Protec Botanica Ltd
Protec Ingredia Limited

Ebong, Fidelis Sameh, Dr
Ebong and Brothers Ltd

Eborall, James Lewis
JLE Trading Limited

Ebubedike, Charles
Clinova Limited

Echeverria, Natalie
Asaya Cosmeceuticals Limited

Wood, Alistair Robin Murray
The Edge Nail & Beauty Limited

Edgecombe, Marian Claire
Inside Trading (Beauty) Ltd

Edgerley, Adam
Tebs Distribution Limited

Edi, Muhammad Zukermi Bin
Nocov Ltd

Eggerton, Michael Stephen
Brodie and Stone PLC

Eggleton, Christopher John
Agenda Salon Concepts Limited

Eggleton, Christopher
Salon Distribution Concepts Ltd

Ejere, Idowu Okheren
Esteem Royale Cosmetics Ltd

El - Bouziani, Soumia
Joddor London Limited

El Arras, Soad
Soadperf Limited

El Houdaigui, Hamza
Moroccan Argan Limited

El Sabagh, Abd Al Halem
El Sabbagh Trading Limited

El Sabbagh, Ziad
El Sabbagh Trading Limited

El-Alaoui, Usaamah
Amalsons Ltd

El-Bacha, Amine
Al-Jazeera Perfumes Ltd

El-Hawary, Gamal Mahmoud
Oud Milano UK Limited

Eldamarawy, Salma
SHL Medical Limited

Elder, Connor Jake
Elder & Co Limited

Eldridge, Lisa
Lisa Eldridge Beauty Ltd

Element, Jessica Grace
Green Jiva Ltd

Eleuterio, Julio Marcel Brugos
Eleuthere Ltd

Elharrak, Yasmin
GameelaCosmetics Ltd

Elkaramany, Tamer Aly Emam Aly
Solarius UK & Overseas Limited

Elliman, Alexander James
Perfumeprice.co.uk Ltd

Elliman, Maryna
Perfumeprice.co.uk Ltd

Elliott, Angela Claire
Aromatic Yogi Ltd

Elliott, Michael
Hemsley James Cosmetics Ltd

Ellis, Michael Peter
Vida Aesthetics Ltd
Vida Skincare Ltd

Ellis, Thomas Malcolm
Value for Money (Cleethorpes) Ltd

Ellithorne, Karen Rae
Spa and Salon Solutions Ltd

Elmizeb, Riyad
L'dreams Limited

Elsheikh, Zuheir
Happy Beauty Life Ltd

Elson, Gary David
446-012 File Limited

Elwen, James
Argan Blossom Ltd

Elzokrod, Tamer Mohamed Hassan
Solarius UK & Overseas Limited

Emadi, Kassi
KSE Cosmetics Ltd

Emelife, Emeka Augustine
Zamoux Cosmetics Limited

Emelife, Oziomachukwu Chikaodili
Zamoux Cosmetics Limited

Emenyonu, Delphine
Eku Skin Care Ltd

Emilio, Eduardo Goncalves
Vida Aesthetics Ltd

Emilio, Eduardo
Vida Skincare Ltd

Emir, Cahit Joe
Gold Class Hair Limited

Emir, Inanch
Gold Class Hair Limited

Enemuo, Chinedu
Ivy Nat Ltd

England, Ben
Eternal Beauty (UK) Ltd

England, Kimberley Anne
Kimibeauty Ltd

Ennis-Cole, Anand
Ekah Foundation C.I.C.

Ennis-Cole, Ramana
Ekah Foundation C.I.C.

Enouf, Stephane Michel
Caudalie UK Limited

Eom, Noella Soo
Five Star International Consulting

Eram, Durrenaz
Green Merchandising Ltd

Ercan, Hasan
Pangaea Laser Ltd

Ergun, Harun Tayfun
Casa Cosmetics Ltd

Ernstberger, Jan Edward
Haircare of Sweden Ltd

Erodotou, Nicholas
Thalia Erodotou Limited

Erodotou, Thalia
Thalia Erodotou Limited

Eruncak, Riza
DS Express Barbering Ltd

Escott, Mike
HABM Ltd

Esdale, Lucy Dolapo
L & L Sunlight Importers and Exporters

Esho, Selina
Heavenly Body Ltd

Esprit, Claudette
Sopureoils Ltd

Kacy, Marie-Claude
The Essence of Esther Ltd

Etim-Ibom, Rose
R & T Natural Cosmetics Ltd

Euen-Gow, Jeffrey
Seventa Image Ltd

Eustace, Tara Ann
Mary Kay Cosmetics (U.K.) Ltd

Euzen, Stephane Paul Regis
Acqua di Parma Limited

Evangelou, Philip
Otonix Limited

Evans, Adrian Paul
Goodscents Limited

Evans, Barbara Jean
Goodscents Limited

Evans, Jacqueline
Risa Lux Ltd

Evans, John Albert Charles
Modernist Fragrance Ltd.

Evans, Lucy Victoria
Loaded Cosmetics Limited

Evans, Mark Edward
Heir & Grace Ltd

Evans, Paul Haydn
Rejuvapen UK Ltd

Evans, Richard Graham
Hughes Evans Essentials Ltd

Evans, Sarah Louise
PLBrands Limited

Evelyn, Sonia Rosalind
Ensley and Ensley Limited

Extremera Junquera, Enrique
Dorian House Marketplace Ltd

Piper, Roland
The Eyelash Design Co Ltd

Piper, Beverly Alison
The Eyelash Design Co Ltd

Eyo-Ephraim, Irene
Lipstick and Black Coffee Ltd

Ezirim, Chimezie
Otterganics Ltd

Fadelli, Celso
Intertrade Group Ltd

Asharia, Fidahusein Gulamali
B.Fairall (UK) Limited

Janmohamed, Moshin
B.Fairall (UK) Limited

Fairbrass, Jack Craig
Koutos Limited

Fakhroo, Reem
Farah Organics Ltd

Fakhruddin, Asgar
Sterling Fragrances International

Fakhruddin, Husainy
Sterling Fragrances International

Fakhruddin, Mohammed Husain
Sterling Fragrances International

Fall, Sean Jean
Janou Brand Limited

Fan, Xintong
Werson International Ltd

Fang, Genming
Seigur Rose International Group Co., Ltd

Faniku, Dorinda Eno-Young
Tauri Corporation Limited

Farah, Faiza
Natrorg Ltd

Farah, Michael Maurice
Choice of Nature Limited

Farahi, Elham, Dr
UK Natural Serenity Ltd

Farid, Bushra
Aquapurity Ltd

Farjon, Lionel
Pilaten EU Ltd

Farkas, Annamaria
Crystal Nails No1 Ltd
Crystalnails4u Ltd

Farmbauer, Manuela
Solution Cosmetic Ltd

Farooq, Zubair
Smellycat Ltd

Farrow, Rachael
Oils4life Limited

Fashandi, Celina Sohelia
Firecrest Communications Ltd

Fatunke, Oyinlola Omowunmi
Honeystyle Limited

Faucitt, Daniel James
London International Inflammation Foundation
Regima Medic Ltd
Regima UK Ltd
Regima Zone Ltd
Regima@Dr H Ltd

Faucitt, Jacqueline
Regima Medic Ltd
Regima UK Ltd
Regima Zone Ltd

Faucitt, Peter Andrew
Regima Medic Ltd
Regima UK Ltd

Faure Rolland, Andrea
Bedrock Trade Ltd

Fayazdastjerdi, Ahmad
British American Solutions Ltd

Fazwani, Sinnan
Royce Health Sciences Ltd

Featherstone, Danielle Michelle
Strip Distribution Limited

Featherstone, Maria Louise
Strip Distribution Limited

Feeney, Andrea Jean
Pause Skincare Limited

Feeney, Nicholas John
Pause Skincare Limited

Felstead, Oliver
Eloise Group Ltd
Wonder and Wild Ltd

Feltamo, Zerthun
Peau Royale Limited

Feng, Yun
Jas Etrading Ltd

Fenton, Julia Alison
SKN Rehab Limited

Ferdek-Guzik, Julia
Pherolec Global Ltd

Ferguson, Anna
Fragrance Group London Ltd

Ferguson-Quilter, Charlotte Rebecca
Disciple Skincare Limited

Fergusson, Irene
Fabdoo Limited

Fergusson, Kenneth
Fabdoo Limited

Fermin, Felipe
US Beauty Store Limited

Fernandes, Emanuel Pedro Andrade
Julien Miguel Ltd

Fernandes, Vanessa Pinho
Naya London Ltd

Ferrara-Bardile Muller, Maria Anna
Ferrara-Bardile Ltd

Ferrari, Dario
Intercos UK Ltd

Ferreira de Souza, Antonio
Trading Corporation International Export and Import

Ferrier, Rhodri Andrew
Greenery Skincare Limited
Mintology Limited
Truity Limited

Fessaha, Robel
Trinity General Trading Ltd

Fevre, Quentin
Beauty and Trade Ltd

Fewtrell, James
Zest Cosmetics Limited

Fiaz, Rabia
Blossom Organics Limited

Ficzu, Gergo
FG Traders Ltd

Field, Andrew John Stanley
Aspects Beauty Co Ltd

Field, Daniel
Organic and Mineral Salons Ltd

Fieldgrass, Theo
Aesthetic Brands (Distribution and Management)

Fields, Ingrid
Candii Bath Limited

Fincher, Oliver James Markham
Haircosmetics (Sunderland) Ltd

Findrik, Branislav
Cheap Cosmetic Ltd

Fiori, Loredana Angela
Flores Brand Works Limited

Fischer, Jacob
Highbase Market Limited

Fisher McRoberts, Kirsty Patricia
Lady Smidgeton's Apothecary Ltd

Fisher, Dean
R & B Hair Extensions Limited

Fisher, Nicole
Body of Work Beauty Ltd
Liquor Lips Ltd

Fisher, Peter
French Beauty Expert Ltd

Fishlock, Sandra
Teoxane UK Limited

Fivey, Peter
Hazellbrook Limited

Flanagan, Gemma
Bloom Artisan Brands Limited

Flax, Jonathan
Star Pearls Ltd

Fleming, Andrew John
Tyn y Ddol Enterprises Ltd

Fleming, Karen Marion
Tyn y Ddol Enterprises Ltd

Flemming, Janet Elizabeth
Al Janan Fragrances Limited

Fletcher, Jane Gillian
Sundome Leisure Products Ltd

Fletcher, Jane
Fish London Limited

Fletcher, Joe
CJ Cosmetics Ltd

Fleury-Richards, Karine
Flores Brand Works Limited

Flook, Richard
HCT Beauty Ltd
HCT Europe Limited
NB Beauty Limited

Florin, Dumitrascu
Beauty Camp Profesional Ltd

Floyd, Generald
Humanity Cosmetics Limited

Floyd, Ruth Elizabeth
Elko Electrical Ltd.

Foa, Attilio
Sun-Glo Limited

Foad, LeOne Rachel
Foad Wax Limited

Foad, Patt
Foad Wax Limited

Fofana, Mona
Honey Corn Limited

Folaron, Anita Katarzyna
Facecharm Ltd

Foot, George William
Mupe Ltd

Foot, Stephen Karl
Mupe Ltd

Foqaha, Abdullah Harbi
ED Trading & Consultancy Ltd

Ford, Kelly
Wheesht Ltd

Ford, Mark
Jax of London Ltd

Ford, Stephen Kelsey
Dr. Organic Limited
Optima Consumer Health Limited

Forde, Sabrina
Blk Oil Limited

Forma, Ewelina Barbara
Klean Skincare Ltd

Fornoles, Adielmofranches
Frontrow International UK Ltd

Forrest, Ryan
Faceoff Limited

Forte, Irene Alisea
Forte Organics Ltd

Fouda, Ibrahim Abdelrazik Albayoomi
Evorin Pharma Limited

Fourie, Stephan
Fourie Hair Limited

Foxley, Michael
Fox Group International Ltd
Revolax Ltd

Frackowiak, Ireneusz
Victoire Limited

France, Mark
Goldeivy London Lashes Ltd

Francis, Alison Helen
A.H. Francis Professional Beauty Ltd

Francis, Clare Elizabeth
Niche Aromas Ltd
T.L.C. (Total Luxury Cosmetics) Ltd

Francis, Glen Junior
Burton Blackmore International Ltd

Francis, Latoya Lovitta
Leicala Natural Products Ltd

Francis, Thomas Trevor, Dr
Winchpharma (Consumer Healthcare) Ltd

Francis, Victor
Viib Limited

Francois-Friis, Olav
Danlab Ltd.

Frand, Esther
Texthold Ltd

Franz, Ernesto
Nat & Co Limited

Frape, Nina Mellissa
Bush Oil Limited

Fraser, Malvina
Malvina Skin Care Limited

Freeman, Lawrence
Pampering Pattie International Ltd

Freer, David
Essential Oils Direct Ltd

Freimanis, Rudolfs
Duron Ltd

French, Carl Stuart
Sunspa Europe Limited
Sunspa UK Limited

French, Christina
Essench Cosmetics Ltd

French, Iman Shakera Shakelle
Lavish Lashes Ltd

Frend-Bullock, Rhianna Dawn
Love Henna Brows Limited
Ultimate Henna Brows Ltd

Freund, Christiane
Parfums Christian Dior (U.K.) Ltd

Munteanu, Simona-Codruta
Simona Fridrich Limited

Frimpong, Eden
Beauty and Trade Ltd

Frimpong, Sandra
SA Plus Enterprise Ltd

Fritz, Claire
Storm of UK Limited

Frost, Martyn Simon
Bigteal Industries Limited

Frost, Michele Elise Sarah
Amahla Limited

Fugate, Ronald Lee
Perricone MD Cosmeceuticals UK Ltd

Fuher, David
On-Top Skincare Limited

Fujiwara, Ayaka
Genten Skincare Ltd

Fuller, Mary Elizabeth
Cheet Beauty Ltd

Fullman, Jason
Turning Tides Ltd

Fung, Ka Wai
Ample Biotechnology UK Co. Ltd

Funk, Howard
TRS & Co (Europe) Limited

Furaha, Theresa Lydie
Hubert & Emilie Ltd

Furber, Edward Richard Alexander
Ellipsis Brands Limited

Furber, Frederick Peter
Ellipsis Brands Limited

Furini, Joseph
Sun Spirit Skincare Limited

Gabriel, Noella
E.J. Contracts Limited

Gadegaard, Jens
Web Store Group Limited

Gadsby, Robin Ivan
Ink Oil Limited

Gaj Komincz, Katarzyna
Design4nails Ltd

Galaiya, Sunil
Ximtrade (UK) Ltd

Galantic, John Stephen
Chanel Limited

Gallagher, Megan Katie
Beached Limited

Gallemore, John Andrew
ESPA International (UK) Ltd
M Beauty Ltd
Mama Mio Limited

Galvin, Louise
Louise Galvin Limited

Gamble, Sheree Anne
Revoke Ltd.

Gambrill, Kevin Michael
Australian Bodycare U.K. Ltd
Beauty & Skincare Essentials Ltd
Essential Bodycare Limited

Gamliel, Gilad Avi
Gaya Minerals Limited

Gamliel, Shahar
Gaya Cosmetics Limited
Gaya Minerals Limited

Gandhi, Anoj Navnitlal
Gold 22 (UK) Limited
Sai Enterprise Limited

Gandhi, Manoj Navnitlal
Gold 22 (UK) Limited
Sai Enterprise Limited

Gandhi, Sunny Anooj
Great London Beauty Limited

Gandhi, Vijay Pal
Holy Group Limited

Gangat, Bilal Mohammed
Azhar Academy Limited

Gangat, Ismail
Azhar Academy Limited

Gangat, Maksud Ahmed
Azhar Academy Limited

Gao, Xiangyu
Aeroeco Co Ltd

Garcia, Paul
Adelphi Corporation Limited

Gare, Sarah Louise
Funky Skincare Limited

Garek, Christopher
Space Brands Limited

Garel, Olivier Gilbert
Brand Evangelists for Beauty Ltd

Garhy, Ahmed
Prevura Ltd

Garofalo, David Victor
Valorem Capital One Ltd

Garrard, Kirsty Jade
Stolen Beauty Limited

Garside, Sarah Ann
Allure Cosmetics Ltd

Garston, Clive Richard
Warpaint London PLC

Gartside, James Howard
Simply Squirrel Limited

Gashi, Drena
Marrouge Limited

Gashi, Silva
Light Up Skincare Ltd

Gatongi, Francis Nderitu
MWK Cosmetics (UK) Ltd

Gaur, Ankit, Dr
Feel Good Products Limited

Gayle, Charesa
Butter Park Ltd

Gazzard, Matthew
Fish London Limited

Ge, Lili
Chinese Gentry Limited

Geary, Julita Joanna, Dr
All Naturals Beauty Limited

Geaves, Chris Paul
446-012 File Limited

Geden, John Harold Charles
Wisp Care Products Limited

Gedman, Paul Jonathan
ESPA International (UK) Ltd
Mama Mio Limited

Gelderd, Lee Graham
Karium Ltd

Gendis, Marlena Anna
Liluna-Organics Ltd

George, Desmond
Zimmerglobal Ltd

George, Hannah
Ethnoceuticals Limited

Georgiou, Antigone
Season of Beauty Limited

Gerrard, Paul Marc
Someplace Nice Limited

Gerrie, Andrew Martin
Balmonds Skincare Ltd

Gersten, Richard
This Works Products Limited

Ghabat, Gawan
Gxskin Limited

Ghafoor, Naeem
Herbal Hakeem Ltd

Ghafoor, Smara
Herbal Hakeem Ltd

Ghag, Anita, Dr
Complexi-Light Ltd

Ghag, Opreet
Complexi-Light Ltd

Gharehbaghi, Behzad
Ring in Ring Ltd

Gharib, Ahmad
SS Wholesaler Limited

Gharibavi, Mehdi
Misawa Healthcare Ltd

Ghenai, Neda Sarah
Narges Beauty Limited

Ghiaroni, Andrea
Itala Group Ltd

Ghircoias, Radu Mihai
Romade Limited

Ghouini, Soumia
Lushes Ltd

Giacone, Gianfranco
Timeless Temple Ltd

Giacone, Lucy
Timeless Temple Ltd

Gibbins, Sally Ann
PHB Franchise Limited

Gibbon, Leo William
Iiuvo Limited

Gibbs, Benjamin
G & G Skincare Ltd
Man Mask Ltd

Gibson, Shennell Shenika
S K A Gibson Ltd

Gibson, Dale
DMG Wholesale Limited

Gigurawa Gamage, Chaminda Thushara
Saravio UK Ltd

Gilbert, Christopher
Korebeauty Limited

Gilbert, David Jacob
Wish List Limited

Gilbert, Taekung
Korebeauty Limited

Giles, Clifford Jean-Marie
Corium Health Limited

Giles, David Victor
Rich 101 Ltd

Gilg, Andreas
Lipoid Kosmetik Ltd

Gill, Lyam Pearson
LPG Clinics Wholesale Ltd

Gillam, Christopher Derek
Guinot-Mary Cohr UK Limited

Gilland Robinson, Christine
Ko. Essentials Ltd.

Alers-Hankey, Pamela Noelle
Rhona Gillmore Limited

Gormley, Ryan Samuel
Rhona Gillmore Limited

Gilmore, Helen
Slixir Ltd

Ginda, Samuel
Taylor Grange Cosmetics Ltd

Giri, Amrit
Perfume London Ltd

Girven, Mark
G & G Skincare Ltd
Man Mask Ltd

Gkenou, Stamatia
Olivoderm Cosmetics UK Limited

Glasson, Alun John
H & B Supplies Limited

Glasson, James Bernard
H & B Supplies Limited

Glasson, Susanne Elizabeth
H & B Supplies Limited

Glazer, Donna
ID Skincare Limited

Burgess, Jasmin Danielle
The Glitterati Shop Ltd

Standley, Robert John
The Glitterati Shop Ltd

Bhagat, Kunal
The Glow Jar Ltd

Gnjatovic, Predrag
Loveco Ltd

Gobdon, Ahmed
Beautonic Skincare Ltd

Gobiec, Luiza
Hermossa Limited

Gobiec, Sylwia
Hermossa Limited

Goeke, Marc Ulrich
Headissimo Limited

Gogna, Dhiraj
Eye Kandy Cosmetics Ltd

Gokay, Sherife
Homsense Ltd

Goknel, Ozgur
Vivatinell Limited

Goldberg, Edward Barry
Aro-Matic (Scotland) Ltd

Golding, Jasmine
Contour and More London Ltd

Goldman, Andrew Stansfield
Vita Liberata Limited

Gomez, Maria-Victoria Victoria
Grandelash MD UK Ltd

Gomez, Monique Julia
Grandelash MD UK Ltd

Gomori, Adrienn
Laguna Organa Ltd

Goncalves Segredo, Arnesto
Avee Ltd

Gonzalez Antonete, Susana
Quelsa Ltd

Gonzalez, Jorge Minguez
J & W Distribution Limited

Gooby, Imogen
R & B Hair Extensions Limited

Goode, George
Skin Enrich Limited

Goode, Kristie Victoria
Feelgoode Ltd

Gooden-Jones, Michelle
Soybalm Ltd

Goodison, Eve Natasha
Five Elements Healthcare Ltd

Goodridge, Mark
Purelonia Ltd

Goodson, Kevin Joseph
Mono Naturoils Ltd

Goodson, Tracy
Mono Naturoils Ltd

Gook, Simon
Pole Position (Licensing) Ltd

Goonesekera, Kumarini Maria
Sash Products Limited

Gopal Laxminarayan, Zanvar
Garron Labs Private Limited

Gordon, James Webster
Muchacho (London) Limited

Gordon-Smith, Heidi
11:11 Limited

Gorskov, Oleg
Almcells Bioscience Ltd.

Gossain, Jagdeep Balram
Sportclinix Labs Ltd.

Gossain, Jagdeep Balram, Dr
Pharmaclinix Limited

Gossain, Shashi Kiran
Pharmaclinix Limited
Sportclinix Labs Ltd.

Gossain, Shiv Nandan
Pharmaclinix Limited

Gould, Stephen
Can Celebrity Brands Limited

Gouzd, Magdalena
Skinlab Medical Ltd

Gouzd, Malgorzata
Skinlab Medical Ltd

Govani, Mohamed Zahid
Trollion Limited

Govani, Mohammad Maisam
Southend Hair and Beauty Ltd

Govani, Mohammad Zohair
Essex Beauty Palace Ltd

Govani, Shafiq
Trollion Limited

Govindarajula, Santoshi Vasantha
Biogene Group Limited

Goyal, Neha
Elegance By London Limited

Goyal, Vidya Bhushan
Ru Si Lacquers Global Ltd.

Goyal, Vikas
Elegance By London Limited

Grainger, Scott
Cont-Hemp-Orary Ltd
Cont-Hemp-Orary Skincare Ltd
Raisingthebaruk Ltd

Grand, Sarah Louise
Little Duckling Soaps Ltd

Grandison, Dennis N/A
Grand By Designs Limited

Grandison, Shenston N/A
Grand By Designs Limited

Granger, Luke Henry James
Cosmetic Traders Limited
Electimuss Limited

Grant, Alan
Aromabar (Scotland) Ltd

Grant, Brian
Standfast Solutions International Ltd

Grant, Catherine
Aromabar (Scotland) Ltd

Grant, Connor
Conscience Clear Tan Limited

Grant, Priscilla
Myrrh & Co. Limited

Grant-Jones, Jake Daniel Luke
Beard and Bones UK Limited

Grass, Brian Lee
Hot (UK) Limited

Grasso, Seanne
Otonix Limited

Gray, Nathan Jerome
Essence Room Ltd

Grayson, Collin
Ava Corporations Ltd
Lamer & Ava Healthcare Ltd

Swift, Ben
The Great British Bee Co Ltd

Grebliunas, Giedrius
Farmavita Ltd

Green, Kenneth Charles
Kenneth Green Associates Ltd

Stanton, Brian John
Kenneth Green Associates Ltd

Stokes, Philip John
Kenneth Green Associates Ltd

Green, Alan
T A Trading Ltd

Green, Gary Michum
72 Hair Limited
72 Hair Retail Limited
Green & Dionisi Ltd

Green, John
General Shop Ltd

Green, Kenneth Charles
Boutique Perfumes Limited
Classic Beaute Limited

Green, Laurence Edward Raymond
Ozprodz Limited

Green, Louise Mary
Beauty Without Cruelty Limited
Ultra Glow Cosmetics Limited

Green, Matthew Jamie
72 Hair Limited
72 Hair Retail Limited

Green, Nicholas Luke
72 Hair Limited
72 Hair Retail Limited

Green, Roger Emanuell
Annexa Solutions Limited

Green, Susan Esther
Boutique Perfumes Limited
Classic Beaute Limited

Green-Armytage, Jock
Karium Ltd

Greene-Smith, Donniece
Eden's Legends Limited

Bridger, Julie
The Greenfrog Soap Co Ltd

Bridger, Nicholas
The Greenfrog Soap Co Ltd

Gregory, Julian
C-Bombe Limited

Grewal, Delysia Kaur
Chando-UK Ltd

Griffin, Monigho
Monshea Limited

Griffiths, Madeline Lucy
Elysian Design Limited

Grigore, Madalin Iustin
Justins Essentials Ltd

Grime, Katie
In & Outbrands Ltd

Grimes, Ashleigh Shantelle
Oatany Ltd

Grimes, Daniel
HD Cosmetics Ltd

Griskevica, Vlada
Nutrics Ltd

Grobler, Jacobus Nicolas Steyn
Aqua Qualia Limited

Groden, Steven David
Arnest International Limited
Sanmex International Limited

Grogan, Alexander Joseph
Mancave Limited

Grogan, Mark Anthony
Mancave Limited

Grogan, Sarah Elizabeth
Mancave Limited

Grogan, Simon Derry
Cosmetronic Global Limited

Grojnowski, Emma
Hydracol Pty Ltd

Groleau, Guillaume
Cosmetics Wholesale Limited

Gros, Bertrand Henry
Chanel Limited

Grosjean, Romain
Olo Edt Ltd

Grossman, Aaron
Beauty Brand (Europe) Ltd

Grossnass, Dov
Gelmoment Limited

Grostina, Gita
Baltica Beauty Professional Ltd

Gualtieri, Gualtiero
Florals of London Limited

Gubin, Leonid
Bonitec Ltd

Guerin, Jean-Baptiste
Jaspmab Ltd

Guha, Sujata Keshvan
Varana UK Limited

Guillard, Catherine
Nature et Bien-Etre Limited

Gulati, Amarjeet Singh
Gold 22 (UK) Limited

Guliker, Richard
Balmain Hair UK Ltd

Guliker, Steward Anton
Balmain Hair UK Ltd

Gunningham, Christine Louise
Cosma Fragrances Limited

Guo, Wei
UK Cosmetic Formula Limited

Gupta, Deep
Predator Trading Limited

Gupta, Gaurav
Dilmaherbals Limited

Gupta, Manoj
Cherie Cosmetics Limited

Gurcan, Emre
Aether Elements Ltd

Gurska, Marius Valentino
Deja Vu International Ltd

Gursoy, Akin
Ether Cosmetics Ltd

Gurt, Ben
Selective Fragrances Ltd

Guru, Gurmukh Singh
GS Fragrances Limited

Gut, Katarzyna Wiktoria
Tiyati Ltd

Gylsen, Louise Cng
Gallya Deelya Ltd.

Haar-Jorgensen, Donna Lesley
Nails & London Holdings Ltd

Habib Pourian, Nima
UK Skinlabs Limited

Habib, Nima
Dr.K Skinlab Ltd

Hagon, Paul George
Warpaint London PLC

Hai, Ofer
I.S.O.D Limited

Haider, Mubeen
Batalveez Ltd

Haider, Syed Mohammed Imran
Spice Fragrances Ltd

Haidzir, Heidi Shafiq
Pinklady International Ltd

Abdulla, Mehboob Mohammed Hussein
The Hair & Cosmetic Co Ltd

Birch, Sarah
The Hair Wardrobe Ltd

Haji, Haydar Jalil
Vanilla Blanc Limited

Hajij, Zakaria
Moroccan Attlas Ltd

Hajnal, Peter
Victoria Pharma London Ltd

Chaudhry, Salma
The Halal Cosmetics Co Ltd

Halaziuk, Ihor
Les Lilas Limited

Hall, Justin Oliver
Roccotek Limited

Hall, Lucy Katherine
Mediskin Pro Limited

Hall, Marie Elizabeth
Bloom Remedies Ltd

Hall, Stephen Richard
Bloom Remedies Ltd

Hallenbeck, Stephen
Vita Liberata Limited

Halliwell, Alison
Pareto Cosmedics Ltd

Hallmark, Robert Spencer
Gruhme UK Limited

Halsall, Neil Paul
Green World Spa Products Ltd

Hamada, Shigeru
Saravio UK Ltd

Hamade, Naim
NXSK UK Ltd

Hamandi, Nader
Spaquashop Ltd

Hamdan, Ahmed Ali
Sopure London Limited

Hamdan, Ali
Sopure London Limited

Hamdoune, Sarah
Najah Ltd

Hamid, May
Argan Liquid Gold Limited

Hamidi, Fazel
Ahwaz Ltd

Hamilton, Jonathan Remington
Mr Carters Essentials Limited

Hamilton, Lonnee Eileen
Madame Laveau Ltd

Hammer, George Christopher
Cosmolab Limited
Urban Retreat Products Limited

Hammersley, Benjamin David
Karium Ltd

Hammon, Izabelle Barbara
Calbrook Cosmetics UK Ltd

Hammond, Glen
Aster & Bay Ltd.

Hamon, Corentin Jacques Octave
Hamon Concepts Limited

Hamre, Kjetil
Oyemam Ltd

Hamre, Pearl Florence
Oyemam Ltd

Hancock, Angela Jayne
Gilmor Hair and Beauty (Newport) Ltd

Hancock, Mark Andrew
Gilmor Hair and Beauty (Newport) Ltd
Salon Distribution Concepts Ltd

Hancock, Sarah
Skin & Tonic London Ltd

Hancock, Thomas Andrew
Gilmor Hair and Beauty (Newport) Ltd

Handley, Alfred
Image Hub Limited

Handley, Juliet Anne
Image Hub Limited

Hanif, Navid
Herb Stuff Limited

Hanna, Haidy Adel Labib
London Links Trading Limited

Hanover, Brian Jason
Azzy London Ltd

Hanover, Mary Gale
Azzy London Ltd

Survila, Jonas
Philip Hansard Limited

Hansen, Tommy Henning
Emma Danmark Ltd
Emma Group Ltd
Emma Prime Ltd
EmmaDK Ltd
Eurohandle Ltd

Hanson, Faith Elizabeth
Ethical House Ltd

Hanumanth Kumar, Darshan, Dr
Sai Darshan Limited

Haralambus, Frixos
Simple Beauty (UK) Limited

Harbon, Sarah Anne
Benefit Cosmetics Limited

Harding, David
L.A. Professional Cosmetic Labs Ltd.

Harding, Pauline Audrey
Shure Enterprises (UK) Limited

Harding-Smolik, Jakub
Prispens Limited

Harding-Smolik, Jane
Prispens Limited

Haringman, Michael Stephan
E.J. Contracts Limited

Hariri, Mohammad
Retailwolfs Ltd

Haritash, Abhishek
Deism IT Solutions Ltd

Gray, Anne Theresa
The Harley Street Fulfilment Co Ltd

Harley, Thomas David
MEA Health and Wellness Ltd

Harman, Gabriella Bethany Tamsin
Dermamaitre Ltd.

Harper, Carol Ann
PH Group UK Limited

Harper, Lee Paul
Darklake Limited
PH Group UK Limited

Harper, Paul Dennis
PH Group UK Limited

Harries, Jonathan Jacob
Shine Shampoo Bars Ltd

Harrington, Sean
E.J. Contracts Limited

Harris, Andrew, Dr
Carr Greens Limited

Harris, Jessica
Pretty Silhouette Limited

Harris, Rachel Susan
Brand Evangelists for Beauty Ltd

Harris, Robert Llewellyn
Mann & Noble Europe Limited

Harris, Tasha
GroundedBodyScrub Limited

Harrison, David John
Capital (Hair and Beauty) Ltd

Harrison, Deborah
Pricecheck Toiletries Limited

Harrison, Jonathan Edward
Pricecheck Toiletries Limited

Harrison, Kiera Louise
Prossentials Ltd

Harrison, Peter Walter
Polar Export Services Limited

Harrison-Mellon, Einna Mildred
Shebelle Limited

Cheema, Jagdeesh Singh
David Hart (Santo) Limited

Cheema, Kirandeep Singh
David Hart (Santo) Limited

Hart, Adam Charles
ACH Cosmetics Limited

Harte, Maria
Hexbomb Ltd

Hartill, Debbie
Fragrance Samples UK Limited

Hartill, Greg Jonathan
Fragrance Samples UK Limited

Harvey, Marcia
Stroppy Ltd

Harvey, Matthew James Richard
Dr. Organic Limited
Optima Consumer Health Limited

Harwell, Lara
Laldhinio Limited

Harwood, Karen Victoria
Oodiee Limited

Hasan, Farhana
Medora of London Limited

Hasan, Mahmudul
Hill and Dale Limited

Hasan, Nazmul
Greenleaf Luton Limited

Hassan, Mark
Ideal Beauty Products Limited

Hatfield, Cherise
Style Cosmetics Limited

Hatfield, David Paul
Bulldog Skincare Limited

Hawash, Tbarak
Kenzak Beauty and Jewellery Ltd

Hawke, Antonia Jane
Beauty Science UK Ltd

Hawker, Richard McDonald
Hemp Earth Ltd

Hawkins, Neville Duncan
Highfields Health Limited

Hawkins, Nicholas Andrew
Myriad Skincare Limited

Hawkins, Olutumininu Olufolabomi, Dr
Highfields Health Limited

Hawthornthwaite, Michael
Beauty Fort Limited

Haxby, Phyllis
Face Lace Limited

Hayat, Abdul-Qadeer, Dr
Tradinguk55 Limited

Hayden, Andrew Gavin
Perfectly Natural Limited

Hayden, Slavka
Perfectly Natural Limited

Haydon, Colette Marguerite Louise
Lixir Skin Limited

Haydon, James Henri, Dr
Lixir Skin Limited

Haydon, Roxanne Louise
Lixir Skin Limited

Haydon, Walter John
Lixir Skin Limited

Hayer, Mandeep
Vasuda Beauty Limited

Hayes, Howard
HQPS Ltd

Hayes, Samantha Elaine
Reimiece Ltd

Hayes, Winston James
BSB Global Limited

Hazell, Lloyd
GroundedBodyScrub Limited

He, Tingting
UK Deer Running Co., Ltd

Head, Emilia Sophia Mary Primrose
Emilia's Handmade Bath and Body Ltd

Head, Megan
Megaco Limited
Tobco Limited
Tommco Limited

Head, Moira
Tommco Limited

Head, Tobias
Megaco Limited
Tobco Limited

Heaps, Brett
Perfume Addict (UK) Ltd

Heasman, Jacqueline Ann
First Choice Hair & Beauty Ltd

Heasman, Nigel John
First Choice Hair & Beauty Ltd

Powell, Hayley Rebecca
The Heath Consumables Ltd

Heather, David Christopher
TA-65 (UK) Wholesale Limited

Heatherington, Darren James
KD Cosmetics (Midlands) Ltd

Heaven, Beau
Geeza Cosmetics Ltd

Hecht, Matthias
M & H Cosmetic Limited

Hegarty, Generald Patrick
Beauty Solutions Limited
Beauty Systems Group Ltd.
Specialist Hair Products Ltd

Hein, Emily
Emortal Maquillage Ltd

Helimi, Nor Faiz Bin Ahmad
RR Cosmeceuticals (UK) Ltd

Helliwell, Darren
Hair Operating Products Ltd

Helliwell, Janet Elizabeth
Hair Operating Products Ltd

Helsby, Patricia Anne
Pink Cosmetics London Limited

Helt, Holly Anne
11:11 Limited

Helvadjian, Mark
Scrubd Ltd

Hemsley, Joe Daniel
Hemsley James Cosmetics Ltd

Henders, Daniel Thomas
Beard and Bones UK Limited

Henderson, Karema
Sassy Hair & Beauty Supplies Ltd

Hendrickx-Butt, Maximiliana Theresia Henrica
Haltrade UK Ltd

Henriot, Loic Pierre Marie
Acqua di Parma Limited
Fresh Cosmetics Limited
Guerlain Limited
LVMH Fragrance Brands UK Ltd
Make Up for Ever U.K. Limited
Parfums Christian Dior (U.K.) Ltd

Henry, Eric
Beaute Prestige International Ltd

Henry, Jemel
Beyond Hair Ltd

Henry, Maxamillion
Sphere 7 Lab Ltd

Henry-Ledgister, Caroline Maurwen
Leicala Natural Products Ltd

Henshaw, Laura
Belfast Beard Co Ltd

Rowse, Richard Montague
Camilla Hepper Sales Limited

Hepurker, Bulent
Naturenk Ltd

Herdman, David George
Beautypro Ltd
Evanesce Ltd

Hernandez Garcia, Jose Maria
Equisalud Ltd

Hernandez Guaitolini, Sabrina Sonia
SGHP Ltd

Celio, Giuseppe Gabrielle
Carolina Herrera UK Ltd

Hetherington, Eleanor Lunaria
Magpie's Ocean Ltd

Hetherington, Paul Anthony
L'Anza Europe Limited

Hewett, Paul David
Calmer Solutions Limited

Hewett, Victoria Lynne
Calmer Solutions Limited

Hewitt, John Guy
Anglo Indian Trading Limited

Hey, Lucy Mary
Wonder and Wild Ltd

Heywood, Suzanne Elizabeth
Chanel Limited

Higginson, James Edward
Aroma Actives Limited

Higham, Beverley Ann
Guerison Skin Solutions Ltd

MacDonald, Angus Francis
The Highland Soap Co. Limited

MacDonald, Archibald Sven
The Highland Soap Co. Limited

Parton, Emma
The Highland Soap Co. Limited

Higley, Andrew John
Essential Cosmetics Ltd

Hili, Lawrence
Starcount Limited
Worth Worldwide Property Ltd

Hill, Alyssa Daphiny Fernandes
Lucy Beauty Products Ltd

Hill, Stuart Colin Parkinson
Dermalogica (UK) Limited

Hillyard-Miller, Christopher John
Acti Laboratories UK Ltd

Hillyard-Miller, James Hugo
Acti Laboratories UK Ltd

Hilson, Lucy
SKN Rehab Limited

Hilton, Nicholas Anthony
Gordon-McCarthy Limited

Hin, Thomas
Velvet Bee Co Ltd

Hirano, Keiichiro
Pota Nini Limited

Hirsch, Kevinn Cayuti
Republik Inc Limited

Hiyama, Yoshio
Hisamitsu Pharmaceutical UK Ltd
Hisamitsu UK Limited
Salonpas UK Limited

Ho, Yu Ping
Eileen Group (UK) Ltd

Ho, Zala Markovic
Skincare 18 Ltd

Hoang, Paul Anh
P.T & Co Ltd

Hocaoglu, Funda
Cosmos Cosmetics Limited

Hodkinson, Paige Any
Lashline Ltd

Hodzheva, Demet
D'val Ltd

Hogg, Alison
Vita Liberata Limited

Hogg, Eunice
Nature-Solves Ltd

Hogg, William Graham
Nature-Solves Ltd

Hoja, Wojciech
Polish Cosmetics Distribution Centre UK

Holcombe, Miriam
Mimm Organics Ltd

Holdsworth, Nicholas Godfrey
Wharfedale Herbal Ltd

Van Der Berg, Engela Elizabeth
The Holistic Natural Wellbeing Co Ltd

Holland, Dean
BLK Cosmetics Limited

Hollis, Cheryll Lynn
Bodygold Limited

Hollis, Tammy Marie
Lipolift Ltd

Holmes, Karon
Ciao Brow Henna Limited

Holmes, Lauren Kate
Planet Sparkle Ltd

Holmes, Nilam
Neete Holdings Limited

Holmes, Peter James
Neete Holdings Limited

Holmes, Vicky
UK MUA Limited

Holtom, George Philip
Irregular Cosmetics Co Ltd

Honari Sharif, Raheleh
Medical Technology Caraco (MYC) Ltd.

Hood, James
James & Jake Ltd

Hood, Sarah Louise
James & Jake Ltd

Hoolihan, Thomas Joseph
Monat Global UK Ltd

Hooper, Sophie Helen
Stuff of Life Limited

Hopkins, Jurema Mendes
Juju Beauty Care Ltd

Hoque, Jahidul
Health-Beauty Ltd

Hoque, Mohammed Anwarul
MH Exports Limited

Horea, Daniel
Pro Brands (UK) Ltd

Horgan-Novarro, Elizabeth Catherine
Maison Danu (UK) Ltd

Hornigold, Elizabeth Katharine
L'Anza Europe Limited

Hornigold, Hilton
L'Anza Europe Limited

Horvath, Laszlo
Endetrox Ltd.

Hoskin, Nikita
Skin Chef Limited

Hossain, Mohammad Moazzem
Beauty The Divine Ltd

Hossain, Rejwana
Sweet Pea Soaps Co Ltd

Hosseini, Caesar
CH General Traders Limited

Hostalery, Philippe
Lab Brands Limited

Houlden, Michael Edward
Pure Thoughts Ltd

Housen-Lewis, Marlon Stefan
True Hemp Ltd

Housen-Lewis, Michael Anthony
True Hemp Ltd

Hovey, Lucy Elizabeth Howell
REN Skincare Limited
Ren Ltd

Howard-Flemming, Aadam
Al Janan Fragrances Limited

Howieson, Joy Elizabeth
Haych Cosmetics Limited
Project Cosmetics Limited

Howlett, Lawrence Marc
On-Top Skincare Limited

Hristov, Stoyan
TM Brands Limited

Hristudor, Constantin Eduard
Organic Iway Ltd

Hu, Qiong
Inbeauting Ltd

Huang, Ruihuan
Ijapan Ltd

Huang, Ssu-Ying
Mooi-H Ltd

Huettemann, Anisoara
Photics Skincare Ltd

Hughes, Amy Louise
Salon Supplies 365 Limited

Hughes, Elizabeth Ann
Cloud 19 Limited

Hughes, Geoffrey William Edward
Salon Supplies 365 Limited

Hughes, John William
Cloud 19 Limited

Hughes, Patricia Anne
Salon Supplies 365 Limited

Hughes, Rupert Harry Alwyn
Cool Blades Limited

Hughes, Russell Paul
Hughes Evans Essentials Ltd

Hulott, Claire Ann
Chulo Naturals Ltd

Humayun, Shafqat Ullah
Wrap N Pack Ltd

Hume, Graeme Paul
Earth Aid Group Limited
Organii Limited
Pravera Ltd
Siam Skin Ltd

Humphries, Jason
Good Pharma Dermatology Ltd

Hung, Choi Yung
Guess Her Secret Limited

Hunston, Paula
Nogender London Ltd

Hunter, Andrew Christopher
Green Jiva Ltd

Hurd, Kim
Elemental Herbology Limited

Hurley, Jessica
Pennies and Feathers Limited

Hurst, Claire Janine
Clever Skin Co Limited

Hurst, Joanne Sarah
International Trade Corporation Ltd
Lustra Beauty Limited
Pouty Lipzz Limited

Husbands, Kim Marguerite
Insta-Jell Cosmetics Ltd

Hussain, Abid
Asian Fashions Ltd

Hussain, Adeeba
Elleshouse Ltd

Hussain, Adill
Beauty Cosmetics (Bristol) Ltd
Beauty Cosmetics (Luton) Ltd
Beauty Cosmetics (Nottingham) Ltd

Hussain, Ajaz-Ahmad
Prostar Trending Online Ltd

Hussain, Bilal
Maryam Imports & Exports Ltd

Hussain, Fakhreddin Saifaddin Hussain
Silk Route Impex Limited

Hussain, Gulzar
Tawakkal Perfumes Ltd

Hussain, Jamal
Maryam Imports & Exports Ltd
Silk and Bubble Limited

Hussain, Mushtaq
New York 77 Ltd

Hussain, Nassar Mahmood
Need4health Limited

Hussain, Omar Saleh
Maryam Imports & Exports Ltd

Hussain, Sagira
Three Organics Ltd

Hussain, Samsara
Real Cosmetics Ltd

Hussain, Tonima
Beauty By Aliyah Ltd

Hussain, Umar
Vogue Cosmetics Ltd

Hussain, Zahra
APC (UK) Limited

Hussain, Zakir Maqsood
Zero Cosmetics UK Limited

Hussein, Mohammad Amir
Velvet Vapours UK Limited

Husseinbhai, Alefiyah Zoher Anverali
My Perfumes London Ltd

Hutchings, Susan
Synlatex Limited

Hutchinson, Diane
Icilda's Ltd

Hutchinson, Holly Elizabeth Marion
Memoize Parfum Ltd

Hutchison, Colin Anthony
Bulldog Skincare Limited

Hutchison, John
Fragrance de Maison Limited

Huys, Luc
Johnson & Johnson Limited

Hwang, Dong Young
Salon Theory Ltd

Iaghanashvili, Diana
Sambio Ltd

Ibanez, Dominique
Colbico Limited

Ibanez, Elmarie
EL Companies Ltd

Ibiks-Ibikunle, Stacy Salisha
Chic Clothing Limited

Ibom, Tracy
R & T Natural Cosmetics Ltd

Ibrahim, Asghar Adam Ali
Nabeel Perfumes International Ltd

Ibrahim, Ayesha
Honey Corn Limited

Ibrahim, Ibrahim Ahmed
Jedidiah Group Ltd

Ibrahim, Mohamed Islam
SHL Medical Limited

Ibrahim, Sherif
Mounir's Ltd

Nordstrom, James Alan
The Icon Consultancy Ltd

Sweet, Samantha Jane
The Icon Consultancy Ltd

Sweet, Samuel Whitney
The Icon Consultancy Ltd

Ifsasse, Abderrahmane
WGTSS Ltd

Igbon-Woods, Hannah
Plectra Polish Limited

Ige, Mohamed Ahmed
Nomad Care Ltd

Ige, Olamide Rachael
Bemi Banks Cosmetics Ltd

Iger, Ian
Loles Cosmetics UK Limited

Ijaz, Muhammad
Be Savvy Ltd

Ikusika, Oludamola
Delmoss Ltd

Ilbrink, Evert Gerhardus Helena Mechtildis
XIP Professional Ltd

Ileri, Nasir
Ileri Trading Limited

Coulton, Holly Anna
The Ilex Wood Ltd

Ilic, Daniel Z
Indigo Direct Ltd

Iliev, Emil Genadiev
Essential Oil Sell Ltd

Imam, Mohamed Said Moustafa Ahmed, Dr
Imamcom Ltd

Imhotep Amonra, Lord Pharaoh
Egyptian Magic Ltd

Inam, Asif
Maryam Imports & Exports Ltd

Indzhov, Vladislav Mihaylov
Elinor-UK Ltd

Ingelfinger, Thomas
Beiersdorf UK Ltd.

Ingham, Sinead
Flo with It Ltd

Ingram, Alan David
Drammock International Limited

Intek, Karolina
Skinsider Cosmetics Ltd

Intek, Krzysztof
Skinsider Cosmetics Ltd

Iqbal, Adnan
AIGC Limited

Iqbal, Aisha
Naturyl Glow Ltd

Iqbal, Ammer
Beauty Forever Cosmetics Ltd
Beauty Forever Limited

Iqbal, Hassan
Beauty Healthcare Ltd

Iqbal, Jawid
Razaq & Iqbal Limited

Iqbal, Junaid
Z & J Enterprises Limited

Iqbal, Khurram
KMZA Enterprises Ltd

Iqtidar, Shahana
U 2 Shine Limited

Ireland, Sarah Louise
Sarah Ireland Perfumes Ltd

Irfan, Ali
Fragrance Souk Limited

Hodge, Jonathan
Alexander Iris Solutions Ltd

Irungu, Climate
Hy-Brd Ltd

Irvine, Noel David King
Excellent Edges Ltd

Isaacs, Elliot James
Pangaea Laser Ltd

Isaacs, Nadine Inez
Norm and Glo Limited

Ishaq, Mohammed Faisal
Exotic Fragrance Ltd

Iskander, Sara
Dazzle Dee Ltd

Islam, Hamzah
Body Care Brand Development Ltd

Islam, MD Tanjil
Imxpo Ltd

Islam, MD Zahir
Rektaz Ltd

Islam, Safiul
Shopti UK Limited

Islam, Shariful
S.I Attar Ltd

Ismail, Hamze
Geeza Cosmetics Ltd

Ismail, Mohd Shukri
Veels UK Limited

Ismail, Naeem
Irum Cosmetics Ltd

Ismail, Wagma, Dr
Dermaperfetca Ltd

Ismiel, Sue
SI & D (UK) Limited

Ismiel-Nash, Nadine
SI & D (UK) Limited

Isobe, Yuichi
Hisamitsu Pharmaceutical UK Ltd
Hisamitsu UK Limited
Salonpas UK Limited

Itani, Abdul
Shyline Ltd

Iwuajoku, Adaaku
CFBP Ltd
Derma Organics by CFBP Ltd

Iyalla, Tamunoiyewuna Esther
Floest Beauty Solutions Ltd

Jabeur, Mickael Karim
Al-Abideen Perfumes Ltd

Jackaman, Grace
Amazingface Limited

Jackel, Ingrid Karine
Yes To Carrots UK Limited

Jackson, Andrew James Benjamin
Aspects Beauty Co Ltd

Jackson, Andrew
Soapy J Limited

Jackson, Duncan Andrew
County Sales Limited

Jackson, James Leonard Thomas
Aspects Beauty Co Ltd

Jackson, Michael
Mitonia Co Ltd

Jackson-Hill, Jill Adrienne
Aspects Beauty Co Ltd

Jacob, David
Perfumes Logistics & Distribution

Jacob-Karol, Rahel
Perfumes Logistics & Distribution

Jafar, Zarlasht
Zero Cosmetics UK Limited

Jafer Naji, Iman
IJN Pure Oils Ltd

Jaff, Aran
Orrwa Pharma Health & Beauty Ltd

Jafri, Syed Muhammad Amir Ali, Dr
Connessioni UK Limited

Jagger, Lufric Demetrius Jasper
Zarvis London Limited

Jagodaarachchi, Dimuth Prasanna
BC (PVT) Ltd

Jahangir, Mohammed
Fragrance World Ltd

Jain, Amit Ashok
Gen Next Ltd

Jain, Ashish Kumar
Lifestyle International Ltd

Jain, Binal
Meet T Needs Limited

Jain, Nitin
Iberia Skin Brands Ltd

Jain, Ruchika
Smiles Glasgow Limited

Jain, Samita
Lifestyle International Ltd

Jain, Vikram
Smiles Glasgow Limited

Jakobsson, Julia Ida
Gorillacare Ltd

Jalloh, Selina Zina
Sopureoils Ltd

Jama, Saed Mohamed
Luban & Murr Ltd

James Kraan, Dennes Johannes
Tabitha JK Limited

James Kraan, Tabitha Heather
Tabitha JK Limited

Jameson, Samantha Miranda
Beauty Stable Ltd

Jamil, Abu Sayeed
Miss Glamm Limited

Jan, Shazia
Sjonlineuk Ltd

Jan, Zahra
Z Online Ltd
Zjonline Ltd

Janakiraman, Vijairahul
Valma Consumer Co Ltd

Janaway, Graham Millis
Graham Hair and Beauty Limited

Jandu, Manveer
Super Natural Apothecary Ltd.

Jangaria, Jamila
Maraki International Limited

Janicka, Helena
Wild Kynd Ltd

Janmohamed, Khairunnisha
Janson Limited

Janmohamed, Riyaz
Janson Limited

Jansari, Rannesh
Fushi Wellbeing Limited

Jarman, Lewis
Siwel Trading Ltd

Jarosz, Aneta
Glossy Center Limited

Jassey, Djibi
Atlantic Beauty Store Limited

Jassi, Rajinder
Pennystore Limited

Jaswan Singh, Parvin Kaur
Cosmetolife Limited

Jatania, Mitesh Devshi
Winter Hill No.2 Limited

Jatania, Pravin Chandra Devshi
Winter Hill No.2 Limited

Jatania, Vibhaker Devshi
Emvi Limited
Winter Hill No.2 Limited

Javed, Fariza
Beautivate Ltd

Javed, Perveen
Land of Beauty Supplies Ltd

Javed, Somia
Gulz Cosmetics Ltd

Javidmehr, Ali
Contemporary Cosmetic Enterprise Ltd

Jawad, Ali
AJ Metals Ltd.
Hansraj House Limited

Jawo, Adebanji Olufaderin
Bodyhug Limited

Jawo, Florence Taiwo
Bodyhug Limited

Jayanetti, Dilani Nirosha
BC (PVT) Ltd

Jayasinghe, Dilshani Buddhika
Lanko Naturals-UK (PVT) Ltd

Jayasinghe, Dilshara Rashmika
Lanko Naturals-UK (PVT) Ltd

Jayasinghe, Ranjith
Lanko Naturals-UK (PVT) Ltd

Jeffrey, Lucy Victoria
Bare Kind Limited

Jeffs, Matthew David
Askett & English Ltd

Jenkins, Anthony George
Glow Consumer Products UK Ltd

Jenkins, Justine Elizabeth
Just Cosmetics Ltd

Jenkins, Sharron
Kalabash Limited

Jenner, Alan John
Kent Cosmetics Limited
Northdown Cosmetics Limited

Jenner, April Louise
Amor Beauty Cosmetics Ltd
Saint and Sinner Cosmetics Ltd

Jenner, David James
Kent Cosmetics Limited
Northdown Cosmetics Limited

Jenner, Diana
Aurum D Limited

Jerrard, Alison Louise
Nailzee Ltd

Jeyadeesan, Kandiah Ampalam
Beauty Complex Europe Ltd

Jhally, Jasjinder Singh
JSProfessionnel Limited

Jia, Yi
Skinkode Ltd

Jia, Zhongshi
Jacob's Well Limited

Jiang, Ruizi
Jia Bo Rui International Trade Ltd

Jibril, Osman
Jayeed Perfumes Ltd

Jimenez Sanchez, Francisco Javier
Vikenias UK Ltd

Jivani, Nikhar
Dream Glow Ltd

Joao, Miguel
ANGMG Ltd

Joenoes, Kusmijaty
Evany Personal Care Limited

Joenoes, Mardijaty
Evany Personal Care Limited

John, Mazel Caryl
GoodNaturedSkincare Ltd

John, Melissa Emily Francis
Cosmetic Doctor at Work Ltd

Johns, Lauren
Beau Belle Brushes Ltd

Johns, Leanne Peta
Sloane Home Ltd

Johnson, Christopher Mark
1962 Ltd

Johnson, Craig
CM Hair & Beauty Supplies Ltd
Hairdye Direct Limited

Johnson, George
Dojah Limited

Johnson, Hannah
Rosse Beau Ltd

Johnson, Kathryn Elizabeth
Eye Love Beauty (Chester) Ltd

Johnson, Matthew Michael
Modern Man Ltd

Johnson, Miles Stanley Clewley
Elemental Herbology Limited

Johnson, Natalie
East Cosmetics Limited

Johnson, Olubunmi Oyetoun
Orikii Naturals Ltd

Johnson, Paul Brian
Zivi Cosmetics Ltd

Johnson, Phillip
Elegant Boss Ltd

Johnson, Samuel Thomas
Fegoo Limited

Johnson-Francis, Charmayne
Burton Blackmore International Ltd

Jokovic, Budimir
Bolm4 Limited

Jolly, Allie
Dermura Skin Ltd

Jonblat, Kamel Malek
South West Aesthetics Ltd

Jones, David Leigh
Leigh Jones & Associates Ltd

Jones, Sonia Margaret
Leigh Jones & Associates Ltd

Jones, David Bradley
Facemane Ltd

Jones, Hilary Anita
Lush Ltd.

Jones, Jeffrey Stewart
Cannamplify Ltd

Jones, Laura Deanne
Lagoon Soaps Limited

Jones, Laura
Beautiful By Nature Ltd
Omaoli Limited

Jones, Mark Lloyd
Geek's Cosmetics Ltd

Jones, Michael Brian
Hair Dressing Supplies Lincoln Ltd

Jones, Nicholas Keith Arthur
Cowshed Products Limited
Neville Cut and Shave Limited

Jones, Teresa
Kidlex Limited

Jones, Thomas, Prof
Julie's Natural Health Ltd

Joore, Johannes
Jonatho Ltd

Jooste, Charmaine, Dr
London International Inflammation Foundation

Joosub, Adam
Eau de Parfum Limited

Jorda Brase, Olga
Nacho Vidal Distribuciones 2 Ltd

Jorda Gonzalez, Ignacio
Nacho Vidal Distribuciones Ltd

Jordan, Margaret
Margaret Jordan Cosmetics Ltd

Jordan, Immaculata Ngozika
Zee Sales Limited

Jordan, William Lawrence
Abbliss Limited

Jose, James Benjamin
Tansi Packaging Solutions Ltd

Jost, Charlotte
Morgan Jost Ltd

Jothinathan, Nishanthan
Anglia Enterprise (UK) Limited
Euroluxe Enterprise UK Ltd

Jowers, Kirk Lincoln
Doterra (Europe) Ltd

Jowkar, Afsana
Sabeauti Ltd.

Jowle, Katherine
Perfume Supplies Limited

Judge, Tessa Nathene
Hot (UK) Limited

Judkowski, Mark
Clean & Care Facilities Management

Juliani, Emerson Diones
Nov'max Keratin Limited

Juliani, Esther Suzannah
Nov'max Keratin Limited

Junday, Narianne Nirpal Kaur
NJ Apparel Ltd.

Kaczan, Robert
MLM Cosmetics Ltd

Kadier, Salahadeen
Linrose Care Ltd

Kadosh, Nir
Sur Trading Limited

Kadri, Olaitan Oluwaseun
Earthly Pleasures Ltd

Kadro, Yousef
International Integrated Solutions Co

Kaedbey, Chafic, Dr
South West Aesthetics Ltd

Kahai, Hartej Singh
HSK Enterprises Ltd

Kahn, Naftoli
SZ Beauty Limited

Kahn, Sarah Zelda
SZ Beauty Limited

Kaigorodcev, Aleksandr
Aromeco Limited

Kalvei, Gabrial, Sir
Gabriel Kalevi Ltd

Kalia, Saba
Unified Commerce Limited

Kalkowska, Patrycja
Cosmetic Hooligans Ltd

Kalla, Mohamed Ameen
M & M Cosmetics Limited

Kallon, Ismael
Karina Enterprise Ltd

Kalnina, Santa
Arlenne Ltd

Kalogiannidis, Dimitris, Dr
Veramic Limited

Kalogiannidis, Irene
Veramic Limited

Kalyanji, Hiten
Ascenttial Ltd

Kandohla, Ravinder
Madre Skincare Limited

Kandrac, Elise Bari
Potion Dynamo Limited

Kanfer, Joseph Samuel
Gojo Industries - Europe Ltd

Kangellaris, Barrie Kyriaco
BS Supply Ltd

Kapadiya, Nitinkumar Kumar
Himalaya Enterprise Limited

Kaplinsky, Natasha Margaret
Q River Limited

Kar, Saumen
London Ethnic Ltd

Kara, Gokhan
Invicta Cosmetics Limited

Karabulut, Niyazi Alpaslan
Rosense (UK) Ltd

Kardzhieva, Raya
Biotrade Cosmeceuticals Ltd

Kargozar, Saeid
Luxmeticgroup Limited

Karia, Jagdish Prabhudas
Affinity Fragrances Limited

Karia, Mala Jagdish
Affinity Fragrances Limited

Karia, Vishal
Affinity Fragrances Limited

Karim, Arsalan
Clinova Limited

Akhtar, Yasmin
Yasmin Karimi Ltd

Karlinski, Krzysztof
Wellness Style Limited

Karlo, Anna Vanessa
Khali Min Limited

Karolia, Salma
SK Network Ltd

Kasdi, Assia, Dr
Oxmetics Ltd

Kaseda, Kuniyoshi
Saravio UK Ltd

Kasparides, Claudia Anna Luise
Essence Pur Ltd.

Kassam, Iram Nadia Xeynah
Just Beautiful Skin Ltd

Kassamali, Muhammadali
Magnum Beauty International Ltd

Kaur, Jagdish
Vasuda Beauty Limited

Kaur, Jaspal
Apsara Cosmetics Ltd

Kaur, Jaspreet
Trichy Ltd

Kaur, Manjit
Birch & Hayer Ltd

Kaur, Taranjot
Fandealtastic Limited

Kava, Hansa
Ve-Glam Limited

Kavlanekar, Snehal
Concept Healthcare Limited

Kay, Philippa
In & Outbrands Ltd

Kaymakam, Gokmen
Per Capelli Ltd

Kayrouz, Abraham
JMAR Op No 2 Ltd

Kazer, Antony Charles
Lukony Ltd

Kazumba Tshinkanka, Guy Jonathan
Spktra Limited

Kearns, David Thomas
I Love Cosmetics Limited

Keeble, Christopher John
Pharma Medico Limited

Kefli, Selim
By Mia Cosmetics Ltd

Kelby, Stephanie Jane
Pure Savvy Limited

Kelby, Stephen Anthony
Pure Savvy Limited

Kelendar, Hisham Ahmad
Zajil Limited

Kelleher, Timothy Anthony
Profile Hair & Skin Care Ltd

Kelly, Jamie Robert
Roja Dove Limited

Kelly, Jennifer
J's Luxury Perfumery Ltd

Kelly, Matthew
Lozano Skincare Ltd

Kelly, Rachel Elizabeth
Earth Mother Limited

Kelly-Morris, Joanna Helen
Earth Mother Limited

Kemp, Derek John
Adel Professional Limited

Kemp, Oliver Benjamin
Adel Professional Limited

Kempson, Pascal
Doyle's Group Ltd
Regista Fragrance Ltd

Kenawy, Walid
Secret Line Ltd

Kennedy, Andrew Martin
Hera Beauty Ltd

Kentish, Caroline Frances
Jica Beauty Products Limited
Kenbar Beauty Products Limited

Kenyon, Anastasia Catherine Alexandra
Make It Up Limited

Keogh, Claudia
Honeypie Minerals Limited

Keogh, Daniel Paul
Worldwide International Retail Ltd

Keong, Eric Wee Shou
J & W Distribution Limited

Kerim, Shikar
Shama Pharma Ltd

Kersten, Dirk Willibrord
XIP Professional Ltd

Keshavji, Nasmin
Stylish & Luxurious Limited

Keskin, Mehmet
Vision Trading Limited

Keswani, Prakash Narayandas
Mayfair Export UK Ltd

Khadiya, Tarun
Man & Diva's Ltd

Khan, Abdullah
Actuate Services (GB) Ltd

Khan, Ajaz Ahmad
CBee (Europe) Limited

Khan, Alina
4symbols Ltd

Khan, Fasil
Suave Cents Limited

Khan, Ishtiaq Ahmed
Naturyl Glow Ltd

Khan, Kyjar
S Beauty Ltd

Khan, MD Sadiqur Rahman
Beehive Cosmetics UK Limited

Khan, Mohammed Abdul-Quddus
Naturyl Glow Ltd

Khan, Mohammed Rafiq
Goldstone Perfumes Limited

Khan, Mohammed Rashid
Oudh Al Aasmah Perfume UK Ltd

Khan, Mojammel Hoque
United Solutions (UK) Limited

Khan, Noman
Botanika Group Ltd

Khan, Reema Adnan
Crescent Soaps Ltd

Khan, Surat Samavi Aziz
Janou Brand Limited

Khanani, Zeeshan Haroon
Need4health Limited

Khanna, Arjun
Herbline U.K. Limited

Khanum, Zahura
Iattar Perfume Oils Ltd

Khatib, Mustapha
Salon Professional London Ltd

Khatri, Sanjay
Scent N Essence UK Ltd

Khattak, Mussarat Fawad, Dr
Alizcare Limited

Khatun, Rajia
Halal Beauty Co Ltd

Khayati, Moulay Driss
Neopilina Moda Ltd

Khder, Peshran
Roz Cosmetics Ltd

Kheiry, Kheiry
Belgravia London Ltd

Khusar, Madiha
LYF Cosmetics Limited

Kibuuka, Nassaka Stella
Naiga Naturals Ltd

Kieda, Agata
Iberia Skin Brands Ltd

Kiiru, Jeremiah Nguru
Harvey Pharma Ltd

Kilci, Mustafa Nejat
Ersag UK Limited

Kilner, Nicola Leanne
Deciem UK Ltd.

Kim, Diane
Space Brands Limited

Kimfumu, Princess Luila Clementina
Albertina Dorosario Ltd

Godlington, Britt
The Kind Planet Co Ltd

Godlington, Kevin Francis
The Kind Planet Co Ltd

Kindersley, Anabel
Neal's Yard (Natural Remedies) Ltd

Kindersley, Barnabas Guy
Neal's Yard (Natural Remedies) Ltd
Neal's Yard Remedies (Home) Ltd
Neal's Yard Remedies (International) Ltd

Kindersley, Peter David
Neal's Yard (Natural Remedies) Ltd
Neal's Yard Remedies (Home) Ltd
Neal's Yard Remedies (International) Ltd

King, James Robert
Very British Baby International Ltd

King, Natasha Rebecca Anne
ORA Naturals Limited

King, Sheila Heather
Eternal Beauty (UK) Ltd

Hill, Andrew Steven
The King of Shaves Co Ltd

King, Douglas Richard John
The King of Shaves Co Ltd

King, William Ashley
The King of Shaves Co Ltd

Kachra, Metish
The King of Sytle Ltd

Kingham, John Charles
Amber House Limited
Square Spots Limited

Kingham, Sophie
Amber House Limited

Kingsley, Natalie Ursula
Aesthetic Brands (Distribution and Management)

Kingston, Kamila
White Lotus Anti Aging Ltd

Kinnear, Adam
Jakor Limited

Kirby, Gregory Thomas
My SNS Academy UK Ltd
SK Flawless Dipping Powder Ltd

Kirkby, Louise
Plane Luxuries Limited

Kirkman, James
Hekiti Cosmetics Ltd

Kirsop, Martin Brian
Green Harmony Limited

Kita, Waldemar Stanislaw
Vivacy Laboratoires Ltd

Haigh, Michelle
The Kitchen Witch Aromatherapy Ltd

Kizhakkepurath Mohiyudeen, Khajahussain
Choize Ltd

Klados, Charalabos
Colgate-Palmolive (U.K.) Ltd

Breuer, Moses
Jennifer Klar Ltd

Klaus, Dana
Alpha Auriga Limited

Klocek, Henry Stanislaw
Polex Limited

Klocek, Mark Henryk
Polex Limited

Klocek, Martin
Polex Limited

Klocek, Peter Adonis
Polex Limited

Klosinski, Rafal
Polcosmetics Ltd

Klue, Clarise
Cosmic Eyes Ltd

Klufio, Augustus Wynn
Akoma International (UK) Ltd

Kminek, Ales
Clearance Masters Ltd

Salmon, Daniel Edward
Amelia Knight Holdings Limited

Salmon, David Brinley
Amelia Knight Holdings Limited

Salmon, Lynn
Amelia Knight Holdings Limited

Salmon, Mark Winston
Amelia Knight Holdings Limited

Salmon, Paul James
Amelia Knight Holdings Limited

Salmon, Tiffany Lynn
Amelia Knight Holdings Limited

Salmon, Daniel Edward
Amelia Knight Limited

Salmon, David Brinley
Amelia Knight Limited

Salmon, Lynn
Amelia Knight Limited

Salmon, Mark Winston
Amelia Knight Limited

Salmon, Paul James
Amelia Knight Limited

Salmon, Tiffany Lynn
Amelia Knight Limited

Knight, Charlotte
Brand Agency (London) Limited
Lottie London Limited

Knowles, Andrew
Cosmetica Natural Oils Ltd

Knowles, Stuart Thomas Gortley
XL Marketing Ltd.

Knox, Wesley David
Essentials4men Ltd

Khan, Yousaf
J Kobain London Ltd
J Kobain Ltd

Koc, Zhanna
JK Hair & Beauty Salon Supplies Ltd

Kochak, Aref Ghaffarzadeh Artloui
Droplet Cosmetics Limited

Hartley, Zayaahn
The Koha Beauty Co Ltd

Kohavi, Ilana
Moyou Ltd

Kohl, Roland
Skinsense Ltd

Kohli, Manjinder Kaur
M & N Traders Limited

Komincz, Piotr
Design4nails Ltd

Kongnurat, Chananchida
Kovet Kit Ltd

Kooner, Malkiat
Miracle8 Ltd

Koranteng, Benedicta
Atarah Beauty Collection Ltd

Korytakova, Veronika
B.Me Skincare Ltd

Koshbakov, Dastan
Omega Flax Limited

Kosmala, Tomasz
Thomas Kosmala Parfums Ltd

Kotecha, Jayshyam
Acering Limited

Kotecha, Kamal Vandravan
Acering Limited

Kotecha, Kashmira
Acering Limited

Kotecha, Liam
Acering Limited

Kotecha, Minal
Acering Limited

Kotecha, Paresh Kumar
Acering Limited

Kotecha, Ravi
Acering Limited

Kotek, Patricia
Belensa Limited

Kouma, Desiree Talleu
Nefert Ltd

Kozenevska, Olga
Fillers Pro Ltd

Kozenevski, Aleksandr
Fillers Pro Ltd

Kozlowska, Marta Janina
Smart Skin Limited

Krakowska, Aleksandra Ewa
Bubble-Bubble Ltd

Krause-Neufeldt, Kerryne
Eyeslices UK Limited

Krawczyk, Michal Arkadiusz
W8T Ltd

Krok, Paul Anthony
Bonfit UK Limited

Krolikowska, Beata
Peters Cosmet Ltd

Krueger, Britta
Flirties Products and Training Ltd

Krynska, Katarzyna
Best Pure Natural Products Ltd

Kryvenko, Valentyna
Valya Beauty Cosmetics Ltd

Kseib, Anthony Adel
General Healthcare Limited

Kseib, Anthony
La Generale Limited

Kseib, Antoinette
General Healthcare Limited
La Generale Limited

Kuba, Bratlomiej
Vancooler Ltd

Kubaczka, Sebastian Rafal
Shori Ltd

Kubair, Anirudha
Holy Lama Naturals Ltd

Kubair, Gouri
Holy Lama Naturals Ltd

Kubanza, Mylene Larisa
Afrocare Ltd

Kujawski, Adam
AK Wholesale Limited

Kujore, Daniel
Lady T Limited

Kuliberda, Tomasz
Colwayland Co Ltd

Kulwicki, Sebastian
Cazza Professional Ltd

Kumar, Ajay, Dr
Herc Ltd.

Kumar, Devinder
DKB Essentials Ltd

Kumar, Diksha
Elegance Gel UK Ltd

Kumar, Narinder
Herc Ltd.

Kumar, Ravi
Scentric Ltd

Kumar, Sunil
Sunrise Essential Oil Limited

Kuntes, Emel
Emel Trade Ltd

Kurisaka, Mai
World Links Europe Limited

Kusmirek, Jan Brian
Somerset Perfumery Ltd

Kuti, Attila Istvan
Aeden UK Ltd

Kwasniewska, Dorota
Genixo Ltd

Kwiecinski, Tomasz
Holistic Plant Technologies Ltd

Kwon, Hyojin
Tonic15 Ltd

Kyei, Kwaku Korankye
VR Consult Limited

Kynaston, Florence
Fem Distribution Limited

Kyriacos, Constantinos
Constantine K Ltd

Kyriacou, Katerina
BS Supply Ltd

Pond, James
Natascha Lacombe Cosmetics Ltd

Ladak, Rizwan
Project 1 Skincare Ltd
Royce Health Sciences Ltd

Ladebat, Noel
N & L Cosmetic Limited

Lagbaj, Oussama
Mamondo Fragrance and Beauty Ltd

Lagutins, Konstantins
L'Revolution Beauty Ltd

Lahai-Taylor, Jeannette, Dr
Ibeautify Ltd

Lai, Mingli
WH Corporation (UK) PTE. Ltd

Laird, Ian
Incorporated Perfumery Distribution

Laird, Sally Kate
Crystal Spring Consumer Division Ltd

Laird, Stuart Wilson
Crystal Spring Consumer Division Ltd

Laird, Thomas James
Crystal Spring Consumer Division Ltd

Laitphlang-Williams, Joshua
Samla Tribe Limited

Lajous, Luis
Beaming White Ltd
Moderna Aesthetics Ltd
Whitening World Ltd

Laker, Sophie Nicole
Co Beauty Ltd

Lakhwani, Johnny Mohan
Iam Finance Limited

Lakhwani, Kishore Kumar Mohan
Macks Ltd.

Lalji, Ali Mehdi
Alsons Beauty Ltd.

Lalji, Kumail Hassan
Alsons Beauty Ltd.

Lalji, Mohamed
Alvor Limited
Honeypot Cosmetics (Wholesale) Ltd

Lalji, Mustafa
Alvor Limited
Honeypot Cosmetics (Wholesale) Ltd

Lalji, Muzafferali
Alvor Limited
Honeypot Cosmetics (Wholesale) Ltd

Lalvani, Tara, Dr
Beautifect Ltd

Lam, Chan Va
Ank Innovation Limited
Green Breeze Ambient (UK) Ltd

Lam, Sio Peng
Green Breeze Ambient (UK) Ltd

Lam, Siu Kuen Michelle
C & A International Trading Ltd

Gambrill, Kevin Michael
Ken Lamacraft Marketing Ltd

Peerless, Fiona McMillan
Ken Lamacraft Marketing Ltd

Lamb, Danielle
Mindful Soulful Limited

Lamb, Hannah
Arvense Skin Care Ltd

Lamb, Lisa Robyn
Tiarna Ltd

Lambat, Ebrahim
7th Heaven Scents Ltd

Lambert, Erik
R & R Global Consumer Healthcare Ltd

Lamont, Angela
ABX Beauty Limited

Lamont, Iain Robert
ABX Beauty Limited

Lampman, George
Dinair Airbrush Makeup Systems Ltd

Lamrani, Ibrahim
Lamari London Ltd

Lancaster, Corrina
Amber House Limited

Landreth-Smith, Joseph
Ko. Essentials Ltd.

Landreth-Smith, Megan
Ko. Essentials Ltd.

Lane Fox, Martha, Baroness
Chanel Limited

Lane, Alexandra
Amor et Psyche Ltd

Lane, Wendy Louise
Meadow Skincare Limited

Langer, Wolfram
Lab Brands Limited

Langmuir, Alexander James MacGillivray
Karium Ltd

Lansbury, Andrea Dawn
Benefit Cosmetics Limited

Lanza, Giovanna Vincenza
Hair There & Everywhere Hair & Beauty

Lanzante, Giuseppe
Joseph Lanzante Products Ltd

Randhawa, Kuldeep
Joseph Lanzante Products Ltd

Lapeyre, Jerome
Jerome Fashion Ltd

Laporte, Julien Philippe Noel Henry
Un Air D'Antan Limited

Laporte, Sophie Christine
Un Air D'Antan Limited

Laskaris, Panagiotis
Fysifarm Limited

Denton, Charles James
Erno Laszlo Group Ltd

Allegaert, Hans
Erno Laszlo Group Ltd

Zhao, Hanxi
Erno Laszlo Group Ltd

Tuchman, Avery
Erno Laszlo Group Ltd

Latchford, Amanda
Fleuroma Limited

Latham, Jody Lee
UK Fillers Ltd

Lau, Michael Pui Hing, Dr
Claracutis, Ltd

Lau, Wing Hang
Double Skies Limited

Lyu, Yang
Estee Lauder (UK) International Group

Day, Alison Claire
Estee Lauder Cosmetics Limited

Prouve, Marc Cedric Yann
Estee Lauder Cosmetics Limited

Warnery, Philippe Michel
Estee Lauder Cosmetics Limited

Travis, Tracey Thomas
Estee Lauder Cosmetics Limited

Launsky, Peter
Hempo Logical International Ltd

Laurie, Stephen McDonald
Imijo Ltd

Makki, Abeer
The Lavender Concept Ltd

Laville, Charlene
Nizz Cosmetics Ltd

Law, Yuen Yan
Bellissimo Fashion Ltd
Oasis Beauty Distribution Ltd

Lawal, Yetunde
Virgovogue Ltd

Lawrence, Andrea
Oya 9 Ltd

Lawton, Jeremy
Argan Secrets Limited

Lawuo-Meena, Hellen
Daughter of The Soil Limited

Lay, GA Ning
Alihair Ltd

Laycock, Joe
Diet Plan Unique Ltd

Lazar, Adrian-Marcel
Lam Cosmetics Ltd

Le ROI, Scott Alexander
Glitterfreaks Limited

Le Vaillant de Chaudenay, Alexandre Jean
Sisley UK Limited

Le, Trang Huyen Thi
Eifelcorp Consumer Care Ltd
Elie Consumer Care Ltd

Le, Vu-Hoang
Eblouir Group Ltd

Leach, Alexander Ian
Neal's Yard (Natural Remedies) Ltd

Leach, Timothy Alan Baylor
Neal's Yard (Natural Remedies) Ltd

Leach, Tommy Bernard
Man'd Skincare Ltd
Recruit Skincare Ltd

Leal Herrera, Maria Eugenia
Laurens Cosmetics UK Limited

Leatham-Leacock, Cerise
Sheasecrets Ltd

Lebedeva, Elena
40075 Limited

Ledes, Leslie Bayly
Fashion Fragrances & Cosmetics UK Ltd

Ledgister, Leighton Wellesley
Leicala Natural Products Ltd

Lee, Adrian Jin Jia
So Susan Limited

Lee, Brian. Dean
Brooks Aesthetics Clinic Ltd

Lee, Candice Amanda
Butterflyy Productions Ltd

Lee, Chloe
Dunstan and Burr Ltd

Lee, David Alexander
RDC (UK) Limited

Lee, Eun Joo
Boylondon Holdings Limited

Lee, Geon
Pharmdex UK Ltd

Lee, Jonathan Richard
Classic Beaute Limited

Lee, Kaman
Maskhouse Wholesale Limited

Lee, Lisa
Rokka Imagine Ltd

Lee, Marc Geoffrey
Patagonia Consult Limited

Lee, Margaret Joan
Brooks Aesthetics Clinic Ltd

Lee, Yae Sel
Cadden & Lee Limited

Lee-Thompson, Karen
Beauty Consociare Ltd

Leetham, Samuel
Bear Journal Limited

Kravitz, Adrianna
The Legends London Limited

Leguen, Laura Jane
Husaco Ltd

Lei, Yan
Sparking-Jy International Trading Co.,

Leibovic Farrar, Anabel
Jigu Corporation Limited

Leicester, John William
Ila Asia Limited
Ila Pothecary Limited

Leitner, Martin
Bali Secrets Ltd

Lekeux, Lynsey
Le Keux Vintage Enterprises Ltd

Raetz, Arnold
The Lemon Tree Beauty Limited

Lendvayne Szantai-Kis, Hajnalka
Novumis Ltd

Leon, Jody
Vilasa Limited

Leon, Lynne
Vilasa Limited

Leppinen, David, Dr
Garnier & Hemo Healthcare Ltd
Hemo Bioscience Ltd

Leprince, Damien
AM Botanical Limited

Lerner, Mark Steven
Gojo Industries - Europe Ltd

Lesdos, Denis Bernard Charles Jean, Dr
Hild International Group Ltd

Leung, Elaine Chi Kit
Natural Skincare London Ltd

Leung, Vivien
Rewind Botanics Limited

Leverett, Christopher Allen
Wild Earth Botanicals Ltd

Levin, Aaron
Oscar & Louis Limited

Levin, Scott
Gojo Industries - Europe Ltd

Lewis, Deborah Ann
Clarins (U.K.) Limited
Talza Limited

Li Volsi, Angelo
Infinityredox Holdings Limited

Li, Beibei
Trade Mall Limited

Li, Huanhuan
Beauty Code Limited

Li, Keya
Cosplus International Ltd

Li, Qihang
One Flower Qinga Limited

Li, Shengli
Echo Hair Limited

Li, Teng
Lee Gallop Enterprise Ltd

Li, Wei
Rooster & Rooster Ltd.

Li, Xianlin
VIS International Corporation Ltd

Li, Yiwei
Foodprint Network Ltd

Li, Yujuan
JZM International Limited

Licence, Timothy William
Plush Soap Ltd

Licence, Wendy Patricia
Plush Soap Ltd

Lightowlers, Michael Henryk
Dr. Organic Limited
Optima Consumer Health Limited

Limbachia, Amita
Lava Jai Limited

Lin, Huaqing
Indiggle Limited

Lin, Shaoyan Yan
Cherry Cherry Fashion Ltd

Lin, Zhe
Egg Pillow Limited

Lin, Zhentao
Indiggle Limited

Lin, Zhong Wu
Asel Ltd

Linnegar, Brian
Bragarlin Limited

Lipsitz, David Melvin
Re:New Beauty Ltd

Lipsitz, Richard
Re:New Beauty Ltd

Little, Ian
Little Enterprises (NI) Ltd

Little, Rod Ryan
Bulldog Skincare Limited

Littler, Anthony James
McCoey & Co. Limited

Littler, Jonathan Mark
McCoey & Co. Limited

Littlewood, Marie
N.S.I. (U.K.) Limited

Liu, Chen
Vilai Europe Trading Limited
Vivlai Europe Trading Limited

Liu, Jianhua
Legendbio Beauty Group Limited

Liu, Jingwen
Faye Florais Global Holdings., Ltd

Liu, Min
UK Vimin Industry Co., Limited

Liu, Shenglong
H.H.L.Brothers Limited

Liu, Weihong
UK Beauty Cosmetics International Group

Liu, Xiangrong
Fragrant Spa Limited

Liu, Yanyan, Lady
K. S. D Beauty Zone Ltd

Livesey, James Edward
Beiersdorf UK Ltd.

Llewellyn, Dionne
Tailord Chic Ltd

Llorente Coto, Ainhoa, Dr
Jigu Corporation Limited

Lo Bue, Robert John Michael
Guestproud Ltd

Lobah, Arnold
Yellbird Limited

Lobashkov, Victor
Sanmex International Limited

Raines, Julie
Charlie Locks Ltd

Raines, Mark Andrew
Charlie Locks Ltd

Lockton, Dean Austin
Protec Botanica Ltd

Lockyer, Brett Eric, Dr
Bubbleworks Limited

Lombardi, Gianmauro
Mayjoy The Perfumer Ltd

Hasan, Farhana
The London Cosmetics Co Ltd

Rizvi, Syed Hasan
The London Cosmetics Co Ltd

Rizvi, Syed Rizwan Hasan
The London Cosmetics Co Ltd

Bodmer, Catkin
The London Skincare Co Ltd.

Long, Christopher
London Bathers Limited

Long, Derek
Pet Scentuary Ltd

Long, Susan Mary
Pet Scentuary Ltd

Longden, Christopher David
GDT Global Limited

Longhi, Katherine
Katherine Longhi Ltd

LooSeniore, John Colin
Beegood Enterprises Limited

Looker, Carmen Corinna
C Looker Ltd

Lopardi, Mariangela
Mandragora Ltd

Lopes, Jose Maria
Trading Corporation International Export and Import

Lopes, Robson Goncalves
Beauty Kosmetika Ltd
Hairshine UK Ltd

Lopez Alvarez, Juan Antonio
Seventa Image Ltd

Louriki, Sofiane Abdelaziz
Sofil Cosmetic Ltd

Frenkel, Andre
The Lovely Distribution Co Ltd

Lowdon, Andrew
La Tips Limited

Lowdon, Antonia
La Tips Limited

Lu, Ning
Bonroy International Limited

Lu, Qian
LCB Trading (UK) Limited

Lu, Yi
Tothun Group UK Ltd

Lu, Yimin
Alihair Ltd

Lubezky, Tamir
TLC - Tender Loving Care UK Ltd

Ludbrook, James David
Yorkshire Beard Co Ltd

Ludzhev, Sergey
Refan UK Ltd

Lueck, Ruth Amelia
Super Yacht Spa Ltd

Lui, Xeng Su
Helen Gel Colour Ltd

Luika, Erlands
Earthbreath Ltd

Lukaitis, Natalie
Wild Things Cosmetics Ltd

Lukic, Zoe
Bad Mermaid Limited

Luksas, Karolis
Buy It Out Ltd

Lulat, Zuber
Adam Michaels Group Ltd

Lunt, Tymeika Marie
Boundless Beauty Ltd

Luo, Fei
Aurelia Skincare (International) Ltd
Aurelia Skincare Limited

Luo, Yang
Ank Innovation Limited

Luotiene, Irma
Organic Stuff Limited

Luxton, Chloe Liz Warwick
Bramley Products Ltd

Lycett-Green, John Peregrine
DLG Partners Limited

Lynch Staunton, Graham Murray
Fine Fragrances and Cosmetics Ltd
Lynch-Staunton Cosmetics Ltd
Vivalis Beauty Limited
Vivalis Limited

Lynch Staunton, Susan Angela
Fine Fragrances and Cosmetics Ltd
Purple Tree Skincare Limited
Vivalis Limited

Lynch, Mark
USA Hair Extensions Ltd

Lynch, Victoria
Additional Lengths Ltd

Lynch-Staunton, Graham Murray
Fade Out Limited
Purple Tree Skincare Limited

Lynch-Staunton, Susan Angela
Fade Out Limited
Lynch-Staunton Cosmetics Ltd
Vivalis Beauty Limited

Lyons, Caroline
Lotus Cosmetics Ltd

Lyons, Jeffred
Lyons Men's Grooming Ltd

Lyons, Robert James
Janiro Ltd

Lythe, Amanda Jane
Pricecheck Toiletries Limited

Lythe, Mark Andrew
Pricecheck Toiletries Limited

Maakrun, Samea
Sasy N Savy Ltd

Maat, Hubert Willem
Inovair Limited

MacDonald, Seonaid
Maringo Ltd

MacDonough, Colette Frances
Hive of Beauty Limited

MacDonough, Stephen James
Hive of Beauty Limited

MacGregor, Rosemary
Arbar Ltd

MacKay, Benjamin Alastair
Uppercut Deluxe Co Limited

MacKenzie, Alan Grant
Wild Organics Limited

MacKenzie, Mali
MacKenzie Cosmetics Limited

MacLeod, Eoin Alan
Trading Scents (2014) Limited
Trading Scents Group Limited
Trading Scents Limited
Unique Fragrances Limited
Warpaint Cosmetics (2014) Ltd
Warpaint Cosmetics Group Ltd
Warpaint Cosmetics Limited
Warpaint London PLC

MacTavish, Alexander Stuart
Seascape Island Management Ltd

Machado Dos Santos, Marlus Filipe
Moda Exportation Limited

Mack, Kimberley
Perfect Look & Health Ltd

Mack, Stephen
Perfect Look & Health Ltd

Mackie, Marc Alexander Rene, Dr
Allied Warden Marketing Ltd

Mackintosh, Haley
Sang Real Tattoo Ltd

Macknay, Tom
Space Brands Limited

Macmillan, Stuart Alexander
Monat Global UK Ltd

Macpherson Guy, Talitha Rachel Delcena
Raebeauty Ltd

Macpherson Le Maire, Thomas Richard
Macden Beauty Ltd

Magembe, Elibariki Robert
Daughter of The Soil Limited

Magembe, Maria Kaitamalya
Daughter of The Soil Limited

Magliacano, Marc
Blissworld Limited

Magnani, Lucia
GVM Long Life Formula UK Ltd

Magne, Didier Rene Serge
We Concept Ltd

Maguhn Elie, Jessy Alexandra
Kounga Ltd

Mahdi, Liban
Soulful Beauty Ltd

Maher, Ali
Thiossane Ltd

Maher, Rachel Claire
Joy Limited
Star Qualities Ltd

Mahmood, Asad
Home & Bodycare Limited

Mahmoud, Ahmed, Dr
Bioxane Ltd

Mahmud, Hasan
Unac Salon Supplies Limited

Mahomed, Osman Imtiaz Mussa
Select & Bargain Ltd

Mahroos, Mariam
MB Professional Beauty Ltd

Mahrotri, Shaan
Cannamplify Ltd

Mai, Leyla
Villainelle Ltd

Maidment, Andrew
Lavant Beauty and Personal Care Ltd

Maj, Slawomir Leszek
Direct Trade Limited

Majed Ali Barakat, Areej
Universe Cosmetics Limited

Majeed, Abdul
Hair Ornaments UK Limited

Majeed, Mahmood Qasim, Dr
MQS Group London Limited

Majid, Mohammed Ahmed
Golden Rose Limited
Southend Hair and Beauty Ltd

Makki, Mansour Nassif
Makki Cosmetics Limited

Makowski, Damian
Green Essence Ltd

Makwana, Reenal Rakesh
4R Guest Supplies Limited

Malek, Shahid
Adam Michaels Group Ltd

Malhotra, Sunny
Ombre Cosmetics Limited
Ombre Paris Limited

Mali, Hemangini
Hemangini Limited

Malik, Henaa
Preen Queen Limited

Malik, Kauser Perveen
Bizi Bazzar Limited

Malik, Mavesh
Organica Skincare Ltd

Malik, Nazila
SFL Group Ltd

Malik, Razia
Razias London Ltd

Malikzada, Zmary
VevBeautyCosmeticsTrading Ltd

Malim, Mohammed
Orit Limited

Malka, Marc
Universal Design Promotion Ltd

Malle, Pierre Frederic Serge Louis Jacques
Editions de Parfums Limited

Mallipal, David Krishna
L'Amour Cosmetics London Ltd

Malone, Giles Addis
CBee (Europe) Limited

Malone, John Anthony
Excel (GS) Limited

Malone, Paul Andrew
Excel (GS) Limited

Mamade, Yassin Bhadurali
Neo Cosmetics Limited

Mammon, Oliver David Sacha
C-Bombe Limited

Managera, Mohmad Shoeb
4 Corners Distribution Ltd

Manchester, Joanne Linda
Joanna Naturals Limited

Mandanka, Kanjikumar
Ved Healthcare Limited

Manev, Zvezdana
DLM Trade Limited

Mangham, Dale
Beauty Leisure Industry Supplies and Services

Morris, Zarina Zarina
The Manhattan Group Ltd.

Mann, Aman
Bath Bombs and Beyond Limited

Mann, Anthony Robert
MH Products Limited

Mann, Tracey
Perricone MD Cosmeceuticals UK Ltd

Manning, Joseph Daniel
Chaleur Ltd

Manson, Yaa Boatemaa
Nova Bleu Cosmetics Limited

Mansour, Khaldoon
International Integrated Solutions Co

Mansour, Lilah
Lbeautie Ltd

Manu, Usha
Kaxton Limited

Maqsood Hussain, Nabila
Zero Cosmetics UK Limited

Marcelja Paravic, Ivona
Beautyline Limited

Marchetti, Giulio
Paliano Ltd

Marcinkeviciene, Inga
Inga Permanent Make Up Limited

Marcinkevicius, Darius
Inga Permanent Make Up Limited

Marco, De Franco
Scontimania Online SRL Limited

Marcroft, Catherine Grace
Zoe Balm Ltd

Marecaux, Django
Claracutis, Ltd

Maree Sime, Teresa
Lovoir Ltd

Maree, Don Wessel
Alumier Labs UK Limited

Marei, Jehan
Khali Min Limited

Margis, Eriks
Trade Dream Ltd

Marinkovich, Julia Katherine
JMAR Op No 2 Ltd

Marino, Giuseppe
Kamarino Limited

Brooks, Warren
Alexandra de Markoff Limited

Mihoc, Paul
Paul Marney & Co Ltd

Marouani, Rachel Gina
Make Up for Ever U.K. Limited

Marrone, Margo
Unicorn Magic Enterprises Ltd

Marrone, Roksana
Unicorn Magic Enterprises Ltd

Marsalek, David
H2 World Health and Beauty Co Ltd

Marshall, Gary
Anatomicals London (England, The World, The Universe-Known and Unknown)

Marshall, Paul
Anatomicals London (England, The World, The Universe-Known and Unknown)

Marszalek, Krystyna
Chirp Body Ltd

Martin, Amy
Martha & Daughter Limited

Martin, Charlotte Elena
Crypt Doll Ltd
Cursed Cosmetics Ltd
Pixie Crypt Ltd

Martin, Cheryl Lynn
Harpar Grace International Ltd

Martin, Heather
Rock Beauty Junkie Limited

Martin, Kayley Louise
Flutter Cosmetics Limited

Martin, Sally Martha
Martha & Daughter Limited

Martin, Shelley
He-Shi Enterprises Ltd

Martin, Victoria Kai Wai
Crane and Peach Limited

Martin-De Lapa, Daniel Marc
OPA Botanicals Ltd

Martinez, Claude Marie Joseph
Parfums Christian Dior (U.K.) Ltd

Martinez, Jose
Maverick Hair & Beauty Ltd
Seadrift Trading Limited

Martinez de San Vicente, Javier
Kounga Ltd
Nukua Limited

Martins, Vladimir Aleixo
HT Cosmetics Ltd

Mas, Christian, Monsieur
Eurocosmetics Limited

Mas, Frederic, Monsieur
Eurocosmetics Limited

Maser, Nicholas John
Bes Hair Products Limited

Maser, Tara Louise
Bes Hair Products Limited

Mashru, Alka Jayant
Mashco Limited

Mashru, Jayant Kumar Gokaldas
Mashco Limited

Maskell, Sarah
Beauty Trinity UK Limited

Maskill, Andrew Nicholas
African Garden Limited

Mason, Daniel Luke
HBD International Limited

Mason, Jane Mary
Natural Birthing Co Ltd

Mason, Paul
HBD International Limited

Mason, Robert John
Jaydaw Limited

Mason, Sharon
Direct Salon Limited

Mason, Sukhdeep Singh
M Cosmetics Distribution Ltd

Massie, Keith James
Dermaenhance Ltd.

Masters, Nicholas
Dea Disir Ltd

Mastoras, Dimitrios
Olivoderm Cosmetics UK Limited

Mat-Ali, Ezam
Marina Muda Ltd

Mateen, Ozair
Color Studio Ltd

Mather, Christopher John
Hair Fantastic Retail Limited

Mather, Deborah Tracy Denise
Hair Fantastic Retail Limited

Mather, Elaine
Dreamweave Products Ltd

Mather, Steven
Dreamweave Products Ltd

Mathers, Charles Rodney
CRM Trading Limited
Glendale Group Limited
Glendale S/S Limited

Mathers, Reamann Gearoid
Mil Iocshlainte, All Natural Balms Ltd

Mathers, Sinead
Mil Iocshlainte, All Natural Balms Ltd

Mathew, Saji
Juliajosh Limited

Mathew, Susan Saji
Juliajosh Limited

Matloob, Zain
Boutique Fragrances Ltd

Matthews, Dougal Jonathan
Fab Professional Hair Supplies Ltd

Matthews, Geoffrey Howard
Aspects Beauty Co Ltd

Matthews, Ian
Skin Sanity Limited

Matthews, Van Geel
Body Beauty Wholesale Exporters Ltd

Matvejevs, Ilja
Hempia Limited

Matyas, Dora
Scented Home Limited

Matytsine, Alexandre
Arnest International Limited
Sanmex International Limited

Mauger, Laurent Richard
Cosma Fragrances Limited

Maughan, Gregg Elliott
Forever Living Products Ireland Ltd

Maughan, Rex
Forever Living Products Ireland Ltd

Maxted, Donna Juliette
Kirimi Limited

Maxted, Robin Hugh
Kirimi Limited

Maxwell Smith, Susan Barbara
Antiageing Haircare Specialists Ltd

Maxwell, Alan Stuart
Ozprodz Limited

Maxwell, Joanna
Savvy & Shine Ltd

Maxwell, Tom
Savvy & Shine Ltd

Mayasi, Roberta Regine
Imaage Ltd

Mayo, Freya Alice
B & F Ventures Ltd

Mbemba Nseko Mayala, Bibish
Kitoko Make Up Ltd

McArdle, Laura, Dr
Winkies Limited

McArdle, Mai Phan
Orca Distributor Ltd

McBeath, Innes Archibald Wilson
Innes McBeath Sourcing Ltd.

McBeath, Susan Valerie
Innes McBeath Sourcing Ltd.

McBride Jr, Cornell
Design Essentials Limited

McBride Sr, Cornell
Design Essentials Limited

McBride, Garry
Swipes Fragrance Ltd

McCall, Euan David
Jorum of Scotland Limited

McCann, Calumn John
Death Head Beard Co Ltd

McCarthy, Claire Louise
Elite Salon Solutions Limited

McCarthy, John Nigel St. Ledger
Gordon-McCarthy Limited

McCarthy, Nigel William
Arosci Trading Limited
McCarthy Inter Africa Ltd

McCarthy, Timothy Patrick
Elite Salon Solutions Limited

McCloy, Charles
CHM Holdings Ltd

McCormick, Shanna
Dead Pretty Official Ltd

McCrumlish, Helen
Lacomo Beauty Ltd

McCrumlish, Paschal
Lacomo Beauty Ltd

McDermott, Andrew James
Bessacarr Ltd

McDermott, Edward Ternie
Adel Professional Limited

McDermott, Lisa
Beautessential Limited

McDermott, Patrick John
Diva Cosmetics Limited

McDonald, Mark Andrew
Mark McDonald Consultancy Ltd

McDonald-Bing, Felicity
Felicity McDonald Organics Ltd

Vickers, Julian
Felicity McDonald Organics Ltd

McDonnell, Catriona
Beautifully Bliss Ltd

McDonnell, Louise
LMD Cosmetics Ltd

McEwan, David Andrew
XY Skin Ltd

McEwen, Oluwatimilehin Marian
Stonera Ltd

McGlynn, Brian William
Mancave Limited

McGovern, Julie
Prezance Ltd

McGowan, Chris
Directfrom Ltd

McGowan, Lee
Party Supplies and More Ltd

McGrath, John Christopher
Meller Design Solutions Ltd

McGuire, Caroline Ann
Lock Stock & Barrel Grooming Co Ltd

McGuirk, Patrick Daniel
Saltee Skincare Limited

McGurk, Una
Revive Express Beauty Ltd

McHugh, Megan Kaytie
Organic Skincare Originals Ltd

McIntosh, Alison
Alimacskincare Limited

McIntosh, Jacqui
305 Professionals Ltd

McIntosh, Taylor Phillipa
Gattino Cosmetics Ltd

McIvor, Terence, Dr
Fasa Capillago Limited
Hydro Fresh Ltd
Quanis Cosmetic Limited

McKay, Brian Francis
Cannabinoid Oil Solutions Ltd
Portobello Organics Ltd
Tetra Hydro Cannabinoid Oils Global Ltd

McKay, Craig
Biologico Cosmetics Limited

McKell, Marie Claire
Dance on Tan Limited

McKenzie, Verna Angela
Afro Hair and Beauty International

McKnight, Samuel
SMCK Hair Care Products Ltd
SMCK Limited

McLaughlin, Stephen
Hive of Beauty Limited

McLean, Georgina Avalina
Avelena Ltd

McLeary, Lloyd
Direct Salon Limited

McLoughlin, Brendan
Hazellbrook Limited

McMahon, Oliver
Laurelle London Ltd

McManigan, Rory Fergus
Pure Products Limited

McMurray, Hilary Hanna
He-Shi Enterprises Ltd

McMurray, William James
He-Shi Enterprises Ltd

McPake, Jill
Acorn Brokerage Limited

McPake, Lawrence
Acorn Brokerage Limited

McPhee, Peter Jonathan
Cowshed Products Limited
Neville Cut and Shave Limited

McStravick, Angela
Lash House Eyelash Extensions Supplies

Mears, Richard John
Cult 51 Ltd
Instant Effects Ltd

Mecheri, Kamel
Kerria, Limited

Mecheri, Keiko
Kerria, Limited

Megas, Michalakis Nestor
GP Mediplus Ltd

Meggiorini, Giovanni
Valma Consumer Co Ltd

Megoran, Tracy
Green Ladies N.I Ltd

Mehmet, Altug Erdal
Per Capelli Ltd

Mehmet, Nevzat Hakan
NMB Property Limited

Mehmood, Abid
Multi Imports Limited

Mehmood, Hamza
AHS Services Ltd

Mehmood, Suleman
Vibrantz Cosmetics Ltd

Mehra, Sanjiv
EOS Products Limited

Mehta, Akash
Leela Living Limited

Mehta, Dilesh Bhogilal
DNA Beauty Group Ltd.
Fragranceexpert Limited
House of Worth Limited
S A Designer Parfums Limited
Shaneel Enterprises Limited

Mehta, Hardik
Sanchi Corp Limited

Mehta, Hitesh Bhogilal
Fragranceexpert Limited
House of Worth Limited
S A Designer Parfums Limited
Shaneel Enterprises Limited

Mehta, Jignesh Pravinkumar
Worth Worldwide Property Ltd

Mehta, Nikita
Leela Living Limited

Mehta, Pranavkumar Satishchandra
GS7 IT Consultants Ltd

Meisheri, Jinali
P P Oil UK Limited

Melano, Massimiliano
2M PH. Intl. Limited

Melia, Donna Marie
Dont Poke It Ltd

Melik, Martin
Mehron Limited

Melkonian, Lara
Espoir Beauty Ltd

Memarian, Pedram
Charlize London Ltd

Memarian, Roxanne
Charlize London Ltd

Member, Mohamad
MM Product Trading UK Limited

Mendes, Anastasia Leonara
Comedic Limited

Mendes, Eva Octaviana
Menco International Limited

Mendes, Jeronimo Cirilo
Comedic Limited

Mendes, Sharon Lillian
Comedic Limited

Mendes, William Spencer
Comedic Limited
Menco International Limited

Mendoza, Paul
Kidlex Limited

Mensa-Bonsu, Kwame Owusu Agyeman
Stenko Ltd

Mensah Nash, John
Bohdidharma Perfume UK Limited

Mensah, Albert
Me Sentir Ltd.

Mensah, Ebenezer
Me Sentir Ltd.

Mensah, Gabriel
Me Sentir Ltd.

Mercik, Grzegorz Gabriel
Dr. Gabriela Ltd

Mason, Dominic Benjamin
Linda Meredith Skin Care Ltd

Meredith, Linda
Linda Meredith Skin Care Ltd

Merrett, Emma Louise
S & E Ventures Ltd

Merrett, Sally Elizabeth
Bath Spa Skincare Limited

Meszaros, Adrian
Brain Burgeon Ltd

Meyer, Aniela
Diva Deva UK Limited

Meysselle, Arnaud Maurice Jean
REN Skincare Limited
Ren Ltd

Mezare, Gija
Gajas Gift Limited

Mhamead, Koubi
IR International Ltd

Miah, Nazir
Kamila Health & Beauty Ltd

Miah, Runu
Karaama Fragrances Ltd

Michaels, Doris Mary Edema
Doris Michaels Cosmetics Ltd

Michel Sanchez, Alondra Del Rocio
AM Botanical Limited

Miezitis, Edgars
Beard Nature Limited

Mikulski, Bartlomiej
Shop4stocks Limited

Millen-Gordon, Lydia Elise
LEM Beauty Ltd

Miller, Jamie
My Pink Ltd

Miller, Ross
Indulge Therapeutics UK Ltd

Millie-James, Karen
Global Beautique Limited

Milner, Paul Andrew
Pam Trading Limited

Milner, Robert Lee
Amberhue Limited

Milton, Maxine Ann
Perfume Bodega Dist. Ltd

Milward, Stephen
Hair from India Limited

Banica, Ionut Bogdan
The Mine of Goods Ltd

Zayd-Aziz, Saphora Bint
The Mink Company U.K Ltd

Minto, Adam Nicholas
Revolution Beauty Limited

Mir, Gisele
Cool Essentials Limited

Mirbod, Parisa
Florence Consumer Products Ltd

Mirzaee Ghomi, Mehrdad
Foundation Brands Ltd

Mirzaee-Ghomi, Mehrdad
Amalgamated Euro Products UK Ltd

Miskell, Charlotte Emily
Niko Pro Limited

Misra, Renu
Ayursavvyveda Limited

Mistry, Rajendra Naranbhai
Pro Impressions (UK) Limited

Mitchell, Asmara
Muamko Uzuri Limited

Mitchell, Brett Anthony
MGC Pharma (UK) Ltd

Mitchell, Daniel Derek
Brodie and Stone PLC

Mitchell, Ian Anton
Wholesale Hair Extensions Ltd

Mitchell, Kelly
Kandi Apple Limited

Mitchell, Lorna
KMI Brands Limited

Mitchell, Simon Jonathan
Evans Close Limited

Mitha, Farzana
Aqua Bleu Limited

Mitra, Sanjay
Bellissimo GmbH International Ltd

Mitroulas, Arthur
A Beauty Story Ltd

Mixeras, Lucie Anais Nathalie
Lanmix Enterperises Ltd

Mizejewska, Natalia
NM Beauty Industries Ltd

Mji, Nolitha, Dr
Rabimed International Limited

Mngxitama, Annette
Flores Distribution Limited

Mngxitama, Lumka
Flores Distribution Limited

Mockford, Deborah Joan
Global Essence UK Ltd

Mockford, Jennifer
Functional Skincare Ltd

Mockford, Mike Alexander
Functional Skincare Ltd

Mockford, Mike
TheGoodSkinCo Ltd

Mockford, Stephen
Functional Skincare Ltd

Hudson, Richard
The Modern Man Project Ltd

Moerl, Sascha
EOB Distribution Ltd

Barr, Victoria Jane
The Moffat Perfume Co Ltd

Mognol, Andrea
Nat & Co Limited

Mohamed Hanif, Shareezma Shishani Binti
Boost Balm Ltd

Mohamed Qhatit, Aiman Ahmed
Organic Land Global Ltd

Mohamed Thahir, Mohamed Inshaf
Iras Trading Ltd

Mohamed Thahir, Mohamed Shiraz
Iras Trading Ltd

Mohamed, Abdirahman
Mahiri Africa Ltd

Mohamed, Gulam Ahmed
UK Make Up Limited

Mohamed, Khaled Mouloud Haj
Dermica Laboratoires UK Ltd

Mohamed, Shazia
Array of Scents Ltd
Esscential Ltd

Mohamoud, Sahra
Adoris UK Ltd

Mohamud, Marian
Nurologie Ltd

Mohanna, Mariam Kamel
Lavant Beauty and Personal Care Ltd

Mohd Sanusi, Zainas Sadeken
Just Beautiful Skin Ltd

Moilanen, Meeri
Botany Squared Limited

Molenda-Skowronek, Anna Maria
Coslab Ltd

Mollett, Jeffrey Wayne
Jeunvie Ltd

Mollison, Mary
Fizz 'n' Bliss Ltd

Molloy, Julie
Nut Dust Ltd

Molyneux, David Anthony
Lavy Sprays International Ltd

Monan, Robert Lee-Roy
Strdom Ltd

Monassebian, Bijan
Prema Naturals Limited

Monassebian, Dalia
Prema Naturals Limited

Monckton, Polly
Espoir Beauty Ltd

Mondin, Jean Daniel Dominique, Dr
Guinot-Mary Cohr UK Limited

Mondor, Geoffray
Mondor & Bache Ltd

Monga, Samir
Pure & Sure Limited

Monger, Joel
HBDeadSea-UK.Com Limited

Monroe, Cheryl Elaine
Mary Kay Cosmetics (U.K.) Ltd

Montenegro Leon, Alvaro
Nukua Limited

Montenovesi, Carlo Giuseppe
GVM Long Life Formula UK Ltd

Mooney, Marette
He-Shi Enterprises Ltd

Moorcraft, Pedro Lopes Dias
Fols for Men Ltd

Moore, Christopher John Liebe
Simply Nature Ltd.

Moore, Kerry Ann
Amly Limited

Moore, Susan
Logical Content Ltd

Moore, Terence Frederick
Logical Content Ltd

Moore, William
Logical Content Ltd

Moorehead, Simon Charles Wheeler
Pippa Beauty Limited
Prism Parfums Limited

Moores, Philip St John
Glorious Brands Ltd.

Moores, Tracy Jane
Glorious Brands Ltd.

Moorfield, Rebecca
California Glow Ltd

Moosa, Baneen Fatima
London Outlet Store Limited

Moran, Julia
Lash Authority Ltd

Moran, Lee
Multitude Makeup Ltd

Morea, Lucas Abel
Valentia Skincare Limited

Moreau, Philip
Edward London Ltd

Morgan, Guy
Guy Morgan Apothecary Limited

Morgan, Aminah
A Pony Called Steve Ltd

Morgan, Callum
Contour and More London Ltd

Morgan, Catherine Lara
Functional Fragrances Ltd

Morgan, Georgina
Morgan Jost Ltd

Morgan, Michael Richard
Vir Original Limited

Morris, Geoffrey Peter
Beauty Innovator 2012 Ltd.

Morris, Kerstina Joanne
SKN Rehab Limited

Morris, Michelle
Heyvega Ltd

Morrison, Deborah Christine
Angel Remy Ltd

Morrison, James
Swan Leigh Cosmetics Ltd

Morrow, Geoffrey Stanton
YJX Group PLC

Morrow, Leslie John
Irregular Cosmetics Co Ltd

Morrow, Rachel Lesley
Irregular Cosmetics Co Ltd

Mortimer, Susan
HG-UK (Pty) Ltd

Morton, Angie Frances
Irregular Cosmetics Co Ltd

Moser, Philip
Labo Nine Limited

Moss, Emma Jane
Prima Makeup Ltd

Moss, Hollie
Natural Pal Limited

Moss, Sara Ellen
Le Labo UK Limited

Moss, Simon
Prima Makeup Ltd

Mottram, Paul
Beautywise Limited
Delights Beauty Co Ltd
Drammock International Limited

Mottram, Susan
Drammock International Limited

Mousa, Seham
N18 Ltd

Moussazadeh, Ali
Paradise Organics London Ltd

Moutousamy, Phillipe Anthony
Sunscreen X Limited

Moutrikas, Stavros
Natur Life Ltd

Petherbridge, David Andrew
Sue Moxley Beauty Limited

Browne, Andrew Graham
Sue Moxley Beauty Limited

Moxley, Susan Anne
Sue Moxley Beauty Limited

Van Day, David
Sue Moxley Beauty Limited

Moya Soria, Francisco-Javier
Eden Perfumes Limited

Moynihan, Carl Michael
L.A.Tanning Co Ltd

Moynihan, Daniel Michael
L.A.Tanning Co Ltd

Muabinga, Nella Mayitane
Kitoko Make Up Ltd

Muchova, Zuzana
Sweet Lilli Ltd

Muddei, Sarah
Fin Perri Ltd

Mughal, Saira Akram
Inshirah Enterprises Limited

Muguiyi, Casha Catherine
Sassy N Trendy Cosmetics Ltd

Muis, Erlinda
Isobel C Professional Cosmetics Ltd

Mukacyubahiro, Aline
Landional Ltd

Mulholland, Jenna
DMK Distribution (NI) Ltd

Mulholland, Mark
DMK Distribution (NI) Ltd

Mulholland, Peter
Top Brands Australia Limited

Mulkern, Debbie
Wisp Care Products Limited

Mulla, Soieb
Al Sunnah Perfumes (Wholesale) Ltd

Mulligan, Bernadette Ann
Love Henna Brows Limited
Ultimate Henna Brows Ltd

Mulligan, Wayne
Refan Portadown Limited

Mumvadi, Mata Marielle
Mata Labs Cosmetics Ltd

Munir, Faizaan Ahmed
Medivas Herbals Ltd

Munro, Derek
SMC Cosmetics (UK) Ltd

Munro, Roy Robinson
SMC Cosmetics (UK) Ltd

Munshi, Javid Ibrahim
Euro Aromas Limited

Munshi, Khalid
Euro Aromas Limited

Munshi, Mohsin
Trending Scents Ltd.

Murphy, Anne Louise
Boots International Limited

Murphy, Ian
Bullet and Bone Limited

Murphy, Shelly
Shhh-Holistic Limited

Murray, Darren Clarke
Euro Healthcare Services Ltd
Eurocare Impex Services Ltd

Murray, Jennifer
Serendipity (N.I.) Ltd

Murray, John David
Euro Healthcare Services Ltd
Eurocare Impex Services Ltd

Murray, Jonathan Conrad
Euro Healthcare Services Ltd
Eurocare Impex Services Ltd

Murray, Linda
Euro Healthcare Services Ltd
Eurocare Impex Services Ltd

Murray, Stephanie
Ekoderma Ltd

Murrell, Lauren
By Sarah Limited

Murrell, Sarah
By Sarah Limited

Murrie, Yvonne Nellie
Custom Tan UK Limited

Mursaleen, Hamza
House of Oud Perfumes Limited
Majestic Company London Ltd
Oudh Co Ltd
Signature Fragrances London Ltd

Murton, Samantha
Be Fast Innovation Services Ltd

Musali, Ibrahim
Oud Milano UK Limited

Musareg, Ehab Mohammed Abdulwali Said
Sirra Limited

Musat, Marian Gabriel
MGM UK Limited

Muscat, Jerome Peter
Neroli Limited

Muscat, Terri
Neroli Limited

Muse, Jamal
Fin Perri Ltd

Mushapho, Dikeledi Nkele
Mahogany Crownz Ltd

Mushtaq, Qaiser
Vibrantz Cosmetics Ltd

Musiani, Silvia
Itala Group Ltd

Mustafa, Ali
Celeb Products Ltd

Mustafa, Ghulam
Be Fairall Limited

Mustafa, Seefat
Posh Gift Ltd

Muzongo, Masota
Valencia Cy Makeup Ltd

Mwale, Loyce
VI Beauty Ltd

Mwangi, Nelly Wanjiru
Mise N Ltd

Mwanje, Joshua
Beauty Avenue Limited

Mxonywa, Sisanda
Renaissance Manyane Global Group Ltd

Wedderburn, Jennifer
Jennifer Myers Limited

Mykolaitis, Karolis
KMY Group Ltd

Mysore Jagadishwara, Shruthi
Sai Darshan Limited

Naake, John Lloyd
Underground Girl London Ltd

Nabi, Youcef
Orveda Limited
Orveda UK Limited

Nadeena, Tatiana
Venus Beauty Limited

Nader, Basil Saad Abdulwahab
Bloom International Group Ltd

Nadvirny, Taras Andrew
Cor Europe Limited

Nagamah, Avinash
Online Motions Limited

Nahar, Sharmin
Diverse Solution Ltd

Naidu, Naliandra
Seaside Investments Ltd

Nguyen, Thi-Huong Thao
The Nail & Beauty Link Limited

Phan, Van Tuan
The Nail & Beauty Link Limited

Nail, Ali
Wonderful Life PHBS Ltd

Nair, Rohit
Valentia Skincare Limited

Nalakath, Sadat Yoonus
Liza Organics Ltd

Nambili, Twamanguluka Ndayaamena
Pheora Rucci Limited

Namdeo, Divya
Viridian Leaf Limited

Nana, Florentine Akouvi
Floest Beauty Solutions Ltd

Nandwani, Bhagwan Philip
Transeur Export Finance Co. Ltd

Nandwani, Gobind Hemandas
Transeur Export Finance Co. Ltd

Nandwani, Sajni Gobind
Transeur Export Finance Co. Ltd

Naoum, Bahaa Tharwat Saad, Dr
London Links Trading Limited

Narayanan, Senthur Pandian
Arabian Aroma Limited
Jass Perfumes Limited

Narita, Virgil Nicolae
Narizaonline Ltd

Nartey, Henrietta
H07CNN Limited

Naseer, Syed Umair
Le-Vap Limited

Nashte, Rushikesh Vishwanath
Ru Si Lacquers Global Ltd.

Nasser, Gulam
Beauty Wholesale Limited
Mamado International Limited

Nasser, Kumail
Kaniz International Limited
Kaniz Organics Limited
Vivora Limited

Nasser, Waziri
Nasser Waziri Ltd

Natty, Rochelle
Rochelle Natty Business Group Ltd

McGillivray, Amanda Jane
The Natural Skincare Co Ltd.

Naveed, Muhammad Aamir
Be Savvy Ltd

Naveenan, Theviya
Whimsical Beauty Ltd

Nawathe, Parag Pramod
Pur3 Health Limited

Nawathe, Prajakta Parag
Pur3 Health Limited

Naylor, David Geoffrey
DHB (UK) Ltd.

Naylor, Philip John
Bits4hair Limited
Branded Hair Limited

Naylor, Phillip John
Salon Focus Ltd

Nayyar-Kamdar, Namrata
Plenaire Limited
Shalohm Ltd

Nazer, Zeina
Jardins D'Eden Ltd

Nazir, Balqees
Comfortz Ltd

Ncube Goremucheche, Thembelihle
Goodangels Ltd

Ndebele, Nokuthula Pambano
Ex'klusive Products Ltd

Ndhlovu, Linda
Trelux Limited

Ndhlovu, Russell
Hidden for Purpose Ltd

Neagu, Marius Catalin
Olfacstory Parfums Limited

Neal, Catherine
Newincco 2301 Limited

Neale, Katrina Anne
Global Essence UK Ltd

Nebeolisa, Ikechukwu
Reliance HBC UK Ltd

Nebeolisa, Ujunwa Comfort
Reliance HBC UK Ltd

Nehme, Elie
Artifact Skin Co Ltd

Nelson, Jacqueline
Neolox Ltd

Nelson, Marcus
Neolox Ltd

Nessa, Shahida
Lashflix Limited

Neufeldt, Tobias
Eyeslices UK Limited

Hampton, Anthony Michael
Suzanne Neville Fragrance Ltd

Newark, Robert Newark
Pro Bright Ltd

Newberry, Colette
Brand Evangelists for Beauty Ltd

Newborough, Robert Vaughan, Lord
Rhug Organic and Natural Ltd

Newman, Hannah
There-There Baby Ltd

Newton, Dean Giles
Sulis Minerva Limited

Newton, Yolande Maria Nadine
Herbalise Limited

Nguyen, Anh Thi Phuong
Muse and Rose Limited

Nguyen, Anh
Elite Capital Limited

Nguyen, Giao Quynh
G.Q Homes Ltd

Nguyen, Phuoc Tung
Jan Nails & Beauty Suppliers Ltd

Nguyen, Quang Minh
Aysthetics Limited

Nguyen, Thi Hong Nhung
Asia Nails and Beauty Supply Ltd

Niblock, Michael
Healthcare Wholesale Ltd

Nichol, Jack Paul
Diamond Smile NE Limited

Nicholas, Ieuan Arwel
Wellbeing Skincare Limited

Nicholas, Paul
Nicholas Fragrances Ltd

Nicholas, Peter
Hi Life Health and Beauty (UK) Ltd

Nicholas, Sarah Frances
VR Consult Limited

Nicholls, Melanie
Rembrandt London Limited

Nicholls, Simon George
Lush Ltd.

Nicholls, Steven Mark
Neora UK Limited

Nicholson, Alison
Innocent Alchemy Ltd

Nicholson, Laura Anne
BM Beauty Ltd.

Nicholson, Margery
From Mini Acorns Ltd

Nicholson, Rebecca
Summerlilly Limited

Nicholson, Sherine
From Mini Acorns Ltd

Nicola, Nicholas
A Essentials Limited

Nicolaisen, Paul
Sunspa Europe Limited

Nicolaou, Christopher Nicholas
Hairco Hair & Beauty Ltd

Nicolay, Olivier
Chanel Limited

McCann, Johanna Claire Krogh
JO Nielsen Limited

Nikolov, Vladimir
Nika Cosmo Group Ltd

Nikolova, Zdravka
Nika Cosmo Group Ltd

Nikroodaryani, Hossein
British American Solutions Ltd

Niksarli, Mustafa Halit
Colour Life Limited

Nimako, Isaiah
Asase Tree Ltd

Niner, Bradley
Salon Distribution Concepts Ltd

Niu, Feng
Antian World Limited

Njoku, Jennifer Jean
Natural Jeanius Ltd

Nkomo, Mufadzi
African Wild Organics Ltd

Nkouele, Juniore Ghislaine
Binaya Solution Ltd

Noble, Anthony Hayden
Spa Voyage Limited
Wild Brands Limited

Nogueira Gomes de Lemos, Antonio Julio
Julio & Ejder Ltd

Nordstrom, James Alan
Lash Authority Ltd
Sweet Squared Limited
Wax Authority Limited

Norlain, Guillemette
LVMH Fragrance Brands UK Ltd

Northover, Grant
Red Hot Products Limited
P.H.A.B Wholesale Limited

Northover, Jane
P.H.A.B Wholesale Limited

Nouri, Sam
Maskologist Ltd

Novak, Istvan
Hahydra Technologies Ltd

Novella, Salma
Minxx Lashes Ltd

Novokhatska, Olga
Larisa Markus Limited

Nowacka, Anna
Nail Island Ltd

Nowak, Patrycja Jolanta
La Beauty Labs Ltd.

Nowakowski, Marcin Henryk
Nomalogic Ltd

Nowosz, Stefan
St-Creation Ltd

Nurey, Abdisamad Madey
Thrillage Ltd.

Nurmahomed, Umar Liyakat
Ella Nur Ltd

Nwafor, Ada
Ude Cosmetics Limited

Nwike, Martin
Two Daughters Limited

Athanasi, Katerina
The Nyasa Organics Limited

Grigorova, Maria Hristova
The Nyasa Organics Limited

Nyman, Fleur
Classic Beaute Limited

O' Conghaile, Sean
Tir Chonaill London Ltd

O'Boyle, Deborah
Primoil Limited

O'Brien, Michael Andre
EOB Distribution Ltd

O'Brien, Mike
UK Elements of Beauty Ltd

O'Connor, Blue Robert John
King's Vegan Grooming Ltd

O'Connor, Daniel Mark
DMG Wholesale Limited

O'Connor, Jessica
Make Up Madness Ltd

O'Connor, Lisa Frances
Amly Limited

O'Connor, Sarah Louise
Dots for Spots Ltd

O'Donovan, Kayleigh
House of Vanity Limited

O'Hart, Martin
Revive Express Beauty Ltd

O'Malley, Stuart
Beautiful By Nature Ltd
Omaoli Limited

O'Malley, Tara Louise
Good By Nature Ltd

O'Neill, Assumpta
Everyday Cosmetics Ltd

O'Neill, Jennifer
Essench Cosmetics Ltd

O'Reilly, Chimene
Cor Cosmetics Limited

O'Rourke, Eloise Megan
Eloise M Beauty Ltd

O'Shea, John, Dr
Good Pharma Dermatology Ltd

O'Sullivan, Brian, Dr
Five Dot Botanics Limited

O'Sullivan, Evbi
Berry Inc Ltd
Evbioo Ltd

O'Sullivan, Zaffrin Aysha
Five Dot Botanics Limited

Obeed, Muthana
Florence Health & Beauty Ltd

Occelli, Orianne Christine
W-Healthy Aging Limited

Oddoye, Okpoti George Jeremy
Plenteous Ltd

Odonovan, Sereta
Serenityhands Ltd

Odufuwa, Adeyosola Adeyoyin
La Bello Beauty Limited

Odularu, Clara
Sebaroyale Ltd

Odutola, Olufemi
Plants Work Limited

Oduyemi, Aanuoluwa
Vetivert & Co Ltd

Ofoegbu, Ijeoma Grace
Gracy Hair and Makeup Ltd

Ogawa Gnjatovic, Atsuko
Loveco Ltd

Ogbunude, Viola
Body Organics Limited

Ogden, Cheryl Dawn
Moyra UK Ltd

Ogden, Michael
Beauty Spot Holdings Limited

Ogden, Rosemary Sarah
Beauty Spot Holdings Limited

Ogebule, Alice Adebola
Lady T Limited

Ogebule, Olubunmi Omotunde
Lady T Limited

Ogebule, Omolade Margaret
Lady T Limited

Oglou, Ertugrul Salich
Modazi Ltd

Ogrodnik, Lukasz
Luuann Limited

Ogunbambi, Mariam
Bambi & Co Ltd

Ogunbambi, Rafiqat
Bambi & Co Ltd

Ogunbanjo, Olutoyin Adebimpe
Yejisu Innovation Ltd

Ogunrinde, Abiola
Dudu-Osun Limited

Ogunrinde, Oladipo Demilade
Dudu-Osun Limited

Ojha, Manoj
Lax Group Co Ltd

Ojolo, Ibukunoluwa Oluwatimileyin
Timi's Cosmetics Ltd

Ojuroye, Ayodeji Adedeji
TLGrooming Limited

Okafor, Emeka
Body Month Ltd

Okawa, Cary
Arbonne UK Limited

Okeke, Nneoma Chibudibia, Dr
Freshly Whip'd Limited

Olafsson, Frosti
Bioeffect Limited

Olaru, Claudiu Iulian
Britexim Ltd

Oldham, Lucy
La Maison Hedonique Limited

Oleary, Libby Kate
LK Beauty Ltd

Oleh, Adora
Adora Beauty Limited

Olesiejuk, Wojciech Pawel
Greenpol Distribution Ltd

Olikkathodi, Rafeeque
Choize Ltd

Oliver, Andrew William
A W Oliver & Co Ltd

Oliver, Andrew
Oliver & Taylor Ltd

Oliver-Wallace, Ebun
Bluebells Hair Boutique Ltd

Ollendorff, Malgorzata
Kor Cosmetics Ltd

Olney, Michael Charles
Santiago Distribution Limited

Olorunfemi, Sherif Adebayo
Ashymo Ltd

Olugunna, Titilayo
Arewa Styles Limited

Olusanya, Oyindamola Sukurat
Shea Touch Ltd

Olusesan, Abiodun
Radiant Glow Beauty UK Ltd

Olusesan, Elizabeth
Sublime Cosmetics UK Ltd

Oluwadare, Chrissi Tomiwa, Dr
Lilies of The Valley Cosmetics Ltd

Omar, Aihd
San & Amad General Trade Co Ltd
Tina Trading Co Ltd

Omar, Amani
Perfumez Limited

Omar, Salman
Trade Giant Limited

Omara, Sean
Icebox Brands EU Limited

Omer Abdella, Abdella
Dabrimela Limited

Omosebi, Morakinyo Oreoluwa
Afthrone Ltd

Onemokpe, Bemigho Jennifer
Ruby Concepts Ltd

Ong, Ivan
Viral Solutions General Trading Ltd

Oniyide, Adebayo Adepegba
Doyin Tradings UK Limited

Onofriescu, Iuliana
Lovalova Ltd
NOP Cosmetics Ltd

Onuba, Nnenna
LBB Skin Ltd

Fox, Jayne Elizabeth
The Orange Square Co Ltd.

Hawksley, Christopher Michael
The Orange Square Co Ltd.

Orasmae, Tiina
Meder Beauty International Ltd
Strategy M Ltd

Oreilly, Bruno Diaouga
France Parfums International Ltd

Orencyr, David
Bellapierre Cosmetics Limited

Orji, Jennifer Uchenna
Miracle Herbs & Fruits Cosmetics Ltd

Ormrod, John Philip
Naturally By Nature Ltd

Osak, Adam Krzysztof
Shori Ltd

Osato, Paris
Dos Osatos International Ltd

Osazuwa, Iyobo
B & D Fragrance Limited Co Ltd

Osborne, Audrey
Paradoxx Ltd

Osborne, Jonathan James
Bond Street Cosmetics Limited

Osei, Kofi Asiama
Enimarkets Ltd

Osman, Nabeela Wahid
NABS Promotions Limited

Osmond, Daniel David Crispin
Cornish Beard Co Ltd

Osseiran, Salaheddine Nizam
KPACA Limited

Ostermayr, Andreas
Beiersdorf UK Ltd.

Ostrowski, Alexander Generald
Supernova UK Pty Ltd

Osumanu, Ishawu
Ish Products Ltd

Otcu, Doruk
Relaxa Trading Ltd

Otley, Richard Reverdy
Karium Ltd

Oualnan, Karim
Pure Skincare London Ltd

Afaq, Ahmer
The Oud & Musk UK Ltd

Ousley, Dina
Dinair Airbrush Makeup Systems Ltd

Ovens, Anne-Marie
Anne Marie Beauty Products (U.K.)

Owen, David Neil
Spa Skincare Limited

Owen, Tiantian
Maxibay Limited

Owino, Ruth
Dermashack Limited

Owusu-Dickson, Leticia Dorothy
Dorothy Hair and Beauty Shop Ltd

Oxley, Peter
Scented Sachets (London) Ltd.

Oyetunji, Omolade Olayemi
Tassels UK Ltd

Oyewole, Maggie
Kiddeo Limited

Oygur, Adem
Adem Oygur Ltd

Ozkol, Onur
Naturela Limited

Ozumba, Michael Chiefozie
Huskie London Ltd

Pace, Christopher James
Healthcare Procurement Services Ltd

Pachacama, Jose
Moor Direct Ltd

Pacheco, Selma de Fatima Goncalves
My7heavens Ltd

Pachonski, Andrzej Stanislaw
A S Pacho Ltd

Padia, Ashwin Karsandas
Asante Distributors Limited

Pagarkar, Firoz Ibrahim
Brands Gallery Ltd

Pagayon, Jasmine
Scent Angels UK Ltd

Pagiryte, Sandra
J26 Limited

Pagliarulo, Rocky
Demert Brands EU Ltd

Paier, Victoria
Glamn Holding Ltd

Pailor, Robert Michael
P.R. Professional Salon Supplies Ltd

Pal, Claudiu Ionut
Interall Ltd

Palestini, Francesco
Easybusiness24 Ltd

Paling, Richard John
Pern Consumer Products Limited

Palmer, Gabrielle Lydia
Pure Natural Therapy Ltd

Palmer, Stephanie Mary
Shimmer and Shine Cosmetics Ltd

Pan, Kai
TheGlobalTrading Ltd

Pan, Yu
Qing Ltd

Panchal, Anjlee Virendra
Master Beauty Limited

Panchal, Nikunj Harishankar
PSR Wellness Limited

Panesar, Isha
Isha Cosmetics Limited

Pankhania, Minesh Bachoo
Nekta Botanics Ltd

Papanicolaou, Rhea Maria
Caarmi Ltd

Papdi, Adrienn
Beauty Avenue Limited

Paprzycki, Dariusz
Shave Algorithm Ltd

Paradisgarten, Michelle
Pellitier & Perkins Limited

Bridgman, Jeremy Patrick
The Parfum Club Ltd

Bridgman, Mark Edward
The Parfum Club Ltd

Olmos, Claudia Virginia
The Parfum Club Ltd

Parikh, Viral
Reliant Overseas UK Limited

Parimelalagan, Rasiah
Xpoze International Limited

Park, Jun Han
ENS Europe Limited

Park, Tule
We Concept Ltd

Park, Yong Chin
Universal Beauty Products Europe Ltd

Parker, David John
Beegood Enterprises Limited

Parker, Jeffrey
Toppers Nails Limited

Parker, Richard
Rationale Skincare Limited

Parkhouse, Fiona
Beauty Buddy Limited

Parkhouse, Richard
Beauty Buddy Limited

Parkinson, Amanda
Healthpoint Limited

Parlak, Ahmet Hamdi
Cosimpex Ltd

Parsonage, Rachel Lisa
KMI Brands Limited

Partouche, Avishai
Beauty Premier Limited

Partoush, Uriya
Beauty Premier Limited

Partridge, Naomi Joy
Ko. Essentials Ltd.

Partridge, Thomas Michael
Ko. Essentials Ltd.

Pascovski, Claudiu Victorian
Privilago Fashion Ltd

Pasha, Nadeem
Passion 4 Health International Ltd

Patel, Ajitkumar
Jazzy Hair Limited
Sharp's Global Trading Limited

Patel, Ami Kalpitkumar
Hair and Cosmetics Wholesale Ltd

Patel, Anish
Londonscentsuk Limited

Patel, Ankit [6-1985]
K2 Supplies Ltd

Patel, Ankit [6-1989]
Eukes Global Limited

Patel, Aryanish
Navya Innoveda Ltd

Patel, Bhavesh Rajesh
Fragrance London Limited

Patel, Bijal
Republic Cosmetics UK Ltd

Patel, Bina Hitesh
Fair Pharm Limited

Patel, Chandu
Republic Cosmetics UK Ltd

Patel, Chhayaben
L'Amour Cosmetics London Ltd

Patel, Chirag Pramod
Greenwise Distribution Ltd

Patel, Dhanush
Comglobal Limited

Patel, Dipen
SYN-RG Trading Ltd

Patel, Divyesh Kumar
Pharmadose Limited

Patel, Gaumish
Beauty Magasin Ltd

Patel, Habib
Sublyme Cosmetics Limited

Patel, Harishkumar Pravinchandra
Real Looks Limited

Patel, Havan
Londonscentsuk Limited

Patel, Hetal Chiragkumar
Divit Beauty Ltd

Patel, Himanshu
Cleanux Chemicals Ltd

Patel, Hitendra
Smartway Pharma Limited

Patel, Hitesh Vanmali
Fair Pharm Limited

Patel, Kalpeshkumar
Beautiful World Limited

Patel, Kamini
Republic Cosmetics UK Ltd

Patel, Kamlesh
Dermatx Ltd

Patel, Kayleigh
Ukin Ltd

Patel, Krishan Janak
Pharmadose Limited

Patel, Mr Jayantilal Dullabhbhai
Veridot Asset Dna Limited

Patel, Mrs Nirmalaben Jayantilal
Veridot Asset Dna Limited

Patel, Nasim Akhtar
Adam Michaels Group Ltd

Patel, Nilam
L'Amour Cosmetics London Ltd

Patel, Purgent Vinubhai
Ruxley Medical Aids Limited

Patel, Rajesh Rameshbhai
Fragrance London Limited

Patel, Rupeshkumar Dinubhai
Medipro Pharma Limited

Patel, Rushisagar Rameshbhai
Yaami's Fashion Beauty & Cosmetics UK

Patel, Sanjay Chandubhai
ASVR Bebidas Limited

Patel, Svikrut
Pharmadose Limited

Patel, Vijanti Ajit
Sharp's Global Trading Limited

Patel, Vijanti Ajitkumar
Jazzy Hair Limited

Patel, Wasim
Supreme Beard Ltd

Patrick, Andrew
Alliance SG Limited
Mob Cosmetics Limited

Patroiu, Maria Gabriela
Gabriellas Beauty Ltd

Patten, Dominic Anton
L'Anza Europe Limited

Patten, Victoria Jane
L'Anza Europe Limited

Patterson, Victoria Louise
S & P Cosmetics Limited

Pattison, Tristan Richard
International Hair Cosmetics Ltd

Pattni, Minesh Rasiklal
Comfort Click Limited

Paudel, Anuj
Cosmetics Online Limited

Paul, Harold John Christopher
Latam HQ Health Ltd

Paul, Simon John Christopher
Latam HQ Health Ltd

Paulson, Nicola Eleanor
Dermaenhance Ltd.

Paun, Dorin Eliodor
Pavone Profumi SRL Ltd

Paus, Pontine Cecilie Alexandra
Dr.Lipp Ltd

Pavlou, Mario
Gymbar Limited

Pavlova, Vania
Lino Rose Ltd

Pavlovsky, Bruno Andre Jean
Chanel Limited

Pawelek, Stanislaw
Top Beauty Brands Ltd

Payne, Danica
Danica Payne Ltd

Pazdanska, Wioletta
Loopy Hair & Beauty Ltd

Peace, Sarah Oludamilola
Yejisu Innovation Ltd

Peacock, Nadia Ann
F.D.D. International Limited

Pearce, Alexander Leonard
Samla Tribe Limited

Pearce, Michael
Esspire Limited

Pearce, Terence
Luxe Associates Ltd

Pearman, Georgina
Hundred Acres Apothecary Ltd

Pearman, Sam
Hundred Acres Apothecary Ltd

Pearson, Andrew James
SMC Cosmetics (UK) Ltd

Pearson, Donna
100% Vegan Skincare Limited

Pearson, Michael Norman
Pearson Cosmetics Limited
SMC Cosmetics (UK) Ltd

Pearson, Savannah
Lux Aesthetics Hull Ltd

Peberdy, David Anthony
White Rose Aromatics Limited

Peberdy, Suzanne Margaret
White Rose Aromatics Limited

Pedersen, Roxanne
Rawly Processed Ltd.

Peerless, Fiona McMillan
Australian Bodycare U.K. Ltd
Beauty & Skincare Essentials Ltd
Essential Bodycare Limited

Pekinel, Harika
Nanosafe Ltd.

Penkul, Alexander Stewart
Occo London Limited

Penney, Sarah Jane
Orange Balloon Ltd

Perez, Alfonso Perez
Hugworld Cristalinas UK Ltd

Jalal, Farzeen
The Perfect Lady Ltd

Perfitt, Raoul John
Herb U.K. Limited
Organic Colour Systems Limited

Akhtar, Saheel Haroon
The Perfumer Ltd

Perkins, Colin
Hair for Men Products Ltd

Perman, Timothy James
Fish London Limited

Perris, Gian-Luca
Incorporated Perfumery Distribution

Perris, Michele
Incorporated Perfumery Distribution

Persaud, Anna Devi
This Works Products Limited

Peters, Philip David
Leading National Training Ltd

Petkov, Dimitar
QZE Limited

Petkov, Dobri Todorov
Regal Skincare Ltd

Petropoulakis, Georghios
GP Mediplus Ltd

Petrou, Vasiliki
REN Skincare Limited
Ren Ltd

Pettit, Matthew
Unilux Trading Ltd

Phan, Van Tuan
Kiara Sky Professional Nail Distribution

Pharand, Georges
Fragrance Factory Limited

Phillips, Dominic Beavis Blake
Lola's Apothecary Ltd

Phillips, Grania Tiffany
Lola's Apothecary Ltd

Phillips, Jonathan Taylor
Canna Biology Distributing Ltd

Phillips, Katherine
This Works Products Limited

Phillips, Luke
Company NBN Limited

Phillips, Mark William
Piggy Paint UK Ltd

Phillips, Mark
Niki & Co Ltd

Phillips, Michael
Fragrancekent (UK) Ltd

Phillips, Natalie Rebecca
Piggy Paint UK Ltd

Phillips, Simon Blake
Lola's Apothecary Ltd

Pian, Deoclides Jandir
Gold Pillar Holding Ltd

Piboonswasdi, Chantarach
Comets Intertrade Co Ltd

Pica, Daniele
Mandragora Ltd

Piccirillo, Guiseppe
Axa Beauty World Limited

Piccirilo, Giuseppe
Hair Passion Limited

Pickerill, Andrew
Potteries Transport Services Ltd

Pickering, Angela
Angela Pickering Limited

Pickthall, Christopher
Yu Parfums Ltd

Pickthall, Nicholas
Yu Parfums Ltd

Pietarinen, Satu
Sangels Limited

Pieter, Alex
Sweet Lilli Ltd

Pietka, Sylwia Krystyna
Wake Up Beauty Ltd

Pietruszka, Miroslaw Roman
Cosmetics 4U Limited

Pilcher, Colin
Dolly Custard Ltd

Pilcher, Terasa Christine
Dolly Custard Ltd

Pina, Bruna Rossana
Golden Vanity Ltd

Pinder, Richard John
Inspired by RJP Limited

Pinder-White, Jonathan Charles
Azur Interiors Limited

Pindoria, Kaushal
Trulips Ltd

Pindoria, Sarita
Pharmaclinix Limited

Pinho Leite Da Costa, Zeferino
Kservices Group Ltd

Pintea, Krisztian
Marcman Perfume Ltd

Pisu, Giovanni
Maximaliste Limited

Pitayanukul, Sydwat Andrew Chiu-Mo
Adonis Skin Ltd

Pitchaimuthu, Sudhakar, Dr
Spruce Vita Limited

Pitsiali, Flora
Oxygen Skin Care - London Ltd

Pitzus, Simon Antony
Scent Retail Ltd

Plant, Bridget Emma
Cochabamba Parfums Limited

Plastow, Margaret Jean
Joy Limited

Plewka, Martyna Helena
Forest Hive Ltd

Plomarteli, Maria
Innon Vision Limited

Plumley-Korab, Bethany
Clean Living Ltd

Pochin, James Patrick
M Beauty Ltd

Pocock, Rebecca Ann
Pococks Absolute Rose Ltd

Pocock, Stewart James
Pococks Absolute Rose Ltd

Poddar, Dilip Kumar
Emita Europe Limited

Pollalis, Athanasios
Miraculous UK Ltd

Pollard, Andrew Miles
Marksman Green Ltd

Pollyn, Douglas Apabara
Eku Skin Care Ltd

Pons Ester, Pedro Miguel
Aromaderme UK Limited

Poole, Andrew Charles William
Mellor & Russell Direct Distribution Ltd

Pooley, Samantha Robyn
Beauty Mastery Ltd.

Pop-Pecev, Risto
Slim Line Club UK Ltd

Popa, Catalin-Leonard
Ned London Limited

Popat, Anish
Beauty Africa Limited

Popat, Ashna
Beauty Africa Limited

Pope, Gary Vincent
Nouvriet Boutros (UK) Ltd

Popov, Daniela
Use Natural Ltd

Popov, Marin Angelov
Quality Brand MG Ltd

Popple, Alex
Flowery Whiff Limited

Popple, Carolyn
Flowery Whiff Limited

Porter, Akil
L.P Cosmetics Ltd

Posner, Daniella Harriet
C-Bombe Limited

Rashid, Soran
Sara Post Ltd

Postir, Giangiacomo
Doers Skincare Limited

Poucher, Jake Alexander
JP Products and Services Ltd

Povey, Dan
Nuke Manufacturing, Distribution & Investments

Powell, Claire
Can Celebrity Brands Limited

Powell, Colin
Hairganic Limited

Powell, Marie Ann
Aromaclub Handmade Skincare Ltd

Power, Zoe
Naturally Untamed Ltd

Powers, Michael
Autoscentsco Ltd

Poy, Glenn Derrick
Dermalogica (UK) Limited

Pozo Caballero, Marcos David
Wisdom of Nature Limited

Prangell, Joanne Claire
Fizzy Peach Ltd

Prasad, Ravi
Varana UK Limited

Prato-Scarlett, Simon
Fatale Cosmetics Limited

Pratt, Dean
Colgate-Palmolive (U.K.) Ltd

Prayoonkham, Thanaphon
AMS-Uhren Ambiente mit Style Ltd

Premji, Sadikally Gulamabbas
American Cosmetics Limited

Prendergast, Edmund Anthony
Ossulstone Hundred Limited

Prendergast, Samantha Jane
Krizma Cosmetics Ltd

Prepok, Adrienn
Raynolds Ltd

Khaldi, Sara
The Prescripteur Ltd

Presswell, James Stephen
International Trade Corporation Ltd
Lustra Beauty Limited
Pouty Lipzz Limited

Presswell, June Linda
International Trade Corporation Ltd
Lustra Beauty Limited
Pouty Lipzz Limited

Presswell, Roy Henry
International Trade Corporation Ltd
Lustra Beauty Limited
Pouty Lipzz Limited

Preston, Trieu Hai
Lisa Preston Ltd

Preston, Arabella Charlotte
Votary Limited

Preston, Jack
Prestonelite Limited

Preston, Julie Carolyn
Serendipity Herbals Ltd

Priadka, Anna
Makeup54 Ltd

Price, Caroline
Discounted Cosmetics Limited

Price, Gareth
Strip Distribution Limited

Price, Paul Bryan
Beiersdorf UK Ltd.

Price, Stephen Ronald
Dr. Organic Limited
Optima Consumer Health Limited

Priestman, John Kenneth
QOD UK Ltd

Prigarska, Linda
Gajas Gift Limited

Prince Alison, Onuoha
Onamex Ltd

Pringle, Matthew James
4M Cosmetics Limited

Prinz, Andreas
Croma-Pharma Limited

Prinz, Gerhard
Croma-Pharma Limited

Prive, Gael Vanessa
Goldshore (UK) Limited

Prive, Philippe Henri
Goldshore (UK) Limited

Probert, Victoria Elizabeth
Nouela Organics Ltd

Procter, Doris Andrew
Procter & Procter Limited

Procter, Dorris
Norpro Limited

Prodniece, Vita
Moor Direct Ltd

Prosenko, Andrey
Droplet Cosmetics Limited

Protopapas, Katerina Androulla
Kiki Body Limited

Prus, Marcin
Organic Professional Ltd

Pumphrey, Janey Emma
Aspects Beauty Co Ltd

Purcell, Kieran Elizabeth
Uppercut Deluxe Co Limited

Aragon, Neil
The Pure Body Skin Care Ltd

Purewal, Parveen Kaur
Instant Beauty UK Limited

Purewal, Terjinder-Deep Singh
Zaliant Skincare Limited

Puthyia Purayil, Thanveer Ahammed
Feel and Heal UK Limited

Puttick, Laura Kay
Regima Zone Ltd

Pyle, Colin
Disciple Skincare Limited

Pyneeandy, Zoe
Sucre By Zoe Skincare Limited

Pytel, Jedrzej Michal
ULB Limited

Qadir, Asif
Disley Limited

Qaiser, Rozina
Orgreen Naturals Ltd

Qasim, Mohammed Luqman
Luqs Womenswear Ltd

Qawas, Abdulsamad
Oud Milano UK Limited

Qayyum, Tahir
Hair & Skin Care Ltd

Qerimi, Fatjon
Albland Limited

Qian, Fuwei Qian
Dily Oka International Group Co., Ltd

Qiao, Huihui
Direct Trade Limited

Qiu, Connor, Dr
Dr. Twilight Ltd

Quaddus, Azr Abdul
Amaani Q Ltd

Quartrmaine, Clare Louise
Fatale Cosmetics Limited

Quida, Ariana Fernanda Paranhos
Nature Scents Limited

Quinn, Elizabeth
Mary Jean Limited

Quinn, Eoin
Labapothecary Ltd.

Quinn, Jade Anike
Rose & Thorn Ltd

Quinn, Leslie Thomas
Mary Jean Limited

Quinn, Victoria
Fox Group International Ltd
Revolax Ltd

Majoros, Agnes Renata
The Quint Essence Lab Ltd

Varro, Attila
The Quint Essence Lab Ltd

Quintard, George George
Prestige Perfumes Limited

Qureshi, Myra Husain
Conatural Ltd

Qureshi, Nausheen
Elequra Limited

Racca, Cristina
Pispo Ltd

Rach, Sunny Nalin
Enfield Distribution Ltd

Radford, John Lawrence
Natural Birthing Co Ltd

Radia, Amish Rajnikant
Anar Naturals Limited

Radia, Rinku Ramesh
Fragrance Plus Limited

Radziszewska, Karolina Urszula
Liolax Limited

Rae, Gavin Paul
RMG Hair Limited

Rae, Martin Andrew
RMG Hair Limited

Raffiq, Mohamed Ali Roshanali
AMF Distribution Limited

Rafi, Yasir
Attar Mist Ltd

Rafie, Helen
Heavenly Riches Limited

Rafiq, Sohail
Allure Beauty Supplies Ltd

Rafiq, Zeba
Z & J Enterprises Limited

Ragbir, Jai Indar
Deo Beauty Products Limited

Ragbir, Sergio
Deo Beauty Products Limited

Rahimtoola, Abbas
Herbal Essentials UK Limited

Rahimtoola, Aly
Herbal Essentials UK Limited

Rahman, Ashadur
Our-Scent Ltd

Rahman, Ashrafur
AR Scents Limited

Rahman, Farjana Lisa
Rawmans Ltd

Rahman, Habibur
Lienex Beauty London Ltd

Rahman, Kazi Mohammed Abidur
Kazi Brothers Group Limited

Rahman, Kazi Mohammed Ashiqur
Esem International Ltd

Rahman, Mohammed Dinar Saddiqur
MD-101 Ltd

Rahman, Mohammed Emadur
Rich & Ruitz Perfume Industry Ltd

Rahman, Moniza
Liza Organics Ltd

Rahmani, Marzia
Real Skin Pickle Ltd

Raihan, MD Mushfiq
Supply Zoom Ltd

Raja, Aarzu
Duo Beauty Products Limited
Gemini Beauty Products Ltd

Raja, Kahinaat
Duo Beauty Products Limited
Gemini Beauty Products Ltd

Rajani, Ashokkumar Haridas
Denbond Pharmaceuticals Ltd

Rajani, Rekha Ashok
Denbond Pharmaceuticals Ltd

Raji, Sukurat Omolara
La Bello Beauty Limited

Rakadjiev, Dian Pentchev
Refan UK Ltd

Rakhmonova, Dilafruz
Monrone Health Ltd

Rakoto, Albert Marie Hanitra
Kayanna Ltd

Rall, Surinder Kaur
Khushi Skincare Limited

Ralph, Malcolm Arnold
Galactix Ltd

Ramanan, Sudhakar
Spruce Vita Limited

Ramjohn, Candy Ria
Chic Clothing Limited

Ramma, Armands
Traderuk Limited

Rampley, Cordelia Petra Nadine, Dr
Oxmetics Ltd

Rampton, Lionel Philip
Brandcare Group Limited

Ramsay, Georgina Louise
Joy Limited

Ramsay-Peters, Ander Anneka Sheila
Serenityy Ltd

Ramsbottom, Amanda
North West Cosmetics Limited

Randall, Jeremy Anthony Philip
Lubatti Limited

Rankin, Harold Reid
Emuology UK 2017 Limited

Rankin, Therese Catherine
Apotheca London Skincare Ltd

Ranno, Consolazione
Sikania Ltd

Rapley, Ian Andrew
ID Skincare Limited

Rashad, Farzad
Alwais Ltd

Rashid, Mohammed Shakil
Select & Bargain Ltd

Rashid, Oleur
HE Products Ltd

Rashkov, Boris
Rashimex Trading Limited

Rasool, Adal
Splashes & Spills Ltd.

Rasool, Mohammed Adnan
Splashes & Spills Ltd.

Rasquinet, Patrick Nicolas Edouard Jacques
La Prairie (UK) Limited

Rasul, Mahmud Ur
Square Wholesale Ltd

Raszewski, Mariusz Lucjan
Optimavia Ltd

Ratcliffe, John Douglas
Pink Cosmetics London Limited

Ratnani, Vinod
Mayfair Export UK Ltd

Rattan, Vanita
Pharmaclinix Limited

Ravensdale, Marta Joanna
Zojo. The Gorgeousness Co Ltd

Rawle, Andrew Thomas
Beiersdorf UK Ltd.

Rawlins, Steven Antony
Rooster & Rooster Ltd.

Rawlinson, Stephen Anthony
Mehron Limited

Rawson, Kim Patrick
Asante Distributors Limited

Rayani, Mahmoud Jiva
Asante Distributors Limited

Raymond, Joseph Marc, Sir
Giva Solution Ltd

Raynsford, Jessica
Look Lovable Ltd.

Raza, Malik Ahsan
H & R Cosmetics Ltd

Razaq, Mohammed
Razaq & Iqbal Limited

Read, Lucy
La Personal Products Ltd

Reay, Kimberley
20seven Limited

Reay, Lauren
20seven Limited

Rebatchi, Mohamed-Lamine
Rebatchi Perfums Ltd

Rechtman, Anthony
Total Beauty Network (UK) Ltd

Reddyhoff, Adam
Hoff Beards Limited

Redstone, Laura Jane
For All Dogkind Limited

Reeve, Alison Suzanne
Palmsextra Limited

Reeve, Linda Jean
Palmsextra Limited

Reeve, Robert George
Palmsextra Limited

Rehman, Ubaid Ur
David & Co. Traders Ltd

Rehman, Waqar
S & G Supplies Ltd

Reid, Christopher
Humanity Cosmetics Limited

Reid, Colin
Paradoxx Ltd

Reilly, Paul Stephen
Balmain Hair UK Ltd

Rejza, Krzysztof Tadeusz
Aga Cosmetics Ltd

Remblance, Scott Stanley
Beautiful Body Limited

Ren, Zhen
Reneebeauty Limited

Renaud, Jessica
Renski Limited

Renda, Alison Marianne
New Era Hair Ltd

Renda, Eddie Patrick
JGR UK Distributions Limited
New Era Hair Ltd

Resch, Roland
Beard Zone Ltd

Revesz, Attila
Raynolds Ltd

Reviron, Sylvain
Reviron Limited

Rezaei, Ali
Aurum Argan Ltd

Rezine, Mohammed
OrganicBeautyshop Ltd

Rhoden, Fiona
Chief Cosmetics Ltd

Rhodes, Simon Timothy
Dee Doo Limited

Rhodes, Suzan
Dee Doo Limited

Beggin, Carolyn Vivienne
Charlotte Rhys UK Limited

McDermott, Shaun
Charlotte Rhys UK Limited

Spyropoulos, Janet Mary
Charlotte Rhys UK Limited

Riaz, Nabila
Seed Fashion and Beauty Incubator Ltd

Ribeiro Kerr, Paula Jane
Evagray Limited

Ricci, Kiera
Toggle Genetica Group Limited

Ricciardo, Antonio
Easybusiness24 Ltd

Rice, Graham
Johnson & Johnson Limited

Richards, Edward
Nanat Limited

Richards, Kate
Nanat Limited

Richardson, Paul John
Ohsho Ltd

Richardson, Raphael
Infini Lab Ltd

Richardson, Samuel James Ivo
Saltee Skincare Limited

Richmond, Anna Maria Adelaide
Pommade Divine Skincare Ltd

Ricketts, Anthony
Silk Oil of Morocco UK Limited

Ricketts, Christina
Silk Oil of Morocco UK Limited

Ridvan, Arslan
Onna Export Import Ltd

Riedner, Thomas
Beiersdorf UK Ltd.

Rieman, Jane Vanessa
Nu Essence Limited

Riera Sucre, Pedro Jose
Laurens Cosmetics UK Limited

Rigby, Charlotte Frances
Sci Check Limited

Rigby, Lauren Victoria
Sci Check Limited

Rigby, Sophie Alexandra
Sci Check Limited

Riley, Charlotte
Benefit & Riley Healthcare Ltd
Riley & Sons Ltd

Rimkeviciene, Silva
Beauty Expression (UK) Limited

Rimkevicius, Feliksas
Beauty Expression (UK) Limited

Rippon, David John
L'Anza Europe Limited

Rishi, Vikas
Dazzlers & Toppers PTL Ltd

Rix, Caroline Beverly
Simlar 2 Limited

Rizvi, Syed Hassan Haider
Excelcia Limited

Rizzelli, Antonio Lloyd
Kanj Wholesale Ltd

Roach, John
UK Brand Holdings Ltd

Roath, Kate
Wild Source Apothecary Ltd

Robba, Stefano, Dr
Hairya Ltd

Robbins, Sharon Virginia
Star Qualities Ltd

Robert, Julien Jean Maxime
Robert Cosmetics Limited

Roberts, Michael Vann
MV Roberts & Co (UK) Ltd

Trout, Lawrence Philip
MV Roberts & Co (UK) Ltd

Glancey, Generald Robert, Dr
Rita Roberts Cosmetics Limited

Glancey, Liudmilla Pentcheva
Rita Roberts Cosmetics Limited

Upchurch, Rita Yvonne
Rita Roberts Cosmetics Limited

Roberts, Alexandra May Howard
Dacre Skincare Limited

Roberts, Ariel
Loop Beauty Limited

Roberts, Chantelle
Njubien Ltd

Roberts, Peter Daryl
Skinmed Ltd
Skinvital Ltd

Roberts, Robert Philip
Wash Your Mouth Out Ltd

Robertson, Anthony John
Pharmacare (Europe) Limited

Robertson, Fay
Cassolette & Co (Sales & Marketing)

Robertson, Paris
Bath Bombs and Beyond Limited

Robertson-Marriott, Francis
Spring and Underworld Ltd

Robh, Badhol Umor
Robh Scrub Limited

Robinson, Christopher
Allied Aerosols Limited
Allied Fragrances Limited

Robinson, David Raymond
Corium Health Limited

Robinson, Felix
Sheacare Cosmetics Limited

Robinson, Jemma
Bluesky Cosmetics UK HQ Ltd

Robinson, Malika
Maliboo Hair and Cosmetics Ltd

Robinson, Sally Anne
Dynamic Skincare Ltd

Robson, Daniel
Hotel Essentials Ltd

Robson, Neil Ian
Dug and Bitch Ltd

Rochell, Luke Daniel
B Luxury Scents Ltd

Rochford, Jason Robert
Soak Rochford Ltd

Rodgers, Antony Alaric
ID Aromatics Limited

Rodol, Neil
Outdoor Girl Limited
Warpaint London PLC

Rodriguez Sone, Guillermo Ramon
Capital Import & Export Co. Ltd

Roe, Brian Generald Clifford
Ink Oil Limited

Roger Jara, Joan Albert
Albert Roger & Partner France Ltd

Bakouch, Guillaume Sylvain Samuel
Albert Roger & Partner France Ltd

Roger Jara, Joan Albert
Albert Roger Benelux Limited
Iconic Beauty London Limited
Miss Vivien Ltd
Wafson Ltd
Albert Roger Limited
Albert Roger Portugal Limited

Rogers, James
Original Additions (Beauty Products)

Rogers, Keith James
Mesoskinline (UK) Limited

Rogers, Mark Adam
Filberts Bees Limited

Rogers, Paul
On & Off Beauty Ltd

Rogers, Philada Rose
Filberts Bees Limited

Rogers, Vanessa Stella Randall
Mesoskinline (UK) Limited

Rogerson, Atanaska
Aurora Spa Health and Beauty Ltd

Rogerson, Stephen
Aurora Spa Health and Beauty Ltd

Rollason, William
Elemental Herbology Limited

Rollocks, Godwyn Joseph Orlando Roy
Green Guru Enterprises Ltd.

Romanova, Karina
Rouge Bunny Rouge UK Limited

Romanowicz, Piotr Marian
Coll Gen Limited

Nooraldin Moosa, Ramin
Rogia Romini Limited

Roozendaal, Henricus Simon
Crete Online Ltd.

Rosa, Ana Lucia
Ivaxane UK Ltd

Rosas Morales, Henry Alexander
Alton Trading Ltd

Rose, David Alan
D & L Hair Products Limited

Rose, Jonathan Russell
D & L Hair Products Limited

Rose, Lorraine Sandra
D & L Hair Products Limited

Kayser, Fenella
The Rosebud Perfume Co Ltd

Son, Covey
JC Rosedale Co Ltd

Rosedam, Denise
Beauty Link Wholesale Ltd

Rosedam, Robert Raymond
Beauty Link Wholesale Ltd

Roselie, Molly Rita
National Supplement Beauty Solutions

Ross, Andrew
Larmed Limited

Rossidis, Freda
Mr. Smith Products UK Ltd

Rossiter, Thomas Anthony
Intercos UK Ltd

Rostaminia, Behzad
Step International Cosmetic Ltd

Rother, Dalis Guisel
MDistributor Hair and Beauty Products

Rothstein, Mindy Eileen
Very British Baby International Ltd

Rougeot, Jean Andre
Benefit Cosmetics Limited

Routley, Shirley May
Somerset Perfumery Ltd

Rouvali, Maria
Bespoke Mr Ltd

Rowe, Jason
Lovorika London Limited

Rowe, Joshua
Intermercantile Limited

Rowe, Nathan Alexander
True Hemp Ltd

Roy-Jones, Pamela
Classic Beaute Limited

Royle, Graham
I Love Cosmetics Limited
Sculptola Ltd

Royle, Nicola Rachel
Sculptola Ltd

Rozenberga, Baiba
Diymonde Corporation Limited

Rozidar, Tengku
Haltrade UK Ltd

Rozman, Maks
Quality Check Ltd

Ruane, Melissa
Blissible Ltd

Rubani, Adeel
Be Fairall Limited

Rubaszewska, Klaudia
Dunia Organic Ltd

Rudd, Anthony Colin
Dermalogica (UK) Limited

Rudgalvis, Edgars
Cosmetics Wholsale Ltd

Rudoe, Laura Francesca
Good Ventures Limited

Kaposts, Artis
J. Rudzitis Ltd

Rueda Hernando, Miguel
Karium Ltd

Ruff, Lothar
Anglia-Perfumery Ltd.

Rujbally, Mohammad Shawood
Hanana Traders Ltd

Rumble, Olga Jane
Rose Tree Enterprises Ltd.

Rupina, Irina
Arna Group Ltd

Ruprecht, Stefan
Com4hospitality Ltd.

Rusiecki, George Henry
Azur Interiors Limited

Aitken, Brian
Jerome Russell Limited

Cunniffe, Sheena Johnston
Jerome Russell Limited

MacDonough, Colette Frances
Jerome Russell Limited

MacDonough, Stephen James
Jerome Russell Limited

McLaughlin, Stephen
Jerome Russell Limited

Russell, Chinwe Mercy
Sheabynature Ltd

Russell, Michelle
Dream Skin Ltd

Russell, Mikhaila Antoinette
Haybae Cosmetics Ltd

Russon-Taylor, Imogen
Kingdom Scotland Limited

Rusu, Adina
Cadyle Ltd

Rutka, Katarzyna
Perezoso Limited

Rutter, James Alistair
Mainline Marketing U K. Ltd

Rutter, Peter
Mainline Marketing U K. Ltd

Rutter, Robert Edward
Mainline Marketing U K. Ltd

Rutter, Vivien Grace
Mainline Marketing U K. Ltd

Ryan, Mark
Natural British Limited

Ryan, Michael
Healthpoint Limited

Rydell, Joseph
Carr Greens Limited

Rzepkowska, Elzbieta Monika
Think Be Nature Ltd

Sabesan, Ragini
Pound Ring Ltd

Sabi, Olu
Yehmea Limited

Sabiketi Lesdos, Antoinette
Hild International Group Ltd

Sackey, Isaac Abednego
Glow Investment Ltd

Sader, Ebrahim Hasan
Azhar Academy Limited

Sadiq, Amina
Yummy Home Ltd

Sadiq, Nabila
Yummy Home Ltd

Sadiq, Naseem
Yummy Home Ltd

Sadler, Keith John
Warpaint London PLC

Sadlier, Alexander
Hotel Essentials Ltd

Sadni, Tarik
Argan Care Ltd

Safadi, Sami
Biovate Limited

Safaie, Pejman
Bod Beauty Ltd

Saffell, Ada Aurelia
Tarsago Ltd

Jackson Burks, Abigail Louise
The Sage Apothecary Limited

Sahin, Hasan
Sahinler Limited

Sahney, Jasbir Kaur
P.S. Sahney & Co Limited

Sahney, Jasprit Kaur
P.S. Sahney & Co Limited

Sahney, Gursharn Singh
Sahney Siblings Limited

Sahney, Jasprit Kaur
Sahney Siblings Limited

Sahni, Shiv
Bion Corporation Limited

Sai Mui, Cheung
Always 20 Limited

Sajawal, Henna Irum Amin
Chit.Ka Ltd

Salama, Mona Mahmoud Saad
Evoiq International Ltd

Salamathullah, Mohammed
Birmingham Fragrances Ltd

Saleem, Rabiya
Radiant and Refined Limited

Saleem, Rozina
A.R Cosmetics Limited

Saleem, Zara
Delhicious Ltd

Salem, Nathan
Salem Stores Ltd

Salem, Salem Hesham Mohamed
SA & A Ltd

Salhov, Efraim
Opatra Limited

Salichou, Maria, Dr
In Situ Cosmetics Ltd

Salih, Yucem
Per Capelli Ltd

Salim, Ilyas Mohammed
Parker & Moses Ltd

Sall, Ibrahima
Thiossane Ltd

Salman, Lior
Wizer Ltd

Salmon, Nicola Helena
Just Acrylics Ltd

Salmon, Thomas Arthur
Beautonomy Limited

Samer Fahem, Stephanie
Saroza Limited

Sampson, Danielle
Lush Lashes London Limited

Samyn, Jean-Christophe
Caudalie UK Limited

Samyshkina, Natalia
Elitelashes Ltd

Chaudhri, Jalil Ahmed
Leonora Sanche Cosmetics Ltd

Simon-Sanchez, Nila Leonor
Leonora Sanche Cosmetics Ltd

Chaudhri, Jalil Ahmed
Leonora Sanche Limited

Simon-Sanchez, Nila Leonor
Leonora Sanche Limited

Sandhu, Ben David
Myego Ltd

Sandler-Vallance, Daniel
Daniel Sandler Ltd

Saragossi, Nicola
Daniel Sandler Ltd

Sandler-Vallance, Simon
Blossom Colour Limited

Sangerwal, Basir
Best Choice FMCG Ltd

Sanghera, Raghbir
K2Y Limited

Sankey, Gordon Ian
Ambassadors Choice Limited

Sanson, David Alan
Pern Consumer Products Limited

Sanson, Edward Alexander
11:11 Limited

Santini, Daniel
Santini Trade Ltd.

Santo, Doron
Onsen Secret UK Ltd

Saragossi, Mark
Blossom Colour Limited

Saragossi, Nicola
Blossom Colour Limited

Sardar, Tabbita
MNF Commodities Ltd

Sardo, Jessica Stephanie
L'Art & La Matiere Limited

Sarfati, David
Repechage Europe Limited

Sarfati, Shiri
Repechage Europe Limited

Sargeant, David John
Spa Therapies Ltd

Sargeant, Tracey Marie
Spa Therapies Ltd

Sargent, Nicola
Miya Hair Limited

Sarkar, Abm Kamran
Trade Giant Limited

Sarwar, Jabir Hussain
Pak Beauty Ltd

Sarwar, Waseem
Fragrance Express Limited

Satchell, Edward William
Fleuroma Limited

Sathi, Sarmin Sultana
CNI Services Limited

Saulenas, Darius
Rupitex Limited

Saunders, Jake Thomas
Wild Violet X Limited

Savani, Priya Ramesh
Ibeautheart Limited

Sawers, Kenny
Chintys Ltd

Scarlett-Hudson, Kyio
Hudsonry Ltd

McCubbin, Sarah Elizabeth
The Scent Edit Limited

Tahir, Arfan
The Scent Factory Limited

Scetbon, Guy
Bellapierre Cosmetics Limited

Schapera, Steven Lorn
Lab Brands Limited

Schaverien, Robert Barry John
Blissworld Limited

Schleider, Helene
Les Petits Parfums Limited

Schlick, Pal
Splendor Europe Ltd.

Schneider, Anu
Beautysugaring Limited

Schoeller, Martin
Croma-Pharma Limited

Schofield, Paul Richard
Drammock International Limited

Schultz, Derrick Andrew
Damrick's White Bunny Ltd

Schutz, Elzbieta Malgorzata
Peters Cosmet Ltd

Schwartz, Jean-David
Arbonne UK Limited

Schwenke, Lionel Edmond Rene
Canna Biology Distributing Ltd

Scott, Daniel John
Wizard Brands Limited

Scott, Deborah Annette
SKN-RG Ltd

Scott, Jeremy Patrick
Ashley & Co UK Ltd

Scott, Kirsty Justine
Simply Pure Skincare Ltd

Scott, Paul
Cult Candy Limited

Scott, Robert
SKN-RG Ltd

Scott-Weeks, Katherine Amelia Rose
Scott Weeks Enterprises Ltd

Sear, Rowan Louise
Eleven Eleven Cosmetics Ltd

Sear-Mayes, David James
Pixie Lott Paint Limited

Sear-Mayes, Siobhan
Impulse Global Solutions Ltd

Sebagh, Jean-Louis
Cosmetic Doctor at Work Ltd

Seban, Jean-Luc
Paris Elysees Holding Ltd.

Sebastian, Sage
Exbrands Ltd

Sefi, Zed Tereq
Perfume Brands Limited

Segev, Nativ
MGC Pharma (UK) Ltd

Sekander, Yousaf Mohammed
Bullingberg Limited

Sekhon, Lakhwinder Singh
Art Creative Limited

Sekine, Motonobu
Takasago (U.K.) Limited

Selim, Erol
E-MO Nails Ltd

Selim, Monika
E-MO Nails Ltd

Sellers, Janet Susan
Sandaig Ltd

Sellers, Jonathan Noel
Sandaig Ltd

Selman, Ali
MSD Trading Services Limited

Semler-West, Charlotte
Votary Limited

Sengul, Lubna
Organica Skincare Ltd

Sentance, Emma
Lush Lashes London Limited

Serebrjakova, Jelena
Wild Beauty Ltd

Serima-Fowler, Rumbidzai
Mimi's Organics Ltd

McPeake, James Anthony
The Serious Skin Care Co Ltd.

Sert, Huseyin
Kozmar International Limited

Serwaah, Hannah
Enimarkets Ltd

Severigny, Chloe
Beauty Everich Ltd

Seyda, Stefanie
Headissimo Limited

Shabbir, Shahid
50shadez Ltd

Shabir, Mohammed Shamas
City Beauty Supplies (UK) Ltd

Shafique, Mohammed
Natural Touch Enterprises Ltd

Shah, Alpan
DealsRUsOnline Ltd

Shah, Amna
Aabis Duty Free Limited
F A Commodities Ltd

Shah, Anoop Shashikant
Medipro Pharma Limited

Shah, Asad Ali
Unique Cosmetics Limited
Zainab Limited

Shah, Ashok Virpal
Beauty Kosmetika Ltd

Shah, Asif Haidra Ali
Unique Cosmetics Limited
Zainab Limited

Shah, Devendra, Dr
Healthcare Wholesale Ltd

Shah, Dinesh Chhabildas
Universal Toiletries Corporation Ltd

Shah, Fatima
F A Commodities Ltd

Shah, Hassan
Aabis Duty Free Limited

Shah, Iffat
Sias Corp Limited

Shah, Jaichand Hemraj
Shilcroft Limited

Shah, Jayshree Dinesh
Universal Toiletries Corporation Ltd

Shah, Karan
Universal Toiletries Corporation Ltd

Shah, Neel Rameshchandra
Sanay Ltd

Shah, Pooja
P & M Beauty Ltd

Shah, Pradip Kumar Mohanlal
Shilcroft Limited

Shah, Prince
P P Oil UK Limited

Shah, Sudhir Punja
P & M Beauty Ltd

Shah, Tushar Vinodchandra
Medipro Pharma Limited

Shah, Vaishaliben
Krish Shoppers Ltd

Shaheen, Sundas
Eva Cosmetics Ltd

Shahid - Humayun, Maliha
Wrap N Pack Ltd

Shakoor, Moheen
Zarahs World Ltd

Shaltoot, Amr
Odeferus Limited

Shamwana, Chakomba
Duke of Charm Limited

Shan, Rizwan
Simple Hair Limited

Shantonas, Mel
Alpha La Roche Limited

Shapovalova-Peters, Tatiana
Leading National Training Ltd

Sharf, Roei
RMD Global OYB Limited
RMD Global Wholesale Limited

Sharifian, Ahmad
Medical Technology Caraco (MYC) Ltd.

Sharma, Mokshika
Deism IT Solutions Ltd

Sharma, Ridhima
Iberia Skin Brands Ltd

Sharma, Vismay
L'Oreal (U.K.) Limited

Sharman, Heather
Rainbow Cosmetics (Manchester) Ltd

Sharman, John William
Rainbow Cosmetics (Manchester) Ltd
Ringley Trading Limited
SES Wholesale Limited

Sharman, Stephanie
Skinjam Cosmetics Limited

Sharman, Stephen John
Rainbow Cosmetics (Manchester) Ltd

Sharp, James Meenan
Sandaig Ltd

Sharp, Melanie Joy
Sandaig Ltd

Sharp, Samantha Louise
It Worx Cosmetics Limited

Sharpe, Frederick Augustus Fenton
Blank Factory Limited

Shaughnessy, Howard
Fragrance Factory Limited

Shaukat, Adnan
Leslie International Ltd

Shaukat, Rizwan
Leslie International Ltd

Shaw, Adam
Shaw International Ltd

Shaw, Andreea Gabriela
Aqolade Ltd

Shaw, Diane
N.S.I. (U.K.) Limited

Shaw, Jason Andrew
N.S.I. (U.K.) Limited

Shaw, Jonathan Simon
Fatale Cosmetics Limited

Shaw, Simon Raymond
Mega Mane Limited

Shaw, Vincent Graham
Chanel Limited

Shawwa, Jaafar
Spree Trading Ltd

Shawwa, Rabie
Spree Trading Ltd

Sheard, Gary, Dr
Dermaloch Limited

Shears, Gareth Edward
S & P Cosmetics Limited

Sheehan, Michael Thomas
Beautyge Fragrances Holdings Ltd

Sheehan, Nicola
F.D.D. International Limited

Sheena, Abraham Albert
Cancun Collection Limited

Sheena, Claudia Martine Hannah
Cancun Collection Limited

Sheikh, Abeda
HE Products Ltd

Sheikhali, Osman
Mahiri Africa Ltd

Shergill, Natasha Jasmine
NRS Cosmetics Ltd

Sheriff, Michael Anthony
Mirimiri Limited

Sherwood, Katarzyna Monika
Shhuk Ltd

Shi, Guangwei
UK Irelia Co Ltd

Shidiak, Antoun Yousif
Eden Perfumes Limited

Shields, Paul
JS Marketing (N.I.) Limited

Shields, Sinead Mary
JS Marketing (N.I.) Limited

Shiers, Margaret
Phoenix Beauty Ltd

Shima, Wendy
Puff & Petals Ltd.

Shipton, Brad
Luxury Personal Care Ltd

Shipton, Bradley John
Luxurious Personal Care Ltd

Shipton, James
Luxurious Personal Care Ltd
Luxury Personal Care Ltd

Shirazi, Donya Shadeh
Jeunvie Ltd

Shirazi, Hanaha-Mae
Jeunvie Ltd

Shirazi, Melodie Lily
Jeunvie Ltd

Shire, Hebo
Sophistique Beauty Ltd

Shiri, Sasi
I.S.O.D Limited

Shirzad, Abdul Wadood
Paiman Limited

Shkukani, Nadir
Amelgo Ltd

Shoaib, Abid
Burly Cosmetics Ltd

Shode, Olufemi Olukayode, Dr
Yejisu Innovation Ltd

Shode, Oluyemisi Olabisi, Dr
Yejisu Innovation Ltd

Shonn, Richard Lee
Zipco Limited

Shonn, Steven Martin
Zipco Limited

Shortt, Stephen Peter
Shortt Investments2 Limited

Shread, Claire
Daly Beauty Limited

Shrestha Dali, Rakhi
Nakkali Limited

Shukla, Dina Hiteshkumar
Beauty Full Ltd

Shumon, Kamal Hassan
Aurum Essence Ltd

Si-Ahmed, Amy Christiansen
Sana Jardin (UK) Limited

Siano, Antonio
Gluedon Ltd

Sibanda, Kudzai
Wuyu Mother and Baby Ltd

Siddiqua, Shirin Ayesha
London Export Ltd

Sidhu, Jotinder Singh
Mystique Swan Ltd

Sidibe, Sira
Bemysoul Ltd

Sieniuc, Anita
FM Cosmetics UK Ltd

Sieniuc, Karol
FM Cosmetics UK Ltd

Sieracki, Konrad Tadeusz
Business Angels Syndicate Ltd

Silcock, Andrew Murray McLean
Bush Oil Limited

Silmbrod, Sonja
Wholesale Hair Extensions Ltd

Silva, Glaci Braga
Glaci Natural Ltd

Silva, Joanna Wiktoria
Elan Skincare Ltd

Silver, Jill
Product World Limited

Silver, Steven
Product World Limited

Silvester, Daniel Jon
F.D.D. International Limited

Simango, Olvera Maitigere
Masculin Limited

Simon, Loic Guy Bernard
Leixaco Trading Ltd

Simon-Cort, Mellisa
Only Perfection Ltd

Simonova, Milada
Neonails Ltd

Simonson, James Alexander
Sub Tropic Limited

Simonson, John Allan
Sub Tropic Limited

Simpkin, Kelly Elizabeth
We Two By Kelly Simpkin Ltd

Simpson, Cheryl
Pretty Silhouette Limited

Simpson, Michael
Effective and Simple Ltd

Simpson, Rochelle
Billionhaire Limited

Sinca, Daiana Mihaela
Privilago Fashion Ltd

Singh Dooa, Jasvinder
Dooa Capital Limited

Singh, Gaganmeet
Beverly Beauty & Fragrances Ltd

Singh, Harinder Paul
Beauty Star Limited

Singh, Irena
Bellevue of London Ltd.

Singh, Jagdeep
Beard Gang Ltd

Singh, Jagdeesh
Cosmetolife Limited

Singh, Omkar
Fandealtastic Limited

Singh, Ranjit Kaur
Beauty Star Limited

Singh, Ricardo Reza Krishna Menon
Bellevue of London Ltd.

Singh, Richard
Iiuvo Limited

Singh, Sharnjit
BSB Fashion Limited

Sinko, Monika
Simona Beauty Store Ltd

Sirop, Jean-Claude
Thalgo UK Limited

Siwak, Waldemar
Aube Laboratories Ltd

Skeffington, David
Discounted Cosmetics Limited

Skelding, Timothy
Perfume Outlet Ltd

Skermer, Emma Louise Maxfield
Hadley and Reed Ltd

Collins, Barrie Christie
The Skin Care Co Ltd

Collins, Rebecca Laura
The Skin Care Co Ltd

Bagley, Andrew John
The Skincare Sanctuary Limited

Bagley, Sarah Edwina
The Skincare Sanctuary Limited

Keech, Joseph John
The Skincare Sanctuary Limited

Powell, Cliff Lewis
The Skincare Sanctuary Limited

Skingsley, Geoffrey Christopher
L'Oreal (U.K.) Limited

Jordan, Marcus Andrew
The Skinsmith Limited

Jordan, Tracy Jayne
The Skinsmith Limited

Skopalova, Daniela
Green Harmony Limited

Skwarek, Grzegorz
Noyras Ltd

Skwiot, Dawid Pawel
Roxie Cosmetics Ltd

Slaoui, Mohammed
Margan Oil Ltd

Sleath, Damien Paul Richmond
Damrick's White Bunny Ltd

Sledzianowska, Magdalena
Meddiamonds Ltd

Sleet, Harry Anthony
Capital (Hair and Beauty) Ltd
Salon Connection (Wales) Ltd

Slevoaca, Vasile
Bibishor Limited

Sliufko, Christopher Harry
Ray & Company (Hairdressers Sundries Men)

Sliufko, Olivia Mary
Ray & Company (Hairdressers Sundries Men)

Sliufko, Paul Anthony Garth
Ray & Company (Hairdressers Sundries Men)

Sliufko, Thomas Guy
Ray & Company (Hairdressers Sundries Men)

Sliwinska-Skwiot, Roksana Ewa
Roxie Cosmetics Ltd

Small, Everton
Rosse Beau Ltd

Smedley, Georgina
Piggy Paint UK Ltd

Smedley, Jason Kenneth
Piggy Paint UK Ltd

Smit, Dagmar
Elegantes London Limited

Smit, Thomas
Elegantes London Limited

Smith, Thomas
TPC Smith Limited

Smith, Andrew James
Moyy Limited

Smith, Ashley Howard
Nail Perfection Limited

Smith, Chloe Ellen
Line21 Ltd.

Smith, Colin
Genetiq Lab Limited

Smith, Daniel
Mesostrata Limited

Smith, Eilidh Janet
EJS Brand Management Limited

Smith, Graham Michael
SB Beauty Marketing Limited

Smith, Ian Elliot
2B Enterprises Limited

Smith, Kevin
Available Beauty Ltd

Smith, Lee Jason
Stantondown Limited

Smith, Matthew Nathaniel
Eden's Legends Limited

Smith, Michael Charles
Amaffi London Limited

Smith, Murray Moyle
Doterra (Europe) Ltd

Smith, Nancy Tanscia
B. Silki Naturally Ltd

Smith, Nathan Paul
Photics Skincare Ltd

Smith, Nicholas Alan
Walking Pet Balloons (UK) Ltd

Smith, Nicholas William
Walking Pet Balloons (UK) Ltd

Smith, Paul David
Mypure Limited

Smith, Philip John
FreshBreathOnline Limited

Smith, Phillip
Magpie Holdings Ltd

Smith, Renford
Afro Hair and Beauty International

Smith, Richard James
Fragrance Group London Ltd

Smith, Robert Peter
Nectar International Limited

Smith, Simon
Worldwidegoodstraders Ltd

Smith, Steven
Dilecta Cosmetics Limited

Smith, Stewart Leslie
Stantondown Limited

Smith, Terence
Stantondown Limited

Smith, Tracey Anne
Ashmira Botanica Ltd

Smolen-Kenawy, Aneta
Secret Line Ltd

Snowdon, Ben Alan
Lock Stock & Barrel Grooming Co Ltd

Snyman, Jan Harm
Lyal Intertrading Ltd

Whip, Casey
The Soap Industry Limited

McCaffrey, Josephine Anne
The Soap and Candle Co Ltd

McCaffrey, Paul David
The Soap and Candle Co Ltd

Soares Bento, Jose Maria
Guilty Fashion Ltd

Soares, German Antonio
Crazy Smiles Group Ltd

Sobell, Bianca Jane
Powered By Nature Cosmetics Ltd

Sobowale, Alix
Precision Brows and Lashes Ltd

Sodha, Naina
Asurex Limited

Sodha, Pankaj
Asurex Limited

Sogaard, Tina
My Beauty World Ltd

Sohail, Ammar
Bays International Limited

Sohail, Bashaar
Bays International Limited

Sokhi, Kuldip Kaur
Elite Beauty (London) Limited

Solanki, Vijay Kumar
Vidology Group Ltd

Soldanski, Dawid
Indigo Nails Online Shop Ltd.

Soldatova, Jelena
Lactura Ltd

Soldatova, Tatjana
Lactura Ltd

Solomon, David Frederick
Vita Liberata Limited

Soltan Talib, Abdul Rahman
Sipro (UK) Ltd

Soltan Talib, Abdullah
Sipro (UK) Ltd

Soltan Talib, Noraini Binti
Sipro (UK) Ltd

Soma, Mitesh
Jivesse Limited

Sonchhatla, Akhil
Fuzzique Limited

Soni, Chanchal
Perfume Essence Ltd

Sonia, Kazi-Tani
Les Laboratoires ILP UK Ltd

Sopel, Wiktor
Nomalogic Ltd

Soper, Roger William
Fragrance and Gifts Limited

Sopyte, Monika
Dimonauk Ltd

Soremekun, Nicola Jade
Manicure You Ltd

Soremi, Alexandra
Ansor Supplies Ltd

Sorensen, Lars Soren
TWC Products Limited

Soumano, Penda
Ellya UK Ltd

Spears, Elizabeth Jane
Star Qualities Ltd

Spears, Leslie George
Joy Limited
Star Qualities Ltd

Speirs, Melvyn Alexander
Arrow Hair & Beauty Supplies Ltd

Spilotopoulou, Sophia
Korres International Limited

Spina, Ivan
Empire Worldwide Ltd

Spinks, Kelly Louise
Meadow Skincare Limited

Adam Ali Ibrahim, Mustafa Asghar
The Spirit of Dubai Limited

Ali, Howaida Asgher Adam
The Spirit of Dubai Limited

Ibrahim, Asghar Adam Ali
The Spirit of Dubai Limited

Spital, Jonathan
Aesthetic Cosmetic Ltd

Spitzer, Romain
LVMH Fragrance Brands UK Ltd

Sproston, Generaldine
Woodwood Limited

Squires, Richard
Beauty Senses Limited

Sriperambuduru, Divakar
Biogene Group Limited

St Pierre, Zoe
Hello Dame London Ltd

Stafford, Laura Janet
Dermura Skin Ltd

Stafford, Lee Samuel
On-Top Skincare Limited

Stainrod, Latoya Nekoya
Niquel Ltd

Stainsby, Gary John
Mitvana and Biological Industries Ltd

Stainsby, Ryan John
Mitvana and Biological Industries Ltd

Stamerra, Giorgio
Amassuna Limited

Stammer, James
Original Additions (Beauty Products)

Stan, Laura Maria
Pellitier & Perkins Limited

Stanbury, Sophie
Glamrolls Limited

Stanford, Bill
Forever Young Cosmetics UK Ltd

Stangerean, Beatrix
Marcman Perfume Ltd

Stanton, Brian John
Classic Beaute Limited
Guerlain Limited

Starczewski, Jaroslaw
Control Cosmetics Ltd

Steadman, Clare Louise
Kokolokahi Limited
Shared Beauty Secrets Limited
Shared Beauty Secrets Spas Ltd

Steele, Michael John Quentin
European Essential Oils (UK) Ltd

Steele, Sheila Joyce
Mint Julip Ltd

Stefanidis-Vlad, Bogdan
Sweet Arabian Ltd

Stefanova, Zdravka
P & Z Solutions Limited

Stenbaek, Signe Kurup
Luxuryscope London Limited

Stennett, David Arnold
Headlines (Hair & Beauty Supplies)

Stephen, Mary
Elie Consumer Care Ltd
Revlon & Elie Healthcare Ltd

Stephen, Penelope Anne
Penny Price Aromatherapy Ltd

Stephen, Robert, Revd Dr
Penny Price Aromatherapy Ltd

Stephenson, John Phillip
Markwins Beauty Brands International
Markwins Beauty Products Ltd

Stephenson, Norville
Noa London Ltd

Stern, David Lawrence
Crabtree & Evelyn (Overseas) Ltd

Stewart, Iryna
Iryna Stewart Ltd

Stewart, Ian Colin
Delights Beauty Co Ltd

Stewart, Iryna
Rederm Limited

Stewart, Janet
Serendipity (N.I.) Ltd

Stewart, Ronan
Conscience Clear Tan Limited

Stibbs, Charlotte Joan Mary
Semy-Estoiles Limited

Stibbs, Patricia Mary Ann
Semy-Estoiles Limited

Stibbs, Timothy Paul Charles
Semy-Estoiles Limited

Stimpson, Paul
Lozano Skincare Ltd

Stinson, Linda Jane
LMD Cosmetics Ltd

Stirling, David
Doterra (Europe) Ltd

Stojek, Kinga
Given By Nature Limited

Stokes, Philip John
Boutique Perfumes Limited
Classic Beaute Limited

Simon, Lauren Belinda
Lauren Stone Limited

Stooks, Timothy David
Beauty Innovator 2012 Ltd.

Stopp, Catherine
Q River Limited

Strang, Sarah Anne
Spa Voyage Limited
Wild Brands Limited

Stratulat, Florin
Makeup Boutique Limited

Straume, Gatis
Original Taste Ltd

Straus, Daniel Reuben
Lipoid Kosmetik Ltd
Protec Botanica Ltd
Protec Ingredia Limited

Streimikis, Kestutis
Saveasy Ltd.

Stroud, Christian Forrest
Egyptian Magic Ltd

Stroud, Christopher John
Brambles Farm Ltd

Stroud, Damian Richard
Mancave Limited

Stroud, Jacqueline Lander
Brambles Farm Ltd

Strzalkowski, Michal
East Garden Ltd

Strzelecki, Wojciech
Love Little Prices Ltd

Stubley, Nigel de Lisle
Nature's Dream Limited

Studd, Trevor
BBA Products Limited

Babic, Zeljko
The Style Factory Limited

Radanovic, Ljubomir
The Style Factory Limited

Vukasinovic, Ratko
The Style Factory Limited

Subramanian, Karthikeyan
Spice International Trading Co Ltd

Subramaniyam, Rishanthini
Rishi Human Hair Extensions Wholesale

Sudnik, Janet
J S Trading (UK) Limited

Sudworth, Daryl John
Anglo Indian Trading Limited

Sugg, Zoe Elizabeth
ZS Beauty Ltd

Sujanani, Renuka
Impressions Beauty Limited

Sukdao, Wesley Timothy
Emma Victoria Cosmetics Ltd

Suleyman, Asiye
Fashion Conspiracy Ltd

Suliteanu, David
Kendo Brands Limited

Sulkhanishvili, Giorgi
Sambio Ltd

Sullivan, Ronald Thomas
Cosmeceuticals Limited

Sultan, Subhi
Pink Empire Limited

Sultana, Nahid
NS Brands International Ltd

Sultana, Nigar
Alianaz Ltd.

Summer, Nicola
International Hair Cosmetics Ltd

Summerlee, Mishah
Phoenix Hair & Beauty (Ely) Ltd

Summerlee, Sandra May
Phoenix Hair & Beauty (Ely) Ltd

Summerlee, Tegan
Phoenix Hair & Beauty (Ely) Ltd

Sun, Jing
Smuccii Trading Ltd

Sun, Min
Uni Supply Ltd

Sunami, Seitaro
Globe Intraworks Limited

Sunka, Asif Taiyab
Eau de Parfum Limited

Suo, Shuhui
Style4you Ltd

Surridge, Alison Mary
Clarins (U.K.) Limited
Talza Limited

Sutcliffe, Arthur
JGR UK Distributions Limited

Sutcu, Fatih Mehmet
CC Dist UK Ltd

Sutherland, Euan Angus
DKH Retail Limited

Sutherland, Tovah
Nevah Rose Ltd

Sutherland, Wayne Arthur
Prezance Ltd

Svampane, Evita
Aroma Dead Sea Limited

Swain, Claudia Alice
Sun Jelly Ltd

Swales, John Mark
Beached Limited

Swaminathan, Vengadan
HFC Prestige Products Limited

Swan, Eliot
Arnest International Limited
Sanmex International Limited

Sweet, Samantha
Lash Authority Ltd
Sweet Squared Limited
Wax Authority Limited

Sweet, Samuel
Lash Authority Ltd
Sweet Squared Limited
Wax Authority Limited

Sweetland, Carolina Aliling
Silk Lounge Beauty Ltd

Swift, Benjamin
GBBC Ltd

Swift, Catherine
Swift Retail Limited

Swift, Ryan
Swift Retail Limited

Syed, Arif Jamal
AJS Marketing Limited

Syed, Zuhaib Babar
Dr Sun Limited

Szabo, Tibor Janos
Arahant Ltd

Szalka, Artur
Adwa Impex Ltd

Szczesny, Mariusz
Age Infinite Ltd
Genixo Ltd

Szczubelek, Gabriela
Gabs Cosmetologist Limited

Szucs, Attila
Barbers House Ltd

Szucs, Sandor
Protective World Ltd

Szydlowska, Jolanta
Given By Nature Limited

Szynkaruk, Przemyslaw Marcin
Sueno Cosmetics Ltd

Szyszka, Natalia
Natcare Beauty Ltd

Tagliente Halilaj, Ermela
Les Blanches Limited

Taha, Ali
Laila Cosmetics Limited

Tahir, Akhtar Ali
Fit Brands (UK) Ltd

Tahir, Uzma
Beautybaseuk Ltd

Tahvanainen, Mirka Lotta Irene
Mirtas Cosmetics Ltd

Tai, Chung Nam Jason
Egg Pillow Limited

Bazazi, Amir Ali
Stella Tailor Ltd

Lee, Seulgi
Stella Tailor Ltd

Takac, Michal
Zerocann Ltd

Takacs, Peter Laszlo
One Green Lab Ltd

Talgaswatta, Yashara Rukshani
Sunrise Essential Oil Limited

Tan, Erika
Bracknell Gardens Ltd

Tanaka, Itsumi
Grautrans Limited

Tanani, Youness, Dr
SPTB Ltd

Tang, Rachel Kit Yee
Kityee Limited

Tanser, Mark James
11:11 Limited

Tant, Angela
Bouffe Limited

Tanturk, Mehmet
Nanosafe Ltd.

Tanveer, Muhammad Haroon
Jay Kay Wholesale Ltd

Tao, Ningning
Aquabeauty Limited

Targosz, Rafal
BeautyEmpireUK Ltd

Tariq, Almas
Connessioni UK Limited

Tariq, Hussna
Niya Cosmetics Ltd

Tarling, Elspeth
Creative Colours International Ltd

Tarling, Simon James
Creative Colours International Ltd

Tavares Veloso, Bianca
Brazilian Kimberlite Clay Ltd

Tay, Joyce Zi Yan
Crane and Peach Limited

Tayefi Nasrabadi, Vahid, Dr
Natural Serenity Ltd

Taylor, Christopher Mark
Eve Taylor (London) Limited

Taylor, Alan Leslie
Eve Taylor (London) Limited

Taylor OBE, Evelyn May
Eve Taylor (London) Limited

Taylor, Abigail Deborah Marie
Haresgraces Limited

Taylor, Alan Leslie
Good Skin Care Co Ltd

Taylor, Brittany Dominique
Haresgraces Limited

Taylor, Callan Joel
Ecocare Organic Limited

Taylor, Charlotte Noel
Nowdynamic Ltd.

Taylor, Christopher Mark
Good Skin Care Co Ltd

Taylor, Craig John
Hadley and Reed Ltd

Taylor, Evan
Urban Altar Ltd

Taylor, Evelyn May
Good Skin Care Co Ltd

Taylor, Jimmy
Bigben Healthcare Limited

Taylor, Judith Ann
Dermaenhance Ltd.

Taylor, Keith Adrian
Nowdynamic Ltd.

Taylor, Krista Louise
Scence Ltd

Taylor, Philip William
Carbon Theory Limited

Taylor, Raymond Neil
Good Skin Care Co Ltd

Taylor, Richard Alexander
Shhuk Ltd

Taylor, Sharon Muriel
Haresgraces Limited

Taylor, Shirley Jean
Beautytrade Limited

Taylor, Steven Russel
Lash House Eyelash Extensions Supplies

Taylor, William Paul
Beautytrade Limited

Taylor-Brewin, Katherine Jane
Bioactivebeauty Ltd

Tayne, Bradley George
Outcome Zero Ltd

Tayne, Geneva
Outcome Zero Ltd

Tayyeb, Zeeshan
Petersham Ventures Ltd

Te Reo, Hana
Ha-Derma Limited

Teague, Mary Angela
RX Cosmetics Limited

Teal, Anna
Aroma Actives Limited

Teasdale, Louise
Bleach Makeup Limited

Teasdale, Samantha
World Wide Gifts Limited

Tefra, Bertrand Albert Francois
Parfums Christian Dior (U.K.) Ltd

Telang, Praveen
Aneen Ventures Limited

Telfer, Joseph
Respect Male Grooming Ltd.

Teller, Jonathan
EOS Products Limited

Tentunian, Roland
Florascent Duftmanufaktur Ltd

Teoh, Lee
Shop Beauty Ltd

Terlecka, Monika
Indigo Nails Online Shop Ltd.

Testolin, Luigi
Garda Service Ltd

Tevendale, Gayle
Warehouse.5 Limited

Tevendale, William Ross
Warehouse.5 Limited

Thakrar, Atul
Pebbles Creative Ltd
Pink Parasol Ltd
Rock Perfumes Ltd
Scent Global Ltd

Thakrar, Dipak Maganlal
Jigsaw International Holdings Ltd

Thakrar, Nayan
Bluestar Enterprise Limited
Eden Brands Limited
Eden Parfums Limited
Edenwest Limited
Imperial Pharmaceuticals Ltd

Thakrar, Shivani
Imperial Pharmaceuticals Ltd

Thalgaswatta, Yashara Rukshani
Kiara Beauty Ltd

Thans, Matthias
Contrast Cosmetics Ltd.

Tharratt, James Daniel
P & P Cosmetics Ltd

Tharwat Naium, Bahaa, Dr
Export Solutions (International) Ltd

Thayakaran, Gayathri
Buy Perfumes London Limited

Theodorou, Alexander Gregory
Republik Inc Limited

Theofanous, Alexandros Panayioti
Brand Evolution (Europe) Ltd
Glitterati Distributions Ltd

Theofanous, Anna
Brand Evolution (Europe) Ltd
Glitterati Distributions Ltd

Therre, Markus
Beatnut Butter Ltd

Thomas, Amber
ASR Aesthetics Ltd

Thomas, Amir
Mane Love Ltd

Thomas, Lorraine Amanda
Lollipop Treats Ltd

Thomas, Titty Pappachen
Heavenly Fragrance (UK) Ltd

Thompson, Cathryn Margaret
Zurego Limited

Thompson, David Paul
Inside Trading (Beauty) Ltd

Thompson, Leigh
LTSC Ltd

Thompson, Mark
Company NBN Limited

Thompson, Nicholas John
Zurego Limited

Thomson, Colin Harvey
CHT Supplies Limited

Thomson, Karen King
CHT Supplies Limited

Thorley, Melya Margaret
Melya & Co. Trading Ltd.

Thorne, Christopher Ronald
Johnson & Johnson Limited

Thornton, Christine Ruth
True Skincare Limited

Thornton, Emma Louise
True Skincare Limited

Thukral, Aseem
Great London Beauty Limited

Thwaites, Shaun Robert
Glam Wholesale Limited

Tickler, Simon Andrew
Salon Success Limited

Tierney, John Peter Francis
PHB Franchise Limited

Tiffin, Julia Susan
Afex Skin Care Ltd

Tiffin, Robert George
Afex Skin Care Ltd

Tillotson, Mark John
Beauty Leisure Industry Supplies and Services

Tillyer, Mark
Inspired Hair Supplies Limited

Timbrell, Adam
Sasha Hair & Beauty Ltd

Toa, Sim Hui
Cherry Cherry Fashion Ltd

Tobitt, Stephen Henry
Neal's Yard (Natural Remedies) Ltd

Todd, Graeme
Natures Merchant Ltd

Tokatly, Taher
Beauty Oasis Ltd

Toland, James
MJL Products Ltd

Tolhurst, Samuel Thomas
STT Industries Ltd.

Tomlinson, David Guy
Absolute Cosmetic Essentials Ltd

Tomsa, Dan
Previa UK Ltd

Tone, Andrew
Steam Cream Limited

Tong, Barry Keith
Natural Birthing Co Ltd

Toofail, Shaenaze
Belgrave Traders Ltd

Toor, Ramzia
Suvaz Linen UK Ltd

Topping, Lisa
Synlatex Limited

Tordjmann, Julien Telesphore
4T Medical Ltd

Tordjmann, Laure Rolande Elisabeth
4T Medical Ltd

Torlop, Christopher
Global Hair Care Limited

Torres, Viviana
Miss Vivien Ltd

Toth, Barbara
B & O Natural Cosmetics Ltd

Touhami, Ramdane
Buly UK Limited

Toure, Djibril Fode
Toure Ltd

Toure, Lassina Karamoko
Noli Distribution Ltd

Town, Bryde Grace
Natural Pal Limited

Townley, Clare Elizabeth
Leclair Cosmetics Limited

Townsend, Caroline Susannah
Natural Vitale Limited

Toyra, Kayleigh Alexandra
Sweden Eco Limited

Trabal Ogazon, Pilar
Puig UK Limited

Traboulssi Barake, Abdelrahman
Herbaleva Ltd

Trajchev, Lazar
Renibo Ltd

Trajkovic, Jelena
West Three Trading Limited

Trajkovic, Zoran
West Three Trading Limited

Trakulchang, Ruethairat
Medileen UK Ltd

Tran, John Quoc
TJ Nail Supplies Ltd

Tran, Son Thanh
Parkside Nails Supplies Ltd

Tran, Tuan
Lahang Ltd

Travis, Tracey Thomas
Le Labo UK Limited

Traynor, David Thomas
Winchpharma (Consumer Healthcare) Ltd

Tremain, Tony Stephen
PH Group UK Limited

Trieu, Guy
CHK (UK) Ltd

Trifonov, Tinko
Vickie's Boutique Ltd

Trimble, Freddie Peter
Wildmint Cosmetics Limited

Trimming, James Watson
Existo Limited

Trinh, Lam Van
No.1 Nail Supply Limited

Trixl, Bernahrd
Madison Steward Ltd

Bersch, Paulette
Geo. F. Trumper (Perfumer and Products)

Cherchi Bersch, Sebastian
Geo. F. Trumper (Perfumer and Products)

Trytko, Marcin
Home Design 24 Ltd

Tsang, Fey
Laogong Laopo Limited

Tsang, Irene
Medileen UK Ltd

Tsompanidis, Theodoros
Atlas Global Trade Ltd

Tubb, Benjamin Clive
FB Beauty Ltd

Tuke, Charles William
KPACA Limited

Tullett, Malcolm
Info Cosmetics Limited

Tumber, Jane Elizabeth
Value for Money (Cleethorpes) Ltd

Tunstall, Paul William
Natrelle Limited

Turan, Omur
Petersham Ventures Ltd

Turner, Clair
Wealden Aesthetics Limited

Turner, Edward
Nail Art Direct Ltd

Turner, Rodney David
Innovaderma PLC

Turner, Tracy Ann
Plantain Essential Oils Ltd

Tydeman, Victoria Louise
Oodiee Limited

Uche-Amadi, Doris Balafama
Ladorisa Limited

Uddin, Ala
Shahadah Ltd

Uddin, MD Kamal
Expo Deal Ltd

Uddin, Mohammed Monir
Total Salon Supplies Limited

Uddin, Mohammed Nizam
Our Choice Gift Limited

Uddin, Nasir
Miy Sofiyah Limited

Uddin, Suraiya
Shahadah Ltd

Ueber, Klaus Georg
Body Reform Limited

Ugrin, Gyorgy
Foramca Ltd

Uhliar, Pavel
Pro Esthe Ltd.

Ullah, Asmat
New Horizons (UK) Ltd

Ullah, Mohammad Shahid
Hasanah Global Ltd

Ullah, Saleem
Rapsodi London Ltd

Umarji, Naeem Inayat Mohmad
La Fumes Ltd

Unadkat, Shaini Harman Jasraj
Fragrance Plus Limited

Unimke, Jonathan Ashvin
Ark Inta Ltd

Unwin, Charles Stephen
Ris Healthcare Limited

Unwin, Stephen Ronald
Ris Healthcare Limited

Uperenko, Oleg
Angsana Ltd

Urban, Nicolas
La Boutique du Discount Ltd.

Urbano, Paolo, Dr
Five Star International Consulting

Urdaneta Fuenmayor, Luis Emiro
Monat Global UK Ltd

Urdaneta, Francisco Javier
Monat Global UK Ltd

Urdaneta, Rayner
Monat Global UK Ltd

Urhan, Harun Resit
Urhan Group Limited

Ursu, Irina
MGM UK Limited

Usher, Alexander James
Butterwhips Ltd

Usher, Victoria May
Butterwhips Ltd

Ustaszewski, Krzysztof Jaroslaw
Sueno Cosmetics Ltd

Uttam-Chandani, Kishin
Ekah Foundation C.I.C.

Uzunov, Svetoslav
Mellor & Russell Direct Distribution Ltd

Vadaniuc, Dorel
NOP Cosmetics Ltd

Vadera, Sanjay Jayantilal
BKSL Limited
Churchill Motley Limited
Fragrance & Beauty Creations Ltd
Fragrance Acquisitions Limited
Fragrance and Beauty Limited
Per-Scent Fine Limited
Per-Scent Group Limited
Per-Scent Limited
Yu Parfums Ltd

Vadera, Vipul Jayantilal
Churchill Motley Limited
Fragrance Acquisitions Limited
Fragrance and Beauty Limited
Per-Scent Fine Limited
Per-Scent Group Limited
Per-Scent Limited
Yu Parfums Ltd

Vadims, Babkins
V@M Limited

Vahtre, Madis Marius
Orien Beauty & Selfcare Ltd

Valambia, Bhash
Plan Target Limited

Valeisa, Kayleigh
Valiscious Limited

Van Huizen, Gerardus Johannes
Grimas.co.uk Limited

Van Laar, Gerrit
Perfume World Limited

Van Laere, Jean-Pierre Aime
NYDG UK Limited

Van Ocken, Heidi
Salon Success Limited

Van Rosenveldt, Anna Marie
Beauty Solutions Trading Ltd

Van Ruymbeke, Astrid
Arbonne UK Limited

Vandegrift, Susan
Perricone MD Cosmeceuticals UK Ltd

Vans Agnew, Hamish Michael
Capital (Hair and Beauty) Ltd
Pompadour Laboratories Limited

Vans Agnew, Peter Ross
Capital (Hair and Beauty) Ltd
Pompadour Laboratories Limited
Salon Connection (Wales) Ltd

Vans Agnew, Rachel Generaldine
Capital (Hair and Beauty) Ltd

Vans Agnew, Sally Jane
Capital (Hair and Beauty) Ltd

Varano, Antonio Della Virgiliana
Lab Brands Limited

Vasilescu, Ioana Francisca
Lime and Lead Global Ltd

Vasileva, Elena
Swiss Cosmetic Distribution Ltd

Vasilj, Ivan
Official IV Ltd

Vasilovska, Ralitsa Hristova
Le Lissage UK Limited

Vassiliou, Charalambos
Oxygen Skin Care - London Ltd

Vaughan, Hannah Elizabeth
Stroppy Ltd

Vavere, Valts
Calestio Ltd

Vegetti, Luca
GVM Long Life Formula UK Ltd

Vegh, Tamas
Parfume-Mania Ltd

Vekaria, Chandrikaben Karsan
50shadez Ltd

Vekaria, Lalji Premji
Comglobal Limited

Veligura, Dmitry
Triaton Ltd

Dompreh, Venessa
Ruth Venessa Services Ltd

Venguswamy, Kannuswamy
Tioluxe Europe Limited

Venzo, Giorgio
Simple Bargain Limited

Verier, Alexander Peter
Blank Factory Limited

Burke, Anthony Michael
The Very Essence Ltd

Burke, Gemma Leanne
The Very Essence Ltd

Burke, Lisa Jane
The Very Essence Ltd

Goodman, Martin Julian
The Very Nature Limited

Vickers, Victoria
Nail Creation UK Distribution Ltd

Vidakis, Dimitrios
Korres International Limited

Vieira Rego, Ricardo
Acquaderm Ltd

Viellard, Ulric
Ulric de Varens UK Limited

Vieth, Christopher
E.J. Contracts Limited

Villecco, Carmine
JNVshop La Piazza Delle Idee Ltd

Villecco, Jeanith Calvo
JNVshop La Piazza Delle Idee Ltd

Vilnerova, Simona
Tattva Ltd.

Vincent, Oluwakemi Mary
Aroma of Grace Ltd

Vinciguerra, Jean-Louis
Oh My Scent Limited

Vinciguerra, Nathalie
Oh My Scent Limited

Vingrovski, Guy
Searching Plants Ltd

Vinklerova, Iveta
Ha-Derma Limited

Violante, Guiseppe Andrea
Acqua di Parma Limited

Virdee, Birpal Singh
SYN-RG Trading Ltd

Vitola, Ketija
K. V. Fair Trades Limited

Vivek, Sharma
Garron Labs Private Limited

Vlahakis, Gail Anne
Serengeti Skincare Limited

Voica, Ecaterina
NA Medical Care Ltd

Von Pfefer, Alexis Rosalia
Lex Roris Ltd

Von Wulffen, Philip
Oh My Scent Limited

Vorbach, Sarah
Face Boutique Limited

Vowles, James Harding
Active Skincare Limited

Vu, Diu Hien
Eutek Group Limited

Vu, Nicolas Ngoc
Orveda Limited

Vyas, Ajay
MYNC Brands Limited

Vyas, Harishkumar Natvarlal
Vyas International Ltd

Vyas, Ruchi
Euro Perfumes (UK) Ltd

Wade, Barry Douglas
Bond Street Cosmetics Limited

Wade, Joshua
Skin & Tonic London Ltd

Wadhwani, Vijay
Ives Lab Ltd

Wafiullah, Salman
Moxxy Limited

Wainman, Nina Leora
Hemp Earth Ltd

Wainwright, Natasha Amy
Multitude Makeup Ltd

Waites, Anthony
Deity World Ltd

Walcott, Shinel
Hidden for Purpose Ltd

Waleed Al-Hity, Shehed Abdulmajeed
Uni London Limited

Walentynowicz, Adam
Blue Rose Shop Ltd

Waling, Robert William
Healthpoint Limited

Walji, Aly
Project 1 Skincare Ltd

Walker, Debra Jayne
Debra Jayne Walker Limited

Walker, Fay Rochelle
Ethereal Beauty Ltd

Walker, Francis John Elliot
Global Luxury Beauty Ltd

Walker, Jon
Hair Contrast UK Limited

Walker, Jonathan
Salon Depot Ltd

Walker, Lee Philip
Pricecheck Toiletries Limited

Walker, Nathan
Natural Health Harmony Group Ltd

Walkowiak, Tomasz
P & T PL Ltd

Wallace, Fiona
Lash Authority Ltd
Wax Authority Limited

Wallace, Simon Richmond
Lesimone Global Limited

Wallace-Jones, Matthew
Komodo Skincare Ltd

Waller, David
Aroma Actives Limited

Walrond, Sherine
Ivy Wild Ltd

Walsh, Richard William
Reminiscents of Didsbury Ltd

Walsh, Richard, Dr
Regis Personal Care Ltd

Walters, Emma Morag Dorothy
HFC Prestige Products Limited

Walton, Graham
Aya Natural (UK) Limited

Wan, Lingling
United Mart (UK) Limited

Wang, Aibing
UK Ailise Biotechnology Trade Ltd

Wang, Calvin
SMC Cosmetics (UK) Ltd

Wang, Chaofeng
Unineed Limited

Wang, Dongyang
Caprise Limited

Wang, Efon
Profusion Cosmetics UK Ltd

Wang, Fei
Deewin Stomatology Research Center Co.,

Wang, Junhui
Shuhui Limited

Wang, Lu
Potions & Possibilities Ltd

Wang, Qian
Boz Ego Ltd

Wang, Shih-Chieh
Gel Labs Limited

Wang, Zhou, Doctor
Vereer Limited

Ward, Alan Butler
Hair Cosmetics Limited

Ward, Christopher John
UK Vietnam Trade Ltd

Ward, Jonathan Mark
Hair Cosmetics Limited

Ward, Jonathan
JWWJ Limited

Ward, Marc Bernard Alexander
EnhanceColor Limited

Ward, Paul Anthony
Maverick Hair & Beauty Ltd

Ward, Stephen Paul
UK Vietnam Trade Ltd

Wareham, Victoria
Pretty Silhouette Limited

Waring, William Banks
Nectar International Limited

Warner, Corbey Michael, Dr
Adorexo Ltd

Warnery, Philippe Michel
Aveda Limited
Editions de Parfums Limited
Le Labo UK Limited

Wasfy, Alan
Tryon Products Limited

Wasserman, Scott
Cosmetic Alchemy Ltd
Scope Cosmetics Ltd

Waterman, Gail Marie
Waterman Corporate Enterprises Ltd

Waterman, Matt Luca
Waterman Corporate Enterprises Ltd

Watkins, Malcolm Peter
Bouffe Limited

Watkins, Mollie Rebecca
Wat Cosmetics Ltd

Watson, Bryony Letitia
B & F Ventures Ltd

Watson, James
Trade Smart Marketing Limited

Watson, Luckiva Malika
876 Skin Beauty Limited

Watson, Ruth
Watsoap.Com Limited

Watt, Sheree Carissa
Ismile Beauty Ltd

Watters, Andrea Margaret
Angel Lash Limited

Watts, Vivian James
Hommage International Ltd

Way, Stephen Robert
Joy Limited
Star Qualities Ltd

Wearing, Keith
Think Beauty Online Limited

Weaver, Ashley
Gordon-McCarthy Limited

Weaver, Michaela
Toppers Nails Limited

Webb, Anthony Reginald
K.B. Salon Supplies Limited

Webb, Robert
Salon Ambition Limited

Webb, Simon Nicholas
Salon Ambition Limited

Webber, Emma Kate
Natural Spa Factory Limited

Webster, Florence Verity Alice
Florence Verity Limited

Wee, Lay Shuan
Colourscent Limited

Wei, Ching-Peng
Forderma Laboratory Ltd.

Wei, Liangshen, Dr
Cambridge Sprouts Limited

Wei, Yuezhu
Bonroy International Limited

Weigall, Paul Jonathan Stewart
Just The Product Ltd

Weir, John Paul
Pixie Dust Products Limited

Weir, Laura
Pixie Dust Products Limited

Weir, Tanya
Xhorah Skincare Ltd

Weiss, Samuel Scott
Uppercut Deluxe Co Limited

Wellings, Luke George William
Cozmetica UK Ltd

Welsh, Caitlin
Bedfordshire Beard Co. Limited

Weng, Dier
Goodsky Co., Ltd.

Went, Klaus
Liqwd Limited

Wertheimer, Aron
YSL Trading Ltd

Wescott, Stephen Robert
Ambassadors Choice Limited

Westbrooke, Sophie
S & E Ventures Ltd

Westcott, Guy James Roger
Pearl & Rocky Limited

Westoll, Caroline Mary
Salt and Pamper Limited

Westoll, Mark Graham
Salt and Pamper Limited

Westwood, Jason Nevada
CFN 1 Limited

Westwood, Kathleen
K Co Cosmetics Ltd

Weymouth, Carola Margarete
Luxuryscope London Limited

Wheeler, Gabriella
Amaxa Ltd

Wheeler, Jane
Clink Street FX Ltd

Wheeler, Steven
Clink Street FX Ltd

Barton, Mark
The Whimsical Beard Co Ltd

White, Kevin
Juni Cosmetics Limited

White, Livingston Anthony
Clarendon of London Limited

White, Madeleine
Juni Cosmetics Limited

White, Nicholas James Mark
One Beauty Ltd

White, Paul Douglas
Escentric Ltd

White, Priti
One Beauty Ltd

White, Sonia Myung-Hee
Balm Balm Limited

White, Suzanne
Juni Cosmetics Limited

White, Thomas
Resquire Health & Beauty Ltd

Whitehurst, Peter Lewis
Nature's Dream Limited

Whiting, Stephen
Fade The Itch Ltd

Whyers, Rosalind Annette
Transformulas International Ltd
Transformulas Limited

Whyte, Simona
Gifts of Earth Ltd

Wijesena, Sujith Nayanapriya
Hampton Brands Limited

Wikner, Anders
Abington Cosmetics Ltd

Wild, Fredrick
Splash Cosmetics Ltd

Wild, Hannah
Splash Cosmetics Ltd

Wild, Jane Debra
TRS & Co (Europe) Limited

Sorensen, Lars Soren
The Wildsmith Collection Ltd

Wilhelm, Daniel
Pandorra Ltd.

Wilken, Angela June
Smooth Image Beauty Limited

Wilkins, Jayne Elizabeth
Brambles Farm Ltd

Wilkins, Robin Rhys
Up Roar Ltd.

Wilkins, Ross Generald
Bio Global Limited

Wilkins, Shaun Michael
Brambles Farm Ltd

Wilkinson, Paul William
Cosmeceuticals Limited
Minmar (1008) Limited

Willcox, Gary John
Jo Loves (Wholesale) Limited

Willcox, Joanne Lesley
Jo Loves (Wholesale) Limited

Lees, Anthony Richard
Dennis Williams Limited

Lees, Arron Richard
Dennis Williams Limited

Lees, Pamela Briony
Dennis Williams Limited

Williams, Andrew Ian
Lescaro Health Limited

Williams, Athena
HG-UK (Pty) Ltd

Williams, Bethan
Luxury Consulting by Bethan Williams

Williams, Claire Elizabeth
Wow Facial Ltd

Williams, Elisabeth Jane
Beyond Glamour Ltd

Williams, Empress-Shera
Egotistic Hair & Beauty Ltd

Williams, Harry Forrester
Winning Lines Limited

Williams, Jasmine Catherine
True Mia Limited

Williams, Jen
Nova Cellulis Ltd

Williams, Kristin Lee
Glitterfreaks Limited

Williams, Leslie Glyndon Henry
Lescaro Health Limited

Williams, Marva Dione
Beauty Stable Ltd

Williams, Paul
Gentle Beauty Co Ltd

Willis, Nicola Waring, Dr
Skin Sanity Limited

Willison-Holt, Helen Marie
It Worx Cosmetics Limited

Wilson, Benjamin Piers
Bare Cosmetics Ltd

Wilson, Chris
Califa Ltd

Wilson, Christopher John
Beauty Leisure Industry Supplies and Services

Wilson, Clifford John
Firecrest Communications Ltd

Wilson, Daniel
Scented LDN Limited

Wilson, Jacqueline Hilda
Hair North East Limited

Wilson, Linda
HQPS Ltd

Wilson, Paul [11-1976]
Bullet and Bone Limited

Wilson, Paul [3-1984]
B2B Beauty UK Limited

Wilson, Redwood
Deity World Ltd

Wilson, Thomas
Hair North East Limited

Wilton, Christina Marie
Crane + Wilton Ltd

Swift, Ben
The Wiltshire Beekeeper Ltd

Winch, Nathan Joseph
Barnsley Card Ltd

Winnington, David St. John
Haircosmetics (Sunderland) Ltd

Winstanley, Joe
Smell Neutralizer Ltd

De Winter, Daniele Sylvie Valentine Michaela-Josephine, Lady
Daniele de Winter Monaco-UK Ltd

Winter, Susan Jane
Neal's Yard (Natural Remedies) Ltd

Wiszniewski, Mark Henrik
Sun Lounge Supplies Limited

Wittke, Cornelia Erika Gabriele
Beauty Ideas Group Limited

Wium-Andersen, Kim
Danlab Ltd.

Wlazlo, Krystian
Hermossa Limited

Wogman, Nathan Simon
C-Bombe Limited

Wojciechowska, Beata Marta
M.S.S (Micro Scientific Services)

Wojcik, Edyta Katarzyna
Tibetan Cosmetics Ltd

Wojcik, Michal Piotr
Tibetan Cosmetics Ltd

Wolfram, Zoe
Zoeva UK Limited

Wolski, Stanislaw
MS Rarytas Ltd

Womersley, Robin Neil
Healthpoint Limited

Woname, Edna Agyeman
K3W Trading Limited

Wong, Hing Yu
Riviere Groupe (Europe) Ltd

Wong, Nicole
Janiro Ltd

Wong, Su Yeon Sylvia
SU Labs Limited

Wong, Yiu Chun
Good Beauty International Holding

Wonta, John
Green World Spa Products Ltd

Wood, John Paul
Collier & Wood Ltd

Wood, Jonathan
Iiuvo Limited

Wood, Karen
Tannovation Laboratories Ltd

Wood, Mark Alexander
Original Additions (Beauty Products)

Wood, Samuel
Lueno Cosmetics Limited

Woodall, Philip John
Export Solutions (International) Ltd
MNM International UK Limited

Woodcock, Steven
IDK Balms Ltd

Woodhall, Philip John
London Links Trading Limited

Woodhead, Christopher
Evanesce Ltd

Woods, Danika Lili
Exentrique Limited

Woods, Edward Philip
Spa and Salon Solutions Ltd

Woolfson, Eric Kevin
Sanmex International Limited

Woolley, Esther Marie
Esthermarie Limited

Woolvett, Joanna Kate
Buff Natural Body Care Ltd

Wormser, Alan Robert
FB Beauty Ltd

Wormser, David Lewis
FB Beauty Ltd

Worsey, Samantha Elisabeth Mary
Southsea Bathing Hut Limited

Wragg, Darren
Nail Creation UK Distribution Ltd

Wray, Andrew Sean
TLY Supplies Ltd

Wray, Xiao Yan
TLY Supplies Ltd

Wright, Colin Vincent
Nature's Dream Limited

Wright, Karl
Thrifty Limited

Wright, Kate
Honor London Limited

Wright, Lee Steven
Wrimes Cosmetics Ltd

Wright, Martin Stephen Northcote
Karium Ltd

Wright, Sam
Thrifty Limited

Wright, Steven Michael
Essential Beauty Supplies Ltd

Wu, Yin Yin
La Loire Ltd

Wu, Ying
Envision International Co., Ltd

Wu-Kosinski, Grzegorz
Lashflix Limited

Xassan Libane, Idil
So Boujee Limited

Xassan Libane, Saleban
So Boujee Limited

Xiong, Tao
Mad Beauty Limited

Xu, Jian
Sinoeast XJ Ltd

Xun, Xun
Lulu Tanner Limited

Yacoubian, Paul
Fragrance Group London Ltd

Yahya, Sameer Mahmood
Boost Balm Ltd

Yakin, Muhterem
JJ Promotions Limited

Yakoob, Ajmal
Cosmetics R Us 1 Limited

Yakoobi, Saeed
Sabeauti Ltd.

Yan, Shuangxing
Konya Food Biotechnology Co., Ltd

Yang, Chunxiang
Green Mass Limited

Yang, Mignon
My London Trade Ltd

Yang, Yujuan
Lins Bros Limited

Yasin, Mollah MD Hamim
Sherhind Accessorize Limited

Yasir Rafi, Humaira
Attar Mist Ltd

Yasir, Muhammad Umair
Hasanah Global Ltd

Yassin, Mohammed Fakhir Hashim
Omprus Limited

Yates, Emma Victoria, Dr
Emma Victoria Cosmetics Ltd

Yates, Steven
Yazmae Cosmetics Limited

Yates-Lee, Gemma Cluness
Yates-Lee and Burnett Limited

Ye, Honghua
Bluesky Cosmetics UK HQ Ltd

Ye, Siyang
Catalina Beauty Group Limited

Yeboaa, Jamielee Akosua
S T K Brows Limited

Yedoh, Hermann, Dr
Generic Physics Limited

Yee, Kelly
Fruu Cosmetics Limited

Yeh, Theresa
Ila Asia Limited

Yener, Dogan
Pera Cosmetics Ltd

Yerlett, Claire
Earthkind Ltd

Yesner, Malcolm
Pinnacle Pharma Limited

Ygartua, Ramon Carl
Salon Supplies 365 Limited

Yorachi, Ham Mukama
Drugget Ltd

York, Alan Edward
Global Essence UK Ltd

Yosef, Yaniv
Beauty and More 2000 Ltd

You, Bing
Cosnique Group Holdings Ltd

Young, Gary Alan
Younghair AB Ltd

Young, Hazel Jean
Kent Cosmetics Limited
Northdown Cosmetics Limited

Yourdi, Marlene
Alico Exports Limited

Yousfzai, Obidullah
Kandahar Trading Limited

Yovkova Telang, Anastasiya
Aneen Ventures Limited

Yu, Christopher
United Perfumes Limited

Yu, Xiaomei
Ecooner Cosmetics London Ltd

Yu, Xiaoxiao
A Rebours Limited

Yu, Xin
Crabtree & Evelyn (Overseas) Ltd

Yuan, Ding
Eloise Group Ltd
Mepro Cosmetic Ltd

Yuan, Xubin
Dermacure Aesthetics Limited

Yukimoto, Takashi
Busy Bee Personal Care Limited

Yule, Elsa Jane
Liplast Ltd

Yusuf, Hamzah
Niya Cosmetics Ltd

Yusuf Jnr, Ibrahim Junior
Ibrahim Yusuf and Sons Ltd

Yusuf, Aziza
Ibrahim Yusuf and Sons Ltd

Yusuf, Ibrahim Ibrahim
Ibrahim Yusuf and Sons Ltd

Yuval, Amnon
C Distribution UK Limited

Zachariou, Georgios
Natur Life Ltd

Zafar, Maleeha, Dr
Dr. Twilight Ltd

Zahatlanova, Marcela
Nextporter Ltd.

Zaidi, Syeda Asma
Colour Lux Cosmetics Ltd

Zaki, Diana
Dazzle Dee Ltd

Zaman, Arif
Zamantraders Limited

Zandi Goharrizi, Afsaneh
Gentille Limited

Zarrai, Hafssa
So Boujee Limited

Zarroug, Osman Hamza Osman
Zarroug Limited

Zartaloudi, Kyriaki
Sandine Zartaux Holding Ltd
Swiss Pharma Dynamic Ltd

Zawada, Malgorzata Alina
Souvre UK Ltd

Zdanowska, Beata
Le Glamour UK Ltd

Zeb, Rizwan
Into Exports Limited

Zedki, Mohamad
Razzo Limited

Farah, Amina
Naseem Zeenah Natural Cosmetics Ltd

Zeijpveld, Roelof
Hot (UK) Limited

Zelkin, Valecia Eunice
Eyeslices UK Limited

Zeng, Xiurong
MQL International Ltd

Zhan, Lily
Lilyz Cosmetics UK Ltd

Zhang, Binrui
Photonic Limited

Zhang, Haiyan
Dear Body Limited

Zhang, Jinqi
Dreamage Ltd.

Zhang, Jun
Valerie Lady Co., Ltd

Zhang, Lei
UK Lemenic International Medical Group

Zhang, Li
UK Aimutaike Electronics Co., Ltd

Zhang, Shubi
Eblouir Group Ltd

Zhang, Shuqi
Ladyology Limited

Zhang, Wanjun
Ovis Liv Limited

Zhang, Xiaofeng
South China Bio-Pharma Co Ltd.

Zhang-Cribbin, Deyi
Better Nature International Ltd

Zhao, Dan
Foreverbeyoung Ltd

Zhao, Lei
Crabtree & Evelyn (Overseas) Ltd

Zheng, Lei
Sun Light EU Trading Ltd

Zheng, Lijun
Aiweisier Limited

Zhou, Dong
Treas Biotechnology UK Ltd

Zhou, Qin
Eleu Beauty Ltd

Zhou, Weijun
Lucas Haynes Limited

Zhou, Weiyan
Agoda Limited

Zhu, Feilin
CZ Cosmetics Ltd.

Zhuo, Yongman
Bortlam Postpartum Restore Health Management (International) Chain Co.,

Zidi, Cendesse
Trees of Beauty Ltd

Zielinski, Krzysztof
Genixo Ltd

Zieseniss, Naomi
Zieseniss Limited

Zimbler, Paul
North One Limited

Zinga, Jacinthe Manga
Etonigbo Limited

Zlidne, Juris
ShopAndEnjoy111 Limited

Zochowski, Rafal Marcin
Beautifull Planet Ltd

Zomer, Roby Reuven
MGC Pharma (UK) Ltd

Zou, Sheng Li
Hanfan (UK) Limited

Zoumaras, Anna
Bisch Limited

Zsolt, Janos
Bioaqua -Biotechnology Ltd.

Zuchlinski, Radoslaw
Souvre UK Ltd

Zucker, Denise
Ecobeauty Ltd

This page is intentionally left blank

Standard Industrial Classification
excluding
Wholesale of perfume and cosmetics

01250 Growing of other tree and bush fruits and nuts
Margan Oil Ltd

01490 Raising of other animals
Wiltshire Beekeeper Ltd

10410 Manufacture of oils and fats
African Wild Organics Ltd
Earth Goddess Ltd
Hedgerow Medicine Chest Ltd

10512 Butter and cheese production
Asase Tree Ltd

10710 Manufacture of bread; manufacture of fresh pastry goods and cakes
CBD Bakes Ltd

10831 Tea processing
Zyzven Naturals Cosmetics Ltd

10860 Manufacture of homogenized food preparations and dietetic food
Easybusiness24 Ltd
Eloise Group Ltd

10890 Manufacture of other food products n.e.c. [26]
Aqolade Ltd
Ava Corporations Ltd
Benefit & Riley Healthcare Ltd
Bigben Healthcare Limited
Clarins & Felix Healthcare Ltd
Eifelcorp Consumer Care Ltd
Elie Consumer Care Ltd
Elliott Nutrition Ltd
Felix Medical Group Ltd
Florence Health & Beauty Ltd
Flynn Group of Companies Ltd
Galaxy Grooming Limited
Garnier & Hemo Healthcare Ltd
Grooming Galaxy Limited
Hemo Bioscience Ltd
Infinityredox Holdings Limited
Jardins D'Eden Ltd
Julie's Natural Health Ltd
Lamer & Ava Healthcare Ltd
Nars & Elliott Healthcare Ltd
Natural Vitale Limited
Organic Stuff Limited
Regis Personal Care Ltd
Revlon & Elie Healthcare Ltd
Riley & Sons Ltd
Rimmel & Flynn Healthcare Ltd

11040 Manufacture of other non-distilled fermented beverages
Lese & Lista Ltd

11050 Manufacture of beer
Sloane Home Ltd

13923 manufacture of household textiles
Vancooler Ltd

13990 Manufacture of other textiles n.e.c.
Aeroeco Co Ltd

14132 Manufacture of other women's outerwear
Brands Gallery Ltd
Risa Lux Ltd

14142 Manufacture of women's underwear
Guilty Fashion Ltd
Thrifty Limited

14190 Manufacture of other wearing apparel and accessories n.e.c.
Boylondon Holdings Limited
Caarmi Ltd
Galaxy Grooming Limited
Grooming Galaxy Limited
Spartzy Lifestyle Brands Ltd

14390 Manufacture of other knitted and crocheted apparel
Ethical House Ltd

15120 Manufacture of luggage, handbags and the like, saddlery and harness
Beautifect Ltd
UK Deer Running Co., Ltd

15200 Manufacture of footwear
Boylondon Holdings Limited
SPTB Ltd

17220 Manufacture of household and sanitary goods and of toilet requisites
Aiweisier Limited
Chinese Gentry Limited
Green Mass Limited
Lese & Lista Ltd
Luxurious Personal Care Ltd
Luxury Personal Care Ltd
Morgan Jost Ltd

18121 Manufacture of printed labels
Nuke Manufacturing, Distribution & Investments

18129 Printing n.e.c.
Hasanah Global Ltd

18130 Pre-press and pre-media services
Ruth Venessa Services Ltd

20140 Manufacture of other organic basic chemicals
CFBP Ltd
Colourscent Limited
Derma Organics by CFBP Ltd
Organic Cosmetic Products Ltd

20411 Manufacture of soap and detergents [49]

All Naturals Beauty Limited
Aromabar (Scotland) Ltd
B.Me Skincare Ltd
Berry Inc Ltd
Biologico Cosmetics Limited
Bloomtown Ltd
Chinese Gentry Limited
Cleanux Chemicals Ltd
Conatural Ltd
Cosmetic Hooligans Ltd
Dee Doo Limited
Elinor-UK Ltd
Emilia's Handmade Bath and Body Ltd
Emma Victoria Cosmetics Ltd
Ersag UK Limited
Estela Dermocosmetics Ltd
Evbioo Ltd
Fysifarm Limited
Genten Skincare Ltd
GoodNaturedSkincare Ltd
Harmonious Brown Limited
Heavenly Fragrance (UK) Ltd
Hempia Limited
Highland Soap Co. Limited
Holistic Plant Technologies Ltd
Icilda's Ltd
Sarah Ireland Perfumes Ltd
Kalabash Limited
Ko. Essentials Ltd.
Kokoa UK Limited
Lady Smidgeton's Apothecary Ltd
Loveve. Ltd
MWK Cosmetics (UK) Ltd
Magpie's Ocean Ltd
Meadow Farm Friends Ltd
Molecula Ltd
Natural British Limited
Nu-E55ence Ltd
Orikii Naturals Ltd
Quint Essence Lab Ltd
R & T Natural Cosmetics Ltd
SGHP Ltd
Sankofa Heritage Ltd
Sheabynature Ltd
Sikania Ltd
Sisi Cosmetics Ltd
TAC Perfumes & Cosmetics (UK) Ltd
Universal Toiletries Corporation Ltd
Zyzven Naturals Cosmetics Ltd

20412 Manufacture of cleaning and polishing preparations

Cleanux Chemicals Ltd
Eku Skin Care Ltd

20420 Manufacture of perfumes and toilet preparations [192]

11:11 Limited
A Natural Treat Limited
Adam Michaels Group Ltd
Ahwaz Ltd
Ajmal Perfume (UK) Limited
Al-Jazeera Perfumes Ltd
Alkaiser Perfumes Ltd
Arbar Ltd
Arizona Botaniq Limited
Aromabar (Scotland) Ltd
Askett & English Ltd
Aube Laboratories Ltd
Ava Corporations Ltd
B Luxury Scents Ltd
B. Silki Naturally Ltd
Beard Nature Limited
Beauty Alliance International Ltd
Bedeaux Ltd
Benefit & Riley Healthcare Ltd
Berry Inc Ltd
Bigben Healthcare Limited
Biologico Cosmetics Limited
Blank Factory Limited
Bloom Remedies Ltd
Bloomtown Ltd
Body Reform Limited
Andre Boyard Perfumes Limited
Bubble-Bubble Ltd
Clarins & Felix Healthcare Ltd
Contour and More London Ltd
Coriungo Limited
Cosmetic Hooligans Ltd
Cosmos Cosmetics Limited
Cutelovelee Limited
Dermafood Limited
Dermamaitre Ltd.
Designer Fragrances Limited
Dilecta Cosmetics Limited
Dr. Organic Limited
Dreamweave Products Ltd
Eabir Ltd
Eden's Legends Limited
Eifelcorp Consumer Care Ltd
Elan Skincare Ltd
Elegant Boss Ltd
Elequra Limited
Eleuthere Ltd
Elie Consumer Care Ltd
Elinor-UK Ltd
Elliott Nutrition Ltd
Ethical House Ltd
Evoiq International Ltd
Excel (GS) Limited
Face Boutique Limited
Fashion Fragrances & Cosmetics UK Ltd
Felix Medical Group Ltd
Flowery Whiff Limited
Flynn Group of Companies Ltd
Foad Wax Limited
Forte Organics Ltd
Fragrant Spa Limited
Freshly Whip'd Limited
Fysifarm Limited
G & G Skincare Ltd
Garnier & Hemo Healthcare Ltd
Glad Gent Ltd
Good By Nature Ltd
Good Skin Care Co Ltd
Gracetree Ltd
Green Jiva Ltd
Green Ladies N.I Ltd
Green Mass Limited
Hamiltons of Canterbury Ltd
Haych Cosmetics Limited
Heavenly Fragrance (UK) Ltd
Hemo Bioscience Ltd
Herc Ltd.
Highland Soap Co. Limited
Hoff Beards Limited
Holistic Plant Technologies Ltd
Honey Corn Limited
Iam By Nature Ltd.
Icebox Brands EU Limited
Icilda's Ltd
Image Hub Limited
Inovair Limited
Sarah Ireland Perfumes Ltd
Irregular Cosmetics Co Ltd
Jardins D'Eden Ltd
Jean Christian Perfumes Ltd
Jorum of Scotland Limited
Julie's Natural Health Ltd
Juni Cosmetics Limited
Karaama Fragrances Ltd
Kehal Ltd
Khali Min Limited
Khushi Skincare Limited
Kingdom Scotland Limited
Ko. Essentials Ltd.
Thomas Kosmala Parfums Ltd
LTSC Ltd
La Maison Hedonique Limited
Ladd Cosmetics Ltd
Lamer & Ava Healthcare Ltd
Lese & Lista Ltd
Lex Roris Ltd
Libhairation Ltd
Lola's Apothecary Ltd
Lumine Beauty Ltd
Lush Ltd.
Luxurious Personal Care Ltd
Luxury Personal Care Ltd
MWK Cosmetics (UK) Ltd
Madre Skincare Limited
Magpie's Ocean Ltd
Majestic Company London Ltd
Man Mask Ltd
Manhattan Group Ltd.
Mary Jean Limited
Maskologist Ltd
Mast - Art Group Limited
Mata Labs Cosmetics Ltd
Meadow Farm Friends Ltd
Meek and Mild Essentials Ltd
Doris Michaels Cosmetics Ltd
Mint Julip Ltd
Molecula Ltd
Mono Naturoils Ltd
Moyy Limited
Myroo Ltd
Nars & Elliott Healthcare Ltd
Natural Sheaness Ltd
Natural Skincare London Ltd
Neal's Yard (Natural Remedies) Ltd
Nectar International Limited
Neville Cut and Shave Limited
A W Oliver & Co Ltd
Oliver & Taylor Ltd
Omprus Limited
One Green Lab Ltd
Organic Stuff Limited
Orikii Naturals Ltd
Pandorra Ltd.
Penny Price Aromatherapy Ltd
Phyto Pharm Limited
Phyto Pharma Limited
Potions & Possibilities Ltd
Prispens Limited
Project Cosmetics Limited
Quint Essence Lab Ltd
Radiant Glow Beauty UK Ltd
Razias London Ltd
Regis Personal Care Ltd
Revlon & Elie Healthcare Ltd
Riley & Sons Ltd
Rimmel & Flynn Healthcare Ltd
Ring in Ring Ltd
Ru Si Lacquers Global Ltd.
Sandine Zartaux Holding Ltd
Scence Ltd
Sheabynature Ltd
Sikania Ltd
Sipro (UK) Ltd
Sloane Home Ltd
Soak Rochford Ltd
South West Aesthetics Ltd
Sphere 7 Lab Ltd
Splash Cosmetics Ltd
Stantondown Limited
Lauren Stone Limited
Sub Tropic Limited
Sweet Arabian Ltd
Swiss Pharma Dynamic Ltd
TAC Perfumes & Cosmetics (UK) Ltd
TWC Products Limited
Eve Taylor (London) Limited
TheManeCo Ltd
Three Organics Ltd
Trees of Beauty Ltd
Geo. F. Trumper (Perfumer and Products)
Twelve Beauty Ltd
Un Air D'Antan Limited
Universal Toiletries Corporation Ltd
Vetivert & Co Ltd
Villa Sauod Ltd
Waterman Corporate Enterprises Ltd
Wheesht Ltd
Wildsmith Collection Limited
Wonder and Wild Ltd
Wrimes Cosmetics Ltd
Zahrat Alqurashi Ltd
Zoe Lane Ltd

20530 Manufacture of essential oils [16]

Asase Tree Ltd
B Luxury Scents Ltd
Bortlam Postpartum Restore Health Management (International) Chain Co.,
Colourscent Limited
Earth Goddess Ltd
Evbioo Ltd
Good Skin Care Co Ltd
Heavenly Fragrance (UK) Ltd
Ink Oil Limited
Jufa Cosmetics Ltd
Karaama Fragrances Ltd
Natural Health Harmony Group Ltd
Nouela Organics Ltd
TAC Perfumes & Cosmetics (UK) Ltd
Eve Taylor (London) Limited
Trees of Beauty Ltd

20590 Manufacture of other chemical products n.e.c.
Amor et Psyche Ltd
Catalina Beauty Group Limited
Chinese Gentry Limited
Elinor-UK Ltd
Ersag UK Limited
Green Mass Limited
Hahydra Technologies Ltd
Innocent Alchemy Ltd
SK Network Ltd

21100 Manufacture of basic pharmaceutical products [19]
Afro Hair and Beauty International
Atlantis Research Limited
Brazilian Kimberlite Clay Ltd
Dermaperfetca Ltd
Ether Cosmetics Ltd
Florence Health & Beauty Ltd
Great British Bee Co Ltd
Hahydra Technologies Ltd
Hydro Fresh Ltd
Ibeautify Ltd
Muamko Uzuri Limited
Nocov Ltd
Pharmacare International Ltd
Royce Health Sciences Ltd
SK Network Ltd
Sandine Zartaux Holding Ltd
Solarius UK & Overseas Limited
Swiss Pharma Dynamic Ltd
Winchpharma (Consumer Healthcare) Ltd

21200 Manufacture of pharmaceutical preparations
Asaya Cosmeceuticals Limited
Beegood Enterprises Limited
Evorin Pharma Limited
GBBC Ltd
SKN-RG Ltd
Sandine Zartaux Holding Ltd
Skindoc Formula Limited
Swiss Pharma Dynamic Ltd

22290 Manufacture of other plastic products
Sipro (UK) Ltd

23990 Manufacture of other non-metallic mineral products n.e.c.
Honeypie Minerals Limited

24410 Precious metals production
Trading Corporation International Export and Import

28290 Manufacture of other general-purpose machinery n.e.c.
Nota Nota Limited

31010 Manufacture of office and shop furniture
Ayhamco Limited

32120 Manufacture of jewellery and related articles
Aromatic Yogi Ltd
Iam By Nature Ltd.
Velvet Bee Co Ltd

32130 Manufacture of imitation jewellery and related articles
New Aesthetic Ltd

32300 Manufacture of sports goods
Galaxy Grooming Limited
Grooming Galaxy Limited
Guilty Fashion Ltd
Nuke Manufacturing, Distribution & Investments

32500 Manufacture of medical and dental instruments and supplies
Beaming White Ltd
Misawa Healthcare Ltd
Moderna Aesthetics Ltd
Passion 4 Health International Ltd
Skins Sexual Health Limited
Solarius UK & Overseas Limited
Toggle Genetica Group Limited
Whitening World Ltd

32990 Other manufacturing n.e.c. [48]
Argan Liquid Gold Limited
Asaya Cosmeceuticals Limited
Bath Bombs and Beyond Limited
Beard Nature Limited
Beautx Ltd
Beautyline Limited
Belfast Beard Co Ltd
Biodeb Beauty Ltd
C-Bombe Limited
Chulo Naturals Ltd
Clink Street FX Ltd
Cath Collins Devon Ltd
Damrick's White Bunny Ltd
Dermatx Ltd
Eden's Daughter Limited
Ezili Botanicals Limited
Firecrest Communications Ltd
H & R Cosmetics Ltd
In Situ Cosmetics Ltd
L'Amour Cosmetics London Ltd
Liplast Ltd
Lotus Cosmetics Ltd
Guy Morgan Apothecary Limited
Neal's Yard (Natural Remedies) Ltd
New Aesthetic Ltd
Nixsi Limited
Nyasa Organics Limited
Orveda Limited
Pennies and Feathers Limited
Pommade Divine Skincare Ltd
Potions & Possibilities Ltd
Prispens Limited
Project 1 Skincare Ltd
Pure Natural Therapy Ltd
RHI By ROC Ltd
Rewind Botanics Limited
Salus Cutis Ltd
Leonora Sanche Cosmetics Ltd
Sheacare Cosmetics Limited
Shebelle Limited
Skin & Tonic London Ltd

Skinjam Cosmetics Limited
Space Brands Limited
Wild Beauty Ltd
Winter Hill No.2 Limited
Wuyu Mother and Baby Ltd
Yejisu Innovation Ltd
Zarvis London Limited

38210 Treatment and disposal of non-hazardous waste
AJ Metals Ltd.

42990 Construction of other civil engineering projects n.e.c.
Hild International Group Ltd

43290 Other construction installation
EnhanceColor Limited
Mega Direct Limited

43390 Other building completion and finishing
Emel Trade Ltd
Home Design 24 Ltd
Tir Chonaill London Ltd

43999 Other specialised construction activities n.e.c.
Cadyle Ltd

45111 Sale of new cars and light motor vehicles
Adnoz Limited

45112 Sale of used cars and light motor vehicles
Adnoz Limited
Adwa Impex Ltd
MSD Trading Services Limited

45200 Maintenance and repair of motor vehicles
Sheyton Ltd

45310 Wholesale trade of motor vehicle parts and accessories
IBS Shopeye World Ltd
International Traders House P.I.T.

45320 Retail trade of motor vehicle parts and accessories
Bedrock Trade Ltd
Swiss Trading .UK. Ltd

46110 Agents selling agricultural raw materials, livestock, textile raw materials and semi-finished goods
Calestio Ltd
Farmers Pure Organics Ltd
My London Trade Ltd

46120 Agents involved in the sale of fuels, ores, metals and industrial chemicals
AJ Metals Ltd.
Rashimex Trading Limited
Trading Corporation International Export and Import

46140 Agents involved in the sale of machinery, industrial equipment, ships and aircraft
AJ Metals Ltd.
Eutek Group Limited
Fit Brands (UK) Ltd

46150 Agents involved in the sale of furniture, household goods, hardware and ironmongery
Feel Good Products Limited
Paul Marney & Co Ltd
Sharp's Global Trading Limited

46160 Agents involved in the sale of textiles, clothing, fur, footwear and leather goods [28]
Aamir Traders Ltd
Adraji Ltd
Aeroeco Co Ltd
Arowell Products Ltd
Beard Gang Ltd
C & P Neptune Ltd
David Dinero Ltd
Golden Vanity Ltd
Healtholozy UK Limited
Hidden for Purpose Ltd
Jerome Fashion Ltd
Just Do You Limited
Lahang Ltd
Lyons Pride Limited
Moor Direct Ltd
My London Trade Ltd
Neopilina Moda Ltd
Oakhill Luxury Ltd
Onyx Clothing Ltd
Pennystore Limited
Pretty Silhouette Limited
Sherhind Accessorize Limited
Strdom Ltd
Thrillage Ltd.
Trade Anchor Limited
Trade Mall Limited
UK Deer Running Co., Ltd
Winkies Limited

46170 Agents involved in the sale of food, beverages and tobacco [13]
Arowell Products Ltd
British American Solutions Ltd
Cannamplify Ltd
Eutek Group Limited
H2 World Health and Beauty Co Ltd
Mayfair Export UK Ltd
Sandgroper Limited
Shori Ltd
Tothun Group UK Ltd
Trade Giant Limited
Triaton Ltd
Velvet Vapours UK Limited
Zoee Cosmetics Co., Ltd

46180 Agents specialised in the sale of other particular products [36]
100% Vegan Skincare Limited
Argan Blossom Ltd
Barbers Warehouse Ltd
Beauty Solutions Trading Ltd
Bespoke Hospitality Supplies Ltd
Biogene Group Limited
Biovate Limited
Cosmetolife Limited
DLG Partners Limited
Enhance You Ltd
Enhancing You Limited
Express Online Superstore, London Ltd
Feel and Heal UK Limited
GP Mediplus Ltd
Gentille Limited
Green Ladies N.I Ltd
Hairways 77 Limited
Leigh Jones & Associates Ltd
Lime and Lead Global Ltd
London Health Sciences Ltd
Loopy Hair & Beauty Ltd
Mabxclusive Limited
Maliboo Hair and Cosmetics Ltd
Modazi Ltd
Monrone Health Ltd
Nut Dust Ltd
Oasis Beauty Distribution Ltd
Only Perfection Ltd
Otonix Limited
Procter & Procter Limited
Quelsa Ltd
Resquire Health & Beauty Ltd
Shhh-Holistic Limited
Takasago (U.K.) Limited
Trade Giant Limited
UK Esthetics Ltd

46190 Agents involved in the sale of a variety of goods [92]
305 Professionals Ltd
Aamir Traders Ltd
Always 20 Limited
Bbeauty Lounge Cosmetics Ltd
Bbeauty Lounge Limited
Bespoke Hospitality Supplies Ltd
Bloom International Group Ltd
Bluesky Cosmetics Limited
Bristol Consumer Health Ltd
Colwayland Co Ltd
Cuelyine Limited
D'Zario UK Ltd
DLG Partners Limited
DYB Tarding Ltd
Diet Plan Unique Ltd
Dily Oka International Group Co., Ltd
Dojah Limited
Double Skies Limited
Elite Capital Limited
Enhancing You Limited
Export Solutions (International) Ltd
Express Online Superstore, London Ltd
Faye Florais Global Holdings., Ltd
Feel and Heal UK Limited
Floest Beauty Solutions Ltd
Fox Group International Ltd
Global One Wholesale Ltd
Golden Vanity Ltd
Gracy Hair and Makeup Ltd
H2 World Health and Beauty Co Ltd
Hairya Ltd
Hedgerow Medicine Chest Ltd
Hempia Limited
Hempo Logical International Ltd
Inbeauting Ltd
Ish Products Ltd
JNVshop La Piazza Delle Idee Ltd
JZM International Limited
Jaydaw Limited
Leigh Jones & Associates Ltd
KMZA Enterprises Ltd
Konya Food Biotechnology Co., Ltd
Lavender Concept Ltd
Lienex Beauty London Ltd
Lime and Lead Global Ltd
Line21 Ltd.
London Heartbeat Ltd
Loopy Hair & Beauty Ltd
Lukony Ltd
Lulu Tanner Limited
Luxury Consulting by Bethan Williams
Lyons Pride Limited
MM Product Trading UK Limited
Mabxclusive Limited
Mine of Goods Ltd
Mr Carters Essentials Limited
My Beauty World Ltd
My London Trade Ltd
Nanosafe Ltd.
Onamex Ltd
Oud & Musk UK Ltd
Paliano Ltd
Pavone Profumi SRL Ltd
Procter & Procter Limited
Pure Body Skin Care Ltd
Pure Natural Therapy Ltd
Quelsa Ltd
Rabimed International Limited
Renaissance Manyane Global Group Ltd
Reneebeauty Limited
Rexez Ltd
Sanay Ltd
Sandgroper Limited
Seigur Rose International Group Co., Ltd
Shhh-Holistic Limited
Sirra Limited
Standfast Solutions International Ltd
Storm of UK Limited
Surreal Health & Beauty Ltd
Think Be Nature Ltd
Tioluxe Europe Limited
Trade Anchor Limited
Trade Giant Limited
UK Deer Running Co., Ltd
UK Lemenic International Medical Group
UK Vietnam Trade Ltd
Universal Toiletries Corporation Ltd
Urhan Group Limited
VY Club Limited
Vidology Group Ltd
Zajil Limited
Zieseniss Limited

46210 Wholesale of grain, unmanufactured tobacco, seeds and animal feeds
Hempo Logical International Ltd
Himalaya Enterprise Limited
Parker & Moses Ltd

46220 Wholesale of flowers and plants
Asante Distributors Limited
Hemp Earth Ltd

46240 Wholesale of hides, skins and leather
Coveti Limited

46310 Wholesale of fruit and vegetables
Africa's Best Artisans Limited
Earthbreath Ltd
Healthology UK Limited
Nutrics Ltd
Portland House International Trading
WGTSS Ltd

46320 Wholesale of meat and meat products
Adible Limited
Jia Bo Rui International Trade Ltd
MS Rarytas Ltd
Unidus Limited

46330 Wholesale of dairy products, eggs and edible oils and fats
Always 20 Limited
W. S Argan Limited
Herbaleva Ltd
Lanko Naturals-UK (PVT) Ltd
Monarch Health & Beauty Ltd.
P P Oil UK Limited
Qiaochu Trading Co. Ltd
United Solutions (UK) Limited

46341 Wholesale of fruit and vegetable juices, mineral water and soft drinks [12]
Bedrock Trade Ltd
Endetrox Ltd.
Haltrade UK Ltd
Herbaleva Ltd
MEA Health and Wellness Ltd
MS Rarytas Ltd
Monrone Health Ltd
NXSK UK Ltd
Rexcel Trading Ltd
Tradinguk55 Limited
WGTSS Ltd
Wisdom of Nature Limited

46342 Wholesale of wine, beer, spirits and other alcoholic beverages [11]
Always 20 Limited
Ark Inta Ltd
Asante Distributors Limited
Europebro Wholesalers Ltd
Jia Bo Rui International Trade Ltd
Kanj Wholesale Ltd
Santa Code Limited
Sloane Home Ltd
Square Wholesale Ltd
Tioluxe Europe Limited
Vett Limited

46350 Wholesale of tobacco products
Hempo Logical International Ltd
P & T PL Ltd
Square Wholesale Ltd
Velvet Vapours UK Limited

46360 Wholesale of sugar and chocolate and sugar confectionery [10]
Azhar Academy Limited
CC Dist UK Ltd
Eurasia Property Limited
FM Cosmetics UK Ltd
Feinkost & Getranke Ltd
Krish Shoppers Ltd
Mayfair Export UK Ltd
NXSK UK Ltd
Rexcel Trading Ltd
United Solutions (UK) Limited

46370 Wholesale of coffee, tea, cocoa and spices [25]
Bedrock Trade Ltd
Coffeinium Germania Ltd
Equisalud Ltd
FM Cosmetics UK Ltd
Feinkost & Getranke Ltd
Green Essence Ltd
Haltrade UK Ltd
Hemp Earth Ltd
Holy Lama Naturals Ltd
Inshirah Enterprises Limited
International Integrated Solutions Co
Konya Food Biotechnology Co., Ltd
Krish Shoppers Ltd
Lienex Beauty London Ltd
MEA Health and Wellness Ltd
Paul Marney & Co Ltd
Mayfair Export UK Ltd
Mooi-H Ltd
NXSK UK Ltd
Nasser Waziri Ltd
Natures Merchant Ltd
Nextporter Ltd.
Slim Line Club UK Ltd
Spice International Trading Co Ltd
Spruce Vita Limited

46380 Wholesale of other food, including fish, crustaceans and molluscs
Amalsons Ltd
Fashion Conspiracy Ltd
Honey Corn Limited
Jia Bo Rui International Trade Ltd
Miraculous UK Ltd
YSO Import-Export Limited

46390 Non-specialised wholesale of food, beverages and tobacco [33]
Alpha Auriga Limited
Antian World Limited
Asadilari Limited
Biogene Group Limited
Pazery Bouffard and Co Ltd
CC Dist UK Ltd
Deism IT Solutions Ltd
Direct Trade Limited
Earthbreath Ltd
Gordon-McCarthy Limited
Greenpol Distribution Ltd
Imijo Ltd
Jacob's Well Limited
Jaydaw Limited
MQS Group London Limited
Maryam Imports & Exports Ltd
Miraculous UK Ltd
Natures Merchant Ltd

Need4health Limited
Nomalogic Ltd
PSM Vision Limited
Parker & Moses Ltd
Peters Cosmet Ltd
Pure & Sure Limited
Razaq & Iqbal Limited
Shori Ltd
Slim Line Club UK Ltd
Square Wholesale Ltd
TM Brands Limited
TheGlobalTrading Ltd
Uni Supply Ltd
Wisdom of Nature Limited
Ximtrade (UK) Ltd

46410 Wholesale of textiles [30]
Agoda Limited
Arewa Styles Limited
Bemysoul Ltd
Bespoke Hospitality Supplies Ltd
Binaya Solution Ltd
Blink Street Limited
Calestio Ltd
Clearance Masters Ltd
Eacho Green Ltd
Giva Solution Ltd
H.H.L.Brothers Limited
Hasanah Global Ltd
Hidden for Purpose Ltd
Iras Trading Ltd
Kayanna Ltd
Lady T Limited
Lyons Pride Limited
Mayfair Gate Limited
Me Sentir Ltd.
Modazi Ltd
Moffat Perfume Co Ltd
Oakhill Luxury Ltd
Official IV Ltd
Oscar & Louis Limited
Relaxa Trading Ltd
Seba Trade Limited
Suvaz Linen UK Ltd
Theodory Ltd
Trollion Limited
WGTSS Ltd

46420 Wholesale of clothing and footwear [141]
9 Silk Gates Ltd
Aamir Traders Ltd
Albland Limited
Alizcare Limited
Antian World Limited
Arewa Styles Limited
Asel Ltd
Asian Fashions Ltd
Beauty The Divine Ltd
Bellissimo GmbH International Ltd
Beta Novis Limited
Bibishor Limited
Binaya Solution Ltd
Blink Street Limited
Blue Rose Shop Ltd
Bluebells Hair Boutique Ltd
Boylondon Holdings Limited
Brands Gallery Ltd
C & A International Trading Ltd
C & P Neptune Ltd
Calestio Ltd

Chaleur Ltd
Chanel Limited
Cherry Cherry Fashion Ltd
Chic Clothing Limited
Clickpoint Limited
Coveti Limited
Cutelovelee Limited
D'val Ltd
DKH Retail Limited
DYB Tarding Ltd
Deewin Stomatology Research Center Co.,
David Dinero Ltd
Diverse Solution Ltd
Dont Poke It Ltd
Dorian House Marketplace Ltd
Eacho Green Ltd
Enimarkets Ltd
Essentials4men Ltd
Ethical House Ltd
Exbrands Ltd
FG Traders Ltd
Faceoff Limited
Farshety Ltd
Fashion Conspiracy Ltd
Simona Fridrich Limited
Garda Service Ltd
Giva Solution Ltd
Global One Wholesale Ltd
Glochina Trading UK Ltd.
Glow Investment Ltd
Gluedon Ltd
Grand By Designs Limited
Carolina Herrera UK Ltd
Hidden for Purpose Ltd
Honeystyle Limited
IBS Shopeye World Ltd
Imijo Ltd
Imxpo Ltd
In & Outbrands Ltd
International Traders House P.I.T.
Ital Living Market Ltd
Jerome Fashion Ltd
Julio & Ejder Ltd
KMZA Enterprises Ltd
Kandi Apple Limited
Kanj Wholesale Ltd
Kaxton Limited
Kayanna Ltd
Jennifer Klar Ltd
Ladorisa Limited
Lady T Limited
Lahang Ltd
Landional Ltd
Lee Gallop Enterprise Ltd
Leixaco Trading Ltd
Leslie International Ltd
Loaded Cosmetics Limited
London Export Ltd
MGM UK Limited
MNF Commodities Ltd
MSD Trading Services Limited
Me Sentir Ltd.
Medna Fashions Ltd
Mine of Goods Ltd
Moda Exportation Limited
Mooi-H Ltd
Moor Direct Ltd
Muchacho (London) Limited
My7heavens Ltd
NJ Apparel Ltd.
NS Brands International Ltd
Oakhill Luxury Ltd

Official IV Ltd
Onamex Ltd
Onlinexclusive Limited
Only Perfection Ltd
Orit Limited
Oscar & Louis Limited
Ossulstone Hundred Limited
Pennystore Limited
Perfect Lady Ltd
Pinklady International Ltd
Posh Gift Ltd
Pretty Silhouette Limited
Qiaochu Trading Co. Ltd
Reetal Development Co Ltd
Renski Limited
Revoke Ltd.
Roccotek Limited
Rose & Thorn Ltd
SPTB Ltd
Leonora Sanche Limited
Seaside Investments Ltd
Seba Trade Limited
Sheyton Ltd
Shop4stocks Limited
Shuhui Limited
Spartzy Lifestyle Brands Ltd
Strdom Ltd
Stroppy Ltd
Style Factory Limited
Swiss Trading .UK. Ltd
Tailord Chic Ltd
Theodory Ltd
Thrifty Limited
Thrillage Ltd.
Trade Mall Limited
Trelux Limited
Trinity General Trading Ltd
US Beauty Store Limited
United Mart (UK) Limited
United Nomads Limited
Valerie Lady Co., Ltd
Varana UK Limited
Veels UK Limited
Viridian Leaf Limited
W8T Ltd
Wonderland Sales Ltd
World Wide Gifts Limited
Yaami's Fashion Beauty & Cosmetics UK

46431 Wholesale of audio tapes, records, CDs and video tapes and the equipment on which these are played
ANGMG Ltd
Age Infinite Ltd
Clearance Masters Ltd
Europebro Wholesalers Ltd
Gluedon Ltd
Hill and Dale Limited
Wonderland Sales Ltd

46439 Wholesale of radio, television goods & electrical household appliances (other than records, tapes, CDs) [16]
DYB Tarding Ltd
Farshety Ltd
Glow Investment Ltd
Gluedon Ltd
Hot (UK) Limited
Jonatho Ltd
K Wholesale Limited
La Boutique du Discount Ltd.

Mashco Limited
Mine of Goods Ltd
Onamex Ltd
Paradoxx Ltd
Reetal Development Co Ltd
SHH Logistics Ltd
Scontimania Online SRL Limited
Wonderland Sales Ltd

46440 Wholesale of china and glassware and cleaning materials
CBee (Europe) Limited
Enimarkets Ltd
FM Cosmetics UK Ltd
Green World Spa Products Ltd
Iras Trading Ltd
Multi Imports Limited

46460 Wholesale of pharmaceutical goods [138]
2M PH. Intl. Limited
A B International Limited
Alizcare Limited
Allied Warden Marketing Ltd
Almirall Limited
Amaxa Ltd
Asaya Cosmeceuticals Limited
Aviva Health Solutions Limited
Bbeauty Lounge Limited
Beegood Enterprises Limited
Beiersdorf UK Ltd.
Bessacarr Ltd
Best-Bio Ltd
Bio Global Limited
Biovate Limited
Bioxane Ltd
Mark Birch Hair Ltd
A & P Blickling Ltd
Blink Street Limited
Bluesky Cosmetics Limited
Boots International Limited
Bristol Consumer Health Ltd
Chronicles Medical Consulting Ltd
Clinova Limited
Colgate-Palmolive (U.K.) Ltd
Coriungo Limited
Croma-Pharma Limited
DLG Partners Limited
Dacre Skincare Limited
Dilmaherbals Limited
Drugget Ltd
Esthetica Pure Ltd
Eurocare Impex Services Ltd
Evorin Pharma Limited
Fair Pharm Limited
Feel and Heal UK Limited
Five Star International Consulting
Florence Health & Beauty Ltd
Foreverbeyoung Ltd
Fox Group International Ltd
FreshBreathOnline Limited
Frontrow International UK Ltd
GBBC Ltd
GP Mediplus Ltd
General Shop Ltd
Generic Physics Limited
Goldshore (UK) Limited
Great British Bee Co Ltd
Green Guru Enterprices Ltd.
Hampton Brands Limited
Harvey Pharma Ltd

Healthcare Procurement Services Ltd
Healtholozy UK Limited
Healthpoint Limited
Herbaleva Ltd
Here We Flo Ltd
Hisamitsu Pharmaceutical UK Ltd
Hisamitsu UK Limited
Iam Finance Limited
Iberia Skin Brands Ltd
Imamcom Ltd
Imperial Bioscience Ltd
Ivee Group Ltd
Leigh Jones & Associates Ltd
K588 Limited
Lambsmead Limited
Laogong Laopo Limited
Larmed Limited
Latam HQ Health Ltd
Layan Pharma Ltd
Legendbio Beauty Group Limited
Lionmark Limited
London Health Sciences Ltd
Luban & Murr Ltd
M & N Traders Limited
MGC Pharma (UK) Ltd
MQS Group London Limited
Macks Ltd.
Mast - Art Group Limited
Mayfair Export London Limited
Medica Ltd
Medipro Pharma Limited
Microskin Cosmeceuticals UK Ltd
Minmar (1008) Limited
Modern Innovations Limited Ltd
Nasser Waziri Ltd
Natures Merchant Ltd
Neolife International Ltd
Novmedic Limited
Optima Consumer Health Limited
Orange Square Co Ltd.
Organic Iway Ltd
Oscar & Louis Limited
Perricone MD Cosmeceuticals UK Ltd
Pharma Medico Limited
Pharmacare International Ltd
Pharmadose Limited
Pharmdex UK Ltd
Pinklady International Ltd
Pispo Ltd
Sara Post Ltd
Prema Naturals Limited
Pricecheck Toiletries Limited
Pure Skincare Limited
RR Cosmeceuticals (UK) Ltd
Rabimed International Limited
Rexcel Trading Ltd
Ris Healthcare Limited
Riviere Groupe (Europe) Ltd
Rogia Romini Limited
Royce Health Sciences Ltd
SHL Medical Limited
Salonpas UK Limited
Sanay Ltd
Sawa Trading & Shipping Ltd
Secret Line Ltd
Skindoc Formula Limited
Skinlab Medical Ltd
Solarius UK & Overseas Limited
South China Bio-Pharma Co Ltd.
TA-65 (UK) Wholesale Limited
Teoxane UK Limited
Tetra Hydro Cannabinoid Oils Global Ltd

Treas Biotechnology UK Ltd
Triaton Ltd
UK Beauty Cosmetics International Group
UK Heluns Industry Co., Ltd
UK Lemenic International Medical Group
UK Vimin Industry Co., Limited
Uni Supply Ltd
Unidus Limited
Ved Healthcare Limited
Veramic Limited
Victoria Pharma London Ltd
Vivacy Laboratoires Ltd
Winchpharma (Consumer Healthcare) Ltd
Zarroug Limited
Zerocann Ltd

46470 Wholesale of furniture, carpets and lighting equipment
Asel Ltd
Kathy Salon Equipment Limited
Paul Marney & Co Ltd
Mooi-H Ltd
My Pure Life-Style Limited
Spaquashop Ltd
Viridian Leaf Limited

46480 Wholesale of watches and jewellery [55]
AMS-Uhren Ambiente mit Style Ltd
ANGMG Ltd
Albland Limited
Arewa Styles Limited
Bluebells Hair Boutique Ltd
Chanel Limited
Cherry Cherry Fashion Ltd
Chic Clothing Limited
Choize Ltd
David Dinero Ltd
Dont Poke It Ltd
Dorian House Marketplace Ltd
Double Skies Limited
Express Online Superstore, London Ltd
Simona Fridrich Limited
Garda Service Ltd
Glochina Trading UK Ltd.
Glow Investment Ltd
Grand By Designs Limited
Honeystyle Limited
In & Outbrands Ltd
Julio & Ejder Ltd
Just Do You Limited
Kandi Apple Limited
Kitchen Witch Aromatherapy Ltd
Ladorisa Limited
Lady T Limited
Liolax Limited
Luuann Limited
MGM UK Limited
Maximaliste Limited
Medna Fashions Ltd
Modern Innovations Limited Ltd
Moor Direct Ltd
My7heavens Ltd
NJ Apparel Ltd.
Ned London Limited
Neopilina Moda Ltd
Official IV Ltd
Orit Limited
Pennystore Limited
Posh Gift Ltd
Pretty Silhouette Limited

Rogia Romini Limited
Leonora Sanche Limited
Sangels Limited
Shuhui Limited
Smuccii Trading Ltd
Stroppy Ltd
Stylish & Luxurious Limited
Tailord Chic Ltd
Tioluxe Europe Limited
Trading Corporation International Export and Import
Valerie Lady Co., Ltd
W8T Ltd

46491 Wholesale of musical instruments
Leslie International Ltd

46499 Wholesale of household goods (other than musical instruments) n.e.c [54]
Age Infinite Ltd
Asel Ltd
Basic Needs Ltd
Beiersdorf UK Ltd.
Big Wholesale Co Ltd
Blk Deer Co. Ltd
Buy It Out Ltd
CBee (Europe) Limited
Clean Living Ltd
Clearance Masters Ltd
Colgate-Palmolive (U.K.) Ltd
County Sales Limited
DealsRUsOnline Ltd
Disley Limited
Enimarkets Ltd
Ersag UK Limited
Evany Personal Care Limited
Faceoff Limited
Fit Brands (UK) Ltd
General Shop Ltd
Goodsky Co., Ltd.
Iam Finance Limited
Imijo Ltd
Jaydaw Limited
L'Art & La Matiere Limited
Loveco Ltd
Luban & Murr Ltd
MGM UK Limited
MNF Commodities Ltd
Macks Ltd.
Mancave Limited
Morgan Jost Ltd
NA Medical Care Ltd
Neal's Yard Remedies (Home) Ltd
Neal's Yard Remedies (International) Ltd
Neolife International Ltd
Outcome Zero Ltd
Pricecheck Toiletries Limited
Reetal Development Co Ltd
Reliance HBC UK Ltd
Soak Rochford Ltd
Spaquashop Ltd
Sparking-Jy International Trading Co.,
St-Creation Ltd
TRS & Co (Europe) Limited
Tassels UK Ltd
Texthold Ltd
Trollion Limited
UK Aimutaike Electronics Co., Ltd
UK Lemenic International Medical Group
Valma Consumer Co Ltd
Vyas International Ltd

Xpoze International Limited
Yummy Home Ltd

46510 Wholesale of computers, computer peripheral equipment and software [11]
Avee Ltd
Bibishor Limited
Buy It Out Ltd
Eukes Global Limited
Jonatho Ltd
Luuann Limited
Novumis Ltd
Raynolds Ltd
Roccotek Limited
Scontimania Online SRL Limited
Sirra Limited

46520 Wholesale of electronic and telecommunications equipment and parts [22]
Ark Inta Ltd
Avee Ltd
Bbeauty Lounge Cosmetics Ltd
Bbeauty Lounge Limited
Best-Bio Ltd
Bio Global Limited
Bluesky Cosmetics Limited
C & P Neptune Ltd
FG Traders Ltd
Goodsky Co., Ltd.
Jonatho Ltd
Luuann Limited
M & M Import Ltd
Misawa Healthcare Ltd
Reliant Overseas UK Limited
Rexez Ltd
Roccotek Limited
Spaquashop Ltd
Tailord Chic Ltd
Texthold Ltd
Valerie Lady Co., Ltd
Z Online Ltd

46610 Wholesale of agricultural machinery, equipment and supplies
Adwa Impex Ltd

46620 Wholesale of machine tools
9 Silk Gates Ltd
A Beauty Story Ltd
Adwa Impex Ltd

46630 Wholesale of mining, construction and civil engineering machinery
Spree Trading Ltd

46640 Wholesale of machinery for the textile industry and of sewing and knitting machines
Medora of London Limited

46650 Wholesale of office furniture
Barbers Warehouse Ltd
DealsRUsOnline Ltd
Jaspmab Ltd
Monrone Health Ltd

46660 Wholesale of other office machinery and equipment
Barbers Warehouse Ltd
Deewin Stomatology Research Center Co.,

46690 Wholesale of other machinery and equipment
3D Lifestyle Ltd
9 Silk Gates Ltd
A Beauty Story Ltd
Nevitrade Ltd
Rejuvapen UK Ltd
Spree Trading Ltd
Triaton Ltd

46711 Wholesale of petroleum and petroleum products
MQS Group London Limited

46719 Wholesale of other fuels and related products
Sirra Limited

46740 Wholesale of hardware, plumbing and heating equipment and supplies
Krish Shoppers Ltd

46750 Wholesale of chemical products [15]
Beard Gang Ltd
Best-Bio Ltd
Bio Global Limited
Body Beauty Wholesale Exporters Ltd
Capital Import & Export Co. Ltd
Euro Aromas Limited
Evorin Pharma Limited
Hydro Fresh Ltd
Iam Finance Limited
London Cosmetics Co Ltd
Macks Ltd.
Rock Beauty Junkie Limited
Ru Si Lacquers Global Ltd.
South China Bio-Pharma Co Ltd.
Valma Consumer Co Ltd

46760 Wholesale of other intermediate products
Directfrom Ltd
Green World Spa Products Ltd
Healthcare Wholesale Ltd
Love Little Prices Ltd
Serendipity (N.I.) Ltd
South China Bio-Pharma Co Ltd.
Winchpharma (Consumer Healthcare) Ltd

46770 Wholesale of waste and scrap
Leslie International Ltd
Unidus Limited

46900 Non-specialised wholesale trade [116]
Acering Limited
Adams General Ltd
Aeden UK Ltd
Alianaz Ltd.
Alpha Auriga Limited
Atlas Global Trade Ltd
Azhar Academy Limited
BS Supply Ltd
Barnsley Card Ltd
Beauty and Trade Ltd
Beautypro Ltd
Beiersdorf UK Ltd.
Blk Deer Co. Ltd
Bluebells Hair Boutique Ltd
Bonroy International Limited
Box of Beauty Ltd
Brands Gallery Ltd
Bristol Consumer Health Ltd
Bubble-Bubble Ltd
C & A International Trading Ltd
CC Dist UK Ltd
Cazza Professional Ltd
Complete Healing Limited
Concept Healthcare Limited
Crazy Smiles Group Ltd
Cyrano Limited
D'Zario UK Ltd
David & Co. Traders Ltd
Direct Trade Limited
Directfrom Ltd
Duke of Charm Limited
EB Stores Ltd
ED Trading & Consultancy Ltd
Eileen Group (UK) Ltd
Eloise Group Ltd
Eukes Global Limited
Eurasia Property Limited
Fillers Pro Ltd
Foramca Ltd
Fragrance and Gifts Limited
Fragrance de Maison Limited
GP Mediplus Ltd
Golo Hair & Beauty Limited
Gracy Hair and Makeup Ltd
Graham Hair and Beauty Limited
Greenpol Distribution Ltd
Hairenvy Boutique Limited
Haltrade UK Ltd
Holy Group Limited
IBS Shopeye World Ltd
Imaage Ltd
Impulse Global Solutions Ltd
Inshirah Enterprises Limited
International Traders House P.I.T.
J26 Limited
Jouer Jouer Limited
K3W Trading Limited
KSE Cosmetics Ltd
Kanj Wholesale Ltd
Kounga Ltd
La Bello Beauty Limited
Lavish Lashes Ltd
Layan Pharma Ltd
Lee Gallop Enterprise Ltd
Leixaco Trading Ltd
Live Rich Academy Limited
London Health Sciences Ltd
Lovalova Ltd
Loveco Ltd
MS Rarytas Ltd

MSD Trading Services Limited
Mashco Limited
Mayfair Gate Limited
Meddiamonds Ltd
Mondor & Bache Ltd
N18 Ltd
NOP Cosmetics Ltd
National Supplement Beauty Solutions
Neo Elegance Ltd
Nomalogic Ltd
Nukua Limited
Oasis Beauty Distribution Ltd
Paint It Orange Ltd
Pink Empire Limited
Pizzaz Ventures Limited
Portland House International Trading
Pricecheck Toiletries Limited
Protective World Ltd
Reliant Overseas UK Limited
Rogia Romini Limited
SA & A Ltd
Sai Enterprise Limited
Sawa Trading & Shipping Ltd
Scented Sachets (London) Ltd.
Seba Trade Limited
SeductiveDirect Ltd
Serendipity (N.I.) Ltd
Simple Bargain Limited
Smuccii Trading Ltd
Spice International Trading Co Ltd
Spree Trading Ltd
Stroppy Ltd
Style4you Ltd
Sunrise Essential Oil Limited
TM Brands Limited
TheGlobalTrading Ltd
Trade Anchor Limited
UK Esthetics Ltd
Urhan Group Limited
Vyas International Ltd
W8T Ltd
Whimsical Beauty Ltd
Wild Violet X Limited
World Links Europe Limited
World Wide Gifts Limited
Zarvis London Limited

47110 Retail sale in non-specialised stores with food, beverages or tobacco predominating
Amalsons Ltd
Comfort Click Limited
Frontrow International UK Ltd
Holy Group Limited
Lanko Naturals-UK (PVT) Ltd
Liquor Lips Ltd
Young Now Ltd

47190 Other retail sale in non-specialised stores [48]
A Beauty Story Ltd
Active Skincare Limited
Alayna Cosmetics and Beauty Ltd
Alizcare Limited
Bedeaux Ltd
Bendito Trading Limited
Coveti Limited
Crazy Smiles Group Ltd
EB Stores Ltd
Floest Beauty Solutions Ltd
Herbalise Limited

Hudsonry Ltd
K2Y Limited
K3W Trading Limited
Lavelle Store UK Ltd
Lavish Lashes Ltd
Lionmark Limited
Liza Organics Ltd
London Heartbeat Ltd
Doris Michaels Cosmetics Ltd
Miracle8 Ltd
Muamko Uzuri Limited
Mupe Ltd
Nanosafe Ltd.
Natural Jeanius Ltd
Oud & Musk UK Ltd
Party Supplies and More Ltd
Perfume Outlet Ltd
Phi Advisory & Consulting Ltd
Sara Post Ltd
Pound Ring Ltd
Prevura Ltd
Prima Makeup Ltd
Pure Natural Therapy Ltd
Razaq & Iqbal Limited
Reimiece Ltd
Sabeauti Ltd.
Salem Stores Ltd
Skin Chef Limited
Sueno Cosmetics Ltd
Tiyati Ltd
Trimmz Ltd
Un Air D'Antan Limited
Varana UK Limited
Whimsical Beauty Ltd
Wipes Direct Ltd
World Links Europe Limited
Yummy Home Ltd

47210 Retail sale of fruit and vegetables in specialised stores
Nutrics Ltd

47240 Retail sale of bread, cakes, flour confectionery and sugar confectionery in specialised stores
Portobello Organics Ltd

47250 Retail sale of beverages in specialised stores
Vett Limited

47260 Retail sale of tobacco products in specialised stores
Le-Vap Limited

47290 Other retail sale of food in specialised stores
Amalsons Ltd
Colwayland Co Ltd
Crete Online Ltd.
Earthly Pleasures Ltd
Equisalud Ltd
Fashion Conspiracy Ltd
General Shop Ltd
P P Oil UK Limited
Watsoap.Com Limited

47300 Retail sale of automotive fuel in specialised stores
Holy Group Limited

47410 Retail sale of computers, peripheral units and software in specialised stores
A S Pacho Ltd
Tothun Group UK Ltd

47421 Retail sale of mobile telephones
Avee Ltd

47429 Retail sale of telecommunications equipment other than mobile telephones
Rexez Ltd
Swiss Trading .UK. Ltd

47510 Retail sale of textiles in specialised stores
Adraji Ltd
Bemysoul Ltd
Hekiti Cosmetics Ltd
Kaxton Limited
Manhattan Group Ltd.
Oh So Locks Ltd
Leonora Sanche Limited
Wipes Direct Ltd

47540 Retail sale of electrical household appliances in specialised stores
JZM International Limited
Shaw International Ltd
Wizer Ltd

47599 Retail of furniture, lighting, and similar (not musical instruments or scores) in specialised store
Home Design 24 Ltd
Itala Group Ltd
My Pure Life-Style Limited
Yummy Home Ltd

47610 Retail sale of books in specialised stores
Greenleaf Luton Limited
Hill and Dale Limited

47640 Retail sale of sports goods, fishing gear, camping goods, boats and bicycles
BSB Fashion Limited

47650 Retail sale of games and toys in specialised stores
Hairya Ltd
Sara Post Ltd
Scontimania Online SRL Limited
ZZ Traders Ltd

47710 Retail sale of clothing in specialised stores [26]
Asian Fashions Ltd
BSB Fashion Limited
Beard and Bones UK Limited
Bloomtown Ltd
Body of Work Beauty Ltd
Chanel Limited
Duke of Charm Limited
Earthly Pleasures Ltd
Essentials4men Ltd
Ex'klusive Products Ltd
Feel Good Products Limited
Greenleaf Luton Limited
Hekiti Cosmetics Ltd
Carolina Herrera UK Ltd
Hill and Dale Limited
Itala Group Ltd
K Wholesale Limited
Melanative Ltd
NJ Apparel Ltd.
NS Brands International Ltd
Onyx Clothing Ltd
Privilago Fashion Ltd
Sphere 7 Lab Ltd
Suvaz Linen UK Ltd
Theodory Ltd
United Nomads Limited

47721 Retail sale of footwear in specialised stores
Feel Good Products Limited

47730 Dispensing chemist in specialised stores
Medipro Pharma Limited
Pharmadose Limited
Rabimed International Limited
Shilcroft Limited

47749 Retail sale of medical and orthopaedic goods in specialised stores (not incl. hearing aids) n.e.c. [12]
Ibeautify Ltd
Imamcom Ltd
Infini Lab Ltd
Medica Ltd
Medical Technology Caraco (MYC) Ltd.
Organic Iway Ltd
Pharmacare International Ltd
Purederma Ltd
South West Aesthetics Ltd
Sparking-Jy International Trading Co.,
Victoria Pharma London Ltd
Vivacy Laboratoires Ltd

47750 Retail sale of cosmetic and toilet articles in specialised stores [583]
2B Enterprises Limited
305 Professionals Ltd
4symbols Ltd
876 Skin Beauty Limited
AJS Marketing Limited
AM Botanical Limited
Abington Cosmetics Ltd
Acqua di Parma Limited
Chris Adams Perfumes Ltd
Adem Oygur Ltd
Aeden UK Ltd
Aether Elements Ltd

African Wild Organics Ltd
Afthrone Ltd
Aga Cosmetics Ltd
Aglory Merchant Enterprises Ltd
Ahoaloe Cosmetics Limited
Ahwaz Ltd
Al Masiya Cosmetic Ltd
All Naturals Beauty Limited
Amassuna Limited
Amelgo Ltd
Anatomicals London (England, The World, The Universe-Known and Unknown)
Aneen Ventures Limited
Anita Brows Cosmetics Limited
Apotheca London Skincare Ltd
Apsara Cosmetics Ltd
Aqolade Ltd
Aquapurity Ltd
Arabian Aroma Limited
Arbar Ltd
Argan Blossom Ltd
W. S Argan Limited
Argan Liquid Gold Limited
Arizona Botaniq Limited
Aroma Dead Sea Limited
Aromaclub Handmade Skincare Ltd
Ars Nova (UK) Limited
Asifall Ltd
Atkinson London 1799 Ltd
Aurelia Skincare (International) Ltd
Aurelia Skincare Limited
Aurora Spa Health and Beauty Ltd
Aurum Argan Ltd
Axa Beauty World Limited
Azzy London Ltd
B. Silki Naturally Ltd
B.Me Skincare Ltd
BU Cosmetics Limited
Bad Mermaid Limited
Barbers House Ltd
Barefaced Beauty Ltd
Batalveez Ltd
Be Savvy Ltd
Beached Limited
Beard Zone Ltd
Beard and Bones UK Limited
Beatnut Butter Ltd
Beautifect Ltd
Beautiful By Nature Ltd
Beautx Ltd
Beauty Africa Limited
Beauty Bash Limited
Beauty Science UK Ltd
Beauty Stable Ltd
Beautybaseuk Ltd
Beautysugaring Limited
Beautyzon Limited
Beehive Cosmetics UK Limited
Bel Corporation Ltd
Bellapierre Cosmetics Limited
Bellevue of London Ltd.
Bemysoul Ltd
Bendito Trading Limited
Bioaqua -Biotechnology Ltd.
Biogene Group Limited
Biola Beauty Ltd
Biologico Cosmetics Limited
Biotrade Cosmeceuticals Ltd
Bisch Limited
Bizi Bazzar Limited
Blank Factory Limited
A & P Blickling Ltd

Blissible Ltd
Blissworld Limited
Blossom Organics Limited
Bluesky Products Limited
Body Beauty & Hair Ltd
Body Month Ltd
Body Reform Limited
Body Shop International Ltd
Body of Work Beauty Ltd
Botanik Beauty Limited
Botanika Group Ltd
Botany Squared Limited
Bramley Products Ltd
Brazilian Kimberlite Clay Ltd
Bubbleworks Limited
Bullingberg Limited
Butter Park Ltd
Butterwhips Ltd
By Sarah Limited
CFBP Ltd
CJ Cosmetics Ltd
CZ Cosmetics Ltd.
Calmer Solutions Limited
Cambridge Sprouts Limited
Cancun Collection Limited
Steven Carey Hair & Beauty Ltd
Carr Greens Limited
Chanson Worldwide Limited
Cheet Beauty Ltd
Ches Editions Ltd
Chintys Ltd
Choize Ltd
Ciao Brow Henna Limited
Cleardot Group Ltd
Cath Collins Devon Ltd
Alia Collyns Cosmetics Ltd
Color Studio Ltd
Colour Lux Cosmetics Ltd
Colourscent Limited
Comets Intertrade Co Ltd
Comfort Click Limited
Complexi-Light Ltd
Conatural Ltd
Contemporary Cosmetic Enterprise Ltd
Contour and More London Ltd
Cool Blades Limited
Coriungo Limited
Cornish Beard Co Ltd
Cosmetics Online Limited
Cosmetics Store Ltd
Cosmetics of London Chelsie Ltd
Cosmetiqa Ltd
Cosmos Cosmetics Limited
Cosnique Group Holdings Ltd
Cowshed Products Limited
Cozmetica UK Ltd
Crivalis Ltd
Cuelyine Limited
Curl Coach Ltd
Custom Tan UK Limited
DC Salon Products Ltd
DS Express Barbering Ltd
Dabrimela Limited
Dacre Skincare Limited
Dance on Tan Limited
Delhicious Ltd
Derma Organics by CFBP Ltd
Design4nails Ltd
Dilecta Cosmetics Limited
Dily Oka International Group Co., Ltd
Dimonauk Ltd
Diymonde Corporation Limited

Dooa Capital Limited
Dorothy Hair and Beauty Shop Ltd
Dr. Gabriela Ltd
Dudu-Osun Limited
Dufeal Your Best Beauty Ltd
Dunia Organic Ltd
Duo Beauty Products Limited
ENS Europe Limited
East Cosmetics Limited
East End Cosmetics Limited
East To West Lifestyle Co Ltd
Eblouir Group Ltd
Eco Twinkle Ltd
Egotistic Hair & Beauty Ltd
Eku Skin Care Ltd
Elan Skincare Ltd
Electimuss Limited
Elegant Boss Ltd
Elemental Herbology Limited
Eleuthere Ltd
Eleven Eleven Cosmetics Ltd
Emel Trade Ltd
Emma Victoria Cosmetics Ltd
Equisalud Ltd
Esem International Ltd
Essench Cosmetics Ltd
Essex Beauty Palace Ltd
Esspire Limited
Esteem Royale Cosmetics Ltd
Ether Cosmetics Ltd
Ethereal Beauty Ltd
Ethnoceuticals Limited
Evanesce Ltd
Exoditi Limited
Ezili Botanicals Limited
Face Fodder Limited
Facemane Ltd
Fandealtastic Limited
Farah Organics Ltd
Fashion Fragrances & Cosmetics UK Ltd
Fatale Cosmetics Limited
Faye Florais Global Holdings., Ltd
Firecrest Communications Ltd
Florence Verity Limited
Flower Cosmetic Ltd
Flowery Whiff Limited
Foad Wax Limited
Fols for Men Ltd
Foreverbeyoung Ltd
Fragrance World Ltd
Fragrant Spa Limited
France Eclavour Cosmetic Ltd
Franok Business Solutions Ltd
Fresh Cosmetics Limited
Freshly Whip'd Limited
From Mini Acorns Ltd
Frontrow International UK Ltd
Funky Skincare Limited
Fushi Wellbeing Limited
Fysifarm Limited
G & G Skincare Ltd
Galenti Limited
Gel Labs Limited
Gemini Beauty Products Ltd
Genten Skincare Ltd
Gentle Beauty Co Ltd
Glad Gent Ltd
Glamn Holding Ltd
Global Luxury Beauty Ltd
Glow Jar Ltd
Golden Rose Limited
Goldstone Perfumes Limited

Gracetree Ltd
Grand Beaute Ltd
Green Jiva Ltd
Gridt Beauty Ltd
GroundedBodyScrub Limited
Guerison Skin Solutions Ltd
HBD International Limited
HFC Prestige Products Limited
HT Cosmetics Ltd
Hair & Skin Care Ltd
Hairshine UK Ltd
Hamiltons of Canterbury Ltd
Hansraj House Limited
Haych Cosmetics Limited
Hekiti Cosmetics Ltd
Helen Gel Colour Ltd
Helia-D UK Ltd
Hello Dame London Ltd
Hemangini Limited
Hempia Limited
Hemsley James Cosmetics Ltd
Herbalise Limited
Carolina Herrera UK Ltd
Highland Soap Co. Limited
Hommage International Ltd
Honey Corn Limited
Honeypie Minerals Limited
House of Vanity Limited
Hy-Brd Ltd
I.S.O.D Limited
Icilda's Ltd
Ileri Trading Limited
Ilex Wood Ltd
Ilys Organic Ltd
Imamcom Ltd
Insta-Jell Cosmetics Ltd
Intertrade Group Ltd
Iras Trading Ltd
Sarah Ireland Perfumes Ltd
Ismile Beauty Ltd
Itala Group Ltd
Ivaxane UK Ltd
Ives Lab Ltd
Janou Brand Limited
Jardin de Parfums Ltd
Jardins D'Eden Ltd
Jax of London Ltd
Jeunvie Ltd
Jigu Corporation Limited
Jivesse Limited
Josie Rose Ltd
Joyganics Ltd
Juju Beauty Care Ltd
Juni Cosmetics Limited
Just Acrylics Ltd
K Wholesale Limited
K. S. D Beauty Zone Ltd
K2Y Limited
K588 Limited
KSE Cosmetics Ltd
Kailijumei Ltd
Kavali Cosmetics Limited
Kazi Brothers Group Limited
Kendo Brands Limited
Khali Min Limited
Kimibeauty Ltd
Klean Skincare Ltd
J Kobain London Ltd
J Kobain Ltd
Kokoa UK Limited
Korban Beauty Limited
Kservices Group Ltd

L'Oreal (U.K.) Limited
L.A. Professional Cosmetic Labs Ltd.
L.P Cosmetics Ltd
LEM Beauty Ltd
LIV Organic Co Ltd
LTSC Ltd
La Beauty Labs Ltd.
La Maison Hedonique Limited
Natascha Lacombe Cosmetics Ltd
Ladd Cosmetics Ltd
Lady Smidgeton's Apothecary Ltd
Lashflix Limited
Leicala Natural Products Ltd
Les Lilas Limited
Lesimone Global Limited
Lex Roris Ltd
Liaver Limited
Libhairation Ltd
Lino Rose Ltd
Lins Bros Limited
Liquor Lips Ltd
Little Duckling Soaps Ltd
Livoliv Cosmetics Ltd.
Lixir Skin Limited
London Outlet Store Limited
Londonscentsuk Limited
Lore Originals Limited
Loveliness Limited
Lovoir Ltd
Lozano Skincare Ltd
Luban & Murr Ltd
Luxurious Personal Care Ltd
Luxury Personal Care Ltd
MB Promotion Ltd.
MD-101 Ltd
MTIstanbul Ltd
MWK Cosmetics (UK) Ltd
Macial Ltd
Madame Laveau Ltd
Make Up Madness Ltd
Makeup Boutique Limited
Man Mask Ltd
Manhattan Group Ltd.
Manicure You Ltd
Marcman Perfume Ltd
Marrouge Limited
Martha & Daughter Limited
Mary-Jane's Beauty Ltd
Maskologist Ltd
Mast - Art Group Limited
Mata Labs Cosmetics Ltd
Felicity McDonald Organics Ltd
Meadow Farm Friends Ltd
Meadow Skincare Limited
Mega Mane Limited
Meilikki Ltd
Merumaya Limited
Metropolitan Beauty Ltd.
Meviq Ltd
Mink Company U.K Ltd
Miracle Herbs & Fruits Cosmetics Ltd
Miss Glamm Limited
Misspap X Bperfect Limited
Mitvana and Biological Industries Ltd
Miya Hair Limited
Mlle Cosmetics Co Ltd
Modazi Ltd
Modern Man Ltd
Mono Naturoils Ltd
Moore Cosmetics Ltd
Moyy Limited
Mr Carters Essentials Limited

Mupe Ltd
My Meghan Ltd
My Pure Life-Style Limited
Jennifer Myers Limited
Nail & Beauty Link Limited
Nailzee Ltd
Nanat Limited
Natcare Beauty Ltd
Natural Skincare London Ltd
Natural Spa Factory Limited
Natural Vitale Limited
Naturally Untamed Ltd
Naturity Cosmetics Ltd
Navya Innoveda Ltd
Neal's Yard (Natural Remedies) Ltd
Nika Cosmo Group Ltd
Nizz Cosmetics Ltd
Noa London Ltd
Noble Soap Limited
Noli Distribution Ltd
Nut Dust Ltd
OPA Botanicals Ltd
Oh So Locks Ltd
Olivoderm Cosmetics UK Limited
Omaoli Limited
Omprus Limited
Only Perfection Ltd
Onya Limited
Orange Square Co Ltd.
Organic Cosmetic Products Ltd
Organic Iway Ltd
Organic Professional Ltd
Organic Stuff Limited
Organica Skincare Ltd
Orikii Naturals Ltd
Orit Limited
Otterganics Ltd
Outcome Zero Ltd
Oxmetics Ltd
Oya 9 Ltd
P & T PL Ltd
PL Distribution Ltd
Paint It Orange Ltd
Parfums Christian Dior (U.K.) Ltd
Pause Skincare Limited
Pennies and Feathers Limited
Penny Price Aromatherapy Ltd
Perfume Outlet Ltd
Pheora Rucci Limited
Phyto Pharm Limited
Pink Empire Limited
Plane Luxuries Limited
Ploom (U.K.) Limited
Polcosmetics Ltd
Predator Trading Limited
Preen Queen Limited
Prima Makeup Ltd
Prime Skincare Ltd
Prismologie International Ltd
Prispens Limited
Pro Brands (UK) Ltd
Pro Bright Ltd
Project Cosmetics Limited
Puff & Petals Ltd.
Pur3 Health Limited
Pure Savvy Limited
Pure Skincare Limited
Pure Thoughts Ltd
Quality Brand MG Ltd
R & T Natural Cosmetics Ltd
REN Skincare Limited
RHI By ROC Ltd

RX Cosmetics Limited
Rawmans Ltd
Real Cosmetics Ltd
Real Looks Limited
Relaxa Trading Ltd
Reminiscents of Didsbury Ltd
Ren Ltd
Renibo Ltd
Reveal Naturals Ltd
Rishi Human Hair Extensions Wholesale
Rock Beauty Junkie Limited
Romade Limited
Roots Are Remedies Ltd
JC Rosedale Co Ltd
Rosse Beau Ltd
Ru Si Lacquers Global Ltd.
Rub-a-Dub Scrub Ltd
SGHP Ltd
SKN-RG Ltd
SPTB Ltd
SU Labs Limited
Sabeauti Ltd.
Sage Apothecary Limited
P.S. Sahney & Co Limited
Salon Professional London Ltd
Samla Tribe Limited
Leonora Sanche Cosmetics Ltd
Daniel Sandler Ltd
Saveasy Ltd.
Seed Fashion and Beauty Incubator Ltd
Select & Bargain Ltd
Serenityy Ltd
Sharp's Global Trading Limited
Shebelle Limited
Silk and Bubble Limited
Simply Nature Ltd.
Sisi Cosmetics Ltd
Skin & Tonic London Ltd
Skinkode Ltd
Skins Sexual Health Limited
Skinsider Cosmetics Ltd
Skintel Cosmetics Ltd
Slixir Ltd
Smart Skin Limited
Smiles Glasgow Limited
Soapy J Limited
Solo Skin London Ltd
Someplace Nice Limited
Sophistique Beauty Ltd
Sopureoils Ltd
Soul Cosmetics Limited
South West Aesthetics Ltd
Southend Hair and Beauty Ltd
Southsea Bathing Hut Limited
Spa Pro Ltd
Sphere 7 Lab Ltd
Spirit of Dubai Limited
Spktra Limited
Splendor Europe Ltd.
St-Creation Ltd
Sun Jelly Ltd
Sun Spirit Skincare Limited
Sun-Glo Limited
Super Natural Apothecary Ltd.
Supernova UK Pty Ltd
Sweet Arabian Ltd
Tabitha JK Limited
Stella Tailor Ltd
Tanovation Ltd
Tansi Packaging Solutions Ltd
Tententen Limited
Thalasso Ltd

TheManeCo Ltd
Thiossane Ltd
This Works Products Limited
Three Organics Ltd
Timeless Temple Ltd
Tonic15 Ltd
Top Beauty Brands Ltd
Top Beauty Limited
Toppers Nails Limited
Total Beauty Ltd
Trees of Beauty Ltd
Trending Scents Ltd.
Trimmz Ltd
True Hemp Ltd
True Skincare Limited
Trulips Ltd
Tryon Products Limited
UK Aimutaike Electronics Co., Ltd
UK Cosmeticz International Ltd
UK Esthetics Ltd
UK Heluns Industry Co., Ltd
UK Vimin Industry Co., Limited
US Beauty Store Limited
Ude Cosmetics Limited
Un Air D'Antan Limited
Underground Girl London Ltd
Unicorn Magic Enterprises Ltd
United Nomads Limited
United Solutions (UK) Limited
Uoma Beauty Group Limited
Uppercut Deluxe Co Limited
VI Beauty Ltd
Valentia Skincare Limited
Valma Consumer Co Ltd
Ve-Glam Limited
Venkh Retail Ltd
Vesta London Beauty Ltd
Vetivert & Co Ltd
Vett Limited
Vitaglow Ltd
Vivacy Laboratoires Ltd
Votary Limited
Vtessia Cosmetic Ltd
WH Corporation (UK) PTE. Ltd
Walk on Gold Limited
Watsoap.Com Limited
We Concept Ltd
Wellbeing Skincare Limited
Wellness Style Limited
Werson International Ltd
White Lotus Anti Aging Ltd
Wild Beauty Ltd
Wild Kynd Ltd
Wildmint Cosmetics Limited
Wipes Direct Ltd
Wizer Ltd
Wonder and Wild Ltd
Wonderful Life PHBS Ltd
Woodwood Limited
Yehmea Limited
Yejisu Innovation Ltd
Young Now Ltd
Younghair AB Ltd
Ibrahim Yusuf and Sons Ltd
Zarvis London Limited
Zed Beauty Ltd
Naseem Zeenah Natural Cosmetics Ltd
Zyzven Naturals Cosmetics Ltd

47770 Retail sale of watches and jewellery in specialised stores
Asian Fashions Ltd

Choize Ltd
Diymonde Corporation Limited
Kenzak Beauty and Jewellery Ltd
Maximaliste Limited
Onlinexclusive Limited
Saroza Limited

47781 Retail sale in commercial art galleries
Hubert & Emilie Ltd

47789 Other retail sale of new goods in specialised stores (not commercial art galleries and opticians) [12]
305 Professionals Ltd
Bad Mermaid Limited
Beauty Spot Holdings Limited
Bendito Trading Limited
Complete Healing Limited
Crabtree & Evelyn (Overseas) Ltd
D'Zario UK Ltd
Earthly Pleasures Ltd
Kailijumei Ltd
Tebs Distribution Limited
Wonderful Life PHBS Ltd
Zerocann Ltd

47810 Retail sale via stalls and markets of food, beverages and tobacco products
Boutique Parfum Limited
Liquor Lips Ltd
RSJ Trading Limited

47820 Retail sale via stalls and markets of textiles, clothing and footwear
Chic Clothing Limited
Dear Body Limited
Elysian Design Limited
Hadley and Reed Ltd
Les Blanches Limited
Look Fab Limited
Me Sentir Ltd.
Thrillage Ltd.

47890 Retail sale via stalls and markets of other goods [29]
Back To Eve Ltd
Cazza Professional Ltd
Crivalis Ltd
Damrick's White Bunny Ltd
Eco Twinkle Ltd
Evanto Fragrance Limited
Filberts Bees Limited
Great British Bee Co Ltd
Hudsonry Ltd
J's Luxury Perfumery Ltd
La Bello Beauty Limited
Lola's Apothecary Ltd
Loveve. Ltd
Mary Jean Limited
NA Medical Care Ltd
ORA Naturals Limited
Olfactive Thirty Eight Fragrances
Opatra Limited
Parfum Club Ltd
Pizzaz Ventures Limited
Reimiece Ltd
Scence Ltd
Scent Angels UK Ltd
Simply Pure Skincare Ltd

Skinjam Cosmetics Limited
Southsea Bathing Hut Limited
Ve-Glam Limited
Vitaglow Ltd
Wiltshire Beekeeper Ltd

47910 Retail sale via mail order houses or via Internet [297]
AHS Services Ltd
Actuate Services (GB) Ltd
Aeden UK Ltd
Aether Elements Ltd
Africa's Best Artisans Limited
Akoma International (UK) Ltd
Alayna Cosmetics and Beauty Ltd
Albertina Dorosario Ltd
Alianaz Ltd.
All-Around Infinity Limited
Amassuna Limited
Angel Remy Ltd
Aqolade Ltd
Arizona Botaniq Limited
Aroma Actives Limited
Aromabar (Scotland) Ltd
Art-Eclair Limited
Askett & English Ltd
B & O Natural Cosmetics Ltd
B. Silki Naturally Ltd
BM Beauty Ltd.
Back To Eve Ltd
Bad Mermaid Limited
Barbers House Ltd
Base Pro Artists Ltd
Beard Gang Ltd
Beard Zone Ltd
Beautifect Ltd
Beautivate Ltd
Beauty Camp Profesional Ltd
Beauty Center Ltd
Beauty Expression (UK) Limited
Beautysugaring Limited
Berry Inc Ltd
Blk Deer Co. Ltd
Blk Oil Limited
Bluesky Cosmetics UK HQ Ltd
Botany Squared Limited
Boutique Parfum Limited
Brain Burgeon Ltd
Cambridge Sprouts Limited
Cazza Professional Ltd
Chanson Worldwide Limited
Chronicles Medical Consulting Ltd
Color Studio Ltd
Comfort Click Limited
Comglobal Limited
Contour and More London Ltd
Cool Blades Limited
Cool Essentials Limited
Cosmetiqa Ltd
Cosmos Cosmetics Limited
Cosnique Group Holdings Ltd
Cosplus International Ltd
Cult Candy Limited
Custom Tan UK Limited
Cutagen Ltd
Cyrano Limited
Damrick's White Bunny Ltd
Dee Doo Limited
Dermamaitre Ltd.
Design4nails Ltd
Dily Oka International Group Co., Ltd
Dimonauk Ltd

Diverse Solution Ltd
Dr. Twilight Ltd
Dr.K Skinlab Ltd
Dreamweave Products Ltd
Duke of Charm Limited
Duo Beauty Products Limited
Dupeshop Ltd
EB Stores Ltd
Earthbreath Ltd
Eco Twinkle Ltd
Ekah Foundation C.I.C.
Elder & Co Limited
Eleuthere Ltd
Elite Capital Limited
Ellipsis Brands Limited
Elysian Design Limited
Essential Oil Sell Ltd
Essentials4men Ltd
Eternal Beauty (UK) Ltd
Eternal Hair & Beauty Limited
Evanto Fragrance Limited
Evbioo Ltd
Express Hair and Beauty Supply Ltd
Ezili Botanicals Limited
Farmavita Ltd
Fatale Cosmetics Limited
Ferrara-Bardile Ltd
Firecrest Communications Ltd
Foramca Ltd
Foreverbeyoung Ltd
France Parfums International Ltd
Franok Business Solutions Ltd
From Mini Acorns Ltd
G & G Skincare Ltd
Gallya Deelya Ltd.
Gel Labs Limited
Gentel Works Ltd
Genten Skincare Ltd
Glow Jar Ltd
Good By Nature Ltd
Green Essence Ltd
Green Ladies N.I Ltd
H & R Cosmetics Ltd
H.H.L.Brothers Limited
Hahydra Technologies Ltd
Harmonious Brown Limited
Hedgerow Medicine Chest Ltd
Helia-D UK Ltd
Herbalise Limited
Highfields Health Limited
Holistic Plant Technologies Ltd
Holy Lama Naturals Ltd
Hommage International Ltd
Honeystyle Limited
House of Kendra Ltd
House of Vanity Limited
Hudsonry Ltd
Humanity Cosmetics Limited
Hundred Acres Apothecary Ltd
Iam By Nature Ltd.
Infini Lab Ltd
Innocent Alchemy Ltd
Inside Trading (Beauty) Ltd
InternationalBeautyLondon Ltd
Irum Cosmetics Ltd
Ish Products Ltd
J's Luxury Perfumery Ltd
Jacob's Well Limited
Jas Etrading Ltd
Juliajosh Limited
Juni Cosmetics Limited
K3W Trading Limited

KM Cosmetics Distribution Ltd
KMY Group Ltd
Kailijumei Ltd
Kamila Health & Beauty Ltd
Kaniz International Limited
Kaniz Organics Limited
Kimibeauty Ltd
Kind2 Limited
Ko. Essentials Ltd.
Koha Beauty Co Ltd
L'Art & La Matiere Limited
LMS Brands Ltd.
LTSC Ltd
La Bello Beauty Limited
Ladyology Limited
Laldhinio Limited
Lam Cosmetics Ltd
Landional Ltd
Latam HQ Health Ltd
Le Pure Limited
Lesimone Global Limited
Lex Roris Ltd
Liluna-Organics Ltd
Lino Rose Ltd
Lins Bros Limited
Lixir Skin Limited
Lola's Apothecary Ltd
London Ethnic Ltd
Loopy Hair & Beauty Ltd
Lovalova Ltd
Loveco Ltd
Loveve. Ltd
Lovoir Ltd
Lozano Skincare Ltd
Lulu Tanner Limited
Luxuryscope London Limited
Mabxclusive Limited
Madame Laveau Ltd
Madre Skincare Limited
Makeup Boutique Limited
Man Mask Ltd
Mandragora Ltd
Maskologist Ltd
Doris Michaels Cosmetics Ltd
Miracle8 Ltd
Miss U Cosmetics Limited
Molecula Ltd
Mondor & Bache Ltd
Moroccan Attlas Ltd
Mr Carters Essentials Limited
Mupe Ltd
Myroo Ltd
NOP Cosmetics Ltd
Nail Art Direct Ltd
Nanosafe Ltd.
Natural Beauty Import Limited
Natural Skincare London Ltd
Nature-Solves Ltd
Need4health Limited
Neete Holdings Limited
Neopilina Moda Ltd
Neville Cut and Shave Limited
Nika Cosmo Group Ltd
Niko Pro Limited
Noli Distribution Ltd
Nu Essence Limited
ORA Naturals Limited
Oasis Beauty Distribution Ltd
Okmarket24 Ltd
Olfactive Thirty Eight Fragrances
Olivoderm Cosmetics UK Limited
Onlinexclusive Limited

Onsen Secret UK Ltd
Paradise Organics London Ltd
Party Supplies and More Ltd
Pavone Profumi SRL Ltd
Perfume Outlet Ltd
Peters Cosmet Ltd
Pharma Medico Limited
Pharmdex UK Ltd
Pheora Rucci Limited
Phyto Pharm Limited
Pinklady International Ltd
Pizzaz Ventures Limited
Plant Me Botanics Ltd
Plush Soap Ltd
Polcosmetics Ltd
Potions & Possibilities Ltd
Prime Skincare Ltd
Prismologie International Ltd
Pur3 Health Limited
Pure Skincare Limited
Quint Essence Lab Ltd
R & B Hair Extensions Limited
R & T Natural Cosmetics Ltd
RHI By ROC Ltd
Real Cosmetics Ltd
Reimiece Ltd
Renibo Ltd
Rewind Botanics Limited
Roxie Cosmetics Ltd
SB Selected Beauty Ltd
SU Labs Limited
Salem Stores Ltd
Salt and Pamper Limited
Leonora Sanche Cosmetics Ltd
Scence Ltd
Scent Angels UK Ltd
Sebaroyale Ltd
Serendipity (N.I.) Ltd
Seventa Image Ltd
Shop Beauty Ltd
Sikania Ltd
Simply Pure Skincare Ltd
Slim Line Club UK Ltd
Slixir Ltd
Sopureoils Ltd
Spartzy Lifestyle Brands Ltd
Spruce Vita Limited
Stonera Ltd
Sun-Glo Limited
Supernova UK Pty Ltd
TM Brands Limited
Tarsago Ltd
Tebs Distribution Limited
Temple Spirit Ltd
Thai Wellness Ltd
Thrifty Limited
Top Beauty Limited
Toppers Nails Limited
Trimmz Ltd
Trollion Limited
UK Aimutaike Electronics Co., Ltd
UK Heluns Industry Co., Ltd
UK Vimin Industry Co., Limited
Uni Supply Ltd
Unineed Limited
Uoma Beauty Group Limited
Urhan Group Limited
VY Club Limited
Valya Beauty Cosmetics Ltd
Vancooler Ltd
Ve-Glam Limited
Vetivert & Co Ltd

Victoire Limited
Vida Aesthetics Ltd
Vida Skincare Ltd
Vision Trading Limited
Vitaglow Ltd
Vivora Limited
Vlinder Cosmetics Ltd
Walking Pet Balloons (UK) Ltd
Winkies Limited
Wizer Ltd
Woldscot Limited
World Links Europe Limited
Wrap N Pack Ltd
Wrimes Cosmetics Ltd
Yellbird Limited
Yorkshire Beard Co Ltd
Zest Cosmetics Limited

47990 Other retail sale not in stores, stalls or markets [52]
Acti Laboratories UK Ltd
Age Infinite Ltd
Alayna Cosmetics and Beauty Ltd
Aqua Bleu Limited
Bibishor Limited
Bodyhug Limited
Buy It Out Ltd
Complete Healing Limited
Cosmetolife Limited
Crazy Smiles Group Ltd
Crivalis Ltd
Foramca Ltd
France Parfums International Ltd
A.H. Francis Professional Beauty
Glow Jar Ltd
GoodNaturedSkincare Ltd
Green Essence Ltd
Gruhme UK Limited
H & R Cosmetics Ltd
Hemsley James Cosmetics Ltd
Imaage Ltd
Imxpo Ltd
Ital Living Market Ltd
JZM International Limited
Jouer Jouer Limited
LIV Organic Co Ltd
Lam Cosmetics Ltd
Lavy Sprays International Ltd
Liza Organics Ltd
Lovoir Ltd
Maliboo Hair and Cosmetics Ltd
Miracle8 Ltd
Mondor & Bache Ltd
Multitude Makeup Ltd
Natural Sheaness Ltd
Nekta Botanics Ltd
New Aesthetic Ltd
Nomalogic Ltd
Online Motions Limited
Privilago Fashion Ltd
Real Cosmetics Ltd
JC Rosedale Co Ltd
Scent Angels UK Ltd
Shaw International Ltd
Simply Nature Ltd.
Storm of UK Limited
Stylish & Luxurious Limited
Temple Spirit Ltd
True Skincare Limited
VY Club Limited
Whimsical Beauty Ltd
Yazmae Cosmetics Limited

49320 Taxi operation
Beauty Camp Profesional Ltd

49390 Other passenger land transport
Shadi's Hairdresser Ltd

49410 Freight transport by road
Beauty Camp Profesional Ltd
A & P Blickling Ltd
KMY Group Ltd
Shop4stocks Limited

50100 Sea and coastal passenger water transport
Sandaig Ltd

50200 Sea and coastal freight water transport
Sandaig Ltd

51102 Non-scheduled passenger air transport
Andre Boyard Perfumes Limited

51210 Freight air transport
Shop4stocks Limited

52219 Other service activities incidental to land transportation, n.e.c.
Nevitrade Ltd

52241 Cargo handling for water transport activities
Renaissance Manyane Global Group Ltd

52242 Cargo handling for air transport activities
Renaissance Manyane Global Group Ltd

52290 Other transportation support activities
Export Solutions (International) Ltd
Nevitrade Ltd
Pavone Profumi SRL Ltd
Rupitex Limited

53202 Unlicensed carriers
Enfield Distribution Ltd

55100 Hotels and similar accommodation
Exa World Ltd

55209 Other holiday and other collective accommodation
Tyn y Ddol Enterprises Ltd

56102 Unlicenced restaurants and cafes
Portobello Organics Ltd

56103 Take-away food shops and mobile food stands
Ayhamco Limited

56290 Other food services [29]
Adible Limited
Ava Corporations Ltd
Benefit & Riley Healthcare Ltd
Bigben Healthcare Limited
Bion Corporation Limited
Clarins & Felix Healthcare Ltd
Cosmetics Wholesale Limited
Eifelcorp Consumer Care Ltd
Elie Consumer Care Ltd
Elliott Nutrition Ltd
Farmers Pure Organics Ltd
Felix Medical Group Ltd
Flynn Group of Companies Ltd
Garnier & Hemo Healthcare Ltd
Hemo Bioscience Ltd
Hubert & Emilie Ltd
Inshirah Enterprises Limited
Julie's Natural Health Ltd
Lamer & Ava Healthcare Ltd
Nars & Elliott Healthcare Ltd
Nekta Botanics Ltd
Regis Personal Care Ltd
Revlon & Elie Healthcare Ltd
Riley & Sons Ltd
Rimmel & Flynn Healthcare Ltd
Serenityhands Ltd
Spice International Trading Co Ltd
Trade Mall Limited
United Mart (UK) Limited

58110 Book publishing
Azhar Academy Limited
Katherine Longhi Ltd
Sangels Limited

59132 Video distribution activities
Live Rich Academy Limited

61100 Wired telecommunications activities
Zipco Limited

61900 Other telecommunications activities
Zipco Limited

62012 Business and domestic software development
Dr Sun Limited
Neonails Ltd
P P Oil UK Limited

62020 Information technology consultancy activities
Adible Limited
Aeroeco Co Ltd
ED Trading & Consultancy Ltd
Raynolds Ltd
Storm of UK Limited
Tassels UK Ltd
Tothun Group UK Ltd

62090 Other information technology service activities
Allied Warden Marketing Ltd
Deism IT Solutions Ltd
Foodprint Network Ltd
La Beauty Labs Ltd.
Rupitex Limited
Sai Darshan Limited
Unigrand Group Limited

63110 Data processing, hosting and related activities
All-Around Infinity Limited

63120 Web portals
Beauty Bash Limited
Boutique Parfum Limited
Farshety Ltd
Grautrans Limited
Jaspmab Ltd
KMY Group Ltd
La Beauty Labs Ltd.

63990 Other information service activities n.e.c.
Globe Intraworks Limited
Nota Nota Limited
Protective World Ltd

64201 Activities of agricultural holding companies
Hild International Group Ltd

64204 Activities of distribution holding companies
Atlas Global Trade Ltd
Salus Cutis Ltd

64205 Activities of financial services holding companies
Magpie Holdings Ltd

64209 Activities of other holding companies n.e.c.
Beauty Spot Holdings Limited
Emma Danmark Ltd
Emma Group Ltd

64304 Activities of open-ended investment companies
Nocov Ltd

64306 Activities of real estate investment trusts
Iberia Skin Brands Ltd

64921 Credit granting by non-deposit taking finance houses and other specialist consumer credit grantors
Bluestar Enterprise Limited

68100 Buying and selling of own real estate
Burton Blackmore International Ltd
Collection 1212 Limited
Kservices Group Ltd
Sipro (UK) Ltd

68209 Other letting and operating of own or leased real estate
Allied Aerosols Limited
David & Co. Traders Ltd
Euro Healthcare Services Ltd
Jazzy Hair Limited
Neonails Ltd
Tansi Packaging Solutions Ltd

68310 Real estate agencies
AAA Edinburgh Ltd
Allied Warden Marketing Ltd

68320 Management of real estate on a fee or contract basis
Collection 1212 Limited
Diverse Solution Ltd
Kservices Group Ltd

69201 Accounting and auditing activities
C Looker Ltd
Plan Target Limited
Rashimex Trading Limited

69203 Tax consultancy
Plan Target Limited
Rashimex Trading Limited

70100 Activities of head offices
Acti Laboratories UK Ltd
Beta Novis Limited
Glamn Holding Ltd
Intertrade Group Ltd
Muamko Uzuri Limited
Paris Elysees Holding Ltd.
Salus Cutis Ltd
Toppers Nails Limited
Winter Hill No.2 Limited

70210 Public relations and communications activities
A Rebours Limited
Lavender Concept Ltd
London Ethnic Ltd

70221 Financial management
Emma Prime Ltd
Plan Target Limited

70229 Management consultancy activities other than financial management [47]
All-Around Infinity Limited
Ars Nova (UK) Limited
Asadilari Limited
Bbeauty Lounge Cosmetics Ltd
Beauty Solutions Trading Ltd
Biovate Limited
Pazery Bouffard and Co Ltd
C Beauty Agency Limited
CNI Services Limited
Cannamplify Ltd
Cosmelinks Consultancy Ltd
Cosmetiques de France Ltd.
Dermafrance Ltd.
Diymonde Corporation Limited
ED Trading & Consultancy Ltd
Emma Prime Ltd
EmmaDK Ltd

Eurohandle Ltd
Franok Business Solutions Ltd
G.Q Homes Ltd
Glamn Holding Ltd
Hild International Group Ltd
Jedidiah Group Ltd
KPACA Limited
Latam HQ Health Ltd
Leading National Training Ltd
Les Blanches Limited
Medora of London Limited
Megaco Limited
Miraculous UK Ltd
New Horizons (UK) Ltd
Novumis Ltd
Peters Cosmet Ltd
Pharmafrance Ltd.
Phi Advisory & Consulting Ltd
Rosense (UK) Ltd
SHH Logistics Ltd
Sanchi Corp Limited
Seed Fashion and Beauty Incubator Ltd
Splendor Europe Ltd.
Standfast Solutions International Ltd
Surreal Health & Beauty Ltd
Tobco Limited
Tommco Limited
Tyn y Ddol Enterprises Ltd
VNS London Limited
Vancooler Ltd

71122 Engineering related scientific and technical consulting activities
Cosnique Group Holdings Ltd
Infinityredox Holdings Limited
Pherolec Global Ltd
Phi Advisory & Consulting Ltd
SHH Logistics Ltd

71129 Other engineering activities
Pherolec Global Ltd

71200 Technical testing and analysis
Tassels UK Ltd

72110 Research and experimental development on biotechnology [10]
Almcells Bioscience Ltd.
Bioaqua -Biotechnology Ltd.
Clinova Limited
Imperial Bioscience Ltd
MGC Pharma (UK) Ltd
Medical Technology Caraco (MYC) Ltd.
Spruce Vita Limited
Treas Biotechnology UK Ltd
UK Irelia Co Ltd
Zoee Cosmetics Co., Ltd

72190 Other research and experimental development on natural sciences and engineering
Atlantis Research Limited
Cannabinoid Oil Solutions Ltd
Clinova Limited
Imperial Bioscience Ltd
In Situ Cosmetics Ltd
Infinityredox Holdings Limited
Inovair Limited
Tiyati Ltd

73110 Advertising agencies
Ayhamco Limited
Gazelli International Limited
Glochina Trading UK Ltd.
London Ethnic Ltd
MB Promotion Ltd.
Pink Empire Limited
Velvet Bee Co Ltd

73200 Market research and public opinion polling
Rapsodi London Ltd
Tattva Ltd.

74100 Specialised design activities
Dr. Twilight Ltd
Hamiltons of Canterbury Ltd
JWWJ Limited
Think Be Nature Ltd
Veels UK Limited

74209 Photographic activities not elsewhere classified
Veels UK Limited

74300 Translation and interpretation activities
B & O Natural Cosmetics Ltd

74909 Other professional, scientific and technical activities n.e.c. [11]
ABX Beauty Limited
Allure Cosmetics Ltd
BSB Fashion Limited
Gallya Deelya Ltd.
Generic Physics Limited
Hydro Fresh Ltd
Innocent Alchemy Ltd
Meder Beauty International Ltd
SGHP Ltd
Tiyati Ltd
VNS London Limited

74990 Non-trading company
Arowell Products Ltd
D'val Ltd
Eleven Eleven Cosmetics Ltd

77390 Renting and leasing of other machinery, equipment and tangible goods n.e.c.
3D Lifestyle Ltd
Cyrano Limited

78101 Motion picture, television and other theatrical casting activities
Relaxa Trading Ltd

78200 Temporary employment agency activities
Alpha Auriga Limited
Liolax Limited

78300 Human resources provision and management of human resources functions
Katherine Longhi Ltd
Tyn y Ddol Enterprises Ltd

79110 Travel agency activities
Hasanah Global Ltd

79120 Tour operator activities
Agoda Limited

80200 Security systems service activities
Ileri Trading Limited

80300 Investigation activities
Pandorra Ltd.

81210 General cleaning of buildings
Hubert & Emilie Ltd

81222 Specialised cleaning services
Clean & Care Facilities Management

81299 Other cleaning services
D'val Ltd

81300 Landscape service activities
Mlaveau Cuban Origins Ltd

82110 Combined office administrative service activities
Dimonauk Ltd

82200 Activities of call centres
Ark Inta Ltd

82301 Activities of exhibition and fair organisers
Moroccan Golden Sands Ltd
Secret Line Ltd

82920 Packaging activities
International Integrated Solutions Co
Mata Labs Cosmetics Ltd
Tansi Packaging Solutions Ltd
UK Beauty Cosmetics International Group

82990 Other business support service activities n.e.c. [43]
Arahant Ltd
Ars Nova (UK) Limited
Available Beauty Ltd
Bambi & Co Ltd
Beauty Spot Holdings Limited
Beltech Limited
Bonroy International Limited
Colgate-Palmolive (U.K.) Ltd
Dermacure Aesthetics Limited
Export Solutions (International) Ltd
France Parfums International Ltd
Fuzzique Limited
Gentel Works Ltd
Glow Beauty Shop Ltd
Hommage International Ltd
House of Worth Limited
Kalabash Limited
Ladyology Limited
Lambsmead Limited
Light Up Skincare Ltd
Liolax Limited
Meddiamonds Ltd

NS Brands International Ltd
Nail Island Ltd
Nature et Bien-Etre Limited
Nizz Cosmetics Ltd
Noa London Ltd
Novumis Ltd
Paragon Enterprise Limited
Patagonia Consult Limited
Perfume Lab Limited
Pharmacare (Europe) Limited
Quality Check Ltd
Real Looks Limited
Republic Cosmetics UK Ltd
Rose Tree Enterprises Ltd.
S A Designer Parfums Limited
Salon Success Limited
Season of Beauty Limited
Secret Line Ltd
Sheabynature Ltd
Strdom Ltd
Sunrise Essential Oil Limited

84120 Regulation of health care, education, cultural and other social services, not incl. social security
Dermica Laboratoires UK Ltd
G.Q Homes Ltd

84220 Defence activities
Pandorra Ltd.

85100 Pre-primary education
Yehmea Limited

85320 Technical and vocational secondary education
Beauty Mastery Ltd.
Ciao Brow Henna Limited
Farmavita Ltd

85410 Post-secondary non-tertiary education
Penny Price Aromatherapy Ltd

85520 Cultural education
Sankofa Heritage Ltd
St-Creation Ltd

85590 Other education n.e.c. [16]
B2B Beauty UK Limited
Mark Birch Hair Ltd
Cambridge Sprouts Limited
Deltagamma Limited
Ekah Foundation C.I.C.
Eternal Beauty (UK) Ltd
Eyelash Design Co Ltd
Flower Cosmetic Ltd
My SNS Academy UK Ltd
Precision Brows and Lashes Ltd
SK Flawless Dipping Powder Ltd
Sansuri Hair & Beauty Supplies and Training
Spa Pro Ltd
Sweet Squared Limited
Tattva Ltd.
Valiscious Limited

85600 Educational support services
Agoda Limited
Alianaz Ltd.
Dermacure Aesthetics Limited
Egotistic Hair & Beauty Ltd
Live Rich Academy Limited
Medical Technology Caraco (MYC) Ltd.
Yehmea Limited

86101 Hospital activities
Deltagamma Limited
Sai Darshan Limited

86102 Medical nursing home activities
Bortlam Postpartum Restore Health Management (International) Chain Co.,

86210 General medical practice activities
Zarroug Limited

86220 Specialists medical practice activities
Mark Birch Hair Ltd
Ibeautify Ltd
Seigur Rose International Group Co., Ltd
Toggle Genetica Group Limited

86900 Other human health activities [20]
3D Lifestyle Ltd
Allies Network Ltd
Bayan Ltd
Beauty Mastery Ltd.
Belfast Beard Co Ltd
Birch & Hayer Ltd
Bluesky Products Limited
Calmer Solutions Limited
Ekah Foundation C.I.C.
Etonigbo Limited
Irum Cosmetics Ltd
MGC Pharma (UK) Ltd
Medipro Pharma Limited
NA Medical Care Ltd
Pharmadose Limited
Project 1 Skincare Ltd
Roots Are Remedies Ltd
Shama Pharma Ltd
Skins Sexual Health Limited
Victoria Pharma London Ltd

87300 Residential care activities for the elderly and disabled
Serenityhands Ltd

90030 Artistic creation
Bath Bombs and Beyond Limited
Bedeaux Ltd
Bespoke Mr Ltd
Lipstick and Black Coffee Ltd
Njubien Ltd
Tattva Ltd.

93130 Fitness facilities
Look Fab Limited

93199 Other sports activities
Perfect Lady Ltd
Renski Limited

95210 Repair of consumer electronics
Shaw International Ltd

96020 Hairdressing and other beauty treatment [120]

100% Vegan Skincare Limited
876 Skin Beauty Limited
ASR Aesthetics Ltd
Adorexo Ltd
Afro Hair and Beauty International
Allure Cosmetics Ltd
Aneen Ventures Limited
Aurora Spa Health and Beauty Ltd
Aurum D Limited
Barbers House Ltd
Bayan Ltd
Beauty By Aliyah Ltd
Beauty Mastery Ltd.
Beauty Royale Ltd
Beautyline Limited
Beautysugaring Limited
Belfast Beard Co Ltd
Billionhaire Limited
Bioaqua -Biotechnology Ltd.
Birch & Hayer Ltd
Blissworld Limited
Bluesky Products Limited
Body Beauty & Hair Ltd
Boundless Beauty Ltd
Brambles Farm Ltd
Butterflyy Productions Ltd
CH General Traders Limited
Contemporary Cosmetic Enterprise Ltd
Cosmetiqa Ltd
Curl Coach Ltd
Custom Tan UK Limited
Cxlture Cosmetics Ltd
Dead Pretty Official Ltd
Death Head Beard Co Ltd
Dermica Laboratoires UK Ltd
Divine Natural Limited
Dorothy Hair and Beauty Shop Ltd
Dufeal Your Best Beauty Ltd
Elegant Boss Ltd
Emel Trade Ltd
Exa World Ltd
Facil Haircare Ltd
Farmavita Ltd
Floest Beauty Solutions Ltd
Flower Cosmetic Ltd
A.H. Francis Professional Beauty
From Mini Acorns Ltd
Gabriellas Beauty Ltd
S K A Gibson Ltd
GoodNaturedSkincare Ltd
Hair & Skin Care Ltd
Herb U.K. Limited
House of Vanity Limited
Huskie London Ltd
Imaage Ltd
Indigo Nails Online Shop Ltd.
Initiative (UK) Limited
Ivy Wild Ltd
JK Hair & Beauty Salon Supplies Ltd
KMC's Fabulous Cosmetics Ltd
Kimibeauty Ltd
Kizzle Beauty Ltd
Kokoa UK Limited
Konya Food Biotechnology Co., Ltd
LK Beauty Ltd
Landermark Ltd
Lanmix Enterperises Ltd
Le Keux Vintage Enterprises Ltd
Lemon Tree Beauty Limited
Libhairation Ltd
Lollipop Treats Ltd
Look Fab Limited
Louts Remit Beautiful International Group Co.,
Lumine Beauty Ltd
Lux Aesthetics Hull Ltd
Lyons Men's Grooming Ltd
Mahogany Crownz Ltd
Maliboo Hair and Cosmetics Ltd
Mesoskinline (UK) Limited
Mlaveau Cuban Origins Ltd
Nail Island Ltd
Ned London Limited
Neonails Ltd
Neville Cut and Shave Limited
Nicfead Cosmetics & Fragrance Ltd
Nouvriet Boutros (UK) Ltd
Nov'max Keratin Limited
Oh So Locks Ltd
Organic Colour Systems Limited
Oya 9 Ltd
Danica Payne Ltd
Pink Lush Lips Ltd
Preen Queen Limited
Privilago Fashion Ltd
Rose & Thorn Ltd
Rosse Beau Ltd
Sage Apothecary Limited
Salon Professional London Ltd
Sansuri Hair & Beauty Supplies and Training
Seigur Rose International Group Co., Ltd
Sfera London Limited
Shadi's Hairdresser Ltd
Sisi Cosmetics Ltd
Spa Pro Ltd
Sun-Glo Limited
Sweet Pea Soaps Co Ltd
Tauri Corporation Limited
Thalasso Ltd
Timeless Temple Ltd
Toggle Genetica Group Limited
Valya Beauty Cosmetics Ltd
Ruth Venessa Services Ltd
Vida Aesthetics Ltd
Vida Skincare Ltd
Wake Up Beauty Ltd
Wheesht Ltd
Wonderful Life PHBS Ltd
Yaami's Fashion Beauty & Cosmetics UK
Zee Sales Limited
Zoee Cosmetics Co., Ltd

96040 Physical well-being activities

Afro Hair and Beauty International
Bortlam Postpartum Restore Health Management (International) Chain Co.,
LIV Organic Co Ltd
Someplace Nice Limited
Temple Spirit Ltd
Thai Wellness Ltd

96090 Other service activities n.e.c. [23]

Almcells Bioscience Ltd.
BU Cosmetics Limited
Butterflyy Productions Ltd
Cosmelinks Consultancy Ltd
Croma-Pharma Limited
Dacre Skincare Limited
Ebong and Brothers Ltd
Fox Group International Ltd
Gallya Deelya Ltd.
Garda Service Ltd
HT Cosmetics Ltd
Ijapan Ltd
Imxpo Ltd
Kitchen Witch Aromatherapy Ltd
Misawa Healthcare Ltd
P & Z Solutions Limited
Perfect Lady Ltd
Rosse Beau Ltd
SeductiveDirect Ltd
Timeless Temple Ltd
Vida Aesthetics Ltd
Vida Skincare Ltd
Ibrahim Yusuf and Sons Ltd

98000 Residents property management

G.Q Homes Ltd

99999 Dormant company

Eleven Eleven Cosmetics Ltd
Miracle Herbs & Fruits Cosmetics Ltd

This page is intentionally left blank

Printed in 8pt Nimbus Sans L

Designed by URW++ Design and Development GmbH

Dellam Publishing Limited

2 Heath Drive, Sutton, Surrey, SM2 5RP

Fax: 020 8770 7478   email: enquiries@dellam.com

SAN: 0177881   EAN/GLN: 5030670177882

www.ingramcontent.com/pod-product-compliance
Lightning Source LLC
Chambersburg PA
CBHW081104080526
44587CB00021B/3439